Langenscheidt's Pocket Korean Dictionary

Korean-English
English-Korean

Edited by the
Langenscheidt Editorial Staff

LANGENSCHEIDT
NEW YORK · BERLIN · MUNICH

Compiled by LEXUS *with*

Kim Jin Heui 김 진희
Jiyoung Nam 남 지영
Okjoo Lee 이 옥주
Dr Judith Cherry, MBE
Dr Michael Finch

General editor: Peter Terrell

Printed in Germany

Preface

Here is a new dictionary of English and Korean, a tool with some 40,000 references for those who work with the English and Korean languages at beginner's or intermediate level.

Focusing on modern usage, the dictionary offers coverage of everyday language, including vocabulary from areas such as computers and business.

The Korean in this dictionary is written both in Korean script and in a romanized pronunciation system - a specially modified version of McCune-Reischauer.

The two sides of this dictionary, the English-Korean and the Korean-English, are quite different in structure and purpose. The English-Korean is designed for productive usage, for self-expression in Korean. The Korean-English is a decoding dictionary, a dictionary to enable the native speaker of English to understand Korean.

Clarity of presentation has been a major objective. The editors have provided the means to enable you, the user of the dictionary, to get straight to the translation that fits a particular context of use. Is the *mouse* you need for your computer, for example, the same in Korean as the *mouse* you don't want in the house? Is *flimsy* referring to furniture the same in Korean as *flimsy* referring to an excuse? The English-Korean dictionary is rich in sense distinctions like this – and in translation options tied to specific, identified senses.

Grammatical or function words are treated in some detail, on both the English-Korean and the Korean-English sides. And a large number of idiomatic phrases are given to show how the two languages correspond in context.

All in all, this is a book full of information, which will, we hope, become a valuable part of your language toolkit.

Contents

How to use the dictionary

To get the most out of your dictionary you should understand how and where to find the information you need. Whether you are yourself writing a text in Korean or wanting to understand a text in Korean, the following pages should help.

1. How and where do I find a word?

1.1 English headwords. The English word list is arranged in alphabetical order.

Sometimes you might want to look up terms made up of two separate words, for example **antivirus program**, or hyphenated words, for example **absent-minded.** These words are treated as though they were a single word and their alphabetical ordering reflects this. Compound words like **bookseller**, **bookstall**, **bookstore** are also listed in alphabetical order.

The only exception to this strict alphabetical ordering is made for English phrasal verbs - words like **♦go off**, **♦go out**, **♦go up**. These are positioned directly after their main verb (in this case **go**), rather than being scattered around in alphabetical positions.

1.2 Korean headwords. The Korean word list is arranged in English alphabetical order by being sorted on the romanization system. The Hangul romanization chart on pages 15-19 will help with this.

You will need to remember the following special points about the alphabetical ordering of the Hangul romanization system:

i) ŏ and ŭ are each treated as separate vowels and are listed before o and u respectively

ii) words starting with ch' are listed after words starting with ch

iii) words starting with k' are listed after words starting with k

iv) words starting with p' are listed after words starting with p

v) words starting with t' are listed after words starting with t

vi) when an apostrophe occurs within a word it is handled as coming after z, so, for example, a typical sequence is:

choripsshigŭi 조립식의 prefabricated
chorip tanwi 조립 단위 module
chorip'ada 조립하다 assemble, set up

vii) romanization can change according to the position of a Korean letter in a word. So, for example, the *p* in

ip 입 mouth

will become a *b* in

ibŭl tamulda 입을 다물다 clam up, keep silent

This means that some phrases in an entry may have a romanization that differs from the main headword. And some compound words may be listed at some distance from the headword.

The chart on pages 15-19 shows which letters are liable to these changes.

viii) Some commonly used phrases or expressions are entered in their alphabetical position rather than under the main term from which they are derived. For example:

majayo! 맞아요! that's it!, that's right!

will be found under maj... and not under

mat-tta 맞다 be right

ix) Some roman letters (including: b, d, g, j, r,) are not used to start words in the romanization system used in this dictionary. However, important suffixes or infixes may begin with some of these letters. These suffixes and infixes have been listed in a block at the end of the preceding letter of the roman alphabet. For example:

...dŏrado ...더라도 even though

is listed in a block at the end of letter C (since there is no letter D).

1.3 Running heads. If you are looking for an English or a Korean word you can use the **running heads** printed in bold in the top corner of each page. The running head on the left tells you the *first* headword on the left-hand page and the one on the right tells you the *last* headword on the right-hand page.

2. Swung dashes

2.1 A swung dash (~) replaces the entire headword when the headword is repeated within an entry:

sly kyohwarhan 교활한; ***on the*** ~ nam mollae saltchak 남 몰래 살짝

Here ***on the*** ~ means ***on the sly***.

2.2 When a headword changes form in an entry, for example if it is put in the past tense or in the plural, then the past tense or plural ending is added to the swung dash - but only if the rest of the word doesn't change:

fluster *v/t* tanghwanghage hada 당황하게 하다; ***get ~ed*** tanghwanghada 당황하다

But:

horrify: ***I was horrified*** ch'unggyŏktchŏgiŏssŏyo 충격적이었어요

♦**come back** toraoda 돌아오다; ***it came back to me*** tashi saenggangnassŏ 다시 생각났어

2.3 Headwords made up of two, or sometimes three, words are replaced by a single swung dash:

♦**hold on** *v/i* (*wait*) kidarida 기다리다; TELEC kkŭntchiank'o it-tta 끊지않고 있다; ***now ~ a minute!*** chamkkanman kidaryŏ poseyo! 잠깐만 기다려 보세요!

♦**come in on**: ~ ***a deal*** kŏraee ch'amgahada 거래에 참가하다

3. What do the different typefaces mean?

3.1 All Korean and English headwords and the Arabic numerals differentiating English parts of speech appear in **bold**:

alcoholic **1** *n* alk'o-ol chungdoktcha 알코올 중독자 **2** *adj* alk'o-olssŏng-ŭi 알코올성의

3.2 *italics* are used for:

a) abbreviated grammatical labels: *adj, adv, v/i, v/t* etc

b) all the indicating words which are the signposts pointing to the correct translation for your needs

mailbox (*in street*) uch'et'ong 우체통; (*of house*) up'yŏnham 우편함; COMPUT meilbakssŭ 메일박스

Thai 1 *adj* T'aegugŭi 태국의 **2** *n* (*person*) T'aegugin 태국인; (*language*) T'aegugŏ 태국어

serve 1 *n* (*in tennis*) sŏbŭ 서브 **2** *v/t food, meal* naeda 내다; *person, guests* shijungdŭlda 시중들다; *customer in shop* moshida 모시다; *one's country, the people* pongsahada 봉사하다

hwamulsshil 화물실 hold (*on ship, plane*)

yŏbo 여보 honey (*form of address to husband*)

3.3 All phrases (examples and idioms) are given in ***secondary bold italics***:

ch'aegim 책임 responsibility; accountability; ***...e ch'aegimi it-tta*** ...에 책임이 있다 be responsible for

knowledge chishik 지식; ***to the best of my ~*** naega algo itkkironŭn 내가 알고 있기로는; ***have a good ~ of*** ...e chŏngt'onghada ...에 정통하다

3.4 Normal typeface is used for the translations.

3.5 If a translation is given in italics, and not in the normal typeface, this means that the translation is more of an *explanation* in the other language and that an explanation has to be given because there is no real equivalent:

walk-up *n ellibeit'ŏga ŏmnŭn ap'at'ŭ* 엘리베이터가 없는 아파트

kkakttugi 깍두기 *spicy, pickled white radish*

4. What do the various symbols and abbreviations tell you?

4.1 A solid black lozenge is used to indicate a phrasal verb:

♦***auction* off** kyŏngmaehada 경매하다

4.2 A white lozenge ◊ is used to divide up longer entries into more easily digested chunks of related bits of text:

a, an ◊ (*no equivalent in Korean*): ***a book about Korea*** Han-guge kwanhan ch'aek 한국에 관한 책; ***he bought a car*** kŭnŭn ch'arŭl sassŏyo 그는 차를 샀어요 ◊ (*with a measure word*) hanaŭi 하나의, han 한; ***a cup of coffee*** k'ŏp'i han chan 커피 한 잔; ***five men and a woman*** tasŏt namjawa han yŏja 다섯 남자와 한 여자 ◊ (*per*) han 한; ***$50 a ride*** han pŏne 50tallŏ 한 번에 50달러; ***$15 a head*** han saram tang 15tallŏ 한 사람 당 15달러

It is also used, in the Korean-English dictionary, to split translations within an entry when the part of speech of each translation is different:

kŭndae 근대 modern times ◊ modern

kŏmsa 검사 examination (*of patient*); prosecutor ◊ exploratory

4.3 The abbreviation F tells you that the word or phrase is used colloquially rather than in formal contexts. The abbreviation V warns you that a word or phrase is vulgar or taboo. Be careful how you use these words. The abbreviation H means that the word is used to make yourself humble before the person you are speaking to.

4.4 A colon before an English or Korean word or phrase means that usage is restricted to this specific example (at least as far as this dictionary's choice of vocabulary is concerned):

accord: ***of one's own*** ~ chabaltchŏgŭro 자발적으로

shisok 시속: ***shisok 150mairŭi sokttoro*** 시속 150마일의 속도로 at a speed of 150 mph

4.5 The letters X and Y are used to indicate insertion points for other words if you are building a complete sentence in Korean, for example:

glue 1 *n* p'ul 풀 **2** *v/t* p'ullo puch'ida 풀로 붙이다; ~ ***X to Y*** Xŭl / rŭl Ye p'ullo puch'ida X을 / 를 Y에 풀로 붙이다

Suspension points (...) are used in a similar way:

♦ **major in** ...ŭl/rŭl chŏn-gonghada ...을 / 를 전공하다

5. Does the dictionary deal with grammar too?

5.1 All English headwords are given a part of speech label, unless, in normal modern English, the headword is only used as one part of speech and so no confusion or ambiguity is possible. In these cases no part of speech label is needed.

abolish p'yejihada 폐지하다

lastly majimagŭro 마지막으로

But:

glory *n* yŏnggwang 영광 (*n* given because 'glory' could be a verb)

own[1] *v/t* soyuhada 소유하다 (*v/t* given because 'own' is also an adjective)

5.2 Korean headwords are not given part of speech labels. Where their English translations are of more than one part of speech, these are separated by a white lozenge. For example:

Sŏyang 서양 the West ◊ Western

5.3 Where a Korean word has a grammatical function, this is illustrated:

...nŭn ...는 (*forms adjectives*): ***nurŏputtchiannŭn*** 눌어붙지 않는 nonstick

...rŭl ...를 *object particle*

...get... ...겠... shall (*indicates future tense, intention, or supposition*)

5.4 Particles

Particles such as **...rŭl** ...를, **...ŭl** ...을 or **...e** ...에 are included with translations in the English-Korean half of the dictionary:

correspond ... ~ ***to*** ...e haedanghada ...에 해당하다

♦**count on** ...ege kidaeda ...에게 기대다

infer: ~ ***X from Y*** Yesŏ Xŭl / rŭl ch'uronhada Y에서 X을 / 를 추론하다

This shows you the ending that is needed when you are building a sentence in Korean.

Some particle endings have more than one version. For example, **ŭl** is used after consonants and **rŭl** after vowels.

These particles are mostly omitted on the Korean-English side of the dictionary.

6. hada 하다

In the English-Korean dictionary an appropriate form of the verb **hada** 하다 'to do' is used to mark the insertion point for any verb that would be used in a real sentence. For example:

when... **2** *conj* ...hal ttae ...할 때

about ... ***be ~ to ...*** mak ...haryŏgo hada 막 ...하려고 하다

can[1] ◊ (*ability*) ...hal su it-tta ...할 수 있다

These forms are used to show a general structure, which, in a particular example, may become, say:

can you hear me? nae marŭl tŭrŭl su issŏyo? 내 말을 들을 수 있어요?

In the Korean-English part of the dictionary, the verb **hada** is removed in such cases and only the element which would be common to any verbal insertion is left:

ttae ... ***-l ttae*** -ㄹ때 when

su 수: ***...l su it-tta*** ...ㄹ 수 있다 can; ***...l su ŏptta*** ...ㄹ 수 없다 cannot

7. English adjectives and Korean descriptive verbs

In general the English-Korean dictionary will give an adjectival form that corresponds to an English adjective. For example:

pretty yeppŭn 예쁜

In Korean these adjectives are formed from "descriptive verbs". The form of the descriptive verb that corresponds to an English adjective is made by adding **n** ㄴ to the verb stem:

yeppŭ 예쁘 + ㄴ = 예쁜 pretty

Where in English "is pretty" is formed from the verb "be" + the adjective "pretty", in Korean it is formed by the single descriptive verb **yeppŭda** 예쁘다 be pretty.

that little girl is wearing a very pretty hat
chŏ chagŭn yŏja aiga aju yeppŭn mojarŭl ssŏssŏyo
저 작은 여자 아이가 아주 예쁜 모자를 썼어요

those flowers are really pretty
저꽃이 참 예뻐요
chŏ kkoch'i ch'am yeppŏyo

Korean personal pronouns

As a result of Confucian cultural influence on Korean society and language, personal pronouns and the way in which they are used in Korean reflect a concern for relative seniority and status. There is a large variety of forms of pronouns. The following table provides a basic outline (but is not exhaustive).

	I	you	she / he
plain	na / nae 나 / 내	nŏ / ne 너 / 네	i / kŭ / chŏ saram 이 / 그 / 저 사람
humble	chŏ / che 저 / 제		
honorific		sŏnsaeng(nim) 선생(님); tangshin 당신	i- / kŭ- / chŏ-bun 이 / 그 / 저분

	we	you	they
plain	uri 우리	nŏhŭi(dŭl) 너희(들)	i / kŭ / chŏ saramdŭl 이 / 그 / 저 사람들
humble	chŏhŭi(dŭl) 저희(들)		
honorific		sŏnsaeng(nim)dŭl 선생(님)들	i- / kŭ- / chŏ-bundŭl 이 / 그 / 저분들

I

When referring to oneself before equals and juniors the plain form **na** 나 may be used (**nae** 내 with the subject particle **ka** 가). When speaking to an older person or someone in seniority, the humble term **chŏ** 저 is used (**che** 제 with the subject particle **ka** 가).

You (singular)

The term **nŏ** 너 (**ne** 네 with the subject particle **ka** 가) may only be used by adults to young children, by older siblings to younger siblings or between intimate friends.

Although **tangshin 당신** is considered a respectful form of you, its use is somewhat restricted and it should definitely not be used when speaking to older people. Koreans generally avoid using *you* when speaking to people with whom they are not familiar and address each other with appropriate titles such as **sŏnsaengnim 선생님** (sir, a polite form), **ajŏsshi 아저씨** (used to address men), **ajumma 아줌마** (used to address women), **samonim 사모님** (madam, a polite form), and so on. Actual job titles can also be used as a form of address together with the honorific ending **nim 님**. For instance you could address someone as 'doctor, taxi-driver, professor, manager etc'.

She / he

These forms are not really simple pronouns but a combination of the demonstrative forms **i 이** (this), **kŭ 그** (that), and **chŏ 저** (that over there) and the words **saram 사람** (person) and **pun 분** (*respectful* person). The terms **i 이**, **kŭ 그**, and **chŏ 저** may also be used with other words such as **yŏja 여자** (woman), **agasshi 아가씨** (young lady), **ajŏsshi 아저씨** (uncle) and so on to form alternative equivalents to *she/he* in English. They may also be used with the word **kŏt 것** (thing) to form the demonstrative pronouns *this*, *that*, and *that over there*. The terms **kŭnŭn 그는** and **kŭnyŏnŭn 그녀는** are also used in written Korean to indicate *he* and *she* respectively.

We

Korean also uses **uri 우리** and derivatives where English uses *I* or *my* etc:

uri abŏji 우리 아버지 my father (literally: our father)

This reflects the tendency for Koreans to emphasize the group over the individual.

You (plural)

The same as *you* (singular) with the addition of the plural suffix **-dŭl 들**. The same restrictions on usage also apply.

They

The same as *she/he* with the addition of the plural suffix **-dul 들**.

Finally, it is important to remember that, in Korean, the subject of a sentence is often omitted, providing that context removes any ambiguity.

Here are some examples of the use and omission of personal pronouns in Korean:

ŏdi kaseyo?
어디가세요
where are you going? (*you* omitted)

hak-kkyo-e kassŏyo
학교에 갔어요
I / he / she / we / they went to school (subject omitted)

ajŏsshi, naeil Sŏure kaseyo?
아저씨, 내일 서울에 가세요?
are you going to Seoul tomorrow? (ajŏsshi used in place of *you*)

nega haenni?
네가 했니?
did you do it? (adult to a child; *it* omitted)

kŭbuni osyŏssŏyo
그분이 오셨어요
he came (use of the honorific form, showing respect)

kwajangnim, k'ŏp'i han chan hashigessŏyo?
과장님, 커피 한 잔 하시겠어요?
would you like a cup of coffee? (kwajangnim is a common title for a department manager)

The pronunciation of Korean

Vowels

ㅏ	a	as in c*a*t longer as in f*a*ther when coming at the end of a word or when coming before a syllable that starts with a vowel or a *y* (eg: **ch'uk'ayŏn 축하연**)
ㅓ	ŏ	a short *o* sound as in f*au*lt or the British pronunciation of n*o*t
ㅗ	o	a longer *o* sound as in *o*we
ㅜ	u	as in d*o*
ㅡ	ŭ	a short sound as in heav*e*n
ㅣ	i	a short *i* as in t*i*n longer as in s*ee* when coming at the end of a word or when coming before a syllable starting with a vowel or a *y* (eg: **p'iano 피아노**)
ㅐ	ae	as in b*ea*r or h*ai*ry but without any *r* sound
ㅔ	e	as in *e*delweiss
ㅑ	ya	as in *ya*m as in *ya*rd but without the *r* sound when it comes at the end of a word or before a vowel or before the letter *h*
ㅕ	yŏ	as in *Yo*rk but without the *r* sound
ㅛ	yo	as in *yo*del
ㅠ	yu	as in *you*
ㅒ	yae	as in *yea*h
ㅖ	ye	as in *Ya*le
ㅘ	wa	as in abatt*oi*r
ㅙ	wae	as in *wh*ere

ㅚ	oe	as in *way* but sometimes shorter as in *whe*n
ㅝ	wŏ	as in *wa*sh
ㅞ	we	as in *way*
ㅟ	wi	as in *wi*nd longer as in *wee* when coming at the end of a word or when coming before a syllable that starts with a vowel or a *y* (eg: **kwiyŏun 귀여운**)
ㅢ	ŭi	officially pronounced uh-ee; but Koreans often say this as in Y*a*le

Consonants

ㄱ	at the start and the end of a word	k	강 kang 시작 shijak	between a *k* and a *g*
	vowel + ㄱ + vowel	g	가구 kagu	
	ㄴ,ㄹ,ㅁ, ㅇ + ㄱ + vowel	g	설계도 sŏlgyedo	
ㄴ		n	나 na	
ㄷ	at the start and the end of a word	t	달 tal 곧 kot	between a *t* and a *d*
	vowel + ㄷ + vowel	d	바둑 paduk	
	ㄴ, ㄹ, ㅁ, ㅇ + ㄷ + vowel	d	날다 nalda	
ㄹ	at the start of a word	l	라디오 ladio	for loan words, it is between an *l* and an *r*; we have used an *l*
	at the end of a word	l	달 tal	
	vowel + ㄹ + vowel	r	사랑 sarang	
	ㄹ + consonant	l	물건 mulgŏn	
ㅁ		m	밤 pam	

→

ㅂ	at the start and the end of a word	p	보리 pori 밥 pap	between a *p* and a *b*
	vowel + ㅂ + vowel	b	아버지 abŏji	
	ㄴ, ㄹ, ㅁ, ㅇ + ㅂ + vowel	b	담배 tambae	
ㅅ		s	상표 sangp'yo	as in *s*aint
	ㅅ + ㅣ, ㅒ, ㅑ, ㅕ, ㅛ, ㅠ, ㅖ, ㅟ	sh	신 shin 섀시 shyaeshi 쉬다 shwida	
	at the end of a word	t	것 kŏt	
ㅇ	at the start of a word	silent	아버지 abŏji	a filler letter
	at the end of a word	ng	자랑 charang	as in you*ng*
ㅈ	at the start of a word	ch	자유 chayu	as in *j*ade but between a *ch* and a *j*
	at the end of a word	t	낮 nat	
	vowel + ㅈ + vowel	j	자주 chaju	
	ㄴ,ㄹ, ㅁ,ㅇ + ㅈ + vowel	j	반지 panji	
ㅊ		ch'	차 ch'a	as in *ch*urch but pronounced more strongly
	at the end of a word	t	닻 tat	
ㅋ		k'	코 k'o	as in *k*ing, but pronounced more strongly
	at the end of a word	k	부엌 puŏk	as in coo*k*

→

ㅌ		t'	타다 t'ada	as in *t*errace, but pronounced more strongly
	at the end of a word	t	논밭 nonbat	as in fla*t*
ㅍ		p'	파란 p'aran	as in *p*opstar, but pronounced more strongly
	at the end of a word	p	입 ip	as in hip
ㅎ	at the start of a word	h	하늘 hanŭl	as in *h*ello

The four consonants ch', k', t' and p' (known as aspirated consonants) are pronounced with a stronger puff of breath than their basic equivalents (ch, k, t and p). If you hold your palm in front of your face when speaking these consonants you should be able to feel your breath.

Double consonants

These are also known as 'tense consonants'. They are pronounced with more force than their single equivalents.

ㄲ	kk	깨다 kkaeda	as in book *k*eeper
ㄸ	tt	때 ttae	as in hit *t*en
ㅃ	pp	빠른 (pparŭn)	as in top *p*eople
ㅆ	ss	쌀 (ssal)	as in those *s*ongs
ㅉ	tch	짜르다 (tcharŭda)	as in that *j*udge

General notes on the pronunciation system

Double vowels are each given their full value. So, for example, **p'yeam** is pronounced 'p'yay-am' and **uul** is pronounced 'oo-ool'.

g is always as in *g*ive, not as in *g*in
s is always as in loo*s*e, not as in lo*s*e

There is no stress in Korean, so give equal weight to all syllables.

What is written and what is said

There are many combinations of Korean consonants or of

vowels plus consonants that, taken together, create a sound that is not reflected in the actual Korean script. So, for example, in:

관점 **kwantchŏm** point of view
the letter ㅈ (ch/j) is actually pronounced ㅉ (tch)

맞다 **mat-tta** be right
the letter ㄷ (t) is actually pronounced ㄸ (tt)

고압선용 철탑 **koapssŏnnyong ch'ŏlt'ap** electricity pylon
the letter 용 (yong) is actually pronounced 뇽 (nyong)

학교 **hak-kkyo** school
the letter ㄱ (k/g) is actually pronounced ㄲ (kk)

괴롭히다 **koerop'ida** trouble
the letter ㅂ (p/b) is actually pronounced ㅍ (p')

괜찮다 **kwaench'ant'a** be OK, be alright
the letters 찮 (ch'an) and 다 (ta) are actually pronounced ch'ant'a

The romanization system used in this dictionary reflects this feature of Korean pronunciation.

Abbreviations

adj	adjective
adv	adverb
ANAT	anatomy
BIO	biology
BOT	botany
Br	British English
CHEM	chemistry
COM	commerce, business
COMPUT	computers, IT term
conj	conjunction
EDU	education
ELEC	electricity, electronics
euph	euphemistic
F	familiar, colloquial
fig	figurative
FIN	financial
fml	formal usage
GRAM	grammar
H	humble, showing humility to the listener
hum	humorous
interj	interjection
LAW	law
MATH	mathematics
MED	medicine
MIL	military
MOT	motoring
MUS	music
n	noun
NAUT	nautical
pej	pejorative
PHOT	photography
PHYS	physics
POL	politics
prep	preposition
pron	pronoun
PSYCH	psychology
RAD	radio
RAIL	railroad
REL	religion
s.o.	someone
SP	sports
sth	something
TECH	technology
TELEC	telecommunications
THEA	theatre
TV	television
V	vulgar
v/i	intransitive verb
v/t	transitive verb
→	see
®	registered trademark

A

aak 아악 court music
abŏji 아버지 father
ach'i 아치 arch
ach'im 아침 morning; breakfast; ***ach'ime*** 아침에 in the morning; ***ach'imŭl mŏktta*** 아침을 먹다 have breakfast
ach'ŏm 아첨 flattery
ach'ŏmhada 아첨하다 flatter, butter up
ach'ŏmhanŭn 아첨하는 flattering
ach'ŏmkkun 아첨꾼 flatterer; yesman
adamhan 아담한 compact; small
adongbok 아동복 children's clothes
adŭl 아들 son; boy
aech'ŏroun 애처로운 pathetic; touching
aedo 애도 condolences
aeguk-kka 애국가 national anthem
aeguksshim 애국심 patriotism
aeguktcha 애국자 patriot
aeguktchŏgin 애국적인 patriotic
aehoga 애호가 fan; devotee; connoisseur; ***ch'a aehoga*** 차 애호가 avid tea drinker
aehohada 애호하다 be fond of
aein 애인 lover; sweetheart; boyfriend; girlfriend
aejijungjihada 애지중지하다 pamper
aejŏng 애정 affection, fondness
aejŏng-i innŭn 애정이 있는 loving
aek 액 fluid
aekch'e 액체 liquid
aekkŭlk'e hanŭn 애끓게 하는 heartbreaking
aekssellŏreit'ŏ 액셀러레이터 gas, accelerator
aekssellŏreit'ŏ p'edal 액셀러레이터 페달 gas pedal, accelerator
aektchŏng p'yoshi changch'i 액정 표시 장치 LCD, liquid crystal display
aelbŏm 앨범 (photograph) album
aemaehan 애매한 evasive
aemaemohohan 애매모호한 ambiguous; noncommittal
aemp'ŭ 앰프 amplifier
aemu 애무 caress
aemuhada 애무하다 caress; kiss; pet
aengk'ŏ 앵커 anchor man
aengmusae 앵무새 parrot
aengmyŏnkka 액면가 face value
aengmyŏn kŭmaek 액면 금액 denomination FIN
aenimeishyŏn 애니메이션 animation
aep'ŭt'ŏ shyeibŭ loshyŏn 애프터 셰이브 로션 aftershave
aep'ŭt'ŏ sŏbisŭ 애프터 서비스 after sales service
aerosahang 애로사항 bottleneck; logjam
aesŏk'ada 애석하다 be regrettable; ***...dani aesŏk'agunyo*** ...다니 애석하군요 it's a pity that ...
aessŭda 애쓰다 make an effort; ***kŭnyŏnŭn ihaeharyŏgo aessŏt-tta*** 그녀는 이해하려고 애썼다 she was struggling to understand; ***...gi wihae mopsshi aessŭda*** ...기 위해 몹시 애쓰다 take great pains to ...
aet'age parada 애타게 바라다 long for; ***muŏt hanŭn kŏsŭl aet'age parada*** 무엇 하는 것을 애타게 바라다 be longing to do sth
aet'ajŏgin 애타적인 altruistic
aet'onghan 애통한 tragic *voice*
aewandongmul 애완동물 pet (*animal*)
aeyong 애용 patronage, custom
agami 아가미 gill
agasshi 아가씨 ma'am; miss (*unmarried woman*)
agi 아기 baby
agŏ 악어 alligator; crocodile
agŭi 악의 ill will; malice
agŭiga ŏmnŭn 악의가 없는 inoffensive

agŭi innŭn 악의 있는 malevolent; malicious
agŭi-ŏmnŭn kŏjinmal 악의없는 거짓말 white lie
agun 악운 bad luck; devil's own luck
agyong 악용 abuse
ahop 아홉 nine
ahop pŏntchaeŭi 아홉 번째의 ninth
ahŭn 아흔 ninety
ahŭn pŏntchaeŭi 아흔 번째의 nintieth
ai 아이 child, kid
aiemep'ŭ 아이엠에프 IMF
aik'on 아이콘 icon COMPUT
aik'yu 아이큐 IQ
Aillaendŭ 아일랜드 Ireland ◊ Irish
airainŏ 아이라이너 eyeliner
airisŭ 아이리스 iris BOT
airŏni 아이러니 irony
aishyaedou 아이섀도우 eyeshadow
aishyop'inghada 아이쇼핑하다 go window-shopping
aisŭ hak'i 아이스 하키 (ice) hockey
aisŭ k'eik'ŭ 아이스 케이크 Popsicle®, ice lolly
aisŭ k'ŏp'i 아이스 커피 iced coffee
aisŭ k'ŭrim 아이스 크림 ice cream
aisŭ k'ŭrim kage 아이스 크림 가게 ice-cream parlor
aisŭ pakssŭ 아이스 박스 icebox, refrigerator
ajaeng 아쟁 (seven-stringed) zither
ajang-ajang kŏt-tta 아장아장 걷다 toddle
...ajida ...아지다 become ..., get ...
ajik 아직 yet, so far; ***kŭ saramŭn yŏgi wassŏyo? – ajik*** 그 사람은 여기 왔어요? – 아직 is he here yet? – not yet
ajiktto 아직도 still, even now
ajirang-i 아지랑이 haze
ajŏsshi 아저씨 uncle (*friendly form of address for men who are not actually related*)
aju 아주 extremely, very; completely
aju choŭn 아주 좋은 amazing, excellent
aju manŭn 아주 많은 a huge amount of
ajumma 아줌마 aunt (*friendly form of address for women who are not actually related*)
ajumoni 아주머니 *polite form of* ***ajumma***
ak 악 evil; vice
akch'wi 악취 stench
akdan 악단 band, group
akkaptta 아깝다 be regrettable
akkida 아끼다 stint on, be mean with; hold dear; ***noryŏgŭl akkiji ant'a*** 노력을 아끼지 않다 be unstinting in one's efforts
ak-kki 악기 (musical) instrument
ak-kkiŭi ŭmŭl match'uda 악기의 음을 맞추다 tune up
akkyŏ ssŭda 아껴 쓰다 stretch, eke out
akppo 악보 sheet music, score
akssent'ŭ 악센트 accent, stress
akssŏng-ŭi 악성의 malignant *tumor*
akssu 악수 handshake
akssuhada 악수하다 shake hands
aktchang 악장 movement MUS
aktchŏn kot'u 악전 고투 struggle, hard time
akttang 악당 villain, scoundrel
ak'ada 악하다 be evil; be immoral
ak'wa 악화 decline, worsening
ak'wadoeda 악화되다 deteriorate; decline, get worse (*of health*)
ak'washik'ida 악화시키다 aggravate
al 알 egg
alda 알다 know; understand, see; appreciate, acknowledge; be aware of; ***naega algo itkkironŭn*** 내가 알고 있기로는 to the best of my knowledge; ***naega al pa anida*** 내가 알 바 아니다 for all I care; ***naega alkke mwŏya!*** 내가 알게 뭐야! I don't give a damn!; ***naega anŭn han*** 내가 아는 한 as far as I know; ***naega anŭn paronŭn*** 내가 아는 바로는 for all I know
algaeng-i 알갱이 grain (*of rice*); ***chagŭn algaeng-i*** 작은 알갱이 granule
algi shwiun 알기 쉬운 clear, lucid
alk'o-ol 알코올 alcohol
alk'o-ol chungdoktcha 알코올 중독자 alcoholic
alk'o-olssŏng-ŭi 알코올성의 alcoholic

alk'oori ŏmnŭn 알코올이 없는 nonalcoholic
allak 안락 comfort
allak'an 안락한 comfortable
allakssa 안락사 euthanasia
allakssa shik'ida 안락사 시키다 put away, put down *animal*
allak ŭija 안락 의자 armchair
allanggŏrinŭn 알랑거리는 slimy, smarmy
allerŭgi 알레르기 allergy; ***...e allerŭgi panŭng-i it-tta*** ...에 알레르기 반응이 있다 be allergic to
allibai 알리바이 alibi
allida 알리다 inform
allim 알림 announcement
alluminyum 알루미늄 aluminum
allyak 알약 tablet
allyŏjida 알려지다 break, become known
allyŏjin 알려진 noted
allyŏjuda 알려주다 inform; ***Xege Yrŭl allyŏjuda*** X에게 Y를 알려주다 inform X of Y
allyŏjum 알려줌 hint
almajŭn 알맞은 proper, fitting
almat-tta 알맞다 be proper, be fitting
almomŭi 알몸의 nude
alp'abesŭi 알파벳의 alphabetical
alp'abet 알파벳 alphabet
am 암 cancer
ama 아마 probably; perhaps
amach'uŏ 아마추어 layman; amateur
amado 아마도 perhaps, maybe; probably; presumably
amch'o 암초 reef
amdamhan 암담한 dark, grim
Amerik'a 아메리카 America ◊ American
Amerik'a Haptchungguk 아메리카 합중국 United States (of America)
Amerik'ain 아메리카인 American
amgihada 암기하다 memorize
amho 암호 password
amhŭk 암흑 darkness, blackness
amhŭk-kka 암흑가 underworld (*criminal*)
Amit'abul 아미타불 Amitabha Buddha
amk'ae 암캐 bitch (*dog*)
amk'ŏt 암컷 female (*animal, plant*)
ammal 암말 mare
ammŏri 앞머리 fringe (*hair*)
ammun 앞문 front door
amnae 암내 body odor
amnyang 암양 ewe
amnyŏgŭl kahada 압력을 가하다 pressure, force
amnyŏk 압력 pressure
amnyŏk tanch'e 압력 단체 pressure group, lobby
amnyu 압류 seizure, impounding
amnyuhada 압류하다 seize, impound
amnyuri 앞유리: (***chadongch'a***) ***amnyuri*** (자동차) 앞유리 windshield
amondŭ 아몬드 almond
amp'yosang 암표상 scalper
amsae 암새 hen (*of bird*)
amsal 암살 assassination
amsalbŏm 암살범 assassin
amsalttan 암살단 hit squad
amsan 암산 mental arithmetic
amsarhada 암살하다 assassinate
amshi 암시 pointer; hint
amshihada 암시하다 imply; point to; indicate
amshijang 암시장 black market
amso 암소 cow
amssasŭm 암사슴 doe
amt'ak 암탉 hen (*of chicken*)
amt'waeji 암퇘지 sow
amu 아무 any; none; anyone; so-and-so; ***amu ch'yok'ollitto*** 아무 쵸콜릿도 (+ *negative verb*) none of the chocolate; ***amu kŏktchŏng ŏmnŭn*** 아무 걱정 없는 carefree
amudo 아무도 (+ *negative verb*) nobody
amu ...do 아무 ...도 (+ *negative verb*) any ...at all; ***amu saenggaktto ŏpsshi*** 아무 생각도 없이 without any thought at all; ***kŭnŭn amu yŏngojado ŏptta*** 그는 아무 연고자도 없다 he doesn't have any family
amugae 아무개 so-and-so; any person
amugaemunja 아무개문자 wildcard character COMPUT
amu kŏt 아무 것 (+ *negative verb*) nothing, not any
amu kot 아무 곳 anywhere

amuri 아무리: ***amuri k'ŭda / puyuhada hadŏrado*** 아무리 크다 / 부유하다 하더라도 however big / rich they are
amurŏk'e 아무렇게 in whatever way
amurŏk'ena hanŭn 아무렇게나 하는 offhand
amurŏn 아무런 any; ***amurŏn chuŭirŭl haji ant'a*** 아무런 주의를 하지 않다 not take any notice of
amu ttae 아무 때 any time; ***chŏnŭn amu ttaerado chossŭmnida*** 저는 아무 때라도 좋습니다 any time is alright with me
amut'ŭn 아무튼 anyway
an 안 inside; ***...(ŭ)ro anŭl taeda*** ...(으)로 안을 대다 line with; insulate with
an... 안 ... (*negating particle*): ***wae hak-kkyoe anwassŏyo?*** 왜 학교에 안왔어요? why didn't you come to school?
anae 아내 wife
anaewŏn 안내원 tour operator
anallogŭ 아날로그 analog
ana ollida 안아 올리다 scoop up
anaunsŏ 아나운서 announcer
anbu 안부 (kind) regards; ***Minaege anbu chŏnhae chuseyo*** 민아에게 안부 전해주세요 give my regards to Mina
ando 안도 relief; ***andoŭi hansumŭl shwida*** 안도의 한숨을 쉬다 heave a sigh of relief
andwaetkkunyo! 안됐군요! what a pity!; ***kŭ yŏjaga andwaetkkunyo*** 그 여자가 안됐군요 I feel sorry for her
...ane ...안에 in; ***tu shigan ane*** 두 시간 안에 in two hours (from now)
anemone 아네모네 snowdrop
...anesŏ ...안에(서) in
an-gae 안개 fog
an-gae kkin 안개 낀 foggy; misty
anggap'ŭmŭl hada 앙갚음을 하다 pay back, get even with
angk'orŭ 앙코르 encore
angma 악마 devil, demon
angmong 악몽 nightmare
angmulda 악물다 clench
angmyŏng nop'ŭn 악명 높은 infamous, notorious
an-gwa ŭisa 안과 의사 ophthalmologist
an-gyŏng 안경 glasses
an-gyŏngsang 안경상 optician
anida 아니다 be not; no; ***igŏshi anira chŏgŏt*** 이것이 아니라 저것 not this one, that one; ***usŭl iri anida*** 웃을 일이 아니다 it's not funny
anihage nak-kkwanjŏgin saenggak 안이하게 낙관적인 생각 wishful thinking
anikkoun saram 아니꼬운 사람 creep, jerk
anin 아닌 no
anio 아니오 no
anjang 안장 saddle
anjŏlbujŏl mot'ada 안절부절 못하다 be in a flap; get the jitters; fidget
anjŏlbujŏl mot'anŭn 안절부절 못하는 jittery; uptight
anjŏn 안전 safety
anjŏnbelt'ŭ 안전벨트 safety belt
anjŏngdoeda 안정되다 stabilize, steady, become stable
anjŏngdoen 안정된 stable, balanced
anjŏngshik'ida 안정시키다 stabilize, steady, make stable
anjŏngssŏng 안정성 stability
anjŏn-gun 안전군 security forces
anjŏng yoppŏp 안정 요법 rest cure
anjŏnhada 안전하다 be safe; be secure
anjŏnhage 안전하게 safely
anjŏnhage hada 안전하게 하다 secure, make safe
anjŏnhaji anŭn 안전하지 않은 unsafe
anjŏnhan 안전한 safe, secure
anjŏn helmet 안전 헬멧 crash helmet
anjŏnp'in 안전핀 safety pin
anjŏnssŏng 안전성 safety, security
anjŏnŭl saenggak'anŭn 안전을 생각하는 safety-conscious
anjŏn usŏn 안전 우선 safety first
ankkam 안감 lining
anma 안마 massage
anmadang 안마당 courtyard
anmahada 안마하다 massage
anmasa 안마사 masseur; masseuse
anmogi nop'ŭn 안목이 높은

discerning
anmu 안무 choreography
anmuga 안무가 choreographer
annae 안내 directions, guidance
annaech'aektcha 안내책자 handbook
annaehada 안내하다 direct, guide
annaeja 안내자 guide; usher
annaesŏ 안내서 guide(book)
annae tesŭk'ŭ 안내 데스크 reception desk
annaewŏn 안내원 courier
annyŏng 안녕 hello, hi; goodbye, so long
annyŏnghaseyo 안녕하세요 good morning; good afternoon; good evening
annyŏnghi chumushipsshiyo 안녕히 주무십시요 good night
annyŏnghi chumusyŏssŏyo 안녕히 주무셨어요 good morning (*on waking up*)
annyŏnghi kaseyo 안녕히 가세요 goodbye (*polite*, *to person leaving*)
annyŏnghi kyeseyo 안녕히 계세요 goodbye (*polite*, *to person staying*)
anppang 안방 master bedroom; living room
ansaek 안색 coloring, complexion
anshikch'ŏ 안식처 haven
anshim 안심 peace of mind; relief
anshimhada 안심하다 feel easy; feel safe
anshimhanŭn 안심하는 secure
anshimshik'ida 안심시키다 reassure
anshingnyŏn 안식년 sabbatical
ansŏng match'umŭi 안성 맞춤의 tailor-made *fig*
antchŏgŭro 안쪽으로 inward
antchoge(sŏ) 안쪽에(서) in back, out the back
antchok 안쪽 inside, nearside
antchok kil 안쪽 길 inside lane
antchuin 안주인 hostess
antchumŏni 안주머니 inside pocket
antta 안다 hug
antta 앉다 sit, sit down; settle, alight
anttŭl 안뜰 courtyard, quadrangle
ant'a 않다 be not; do not; ***...e ikssuk'aji ant'a*** ...에 익숙하지 않다 not be familiar with
ant'ena 안테나 antenna
anŭi 안의 internal
anŭk'an 아늑한 cozy, snug
anŭn ch'e hanŭn saram 아는 체 하는 사람 know-it-all
anŭro 안으로 inside, indoors ◊ into
ap 앞 front
apch'ukttoen 압축된 compact
apch'uk'ada 압축하다 compress; condense
appa 아빠 dad, pop
appak'ada 압박하다 oppress
appubun 앞부분 opening, beginning
app'in 압핀 thumbtack
ap sŏn 앞 선 advanced
apssŏ kada 앞서 가다 lead the way, lead
apssŭng 압승 landslide victory
apssuhada 압수하다 confiscate
aptchang sŏda 앞장 서다 lead on, go ahead
aptchehada 압제하다 tyrannize
aptchŏng 압정 tack
...aptchoge(sŏ) ...앞쪽에(서) before; in front of, at the front of
aptchogŭi 앞쪽의 front
aptchul 앞줄 front row
aptchwasŏk sŭnggaek 앞좌석 승객 front seat passenger
apttodanghada 압도당하다 dazzle; overwhelm
apttohada 압도하다 dominate; overwhelm
apttohanŭn 압도하는 devastating
apttwiro 앞뒤로 back and forth, to and fro
ap'ahada 아파하다 be in pain; ***ap'asŏ momŭl kuburida*** 아파서 몸을 구부리다 double up in pain; ***ap'ayo?*** 아파요? is it sore?; ***momi ap'ayo?*** 몸이 아파요? are you ill?
ap'at'ŭ 아파트 apartment
ap'at'ŭ tanji 아파트 단지 apartment block
ap'e 앞에 be ahead of
ap'e(sŏ) 앞에(서) in front; at the front
ap'i poiji annŭn 앞이 보이지 않는 blind *corner*
ap'ŭda 아프다 ache, hurt

Ap'ŭganisŭt'an 아프가니스탄 Afghanistan ◊ Afghan
ap'ŭi 앞의 preceding
ap'ŭm 아픔 ache, pain; discomfort
ap'ŭn 아픈 sick; painful, sore
Ap'ŭrik'a 아프리카 Africa ◊ African
Ap'ŭrik'a saram 아프리카 사람 African
ap'ŭro 앞으로 forward; onward
arabia suttcha 아라비아 숫자 digit; Arabic numbers
Arabin 아랍인 Arab
Arabŏ 아랍어 Arabic (*language*)
araboda 알아보다 check; check out; recognize, identify
arabol su innŭn 알아볼 수 있는 recognizable; discernible
arach'aeda 알아채다 notice; take note of; detect; sense; spot
arach'arida 알아차리다 perceive; become aware of; interpret
arae 아래 the lower part ◊ under, below
araech'ŭng-ŭi 아래층의 downstairs
araech'ung-e(sŏ) 아래층에(서) downstairs
...araee(sŏ) ...아래에(서) below, under; lower than
araetchogŭro 아래쪽으로 down, downward
araet saram 아랫 사람 subordinate
araet-tchoge(sŏ) 아랫쪽에(서) below
arae-ŭi 아래의 subordinate
aranaeda 알아내다 find out; identify
ara nuwŏ it-tta 앓아 누워 있다 be confined to one's bed
ara tŭt-tta 알아 듣다 catch, hear
Arŭhent'ina 아르헨티나 Argentina ◊ Argentinian
arŭmdaptta 아름답다 be beautiful
arŭmdaum 아름다움 beauty
arŭmdaun 아름다운 beautiful, lovely; fond *memories*
arŭn-gŏrida 아른거리다 shimmer
aryak 알약 pill
Ashia 아시아 Asia ◊ Asian
Ashiain 아시아인 Asian
asŭp'alt'ŭ 아스팔트 asphalt, pavement
asŭp'aragŏsŭ 아스파라거스 asparagus
asŭp'irin 아스피린 aspirin
asurajang 아수라장 pandemonium
ausŏng 아우성 outcry
...aya handa ...아야 한다 have to, must; be bound to
...ayaman hada ...아야만 하다 have (got) to; should, must
ayŏn 아연 zinc

CH

cha 자 ruler
chaa 자아 self; ego
chabach'aeda 잡아채다 snatch; pull away
chabadangginŭn kori 잡아당기는 고리 ring-pull
chabaek 자백 confession
chabaek'ada 자백하다 confess
chabaltchŏgin 자발적인 spontaneous; voluntary
chabaltchŏgŭro 자발적으로 of one's own accord
chabamŏktta 잡아먹다 prey on, feed on; absorb
chabang 자방 ovary (*of plant, flower*)
chaba ppoptta 잡아 뽑다 pull up *plant*
chaba tanggida 잡아 당기다 pull; tug, haul
chaba t'ada 잡아 타다 catch *bus etc*
chabi 자비 mercy
chabiroun 자비로운 merciful
chabon 자본 capital, money
chabon chŭngga 자본 증가 capital growth
chabon-ga 자본가 capitalist
chabonjuŭi 자본주의 capitalism
chabonjuŭija 자본주의자 capitalist, believer in capitalism
chabonjuŭijŏk 자본주의적 capitalist
chabushim 자부심 ego, self-esteem
chach'aek 자책 remorse
chach'i 자치 autonomy
chach'wi 자취 mark, trace
chach'wi-rŭl kamch'uda 자취를 감추다 disappear, run away
chada 자다 sleep; drop (*of wind*)
chadong 자동 automatic movement; intransitivity ◊ automatic
chadong chŏmmyŏl changch'i 자동 점멸 장치 flasher, direction indicator
chadong chojong changch'i 자동 조종 장치 autopilot
chadongch'a 자동차 automobile; motor vehicle
chadongch'a haengnyŏl 자동차 행렬 motorcade
chadongch'a sanŏp 자동차 산업 automobile industry
chadongch'a suriso 자동차 수리소 garage (*for repairs*)
chadonghwa 자동화 automation
chadonghwahada 자동화하다 automate
chadongkigye 자동기계 automatic
chadong ondo chojŏl changch'i 자동 온도 조절 장치 thermostat
chadong p'anmaegi 자동 판매기 vending machine
chadongsa 자동사 intransitive verb
chadong sohwa changch'i 자동 소화 장치 sprinkler
chadong taech'e 자동 대체 banker's order
chadong-ŭngdapkki 자동응답기 answerphone
chadong-ŭro 자동으로 automatically
chadu 자두 plum
chae 재 ash; ashes
chaebaech'ihada 재배치하다 relocate
chaebaeyŏrhada 재배열하다 rearrange
chaebal 재발 relapse
chaebangmun 재방문 follow-up visit
chaebangsong 재방송 repeat, rerun
chaebarhada 재발하다 recur
chaebarhanŭn 재발하는 recurrent
chaebŏl 재벌 conglomerate
chaebongsa 재봉사 tailor
chaebongt'ŭl 재봉틀 sewing machine
chaebongt'ŭllo paktta 재봉틀로 박다 machine
chaech'aegi 재채기 sneeze
chaech'aegihada 재채기하다 sneeze

chaech'ep'ohada 재체포하다 recapture
chaech'i 재치 tact; wit; witticism
chaech'i innŭn 재치 있는 tactful; quickwitted; witty
chaech'i innŭn mal 재치 있는 말 quip
chaech'i ŏmnŭn 재치 없는 tactless
chaech'ŏng 재청 encore
chaech'ok'ada 재촉하다 hurry up
chaeda 재다 take *temperature*
chaedan 재단 foundation, organization
chaegae 재개 renewal
chaegaebarhada 재개발하다 redevelop
chaegaehada 재개하다 renew, resume
chaegaejanghada 재개장하다 reopen
chaegal 재갈 gag; ***chaegarŭl mullida*** 재갈을 물리다 gag
chaegŏmt'o 재검토 review (*of situation*)
chaegŏmt'ohada 재검토하다 review *situation*
chaegŏnhada 재건하다 reconstruct
chaegŏrae 재거래 repeat business
chaego chŏngni seil 재고 정리 세일 clearance sale
chaegohada 재고하다 reconsider
chaego josa 재고 조사 stocktaking
chaegŭro mirŏ ollida 잭으로 밀어 올리다 jack up
chaegyoyuk kwajŏng 재교육 과정 refresher course
chaehae 재해 disaster
chaehae chiyŏk 재해 지역 disaster area
Chaehŏnjŏl 재헌절 Constitution Day
chaehoe 재회 reunion
chaehoehada 재회하다 reunite
chaehonhada 재혼하다 remarry
chaehyŏnhada 재현하다 reproduce; reconstruct *crime*; return (*of doubts etc*)
chaeil kyop'o 재일 교포 Korean resident in Japan
chaemi kyop'o 재미 교포 Korean resident in the USA
chaejalgŏrida 재잘거리다 yap
chaejin 재진 follow-up visit
chaejŏng 재정 finance ◊ financial
chaejŏngga 재정가 financier
chaejŏngnihada 재정리하다 readjust; reschedule; rearrange
chaejŏgŭnghada 재적응하다 readjust (*to conditions*)
chaejŭ 재즈 jazz
chaeju nŏmkki 재주 넘기 somersault
chaeju nŏmtta 재주 넘다 somersault
chaejurŭl purida 재주를 부리다 juggle; deal with
chaek 잭 jack (*for car, in cards*)
chaek'it 재킷 jacket
chaem 잼 conserve; jelly
chaemi 재미 fun, amusement
chaemiinnŭn 재미있는 amusing, entertaining; interesting
chaemiinnŭn saram 재미있는 사람 clown, joker
chaemi ŏmnŭn 재미없는 uninteresting
chaemiro 재미로 for fun, for kicks
chaemok 재목 lumber
Chaemubu 재무부 Ministry of Finance
Chaemujanggwan 재무장관 Secretary of the Treasury
chaemujanghada 재무장하다 rearm
chaemul 재물 worldly goods
Chaemusŏng 재무성 Treasury Department
chaengban 쟁반 tray
chaenggi 쟁기 plow
chaengtchŏm 쟁점 issue, matter
chaeng-ŭi 쟁의 dispute
chaenŭng 재능 flair, talent
chaenŭng-innŭn 재능있는 talented
chaeŏjida 재어지다 measure
chaeppalli 재빨리 quickly, swiftly
chaepparŭge tolda 재빠르게 돌다 spin around
chaepparŭn 재빠른 agile, nimble
chaepssage umjigida 잽싸게 움직이다 move quickly, zap along
chaep'an 재판 judgment LAW; reprint; ***Xŭl / rŭl chaep'ane kŏlda*** X을 / 를 재판에 걸다 take X to court
chaep'anhada 재판하다 judge; try LAW; reprint

chaep'ojanghada 재포장하다 resurface
chaep'yŏnsŏng 재편성 reorganization
chaep'yŏnsŏnghada 재편성하다 reorganize
chaeryang 재량 discretion; ***tangshinŭi chaeryang-ŭro*** 당신의 재량으로 at your discretion
chaeryo 재료 ingredient; material
chaesaeng 재생 replay, playback; reproduction
chaesaeng iyong 재생 이용 recycling
chaesaeng iyonghada 재생 이용하다 recycle
chaesaengshik 재생식 reproduction; breeding
chaesaengshik'ada 재생식하다 reproduce; breed
chaesaengshik'anŭn 재생식하는 reproductive
chaesan 재산 means; possessions; assets
chaesangyŏnghada 재상영하다 rerun
chaesan kwalli sangt'aee noyŏ itta 재산 관리 상태에 놓여 있다 be in receivership
chaesayonghada 재사용하다 reuse
chaesayong-i kanŭnghan 재사용이 가능한 reusable
chaeshihap 재시합 replay
chaeshihap'ada 재시합하다 replay
chaesuŏmnŭn saram 재수없는 사람 jinx (*person*)
chaesuŏpkkun! 재수없군! hard luck!
chaettŏri 재떨이 ashtray
chaet'onghap'ada 재통합하다 reunite
chaet'ujahada 재투자하다 reinvest, plow back
chaewŏjuda 재워주다 put up
chaewŏn 재원 financial resources
chaga chejak yŏnghwa 자가 제작 영화 home movie
chagae 자개 mother-of-pearl
chagae changshik 자개 장식 mother-of-pearl inlay
chagajida 작아지다 grow smaller; ***chŏmjŏm chagajida*** 점점 작아지다 dwindle
chagal 자갈 gravel; shingle; pebble; gravestone
chagayong unjŏnsa 자가용 운전사 chauffeur
chagi 자기 china (*pottery*); honey, darling; magnetism ◊ magnetic
chagi chabon 자기 자본 equity capital
chagi chashin 자기 자신 oneself
chagi chungshimŭi 자기 중심의 egocentric
chagi kŭrŭt 자기 그릇 china (*material*)
chagi manjok 자기 만족 complacency
chagi manjoktchŏgin 자기 만족적인 complacent
chagi maŭmdaerohada 자기 마음대로 하다 have one's (own) way
chagi pang-ŏ 자기 방어 self-defense
chagi ponwiŭi 자기 본위의 self-centered
chagi pulsshin 자기 불신 self-doubt
chagi sŏnjŏn-ga 자기 선전가 exhibitionist
chagi suyang 자기 수양 self-discipline
chagiya! 자기야! darling!
chagŏp inbu 작업 인부 workman
chagŏp kongjŏngdo 작업 공정도 flowchart
chagŏpsshil 작업실 studio
chagŏptchang 작업장 workshop
chagŏpttae 작업대 work bench
chagŏp yŏn-gu 작업 연구 work study
chagŭk 자극 spur, incentive
chagŭk'ada 자극하다 rouse, stimulate; spur on; arouse
chagŭk'anŭn 자극하는 provocative; controversial; pungent
chagŭktchŏgin 자극적인 electric *atmosphere*; stimulating; provocative, alluring; sharp *taste*
chagŭm 자금 fund
chagŭmahan 자그마한 diminutive; insignificant
chagŭm chiwŏnŭl hada 자금 지원을 하다 finance

chagŭm pujogŭro pullihan 자금 부족으로 불리한 underfunded
chagŭmsŏng 자금성 forbidden city
chagŭmŭl taeda 자금을 대다 bankroll
chagŭn 작은 little, small; low
chaguk 자국 mark, trace; one's own country; ***chagugŭl naeda*** 자국을 내다 mark, stain; ***nullŏ tchigŭn chaguk*** 눌러 찍은 자국 imprint
chagumnong 자급농 subsistence farmer
chagung 자궁 uterus, womb
chagung chŏkch'ulssul 자궁 적출술 hysterectomy
chagungam kŏmsa 자궁암 검사 cervical smear
chagungnada 자국나다 mark, become stained
chagyŏgi innŭn 자격이 있는 eligible
chagyŏgi ŏmnŭn 자격이 없는 ineligible; unqualified
chagyŏgŭl chuda 자격을 주다 entitle, qualify
chagyŏgŭl ŏt-tta 자격을 얻다 qualify
chagyŏk 자격 qualification; ***...l chagyŏgi it-tta*** ...ㄹ 자격이 있다 be qualified to ...; ***tongdŭnghan / tarŭn chagyŏgida*** 동등한 / 다른 자격이다 be on the same / a different footing
chagyŏktchŭng 자격증 certificate
chagyŏktchŭng-i innŭn 자격증이 있는 qualified
chagyong 작용 action; operation; function
chahoesa 자회사 subsidiary; wholly owned subsidiary
chainhada 자인하다 acknowledge, admit; ***choerŭl chainhada*** 죄를 자인하다 incriminate oneself
chainhanŭn 자인하는 self-confessed
chajangga 자장가 lullaby
chaje 자제 self-control
chajehada 자제하다 control oneself, restrain oneself
chajehanŭn 자제하는 lowkey
chajilgurehan changshin-gu 자질구레한 장신구 knick-knacks; trinket
chajinhaesŏ hada 자진해서 하다 volunteer
chajŏng 자정 midnight; ***chajŏng-e*** 자정에 at midnight
chajŏn-gŏ 자전거 bicycle
chajŏn-gŏ haendŭl 자전거 핸들 handlebars
chajŏn-gŏrŭl t'ada 자전거를 타다 bike; pedal
chajonshim 자존심 pride, self-respect
chajŭn 잦은 frequent
chaju 자주 often
chaju ch'at-tta 자주 찾다 frequent, visit
chaju onŭn 자주 오는 frequent
chajuppich'ŭi 자주빛의 purple
chak-kka 작가 writer; scriptwriter; author
chak-kkak'ada 착각하다 mistake, confuse
chak-kkok 작곡 composition
chak-kkok-kka 작곡가 composer
chak-kkok'ada 작곡하다 compose
chakppyŏl insa 작별 인사 parting greeting; ***nuguege chakppyŏl insarŭl hada*** 누구에게 작별 인사를 하다 say goodbye to s.o.
chakp'um 작품 work (*literary, artistic*)
chakssa chak-kkok-kka 작사 작곡가 songwriter
chakssaga 작사가 lyricist
chakssal 작살 harpoon
chakssihada 작시하다 rhyme
chakssŏnghada 작성하다 draw up, write; ***ch'ogorŭl chakssŏnghada*** 초고를 작성하다 draft
chaktchŏnghada 작정하다 decide, determine; ***muŏsŭl haryŏgo chaktchŏnghada*** 무엇을 하려고 작정하다 be intent on doing sth; ***X hanŭn kŏsŭl chaktchŏnghada*** X 하는 것을 작정하다 set out to do X
chaktchŏng-ida 작정이다 intend; ***muŏsŭl hal chaktchŏng-ida*** 무엇을 할 작정이다 intend to do sth
chaktchŏn kiji 작전 기지 base MIL
chaktta 작다 be small, be little
chakttonghada 작동하다 go, function; perform; engage, kick in

chakttong pullyang 작동 불량 malfunction
chakŭktche 자극제 stimulant
chak'uji 자쿠지 jacuzzi, whirlpool
chal 잘 well; nicely
chal allyŏjin 잘 알려진 well-known
chal anŭn 잘 아는 familiar
chal arajunŭn 잘 알아주는 sympathetic, understanding
chal cha 잘 자 good night (*informal*)
chal hada 잘 하다 do well; ***na-ege marŭl chal haet-tta*** 내게 말을 잘 했다 good thing you told me
chal igŭn 잘 익은 well-done *food*
chal ihaehada 잘 이해하다 sympathize with
chal ijŏbŏrinŭn 잘 잊어버리는 forgetful
chal it-tta 잘 있다 be well
chaljalmot 잘잘못 right and wrong
chal kakkuŏjin 잘 가꾸어진 in good condition
chal kŏnjodoen 잘 건조된 seasoned *wood*
challabŏrida 잘라버리다 slash
challanaeda 잘라내다 cut off
challan ch'ŏk'anŭn 잘난 척하는 pretentious
challanoŭn ppang 잘라놓은 빵 sliced bread
chal mandŭrŏjin 잘 만들어진 well-made
chal minnŭn 잘 믿는 credulous
chalmot 잘못 error; wrong ◊ wrongly; badly; ***nŏŭi / naŭi chalmoshida*** 너의 / 나의 잘못이다 it's your / my fault
chalmot chidodoen 잘못 지도된 misguided
chalmot chun 잘못 준 misplaced
chalmot ch'ŏltchahada 잘못 철자하다 misspell
chalmot haesŏk'ada 잘못 해석하다 misinterpret, misconstrue
chalmot iltta 잘못 읽다 misread
chalmot kŏllin chŏnhwa 잘못 걸린 전화 wrong number
chalmot kyesanhada 잘못 계산하다 miscalculate
chalmot match'uda 잘못 맞추다 mismatch
chalmot p'andanhada 잘못 판단하다 misjudge
chalmot saenggak'ada 잘못 생각하다 be under a misapprehension
chalmot sayonghada 잘못 사용하다 misuse
chalmot taruda 잘못 다루다 mishandle
chalmot-ttoeda 잘못되다 go wrong; ***mwŏga chalmot twaennayo?*** 뭐가 잘못 됐나요? is something wrong?
chalmot-ttoen 잘못된 wrong; unfortunate
chalmot-ttoen haesŏk 잘못된 해석 misinterpretation
chalmot-ttoen inswae 잘못된 인쇄 misprint
chalmot-ttoen unyŏng 잘못된 운영 mismanagement
chalmot unyŏnghada 잘못 운영하다 mismanage
chal nan ch'ehanŭn 잘 난 체하는 smug
chal padadŭrida 잘 받아들이다 be receptive to
chal saenggin 잘 생긴 good-looking
chal sagwida 잘 사귀다 cultivate *person*
chal salp'yŏboda 잘 살펴보다 study, examine
chal songnŭn 잘 속는 gullible
chal sonjildoen 잘 손질된 well groomed
chal tadŭmŏjin 잘 다듬어진 polished, accomplished
chal toeda 잘 되다 work, succeed; work out, be successful
chal tolbonŭn 잘 돌보는 caring
chal tolbwajunŭn 잘 돌봐주는 obliging
chal tolda 잘 돌다 negotiate
chal towajunŭn 잘 도와주는 supportive
chal ttaragada 잘 따라가다 stick to
cham 잠 sleep
chamae toshi 자매 도시 twin town
chamagŭl talda 자막을 달다 subtitle
chamak 자막 subtitle
chaman 자만 conceit
chamanhanŭn 자만하는 conceited

chamanshim 자만심 vanity
chambok'ada 잠복하다 lurk
chamdŭlda 잠들다 fall asleep
chamgida 잠기다 fasten
chamgŭda 잠그다 fasten; lock; turn off *faucet*
chamhaengssŏng-ŭi 잠행성의 insidious
chami kkaeda 잠이 깨다 wake (up)
chami tŭlda 잠이 들다 drop off; go to sleep
chamjaehada 잠재하다 lurk
chamjaejŏgin 잠재적인 potential, possible
chamjaejŏgŭro 잠재적으로 potentially
chamjaeryŏk 잠재력 potential, possibilities
chamjarie tŭlda 잠자리에 들다 go to bed
chamkkan 잠깐 a bit, a while
chamkkanmanyo 잠깐만요 just a second
chamkkan tong-anŭi 잠깐 동안의 fleeting
cham mot irunŭn 잠 못 이루는 sleepless
chamot 잠옷 pajamas; nightshirt; nightdress
chamot paji 잠옷 바지 pajama pants
chamot wit-ttori 잠옷 윗도리 pajama jacket
chamshi antta 잠시 앉다 perch, sit
chamshi chungdandoem 잠시 중단됨 lull, break
chamshidong-an 잠시동안 briefly
chamshi hu 잠시 후 a little later; ***nanŭn chamshi hue kŏgi toch'ak'al kŏmnida*** 나는 잠시 후에 거기 도착할 겁니다 I'll be there in a bit
chamshi mŏmum 잠시 머뭄 stopover
chamshi mŏmurŭda 잠시 머무르다 stop over
chamshinham 참신함 novelty
chamshi tong-an 잠시 동안 for a while, for a moment
chamsu 잠수 dive (*underwater*)
chamsubu 잠수부 diver, frogman
chamsuhada 잠수하다 dive, submerge; go diving
chamsuham 잠수함 submarine
chamulssoe 자물쇠 bolt; lock
chamulssoe chejogong 자물쇠 제조공 locksmith
chamulssoeŭi pŏnho 자물쇠의 번호 combination (*of safe*)
chamyŏnghan 자명한 self-evident
chamyŏngjong shigye 자명종 시계 alarm clock
chan 잔 cup; tumbler; ***... han chan*** ...한 잔 a drink of; a glass of; a cup of
chanaegŭl ch'ogwahanŭn inch'ul 잔액을 초과하는 인출 overdraft
chanaekppoda tŏ inch'urhada 잔액보다 더 인출하다 have an overdraft; ***...esŏ chanaekppoda tŏ inch'ulshik'ida*** ...에서 잔액보다 더 인출시키다 overdraw
chanch'itssang 잔칫상 spread, meal
chandi 잔디 lawn; (piece of) turf
chandibat 잔디밭 turf, grass
chandi kkangnŭn kigye 잔디 깎는 기계 lawn mower
chandon 잔돈 change, loose change
chang 장 chief, head; sheet (*of paper*); chapter; scene (*in theater*); exposure (*on film*); copy; ice rink ◊ *countword for paper and thin flat objects*
chang-ae 장애 problem; disorder MED; hitch; hindrance; obstacle; burden
chang-aemul 장애물 stumbling-block; blockage; hurdle SP
chang-aemul kyŏnggi 장애물 경기 steeplechase (*athletics*)
chang-aemul kyŏngju 장애물 경주 hurdles
chang-aemul kyŏngjuja 장애물 경주자 hurdler
chang-aemul kyŏngjuma 장애물 경주마 jumper (*horse*)
chang-aemul ttwiŏnŏmkki 장애물 뛰어넘기 show jumping
chang-aeŏpsshi 장애없이 without a hitch
chang-ak'ada 장악하다 take over; ***muŏsŭl chang-ak'ada*** 무엇을 장악하다 tighten one's grip on sth

changbi 장비 equipment, plant; kit
changboda 장보다 do one's shopping
changbu 장부 accounts book; (real) man; ***changburŭl sogida*** 장부를 속이다 fiddle the accounts
changch'i 장치 apparatus, equipment; device; system
changgap 장갑 glove
changgapch'a 장갑차 armored vehicle
changgi 장기 Korean chess
changgijŏgin 장기적인 long-range; ***changgijŏgŭro*** 장기적으로 in the long term
changgiŭi 장기의 long-term
changgŏriŭi 장거리의 long-distance
changgo 장고 hourglass drum
changgun 장군 general MIL; checkmate
changgunp'ul 장군풀 rhubarb
changgwan 장관 minister, secretary; spectacle
changgwan-ŭi 장관의 ministerial
changgyo 장교 officer MIL
changhak-kkŭm 장학금 grant, scholarship
changhwa 장화 boot
chang-in 장인 craftsman; father-in-law
chang-in ŏrŭn 장인 어른 father-in-law
changjŏng 장정 binding; epic journey
changjŏngbon 장정본 hardback (*book*)
changjŏnhada 장전하다 load *gun*
changjo 장조 major MUS
changjogŭi paltchŏnŭl hada 장족의 발전을 하다 make great strides
changk'waehan 장쾌한 stirring
changma 장마 the rains
changmach'ŏl 장마철 rainy season
changmi 장미 rose
changmun 작문 composition, essay
changmyŏn 장면 scene
changnaesŏng ŏmnŭn chigŏp 장래성 없는 직업 dead-end job
changnaeŭi hŭimang 장래의 희망 expectations
changnan 장난 prank; ***nuguege changnanjirŭl hada*** 누구에게 장난질을 하다 play a trick on s.o.; ***chitkkujŭn changnan*** 짓궂은 장난 practical joke
changnanch'ida 장난치다 fool around
changnankkam 장난감 toy
changnankkurŏgi 장난꾸러기 little rascal, cheeky child
Changno Kyohoe 장로 교회 Presbyterian Church
changnong 장롱 chest, box
changnyeshik 장례식 funeral
changnyŏhan 장려한 magnificent
changnyŏn ŏnjen-ga 작년 언젠가 sometime last year
chang-ŏ 장어 eel
chan-go 잔고 balance
chan-go chohoe 잔고 조회 bank statement
chan-goran 잔고란 debit
chan-gorane kiip'ada 잔고란에 기입하다 debit
chang pon mulgŏn 장 본 물건 shopping, purchases
changp'a 장파 long wave
changp'yŏn yŏnghwa 장편 영화 movie; feature
changsahada 장사하다 trade, do business
changshik 장식 decoration, decor
changshik-kka 장식가 painter
changshiktchang 장식장 cabinet
changshik'ada 장식하다 embellish, adorn
changshingnyong-ŭi 장식용의 ornamental
changshin-gu 장신구 accessory
changso 장소 place, spot; site; venue; room, space; ***...ŭl / rŭl wihan changsoga ŏptta*** ...을 / 를 위한 장소가 없다 there's no room for
changsshik 장식 décor
changsshikp'um 장식품 ornament
changsshik'ada 장식하다 decorate
changtchŏm 장점 merit, strength
changttae nop'i ttwigi 장대 높이 뛰기 polevault
changt'ip'usŭ 장티푸스 typhoid
chang-ŭisa 장의사 mortician
chanhae 잔해 wreck, wreckage

chaninhada 잔인하다 be cruel
chaninhage 잔인하게 brutally
chaninham 잔인함 cruelty; brutality; ferocity
chanmorae 잔모래 grit (*for roads*)
chansorihada 잔소리하다 go on at, nag
chansorihanŭn 잔소리하는 nagging
chanttŭk mŏktta 잔뜩 먹다 eat one's fill
chanyŏgŭm 잔여금 balance, remainder
chanyŏmul 잔여물 residue
chaoesŏn 자외선 ultraviolet rays
chapch'o 잡초 weed
chapkki 잡기 catch
chap-ppi 잡비 incidental expenses
chapssŏk 잡석 rubble
chaptchi 잡지 magazine, journal
chaptchong 잡종 hybrid
chaptchonggyŏn 잡종견 mongrel
chaptta 잡다 catch; seize; hold
chapttahan kŏttŭl 잡다한 것들 odds and ends, little jobs
chapttam 잡담 chat, small talk
chapttamhada 잡담하다 chat, gossip
chapttongsani 잡동사니 odds and ends; paraphernalia
chap'an 자판 dial, face
chap'an-gi 자판기 vending machine
chap'ojagishig-ŭi haengdong 자포자기식의 행동 an act of desperation
chap'yetchŭng-ŭi 자폐증의 autistic
charada 자라다 grow; ***chal charada*** 잘 자라다 flourish
charak 자락 patch (*of fog*)
charanada 자라나다 grow up
charang 자랑 pride
charanghada 자랑하다 boast
charang kŏri 자랑 거리 boast
charangsŭrŏpkke 자랑스럽게 proudly
charangsŭrŏptta 자랑스럽다 be proud
charangsŭrŏun 자랑스러운 proud
charhada 잘하다 be good at
charhan hŭngjŏng 잘한 흥정 bargain, good deal
chari 자리 place, seat; floor mat
charijaptta 자리잡다 settle down, calm down (*in lifestyle*)
charirŭl mandŭlda 자리를 만들다 move up, make room
charŏ kada 자러 가다 go to bed
charŭda 자르다 carve; cut
charŭgi 자르기 cut; carve *meat*
charu 자루 hilt; shaft ◊ *countword for pencils, brushes, pens, chalk, scissors, rifles etc*
charyo 자료 materials; data
chasal 자살 suicide
chasan 자산 asset
chasan sodŭksse 자산 소득세 capital gains tax
chasarhada 자살하다 commit suicide
chase 자세 position, posture
chasehada 자세하다 be detailed
chasehage 자세하게 in detail
chasehan chosa 철저한 조사 investigation, probe
chasehan naeyong 자세한 내용 detail
chasehi chosahada 자세히 조사하다 scrutinize, probe
chasehi poda 자세히 보다 peer; study, pore over
chashik 자식 offspring
chashin 자신 self-confidence; ***chashinŭl ŏktchehal su ŏpkke toeda*** 자신을 억제할 수 없게 되다 lose control of oneself, get angry, get upset
chashin innŭn 자신 있는 self-confident, self-assured
chashini nŏmch'yŏboinŭn 자신이 넘쳐보이는 flamboyant
chasŏjŏn 자서전 autobiography
chasŏk 자석 magnet
chasŏn 자선 charity; philanthropy
chasŏn-ga 자선가 philanthropist
chasŏnshimi manŭn 자선심이 많은 charitable
chasŏn tanch'e 자선 단체 charity (*organization*)
chasŏnŭi 자선의 charitable
chason 자손 descendant
chasonida 자손이다 be descended from
chasu 자수 embroidery
chasusŏnggahan saram 자수성가한 사람 self-made man

chattchip 찻집 tearoom
chattchujŏnja 찻주전자 teapot
chat'aek kŭnmu 자택 근무 work from home
chaŭishigi kanghan 자의식이 강한 self-conscious
chaŭm 자음 consonant
chawihada 자위하다 masturbate
chawŏn 자원 resource
chawŏn ipttaehada 자원 입대하다 enlist
chawŏnja 자원자 volunteer
chawŏn kogal 자원 고갈 a drain on resources
chawŏn pohoronja 자원 보호론자 conservationist
chayŏn 자연 nature
chayŏng-ŭi 자영의 self-employed
chayŏn kwahak 자연 과학 natural science
chayŏn kwahaktcha 자연 과학자 natural scientist
chayŏn pohogu 자연 보호구 nature reserve
chayŏnsa 자연사 natural death
chayŏn shikp'um 자연 식품 whole food
chayŏnsŭrŏpkke 자연스럽게 naturally
chayŏntchŏgin 자연적인 natural *death*
chayŏnŭi 자연의 natural *resources etc*
chayu 자유 freedom, liberty
chayujuŭiŭi 자유주의의 liberal
chayu kyeyagŭi 자유 계약의 freelance
chayuro 자유로 at liberty
chayurowajin 자유로와진 emancipated, liberated
chayu shijang kyŏngje 자유 시장 경제 free market economy
chayuŭi 자유의 free, at liberty
chayuŭi yŏshinsang 자유의 여신상 Statue of Liberty
che 제 my; ***kŭ sŭt'eik'ŭnŭn che kŏshimnida*** 그 스테이크는 제 것입니다 the steak is for me
chean 제안 approach, arrival; motion, proposal; suggestion
cheanhada 제안하다 advance, propose, suggest; hold out, offer
cheap'ada 제압하다 restrain
chebal 제발 please, kindly
chebang 제방 river bank
chebi 제비 swallow
chebikkot 제비꽃 violet
chebinghada 제빙하다 de-ice
chebingje 제빙제 de-icer
chebi ppopkki 제비 뽑기 raffle, draw
chebirŭl ppoptta 제비를 뽑다 draw
chebok 제복 uniform
chebyŏng 제병 wafer
chech'oje 제초제 weedkiller
chech'uran 제출안 submission
chech'urhada 제출하다 bring in, introduce; hand in; send in; submit, lodge; ***chŭnggŏrŭl chech'urhada*** 증거를 제출하다 produce evidence
chedae 제대 discharge (*from the army*)
chedaero 제대로 properly
chedan 제단 altar
chedop'an 제도판 drawing board
chegihada 제기하다 raise, bring up *question*
chegirŏl 제기랄 damn!
chegŏ 제거 removal, elimination
chegŏhada 제거하다 eliminate, root out
chegong 제공 offer
chegonghada 제공하다 offer, provide; ***chinael kosŭl chegonghada*** 지낼 곳을 제공하다 accommodate
chegop 제곱 square MATH
chegopkkŭn 제곱근 square root
chegugŭi 제국의 imperial
cheguk 제국 empire
cheguryŏk 제구력 control
chegwajŏm 제과점 confectioner's
chehada 제하다 allow; calculate
chehan 제한 restriction; qualification
chehandoen 제한된 confined *space*; qualified, limited
chehan-guyŏk 제한구역 restricted area
chehanhada 제한하다 confine, restrict; qualify
chehan pŏmwi 제한 범위 parameter

chehan shigan 제한 시간 time limit
che himŭro kkuryŏnagada 제 힘으로 꾸려나가다 fend for oneself
che himŭro ŏdŭn 제 힘으로 얻은 well-earned
cheil 제일 best
cheil choahanŭn 제일 좋아하는 favorite
cheja 제자 disciple
chejae 제재 sanction, penalty
chejak 제작 production
chejaktcha 제작자 producer
chejak'ada 제작하다 produce
chejarie tollyŏnot'a 제자리에 돌려놓다 put back, replace
chejŏnghada 제정하다 enact *law*; legislate
chejŏngshin 제정신 sanity
chejŏngshinŭi 제정신의 sane, lucid
chejŏngshinŭl ilt'a 제정신을 잃다 go insane; be beside oneself
chejohada 제조하다 manufacture
chejoŏp 제조업 manufacture; manufacturing
chejoŏptcha 제조업자 manufacturer
chel 젤 gel
chemŏt-ttaeroin 제멋대로인 wanton; wayward
chemok 제목 title, name; ***...(i)ranŭn chemogŭi*** ...(이)라는 제목의 entitled, called; ***chagŭn chemok*** 작은 제목 subheading
chemot-ttaero nolda 제멋대로 놀다 run wild
chemoyongp'um 제모용품 hair remover
chemul 제물 sacrifice
chemyŏngshik'ida 제명시키다 drop
chenjang! 젠장! damn it!
cheŏ 제어 control
cheŏban 제어반 control panel
cheŏhada 제어하다 bring under control
cheoehada 제외하다 eliminate, rule out; exclude, leave out
cheoehago 제외하고 aside from, except for; excluding
cheoeshik'ida 제외시키다 leave out; ***chŏnŭn i iresŏ cheoeshik'yŏ chushipsshio*** 저는 이 일에서 제외시켜 주십시오 leave me out of this
cheppang-ŏptcha 제빵업자 baker
chep'um 제품 product; goods; wares
chero sŏngjang 제로 성장 zero growth
chesa 제사 ancestral rite
Chesam Segye 제3 세계 Third World
cheshigane 제시간에 promptly, on time; ***cheshigan ane hada*** 제시간 안에 하다 make it, get there on time
cheshihada 제시 하다 put in *request*
chesŏlgi 제설기 snowplow
chet'ŭ enjin 제트 엔진 jet engine
chet'ŭgi 제트기 jet
cheŭi 제의 proposition
cheŭihada 제의하다 make overtures to
chewang chŏlgae 제왕 절개 Cesarean section
cheyagŭi 제약의 pharmaceutical
cheyak 제약 pharmaceuticals
chiap 지압 acupressure massage
chibae 지배 control; domination
chibaehada 지배하다 control, be in control of; dominate
chibaehanŭn 지배하는 ruling
chibaein 지배인 manager
chibaejŏgin 지배적인 domineering
chibaejŏk ikkwŏn 지배적 이권 controlling interest
chibang 지방 region; province; fat (*on meat*) ◊ regional; local
chibang chach'i 지방 자치 local government
chibang-i manŭn 지방이 많은 fatty
chibang kŏmsa 지방 검사 DA, district attorney
chibang punkkwŏnhwa hada 지방 분권화 하다 decentralize
chibang saram 지방 사람 local; inhabitant
chibang t'ŭkssanmul 지방 특산물 local produce
chiban il 집안 일 chore; housework
chibe 집에 home, at home
chibesŏ mandŭn 집에서 만든 homemade
chibŏdŭlda 집어들다 hold
chibŏmnŭn 집없는 homeless
chibŏ nŏt'a 집어 넣다 get in; store;

fit in
chibŏ tŭlda 집어 들다 pick up
chibu 지부 branch, chapter
chibul 지불 payment, settlement
chibul nŭngnyŏgi innŭn 지불 능력이 있는 solvent
chibul ponggŭp ch'ongaek 지불 봉급 총액 payroll
chibul pullŭng-ŭi 지불 불능의 insolvent
chibung 지붕 roof
chibung kkokttaegi 지붕 꼭대기 ridge (*of roof*)
chiburhada 지불하다 pay, pay up, settle
chiburin 지불인 payer
chibyohan 집요한 persistent
chich'e 지체 delay, holdup
chich'ehada 지체하다 delay, wait
chich'eshik'ida 지체시키다 detain, delay
chich'ida 지치다 tire, flag
chich'ige hada 지치게 하다 tire, wear out, exhaust
chich'ige hanŭn 지치게 하는 tiring, exhausting, wearing
chich'il chul morŭnŭn 지칠 줄 모르는 tireless, inexhaustible
chich'im 지침 pointer; guidelines
chich'in 지친 run-down, worn out, pooped
chich'ul 지출 expenditure
chida 지다 lose; get a beating; go down (*of sun*); be out (*of sun, flower*)
chidae 지대 zone
chido 지도 map; leadership
chidoch'aek 지도책 atlas
chidoja 지도자 leader; mastermind
chidoja sŏn-gŏ hoeŭi 지도자 선거 회의 leadership contest
chidok'ada 지독하다 be vicious; be terrible; be tough
chidok'age 지독하게 terribly, atrociously; viciously
chidoryŏk 지도력 leadership skills
chigagi innŭn 지각이 있는 conscious, aware
chigak 지각 awareness; insight
chigak'ada 지각하다 be delayed
chigap 지갑 billfold, pocketbook
chigech'a 지게차 forklift truck
chigŏbtchŏgin 직업적인 professional
chigŏp 직업 employment; job; profession; trade
chigŏp annaeso 직업 안내소 employment agency
chigŏp manjoktto 직업 만족도 job satisfaction
chigŏpssang-ŭi 직업상의 vocational
chigohan 지고한 lofty, high
chigo it-tta 지고 있다 be behind
chigŭjaegŭhyŏng 지그재그형 zigzag
chigŭjaegŭro umjigida 지그재그로 움직이다 zigzag
chigŭjaegŭshigŭi 지그재그식의 erratic
chigŭlgŏrida 지글거리다 sizzle
chigŭm 지금 now, currently, at present; ***paro chigŭm*** 바로 지금 right now
chigŭmbut'ŏ 지금부터 from now on
chigŭmkkaji 지금까지 ever; yet, so far
chigŭmtchŭm 지금쯤 by now
chigŭmŭi 지금의 current
chigŭmŭn 지금은 at the moment
chigŭp'ada 지급하다 issue
chigu 지구 earth; globe
chigubon 지구본 globe
chiguin 지구인 inhabitant of earth
chiguryŏk 지구력 endurance
chigwŏn 직원 attendant; staff; personnel
chigyŏng 지경 boundary; verge; ...ㄹ 지경이다 ***...l chigyŏng-ida*** be on the verge of
chigyŏwŏhada 지겨워하다 loathe
chiha 지하 underground
chiha ch'anggo 지하 창고 vault, cellar
chihach'ŏl 지하철 subway RAIL
chihach'ŭng 지하층 basement
chihado 지하도 underpass
chihaesŏ 지하에서 underground
chihashil 지하실 cellar, basement
chihasumyŏn 지하 수면 waterline
chiha undong 지하 운동 underground activities
chihwihada 지휘하다 conduct MUS
chihwija 지휘자 conductor
chihye 지혜 wisdom

chihyŏng 지형 terrain
chijang-ŭl pat-tta 지장을 받다 suffer
chiji 지지 support, backing
chijida 지지다 fry
chijihada 지지하다 support; endorse; confirm, stand by
chijija 지지자 supporter, follower; following
chijil 지질 geology (*of area*) ◊ geological
chijin 지진 earthquake
chijinhak 지진학 seismology
chijirhak 지질학 geology (*subject*)
chijirhaktcha 지질학자 geologist
chijirhaktchŏk 지질학적 geological
chijŏbunhada 지저분하다 be messy; be filthy
chijŏbunham 지저분함 disorder, untidiness
chijŏgwida 지저귀다 chirp; twitter
chijŏk'ada 지적하다 point out
chijŏm 지점 branch
chijŏmjang 지점장 branch manager; ***ŭnhaeng chijŏmjang*** 은행 지점장 bank manager
chijŏnghada 지정하다 designate
chiju 지주 land owner
chik kangha 직 강하 plummet
chik-kkagŭro 직각으로 at right-angles to
chik-kkak 직각 right-angle
chik-kkwan 직관 intuition
chik-kkyŏng 직경 diameter
chikssagak'yŏng 직사각형 rectangle
chikssa kŏriesŏ 직사 거리에서 at point-blank range
chiktchang-e it-tta 직장에 있다 be at work
chiktchŏp 직접 in person, personally
chiktchŏptchŏgin 직접적인 direct
chiktchŏptchogŭro 직접적으로 firsthand ◊ at first hand
chik'aeng pihaenggi 직행 비행기 through flight
chik'aeng-ŭi 직행의 direct, nonstop
chik'aeng-ŭro 직행으로 nonstop
chik'aeng yŏlch'a 직행 열차 through train
chik'am 직함 title, form of address
chik'ang 직항 direct flight
chik'ida 지키다 defend; keep to; guard; keep *promise*
chik'yŏboda 지켜보다 watch; monitor; keep an eye on, look after
chil 질 vagina
chilbyŏng 질병 disease
chilch'aek'ada 질책하다 rebuke
chilch'ŏk'an 질척한 slimey
chilgin 질긴 stout; tough
chilgŏp'age hada 질겁하게 하다 appall
chiljil kkŭlda 질질 끌다 drag on
chillajŭn 질낮은 mediocre
chillida 질리다 be fed up with
chillin 질린 fed up
chillo 진로 path
chillyobi 진료비 fee
chillyo kwajŏng 진료 과정 course of treatment
chillyoso 진료소 clinic; infirmary
chilmŏjida 짊어지다 hump; shoulder *burden*
chilmun 질문 question
chilmunhada 질문하다 ask; question
chilmunsŏ 질문서 questionnaire
chilso 질소 nitrogen
chilsshik 질식 suffocation
chilsshik shik'ida 질식 시키다 smother; suffocate
chiltchu 질주 sprint
chiltchuhada 질주하다 race, sprint; tear; gallop
chilt'u 질투 jealousy
chilt'uhada 질투하다 be jealous; be jealous of
chilt'uhanŭn 질투하는 jealous
chilt'ushim 질투심 jealousy
chim 짐 load, burden; belongings; ***chim kkurida*** 짐 꾸리다 pack
chimjak'ada 짐작하다 suspect
chimmach'a 짐마차 cart
chimsŭng 짐승 beast
chimun 지문 fingerprint
chimyŏng subaedoen 지명 수배된 wanted
chin 진 gin; resin
chinach'ida 지나치다 exceed, overdo
chinach'ige 지나치게 overly; unduly
chinach'ige pohohada 지나치게 보호하다 overprotect
chinach'ige sŏlch'inŭn 지나치게 설치는 hyperactive

chinach'in 지나친 drastic, excessive, undue
chinach'yŏ kada 지나쳐 가다 turn away
chinaeda 지내다 celebrate; get along, progress; ***yojŭm musŭn irŭl hamyŏ chinaeshimnikka?*** 요즘 무슨 일을 하며 지내십니까? what are you up to these days?
chinagada 지나가다 pass; pass by, go by; get on; ***ttwiŏsŏ / kŏrŏsŏ chinagada*** 뛰어서 / 걸어서 지나가다 run / walk past
chinan myŏch'il 지난 며칠 the past few days
chinan pŏne 지난 번에 last time
chinap 진압 repression
chinap'ada 진압하다 suppress, put down
chinasŏ 지나서 beyond; past, by
chinbo 진보 advance
chinbohada 진보하다 advance, progress
chinbojŏgin 진보적인 progressive
chinbuhan 진부한 trite; corny; stale *news*; ready-made *solution*
chinch'arhada 진찰하다 examine
chinch'ŏkttoeda 진척되다 get on, make progress
chinch'ul 진출 penetration
chinch'urhada 진출하다 penetrate; ***uri t'imŭn chun-gyŏlssŭngjŏne chinch'urhaet-tta*** 우리 팀은 준결승전에 진출했다 our team has gotten through to the semi-final
chinch'wijŏgin 진취적인 enterprising, dynamic, go-ahead
chinch'wijŏk kisang 진취적 기상 enterprise, initiative
chindansŏ 진단서 medical certificate
chindo 진도 rate
chindoga nagada 진도가 나가다 progress
chindong 진동 vibration
chindonghada 진동하다 pulsate; rock
ching 징 gong
chingbyŏng 징병 draft MIL
chingbyŏnghada 징병하다 draft MIL
chingbyŏng kip'ija 징병 기피자 draft dodger
chinggyehada 징계하다 discipline
chinggyeŭi 징계의 disciplinary
chin-gihan 진기한 rare
chingjip-ppyŏng 징집병 draftee
chingmul 직물 fabric, textile; texture
chingmu naeyong sŏlmyŏngsŏ 직무 내용 설명서 job description
chingmurŏp 직물업 textile business; textiles
chingmyŏnhada 직면하다 face
chingnŭng 직능 function
chingnyu 직류 direct current
chin-gong 진공 vacuum
chin-gong ch'ŏngsogi 진공 청소기 vacuum cleaner
chin-gonggwan 진공관 vacuum flask
chin-gongp'ojang-ŭi 진공포장의 vacuum-packed
chingse 징세 taxation
chingsuhada 징수하다 levy
chinhaeng 진행 progress
chinhaeng chung-ida 진행 중이다 be under way
chinhaengdoeda 진행되다 proceed; progress; come along
chinhaenghada 진행하다 advance, go on; front TV
chinhaenghanŭn 진행하는 progressive
chinhan 진한 dark; deep *color*; strong *tea etc*
chinhongsaegŭi 진홍색의 crimson
chinhŭk 진흙 clay; mud
chinhŭkt'usŏng-iŭi 진흙투성이의 muddy
chinhwa 진화 evolution
chinhwahada 진화하다 evolve
chinida 지니다 assume
chinigo tanida 지니고 다니다 carry around
chinimno 진입로 access road
chinji 진지 position
chinjihage 진지하게 in earnest; ***nugurŭl chinjihage saenggak'ada*** 누구를 진지하게 생각하다 take s.o. seriously
chinjihan 진지한 earnest, serious
chinjŏlmŏri nanŭn 진절머리 나는 disgusting, repulsive

chinjŏng 진정 lull
chinjŏngdoeda 진정되다 quieten down
chinjŏngje 진정제 sedative, tranquilizer
chinjŏngshik'ida 진정시키다 control; pacify; soothe; defuse; keep down *costs*
chinjŏngŭro 진정으로 seriously
chinjŏ piŏ 진저 비어 gingerbeer
chinju 진주 pearl
chinmi 진미 delicacy
chinp'um 진품 rarity
chinshil 진실 truth
chinshillo 진실로 truly; sincerely
chinshimiya 진심이야 I'm serious
chinshimŭi 진심의 whole-hearted
chinshimŭro 진심으로 sincerely
chinshirhada 진실하다 be truthful, be sincere
chinshirŭl iptchŭnghada 진실을 입증하다 vindicate
chinsu 진수 launch
chinsuhada 진수하다 launch
chinsul 진술 statement
chinsushik 진수식 launch ceremony
chinsusŏn 진수선 launch
chintcha 진짜 the real thing ◊ authentic, genuine; original; real; truthful
chint'ang surŭl mashida 진탕 술을 마시다 go on a bender
chint'oeyangnan 진퇴양난 dilemma; deadlock
chint'ongje 진통제 painkiller
chint'onik 진토닉 gin and tonic
chinŭng 지능 intelligence, brains
chinŭrŏmi 지느러미 fin
chinwŏnji 진원지 epicenter
chinyŏl 진열 display; ***chinyŏldoen*** 진열된 in the window
chinyŏltchang 진열장 display cabinet
chinyŏlttae 진열대 stall
chinyŏrhada 진열하다 display, lay out
chiŏnaen iyagi 지어낸 이야기 story
chiok 지옥 hell
chip 집 home; house; collection (*of writings*); straw
chipch'ak'ada 집착하다 cling to
chipkke 집게 tongs
chipkkebal 집게발 pincers
chipkke sonkkarak 집게 손가락 forefinger, index finger
chipkkwŏnhanŭn 집권하는 in power
chipkkyŏltchi 집결지 rendez-vous
chipp'iltcha 집필자 author
chipsaram 집사람 wife
chipsshi 집시 gipsy
chiptchŏk hoero 집적 회로 integrated circuit
chiptchung 집중 concentration
chiptchunghada 집중하다 concentrate
chiptchungjŏgin 집중적인 intensive
chiptchung kangjwa 집중 강좌 crash course
chiptchung kyŏrŭihada 집중 결의하다 centralize
chiptchung k'osŭ 집중 코스 intensive course
chiptchung sagyŏk 집중 사격 burst
chiptchungshik'ida 집중시키다 concentrate
chiptchuso 집주소 home address
chipttan 집단 circle, set, group
chipttanjŏgin 집단적인 collective
chipttan p'ok'aeng-ŭl kahada 집단 폭행을 가하다 lynch
chipttŭri 집들이 housewarming
chip'aeng yuye 집행 유예 probation; reprieve
chip'ang-i 지팡이 walking stick
chip'ap 집합 set MATH
chip'atchang 집하장 terminal
chip'apch'e 집합체 complex
chip'ŏ 지퍼 zipper
chip'ŏrŭl chamgŭda 지퍼를 잠그다 zip up
chip'ŏrŭl yŏlda 지퍼를 열다 unzip
chip'oe 집회 congregation REL
chip'ŭch'a 지프차 jeep
chip'ye 지폐 (bank) bill
chip'yŏngsŏn 지평선 horizon
chip'yo 지표 barometer *fig*
chirado 지라도: ***...l chirado*** ...ㄹ 지라도 while; although; even though
chire 지레 lever
chirhwan 질환 condition MED
chiri 지리 geography
chirijŏk 지리적 geographical

chirimyŏllŏrhan 지리멸렬한 scrappy
chiroe 지뢰 mine
chiroepat 지뢰밭 minefield
chiroe t'amsaekssŏn 지뢰 탐색선 minesweeper
chirŭi 질의 vaginal
chirŭmkkil 지름길 short cut
chiruhada 지루하다 be tedious; drag
chiruhaejida 지루해지다 be bored
chiruhaesŏ mich'ilkkŏt kat'ŭn 지루해서 미칠것 같은 deadly, boring
chiruhan 지루한 boring, dull
chiryu 지류 tributary
chisa 지사 governor
chisang 지상 the ground ◊ ground; earthly, terrestrial
chisang kŭnmuwŏn 지상 근무원 ground crew; ground staff
chisang kwanje 지상 관제 ground control
chishigi innŭn 지식이 있는 knowledgeable
chishigin 지식인 intellectual
chishiginŭi 지식인의 intellectual, highbrow
chishihada 지시하다 instruct
chishik 지식 knowledge, learning
chishi sahang 지시 사항 instruction
chisŏng 지성 intellect
chisŏng-in 지성인 intellectual
chisok 지속 persistence
chisok kigan 지속 기간 duration
chisoktchŏgin 지속적인 enduring; persistent
chisokttoeda 지속되다 last
chisok'ada 지속하다 persist; maintain; sustain
chitchŏgin 지적인 intellectual
chitchŏgŭro 지적으로 mentally
chitkkujŭn 짓궂은 mischievous
chit-tta 짖다 bark
chit'aenghada 지탱하다 bear, hold, support
chit'ŭm 짙음 depth
chit'ŭn 짙은 thick
chiuda 지우다 erase, delete; scrap; remove; blot out *memory*
chiugae 지우개 eraser
chiwi 지위 position; status, standing
chiwŏn 지원 application; backup
chiwŏnhada 지원하다 apply for
chiwŏnsŏ 지원서 application form
chiyŏgŭi 지역의 regional
chiyŏk 지역 area; region; district; quarter
chiyŏk pŏnho 지역 번호 area code
chiyŏnshik'ida 지연시키다 stall
chŏ 저 ㅂ I; me; mine; that
chŏ araee 저 아래에 down there
chŏbŏduda 접어두다 put aside; ***chinan irŭn kŭnyang chŏbŏduja*** 지난 일은 그냥 접어두자 let bygones be bygones
chŏbŏ nŏt'a 접어 넣다 tuck in
chŏbŭn chari 접은 자리 fold
chŏch'eontchŭng 저체온증 hypothermia
chŏch'uk ŭnhaeng 저축 은행 savings bank
chŏch'uk'ada 저축하다 save
chŏdang 저당 mortgage
chŏdang chap'ida 저당 잡히다 mortgage; pawn
chŏgiap 저기압 depression, low
chŏgiap chidae 저기압 지대 low-pressure area
chŏgi araetchoge 저기 아래쪽에 down there
chŏgŏdo 적어도 at least
chŏgŏduda 적어두다 note down
chŏgŏsŭn muŏshimnikka? 저것은 무엇입니까? what is that?
chŏgŏt 저것 that one
chŏgoesŏnŭi 적외선의 infra-red
chŏgori 저고리 short jacket
chŏgŭmhada 저금하다 put aside, save
chŏgŭn 적은 small; slight; a small number of
chŏgŭnghada 적응하다 adapt, acclimatize
chŏgŭngnyŏgi innŭn 적응력이 있는 adaptable
chŏgŭngshik'igi 적응시키기 conditioning
chŏgŭng-ŭl mot'anŭn 적응을 못하는 maladjusted
chŏgyŏkppyŏng 저격병 sniper
chŏgyongdoeda 적용되다 apply; apply to
chŏgyonghada 적용하다 apply
chŏhadoeda 저하되다 slip, decline

chŏhang 저항 resistance
chŏhanghada 저항하다 resist
chŏhangnyŏgi innŭn 저항력이 있는 resistant
chŏjak-kkwŏn 저작권 copyright
chŏjang 저장 store, stock
chŏjanghada 저장하다 store; preserve; save COMPUT
chŏjangshikp'um 저장식품 preserves
chŏjang t'aengk'ŭ 저장 탱크 tank
chŏjangt'ong 저장통 bin
chŏji 저지 jersey; lowlands
chŏjibang-ŭi 저지방의 low-fat
chŏjihada 저지하다 save
chŏjil 저질 mediocrity
chŏjŏllo 저절로 by itself
chŏjo 저조 low
chŏjŭl tchada 젖을 짜다 milk
chŏjŭl tteda 젖을 떼다 wean
chŏjŭn 젖은 soggy
chŏju 저주 curse
chŏjuhada 저주하다 curse
chŏk 적 enemy; adversary
chŏkch'urŭi 적출의 legitimate
chŏk-kkŭktchŏgin 적극적인 positive
chŏkkŭk p'anmae 적극 판매 hardsell
chŏkppŏbŭi 적법의 legitimate
chŏksshida 적시다 soak
Chŏksshiptcha 적십자 Red Cross
chŏksshiŭi 적시의 timely
chŏkssŏng 적성 aptitude
chŏktaeshim 적대심 antagonism
chŏktcha 적자 deficit
chŏktchaehada 적재하다 load; carry
chŏktchaehan 적재한 laden
chŏktchaga nada 적자가 나다 in the red
chŏktcha saengjon 적자 생존 survival of the fittest
chŏktchŏrhan 적절한 appropriate; right; pertinent
chŏktta 적다 take notes
chŏkttaejŏgin 적대적인 hostile
chŏkttaeshim 적대심 hostility
chŏkttanghada 적당하다 be suitable; be adequate
chŏkttanghage 적당하게 moderately; in moderation
chŏkttanghan 적당한 adequate; moderate; reasonable; decent; suitable
chŏkttanghi hada 적당히 하다 moderate
chŏktto 적도 equator
chŏk'alloriŭi 저칼로리의 low-calorie
chŏk'ap'ada 적합하다 be suited for, be cut out for
chŏk'ap'age 적합하게 properly
chŏk'ap'an 적합한 morally fit
chŏk'apssŏng 적합성 compatibility
chŏl 절 clause; passage; verse; bow, obeisance; Buddhist temple
chŏlbak'an 절박한 imminent
chŏlbyŏk 절벽 cliff
chŏlch'a 절차 procedure
chŏlch'wisŏn 절취선 perforations
chŏlgae 절개 incision
chŏlgyohada 절교하다 drop
chŏllŭmbariŭi 절름발이의 lame
chŏllŭmgŏrida 절름거리다 hobble
chŏllyak 전략 strategy
chŏllyaktchŏgin 전략적인 strategic
chŏllye ŏmnŭn 전례 없는 unheard-of, unprecedented
chŏllyŏm 전렴 commitment
chŏllyu 전류 current ELEC
chŏlmang 절망 despair
chŏlmanghada 절망하다 despair; ***chŏlmanghayŏ*** 절망하여 in despair
chŏlmangjŏgin 절망적인 desperate
chŏlmtta 젊다 be young
chŏlmŭn 젊은 young, youthful
chŏlmŭni 젊은이 youth, youngster, young man
chŏlmyohan 절묘한 exquisite
chŏlp'andoen 절판된 out of print
chŏlsshirhan 절실한 pressing
chŏltchŏng 절정 climax; high point; summit; height
chŏltchŏng-e tarhada 절정에 달하다 culminate in
chŏlttae absolutely; ***chŏlttae andoemnida!*** 절대 안됩니다! absolutely not!
chŏlttaejŏgin 절대적인 absolute; ***chŏlttaero amuegedo iyagihaesonŭn andoemnida*** 절대로 아무에게도 이야기해서는 안됩니다 on no account must you tell anybody

chŏlttanhada 절단하다 sever; amputate
chŏlttotchoe 절도죄 larceny
chŏlttuk-kkŏrim 절뚝거림 limp
chŏm 점 dot; spot; mole; ***mŏnji han chŏm ŏmnŭn*** 먼지 한 점 없는 spotless
chŏmaek 점액 mucus
chŏmanje 점안제 drops
chŏmch'ajŏgin 점차적인 gradual
chŏmch'ajŏgŭro 점차적으로 gradually
chŏmch'ajŏgŭro ŏpssŏjida 점차적으로 없어지다 peter out
chŏmgŏm 점검 inspection
chŏmgŏmhada 점검하다 check; inspect; vet
chŏmho 점호 roll call
chŏmhwa changch'i 점화 장치 ignition
chŏmhwahada 점화하다 set off *explosion*
chŏmhwajŏn 점화전 spark plug
chŏmhwa p'ullŏgŭ 점화 플러그 (spark) plug
chŏmida 저미다 mince
chŏmjaeng-i 점쟁이 fortune-teller
chŏmjanch'i mot'an 점잖지 못한 indecent
chŏmjanŭn 점잖은 gentle
chŏmjŏk 점적 drip
chŏmjŏm 점점 by degrees, gradually; ***chŏmjŏm tŏ manŭn hakssaengdŭl / shigan*** 점점 더 많은 학생들 / 시간 more and more students / time; ***chŏmjŏm ch'uwŏjida / tŏwŏjida*** 점점 추워지다 / 더워지다 be getting colder / warmer; ***chŏmjŏm sarajida*** 점점 사라지다 die away; fade away; slowly disappear
chŏm kŭlkkol 점 글꼴 bitmap font
chŏmnŭn 접는 folding
chŏmnyŏng 점령 capture; occupation
chŏmnyŏnghada 점령하다 capture; occupy
chŏmp'ŏ 점퍼 jumper COMPUT
chŏmp'o 점포 booth
chŏmshim 점심 lunch
chŏmshimshigan 점심시간 lunch break, lunchtime
chŏmsŏn 점선 dotted line
chŏmsŏngga 점성가 astrologer
chŏmsŏng komu 점성 고무 gum
chŏmsŏngsul 점성술 astrology; horoscope
chŏmsŏni tchik'in 점선이 찍힌 perforated
chŏmsu 점수 point
chŏmtcha 점자 braille
chŏmwŏn 점원 assistant; clerk
chŏmyŏnghan 저명한 distinguished, eminent
chŏn 전 pancake (*Korean-style*)
chŏn(ŭi) 전(의) preceding; front; former ◊ before; ago
chŏnaegŭl naeda 전액을 내다 pay in full
chŏnap 전압 voltage
chŏnbanjŏgin 전반적인 overall
chŏnbŏnŭi 전번의 last
chŏnbo 전보 telegram
chŏnbok 전복 overthrow
chŏnbokshik'ida 전복시키다 bring down, topple
chŏnbok'ada 전복하다 overthrow, overturn
chŏnbu 전부 in all; all of it; altogether
chŏnbuin 전부인 ex-wife
chŏnbuŭi 전부의 complete
chŏn chong-ŏbwŏn 전 종업원 workforce
chŏnch'a 전차 streetcar
chŏnch'ae 전채 appetizer, hors d'oeuvre
chŏnch'e 전체 whole; ***Miguk chŏnch'e*** 미국 전체 the whole of the United States
chŏnch'ejŏgin 전체적인 general
chŏnch'ejŏgŭro 전체적으로 throughout
chŏnch'ejuŭi 전체주의 totalitarianism
chŏnch'ejuŭiŭi 전체주의의 totalitarian
chŏnch'eŭi 전체의 entire; overall; total
chŏnch'isa 전치사 preposition
chŏndaehada 전대하다 sublet
chŏndal sudan 전달 수단 vehicle

(*for information*)
chŏndan 전단 leaflet
chŏndangp'o 전당포 pawnshop
chŏndangp'o chuin 전당포 주인 pawnbroker
chŏndarhada 전달하다 communicate; deliver
chŏndoga ch'angch'anghan 전도가 창창한 promising
chŏndohada 전도하다 conduct ELEC; evangelize
chŏndŭnggat 전등갓 lampshade
...chŏne ...전에 before ◊ previously; ***3il chŏne*** 3일 전에 3 days ago; ***...gi chŏne*** ...기 전에 before ...ing
chŏn-gaehada 전개하다 develop, pan out
chŏng-aek 정액 semen, sperm
chŏngbaksshik'ida 정박시키다 moor
chŏngbaktchang 정박장 berth, moorings
chŏngbandaeŭi 정반대의 diametrically opposed
chŏngbidoeda 정비되다 be in good order
chŏngbigong 정비공 fitter
chŏngbiwŏn 정비원 ground staff
chŏngbo 정보 information, data, intelligence
chŏngbo chegongja 정보 제공자 informant, source
chŏngboga manŭn 정보가 많은 informative
chŏngbok 정복 conquest; mastery
chŏngbo kigwan 정보 기관 intelligence service
chŏngbo kisul 정보 기술 IT, information technology
chŏngboktcha 정복자 conqueror
chŏngbo kwahak 정보 과학 information science
chŏngbo kwahaktcha 정보 과학자 information scientist
chŏngbok'ada 정복하다 conquer
chŏngbu 정부 government; mistress; ***chŏngbu kyugyŏge ttarŭda*** 정부 규격에 따르다 conform to government standards
chŏngch'aek 정책 policy
chŏngch'ahada 정차하다 call at
chŏngch'ak'ada 정착하다 settle; settle down
chŏngch'al 정찰 reconnaissance
chŏngch'i 정치 politics
chŏngch'iga 정치가 politician, statesman
chŏngch'i hŏn-gŭm 정치 헌금 political donation
chŏngch'ijŏgin 정치적인 political
chŏngch'ijŏk mangmyŏng-ŭl shinch'ŏnghada 정치적 망명을 신청하다 seek political asylum
chŏngch'ŏo 정처 fixed place; ***chŏngch'ŏŏpsshi pangnanghada*** 정처없이 방랑하다 drift
chŏngdang 정당 party
chŏngdanghage 정당하게 justifiably; justly
chŏngdanghan 정당한 legitimate; above board
chŏngdanghwa 정당화 justification
chŏngdanghwahada 정당화하다 justify
chŏngdanghwa hal su innŭn 정당화할 수 있는 justifiable
chŏngdang kangnyŏng 정당 강령 party platform
chŏngdo 정도 degree; ***50 chŏngdo*** 50정도 50 or so, about 50; ***i chŏngdoro k'ŭda / noptta*** 이 정도로 크다 / 높다 this big / high; ***i chŏngdo sokttomyŏn*** 이 정도 속도면 at this rate
chŏngdondoen 정돈된 straight, tidy
chŏngdonhada 정돈하다 clear up, tidy
chŏngdorŭl ttŏrŏttŭrida 정도를 떨어뜨리다 downgrade
chŏnggage 정각에 on time
chŏnggak tu shie 정각 두 시에 at two o'clock prompt
chŏnggang-i 정강이 shin
chŏnggi hanggongp'yŏn 정기 항공편 scheduled flight
chŏnggi iptchangkkwŏn 정기 입장권 season ticket
chŏnggijŏgŭro 정기적으로 periodically
chŏnggijŏn 정기전 fixture
chŏnggi kanhaengmul 정기 간행물 periodical

chŏnggi kudok 정기 구독 subscription
chŏnggi kudoktcha 정기 구독자 subscriber
chŏnggi kudok'ada 정기 구독하다 subscribe to
chŏnggisŏn 정기선 liner
chŏnggi sŭngch'akkwŏn 정기 승차권 season ticket
chŏnggŏjang 정거장 depot RAIL
chŏnggwansa 정관사 definite article
chŏnggyohage hada 정교하게 하다 refine
chŏnggyohan 정교한 sophisticated; fine *print*
chŏnggyosujik 정교수직 chair
chŏnggyuŭi wich'ie 정규의 위치에 onside
chŏnghada 정하다 set, fix
chŏnghaptchŏgin 정합적인 coherent
chŏnghwahada 정화하다 purify
chŏnghwak 정확 accuracy, precision
chŏnghwak'ada 정확하다 be right
chŏnghwak'age 정확하게 precisely
chŏnghwak'an 정확한 accurate; definite; exact
chŏnghwak'i 정확히 exactly; punctually, on the dot
chŏnghwak'i aranaeda 정확히 알아내다 pinpoint
chŏnghyŏng oekkwaŭi 정형 외과의 orthopedic
chŏn-gi 전기 electricity, power; biography
chŏn-gi ch'ŏngsogi 전기 청소기 hoover
chŏn-giga t'onghago innŭn 전기가 통하고 있는 live *wire*
chŏn-gi kisa 전기 기사 electrician
chŏn-gi papssot 전기 밥솥 (electric) rice cooker
chŏn-girŭl t'onghage hada 전기를 통하게 하다 electrify
chŏn-gisŏn 전기선 power line
chŏn-gisŏnyong komut'eip'ŭ 전기선용 고무테이프 friction tape
chŏn-gi somoga chŏgŭn shiganŭi 전기 소모가 적은 시간의 off-peak electricity
chŏn-gi tamnyo 전기 담요 electric blanket
chŏngit-tchul 전깃줄 wire
chŏn-giŭi 전기의 electric, electrical
chŏn-gi ŭija 전기 의자 electric chair
chŏngja 정자 sperm
chŏngja ŭnhaeng 정자 은행 sperm bank
chŏngje 정제 tablet
chŏngjehada 정제하다 refine
chŏngje sŏlt'ang 정제 설탕 confectioners' sugar
chŏngjeso 정제소 refinery
chŏngji 정지 halt; suspension
chŏngjihan 정지한 stationary
chŏngjik 정직 honesty, integrity
chŏngjik'ada 정직하다 be on the level
chŏngjik'an 정직한 honest
chŏngji pŏt'ŭn 정지 버튼 off switch
chŏngjishik'ida 정지시키다 suspend; ***chiburŭl chŏngjishik'ida*** 지불을 정지시키다 stop a check
chŏngjŏn 정전 power cut, power outage
chŏngjŏn-gi 정전기 static ELEC
chŏngjong 정종 distilled rice wine
chŏngjunghage 정중하게 respectfully
chŏngjunghan 정중한 courteous; deferential; gallant
chŏngkka 정가 net COM
chŏngkkwŏn 정권 regime
chŏngk'ŭ p'udŭ 정크 푸드 junk food
chŏngmaek 정맥 vein
chŏngmaeng-naeŭi 정맥내의 intravenous
chŏngmal 정말 truth; fact ◊ truly, really; quite; very
chŏngmallo 정말로 actually; really; sure enough
chŏngmil chosahada 정밀 조사하다 investigate in detail
chŏngmil kŏmsahada 정밀 검사하다 overhaul
chŏngmil kŏmt'ohada 정밀 검토하다 overhaul
chŏngmun 정문 front entrance
chŏngmyŏn 정면 façade
chŏngmyŏnch'ungdorŭi 정면충돌의 head-on
chŏngnarahan 적나라한 naked *truth*,

aggression; stark
chŏngnyŏgŭl tahada 정력을 다하다 burn oneself out
chŏngnyŏltchŏgin 정열적인 passionate
chŏngnyŏn 정년 retirement age
chŏngnyujang 정류장 (bus) depot; (bus) shelter; (bus) stop
chŏngnyu ktchŏm 정육점 butcher's
chŏngnyuktchŏm chuin 정육점 주인 butcher
chŏng-ŏri 정어리 sardine
chŏng-o 정오 midday
chŏn-gongdae 천공대 drilling rig
chŏn-gonghada 전공하다 specialize; specialize in; major in
chŏngsa 정사 love affair
chŏngsang 정상 norm; peak, summit; tip; pinnacle ◊ normal; ***chŏngsang-e orŭda*** 정상에 오르다 get to the top
chŏngsanghwahada 정상화하다 normalize
chŏngsang sangt'ae 정상 상태 normality
chŏngsang-ŭro 정상으로 normally
chŏngshigŭi 정식의 proper, real
chŏngshik 정식 set meal
chŏngshin 정신 mind; soul, spirit ◊ psycho-, mental; ***chŏngshini mŏnghada*** 정신이 멍하다 my mind's a blank
chŏngshinbunsŏk 정신분석 psychoanalysis
chŏngshin chang-aega innŭn 정신 장애가 있는 mentally handicapped
chŏngshin ch'angnane kŏllin 정신 착란에 걸린 demented
chŏngshin ch'angnanŭi 정신 착란의 delirious
chŏngshin ch'arige hada 정신 차리게 하다 bring around
chŏngshini mŏnghan 정신이 멍한 dazed
chŏngshini nagada 정신이 나가다 be out of one's mind
chŏngshin isang 정신 이상 insanity
chŏngshin isang-ŭi 정신 이상의 disturbed
chŏngshin kamŭng 정신 감응 telepathy
chŏngshin kamŭng-ŭi 정신 감응의 telepathic
chŏngshinkkwaŭi 정신과의 psychiatric
chŏngshinkkwa ŭisa 정신과 의사 psychiatrist
chŏngshinŏpsshi chikkŏrida 정신없이 지껄이다 rave on mindlessly
chŏngshin pagyaktcha 정신박약자 imbecile
chŏngshinppyŏng 정신병 mental illness
chŏngshinppyŏng-i innŭn 정신병이 있는 mentally ill
chŏngshinppyŏngja 정신병자 psychopath
chŏngshinppyŏng-ŭi 정신병의 mental, crazy
chŏngshinppyŏng-wŏn 정신병원 asylum, mental hospital
chŏngshin punsŏk 정신 분석 psychoanalysis
chŏngshin punsŏk haktcha 정신 분석 학자 psychoanalyst
chŏngshin punsŏk'ada 정신 분석하다 psychoanalyse
chŏngshin punyŏltchŭng 정신 분열증 schizophrenia
chŏngshin punyŏltchŭng hwanja 정신 분열증 환자 schizophrenic patient
chŏngshin punyŏltchŭng-ŭi 정신 분열증의 schizophrenic
chŏngshin sangt'ae 정신 상태 mental state
chŏngshintchŏgin 정신적인 spiritual; platonic
chŏngshintchŏk chang-aega innŭn 정신적 장애가 있는 mentally handicapped
chŏngshintchŏk hakttae 정신적 학대 mental cruelty
chŏngshinŭi 정신의 mental
chŏngshinŭihak 정신의학 psychiatry
chŏngsŏnhan 정선한 select, exclusive
chŏngt'ong 정통 familiarity
chŏngt'onghada 정통하다 know; have a good knowledge of; master; be a master of

chŏng-ŭi 정의 justice; definition
chŏng-ŭirŭl naerida 정의를 내리다 define
chŏn-gŭk 전극 electrode
chŏn-gu 전구 light bulb
chŏn-gun 전군 the forces MIL
chŏng-wŏn 정원 garden
chŏng-wŏnnyong kawi 정원용 가위 clippers
chŏng-wŏnsa 정원사 gardener
chŏng-ye 정예 elite
chŏng-yeŭi 정예의 elite
chŏn-gyŏng 전경 foreground
chŏnhada 전하다 pass on, relay
chŏnhaejuda 전해주다 pass, hand
chŏnhanŭn mal 전하는 말 message
chŏnhuŭi 전후의 postwar
chŏnhwa 전화 telephone; phone call; ***chŏnhwarŭl ssŏdo toemnikka?*** 전화를 써도 됩니까 can I use the phone?
chŏnhwabŏnhobu 전화번호부 phone book
chŏnhwahada 전화하다 phone, call
chŏnhwa kŏlda 전화 걸다 phone
chŏnhwa kyohwan-guk 전화 교환국 telephone exchange
chŏnhwan 전환 change; changeover; conversion
chŏnhwanjŏm 전환점 turning point
chŏnhwa pŏnho 전화 번호 telephone number
chŏnhwa pŏnhobu 전화 번호부 telephone directory
chŏnhwa p'anmae 전화 판매 telesales
chŏnhwarŭl hada 전화를 하다 make a telephone call
chŏnhwarŭl kkŭnt'a 전화를 끊다 hang up
chŏnhwarŭl kŏlda 전화를 걸다 call; telephone; dial
chŏnhwarŭl pat-tta 전화를 받다 answer the telephone
chŏnhyang 전향 convert
chŏnhyangshik'ida 전향시키다 convert *person*
chŏnhyŏ 전혀 entirely, completely, utterly; ***chŏnhyŏ ...ji ant'a*** 전혀 ...지 않다 be anything but; do anything but; ***chŏnhyŏ kwanshimi ŏpssŏ*** 전혀 관심이 없어 I couldn't care less
chŏnhyŏng 전형 stereotype
chŏnhyŏngjŏgin 전형적인 typical
chŏnimja 전임자 predecessor
chŏnja 전자 the former; electron ◊ electronic
chŏnja chep'um 전자 제품 electrical appliance
chŏnja chŏngbo ch'ŏri 전자 정보 처리 EDP, electronic data processing
chŏnjaeng 전쟁 war; warfare
chŏnjaeng chŏnŭi 전쟁 전의 prewar
chŏnjaeng p'oro 전쟁 포로 prisoner of war
chŏnjaengt'ŏ 전쟁터 battlefield, battleground
chŏnjaeng-ŭi ch'amsa 전쟁의 참사 horrors of war
chŏnja keship'an 전자 게시판 bulletin board
chŏnja konghak 전자 공학 electronics
chŏnja k'adŭ 전자 카드 smart card
chŏnja orak 전자 오락 electronic game
chŏnjarenji 전자렌지 microwave
chŏnja sanŏp 전자 산업 electronics industry
chŏnja up'yŏn 전자 우편 electronic mail
chŏnje chŏngch'i 전제 정치 tyranny
chŏnjejokkŏn 전제조건 prerequisite
chŏnji 전지 battery
chŏnjin 전진 advance
chŏnjinhada 전진하다 advance; move on
chŏnjip 전집 collected works
chŏnjugok 전주곡 prelude
chŏnkkwa 전과 criminal record
chŏnmang 전망 prospects
chŏnmang-i choŭn chijŏm 전망이 좋은 지점 vantage point
chŏnmŏgi twaeji 젖먹이 돼지 sucking pig
chŏnmun 전문 specialty
chŏnmun chishik 전문 지식 expertise
chŏnmun-ga 전문가 expert, specialist

chŏnmun-gaŭi ch'unggo 전문가의 충고 expert advice
chŏnmunindaptchi anŭn 전문인답지 않은 unprofessional
chŏnmunjik chongsaja 전문직 종사자 professional
chŏnmunjŏgin 전문적인 professional
chŏnmunjŏgŭro 전문적으로 professionally
chŏnmun kisul 전문 기술 expertise
chŏnmunsŏng 전문성 technicality, technical nature
chŏnmunŭi 전문의 technical
chŏnmunŭro hada 전문으로 하다 specialize; specialize in
chŏnmun yong-ŏ 전문 용어 terminology, jargon
chŏnmyŏlshik'ida 전멸시키다 exterminate, wipe out
chŏnmyŏnjŏgin 전면적인 sweeping
chŏnnamp'yŏn 전남편 ex-husband
chŏnnamu 전나무 fir
Chŏnnŭngja 전능자 the Almighty
chŏnnŭn pae 젓는 배 rowboat
chŏnnyŏm 전념 dedication
chŏnnyŏmhada 전념하다 dedicate oneself to; keep one's mind on; concentrate
chŏnnyŏmhanŭn 전념하는 single-minded, dedicated
chŏnsa 전사 warrior, fighter
chŏnsanhwahada 전산화하다 computerize
chŏnsegi 전세기 charter flight
chŏnsegŭm 전세금 deposit money for a lease on an apartment
chŏnsegyeŭi 전세계의 global
chŏnse naeda 전세 내다 charter
chŏnse not'a 전세 놓다 lease an apartment on a deposit basis
chŏnshi 전시 display; exhibition; wartime
chŏnshiganjero 전시간제로 full time
chŏnshiganjeŭi 전시간제의 full-time
chŏnshihada 전시하다 display, show, exhibit
chŏnshindaeŭi 전신대의 full-length
chŏnshinju 전신주 telegraph pole
chŏnshin mach'wi 전신 마취 general anesthetic
chŏnship'um 전시품 exhibit
chŏnsŏl 전설 legend
chŏnsŏljŏgin 전설적인 legendary
chŏnsŏn 전선 front MIL, (*of weather*); cord; cable
chŏnsŏnggi 전성기 heyday
chŏnsonghada 전송하다 export COMPUT
chŏnsongnyŏgŭro hada 전속력으로 하다 flat out
chŏnsul 전술 tactics
chŏnsultchŏgin 전술적인 tactical
chŏntchŏk 전적 complete, whole; ***chŏntchŏgŭro matsŭmnida*** 전적으로 맞습니다 that's absolutely right
chŏnt'ong 전통 tradition
chŏnt'ongjŏgin 전통적인 traditional, conventional
chŏnt'ongjŏgŭro 전통적으로 traditionally
chŏnt'u 전투 battle; combat; hostilities
chŏnt'ugi 전투기 fighter (*airplane*)
chŏnŭi 전의 former
chŏnŭnghan 저능한 retarded
chŏnya 전야 eve
chŏnyŏge 저녁에 in the evening
chŏnyŏk 전역 evening; all parts; ***Hanguk chŏnyŏgŭl yŏhaenghada*** 한국 전역을 여행하다 travel all over Korea
chŏnyŏk shikssa 저녁 식사 supper
chŏnyŏm 전염 transmission
chŏnyŏmdoenŭn 전염되는 contagious
chŏnyŏmppyŏng 전염병 plague
chŏnyŏmshik'ida 전염시키다 transmit *disease*
chŏnyŏmssŏng-ŭi 전염성의 infectious
chŏnyul 전율 thrill
chŏŏgada 저어가다 row
chŏpch'aktche 접착제 adhesive
chŏpch'ak'ada 접착하다 bond, stick
chŏpch'ok 접촉 contact; touch
chŏpch'ok yŏng-yŏk 접촉 영역 interface
chŏpch'ok'ada 접촉하다 approach, contact; touch
chŏpkkŭn 접근 access
chŏpkkŭnhada 접근하다 access

chŏpkkŭn pangbŏp 접근 방법 approach
chŏppuchi'gi 접붙이기 graft BOT
chŏpssi 접시 plate
chŏpssogŭl kkŭnt'a 접속을 끊다 go off-line
chŏpssokssa 접속사 conjunction GRAM
chŏpssoksshik'ida 접속시키다 connect
chŏpssu kyewŏn 접수 계원 desk clerk
chŏpssok'ada 접속하다 interface; connect with; go on-line to
chŏpssuwŏn 접수원 receptionist
chŏptchi 접지 ground ELEC
chŏptchihada 접지하다 ground ELEC
chŏptta 접다 fold; fold up; turn down
chŏpttusa 접두사 prefix
chŏp'ae it-tta 접해 있다 border
chŏp'ida 접히다 fold up
chŏp'yŏnŭro 저편으로 beyond
chŏrhoehada 철회하다 retrograde
chŏrida 절이다 marinate; pickle
chŏrim 저림 pins and needles
chŏrŏn! 저런! good heavens!
chŏryak 절약 economy; saving
chŏryakpun 절약분 saving
chŏryak undong 절약 운동 economy drive
chŏryak'ada 절약하다 economize; economize on, save
chŏryak'anŭn 절약하는 economical, thrifty
chŏryak'yŏng 절약형 economy size
chŏryŏn 절연 insulation
chŏryŏnhada 절연하다 insulate; sever
chŏsok'an 저속한 vulgar
chŏsŭng 저승 underworld
chŏsuji 저수지 reservoir
chŏtkkarak 젓가락 chopsticks
chŏtkkasŭm 젖가슴 bosom, breast
chŏtkkoktchi 젖꼭지 nipple; teat
chŏt-tta 젖다 get wet
chŏt-tta 젓다 paddle
chŏt'aek 저택 mansion
chŏŭi 저의 H my
chŏŭm poepkkessŭmnida 처음 뵙겠습니다 how do you do (*formal greeting used on first meeting*)
chŏŭmŭi 저음의 deep; bass
chŏul 저울 scales
chŏ wie 저 위에 over there
cho 조 trillion; millet; article, clause; dynasty; tune; air
choahada 좋아하다 like, be fond of; ***muŏt hanŭn kŏsŭl choahada*** 무엇 하는 것을 좋아하다 like to do sth; ***Xŭl / rŭl Ypoda tŏ choahada*** X을 / 를 Y보다 더 좋아하다 prefer X to Y
choajida 좋아지다 pick up, improve; ***nŏn uni choassŏ*** 넌 운이 좋았어 you were lucky
choayo 좋아요 right, OK
chobashimhada 조바심하다 be on tenterhooks
chobŭn 좁은 narrow
chobŭn kil 좁은 길 lane
chobumo 조부모 grandparents
choch'a 조차 even, into the bargain; ***choch'a ant'a*** 조차 않다 not even
choch'ado 조차도 even; ***naŭi abŏji choch'ado*** 나의 아버지 조차도 even my father
choch'i 조치 step, measure
choch'wirŭl ch'wihada 조취를 취하다 take action
choe 죄 sin; guilt, responsibility
choe chit-tta 죄 짓다 sin
choe chiŭn 죄 지은 guilty
choech'aek-kkam 죄책감 guilt; ***...e taehae choech'aek-kkamŭl nŭkkida*** ...에 대해 죄책감을 느끼다 feel bad about, feel guilty about
choein 죄인 sinner
choemsoe 죔쇠 clamp
choemsoero choeda 죔쇠로 죄다 clamp
choeoehada 제외하다 rule out
choerŭl ssŭiuda 죄를 씌우다 incriminate
choesonghamnida 죄송합니다 excuse me; I beg your pardon
choesu 죄수 prisoner
choesu hosongch'a 죄수 호송차 patrol wagon
chogaek 조객 mourner
chogak 조각 bit; piece; slice; fragment; shred; lump; carving, sculpture; ***p'ai / ppang han chogak***

파이/빵 한 조각 a piece of pie/bread
chogak-kka 조각가 sculptor
chogak kŭrim match'ugi 조각 그림 맞추기 jigsaw (puzzle)
chogak naeda 조각 내다 shred
chogakp'um 조각품 sculpture
chogamdok 조감독 assistant director
chogangnada 조각나다 splinter
choging 조깅 jog; jogging
chogingbok 조깅복 jogging suit
choginghada 조깅하다 go for a run, jog
choging shyujŭ 조깅 슈즈 jogger
chogok 조곡 suite MUS
chogŭm 조금 a bit, a little; a bit of; just a couple ◊ any ◊ some; slightly; ***ppang/p'odoju chogŭm*** 빵/포도주 조금 a little bread/wine
chogŭmaham 조그마함 modesty
chogŭmahan 조그마한 tiny; modest
chogŭmdo 조금도 (not) at all, in the least, in the slightest; ***chogŭmdo animnida*** 조금도 아닙니다 not in the slightest
chogŭmsshik 조금씩 little by little
chogŭmsshik tonŭl naeda 조금씩 돈을 내다 chip in
chogŭmŭi 조금의 a few
chogŭmŭn 조금은 little
chohabe kaip'aji anŭn 조합에 가입하지 않은 non-union
chohang 조항 article, clause, section; provision
chohap 조합 association; union; partnership
chohoe 조회 reference
chohoehada 조회하다 refer to
chohwa 조화 harmony; reconciliation
chohwadoen 조화된 harmonious
chohwashik'ida 조화시키다 harmonize; reconcile
chohyŏngjŏgin 조형적인 figurative
choida 조이다 tie
chojak 조작 mockery; fabrication
chojak'ada 조작하다 manufacture; fix; manipulate
chojanghada 조장하다 further *cause*
chojap'an 조잡한 crude
chojeshil 조제실 dispensary
chojik 조직 organization; system; organ ANAT; tissue
chojiktcha 조직자 organizer
chojiktchŏgin 조직적인 systematic
chojik'ada 조직하다 organize
chojŏng chohwa 조정 조화 coordination
chojŏng chohwashik'ida 조정 조화시키다 coordinate
chojŏnghada 조정하다 set, adjust
chojŏrhada 조절하다 tune up
chojong 조종 operation; manipulation; aviation
chojong changch'i 조종 장치 controls
chojonghada 조종하다 operate; manipulate; steer; pilot
chojonghanŭn 조종하는 manipulative
chojongsa 조종사 pilot
chojongshil 조종실 cockpit; flight deck
chokki 조끼 vest
chokkŏn 조건 condition, requirement; ***...ranŭn chokkŏnŭro*** ...라는 조건으로 on condition that
chokkŏnbuŭi 조건부의 conditional
chokkŏnppŏp 조건법 conditional
chokppo 족보 genealogy book
choktchang 족장 chief
choktchebi 족제비 weasel
choktchipkke 족집게 tweezers
chok'a 조카 nephew
chok'attal 조카딸 niece
chok'ŏ 조커 joker
chol 졸 pawn
cholda 졸다 doze, snooze
cholgi 졸기 doze, snooze
chollamaeda 졸라매다 fasten tightly; ***hŏrittirŭl chollamaeda*** 허리띠를 졸라매다 tighten one's belt *fig*
chollida 졸리다 be sleepy
chollin 졸린 sleepy
choltchak 졸작 trash
chom 좀 some; something; ***chom hashigessŏyo?*** 좀 하시겠어요? would you like some?
chomajomahage hanŭn 조마조마하게 하는 nerve-racking
choman-gan 조만간 sooner or later
chomirhada 조밀하다 be dense; ***in-***

guga chomirhan 인구가 조밀한 densely populated
chomiryo 조미료 seasoning; flavoring
chommŏgŭm 좀먹음 erosion *fig*
chommŏktta 좀먹다 erode *fig*
chomttoduktchil 좀도둑질 pilfering
Chomultchu 조물주 the Creator
chomyŏng 조명 lighting
chomyŏnghada 조명하다 illuminate, light
chomyŏngt'an 조명탄 flare
chonan 조난 disaster; accident
chonan sangt'aeŭi 조난 상태의 in distress
chonan shinho 조난 신호 distress signal
chong 종 species; bell
chong-ari 종아리 calf
chongbŏm 종범 accessory LAW
chongdalssae 종달새 lark
chonggi 종기 boil
chonggyo 종교 religion
chonggyojŏgin 종교적인 religious; sacred
chonghap pohŏm 종합 보험 comprehensive insurance
chong-i 종이 paper; ***chong-i han chang*** 종이 한 장 a piece of paper
chong-i kabang 종이 가방 paper bag
chong-ik'ŏp 종이컵 paper cup
chong-i mukkŭm 종이 묶음 pad
chong-ip'yojiŭi yŏmkkap'an ch'aek 종이표지의 염가판 책 paperback
chong-iro mandŭn 종이로 만든 (made of) paper
chong-i ullida 종이 울리다 chime
chongma 종마 stallion
chongnyang 종양 growth, tumor
chongnyohada 종료하다 log off; shut down
chongnyonaeda 종료내다 shut down
chongnyu 종류 kind, sort; ***chŏgŏsŭn ŏttŏn chongnyuŭi kaeimnikka?*** 저것은 어떤 종류의 개입니까? what kind of dog is that?; ***oman chongnyuŭi saram*** 오만 종류의 사람 all kinds of people
chongŏbwŏn 종업원 worker
chongŏbwŏn ch'ongsu 종업원 총수 payroll
chongp'a 종파 denomination
chongsahada 종사하다 practice
chongtchŏm 종점 terminus
chong-ŭl ch'yŏsŏ pullŏjuseyo 종을 쳐서 불러주세요 please ring for attention
chon-gyŏng 존경 respect
chon-gyŏnghada 존경하다 respect, have a great regard for
chon-gyŏnghanŭn sŏnsaengnim-kke 존경하는 선생님께 Dear Sir
chonham 존함 name
chonjae 존재 being, existence
chonjaehada 존재하다 exist
chonjaerŭl mit-tta 존재를 믿다 believe in
chonjunghada 존중하다 respect
chonŏm 존엄 dignity
choŏn 조언 advice; hint; pointer; ***nuguŭi choŏnŭl padadŭrida*** 누구의 조언을 받아들이다 take s.o.'s advice
choŏnhada 조언하다 advise
choŏp tanch'uk'ada 조업 단축하다 be on short time
chopch'ok'aji ank'o chinaeda 접촉하지 않고 지내다 be out of touch
choptta 좁다 be narrow
chop'ap pubun 접합 부분 joint
chorangmal 조랑말 pony
choribnyongp'um 조립용품 kit
choribŏp 조리법 recipe
choribŭi 조립의 modular
choriga sŏnŭn 조리가 서는 coherent
chorip 조립 assembly
chorip kongjang 조립 공장 assembly plant
choripsshigŭi 조립식의 prefabricated
chorip tanwi 조립 단위 module
chorip'ada 조립하다 assemble, set up
chorŏp 졸업 graduation
chorŏpssaeng 졸업생 graduate
chorŏp'ada 졸업하다 graduate
chorong 조롱 mockery; taunt
choronghada 조롱하다 ridicule; ***hyungnaenaemyŏ choronghada*** 흉내내며 조롱하다 mock

chorŭda 조르다 press for; badger; pester
choryŏktcha 조력자 mentor
choryu 조류 current; tide; birds, fowls
choryu poho kuyŏk 조류 보호 구역 bird sanctuary
choryuŭi naejang 조류의 내장 giblets
chosa 조사 investigation; scrutiny; survey
chosadan 조사단 panel
chosahada 조사하다 examine, investigate; survey
chosang 조상 ancestor; ancestry
chosang sungbae 조상 숭배 ancestral worship
chosanwŏn 조산원 midwife
chose 조세 tax; taxes; taxation
choseŭi 조세의 fiscal
choshim 조심 caution
choshimhada 조심하다 take care; guard against; beware of; ***kyedanŭl choshimhaseyo!*** 계단을 조심하세요! mind the step!
choshimsŏng innŭn 조심성 있는 guarded, careful
choshimsŏng ŏmnŭn 조심성 없는 careless
choshimsŭrŏpkke 조심스럽게 carefully
choshimsŭrŏun 조심스러운 cautious
chosŏkp'a 조석파 tidal wave
Chosŏn Minjujuŭi Inmin Konghwaguk 조선 민주주의 인민 공화국 Democratic People's Republic of Korea, DPRK
chosŏnso 조선소 dockyard
choso 조소 ridicule
chosu 조수 assistant; tide
chosuga 조숙아 premature baby
chosuk'an 조숙한 precocious
chot 좆 V prick
chot'a 좋다 be good; ***...do chot'a*** ...해도 좋다 may
choŭn 좋은 good; ***choŭn shiganŭl ponaeda*** 좋은 시간을 보내다 have a good time
choyak 조약 treaty
choyonghada 조용하다 be quiet
choyonghaejida 조용해지다 quieten down, settle down
choyonghage 조용하게 in silence
choyonghage hada 조용하게 하다 quieten down
choyongham 조용함 hush
choyonghan 조용한 quiet; silent
choyonghi! 조용히! hush!, silence!
choyonghi hada 조용히 하다 be quiet, shut up; ***chom choyonghi hae!*** 좀 조용히 해! just be quiet!
choyurhada 조율하다 tune
chŭbi manŭn 즙이 많은 juicy
chŭk 즉 namely
chŭk-kkaktchŏgin 즉각적인 speedy, prompt; instant
chŭksshi 즉시 instantly; on the spot, straight away
chŭksshiro 즉시로 immediately
chŭksshiŭi 즉시의 immediate
chŭkssŏgesŏ chit-tta 즉석에서 짓다 improvize, wing it
chŭkssŏgesŏ mandŭlda 즉석에서 만들다 improvize
chŭkssŏgŭi 즉석의 off the cuff
chŭkssŏk shikp'um 즉석 식품 fast food
chŭk'ŭ 즈크 canvas
chŭk'ŭng-ŭro hada 즉흥으로 하다 improvize
chŭlgida 즐기다 enjoy; relish
chŭlgŏpkke chinaeda 즐겁게 지내다 enjoy oneself
chŭlgŏpkke hada 즐겁게 하다 entertain; ***urinŭn chŏngmal chŭlgŏpkke ponaessŏyo*** 우리는 정말 즐겁게 보냈어요 we had a lovely time
chŭlgŏptta 즐겁다 be delightful, be pleasant
chŭlgŏum 즐거움 enjoyment; amusement
chŭlgŏun 즐거운 enjoyable; pleasing
chŭlgŏun Sŏngt'ani toegirŭl paramnida! 즐거운 성탄이 되기를 바랍니다! Merry Christmas!
chŭngbalshik'ida 증발시키다 vaporize
chŭngbarhada 증발하다 evaporate
chŭngga 증가 increase
chŭnggahada 증가하다 increase
chŭnggahanŭn 증가하는 increasing

chŭnggashik'ida 증가시키다 increase, step up
chŭnggi 증기 vapor
chŭnggŏ 증거 evidence, proof
chŭnggŏrŭl taeda 증거를 대다 substantiate
chŭnghu 증후 symptom; ***...ŭi chŭnghurŭl poida*** ...의 증후를 보이다 be symptomatic of
chŭng-in 증인 witness
chŭng-insŏk 증인석 witness stand
chŭng-inŭro sŏmyŏnghada 증인으로 서명하다 witness
chŭng-inŭro sŏmyŏngham 증인으로 서명함 witness
chŭng-inŭro sŏnsŏhada 증인으로 선서하다 swear in as a witness
chŭngjŏnghada 증정하다 present
chŭngjobu 증조부 great-grandfather
chŭngjomo 증조모 great-grandmother
chŭngkkwŏn kŏraeso 증권 거래소 stock exchange
chŭngkkwŏn shijang 증권 시장 stock market
chŭngkkwŏn shijang punggoe 증권 시장 붕괴 stockmarket crash
chŭngmyŏnghada 증명하다 prove; validate, verify
chŭngmyŏngsŏ 증명서 certificate; ID
chŭng-ŏn 증언 evidence
chŭng-ŏnhada 증언하다 testify, give evidence
chŭng-o 증오 hatred, animosity
chŭngp'ok'ada 증폭하다 amplify
chŭngsangŭl poida 증상을 보이다 be sickening for
chŭngsŏ 증서 diploma
chŭngson 증손 great-grandchild
chŭng-wŏn-gun 증원군 reinforcements
chu 주 note; province, state; week; Lord
chubang 주방 kitchen
chubangjang 주방장 chef
chubangyong seje 주방용 세제 dishwashing liquid
chubu 주부 housewife
chubyŏn 주변 perimeter
chubyŏn changch'i 주변 장치 peripheral COMPUT
chuch'a 주차 parking
chuch'a changso 주차 장소 parking place
chuch'adae 주차대 rack
chuch'agŭmji 주차금지 no parking
chuch'ahada 주차하다 park
chuch'ajang 주차장 parking lot
chuch'a wiban tansogwŏn 주차 위반 단속원 traffic warden
chuch'a wiban ttaktchi 주차 위반 딱지 parking ticket
chuch'a yogŭmgi 주차 요금기 parking meter
chuch'eŭishik 주체의식 sense of independence and sovereignty; ***kungmin chuch'eŭishik*** 국민 주체의식 sense of national identity
chuch'iŭi 주치의 family doctor
chuda 주다 give; assign; allow; give away
chudang 주당 weekly rate
chudo 주도 initiative
chudoen 주된 main
chudohada 주도하다 lead the way
chudojŏgin 주도적인 leading
chudokkwŏn 주도권 supremacy
chudoro 주도로 main road
chudung-i 주둥이 muzzle, snout; spout
chudun-gun 주둔군 garrison
chugan 주간 weekly
chugan kongnyŏn 주간 공연 matinée (*of play*)
chugan kosok toro 주간 고속 도로 interstate
chugan sangnyŏng 주간 상영 matinée (*of movie*)
chuga toeŏ it-tta 주가 되어 있다 predominate
chugida 죽이다 kill; deaden
chugijŏgin 주기적인 periodic
chugŏganŭn 죽어가는 dying
chugŏŭi 주거의 residential
chugŭl unmyŏng 죽을 운명 mortality
chugŭm 죽음 death
chugŭn 죽은 dead
chugŭndŭshi choyonghan 죽은듯이 조용한 deadly quiet
chugŭnkkae 주근깨 freckle

chugŭn saram 죽은 사람 the deceased
chugŭp 주급 weekly payment
chugwanjŏgin 주관적인 subjective
chugyŏ ŏpssaeda 죽여 없애다 eliminate, kill
chugyo 주교 bishop
chuhaeng 주행 run, drive
chuhaeng anjŏngssŏng 주행 안정성 road holding
chuhaeng kŏrigye 주행 거리계 odometer
Chuhan Migun 주한 미군 American Military Forces in Korea
chuhongsaek 주홍색 scarlet
chuhwangsaek 주황색 orange (*color*)
chuhyŏng 주형 cast, mold
chuin 주인 host; landlord; owner, master; mistress
chuin ŏmnŭn 주인 없는 stray (*dog*)
chuip 주입 injection; transfusion
chuipkku 주입구 inlet
chuip'ada 주입하다 infuse; instil; indoctrinate; pump; ***konggirŭl chuip'ada*** 공기를 주입하다 inflate; pump up
chujang 주장 case, argument; claim, assertion; allegation; team captain
chujanghada 주장하다 argue; claim, insist, maintain; ***chagirŭl chujang-hada*** 자기를 주장하다 assert oneself
chujangdoen 주장된 alleged
chuje 주제 motif; topic
chujega 주제가 theme song
chujenŏmŭn 주제넘은 uncalled-for
chujŏhada 주저하다 waver
chujŏhanŭn 주저하는 tentative
chujŏnja 주전자 kettle; jug; teapot; coffee pot
chujohada 주조하다 cast *metal*
chujo kongjang 주조 공장 foundry
chuju 주주 shareholder, stockholder
chujung-e 주중에 midweek
Chu Kidomun 주 기도문 Lord's Prayer
chuktta 죽다 die; ***algo ship'ŏ chuk-kket-tta*** 알고 싶어 죽겠다 I'm dying to know; ***amŭro chuktta*** 암 으로 죽다 die of cancer
chuk'ŭ pakssŭ 주크 박스 jukebox
chul 줄 column, line; file; strap; string; ***chul chiŏ*** 줄 지어 in single file; ***han churŭi kyedan*** 한 줄의 계단 flight (of stairs); ***churŭl ch'ida*** 줄을 치다 rope off; ***churŭl sŏda*** 줄을 서다 stand in line
chulda 줄다 decrease, diminish
chuldambaerŭl p'iuda 줄담배를 피우다 chain smoke
chuldambaerŭl p'iunŭn saram 줄담배를 피우는 사람 chain smoker
chulgi 줄기 stalk, stem; trunk; wisp
chulgot 줄곧 all the time; ***chulgot irhayŏ*** 줄곧 일하여 on the go
chulja 줄자 tape measure
chuljabŭn 줄잡은 conservative
chullŏmkki chul 줄넘기 줄 skipping rope
chullŏmkkihada 줄넘기하다 skip
chulmunŭi 줄무늬 stripe
chulmunŭi ŏlluk 줄무늬 얼룩 streak
chulmunŭi-ŭi 줄무늬의 striped
chul sŏda 줄 서다 line up
chult'agi chul 줄타기 줄 high wire
chumal 주말 weekend; ***chumare*** 주말에 on the weekend
chumnenjŭ 줌렌즈 zoom lens
chumnenjŭro match'uda 줌렌즈로 맞추다 zoom in on
chumŏk 주먹 fist
chumŏk k'oŭi 주먹코의 snub-nosed
chumŏktchil 주먹질 punch, thump
chumŏni 주머니 pouch, bag; pocket
chumŏnik'al 주머니칼 pocketknife
chumoja 주모자 ringleader
chumok 주목 attention, notice; ***mut saramŭi chumogŭl pat-tta*** 뭇 사람의 주목을 받다 be in the limelight
chumok'ada 주목하다 pay attention
chumok'ae chushipsshio 주목해 주십시오 your attention please
chumok'al manhan 주목할 만한 remarkable; notable; noticeable
chumun 주문 order; magic spell; ***chumune match'uda*** 주문에 맞추다 fill an order
chumunhada 주문하다 order
chunbi 준비 preparation
chunbidoen 준비된 ready; ***muŏsŭl hal chunbiga toeŏ it-tta*** 무엇을 할

준비가 되어 있다 be prepared to do sth, be willing to do sth
chunbihada 준비하다 arrange, fix; prepare; get ready
chunbihaesŏ 준비해서 in preparation for
chunbihanŭn tan-gye-esŏ 준비하는 단계에서 at the planning stage
chunbi undong-ŭl hada 준비 운동을 하다 warmup
chung 중 Buddhist monk; middle ◊ among; out of; in ◊ while; ***yŏl kae chung han kae*** 열 개 중 한 개 one in ten; ***...ŭi chung-ang-esŏ*** ...의 중앙에서 in the middle of; ***...chung-e*** ...중에 in the middle of
chung-ang 중앙 center ◊ central
chung-ang anjŏn changch'i 중앙 안전 장치 central locking
chung-ang chamgŭm changch'i 중앙 잠금 장치 central heating
chung-ang ch'ŏri changch'i 중앙 처리 장치 CPU, central processing unit
chung-ang pullidae 중앙 분리대 median strip
chung-ang ŭnhaeng-ŭi kibon kŭmni 중앙 은행의 기본 금리 base rate
chungbokdoeda 중복되다 overlap
chungch'ŭnghyŏng-ŭi ap'at'ŭ 중층형의 아파트 duplex (apartment)
chungch'ujŏgin 중추적인 spinal
chungdaehada 중대하다 be important; ***...ranŭn kŏsŭn kŭk'i chungdaehamnida*** ...라는 것은 극히 중대합니다 it is vital that
chungdaehan 중대한 significant, momentous; great; grave
chungdan 중단 disruption, interruption; pause
chungdanhada 중단하다 interrupt; cease; pause; cut out; ***chamshi chungdanhada*** 잠시 중단하다 take a break
chungdan ŏmnŭn 중단 없는 non-stop
chungdan ŏpsshi 중단 없이 non-stop
chungdanshik'ida 중단시키다 cease; pause; disrupt, interrupt; disconnect
chungdo-e 중도에 midway
chungdogida 중독이다 be addicted to
chungdok 중독 addiction
chungdokssŏng-ida 중독성이다 be addictive
chungdoktcha 중독자 addict
Chungdong 중동 Middle East ◊ Middle Eastern
chungdop'a 중도파 center group, center party
chungdŭng kyoyuk 중등 교육 secondary education
chunggae 중개 mediation; ***...saiŭi chunggae yŏk'arŭl hada*** ...사이의 중개 역할을 하다 bridge *fig*
chunggaehada 중개하다 mediate
chunggaeja 중개자 go-between
chunggaeŏp 중개업 agency
chunggaeŏptcha 중개업자 broker
chunggan chijŏmŭi 중간 지점의 halfway
chunggane 중간에 halfway
chunggan hyushik 중간 휴식 half time
chunggan irŭm 중간 이름 middle name
chunggankkŭp 중간급 middleweight
chunggan k'ŭgi 중간 크기 medium size
chunggansaegŭi 중간색의 neutral *color*
chunggan sang-in 중간 상인 middleman
chungganŭi 중간의 middle; medium; intermediate
chunggoro 중고로 secondhand
chunggoŭi 중고의 secondhand
Chunggug-ŏ 중국어 Chinese (*language*)
Chungguk 중국 China ◊ Chinese
Chungguk pont'o 중국 본토 mainland China
Chungguk pukkyŏngŏ 중국 북경어 Mandarin (*language*)
Chungguk saram 중국 사람 Chinese (*person*)
chunggyehada 중계하다 relay
chunggyein 중계인 contact
chunghan 중한 heavy
chunghon 중혼 bigamy

chunghwahada 중화하다 counteract
chunghwanjashil 중환자실 intensive care (unit)
chung-ida 중이다: ***kŭgŏsŭn kŏmt'o / chosa chung-ida*** 그것은 검토 / 조사 중이다 it is under review / investigation
chungjae 중재 intervention; mediation; arbitration
chungjaehada 중재하다 intervene; intercede; arbitrate, mediate
chungjaein 중재인 mediator, intermediary
chungji 중지 cessation
chungjihada 중지하다 discontinue; abort
chungjishik'ida 중지시키다 break up
chungjoe 중죄 felony
chungmae kyŏrhon 중매 결혼 arranged marriage
chungnibŭi 중립의 neutral
chungnip 중립 neutrality; ***chungnibe*** 중립에 in neutral
chungnipssŏng 중립성 neutrality
chungniptchŏgin 중립적인 nonaligned
chungnip wich'i 중립 위치 neutral
chungnyang ch'ogwaŭi 중량 초과의 overweight
chungnyŏk 중력 gravity
chungnyŏn 중년 middle age ◊ middle-aged
chungnyohada 중요하다 matter, be important
chungnyohan 중요한 important
chungnyong 중용 moderation
chungnyosŏng 중요성 importance
chung-ŏlgŏrida 중얼거리다 mumble, mutter
chungp'a 중파 medium wave
chungsa 중사 sergeant
chungsanch'ŭng 중산층 middle classes
chungsang 중상 slander
chungsanghada 중상하다 slander
chungsang moryak 중상 모략 smear campaign
chungsanmo 중산모 top hat
Chungse 중세 Middle Ages ◊ medieval
chungshimbue innŭn 중심부에 있는 central
chungshimdae 중심대 crossbar
chungshimga 중심가 main street
chungshimji 중심지 center (*region*)
chungshimjŏk 중심적 central; ***muŏse chungshimjŏgida*** 무엇에 중심적이다 be central to sth
chungshimŭi 중심의 central
chungshimŭl tuda 중심을 두다 center on
chungso kiŏp 중소 기업 small and medium industry
chungt'ae 중태 serious condition MED
chungt'ae-esŏ pŏsŏnan 중태에서 벗어난 out of danger MED
chungt'oehada 중퇴하다 drop out
chungt'oeja 중퇴자 dropout
chung-wi 중위 (first) lieutenant
chun-gyŏlssŭng 준결승 semifinal
chung-yohada 중요하다 be important
chung-yohan 중요한 important, crucial
chung-yo insa 중요 인사 very important person
chung-yo shinch'e kigwan 중요 신체 기관 vital organs
chunim 주님 Lord (Jesus)
chunjun-gyŏlssŭng 준준결승 quarter-final
chunjun-gyŏlssŭng chinch'ultcha 준준결승 진출자 quarter-finalist
chun kunsajŏgin 준 군사적인 paramilitary
chun kunsayowŏn 준 군사요원 paramilitary
chunŏmhan 준엄한 austere
chunsŏrhada 준설하다 dredge
chunsuja 준수자 conformist
chun ŭiryo hwalttong chongsaja 준 의료 활동 종사자 paramedic
chuŏ 주어 subject GRAM
chup'asu 주파수 frequency
chu(rib)ŭi 주(립)의 state, provincial
churi chida 줄이 지다 be streaked with
churida 줄이다 reduce; turn down *volume, heating*; cut down, cut down on; cut short; shorten; narrow
churin irŭm 줄인 이름 diminutive

churŏdŭlda 줄어들다 go down; die down; shrink
churŏdŭrŏ it-tta 줄어들어 있다 be down (*of numbers, amount*)
churo 주로 mainly
churŭm 주름 pleat; crease; wrinkle
churŭm changshik 주름 장식 ruffle
churŭm chegŏsul 주름 제거술 facelift
churŭmjida 주름지다 wrinkle
churŭmjige hada 주름지게 하다 wrinkle
churyehada 주례하다 marry
churyŏssŭda 줄여쓰다 abbreviate
churyu p'anmaejŏm 주류 판매점 liquor store
chusa 주사 injection
chusagi 주사기 syringe
chusahada 주사하다 inject
chusa panŭl 주사 바늘 hypodermic needle
chusawi 주사위 dice
chushik 주식 stock, share
chushik chungmae-in 주식 중매인 stockbroker
chushik hoesa 주식 회사 stock company
chushik shijang 주식 시장 (stock) market
chusŏk 주석 gloss, explanation; tin
chuso 주소 address
chusorok 주소록 address book; mailing list
chusorŭl ssŭda 주소를 쓰다 address *letter*
chuso sŏngmyŏngnok 주소 성명록 directory
chut'aek 주택 housing
chut'aek sajŏng 주택 사정 housing conditions
chut'aek tanji 주택 단지 housing project
chuŭi 주의 attention; warning; notice
chuŭi chuda 주의 주다 tick off
chuŭigip'ŭn 주의깊은 attentive, watchful
chuŭihada 주의하다 pay attention, take notice of
chuŭi kipkke saenggak'ada 주의 깊게 생각하다 mull over
chuŭirŭl kiurida 주의를 기울이다 pay attention
chuŭirŭl kkŭlda 주의를 끌다 draw attention
chuŭirŭl tollida 주의를 돌리다 sidetrack
chuŭishik'ida 주의시키다 caution
chuwi 주위 perimeter, periphery ◊ around; ***chuwie*** 주위에 around, in the area
chuwiŭi 주위의 surrounding
chuwŏ moŭda 주워 모으다 gather up
chuwŏ ollida 주워 올리다 pick up
chuya p'yŏngbunshi 주야 평분시 equinox
chuyŏnhada 주연하다 star
chuyŏnŭro hada 주연으로 하다 feature; star
chuyohan 주요한 main, major; predominant
chuyo shikp'um 주요 식품 staple food
chuyoshikttan 주요식단 staple diet
chuyu p'ŏmp'ŭ 주유 펌프 gas pump
chuyuso 주유소 gas station
chwach'ŭk haendŭl unjŏn 좌측 핸들 운전 left-hand drive
chwach'ugŭi 좌측의 port; left-hand
chwadamhoe 좌담회 talk show
chwagol shin-gyŏngt'ong 좌골 신경통 sciatica
chwaigŭi 좌익의 left-wing
chwaik 좌익 left wing ◊ left-wing
chwajŏl 좌절 frustration; setback; discouragement
chwajŏlsshik'ida 좌절시키다 frustrate; defeat; foil, thwart
chwajŏrhada 좌절하다 collapse; go to pieces; get discouraged
chwaumyŏng 좌우명 motto
chwayak 좌약 suppository
chwi 쥐 mouse; rat
chwikkori 쥐꼬리 rat tail
chwikkorimanhan 쥐꼬리만한 derisory, paltry
chyusŭ 쥬스 juice

CH'

ch'a 차 vehicle; car; tea; ***ch'aro teryŏjuda*** 차로 데려다주다 drive, take by car; ***ch'arŭl t'ago kabŏrida*** 차를 타고 가버리다 drive away
ch'abŏrida 차버리다 ditch, jilt
ch'abunhan 차분한 placid, serene; imperturbable
ch'abyŏl 차별 discrimination
ch'abyŏrhada 차별하다 differentiate between; discriminate against
ch'ach'a 차차 by degrees
ch'ach'ang 차창 car window; bus window; train window
ch'ach'e 차체 bodywork
ch'ach'e kongjang 차체 공장 body shop
ch'ach'uk 차축 axle
ch'ada 차다 be filled, be packed; be satisfied; expire; kick; reject
ch'adanhada 차단하다 block out; exclude
ch'ado 차도 driveway
ch'adorŭl poida 차도를 보이다 make progress (*in health*)
ch'ado tchogŭi 차도 쪽의 offside MOT
ch'ae 채 bat ◊ *countword for buildings*
ch'aegim 책임 responsibility; accountability; ***...e ch'aegimi it-tta*** ...에 책임이 있다 be responsible for; ***ch'aegimŭl chida*** 책임을 지다 be held accountable for, answer for; ***ch'aegimŭl chŏn-gahada*** 책임을 전가하다 pass the buck
ch'aegimi innŭn 책임이 있는 responsible
ch'aegimi mugŏun 책임이 무거운 responsible *job*
ch'aegimja 책임자 person in charge; ***ch'aegimjarŭl mannal su issŭlkkayo?*** 책임자를 만날 수 있을까요? can I see the manager?
ch'aegim pohŏm 책임 보험 liability insurance
ch'aegurhada 채굴하다 mine for
ch'aegwangch'ang 채광창 skylight
ch'aegwŏnja 채권자 creditor
ch'aek 책 book
ch'aek-kkabang 책가방 school bag
ch'aekkwŏn 채권 bond
ch'aekssang 책상 desk
ch'aektchang 책장 bookcase
ch'aek k'ŏbŏ 책 커버 dust jacket
ch'aemp'iŏn 챔피언 champion
ch'aemuja 채무자 debtor
ch'aeng 챙 visor
ch'aenggyŏduda 챙겨두다 set aside
ch'aengnyak 책략 maneuver
ch'aenŏl 채널 channel
ch'aeshigŭi 채식의 vegetarian
ch'aeshiktchuŭija 채식주의자 vegetarian
ch'aesŏktchang 채석장 quarry
ch'aetchiktchil 채찍질 beating; whip
ch'aetchiktchirhada 채찍질하다 whip, beat
ch'aet'aek 채택 choice, selection; adoption
ch'aet'aek'hada 채택하다 select, choose; adopt
ch'aeuda 채우다 complete, fill out; do up, fasten; fill; chill
ch'aewŏ nŏt'a 채워 넣다 stuff
ch'agaptta 차갑다 be cold; be coldhearted
ch'agaun 차가운 cold; cool
ch'age hada 차게 하다 chill
ch'agi 차기 kick
ch'ago 차고 (parking) garage
ch'agwandan 차관단 consortium
ch'agyonghada 착용하다 put on; wear; ***anjŏnbelt'ŭrŭl ch'agyonghashio*** 안전벨트를 착용하시오 fasten your seatbelt
ch'ai 차이 difference; ***amurŏn ch'aiga ŏptta*** 아무런 차이가 없다 it

doesn't make any difference
ch'ajaboda 찾아보다 look; look up; look out for
ch'ajabogi 찾아보기 index
ch'ajagada 찾아가다 pay a visit to
ch'ajanaeda 찾아내다 dig out; dig up
ch'ajang 차장 conductor (*on train*)
ch'aja tanida 찾아 다니다 scour, search
ch'ajihada 차지하다 occupy, take up
ch'ajŭngnanŭn kŏt 짜증나는 것 irritation
ch'akch'wi 착취 exploitation
ch'akch'wihada 착취하다 exploit; ***tonŭl ch'akch'wihada*** 돈을 착취하다 bleed, drain *fig*
ch'ak-kkak 착각 delusion
ch'ak-kkak'ada 착각하다 mistake; ***nŏn sŭsŭro ch'ak-kkak'ago innŭn kŏya*** 넌 스스로 착각하고 있는 거야 you're deluding yourself
ch'akssaek 착색 stain (*for wood*)
ch'akssaek'ada 착색하다 stain *wood*
ch'aksshi 착시 optical illusion
ch'aksshirhan saenghwarŭl hada 착실한 생활을 하다 go straight
ch'akssŏk'ayŏ chushipsshio 착석하여 주십시오 please take a seat
ch'akssuhada 착수하다 start, commence; mount; launch; ***chinjihage ch'akssuhada*** 진지하게 착수하다 start in earnest; knuckle down
ch'aktchap'an 착잡한 complex; ***nanŭn kŭege ch'aktchap'an shimjŏng-ŭl kajigo it-tta*** 나는 그에게 착잡한 심정을 가지고 있다 I have mixed feelings about him
ch'ak'an ch'ŏk'anŭn saram 착한 척하는 사람 goody-goody
ch'algwasang 찰과상 graze
ch'alk'ak'anŭn soriga nada 찰칵하는 소리가 나다 click
ch'alssak ch'ida 찰싹 치다 swat
ch'alssak ttaerida 찰싹 때리다 slap, cuff
ch'alssak ttaerim 찰싹 때림 blow, cuff
ch'am 참 truth ◊ true ◊ truly; what!
ch'amara! 참아라! just be patient!
ch'amch'i 참치 tuna
ch'amga 참가 participation
ch'amgahada 참가하다 enter; participate; play in; ***kŏraee ch'amgahada*** 거래에 참가하다 come in on a deal
ch'amgaja 참가자 entrant, participant; entry
ch'amgashik'ida 참가시키다 enter
ch'amgohada 참고하다 consult
ch'amgo tosŏ 참고 도서 reference book
ch'am-gyŏn chal hanŭn saram 참견 잘 하는 사람 busybody
ch'amgyŏnhada 참견하다 poke one's nose into
ch'amgyŏnhagi choahanŭn 참견하기 좋아하는 nosy
ch'amho 참호 trench
ch'a mŏlmi 차 멀미 car sickness
ch'amp'ae 참패 thashing, massacre SP
ch'amp'aeshik'ida 참패시키다 thrash SP
ch'amsae 참새 sparrow
ch'amshinhan 참신한 refreshing; gratifying
ch'amsŏk 참석 attendance
ch'amsŏktcha 참석자 turnout
ch'amsŏk'ada 참석하다 attend, be present; ***chamkkan ch'amsŏk'ada*** 잠깐 참석하다 put in an appearance
ch'amsŏn 참선 meditation (*Buddhism*)
ch'amsŏnhada 참선하다 meditate (*Buddhism*)
ch'amtta 참다 contain, repress; contain oneself; stand, tolerate; stomach
ch'amŭlssŏng 참을성 patience
ch'amŭlssŏng innŭn 참을성 있는 patient
ch'amŭlssŏng itkke 참을성 있게 patiently
ch'amŭlssŏng ŏmnŭn 참을성 없는 impatient
ch'amŭl su innŭn 참을 수 있는 tolerable
ch'amŭl su ŏmnŭn 참을 수 없는 intolerable
ch'amŭro 참으로 vitally
ch'amyŏhada 참여하다 take part in

ch'anban yangnon 찬반 양론 the pros and cons
ch'angbaek 창백 pallor
ch'angbaek'an 창백한 pale, pasty
ch'anggo 창고 depot, warehouse; storehouse; stockroom; ***...ch'anggo-e nŏ-ŏ pogwanhada*** ... 창고에 넣어 보관하다 put in storage
ch'anggu 창구 wicket, window
ch'angja 창자 bowels, gut
ch'angjaktcha 창작자 author
ch'angjo 창조 creation
ch'angjohada 창조하다 create
ch'angjoja 창조자 creator
ch'angjojŏgin 창조적인 creative
ch'angjomul 창조물 creation, work
ch'angmun 창문 window
ch'angmunŭl yŏrŏ chushigessŭmnikka? 창문을 열어 주시겠습니까? would you mind opening the window?
ch'angnyŏ 창녀 prostitute, hooker
ch'angnyuk 착륙 landing, touchdown
ch'angnyuk changch'i 착륙 장치 undercarriage, landing gear
ch'angnyukshik'ida 착륙시키다 land
ch'angnyuk'ada 착륙하다 land, touch down
ch'angshija 창시자 originator
ch'angsŏltcha 창설자 creator, founder
ch'angt'ŏk 창턱 windowsill
ch'ang-ŭijŏgin 창의적인 inventive
ch'ang-yuri 창유리 pane, windowpane
ch'anmija 찬미자 admirer
ch'annip 찻잎 tea leaf
ch'ansa 찬사 compliment
ch'ansahada 찬사하다 compliment, pay a compliment
ch'ansahanŭn 찬사하는 complimentary
ch'ansŏnghada 찬성하다 approve; approve of; be in favor of
ch'ansongga 찬송가 hymn
ch'antchang 찬장 cupboard (*in kitchen*); sideboard
ch'a pongji 차 봉지 teabag
ch'apssal 찹쌀 glutinous rice, sticky rice
ch'ap'okttŭng 차폭등 sidelight
ch'arida 차리다 prepare *meal*; set up *shop*; dress up; keep; collect *one's senses*; take care; preserve; ***ch'arin kŏn optchiman mani tŭseyo*** 차린 건 없지만 많이 드세요 please help yourself
ch'aryang 차량 railroad car, carriage
ch'aryang kujo hoesa 차량 구조 회사 wrecking company
ch'aryang kyŏninso 차량 견인소 pound (*for cars*)
ch'aryang tŭngnok pŏnho 등록 번호 license plate number
ch'arye 차례 turn, act; ***nŏŭi ch'arye*** 너의 차례 over to you; ***ch'arye ch'aryero*** 차례 차례로 in turns; ***che ch'aryeimnida*** 제 차례입니다 it's my turn; ***tangshin ch'aryeyeyo*** 당신 차례예요 it's your turn
ch'aryŏ iptta 차려 입다 dress up; ***mŏttchige ch'aryŏ iptta*** 멋지게 차려 입다 get dolled up
ch'aryŏnaeda 차려내다 serve up
ch'a sech'ŏk 차 세척 car wash
ch'asŏn 차선 (*traffic*) lane
ch'atchan 찻잔 teacup
ch'atkki himdŭn 찾기 힘든 elusive
ch'atssutkkarak 찻숟가락 teaspoon
ch'attchan set'ŭ 찻잔 세트 tea service, tea set
ch'attchŏmja 차점자 runner-up
ch'at-tta 찾다 find; look for; search for *place*
ch'ayang 차양 awning
ch'ayongja 차용자 tenant
ch'e 체 sieve, strainer; pretense
ch'ege 체계 system
ch'egejŏgŭro 체계적으로 systematically
ch'egyŏk 체격 physique, build
ch'ehada 체하다 pretend
ch'ehŏm 체험 experience
ch'ehyŏng 체형 corporal punishment
ch'ein 체인 chain
ch'einjom 체인점 chain (*of stores*)
ch'eisŏ 체이서 chaser
ch'ejil 체질 constitution
ch'ejo 체조 gymnastics

ch'ejobok 체조복 leotard
ch'ejung kwadaŭi 체중 과다의 overweight
ch'ejung midarŭi 체중 미달의 underweight
ch'ejung-ŭl nŭrida 체중을 늘이다 put on weight
Ch'ek'o 체코 Czech
Ch'ek'o konghwaguk 체코 공화국 Czech Republic
Ch'ek'oŏ 체코어 Czech (*language*)
Ch'ek'o saram 체코 사람 Czech (*person*)
ch'ek'ŭaut'ada 체크아웃하다 check out
ch'ek'ŭinhada 체크인하다 check in
ch'ek'ŭ munŭi 체크 무늬 check pattern
ch'ek'ŭ munŭiŭi 체크 무늬의 checked
ch'ek'ŭp'oint'ŭ 체크포인트 checkpoint
ch'ello 첼로 cello
ch'emyŏnŭl ch'arinŭn 체면을 차리는 image-conscious
ch'emyŏnŭl ilt'a 체면을 잃다 lose face; be in the doghouse
ch'emyŏnŭl sonsangshik'ida 체면을 손상시키다 degrade; ***chagiŭi ch'emyŏnŭl sonsangshik'ida*** 자기의 체면을 손상시키다 compromise oneself
ch'emyŏnŭl sonsangshik'inŭn 체면을 손상시키는 degrading
ch'enae 체내 inside the body; ***ch'enaee(sŏ)*** 체내에(서) internally; ***ch'enae pangsanŭng punp'o sajin*** 체내 방사능 분포 사진 scan MED
ch'enap 체납 delinquency
ch'enyŏmhanŭn 체념하는 resigned
ch'eŏ lip'ŭt'ŭ 체어 리프트 chair lift
ch'ep'o 체포 arrest
ch'ep'ohada 체포하다 arrest, pick up
ch'ero ch'ida 체로 치다 sift
ch'eryŏginnŭn 체력있는 athletic
ch'eryŏk 체력 stamina
ch'eryu 체류 residence, stay
ch'esŭ 체스 chess
ch'esŭp'an 체스판 chessboard
ch'eyuk 체육 gym, gymnastics
ch'eyuk-kkwan 체육관 gym, gymnasium
ch'eyuk kyosa 체육 교사 gymnast
ch'ia 치아 teeth ◊ dental
ch'ia kŏmsa 치아 검사 dental checkup
ch'ida 치다 hit, knock; buffet; count, include; strike (*of clock*); crash (*of thunder*); draw *curtain*; pitch *tent*; take *exam*
ch'igi 치기 slap, blow
ch'igwan 치관 crown
ch'ijanghada 치장하다 preen oneself
ch'ijil 치질 piles
ch'ijŭ 치즈 cheese
ch'ijŭbŏgŏ 치즈버거 cheeseburger
ch'ijŭk'eik 치즈케익 cheesecake
ch'ikkwa 치과 dental clinic
ch'ikkwa ŭisa 치과 의사 dentist
ch'ik'yŏ ollagan 치켜 올라간 slanting
ch'il 칠 seven; paint; varnish; laquer; ***ch'il chu-ŭi*** 칠 주의 wet paint
ch'ilgi 칠기 lacquerware
ch'ilmyŏnjo 칠면조 turkey
ch'ilp'an 칠판 blackboard
ch'ilsship 칠십 seventy
ch'im 침 saliva; acupuncture
ch'ima 치마 skirt
ch'imbŏm 침범 invasion; intrusion
ch'imbŏmhada 침범하다 invade; intrude
ch'imch'ak 침착 calm, composure; poise
ch'imch'ak'ada 침착하다 keep one's cool
ch'imch'ak'age hae! 침착하게 해! steady on!
ch'imch'ak'age it-tta 침착하게 있다 keep calm; keep one's wits about one
ch'imch'ak'am 침착함 presence of mind
ch'imch'ak'an 침착한 calm, composed; poised; unflappable
ch'imch'ehada 침체하다 stagnate
ch'imch'ehan 침체한 stagnant
ch'imdae 침대 bed
ch'imdaebo 침대보 bedspread
ch'imdaech'a 침대차 sleeping car
ch'imdaech'atkkan 침대찻간

couchette
ch'imdaek'an 침대칸 berth
ch'imdaeppo 침대보 cover, blanket
ch'imgu 침구 bedclothes
ch'imha 침하 subsidence
ch'imhaehada 침해하다 encroach on *rights*
ch'imip 침입 break-in, raid
ch'imiptcha 침입자 intruder, raider
ch'imip'ada 침입하다 encroach on; trepass; infiltrate; break in; raid
ch'imjŏnmul 침전물 sediment
ch'immugŭl chik'ida 침묵을 지키다 stay silent
ch'immuk 침묵 silence
ch'immukshik'ida 침묵시키다 silence
ch'imnyak 침략 invasion
ch'imnyak'ada 침략하다 invade
ch'imnyŏpssu 침엽수 conifer
ch'imp'anji 침팬지 chimpanzee
ch'imshik 침식 erosion
ch'imshik'ada 침식하다 erode
ch'imshil 침실 bedroom
ch'imsul 침술 acupuncture
ch'imt'u 침투 penetration
ch'imŭl hŭllida 침을 흘리다 dribble
ch'imŭl paet-tta 침을 뱉다 spit
ch'imurhae it-tta 침울해 있다 be gloomy, feel down
ch'imurhage nŭkkida 침울하게 느끼다 be feeling low
ch'imurhan 침울한 melancholy; dismal; sullen; somber
ch'imyŏngjŏgin 치명적인 fatal, lethal; devastating, shattering
ch'imyŏngsang-ŭi 치명상의 fatally injured
ch'inaehanŭn 친애하는 dear
ch'inbumo 친부모 biological parents
ch'inch'ŏgi toenŭn 친척이 되는 related
ch'inch'ŏk 친척 relative, relation
ch'ingch'an 칭찬 praise
ch'ingch'anhada 칭찬하다 praise; pay a compliment
ch'ingch'anhal manhan 칭찬할 만한 creditable; praiseworthy
ch'ingho 칭호 form of address
ch'ing-ŏlgŏrida 칭얼거리다 whine, complain
ch'ingsong 칭송 applause, praise
ch'ingsonghada 칭송하다 applaud, praise
ch'in-gŭnhan 친근한 familiar, friendly
ch'in-gu 친구 friend, buddy
ch'in-guga toeda 친구가 되다 make friends
ch'in-gyo moim 친교 모임 get-together
ch'inhada 친하다 be close; ***Xwa / kwa ch'inhage toeda*** X와 / 과 친하게 되다 be friendly with X, be friends with X
ch'inhan 친한 friendly; close
ch'inhwan-gyŏngjŏgin 친환경적인 environmentally friendly
ch'inhwan-gyŏng sech'ŏktche 친환경 세척제 biological detergent
ch'injŏl 친절 kindness
ch'injŏrhada 친절하다 be kind
ch'injŏrhage 친절하게 kindly; ***nuguege ch'injŏrhage hada*** 누구에게 친절하게 하다 do s.o. a good turn
ch'injŏrhan 친절한 kind
ch'inmogŭi 친목의 social
ch'insuk'am 친숙함 intimacy
ch'insuk'an 친숙한 intimate
ch'iŏ nŏmŏttŭrida 치어 넘어뜨리다 knock over; run over
ch'iŏridŏ 치어리더 cheerleader
ch'ip 칩 chip
ch'irhada 칠하다 paint
ch'irhŭk 칠흑 pitch black
ch'irŭda 치르다 pay; take *examination*; undergo; hold *ceremony*
ch'irwŏl 칠월 July
ch'iryo 치료 cure; treatment; therapy
ch'iryo chŏnmun-ga 치료 전문가 therapist
ch'iryohada 치료하다 treat; cure
ch'iryoŭi 치료의 therapeutic
ch'isŏk 치석 plaque
ch'isot-tta 치솟다 rocket, soar, shoot up
ch'issu 치수 size; measurements
ch'issurŭl chaeda 치수를 재다 measure
ch'itssol 칫솔 toothbrush

ch'it'ong 치통 toothache
ch'iuda 치우다 brush; clear; remove; put away
ch'iyak 치약 toothpaste
ch'iyŏl kyojŏnggi 치열 교정기 brace
ch'iyŏrhan 치열한 cut-throat
ch'iyok 치욕 a disgrace; ***ch'iyoktchŏgin iriyeyo*** 치욕적인 일이에요 it's a disgrace
ch'iyokssŭrŏpkke 불명예스럽게 disgracefully, shamefully
ch'ŏbanghada 처방하다 prescribe
ch'ŏbangjŏn 처방전 prescription
ch'ŏbŏl 처벌 punishment; penalty
ch'ŏbŏrhada 처벌하다 punish; penalize
ch'ŏbun 처분 disposal
ch'ŏbunhada 처분하다 dispose of; part with
ch'ŏhada 처하다 run into
ch'ŏhyŏng 처형 sister-in-law (*wife's elder sister*)
ch'ŏje 처제 sister-in-law (*wife's younger sister*)
ch'ŏjida 처지다 hang down; ***ch'uk ch'ŏjida*** 축 처지다 sag (*of ceiling, rope*)
ch'ŏk 척 *countword for boats*
ch'ŏkch'u 척추 spine
ch'ŏkch'u chiapssa 척추 지압사 chiropractor
ch'ŏkch'udongmul 척추동물 vertebrate
ch'ŏkch'ugol 척추골 vertebra
ch'ŏkch'uŭi 척추의 spinal
ch'ŏktto 척도 yardstick, criterion
ch'ŏk'ada 척하다 pretend, play-act
ch'ŏl 철 season, period
ch'ŏlgap sang-ŏ aljŏt 철갑 상어 알젓 caviar
ch'ŏlgongso 철공소 ironworks
ch'ŏlgŭn k'onk'ŭrit'ŭ 철근 콘크리트 reinforced concrete
ch'ŏlk'ŏdŏnghanŭn sori 철커덩하는 소리 clang
ch'ŏlk'ŏdŏnghanŭn soriga nada 철커덩하는 소리가 나다 clang
ch'ŏlmang 철망 wire netting
ch'ŏlmul 철물 hardware
ch'ŏlmultchŏm 철물점 hardware store
ch'ŏlssa 철사 wire
ch'ŏlssŏk ttaerida 철썩 때리다 whack
ch'ŏlssu 철수 withdrawal
ch'ŏlssuhada 철수하다 withdraw (*of troops*)
ch'ŏlssushik'ida 철수시키다 withdraw *troops*
ch'ŏltcha 철자 spelling
ch'ŏltchahada 철자하다 spell
ch'ŏltcha hwagin 철자 확인 spellcheck
ch'ŏltcha hwagin togu 철자 확인 도구 spellchecker
ch'ŏltchŏhage 철저하게 thoroughly
ch'ŏltchŏhan 철저한 thorough; exhaustive
ch'ŏltchŏhi chosahada 철저히 조사하다 look through
ch'ŏltto 철도 rail; railroad; track
ch'ŏma 처마 eaves
ch'ŏmbusŏ 첨부서 covering letter
ch'ŏmdan kisul 첨단 기술 high technology, high tech
ch'ŏmdanŭi 첨단의 leading-edge
ch'ŏmgaje 첨가제 (food) additive
ch'ŏn 천 cloth; thousand
ch'ŏ-nam 처남 brother-in-law (*wife's younger brother*)
ch'ŏnbak'an 천박한 shallow, superficial; small-minded
ch'ŏnch'amanbyŏrijiyo 천차만별이지요 it varies
ch'ŏnch'ŏnhi 천천히 slowly
ch'ŏnch'ung 촌충 tapeworm
ch'ŏndung 천둥 thunder
ch'ŏngbaji 청바지 jeans
ch'ŏngbu sarinja 청부 살인자 hitman
ch'ŏngch'ŏnbyŏngnyŏk-kkwa kach'i 청천벽력과 같이 like a bolt from the blue
ch'ŏngch'un-gi 청춘기 youth (*age*)
ch'ŏngch'wihada 청취하다 tune in to
ch'ŏngch'wija 청취자 listener; audience (*of radio program*)
ch'ŏngdong 청동 bronze
ch'ŏngdongsaek 청동색 bronze
ch'ŏnggak chang-ae 청각 장애 deafness

ch'ŏngganghada 청강하다 audit
ch'ŏnggangsaeng 청강생 auditor
ch'ŏnggu 청구 claim
ch'ŏngguhada 청구하다 charge; claim
ch'ŏnggusŏ 청구서 bill
ch'ŏnggyŏl 청결 purity
ch'ŏnggyodo 청교도 puritan
ch'ŏnghada 청하다 request
ch'ŏnghon 청혼 proposal
ch'ŏnghonhada 청혼하다 propose
ch'ŏngja 청자 celadon ware
ch'ŏngjin-gii 청진기 stethoscope
ch'ŏngjinhada 청진하다 sound
ch'ŏngjung 청중 audience
ch'ŏngnokssaek 청록색 turquoise
ch'ŏngnyang ŭmnyo 청량 음료 soft drink
ch'ŏngnyŏk 청력 hearing
ch'ŏng-ŏ 청어 herring
ch'ŏn-gonggi 천공기 drill
ch'ŏngsajin 청사진 blueprint
ch'ŏngsan 청산 settlement; liquidation
ch'ŏngsanhada 청산하다 go into liquidation; settle; write off
ch'ŏngsobu 청소부 cleaner
ch'ŏngsohada 청소하다 clean; clean up; rub down; ***kkaekkŭt'age ch'ŏngsohada*** 깨끗하게 청소하다 clean out *room*, *closet*
ch'ŏngsohanŭn ajumma 청소하는 아줌마 cleaning woman
ch'ŏngsokkwa 청소과 sanitation department
ch'ŏngsonyŏn 청소년 adolescents, juveniles ◊ juvenile, adolescent
ch'ŏngsonyŏn pihaeng 청소년 비행 youthful misdemeanors
ch'ŏnguk 천국 heaven
Ch'ŏng-wadae 청와대 The Blue House (*South Korean President's residence*)
ch'ŏng-wŏnsŏ 청원서 petition
ch'ŏnhamujŏgŭi 천하무적의 unbeaten
ch'ŏnhan 천한 humble, menial
ch'ŏnjae 천재 genius
ch'ŏnjaejibyŏn 천재지변 catastrophe, disaster
ch'ŏnjang 천장 ceiling
ch'ŏnjang-ŭi nop'i 천장의 높이 headroom
Ch'ŏnji ch'angjo 천지 창조 Creation REL
ch'ŏnjinhan 천진한 childlike; disarming
Ch'ŏnjugyo 천주교 Roman Catholicism
Ch'ŏnjugyo shinja 천주교 신자 Catholic
Ch'ŏnjugyoŭi 천주교의 Catholic
ch'ŏnmagŭl ch'ida 천막을 치다 camp
ch'ŏnmak 천막 tent
ch'ŏnmaneyo 천만에요 you're welcome
ch'ŏnmunhak 천문학 astronomy
ch'ŏnmunhaktcha 천문학자 astronomer
ch'ŏnmunhaktchŏgin 천문학적인 astronomical
ch'ŏnnyŏn 천년 millennium
ch'ŏn pŏntchaeŭi 천 번째의 thousandth
ch'ŏn pŏnŭi 천 번의 thousandth
ch'ŏnshik 천식 asthma
ch'ŏnsŏng 천성 nature, disposition
ch'ŏntchogak 천조각 pad, wad
ch'ŏnyŏ 처녀 virgin (*female*)
ch'ŏnyŏ hanghae 처녀 항해 maiden voyage
ch'ŏnyŏndu 천연두 smallpox
ch'ŏnyŏn kassŭ 천연 가스 natural gas
ch'ŏrhada 철하다 file
ch'ŏrhak 철학 philosophy
ch'ŏrhaktcha 철학자 philosopher
ch'ŏrhatchŏgin 철학적인 philosophical
ch'ŏrhoehada 철회하다 pull out; withdraw; backpedal; dispense with, waive
ch'ŏrihada 처리하다 take care of, deal with; cope with; cope; process; transact
ch'ŏrŏm 처럼 as, like
chŏryak'ada 절약하다 economize
ch'ŏshinhada 처신하다 conduct oneself
ch'ŏt 첫 first; ***...ŭi ch'ŏtchaenare*** ...의 첫째날에 on the 1st of ...

ch'ŏt-tchaero 첫째로 in the first place
ch'ŏtwŏlgŭp 첫 월급 starting salary
ch'ŏŭm 처음 start
ch'ŏŭmbut'ŏ 처음부터 initially; from the start
ch'ŏŭmbut'ŏ shijak'ada 처음부터 시작하다 start from scratch
ch'ŏŭmenŭn 처음에는 originally, at first
ch'ŏŭmŭi 처음의 first
ch'ŏŭmŭro 처음으로 first; the first time
ch'o 초 candle; excerpt; second; draft; vinegar; beginning, early part ◊ ultra-; ***yuwŏl ch'oe*** 유월 초에 in early June
ch'oboja 초보자 beginner
ch'och'im 초침 second hand (*on clock*)
ch'odae 초대 invitation
ch'odaehada 초대하다 invite
ch'odŭnghak-kkyo 초등학교 elementary school, infant school
ch'odŭnghak-kkyo kyosa 초등학교 교사 elementary teacher
ch'oe-agŭi sangt'ae-enŭn 최악의 상태에는 if the worst comes to worst
ch'oe-ak 최악 the worst
ch'oech'ŏmdan 최첨단 frontier
ch'oech'ŏmdanŭi 최첨단의 state-of-the-art
ch'oech'oŭi 최초의 original; initial
ch'oedae 최대 maximum; ***...ŭl ch'oedaehan hwaryonghayŏ kkŭrŏnaeda*** ...을 최대한 활용하여 끌어내다 make the most of
ch'oedaehanŭi 최대한의 utmost
ch'oedaehanŭro 최대한으로 at the outside
ch'oedaehanŭro iyonghada 최대한으로 이용하다 make the best of
ch'oedaehwahada 최대화하다 maximize
ch'oedae saengsannyŏk 최대 생산력 capacity
ch'oedae sobiryang 최대 소비량 peak consumption
ch'oedaeŭi 최대의 maximum
ch'oego 최고 the best
ch'oegoch'i 최고치 peak
ch'oegoch'ie tarhada 최고치에 달하다 peak
ch'oegogŭbŭi 최고급의 first-rate
ch'oego hando 최고 한도 ceiling, limit
ch'oego kyŏngnyŏngja 최고 경영자 CEO, Chief Executive Officer
ch'oego p'umjil pojŭng kigan 최고 품질 보증 기간 best before date
ch'oego saryŏnggwan 최고 사령관 commander-in-chief
ch'oego suwi 최고 수위 high water
ch'oegoŭi 최고의 best; top; terrific
ch'oegoŭmbuŭi 최고음부의 treble
ch'oegowiŭi 최고위의 supreme
ch'oegŭn 최근 newly
ch'oegŭne 최근에 recently; lately
ch'oegŭnŭi 최근의 recent; latest
ch'oehu t'ongch'ŏp 최후 통첩 ultimatum
ch'oehuŭi kyŏng-ŭi 최후의 경의 last respects; ***nuguege ch'oehuŭi kyŏng-ŭirŭl p'yohada*** 누구에게 최후의 경의를 표하다 pay one's last respects to s.o.
ch'oejŏgŭi 최적의 optimum
ch'oejŏk 최적 optimum
ch'oejŏng-ŭi 최종의 final
ch'oejŏ ponggŭp 최저 봉급 minimum wage
ch'oejŏ saenghwal sujun 최저 생활 수준 subsistence level
ch'oejŏŭi 최저의 rock-bottom
ch'oejong 최종 the last; the end ◊ final
ch'oejong kyŏlkwa 최종 결과 end result
ch'oejong myŏngdan 최종 명단 shortlist
ch'oejong sayongja 최종 사용자 end-user
ch'oejongsuro 최종수로 at the last count
ch'oemyŏnsul 최면술 hypnosis
ch'oemyŏnsurŭl kŏlda 최면술을 걸다 hypnotize
ch'oemyŏn yoppŏp 최면 요법 hypnotherapy
ch'oerugasŭ 최루가스 tear gas

ch'oesang-ŭi 최상의 top, best; ultimate
ch'oeshin chŏngborŭl chuda 최신 정보를 주다 update
ch'oeshinŭi 최신의 latest; up-to-date
ch'oeshin yuhaeng-ŭi 최신 유행의 trendy
ch'oesŏnŭl tahada 최선을 다하다 do one's best
ch'oeso 최소 minimum
ch'oesohanŭi 최소한의 minimum
ch'oesohwahada 최소화하다 minimize
ch'oesoryang 최소량 least
ch'oesoŭi 최소의 minimal
ch'oeusŏn sahang 최우선 사항 priority
ch'ogangdaeguk 초강대국 superpower
ch'ogi 초기 infancy
ch'ogiŭi 초기의 early, first
ch'ogo 초고 draft
ch'ogosok yŏlch'a 초고속 열차 bullet train
ch'ogwahada 초과하다 exceed; overrun *time*
ch'ogwahanŭn 초과하는 in excess of
ch'ogwa kŭnmu 초과 근무 overtime
ch'ogwa suhamul 초과 수하물 excess baggage
ch'ogwa yogŭm 초과 요금 excess fare
ch'ohyŏndaejŏgin 초현대적인 futuristic
ch'o ilkki 초 읽기 countdown
ch'oinjŏgin 초인적인 enormous
ch'oinjong 초인종 doorbell
ch'ojayŏnjŏgin 초자연적인 supernatural
ch'ojŏnyŏge 초저녁에 at nightfall
ch'ojohaehada 초조해하다 panic, flap
ch'ojohan 초조한 edgy
ch'ok-kkam 촉감 (sense of) touch
ch'okppak'an 촉박한 tight (*of time*)
ch'okssu 촉수 tentacle
ch'oktchin 촉진 boost
ch'oktchinhada 촉진하다 promote, foster
ch'oktchinje 촉진제 catalyst
ch'oktchinshik'ida 촉진시키다 boost
ch'ok'ollit 초콜릿 chocolate
ch'ok'ollit k'eik 초콜릿 케익 chocolate cake, brownie
ch'ok'ŭ 초크 choke
ch'ong 총 gun
ch'ong-aek 총액 total amount of money
ch'ong-al 총알 bullet; shotgun pellet
ch'ongbiyong 총비용 capital expenditure
ch'ongch'e 총체 the whole, all
ch'ongch'ong kŏrŭmŭro kada 총총 걸음으로 가다 trot
ch'onggak 총각 bachelor
ch'onggak p'at'i 총각 파티 stag party
ch'onggi hyudaeja 총기 휴대자 gunman
ch'onggye 총계 total; sum; gross
ch'onghoe 총회 general meeting
ch'ongkyŏlssan 총결산 bottom line
ch'ongmae k'ŏnbŏt'ŏ 촉매 컨버터 catalytic converter
ch'ongmyŏngham 총명함 intelligence, brightness
ch'ongmyŏnghan 총명한 intelligent, bright
ch'ongsang 총상 gunshot wound
ch'ongsarhada 총살하다 shoot dead
ch'ongsŏn-gŏ 총선거 general election
ch'ongssori 총소리 gunshot
ch'ongŭk 촌극 sketch THEA
ch'onssŭrŏun 촌스러운 provincial, parochial
ch'onsŭrŏpkke hwaryŏhan 촌스럽게 화려한 gaudy
ch'onsŭrŏun 촌스러운 dowdy
ch'oraehada 초래하다 bring, create; incur
ch'orahan 초라한 humble
ch'osanghwa 초상화 portrait
ch'oshimja 초심자 novice
ch'osohyŏng 초소형 miniature, midget
ch'ossŭngttal 초승달 new moon
ch'otchŏm 초점 focus; ***ch'otchŏmi mat-tta / mat-tchi ant'a*** 초점이 맞다 / 맞지 않다 be in focus / out of focus; ***ch'otchŏmŭl match'uda*** 초점을 맞추다 focus on

ch'ot-ttae 촛대 candlestick
ch'oŭmp'a 초음파 ultrasound
ch'oŭmsok 초음속 supersonic speed ◊ supersonic
ch'owŏltchŏgin 초월적인 transcendental
ch'owŏn 초원 meadow
ch'oyŏn 초연 première
ch'oyŏnhan 초연한 aloof, remote
ch'ŭktchŏng 측정 measurement, reading
ch'ŭktchŏnghada 측정하다 gauge
ch'ŭktchŏngppŏp 측정법 system (of measurement)
ch'ŭng 층 layer; floor; tier; deck
ch'ŭnggye 층계 the stairs
ch'ŭnggyech'am 층계참 landing
ch'ubang 추방 exile; expulsion
ch'ubanghada 추방하다 exile; ***t'up'yoe ŭihae ch'ubanghada*** 투표에 의해 추방하다 vote out
ch'ubangja 추방자 exile
ch'ubun 추분 the autumnal equinox
ch'uch'ŏn 추천 recommendation, endorsement
ch'uch'ŏnhada 추천하다 recommend, endorse
ch'uch'ŏnsŏ 추천서 reference
ch'uch'ŏntchang 추천장 testimonial
ch'uch'ŭk 추측 guess; conjecture; speculation
ch'uch'ŭk'ada 추측하다 expect; gather; speculate; guess
ch'uch'ul 추출 extraction
ch'udohada 추도하다 mourn
ch'uga 추가 addition, supplement ◊ additional, extra
ch'uga-aek 추가액 supplement FIN
ch'ugahada 추가하다 add
ch'uga hangmok 추가 항목 add-on
ch'uganp'an 추간판 slipped disc
ch'ugaro 추가로 in addition
ch'uga yogŭm 추가 요금 extra charge
ch'ugu 추구 search; pursuit
ch'uguhada 추구하다 pursue; search for; seek
ch'ugyŏk 추격 chase
ch'uhu t'ongjiga issŭl ttaekkaji 추후 통지가 있을 때까지 until further notice
ch'ujap'an 추잡한 lewd
ch'ujinhada 추진하다 propel, drive; go ahead with; set things in motion
ch'ujinnyŏk 추진력 driving force
ch'ujŏk 추적 pursuit
ch'ujŏktcha 추적자 pursuer
ch'ujŏk'ada 추적하다 pursue; stalk; trace
ch'ujŏng 추정 presumption
ch'ujŏngdoeda 추정되다 be presumed; ***muŏshi ...ttaemunŭro ch'ujŏngdoeda*** 무엇이 ...때문으로 추정되다 attribute sth to ...
ch'ujŏnghada 추정하다 presume
ch'ukch'ŏk 축척 scale
ch'ukch'ŏk tomyŏn 축척 도면 scale drawing
ch'ukch'uk'age hada 축축하게 하다 dampen, moisten
ch'ukch'uk'an 축축한 damp, moist
ch'uk-kka 축가 carol
ch'uk-kku 축구 soccer
ch'uk-kku sŏnsu 축구 선수 soccer player
ch'uk-kkugong 축구공 football, ball
ch'ukppok'ada 축복하다 bless
ch'ukssohada 축소하다 cut back
ch'uktche 축제 carnival; festival; feast
ch'uktcheŭi 축제의 festive
ch'uk'a 축하 congratulations
ch'uk'ahada 축하하다 celebrate; congratulate
ch'uk'a haengsa 축하 행사 festivities
ch'uk'ahamnida 축하합니다 congratulations on
ch'uk'ayŏn 축하연 celebration
ch'ulbal 출발 departure; starting; start; ***choŭn / nappŭn ch'ulbarŭl hada*** 좋은/나쁜 출발을 하다 get off to a good/bad start; ***sae ch'ulbal*** 새 출발 a new departure
ch'ulbal shigak 출발 시각 departure time
ch'ulbal shigan 출발 시간 flight time
ch'ulbaltchŏm 출발점 starting point; threshold
ch'ulbarhada 출발하다 leave, go; depart; set off
ch'ulgŭnhada 출근하다 go to work

ch'ulgu 출구 exit
ch'ullabwŏn 출납원 cashier
ch'ullyŏk 출력 output
ch'ullyŏk'ada 출력하다 output
ch'ulmahada 출마하다 run, stand; ***taet'ongnyŏnge ch'ulmahada*** 대통령에 출마하다 run for President
ch'ulp'an 출판 publication
ch'ulp'andoeda 출판되다 be published, be out
ch'ulp'anhada 출판하다 publish
ch'ulp'anŏp 출판업 publishing
ch'ulp'anŏptcha 출판업자 publisher (*person*)
ch'ulp'ansa 출판사 publisher (*company*)
ch'ulsan hyuga 출산 휴가 maternity leave
ch'ulssaeng chŏnŭi 출생 전의 prenatal
ch'ulssaeng chŭngmyŏngsŏ 출생 증명서 birth certificate
ch'ulssaengguk 출생국 native country
ch'ulssaengji 출생지 birthplace
ch'ulssaengnyul 출생률 birthrate
ch'ulssaeng-ŭi 출생의 native
ch'ulssan 출산 birth
ch'ulssan chŏnŭi 출산 전의 antenatal
ch'ulssanhada 출산하다 bear *child*
ch'ulsshihada 출시하다 appear, come out; bring out; release
ch'ulsshinida 출신이다 originate, come from
ch'ulsshin sŏngbun 출신 성분 background
ch'ulssŏk 출석 attendance
ch'ultchang 출장 business trip
ch'ultchŏnhada 출전하다 compete; go in for, enter
ch'ulttongshik'ida 출동시키다 call out
ch'ulttu 출두 appearance (*in court*)
ch'ulttuhada 출두하다 appear (*in court*); report
ch'ult'oegŭn shigan 출퇴근 시간 rush hour
ch'ult'oegŭn shigan kirok-kkye 출퇴근 시간 기록계 time clock
ch'um 춤 dance
ch'umch'uda 춤추다 dance
ch'unbun 춘분 the spring equinox
ch'ungbunhada 충분하다 be sufficient; be satisfactory; ***kŭgŏllo ch'ungbunhamnida*** 그걸로 충분합니다 that should be enough
ch'ungbunhage 충분하게 sufficiently
ch'ungbunhan 충분한 enough
ch'ungbunhan yang 충분한 양 enough
ch'ungbunhi 충분히 duly; enough
ch'ungch'i 충치 cavity
ch'ungch'iga saenggida 충치가 생기다 decay (*of teeth*)
ch'ungdol 충돌 collision; crash; conflict; impact
ch'ungdolshik'ida 충돌시키다 crash
ch'ungdong 충동 urge; impulse; ***ch'ungdongjŏgŭro muŏsŭl hada*** 충동적으로 무엇을 하다 do sth on an impulse
ch'ungdongjŏgin 충동적인 impulsive
ch'ungdong kumae 충동 구매 impulse buy
ch'ungdongtchŏgŭro 충동적으로 on the spur of the moment
ch'ungdorhada 충돌하다 crash; collide with, hit; clash; be at odds with
ch'unggo 충고 used, secondhand; advice; warning
ch'unggohada 충고하다 advise *caution etc*
ch'unggo han madi 충고 한 마디 piece of advice
ch'unggyŏgesŏ pŏsŏnaji mot'ada 충격에서 벗어나지 못하다 be in shock
ch'unggyŏgŭl pat-tta 충격을 받다 be shocked; be flabbergasted
ch'unggyŏk 충격 blow, shock
ch'unggyŏktchŏgin 충격적인 shocking, horrifying
ch'unghyŏldoen 충혈된 bloodshot
ch'ungjŏnhada 충전하다 charge *battery*
ch'ungjokshik'ida 충족시키다 meet, satisfy
ch'ungmanhada 충만하다 be full, be

filled; ***hwalgiga ch'ungmanhan*** 활기가 충만한 exuberant
ch'ungmyŏn 측면 side
ch'ungnongtchŭng 축농증 sinusitis
ch'ungshil 충실 fidelity, faithfulness
ch'ungshimŭro 충심으로 heartily, cordially
ch'ungshirhada 충실하다 stick by; be faithful, be loyal; ***sangdaeege ch'ungshirhada*** 상대에게 충실하다 be faithful to one's partner
ch'ungshirhan 충실한 faithful, staunch
ch'ungsŏngshim 충성심 sense of loyalty; ***kiŏbe taehan ch'ungsŏngshim*** 기업에 대한 충성심 sense of corporate loyalty
ch'ungsŏngsŭrŏun 충성스러운 loyal
ch'ungsu 충수 appendix
ch'ungsuyŏm 충수염 appendicitis
ch'uŏk 추억 memory
ch'up'a 추파 leer
ch'urak 추락 crash, fall
ch'urak'ada 추락하다 crash
ch'urhanghada 출항하다 sail, depart
ch'urhyŏl 출혈 bleeding; hemorrhage
ch'urhyŏn 출현 arrival, appearance
ch'urhyŏrhada 출혈하다 bleed; hemorrhage
ch'urimmun 출입문 door; entrance; exit
ch'urimul 추리물 whodunnit
ch'urip 출입 access
ch'uripkku 출입구 doorway
ch'urip kŭmji 출입 금지 off limits; no trespassing
Ch'urip Kwalliguk 출입 관리국 Immigration Bureau
ch'urip'ang kŭmji 출입항 금지 ban, embargo
ch'uron 추론 deduction, conclusion; line of reasoning
ch'uronhada 추론하다 deduce; infer
ch'uryŏn 출연 appearance (*on TV etc*)
ch'uryŏnaeda 추려내다 remove, weed out
ch'uryŏnhada 출연하다 appear (*on TV etc*)
ch'uryŏnjin 출연진 cast (*of play*)
ch'usangjŏgin 추상적인 abstract
ch'ushin 추신 PS, postscript
Ch'usŏk 추석 Harvest Festival
ch'usu 추수 harvest
Ch'usu Kamsajŏl 추수 감사절 Thanksgiving (Day)
ch'uun 추운 cold; freezing
ch'uwi 추위 cold; ***chŏnŭn mopsshi ch'uwŏyo*** 저는 몹시 추워요 I'm freezing cold
ch'uwŏrhada 추월하다 pass MOT
ch'waryŏng 촬영 photography
ch'waryŏnghada 촬영하다 film, shoot
ch'waryŏngjangso 촬영장소 set (*for movie*)
ch'waryŏng kisa 촬영 기사 cameraman
ch'wich'im shigan 취침 시간 bedtime
ch'widŭk'ada 취득하다 take
ch'wigŭp 취급 treatment
ch'wigŭp chuŭi 취급 주의 handle with care!
ch'wihada 취하다 get drunk
ch'wihan 취한 high, loaded, stoned
ch'wihyang 취향 taste
ch'wiimshigŭl kŏhaenghada 취임식을 거행하다 inaugurate
ch'wiji akttan 취주 악단 brass band
ch'wijung-ŭi 취중의 drunken
ch'wimi 취미 pastime, hobby
ch'wiso 취소 cancellation; withdrawal
ch'wisohada 취소하다 cancel; withdraw; tear up
ch'yat'ŭ 차트 chart, map

...dago hani ...다고 하니 that
...dani ...다니 that
...dŏrado ...더라도 even though
...do ...도 as well, also
...do ŏptta ...도 없다 without any ... at all
...dorok ...도록 so that, in order to; till; as ... as possible
...dŭshi ...듯이 like, as; as if

E

...e ...에 in; at; on; for; ***...e ch'aegimi it-tta*** ...에 책임이 있다 be responsible for
...eda(ga) ...에다(가) at; in; on
...ege ...에게 to (*a person*)
...egesŏ ...에게서 from (*a person*)
Eijŭ 에이즈 Aids
Eijŭ yangsŏng panŭng 에이즈 양성 반응 HIV-positive
eksŭsedae 엑스세대 (X-세대) generation X (*Korea's contemporary youth without the same values and sense of purpose as their parents*)
ellibeit'ŏ 엘리베이터 elevator
emt'i 엠티 MT, Membership Training (*for college freshmen*)
en 엔 yen FIN
enamel 에나멜 enamel
enamel kajuk 에나멜 가죽 patent leather
enjin 엔진 engine, motor
enjin ttukkŏng 엔진 뚜껑 hood MOT
enŏji 에너지 energy, power
enŏjirŭl chŏryak'anŭn 에너지를 절약하는 energy-saving
ensedae 엔세대 (N-세대) networking generation (*via internet and cell phone*)
ent'ŏ k'i 엔터 키 enter key
eŏk'on 에어콘 air-conditioning
eŏrobik 에어로빅 aerobics
ep'isodŭ 에피소드 episode
ep'it'aijyŏ 에피타이저 appetizer, starter
erŏ 에러 error COMPUT
erŏ mesiji 에러 메시지 error message
...esŏ ...에서 in; at; on; from
...esŏbut'ŏ ...에서부터 from ... onward
esŭk'ŏlleitŏ 에스컬레이터 escalator
ewŏssada 에워싸다 encircle

...ga ...가 *subject particle* → **...ka** ...가
...get... ...겠... shall (*indicates future tense, intention or supposition*)
...gi ...기 위해 in order to
...go ...고 and

H

habanshin mabihwanja 하반신 마비환자 paraplegic
habŭidoen 합의된 concerted
habŭihada 합의하다 agree, agree on
habu chojik 하부 조직 infrastructure
habu kujo 하부 구조 infrastructure (*of organisation*)
hach'anŭn 하찮은 insignificant
hach'ŏnghada 하청하다 subcontract
hach'ŏng-ŏptcha 하청업자 subcontractor
hada 하다 ◊ do; make; play; put on ◊ (*makes nouns into verbs*): ***saranghada*** 사랑하다 love ◊ ***...ge hada*** ...게 하다 make; let; ***nugurŭl haengbok'age hada*** 누구를 행복하게 하다 make s.o. happy
hadan 하단 bottom, lower part; ***hwamyŏnŭi hadane*** 화면의 하단에 at the bottom of the screen
hadŭ k'ap'i 하드 카피 hard copy
hadŭ tisŭk'ŭ 하드 디스크 hard disk
hadŭweŏ 하드웨어 hardware
hae 해 harm; ***haerŭl ip'ida*** ...에 해를 입히다 be to the detriment of
haeansŏn 해안선 coastline; waterline
haebalgodo 해발고도 altitude
haebang 해방 emancipation, liberation
haebanghada 해방하다 emancipate, liberate
haeboda 해보다 try
haebuhak 해부학 anatomy
haebyŏn 해변 beach; ***haebyŏne*** 해변에 at the seaside
Haebyŏngdae 해병대 Marine Corps
haebyŏnkka 해변가 seaside
haebyŏn lijot'ŭ 해변 리조트 seaside resort
haech'ehada 해체하다 break up; take down
haech'ibaek 해치백 hatchback
haech'ida 해치다 harm, impair
haech'iuda 해치우다 finish off *task*; kill, do away with
haech'o 해초 seaweed
haech'ung 해충 vermin
haedanghada 해당하다 correspond to
haedap 해답 answer, solution
haedo 해도 chart
haedoktche 해독제 antidote
haedok'ada 해독하다 decode
haego 해고 dismissal
haegohada 해고하다 fire; lay off
haegol 해골 skeleton; skull
haegoshik'ida 해고시키다 dismiss
haegŭi 핵의 nuclear
haegŭm 해금 two-stringed fiddle
haegun 해군 navy; marine
haegun taejang 해군 대장 admiral
haegun kiji 해군 기지 naval base
haegyŏl 해결 fix, solution; resolution (*of problem*)
haegyŏlch'aek 해결책 solution
haegyŏrhada 해결하다 settle, sort out, clear up; work out, crack, solve
haegyŏrhal su innŭn 해결할 수 있는 solvable
haegyŏri kollanhan 해결이 곤란한 difficult, knotty *problem*
haehak 해학 humor
haehyŏp 해협 strait
haejil muryŏp 해질 무렵 sunset, dusk; ***haejin hue*** 해진 후에 after sunset
haejŏkp'an 해적판 pirated version
haek 핵 nucleus ◊ nuclear
haek enŏji 핵 에너지 nuclear energy
haek konggyŏk'ada 핵 공격하다 make a nuclear strike
haek mugi 핵 무기 nuclear weapons
haek mullihak 핵 물리학 nuclear physics
haek punnyŏl 핵 분열 nuclear fission
haek p'yegimul 핵 폐기물 nuclear waste

haeksshim 핵심 core; heart, nub
haeksshimbu 핵심부 heart, center
haeksshimch'ŭng 핵심층 hard core
haeksshimjŏgin 핵심적인 essential, key
haekssŭregi 핵쓰레기 atomic waste
haek'ŏ 해커 hacker
haelssuk'an 핼쑥한 ghastly
haem 햄 ham
haema 해마 walrus
haembŏgŏ 햄버거 hamburger
haemsŭt'ŏ 햄스터 hamster
haemyŏnghada 해명하다 explain, shed light on
haenaeda 해내다 beat; argue down; succeed; accomplish; ***chal haenaeda*** 잘 해내다 do well
haenagada 해나가다 carry on
haendŭbaek 핸드백 purse, pocket book, *Br* handbag
haendŭl 핸들 (steering) wheel
haendŭp'on 핸드폰 cell phone
haeng 행 for, bound for; ***Sŏurhaeng pihaenggi*** 서울행 비행기 a plane bound for Seoul
haengbok 행복 happiness, well-being
haengbok'ada 행복하다 be happy
haengbok'age 행복하게 happily
haengbok'an 행복한 happy
haengdong 행동 act, deed; behavior
haengdonghada 행동하다 act, behave
haengdong pangch'im 행동 방침 course of action
haenggŭllaidŏ 행글라이더 hang glider
haenghada 행하다 render
haengjin 행진 march, procession
haengjinhada 행진하다 march, parade
haengjŏng 행정 administration
haengjŏnggwan 행정관 administrator
haengjŏng kuyŏk 행정 구역 precinct, district
haengjŏng samu 행정 사무 civil service
haengju 행주 dishcloth
haengnakkaek 행락객 vacationist
haengno 행로 course
haengnyŏl 행렬 procession
haengsa 행사 event; function; events; observance
haengsa wiwŏn 행사 위원 marshal
haengsŏng 행성 planet
haeng-un 행운 good fortune; ***haeng-uni itkkirŭl!*** 행운이 있기를! all the best!
haeng-unŭl kajyŏonŭn 행운을 가져오는 lucky
haeng-unŭl pilda 행운을 빌다 wish good luck
haeng-wi 행위 conduct; deed
haeoe 해외 abroad
haeoe kyop'o 해외 교포 overseas Koreans
haep'ari 해파리 jellyfish
haeri 해리 nautical mile
haeroun 해로운 harmful, damaging
haesam 해삼 sea cucumber, sea slug
haesan 해산 childbirth; confinement
haesangdo 해상도 resolution (*of monitor*)
haesang kyot'ong 해상 교통 shipping
haesanhada 해산하다 give birth; disperse *crowd*; dissolve *assembly*
haesanmul 해산물 seafood
haeshigye 해시계 sundial
haesŏk 해석 interpretation
haesŏk'ada 해석하다 interpret
haesŏl 해설 commentary
haesŏltcha 해설자 commentator
haetppit 햇빛 sunshine
haetppyŏch'e t'ada 햇볕에 타다 tan, go brown
haetppyŏch'e t'aeuda 햇볕에 태우다 get a suntan
haetppyŏch'ŭl tchoeda 햇볕을 쬐다 sunbathe
haetppyŏt'e(sŏ) 햇볕에(서) in the sun
haeunhoesa 해운회사 shipping company
haeyang 해양 ocean, sea
hagang 하강 fall, descent
haganghada 하강하다 descend
hagŭp 하급 low class
hagu 하구 estuary
hagwi 학위 degree
hagwirŭl ttada 학위를 따다

graduate, get one's degree
hagwŏn 학원 academy; institute
hahyang shiseŭi shijang 하향 시세의 시장 bear market
haip'ai 하이파이 hi-fi
haip'ŏt'ekssŭt'ŭ 하이퍼텍스트 hypertext
hairait'ŭ 하이라이트 highlight
hak 학 crane (*bird*)
hak-kki 학기 semester
hak-kkŭp 학급 class
hak-kkwa 학과 department
hak-kkyo 학교 school
hak-kkyo sŏnsaengnim 학교 선생님 schoolteacher
hak-kkujŏgin 학구적인 academic
hakppi 학비 tuition fee
hakppu 학부 faculty
hakssaeng 학생 pupil, student
hakssaeng kunsa kyoryŏndan 학생 군사 교련단 cadet corps
hakssaeng undong 학생 운동 student movement
hakssal 학살 slaughter
hakssaltcha 학살자 killer, murderer
hakssarhada 학살하다 slaughter
hakssŭp 학습 learning
hakssŭp kokssŏn 학습 곡선 learning curve
haktcha 학자 scholar
haktchang 학장 dean
hakttae 학대 abuse; maltreatment
hakttaehada 학대하다 abuse; maltreat
hakttong 학동 schoolchildren
hak'oe 학회 institute
hal il ŏmnŭn 할 일 없는 unoccupied
halkkamalkka saenggak'ada 할까말까 생각하다 think about doing
halkki 핥기 lick
halk'wida 할퀴다 claw; scratch
halk'wigi 할퀴기 scratch
hal marŭl irŭn 할 말을 잃은 speechless
halmŏni 할머니 grandmother, granny
hal su ŏpsshi ... 할 수 없이 ... have to ..., be compelled to ...
haltta 핥다 lick
halttanghada 할당하다 assign; commit
halt'amŏktta 핥아먹다 lap up, drink
hama 하마 hippopotamus
hamburo manjida 함부로 만지다 tamper with
hamburo taruda 함부로 다루다 mishandle
hamch'uk 함축 implication
hamch'uktchŏgin 함축적인 implicit
hamdae 함대 fleet
hamjŏng 함정 pitfall; trap; ***nugurŭl hamjŏng-e ppattŭrida*** 누구를 함정에 빠뜨리다 set a trap for s.o.; ***hamjŏng-e ppajida*** 함정에 빠지다 be trapped
hamkke 함께 with, along with ◊ together
hamkke hada 함께 하다 share *feelings*
hamkke nanuda 함께 나누다 share; ***hamkke ssŭda*** 함께 쓰다 share *room etc*
hamnihwahada 합리화하다 rationalize
hamnijŏgin 합리적인 rational
hamnisŏng 합리성 rationality
hamnyuhada 합류하다 join
hamonik'a 하모니카 harmonica, mouthorgan
hamppak chŏt-tta 함빡 젖다 be wet through
han 한 limit; ***...nŭn han*** ...는 한 so long as
hana 하나 one; single; ***hananŭn ..., namŏjinŭn ...*** 하나는 ..., 나머지는 ... one ..., the others ...
hanaga toen 하나가 된 united
hanasshik 하나씩 one by one
hanbam chung-e 한밤 중에 in the middle of the night
hanbŏn 한번 one time, once
hanbŏn tŏ 한번 더 once more
hanbok 한복 Korean costume
hanch'ang ttaeida 한창 때이다 be in one's prime
hando 한도 limit; ***muŏsŭl handoro chŏnghada*** 무엇을 한도로 정하다 draw the line at sth
handoga ŏmnŭn 한도가 없는 open-ended
...handokkajinŭn ...한도까지는 to such an extent that

hangahan ttaee 한가한 때에 in an idle moment
hang-ari 항아리 storage jar
han-gaunde 한가운데 center, middle
han-gaundero tuda 한가운데로 두다 center, put in the center
hangbok 항복 surrender
hangbok'ada 항복하다 surrender, capitulate, give in
hangbyŏnhada 항변하다 plead; ***yujoe / mujoerŭl hangbyŏnhada*** 유죄/무죄를 항변하다 plead guilty / not guilty
hangch'e 항체 antibody
hanggong 항공 aviation, flight
hanggongbonghamnyŏpssŏ 항공봉함엽서 air letter
hanggonggi 항공기 aircraft
hanggonghak 항공학 aeronautics
hanggong kyot'ong 항공 교통 air traffic
hanggong kyot'ong kwanje 항공 교통 관제 air-traffic control
hanggong kyot'ong kwanjewŏn 항공 교통 관제원 air-traffic controller
hanggongmoham 항공모함 aircraft carrier
hanggongp'yŏn 항공편 flight
hanggongp'yŏn pŏnho 항공편 번호 flight number
hanggongp'yŏnŭro 항공편으로 by air
hanggongsa 항공사 airline
hanggongsajin 항공사진 aerial photograph
hanggong-ujugonghak 항공우주공학 aerospace industry
hanggong unsonghada 항공 운송하다 fly; send by air
hanggong-up'yŏnŭro 항공우편으로 by airmail
hanggu 항구 harbor; port
hanggudoshi 항구도시 seaport
hanghae 항해 voyage, sea journey
hanghaehada 항해하다 navigate; sail
hanghaesa 항해사 navigator; mate
hanghaesul 항해술 navigation
han-gi 한기 chill
han-gil 한길 mainroad
hangmok 항목 item
hangmokppyŏl kwanggo 항목별 광고 classified advertisement
Hangmu 학무 Crane Dance
hangmun 학문 scholarship
hangnoesŏ pŏsŏnada 항로에서 벗어나다 stray off course
hangnyŏn 학년 academic year; form, class
han-gŏrŭm naedidida 한걸음 내디디다 take a step
hangsaeng multchil 항생 물질 antibiotic
hangsang 항상 always; ***tang-shinŭn / kŭnŭn hangsang kŭrŏch'ana!*** 당신은/그는 항상 그렇잖아! that's typical of you/him!
hangso 항소 appeal LAW
hangsohada 항소하다 appeal LAW
hangssok kŏri 항속 거리 range
hang-ŭi 항의 protest; uproar
hang-ŭihada 항의하다 protest
han-gŭl 한글 hangul, Korean script
Han-gugŏ 한국어 Korean (*language*)
Han-guk 한국 (South) Korea ◊ (South) Korean
Han-guk-kkye 한국계 Korean descent
Han-guk Pangsong Kongsa 한국 방송 공사 Korean Broadcasting System, KBS
Han-guk saram 한국 사람 (South) Korean
Han-gukssan 한국산 made in Korea
han-gye 한계 limit, limitation; ***han-gyee irŭda*** 한계에 이르다 reach one's limit
han-gyerŭl chŏnghada 한계를 정하다 delimit
hangyŏul 한겨울 midwinter
hanjŏngdoen 한정된 restricted
hanjŏnghada 한정하다 limit
hankkŏbone 한꺼번에 in one, at once
han kyŏure 한 겨울에 in the depths of winter
han myŏng kŏnnŏ 한 명 건너 every other person
hannaeng chŏnsŏn 한랭 전선 cold front
hannyŏrŭm 한여름 midsummer
hanŏmnŭn 한없는 unlimited

han pamtchung-e 한 밤중에 in the middle of the night
han p'an taegyŏl 한 판 대결 showdown
hanp'yŏnŭronŭn ..., tarŭn hanp'yŏnŭronŭn 한편으로는..., 다른 한편으로는 on the one hand ..., on the other hand
hansanhan ttae 한산한 때 offpeak
hanshi 한시 hanshi (*poem in Chinese characters*)
hanshimhan 한심한 pitiful
hansum 한숨 sigh
hansum chada 한숨 자다 take a nap
hansum chit-tta 한숨 짓다 sigh
hantcha 한자 Chinese character
hantchogŭro kiurŏjin 한쪽으로 기울어진 lop-sided
hanttae(e) 한때(에) once, formerly; ***hanttae nanŭn kŭrŭl choa-haessŏt-tta / arassŏt-tta*** 한때 나는 그를 좋아했었다 / 알았었다 I used to like / know him
hant'anhada 한탄하다 deplore
hant'anhal 한탄할 deplorable
hant'ŏk naeda 한턱 내다 pick up the tab; treat
hanŭisa 한의사 Chinese herbal medicine practitioner
hanŭiwŏn 한의원 Chinese medicine clinic
hanŭl 하늘 sky; ***hanŭl wie*** 하늘 위에 up in the sky; ***hanŭl nopkke*** 하늘 높게 high in the sky
Hanŭnim 하느님 God
hanyak 한약 Chinese herbal medicine
hanyakppang 한약방 Chinese herbal pharmacy
Hanyang 한양 Hanyang (*Choson name for Seoul*)
hanyŏ 하녀 maid (*servant*)
hapch'ang 합창 chorus, refrain
hapch'angdan 합창단 choir, chorus
hapch'ida 합치다 combine; merge
hapch'yŏjida 합쳐지다 join, meet
Hapkkido 합기도 Hapkido (*martial art*)
hapkkŭm 합금 alloy
hapkkye 합계 total
hapkkyehada 합계하다 add up
hapkkyŏktchŏm 합격점 pass mark
hapkkyŏk'ada 합격하다 pass *examination*
hap-ppŏp 합법 legality
hap-ppŏp t'ujaeng 합법 투쟁 work-to-rule
hap-ppŏptchŏgin 합법적인 lawful, legal
hap-ppŏp'wahada 합법화하다 legalize
hap-ppyŏng 합병 merger
hap-ppyŏnghada 합병하다 amalgamate, merge; annex; unite
hap-ppyŏngtchŭng 합병증 complications MED
happ'an 합판 plywood
hapssŏng 합성 synthesis; composition
hapssŏngmul 합성물 compound
haptcha hoesa 합자 회사 joint-stock company
haptchak t'uja 합작 투자 joint venture
hapttanghada 합당하다 be appropriate; ***kŭnŭn hapttanghan taeurŭl padat-tta*** 그는 합당한 대우를 받았다 he got what he deserved
hap'ŭ 하프 harp
hap'um 하품 yawn
hap'umhada 하품하다 yawn
harabŏji 할아버지 grandfather, grandad
harak 하락 fall, drop
harak'ada 하락하다 fall, drop
harin 할인 discount
harinhada 할인하다 discount; ***ishibul harinhayŏ*** 20불 할인하여 $20 discount
harinkka(gyŏk) 할인가(격) bargain price
harinkkwŏn 할인권 discount voucher
harin p'anmae 할인 판매 sale
harirŏmnŭn 하릴없는 unavoidable
haru 하루 day; ***harue sebŏnŭi hanggongp'yŏn*** 하루에 세번의 항공편 three flights a day
haru chong-il 하루 종일 all day
haru kŏnnŏ 하루 건너 every other day

haruppamŭl chinaeda 하룻밤을 지내다 stay overnight
haru shwida 하루 쉬다 take a day off
haryŏgo momburimch'ida 하려고 몸부림치다 struggle to do
haryŏgo noryŏk'ada 하려고 노력하다 strive to do
hasan 하산 descent
hasu 하수 sewage
hasu ch'ŏrijang 하수 처리장 sewage plant
hasugin 하숙인 lodger
hasugu 하수구 drain
hasugwan 하수관 sewer
hasuk 하숙 board and lodging
hasukssaeng 하숙생 boarder
hasuktchip 하숙집 boarding house
hasuk'ada 하숙하다 board with
hat ch'ok'ollit 핫 초콜릿 hot chocolate
hattogŭ 핫도그 hot dog
hat'ŭ 하트 hearts
hawi 하위 low rank
Hawŏn 하원 House of Representatives
hayan 하얀 white
hayan saek 하얀 색 white
hayat'a 하얗다 be white
hayŏt'ŭn 하여튼 anyhow
hearil su ŏmnŭn 헤아릴 수 없는 impenetrable; inestimable
hebikkŭp 헤비급 heavyweight
hech'yŏnagada 헤쳐나가다 wriggle out of
heding 헤딩 header (*in soccer*)
hedŭp'on 헤드폰 earphones
hedŭrait'ŭ 헤드라이트 headlamp, headlight
hellik'opt'ŏ 헬리콥터 helicopter, chopper
hellik'opt'ŏ nalgae 헬리콥터 날개 rotor blade
helmet 헬멧 helmet
helssŭ k'ŭllŏp 헬스 클럽 fitness center, health club
hemaeda 헤매다 stray
hengguda 헹구다 rinse
heŏdŭraiŏ 헤어드라이어 hairdryer
heŏjida 헤어지다 break up, part
heŏsŭp'ŭrei 헤어스프레이 (hair) lacquer
heroin 헤로인 heroin
hiashinsŭ 히아신스 hyacinth
hiiing! 히이잉! neigh!
him 힘 energy; might; power; strength; impetus
himch'an 힘찬 forceful
himdŭlda 힘들다 be difficult; be arduous
himdŭn 힘든 difficult; strenuous
himdŭnŭn 힘드는 painstaking, laborious
himgyŏun 힘겨운 heavy, profuse
himinnŭn 힘있는 mighty; firm
himŏmnŭn 힘없는 weak, feeble
himssen 힘센 strong
himtchul 힘줄 tendon
himŭl ppaeda 힘을 빼다 relax
hinghinggŏrida 힝힝거리다 neigh
hint'ŭ 힌트 hint
hisŭt'eri 히스테리 hysteria, hysterics
hisŭt'erisŏng-ŭi 히스테리성의 hysterical
hit'ŭ 히트 hit MUS
hit'ŭgok sunwi 히트곡 순위 the charts
hŏbihada 허비하다 fritter away, waste
hŏbŭ 허브 herb
hŏbŭ ch'a 허브 차 herbal tea
hŏga 허가 permission, approval
hŏgabat-tta 허가받다 receive permission
hŏgahada 허가하다 clear, authorize; grant; ***ipkkugŭl hŏgahada*** 입국을 허가하다 admit to a country; ***tŭrŏonŭn kŏsŭl hŏgahada*** 들어오는 것을 허가하다 admit, allow in
hŏga pat-tta 허가 받다 be licensed; be authorized
hŏgasŏ 허가서 permit
hŏgatchŭng 허가증 license, permit
hŏgu 허구 fabrication; fiction; lie
hŏhwangdoen iyagi 허황된 이야기 farfetched story
hŏksshin-ga 혁신가 innovator
hŏlda 헐다 demolish
hŏlgŏpkke 헐겁게 loosely
hŏlgŏun 헐거운 loose
hŏlkkap 헐값 dirt-cheap price

hŏllanshik'ida 혼란시키다 confuse
hŏllŏnghan 헐렁한 baggy; roomy; floppy
hŏlttŏgida 헐떡이다 be winded
hŏlttŏk-kkŏrida 헐떡거리다 gasp, puff
hŏlttŭnnŭn 헐뜯는 disparaging
hŏlttŭt-tta 헐뜯다 slander; malign
hŏmak'an 험악한 forbidding; inclement; unsavory
hŏmdam 험담 gossip
hŏmhan pawi 험한 바위 crag
hŏmulda 허물다 pull down
hŏmurŏjida 허물어지다 disintegrate
hŏmurŏjin 허물어진 dilapidated
hŏmurŏmnŭn 허물없는 candid, frank; familiar
hŏnbyŏng 헌병 MP, military police
Hŏnggari 헝가리 Hungary ◊ Hungarian
hŏnggŏp(tchogak) 헝겊(조각) patch
hŏnggŏp'ŭl taeda 헝겊을 대다 patch
hŏngk'ŭrŏjige hada 헝클어지게 하다 ruffle
hŏngk'ŭrŏjin 헝클어진 disheveled
hŏnhyŏltcha 헌혈자 blood donor
hŏnppŏp 헌법 constitution
hŏnppŏpssang-ŭi 헌법상의 constitutional
hŏnshiltchŏgŭro 현실적으로 in practice
hŏnshin 헌신 commitment, devotion; donation
hŏnshinjŏgida 헌신적이다 be devoted to
hŏnshinjŏgin 헌신적인 devoted
hŏp'ung 허풍 tall story; hot air
hŏp'ungjang-i 허풍잡이 show-off
hŏp'ung-ŭl ttŏlda 허풍을 떨다 exaggerate; boast, brag, talk big
hŏrak 허락 permission
hŏrak'ada 허락하다 allow, permit
hŏri 허리 waist
hŏrirŭl p'yŏda 허리를 펴다 straighten up
hŏrisŏn 허리선 waistline
hŏritti 허리띠 belt
hŏrŏppajin 헐어빠진 dilapidated
hŏrŭmhan 허름한 run-down
hŏse 허세 bravado
hŏshigŏmnŭn 허식없는 unpretentious
hŏshik 허식 affectation
hŏshim t'anhoe 허심 탄회 candor
hŏshimt'anhoehada 허심탄회하다 be open-minded
hŏsuabi 허수아비 scarecrow
hŏsuk'ihan 허스키한 husky *voice*
hŏtchŏm 허점 blind spot; loophole
hŏtkkallida 헛갈리다 mix up, confuse
hŏtkkan 헛간 barn
hŏtkkich'imhada 헛기침하다 clear one's throat
hŏtppae purŭm 헛배 부름 wind, flatulence; gas
hŏtssomunŭl p'ŏttŭrinŭn saram 헛소문을 퍼뜨리는 사람 scaremonger
hŏtssorihada 헛소리하다 rave; ramble
hŏtssugo 헛수고 vain effort; ***kŭdŭrŭi noryŏgŭn hŏtssugoro torakat-tta*** 그들의 노력은 헛수고로 돌아갔다 their efforts were in vain
hŏt-ttidida 헛디디다 lose one's footing, stumble
hŏt-ttoege 헛되게 in vain
hŏt-ttoen 헛된 vain
hŏt'ŭn sori 허튼 소리 nonsense, hokum
hŏyak 허약 infirmity
hŏyak'ada 허약하다 be frail
hŏyak'an 허약한 infirm; delicate; puny
hŏyŏngshim 허영심 vanity; ***hŏyŏng-shimi manŭn*** 허영심이 많은 vain
hŏyongdoel su innŭn 허용될 수 있는 permissible
hŏyong pŏmwi 허용 범위 latitude
ho 호 issue, edition
hobak 호박 pumpkin; amber
hobŏk'ŭrap'ŭt'ŭ 호버크라프트 hovercraft
hoch'ik'isŭ 호치키스 stapler
hoch'ik'isŭ al 호치키스 알 staple
hoch'ik'isŭro tchiktta 호치키스로 찍다 staple
hoch'ulgi 호출기 pager, bleeper
hoch'ul shigan 호출 시간 access time
hoch'urhada 호출하다 summon;

page, bleep
hodoege kkujit-tta 호되게 꾸짖다 scold severely, chew out
hodohada 호도하다 gloss over, whitewash
hodu 호두 walnut
hodu kkanŭn kigu 호두 까는 기구 nutcracker
hoe 회 round, heat; raw fish
hoebanjugŭl parŭda 회반죽을 바르다 plaster
hoebanjuk 회반죽 plaster; mortar
hoebi 회비 fee
hoebok 회복 recovery
hoebok-kki 회복기 convalescence
hoeboktoeda 회복되다 revive, recover
hoebok'ada 회복하다 rebuild; recover; ***kŭŭi hoebogŭn sunjorowat-tta*** 그의 회복은 순조로왔다 he has made a good recovery; ***kŏn-gang-ŭl hoebok'ada*** 건강을 회복하다 convalesce
hoebok'al su ŏmnŭn 회복할 수 없는 incurable
hoegohae pomyŏn 회고해 보면 in retrospect
hoegojŏn 회고전 retrospective
hoegorok 회고록 memoirs
hoegwisŏn 회귀선 tropics
hoegye 회계 accounts
hoegyejangbu 회계장부 accounts book; ***hoegyejangburŭl chŏngnihada*** 회계장부를 정리하다 do the books; ***hoegye kyŏlssanhada*** 회계 결산하다 balance the books
hoegyesa 회계사 accountant
hoegye tamdangja 회계 담당자 treasurer
hoegye yŏndo 회계 연도 fiscal year, financial year
hoehwa 회화 conversation; picture
hoehwa chakp'um 회화 작품 painting
hoejin 회진 round
hoejŏn 회전 revolution, rotation, turn, rev
hoejŏnhada 회전하다 turn, rotate, swivel
hoejŏn mongma 회전 목마 carousel
hoejŏnmun 회전문 revolving door
hoejŏnshik kŏnjogi 회전식 건조기 tumble-dryer
hoejŏnshik'ida 회전시키다 spin; swing, turn
hoejung chŏndŭng 회중 전등 flashlight
hoek 획 stroke (*in writing*)
hoekch'aek'ada 획책하다 plot
hoek-kkijŏgin 획기적인 epoch-making
hoekttŭk'ada 획득하다 acquire, obtain
hoengdan 횡단 crossing
hoengdan podo 횡단 보도 crosswalk
hoenggyŏngmak 횡격막 diaphragm ANAT
hoengjae 횡재 windfall
hoengnyŏng 횡령 embezzlement
hoengnyŏnghada 횡령하다 embezzle
hoengp'orŭl purinŭn 횡포를 부리는 dictatorial
hoengsŏlsusŏl 횡설수설 gibberish; rambling
hoe-oribaram 회오리바람 whirlwind, tornado
hoep'i 회피 evasion
hoep'ihada 회피하다 evade
hoero 회로 circuit
hoero ch'adan-gi 회로 차단기 circuit breaker
hoero kyegip'an 회로 계기판 circuit board
hoesa 회사 business, company, firm; ***hoesa piyong-ŭro*** 회사 비용으로 at the company's expense
hoesa chibunŭl sadŭrida 회사 지분을 사들이다 buy out *company*
hoesa ch'a 회사 차 company car
hoesaek 회색 gray
hoesang 회상 reminiscence
hoesanghada 회상하다 recollect
hoesapŏp 회사법 company law
hoesonghada 회송하다 forward *letter*
hoessu 횟수 frequency
hoeŭi 회의 meeting, conference; assembly; council; ***kŭnŭn hoeŭi chung-ida*** 그는 회의 중이다 he's in a meeting

hoeŭijŏgin 회의적인 skeptical
hoeŭiron 회의론 skepticism
hoeŭironja 회의론자 skeptic
hoeŭishil 회의실 conference room
hoewŏn 회원 member; membership
hoewŏn su 회원 수 membership, number of members
hoewŏntchŭng 회원증 membership card
hoeyujŏgin 회유적인 conciliatory
hogak 호각 whistle
hogami kanŭn 호감이 가는 likable, amiable
hogamŭl kajida 호감을 가지다 be well disposed toward
hogishim 호기심 curiosity; ***hogishimesŏ*** 호기심에서 out of curiosity
hogishim manŭn 호기심 많은 curious, inquisitive
hogishimŭl chagŭk'anŭn 호기심을 자극하는 intriguing
hogŭn 혹은 or
hohŭp 호흡 breathing
hohŭp kollan 호흡 곤란 breathlessness
hohwandoeji annŭn 호환되지 않는 incompatible
hohwanhal su innŭn 호환할 수 있는 compatible
hohwan pulganŭng 호환 불가능 incompatibility
hohwansŏng 호환성 compatibility
hohwaroptta 호화롭다 be luxurious
hohwaroun 호화로운 de luxe
hoil 호일 foil
hojŏ 호저 porcupine
hojŏk 호적 census registration; census register
hojŏkssurŭl mannada 호적수를 만나다 meet one's match
hojŏn 호전 improvement, upturn
hojŏnjŏgin 호전적인 belligerent
hojŏnshik'ida 호전시키다 turn around
Hoju 호주 Australia ◊ Australian
Hojuin 호주인 Australian
hojumŏni 호주머니 pocket
hok 혹 bump, lump; hump
hokp'yŏnghada 혹평하다 criticize severely
hoksshi 혹시: ***hoksshi kŭga ttŏnassŭltchi morŭgessŭmnida*** 혹시 그가 떠났을지 모르겠습니다 I don't know whether he has left
hokttok'an 혹독한 brutal
hol 홀 hall
hollan 혼란 confusion, muddle; unrest; turmoil
hollanhada 혼란하다 be confused; be chaotic
hollanshik'ida 혼란시키다 confuse
hollansŭrŏpda 혼란스럽다 be topsy-turvy
hollansŭrŏun 혼란스러운 shaken; topsy-turvy
hollansŭrŏwŏ hada 혼란스러워 하다 be mixed up
hollo 홀로 by itself
hollograem 홀로그램 hologram
hollye 혼례 marriage
holssu 홀수 odd number
holssusŏn 홀수선 waterline
holtchak-kkŏrida 홀짝거리다 sip
holtchuk'an 홀쭉한 sunken
holttak panhada 홀딱 반하다 be infatuated with, have a crush on
holttak pŏsŭn 홀딱 벗은 stark naked
holttak ppajida 홀딱 빠지다 dote on
hom 홈 rut
homil 호밀 rye
homil ppang 호밀 빵 rye bread
hom kyŏnggi 홈 경기 home match
hom kyŏnggijang-esŏ 홈 경기장에서 at home SP
homo 호모 fag *pej*
homp'eiji 홈페이지 home page
homt'ong 홈통 gutter (*on roof*)
hondonghada 혼동하다 confuse
hongbo 홍보 PR, public relations
hongch'a 홍차 black tea
hongch'ae 홍채 iris (*of eye*)
hongdŭngga 홍등가 red light district
honghap 홍합 mussel
hong-igin-gan 홍익인간 devotion to the welfare of mankind
hongjo 홍조 blush
hongjorŭl ttin 홍조를 띤 rosy
Hong Kilttong 홍 길동 Hong Kiltong (*Korean Robin Hood*)
Hongk'ong 홍콩 Hong Kong
hongnyŏk 홍역 measles

hongsu 홍수 flood
hon-gyo 혼교 promiscuity
honhammul 혼합물 concoction, mixture
honhap 혼합 blend, mixture; hybrid; solution
honhap'ada 혼합하다 blend
honja 혼자 alone; on my/her etc own
honjap 혼잡 congestion
honjap'ada 혼잡하다 be congested; be disordered
honjasŏ 혼자서 single-handedly; by oneself; ***honjasŏ ŏtchŏl su ŏmnŭn*** 혼자서 어쩔 수 없는 alone and helpless
honjŏn(ŭi) 혼전(의) premarital
honsŏn 혼선 interference
honsu sangt'ae 혼수 상태 coma; trance; ***honsu sangt'aee ppajida*** 혼수 상태에 빠지다 go into a trance; lapse into a coma
hop 홉 hop BOT
horabi 홀아비 widower
horanggashinamu 호랑가시나무 holly
horang-i 호랑이 tiger
horihorihan 호리호리한 lanky
horŭmon 호르몬 hormone
hosohada 호소하다 appeal for; complain of
hosonghada 호송하다 convoy
hosŭ 호스 hose
hosŭt'essŭ 호스테스 hostess, escort
hosu 호수 lake
hot'el 호텔 hotel; ***hot'ere muktta*** 호텔에 묵다 stay in a hotel
hot'el chong-ŏbwŏn 호텔 종업원 maid
hot'ong-ŭl ch'ida 호통을 치다 bawl out
hoŭi 호의 favor; goodwill; ***nuguege hoŭirŭl pep'ulda*** 누구에게 호의를 베풀다 do s.o. a favor
hoŭijŏgin 호의적인 favorable
hoŭng 호응 response
howihada 호위하다 escort, convoy
hŭbip 흡입 suction
hŭbipkki 흡입기 inhaler
hŭbip'ada 흡입하다 inhale
hŭbyŏn 흡연 smoking
hŭbyŏnja 흡연자 smoker
hŭbyŏnshil 흡연실 smoking compartment
hŭgin 흑인 black, negro
hŭibak'an 희박한 thin, rare; sparse; ***in-guga hŭibak'an*** 인구가 희박한 sparsely populated
hŭida 희다 white ◊ be white
hŭigok 희곡 drama
hŭigŭk 희극 comedy
hŭimang 희망 hope
hŭimang-e ch'an 희망에 찬 hopeful
hŭimanghada 희망하다 hope
hŭimang-ŭl irŭn 희망을 잃은 hopeless
hŭimihaejida 희미해지다 fade
hŭimihan 희미한 faint
hŭimihan pit 희미한 빛 glimmer
hŭisa 희사 donation
hŭisaeng 희생 cost; sacrifice; death toll; victim
hŭisaenghada 희생하다 make sacrifices; sacrifice
hŭisaengja 희생자 victim
hŭisaengshikida 희생시키다 victimize
hŭisaengnyang 희생양 scapegoat
hŭisahada 희사하다 donate
hŭi-yŏmŏlgŏn 희여멀건 wishy-washy
hŭk 흙 soil, earth
hŭktcharo 흑자로 in the black FIN
hŭlkkŭt poda 흘끗 보다 catch sight of, catch a glimpse of
hŭllida 흘리다 shed *blood, sweat, tears*; spill *water*
hŭm 흠 blemish, flaw; blot; groove; nick, cut
hŭmjabŭlde ŏmnŭn 흠잡을데 없는 faultless
hŭmjaptta 흠잡다 find fault with
hŭmnaeda 흠내다 blemish
hŭmŏmnŭn 흠없는 flawless
hŭmppŏk chŏjŭn 흠뻑 젖은 dripping, soaking wet
hŭmppŏk chŏksshida 흠뻑 적시다 drench
hŭmppŏk chŏt-tta 흠뻑 젖다 get drenched
hŭmtchibŏmnŭn 흠집없는 unscathed
hŭndŭlda 흔들다 shake; swing; wave; wiggle; undermine; ***Xŭl/rŭl toege***

hŭndŭlda X을/를 되게 흔들다 give X a good shake
hŭndŭlgŏrida 흔들거리다 rock; roll; sway; swing; wag
hŭndŭlgŏrinŭn 흔들거리는 shaky
hŭndŭllida 흔들리다 shake; vibrate; tremble
hŭndŭl ŭija 흔들 의자 rocking chair
hŭngbun 흥분 excitement, kick, thrill; stimulation
hŭngbundoeda 흥분되다 be excited
hŭngbunhada 흥분하다 get excited; ***nŏmu hŭngbunhaji maseyo!*** 너무 흥분하지 마세요! don't get excited!, take it easy!
hŭngbunshik'ida 흥분시키다 excite
hŭngbunshik'inŭn 흥분시키는 exciting
hŭngch'ŏngmangch'ŏng shyop'ing-ŭl hada 흥청망청 쇼핑을 하다 go on a shopping spree
hŭngjŏnghada 흥정하다 bargain
hŭngmijinjinhan 흥미진진한 very interesting
hŭngmi kkŭlda 흥미 끌다 intrigue
hŭngmirŭl irŭk'ige hada 흥미를 일으키게 하다 interest; arouse interest
hŭngmirŭl kajida 흥미를 가지다 take an interest in
hŭngmirŭl todunŭn 흥미를 돋우는 compelling
hŭnhaji anŭn 흔하지 않은 uncommon
hŭnjŏk 흔적 trace; trail; vestige
hŭnŭjŏk-kkŏrinŭn 흐느적거리는 limping
hŭnŭkkim 흐느낌 sob
hŭnŭkkyŏ ulda 흐느껴 울다 sob
hŭpssuhada 흡수하다 absorb
hŭpssussŏng-ŭi 흡수성의 absorbent
hŭrida 흐리다 be cloudy
hŭrige hada 흐리게 하다 blur; dim
hŭrim 흐림 blur
hŭrin 흐린 cloudy; misty; overcast
hŭrit'aejida 흐릿해지다 blur
hŭrit'an 흐릿한 dim; fuzzy; vague; glazed
hŭrŭda 흐르다 run, flow; stream
hŭrŭm 흐름 current; flow
hŭrŭnŭn 흐르는 flowing; runny
hŭryŏjida 흐려지다 mist over
hŭryŏjin 흐려진 misty; ***ont'ong hŭryŏjida*** 온통 흐려지다 cloud over
hŭt'ŏjida 흩어지다 disperse, scatter
hŭt'ŏjin 흩어진 scattered
hŭt'ŭrŏjin 흐트러진 disheveled
huban 후반 second half
hubida 후비다 dig up; grub; ***k'orŭl hubida*** 코를 후비다 pick one's nose
hubo 후보 nominee
huboja 후보자 candidate
hubo sŏnsu 후보 선수 reserve SP
hubul 후불 deferred payment; ***nanŭn hubullo chigŭppannŭnda*** 나는 후불로 지급받는다 I'm paid in arrears
huch'ŏnssŏng myŏnnyŏk kyŏlp'iptchŭng 후천성 면역 결핍증 Aids, acquired immune deficiency syndrome
huch'u 후추 pepper
hudae 후대 posterity
hudu 후두 larynx
hududuk ttŏrŏjida 후두둑 떨어지다 patter
hududuk'anŭn sori 후두둑하는 소리 patter, pattering sound
huduyŏm 후두염 laryngitis
hue 후에: ***...n(ŭn) hue*** ...ㄴ(은) 후에 since; after
hugak 후각 sense of smell
hugi 후기 epilog
hugyŏnin 후견인 guardian
huhoe 후회 penitence
huhoehada 후회하다 regret; repent
huhoesŭrŏpkkedo 후회스럽게도 regretfully, sadly
huim(ja) 후임(자) successor
huimjaga toeda 후임자가 되다 succeed *person*
huja 후자 the latter
hujin 후진 reverse (gear)
hujinhada 후진하다 reverse, back
hujinshik'ida 후진시키다 reverse, back
huk p'unggim 훅 풍김 whiff
hullyŏn 훈련 drill, exercise; training
hullyŏnhada 훈련하다 practice, drill; train
hullyŏn kyehoek 훈련 계획 training scheme

hullyŏnsa 훈련사 trainer
hullyŏnshik'ida 훈련시키다 train
hullyunghada 훌륭하다 be magnificent; be worthy; admirable; be noble; be great
hullyunghage 훌륭하게 wonderfully, beautifully
hullyunghan 훌륭한 brilliant, fine; masterly; respectable
hultchŏk-kkŏrida 훌쩍거리다 sniffling, snivelling
hultchŏk ttwida 훌쩍 뛰다 leap
hultta 훑다 thresh; strip; remove
hult'ŏboda 훑어보다 skim through *book*; look over *person*
humch'ida 훔치다 steal
humi 후미 inlet
humijin kot 후미진 곳 cove
hunjang-ŭl suyŏhada 훈장을 수여하다 decorate, award a medal
hunjehada 훈제하다 smoke *ham etc*
hunje soegogi 훈제 쇠고기 pastrami
huraip'aen 후라이팬 frying pan
Hurench'ihurai 후렌치후라이 French fries
huryŏch'ida 후려치다 punch
huryŏm 후렴 refrain MUS
hushik 후식 dessert
hut'ŏptchigŭnhada 후텁지근하다 be sultry (*of weather*)
hut'oe 후퇴 setback; retreat
hut'oehada 후퇴하다 retreat; pull out
huwi 후위 back SP
huwŏn 후원 sponsorship, patronage
huwŏnhada 후원하다 back (up), support; sponsor
huwŏnja 후원자 supporter; sponsor; backer; patron
hwanada 화나다 get angry
hwa 화 anger, annoyance
hwabun 화분 pollen; flowerpot
hwabunnyang 화분량 pollen count
hwabyŏng 화병 vase; hypochondria
hwach'a 화차 wagon
hwach'anghada 화창하다 be bright, be sunny
hwach'anghan nalssi 화창한 날씨 Indian summer
hwadan 화단 flowerbed
hwadŏk 화덕 furnace
hwaek sugŭrida 홱 수그리다 duck
hwaek tanggida 홱 당기다 yank, jerk
hwaetppul 횃불 torch (*with flame*)
hwaet-ttae 횃대 perch
hwaet-ttaee antta 횃대에앉다 perch
hwaga 화가 painter, drawer
hwaga ch'isot-tta 화가 치솟다 flareup
hwaga nada 화가 나다 get angry, get worked up
hwaga nan 화가 난 angry, sore
hwagang-am 화강암 granite
hwagin 확인 inspection; confirmation; identification; OK COMPUT
hwaginhada 확인하다 check; confirm; identify; check for; query
hwaginhae tuda 확인해 두다 keep a check on
hwahae 화해 reconciliation; settlement
hwahaehada 화해하다 make up; be reconciled
hwahaeshik'ida 화해시키다 reconcile
hwahak 화학 chemistry
hwahak chep'um 화학 제품 chemical
hwahaktcha 화학자 chemist
hwahaktchŏn 화학전 chemical warfare
hwahak yoppŏp 화학 요법 chemotherapy
hwahwan 화환 garland, wreath
hwail 화일 file COMPUT
hwail maenijŏ 화일 매니저 file manager
hwajae 화재 fire, blaze
hwajae kyŏngbogi 화재 경보기 fire alarm
hwajae p'inan changch'i 화재 피난 장치 fire escape
hwajang 화장 cremation; make-up; beauty care
hwajangdae 화장대 dressing table
hwajanghada 화장하다 cremate; put on make-up
hwajangjang 화장장 crematorium
hwajangji 화장지 tissue; toilet paper
hwajangp'um 화장품 make-up;

cosmetics
hwajangshil 화장실 restroom, bathroom; toilet
hwaje 화제 topic
hwajerŭl pakkŭda 화제를 바꾸다 change the subject
hwak ch'isosŭm 확 치솟음 blaze
hwak-kkohan 확고한 strong, definite, determined, firm
hwakkobudonghan 확고부동한 unswerving
hwaksshilssŏng 확실성 certainty; inevitability
hwaksshin 확신 certainty; confidence
hwaksshine ch'an 확신에 찬 assured
hwaksshinhada 확신하다 be positive; firmly believe; ***Xŭl / rŭl hwaksshinhaji mot'ada*** X을 / 를 확신하지 못하다 be uncertain about X
hwaksshinhanŭn 확신하는 certain, sure
hwaksshinshik'ida 확신시키다 convince
hwaksshirhada 확실하다 be certain, be definite
hwaksshirhage 확실하게 reliably
hwaksshirhan 확실한 marked, definite
hwaksshirhi 확실히 certainly definitely; decidedly; doubtless
hwakssŏnggi 확성기 loudspeaker
hwaktae 확대 zoom in
hwaktchang 확장 expansion; extension
hwaktchanghada 확장하다 expand; diversify
hwaktchang k'adŭ 확장카드 expansion card COMPUT
hwaktchŏngdoeda 확정되다 be finalized
hwaktchŏng kŭmaek 확정 금액 sum insured
hwaktchŭng 확증 confirmation
hwaktchŭnghada 확증하다 confirm
hwakttae chŏgyonghada 확대 적용하다 stretch *rules*
hwakttaehada 확대하다 blow up, enlarge; magnify; escalate
hwak t'ŭin 확 트인 panoramic
hwal 활 bow MUS
hwalbarhada 활발하다 be lively, be brisk
hwalgangno 활강로 chute
hwalgang sŭk'i 활강 스키 downhill skiing
hwalgi 활기 vigor, energy
hwalgi ch'an 활기 찬 lively
hwalgirŭl purŏnŏt'a 활기를 불어넣다 enliven
hwalgonghada 활공하다 glide
hwallyŏk 활력 drive, energy; vitality
hwalsŏng 활성 active COMPUT
hwaltcha 활자 moveable type
hwaltchak p'in 활짝 핀 in full bloom
hwaltchak ut-tta 활짝 웃다 beam, smile
hwaltchuro 활주로 runway, tarmac
hwalttong 활동 activity, action
hwalttongga 활동가 activist
hwalttong hoewŏn 활동 회원 active member
hwalttongjŏgin 활동적인 active; energetic, dynamic
hwamul 화물 freight; shipment, consignment
hwamulch'a 화물차 freight car; truck
hwamul pihaenggi 화물 비행기 freight plane
hwamulsŏn 화물선 freighter
hwamulsshil 화물실 hold (*on ship, plane*)
hwamul unbanttae 화물 운반대 pallet
hwamul unsongnyo 화물 운송료 freight (costs)
hwamul yŏlch'a 화물 열차 freight train
hwamyŏn 화면 screen; ***hwamyŏnsang-e*** 화면상에 on screen
hwamyŏne p'yoshihada 화면에 표시하다 display
hwamyŏn pohogi 화면 보호기 screen saver
hwanada 화나다 be annoyed; get annoyed, blow up
hwanaege hada 화내게 하다 anger
hwanan 화난 exasperated
hwanbul 환불 refund, rebate
hwanbul pulgaŭi 환불 불가의

nonreturnable *deposit*
hwanburhada 환불하다 refund
hwandae 환대 hospitality
hwandaehanŭn 환대하는 hospitable
hwandŭnggi p'illŭm k'arusel 환등기 필름 카루셀 carousel (*for slides*)
hwan-gap 환갑 sixtieth birthday (*61st birthday in the West, since Koreans are one year old at birth*)
hwangdal 황달 jaundice
hwangdodae 황도대 zodiac
hwangdodaeŭi shibi kung 황도대의 십이 궁 12 signs of the zodiac
hwanggalssaek 황갈색 buff (*color*)
hwanggŭmshiganttae 황금시간대 prime time
hwanggŭp'i 황급히 in double-quick time
Hwangha 황하 Yellow River
Hwanghae 황해 Yellow Sea
hwanghol 황홀 ecstasy
hwanghorhan 황홀한 ecstatic
hwan-gich'ang 환기창 vent, ventilation window
hwan-gi changch'i 환기 장치 ventilator; ventilation
hwan-gigaeng 환기갱 ventilation shaft
hwan-gihada 환기하다 ventilate
hwan-gishik'ida 환기시키다 air *room*; challenge; evoke
hwangje 황제 emperor
hwangmuji 황무지 desert; wilderness
hwangnyanghan 황량한 bleak, desolate; godforsaken
hwangp'ye chiyŏk 황폐 지역 wasteland
hwangp'yehaejida 황폐해지다 ravaged by war
hwangp'yehan 황폐한 desolate, inhospitable
hwangsae 황새 stork
hwangsaek shinho-e 황색 신호에 at amber (*of traffic light*)
hwangso 황소 bull, ox
hwangsonghada 황송하다 be indebted, be obliged; ***kŭnŭn hwangsonghagedo na-ege marŭl kŏrŏssŏ*** 그가 황송하게도 내게 말을 걸었어 he condescended to speak to me
hwan-gyŏng 환경 conditions; surroundings; environment
hwan-gyŏngboho 환경보호 environmental protection
hwan-gyŏngbohoronja 환경보호론자 environmentalist
Hwan-gyŏngch'ŏng 환경처 Department of the Interior
hwan-gyŏng-oyŏm 환경오염 environmental pollution
hwanhada 환하다 be bright; be open
hwanhage 환하게 brightly
hwanhan 환한 bright, broad *smile*
hwanhi pinnanŭn 환히 빛나는 radiant
hwanho 환호 cheer; cheering; jubilation
hwanhohada 환호하다 cheer
hwanhohanŭn 환호하는 jubilant
hwanhoŭi sori 환호의 소리 hurray
hwanhŭi 환희 joy, delight; rapture
hwanja 환자 patient
hwanjŏnhada 환전하다 exchange
hwanmyŏl 환멸 disillusionment
hwannyul 환율 exchange rate
hwanŏŭm 환어음 bill of exchange
hwanp'unggi 환풍기 ventilation fan
hwansaeng 환생 reincarnation
hwansan 환산 conversion
hwansang 환상 fantasy
hwansangjŏgin 환상적인 fantastic
hwansanhada 환산하다 convert
hwansanp'yo 환산표 conversion table
hwanyŏng 환영 reception, welcome; vision; illusion
hwanyŏnghada 환영하다 welcome
hwanyŏng pannŭn 환영 받는 welcome
Hwaŏmgyŏng 화엄경 Flower Garland Sutra
hwap'urihada 화풀이하다 take it out on
hwarang 화랑 gallery
Hwarangdo 화랑도 Youth Corps
hwarŭl ch'amtta 화를 참다 keep one's temper
hwarŭl naeda 화를 내다 lose one's temper; vent one's anger
hwaryŏhada 화려하다 be sumptuous
hwaryŏhage changshik'an 화려하게

장식한 ornate
hwaryŏham 화려함 splendor
hwaryonghada 활용하다 put to practical use, utilize
hwaryongshik'ida 활용시키다 conjugate
hwasal 화살 arrow
hwasalp'yo kŭlsoe 화살표 글쇠 arrow key COMPUT
hwasan 화산 volcano
hwasang 화상 burn (*injury*)
hwasang hoeŭi 화상 회의 video conference
hwashin 화신 embodiment
hwasŏk 화석 fossil
hwasŏng 화성 harmony
Hwasshi 화씨 Fahrenheit
hwayak 화약 gunpowder
hwayoil 화요일 Tuesday
hwesonhada 훼손하다 mutilate; defame
hwibaryu 휘발유 gasoline, gas
hwich'ŏnggŏrida 휘청거리다 stagger
hwida 휘다 bend, warp
hwidurŭda 휘두르다 brandish; wield; flick
hwigalgyŏ ssŭda 휘갈겨 쓰다 scrawl
hwigehada 휘게하다 warp
hwigi shwiun 휘기 쉬운 pliable
hwijang 휘장 drapery
hwijŏnnŭn kigu 휘젓는 기구 whisk
hwijŏt-tta 휘젓다 stir; whisk
hwik kkŭjibŏnaeda 휙 끄집어내다 pull out, whip out
hwilch'eŏ 휠체어 wheelchair
hwin 휜 bent
hwip'aram 휘파람 whistle
hwip'aramŭl pulda 휘파람을 불다 whistle
hwŏlsshin kŭ chŏne 훨씬 그 전에 long before then
hwŏnhada 훤하다 be broad; be extensive; be well versed in; ***...ŭl / rŭl hwŏnhi alda*** ...을 / 를 훤히 알다 have at one's fingertips
hwŏnhi t'ŭin 훤히 트인 open and bright
hyŏmnyŏktcha 협력자 co-worker, collaborator (*on a project*)
hyŏng 형 elder brother
hyŏnshiljŏgin 현실적인 realistic
hyang 향 incense
hyanggi 향기 aroma, scent; bouquet
hyangginanŭn 향기나는 fragrant
hyanghada 향하다 face
hyanghayŏ 향하여 to; toward; facing
hyangsang 향상 improvement
hyangsangdoeda 향상되다 get better
hyangsanghada 향상하다 improve, progress
hyangsangshik'ida 향상시키다 improve, upgrade
hyangsu 향수 perfume; nostalgia
hyangsuppyŏng-ul alt'a 향수병을 앓다 be homesick
hyang-yŏn 향연 banquet, dinner
hyesŏng 혜성 comet
hyet'aekpat-tchi mot'an 혜택받지 못한 underprivileged
hyŏ 혀 tongue
hyŏbŭihada 협의하다 confer
hyŏksshin 혁신 innovation
hyŏksshinhanŭn hoesa 혁신하는 회사 innovative company
hyŏksshinjŏgin 혁신적인 innovative
hyŏlgi 혈기 blood
hyŏlgu 혈구 corpuscle
hyŏlgwan 혈관 blood vessel
hyŏlgwan ishik 혈관 이식 bypass MED
hyŏllyu 혈류 bloodstream
hyŏlssaegi anjohŭn 혈색이 안좋은 sickly
hyŏltchŏntchŭng 혈전증 thrombosis
hyŏlt'ong 혈통 blood; pedigree
hyŏlt'ong-i punmyŏnghan 혈통이 분명한 pedigree
hyŏmnyŏk kwan-gye 협력 관계 partnership
hyŏmnyŏktcha 협력자 collaborator (*on a project*)
hyŏmnyŏktchŏgin 협력적인 cooperative
hyŏmnyŏk 협력 cooperation
hyŏmnyŏk'ada 협력하다 cooperate; collaborate; ***... wa / kwa hyŏmnyŏk'ayŏ*** ...와 / 과 협력하여 in association with
hyŏmo 혐오 disgust
hyŏmogamŭl irŭk'ida 혐오감을 일으키다 disgust

hyŏmohada 혐오하다 detest
hyŏmosŭrŏun 혐오스러운 disgusting
hyŏmŭi 혐의 charge LAW
hyŏmŭija 혐의자 suspect
hyŏmŭirŭl pannŭn 혐의를 받는 suspected
hyŏn 현 chord
hyŏnak-kki 현악기 stringed instrument
hyŏnak-kki yŏnjuja 현악기 연주자 string player; strings
hyŏnch'ang 현창 porthole
Hyŏnch'ung-il 현충일 Memorial Day
hyŏndae 현대 modern times ◊ modern
hyŏndaehwa 현대화 modernization
hyŏndaehwahada 현대화하다 modernize
hyŏndaejŏgin 현대적인 modern
hyŏndaejŏgŭro pakkuda 현대적으로 바꾸다 modernize
hyŏndaeŭi 현대의 contemporary
hyŏngbu 형부 brother-in-law (*woman's elder sister's husband*)
hyŏnggwang 형광 fluorescence
hyŏnggwangp'en 형광펜 highlighter
hyŏnggwang-ŭi 형광의 fluorescent
hyŏn-gitchŭng 현기증 giddiness; vertigo
hyŏn-gitchŭng-i nada 현기증이 나다 feel dizzy
hyŏngje chamae 형제 자매 brothers and sisters
hyŏngmyŏng 혁명 revolution
hyŏngmyŏngga 혁명가 revolutionary
hyŏngmyŏngjŏgin 혁명적인 revolutionary *ideas*
hyŏngmyŏng-ŭi 혁명의 revolutionary *spirit*
hyŏngmyŏng-ŭl irŭk'ida 혁명을 일으키다 revolutionize
hyŏng-ŏnhal su ŏmnŭn 형언할 수 없는 indescribable
hyŏngp'yŏnŏmnŭn 형편없는 wretched, pathetic; useless; disreputable
hyŏngp'yŏnŏpsshi 형편없이 dreadfully; poorly
hyŏngsa 형사 detective; criminal case
hyŏngsang 형상 figure
hyŏngsasang-ŭi 형사상의 criminal
hyŏngshik 형식 format, make-up; formality
hyŏngshiktchŏgin 형식적인 formal; perfunctory
hyŏngshiktchŏgŭro 형식적으로 formally
hyŏngsŏng 형성 formation
hyŏngsŏnghanŭn 형성하는 formative
hyŏngsŏngshik'ida 형성시키다 mold
hyŏngsu 형수 sister-in-law (*elder brother's wife*)
hyŏngt'ae 형태 form
hyŏn-gŭm 현금 cash; ***kŭ chariesŏ hyŏn-gŭmŭro*** **그 자리에서 현금으로** cash down
hyŏn-gŭm harin 현금 할인 cash discount
hyŏn-gŭm inch'ulgi 현금 인출기 cash machine, ATM
hyŏn-gŭmŭro naeda 현금으로 내다 pay (in) cash
hyŏn-gŭmŭro pakkuda 현금으로 바꾸다 cash *check*
hyŏn-gŭm yuch'urip 현금 유출입 cash flow
hyŏn-gwan 현관 entrance, porch
hyŏng-yongsa 형용사 adjective
hyŏnhaengbŏmŭro 현행범으로 in the very act
hyŏnhaktchŏgin 현학적인 pedantic
hyŏnjae 현재 the present
hyŏnjaehyŏng 현재형 present GRAM
hyŏnjaeronŭn 현재로는 presently, at the moment
hyŏnjaeŭi 현재의 current, present; going
hyŏnjang 현장 scene; ***hyŏnjang-e*(*sŏ*) 현장에(서)** on the scene; on the spot; on site
hyŏnji shigan 현지 시간 local time
hyŏnjŏhan 현저한 remarkable, striking
hyŏnjonhanŭn 현존하는 existing
hyŏnmigyŏng 현미경 microscope
hyŏnmyŏnghada 현명하다 be wise
hyŏnmyŏng-hage 현명하게 wisely
hyŏnmyŏnghan 현명한 clever; sensible; wise; advisable

hyŏnsang 현상 phenomenon; development (*of film*)
hyŏnsanghada 현상하다 develop *film*
hyŏnshil 현실 reality
hyŏnshiltchŏgin 현실적인 realistic
hyŏnshiltchuŭi 현실주의 realism
hyŏnshiltchuŭija 현실주의자 realist
hyŏnsugyo 현수교 suspension bridge
hyŏpkkok 협곡 gorge
hyŏp-ppak 협박 threat, intimidation
hyŏp-ppak p'yŏnji 협박 편지 threatening letter
hyŏp-ppak'ada 협박하다 intimidate, threaten
hyŏpssang 협상 negotiation
hyŏpssangga 협상가 negotiator
hyŏpssanghada 협상하다 negotiate
hyŏpsshimtchŭng 협심증 angina
hyŏptchugok 협주곡 concerto
hyŏpttong 협동 collaboration, cooperation
hyŏpttong chagŏp 협동 작업 teamwork
hyŏpttong chohap 협동 조합 cooperative COM
hyŏpttonghada 협동하다 pull together
hyŏraek kŏmsa 혈액 검사 blood test
hyŏraek saemp'ŭl 혈액 샘플 blood sample
hyŏraek ŭnhaeng 혈액 은행 blood bank
hyŏraek'yŏng 혈액형 blood group
hyŏrap 혈압 blood pressure
hyo 효 filial piety (*Confucian*)
hyokkwaga ŏmnŭn 효과가 없는 ineffective
hyokkwajŏgin 효과적인 effective
hyokkwarŭl churida 효과를 줄이다 counter the effect of
hyomo 효모 yeast
hyoryŏgi innŭn 효력이 있는 effective
hyoryŏgŭl nat'anaeda 효력을 나타내다 take effect
hyoyul 효율 efficiency
hyoyultchŏgin 효율적인 efficient
hyoyurhwa 효율화 rationalization
hyoyurhwahada 효율화하다 rationalize
hyudaep'um pogwanso 휴대품 보관소 checkroom
hyudaeyong-(ŭi) 휴대용(의) portable
hyudaeyong ŭija 휴대용 의자 deckchair
hyuga 휴가 vacation; leave
hyugarŭl kat-tta 휴가를 갖다 take a holiday
hyuga yŏhaenggaek 휴가 여행객 vacationer
hyuge shigan 휴게 시간 intermission, interval
hyugeshil 휴게실 lobby
hyugeso 휴게소 service area
hyuhoe 휴회 recess
hyuhwasan 휴화산 dormant volcano
hyuil 휴일 holiday
hyuji 휴지 toilet paper; waste paper
hyujit'ong 휴지통 wastepaper basket
hyujŏn 휴전 cease-fire; truce; armistice
hyujŏngdoeda 휴정되다 adjourn
hyujŏnsŏn 휴전선 ceasefire line
hyung-ak 흉악 atrocity
hyung-akppŏm 흉악범 thug
hyung-akssŏng 흉악성 enormity
hyung-ak'an 흉악한 hideous
hyunghada 흉하다 be hideous; be unlucky
hyunghan 흉한 ugly
hyungmul 흉물 monstrosity
hyungnae 흉내 impersonation take-off
hyungnaenaeda 흉내내다 imitate, take off, mimic; simulate
hyungnaenaegi 흉내내기 impression, take off
hyungp'ohan 흉포한 ferocious
hyungt'ŏ 흉터 scar; ***hyungt'ŏrŭl namgida*** 흉터를 남기다 leave a scar
hyushik 휴식 rest, respite; ***kabyŏun hyushik shigan*** 가벼운 휴식 시간 coffee break
hyushikch'ŏ 휴식처 resting place; lounge
hyushik-kki 휴식기 break
hyuyangji 휴양지 resort

I

...i ...이 (*subject particle*): ***...i it-tta*** ...이 있다 there is / are
i 이 two ◊ tooth; louse; profit; interest FIN; reason; person ◊ this
ibalssa 이발사 barber
ibanja 입안자 draftsman
ibe taego punŭn pubun 입에 대고 부는 부분 mouthpiece
ibi ttak pŏrŏjin 입이 딱 벌어진 open-mouthed; wide-mouthed
ibŏboda 입어보다 try on
ibŭl tamulda 입을 다물다 clam up, keep silent
ibŭl ttak pŏlligo paraboda 입을 딱 벌리고 바라보다 gape
ibul 이불 coverlet
ibunppŏp 이분법 dichotomy
ibwŏnhada 입원하다 go into hospital
ibwŏn hwanja 입원 환자 in-patient
ibyang 입양 adoption
ibyang-a 입양아 foster child
ibyanghada 입양하다 adopt
ibyŏl 이별 farewell; parting
ich'ajŏgŭro chung-yohan 이차적으로 중요한 of secondary importance
ich'ie matkke 이치에 맞게 reasonably
ich'ŭng ch'imdae 이층 침대 bunk beds
ich'yŏjida 잊혀지다 fall into oblivion
ida 이다 be; ***nanŭn hakssaeng-iyeyo*** 나는 학생이에요 I am a student
idan kiŏ 이단 기어 second gear
ideollogi 이데올로기 ideology
idojŏdo anin kyŏng-u 이도저도 아닌 경우 a borderline case
idong 이동 shift; transfer; mobility
idong chŏnhwa 이동 전화 cell phone
idonghada 이동하다 travel around; change direction
idong-i kanŭnghan 이동이 가능한 mobile
idong musŏn chŏnhwa 이동 무선 전화 cellular phone
idongssŏng 이동성 mobility
idŭgi toeda 이득이되다 be profitable, pay off
idŭngsŏgŭi 이등석의 second class
Idu 이두 Idu (*Silla-Choson writing system*)
iga ŏmnŭn 이가 없는 toothless
iga ppajida 이가 빠지다 be chipped
igida 이기다 win; beat; win out; mix
igijŏgin 이기적인 selfish
igŏt 이것 this ◊ this one
igŏttŭl 이것들 these
igŭllu 이글루 igloo
igŭn 익은 ripe
igŭnishyŏn k'i 이그니션 키 ignition key
iguktchŏgin 이국적인 exotic
igyŏn 이견 different opinion; difference (of opinion)
igyŏnaeda 이겨내다 get over, overcome, surmount
igyodo 이교도 heathen
iha 이하 not exceeding, less than; under, below; the following; ***...iharo*** ...이하로 below
ihae 이해 understanding
ihaeganŭn 이해가는 meaningful
ihaehada 이해하다 understand
ihaengjŏng ssaik'ŭrŭi 이행정 싸이클의 two-stroke
ihaeryŏk 이해력 understanding, comprehension
ihaeshik'ida 이해시키다 make understand; get through
ihaeshimninnŭn 이해심있는 understanding *person*
ihangnyŏn 이학년 sophomore
ihasŏnnyŏm 이하선염 mumps
ihon 이혼 divorce
ihonhada 이혼하다 divorce, get divorced

ihonhan 이혼한 divorced
ihonnam 이혼남 divorcee (*man*)
ihonnyŏ 이혼녀 divorcee (*woman*)
ihuro 이후로 since; ***chinan chu ihuro*** 지난 주 이후로 since last week
iigi andoenŭn 이익이 안되는 uneconomic
iigi ŏmnŭn 이익이 없는 unprofitable
iigi toeda 이익이 되다 benefit
iigŭl naeda 이익을 내다 yield a profit
iigŭl ŏt-tta 이익을 얻다 get a profit; benefit
iigŭl poda 이익을 보다 make a profit
iik 이익 benefit; profit, return
iinyong pang 이인용 방 double room
ija 이자 interest
ijayul 이자율 interest rate
ije 이제 now; no longer, not any more; ***ije kŭmanhae!*** 이제 그만해! I've had enough!, stop!
ijel 이젤 easel
ijiltchŏgin 이질적인 alien
ijinppŏp 이진법 binary system
Ijipt'ŭ 이집트 Egypt ◊ Egyptian
ijŏbŏrida 잊어버리다 forget, lose sight of; lose
ijŏbŏrigo tŭgo kada 잊어버리고 두고 가다 leave behind, forget
ijŏk haeng-wija 이적 행위자 collaborator *pej*
ijŏk'ada 이적하다 transfer
ijŏne 이전에 before; formerly
ijŏngp'yo 이정표 milestone
ijŏnhada 이전하다 relocate
ijŏnŭi 이전의 ex-; previous, prior
ijŭl su ŏmnŭn 잊을 수 없는 unforgettable
iju 이주 migration; emigration; immigration
ijuhada 이주하다 migrate; immigrate
ijuja 이주자 settler, immigrant
ijung chuch'ashik'ida 이중 주차시키다 double park
ijungch'ang 이중창 duo
ijung in-gyŏkja 이중 인격자 two-faced person
ijung inkkyŏk 이중 인격 split personality
ijungju 이중주 duet
ijung kuktchŏk 이중 국적을 dual nationality
ijungt'ŏk 이중턱 double chin
ijung-ŭi 이중의 dual
ijung yuri 이중 유리 double glazing
iju nodongja 이주 노동자 migrant worker
ikki 이끼 moss
ikki kkin 이끼 낀 mossy
ikkŭlda 이끌다 head, lead; steer
ikkŭlgo kada 이끌고 가다 lead up to
ikssahada 익사하다 be drowned
ikssalburida 익살부리다 joke
ikssashik'ida 익사시키다 drown
ikssuk'aejida 익숙해지다 familiarize oneself with, get used to
ikssuk'aji anŭn 익숙하지 않은 unfamiliar; ***...e ikssuk'aji ant'a*** ...에 익숙하지 않다 be unfamiliar with, be unaccustomed to
iktta 익다 get used to; get cooked; ripen
ikttŏn kot 읽던 곳 place (*in a book*)
ik'ida 익히다 familiarize; cook
il 일 affair; business; job; pursuit; work; things; ***ne irina haera!*** 네 일이나 해라! mind your own business!
ilbangjŏgin 일방적인 one-sided, unilateral
ilbang t'onghaengno 일방 통행로 one-way street
ilbanhwa 일반화 generalization
ilbanhwahada 일반화하다 generalize
ilbanin 일반인 civilian
ilbanjŏgin 일반적인 general
ilbanjŏgŭro 일반적으로 generally, in general
ilban sabyŏng 일반 사병 the ranks
ilbŏlle 일벌레 workaholic
ilbo 일보 a step; ***ilbo chiktchŏne it-tta*** 일보 직전에 있다 be on the verge of
Ilbon 일본 Japan ◊ Japanese
Ilbonŏ 일본어 Japanese (*language*)
Ilbon saram 일본 사람 Japanese
ilbubun 일부분 one part, a portion
ilburŏ 일부러 deliberately
ilbu saramdŭl 일부 사람들 some people
ilch'erŭl p'ohamhayŏ 일체를

포함하여 all inclusive
ilch'i 일치 agreement, consensus; match, correspondence
ilch'ihada 일치하다 agree, match, correspond; agree with
ilch'ihanŭn 일치하는 corresponding, matching; coinciding
ilch'ishik'ida 일치시키다 agree; reconcile
ilch'ŭng 일층 first floor
ilch'ul 일출 sunrise
ilda 일다 brew, get up
ilgan shinmun 일간 신문 daily paper
ilgi 일기 diary
ilgido 일기도 weather chart
ilgi yebo 일기 예보 weather forecast
ilgop 일곱 seven
ilgop pŏntchaeŭi 일곱번째의 seventh
ilgŭl kŏri 읽을 거리 reading matter
ilgŭl su innŭn 읽을 수 있는 readable
ilgwa 일과 routine
ilgwal 일괄 package
ilgwaljŏgŭro ch'wigŭp'ada 일괄적으로 취급하다 lump together
ilgwangnyogŭl hada 일광욕을 하다 sunbathe
ilgwanjagŏp yŏl 일관작업 열 assembly line
ilgwansŏng 일관성 consistency
ilgwansŏng innŭn 일관성 있는 consistent
il hoebun 일 회분 installment, episode
iljikssŏnŭro 일직선으로 in a straight line
ilkkaewŏjuda 일깨워주다 remind
ilkke hada 잃게 하다 cost; cause the loss of
ilkki ŏryŏun 읽기 어려운 illegible; unreadable; ***ilkki shwiun*** 읽기 쉬운 legible; easy to read
illanssŏng ssangdung-i 일란성 쌍둥이 identical twins
illyŏk 인력 manpower
illyŏnbŏnho 일련번호 serial number
illyŏne 일년에 in a year, per annum
illyŏne han ponŭi 일년에 한 번의 annual
illyu 인류 human race; humanity; man
illyunch'a 일륜차 wheelbarrow; monocycle
illyuŭi 일류의 first-rate
ilmol 일몰 sunset
ilmyŏn 일면 front page
ilmyŏn kisa 일면 기사 front page news
ilsangjŏgin 일상적인 everyday
ilshijŏk yŏn-gi 일시적 연기 reprieve
ilssang 일상 everyday
ilssangbok 일상복 clothes for everyday wear
ilssangjŏgin 일상적인 routine
ilssangjŏgŭro 일상적으로 as a matter of routine, routinely
ilssang-yong-ŏ 일상용어 vernacular
ilssanhwat'anso 일산화탄소 carbon monoxide
ilssappyŏng 일사병 sunstroke
ilsshibul 일시불 lump sum
ilsshijŏgin 일시적인 temporary, casual
ilsshijŏgŭro 일시적으로 temporarily
ilsshijŏk chŭngga 일시적 증가 temporary increase, bulge
ilsshijŏk pyŏndong 일시적 변동 temporary fluctuation, blip
ilsshijŏk taeyuhaeng 일시적 대유행 passing fad, craze
ilsshik 일식 eclipse of the sun
ilsshirŭl chŏnghada 일시를 정하다 fix a time
ilssohada 일소하다 clean up
ilsson 일손 hand, worker
iltchesagyŏk 일제 사격 volley
iltchi 일지 diary; logbook
...iltchido morŭnda ...일지도 모른다 may, might
iltchigin 일찍인 early
iltchik 일찍 early
iltchŏne 일전에 the other day
iltchŏng 일정 agenda; schedule
iltchŏng-aek 일정액 flat rate
iltchŏngch'i anŭn 일정치 않은 unsettled
iltchŏnghada 일정하다 be regular
iltchŏnghaji anŭn 일정하지 않은 erratic
iltchŏnghan 일정한 particular, specific; regular, uniform
iltchŏng-i kkwak ch'ada 일정이 꽉 차다 booked up

iltchŏng kigan 일정 기간 stint
iltchŏngsang 일정상 on the agenda
iltta 읽다 read
ilttŭngshil 일등실 first class cabin / compartment
ilt'a 잃다 lose
ima 이마 forehead, brow
imbak'an 임박한 pending, impending
imdae 임대 lease
imdae chadongch'a 임대 자동차 rental car
imdaehada 임대하다 lease, rent
imdae kyeyaksŏ 임대 계약서 rental agreement
imdaeryo 임대료 rent
imdaeyong 임대용 for rent
imeil 이메일 e-mail
imeil chuso 이메일 주소 e-mail address
imeillo ponaeda 이메일로 보내다 e-mail, send by e-mail
imeirŭl ponaeda 이메일을 보내다 e-mail, send an e-mail to
imgŭm tonggyŏl 임금 동결 wage freeze
imhak 임학 forestry
imi 이미 already
imiji 이미지 image
imin 이민 emigrant
Imin-guk 이민국 Immigration
iminhada 이민하다 emigrate
imjaga pakkwida 임자가 바뀌다 change hands
immagae 입마개 muzzle
immasŭl tashida 입맛을 다시다 lick one's lips
immu 임무 task, brief; assignment; duty
immyŏng 임명 appointment; posting
immyŏnghada 임명하다 appoint, nominate
immyŏngja 임명자 appointee
imnyŏk 입력 input; enter, return
imnyŏkshik'ida 입력시키다 enter COMPUT; ***k'ŏmp'yut'ŏe imnyŏksshik'yŏ not'a*** 컴퓨터에 입력시켜 놓다 put sth on computer
imnyŏk tanja 입력 단자 input port
imnyŏk'ada 입력하다 enter, key in
imo 이모 aunt (*mother's sister*)
imobu 이모부 uncle (*mother's sister's husband*)
imsanbok 임산복 maternity dress
imsang-ŭi 임상의 clinical
imshi chigwŏn 임시 직원 temporary employee, temp
imshi chŏjangso 임시 저장소 buffer COMPUT
imshijigŭro irhada 임시직으로 일하다 work on a temporary basis, temp
imshijŏgin 임시적인 temporary, provisional
imshin 임신 conception; pregnancy
imshinbu 임신부 expectant mother
imshinhada 임신하다 conceive; be pregnant
imshinhan 임신한 pregnant
imshinjung-ida 임신 중이다 be expecting
imshi pyŏnt'ong 임시 변통 stopgap
imshi sudan 임시 수단 makeshift
imshiŭi 임시의 temporary, acting
imun 이문 margin
...inae-e ...이내에 within
inboisŭ 인보이스 invoice
inbun 인분 (human) feces; portion
Inch'e Myŏnyŏk Kyŏlp'ip Pairŏsŭ 인체 면역 결핍 바이러스 HIV
inch'i 인치 inch
inch'ing taemyŏngsa 인칭 대명사 personal pronoun
inch'ŏk 인척 in-laws
inch'ul 인출 withdrawal
inch'urhada 인출하다 withdraw
indae 인대 ligament
Indian 인디안 (American) Indian
indo 인도 footpath, sidewalk; surrender; India ◊ Indian
Indoch'aina 인도차이나 Indochina ◊ Indochinese
indohada 인도하다 lead, take; extradite; usher in
Indoin 인도인 Indian (*person*)
indojuŭi 인도주의 humanism; humanitarianism
Indoneshia 인도네시아 Indonesia ◊ Indonesian
Indoneshiain 인도네시아인 Indonesian (*person*)
in-gan 인간 human (being)
in-ganjŏgin 인간적인 human,

humane
in-ganssŏng 인간성 humanity, humaneness
in-gan ssŭregi 인간 쓰레기 lowlife
in-girŭl ŏt-tta 인기를 얻다 catch on
ingkko 잉꼬 budgerigar
ingk'ŭ 잉크 ink
ingk'ŭ chet p'ŭrint'ŏ 잉크 젯 프린터 inkjet (printer)
ingmyŏng tong-ŏptcha 익명 동업자 silent partner
ingmyŏng-ŭi 익명의 anonymous
in-gong 인공 man-made
in-gong hohŭpkki 인공 호흡기 respirator
in-gongjinŭng 인공지능 artificial intelligence
in-gongjŏgin 인공적인 artificial
in-gong-wisŏng 인공위성 satellite
in-gong-wisŏng chŏpsshi 인공위성 접시 satellite dish
in-gu 인구 population
in-gu miltto 인구 밀도 population density
ing-yŏ 잉여 surplus
inhaesŏ 인해서: ***kŭgŏsŭ(ro) in-haesŏ*** 그것으로 인해서 so, for that reason
inhwa 인화 print
inhwassŏng(-ŭi) 인화성(의) inflammable
inhyŏng 인형 doll
inishyŏl 이니셜 initial
inishyŏllo ssŭda 이니셜로 쓰다 initial
injae sŭk'aut'ŭ tamdangja 인재 스카우트 담당자 headhunter *fig*
inji 인지 perception
...inji ...인지 if; whether; ***...inji anidŭnji kane*** ...인지 아니든지 간에 whether or not; ***...inji ...inji*** ...인지 ...인지 whether ... or ...
injil 인질 hostage
injilbŏm 인질범 hostage taker
injillo chap'ida 인질로 잡히다 be taken hostage
injŏgi kkŭnk'in 인적이 끊긴 deserted
injŏng 인정 acknowledgment
injŏnghada 인정하다 admit; approve of
injŏng-i manŭn 인정이 많은 philanthropic; benevolent
injŏng-innŭn 인정있는 humane
injŏng ŏmnŭn 인정 없는 inhuman
injŏp'an 인접한 adjacent
injong 인종 race
injong ch'abyŏl p'yeji 인종 차별 폐지 abolish racial discrimination, desegregate
injong ch'abyŏltchŏgin 인종 차별적인 racist
injong ch'abyŏltchuŭi 인종 차별주의 racism
injong ch'abyŏltchuŭija 인종 차별주의자 racist
injong p'yŏngdŭng 인종 평등 racial equality
injoŭi 인조의 artificial
inkki 인기 popularity
inkkiinnŭn 인기있는 fashionable, popular
inkki-it-tta 인기있다 be popular
inkkiŏmnŭn 인기없는 unpopular
inkkirŭl ŏt-tta 인기를 얻다 become popular, take off
ink'yubeit'ŏ 인큐베이터 incubator
inmom 잇몸 gum (*in mouth*)
inmul 인물 character
inp'ŭlle(ishyŏn) 인플레(이션) inflation
inp'ŭlleishyŏnŭl yubarhanŭn 인플레이션을 유발하는 inflationary
inp'yŏnŭro 인편으로 by hand
insa 인사 greeting, bow
insaek'ada 인색하다 be miserly
insaek'an 인색한 mean, stingy; miserly; grudging
insaeng 인생 life
insaeng-ŭl chŭlgida 인생을 즐기다 enjoy life
insahada 인사하다 greet; bow
insakkwa 인사과 personnel; human resources
insam 인삼 ginseng
insang 인상 raise, rise; image, reputation; impression; ***nuguege choŭn / nappŭn insangŭl chuda*** 누구에게 좋은 / 나쁜 인상을 주다 make a good / bad impression on s.o.; ***...(ŭ)n insangŭl pat-tta*** ... ...(으)ㄴ 인상을 받다 I get the impression that

insangjŏgin 인상적인 impressive; imposing, striking
insa pulssŏng 인사 불성 stupor
insa tamdang pujang 인사 담당 부장 personnel manager
inshik 인식 awareness
inshim chot'a 인심 좋다 be generous
inshim choŭn 인심 좋은 generous, good-hearted
inshyullin 인슐린 insulin
insŭt'ŏnt'ŭ k'ŏp'i 인스턴트 커피 instant coffee
insŭt'ŏnt'ŭ shikp'um 인스턴트 식품 convenience food
insu 인수 takeover; factor MATH
insuhada 인수하다 take over
inswae 인쇄 print
inswaegi 인쇄기 printing press
inswaehada 인쇄하다 printout
inswaemul 인쇄물 printed matter
inswaeŏptcha 인쇄업자 printer (*person*)
int'elli 인텔리 egghead; the intelligentsia
int'eriŏ tijain 인테리어 디자인 interior design
int'eriŏ tijainŏ 인테리어 디자이너 interior designer
int'ŏbyu 인터뷰 interview
int'ŏbyuhada 인터뷰하다 interview
int'ŏbyuhanŭn saram 인터뷰하는 사람 interviewer
int'ŏch'einji 인터체인지 interchange
int'ŏk'ŏm 인터컴 intercom
Int'ŏnesŭl tullŏboda 인터넷을 둘러보다 surf the Net
Int'ŏnet 인터넷 Internet; ***Int'ŏnet sangesŏ*** 인터넷 상에서 on the Internet
int'ŏpeisŭ 인터페이스 interface
inwijŏgin 인위적인 artificial, insincere
inyŏmjŏgin 이념적인 ideological
inyong 인용 quotation; extract
inyonghada 인용하다 quote; ***chakkkaŭi kŭrŭl inyonghada*** 작가의 글을 인용하다 quote from an author
inyongmun 인용문 quote (*from author*)
inyong puho 인용 부호 quotation marks
iŏp'on 이어폰 earphones
...iŏsŏ ...이어서 next to
...ioe-e ...이외에 besides, except for
ip 잎 leaf; blade; foliage
ip 입 mouth; ***han ip*** 한 입 a bite, a mouthful; ***nanŭn surŭl ibe taeji anssŭmnida*** 나는 술을 입에 대지 않습니다 I never touch alcohol, I don't drink
ipch'al 입찰 tender; bid
ipch'arhada 입찰하다 bid
ipch'ullyŏk k'odŭ 입출력 코드 access code
ipch'ullyŏk'ada 입출력하다 access
ipkkimŭl pulda 입김을 불다 blow
ipkku 입구 entrance, entry
ipkkuk 입국 arrivals (*at airport*); entry (*to country*)
ipkkuk hŏga 입국 허가 admission (*to country*)
ipkkukpija 입국비자 entry visa
i ppajin chaguk 이 빠진 자국 chip (*in cup etc*)
ip ppakkŭro naeda 입 밖으로 내다 let out *gasp, scream etc*
ip-ppangch'e 입방체 cube
ip-ppang-ŭi 입방의 cubic
ip-ppang yongjŏk 입방 용적 cubic volume
ip-ppang yongnyang 입방 용량 cubic capacity
ip-ppŏp 입법 legislation
ip-ppŏp-ppu 입법부 legislature
ipssahada 입사하다 join
ipssanghan 입상한 prizewinning
ipsshim choŭn 입심 좋은 glib, voluble
ipssŏk 입석 standing room
ipssuhada 입수하다 pick up
ipssul 입술 lip
iptchang 입장 entrance; stance; situation
iptchang hŏga 입장 허가 admission
iptchang kŭmji 입장 금지 no admittance
iptchangnyo 입장료 entrance fee
iptchŭng 입증 verification
iptchŭnghada 입증하다 establish, prove
iptta 입다 wear; put on
ipttaehada 입대하다 enlist

ip'agŭl hŏgahada 입학을 허가하다 admit to school
ip'akkŭm 입학금 fee
ip'ak tŭngnogŭl hada 입학 등록을 하다 register (*for school, university*)
ip'ak tŭngnok 입학 등록 registration (*at school, university*)
ip'ak wŏnsŏ 입학 원서 application form (*for school, university*)
ip'oehada 입회하다 join
ip'oe hŏga 입회 허가 admission
ip'oein 입회인 observer
ip'oerŭl hŏgahada 입회를 허가하다 admit to an organization
ip'ubo 입후보 candidacy
iraero 이래로 since
Irak'ŭ 이라크 Iraq ◊ Iraqi
Iran 이란 Iran ◊ Iranian
irhada 일하다 work
irhoe 일회 one time, once
irhoe pogyongnyang 일회 복용량 a dose
irhoeyong 일회용 disposable, throw-away
irhŭn 일흔 seventy
irhŭn pŏntchaeŭi 일흔 번째의 seventieth
irijŏri kŏnilda 이리저리 거닐다 stroll around
iri kkŭnnada 일이 끝나다 get off (work)
irŏbŏrin 잃어버린 missing
irŏktchŏrŏk 이럭저럭 somehow or other; ***irŏktchŏrŏk ...haenaeda*** 이럭저럭 ...해내다 manage to ... one way or another; ***irŏktchŏrŏk saenghwarhada*** 이럭저럭 생활하다 scrape a living, get by somehow
irŏk'e 이렇게 this way
irŏn 이런 like this; ***irŏn shigŭro irŏnat-tta*** 이런 식으로 일어났다 it happened like this; ***irŏn, irŏn!*** 이런, 이런! well, well!; ***irŏn, sesange!*** 이런, 세상에! (oh) dear!, dear me!
irŏna antta 일어나 앉다 sit up
irŏnada 일어나다 happen; come about; get up, rise
irŏnal kŏt kattchi anŭn 일어날 것 같지 않은 improbable; dim *prospects*
irŏsŏda 일어서다 stand (up), rise
iron 이론 theory
iron mullihak 이론 물리학 theoretical physics
ironsang-ŭro 이론상으로 in theory
irŭda 이르다 come to; reach; carry (*of sound*); range; ***chŏgŏsŭn ch'ilman wŏne irŭnda*** 저것은 70000원에 이른다 that comes to 70,000 won
irŭge 이르게 early
irŭk'ida 일으키다 cause; generate, stir up; cast *doubt*
irŭl shik'ida 일을 시키다 make work
irŭm 이름 name; first name
irŭmppunin 이름뿐인 nominal
irŭmp'yo 이름표 nametag
irŭmŭl chit-tta 이름을 짓다 name; ***Yŭi irŭmŭl ttasŏ Xŭi irŭmŭl chit-tta*** Y의 이름을 따서 X의 이름을 짓다 name X for Y
irŭn 이른 early
irŭn 잃은 lost
iruŏjida 이루어지다 be formed; ***iruŏjyŏ it-tta*** 이루어져 있다 consist of
irwŏl 일월 January
irwŏn 일원 member
irwŏnida 일원이다 belong to, be a member of
irye 이례 exception
iryejŏgin 이례적인 exceptional
iryejŏgŭro 이례적으로 exceptionally
iryŏksso 이력서 résumé
iryoil 일요일 Sunday
iryongp'um 일용품 daily necessity; daily necessities
iryu 이류 inferiority
iryuk 이륙 takeoff, liftoff
iryuk'ada 이륙하다 take off (*of airplane*)
iryu(ŭi) 이류(의) second-rate; inferior
isa 이사 director; move
isa chŏnmun ŏpch'e 이사 전문 업체 movers
isahada 이사하다 move house, move away
isahoe 이사회 board (of directors)
isa hoeŭi 이사 회의 board meeting
isa hoeŭishil 이사 회의실 board room
isahŭl 이사흘 couple of days
isak 이삭 ear (*of grain*)

isanagada 이사나가다 move out
isang 이상 not less than, more than ◊ ideal ◊ strangeness; ***10,000 isangŭro*** 10,000 이상으로 upward of 10,000; ***ch'a-e muŏshin-ga isang-i it-tta*** 차에 무엇인가 이상이 있다 there is something wrong with the car
isanghada 이상하다 be strange
isanghage 이상하게 curiously, strangely
isanghagedo 이상하게도 curiously enough
isangjŏgin 이상적인 ideal
isangjuŭijŏgin 이상주의적인 idealistic
isanhwat'anso 이산화탄소 greenhouse gas
isaoda 이사오다 move in
isatchim unsong-ŏptcha 이삿짐 운송업자 movers
isattchim t'ŭrŏk 이삿짐 트럭 movers' van
ishik chojik 이식 조직 graft
ishik susul 이식 수술 transplant
ishik'ada 이식하다 transplant
iship 이십 twenty
isŏ 이서 endorsement
isŏhada 이서하다 endorse
isŏng 이성 the opposite sex; reason
isŏng-aeŭi 이성애의 heterosexual
issŭl su ŏmnŭn 있을 수 없는 unacceptable
issŭm 있음 presence
issushigae 이쑤시개 toothpick
isŭk'eip'ŭ 이스케이프 escape COMPUT
isŭl 이슬 dew
isŭlbi 이슬비 drizzle
isŭlbiga naerida 이슬비가 내리다 drizzle
Isŭllamgyo 이슬람교 Islam (*religion*)
Isŭllam kuk-kka 이슬람 국가 Islam, Islamic world
Isŭllam minjok 이슬람 민족 Islam (*people*)
Isŭrael 이스라엘 Israel ◊ Israeli
Isŭraerin 이스라엘인 Israeli
itchŏm 이점 advantage; perk; plus
itchogŭro 이쪽으로 this way
itta 잇다 join; inherit; knit together; preserve
it-tta 있다 be; exist; stay; be located; have, possess; ***...i / ga issŭmnikka?*** ...이 / 가 있습니까? do you have ...?; **... it-tta** ...있다 there is / are ◊ (*forms continuous present of action verbs*): ***...go it-tta*** ...고 있다 ...ing; ***nŏnŭn irŭl chinach'ige hago it-tta*** 너는 일을 지나치게 하고 있다 you're overdoing things
it-tta 잊다 forget; get over
it-ttarŭda 잇따르다 follow one after another; ***...ŭl / rŭl it-ttara*** ...을 / 를 잇따라 one after another
it-ttarŭn 잇따른 successive
it'ajŏgin 이타적인 altruistic
it'al 이탈 departure
It'allia 이탈리아 Italy ◊ Italian
It'alliain 이탈리아인 Italian
It'alliaŏ 이탈리아어 Italian (*language*)
it'ŭlmada 이틀마다 every other day
iŭirŭl chegihada 이의를 제기하다 raise an objection, object
iŭirŭl shinch'ŏnghada 이의를 신청하다 take exception, object
iŭmp'yo 이음표 hyphen
iŭn chari 이은 자리 join
iut 이웃 neighborhood; neighbor
iut saram 이웃 사람 neighbor
iut'ada 이웃하다 border on
iwŏl 이월 February
iyagi 이야기 story, tale
iyagihada 이야기하다 tell, narrate
iyagihagi 이야기하기 narration
iyagishigŭi 이야기식의 narrative
iyong 이용 use
iyonghada 이용하다 use, draw on; take advantage of; manipulate
iyu 이유 cause; reason; ***amu iyu ŏpsshi*** 아무 이유 없이 for nothing, for no reason

-ja -자 (*suffix for persons*): ***tokch'angja*** 독창자 soloist; ***tongŏptcha*** 동업자 partner
...jamaja ...자 마자 as soon as

K

...ka ...가 (*subject particle*): ***kŭ che-ŭiga maŭme tŭmnikka?*** 그 제의가 마음에 듭니까 does that offer interest you?
kaap'ada 가압하다 push, pressure
kabal 가발 wig
kabang 가방 bag
kabŏrida 가버리다 go off, leave
kabyŏn 가변 variableness ◊ variable
kabyŏpkke 가볍게 lightly
kabyŏpkke hada 가볍게 하다 lighten
kabyŏptta 가볍다 be light; be slight; be frivolous
kabyŏum 가벼움 lightness
kabyŏun 가벼운 light; airy; dismissive
kach'aŏmnŭn 가차없는 ruthless
kach'i 가치 value, worth, merit
kach'i anŭn 같지 않은 unlike
kach'i chada 같이 자다 sleep with; have sex with
kach'iga it-tta 가치가 있다 be worth; merit; count, be important
kach'iga ŏmnŭn 가치가 없는 worthless
kach'iga orŭda 가치가 오르다 rise in value
kach'iga ttŏrŏjida 가치가 떨어지다 fall in value; depreciate
kach'i hada 같이 하다 join in
kach'i harak 가치 하락 depreciation
kach'i itkke yŏgida 가치 있게 여기다 value, prize
kach'iŏmnŭn 가치없는 worthless
kach'i oda 같이 오다 come along, come too
kach'i put'ŏit-tta 같이 붙어있다 be stuck together
kach'irŭl ttŏrŏttŭrida 가치를 떨어뜨리다 detract from; run down
kach'ŏbun sodŭk 가처분 소득 disposable income
kach'uk 가축 domestic animal; livestock
kach'uk uri 가축 우리 corral
kada 가다 go (*toward listener*); come; get along (*come to party etc*); proceed (*of people*); ***yŏgŭro kanŭn kire issŏyo*** 역으로 가는 길에 있어요 it's on the way to the station
kadak 가닥 strip, strand
kadonghaji mot'age hada 가동하지 못하게 하다 immobilize
kadŭk ch'ada 가득 차다 fill up (*of place*) ◊ full up
kadŭk ch'aeuda 가득 채우다 fill up, top up
kadŭk ch'ait-tta 가득 차있다 be bristling with; be crammed with
kadŭk ch'an 가득 찬 full
kadŭk'an 가득한 full of
kaduda 가두다 lock in
kae 개 dog ◊ *general countword*
kaeam 개암 hazelnut
kaeamnamu 개암나무 hazel (tree)
kaebal 개발 development
kaebaldosangguk 개발도상국 developing country
kaebaltcha 개발자 developer
kaebangdoen 개방된 open *market, society*
kaebarhada 개발하다 develop
kaebarhayŏ iyonghada 개발하여 이용하다 exploit, make use of
kaebyŏltchŏgŭro 개별적으로 individually
kae chul 개 줄 leash
kaech'arhada 개찰하다 punch *ticket*
kaech'ŏk'ada 개척하다 pioneer
Kaech'ŏnjŏl 개천절 National Foundation Day
kaech'uk'ada 개축하다 rebuild
kaeda 개다 clear, clear up (*of weather*); fold
kaegae 개개 individually, one by one
kaegaeŭi 개개의 individual, separate
kaegŭ 개그 gag, joke

kaegulgaegul ulda 개굴개굴 울다 croak (*of frog*)
kaeguri 개구리 frog
kaegwanhada 개관하다 inaugurate
kaehoeshik 개회식 opening ceremony
kaehwahada 개화하다 civilize
kaehyŏk 개혁 reform
kaehyŏk undong 개혁 운동 crusade (*for reform*)
kaehyŏk'ada 개혁하다 reform
kaein 개인 individual ◊ individual, personal
kaeinbisŏ 개인 비서 PA, personal assistant
kaein hwagin pŏnho 개인 확인 번호 PIN, personal identification number
kaeinjuŭi 개인주의 individualism
kaeinjuŭija 개인주의자 individualist
kaein kyosa 개인 교사 (private) tutor
kaein kyosŭp 개인 교습 (private) tuition
kaeintchŏgin 개인적인 personal, private
kaeinŭi 개인의 individual; personal
kaeinyong k'ŏmp'yut'ŏ 개인용 컴퓨터 PC, personal computer
kaeinyong sŭt'ereo 개인용 스테레오 personal stereo
kaejip 개집 kennel
kaejŏng 개정 sitting (*of court*); reform
kaejŏng chungim 개정 중임 session (*of parliament*)
kaejo 개조 conversion; renovation
kaejohada 개조하다 convert; renovate
kaekch'a 객차 car (*of a train*)
kaekkwanjŏgin 객관적인 objective
kaeksshil 객실 cabin
kaekssil tamdangja 객실 담당자 room clerk
kaekwan 개관 survey
kaek'owŏnsung-i 개코원숭이 baboon
kaemi 개미 ant
kae mok-kkŏri 개 목걸이 (dog) collar
kaemyŏnghada 개명하다 rename
kaenbŏsŭ 캔버스 canvas (*for painting*)
kaeng 갱 gang; pit, coal mine
kaengshin 갱신 renewal
kaengshinhada 갱신하다 renew
kaenyŏm 개념 concept
kaeŏp'ada 개업하다 set up (*in business*)
kaesaekki V 개새끼 son of a bitch, bastard
kaeshi 개시 initiation
kaeshihada 개시하다 initiate
Kaeshin-gyo 개신교 Protestantism
kaeŭich'i ank'o 개의치 않고 regardless of
kaeul 개울 stream
kaeyo 개요 outline; syllabus
kage 가게 store
kage chuin 가게 주인 storekeeper
kagi shwiun 가기 쉬운 accessible
kagonghada 가공하다 process *food, raw materials*
kagonghaji anŭn 가공하지 않은 raw *sugar, iron*
kagu 가구 furniture
kagu han chŏm 가구 한 점 a piece of furniture
kagurŭl tŭryŏ not'a 가구를 들여 놓다 furnish
kagyanggakssaek 각양각색 medley, mixture, assortment
kagye 가계 descent, ancestry; housekeeping (*money*)
kagyebu 가계부 housekeeping book
kagyŏgi orŭda 가격이 오르다 appreciate, increase in value
kagyŏgi pissan 가격이 비싼 expensive
kagyŏgŭl maegida 가격을 매기다 price
kagyŏgŭl naerida 가격을 내리다 mark down, reduce the price of
kagyŏgŭl ollida 가격을 올리다 mark up *price*
kagyŏk 가격 cost; price
kagyŏk harin kyŏngjaeng 가격 할인 경쟁 price war
kagyŏk insang 가격 인상 price rise; mark-up
kahada 가하다 inflict
kahok 가혹 severity
kahok'an 가혹한 harsh; oppressive

kaijrŏ oda 가지러 오다 come for; collect
kaip'ada 가입하다 join, become a member
kajami 가자미 turbot
kajang 가장 most, very ◊ wage earner; masquerade
kajang chal naganŭn sangp'yo 가장 잘 나가는 상표 brand leader
kajang chari 가장 자리 edge
kajanghada 가장하다 act; put on; pretend
kajangjari 가장자리 edge; rim; brim; brink; verge
kajang mudobok 가장 무도복 fancy dress
kajang mudohoe 가장 무도회 fancy-dress party
kaji 가지 branch; twig; eggplant
kajida 가지다 own, have; hold; ***iriro kŭgŏsŭl kajyŏda chullaeyo?*** 이리로 그것을 가져다 줄래요? bring it here, will you?
kajigakssaegŭi 가지각색의 miscellaneous
kajigakssaek 가지각색 assortment
kajigo it-tta 가지고 있다 have got
kajigo kada 가지고 가다 take, remove
kajigo nolda 가지고 놀다 toy with
kajirŏ kada 가지러 가다 collect, call for
kajirŏnhi kkot-tta 가지런히 꽂다 put neatly; fix neatly; arrange
kajirŭl ch'ida (가지를) 치다 prune *branch*
kajŏng 가정 assumption; home
kajŏngnyong k'ŏmp'yut'ŏ 가정용 컴퓨터 home computer
kajŏng kyosa 가정 교사 home tutor
kajŏng kyoyuk 가정 교육 upbringing; home education
kajŏngbu 가정부 housekeeper
kajŏnghada 가정하다 assume, suppose
kajŏngjŏgin 가정적인 homeloving, homely
kajŏngnyŏng-i anin 가정용이 아닌 not designed for use in the home
kajŏnjep'um 가전제품 (household) appliance
kajok 가족 family; household
kajok kyehoek 가족 계획 family planning
kajoktchŏgin 가족적인 paternalistic
kajoktchuŭi 가족주의 paternalism
kajuk 가죽 hide, skin (*of animal*); leather
kajuk kkŭn 가죽 끈 lead, leash; (leather) strap
kajyŏoda 가져오다 bring; get, fetch; earn
kak 각 each, every, all; angle
kakkai 가까이 near ◊ about, approximately
kakkaie 가까이에 at hand, to hand ◊ near; ***ŭnhaeng kakkaie*** 은행 가까이에 near the bank
kakkaie(sŏ) 가까이에(서) locally
kakkai hagi shwiun 가까이 하기 쉬운 approachable
kakkai kaji mot'age hada 가까이 가지 못하게 하다 prevent from going near, keep away
kakkai tagagada 가까이 다가가다 approach, draw near
kakkai tagaoda 가까이 다가오다 draw near (*of time*)
kakkaihagi ŏryŏun 가까이하기 어려운 unapproachable
kakkapkke 가깝게 close, near
kakkaptta 가깝다 be close, be near
kakkasŭro 가까스로 scarcely, barely; hardly
kakkasŭro ppajyŏnagada 가까스로 빠져나가다 have a narrow escape (*from arrest*)
kakkasŭro saranamtta 가까스로 살아남다 have a narrow escape (*from death*)
kakkaun 가까운 close, near
kak-kkage 각각에 each
kak-kkagŭi 각각의 each, respective
kak-kkak 각각 each
kak-kki 각기 respectively
kak-kkwang 각광 footlights
kakkŭm 가끔 occasionally, sometimes
kakppon 각본 screenplay
kakssaek 각색 adaptation
kaktcha 각자 each other
kaktchu 각주 footnote

kalbi 갈비 spare ribs, barbecued ribs
kalbippyŏ 갈비뼈 rib
kalbitchim 갈비찜 steamed (beef) ribs
kalbi t'ang 갈비탕 beef rib soup
kalda 갈다 change, replace; grind; sharpen; plow
kalga mŏktta 갉아 먹다 nibble
kalgigalgi tchit-tta 갈기갈기 찢다 tear up
kalgo tadŭmtta 갈고 다듬다 polish up
kalgori 갈고리 hook
kalgyŏ ssŭda 갈겨 쓰다 scribble
kalgyŏ ssŭgi 갈겨 쓰기 scribble
kal kiri mŏlda 갈 길이 멀다 it's a long way off
kalk'wi 갈퀴 rake
kallajida 갈라지다 branch off; diverge
kallajin t'ŭm 갈라진 틈 crevice
kallyak 간략 simplicity; brevity; ***kallyak'i p'yŏnjirŭl ssŭda*** 간략히 편지를 쓰다 drop a line
kallyakhada 간략하다 be simple; be brief
kalmaegi 갈매기 gull; seagull
kalmang 갈망 craving, longing
kalmanghada 갈망하다 crave, long for
kalp'i 갈피 point, sense; ***nae maŭmi kalp'irŭl mot-tchamnŭnda*** 내 마음이 갈피를 못잡는다 my mind is in a whirl
kalsaek 갈색 brown
kalssurok tŏ 갈수록 더 increasingly
kaltchŭng 갈증 thirst
kaltta 갉다 gnaw
kalttae 갈대 reed
kama 가마 kiln
kamang 가망 chance, possibility
kamang-innŭn 가망있는 hopeful, promising
kamang ŏmnŭn 가망 없는 hopeless, useless
kamangsŏng 가망성 probability
kamanhaejuda 감안해주다 make allowances
kamanhi 가만히 still; ***kamanhi issŏ!*** 가만히 있어! keep still!
kamanittchi mot'anŭn 가만있지 못하는 restless
kambang 감방 cell (*for prisoner*)
kamchwŏjin 감춰진 hidden
kamch'altcha 감찰자 inspector (*in factory*)
kamch'o 감초 licorice
kamch'ok 감촉 feeling; touch; ***shilk'ŭwa / myŏn-gwa kat'ŭn kamch'ogida*** 실크와 / 면과 같은 감촉이다 it feels like silk / cotton
kamch'uda 감추다 conceal, cover up; withhold
kamdanghada 감당하다 control
kamdanghal su innŭn / ŏmnŭn 감당할 수 있는 / 없는 controllable / uncontrollable
kamdok 감독 director (*of movie*); direction (*of movie*)
kamdoktcha 감독자 supervisor
kamdok'ada 감독하다 direct *movie*; supervise
kamdongjŏgin 감동적인 emotional, poignant
kamdongshik'ida 감동시키다 move, touch (*emotionally*)
kamdongshik'inŭn 감동시키는 touching
kamgaginnŭn 감각있는 tasteful
kamgagŏmnŭn 감각없는 numb
kamgak 감각 sensation; sense (*sight, touch, smell etc*)
kamgaktchŏgin 감각적인 sensuous
kamgi 감기 cold, chill (*illness*)
kamgida 감기다 close; wind round
kamgie kŏllida 감기에 걸리다 catch a cold
kamgin 감긴 closed
kamgŭm 감금 captivity, confinement; detention
kamgŭmhada 감금하다 confine, imprison
kamgyŏk'ada 감격하다 be thrilled
kamgyŏk'age hanŭn 감격하게 하는 thrilling
kamhaenghae popsshida 감행해 봅시다 let's risk it
kamhi 감히 daringly; ***nega kamhi ŏttŏk'e!*** 네가 감히 어떻게! how dare you!
kamhihada 감히 하다 dare; ***kunŭn kamhi hal su ŏpssŏssŏyo*** 그는

감히 할 수 없었어요 he didn't dare
kamhyŏnghada 감형하다 commute *death sentence*
kamja 감자 potato
kamja ch'ip 감자 칩 potato chip
kamja t'wigim 감자 튀김 French fries; fried potatoes
kamji 감지 perception (*through senses*)
kamjihada 감지하다 perceive (*with senses*)
kamjilnage hanŭn 감질나게 하는 tantalizing
kamjŏng 감정 emotion; valuation
kamjŏngga 감정가 connoisseur
kamjŏng-i sanghagi shwiun 감정이 상하기 쉬운 sensitive
kamjŏngjŏgin 감정적인 emotional
kamjŏng-ŭi p'okppal 감정의 폭발 outburst of emotion
kamjŏng-ŭl ŏngnurŭji mot'ada 감정을 억누르지 못하다 be unable to control one's emotions, be overcome by emotion
kamjŏnsashik'ida 감전사시키다 electrocute
kammiroun 감미로운 mellow
kammiryo 감미료 sweetener (*for drink*)
kammyŏng 감명 deep impression; ***nuguege / muŏse kammyŏng patta*** 누구에게 / 무엇에 감명 받다 be impressed by s.o. / sth
kammyŏng chuda 감명 주다 make an impression
Kamni Kyohoe 감리 교회 Methodist Church
kamok 감옥 prison
kamsa 감사 gratitude; thanks; audit
kamsagwan 감사관 auditor
kamsahada 감사하다 be grateful for; thank; audit
kamsahagedo 감사하게도 thankfully
kamsahal chul morŭnŭn 감사할 줄 모르는 ungrateful
kamsahamnida 감사합니다 thank you (*polite*)
kamsahanŭn 감사하는 thankful
kamsang 감상 sentimentality, sentiment
kamsangjŏgin 감상적인 sentimental
kamshihada 감시하다 monitor, watch; spy on; picket
kamso 감소 decrease, decline
kamsohada 감소하다 decline, decrease
kamsok'ada 감속하다 decelerate, slow down
kamsuhada 감수하다 reconcile oneself
kamsusŏng-i kanghan 감수성이 강한 susceptible
kamsusŏng-i yeminhan 감수성이 예민한 impressionable
kamtta 감다 wind, wind up *clock*; close
kamt'an 감탄 admiration
kamt'anhada 감탄하다 admire
kamum 가뭄 drought
kamwŏn 감원 lay-off, staff cut
kamwŏndoeda 감원되다 be laid off
kamwŏnhada 감원하다 lay off
kamwŏnshik'ida 감원시키다 lay off
kamyŏm 감염 infection
kamyŏmdoeda 감염되다 become infected
kamyŏmdoen 감염된 infected
kamyŏmshik'ida 감염시키다 infect
kamyŏn 가면 mask
ka-myŏng 가명 pseudonym
kan 간 liver (*food*)
kanan 가난 poverty
kananhada 가난하다 be poor
kananhan 가난한 poor, deprived
kanbu 간부 executive
kanch'ŏk'ada 간척하다 reclaim
kanch'ŏnghada 간청하다 implore, plead with
kanch'ŏp 간첩 secret agent, spy
kang 강 river
kang-aji 강아지 puppy, pup; whelp
kangbak kwannyŏm 강박 관념 obsession; compulsion
kangbak kwannyŏme sarojap'in 강박 관념에 사로잡힌 obsessive; compulsive
Kangbuk 강북 Kangbuk (*Seoul, north of the Han river*)
kangbyŏn 강변 riverside
kangch'ŏl 강철 steel
kangdo 강도 intensity; burglar; burglary

kangdojil 강도질 robbery
kangdojirhada 강도질하다 burglarize
kangdo(rŭl) tanghada 강도(를) 당하다 be robbed
kangdŭngshik'ida 강등시키다 downgrade
kanggan 강간 rape
kangganbŏm 강간범 rapist
kangganhada 강간하다 rape
kanggŏnhan 강건한 virile
kanggyŏnghan 강경한 strong, firm
kanggyŏngnonja 강경론자 hardliner, hawk *fig*
kanghada 강하다 be strong
kanghaejida 강해지다 strengthen; harden (*of attitude*); intensify
kanghage 강하게 strongly
kangham 강함 strength, intensity
kanghan 강한 intense, strong, high
Kanghwado 강화도 Kanghwa Island
kanghwahada 강화하다 reinforce; tighten *control*, *security*
kangjangje 강장제 tonic
kangje 강제 force
kangjejŏgin 강제적인 forced
kangjero 강제로 by force; ***Xŭl / rŭl kangjero Yhadorok mandŭlda*** X을 / 를 강제로 Y하도록 만들다 force X to do Y
kangjo 강조 emphasis, accent
kangjohada 강조하다 emphasize; highlight
Kangnam 강남 Kangnam (*Seoul, south of the Han river*)
kangnyŏk shilsshihada 강력 실시하다 forcibly carry out, enforce
kangnyŏk'ada 강력하다 be powerful
kangnyŏk'age 강력하게 violently, very strongly
kangnyŏk'an 강력한 powerful, strong; intense
kangnyŏk'i 강력히 strongly
kangnyŏn 강연 talk, lecture
kangnyŏrham 강렬함 violence (*of gale*)
kangnyŏrhan 강렬한 strong, violent
kang-ŏgwi 강 어귀 river mouth
kangppadak 강바닥 riverbed
kangp'an 강판 grater
kangp'ung 강풍 gale
kangsa 강사 lecturer; instructor
kangse 강세 strength; stress, emphasis; ***tallŏ kangse*** 달러 강세 a run on the dollar
kangse chusik shijang 강세 주식 시장 bull market
kangtchŏm 강점 strong point
kangt'a 강타 blow, punch
kangt'ahada 강타하다 smash, bang
kangt'al 강탈 extortion
kangt'arhada 강탈하다 rob
kang-ŭi 강의 lecture
kang-ŭihada 강의하다 give a lecture, lecture
kang-ŭishil 강의실 lecture hall
kang-u 강우 rainfall
kan-gyŏk 간격 space
kan-gyŏrhage 간결하게 briefly
kan-gyŏrhan 간결한 brief, succinct
kan-gyŏrhi hada 간결히 하다 shorten, trim
kangyohada 강요하다 coerce, force; press, urge; insist on
kanho 간호 care (*of sick person*)
kanho ŏmmu 간호 업무 nursing
kanhosa 간호사 nurse
kanho shilssŭpssaeng 간호 실습생 student nurse
kani ch'imdae 간이 침대 cot
kani maejŏm 간이 매점 kiosk
kani shikttang 간이 식당 snack bar
kanjang 간장 soy sauce; liver ANAT
kanjilppyŏng 간질병 epilepsy
kanjilppyŏng hwanja 간질병 환자 epileptic (*person*)
kanjirida 간질이다 tickle
kanjirŏp'ida 간지럽히다 tickle
kanjirŭi paltchak 간질의 발작 epileptic fit
kanjŏppi 간접비 overhead FIN
kanjŏptchŏgin 간접적인 indirect
kanjŏptchŏgŭro 간접적으로 indirectly
kanjŏrhada 간절하다 be eager, be earnest
kanjŏrhan 간절한 eager
kanjŏrhi 간절히 eagerly
kan kogi 간 고기 ground meat
kanjuhada 간주하다 deem, consider
kannan 갓난 newborn
kannyŏm 간염 hepatitis

kanp'ahanŭn 간파하는 penetrating
kanp'an 간판 notice; signboard (*outside shop*, *on building*); front, cover organization
kansahae poinŭn 간사해 보이는 shifty-looking *person*
kansahan 간사한 shifty, deceitful
kanshik 간식 snack
kanshinhi 간신히 barely, only just
kansŏndoro 간선도로 arterial road
kansŏp 간섭 interference
kansŏp'ada 간섭하다 interfere
kansu 간수 guard
kansuhada 간수하다 store, keep
kanttanhada 간단하다 be simple; be brief
kanttanhage 간단하게 simply
kanttanham 간단함 simplicity
kanttanhan 간단한 simple, straightforward
kanttanhi 간단히 plainly, simply
kant'ong 간통 adultery; ***kant'ongŭl tanghada*** 간통을 당하다 commit adultery
kant'ŏng kwan-gye 간통 관계 adulterous relationship; adultery
kanŭlda 가늘다 be thin
kanŭn 가는 thin; fine
kanŭnghada 가능하다 be possible
kanŭnghage hada 가능하게 하다 allow, enable
kanŭnghan 가능한 possible; ***kanŭnghan han ppalli*** 가능한 한 빨리 as soon as possible; ***kanŭnghan kajang tchalbŭn / pparŭn...*** 가능한 가장 짧은 / 빠른... the shortest / quickest possible
kanŭngssŏng 가능성 possibility; likelihood; ***kanŭngssŏng-i kŏŭi hŭibak'an*** 가능성이 거의 희박한 just remotely possible
kanŭn kire 가는 길에: ***...ro kanŭn kire*** ...로 가는 길에 on the way
kanŭrŏjida 가늘어지다 get thin
kanyalp'ŭn 가냘픈 slender, slight
kap 갑 pack (*of cigarettes*)
kap 값 price
kapkkangnyu 갑각류 shellfish
kap pissan 값 비싼 expensive
kapp'an 갑판 deck NAUT
kapssangsŏn 갑상선 thyroid (gland)
kapsshi pissan 값이 비싼 expensive
kapsshi ssan 값이 싼 inexpensive, cheap
kapssŭl naerida 값을 내리다 knock down, reduce the price of
kaptchagi 갑자기 suddenly, all of a sudden
kaptchakssŭrŏn 갑작스런 sudden, unexpected; abrupt
kaptta 갚다 repay
kap'arŭn 가파른 steep
karaanch'ida 가라앉히다 calm down; sink
kara-anjŭn 가라앉은 subdued
karaantta 가라앉다 go down; subside, settle; cool (down); sink; go under
karaibŭl ot 가라입을 옷 a change of clothes
karaiptta 가라입다 change *clothes*, get changed
karak 가락 tune; pitch; tone
karaok'e 가라오케 karaoke
karat'ada 갈아타다 change *train etc*
karat'agi 갈아타기 change (*in travel*)
karida 가리다 shade; veil *face*, *eyes*
karik'ida 가리키다 indicate, point at
karoch'aeda 가로채다 intercept
karodŭng 가로등 streetlight
karo panghyang-ŭro 가로 방향으로 landscape *print*
karŭch'ida 가르치다 teach; instruct; coach
karŭdsa 가르다 mark out, set apart
karŭma 가르마 part (*in hair*)
karŭmarŭl t'ada 가르마를 타다 part one's hair
karu 가루 powder
karubinu 가루 비누 washing powder
karyŏnaeda 가려내다 sort out
karyŏptta 가렵다 itch
karyŏum 가려움 itch
kasa 가사 lyrics; housekeeping
kasang 가상 imagination
kasang hyŏnshil 가상 현실 virtual reality
kasang konggan 가상 공간 cyberspace
kashi 가시 thorn; spine; splinter; fish bone

kashi ch'ŏlssa 가시 철사 barbed wire
kashige hada 가시게 하다 rinse away *taste*
kasŏkppang 가석방 parole
kasŏl 가설 temporary construction; hypothesis
kasŏl hwaltchuro 가설 활주로 temporary landing strip
kasŏrhada 가설하다 build; suppose
kasok 가속 acceleration
kasokshik'ida 가속시키다 accelerate
kasok'ada 가속하다 accelerate
kasoktto 가속도 rate of acceleration
kassŭ t'aengk'ŭ 가스탱크 gasometer; gas works
kasŭ 가스 gas (*for cooking*)
kasŭk'et 가스켓 gasket
kasŭm 가슴 chest, bust
kasŭmari 가슴앓이 heartburn
kasŭmi mani p'ain 가슴이 많이 파인 low-cut
kasŭmi pinyaka'n 가슴이 빈약한 flat-chested
kasŭmŭl tŭrŏnaen 가슴을 드러낸 bare-chested
kasŭpkki 가습기 humidifier
kasu 가수 singer
kat 갓 traditional horsehair hat
katcha 가짜 fake
katch'uda 갖추다 possess; have in stock
katch'i 같이 as, like; together with
katch'uŏ chuda 갖추어 주다 equip
katkko nolda 갖고 놀다 mess around with
kat-tta 같다 be the same; be equal; be like; come to MATH; be on a par with; it appears that; ***...kŏt kat-tta*** ...것 같다 it seems like
kat'a poida 같아 보이다 seem like
kat'ŏ 가터 garter
kat'ŭn 같은 like, such as ◊ same; equal; identical; ***...wa / kwa kat'ŭn kŏt*** ...와 / 과 같은 것 something like; ***kat'ŭn nop'iŭi*** 같은 높이의 flush, level
kaŭl 가을 fall, autumn
kaun 가운 gown
kaunde 가운데 middle ◊ among, amongst

kawi 가위 scissors
kawiro charŭda 가위로 자르다 cut with scissors, clip, trim
Kaya 가야 Kaya (*Ancient Kingdom*)
kayagŭm 가야금 Kaya zither
kayŏnssŏng-ŭi 가연성의 flammable
kayongssŏng-ŭi 가용성의 soluble
ke 게 crab
kedaga 게다가 besides, moreover
kegŏlssŭrŏpkke 게걸스럽게 ravenously
kegŏlssŭrŏptta 게걸스럽다 be ravenous
kegŏlssŭrŏun 게걸스러운 ravenous
keim 게임 game (*in tennis*)
keim sent'ŏ 게임 센터 amusement arcade
kerilla 게릴라 guerrilla
keshi 게시 notice, bulletin
keshihada 게시하다 post, put up *notice*
keship'an 게시판 bulletin board
...ket ...겠... shall (*indicates future tense, intention or supposition*)
keŭllihada 게을리하다 shirk
keŭrŭda 게으르다 be lazy
keŭrŭm 게으름 indolence
keŭrŭmbaeng-i 게으름뱅이 layabout
keŭrŭn 게으른 lazy
keyangdoeda 게양되다 fly (*of flag*)
ki 기 era; flag; energy
kia 기아 starvation
kiapkkye 기압계 barometer
kiban 기반 basis, footing
kibarhan 기발한 extraordinary, striking
kibarhan saenggak 기발한 생각 inspiration
kibok 기복 ups and downs
kibonjŏgin 기본적인 basic, fundamental
kibonjŏgŭro 기본적으로 basically
kibonkap 기본값 default COMPUT
kibonŭi 기본의 rudimentary, basic
kibsŭ 깁스 plaster cast
kibu 기부 contribution; donation
kibugŭm mojip 기부금 모집 collection (*in church*)
kibuhada 기부하다 contribute, donate
kibuja 기부자 contributor, donor

kibun 기분 mood, frame of mind; ***kibun chŏnhwan*** 기분 전환 diversion, recreation; ***kibun chŏnhwanŭro*** 기분 전환으로 for a change; ***onŭl kibuni ŏttŏseyo?*** 오늘 기분이 어떠세요? how are you feeling today?
kibunjoŭn 기분좋은 agreeable, pleasant
kibun p'ulda 기분 풀다 lighten up
kibun sanghagehada 기분 상하게하다 upset, offend
kibun sanghan 기분 상한 upset; ***kibuni chot'a / nappŭda*** 기분이 좋다 / 나쁘다 be in a good / bad mood; ***kibuni chot'a / p'uri chugŏit-tta*** 기분이 좋다 / 풀이 죽어있다 be in good / poor spirits; ***kibuni karaantta*** 기분이 가라앉다 weigh down (*with worries*); ***kibuni nappŭn*** 기분이 나쁜 bad-tempered, moody
kibunŭl todunŭn 기분을 돋우는 exhilarating
kich'a 기차 train
kich'ayŏk 기차역 railroad station
kich'e 기체 gas (*oxygen etc*)
kich'eŭi 기체의 pneumatic
kich'im 기침 cough
kich'imhada 기침하다 cough
kich'im sorirŭl naeda 기침 소리를 내다 cough (*to get attention*)
kich'im shirŏp 기침 시럽 cough syrup
kich'im yak 기침 약 cough medicine
kich'o 기초 basis; foundations (*of building*) ◊ basic, fundamental
kich'obut'ŏ hada 기초부터 하다 get down to basics
kich'o chagŏp 기초 작업 groundwork
kich'ohada 기초하다 rest on, be based on
kich'ojŏgin 기초적인 basic
kich'oŭi 기초의 rudimentary
kida 기다 crawl
kidae 기대 expectation, hope
kidaeda 기대다 count on, rely on; lean; balance; recline, lie back
kidaedoenŭn 기대되는 prospective
kidaehada 기대하다 expect; look forward to; bank on
kidaeŏ not'a 기대어 놓다 prop; lean
kidarida 기다리다 wait for; wait, hang on
kido 기도 prayer
kidohada 기도하다 pray
Kidok-kkyo 기독교 Christianity ◊ Christian
Kidok-kkyo Ch'ŏngnyŏnhoe 기독교 청년회 YMCA
Kidok-kkyo Pangsong 기독교 방송 Christian Broadcasting System, CBS
Kidok-kkyo shinja 기독교 신자 Christian (*person*)
kidung 기둥 column; pole; stilts; supports
kiga kkŏkkin 기가 꺾인 demoralized
kiga mak'inŭn 기가 막히는 staggering, astonishing
kigabait'ŭ 기가바이트 gigabyte
kigan 기간 period, spell, term
kigan shisŏl 기간 시설 infrastructure (*of society*)
kigo 기고 contribution (*to magazine*)
kigoga 기고가 columnist
kigohada 기고하다 contribute (*to magazine, newspaper*)
kigŭn 기근 famine
kigu 기구 organization; balloon (*for flight*)
kigwan 기관 institution; machinery (*governmental*)
kigwanch'ong 기관총 machine gun
kigwanjiyŏm 기관지염 bronchitis
kigwansa 기관사 driver; engineer (*of train*)
kigwan tanch'ong 기관 단총 submachine gun
kigye 기계 appliance, machine ◊ mechanical
kigye changch'i 기계 장치 mechanism
kigyegong 기계공 mechanic
kigyehwahada 기계화하다 mechanize
kigyejŏgin 기계적인 mechanical
kigyejŏgŭro 기계적으로 mechanically
kigyeryu 기계류 machinery, machines
kigyŏlssu 기결수 convict

kigyo 기교 trick, knack; technique
kihahak 기하학 geometry
kihahaktchŏk 기하학적 geometric(al)
kihan mallyo 기한 만료 expiry
kiho 기호 symbol, character; choice; preference
kihoe 기회 chance, opportunity; ***kihoerŭl chuda*** 기회를 주다 give a break, give an opportunity; ***muŏsŭl hal kihoerŭl kajida*** 무엇을 할 기회를 가지다 get to do sth
kihonja 기혼자 married person
kihon namsŏng 기혼 남성 married man
kihon yŏsŏng 기혼 여성 married woman
kihu 기후 climate
kihyŏng 기형 deformity; freak
kiil 기일 term, condition
kiinhada 기인하다 result from
kiip'ada 기입하다 enter, write down; fill in, fill out
kija 기자 reporter, journalist
kijahoegyŏn 기자회견 press conference
kijang 기장 captain (*of aircraft*)
kijil 기질 disposition, nature
kijinmaektchinhan 기진맥진한 dog-tired
kijŏgwi 기저귀 diaper
kijŏk 기적 miracle
kijŏkkach'i 기적같이 miraculously
kijŏktchŏgin 기적적인 miraculous
kijŏlsshik'ida 기절시키다 stun (*with a blow*)
kijŏrhada 기절하다 pass out, faint
kijo yŏnsŏl 기조 연설 keynote speech
kijŭng 기증 donate
kijŭnghada 기증하다 donate
kijun 기준 standard
kijunggi 기중기 crane; hoist
kikkŏi 기꺼이 gladly, willingly, with pleasure; ***kikkŏi ...hada*** 기꺼이 ...하다 be willing to do
kikkŏi padadŭrida 기꺼이 받아들이다 welcome
kikkwŏn 기권 abstention
kikkwŏnhada 기권하다 abstain
kil 길 route; road; avenue; path; fathom NAUT; ***kirŭl ilt'a*** 길을 잃다 stray, wander away; get lost
kil annaerŭl hada 길 안내를 하다 navigate
kilda 길다 be long
kildŭryŏjin 길들여진 tame
kilge 길게 at length
kilge nŭllida 길게 늘리다 lengthen; pad *speech*
kilge pomyŏn 길게 보면 in the long run
kilkka 길가 roadside
kilmot'ung-i 길모퉁이 corner
kiltŭrida 길들이다 domesticate
kim 김 steam; laver, edible seaweed
kimch'i 김치 kimchee (*spicy pickled cabbage*)
kimi 기미 sign, indication; streak, touch
kimil 기밀 secrecy ◊ secret
kimi sŏrida 김이 서리다 mist up, steam up
kimirŭi 기밀의 classified, confidential
kimppajin 김빠진 bland; flat *beer*
kimppap 김밥 rice rolled in edible seaweed
kimyoham 기묘함 peculiarity, strangeness
kimyohan 기묘한 peculiar; quaint
kin 긴 long, lengthy
kinbak-kkam 긴박감 tension
kin-gŭp 긴급 urgency
kinjang 긴장 tension, strain
kinjangdoeda 긴장되다 tense up; be tense
kinjangdoen 긴장된 tense *muscle*; keyed up
kinjangdoenŭn 긴장되는 tense *moment*
kinjanghan 긴장한 tense *voice, person*
kinjang-ŭl p'ulda 긴장을 풀다 relax, unwind
kinjang-ŭro ttakttak'aejin 긴장으로 딱딱해진 uptight, inhibited
kinjang wanhwa 긴장 완화 détente
kin kŏt'ot 긴 겉옷 gown
kin somaeŭi 긴 소매의 long-sleeved
kinŭng 기능 craft, trade; function
kinŭngk'i 기능키 function key

COMPUT
kinŭng tanwi 기능 단위 unit
kinŭng-ŭl hada 기능을 하다 function as
kinyŏm 기념 commemoration ◊ memorial
kinyŏmbi 기념비 memorial, monument
kinyŏmhada 기념하다 commemorate, mark
kinyŏmil 기념일 (wedding) anniversary
kinyŏmmul 기념물 memento
kinyŏmp'um 기념품 souvenir
kinyŏm tongsang 기념 동상 monument
kinyŏmŭro 기념으로 in commemoration of
kiŏ 기어 gear
kiŏ chŏnhwan changch'i 기어 전환 장치 gear shift
kiŏk 기억 memory
kiŏk yongnyang 기억 용량 storage capacity
kiŏk'ada 기억하다 remember; store COMPUT; ***muŏsŭl kiŏk'ago it-tta*** 무엇을 기억하고 있다 bear sth in mind
kiŏngnyŏk 기억력 memory
kiŏp 기업 corporation ◊ business *ethics*, *style etc*
kiŏpkka 기업가 entrepreneur
kipkke 깊게 deeply
kipkke hada 깊게 하다 deepen
kippŏhada 기뻐하다 be delighted
kippŏhanŭn 기뻐하는 delighted; gleeful
kippŏnalttwida 기뻐날뛰다 exult
kiptta 깊다 be deep
kippŭda 기쁘다 be glad
kippŭge 기쁘게 happily, gladly; pleasantly
kippŭge hada 기쁘게 하다 please
kippŭm 기쁨 joy, delight
kippŭn 기쁜 pleased, glad
kip'i 깊이 depth ◊ deeply, soundly
kip'i chamdŭn 깊이 잠든 fast asleep
kip'ŏgada 깊어가다 draw on, advance
kip'oga saenggida 기포가 생기다 blister (*of paint*)
kip'o sujun-gi 기포 수준기 spirit level
kip'ŭm 깊음 depth
kip'ŭn 깊은 deep, profound
kip'um 기품 nobility; elegance
kip'um innŭn 기품 있는 distinguished, dignified
kip'yoso 기표소 polling booth
kiri 길이 length
kirin 기린 giraffe
kirogŭl kkaenŭn 기록을 깨는 record-breaking
kirok 기록 memo; archives; writing (*script*); ***muŏshi kirogŭl namgida*** 무엇의 기록을 남기다 keep track of sth
kirok munsŏ 기록 문서 record (*written document*)
kirok poyuja 기록 보유자 record holder
kirŭda 기르다 keep; grow; breed
kirŭl kkŏktta 기를 꺾다 daunt, deter, dishearten
kirŭl kkŏngnŭn 기를 꺾는 demoralizing
kirŭm 기름 oil
kirŭmch'irŭl hada 기름칠을 하다 oil
kirŭmgi kkin 기름기 낀 lank, greasy *hair*
kirŭmkki manŭn 기름기 많은 oily, greasy
kirŭmt'ong 기름통 sump
kiryagi p'ungbuhan 기략이 풍부한 resourceful
kiryak 기략 resources
kisa 기사 article (*in newspaper*); engineer; (machine) operator
kisadojŏgin 기사도적인 chivalrous
kisaek 기색 tinge
kisaeng 기생 kisaeng (*traditional female entertainer*)
kisaengch'unggat'ŭn saram 기생충같은 사람 parasite
kisaeng tongshingmul 기생 동식물 parasite
kisa kŏri 기사 거리 copy (*written material*)
kisang 기상 original idea; weather
kisanghak 기상학 meteorology
kisang yebo 기상 예보 weather forecast

kisang yebowŏn 기상 예보원 weatherman
kisŏngbok 기성복 off the peg, ready-to-wear
kiso 기소 prosecution
kisohada 기소하다 prosecute
kisojach'ŭk 기소자측 prosecution
kisŭk 기슭 slope (*of mountain*)
kisu 기수 rider, jockey
kisuk hak-kkyo 기숙 학교 boarding school
kisukssa 기숙사 dormitory
kisul 기술 skill; technique
kisultcha 기술자 technician
kisultchŏgin 기술적인 technical
kisultchŏgŭro 기술적으로 technically
kit 깃 collar
kitchŏm 기점 starting point
kitppal 깃발 flag
kit'a 기타 the rest; and so on; guitar
kit'adŭngdŭng 기타 등등 and so on, et cetera
kit'a yŏnjuga 기타 연주가 guitarist
kit'ŏl 깃털 feather; plumage
kit'ong 기통 cylinder (*in engine*)
kiulda 기울다 slant; tilt; swing (*of public opinion*)
kiulgi 기울기 slope (*of handwriting*)
kiun 기운 energy; vigor; vapor
kiuni nada 기운이 나다 cheer up
kiunŭl naege hada 기운을 내게 하다 cheer up
kiurida 기울이다 devote; tilt; ***kwi kiurida*** 귀 기울이다 prick up one's ears
kiwŏn 기원 origin
kiyŏ 기여 contribution (*to discussion*)
kiyŏhada 기여하다 contribute (*to discussion*)
kkach'ibal 까치발 bracket (*for shelf*)
kkadaroptta 까다롭다 be difficult; be strict; be picky
kkadaroun 까다로운 fussy, picky; tricky
kkaeda 깨다 break *record*; rouse
kkaedarŭm 깨달음 realization; understanding; enlightenment
kkaedat-tta 깨닫다 realize; ***Xŭl / rŭl kkaedatchi mot'ada*** X을 / 를 깨닫지 못하다 be unconscious of X
kkaejida 깨지다 break; shatter
kkaejin 깨진 broken
kkaek-kkaek-kkŏrida 깩깩거리다 squeal
kkaekkŭshi 깨끗이 completely, clean
kkaekkŭt'ada 깨끗하다 be clean; be pure; be chaste
kkaekkŭt'age hada 깨끗하게 하다 clean
kkaekkŭt'an 깨끗한 clean; pure; tidy, neat
kkaengkkaenggŏrida 깽깽거리다 yelp
kkaennip 깻잎 (pickled) sesame leaf
kkaeŏinnŭn 깨어있는 awake
kkaeŏjida 깨어지다 break up (*of ice*)
kkaeŏjigi shiun 깨어지기 쉬운 breakable
kkaettŭrida 깨뜨리다 break; break off *relationship*; terminate
kkaeuch'ida 깨우치다 educate; make realize
kkaeuda 깨우다 wake
kkaji 까지 until; by; no later than; to; up to; ***1989nyŏnkkaji*** 1989년까지 until 1989; ***hot'elkkaji*** 호 텔까지 as far as the hotel
kkakkabŏrida 깎아버리다 shave off *beard*
kkakkanaeda 깎아내다 shave off *from piece of wood*
kkakka tadŭmtta 깎아다듬다 whittle
kkaktta 깎다 cut; trim; shear; shave; sharpen; peel; cut *price*; haggle
kkakttugi 깍두기 *spicy, pickled white radish*
kkalboda 깔보다 criticize, knock
kkalda 깔다 pave
kkalgae 깔개 rug
kkamagwi 까마귀 crow; raven
kkamppagida 깜박이다 flicker, glimmer
kkamppakkŏrida 깜박거리다 twinkle; blink
kkamtchak nollada 깜짝 놀라다 be astonished; ***Xŭl / rŭl kkamtchak nollage hada*** X을 / 를 깜짝 놀라게 하다 give X a fright
kkangch'unggŏrimyŏ ttwiŏdanida 깡충거리며 뛰어다니다 skip around
kkangmarŭn 깡마른 skinny
kkangp'ae 깡패 bully; hoodlum,

gangster
kkangt'ong 깡통 can (*for food*)
kkangt'ong ttagae 깡통 따개 can opener
kkich'ida 끼치다 cause; ***namege p'yerŭl kkich'ida*** 남에게 폐를 끼치다 make a nuisance of oneself, cause trouble; ***kŏktchŏng-ŭl kkich'ida*** 걱정을 끼치다 affect; concern
kkida 끼이다 be wedged; be caught between
kkilkkil ut-tta 낄낄 웃다 giggle
kkik'anŭn sori 끽하는 소리 screech
kkingkkangjok 낑깡족 *orenjijok* wannabes
kkingkkinggŏrida 낑낑거리다 whimper, whine
kkiŏ nŏt'a 끼어 넣다 squeeze in
kkiuda 끼우다 slot in
kkiwŏjida 끼워지다 slot in
kkiwŏnŏtki 끼워넣기 open; retrieve COMPUT
kkiwŏ nŏt'a 끼워 넣다 put, insert; tuck
kkŏjida 꺼지다 blow out, go out (*of candle*); collapse; vanish
kkŏjin 꺼진 dead *battery*, *engine*
kkŏjyŏ it-tta 꺼져 있다 be out (*of light*, *fire*)
kkŏjyŏ pŏrida 꺼져 버리다 buzz off; go out (*of fire*); ***kkŏjyŏ (pŏryŏ)!*** 꺼져 (버려)! beat it!, get lost!
kkŏk-kkŏk-kkŏrinŭn sori 꺽꺽거리는 소리 squawk
kkŏkkŏnaeda 꺾어내다 break off *piece of chocolate etc*
kkŏktta 꺾다 destroy; break off; pluck; dash
kkŏm 껌 chewing gum
kkŏnaeda 꺼내다 take out (*from bag, pocket etc*); ***...e taehan marŭl kkŏnaeda*** ...에 대한 말을 꺼내다 drag in
kkŏptchil 껍질 shell; peel; husk; skin
kkŏrida 꺼리다 shun
kkŏrimch'ik'ada 꺼림칙 하다 feel uncomfortable about
kkobak 꼬박 whole
kkobulgŏrinŭn 꼬불거리는 curly
kkoch'ikkoch'i k'aeda 꼬치꼬치 캐다 poke around
kkoch'i p'ida 꽃이 피다 flower
kkoda 꼬다 twist; ***tarirŭl kkoda*** 다리를 꼬다 cross one's legs
kkoe 꾀 wile, strategem
kkoeda 꾀다 entice; persuade
kkoehada 꾀하다 engineer, contrive
kkoim 꼬임 kink, twist
kkoji 꽂이 rack
kkojiptta 꼬집다 pinch
kkok 꼭 surely; firmly, tightly; exactly
kkoktchi 꼭지 stem; tap, faucet; nipple; handle
kkokttaegi 꼭대기 top, crest
kkokttugaksshi 꼭두각시 puppet
kkolsanaum 꼴사나움 clumsiness
kkoma 꼬마 the little ones; urchin
kkomkkomhan 꼼꼼한 thorough; scrupulous
kkomtchagank'o innŭn 꼼짝않고 있는 stand stock-still
kkomtchak'ada 꼼짝하다 budge, stir; ***kŏgisŏ kkomtchaktto hajima!*** 거기서 꼼짝도 하지마! stay right there!
kkongch'o 꽁초 stub
kkonnip 꽃잎 petal
kkori 꼬리 tail; ***ne kkori pol man-haguna!*** 네 꼴이 볼 만하구나! what a sight you are!
kkorip'yo 꼬리표 tag, label
kkorip'yorŭl puch'ida 꼬리표를 붙이다 label, stick a label on
kkorŭrŭkkŏrida 꼬르륵거리다 rumble
kkoshyŏsŏ ŏdŏnaeda 꼬셔서 얻어내다 wheedle
kkot 꽃 flower; blossom
kkotchangsu 꽃장수 florist
kkot hantabal 꽃 한 다발 a bunch of flowers
kkotkkoji 꽃꽂이 arrangement (*of flowers*)
kkotkkot'an 꼿꼿한 straight (*erect*, *not bent*)
kkotppyŏng 꽃병 vase
kkot-tta 꽂다 attach; pin
kkot-ttabal 꽃다발 bouquet
kkŭch'ŭl maet-tta 끝을 맺다 wind up, finish
kkŭda 끄다 blow out; switch off; be

off; stall
kkŭdŏgim 끄덕임 nod
kkŭdŏmnŭn 끝없는 endless, never-ending
kkŭjibŏ naeda 끄집어 내다 mention, drag up
kkŭl 끌 chisel
kkŭlda 끌다 pull; haul; tow; drag; move slowly; attract; spin out, prolong; appeal to, be attractive to
kkŭlgi 끌기 tow; drag COMPUT
kkŭllida 끌리다 trail, lag behind; be dragged; be attracted to; ***...e(ge) maŭmi kkŭllida*** ...에(게) 마음이 끌리다 be attached to; ***nuguege maŭmi kkŭllida*** 누구에게 마음이 끌리다 be attracted to s.o.
kkŭlt'a 끓다 boil
kkŭmtchigi 끔찍이 terribly; exceedingly; kindly
kkŭmtchik'ada 끔찍하다 be hideous
kkŭmtchik'an 끔찍한 hideous, terrible
kkŭn 끈 band (*material*); lace (*for shoe*); tie, bond; string; strap (*of shoe, dress, bra*)
kkŭndŏktchige toep'urihada 끈덕지게 되풀이하다 persist in
kkŭndŏktchige toep'urihanŭn 끈덕지게 되풀이하는 persistent
kkŭn-gi 끈기 perseverance, persistence
kkŭnimŏmnŭn 끊임없는 continuous, incessant
kkŭnimŏpsshi 끊임없이 incessantly, forever
kkŭnimŏpsshi kyesok'aesŏ 끊임없이 계속해서 on and on, endlessly
kkŭnjilgin 끈질긴 dogged; high-powered *salesman*; nagging *pain*
kkŭnjŏk-kkŏrinŭn 끈적거리는 sticky; tacky; gooey
kkŭnjŏk-kkŭnjŏk'an 끈적끈적한 tacky; gooey
kkŭnmach'ida 끝마치다 finish off *drink, meal, work etc*
kkŭnmaejŭm 끝맺음 finish (*of product*)
kkŭnmat 끝맛 aftertaste (*from food, drink*)
kkŭnnada 끝나다 end, finish; result in; ***ije ta kkŭnnat-tta*** 이제 다 끝났다 it's all over now
kkŭnnaeda 끝내다 finish, conclude; ***ta kkŭnnaebŏrida*** 다 끝내버리다 finish up
kkŭnnaeji anŭn 끝내지 않은 unfinished
kkŭnŏjida 끊어지다 break; blow *fuse*; break off with; be interrupted; run out
kkŭnŏjin 끊어진 dead
kkŭntchiank'o it-tta 끊지않고 있다 hold on TELEC
kkŭntchimalgo kidariseyo 끊지말고 기다리세요 hold the line
kkŭnt'a 끊다 give up, kick; disconnect, cut off; hang up TELEC
kkŭnŭl maeda 끈을 매다 strap on; put on *watch, holster*; lace up
kkŭnŭm 끊음 withdrawal (*from drugs*)
kkŭrida 끓이다 boil, brew
kkŭrŏ antta 끌어 안다 snuggle up to
kkŭrŏjuda 끌어주다 give a tow
kkŭrŏ nŏmch'ida 끓어 넘치다 boil over
kkŭrŏ ollida 끌어 올리다 boost; push up; connect; hitch up; hoist; pull up
kkŭrŏ tanggida 끌어 당기다 pull; drag; retract *undercarriage*
kkŭrŏ tŭrida 끌어 들이다 drag
kkŭt 끝 end, bottom (*of street*); edge; point; nozzle ◊ exit COMPUT; ***yŏnghwarŭl kkŭtkkaji poda*** 영화를 끝까지 보다 watch a movie to the end
kkŭttchangnaeda 끝장내다 put an end to, end
kkŭt'ŭro 끝으로 in conclusion
kkubŏk-kkubŏk cholda 꾸벅꾸벅 졸다 doze off
kkubulkkuburhan 꾸불꾸불한 winding *road*
kkujit-tta 꾸짖다 scold
kkujunhada 꾸준하다 be persistent; persevere, plug away
kkujunhan 꾸준한 unrelenting
kkuk ch'amtta 꾹 참다 stifle

kkul 꿀 honey
kkulkkŏk-kkulkkŏk mashida 꿀꺽꿀꺽 마시다 gulp down
kkulkkulgŏrida 꿀꿀거리다 grunt
kkum 꿈 dream; ambition
kkumgat'ŭn 꿈같은 dreamlike, dream
kkumida 꾸미다 embellish; embroider; exaggerate; make up *story*; decorate
kkumijianŭn 꾸미지 않은 unadorned, undecorated, plain; austere
kkumin iyagi 꾸민 이야기 fiction
kkumin kŏt 꾸민 것 make-believe, pretense
kkumkkuda 꿈꾸다 dream
kkumkkyŏlgat'ŭn 꿈결같은 dreamy *voice*, *look*
kkumt'ŭlgŏrimyŏ naagada 꿈틀거리며 나아가다 wriggle (*along the ground*)
kkumŭl kkuda 꿈을 꾸다 dream
kkumuldaenŭn 꾸물대는 slow
kkumulgŏrida 꾸물거리다 dawdle, move slowly
kkumyŏjin il 꾸며진 일 set-up, frame-up
kkumyŏnaen iyagi 꾸며낸 이야기 yarn, story
kkurida 꾸리다 bundle up
kkurŏmi 꾸러미 bundle
kkurŏmiro ssada 꾸러미로 싸다 parcel up
kkuryŏgada 꾸려가다 manage *money*
kkuryŏnagada 꾸려나가다 manage, get by (*financially*)
kkwae 꽤 quite, fairly
kkwaek-kkwaek ulda 꽥꽥 울다 quack
kkwaenggwari 꽹과리 small gong (*made of brass*)
kkwak 꽉 hard; fast; full; compact; packed
kkwak chaptta 꽉 잡다 grip, clutch
kkwak choenŭn 꽉 죄는 skimpy
kkwak chwida 꽉 쥐다 clasp, squeeze; clench
kkwak ch'ada 꽉 차다 be jam-packed
kkwak ch'ait-tta 꽉 차있다 be jammed (*of roads*)
kkwak ch'an 꽉 찬 completely full
kkwak kkiida 꽉 끼이다 squeeze in
kkwak tŭrŏch'an 꽉 들어찬 chockfull, crowded
kkwemaeda 꿰매다 sew; stitch; darn
kkwemaeŏ talda 꿰매어 달다 sew on
kkyŏantta 껴안다 clasp (*to oneself*)
kŏaegŭi sanggŭm 거액의 상금 jackpot
kŏaegŭi sanggŭmŭl t'ada 거액의 상금을 타다 hit the jackpot
kŏbe chillida 겁에 질리다 be terrified
kŏbe chillin 겁에 질린 panic-stricken
kŏbi manŭn 겁이 많은 easily frightened; spineless; cowardly
kŏbŭl mŏgŭn 겁을 먹은 fearful; cowardly, chicken
kŏbŭl mŏk-kko mullŏsŏda 겁을 먹고 물러서다 chicken out
kŏbuhada 거부하다 veto; reject; refuse
kŏbuk 거북 turtle; tortoise
kŏbukkwŏn 거부권 right of veto
kŏbukssŏn 거북선 turtle ship (*first armored warship*)
kŏbuk'aehada 거북해하다 feel awkward
kŏbuk'an 거북한 awkward, embarrassing
kŏch'ida 걷히다 lift, clear (*of fog*)
kŏch'ilda 거칠다 be rough
kŏch'ilge taehada 거칠게 대하다 manhandle; treat roughly
kŏch'in 거친 rough; coarse; rugged
kŏch'yŏsŏ 거쳐서 by way of, via
kŏdaehada 거대하다 be enormous
kŏdaeham 거대함 enormity
kŏdaehan 거대한 enormous, huge
kŏdŏollida 걷어올리다 roll up *sleeves*
kŏdŭrŭm p'iunŭn 거드름 피우는 pompous
kŏgidaga 거기다가 moreover
kŏin 거인 giant
Kŏjedo 거제도 Koje Island
kŏji 거지 beggar
kŏjinmal 거짓말 lie
kŏjinmarhada 거짓말하다 lie, tell a lie

kŏjit 거짓 pretense
kŏjitmaljaeng-i 거짓말쟁이 liar
kŏjŏ ŏt-tta 거저 얻다 cadge, bum
kŏjŏrhada 거절하다 deny; reject; refuse
kŏjŭ 거즈 gauze
kŏjuhada 거주하다 inhabit; reside
kŏju hŏga 거주 허가 residence permit
kŏjuja 거주자 inhabitant; resident
kŏjuji 거주지 residence (*house etc*)
kŏkkuro 거꾸로 upside down; back to front
kŏkkuro hada 거꾸로 하다 reverse
kŏkkuro toen 거꾸로 된 inverse *order*; reverse
kŏktchŏng 걱정 concern, worry, anxiety
kŏktchŏngdoenŭn 걱정되는 worrying
kŏktchŏnghada 걱정하다 worry; be worried, be concerned
kŏktchŏnghanŭn 걱정하는 concerned, anxious
kŏktchŏngshik'ida 걱정시키다 worry, trouble
kŏktchŏngsŭrŏn 걱정스런 worried
kŏktchŏngsŭrŏptta 걱정스럽다 be worried
kŏlch'ida 걸치다 extend, range; span; throw on *clothes*
kŏlda 걸다 hang; stake; be on (*of brake*)
kŏlle 걸레 cloth; tramp (*woman*)
kŏllejirhada 걸레질하다 mop; swab; wipe
kŏllida 걸리다 catch *illness*; take *time*
kŏllŏnaeda 걸러내다 strain; sift
kŏllyŏ nŏmŏjida 걸려 넘어지다 trip, stumble; trip over, stumble over
kŏllyŏonŭn 걸려오는 incoming *phonecall*
kŏlssang 걸상 stool
kŏlssoe 걸쇠 clasp; latch
kŏlsŭk'aut'ŭ 걸스카우트 girl scout
kŏltchuk'age hada 걸쭉하게 하다 thicken
kŏltchuk'an 걸쭉한 thick
kŏm 검 sword
kŏman 거만 arrogance
kŏmanhada 거만하다 be arrogant
kŏmanhan 거만한 arrogant, stuck-up
kŏmch'algwan 검찰관 public prosecutor
kŏmda 검다 be black; be dark
kŏmgŏ 검거 round-up (*of suspects, criminals*)
kŏmgŏhada 검거하다 round up *suspects, criminals*
kŏmi 거미 spider
kŏmijul 거미줄 cobweb
kŏmjŏngsaek 검정색 black
kŏmmanŭn 겁많은 timid
kŏmmŏgŭn 겁먹은 timid
kŏmmŏktta 겁먹다 be afraid, be scared; get cold feet; be overawed
kŏmmunso 검문소 checkpoint
kŏmnada 겁나다 be frightened; be frightened of
kŏmnage hada 겁나게 하다 terrify
kŏmnage hanŭn 겁나게 하는 terrifying
kŏmnanŭn 겁나는 frightening, unnerving
kŏmnyŏk 검역 quarantine (*for animals*)
kŏmp'yowŏn 검표원 inspector (*on buses*)
kŏmp'yut'ŏ chulp'an 컴퓨터 출판 desktop publishing
k'ŏmp'yut'ŏ ch'ŏriga kanŭnghan 컴퓨터 처리가 가능한 machine-readable
k'ŏmp'yut'ŏŭi sohyŏng ch'ŏrigi 컴퓨터의 소형 처리기 microprocessor
kŏmsa 검사 examination (*of patient*); prosecutor ◊ exploratory
kŏmsaek'ada 검색하다 navigate
kŏmshi 검시 post-mortem
kŏmshigwan 검시관 coroner
kŏmt'ohada 검토하다 go over, check; take stock; consider
kŏmŭn 검은 black
kŏmul 거물 tycoon, big shot
kŏmun-go 거문고 zither
kŏmusŭrehan 거무스레한 swarthy
kŏmusŭrŭmhan 거무스름한 dark, somber
kŏmyŏl chedo 검열 제도 censorship
kŏmyŏrhada 검열하다 censor
kŏnbae 건배! cheers!

kŏnbaehada 건배하다 toast (*drinking*); ***nugurŭl wihae kŏnbaehajago hada*** 누구를 위해 건배하자고 하다 propose a toast to s.o.
kŏnban 건반 keyboard (*of piano*)
kŏnbangjida 건방지다 be forward, be impertinent
kŏnbangjige kulda 건방지게 굴다 get smart with, be cheeky with
kŏnbangjin 건방진 forward, impertinent, insolent
kŏnch'o 건초 hay
kŏnch'oyŏl 건초열 hay fever
kŏnch'ugŏp 건축업 builder (*company*); building trade
kŏnch'ugŏptcha 건축업자 builder (*person*)
kŏnch'uk 건축 building
kŏnch'uk'ak 건축학 architecture (*subject*)
kŏnch'ungmul 건축물 construction, structure
kŏnch'ungnyangshik 건축양식 architecture (*style*)
kŏndal 건달 rogue, good-for-nothing
kŏndubaktchillo 곤두박질로 headlong
kŏn-gang 건강 health; ***tangshinŭi kŏn-gang-ŭl wihae!*** 당신의 건강을 위해! your health!
kŏn-gang chindan 건강 진단 check-up MED
kŏn-gang-e choŭn 건강에 좋은 healthy, wholesome
kŏn-ganghada 건강하다 be healthy
kŏn-ganghan 건강한 fit, healthy
kŏn-gang munje 건강 문제 medical problem
kŏn-gang sangt'ae 건강 상태 condition, state of health
kŏn-gang shikp'um 건강 식품 health food
kŏn-gang shikp'umjŏm 건강 식품점 health food store
kŏnjanghan 건장한 burly
kŏnjŏnhada 건전하다 be wholesome, be healthy
kŏnjŏnhan 건전한 wholesome, healthy; sound
kŏnjogi 건조기 drier; dry season
kŏnjohada 건조하다 be dry, be arid
kŏnjohan 건조한 dry
kŏnmosŭp 겉모습 exterior, façade
kŏnmul 건물 building
kŏnmul chosawŏn 건물 조사원 surveyor
kŏnnejuda 건네주다 hand over, give
kŏnnŏ 건너 over, across
kŏnnŏda 건너다 cross, go across
kŏnnŏgada 건너가다 cross, go across
kŏnnŏ p'yŏn 건너 편 across, on the other side of
kŏnnosŏ 건너서 across
kŏnp'odo 건포도 raisin; currant
kŏnsŏl 건설 construction
kŏnsŏltchŏgin 건설적인 constructive
kŏnsŏrŏp 건설업 construction industry
kŏptchaeng-i 겁쟁이 chicken, coward
kŏptchuda 겁주다 frighten
kŏptchuŏ tchoch'anaeda 겁주어 쫓아내다 scare away
kŏp'um 거품 bubble; foam; froth
kŏp'umnanŭn 거품나는 effervescent
kŏrae 거래 deal; dealing; dealings; business; transaction
kŏraehada 거래하다 deal with; deal in; bank with
kŏraerŭl maedŭp chit-tta 거래를 매듭 짓다 clinch a deal
kŏri 거리 distance; street; ***kŏrie*(*sŏ*)** 거리에(서) in the street
kŏri 걸이 rack
kŏrikkimŏpsshi marhada 거리낌없이 말하다 speak out
kŏrirŭl tuda 거리를 두다 distance oneself
kŏrŏdanida 걸어다니다 walk around
kŏrŏgada 걸어가다 walk away
kŏrŏmaeda 걸어매다 hitch (onto)
kŏrŏ nŏmŏttŭrida 걸어 넘어뜨리다 trip up
kŏrŏsŏ 걸어서 on foot
kŏrŏsŏ kada 걸어서 가다 walk, go on foot
kŏrŏsŏ kŏnnŏda 걸어서 건너다 walk across
kŏrŭda 거르다 filter
kŏrŭm 걸음 step, pace; ***kŏrŭmi nŭrida* / *pparŭda*** 걸음이

느리다/빠르다 be a slow/fast walker
kŏsehada 거세하다 neuter *animal*
kŏsehan hwangso 거세한 황소 steer (*animal*)
kŏshida 것이다: ***...l kŏshida*** ...ㄹ 것이다 shall, will
kŏshiktchŭng 거식증 anorexia
kŏshiktchŭng-ŭl alt'a 거식증을 앓다 be anorexic
kŏshil 거실 living room
kŏsŭllida 거슬리다 grate; jar on
kŏsŭllinŭn 거슬리는 harsh, abrasive
kŏsŭllŏ ollagada 거슬러 올라가다 go back, date back
kŏt 것 thing ◊ (*forms equivalent of relative clause*): ***kŭ sarami naeil olgŏsŭl arayo*** 그 사람이 내일 올것을 알아요 I know that he will come tomorrow; ***nae ch'in-guga ŏjae pyŏngwŏne ibwŏnhan kŏsŭl tŭŏssŏyo*** 내 친구가 어재 병원에 입원한 것을 들었어요 I heard that my friend went into the hospital yesterday; ***chibe iltchik kanŭn kŏsi natkk'essŏyo*** 집에 일찍 가는 것이 낫겠어요 it'd be better to go home early ◊ (*forms equivalent of noun form in ...ing*): ***suhagŭl kon-buhanŭn kŏsi shiptchi anayo*** 수학을 공부하는 것이 쉽지 않아요 studying math is not easy
kŏtch'ire 겉치레 pose, pretense
kŏtkki 걷기 walking
kŏt-tta 걷다 walk
kŏt'ŭronŭn 겉으로는 outwardly, externally
kŏŭi 거의 almost; ***kŏŭi kat-tta*** 거의 같다 be almost like, verge on; ***kŏŭi ŏptta*** 거의 없다 scarcely any; ***kŏŭi ta*** 거의 다 all but, nearly all
kŏul 거울 mirror
kŏwi 거위 goose
kŏyŏk'ada 거역하다 disobey
...ko ...고 and
koa 고아 orphan
koanhada 고안하다 devise
koanmul 고안물 gimmick
koap 고압 high voltage; high pressure ◊ high-voltage; high-pressure
koap kkassŭ 고압 가스 propellant
koapssŏnnyong ch'ŏlt'ap 고압선용 철탑 (electricity) pylon
koawŏn 고아원 orphanage
kobaek 고백 confession
kobaek'ada 고백하다 confess
kobal 고발 accusation
kobarhada 고발하다 charge, accuse
koch'arhada 고찰하다 look at, consider
koch'e 고체 solid mass
koch'ida 고치다 correct; repair
koch'ŭng piltting 고층 빌딩 high-rise building
koch'u 고추 red pepper; chilli
koch'ugaru 고추가루 chilli (pepper) powder
koch'ujang 고추장 red pepper paste
kodae 고대 antiquity ◊ ancient
kodaehada 고대하다 be anxious for
kodo 고도 altitude
kodok 고독 solitude
kodok'ada 고독하다 be solitary; be lonely
kodok'an 고독한 solitary
kodong 고동 beat (*of heart*)
kodongch'ida 고동치다 pulsate (*of heart, blood*)
kodo pulp'ohwa multchil 고도 불포화 물질 polyunsaturate
kodŭn 곧은 straight (*not curly*)
kodŭnghak-kkyo 고등학교 high school
kodŭnghakssaeng 고등학생 high school student
Kodŭng Pŏbwŏn 고등 법원 Supreme Court
kodŭrŭm 고드름 icicle
koemul 괴물 monster
koemulgat'ŭn 괴물같은 monstrous, frightening
koengjanghada 굉장하다 be awesome
koengjanghage 굉장하게 very, terrifically
koengjanghan 굉장한 awesome; terrific; tremendous
koengjanghi 굉장히 greatly; beautifully; tremendously
koeng-ŭm 굉음 boom (*noise*)
koeŏ innŭn 괴어 있는 stagnant
koeroe chŏngbu 괴뢰 정부 puppet government

koerop'ida 괴롭히다 trouble; torment
koerop'im 괴롭힘 harassment
koetcha 괴짜 crank, eccentric
kogaek 고객 customer, client
kogaek kwalli 고객 관리 customer relations
kogaerŭl chŏt-tta 고개를 젓다 shake one's head
kogaerŭl kkŭdŏgida 고개를 끄덕이다 nod one's head
kogi 고기 meat
kogiap 고기압 high pressure (*weather*)
kogohak 고고학 archeology
kogohaktcha 고고학자 archeologist
kogŭl 고글 goggles (*for skiing*)
kogŭp 고급 high class ◊ high-class
kogŭp chaptchi 고급 잡지 glossy (magazine)
koguk 고국 home; native country; ***koguge kada*** 고국에 가다 go home
Koguryŏ 고구려 Koguryo (*Ancient Kingdom*)
kogwihan 고귀한 noble
kogye 곡예 acrobatics
kogyesa 곡예사 acrobat
kogyeyong kŭne 곡예용 그네 trapeze
kogyŏrhan 고결한 virtuous
kohae 고해 confession
kohaehada 고해하다 confess
kohaeshil 고해실 confessional
kohae shinbu 고해 신부 confessor
koham 고함 roar, bellow
koham chirŭda 고함 지르다 yell, cry out
kohamch'ida 고함치다 roar, bellow
kohamch'yŏ purŭda 고함쳐 부르다 yell
kohwan 고환 testicle
kohyang 고향 home; roots
kohyŏrap 고혈압 hypertension
koin 고인 the dead, the deceased; ancient people
koindol 고인돌 dolmen
kojajiljaeng-i 고자질쟁이 telltale
kojajirhada 고자질하다 tell tales, snitch
kojang 고장 breakdown; crash (*of computer*)
kojang suri 고장 수리 troubleshooting
kojang-i nada 고장이 나다 play up; break down; crash COMPUT
kojang-i ŏmnŭn 고장이 없는 trouble-free
kojangna it-tta 고장나 있다 be down, not be working
kojangnan 고장난 out of order, not working
kojibi ssen 고집이 센 stubborn, obstinate
kojip 고집 obstinacy
kojip'ada 고집하다 be stubborn; stand by, adhere to
kojishik'an 고지식한 conservative; straight
kojŏn 고전 classic
kojŏngdoeda 고정되다 be fixed
kojŏngdoen 고정된 fixed *part, exchange rate*
kojŏnghada 고정하다 fasten, fix; ***umjigiji ank'e kojŏnghada*** 움직이지 않게 고정하다 set *broken limb*
kojŏngshik'ida 고정시키다 fix; attach; stabilize; strap in; ***muŏsŭl chejarie kojŏngshik'ida*** 무엇을 제자리에 고정시키다 lock sth in position
Kojosŏn 고조선 Old Choson (*Ancient Kingdom*)
kojup'a 고주파 high-frequency
kokka toro 고가 도로 overpass (*for car*)
kokkurajida 고꾸라지다 fall head over heels
kokssŏn 곡선 curve
koktcho 곡조 tune
koktchoga arŭmdaun 곡조가 아름다운 melodious
kol 골 goal, target
kolbanppyŏ 골반뼈 pelvis
kolch'i ap'ŭn 골치 아픈 troublesome
kolch'itkkŏri 골칫거리 bother, headache
kolch'o 골초 heavy smoker
kolden 골덴 corduroy
kolden paji 골덴 바지 corduroy pants, cords
kolk'ip'ŏ 골키퍼 goalkeeper

kollan 곤란 hardship; embarrassment
kollanaeda 골라내다 pick on; select
kollanhada 곤란하다 be arduous; be awkward
kolmok 골목 alley
kolmok-kkil 골목길 side street
kolmu 골무 thimble
kolp'anji 골판지 corrugated cardboard
kolp'ŭ 골프 golf
kolp'ŭjang 골프장 golf course; golf club
kolp'ŭ k'ŭllŏp 골프 클럽 golf club (*instrument*)
koltcha 골자 core
koltchagi 골짜기 valley
koltchitkkŏri 골칫거리 pest, nuisance
kolttae 골대 goalpost
kolttongp'um 골동품 antique
kolttongp'um sang-in 골동품 상인 antique dealer
kom 곰 bear (*animal*)
komak 고막 eardrum
komapkkedo 고맙게도 thankfully
komapkke yŏginŭn 고맙게 여기는 grateful
komapssŭmnida 고맙습니다 thank you (*polite*)
komaptta 고맙다 thank
komawŏ 고마워 thanks
kombo chaguk 곰보 자국 spot (*caused by measles etc*)
komgomhi saenggak'ada 곰곰히 생각하다 reflect; brood; ponder
komin 고민 distress
komindoenŭn 고민되는 vexed
kominhada 고민하다 worry, fret
kominhage hada 고민하게 하다 concern, worry
komo 고모 aunt (*own, sister of father*)
komobu 고모부 uncle (*father's sister's husband*)
komp'ang-i 곰팡이 mold, mildew
komp'ang-i p'in 곰팡이 핀 moldy
komp'angnae nanŭn 곰팡내 나는 musty
komtta 곪다 go septic
komu 고무 rubber
komu chŏtkkoktchi 고무 젖꼭지 pacifier (*for baby*)
komujul 고무줄 elastic
komul 고물 junk
komul sujipsso 고물 수집소 junkyard
komun 고문 adviser; torture
komunhada 고문하다 torture
komu paendŭ 고무 밴드 rubber band
komu pot'ŭ 고무 보트 inflatable boat
komyŏng-ŭro changshik'ada 고명으로 장식하다 garnish
konbong 곤봉 club, stick
konch'ung 곤충 insect
kong 공 ball (*tennis, golf etc*); zero
kongbaek 공백 blank; empty space; gap
kongbŏm 공범 accomplice
Kongboch'ŏ 공보처 Ministry of Information
kongbu 공부 study, learning
kongbuhada 공부하다 study, learn
kongch'aek 공책 notebook
kongch'ŏga 공처가 henpecked husband
kongch'ŏn 공천 nomination
kongch'ŏnhada 공천하다 nominate
kongch'ŏnja 공천자 nominee; nomination
kongdan 공단 satin
kongdong 공동 cooperation ◊ joint, common
kongdong chŏja 공동 저자 collaborator (*in writing book etc*)
kongdong chŏngnipkkŭm 공동 적립금 kitty, common fund
kongdongch'e 공동체 community
kongdonggigŭm 공동기금 pool, kitty, common fund
kongdong ikkwŏnŭro hada 공동 이권으로 하다 pool, combine, merge
kongdong kujwa 공동 구좌 joint account
kongdong soyuja 공동 소유자 part owner
kongdong-ŭro chŏjak'ada 공동으로 저작하다 collaborate (*on book etc*)
kongdong-ŭro irhada 공동으로 일하다 collaborate, work together
kongdong yŏn-guhada 공동 연구하다 collaborate (*in research*)

kongdŭrin 공들인 elaborate
konggaehada 공개하다 unveil *plans*
konggaejŏgin 공개적인 public
konggaejŏgŭro 공개적으로 publicly
konggae maeip 공개 매입 takeover bid
konggal 공갈 blackmail
konggal ch'ida 공갈 치다 blackmail
konggal ch'inŭn saram 공갈 치는 사람 blackmailer
konggan 공간 space, room
konggi 공기 air; bowl, dish (*for rice*)
konggiga ant'onghanŭn 공기가 안통하는 airtight
konggiga shinsŏnhan 공기가 신선한 airy *room*
konggi tŭril 공기 드릴 pneumatic drill
konggo 공고 notice, announcement
konggohada 공고하다 notify
konggong 공공 public
konggong kigwan 공공 기관 institute (*special home*)
konggong pumun 공공 부문 public sector
konggŭbwŏn 공급원 supplier
konggŭp 공급 supply, provision
konggŭpkkwa suyo 공급과 수요 supply and demand
konggŭpp'um 공급품 supplies
konggŭp'ada 공급하다 supply, provide
konggun 공군 air force
konggun kiji 공군 기지 airbase
konggyŏk 공격 offensive, aggression MIL
konggyŏktchŏgin 공격적인 aggressive
konggyŏk'ada 공격하다 attack, go on the offensive
konghak 공학 engineering
konghang 공항 airport
konghang t'ŏminŏl 공항 터미널 air terminal
konghŏ 공허 vacuum *fig*
konghŏham 공허함 emptiness; vanity (*of hopes*)
konghŏhan 공허한 hollow *words*
konghŏn 공헌 contribution (*of time, effort*)
konghŏnhada 공헌하다 contribute (*with time*)
Konghwadang chijija 공화당 지지자 Republican
Konghwadang-wŏn 공화당원 Republican, member of the Republican party
konghwaguk 공화국 republic
kong-ik saŏp 공익 사업 public utilities
kong-in hoegyesa 공인 회계사 certified public accountant
Kongja 공자 Confucius
kongjakssae 공작새 peacock
kongjang 공장 plant; factory; mill
kongjangjang 공장장 foreman
kongje 공제 deduction (*from salary*)
kongjŏ 공저 collaboration (*on book etc*)
kongjŏnghada 공정하다 be fair, be just
kongjŏnghage 공정하게 fairly, justly
kongjŏnghan 공정한 fair, just
kongjŏnhada 공전하다 idle (*of engine*); orbit
kongjon 공존 coexistence
kongjonhada 공존하다 coexist
kongjŭng 공증 notarization
kongjŭng-in 공증인 notary
kongjung 공중 public; air; midair; ***kongjung-esŏ*** 공중에서 in midair
kongjung chŏnhwa 공중 전화 pay phone
kongjung chŏnhwa pakssŭ 공중 전화 박스 phone booth
kongjung napch'i 공중 납치 hijack
kongjung napch'ibŏm 공중 납치범 hijacker
kongjung napch'ihada 공중 납치하다 hijack
kongjung pihaenghada 공중 비행하다 fly past (in formation)
kongju 공주 princess
kongmin p'yŏngdŭngkkwŏn 공민 평등권 civil rights
kongmohada 공모하다 conspire with, be in cahoots with
kongmul 곡물 cereal (*grain*)
kongmuwŏn 공무원 civil servant, government official
kongnip hak-kkyo 공립 학교 public school

kongno 공로 credit, honor; ***Xe taehan kongnorŭl injŏngpat-tta*** X에 대한 공로를 인정받다 get the credit for X
kongnyŏnhada 공연하다 perform, stage; co-star; be futile
kongnyong 공룡 dinosaur
kong-ŏp 공업 manufacturing
kong-ŏpttanji 공업 단지 industrial estate
kongp'an 공판 trial; ***kongp'an chung*** 공판 중 on trial
kongp'o 공포 horror, terror
kongp'otchŭng 공포증 phobia
kongp'o yŏnghwa 공포 영화 horror movie
kongp'yŏngham 공평함 detachment, objectivity
kongp'yŏnghan 공평한 detached, objective
kongp'yohada 공표하다 declare, state; issue *warning*
kongsa 공사 construction; public and private affairs; minister; ***kongsa chung*** 공사 중 under construction
kongsajang 공사장 building site, construction site
kongsajang inbu 공사장 인부 construction worker
Kongsandang 공산당 Communist Party
Kongsandang-ŭi 공산당의 Communist
kongsang-e chamgida 공상에 잠기다 daydream
kongsang kwahak sosŏl 공상 과학 소설 science fiction
kongsang kwahak sosŏl chaptchi 공상 과학 소설 잡지 science fiction fanzine
Kongsanjuŭi 공산주의 Communism ◊ Communist
Kongsanjuŭija 공산주의자 Communist
Kongsanjuŭiŭi 공산주의의 Communist
kongshihada 공시하다 post, show *profits*
kongshik 공식 formula; formality ◊ formal, official
kongshiktchŏgin 공식적인 state, ceremonial
kongshiktchŏgŭro 공식적으로 officially, strictly speaking; ***kongshiktchŏgŭro allida*** 공식적으로 알리다 officially announce
kongshik'wadoen 공식화된 official, confirmed
kongsŏgin 공석인 vacant
kongsŏk 공석 vacancy
kongsonhada 공손하다 be polite
kongsonhage 공손하게 politely
kongsonhan 공손한 polite
kongsshik pangmun 공식 방문 state visit
kongtcharo 공짜로 for nothing, for free
kongtchŏgin 공적인 official; ***kongtchŏgin changso-e(sŏ)*** 공적인 장소에(서) in public
kongtchŏgŭro 공적으로 formally
kongt'eip'ŭ 공테이프 blank tape
kongt'ong 공통 common *language etc*
kongt'onghada 공통하다 be common
kongt'ong-ŭro 공통으로 in common; ***muŏsŭl nuguwa kongt'ong-ŭro kajigo it-tta*** 무엇을 누구와 공통으로 가지고 있다 have sth in common with s.o.
kong-wŏn 공원 park
kong-ye 공예 craft
kong-yŏn 공연 performance
kon-gyŏng 곤경 impasse; mess; plight
kon-gyŏng-e ch'ŏhada 곤경에 처하다 be in a jam
kon-gyŏng-e ch'ŏhae it-tta 곤경에 처해 있다 be in a fix
kon-gyŏng-esŏ kuhaenaeda 곤경에서 구해내다 bail out *fig*
kong-yŏnhada 공연하다 perform
kong-yŏnja 공연자 performer
koppi 고삐 rein
kopssem 곱셈 multiplication
kopssŭlgŏrida 곱슬거리다 curl
kopssŭlgŏrim 곱슬거림 curl
kopssŭlgŏrinŭn 곱슬거리는 curly; frizzy
kopssŭlgopssŭrhan 곱슬곱슬한 fuzzy

koptta 곱다 be fine; be fair; be pretty; be gentle
kop'ada 곱하다 multiply
kop'umkkyŏgŭi 고품격의 upmarket
kora ttŏrŏjida 곯아 떨어지다 crash out, fall asleep
korae 고래 whale
koraegorae sorich'ida 고래고래 소리치다 rant and rave
koraejabi 고래잡이 whaling
korhamsŏk 골함석 corrugated iron
kori 고리 catch (*locking device*); hook; link; loop
korilla 고릴라 gorilla
korip 고립 isolation
koripsshik'ida 고립시키다 cut off, isolate
koripttoen 고립된 lonely, isolated
korŭda 고르다 pick and choose; plump for
korŭge 고르게 evenly, regularly
korŭji ank'e 고르지 않게 unevenly
korŭji anŭn 고르지 않은 uneven
korŭm 고름 pus
korŭn 고른 even, regular
koryŏ 고려 consideration, thoughtfulness, concern; Koryo (*Kingdom*)
koryŏhada 고려하다 allow for; make allowances; take on board; consider
koryŏhaji ank'o 고려하지 않고 with no regard for
koryŏhal sahang 고려할 사항 consideration, factor
kosaeng 고생 hardship; toil
kosaenghada 고생하다 suffer, be in pain
kosang 고상 elegance
kosanghan 고상한 elegant
kosŏngnŭng 고성능 high performance
kosŏngnŭng-ŭi 고성능의 high-powered
kosogŭro kamtta 고속으로 감다 fast forward
kosohada 고소하다 sue
kosohaehada 고소해하다 gloat; gloat over
kosok ch'asŏn 고속 차선 fast lane
kosok ellibeit'ŏ 고속 엘리베이터 express elevator
kosok kamkki 고속 감기 fast forward
kosok kiŏ 고속 기어 high (gear)
kosokttoro 고속도로 freeway, highway, expressway
kosok yŏlch'a 고속 열차 high-speed train
kosŭmdoch'i 고슴도치 hedgehog
kosu 고수 drummer
kosuhada 고수하다 hold on to *belief*; stick to *story*, *opinion*
kot 곧 soon, in a minute
kot 곳 joint; place; patch; ***...nŭn kot*** ...는 곳 where
kotpparo 곧바로 straight; straight away
kot-tchang 곧장 straight; directly, immediately
kot-tchang tallyŏgada 곧장 달려가다 run directly to; make a beeline for
kot'ong 고통 suffering; distress; agony
kot'ongsŭrŏun 고통스러운 painful; agonizing
koŭiga anin 고의가 아닌 unintentional
koŭijŏgin 고의적인 deliberate
koŭijŏgŭro 고의적으로 deliberately
koŭmŭi 고음의 high-pitched
koun 고운 fine
kowi insa 고위 인사 dignitary
kowi kogwanŭi 고위 고관의 high-level
kowŏn 고원 plateau
koyak'ada 고약하다 be foul; be bad
koyak'an 고약한 ugly; vicious; foul; bad; ***koyak'an naemsaega nada*** 고약한 냄새가 나다 stink, have a foul smell
koyang-i 고양이 cat
koyo 고요 peace; quietness; silence
koyohada 고요하다 be calm
koyohaejida 고요해지다 calm down
koyohan 고요한 still, calm, quiet
koyongdoeda 고용되다 be employed, be on the payroll
koyongdoen 고용된 in the pay of
koyonghada 고용하다 employ, hire
koyong-in 고용인 employee; servant
koyongju 고용주 employer

kŭ 그 the ◊ he; ***kŭ sŭsŭro*** 그 스스로 by himself
kŭbakke 그밖에 everyone else
kŭbakkŭi tarŭn kŏsŭn? 그밖의 다른 것은? anything else?
kŭbu 급우 school friend
kŭbyŏ 급여 allowance (*money*)
kŭ chashin 그 자신 himself
kŭ chik'ue 그 직후에 whereupon
kŭ chŏne paro 그 전에 바로 shortly before that
kŭ chŏngdo 그 정도 thereabouts
kŭ chŏngdo-ŭi 그 정도의 such a ◊ to that extent
kŭ chŏnjue 그 전주에 the week before
kŭ chŏnnal 그 전날 the day before
kŭ chŏnnare 그 전날에 the day before
kŭch'ida 그치다 stop
kŭdŭl 그들 them; they; those
kŭdŭl chashin 그들 자신 themselves
kŭdŭl sŭsŭro 그들 스스로 by themselves
kŭdŭrŭi 그들의 their; those
kŭdŭrŭi kŏt 그들의 것 theirs
kŭgŏllo twaessŏyo 그걸로 됐어요 alright, that's enough!
kŭgŏsŭi 그것의 its
kŭgŏsŭl 그것을 it (*as object*)
kŭgŏsŭn 그것은 it (*as subject*)
kŭgŏt chach'e 그것 자체 itself
kŭgŏttŭl 그것들 they; those (*things*)
kŭgŏt tul ta 그것 둘 다 both of them (*things*)
kŭgŏttŭrŭi 그것들의 those
kŭgot malgo 그곳 말고 not there
kŭgup'a 극우파 right-wing extremism
kŭ hu chulgot 그 후 줄곧 ever since
kŭ hue 그 후에 subsequently; later, afterward
kŭ ihue 그 이후에 after that
kŭjŏkke 그저께 the day before yesterday
kŭjŏ kŭrŏn 그저 그런 satisfactory; so so, average
kŭk 극 pole
kŭkch'anŭi p'yŏng 극찬의 평 rave review
kŭ kose 그 곳에 there
kŭk'i chagŭn 극히 작은 microscopic, minute
kŭk'i chungdaehan 극히 중대한 vitally important
kŭk'wa 극화 dramatization
kŭk'wahada 극화하다 dramatize
kŭk'yŏng 극형 capital punishment
kŭkppi 극비 top secret
kŭkppiŭi 극비의 classified
kŭkppok'ada 극복하다 conquer, overcome
kŭksshimhan 극심한 acute, extreme
kŭksso chŏnja konghak 극소 전자 공학 microelectronics
kŭkssoryang 극소량 iota, grain
kŭktchak-kka 극작가 dramatist
kŭktchang 극장 theater
kŭktchang annaewŏn 극장 안내원 usherette, attendant
kŭktchi 극지 pole ◊ polar
kŭktchŏgin 극적인 dramatic; rousing
kŭktchŏgin sanghwang 극적인 상황 drama, excitement
kŭktta 긁다 scrape; scratch
kŭkttan 극단 extreme; theater company
kŭkttanjŏgin 극단적인 extreme; immoderate
kŭktto 극도 extreme
Kŭkttong 극동 Far East ◊ Far Eastern
kŭkttoŭi p'iro 극도의 피로 exhaustion
kŭlja 글자 character (*in typography*)
kŭlkki 긁기 scratch
kŭlkkol 글꼴 font
kŭlk'in chaguk 긁힌 자국 scrape; scratch
kŭllaidŏ 글라이더 glider
kŭlsseyo 글쎄요 I'm not sure
kŭlsshi 글씨 handwriting
kŭl ssŭgi 글 쓰기 writing
kŭltcha 글자 letter (*of alphabet*)
kŭltchach'e 글자체 script; font
kŭltcha kŭdaero 글자 그대로 literally, to the letter
kŭltcha match'ugi nori 글자 맞추기 놀이 crossword
kŭm 금 gold; break, fracture
kŭmaek 금액 amount

kŭmanduda 그만두다 stop, quit; drop; drop out
kŭmanhan kach'iga it-tta 그만한 가치가 있다 be good value
kŭmbak 금박 gilt
kŭmbal mŏri yŏja 금발 머리 여자 blonde
kŭmbang 금방 directly, immediately
kŭmbung-ŏ 금붕어 goldfish
kŭmdan hyŏnsang 금단 현상 withdrawal symptoms
kŭmgage hada 금가게 하다 crack, fracture
Kŭmgang 금강 Kum River
Kŭmganggyŏng 금강경 Diamond Sutra
kŭmgi 금기 taboo
kŭmgo 금고 safe
kŭmgoe 금괴 gold ingot
kŭmhada 금하다 bar, forbid, ban
kŭmhonshik 금혼식 golden wedding anniversary
kŭmi kada 금이 가다 crack; split up
kŭmi kan 금이 간 cracked
kŭmji 금지 ban, prohibition; ***kŭmnyŏn kŭmji*** 금연 금지 no smoking
kŭmjidoeda 금지되다 be forbidden
kŭmjidoen 금지된 forbidden
kŭmjihada 금지하다 forbid, ban
kŭmjiryŏng 금지령 prohibition
kŭmjŏn tŭngnok-kki 금전 등록기 cash register
Kŭmjuppŏp 금주법 Prohibition
kŭmnyoil 금요일 Friday
kŭmnyu 급류 torrent; rapids
kŭmnyung 금융 finance; funding ◊ financial; monetary
kŭmnyung shijang 금융 시장 money market
kŭmsegongsa 금세공사 goldsmith
kŭmshi ch'omunida 금시 초문이다 that's news to me
kŭmshik 금식 fast (*not eating*)
kŭmsok 금속 metal
kŭmsokssŏng-ŭi 금속성의 metallic
kŭmul 그물 mesh, net
kŭmyŏn 금연 no smoking
kŭmyoktchŏgin 금욕적인 austere
kŭnbon 근본 root; source; origin
kŭnbonjŏgin 근본적인 basic, fundamental
kŭnbonjŏgŭro 근본적으로 radically
kŭnch'in 근친 next of kin
kŭnch'insanggan 근친상간 incest
kŭnch'ŏ 근처 vicinity; ***...ŭi kŭnch'ŏe(sŏ)*** ...의 근처에(서) in the vicinity of; ***kŭnch'ŏe it-tta*** 근처에 있다 be around
kŭndae 근대 modern times ◊ modern
kŭndaeŭi 근대의 modern
kŭndaehwa 근대화 modernization
kŭne 그네 swing
kŭngjŏngjŏgin 긍정적인 positive
kŭn-gŏ 근거 basis, foundation; ground, reason
kŭn-gŏga toeda 근거가 되다 underlie
kŭn-gŏji 근거지 stronghold
kŭn-gŏjirŭl tugo it-tta ...에 근거지를 두고 있다 be based in
kŭn-gŏ ŏmnŭn 근거 없는 groundless, unfounded
kŭn-gyo 근교 environs; suburbs ◊ suburban
kŭnjŏng tchoktchi 근정 쪽지 compliments slip
kŭnjŏp 근접 proximity
kŭnjŏrhada 근절하다 stamp out, eradicate
kŭnmuhada 근무하다 serve
kŭnmu shigan 근무 시간 work hours; work day
kŭnmyŏnhan 근면한 industrious
kŭnŏmhan 근엄한 grave
kŭnsahan 근사한 gorgeous; neat, terrific
kŭnshian 근시안 myopia
kŭnshianjŏgin 근시안적인 shortsighted *fig*; short-term
kŭnshianŭi 근시안의 shortsighted; myopic
kŭnshimhada 근심하다 worry about, have on one's mind
kŭnŭl 그늘 shade; ***kŭnŭre(sŏ)*** 그늘에(서) in the shade
kŭnŭljige hada 그늘지게 하다 eclipse *fig*
kŭnŭljin 그늘진 shady
kŭnŭn 그는 he
kŭnwŏn 근원 origin; source; root
kŭnwŏnjŏgin 근원적인 underlying

kŭnyang 그냥 as it is; just; ***kŭnyang nongdamiyeyo*** 그냥 농담이에요 I was just kidding
kŭnyŏ 그녀 she
kŭnyŏ chashin 그녀 자신 herself
kŭnyŏrŭl 그녀를 her (*object*)
kŭnyŏ sŭsŭro 그녀 스스로 by herself
kŭnyŏŭi 그녀의 her
kŭnyŏŭi kŏt 그녀의 것 hers
kŭnyuk 근육 muscle ◊ muscular
kŭnyuk chŭnggangje 근육 증강제 anabolic steroid
kŭpkkangha 급강하 dive; sudden drop
kŭpkkanghahada 급강하하다 dive; drop suddenly
kŭpssangssŭng 급상승 jump; surge; sudden increase
kŭpssangssŭnghada 급상승하다 jump; increase
kŭpssok naengdong naengjanggo 급속 냉동 냉장고 deep freeze (*with fast freeze capability*)
kŭpssok'ada 급속하다 be rapid, be fast
kŭpssok'i orŭda 급속히 오르다 rise rapidly, spiral
kŭpssŭp 급습 raid
kŭpssŭp'ada 급습하다 raid
kŭpssugwan 급수관 water pipe
kŭptchinjŏgin 급진적인 radical
kŭptchinjuŭi 급진주의 radicalism
kŭptchinjuŭija 급진주의자 radical (*person*)
kŭptchŭng 급증 explosion
kŭp'ada 급하다 be urgent; be impatient; be sudden
kŭp'aeng 급행 express; haste ◊ express; hasty; ***kŭp'aeng yŏlch'a / pŏssŭ*** 급행 열차 / 버스 express train / bus
kŭp'an 급한 urgent; hasty, rash
kŭp'i kada 급히 가다 dash; rush; zoom
kŭraedo 그래도 nevertheless, still, even so
kŭraem 그램 gram
kŭraendŭ p'iano 그랜드 피아노 grand piano
kŭraengk'ŭch'uk 크랭크축 crankshaft
kŭraenyudang 그래뉴당 granulated sugar
kŭraep'ik 그래픽 graphic
kŭraep'ik k'adŭ 그래픽카드 graphics card COMPUT
kŭraep'ikssŭ 그래픽스 graphics
kŭraesŏ 그래서 and; so that; that's why; ***kŭraesŏ?*** 그래서? so what?
kŭraeyaman hada 그래야만 하다 must do, have to do
kŭraeyo 그래요 indeed, really; yes
kŭreihaundŭ 그레이하운드 grayhound
kŭreip'ŭp'ŭrut'ŭ 그레이프프루트 grapefruit
kŭreip'ŭp'ŭrut'ŭ chusŭ 그레이프프루트 주스 grapefruit juice
kŭri 그리 so ◊ there; that direction; ***kŭri manch'i anŭn saram*** 그리 많지 않은 사람 not so many people
kŭrida 그리다 draw; paint
kŭrigo 그리고 and
kŭrigo nasŏ 그리고 나서 then, after that
kŭrim 그림 drawing; picture; illustration
kŭrimch'aek 그림책 picture book
kŭrimgwa kat'ŭn 그림과 같은 picturesque
kŭrimja 그림자 shadow
kŭrim kŭrigi 그림 그리기 painting
kŭrim put 그림 붓 paintbrush
kŭrimŭl kŭrida 그림을 그리다 draw
kŭrimyŏpssŏ 그림엽서 (picture) postcard
Kŭrisŭ 그리스 Greece ◊ Greek
Kŭrisŭdo 그리스도 Christ
Kŭrisŭŏ 그리스어 Greek (*language*)
kŭriwŏhada 그리워하다 miss
kŭrŏch'i anŭmyŏn 그렇지 않으면 otherwise
kŭrŏch'i anŭn kŏt kat'ayo 그렇지 않은 것 같아요 I guess not
kŭrŏch'iman 그렇지만 but
kŭrŏgil paramnida 그러길 바랍니다 I hope so
kŭrŏktchŏrŏk hada 그럭저럭 하다 get by, just manage; ***yŏrŭi ŏpsshi kŭrŏktchŏrŏk hada*** 열의 없이 그럭저럭 하다 plod along, plod on
kŭrŏk'e 그렇게 such; so; ***kŭrŏk'e***

haseyo 그렇게 하세요 do it like that; go ahead; ***kŭrŏk'e manch'i anŭn*** 그렇게 많지 않은 not so much; ***kŭrok'e mani?*** 그렇게 많이? as much as that?; ***kŭrŏl kŏyeyo*** 그럴 거예요 I expect so
kŭrŏlttŭt'an 그럴듯한 probable; plausible
kŭrŏmedo pulguhago 그럼에도 불구하고 nevertheless, nonetheless
kŭrŏmŭro 그러므로 therefore
kŭrŏmyŏnsŏdo 그러면서도 at the same time, however
kŭrŏn 그런 such, of that kind; ***kŭrŏn kŏt kat'ayo*** 그런 것 같아요 it looks that way, I guess so; ***kŭrŏn kyŏng-ue*** 그런 경우에 in that case; ***kŭrŏn sanghwang-esŏnŭn*** 그런 상황에서는 under those circumstances; ***kŭrŏnŭn kwajŏng-e*** 그러는 과정에 in the process
kŭrŏna 그러나 however; whereas; but
kŭrŏnde 그런데 but; and yet; by the way
kŭrŏt'a 그렇다 be that way; be so; be true
kŭrŏt'a hadŏrado 그렇다 하더라도 even so, but then (again)
kŭrŏt'amyŏn 그렇다면 then (*deducing*); if so
kŭrŏt'ŏrado 그렇더라도 though
kŭrol suyŏng 크롤 수영 crawl (*in swimming*)
kŭrosŏ 그로서 as such, in that capacity
kŭrŭl 그를 him
kŭrŭl ssŭda 글을 쓰다 write
kŭrŭrŏnggŏrida 그르렁거리다 purr
kŭrŭt 그릇 bowl, dish ◊ *countword for cooked rice*
kŭrŭttoen 그릇된 false
kŭrup 그룹 group
kŭrut'ŏgi 그루터기 stump
kŭ saie 그 사이에 in the meantime, meanwhile
kŭsŭllida 그슬리다 scorch
kŭsŭllin 그슬린 scorched; charred
kŭ tangshienŭn 그 당시에는 in those days
kŭ taŭmnal 그 다음날 the day after, the next day
kŭ taŭmŭi 그 다음의 following
kŭ ttae 그 때 then, at that time
kŭ ttaeenŭn 그 때에는 by then
kŭt-tta 긋다 strike
kŭŭi 그의 his
kŭŭi kŏt 그의 것 his
kŭŭllida 그을리다 singe
kŭŭrŭm 그을음 soot
kŭ yŏja 그 여자 she
ku 구 nine; sphere; district (*part of a city*)
kuaehada 구애하다 make a pass at
kubich'im 굽이침 swell
kubijida 굽이지다 wind, coil
kubunhada 구분하다 sort
kuburida 구부리다 bend, bend down
kuburigi shwiun 구부리기 쉬운 flexible
kuburŏjida 구부러지다 curve; buckle
kuburŏjin 구부러진 crooked
kubyŏl 구별 distinction; differentiation
kubyŏrhada 구별하다 tell; mark out; differentiate; ***olk'o kŭrŭmŭl kubyŏrhada*** 옳고 그름을 구별하다 know right from wrong
kuch'ehwadoeda 구체화되다 form, take shape, develop
kuch'ehwahada 구체화하다 embody, crystallize
kuch'ejŏgin 구체적인 concrete, specific; definite
kuch'ida 굳히다 cement; harden
kuch'ŏng 구청 district office
kuch'uk'am 구축함 destroyer NAUT
kuch'urhada 구출하다 extricate; release; free
kudŏbŏrin 굳어버린 confirmed, inveterate
kudŏgi 구더기 maggot
kudŏjida 굳어지다 solidify
kudu 구두 shoe
kudusoe 구두쇠 miser
kudu susŏntchip 구두 수선집 heel bar, shoe repairer
kudutppŏp 구두법 punctuation
kuduttchŏm 구두점 punctuation mark
kuduttchŏmŭl tchiktta 구두점을

찍다 punctuate
kugae 구개 palate ANAT
kugang 구강 mouth ◊ oral MED
kugida 구기다 crease, crumple
kugimsal 구김살 crease
Kugŏ 국어 Korean language
kugŏrhada 구걸하다 beg; cadge
kugoe ch'ubang 국외 추방 deportation
kugoero ch'ubanghada 국외로 추방하다 deport
kugŭn 구근 bulb BOT
kugŭpch'a 구급차 ambulance
kugŭp sangja 구급 상자 first aid kit
kugyŏjida 구겨지다 crease; ruffle
kugyŏng 구경 sightseeing; aperture; caliber
kugyŏnghada 구경하다 see; watch; see the sights
kugyŏnghwahada 국영화하다 nationalize
kugyŏngkkun 구경꾼 onlooker
kuhada 구하다 save, rescue; find, come by
kuhoek 구획 block, section
kuibi kanŭnghan 구입이 가능한 obtainable
kuiyong yŏnggye 구이용 영계 broiler (*chicken*)
kujebullŭng-in saram 구제불능인 사람 hopeless case, disaster area
kujech'aek 구제책 remedy
kujik'ada 구직하다 be seeking employment
kujo 구조 set-up; structure; rescue; salvation
kujo chojŏng 구조 조정 structural alteration; shake-up
kujoch'a 구조차 wrecker, recovery vehicle
kujodae 구조대 rescue party
kujohada 구조하다 rescue, salvage
kujowŏn 구조원 lifeguard
kujwa 구좌 account
kujwa pŏnho 구좌 번호 account number
kuk 국 soup
kuk kŭrŭt 국 그릇 soup bowl
kukch'ae 국채 national debt
kukki 국기 (national) flag
kuk-kka 국가 state, nation; national anthem
Kuk-kka Poanppŏp 국가 보안법 National Security Law
kuk-kkaŭi 국가의 national
kuk-kkyŏng 국경 border
kukko 국고 national treasury
kukkun 국군 armed forces
kukppang 국방 national defense
kukppangbi yesan 국방비 예산 defense budget
Kukppangbu 국방부 Department of Defense
Kukppangbuhanggwan 국방부 장관 Defense Secretary
kukppu mach'wi 국부 마취 local anesthetic
Kukssech'ŏng 국세청 Internal Revenue (Service)
kukssu 국수 noodles
kuktcha 국자 ladle; scoop
kuktche 국제 international
kuktchejŏgin 국제적인 international
kuktchejŏgŭro 국제적으로 internationally
kuktche kyŏrhon 국제 결혼 international marriage, mixed marriage
Kuktche Sabŏp Chaep'anso 국제 사법 재판소 International Court of Justice
kuktche suji 국제 수지 balance of payments
Kuktche T'onghwa Kigŭm 국제 통화 기금 IMF, International Monetary Fund
Kuktche Yŏnhap 국제 연합 United Nations
kuktchŏk 국적 nationality
Kuk'oe 국회 Congress; Parliament; National Assembly
kuk'oeŭi 국회의 congressional
kuk'oe ŭisadang 국회 의사당 parliamentary buildings
kuk'oe ŭiwŏn 국회 의원 member of Congress
kuk'oe wiwŏn 국회 위원 congressman
kuk'wa 국화 chrysanthemum
kul 굴 oyster; tunnel; burrow
kulbok'ada 굴복하다 surrender, give in; knuckle under; succumb

kulch'ak changch'i 굴착 장치 (oil) rig
kulch'ak-kki 굴착기 excavator
kulgok 굴곡 twist, bend
kulgŭn kŭlsshich'e 굵은 글씨체 bold *print*
kulkko t'ak'an mokssori 굵고 탁한 목소리 gruff voice
kullida 굴리다 run
kullim 군림 reign
kullimhada 군림하다 reign
kullŏ ttŏrŏjida 굴러 떨어지다 tumble
kullyŏ nŏmŏttŭrida 굴려 넘어뜨리다 roll over
kulttuk 굴뚝 chimney, smokestack; funnel
kultt'uksae 굴뚝새 wren
kumae 구매 purchase
kumaehada 구매하다 buy, purchase
kumaeja 구매자 buyer
kumaesŏrŭl ponaeda 구매서를 보내다 invoice
kumie mat-tta 구미에 맞다 cater for, meet the needs of
kumjurida 굶주리다 starve
kumŏng 구멍 hole; pit; puncture
kumŏng magae 구멍 마개 stopper
kumŏng naeda 구멍 내다 drill; make a hole
kumŏng ttult'a 구멍 뚫다 puncture; punch a hole in
kumyŏng 구명 lifesaving
kumyŏng chokki 구명 조끼 life jacket
kumyŏngjŏng 구명정 lifeboat
kumyŏng tti 구명 띠 life belt
kun 군 the military, army; county; Mr; Lord
kunae 구내 premises; yard
kunae shikttang 구내 식당 canteen (*on the premises*)
kunbi 군비 arms, weapons
kunbongmuhada 군복무하다 do military service
kun chudunji 군 주둔지 garrison
kunch'im hŭllida 군침 흘리다 slobber, drool
kunch'im tolge hanŭn 군침 돌게 하는 mouthwatering
kundae 군대 troops; the services
kundan 군단 corps
kungdung-i 궁둥이 hip; posterior; buttocks
kunggŭktchŏgin 궁극적인 final
kunggŭktchŏgŭro 궁극적으로 eventually
kunggŭmhada 궁금하다 wonder; be anxious about
kunggwŏl 궁궐 palace
kunggwŏlgat'ŭn 궁궐같은 palatial
kunghada 궁하다 be in want; ***toni kunghan*** 돈이 궁한 hard up, broke
kun-gi 군기 colors
kungji 궁지 predicament; ***kungjie moranŏt'a*** 궁지에 몰아넣다 drive into a corner
kungmin 국민 national, citizen; the people
kungmin ch'ongsaengsan 국민 총생산 GNP, gross national product
kungmin t'up'yo 국민 투표 referendum
Kungmubu Changgwan 국무부 장관 Secretary of State
Kungmuch'ongni 국무총리 Prime Minister
kungmul 국물 broth
Kungmusŏng 국무성 State Department
kungnae 국내 domestic
kungnae ch'ongsaengsan 국내 총생산 GDP, gross domestic product
kungnaesŏn pihaenggi 국내선 비행기 domestic flight
kungnaewoeesŏ 국내외에서 at home and abroad
kungnip kong-wŏn 국립 공원 national park
kun-goguma 군고구마 baked sweet potato
kunham 군함 warship
kunin 군인 soldier; serviceman
kunju 군주 monarch
kunjung 군중 crowd, crush
kunppŏp hoeŭi 군법 회의 court martial
kunsa 군사 military affairs ◊ military
kunsal 군살 flab
kunsaryŏk 군사력 military capability
kunsashisŏl 군사시설 military

installation
kunyonggi 군용기 warplane
kupssŭlgŏrinŭn 굽슬거리는 wavy
kuptta 굽다 bake; roast; broil
kup'il su ŏmnŭn 굽힐 수 없는 inflexible
kurhaji ank'o haenaeda 굴하지 않고 해내다 carry on undaunted
kuri 구리 copper
kurŏngt'ŏng-i 구렁텅이 abyss
kurŭda 구르다 roll
kurŭm 구름 cloud
kurŭng 구릉 hill ◊ hilly
kuryŏk 굴욕 humiliation
kuryogŭl chuda 굴욕을 주다 humiliate
kuryokkamŭl katkkehada 굴욕감을 갖게하다 feel humiliated
kuryoktchŏgin 굴욕적인 humiliating
kuryu chung 구류 중 in custody
kuryu chung-ida 구류 중이다 be in custody; be on remand
kuryushik'ida 구류시키다 remand in custody
kusaek 구색 selection, assortment
kusang 구상 framework
Kusegun 구세군 Salvation Army
Kuseju 구세주 Lord of Salvation, Savior
kushik 구식 old-fashioned
kuship 구십 ninety
kusŏge(sŏ) 구석에(서) in the corner
kusŏgŭro molda 구석으로 몰다 corner, drive into a corner
kusŏk 구석 corner
kusŏng 구성 composition, make-up; plot
kusŏngdoeda 구성되다 comprise
kusŏngdoeŏ it-tta 구성되어 있다 be composed of
kusŏnghada 구성하다 compose, constitute, make up, form
kusŏng yoso 구성 요소 component, constituent
kusok'ada 구속하다 tie down, restrict; intern
kusongnyŏgi innŭn 구속력이 있는 binding
kusŭl 구슬 beads
kusŭllida 구슬리다 coax
kusŭlp'ŭn 구슬픈 plaintive
kusŭlp'ŭn sori 구슬픈 소리 wail
kusŭlp'ŭn sorirŭl naeda 구슬픈 소리를 내다 wail
kusul 구술 oral statement ◊ oral *exam*
kusurhada 구술하다 dictate
kut 굿 shaman rite of exorcism
kutkke kyŏlsshimhada 굳게 결심하다 make a firm decision, put one's foot down, be firm
kut-tta 굳다 harden
kut'a 구타 beating
kut'ahada 구타하다 beat up
kut'o 구토 vomit
kuŭn 구운 baked; roasted
kuwŏjida 구워지다 be roasted
kuwŏl 구월 September
kuwŏn 구원 salvation
kuwŏnhada 구원하다 redeem
Kuyak Sŏngsŏ 구약 성서 Old Testament
kuyŏk 구역 territory
kuyŏktchil nanŭn 구역질 나는 disgusting, sick
kwa 과 section, department; faculty; lesson ◊ with ◊ and; as, like
kwabansu 과반수 majority
kwabansuida 과반수이다 be in the majority
kwabu 과부 widow
kwabugat'ŭn shinse 과부같은 신세 grass widow
kwabuhahada 과부하하다 overload
kwadae p'yŏngkkadoen 과대 평가된 overrated
kwadae p'yŏngkkahada 과대 평가하다 overestimate
kwadae sŏnjŏn 과대 선전 hype
kwadahage chibuldoen 과다하게 지불된 overpaid
kwadahan 과다한 excessive
kwadogi 과도기 transitional period
kwadojŏgin 과도적인 transitional
kwaench'ant'a 괜찮다 be OK, be alright; ***kwaench'anayo*** **괜찮아요** it's not bad; that's alright; ***anio, kwaench'ansŭmnida*** **아니오, 괜찮습니다** no, I don't mind; ***tambaerŭl p'iwŏdo kwaench'ank'essŭmnikka?*** **담배를**

피워도 괜찮겠습니까? do you mind if I smoke?
kwaench'anŭn 괜찮은 acceptable
kwaench'anŭn chŏngdoŭi 괜찮은 정도의 decent, acceptable
kwagamhan 과감한 drastic
kwagamhi haeboda 과감히 해보다 venture boldly
kwagŏ 과거 past; civil service examination (*formerly*)
kwagŏe 과거에 in the past
kwagŏ punsa 과거 분사 past participle
kwagŏ shije 과거 시제 past tense
kwagyŏngnonja 과격론자 extremist
kwahak 과학 science
kwahak kisul 과학 기술 technology
kwahak kisul kongp'otchŭng 과학 기술 공포증 technophobia
kwahak kisulsang-ŭi 과학 기술상의 technological
Kwahak-kkisulch'ŏ 과학기술처 Ministry of Science and Technology
kwahaktcha 과학자 scientist
kwahaktchŏgin 과학적인 scientific
kwail 과일 fruit
kwail chyussŭ 과일 쥬스 fruit juice
kwail saellŏdŭ 과일 샐러드 fruit salad
kwaing pogyong 과잉 복용 overdose
kwaing pohohada 과잉 보호하다 overprotect
kwajang 과장 exaggeration; department manager
kwajangdoeda 과장되다 be over the top, be exaggerated
kwajangdoen 과장된 exaggerated; melodramatic, theatrical
kwajanghada 과장하다 exaggerate
kwajanghan sŏnjŏn 과장한 선전 hype
kwajanghayŏ p'yohyŏnhada 과장하여 표현하다 dramatize, exaggerate
kwajaryu 과자류 confectionery
kwaje 과제 project
kwajŏng 과정 process
kwajunghan 과중한 stiff
kwak 곽 carton; holder; tub
kwallamgaek 관람객 visitor (*at exhibition*)
kwallamsŏk 관람석 stand; booth (*at exhibition*)
kwalli 관리 administration; management; mandarin
kwalliin 관리인 administrator; manager; caretaker
kwallija 관리자 administrator; manager
kwalliŭi 관리의 managerial
kwallyŏn 관련 connection, link; involvement; ***...wa / kwa kwallyŏnhayŏ*** ...와 / 과 관련하여 in connection with
kwallyŏndoeda 관련되다 be connected with, be involved in; be relevant; be related
kwallyŏndoen 관련된 related; relevant
kwallyŏni innŭn 관련이 있는 related
kwallyŏni it-tta 관련이 있다 be related to; be relevant to
kwallyŏni ŏmnŭn 관련이 없는 irrelevant
kwallyŏnshik'ida 관련시키다 bring in, involve; connect, link
kwallyŏnssŏng 관련성 relevance
kwallyo 관료 bureaucrat
kwallyoje 관료제 bureaucracy
kwallyojŏgin 관료적인 bureaucratic
kwallyojuŭi 관료주의 bureaucracy, red tape
kwalmok'al manhan 괄목할 만한 spectacular
kwaminhan 과민한 hypersensitive
kwamok 과목 subject (*branch of learning*)
kwan 관 casket, coffin; pipe; tube; crown; mansion
kwanak-kki 관악기 wind instrument
kwanch'al 관찰 observation
kwanch'allyŏgi yerihan 관찰력이 예리한 observant
kwanch'altcha 관찰자 observer
kwanch'arhada 관찰하다 observe
kwanch'ŏng 관청 office, position
kwanch'ŭksso 관측소 observatory
kwandaehada 관대하다 be generous
kwandaehan 관대한 generous; broadminded; lenient; soft; permissive

-kwang -광 enthusiast, fan; craze, mania; ***yŏnghwagwang* / *chaejŭgwang*** 영화광 / 재즈광 movie / jazz freak
kwan-gae 관개 irrigation
kwan-gaehada 관개하다 irrigate
kwan-gaek 관객 spectator
kwan-gaeyong suro 관개용 수로 irrigation canal
kwangbŏmwihan 광범위한 extensive, wide
Kwangboktchŏl 광복절 Liberation Day
kwangbu 광부 miner
kwangch'ŏnsu 광천수 mineral water
kwangch'ŭng 광층 seam (*of ore*)
kwangdaeppyŏ 광대뼈 cheekbone
kwanggagŭi 광각의 wide-angle
kwanggo 광고 advertisement, advert, commercial; advertising
kwanggohada 광고하다 advertise; publicize
kwanggoju 광고주 advertiser
kwanggo munan 광고 문안 advertising copy, text
kwanggo-ŏp 광고업 advertising
kwanggo pangsong 광고 방송 commercial break
kwanggop'an 광고판 billboard
kwanggo p'osŭt'ŏ 광고 포스터 bill, poster
kwanggo taehaengsa 광고 대행사 advertising agency
kwanggyŏng 광경 sight, spectacle
kwanggyŏnppyŏng 광견병 rabies
kwanghwarhan 광활한 vast
kwangjang 광장 square, plaza
kwangkki 광기 madness, insanity
kwangmul 광물 mineral
kwangnaeda 광내다 polish
kwangnŭng 관능 sensuality
kwangnŭngtchŏgin 관능적인 sensual
kwangnyŏn 광년 light year
kwang-ŏp 광업 mining
kwangp'ok'aejida 광폭해지다 go berserk
kwangsan 광산 mine
kwangshinja 광신자 fanatic
kwangshinjŏgin 광신적인 fanatical
kwangsŏk 광석 ore
kwangsŏmnyu 광섬유 fiber optics
kwangsŏmnyuŭi 광섬유의 fiber optic
kwangt'aegi ŏmnŭn 광택이 없는 matt
kwangt'aek nanŭn 광택 나는 glossy
kwangt'aek p'eint'ŭ 광택 페인트 gloss paint
kwangt'aektche 광택제 polish
kwan-gwang 관광 tour; sightseeing
kwan-gwang annaeso 관광 안내소 tourist (information) office
kwan-gwanggaek 관광객 visitor, tourist
kwan-gwanghada 관광하다 tour; go sightseeing
kwan-gwang-ŏp 관광업 tourism
kwan-gwang-ŏptcha 관광업자 tour operator
kwan-gwang yŏhaeng 관광 여행 sightseeing tour
kwan-gye 관계 connection, relationship
kwan-gyedoeda 관계되다 get involved with
kwan-gyedoenŭn 관계되는 concerned, involved
kwan-gyega kkŭnnada 관계가 끝나다 be through, be finished
kwan-gyehada 관계하다 involve, concern; get mixed up with
kwan-gyeŏmnŭn 관계없는 unrelated
kwan-gyeŏpsshi 관계없이 irrespective of
kwan-gyerŭl kkŭnt'a 관계를 끊다 dissociate oneself from
kwanhada 관하다 be related to; ***...e kwanhaesŏ*** ...에 관해서 with regard to; ***i chŏme kwanhaesŏnŭn*** 이 점에 관해서는 in this regard; ***...e kwanhan*** ...에 관한 about, concerning; ***...e kwanhayŏ*** ...에 관하여 concerning; ***muŏse kwanhan kŏshimnikka?*** 무엇에 관한 것입니까? what's it about?
kwanhae tŭt-tta 관해 듣다 hear about
kwanjanori 관자놀이 temple ANAT
kwanjet'ap 관제탑 control tower
kwanjŏl 관절 joint ANAT
kwanjŏllyŏm 관절염 arthritis

kwanjung 관중 crowd, audience
kwanjungsŏk 관중석 auditorium
kwanmok 관목 bush, shrub; shrubbery
kwanmun 관문 gateway
kwannŭngjŏgin 관능적인 erotic; tasty; sexy; sultry
kwannŭngjuŭi 관능주의 eroticism
kwannyong 관용 forgiveness; clemency
kwansa 관사 article
kwanse 관세 customs; duty, tariff
Kwanseguk 관세국 Customs and Tariff Bureau
kwanshim 관심 interest
kwanshimi innŭn 관심이 있는 interested
kwanshimsa 관심사 concern, business
kwanshimŭl kajida 관심을 가지다 care; care about; have an interest in
kwansŭp 관습 custom, convention; institution
kwansŭppŏp 관습법 unwritten law
kwansŭptchŏgin 관습적인 customary; unwritten
kwantchŏm 관점 position, point of view; ***chŏrŏhan kwantchŏmesŏ*** 저러한 관점에서 from that point of view, in that respect
kwant'onghada 관통하다 pierce, penetrate
kwanŭro ponaeda 관으로 보내다 pipe
kwanyŏgŭi hanbokp'an 과녁의 한복판 bull's-eye
kwanyŏgŭl match'uda 과녁을 맞추다 hit the bull's-eye
kwanyŏhada 관여하다 concern oneself with
kwanyŏk 과녁 target
kwanyong 관용 tolerance
kwanyong innŭn 관용 있는 tolerant
kwanyongjŏgin 관용적인 idiomatic
kwanyong-ŏ 관용어 idiom
kwarho 괄호 bracket; parenthesis
kwaro 과로 overwork
kwarohada 과로하다 overwork
kwaroshik'ida 과로시키다 overwork *s.o.*
kwase 과세 taxation
kwashi 과시 demonstration, display
kwashihada 과시하다 parade, flaunt, show off
kwashihanŭn 과시하는 ostentatious
kwashil 과실 malpractice
kwasok 과속 speeding
kwasok pŏlgŭm 과속 벌금 speeding fine
kwasok'ada 과속하다 speed, drive too quickly
kwaso p'yŏngkkahada 과소 평가하다 minimize; undervalue; underestimate
kwasuwŏn 과수원 orchard
kwayuk 과육 pulp
kwedo 궤도 orbit
kweyang 궤양 ulcer
kwi 귀 ear
kwiari 귀앓이 earache
kwich'ank'e hada 귀찮게 하다 bother, disturb
kwich'ank'e kulda 귀찮게 굴다 pester
kwich'ant'a 귀찮다 be a nuisance; ***irŏk'e kwich'anŭl suga!*** 이렇게 귀찮을 수가! what a nuisance!
kwich'anŭn 귀찮은 tiresome, annoying
kwich'ŏng-i ttŏrŏjil ttŭt'an 귀청이 떨어질 듯한 deafening, ear-piercing
kwie kŏsŭllinŭn 귀에 거슬리는 grating; strident; harsh
kwiga 귀가 homecoming
kwigahada 귀가하다 return home
kwiga kire 귀가 길에 homeward (*to own country*)
kwiga mŏn 귀가 먼 hard of hearing
kwigori 귀고리 earring
kwiguk kire 귀국 길에 homeward (*to own country*)
kwihwahada 귀화하다 become naturalized
kwihwan 귀환 return
kwiji 귀지 earwax
kwijok 귀족 aristocrat; nobility
kwijunghada 귀중하다 be precious
kwijunghan 귀중한 precious, valuable
kwijungp'um 귀중품 valuables
kwimŏgŭn 귀먹은 deaf
kwimŏk-kke hada 귀먹게 하다

deafen
kwiri 귀리 oats
kwirŭl tchonggŭt seuda 귀를 쫑긋 세우다 prick up one's ears
kwishin 귀신 ghost
kwishin-gat'ŭn 귀신같은 ghostly
kwitturami 귀뚜라미 cricket (*insect*)
kwiyŏptta 귀엽다 be cute, be lovable
kwiyŏun 귀여운 cute, pretty
kwŏlli 권리 right, claim; title
kwŏllyŏk 권력 power, authority
kwŏllyŏk chipttan 권력 집단 the Establishment
kwŏn 권 bloc ◊ *countword for books*
kwŏnch'ong 권총 pistol, revolver
kwŏnch'ongjip 권총집 holster
kwŏnhada 권하다 offer
kwŏnhan puyŏ 권한 부여 mandate, authority
kwŏnhanŭl chuda 권한을 주다 authorize
kwŏnjwa-esŏ ttŏrŏjida 권좌에서 떨어지다 fall from power
kwŏnt'ae 권태 boredom
kwŏnt'u 권투 boxing
kwŏnt'uhada 권투하다 box SP
kwŏnt'u shihap 권투 시합 boxing match
kwŏnt'u sŏnsu 권투 선수 boxer
kwŏnwi 권위 authority
kwŏnwiinnŭn 권위있는 authoritative, definitive
kwŏnwijaida 권위자이다 be an authority
kwŏnyanggi 권양기 winch, windlass
kwŏnyuhada 권유하다 canvass; drum up
-kye -계: ***chaejŭgye / mayak-kkye*** 재즈계 / 마약계 jazz scene / drugs scene; ***k'ŏmpyut'ŏgye / yŏngŭk-kkye*** 컴퓨터계 / 연극계 the world of computers / the world of the theater
kye 계 credit union; loan club
kyebu 계부 stepfather
kyedan 계단 stair, step
kyedanshik pat 계단식 밭 terraced field
kyeganŭro 계간으로 quarterly
kyegi 계기 gauge
kyegip'an 계기판 dashboard
kyegŏlssŭre mŏktta 게걸스레 먹다 wolf (down)
kyegŭp 계급 class, rank; stripe
kyegŭp chojik 계급 조직 hierarchy
kyegŭp t'ujaeng 계급 투쟁 class warfare
kyehoek 계획 plan; project; strategy
kyehoektchŏgin 계획적인 premeditated
kyehoektchŏgin p'agoe 계획적인 파괴 sabotage
kyehoektchŏgŭro 계획적으로 systematically
kyehoektchŏgŭro p'agoehada 계획적으로 파괴하다 sabotage
kyehoek'ada 계획하다 plan, propose
kyejibae 계집애 little girl; chick, babe
kyejip 계집 female *pej*
kyejŏl 계절 season
kyeju kyŏnggi 계주 경기 relay
kyemo 계모 stepmother
kyemongdoen 계몽된 enlightened, liberal
kyemonghada 계몽하다 enlighten
kyeŏmnyŏng 계엄령 martial law
kyep'i 계피 cinnamon
kyeran 계란 egg
kyeran hurai 계란 후라이 fried egg
kyeryak 계략 plot, conspiracy
kyeryanggi 계량기 meter
kyesan 계산 sum; calculation
kyesandae 계산대 checkout; counter; cash desk
kyesan-gi 계산기 calculator
kyesanhada 계산하다 count, calculate
kyesanjŏgin 계산적인 calculating
kyesansŏ 계산서 bill, check
kyesansŏro ch'ŏngguhada 계산서로 청구하다 bill, invoice
kyesanŭl hal su innŭn 계산을 할 수 있는 numerate
kyesok irŏn sangt'aeramyŏn 계속 이런 상태라면 at this rate; if things go on like this
kyesok ... it-tta 계속 ... 있다 remain, stay
kyesok kajigo it-tta 계속 가지고 있다 hold on to, keep
kyesok myŏt shigan tong-an 계속 몇 시간 동안 for hours on end
kyesok namait-tta 계속 남아있다

hold out
kyesok noryŏk'ada 계속 노력하다 keep (on) trying
kyesok panbok'aesŏ 계속 반복해서 over and over again
kyesok panghaehada 계속 방해하다 keep (on) interrupting
kyesok salda 계속 살다 live on
kyesok seda 계속 세다 keep count of
kyesok shich'ŏnghada 계속 시청하다 follow *TV series, news*
kyesoktchŏgin 계속적인 continual
kyesok ttŏdŭrŏdaeda 계속 떠들어대다 go on about
kyesokttoeda 계속되다 continue
kyesokttoenŭn 계속되는 constant, continuous
kyesok yŏllak'ada 계속 연락하다 keep up with, stay in touch with
kyesok yujihada 계속 유지하다 retain
kyesok'ada 계속하다 continue, carry on; pursue; ***kyesok kŏt-tta / iyagi hada*** 계속 걷다 / 이야기 하다 walk / talk on; ***kyesok ibwŏnhae itkke hada*** 계속 입원해 있게 하다 keep in the hospital
kyesok'aesŏ 계속해서 in succession; perpetually; persistently; continually
kyesok'aesŏ hada 계속해서 하다 persevere
kyesok'aesŏ irŏnada 계속해서 일어나다 follow, dog
kyesŭng 계승 succession (*to the throne*)
kyesŭnghada 계승하다 succeed (*to the throne*)
kyesu 계수 sister-in-law (*younger brother's wife*)
kyeyak 계약 contract, agreement; deal
kyeyak-kkŭm 계약금 down payment, deposit
kyeyakssang-ŭi 계약상의 contractual
kyeyaktcha 계약자 contractor
kyeyak wiban 계약 위반 breach of contract
kyŏdŭrang-i 겨드랑이 armpit
kyŏgillo 격일로 on alternate days
kyŏja 겨자 mustard
kyŏk'an 격한 heated
kyŏkppyŏn 격변 upheaval; revulsion
kyŏkp'ahada 격파하다 whip, defeat
kyŏksshimhan 격심한 vigorous
kyŏktcha 격자 grid
kyŏktta 겪다 go through, experience
kyŏkt'oehada 격퇴하다 repel
kyŏl 결 texture
kyŏlbaek 결백 innocence; purity
kyŏlbaek'an 결백한 innocent; pure
kyŏlbyŏl 결별 separation
kyŏlgŭn 결근 absence
kyŏlgŭnhan 결근한 absent
kyŏlguk 결국 after all, in the end; ***kyŏlguk pyŏng-wŏn shinserŭl chida*** 결국 병원 신세를 지다 wind up in the hospital
kyŏlkkwa 결과 consequence, result; outcome
kyŏlk'o 결코 surely, assuredly
kyŏllon 결론 conclusion; decision; ***kyŏllone irŭda*** 결론에 이르다 come to a decision
kyŏllonŭl naerida 결론을 내리다 conclude, deduce
kyŏlmal 결말 ending; conclusion; upshot
kyŏlmangnyŏm 결막염 conjunctivitis
kyŏlmarŭl chit-tta 결말을 짖다 wind up; tie up the loose ends
kyŏlp'ip 결핍 lack, deficiency
kyŏlp'ipttoeda 결핍되다 be deficient in
kyŏlssandoeda 결산되다 balance
kyŏlsshim 결심 determination, resolution
kyŏlsshimhada 결심하다 decide
kyŏlsshimhan 결심한 determined
kyŏlssŏk 결석 absence
kyŏlssŏk'ada 결석하다 be absent
kyŏlssŏk'an 결석한 absent
kyŏlssok 결속 solidarity
kyŏlssŭng 결승 final
kyŏlssŭngjŏm 결승점 winning post, finish
kyŏlssŭngjŏn 결승전 finals; decider SP
kyŏlssŭngjŏn ch'ultchŏn sŏnsu 결승전 출전 선수 finalist
kyŏlssŭngsŏn 결승선 finishing line

kyŏltchang 결장 colon ANAT
kyŏltchŏm 결점 defect, shortcoming
kyŏltchŏm innŭn 결점 있는 faulty
kyŏltchŏmi innŭn 결점이 있는 defective, faulty
kyŏltchŏng 결정 decision; ***kyŏltchŏng-ŭl hada*** 결정을 하다 make a decision; ***kyŏltchŏng-ŭl naerida*** 결정을 내리다 decide, settle
kyŏltchŏngdoeji anŭn 결정되지 않은 unsettled, undecided
kyŏltchŏnghada 결정하다 decide, determine
kyŏltchŏnghaji mot'ada 결정하지 못하다 be undecided about; be unable to decide
kyŏltchŏngjŏgin 결정적인 conclusive; critical, crucial; definitive
kyŏltchŏngjŏgin kŏmt'o 결정적인 검토 acid test
kyŏltchŏngjŏk shigi 결정적 시기 decisive moment
kyŏlttanssŏng-i ŏmnŭn 결단성이 없는 indecisive
kyŏmja 겸자 forceps
kyŏmson 겸손 humility, modesty
kyŏmsonhada 겸손하다 be humble, be modest
kyŏmsonhan 겸손한 modest, unassuming
kyŏnbon 견본 sample, specimen
kyŏndida 견디다 endure, wear, last; cope; do without; resist
kyŏndil su innŭn 견딜 수 있는 bearable
kyŏndil su ŏmnŭn 견딜 수 없는 unbearable
kyŏndiŏnaeda 견디어내다 withstand
...kyŏng ...경 around, about; ***idal malgyŏng*** 이달 말경 around the end of this month
kyŏngapkkol 견갑골 shoulder blade
kyŏngbi 경비 expenses
kyŏngbirŭl chŏlgamhanŭn 경비를 절감하는 cost-conscious
kyŏngbiwŏn 경비원 security guard; bouncer
kyŏngbŏmtchoe 경범죄 misdemeanor
kyŏngbogi 경보기 alarm
kyŏngboŭm 경보음 alert; signal
kyŏngch'al 경찰 police; cop; ***kyŏngch'are ch'asuhada*** 경찰에 자수하다 give oneself up to the police
kyŏngch'algwan 경찰관 policeman; marshal
kyŏngch'al kuk-kka 경찰 국가 police state
kyŏngch'al kuktchang 경찰 국장 superintendent
kyŏngch'al sarin chŏndam pusŏ 경찰 살인 전담 부서 homicide (department)
kyŏngch'alsŏ 경찰서 police station
kyŏngch'i 경치 landscape; view
kyŏngch'ŏp 경첩 hinge
kyŏngdo 경도 longitude
kyŏnggam sayu 경감 사유 mitigating circumstances
kyŏnggi 경기 game; meet; fight; play; business; things; times
kyŏnggi ch'amgaja 경기 참가자 participant, entrant SP
kyŏnggi ch'imch'e 경기 침체 (economic) downturn
kyŏnggiga p'okttŭnghada 경기가 폭등하다 boom COM
kyŏnggija 경기자 player
kyŏnggijang 경기장 playing field; stadium
kyŏnggi kirok 경기 기록 record SP
kyŏnggi p'okttŭng 경기 폭등 boom
kyŏnggŏnhan 경건한 pious, devout
kyŏnggo 경고 alarm, warning
kyŏnggohada 경고하다 warn, alert; raise the alarm
kyŏnggwa 경과 passage (*of time*)
kyŏnggwahada 경과하다 elapse
kyŏnggwan 경관 officer; sights
kyŏnggye 경계 boundary, limit
kyŏnggyehada 경계하다 be on one's guard against, look out for
kyŏnggyehanŭn 경계하는 alert
kyŏnggyesŏn 경계선 boundary, border
kyŏnghŏm 경험 experience
kyŏnghŏminnŭn 경험있는 experienced
kyŏnghŏmi ŏmnŭn 경험이 없는

inexperienced
kyŏnghŏmŭl ssahŭn 경험을 쌓은 seasoned *traveler etc*
kyŏnghohada 경호하다 escort, act as bodyguard to
kyŏnghowŏn 경호원 bodyguard
kyŏnghyang 경향 tendency; trend
kyŏnghyang-i it-tta 경향이 있다 tend toward; ***...nŭn kyŏnghyang-i it-tta*** ...는 경향이 있다 be liable to
kyŏngjaeng 경쟁 contest; rivalry; competition
kyŏngjaenghada 경쟁하다 compete; rival
kyŏngjaengja 경쟁자 competitor, rival; competitors; the competition
kyŏngjaengjŏgin 경쟁적인 competitive *person*
kyŏngjaengnyŏk innŭn 경쟁력 있는 competitive *bid*
kyŏngjaeng sangdae 경쟁 상대 competitor
kyŏngjak 경작 cultivation
kyŏngjak'ada 경작하다 plow, till; cultivate
kyŏngje 경제 economy
kyŏngje chaptchi 경제 잡지 financial magazine
kyŏngje chejae 경제 제재 economic sanctions
kyŏngjehak 경제학 economics
kyŏngjehaktcha 경제학자 economist
kyŏngjejŏgin 경제적인 economical, cheap
kyŏngjejŏgŭro 경제적으로 economically
kyŏngjejŏk ch'ŭngmyŏn 경제적 측면 economics; financial aspects
kyŏngjeŭi 경제의 economic
kyŏngjŏgŭl ullida 경적을 울리다 hoot, sound one's horn
kyŏngjŏk 경적 horn
kyŏngjŏn 경전 holy scriptures, holy book
kyŏngju 경주 race; racing
kyŏngjuch'a 경주차 racing car
kyŏngjuhada 경주하다 race, run
kyŏngjuja 경주자 runner, athlete; racing driver
kyŏngjujang 경주장 racetrack
kyŏngju k'osŭ 경주 코스 racecourse
kyŏngjuma 경주마 racehorse
kyŏngma 경마 horse race; the races
kyŏngmae 경매 auction
kyŏngmaehada 경매하다 auction
kyŏngmyŏl 경멸 contempt, scorn
kyŏngmyŏrhada 경멸하다 despise; scorn
kyŏngmyŏrhal manhan 경멸할 만한 contemptible
kyŏngmyŏrhanŭn 경멸하는 derogatory; scornful
kyŏngmyŏrŏ 경멸어 pejorative
kyŏngnapkko 격납고 hangar
kyŏngnihayŏ 격리 하여 in isolation
kyŏngni pyŏngdong 격리 병동 isolation ward
kyŏngnishik'ida 격리시키다 isolate
kyŏngno 격노 rage, fury
kyŏngnohada 격노하다 rage, be in a rage
kyŏngnohanŭn 격노하는 furious
kyŏngno shik'ida 격노 시키다 infuriate
kyŏngnye 경례 salute; bow
kyŏngnyehada 경례하다 salute; bow
kyŏngnyerŭl pat-tta 경례를 받다 take the salute
kyŏngnyŏ 격려 boost, encouragement
kyŏngnyŏhada 격려하다 encourage, incite
kyŏngnyŏk 경력 career, profession; experience
kyŏngnyŏl 격렬 intensity
kyŏngnyŏn 경련 convulsion; twitch
kyŏngnyŏng 경영 management (*of big company*)
kyŏngnyŏnghada 경영하다 manage *big company*
kyŏngnyŏnghak 경영학 business studies; management studies
kyŏngnyŏnghak sŏkssa 경영학 석사 Master's in Business Administration, MBA
kyŏngnyŏng-in 경영인 manager, executive; proprietor
kyŏngnyŏngja 경영자 manager (*of company*)
kyŏngnyŏngjin 경영진 management, managers
kyŏngnyŏngju 경영주 manager

(*owner*)
kyŏngnyŏngkkwŏn maemae 경영권 매매 management buyout
kyŏngnyŏng sangdamja 경영 상담자 management consultant
kyŏngnyŏng taehagwŏn 경영 대학원 business school
kyŏngnyŏngt'im 경영팀 management team
kyŏngnyŏni ilda 경련이 일다 twitch; jerk
kyŏng-nyŏnŭi 격년의 biennial
kyŏngnyŏrhada 격렬하다 be violent
kyŏngnyŏrhaejida 격렬해지다 intensify
kyŏngnyŏrhage 격렬하게 furiously, violently; with a vengeance
kyŏngnyŏrham 격렬함 violence
kyŏngnyŏrhan 격렬한 drastic *change*; stormy, turbulent; violent
kyŏngnyŏ yŏnsŏl 격려 연설 pep talk
kyŏngnyuhayŏ 경유하여 via
kyŏngŏnhan 경건한 reverent
kyŏn-gohan 견고한 solid, strong
kyŏngsa 경사 slant; slope
kyŏngsado 경사도 gradient
kyŏngsajida 경사지다 slope; descend
kyŏngsa-myŏn 경사면 side (*of mountain*)
kyŏngshihada 경시하다 downplay
kyŏngŭirŭl p'yohada 경의를 표하다 show respect to
kyŏng-u 경우 case, instance
kyŏn-gwa 견과 nut
kyŏng-wi 경위 inspector
kyŏngyŏng kwalli 경영 관리 running (*of business*)
kyŏnhae 견해 view, opinion
kyŏninhada 견인하다 tow away
kyŏninnyong patchul 견인용 밧줄 towrope
kyŏnje 견제 restraint, brake
kyŏnjŏk 견적 estimate; quotation
kyŏnjŏk'ada 견적하다 quote
kyŏnnunjil 곁눈질 leer
kyŏnnunjirhada 곁눈질하다 look away; sneak a glance at
kyŏnsonhan 겸손한 humble
kyŏnsŭp 견습 probation
kyŏnsŭp kigan 견습 기간 trial period, probation period
kyŏnsŭp kwajŏng 견습 과정 training course
kyŏnsŭpsaeng 견습생 apprentice; trainee
kyŏnuda 겨누다 point
kyŏnyang 겨냥 aim
kyŏnyanghada 겨냥하다 aim (at); measure
kyŏpch'ida 겹치다 clash
kyŏrhaek 결핵 tuberculosis
kyŏrhamŭl koch'ida 결함을 고치다 debug
kyŏrhap 결합 combination
kyŏrhap'ada 결합하다 combine, unite
kyŏrhon 결혼 marriage (*institution*)
kyŏrhon chŭngmyŏngsŏ 결혼 증명서 marriage certificate
kyŏrhon kinyŏmil 결혼 기념일 wedding anniversary
kyŏrhon panji 결혼 반지 wedding ring
kyŏrhon saenghwal 결혼 생활 married life; marriage
kyŏrhon sangdamwŏn 결혼 상담원 marriage counselor
kyŏrhon yego 결혼 예고 banns
kyŏrhonhada 결혼하다 marry, get married
kyŏrhonhan 결혼한 married
kyŏrhonshik 결혼식 marriage, wedding
kyŏrhonshingnal 결혼식날 wedding day
kyŏrhonŭi 결혼의 marital
kyŏron chŏnŭi 결혼 전의 prenuptial
kyŏruda 겨루다 play *opponent*; fight, contest
kyŏryŏnham 결연함 resolution, determination
kyŏtssoe 곁쇠 skeleton key
kyŏt'e(sŏ) 곁에(서) beside, next to
kyŏu 겨우 barely, only just
kyŏul 겨울 winter
kyŏul kat'ŭn 겨울같은 wintry
kyŏul sŭp'och'ŭ 겨울 스포츠 winter sports
kyobok 교복 uniform
kyobok sang-ŭi 교복 상의 tunic
kyoch'a 교차 intersection

kyoch'ahada 교차하다 intersect, cross
kyoch'ajŏm 교차점 junction
kyoch'ak sangt'ae 교착 상태 deadlock
kyoch'aro 교차로 cross street
kyoch'ehada 교체하다 alternate
kyodae 교대 shift; turn; ***kyodaero hada*** 교대로 하다 take turns in doing, do in rotation; ***ch'arŭl kyodaero unjŏnhada*** 차를 교대로 운전하다 take turns at the wheel
kyodaehada 교대하다 relieve, take over from
kyodae kŭnmu 교대 근무 shift work
kyodogwan 교도관 guard
kyodoso 교도소 jail, penitentiary
kyodosojang 교도소장 prison warden
kyogu mokssa 교구 목사 vicar
kyogu mokssagwan 교구 목사관 vicarage
kyohoe 교회 church
kyohun 교훈 moral, message; school motto
kyohwan 교환 exchange, flow
kyohwang 교황 pope
kyohwanhada 교환하다 exchange, trade; ***muŏtkkwa muŏsŭl kyohwanhada*** 무엇과 무엇을 교환하다 trade sth for sth
kyohwan kanŭng t'onghwa 교환 가능 통화 hard currency
kyohwansu 교환수 operator TELEC
kyohwanŭro 교환으로 in exchange; in exchange for
kyohwarham 교활함 cunning
kyohwarhan 교활한 crafty, cunning, sly; devious
kyohyanggok 교향곡 symphony
kyojang 교장 principal (*of school*)
kyoje 교제 contact
kyojehada 교제하다 associate with; keep company
kyojigwŏn 교직원 faculty, teaching staff
kyojik 교직 teaching (*profession*)
kyojŏn 교전 battle; war; hostilities
kyojŏn chung-ida 교전 중이다 be at war
kyojŏng 교정 manipulation
kyojŏnghada 교정하다 manipulate; 교정하다 correct *proofs*
kyojŏngswae 교정쇄 proof (*of book*)
kyokkwa kwajŏng 교과 과정 course (*series of lessons*); curriculum
kyokkwasŏ 교과서 textbook
kyomushil 교무실 staffroom
kyomyohada 교묘하다 be crafty; be clever; ***kyomyohage shiganŭl kkŭlda*** 교묘하게 시간을 끌다 stall, play for time
kyomyohan 교묘한 sneaky, crafty
kyomyohi hoep'ihada 교묘히 회피하다 evade, dodge *responsibility*
kyomyohi umjigida 교묘히 움직이다 maneuver
kyo-oe 교외 suburb
kyop'yŏn 교편 pointer
kyori 교리 dogma
kyoryu 교류 alternating current
kyosa 교사 teacher; academic; teachers; staff
kyosaeng 교생 student teacher
kyosa hullyŏn 교사 훈련 teacher training
kyosarhada 교살하다 strangle
kyoshil 교실 classroom
kyoshin 교신 contact
kyoshinhada 교신하다 contact
kyosŏp 교섭 approach; advance; proposal
kyosu 교수 professor
kyosudae 교수대 gallows
kyosuhyŏng-e ch'ŏhada 교수형에 처하다 string up, hang
kyot'ong 교통 traffic
Kyot'ongbu 교통부 Department of Transportation
kyot'ong ch'ejŭng 교통 체증 traffic jam
kyot'ong honjap 교통 혼잡 jam ; traffic congestion
kyot'ongmang chŏngch'e 교통망 정체 gridlock
kyot'ong p'yojip'an 교통 표지판 signpost
Kyot'ong Pŏpkkyu 교통 법규 Highway Code, rules of the road
kyot'ong shinho 교통 신호 traffic sign

kyot'ong sudan 교통 수단 means of transportation
kyot'ong sun-gyŏng 교통 순경 traffic cop; traffic police
kyoyang-i ŏmnŭn 교양이 없는 lowbrow
kyoyuge kwanhan 교육에 관한 educational
kyoyuk 교육 education; training
kyoyukpat-tta 교육받다 be educated; receive one's training
kyoyukpadŭn 교육받은 educated
kyoyukpat-tchi mot'an 교육받지 못한 uneducated
Kyoyukppu 교육부 Department of Education
kyoyukshik'ida 교육시키다 train
kyoyuk shilssŭpssaeng 교육 실습생 student teacher
kyoyuktchŏgin 교육적인 educational, instructive, informative
kyoyuk'ada 교육하다 educate
kyuch'igŭl ttarŭda 규칙을 따르다 follow the rules, toe the line
kyuch'ik 규칙 rule, regulation
kyuch'iktchŏgin 규칙적인 regular
kyugyŏk'wahada 규격화하다 standardize
kyujehada 규제하다 regulate
kyuje yangmul 규제 약물 controlled substance
kyujŏng 규정 stipulation, condition
kyujŏnghada 규정하다 stipulate, provide for
kyul 귤 mandarin orange
kyumo 규모 size, scale
kyumoga chulda 규모가 줄다 downsize
kyumorŭl churida 규모를 줄이다 downsize
kyundŭnghage 균등하게 equally; ***kyundŭnghage nanuda*** 균등하게 나누다 share out equally
kyunhyŏng 균형 balance, equilibrium; ***kyunhyŏng-ŭl chap-tta*** 균형을 잡다 balance
kyunhyŏng chap'in 균형 잡힌 balanced, well-balanced
kyunyŏl 균열 rift
kyuyul 규율 discipline

K'

k'adŭ 카드 card
k'adŭk'i 카드키 cardkey
k'adŭshik saegin 카드식 색인 card index
k'aeda 캐다 nose about
k'aedi 캐디 caddie
k'aemp'ing 캠핑 camping
k'aemp'ŭ 캠프 camp
K'aenada 캐나다 Canada ◊ Canadian
k'aengk'aeng chit-tta 캥캥 짖다 yap
k'aep 캡 cap
k'aepsshyul 캡슐 capsule
k'ajino 카지노 casino
k'akt'eil 칵테일 cocktail
k'al 칼 knife
k'allal 칼날 blade
k'alla sajin 칼라 사진 color photograph
k'alla t'ellebijŏn 칼라 텔레비젼 color TV
k'allaro toen 칼라로 된 (in) color
k'allori 칼로리 calorie
k'alshyum 칼슘 calcium
k'altchip 칼집 sheath (*for knife*)
K'ambodia 캄보디아 Cambodia ◊ Cambodian
k'amera 카메라 camera
k'an 칸 compartment; panel; section
k'aneishyŏn 카네이션 carnation
k'anmagi 칸막이 partition
k'anmagirŭl hada 칸막이를 하다 partition off
k'ap'e 카페 café
k'ap'ein 카페인 caffeine
k'ap'eini chegŏdoen 카페인이 제거된 decaffeinated
k'ap'irait'ŏ 카피라이터 copy-writer
k'arat'e 카라테 karate
k'aset'ŭ p'ŭlleiŏ 카셋트 플레이어 tape deck
k'auboi 카우보이 cowboy
k'aunt'ŏ 카운터 counter (*in café etc*)
k'aunt'ŭ 카운트 count (*in baseball, boxing*)
k'ech'ŏp 케첩 catsup, ketchup
k'eibŭlk'a 케이블카 cable car
k'eik'ŭ 케이크 cake
k'eisŭ 케이스 case, container
k'i 키 height; key (*on keyboard*); helm
k'ibodŭ 키보드 keyboard
k'iga chagŭn 키가 작은 short
k'iga k'ŭn 키가 큰 tall
k'ikk'ik-kkŏrida 킥킥거리다 titter
k'ik'op'ŭ 킥오프 kickoff
k'ilk'il ut-tta 킬킬 웃다 chuckle
k'illo 킬로 kilo
k'illobait'ŭ 킬로바이트 kilobyte
k'illogŭraem 킬로그램 kilogram
k'illomit'ŏ 킬로미터 kilometer
k'ing saijŭ 킹 사이즈 king-size(d)
k'irŭl ch'ida 키를 치다 key, key in COMPUT
k'isŭ 키스 kiss
k'isŭhada 키스하다 kiss
k'iuda 키우다 raise, bring up *children*
k'ŏbŏ 커버 cover, jacket (*of book*)
k'ŏjida 커지다 grow (*of number, amount*)
k'ŏmp'ŏsŭ 컴퍼스 (pair of) compasses
k'ŏmp'yut'ŏ 컴퓨터 computer
k'ŏmp'yut'ŏ ch'ulp'an 컴퓨터 출판 DTP, desk-top publishing
k'ŏmp'yut'ŏ keim 컴퓨터 게임 computer game
k'ŏmp'yut'ŏ kwahak 컴퓨터 과학 computer science
k'ŏmp'yut'ŏ kwahaktcha 컴퓨터 과학자 computer scientist
k'ŏmp'yut'ŏ sayong 컴퓨터 사용 computing
k'ŏmp'yut'ŏro t'ongjedoenŭn 컴퓨터로 통제되는 computer-controlled
k'ŏnbeiŏ pelt'ŭ 컨베이어 벨트 conveyor belt

k'ŏnbenshyŏn sent'ŏ 컨벤션 센터 convention center
k'ŏndishyŏn 컨디션 condition, shape
k'ŏnssŏlt'ŏnt'ŭ 컨설턴트 consultant, adviser
k'ŏnssŏlt'ŏnt'ŭŏp 컨설턴트업 consultancy (*company*)
k'ŏnt'einŏ 컨테이너 container
k'ŏnt'ŭri myujik 컨트리 뮤직 country and western (music)
k'ŏnyŏng 커녕 to say nothing of; ***...kinŭn k'ŏnyŏng*** ...기는 커녕 let alone
k'ŏp 컵 cup; glass
k'ŏp'i 커피 coffee
k'ŏp'i meik'ŏ 커피 메이커 coffee maker
k'ŏp'i p'ot'ŭ 커피 포트 coffee pot
k'ŏp'i shyop 커피 숍 coffee shop
k'ŏsŏ 커서 cursor
k'ŏt'ŭn 커튼 drapes, curtains
k'o 코 nose; trunk; stitch
k'och'i 코치 coach SP
k'odŭ 코드 code
k'okkiri 코끼리 elephant
k'o kolda 코 골다 snore
k'ok'ain 코카인 cocaine
k'ok'oa 코코아 cocoa
k'ollesŭt'erol 콜레스테롤 cholesterol
k'ol t'aeksshi 콜 택시 radio taxi
k'omidiŏn 코미디언 comedian
k'omp'aekt'ŭ tisŭk'ŭ 콤팩트 디스크 CD, compact disc
k'omp'ŭllekssŭ 콤플렉스 complex PSYCH
k'ondishyŏnŏ 콘디셔너 conditioner
k'ondo 콘도 condo
k'ondom 콘돔 condom, sheath
k'ondominium 콘도미니움 condominium
k'ong 콩 bean; soy bean
k'ongp'at 콩팥 soy and red beans; kidney ANAT
k'onk'ŭrit'ŭ 콘크리트 concrete
k'onmul 콧물 mucus
k'onnoraerro purŭda 콧노래로 부르다 hum
k'onŏk'ik 코너킥 corner kick
k'ont'aekt'ŭrenjŭ 콘택트렌즈 contact lens
k'onyak 코냑 cognac
k'op'i 코피 nosebleed; copy; ***nanŭn k'op'iga nanda*** 나는 코피가 난다 my nose is bleeding
k'orŭk'ŭ 코르크 cork (*material*)
k'orŭk'ŭ magae 코르크 마개 cork (*in bottle*)
k'osŭ 코스 course, track
k'otkkumŏng 콧구멍 nostril
k'otppanggwi kkwida 콧방귀 뀌다 snort (*disdainfully*)
k'otppulsso 코뿔소 rhinoceros
k'otssori 콧소리 twang
k'otssuyŏm 콧수염 mustache
k'ot'inghan 코팅한 laminated
k'ot'ŭ 코트 court SP
k'ŭda 크다 be big
k'ŭge 크게 large ◊ very, highly; greatly; loudly; ***k'ŭge ttŭn*** 크게 뜬 wide-open; ***k'ŭge ut-tta*** 크게 웃다 roar with laughter
k'ŭge hada 크게 하다 enlarge
k'ŭgi 크기 size
k'ŭllaeshik 클래식 classical
k'ŭllarinet 클라리넷 clarinet
k'ŭllenjŏ 클렌저 cleanser
k'ŭllik 클릭 click
k'ŭllik'ada 클릭하다 click on
k'ŭllip 클립 clip; fastener
k'ŭllip-ppodŭ 클립보드 clipboard
k'ŭllŏch'i 클러치 clutch MOT
k'ŭllŏch'irŭl p'ulda 클러치를 풀다 declutch
k'ŭllojŭŏp 클로즈업 close-up
k'ŭn 큰 big, large
k'ŭngk'ŭnggŏrida 킁킁거리다 sniff
k'ŭn haengbok-kkam 큰 행복감 euphoria
k'ŭn saejang 큰 새장 aviary
k'ŭn ton 큰 돈 fortune; big money
k'ŭraek'ŏ 크래커 cracker
k'ŭreyong 크레용 crayon
k'ŭrim 크림 cream
k'ŭrim ch'ijŭ 크림 치즈 cream cheese
K'ŭrisŭmasŭ 크리스마스 Christmas
k'udet'a 쿠데타 coup
k'uk tchirŭda 쿡 찌르다 jab, poke
k'uk'i 쿠키 cookie
k'ullŏp 클럽 club
k'unghanŭn sori 쿵하는 소리 thud, thump
k'ungk'ung kŏt-tta 쿵쿵 걷다 tramp;

trudge
k'up'on 쿠폰 coupon
k'urisŭt'ŏl 크리스털 crystal (*glass*)
k'ushyŏn 쿠션 cushion
k'waehwalhada 쾌활하다 be lively, be vivacious
k'waejŏk'an 쾌적한 delightful
k'waesoktchŏng 쾌속정 speedboat
k'walk'wal hŭllŏnaoda 콸콸 흘러나오다 gush out
k'wang! 쾅! bang!; ***munŭl k'wangk'wang tudŭrida*** 문을 쾅쾅 두드리다 hammer at the door
k'wang pudich'ida 쾅 부딪히다 bang, hit
k'wang tach'ida 쾅 닫히다 bang, be slammed shut
k'wang tat-tta 쾅 닫다 bang, slam shut
k'wijŭ 퀴즈 quiz
k'wijŭ p'ŭro 퀴즈 프로 quiz program
k'wik'wihan 퀴퀴한 moldy, musty
k'yabare 카바레 cabaret
k'yŏda 켜다 switch on *machine*
k'yŏit-tta 켜있다 be on (*of device*)
k'yŏjida 켜지다 be turned on (*of device*)
k'yŏlle 켤레 pair ◊ *countword for shoes and socks*
k'yŏn ch'aero tuda 켠 채로 두다 leave on *machine*
k'yu 큐 cue
k'yureit'ŏ 큐레이터 curator

L

...l ... ㄹ *future particle*
labendŏ 라벤더 lavender
ladiet'ŏ 라디에이터 radiator
ladio 라디오 radio
ladio pangsongguk 라디오 방송국 radio station
laelli 랠리 rally
laem 램 RAM, random access memory
laep 랩 rap MUS
laept'ap 랩탑 laptop
lagŏ piŏ 라거 비어 lager
lago hanŭn kŏsŭn 라고 하는 것은 so-called
laillak 라일락 lilac
laim 라임 lime (*fruit*, *tree*)
laim nokssaek 라임 녹색 limegreen
laining 라이닝 lining
lait'ŏ 라이터 lighter
lait'ŭkkŭp sŏnsu 라이트급 선수 lightweight
lait'ŭ p'en 라이트 펜 light pen
lak 락 rock (music)
lakk'ŭllol 락큰롤 rock'n'roll
laksŭt'a 락스타 rock star
lak'et 라켓 racket
langdebu 랑데부 rendez-vous
lanjeri 란제리 lingerie
laundŭ 라운드 round
launji 라운지 lounge
Laosŭ 라오스 Laos ◊ Laotian
leiausŭl hada 레이아웃을 하다 lay out
leida 레이다 radar
leida yŏngsang 레이더 영상 blip
leijyŏ 레이저 laser
leijyŏ kwangsŏn 레이저 광선 laser beam
leijyŏ p'urint'ŏ 레이저 프린터 laser printer
leisŭ 레이스 lace
lejŏ sent'ŏ 레저 센터 leisure center
lejŭbiŏn 레즈비언 lesbian
lek'odŭ 레코드 record
lemon 레몬 lemon
lemon chussŭ 레몬 주스 lemon juice
lemonch'a 레몬차 lemon tea
lemoneidŭ 레모네이드 lemonade
lench'i 렌치 wrench
lenjŭ 렌즈 lens
lenjŭ k'ong 렌즈 콩 lentil
lenjŭ k'ong sŭp'ŭ 렌즈 콩 스프 lentil soup
lenjŭ ttukkŏng 렌즈뚜껑 lens cover
lep'ot'ŭ 레포트 essay
lesŭlling 레슬링 wrestling
lesŭlling kyŏnggi 레슬링 경기 wrestling bout
lesŭlling sŏnsu 레슬링 선수 wrestler
Libia 리비아 Libya ◊ Libyan
libon 리본 ribbon
libon maedŭp 리본 매듭 bow, knot
lidŭm 리듬 rhythm
lihŏsŏl 리허설 practice; rehearsal
lihŏsŏrhada 리허설하다 rehearse
lik'odŏ 리코더 recorder
lik'yurŭ 리큐르 liqueur
lil 릴 reel
limp'ŭsaem 림프샘 lymph gland
limujin 리무진 limo, limousine
linen 리넨 linen
ling 링 ring
linssŭhada 린스하다 rinse
lipssŭt'ik 립스틱 lipstick
lisait'ŭl 리사이틀 recital
lisepsshyŏn p'at'i 리셉션 파티 reception
lishibŏ 리시버 receiver (*in tennis*)
lit'ŏ 리터 liter
lit'ŭribŏ 리트리버 retriever (*dog*)
lŏm 럼 rum
lŏmp'ŭ sŭt'eik'ŭ 럼프 스테이크 rumpsteak
Lŏndŏn 런던 London
lŏning shyŏch'ŭ 러닝 셔츠 undershirt
lŏp'ŭ 러프 rough (*in golf*)
Lŏshia 러시아 Russia ◊ Russian

Lŏshiain 러시아인 Russian (*person*)
Lŏshiaŏ 러시아어 Russian (*language*)
lobi 로비 lobby
lobot 로봇 robot
lodŭhada 로드하다 load
logo 로고 logo
lok'et 로켓 (space) rocket
lok'ŏ 로커 locker
lol 롤 roll (*of film*)
lollŏ k'osŭt'ŏ 롤러 코스터 roller coaster
lollŏ pŭlleidŭ 롤러 블레이드 roller blade
lollŏ sŭk'eit'ŭ 롤러 스케이트 roller skate
lolppang 롤빵 (bread) roll
lom 롬 ROM, read only memory
lomaensŭ 로맨스 romance; affair
lomaent'ik'ada 로맨틱하다 be romantic
lomaent'ik'an 로맨틱한 romantic
Loma K'at'ollik 로마 카톨릭 Roman Catholic
Loma K'at'ollik-kkyoŭi 로마 카톨릭교의 Roman Catholic
loshyŏn 로션 lotion
lot'ŏri 로터리 traffic circle
loyŏlt'i 로열티 royalty (*on book, recording*)
lubi 루비 ruby
lullet 룰렛 roulette
lum meit'ŭ 룸 메이트 room mate
lum ssŏbissŭ 룸 서비스 room service
lyumat'ijŭm 류마티즘 rheumatism

M

ma 마 jinx, bad luck
mabi 마비 paralysis
mabishik'ida 마비시키다 paralyze
mabŏbe kŏllin 마법에 걸린 spellbound, enraptured
mabŏbŭi 마법의 occult
mabŏp 마법 the occult; witchcraft
mabŏpsa 마법사 wizard
mabu 마부 groom (*for horse*)
mach'al 마찰 friction
mach'i ...ch'ŏrŏm 마치 ...처럼 as though
mach'ida 마치다 end, finish
mach'im 마침 just, exactly
mach'imnae 마침내 finally, at last
mach'imp'yo 마침표 period (*punctuation mark*)
mach'ŏllu 마천루 skyscraper
mach'wihada 마취하다 drug
mach'wije 마취제 anesthetic
mach'wisa 마취사 anesthetist
madi 마디 joint; word; phrase; ***...wa / kwa handu madi marhada*** ...와 / 과 한두 마디 말하다 have a word with
madit'usŏng-iin 마디투성이인 gnarled
madŏbodŭ 마더보드 motherboard
mae 매 hawk
mae- 매 each, every
maeaehago ulda 매애하고 울다 bleat
maebok 매복 ambush
maech'e 매체 medium, vehicle
maech'un 매춘 prostitution
maech'unbu 매춘부 prostitute
maech'un-gul 매춘굴 brothel
maeda 매다 knot; tether, tie up
maedalda 매달다 suspend, hang; ***mok maedalda*** 목 매달다 hang *person*
maedallida 매달리다 cling to
maedalmada 매달마다 monthly
maedarŭi 매달의 monthly
maedogyŏn 맹도견 seeing-eye dog
maedok 매독 syphilis
maedŭp 매듭 knot; decorative tassle
maegagin 매각인 vendor
maehok 매혹 charm; magnetism
maehoksshik'ida 매혹시키다 fascinate
maehoktchŏgin 매혹적인 charming; ravishing; fascinating
maehokttoeda 매혹되다 be fascinated by
maehok'ada 매혹하다 charm
maehyŏng 매형 brother-in-law (*man's elder sister's husband*)
maeil 매일 every day
maeil maeil kyesok'aesŏ 매일 매일 계속해서 day in, day out
maeil pame 매일 밤에 nightly
maeiptcha 매입자 purchaser
maeirŭi 매일의 daily
maejang 매장 department (*of store*); outlet; burial
maejangmul 매장물 deposit
maejil 매질 beating, hiding
maejindoen 매진된 out of stock
maejŏk'ijŭm 매저키즘 masochism
maejŏk'isŭt'ŭ 매저키스트 masochist
maejŏm 매점 bookstall
maejŏmhada 매점하다 buy up
maejŏnghan 매정한 heartless, pitiless
maeju 매주 every week
maejumada 매주마다 weekly
maeju-ŭi 매주의 weekly
makttaehada 막대하다 be huge
maekkŭrŏptta 매끄럽다 be smooth
maekppak 맥박 throb, pulse
maekppak chojŏnggi 맥박 조정기 pacemaker
maektchu 맥주 beer
maek'ŭro 매크로 macro
maemae 매매 marketing ◊ for sale
maemae changso 매매 장소 market-place

maemaeshijang 매매시장 market
maemdom 맴돔 curl
maen araetchok 맨 아래쪽 bottom
maenbarida 맨발이다 be barefoot
maeng-in 맹인 the blind
Maengja 맹자 Mencius
maengjang 맹장 appendix
maengjangnyŏm 맹장염 appendicitis
maengnyŏrhan sokttoro 맹렬한 속도로 at a furious pace
maengnyŏrhi pinanhada 맹렬히 비난하다 hit out at, criticize
maengsehada 맹세하다 swear, promise
maengtchŏm 맹점 blind spot
maenik'yuŏ 매니큐어 manicure; nail polish
maenik'yuŏ chiunŭn yak 매니큐어 지우는 약 nail polish remover
maen katchok 맨 가쪽 bottom
maenmaru 맨마루 bare floor
maen mitppadagŭi 맨 밑바닥의 bottom; lowest
maen twittchogŭi 맨 뒷쪽의 rearmost
maenwiŭi 맨위의 top
maenyŏn 매년 yearly
maenyŏnŭi 매년의 yearly
maenyuŏl 매뉴얼 manual
maepok'ayŏ sŭpkkyŏk'ada 매복하여 습격하다 ambush
maepsshi innŭn 맵시있는 spruce, neat
maeptta 맵다 be hot, be spicy
maep'yogyewŏn 매표계원 booking clerk
maep'yoso 매표소 box office, ticket office
maeryŏginnŭn 매력있는 attractive
maeryŏgi nŏmch'inŭn 매력이 넘치는 glamorous
maeryŏk 매력 appeal, attraction
maeryŏktchŏgin 매력적인 engaging; seductive; cute
maeryodoen 매료된 entranced
maeryohada 매료하다 enchant
maesanggo 매상고 turnover, takings
maesang-ŭl ollida 매상을 올리다 turn over FIN
maeshit'ŭ p'ot'eit'o 매시트 포테이토 mashed potatoes
maesŏun 매서운 severe, strict; piercing
maesŭk'ŏm 매스컴 the media
maesŭk'ŏmŭi kwajang 매스컴의 과장 media hype
maesuhada 매수하다 bribe; corrupt
maet-tta 맺다 form, establish
maet'ŭ 매트 mat
maet'ŭrisŭ 매트리스 mattress
maeu 매우 most, tremendously
maeun 매운 hot, spicy
maeunt'ang 매운탕 spicy fish soup
maewŏl 매월 every month
maeyŏn 매연 fumes
magae 마개 plug
magaerŭl ppoptta 마개를 뽑다 uncork
magaerŭl yŏlda 마개를 열다 unscrew
magamil 마감일 deadline (*day*)
magamshigan 마감시간 deadline (*hour*)
maganaeda 막아내다 keep away, ward off
magarin 마가린 margarine
magi 막이 screen, shield
magu charada 마구 자라다 run wild
magu chitppalp'ida 마구 짓밟히다 be trampled underfoot
magujabiŭi 마구잡이의 haphazard
magutkkan 마구간 stable
magu toradanida 마구 돌아다니다 travel; wander
magu ttaerida 마구 때리다 thrash
magu tudŭlgyŏ p'aeda 마구 두들겨 패다 beat, knock around
magu tudŭrida 마구 두드리다 pound on, hammer on
magwŏnŏptcha 마권업자 bookmaker
magyŏnhan 막연한 indefinable
mahŭn 마흔 forty
mahŭn pŏntchaeŭi 마흔 번째의 fortieth
maik'ŭroch'ip 마이크로칩 microchip
maik'ŭrop'illŭm 마이크로필름 microfilm
maik'ŭrop'ŭrosesŏ 마이크로프로세서 microprocessor

maik'ŭ 마이크 mike, microphone
mail 마일 mile
mail su 마일 수 mileage
majak 마작 mah-jong
majayo! 맞아요! that's it!, that's right!
maji 맏이 the eldest
majihada 맞이하다 meet with
majijak-kkŏrida 만지작거리다 fiddle (around) with
majimagesŏ tu pŏntchae 마지막에서 두 번째 second to last, penultimate
majimagŭi 마지막의 final, last
majimagŭro 마지막으로 finally, lastly
majimak 마지막 last
majimak sudanŭro 마지막 수단으로 as a last resort
majimak sun-gane 마지막 순간에 at the last moment, at the eleventh hour
maji mot'ae 마지 못해 reluctantly
majiro t'aeŏnan 맏이로 태어난 first-born, eldest
majok'ago innŭn 만족하고 있는 contented
majŭl li ŏpssŏ 맞을 리 없어 that can't be right
majuboda 마주보다 face
majuch'ida 마주치다 meet
majuhada 마주하다 confront, face
majungnagada 마중나가다 collect, meet
majung naoda 마중 나오다 pick up, collect
mak 막 membrane; slick; curtain; act
mak haryŏgo hada 막 하려고 하다 be on the point of; ***nanŭn mak ttŏnaryŏdŏn ch'amiŏssŏyo*** 나는 막 떠나려던 참이었어요 I was just about to leave
mak-kkan 막간 interlude
mak-kkŏlli 막걸리 rice wine
makkwŏnŏptcha 마권업자 bookie
makssa 막사 barracks
makssangmak'ae irŭda 막상막하에 이르다 draw level
maksshimhan 막심한 heavy
maktta 막다 block; contain; hold back; prevent
makttae 막대 rod, stick
makttaegi 막대기 bar, stick
makttaegi sat'ang 막대기 사탕 lollipop
makttaehan 막대한 huge, incalculable
makttarŭda 막다르다 be closed off
makttarŭn kil 막다른 길 cul-de-sac
makttarŭn kolmok 막다른 골목 blind alley
mak'ida 막히다 clog up
mak'ige hada 막히게 하다 clog up
mak'im 막힘 congestion
mak'yŏ innŭn kŏt 막혀있는 것 blockage
mal 말 horse; piece (*in board game*); end; word; ***idal mare*** 이달 말에 at the end of this month; ***ch'irwŏl mal*** 칠월 말 at the end of July
malbŏl 말벌 wasp; hornet
malch'amgyŏnhada 말참견하다 chip in, interrupt
malda 말다 stop; ***kŭnŭn kŭgose salge toego marat-tta*** 그는 그곳에 살게 되고 말았다 he finished up living there; ***hwanaeji mallagu*** 화내지 말라구 don't get angry
maldaekkuhada 말대꾸하다 answer back
maldat'um 말다툼 disagreement, squabble
maldat'umhada 말다툼하다 argue, squabble, bicker
maldŏdŭm 말더듬 stammer
maldo andoenda! 말도 안된다! that's out of the question!
maldo an toenŭn sori 말도 안 되는 소리 nonsense
malgajida 맑아지다 settle; brighten up
malgŭm 맑음 brightness; clearness
malgŭn 맑은 clear; pure; fine
malgup 말굽 horseshoe
malgwallyang-i 말괄량이 tomboy
malkkŭmhan 말끔한 trim, neat
malktta 맑다 be clear; be clean; be honest
Malleiŏ 말레이어 Malay (*language*)
Malleishia 말레이시아 Malaysia ◊ Malaysian
Malleishia saram 말레이시아 사람 Malay (*person*)

mallida 말리다 dry; dissuade; break up *fight*
mallin 말린 dried *fruit etc*
mallin chadu 말린 자두 prune
mallo wihyŏp'ada 말로 위협하다 browbeat
malssŏng 말썽 disturbance, trouble; ***malssŏng-ŭl purida*** 말썽을 부리다 cause trouble, make a fuss
malssŏng-i nada 말썽이 나다 get into trouble
malssŏngkkun 말썽꾼 troublemaker
malsso 말소 deletion
malssuga chŏgŭn 말수가 적은 reserved
malssuk'aejida 말쑥해지다 clean up, wash
malssuk'age hada 말쑥하게 하다 smarten up
malttugŭro chijihada 말뚝으로 지지하다 stake, support
malttuk 말뚝 stake, peg
malttuk ult'ari 말뚝 울타리 picket fence
malt'u 말투 speech, way of speaking
Malŭk'ŭsŭjuŭi 마르크스주의 Marxism
mamalleidŭ 마말레이드 marmalade
mamurihada 마무리하다 finalize, round off
man 만 bay, inlet; gulf; ten thousand ◊ after ◊ only, just
manaya 많아야 at (the) most
manbarhada 만발하다 come into full bloom
manch'an 만찬 dinner; feast
manch'an sonnim 만찬 손님 dinner guest
manch'wihan 만취한 drunken
mandŭlda 만들다 ◊ establish, create, form, make ◊ (*causative*): ***...ge mandŭlda*** ...게 만들다 make
mandu 만두 stuffed dumpling
manek'ing 마네킹 mannequin (*for clothes*)
mang-aji 망아지 colt
mangboda 망보다 keep watch
mangbogi 망보기 lookout
mangch'i 망치 hammer
mangch'ida 망치다 destroy; ruin; spoil
mangch'ijirhada 망치질하다 hammer
mangch'yŏnot'a 망쳐놓다 mess up, spoil; ***sŏt'urŭge haesŏ mangch'yŏbŏrida*** 서투르게 해서 망쳐버리다 botch, bungle
manggattŭrida 망가뜨리다 ruin
manghada 망하다 fail, fold
man-gi 만기 termination
man-gidoeda 만기되다 expire
man-giga toeda 만기가 되다 mature; run out
mangmyŏng 망명 exile, asylum
mangmyŏngja 망명자 exile (*person*)
mangnani 망나니 bum (*person*)
man-gok 만곡 bend, sweep
mangsa k'ŏt'ŭn 망사 커튼 net curtain
mangsang 망상 myth
mangshinshik'ida 망신시키다 shame, bring dishonor on
mangsŏrida 망설이다 hesitate; ***tu taean saiesŏ mangsŏrida*** 두 대안 사이에서 망설이다 be torn between two alternatives
mangsŏrim 망설임 hesitation
mang-wŏn-gyŏng 망원경 telescope
mang-wŏn lenjŭ 망원 렌즈 telephoto lens
manhada 만하다 be worth; deserve to; ***ilgŭl / pol manhada*** 읽을 / 볼 만하다 be worth reading / seeing; ***chumŏngmanhan tol*** 주먹만한 돌 a rock the size of your fist
manhwa 만화 cartoon
manhwa chaptchi 만화 잡지 comic (book)
manhwa ch'aek 만화 책 comic book
manhwaran 만화란 comics; comic strip
manhwa yŏnghwa 만화 영화 cartoon
mani 많이 a lot, lots, a good deal; much; ***aju mani*** 아주 많이 very much; ***mani tŭseyo*** 많이 드세요 please help yourself; enjoy
manjang-ilch'ihada 만장일치하다 be unanimous on
manjang-ilch'iro 만장일치로 unanimously
manjang-ilch'iŭi 만장일치의

unanimous
manjida 만지다 touch, feel
manjijak-kkŏrida 만지작거리다 meddle with, tinker with
manjo 만조 high tide
manjok 만족 satisfaction, contentment; pleasure; ***muŏsesŏ manjogŭl nŭkkida*** 무엇에서 만족을 느끼다 get satisfaction out of sth
manjok-kkam 만족감 feeling of satisfaction, fulfillment
manjoksshik'ida 만족시키다 satisfy, gratify
manjoksshik'igi 만족시키기 gratification
manjokssŭrŏun 만족스러운 adequate; fulfilling
manjok'ada 만족하다 be satisfied; content oneself with; feel fulfilled; ***...ŭro manjok'ada*** ...으로 만족하다 make do with
manjok'an 만족한 satisfactory; pleased
manjok'anŭn 만족하는 content
mank'ŭm 만큼 as; ***...mank'ŭm chal hada*** ...만큼 잘 하다 be as good as; measure up to; ***...mank'ŭm mani*** ...만큼 많이 as much as ...
mannada 만나다 meet, meet with; join
mannaeda 맛내다 flavor
mannal kwŏllirŭl kat-tta 만날 권리를 갖다 have access to *one's children*
mannam 만남 meeting
mannasŏ pan-gapssŭmnida 만나서 반갑습니다 pleased to meet you; glad to see you
mannŭn 맞는 correct, right; ***kŭgŏsŭn uriŭi kyehoege tŭrŏ mannŭnda*** 그것은 우리의 계획에 들어 맞는다 it fits in well with our plans
mannŭng 만능 versatility
mannŭng-ŭi 만능의 versatile, all-round
mannŭn saenghwarŭl hada 맞는 생활을 하다 live up to
mannyŏnp'il 만년필 (fountain) pen
mansa 만사 everything
mansa p'yŏnanhan 만사 편안한 hunky-dory
manse! 만세! hurray!
mansŏng-ŭi 만성의 chronic
mant'a 많다 be many
manŭl 마늘 garlic
manŭn 많은 many, a lot of, lots of; much; plenty of; heavy
manŭn chŏngdo 많은 정도 number, quantity
manŭn shigani kŏllinŭn 많은 시간이 걸리는 time-consuming
manura 마누라 wife
manyak ...myŏn 만약 ...면 if; on condition that; ***manyak tarŭn hal iri ŏpttamyŏn*** 만약 다른 할 일이 없다면 if you've got nothing else to do
manyŏ 마녀 witch
manyŏn 만연 spread; diffusion
manyŏn chashil 망연 자실 stupor
manyŏndoen 만연된 widespread
manyŏnhada 만연하다 spread
Map'ia chojik 마피아 조직 the Mafia
marat'on 마라톤 marathon
marhada 말하다 talk; speak; say; tell; ***hago ship'ŭn marŭl hada*** 하고 싶은 말을 하다 have one's say
marhagi choahanŭn 말하기 좋아하는 talkative; communicative
marhanŭn nŭngnyŏk 말하는 능력 speech (*ability to speak*)
marharyŏhada 말하려하다 get at; imply; mean
mari 마리 *countword for animals*
mari andwaeyo 말이 안돼요 not make sense
marihwana 마리화나 marijuana
mari manŭn 말이 많은 talkative
mari nan-gime 말이 난김에 incidentally
maronie yŏlmae 마로니에 열매 horse chestnut
marŭda 마르다 dry; waste away; run out (*of money*)
Marŭk'ŭsŭjuŭija 마르크스주의자 Marxist (*person*)
Marŭk'ŭsŭjuŭiŭi 마르크스주의의 Marxist
marŭl kkŏnaeda 말을 꺼내다 bring up, broach

marŭl kollasŏ ssŭda 말을 골라서 쓰다 put into words, formulate
marŭl ttokttok'i mot'anŭn 말을 똑똑히 못하는 inarticulate
marŭl tŭt-tchi annŭn 말을 듣지 않는 disobedient
marŭl t'ago 말을 타고 on horseback
marŭmjil 마름질 cut
marŭmmokkol 마름모꼴 lozenge
marŭn 마른 dry; thin
marŭn haengju 마른 행주 tea cloth, dishcloth
maru 마루 brow
maru kŏlle 마루 걸레 floor cloth
marutppadak 마룻바닥 floor
maryŏk 마력 horsepower
maryŏnhada 마련하다 lay on, provide
masaji 마사지 massage
mashi chinhan 맛이 진한 rich
mashida 마시다 drink
mashil su innŭn 마실 수 있는 drinkable
mashimaello 마시멜로 marshmallow
mashinnŭn 맛있는 tasty, delicious
mashinŭn mul 마시는 물 drinking water
mashitkke tŭseyo! 맛있게 드세요! enjoy!
mashyŏbŏrida 마셔버리다 consume, drink
masŭk'ara 마스카라 mascara
masŭk'ot'ŭ 마스코트 mascot
masul 마술 magic; conjuring tricks
masuljŏgin 마술적인 magical
masulssa 마술사 magician, conjurer
masurŭi 마술의 magic
mat 맛 flavor, taste; ***ammu mat ŏmnŭn*** 아무 맛 없는 tasteless *food*
match'uda 맞추다 adjust; fit together; be fitting; be appropriate; ***ch'aenŏrŭl match'uda*** 채널을 맞추다 tune in; ***kŭe match'uŏ*** 그에 맞추어 accordingly, appropriately
match'ugi 맞추기 justify *text*
match'umbŏp kŏmsagi 맞춤법 검사기 spell checker
match'um k'ap'et 맞춤 카펫 wall-to-wall carpet
match'um puŏk 맞춤 부엌 fitted kitchen
match'umŭi 맞춤의 custom-made, tailor-made
match'uŏ not'a 맞추어 놓다 set; adjust
matkkida 맡기다 entrust
matpakkuda 맞바꾸다 exchange
matppadach'igi 맞받아치기 tit for tat
matpparam 맞바람 headwind
matppoda 맛보다 taste, sample
matpput'ŏ ssauda 맞붙어 싸우다 grapple with
matssŏda 맞서다 meet, confront, stand up to; retaliate
mattakttŭrida 맞닥뜨리다 meet with
mattanghage 마땅하게 justly, deservedly
mattanghan 마땅한 due, proper
mattanghan shillangkkam 마땅한 신랑감 eligible bachelor
mat-tchi ant'a 맞지 않다 be alien to
mat-tta 맞다 be right; fit, go in; take on *job*; suit; match; strike, hit; meet; be exposed to; encounter; be struck by; get, have; ***mat-tchiyo?*** 맞지요? that's right, isn't it?; ***chal mat-tta*** 잘 맞다 it's a good fit
mat-ttakttŭrida 맞닥뜨리다 encounter
maŭl 마을 village
maŭl saram 마을 사람 villager
maŭm 마음 heart; mind; spirit; ***kŭgŏshi maŭme kŏllyŏssŏyo*** 그것이 마음에 걸렸어요 it has been on my conscience; ***maŭmi t'onghaetkkunyo!*** 마음이 통했군요! you must be telepathic!; ***hyŏmnyŏktchŏgin maŭmŭro*** 협력적인 마음으로 in a spirit of cooperation; ***maŭm p'yŏnhage saenggak'ae!*** 마음 편하게 생각해! relax!
maŭmdaero 마음대로: ***nuguŭi maŭmdaero toeda*** 누구의 마음대로 되다 be at s.o.'s mercy; ***muŏsŭl maŭmdaero hada*** 무엇을 마음대로 하다 be at liberty to do sth; ***maŭmdaero haseyo!*** 마음대로 하세요! do what you like!, suit yourself!; ***Xŭl / rŭl Yŭi maŭmdaero ssŭge hada*** X을 / 를 Y의 마음대로

쓰게 하다 put X at Y's disposal
maŭme mannŭn 마음에 맞는 congenial, pleasant
maŭme p'umtta 마음에 품다 harbor *grudge*
maŭme tŭlda 마음에 들다 be to s.o.'s liking
maŭme tuda 마음에 두다 mind, heed
maŭmi chobŭn 마음이 좁은 narrow-minded
maŭmi mŏrŏjida 마음이 멀어지다 drift apart (*emotionally*)
maŭmi naek'iji annŭn 마음이 내키지 않는 half-hearted; disinclined; listless
maŭmi nŏlbŭn 마음이 넓은 liberal, broad-minded
maŭmi nugŭrŏjida 마음이 누그러지다 relent
maŭmi ŏjirŏun 마음이 어지러운 disturbed, concerned, worried
maŭm kabyŏun 마음 가벼운 light-hearted
maŭmkkŏt tŭlda 마음껏 들다 help oneself
maŭm soge ttŏollida 마음 속에 떠올리다 visualize
maŭmsogŭro 마음속으로 inwardly; privately; mentally
maŭmsshi koun 마음씨 고운 kind-hearted
maŭmŭi 마음의 mental
maŭmŭi sangch'ŏrŭl ibŭn 마음의 상처를 입은 broken-hearted
maŭmŭl chŏnghada 마음을 정하다 make up one's mind
maŭmŭl karaanch'ida 마음을 가라앉히다 pull oneself together, compose oneself
maŭmŭl ŏjirŏp'ida 마음을 어지럽히다 disturb, upset
maŭmŭl ŏjirŏp'inŭn 마음을 어지럽히는 disturbing, upsetting
maŭmŭl pakkuda 마음을 바꾸다 change one's mind
maŭmŭl pakkuge hada 마음을 바꾸게 하다 cause to change his/her mind
maŭmŭl p'yŏnhi noch'i mot'ada 마음을 편히 놓지 못하다 feel ill at ease
maŭmŭl sanghage hada 마음을 상하게 하다 hurt *feelings*
maŭmŭl sarojaptta 마음을 사로잡다 captivate, enthrall
maŭmŭl t'ŏnot'a 마음을 터놓다 come out of one's shell
maundŭ 마운드 mound (*in baseball*)
mausŭ 마우스 mouse COMPUT
mausŭ maet'ŭ 마우스 매트 mouse mat
mayagŭl hada 마약을 하다 be on drugs
mayak 마약 narcotic, drug; dope
mayak kŏrae 마약 거래 drug trafficking
mayak milmaehada 마약 밀매하다 push *drugs*
mayak milmaeja 마약 밀매자 pusher (*of drugs*)
mayak p'anmaeja 마약 판매자 drug dealer
mayak sang-yongja 마약 상용자 drug addict
mayak tansokppan 마약 단속반 narcotics agent
mayak tillŏ 마약 딜러 (drug) dealer
mayonejŭ 마요네즈 mayo, mayonnaise
meari 메아리 echo
medal 메달 medal
medŭlli 메들리 medley
megabait'ŭ 메가바이트 megabyte
meilbakssŭ 메일박스 mailbox
meilmŏji 메일머지 mail merge
meinbodŭ 메인보드 mainboard
Meksshik'o 멕시코 Mexico ◊ Mexican
melodi 멜로디 melody
melodŭramagat'ŭn 멜로드라마같은 melodramatic
melon 멜론 melon
melppang 멜빵 suspenders (*for pants*)
melppang paji 멜빵 바지 dungarees
memo 메모 note; memo
memojich'ŏp 메모지첩 notepad
memori 메모리 memory COMPUT
menyu 메뉴 menu *also* COMPUT
Meri K'ŭrisŭmasŭ 메리 크리스마스! Merry Christmas!

mesiji 메시지 message
mesŭkkŏun 메스꺼운 repulsive
mettugi 메뚜기 grasshopper; locust
meuda 메우다 fill in
mianhae 미안해 (I'm) sorry
mianhamnida 미안합니다 *fml* (I'm) sorry
mibongjŏgŭro koch'ida 미봉적으로 고치다 patch up
mibul 미불 nonpayment
miburŭi 미불의 outstanding *payment*
mich'ida 미치다 become insane; be crazy; reach; happen; match
mich'idŭshi choahada 미치듯이 좋아하다 be mad about, be enthusiastic about
mich'igwang-i 미치광이 lunatic, madman
mich'il tŭshi hwanage hada 미칠 듯이 화나게 하다 madden, infuriate, drive crazy
mich'il tŭshi hwanan 미칠 듯이 화난 mad, angry
mich'il tŭt'an 미칠 듯한 distraught
mich'in 미친 insane, mad, crazy
mich'in tŭshi 미친 듯이 madly, like mad
mich'in tŭt'an 미친 듯한 wild, crazy, frantic
mich'ŏribun 미처리분 backlog
mich'yŏgada 미쳐가다 become insane, go mad
midaji mun 미닫이 문 sliding door
midiŏ 미디어 media
midŏjiji annŭn 믿어지지 않는 incredible, amazing, very good
midŭl manhan 믿을 만한 credible, believable
midŭl su ŏmnŭn 믿을 수 없는 unbelievable; unreliable
midŭm 믿음 belief
midŭng 미등 tail light
migaein 미개인 savage
migaeji 미개지 the wilds
migak 미각 taste (*sense*); palate
Migugin 미국인 American (*person*)
Miguk 미국 USA, America ◊ American
Miguk chung-ang chŏngbobu 미국 중앙 정보부 CIA, Central Intelligence Agency
Miguk kukppangssŏng 미국 국방성 the Pentagon
Miguk nŏguri 미국 너구리 raccoon
Miguk saram 미국 사람 American (*person*)
migyŏltcheŭi 미결제의 unsettled, unpaid
mihaenghada 미행하다 follow, dog
Mihaptchungguk 미합중국 United States of America
mihonŭi 미혼의 unmarried
mijigŭnhan 미지근한 lukewarm, tepid
mijiroŭi yŏhaeng 미지로의 여행 journey into the unknown
mikki 미끼 bait
mikkirŭl mulda 미끼를 물다 bite (*of fish*); get a bite
mikkŭrŏjida 미끄러지다 slip, slither, skid
mikkŭrŏjiji annŭn 미끄러지지 않는 nonslip, nonskid
mikkŭrŏjim 미끄러짐 slip
mikkŭrŏm 미끄럼 skid
mikkŭrŏmt'ŭl 미끄럼틀 slide
mikkŭrŏpkke hada 미끄럽게 하다 lubricate
mikkŭrŏptta 미끄럽다 be smooth; be slippery, be slick
mikkŭrŏun 미끄러운 slippery
mikkŭrojida 미끄러지다 slide, glide
miksŏ 믹서 food mixer
miksŏgi 믹서기 blender
mil 밀 wheat
milbong 밀봉 seal
milbonghada 밀봉하다 seal
milda 밀다 push, shove
milgam 밀감 tangerine
milgi 밀기 pushing
milgoja 밀고자 informer
milgo kada 밀고 가다 push along
milkkaru 밀가루 flour
milkkaru panjuk 밀가루 반죽 dough, pastry; batter
milk'ŭ chyok'ollit 밀크 쵸콜릿 milk chocolate
milk'ŭ shweik'ŭ 밀크 쉐이크 milk shake
milligŭraem 밀리그램 milligram
millim 밀림 jungle
millimit'ŏ 밀리미터 millimeter

millyŏdŭnŭn p'ado 밀려드는 파도 surf
millyŏ it-tta 밀려있다 be behind with; be backed up
millyŏnagada 밀려나가다 surge forward
millyŏp'ada 밀렵하다 poach *rabbits etc*
milmul 밀물 incoming tide
milmurida 밀물이다 the tide is out
milsshil kongp'otchŭng 밀실 공포증 claustrophobia
milssu 밀수 smuggling
milssuhada 밀수하다 smuggle; traffic in
milssuŏptcha 밀수업자 smuggler
miltchip 밀짚 straw (*of wheat etc*)
miltchip chiyŏk 밀집 지역 crowded area
miltchip'an 밀집한 dense
miman 미만 under, below; less than
mimang-ini toen 미망인이 된 widowed
mimyohan 미묘한 subtle, delicate
mimyoham 미묘함 delicacy
minapkkŭm 미납금 arrears
minap'ada 미납하다 be in arrears
minbak 민박 vacation home
minbang-wi 민방위 civil defense
minch'ŏp'an 민첩한 snappy
mindalp'aeng-i 민달팽이 slug
min-gamhada 민감하다 be sensitive
min-gamham 민감함 sensitivity
min-gane ŭihae 민간에 의해 privately
min-ganin 민간인 civilian
min-gan pangsong 민간 방송 commercial television
min-gan pumun 민간 부문 private sector
min-ganŭi 민간의 civil
min-gan yoppŏp 민간 요법 folk medicine
mingk'ŭ 밍크 mink (*fur*)
mingk'ŭ k'ot'ŭ 밍크 코트 mink (coat)
minhwa 민화 folk painting
mini sŭk'ot'ŭ 미니 스커트 miniskirt
minjogŭi 민족의 ethnic
minjok 민족 people; race; tribe
minjokchipttan 민족집단 ethnic group
minjoktchuŭi 민족주의 nationalism
Minju Chayudang 민주 자유당 Democratic Liberal Party
Minjudang 민주당 Democratic Party
minjudang chijija 민주당 지지자 democrat
Minjudang-wŏn 민주당원 Democrat
minjujuŭi 민주주의 democracy
minjujuŭija 민주주의자 democrat
minjujuŭiŭi 민주주의의 democratic
minjung shinhak 민중 신학 people's theology
minmurŭi 민물의 freshwater
minsok ch'um 민속 춤 folk dance
minsok ŭmak 민속 음악 folk music
mint'ŭ 민트 mint
mint'ŭ chyok'ollit 민트 쵸콜릿 mint
minyo 민요 folk song
minyo kasu 민요 가수 folk singer
mirae 미래 future; ***miraeeŭi kyehoek/saenggak*** 미래에의 계획/생각 plan/think ahead
miraehyŏngŭi 미래형의 futuristic
mirhanghada 밀항하다 stow away
mirhangja 밀항자 stowaway
miri 미리 beforehand, in advance
miribogi 미리보기 print preview COMPUT
miri haenghaejida 미리 행해지다 precede
miri mandŭrŏjyŏ innŭn 미리 만들어져 있는 ready-made
miri naeda 미리 내다 advance
miri sŏltchŏngdoen 미리 설정된 default (setting)
mirŏ chech'ida 밀어 제치다 push away
mirŏdakch'yŏ it-tta 밀어닥쳐 있다 be swamped with
mirŏnaeda 밀어내다 shove off, push off; pump
mirŏnŏt'a 밀어넣다 slide; cram
mirŏ puch'ida 밀어 붙이다 squeeze up
mirŏ umjigida 밀어 움직이다 wheel
miro 미로 maze
Mirŭkppul 미륵불 Maitreya Buddha
miruda 미루다 wait
misa 미사 mass

misaegŭi 미색의 off-white
misaengmure ŭihae punhaega toenŭn 미생물에 의해 분해가 되는 biodegradable
misail 미사일 missile
misayŏguŭi 미사여구의 flowery
misehan 미세한 fine
Mishik ch'uk-kku 미식 축구 (American) football
Mishik ch'uk-kku kyŏnggijang 미식 축구 경기장 gridiron
Mishik ch'uk-kku sŏnsu 미식 축구 선수 (American) football player
mishin 미신 superstition
mishinŭl minnŭn 미신을 믿는 superstitious
misŏngnyŏnja 미성년자 minor (*child*)
misŏngnyŏnjaida 미성년자이다 be underage
misŏngnyŏnŭi 미성년의 underage
misŏngsugŭi 미성숙의 immature
miso 미소 smile
misojit-tta 미소짓다 smile; smile at
misshik-kka 미식가 gourmet
misuga 미숙아 premature baby
misuk'an 미숙한 immature, juvenile; unskilled
misulga 미술가 artist, painter
misulgwan 미술관 art gallery
misungnyŏn nodongja 미숙련 노동자 unskilled labor
mit 밑 base, bottom
mitchul kŭt-tta 밑줄 긋다 underline
mitkkŭrim 밑그림 design
mitppadagŭro ttŏrŏjida 밑바닥으로 떨어지다 reach rock bottom
mitppadak 밑바닥 bottom, underside
mit-tta 믿다 believe
mit'e 밑에 underneath; ***chang-ŭi / ŏndŏgŭi mit'e*** 장의 / 언덕의 밑에 at the foot of the page / hill
mit'ing 미팅 meeting, session; blind date
mit'ŏ 미터 meter
mit'ŏppŏbŭi 미터법의 metric
mit'ŭ 미트 mitt
mit'ŭro tŏnjyŏ 밑으로 던져 underarm throwing
mium 미움 hate
miwallyo 미완료 imperfect
miwŏhada 미워하다 hate
miyak'an 미약한 feeble
miyak'an chinghu 미약한 징후 hint
miyongsa 미용사 beautician; hairdresser
miyongshil 미용실 beauty parlor
mŏdŏmnŭn 멋없는 tasteless
mŏgi 먹이 prey
mŏgida 먹이다 feed
mŏgirŭl chuda 먹이를 주다 feed
mŏgŏbŏrida 먹어버리다 consume, eat up
mŏgŏboda 먹어보다 try *food*
mŏgŏ ch'iuda 먹어 치우다 eat up
mŏgŭjan 머그잔 mug
mŏgŭl su innŭn 먹을 수 있는 edible
mŏgŭl su ŏmnŭn 먹을 수 없는 uneatable
mŏk-kkie chot'a 먹기에 좋다 nice to eat
mŏk-kko salda 먹고 살다 live on *food*
mŏktta 먹다 eat, have
mŏlda 멀다 be distant, be remote; be unskilled
mŏlli 멀리 far, far away ◊ remotely
mŏlli ttŏrŏjim 멀리 떨어짐 seclusion
mŏlli ttŏrŏjin 멀리 떨어진 far away, remote
mŏlli ttŏrŏjyŏ hanjŏk'an 멀리 떨어져 한적한 secluded
mŏlli ttŏrojyŏ it-tta 멀리 떨어져 있다 it's a long way off
mŏlli ttwigi 멀리 뛰기 broad jump, long jump
mŏlmiga chal nanŭn 멀미가 잘 나는 squeamish
mŏlt'imidiŏ 멀티미디어 multimedia
mŏmch'uda 멈추다 stop; stall; seize up; put a stop to
mŏmch'uge hada 멈추게 하다 stop, halt, bring to a standstill
mŏmch'ul su ŏmnŭn 멈출 수 없는 remorseless, relentless
mŏmch'um chŏngji 멈춤 정지 no stopping
mŏmch'um shinho 멈춤 신호 stop sign
mŏmch'un 멈춘 be at a standstill
mŏmullŏ it-tta 머물러 있다 stick around

mŏmurŭda 머무르다 stay
mŏn 먼 distant, remote
mŏng 멍 bruise
mŏngch'ŏng-i 멍청이 idiot, dope, jerk
mŏngdŭlda 멍들다 bruise
mŏngdŭlge hada 멍들게 하다 bruise
mŏngdŭn nun 멍든 눈 black eye
mŏng-e 멍에 yoke (*for oxen*)
mŏnghage hada 멍하게 하다 stupefy
mŏnghan 멍한 vacant, blank, absent-minded
mŏngk'i sŭp'aenŏ 멍키 스패너 monkey wrench
mŏngmŏng-i 멍멍이 doggie
mŏngnŭn p'iimyak 먹는 피임약 the (contraceptive) pill
mŏnji 먼지 dirt; grit; dust
mŏnji magi tŏpkkae 먼지 막이 덮개 dust cover
mŏnjirŭl t'ŏlda 먼지를 털다 dust
mŏnji tangnŭn hŏnggŏp 먼지 닦는 헝겊 duster
mŏnjit'usŏng-iŭi 먼지투성이의 dusty
mŏnjŏ 먼저 first
mŏnjŏtppŏnŭi 먼젓번의 past, former
mŏn kose(sŏ) 먼 곳에(서) in the distance
mŏp'in 머핀 muffin
mŏri 머리 head; hair; ***mŏrirŭl tchada*** 머리를 짜다 rack one's brains
mŏriga nappŭn 머리가 나쁜 not clever
mŏriga pŏtkkyŏjinŭn 머리가 벗겨지는 balding
mŏriga saltchak ton 머리가 살짝 돈 be slightly crazy
mŏrihyŏng 머리형 hairstyle, hairdo
mŏri indu 머리 인두 tongs
mŏri kamtta 머리 감다 shampoo
mŏrikkŭch'i tchuppyŏt'aejinŭn 머리끝이 쭈뼛해지는 hair-raising
mŏrik'arak 머리카락 hair
mŏri manŭn lol 머리 마는 롤 roller (*for hair*)
mŏrinmal 머릿말 header (*in text*)
mŏri patch'im 머리 받침 headrest
mŏrip'in 머리핀 hairpin
mŏriro pat-tta 머리로 받다 head *ball*; head-butt; bump one's head
mŏrirŭl charŭda 머리를 자르다 have a haircut, get one's hair cut
mŏrirŭl handae mat-tta 머리를 한대 맞다 get a bump on the head
mŏrirŭl sonjirhada 머리를 손질하다 have one's hair done
mŏri sŭk'ap'ŭ 머리 스카프 headscarf
mŏritkkajuk 머리가죽 scalp
mŏritkkisa 머릿기사 headline
mŏritkkisaro k'ŭge ch'wigŭpttoeda 머릿기사로 크게 취급되다 make the headlines
mŏshinnŭn 멋있는 stylish
mŏsŭl chal naenŭn 멋을 잘 내는 fashionable
mŏtchida 멋지다 be stylish
mŏtchige 멋지게 impeccably
mŏtchin 멋진 smart, elegant; stylish; nice, lovely
mŏt-tta 멎다 let up; stop
mo 모 *countword for tofu*
moanot'a 모아놓다 collect
mobang 모방 imitation, copying; copy
mobanghada 모방하다 imitate, copy
mobang pŏmjoe 모방 범죄 copycat crime
mobil 모빌 cell phone, *Br* mobile
mobŏmjŏgin 모범적인 exemplary
mobŏmŭi 모범의 model, perfect
modakppul 모닥불 camp fire
model 모델 model
modem 모뎀 modem
moderida 모델이다 be a model, model
moderŭl hada 모델을 하다 model *clothes*
modok 모독 violation
modok'ada 모독하다 violate; blaspheme
modŭ 모드 mode COMPUT
modŭn 모든 all; whole; every
modŭn kwanshimŭl ssot-tta 모든 관심을 쏟다 make a fuss of
modu 모두 everyone; all
mogi 모기 mosquito
mogihyang 모기향 mosquito coil
mogijang 모기장 mosquito net
mogi maeida 목이 매이다 choke
mogi marŭda 목이 마르다 be thirsty
mogi t'ada 목이 타다 be parched

mogong 모공 pore
mogŭl charŭda 목을 자르다 decapitate
mogŭl chorŭda 목을 조르다 choke
mogŭl kilge ppaeda 목을 길게 빼다 crane one's neck
mogŭl kkolttak-kkŏrida 목을 꼴딱거리다 gurgle
mogŭl ppida 목을 삐다 have a crick in the neck
mogugŏ 모국어 native language, mother tongue
moguk 모국 native country
mogyeŭi 모계의 maternal
mogyoil 목요일 Thursday
mogyok 목욕 bath
mogyok kaun 목욕 가운 bathrobe
mogyok sugŏn 목욕 수건 bath towel
mogyokt'ang 목욕탕 public bathhouse
mogyokt'ang kkalgae 목욕탕 깔개 bath mat
mogyok'ada 목욕하다 have a bath, bathe
mohŏm 모험 venture; adventure
mohŏmjŏk 모험적 adventurous
mohŏmŭl chŭlginŭn 모험을 즐기는 adventurous *person*
mohŏmŭl hada 모험을 하다 venture; take the plunge
mohoesa 모회사 parent company, holding company
mohohage 모호하게 vaguely
mohohan 모호한 vague
mohyŏng 모형 model, miniature; mock-up
mohyŏng-ŭi 모형의 model
moida 모이다 meet; congregate; accumulate
moim 모임 gathering
moirŭl tchoda 모이를 쪼다 pick at one's food
moisch'yŏraijŏ 모이스쳐라이저 moisturizer
moja 모자 hat
mojaik'ŭ 모자이크 mosaic
mojarada 모자라다 be short of, be wanting in; be stupid
mojaran 모자란 useless
mojaranŭn 모자라는 scarce; ***chigwŏni mojaranŭn*** 직원이 모자라는 short-staffed
mojik 모직 woolen
mojim 모짐 severity
mojin 모진 severe
mojingmul 모직물 woolen fabric
mojohada 모조하다 forge
mojo posŏngnyu 모조 보석류 costume jewelry
mojop'um 모조품 imitation
mojori 모조리 without exception; completely
mok 목 neck; throat
mok 몫 share, quota
mokch'oji 목초지 field
mokch'ugŏptcha 목축업자 stockbreeder
mok-kkŏri 목걸이 necklace, pendant
mok-kkŏrijul 목걸이줄 chain (*jewelry*)
mok-kkong 목공 woodwork
mok-kkwanak-kki 목관악기 woodwind
mok-kkyŏktcha 목격자 (eye)witness
mok-kkyŏk'ada 목격하다 witness
mokkumŏng 목구멍 throat
mokp'yo 목표 objective, goal, target
mokp'yo kŭrup 목표 그룹 target group
mokp'yo magamil 목표 마감일 target date
mokp'yoro hada 목표로 하다 target
mokp'yoro samtta 목표로 삼다 aim at; aim to
mok sat'ang 목 사탕 throat lozenges
mokssa 목사 priest
moksshwin 목쉰 hoarse
mokssŏn 목선 neckline
mokssori 목소리 voice, tone of voice; ***k'ŭn mokssoriro*** 큰 목소리로 in a loud voice
mokssu 목수 joiner, carpenter
moktchae 목재 timber
moktchang 목장 ranch
moktchangju 목장주 rancher
moktchŏgŏ 목적어 object GRAM
moktchŏk 목적 objective, aim; ***.../ moktchŏgŭro*** ...ㄹ목적으로 with a view to
moktchŏktchi 목적지 destination
moktcho pubun 목조 부분 woodwork, wooden part

moktchorŭda 목조르다 throttle
mokttari 목다리 crutch
mokttŏlmi 목덜미 nape of the neck
mokttori 목도리 scarf, muffler
mokt'an 목탄 charcoal
molda 몰다 drive
molgo tanida 몰고 다니다 kick around
mollae 몰래 secretly, privately; furtively
mollae hanŭn 몰래 하는 stealthy
mollae pekkida 몰래 베끼다 (secretly) copy
mollak 몰락 comedown; downfall
Molmon-gyo 몰몬교 Mormonism
molttudoen 몰두된 engrossed in
molttuhada 몰두하다 immerse oneself in; ***ire molttuhada*** 일에 몰두하다 bury oneself in work
molttuhan 몰두한 preoccupied, absorbed
mom 몸 body; ***onmomi ssushida*** 온몸이 쑤시다 it hurts all over
momburimch'ida 몸부림치다 writhe, thrash about; struggle
mome kkok mannŭn 몸에 꼭 맞는 skin-tight
momi choch'i anŭn 몸이 좋지 않은 unwell, poorly
momi chot'a 몸이 좋다 feel well
momi pulp'yŏnhan 몸이 불편한 indisposed, unwell
momi tchibudŭdŭhada 몸이 찌부드드하다 be feeling under the weather
momjorishik'ida 몸조리시키다 take good care of
momkkap 몸값 ransom
mommae 몸매 figure, physique
mommae ch'itssu 몸매 치수 vital statistics
momsŏrich'ida 몸서리치다 shudder
momsusaek'ada 몸수색하다 frisk
momtchibi chagŭn 몸집이 작은 petite
momtchit ŏnŏ 몸짓 언어 body language
momttung-i 몸뚱이 trunk
momŭi 몸의 bodily
momŭl kuburida 몸을 구부리다 slouch; crouch
momŭl umsshirhada 몸을 움씰하다 cringe
momŭro 몸으로 bodily
momyŏnhada 모면하다 escape; avoid, evade
monaegi 모내기 rice planting
Monggo 몽고 Mongolia ◊ Mongolian
mongmarŭda 목마르다 be thirsty
mongmarŭn 목마른 thirsty
mongnoge ollida 목록에 올리다 list, put on a list
mongnok 목록 list, roll, inventory
mongnyuppyŏngja 몽유병자 sleep walker
mongsangga 몽상가 (day)dreamer
mongsanghada 몽상하다 (day)dream
mongttang chŏjŏt-tta 몽땅 젖었다 wet through
moning k'ol 모닝 콜 wake-up call
monit'ŏ 모니터 monitor COMPUT
monmŏri 뭇머리 head
monsun 몬순 monsoon
monsun kyejŏl 몬순 계절 monsoon season
mopsshi 몹시 very, terribly
morae 모래 sand
morae chumŏni 모래 주머니 sandbag
morae ŏndŏk 모래 언덕 sand dune
moraep'an 모래판 sandpit
moraesaegŭi 모래색의 sandy *color*
moranaeda 몰아내다 repel
more 모레 the day after tomorrow
mori 몰이 round-up
morinjŏnghan 몰인정한 inhuman
morŭda 모르다 not know; be ignorant of; not appreciate; ignore; ***morŭgessŭmnida*** 모르겠습니다 I don't know; ***naega kŏŭi morŭnŭn kŏt*** 내가 거의 모르는 것 the little I know ◊: ***...ltchido morŭnda*** ...ㄹ지도 모른다 may, might; ***kŭ yŏjaga kaltchido morŭnda*** 그 여자가 갈지도 모른다 I don't know whether she'll go, she may go
morŭmot'ŭ 모르모트 guinea pig
morŭnŭn 모르는 strange, unknown; ignorant
morŭp'in 모르핀 morphine

moshida 모시다 attend to, serve; accompany, escort
moshinnŭn 멋있는 good-looking *man*
mosŏng 모성 motherhood
mosŏri 모서리 edge
mossaenggida 못생기다 be ugly
mosshi 모씨: ***Pak mosshi*** 박 모씨 a certain Mr Park
mosun 모순 contradiction; discrepancy
mosundoen 모순된 contradictory
mosundoenŭn 모순되는 inconsistent
mot 못 nail; peg
mot... 못... cannot; ***...ji mot'ada*** ...지 못하다 be unable to, cannot
motppoda 못보다 overlook
mot salge kulda 못 살게 굴다 bully
motssaenggin 못생긴 plain, homely
mot-ttoen 못된 nasty; ***mot-ttoen chisŭl hada*** 못된 짓을 하다 be up to something (bad)
mot'age hada 못하게 하다 discourage; stop, prevent
mot'el 모텔 motel
mot'ŏ 모터 motor
mot'ŏbot'ŭ 모터보트 motorboat
mot'o 모토 motto
mot'ung-i 모퉁이 turning, turn, corner
mot'ung-irŭl tolda 모퉁이를 돌다 turn a corner; corner (*of vehicle*)
moŭda 모으다 collect; gather; accumulate; save; ***chogagŭl moŭda*** 조각을 모으다 piece together
moŭi 모의 scheme
moŭihada 모의하다 scheme
moŭiŭi 모의의 mock
moŭm 모음 vowel
moŭn 모은 collected
moyang 모양 appearance, look; shape
moyŏ it-tta 모여 있다 be gathered together; be crowded
moyok 모욕 insult
moyok'ada 모욕하다 insult
moyurŭl mŏgida 모유를 먹이다 breastfeed
mu 무 nil
mu... 무... non...
mu 무 radish
muak 무악 shamanistic music
mubangbiŭi 무방비의 defenseless, unprotected
mubŏbŭi 무법의 disorderly; lawless
mubunbyŏl 무분별 indiscretion
mubunbyŏrhan 무분별한 indiscreet
much'abyŏrŭi 무차별의 indiscriminate
much'aegimhan 무책임한 irresponsible
much'ŏk 무척 extremely; ***much'ŏk ttokttok'an*** 무척 똑똑한 brilliant, very intelligent
much'ŏkch'u tongmul 무척추 동물 invertebrate
mudae 무대 stage
mudae paegyŏng 무대 배경 scenery, scenes
mudang 무당 shaman (*female*)
mudangbŏlle 무당벌레 ladybug
mudan hwoengdan 무단 횡단 jaywalking
mudan kŏjuhada 무단 거주하다 squat (*in building*)
mudan kŏjuja 무단 거주자 squatter
mudan kyŏlssŏk'ada 무단 결석하다 play truant
mudin 무딘 blunt
mudŏm 무덤 grave, tomb
mudŏmdŏmhan 무덤덤한 impervious to
mudŭktchŏm 무득점 love (*in tennis*)
mudujirhada 무두질하다 tan *leather*
muga 무가 shaman song
mugamgak 무감각 insensitivity
mugamgak'an 무감각한 callous, insensitive; numb
muge 무게 weight
mugega nagada 무게가 나가다 weigh
mugero nullyŏjida 무게로 눌려지다 be weighed down with
mugerŭl talda 무게를 달다 weigh
mugi 무기 weapon
mugihanŭro 무기한으로 indefinitely
muginhada 묵인하다 tolerate
mugirŭl ppaeat-tta 무기를 빼앗다 disarm
mugiŭi 무기의 inorganic
mugŏptta 무겁다 be heavy; be important

mugŏun 무거운 heavy
mugŏun 무거운 weighty, hefty
mugonghaeŭi 무공해의 nonpolluting
mugŭbŭi 무급의 unpaid
Mugunghwa 무궁화 Rose of Sharon
mugunghwa nesŭi 무궁화 넷의 four-star
mugwanhada 무관하다 be unrelated; be irrelevant
mugwanshim 무관심 indifference
mugwanshimhan 무관심한 offhand, indifferent
muhaehan 무해한 harmless; inoffensive
muhan 무한 infinity
muhanhan 무한한 infinite
muhanjŏnghan 무한정한 indefinite
muhanŭi 무한의 boundless
muhŏgaŭi 무허가의 unauthorized
muhwagwa 무화과 fig
muhyŏrŭi 무혈의 bloodless
muhyohwahada 무효화하다 invalidate; overrule
muhyorohada 무효로 하다 annul, revoke
muhyoŭi 무효의 invalid, null and void
muilp'unŭi 무일푼의 penniless
muinŭi 무인의 unmanned
mujabihan 무자비한 merciless, remorseless
mujagwi ch'uch'ul kŏmsa 무작위 추출 검사 spot check
mujagwihan 무작위한 arbitrary
mujagwiro 무작위로 at random, willy-nilly; ***mujagwiro kŏmsahada*** 무작위로 검사하다 carry out a spot check
mujagwi saemp'ŭl 무작위 샘플 random sample
mujagwiŭi 무작위의 random
mujang haeje 무장 해제 disarmament
mujang haejeshik'ida 무장 해제시키다 disarm
mujanghan 무장한 armed
mujang kangdo 무장 강도 armed robbery; gunman
mujangshik'ida 무장시키다 arm
mujang-ŭl haejehada 무장을 해제하다 disarm
muji 무지 ignorance
mujigae 무지개 rainbow
mujilssŏ 무질서 lawlessness; confusion; disorder
mujilssŏhan 무질서한 disorganized
mujinjanghan 무진장한 inexhaustible
mujiŭi 무지의 plain
mujŏgŭi 무적의 invincible
mujŏltchehan 무절제한 immoderate
mujŏngbu sangt'ae 무정부 상태 anarchy
mujŏnghan 무정한 unfeeling
mujŏn-gi 무전기 walkie-talkie
mujŏnŭro 무전으로 by radio
mujoeimŭl sŏnŏnhada 무죄임을 선언하다 acquit
mujoero hada 무죄로 하다 acquit, clear
mujoerŭl chŭngmyŏnghada 무죄를 증명하다 exonerate, clear
mujokkŏnŭi 무조건의 unconditional
mujungnyŏgŭi 무중력의 weightless
mujungnyŏk 무중력 weightlessness
mujut'aektcha 무주택자 the homeless
mukke hada 묵게 하다 take in, put up, give accommodation
muk-kke hada 묽게 하다 dilute
mukkŏ not'a 묶어 놓다 tie down
mukkŭm 묶음 packet; ***han mukkŭm*** 한 묶음 batch
mukssang 묵상 meditation
mukssanghada 묵상하다 meditate
muktta 묶다 tie, tie up
mukwanshimhan 무관심한 apathetic
mul 물 water
mulbang-ul p'ojang 물방울 포장 blister pack
mulbinu 물비누 gel, liquid soap
mulbora 물보라 spray
mulch'e 물체 object
mulda 물다 bite
muldŭrida 물들이다 infect
mulgalk'wi 물갈퀴 flipper
mulgalk'wiga tallin 물갈퀴가 달린 webbed
mulgi 물기 nip, bite
mulgŏn 물건 stuff, things
mulgŭn 묽은 thin, watery
mulgŭn sup'ŭ 묽은 수프 broth, soup

mulkka 물가 shore, waterside
mulkkae 물개 seal
mulkkam 물감 paint
mulkkawa yŏndongshik'in 물가와 연동시킨 index-linked
mulkkiga marŭda 물기가 마르다 drain
mulkkirŭl ppaeda 물기를 빼다 drain
mulkkirŭl tudŭryŏ chiuda 물기를 두드려 지우다 blot (dry)
mulkkogi 물고기 fish
mulkkoktchi 물꼭지 faucet
mulkkyŏl 물결 ripple; stream
mulli ch'iryo 물리 치료 physiotherapy
mulli ch'iryosa 물리 치료사 physiotherapist
mullihak 물리학 physics
mullihaktcha 물리학자 physicist
mullŏnada 물러나다 stand down; back away; ***...(ŭ)robut'ŏ mullŏna it-tta*** ...(으)로부터 물러나 있다 keep away from
mullon 물론 certainly, of course, sure; ***mullon andwaeji!*** 물론 안돼지! no way!; ***mullon anijyo!*** 물론 아니죠! of course not!
mulloniji 물론이지 no problem
mullonimnida 물론입니다 please do, by all means
mullyŏjuda 물려주다 hand down; make over
mulmangch'o 물망초 forget-me-not
mulmul kyohwan 물물 교환 barter
mulmul kyohwanhada 물물 교환하다 barter
mulnaeng-i 물냉이 watercress
mulppang-ul munŭi 물방울 무늬 spot (*in pattern*)
mulppurigae 물뿌리개 watering can
multchangnanŭl ch'ida 물장난을 치다 paddle
multchibi saenggida 물집이 생기다 blister
multchil 물질 matter
multchip 물집 blister
multchirŭi 물질의 material
mul t'aengk'ŭ 물 탱크 cistern
mul t'winŭn sori 물 튀는 소리 splash
mulyak 물약 mixture; medicine
mumohan 무모한 reckless
mumyŏng-ŭi 무명의 obscure; anonymous
mun 문 door; ***mune*** 문에 at the door; ***kagega munŭl tadat-tta*** 가게가 문을 닫았다 the store was shut
munbanggu 문방구 stationery
munbanggujŏm 문방구점 stationer's
munch'e 문체 style (*literary*)
mundan 문단 paragraph
mungch'i 뭉치 bundle, wad
mungch'ida 뭉치다 unite together
mungttuk'an 뭉뚝한 stubby
munhagŭi 문학의 literary
munhak 문학 literature
munhak sŏkssa 문학 석사 Master of Arts
munhakssa 문학사 arts degree
munhŏn mongnok 문헌 목록 bibliography
munhwa 문화 culture
Munhwach'eyukppu 문화체육부 Ministry of Culture and Sports
munhwajŏgin 문화적인 cultural
munhwajŏk ch'unggyŏk 문화적 충격 culture shock
Munhwa Pangsong 문화 방송 Munhwa Broadcasting Corporation, MBC
munhwayesul 문화예술 the arts
munjabi 문잡이 doorknob
munjang 문장 sentence
munjangnon 문장론 syntax
munjap'yo 문자표 character set
munje 문제 problem; trouble; question; ***tonŭi munjeida*** 돈의 문제이다 it's a question of money
munje haegyŏl 문제 해결 troubleshooting, problem solving
munje haegyŏlssa 문제 해결사 troubleshooter
munjeŏpsshi 문제없이 without any problems; safely
munjeŭi 문제의 in question
munjillŏ ŏpssaeda 문질러 없애다 rub off
munjillŏ taktta 문질러 닦다 scour
munjirŭda 문지르다 rub, scrub
munkku 문구 phrase
munmaek 문맥 context; ***Xŭl / rŭl munmaege match'wŏ /***

munmaegŭl pŏsŏna poda X을 / 를 문맥에 맞춰 / 문맥을 벗어나 보다 look at X in context / out of context
munmaeng-ŭi 문맹의 illiterate
munmyŏng 문명 civilization
munŏ 문어 octopus
munŏjida 무너지다 fall down, collapse, give way
munŏjilttŭt'an 무너질 듯한 tumbledown
munŏjim 무너짐 crash
munŏttŭrida 무너뜨리다 flatten, knock out
munppŏp 문법 grammar
munppŏpssang-ŭi 문법상의 grammatical
munshin 문신 tattoo
munsŏ 문서 document
munsŏe ŭihan myŏng-ye hweson 문서에 의한 명예 훼손 libel
munsŏ ŏmmu 문서 업무 paperwork
muntcha 문자 character, letter
muntchibang 문지방 doorstep, threshold
mun tudŭrinŭn sori 문 두드리는 소리 knock
munŭi 문의 inquiry
munŭi 무늬 pattern, design
munŭihada 문의하다 inquire
munŭi innŭn 무늬 있는 patterned
munŭng 무능 inability
munŭnghada 무능하다 be incompetent; *muŏsŭl hanŭn kŏse munŭnghada* 무엇을 하는 것에 무능하다 be incapable of doing sth
munŭnghage hada 무능하게 하다 incapacitate; cripple
munŭngnyŏk 무능력 incompetence
munŭngnyŏktcha 무능력자 incompetent, no-hoper
munŭngnyŏk'an 무능력한 incompetent
muŏnŭi 무언의 mute, silent; tacit
muŏshidŭn 무엇이든 whatever; *...nŭn kosŭn muŏshidŭnji* ...는 것은 무엇이든지 whatever
muŏshin-ga 무엇인가 something
muŏt 무엇 something; anything; what
muŏtppodado 무엇보다도 above all
muran-gyŏng 물안경 goggles
mure chamgin 물에 잠긴 waterlogged
muri 무리 group; strain
muri chit-tta 무리 짓다 congregate, form a group
muri choŭn 물이 좋은 freshwater
murie ŏullida 무리에 어울리다 fit in (*with a group*)
murihada 무리하다 be unreasonable
murihage ssŭda 무리하게 쓰다 overuse *machine etc*
murihanŭn 무리하는 compulsive
murihan yogu 무리한 요구 excessive demand, tall order
murijit-tta 무리짓다 group
murirŭl hada 무리를 하다 strain; injure
muri tŭlda 물이 들다 dye; be stained; become infected
murŏboda 물어보다 question, quiz
murŏttŭtda 물어뜯다 bite off
murŭda 무르다 take back; be soft
murŭiktta 무르익다 ripen
murŭl chuda 물을 주다 water *plants, animals*
murŭl naerida 물을 내리다 flush *water*
murŭl t'ada 물을 타다 water down *liquor etc*
murŭl t'wigida 물을 튀기다 splash
murŭmp'yo 물음표 question mark
murŭp 무릎 knee; lap; *murŭp'ŭl kkulk'o* 무릎을 꿇고 down on one's knees
murŭp kkult'a 무릎 꿇다 kneel
murye 무례 rudeness, disrespect
muryehada 무례하다 be rude
muryehan 무례한 rude, disrespectful
muryŏkk'ehada 무력게하다 paralyze
muryŏk'age hada 무력하게 하다 neutralize; overpower
muryŏk'an 무력한 impotent, powerless, helpless
muryŏŭi 무료의 free (*no cost*)
muryo iptchang 무료 입장 admission free
muryo kyŏnbon 무료 견본 free sample
muryoro 무료로 free of charge, for free
muryo t'onghwa 무료 통화 toll-free
muryoŭi 무료의 complimentary, free

musaengmurŭi 무생물의 inanimate
musahada 무사하다 be in safety
musahan 무사한 unharmed
musahi 무사히 safely
musahi chinagada 무사히 지나가다 blow over (*of crisis*)
mushi 무시 disregard
mushihada 무시하다 ignore; dismiss
mushihago 무시하고 in defiance of
mushillonja 무신론자 atheist
mushimushihan 무시무시한 dreadful; lurid; scary
mushin-gyŏnghan 무신경한 insensitive, callous
musŏn chŏnhwagi 무선 전화기 cordless phone; radio telephone
musŏnghan 무성한 overgrown
musŏng-ŭi 무성의 insincerity ◊ silent *movie*
musŏng-ŭihan 무성의한 insincere
musŏnŭi 무선의 wireless
musŏptta 무섭다 be appalling; be frightening
musŏwŏhada 무서워하다 be afraid of, be scared of
musoe 무쇠 cast iron
musoero mandŭn 무쇠로 만든 cast-iron
Musok Shinang 무속 신앙 Shamanism
musŭn 무슨 any; some; what kind of ◊ what; ***musŭn il issŏyo?*** 무슨 일 있어요? what's up?; ***musŭn soriya?*** 무슨 소리야? what are you saying?
musŭngbu 무승부 dead heat
musuhan 무수한 innumerable
musul 무술 martial arts
mut-tta 묻다 ask; ***..ŭi kŭnhwang-ŭl mut-tta*** ...의 근황을 묻다 ask after
muttukttuk'an 무뚝뚝한 surly; brusque
mut'e 뭍에 ashore
mut'e orŭda 뭍에 오르다 go ashore
mut'ong-ŭi 무통의 painless
muŭimi 무의미 nonsense
muŭimihan 무의미한 meaningless, pointless
mu-ŭishik 무의식 the subconscious
muŭishik sangt'aeŭi 무의식 상태의 unconscious
muŭishiktchŏgin 무의식적인 involuntary, unconscious
muyŏk 무역 business, trade
muyŏk chŏnshihoe 무역 전시회 trade fair
muyŏk-kkwan 무역관 trade mission
muyŏk pangnamhoe 무역 박람회 fair, trade show
muyŏk suji 무역 수지 balance of trade
muyŏn hwibaryu 무연 휘발유 unleaded gasoline
muyŏnŭi 무연의 lead-free
muyong 무용 dancing
muyongga 무용가 dancer
mwŏrago? 뭐라고? what?
mwŏragoyo? 뭐라고요? excuse me?
mwŏraguyo? 뭐라구요? pardon me?
myŏlch'i 멸치 anchovies
myŏltchong 멸종 extinction
myŏltchongdoen 멸종된 extinct
myŏltchongshik'ida 멸종시키다 exterminate
myŏltchong wigiŭi p'umjong 멸종 위기의 품종 endangered species
myŏn 면 cotton; aspect; township
myŏndo 면도 shave
myŏndogi 면도기 shaver
myŏndohada 면도하다 shave, have a shave
myŏndohaji anŭn 면도하지 않은 unshaven
myŏndok'al 면도칼 razor
myŏndonal 면도날 razor blade
myŏndoyong pinu 면도용 비누 shaving soap
myŏndoyong sol 면도용 솔 shaving brush
myŏng 명 *countword for people*
myŏngbaek'ada 명백하다 be clear
myŏngbaek'age 명백하게 obviously
myŏngbaek'age hada 명백하게 하다 make plain, make clear
myŏngbaek'i 명백히 evidently, apparently; explicitly
myŏngdanŭi ch'ŏnmŏrie 명단의 첫머리에 at the head of the list
myŏnggihada 명기하다 specify
myŏngham 명함 business card, visiting card
myŏnghwak'age hada 명확하게 하다 clarify

myŏnghwak'am 명확함 clarity
myŏnghwak'an 명확한 definite; articulate
myŏnghwak'i 명확히 expressly, explicitly; ***myŏnghwak'i p'yohyŏnhada*** 명확히 표현하다 express clearly
myŏngjak 명작 masterpiece
myŏngminhan 명민한 intelligent, sharp
myŏngnanghada 명랑하다 be bright; be cheerful
myŏngnyŏng 명령 command, order
myŏngnyŏnghada 명령하다 order, command, instruct
myŏngnyŏngjŏgin 명령적인 dictatorial
myŏngnyŏngppŏp 명령법 imperative GRAM
myŏngsa 명사 noun
myŏngsang 명상 meditation
myŏngsanghada 명상하다 meditate
myŏngserŭl palk'ida 명세를 밝히다 itemize
myŏngsesŏ 명세서 specifications
-myŏnsŏ 면서 (*indicates two parallel actions*): ***mashimyŏnsŏ iyagihap-sshida*** 마시면서 이야기합시다 let's talk over a drink
myŏngsŏk'an 명석한 clear
myŏngsŏng 명성 fame; standing; prestige
myŏngsŏng-i nainnŭn 명성이 나있는 prestigious
myŏng-ye 명예 honor
myŏng-ye hwesonhada 명예 훼손하다 libel
myŏng-ye t'oejiksshik'ida 명예 퇴직시키다 pension off
myŏnhada 면하다 look onto
myŏnhŏ pat-tta 면허 받다 be licensed
myŏnhŏtchŭng 면허증 license
myŏnhoe shigan 면회 시간 visiting hours
myŏnje 면제 immunity
myŏnjedoeda 면제되다 be exempt from
myŏnjedoen 면제된 immune; exempt
myŏnjehae chuda 면제해 주다 exempt from, excuse from
myŏnjŏk 면적 area
myŏnjŏnesŏ 면전에서 in the presence of
myŏnjŏp 면접 interview
myŏnjŏpkkwan 면접관 interviewer
myŏnjŏp'ada 면접하다 interview
myŏnmirhada 면밀하다 be detailed, be meticulous
myŏnmirhan 면밀한 rigorous
myŏnmirhi 면밀히 meticulously
myŏnmyŏch'ŭi 몇몇의 several
myŏn samuso 면사무소 township office
myŏnsejŏm 면세점 duty-free shop
myŏnsep'um 면세품 duty-free (*goods*)
myŏnseŭi 면세의 duty-free, tax-free
myŏnŭnim 며느님 (*polite*) daughter-in-law
myŏnŭri 며느리 daughter-in-law
myŏnŭro mandŭn 면으로 만든 cotton
myŏnyŏgŭi 면역의 immune
myŏnyŏk 면역 immunity
myŏnyŏk ch'egye 면역 체계 immune system
myŏt 몇 how many; how much; ***onŭl myŏch'irijyo?*** 오늘 몇일이죠? what's the date today?
myŏt kae 몇 개 several
myŏt pŏnina kyesok 몇 번이나 계속 time and again
myŏt pun ch'airo 몇 분 차이로 by a couple of minutes
myŏt shiimnikka? 몇 시입니까? what's the time?, what time is it?
myoan 묘안 brainwave
myohage tamtta 묘하게 닮다 have an uncanny resemblance to
myohan 묘한 uncanny
myoji 묘지 cemetery, graveyard
myojong 묘종 seedling (*of plant*)
myomok 묘목 seedling (*of tree*)
myosa 묘사 description
myosahada 묘사하다 describe
myujik'ŏl 뮤지컬 musical (*drama*)
myul 뮬 mule, slipper

N

na 나 I ◊ me ◊ mine
nabang 나방 moth
nabi 나비 butterfly
nabi nekt'ai 나비 넥타이 bow tie
nabip 납입 payment
nabip chabon 납입자본 equity capital
na chashin 나 자신 myself
nach'ehwa 나체화 nude
nach'ejuŭija 나체주의자 nudist
nach'ero 나체로 in the nude
nach'imban 나침반 compass
nach'uda 낮추다 turn down; belittle
nada 나다 it's me ◊ flare up
nadal 낟알 grain
nae 내 my
naebaet-tta 내뱉다 spit out
naebŏrida 내버리다 throw out, dump
naebŏryŏduda 내버려두다 leave alone; leave unattended
naebŏryŏdun 내버려둔 unattended
naebu 내부 inside
naebu chŏngbo 내부 정보 inside information
naebue(sŏ) 내부에(서) inside
naebue innŭn 내부에 있는 inside
naebu haeksshim chipttan 내부 핵심 집단 in-crowd
naebuin 내부인 insider
naebujŏgŭro 내부적으로 internally
naebuŭi 내부의 inner, internal
naeda 내다 provide; serve; spare; give off
naedaboda 내다보다 look out (of)
naedŏnjida 내던지다 fling, throw
naegak 내각 cabinet
naegi 내기 bet, wager; ***...e naegirŭl kŏlda*** ...에 내기를 걸다 bet
naegusŏng-i innŭn 내구성이 있는 durable
naegusŏng-i kanghan 내구성이 강한 resilient
naehyangjŏgin 내향적인 retiring
naeil 내일 tomorrow; ***naeil ach'im*** 내일 아침 in the morning, tomorrow morning; ***naeil i shigankkaji*** 내일 이 시간까지 by this time tomorrow
naejangdoeŏ innŭn 내장되어 있는 built-in
naejangdoeŏ it-tta 내장되어 있다 be supplied with
naejŏn 내전 civil war
naekkwa ŭisa 내과 의사 physician
nae kŏt 내 것 mine
naek'iji annŭn 내키지 않는 reluctant
naeda 내다 pay; ***naega naenda*** 내가 낸다 I'm paying, this is on me
naekkwa chŏnmun ŭisa 내과 전문 의사 internist
naembi 냄비 pot, saucepan
naemilda 내밀다 extend, stretch
naemirhage 내밀하게 in private, privately
naemsae 냄새 smell; odor; scent
naemsaega nada 냄새가 나다 smell, reek
naemsae nanŭn 냄새 나는 smelly
naemsaerŭl mat-tta 냄새를 맡다 smell, sniff
Naemubu 내무부 Department of the Interior
naenae 내내 all the time, all along; ***wŏryoilbut'ŏ kŭmnyoil tong-an naenae*** 월요일부터 금요일 동안 내내 Monday through Friday
naengbang 냉방 air-conditioning
naengbangjung 냉방중 air-conditioned
naengdae 냉대 snub
naengdaehada 냉대하다 snub
naengdam 냉담 reserve, aloofness
naengdamhan 냉담한 unfriendly
naengdong 냉동 freezing
naengdong shikp'um 냉동 식품 frozen food
naengdongshil 냉동실 freezer; freezing compartment
naenghok'age 냉혹하게 in cold

blood
naenghok'an 냉혹한 grim
naenghyŏrhage 냉혈하게 in cold blood
naenghyŏrhan 냉혈한 cold-blooded *fig*
naenghyŏrŭi 냉혈의 cold-blooded
naengjanggo 냉장고 fridge, freezer
naengjŏnghada 냉정하다 be cool, be calm
naengjŏnghan 냉정한 dispassionate, objective; calm, impassive; hardheaded
naengmyŏn 냉면 chilled noodles
naeng-ŏmhan 냉엄한 brutal
naengso 냉소 cynicism
naengsojŏgin 냉소적인 cynical
naeng-yuk 냉육 cold cuts
naenot'a 내놓다 set out; ***p'allyŏgo naenot'a*** 팔려고 내놓다 put up for sale
naepk'in 냅킨 napkin
naeppumtta 내뿜다 blow *smoke*; snort
naep'aenggaech'ida 내팽개치다 throw; toss away
naep'ip 내핍 austerity
naeribeda 내리베다 slash
naerida 내리다 get out (*of car etc*); get off, disembark; come down (*of rain*); lower; wind down; unload; bring in *verdict*; percolate, filter; ***araero naerida*** 아래로 내리다 scroll down
naerige hada 내리게 하다 bring down
naerimak-kkiri toeda 내리막길이 되다 go downhill, decline
naeri tŏpch'ida 내리 덮치다 swoop; swoop down on
naeryŏant'a 내려앉다 subside; descend
naeryŏ chuda 내려 주다 let off (*from car*)
naeryŏdaboda 내려다보다 overlook; look down
naeryŏgada 내려가다 go down, descend, get down
naeryŏga it-tta 내려가 있다 be down
naeryŏjuda 내려주다 drop; ***ch'a-esŏ naeryŏjuda*** 차에서 내려주다 drop off (*from car*)
naeryŏk 내력 personal history, career
naeryŏoda 내려오다 come down
naeryugŭi 내륙의 inland
naeryuk 내륙 interior
naesaek'aji ant'a 내색하지 않다 disguise one's emotions
naeshwida 내쉬다 exhale
naesŏn 내선 extension
naesŏngjŏgin 내성적인 withdrawn; introspective
naetchŏgin 내적인 inner
naetchot-tta 내쫓다 throw out, oust
naeŭi 내의 underwear
naeyŏlssŏng-ŭi 내열성의 heatproof, heat-resistant
naeyŏn-gigwan 내연기관 internal combustion engine
naeyŏnŭi ch'ŏ 내연의 처 common law wife
naeyong 내용 content; contents
nagada 나가다 go out; ***kŭnŭn chigŭm chŏng-wŏne nagait-tta*** 그는 지금 정원에 나가있다 he's out in the garden; ***nagaseyo!*** 나가세요! (get) out!; ***nagayo!*** 나가요! get out!
nagage hada 나가게 하다 let out
naga ttŏrŏjige hada 나가 떨어지게 하다 knock out
nagoja 낙오자 dropout
nagwŏn 낙원 paradise
nagwŏn-gat'ŭn 낙원같은 idyllic
nai 나이 age
nai chigŭt'an 나이 지긋한 elderly
naidŭrŏ kada 나이들어 가다 get on, become old
nai kapssŭl hae! 나이 값을 해! grow up!
naillon 나일론 nylon
naillonŭi 나일론의 nylon
nai tŭlda 나이 들다 age
nait'inggeil 나이팅게일 nightingale
nait'ŭ k'ŭllŏp 나이트클럽 nightclub, nightspot
naje 낮에 by day, in the daytime
najŭn 낮은 low
najŭn kubŭi 낮은 굽의 flat
najŭn tchogŭro 낮은 쪽으로 down
najŭn ŭmjarip'yo 낮은 음자리표 bass clef

najung-e 나중에 later, later on, afterward; ***najung-e poja!*** 나중에 보자! see you later!
najung-e tashi chŏnhwahada 나중에 다시 전화하다 call back TELEC
nakch'ŏnjŏgin 낙천적인 optimistic, happy-go-lucky
nakch'ŏnjuŭi 낙천주의 optimism
nakch'ŏnjuŭija 낙천주의자 optimist
nakka ch'aeda 낚아 채다 nab
nakkda 낚다 fish, angle; lure, entice; ***nakkŭn kŏt*** 낚은 것 catch *fish*
nakkwanjŏgin 낙관적인 optimistic
naksshi 낚시 fishing
naksshihada 낚시하다 fish
naksshippanŭl 낚시바늘 fish-hook
naksshitchul 낚싯줄 fishing line
naksshit-ttae 낚싯대 fishing rod
nakssŏ 낙서 graffiti
nakssŏndoen 낙선된 unsuccessful
nakssŭng 낙승 walkover
naktcherŭl pat-tta 낙제를 받다 flunk
naktchi 낙지 octopus
nakttam 낙담 dismay, disappointment
nakttamhan 낙담한 despondent, dejected; disheartened
nakttamshik'ida 낙담시키다 discourage; dishearten
nakt'ae 낙태 abortion
nakt'aehada 낙태하다 have an abortion
nakt'aeshik'ida 낙태시키다 terminate a pregnancy
nak'asan 낙하산 parachute
nak'asanbyŏng 낙하산병 paratrooper
nak'asanŭro naeryŏoda 낙하산으로 내려오다 parachute down
nak'asanŭro t'alch'urhada 낙하산으로 탈출하다 bail out (*of airplane*)
nak'asanŭro t'uhahada 낙하산으로 투하하다 parachute
nal 날 day; edge (*of knife*); blade
nalda 날다 fly
nalgae 날개 wing
nalgi 날기 flight; flying
nalgŭn 낡은 old; shabby; outmoded
nalkkŏsŭi 날것의 raw
nalktta 낡다 be old; be old-fashioned
nalk'aroptta 날카롭다 be sharp; be incisive; be cutting
nalk'aroun 날카로운 sharp; incisive, penetrating; pointed; searching
nallibŏpssŏk 난리법석 fuss
nallibŏpssŏk ttŏlda 난리법석 떨다 make a fuss
nallich'ida 난리치다 make a fuss; complain
nallida 날리다 spend, blow
nalsshi 날씨 weather
nalsshinhada 날씬하다 be slim
nalsshinhan 날씬한 slim
naltcha 날짜 date
naltchaga chinan 날짜가 지난 out of date
naltcharŭl chŏktta 날짜를 적다 date *document*, put a date on
nalttwimyŏ toradanida 날뛰며 돌아다니다 rampage, go on the rampage
nama it-tta 남아 있다 linger
Namap'ŭrik'a 남아프리카 South Africa ◊ South African
Namap'ŭrik'ain 남아프리카인 South African
Namap'ŭrik'aŭi 남아프리카의 South African
nambi 남비 pan
nambuŭi 남부의 southern
namch'ang 남창 male prostitute
namdongsaeng 남동생 (younger) brother
namdongtchogŭi 남동쪽의 southeast, southeastern
namdongtchogŭro 남동쪽으로 southeast
namdongtchok 남동쪽 southeast
namgida 남기다 leave; ***kŭga namgin tu ttal*** 그가 남긴 두 딸 his two surviving daughters
Namgŭk-kkwŏn 남극권 Antarctic
namgyŏjida 남겨지다 remain
namgyŏ tuda 남겨 두다 leave
Namhae 남해 South Sea, Korean Strait
Namhaedo 남해도 Namhae Island
namhakssaeng 남학생 schoolboy
Namhan 남한 South Korea ◊ South

Korean
Namhanin 남한인 South Korean
namhyang-ŭi 남향의 southerly
namja 남자 man, male
namja ch'in-gu 남자 친구 boyfriend
namjadaum 남자다움 manhood
namjadaun 남자다운 manly; macho; virile
namja hwajangshil 남자 화장실 men's room
namja kanhosa 남자 간호사 male nurse
namja paeu 남자 배우 actor
namja suyŏngbok 남자 수영복 swimsuit
namja undongga 남자 운동가 sportsman
namjit 남짓 more than
Nammi 남미 South America ◊ South American
Nammiin 남미인 South American
Nammiŭi 남미의 South American
nam mollae saltchak 남 몰래 살짝 on the sly
nam morŭge 남 모르게 behind the scenes
namnŭn shigan 남는 시간 spare time
namnuhan 남루한 ragged
namnyŏ konghagŭi 남녀 공학의 coeducational
namŏji 나머지 the rest, remainder
namŏji kŏt 나머지 것 the others
namŏjiŭi 나머지의 surplus
namp'yŏn 남편 husband
namsaek 남색 navy blue
namsŏngdaum 남성다움 virility
namsŏngjŏgin 남성적인 masculine
namsŏngmi 남성미 masculinity
namsŏng-ŭi 남성의 male, masculine
namsŏng uwŏltchuŭija 남성 우월주의자 male chauvinist (pig)
namsŏtchogŭi 남서쪽의 southwest, southwestern
namsŏtchogŭro 남서쪽으로 southwest
namsŏtchok 남서쪽 southwest
namtchoge 남쪽에 to the south of
namtchogŭi 남쪽의 south
namtchogŭro 남쪽으로 south, southward
namtchok 남쪽 south
namtchok chibang 남쪽 지방 south
namtta 남다 be left, remain; ***namŭn kŏshi ŏptta*** 남은 것이 없다 there isn't/aren't any left
namŭn kŏt 남은 것 left-overs
namu 나무 tree; wood
Namu Amit'abul 나무 아미타불 Namu Amit'abul (*Buddhist chant*)
namuga manŭn 나무가 많은 woody
namuga ugŏjin 나무가 우거진 wooded
namu kkŏptchil 나무 껍질 bark
namukkun 나무꾼 woodcutter
namurada 나무라다 reprimand, give a piece of one's mind
namural te ŏmnŭn 나무랄 데 없는 impeccable, irreproachable
namural te ŏpsshi 나무랄 데 없이 impeccably
namuro toen 나무로 된 wooden
namu sangja 나무 상자 crate
namutkkyŏl 나뭇결 grain
namuttalgi 나무딸기 raspberry
namyong 남용 abuse
nan 난 column
nanari 나날이 day by day
nanbang 난방 heating
nanbang changch'i 난방 장치 heating; heater
nanbanggi 난방기 radiator
nanch'ŏhage hada 난처하게 하다 stump, baffle
nanch'ŏhan 난처한 messy, unpleasant
nanch'ŏng chiyŏgesŏ 난청 지역에서 out of earshot
nanch'o 난초 orchid
nan-gan 난간 handrail
nangbi 낭비 waste
nangbibyŏgi shimhan 낭비벽이 심한 spendthrift
nangbiga shimhan 낭비가 심한 wasteful
nangbihada 낭비하다 waste, squander; ***shigan nangbiyeyo*** 시간 낭비예요 it's a waste of time
nan-giryu 난기류 turbulence
nangnongjang 낙농장 dairy
nangsonghada 낭송하다 recite
nanhaehan 난해한 obscure

nanjaeng-i 난쟁이 dwarf
nanjangp'an 난장판 madhouse
nanjap'an 난잡한 promiscuous
nanmin 난민 refugee
nanp'a 난파 shipwreck
nanp'adoeda 난파되다 be shipwecked
nanp'ashik'ida 난파시키다 shipwreck
nanp'ok'age 난폭하게 violently
nanp'ok'age milda 난폭하게 밀다 jostle
nanp'ok unjŏnja 난폭 운전자 road hog
nanp'ok'an 난폭한 rough, rowdy
nanso 난소 ovary
nant'u 난투 scuffle
nanŭn 나는 I
nanuda 나누다 divide, distribute
nanul su innŭn 나눌 수 있는 divisible
nanuŏ chuda 나누어 주다 hand out, deal out
nanutssem 나눗셈 division
naoda 나오다 come out, get out; add up to
naogehada 나오게 하다 flush out
nap 납 lead (*metal*)
napch'i 납치 kidnapping
napch'ibŏm 납치범 kidnapper
napch'ihada 납치하다 abduct, kidnap
nappajida 나빠지다 deteriorate, suffer
nap-ppuhada 납부하다 pay
nappŭda 나쁘다 be wrong, be bad (*morally*)
nappŭge 나쁘게 badly
nappŭge haengdonghada 나쁘게 행동하다 misbehave
nappŭn 나쁜 bad
nappŭn haengdong 나쁜 행동 misbehavior
nappŭn nyŏn V 나쁜 년 bitch *pej*
napsseja 납세자 tax payer
napsse shin-gosŏ 납세 신고서 tax return
napttŭk 납득 understanding
nap'al 나팔 brass trumpet
nara 나라 nation, country
naragada 날아가다 fly away, fly off; fly out
naranhi 나란히 side by side
naraŭi 나라의 national
narŭda 나르다 carry
narŭnhan 나른한 drowsy; weak
narutppae 나룻배 ferry
nasamot 나사못 screw; ***muŏsŭl muŏse nasamosŭro kojŏngshik'ida*** 무엇을 무엇에 나사못으로 고정시키다 screw sth to sth
nasarŭl p'ulda 나사를 풀다 unscrew
nasasan 나사산 thread (*of screw*)
nasŏda 나서다 come out, appear
nasŏnhyŏng kyedan 나선형 계단 winding staircase
nasŏnhyŏng-ŭi 나선형의 spiral
nasŏnhyŏng-ŭi ch'ŭnggye 나선형의 층계 spiral staircase
nat 낮 daylight
nat 낫 scythe
natch'uda 낮추다 lower; keep down
natch'un 낮춘 subdued
natch'uŏ poda 낮추어 보다 look down on
natkke hada 낫게 하다 heal
natssŏn saram 낯선 사람 stranger
nattcham 낮잠 nap
nattchamŭl chada 낮잠을 자다 have a nap
nat-tta 낳다 generate, create; ***airŭl nat-tta*** 아이를 낳다 give birth
nat-tta 낫다 heal, clear up
nat-tta 낮다 be low
nat'a 낳다 bear, give birth to; lay; spawn
nat'aehan 나태한 indolent, idle
nat'anada 나타나다 appear, turn up; manifest itself; haunt
nat'anaeda 나타내다 show, constitute
naŭi 나의 my
ne chashin 네 자신 yourself
Nedŏllandŭin 네덜란드인 the Dutch
Nedŏllandŭŏ 네덜란드어 Dutch (*language*)
Nedŏllandŭŭi 네덜란드의 Dutch
nekt'ai 넥타이 tie, necktie
neon ssain 네온 싸인 neon light
ne paero hada 네 배로 하다 quadruple

ne pal chimsŭng 네 발 짐승 quadruped
ne pŏn 네 번 four times
ne pŏntchaeŭi 네 번째의 fourth
Nep'al 네팔 Nepal ◊ Nepalese
ne ssangdung-i 네 쌍둥이 quadruplets
net 넷 four
net'ŭ 네트 net (*for tennis*)
net'ŭwŏk'ŭ 네트워크 network
nik'el 니켈 nickel
nisŭ 니스 varnish
nisŭrŭl ch'irhada 니스를 칠하다 varnish
nit'ŭ weŏ 니트 웨어 knitwear
...nji ...ㄴ지 → **...inji** ...인지
nŏ 너 (*informal*) you
nŏdobamnamu 너도밤나무 beech
nŏgŭrŏun 너그러운 decent
nŏhŭidŭl chashin 너희들 자신 yourselves
nŏhŭidŭl sŭsŭro 너희들 스스로 by yourselves
nŏkssŭl ilk'e hada 넋을 잃게 하다 devastate
nŏkssŭl ilt'a 넋을 잃다 get carried away
nŏlbi ttwigi 넓이 뛰기 long jump, broad jump
nŏlbŏjida 넓어지다 broaden, widen
nŏlbŭn 넓은 roomy, wide
nŏlbŭn kang-ŏgwi 넓은 강어귀 estuary
nŏlkke 넓게 widely; ***nŏlkke pyŏlch'yŏjin*** 넓게 펼쳐진 a vast expanse of; ***nŏlkke yŏllin*** 넓게 열린 wide-open
nŏlli p'ŏjyŏ innŭn 널리 퍼져 있는 pervasive
nŏlppanji 널빤지 plank
nŏlptta 넓다 be wide, be broad
nŏlp'ida 넓히다 broaden, widen; expand; dilate
nŏmch'ida 넘치다 exceed; overflow; ***kaemidŭllo nŏmch'ida*** 개미들로 넘치다 be teeming with ants; ***...esŏ nŏmch'yŏ hŭrŭda*** ...에서 넘쳐 흐르다 stream out of; ***kangttugi nŏmch'ida*** 강둑이 넘치다 flood its banks; ***kamjŏng-i nŏmch'inŭn*** 감정이 넘치는 effusive
nŏmgida 넘기다 turn; ***...ege kyŏltchŏng-ŭl / mun-jerŭl nŏmgida*** ...에게 결정을 / 문제를 넘기다 refer a decision / problem to
nŏmgyŏjuda 넘겨주다 hand over, surrender
nŏmŏ 넘어 past (*in time*)
nŏmŏjida 넘어지다 fall, trip up; stumble
nŏmŏjim 넘어짐 fall; stumble
nŏmŏsŏ 넘어서 beyond
nŏmŏttŭrida 넘어뜨리다 knock over; ***hŏrŏ nŏmŏttŭrida*** 헐어 넘어뜨리다 knock down
nŏmtta 넘어서다 exceed; be past; go over *mountain*; ***ilgop shiga nŏmŏssŏyo*** 일곱 시가 넘었어요 it's past 7 o'clock
nŏmu 너무 too; far; ***unbanhagie nŏmu mugŏp-tta*** 운반하기에 너무 무겁다 too heavy to carry; ***nŏmu andwaessŏyo*** 너무 안됐어요 that's really too bad; ***nega nŏmu chi-nach'yŏt-tta*** 네가 너무 지나쳤다 you've gone too far; ***kŭdŭlŭn iri nŏmu millyŏ issŏyo*** 그들은 일이 너무 밀려 있어요 they are way behind with their work
nŏmu honjap'an 너무 혼잡한 overcrowded
nŏmu ik'ida 너무 익히다 overdo
nŏmu mani 너무 많이 too much
nŏmu pissan 너무 비싼 too expensive, overpriced
nŏmu ttabunhan irida 너무 따분한 일이다 it's such a bore
nŏngnŏk'an 넉넉한 plentiful
nŏnjishi pich'ida 넌지시 비치다 insinuate, imply
nŏnjishi pich'uda 넌지시 비추다 make out, imply
nŏnŭn 너는 you (*informal*); as for you
nŏptchŏkttari 넓적다리 thigh
nŏrŏsŏ mallida 널어서 말리다 dripdry
nŏt'a 넣다 put in, inject
nŏt'ŭ 너트 nut
nŏŭi 너의 (*informal*) your
no 노 oar; paddle
noajuda 놓아주다 disengage

noa pŏrida 놓아 버리다 let go of
noa tuda 놓아 두다 put
nobaldaebarhada 노발대발하다 be furious with
nobaldaebarhan 노발대발한 livid
noch'ida 놓치다 miss (*not hit*); lose one's hold on; pass up *opportunity*
noch'ŏn k'ap'e 노천 카페 sidewalk café
no chŏt-tta 노 젓다 row *boat*
noch'ul 노출 exposure
noch'uldoen 노출된 revealing
noch'ulshik'ida 노출시키다 expose
noch'urhada 노출하다 expose; ***chinach'ige noch'urhada*** 지나치게 노출하다 overexpose
noch'uri pujok'an 노출이 부족한 underexposed
nodong 노동 labor
nodong chaeng-ŭi haeng-wi 노동 쟁의 행위 industrial action
nodong chohap 노동 조합 labor union
nodong hŏga 노동 허가 work permit
nodong in-gu 노동 인구 workforce
nodongja 노동자 laborer, worker
nodongja kyegŭbŭi 노동자 계급의 working-class
nodongja kyegŭp 노동자 계급 working class
Nodongjŏl 노동절 May Day, Labor Day
nodongjohabŭi chiktchangwiwŏn 노동조합의 직장위원 shop steward
noe chŏnmun oekkwa ŭisa 뇌 전문 외과 의사 brain surgeon
noejint'ang 뇌진탕 concussion
noejol 뇌졸 stroke
noemangnyŏm 뇌막염 meningitis
noemul 뇌물 bribe
noemul susu 뇌물 수수 bribery
noemurŭl chuda 뇌물을 주다 pay off, bribe
noerirŭl ttŏnaji annŭn 뇌리를 떠나지 않는 haunting
noeu 뇌우 thunderstorm
nogaut'ŭ 녹아우트 knockout
nogida 녹이다 melt; dissolve; defrost
nogi sŭlji annŭn 녹이 슬지 않는 rust-proof
nogi sŭn 녹이 슨 rusty
nogo 노고 toil
nogoltchŏgin 노골적인 direct; point-blank; obvious
nogoltchŏgin p'orŭno 노골적인 포르노 hardcore porn
nogoltchŏgŭro 노골적으로 pointblank
nogonhan 노곤한 lethargic
nogŭm 녹음 recording
nogŭmdoen 녹음된 canned
nogŭmgi 녹음기 cassette player; record player
nogŭmhada 녹음하다 tape
nogŭmshil 녹음실 recording studio
nogŭm t'eip'ŭ 녹음 테이프 cassette
nogŭn 녹은 molten
nohau 노하우 knowhow, expertise
noin 노인 geriatric
noinppyŏng-ŭi 노인병의 geriatric
nojang chŏngmaek 노장 정맥 varicose vein
nojo 노조 (labor) union
nok 녹 rust
nok chejŏje 녹 제거제 rust remover
nokch'a 녹차 green tea
nokch'oga toen 녹초가 된 exhausted
nokch'oga toeŏ 녹초가 되어 dead beat, dead tired
nokch'oro mandŭlda 녹초로 만들다 exhaust
nokch'oro mandŭnŭn 녹초로 만드는 grueling
nokkŭn 노끈 cord, string
nokssaegŭi 녹색의 green
nokssŭlda 녹슬다 rust
noktta 녹다 thaw; dissolve; melt
nok'ŭhada 노크하다 knock; ***munŭl nok'ŭhada*** 문을 노크하다 knock at the door
nok'wahada 녹화하다 tape, record
nok'washil 녹화실 recording studio
nolda 놀다 play
nolgo chinaeda 놀고 지내다 loaf around
nolgo innŭn 놀고 있는 idle
nollada 놀라다 marvel at; be surprised
nollage hada 놀라게 하다 surprise; shock; rock
nollapk'e 놀랍게 suprisingly

nolla poida 놀라 보이다 look surprised
nollaptta 놀랍다 be surprising
nollaŭn kŏt 놀라운 것 marvel
nollaun 놀라운 surprising; wonderful; ***...ranŭn kŏsŭn nollaun irida*** ...라는 것은 놀라운 일이다 it's a wonder that ...
nolli 논리 reasoning, argument, logic
nollida 놀리다 make fun of, tease; play a joke on; send up; scoff; quip
nollijŏgin 논리적인 logical
non 논 rice field, rice paddy
nonbat 논밭 rice fields and dry fields
nong-ak 농악 farmer's music
nong-akttae 농악대 traditional farmers' band
nong-aŭi 농아의 deaf-and-dumb
nongbu 농부 farmer
nongch'ukttoen 농축된 concentrated
nongdam 농담 joke
nongdamhada 농담하다 joke, jest
nongdam kŭmanhago 농담 그만하고 joking apart
nongdamŭi p'yojŏk 농담의 표적 butt (*of joke*)
nongdamŭro 농담으로 in jest, jokingly
nongdo 농도 consistency, texture
nongga 농가 farmhouse
nonggu 농구 basketball
nonggyŏng-e almajŭn 농경에 알맞은 arable
nongjang 농장 farm
nongjangmul 농작물 crop
nongjang-ŭi ilkkun 농장의 일꾼 farmworker
nongmal 녹말 cornstarch
nongmin 농민 peasant
nong-ŏbŭi 농업의 agricultural
nong-ŏp 농업 agriculture
nongsa 농사 agriculture, farming; ***nongsa chitkko salda*** 농사 짓고 살다 make a living from farming
nongsanmul 농산물 produce
nong-yang 농양 abscess
nonhada 논하다 argue, reason
nonjaeng 논쟁 argument; debate; controversy
nonjaenghada 논쟁하다 debate
nonjaengjŏgin 논쟁적인 provocative
nonjaeng-ŭi yŏjiga innŭn 논쟁의 여지가 있는 debatable
nonjaeng-ŭl irŭk'inŭn 논쟁을 일으키는 controversial
nonmun 논문 thesis, academic paper
nonp'iksshyŏn 논픽션 nonfiction
nonp'yŏnghada 논평하다 review
nontchŏm 논점 issue, topic
nonŭi 논의 discussion; ***nonŭi sahang*** 논의 사항 the point at issue
nonŭihada 논의하다 discuss
nonŭiŭi yŏjiga ŏmnŭn 논의의 여지가 없는 indisputable
nonyŏn 노년 old age
nopkke 높게 high
noptta 높다 be high
nop'i 높이 height; elevation; altitude; ***nugurŭl nop'i p'yŏngkkahada*** 누구를 높이 평가하다 have a high opinion of s.o.
nop'ida 높이다 increase, turn up; elevate
nop'i ttwigi 높이 뛰기 high jump
nop'ŭn 높은 high
nop'ŭn ponggŭbŭl pat-tta 높은 봉급을 받다 be highly paid
nop'ŭn kubŭi 높은 굽의 high-heeled
nop'ŭn sujun 높은 수준 high (*in statistics*)
norae 노래 song; chant
noraebang 노래방 karaoke room
noraehada 노래하다 sing; chant
noran 노란 yellow
norang 노랑 yellow
noransaegŭro 노란색으로 in yellow
norat'a 노랗다 be yellow
nori 놀이 play ◊ game
norich'in-gu 놀이친구 playmate
norit'ŏ 놀이터 playground
norŭnja 노른자 yolk
norŭnnorŭt'age kuptta 노릇노릇하게굽다 brown (*in cooking*)
norŭnnorŭt'age toeda 노릇노릇하게되다 brown (*in cooking*)
Norŭwei 노르웨이 Norway ◊ Norwegian
Norŭweiin 노르웨이인 Norwegian
Norŭweiŏ 노르웨이어 Norwegian (*language*)
Norŭweiŭi 노르웨이의 Norwegian

noryŏboda 노려보다 glare at
noryŏk 노력 effort, attempt
noryŏk'ada 노력하다 try, exert oneself; ***tangshinŭn tŏ yŏlshimhi noryŏk'aeya hamnida*** 당신은 더 열심히 노력해야 합니다 you must try harder
nosae 노새 mule
nosaganŭi purhwa 노사간의 불화 industrial dispute
nosahyŏbŭihwoe 노사협의회 works council
nosang kangdo 노상 강도 mugger
nosang kangdo haeng-wi 노상 강도 행위 mugging
nosang kangdojirŭl hada 노상 강도질을 하다 mug, rob on the street
nosoe 노쇠 senility
nosoehan 노쇠한 senile
nosuk'ada 노숙하다 sleep rough
notssoe 놋쇠 brass
not'a 놓다 put; put down
not'ŭbuk 노트북 notebook COMPUT
noŭl 노을 twilight
noye 노예 slave
noyŏum 노여움 anger
nŭgŭt'age 느긋하게 in a leisurely way
nŭgŭt'an 느긋한 easy-going, laidback; leisurely
nŭjŏjida 늦어지다 lose
nŭjŏjinda 늦어진다 it's getting late
nŭjŭn 늦은 late, overdue
nŭkkida 느끼다 feel, experience
nŭkkim 느낌 feeling; impression
nŭkkimp'yo 느낌표 exclamation point
nŭkttae 늑대 wolf
nŭl 늘 always, all the time; ***nŭl hanŭn kŏsŭro chushipsshio*** 늘 하는 것으로 주십시오 the usual, please
nŭlda 늘다 expand; mount up; ***op'aundŭga nŭlda*** 5파운드가 늘다 gain 5 pounds
nŭlgŏjida 늙어지다 grow old
nŭlgŭn 늙은 old
nŭlgŭnina chŏlmŭnina ttokkach'i 늙은이나 젊은이나 똑같이 old and young alike
nŭlktta 늙다 grow old
nŭllida 늘리다 extend, roll over; raise; lengthen; let out
nŭlsshinhan 늘씬한 trim
...nŭn ... 는 ◊ (*contrast particle, also used to introduce a topic*): ***nŏnŭn*** 너는 you; as for you; ***...nŭn cheoehago*** ... 는 제외하고 excluding ◊ (*relative*) which; who; whose; ***naega kongbuhanŭn kwamok*** 내가 공부하는 과목 the subject which I'm studying ◊ (*forms adjectives*): ***nurŏputtchi annŭn*** 눌어붙지 않는 nonstick
nŭngdongt'aeŭi 능동태의 active
nŭnggahada 능가하다 surpass, exceed
nŭnggŭlmajŭn usŭm 능글맞은 웃음 smirk
nŭnggŭlmatkke ut-tta 능글맞게 웃다 smirk
nŭngnyŏginnŭn 능력있는 able, skillful
nŭngnyŏgi ŏmnŭn 능력이 없는 incapable; inept
nŭngnyŏgŭl shihŏmhaebonŭn 능력을 시험해보는 challenging
nŭngnyŏk 능력 capability, ability; competence; faculty; ***...l nŭngnyŏgi it-tta*** ...ㄹ 능력이 있다 be capable of ...ing
nŭngnyŏk innŭn 능력 있는 capable, competent
nŭngnyŏng 능력 capacity, ability
nŭngnyul 능률 efficiency
nŭngnyultchŏgin 능률적인 efficient; streamlined
nŭngnyultchŏgŭro 능률적으로 efficiently
nŭngsuk 능숙 proficiency
nŭngsuk'ada 능숙하다 be skilled; ***muŏse nŭngsuk'ada*** 무엇에 능숙하다 be good at sth
nŭngsuk'an 능숙한 skillful, proficient
...nŭn kŏt ...는 것 ◊ (*creates a noun form*) ...ing; ***kongbu hanŭn kŏt*** 공부 하는 것 studying ◊ what; ***kŭgŏshi chega choahanŭn kŏshiyeyo*** 그것이 제가 좋아하는 것이에요 that's what I like

nŭp 늪 swamp
nŭp kat'ŭn 늪 같은 swampy
nŭrida 늘이다 extend, stretch; take down
nŭrida 느리다 be slow; be loose
nŭrige hada 느리게 하다 slow down
nŭrin 느린 slow, sluggish
nŭrin malt'u 느린 말투 drawl
nŭrinnŭrit kada 느릿느릿 가다 crawl
nŭrinnŭrit'age 느릿느릿하게 at a crawl
nŭrin tongjagŭro 느린 동작으로 in slow motion
nŭrŏjida 늘어지다 stretch; sag, hang; ***ch'uk nŭrŏjida*** 축 늘어지다 droop, sag
nŭrŏjin 늘어진 flabby
nŭrŏnada 늘어나다 stretch, give
nŭrŏnot'a 늘어놓다 draw up
nŭrŭmnamu 느릅나무 elm
nŭryŏjida 느려지다 slow down
nŭsŭnhage hada 느슨하게 하다 loosen, slacken
nŭsŭnhan 느슨한 loose, slack; lax
nŭtch'uda 늦추다 slacken
nŭtch'uŏjida 늦추어지다 slacken off
nŭtkkim 느낌 sense, feeling
nŭttcham chada 늦잠 자다 sleep late; oversleep
nŭt-tta 늦다 be late
nubida 누비다 weave; move
nubi ibul 누비 이불 quilt
nubi chaek'it 누비 재킷 quilted jacket
nuch'uham 누추함 squalor
nuch'uhan chip 누추한 집 hovel
nuch'ul 누출 escape, leak
nuch'uldoeda 누출되다 escape
nudŏgiga toeŏ 누더기가 되어 in tatters
nuga 누가 nougat; who; Luke
nugŭrŏjida 누그러지다 ease off
nugu 누구 who; ***igŏsŭn nuguegesŏ on kŏshinji palk'yŏittchi ant'a*** 이것은 누구에게서 온 것인지 밝혀있지 않다 it doesn't say who it's from
nugudo 누구도 any; ***hakssaengdŭl chung kŭ nugudo*** 학생들 중 그 누구도 (+ *negative verb*) none of the students; ***... nugudŭnji ...*** 누구든지 whoever
nuguna 누구나 everybody, everyone
nugun-ga 누군가 somebody; anybody
nugurŭl 누구를 who; somebody
nugurŭl chemŏt-ttaero hage naebŏryŏduda 누구를 제멋대로 하게 내버려두다 leave s.o. to his own devices
nuguseyo 누구세요 hello
nuguŭi 누구의 whose; ***igŏsŭn nuguŭi kŏshimnikka?*** 이것은 누구의 것입니까? whose is this?
nuguŭi kŏt 누구의 것 whose
numyŏng ssŭiuda 누명 씌우다 frame *person*
nun 눈 eye; snow
nunal 눈알 eyeball
nunbora 눈보라 snowstorm
nunbushida 눈부시다 be dazzling; be spectacular
nunbushige hada 눈부시게 하다 dazzle
nunbushige pinnada 눈부시게 빛나다 glare
nunbushin 눈부신 dazzling, spectacular
nunbushinŭn pit 눈부시는 빛 glare
nunch'ich'aeda 눈치채다 observe, notice
nunch'i ŏmnŭn 눈치 없는 clumsy, tactless
nundŏmi 눈더미 drift
nune hwak ttŭinŭn 눈에 확 띄는 glaring
nune kashi 눈에 가시 undesirable element
nune katch'in 눈에 갇힌 snowbound
nune saenggirŭl ilt'a 눈에 생기를 잃다 glaze over (*of eyes*)
nune ttŭida 눈에 띄다 stick out, stand out
nune ttŭige 눈에 띄게 visibly
nune ttŭinŭn 눈에 띄는 visible; ***nŏmu nune ttŭinŭn*** 너무 눈에 띄는 showy
nun-gama chuda 눈감아 주다 overlook
nun-gŭmp'an 눈금판 dial
nuni ch'imch'imhan 눈이 침침한

bleary-eyed
nuni mŏl chŏngdoŭi 눈이 멀 정도의 blinding
nuni naerida 눈이 내리다 snow
nuni onŭn 눈이 오는 snowy *day*
nuni ssain 눈이 쌓인 snowy *field*
nun karigae 눈 가리개 blindfold
nun kkamtchak'al saie 눈 깜짝할 사이에 in a flash
nunkkŏp'ul 눈꺼풀 eyelid
nunkkŭm 눈금 scale
nun maja taranada 눈 맞아 달아나다 elope
nun mŏlge hada 눈 멀게 하다 blind
nun mŏn 눈 먼 blind
nunmul 눈물 tear
nunmulnage komapkkunyo 눈물나게 고맙군요 thanks a bunch
nunmul ŏrin 눈물 어린 tearful
nunmul pang-ŭl 눈물 방울 teardrop
nunmul tchage hanŭn kŏt 눈물 짜게 하는 것 slush *pej*
nunmuri nada 눈물이 나다 water (*of eyes*)
nunmurŭl hŭllida 눈물을 흘리다 be in tears
nunmurŭl taktta 눈물을 닦다 dry one's eyes
nun pushige hanŭn 눈 부시게 하는 blinding
nunsat'ae 눈사태 avalanche
nunsong-i 눈송이 snowflake
nunssaram 눈사람 snowman
nunssŏp 눈썹 eyebrow
nunttŏng-i 눈덩이 snowball
nunttongja 눈동자 pupil (*in eye*)
nunŭi kashi 눈의 가시 pain in the neck (*person*)
nunŭi p'iro 눈의 피로 eye strain
nunŭl karida 눈을 가리다 blindfold
nuptta 눕다 lie, lie down
nurŏputtchi annŭn 눌어붙지 않는 nonstick
nurŭda 누르다 push, press; click COMPUT
nurŭgi 누르기 push COMPUT
nurŭm tanch'ushigŭi 누름 단추식의 push button
nusŏl 누설 disclosure
nusŏldoeda 누설되다 leak out
nusŏrhada 누설하다 divulge
nwiuch'inŭn 뉘우치는 penitent, remorseful
nyŏn 년 year; woman *pej*
Nyujillaendŭ 뉴질랜드 New Zealand
Nyujillaendŭin 뉴질랜드인 New Zealander
nyusŭ 뉴스 news; development; event
nyusŭ pangsonghanŭn saram 뉴스 방송하는 사람 newsreader
nyusŭ pangsong-ŭl hada 뉴스 방송을 하다 newscast
nyusŭ podo 뉴스 보도 news report
Nyuyok 뉴욕 New York

ŏ

Ŏbŏinal 어버이날 Parents' Day
ŏbu 어부 fisherman
-ŏch'i -어치 worth; ***samch'ŏn wŏnŏch'i*** 삼천 원어치 three thousand wons' worth
ŏch'ŏguniŏmnŭn 어처구니없는 absurd
ŏdaept'ŏ 어댑터 adapter ELEC
ŏdi 어디 where; ***ŏdie noŭlkkayo?*** 어디에 놓을까요? where shall I put this?; ***ŏdiesŏ wassŭmnikka?*** 어디에서 왔습니까? where are you from?; ***ŏdiro kamnikka?*** 어디로 갑니까? where are you going?; ***ŏdi tarŭn kosŭro kapsshida*** 어디 다른 곳으로 갑시다 let's go somewhere else; ***ŏdirŭl kadŏrado*** 어디를 가더라도 wherever you go; ***kŭgŏsŭn Hanguk ŏdiena it-tta*** 그것은 한국 어디에나 있다 you find them all over Korea
ŏdidŭnji 어디든지 everywhere, wherever
ŏdin-gae 어딘가에 somewhere
ŏditchŭme(sŏ) 어디쯤에(서) whereabouts, where
ŏdŭl su innŭn 얻을 수 있는 obtainable
ŏdŭl su ŏmnŭn 얻을 수 없는 unobtainable
ŏdŭryŏgo noryŏk'ada 얻으려고 노력하다 strive for
ŏduk'ŏmk'ŏmhan 어두컴컴한 gloomy
ŏdum 어둠 darkness
ŏdumch'imch'imhan 어둠침침한 dim
ŏduptta 어둡다 be dark; be in the dark; be weak
ŏduun 어두운 dark; gloomy
ŏduun pitkkarŭi 어두운 빛깔의 dark-colored
ŏduwŏjida 어두워지다 get dark
ŏgan 어간 stem (*of word*)
ŏgaptchŏgin 억압적인 repressive
ŏgap'ada 억압하다 repress
ŏgŭmni 어금니 molar
ŏgwi 어귀 mouth (*of river*)
ŏgyang 억양 inflection
ŏhagŭi 어학의 linguistic
ŏhoengnyang 어획량 haul (*of fish*)
ŏhwi 어휘 vocabulary
ŏje 어제 yesterday
ŏjetppam 어젯밤 last night
...ŏjida ...어 지다 become ..., get ...
ŏjillŏ noŭn 어질러 놓은 disorderly
ŏjirŏptta 어지럽다 feel faint; be dizzy; be chaotic
ŏjirŏun 어지러운 giddy, faint; messy
ŏjirŭda 어지르다 mess up
ŏjo 어조 tone
ŏkkae 어깨 shoulder; ***ŏkkaerŭl ŭssŭk-kkŏrida*** 어깨를 으쓱거리다 shrug one's shoulders
ŏkssen 억센 strong, tough, robust
ŏkssen sanai 억센 사나이 tough guy
ŏkssugat'ŭn 억수같은 driving, torrential *rain*; (***piga***) ***ŏkssugach'i p'ŏbunnŭnda*** (비가) 억수같이 퍼붓는다 it's pouring (with rain)
ŏktche 억제 constraint, curb, inhibition; restraint
ŏktchedoen 억제된 inhibited
ŏktchedoen p'yohyŏn 억제된 표현 understatement
ŏktchehada 억제하다 check, restrain; control; inhibit; stifle
ŏktchehal su ŏmnŭn 억제할 수 없는 irresistible
ŏktchi 억지 obstinacy
ŏktchiro ppaeda 억지로 빼다 wrench; pull
ŏktchiro ...shik'ida 억지로 ...시키다 compel
ŏlbŏmurida 얼버무리다 manipulate; stall
ŏlda 얼다 freeze
ŏlgul 얼굴 face

ŏlgurŭl pulk'ida 얼굴을 붉히다 blush, go red in the face
ŏlgurŭl tchip'urida 얼굴을 찌푸리다 wince
ŏlk'ida 얽히다 become entangled in
ŏlk'ŭnhage ch'wihan 얼큰하게 취한 tipsy
ŏllida 얼리다 freeze
ŏllon 언론 journalism; the press
ŏllon-gye 언론계 journalism
ŏllonŭi chayu 언론의 자유 free speech
ŏllugi saenggida 얼룩이 생기다 stain
ŏlluk 얼룩 mark; stain; smear; smudge
ŏlluk chegŏje 얼룩 제거제 stain remover
ŏlluktchin 얼룩진 streaky
ŏllungmal 얼룩말 zebra
ŏlma 얼마 how much; how long; how many; how far; ***ŏlma andoenŭn*** 얼마 안되는 not much; ***...ŭn / nŭn ŏlmaimnikka?*** ...은 / 는 얼마입니까? how much is / are ...?
ŏlmana ...? 얼마나 ...? how much?
ŏlmana chaju? 얼마나 자주? how often?
ŏlmana chŏne? 얼마나 전에? how long ago?
ŏlmana kŏllimnikka? 얼마나 걸립니까? how long does it take?
ŏlmana mani? 얼마나 많이? how many?
ŏlp'it poda 얼핏 보다 catch a fleeting glimpse of
ŏmaŏmahan 어마어마한 huge
ŏmch'ŏng manŭn 엄청 많은 an awful lot
ŏmch'ŏngnada 엄청나다 be preposterous
ŏmch'ŏngnage 엄청나게 very, extraordinarily
ŏmch'ŏngnan 엄청난 extraordinary, amazing; preposterous
ŏmhage 엄하게 severely
ŏmhage hada 엄하게 하다 tighten up
ŏmhage tasŭrida 엄하게 다스리다 crack down on
ŏmhan 엄한 grim; strict, tough
ŏmi 어미 ending GRAM
ŏmji sonkkarak 엄지 손가락 thumb
ŏmjunghan 엄중한 stringent
ŏmkkyŏk 엄격 severity; rigor
ŏmkkyŏk'ada 엄격하다 be strict
ŏmkkyŏk'age 엄격하게 strictly; ***kŭgŏsŭn ŏmkkyŏk'age kŭmjidoeŏ it-tta*** 그것은 엄격하게 금지되어 있다 it is strictly forbidden
ŏmkkyŏk'an 엄격한 strict, stern; straitlaced
ŏmma 엄마 mom
ŏmmang-in sangt'ae 엉망인 상태 muddle, mess
ŏmmirhi 엄밀히 strictly, closely
ŏmmu 업무 affair, business
ŏmmuryang 업무량 workload
ŏmmu shigan 업무 시간 office hours
ŏmmu suhaeng 업무 수행 performance
ŏmni 엄니 fang; tusk
ŏmnŭn 없는 no; ***...i / ga ŏmnŭn*** ...이 / 가 없는 without; ***toni hanp'undo ŏmnŭn*** 돈이 한푼도 없는 penniless
ŏmŏni 어머니 mother
ŏmŏnigat'ŭn 어머니같은 motherly
ŏmŏninal 어머니날 Mother's Day
ŏmŏniŭi 어머니의 maternal
ŏmp'o 엄포 bluff; deception
ŏmp'orŭl not'a 엄포를 놓다 bluff
ŏmssuk'ada 엄숙하다 be solemn
ŏmssuk'an 엄숙한 solemn
ŏndŏk 언덕 hill
ŏndŏk kkokttaegi 언덕 꼭대기 hilltop
ŏngdŏng-i 엉덩이 bottom, butt; buttocks
ŏnggida 엉기다 clot, coagulate
ŏngk'ida 엉키다 get tangled up
ŏngmang 엉망 mess
ŏngmangjinch'ang 엉망진창 havoc
ŏngmang-ŭro mandŭlda 엉망으로 만들다 wreck, mess up
ŏngmang-ŭro p'agoehada 엉망으로 파괴하다 wreck
ŏngnullin 억눌린 repressed, pent-up
ŏngnurŭda 억누르다 repress
ŏngnurŭl su ŏmnŭn 억누를 수 없는 irrepressible
ŏngnyuja 억류자 detainee

ŏngttunghada 엉뚱하다 be extraordinary
ŏngttunghan shigane 엉뚱한 시간에 at this unearthly hour
ŏngt'ŏri 엉터리 broken *Korean etc*
ŏn-gŭp 언급 comment, remark; mention; reference
ŏn-gŭp'ada 언급하다 comment, remark; mention; refer to
ŏnje 언제 when; ***...l ttaenŭn ŏnjedŭnji*** ...ㄹ 때는 언제든지 whenever; ***ŏnjedŭn malman haseyo*** 언제든 말만 하세요 I am at your disposal
ŏnjekkajina 언제까지나 forever
ŏnjena 언제나 always, for ever
ŏnjen-ga 언젠가 ever, someday
ŏnŏ 언어 language
ŏnŏ chang-ae 언어 장애 language barrier; speech defect
ŏnŏ ch'iryo chŏnmun-ga 언어 치료 전문가 speech therapist
ŏnŏhaktcha 언어학자 linguist
ŏntchanahada 언짢아하다 mind, object to
ŏnttŭt poda 언뜻 보다 catch sight of
ŏnŭ 어느 what; which; ***ŏnŭ chŏngdo*** 어느 정도 some, a measure of; ***ŏnŭ chŏngdokkaji*** 어느 정도까지 to a certain extent
ŏnŭ han tchogŭi 어느 한 쪽의 either; ***Xna Y chung ŏnŭ hanarado*** X나 Y 중 어느 하나라도 either X or Y
ŏnŭ kŏt 어느 것 which; ***... ŏnŭ kŏshidŭn(ji)*** ... 어느 것이든(지) whichever
ŏnŭ kot 어느 곳 anywhere
ŏnŭnal 어느날 one day
ŏnŭ tchogina 어느 쪽이나 either
ŏpkkŭreidŭ 업그레이드 upgrade
ŏpkkŭreidŭhada 업그레이드하다 upgrade
ŏppŏp 어법 usage
ŏprait'ŭ p'iano 업라이트 피아노 upright piano
ŏprodŭhada 업로드하다 upload
ŏpssaeda 없애다 remove, get rid of
...ŏpsshi ...없이 without; ***...ŏpsshi chinaeda*** ...없이 지내다 do without, go without; ***...ŏpsshi hada*** ...없이 하다 dispense with; ***...ŏpsshi saragada*** ...없이 살아가다 go without
ŏpssŏjida 없어지다 go; disappear; be missing
ŏpssŏsŏ 없어서 for want of
ŏptchillŏjida 엎질러지다 spill
ŏptchirŭda 엎지르다 spill
ŏptchŏk 업적 achievement
ŏptchongbyŏl chŏnhwa pŏnhobu 업종별 전화 번호부 yellow pages
ŏptta 없다 there is no; not have; lack; be out, not be at home; ***k'ŏp'i / ch'aga ŏptta*** 커피 / 차가 없다 there's no coffee / tea; ***nanŭn ŏnŏe sojiri ŏptta*** 나는 언어에 소질이 없다 I'm no linguist
ŏpttŭrida 엎드리다 get down, duck
ŏp'asŭt'ŭrop'i 어파스트로피 apostrophe
ŏribŏngbŏnghage hada 어리벙벙하게 하다 stun
ŏrida 어리다 be very young
ŏridungjŏrhaejin 어리둥절해진 dazed
ŏrimdo ŏpssŏ! 어림도 없어! no way!
ŏrimjimjak 어림짐작 guesswork
Ŏrininal 어린이날 Children's Day
ŏriniyong chwasŏk 어린이용 좌석 child's seat, car seat
ŏrin nom 어린 놈 monkey, young rascal
ŏrinshijŏl 어린시절 childhood
ŏrisŏgŭn 어리석은 stupid, dumb; foolish
ŏrisŏgŭn chit 어리석은 짓 folly
ŏrisŏktta 어리석다 be foolish
ŏritkkwangdae 어릿광대 clown
ŏrŭm 얼음 ice; ***ŏrŭmŭl kyŏt-ttŭryŏ*** 얼음을 곁들여 on the rocks, with ice; ***ŏrŭmŭl nŏhŭn*** 얼음을 넣은 iced
ŏrŭmi ŏrŭn 얼음이 얼은 icy
ŏrŭn 어른 adult, grown-up
ŏrŭn 얼은 frozen
ŏrŭnsŭrŏun 어른스러운 grown-up
ŏryŏmp'ushi nat'anada 어렴풋이 나타나다 loom up
ŏryŏmp'ut'an 어렴풋한 vague
ŏryŏpkke 어렵게 with difficulty
ŏryŏptta 어렵다 be hard, be difficult
ŏryŏum 어려움 difficulty
ŏryŏun 어려운 difficult

ŏsaek'an 어색한 labored
ŏsŏlp'ŭn 어설픈 rough, careless; lame *excuse*
ŏsŏn 어선 fishing boat
ŏsŭllŏnggŏrida 어슬렁거리다 hang about; saunter; prowl
ŏsŭrehage pich'ida 어스레하게 비치다 gleam
ŏsŭrehan pit 어스레한 빛 gleam
ŏsusŏnhada 행동이 어수선다 be in disorder; ***haengdong-i ŏsusŏnhan*** 행동이 어수선한 clumsy
ŏtchaet-ttŭn 어쨌든 regardless; in any case; anyhow; ***ŏtchaet-ttŭn chossŭmnida*** 어쨌든 좋습니다 very well, alright then
ŏtchidoen iriya? 어찌된 일이야? how come?
ŏtchihal parŭl morŭda 어찌할 바를 모르다 be at a loss
ŏtchŏl chul morŭda 어쩔 줄 모르다 be overwhelmed by
ŏtchŏl su ŏmnŭn 어쩔 수 없는 unavoidable
ŏtchŏl su ŏpssŏyo 어쩔 수 없어요 it can't be helped
ŏtchŏnji 어쩐지 somehow, for some unknown reason
ŏtkkallida 엇갈리다 miss (*not meet*)
ŏtkkoja hanŭn 얻고자 하는 acquisitive
ŏttaeyo 것은 how; how about; ***k'ŏp'i han chan ŏttaeyo?*** 커피 한 잔 어때요? how about a cup of coffee?; ***yojŭm ŏttaeyo*** 요즘 어때요? how are things?
ŏttŏk'e 어떻게 how; ***ŏttŏk'e chinaeseyo? – chal issŭmnida*** 어떻게 지내세요? - 잘 있습니다 how are you? – fine; ***ŏttŏk'e saenggak'aseyo?*** 어떻게 생각하세요? what do you think?
ŏttŏk'edŭnji 어떻게든지 somehow
ŏttŏn 어떤 any; some; which; what; what kind of; ***ŏttŏn myŏnesŏnŭn*** 어떤 면에서는 in a way, in certain respects; ***ŏttŏn ŭimiesŏnŭn*** 어떤 의미에서는 in a sense; ***ŏttŏn ...(i)rado*** 어떤 ...(이)라도 whatever; any; ***ŏttŏn chongnyuŭi ...?*** 어떤 종류의 ...? what kind of ...?
ŏttŏn kŏt 어떤 것 something; ***ŏttŏn kŏt?*** 어떤 것? which one?; what kind of thing?
ŏttŏn tarŭn kosesŏ 어떤 다른 곳에서 elsewhere, somewhere else; ***ŏttŏn tarŭn kosŭro*** 어떤 다른 곳으로 elsewhere, somewhere else (*motion toward*)
ŏttŏseyo? 어떠세요? how are you?
ŏt-tta 얻다 get, obtain; earn; gain
ŏullida 어울리다 go with, associate with; mix with; get on with; suit; match
ŏullinŭn 어울리는 matching; suitable
...ŏya handa ...어야 한다 have to, must; be bound to
...ŏyaman hada ...어야만 하다 have (got) to; should, must

O

o 오 five; oh!
oashissŭ 오아시스 oasis
obŏdŭraibŭ 오버드라이브 overdrive
obŭn 오븐 oven
och'an 오찬 lunch
oda 오다 come; fall (*of night*); ***...esŏ oda*** ...에서 오다 come from
odioŭi 오디오의 audio
odishyŏn 오디션 audition
odogado mot'ada 오도가도 못하다 be stranded, be stuck
odohada 오도하다 mislead
odohanŭn 오도하는 misleading
odumak 오두막 hut
odumaktchip 오두막집 shack
oe 외 outside; except; ***Sŏul oegwage*** 서울 외곽에 outside Seoul
oeadŭl 외아들 only son
oebu 외부 outside ◊ external
oebusaram 외부사람 outsider
oech'ida 외치다 cry, exclaim
oech'im 외침 cry, call; scream
oech'yŏ purŭda 외쳐 부르다 cry out
oedongttal 외동딸 only daughter
oegugin 외국인 foreigner
oegugin hyŏmo 외국인 혐오 xenophobia
oegugŏ 외국어 foreign language
oeguk 외국 foreign country ◊ foreign
oeguk'wan 외국환 foreign exchange
oegwan 외관 external appearance
oegwansang-ŭi 외관상의 exterior
oegwanŭl sonsangshik'ida 외관을 손상시키다 disfigure
oegyein 외계인 alien (*from space*)
oegyo 외교 diplomacy ◊ diplomatic
oegyogwan 외교관 diplomat
oegyomyŏnch'aek 외교면책 diplomatic immunity
oegyosul 외교술 diplomacy, tact
oeharabŏji 외할아버지 maternal grandfather
oehwa 외화 foreign currency
oehyangtchŏgin 외향적인 outgoing
oejin 외진 out of the way
oekkwa ŭisa 외과 의사 surgeon
oekkwayong mesŭ 외과용 메스 scalpel
oemu 외무 foreign affairs ◊ foreign
Oemubu 외무부 Department of State
Oemu changgwan 외무 장관 Secretary of State
oemu chŏngch'aek 외무 정책 foreign policy
oemuŏmmu 외무업무 foreign affairs
oemyŏnhada 외면하다 turn away, look away
oensonjabi 왼손잡이 left-handed
oentchoge(sŏ) 왼쪽에(서) on the left
oentchogŭro 왼쪽으로 to the left
oentchok 왼쪽 left
oe pal sŭk'eit'ŭ 외 발 스케이트 scooter (*child's*)
oep'anwŏn 외판원 commercial traveler
oeroptta 외롭다 be solitary, be lonely
oeroum 외로움 loneliness
oeroun 외로운 lonely
oesamch'on 외삼촌 uncle (*mother's brother*)
oesang 외상 credit FIN
oesang kŏrae 외상 거래 charge account
oeshik'ada 외식하다 eat out
oesŏltchŏgin 외설적인 pornographic, obscene
oesungmo 외숙모 aunt (*mother's brother's wife*)
oettan 외딴 isolated, remote
oet'u 외투 overcoat; cloak
oeuda 외우다 memorize
ogap'ada 억압하다 supress
ogoe 옥외 open-air ◊ open air
ohae 오해 misunderstanding, misconception
ohaehada 오해하다 misread, misunderstand

ohiryŏ 오히려 rather, preferably
ohiryŏ naŭn 오히려 나은 preferable
ohu 오후 afternoon; ***ohue*** 오후에 in the afternoon
oi 오이 cucumber
oil 오일 oil
oji 오지 bush, hinterland
ojik 오직 only, solely
ojing-ŏ 오징어 squid
ojŏn 오전 morning; ***ojŏne*** 오전에 in the morning
ojon 오존 ozone
ojonch'ŭng 오존층 ozone layer
ojum nuda 오줌 누다 urinate; pee
okp'yŏn 옥편 Chinese character dictionary
oksshin-gaksshinhada 옥신각신하다 argue, squabble
okssusu 옥수수 maize, corn; sweetcorn
ok'esŭt'ŭra 오케스트라 orchestra
ok'ŭ 오크 oak (*wood*)
ok'ŭnamu 오크나무 oak (tree)
olbarŭda 올바르다 be straight; be upright; be honest
olbarŭge 올바르게 correctly, right
olbarŭn 올바른 right, proper; just
olch'aeng-i 올챙이 tadpole
olgami 올가미 noose
olk'e 올케 sister-in-law (*woman's brother's wife*)
ollagada 올라가다 go up, climb; ***1935nyŏnŭro kŏsŭllŏ ollagasŏ*** 1935년으로 거슬러 올라가서 back in 1935
ollain 온라인 on-line
ollain sŏbissŭ 온라인 서비스 on-line service
olla it-tta 올라 있다 be up (*of prices, temperature*)
ollaoda 올라오다 come up
ollibŭ 올리브 olive
ollibŭ kirŭm 올리브 기름 olive oil
ollida 올리다 raise; ***p'ŏmp'ŭro p'ŏ ollida*** 펌프로 퍼 올리다 pump
ollim 올림 Yours truly, Yours sincerely
Ollimp'ik Keim 올림픽 게임 Olympic Games
olppaemi 올빼미 owl
olt'a 옳다 be right, be correct ◊ OK
omgida 옮기다 move, transfer; carry
omgyŏjigi shwiun 옮겨지기 쉬운 infectious *laughter*
omgyŏt'ada 옮겨타다 transfer
omŭllet 오믈렛 omelet
omŭrida 오므리다 pucker; purse; furl
onch'ŏn 온천 spa
ondo 온도 temperature
ondogye 온도계 thermometer
ondol 온돌 heated floor
ongho 옹호 defense
onghohada 옹호하다 defend
onghoja 옹호자 defender, champion
on-gi 온기 warmth
on-gŏnhan 온건한 moderate
on-gŏnp'a 온건파 moderate party
onhwahan 온화한 mild, gentle; benign
onjŏng 온정 warmth, geniality
onlain 온라인 on-line
onnan chŏnsŏn 온난 전선 warm front
onsang 온상 breeding ground; hotbed
onshil 온실 glasshouse; nursery; conservatory
onshil hyokkwa 온실 효과 greenhouse effect
onsunhan 온순한 gentle, meek
onsu suyŏngjang 온수 수영장 heated swimming pool
ont'ong 온통 entirely
onŭl 오늘 today
onŭl ach'im 오늘 아침 this morning
onŭl chŏnyŏk 오늘 저녁 this evening
onŭllobut'ŏ 오늘로부터 from today on
onŭlnarŭi 오늘날의 present-day
onŭl ohue 오늘 오후에 this afternoon
onŭl pam 오늘 밤 tonight
oppa 오빠 brother (*woman's elder*)
opsshŏn sangp'um 옵션 상품 optional extras
op'era 오페라 opera
op'era haussŭ 오페라 하우스 opera house
op'era kasu 오페라 가수 opera singer
op'era mang-wŏn-gyŏng 오페라 망원경 opera glasses

op'ŏreit'ing shisŭt'em 오퍼레이팅 시스템 operating system
op'ŭnt'ik'et 오픈티켓 open ticket
op'ŭsaidŭ 오프사이드 offside
orae 오래 long, a long while; ***orae chŏne*** 오래 전에 long ago
oraedoen 오래된 old
orae kanŭn 오래 가는 durable
orae kkŭnŭn 오래 끄는 protracted, lengthy
oraen 오랜 old
orae sayonghan 오래 사용한 old, veteran
oraettong-an 오랫동안 for a long time
orak 오락 entertainment, pleasure
oraksshishŏl 오락시설 amenities
oral ssekssŭ 오랄 섹스 oral sex
orangmul 오락물 amusements, games
orenji 오렌지 orange
orenji chyussŭ 오렌지 쥬스 orange juice
orenjijok 오렌지족 rich kids (*of Seoul's wealthy elite renowned for their extravagant lifestyle*)
ori 오리 duck
orient'eishyŏn 오리엔테이션 orientation; induction ceremony
orit'ŏl ibul 오리털 이불 eiderdown, quilt
orit'ŏl p'ak'a 오리털 파카 padded jacket
orŭda 오르다 climb; mount; increase
orŭgajŭm 오르가즘 orgasm
orŭgan 오르간 organ MUS
orŭn 옳은 correct
orŭnp'yŏne 오른편에 on the right-hand side
orŭnsonjabiŭi 오른손잡이의 right-handed
orŭntchogŭro 오른쪽으로 right, to the right
orŭntchok 오른쪽 right; ***orŭntchoge*(*sŏ*)** 오른쪽에(서) on the right; ***orŭntchok panghyangŭro*** 오른쪽 방향으로 on your right hand
oryŏdugi 오려두기 cut COMPUT
oryŏnaeda 오려내다 cut out
oryŏnaen kŏt 오려낸 것 cutting
osan 오산 miscalculation
Oseania 오세아니아 Oceania ◊ Oceanian
oship 오십 fifty
osolkkil 오솔길 alley
ossak'an 오싹한 eerie
Osŭk'a shisangshik 오스카 시상식 Oscars ceremony
osŭl iptta 옷을 입다 dress, get dressed
osŭl ip'ida 옷을 입히다 dress *person*
osŭl pŏtkkida 옷을 벗기다 undress, strip *person*
osŭl pŏt-tta 옷을 벗다 undress, strip
Osŭt'ŭria 오스트리아 Austria ◊ Austrian
ot 옷 clothes; clothing; ***ot hanbŏl*** 옷 한벌 an item of clothing
otchŏm 오점 smear (*on character*)
otkkabang 옷가방 suitcase
otkkaji 옷가지 wardrobe (*clothes*)
otkkam 옷감 material, fabric
otkkŏri 옷걸이 clothes hanger
ot-tchang 옷장 closet
ottŏn 어떤 certain, particular
ot-ttan 옷단 hem
ott'ŏri 옷털이 clothes brush
ot'obai 오토바이 motorbike
ot'ŭmil 오트밀 oatmeal
owŏl 오월 May
oyŏm 오염 pollution; contamination
oyŏmmultchil 오염물질 pollutant
oyŏmshik'ida 오염시키다 pollute, contaminate
oyonghada 오용하다 misuse

P

pa 바 way; thing; crossbar; ***naega al pa anida*** 내가 알 바 아니다 for all I care
pabek'yu 바베큐 barbecue
pabek'yuyong ch'ŏlp'an 바베큐용 철판 barbecue (*equipment*)
pabo 바보 idiot; ***pabojisŭl hada*** 바보짓을 하다 behave like an idiot
pabosŭrŏun 바보스러운 idiotic
pach'ida 바치다 dedicate, devote; donate; sacrifice
pach'im chŏpsshi 받침 접시 saucer
pada 바다 sea; ocean
pada chŏktta 받아 적다 take down, write down
padadŭrida 받아들이다 assimilate; accept; come to terms with; keep down; ***chok'e*** / ***nappŭge padadŭryŏjida*** 좋게 / 나쁘게 받아들여지다 go down well / badly
padadŭril su innŭn 받아들일 수 있는 acceptable; admissible
padagŭl pŏsŏnada 바닥을 벗어나다 bottom out
padajŏktta 받아적다 write down
padak 바닥 floor; bottom; sole (*of foot, shoe*)
padassŭgi 받아쓰기 dictation
padatkkajae 바다가재 lobster
padŭl manhada 받을 만하다 deserve
padŭl manhan 받을 만한 be worthy of, deserve
Paduk 바둑 Go
pae 배 stomach, belly; embryo; ship; pear; ***han pae saekki*** 한 배 새끼 litter (*of animal*); ***pae ane*** 배 안에 on board
paeban 배반 betrayal, treachery
paebanhada 배반하다 betray, doublecross
paebanhanŭn 배반하는 treacherous
paebanja 배반자 traitor
paebuhada 배부하다 distribute
paeburŭda 배부르다 full up (*with food*)
paech'i 배치 layout; batch (*of data*)
paech'idoeda 배치되다 be stationed at
paech'ihada 배치하다 arrange, position
paech'u 배추 Chinese cabbage
paech'ul 배출 exhaust, fumes
paech'ulgu 배출구 outlet (*of pipe*)
paech'ulshik'ida 배출시키다 drain (off)
paedal 배달 delivery
paedalbu 배달부 messenger, courier
paedalch'a 배달차 delivery van
paedal kuyŏk 배달 구역 round (*of mailman etc*)
paedal naltcha 배달 날짜 delivery date
paedanggŭm 배당금 dividend
paedanghada 배당하다 allot
paedarhada 배달하다 deliver
paedarwŏn 배달원 tradesman
paedŭmint'ŏn 배드민턴 badminton
paedŭmint'ŏn kong 배드민턴 공 shuttlecock
Paegak-kkwan 백악관 White House
paegigwan 배기관 exhaust (pipe); waste pipe
paegi kasŭ 배기 가스 exhaust
paegil 백일 100 day ceremony (*after birth*); one hundred and one
paegilmong 백일몽 daydream
paegin 백인 white (*person*)
paegirhae 백일해 whooping cough
paegŏp 백업 backup
paegŏp tisŭk'ŭ 백업 디스크 backup disk
paegŏp tŭraibŭ 백업 드라이브 backup drive; tape drive
paegŏp'ada 백업하다 back up *file*
paegop'ŭda 배고프다 be hungry
paegop'ŭm 배고픔 hunger
paegop'ŭn 배고픈 hungry; ***paega kop'ayo*** 배가 고파요 I'm hungry

paegŭbŏptcha 배급업자 distributor COM
paegŭmnyang 배급량 ration
paegŭp'ada 배급하다 ration
paegu 배구 volleyball
paegwan 배관 plumbing, pipes
paegwangong 배관공 plumber
paegyŏl chŏn-gu 백열 전구 light bulb
paegyŏng 배경 background, setting
paegyŏng ŭmak 배경 음악 soundtrack
paehu 배후 background; rear
paehu-esŏ chojonghada 배후에서 조종하다 pull strings
paejehada 배제하다 exclude
paejŏnban 배전반 switchboard
paek 백 hundred; white; back; bag
paek chunyŏn 백 주년 centenary
paek haendŭ 백 핸드 backhand
paek-kkŭm 백금 platinum
paek-kkwa sajŏn 백과 사전 encyclopedia
paekkop 배꼽 navel
paekppal 백발 white hair; gray hair; ***paekppari toeda*** 백발이 되다 be going gray
paekpparŭi 백발의 gray-haired
paekppunŭi il 백분의 일 hundredth
paekp'odoju 백포도주 white wine
paeksshin 백신 vaccine
paekssŭp'eisŭ k'i 백스페이스 키 backspace (key)
paektcha 백자 white porcelain (*Choson*)
paektcho 백조 swan
paek'ap 백합 lily
paek'wajŏm 백화점 department store
paek'yŏlppyŏng 백혈병 leukemia
paelbŭ 밸브 valve
paem 뱀 snake
paemjang-ŏ 뱀장어 eel
paemŏlmi 배멀미 seasickness
paemŏlmiga nan 배멀미가 난 seasick
paemŏlmihada 배멀미하다 get seasick
paenang 배낭 rucksack; ***paenang maego yŏhaenghada*** 배낭 매고 여행하다 backpack, go backpacking
paenang yŏhaengja 배낭 여행자 backpacker
paendŭ 밴드 (pop) band
paengman 백만 million
paengman changja 백만 장자 millionaire
paengmirŏ 백미러 rear-view mirror
paenmŏri 뱃머리 bow, prow
paennori 뱃놀이 sail
paeran ch'oktchinje 배란 촉진제 fertility drug
paeryŏ 배려 respect; tact; consideration
paesang 배상 compensation, recompense
paesanghada 배상하다 compensate
paeshimwŏn 배심원 juror
paeshimwŏndan 배심원단 jury
paeshimwŏnjang 배심원장 foreman (of the jury)
paesŏhada 배서하다 endorse
paesŏn 배선 wiring
paesok'ada 배속하다 post, transfer, send
paesu 배수 drainage; drains
paesugwan 배수관 drainpipe
paesuro 배수로 drain; storm drain
paetchang 배짱 courage, nerve
paetchi 배지 pin, badge
paet'ajŏgin 배타적인 exclusive
paet'al 배탈 upset stomach
paet'alnada 배탈나다 have an upset stomach
paet'ŏri 배터리 battery
paeŭi k'i 배의 키 rudder
paeŭnmangdŏk 배은망덕 ingratitude
paeuda 배우다 learn
paeuga toeda 배우가 되다 become an actor / actress
paeuja 배우자 partner; spouse
paeunghada 배웅하다 see off
paeyŏng 배영 backstroke
paeyŏrhada 배열하다 arrange, put in order
pagaji kŭltta 바가지 긁다 go on at
pagaji ssŭiuda 바가지 씌우다 overcharge
paguni 바구니 basket
paindŏ 바인더 binder
paiŏ 바이어 buyer

paiollin 바이올린 violin
paiollin yŏnjuja 바이올린 연주자 violinist
paiosŭ 바이오스 BIOS COMPUT
pairŏsŭ 바이러스 virus COMPUT
pairŏsŭ paeksshin p'ŭrogŭraem 바이러스 백신 프로그램 antivirus program
pait'ŭ 바이트 byte
paji 바지 pants
paji ammun 바지 앞문 fly
pak 박 night (*in hotel*)
pakk 밖 outside
pakkach'ŭi 바깥의 outside, external
pakkat'e 바깥에 outside
pakkat myŏn 바깥 면 outside
...pakke ...밖에 outside (of); except
pakkŭro 밖으로 outside
pakkuda 바꾸다 change, exchange; swap; vary; move on
pakkul su innŭn 바꿀 수 있는 interchangeable
pakkuŏ chuda 바꾸어 주다 change *money*
pakkuŏ iptta 바꾸어 입다 change *clothes*
pakkuŏjida 바뀌어지다 change
pakkuŏ not'a 바꾸어 놓다 displace, supplant
pakkuŏ t'ada 바꾸어 타다 change *trains, planes*
pakkwida 바뀌다 switch, change; vary; ***...(ŭ)ro pakkwida*** ...(으)로 바뀌다 give way to, be replaced by
pakkwŏ chuda 바꿔 주다 put through TELEC
pakkwŏt'ada 바꿔타다 transfer
pakkyŏkp'o 박격포 mortar MIL
pakssa 박사 PhD, Doctor of Philosophy
pakssae 박새 tit (*bird*)
pakssa hagwi 박사 학위 doctorate
pakssallaeda 박살내다 write off, wreck
paksshik'an 박식한 erudite
pakssŭ 박스 carton; booth
pakssurŭl ch'ida 박수를 치다 clap, applaud
pakssurŭl ponaeda 박수를 보내다 applaud
paktcha 박자 tempo, beat
paktchwi 박쥐 bat (*animal*)
paktta 박다 drive in *nail*
pakt'arhada 박탈하다 deprive; ***chagyŏgŭl pakt'arhada*** 자격을 박탈하다 disqualify
pakt'eria 박테리아 bacteria
pak'a 박하 mint (*herb*)
pak'ae 박해 persecution
pak'aehada 박해하다 persecute, oppress
pak'ahyang 박하향 peppermint (*flavoring*)
pak'a sat'ang 박하 사탕 mint, peppermint
pak'ida 박히다 lodge (*of bullet, ball*)
pak'odŭ 바코드 bar code
pak'wi 바퀴 wheel; lap, circuit
pak'wi pŏlle 바퀴 벌레 cockroach
pak'wiŭi chungshimbu 바퀴의 중심부 hub
pal 발 foot; paw
palbal 발발 eruption
palba munggaeda 밟아 뭉개다 trample on
palbarhada 발발하다 erupt
palbyŏnghada 발병하다 affect
palch'we 발췌 clip, extract (*from movie*)
palgabŏsŭn 발가벗은 naked; bare
palgajida 밝아지다 brighten up, become more cheerful
palgak 발각 detection
palgi 발기 erection (*of penis*)
palgŭm 밝음 lightness
palgŭn 밝은 bright; light; fair
palgŭp'ada 발급하다 issue, give out
palgul 발굴 excavation
palgurhada 발굴하다 discover; excavate, unearth
palgwang taiodŭ 발광 다이오드 LED, light-emitting diode
palgyŏn 발견 discovery
palgyŏnhada 발견하다 discover, find
palkkarak 발가락 toe
palkke hada 밝게 하다 light up, lighten
palkkŏrŭm 발걸음 tread
palktta 밝다 be bright; be keen; be expert; be cheerful; dawn
palkkŭn hwarŭl naeda 발끈 화를 내다 flare up, fly into a rage

palkkŭt pubun 발끝 부분 toe
palkkŭt'ŭro 발끝으로 on tippy-toe
palkkup 발굽 hoof
palk'ida 밝히다 reveal, make known; express
palk'yŏjunŭn 밝혀주는 revealing
palk'yŏnaeda 밝혀내다 find out, uncover
pallajida 발라지다 straighten out; spread
pallan 반란 mutiny, rebellion
pallanaeda 발라내다 shell; clean; take off; debone
pallan-gun 반란군 rebel troops
pallanŭl irŭk'ida 반란을 이르키다 revolt
palle 발레 ballet
palle muyongga 발레 무용가 ballet dancer
pallerina 발레리나 ballerina
pallonhada 반론하다 dispute; disagree with
palmae 발매 launch; release; sale
palmae ch'uk'ayŏn 발매 축하연 launch; release (*event*)
palmaehada 발매하다 launch; release; bring out
palmok 발목 ankle; ***palmogŭl ppida*** 발목을 삐다 twist one's ankle
palmyŏng 발명 invention
palmyŏngga 발명가 inventor
palmyŏnghada 발명하다 invent
palp'an 발판 scaffolding; stepping stone
palp'o 발포 gunshot
palppyŏng 발병 bout, attack MED
palppyŏnghada 발병하다 break out (*of disease*)
palp'yŏ chuktta 밟혀 죽다 be trampled to death
palp'yo 발표 release; presentation; statement
palssa 발사 blast-off
palssadae 발사대 launch pad
palssadoeda 발사되다 go off (*of gun*)
palssaeng 발생 happening
palssaengshik'ida 발생시키다 generate, produce
palssahada 발사하다 launch
palssan 발산 emission
palssashik'ida 발사시키다 blast off
palsshinŭm 발신음 dial tone
palssong 발송 shipping
palssonghada 발송하다 dispatch, send
palssong-in 발송인 sender
paltchaguk 발자국 footprint
paltchaguk sori 발자국 소리 footstep
paltchak 발작 fit, seizure
paltchaktchŏgin 발작적인 hysterical
paltchin 발진 rash MED
paltchint'ip'usŭ 발진티푸스 typhus
paltchŏn 발전 development; progression
paltchŏn-gi 발전기 dynamo; generator
paltchŏnhada 발전하다 develop; advance, improve
paltchŏnshik'ida 발전시키다 develop, expand
paltchŏnso 발전소 power station
paltta 밟다 tread; tread on; ***chandirŭl paltchi mashiyo!*** 잔디를 밟지 마시요! keep off the grass!
palttalshik'ida 발달시키다 develop; progress
palttŭng 발등 instep
palt'op 발톱 toenail; claw; talon
pam 밤 night; chestnut; ***pame*** 밤에 at night-time, in the night-time; ***pam saie*** 밤 사이에 during the night; ***naeil pam*** 내일 밤 tomorrow night; ***pam nŭjŭn*** 밤 늦은 late (at night); ***pam yŏhaeng*** 밤 여행 travel by night
pambihaenggi 밤비행기 night flight
pamnanu 밤나무 chestnut (tree)
pamsae 밤새 overnight
pan 반 half; ***tushi paniyeyo*** 두시 반이예요 it's half past two
panana 바나나 banana
panbaji 반바지 shorts
panbak 반박 retort
panbak'ada 반박하다 contradict; protest; retort
panbal 반발 backlash
panbok 반복 repetition
panbok'ada 반복하다 repeat; ***muŏsŭl panbok'ada*** 무엇을 반복하다 do sth over (again)

panch'an 반찬 side dish
panch'anggo 반창고 adhesive tape; Band-Aid®
panch'igŭi 반칙의 irregular
panch'ik 반칙 foul
pandae 반대 opposite; objection; opposition
pandaedoeda 반대되다 run counter to
pandaehada 반대하다 object; object to; oppose, resist; contest; ***wae kŭrŭl pandaehanŭn kŏyeyo?*** 왜 그를 반대하는 거예요? what do you have against him?
pandaeja 반대자 opponent; dissident
pandaep'yŏn 반대 편 across
pandaero 반대로 on the other hand; conversely; on the contrary; as opposed to; vice versa
pandae shimmunhada 반대 심문하다 cross-examine
pandae tchogŭi 반대 쪽의 opposite
pandaeŭi 반대의 opposite
pandae ŭigyŏn 반대 의견 dissent
pando 반도 peninsula
pandoch'e 반도체 semiconductor
pandongjuŭija 반동주의자 reactionary (*person*)
pandŭshi 반드시 necessarily; certainly
pang 방 room
pan-gam 반감 antipathy
pang-asoe 방아쇠 trigger
pangbŏp 방법 method; style; formula
pangbu ch'ŏrihada 방부 처리하다 embalm
pangbuje 방부제 preservative
pangch'aek 방책 measure, step
pangch'i 방치 neglect
pangch'ŏp 방첩 counterespionage
pangch'ungje 방충제 insect repellent
pangdaehan 방대한 vast, gigantic
Panggŭlladeshi 방글라데시 Bangladesh ◊ Bangladeshi
panggŭm 방금 just now
panggwang 방광 bladder
panggwanhada 방관하다 stand by (and do nothing)
panggwanja 방관자 bystander
panggwi 방귀 fart
panggwi kkwida 방귀 뀌다 fart
panghae 방해 obstacle; disturbance; ***panghaerŭl pat-tta*** 방해를 받다 suffer a setback
panghaehada 방해하다 disturb; interrupt, disrupt; hinder, impede; jam
panghaehanŭn 방해하는 obstructive
panghaemul 방해물 obstruction; deterrent
panghan 방한 insulation
panghanhada 방한하다 insulate
panghwa 방화 arson
panghwajangch'i 방화장치 incendiary device
panghyang 방향 direction; directions; ***panghyang kamgagŭl irŏbŏrin*** 방향 감각을 잃어버린 disoriented, confused
panghyang p'yoshidŭng 방향 표시등 turn signal
pangjŏk'ada 방적하다 spin
pangjŏngshik 방정식 equation
pangjonghan 방종한 dissolute, loose
pangmang-i 방망이 bat (*in baseball*)
pangmang-iro ch'ida 방망이로 치다 bat
pangmulgwan 박물관 museum
pangmun 방문 door; visit
pangmunhada 방문하다 visit, call on; look in on; look up
pangmyŏrhada 박멸하다 eradicate
pangnanghada 방랑하다 rove, wander
pangnangja 방랑자 drifter, hobo
pang-ŏ 방어 defense; ***pang-ŏhanŭn chasero*** 방어하는 자세로 on the defensive
pang-ŏhada 방어하다 defend
pang-ŏjŏgin 방어적인 defensive
pang-ŏyong-ŭi 방어용의 defensive
pan-gongjuŭi 반공주의 anti-Communism
pangp'ae 방패 shield
pangp'aje 방파제 breakwater
pangsanŭng 방사능 radioactivity
pangsanŭng-i innŭn 방사능이 있는 radioactive
pangsanŭng yoppŏp 방사능 요법

radiotherapy
pangsasŏn 방사선 radiation
pangsasŏng naktchin 방사성 낙진 fallout
pangshik 방식 manner, way; system; method; mode; form; ***iltchŏnghan pangshige ttarŭn*** 일정한 방식에 따른 methodical
pangsong 방송 broadcast; broadcasting; ***pangsong chung-e*** 방송 중에 on the air
pangsongguk 방송국 station RAD, TV
pangsonghada 방송하다 broadcast; transmit
pangsong-in 방송인 broadcaster
pangsong p'ŭrogŭraem chaptchi 방송 프로그램 잡지 listings magazine
pangsongshil 방송실 studio
pangsudoenŭn 방수되는 waterproof
pangsu oet'u 방수 외투 mackintosh
pangsup'o 방수포 tarpaulin
pangsuŭi 방수의 watertight; showerproof
pangt'an chokki 방탄 조끼 armor
pangt'ang 방탕 debauchery
pangt'anghan 방탕한 debauched, dissolute
pang-ŭm 방음 soundproofing ◊ soundproof
pang-ŭm changch'i 방음 장치 muffler MOT
pan-gu 반구 hemisphere
pang-ul 방울 drip, drop
pang-wi 방위 defense
pan-gyŏk 반격 return
pang-yŏnghada 방영하다 televise
panhae it-tta 반해 있다 be stuck on; have a crush on
panhal manhan 반할 만한 adorable
panhang 반항 defiance
panhanghada 반항하다 defy
panhangjŏgin 반항적인 defiant; rebellious
panhayŏ 반하여 contrary to
panhwan 반환 return
panil kŭnmu 반일 근무 part-time job
panilla 바닐라 vanilla
panjagyong 반작용 reaction
panjagyonghada 반작용하다 react
panji 반지 ring
panjirŭm 반지름 radius
panjŏm 반점 spot; blotch
panjŭnghada 반증하다 disprove
panju 반주 accompaniment; backing
panjudan 반주단 backing group
panjuk'ada 반죽하다 knead
panjurŭl hada 반주를 하다 accompany MUS
pannŭn chŭksshiro 받는 즉시로 by return (of mail)
panp'arŭi 반팔의 short-sleeved
pansahada 반사하다 reflect
pansa shin-gyŏng 반사 신경 reflex
pansa undong 반사 운동 reflex reaction
pansonghada 반송하다 send back
pantchagida 반짝이다 shine, gleam; twinkle
pantchak 반짝 glint
pantchak-kkŏrida 반짝거리다 shine; glisten
pantchak-kkŏrinŭn 반짝거리는 shiny
pantchakpantchak pinnada 반짝반짝 빛나다 glitter
pantchak pinnada 반짝 빛나다 glint
panŭi 반의 half
panŭjil 바느질 needlework, sewing
panŭjilkkŏri 바느질거리 sewing
panŭjil yongp'um 바느질 용품 notions
panŭjirhada 바느질하다 sew
panŭl 바늘 needle; stitches
panŭlgwi 바늘귀 eye (*of needle*)
panŭlttam 바늘땀 stitch
panŭm naerimŭi 반음 내림의 flat MUS
panŭm nopkke 반음 높게 sharp MUS
panŭng 반응 reaction
panŭnghada 반응하다 react, respond
panŭnghanŭn 반응하는 responsive
panŭro chŏptta 반으로 접다 fold in half
panŭro hada 반으로 하다 halve
panwŏn 반원 semicircle
panwŏnhyŏngŭi 반원형의 semicircular
panyŏk 반역 treason
panyŏktcha 반역자 rebel
pap 밥 rice

pap kŭrŭt 밥 그릇 rice bowl
pappŭda 바쁘다 be busy; busy oneself with, occupy oneself with; ***...ŭl / rŭl hanŭra pappŭda*** ...을 / 를 하느라 바쁘다 be busy doing ...
pappŭn 바쁜 busy; full
paraboda 바라보다 view
parada 바라다 hope; wish; hope for; wish for; ***...girŭl parada*** ...기를 바라다 may ...; ***nanŭn ...girŭl paramnida*** 나는 ...기를 바랍니다 I wish that ...
paraeda 바래다 fade; take, escort; ***munkkaji paraeda chulkkeyo*** 문까지 바래다 줄께요 I'll see you to the door
paraedajuda 바래다주다 escort
paraen 바랜 faded
paragŏnde 바라건데 hopefully
param 바람 desire, wish; wind; ***parami pulgi shijak'anda*** 바람이 불기 시작한다 it's getting windy; ***parami shimhan*** 바람이 심한 gusty
paramdung-i 바람둥이 womanizer
paramjik'an 바람직한 desirable, advisable
param mach'ida 바람 맞히다 stand up (*on date*)
param multchil 발암 물질 carcinogen
paramnan 바람난 flirtatious
param punŭn 바람 부는 windy
param p'iuda 바람 피우다 have an affair with; fool around; cheat on one's wife
paramsŏng-ŭi 발암성의 carcinogenic
paramŭl p'iuda 바람을 피우다 have an affair; be unfaithful
parhada 발하다 utter
parhaeng 발행 publication
parhaenghada 발행하다 print; issue
parhaeng pusu 발행 부수 circulation
parhwi 발휘 exhibition (*of skill*)
parhwihada 발휘하다 exert; show off; ***chagi nŭngnyŏk isang-ŭl parhwihada*** 자기 능력 이상을 발휘하다 excel oneself
parhyo 발효 fermentation
parhyohada 발효하다 ferment
parik'ang 바리캉 hair clippers
parik'eidŭ 바리케이드 barricade; roadblock
parŏnhada 발언하다 speak; state
paro 바로 properly; directly; ***paro ap'e*** 바로 앞에 straight ahead; ***paro chŏne*** 바로 전에 recently; ***paro kakkaie*** 바로 가까이에 close at hand; ***paro kyŏt'e*** 바로 곁에 close by; ***ŭnhaeng paro yŏp'ye*** 은행 바로 옆에 right next to the bank; ***paro kŭgŏya!*** 바로 그거야! that's right!; ***paro kŭrŏk'e*** 바로 그렇게 just like that, exactly like that; ***paro kŭ saenggak*** 바로 그 생각 the very thought; ***paro kŭ sun-gane*** 바로 그 순간에 at the very moment; ***paro seuda*** 바로 세우다 erect; ***paro sŏ!*** 바로 서! stand up straight!
parŭda 바르다 be straight; be right; stick, paste, plaster; spread; put up *wallpaper*
parŭge hada 바르게 하다 straighten out
parŭl kurŭda 발을 구르다 stamp one's feet
parŭm 발음 pronunciation
parŭmhada 발음하다 pronounce
parŭn 바른 proper, correct; orderly; honest; decent
passak mallida 바싹 말리다 parch
passak marŭda 바싹 마르다 dry up
pasŭk'et 바스켓 basket
pasŭrak-kkŏrida 바스락거리다 rustle
pat 밭 (dry) field
patatkka 바닷가 seaside
patch'imttae 받침대 stand, support, base
pattchul 밧줄 rope
pattchurŭl p'ulda 밧줄을 풀다 cast off
pat-tta 받다 receive, accept; undergo; sustain; butt (*of goat*)
pat'ang 바탕 bout; nature; base; ***...e pat'angŭl tuda*** ...에 바탕을 두다 base on
pat'endŏ 바텐더 bartender
pawi 바위 rock
peda 베다 cut
pegae 베개 pillow
pegaennit 베갯잇 pillowcase
pegi 베기 cut, slash

peil 베일 veil
peisŭ 베이스 bass
pekkyŏ ssŭda 베껴 쓰다 copy
Pelgie 벨기에 Belgium ◊ Belgian
Pelgiein 벨기에인 Belgian
pench'i 벤치 bench
peniŏ happ'an 베니어 합판 veneer
pen sangch'ŏ 벤 상처 cut (*injury*)
peŏnaeda 베어내다 cut off
peŏring 베어링 bearing TECH
peranda 베란다 balcony; veranda
pesŭt'ŭsellŏ 베스트셀러 best-seller
pet'erang 베테랑 veteran
Pet'ŭnam 베트남 Vietnam ◊ Vietnamese
Pet'ŭnamin 베트남인 Vietnamese
Pet'ŭnamŏ 베트남어 Vietnamese (*language*)
pi... 비... non..., un...
pi 비 rain
pibang 비방 slur, defamation
pibanghanŭn 비방하는 defamatory
pibarame shidallin 비바람에 시달린 weather-beaten
pibi kkoda 비비 꼬다 squirm (*in embarrassment*)
pibimppap 비빔밥 rice mixed with meat and vegetables
pibŏnida 비번이다 be off duty
pich'amhada 비참하다 be miserable
pich'ida 비치다 flash
pich'inŭn 비치는 see-through
pich'ŭl naeda 빛을 내다 glow
pich'ŭl naenŭn 빛을 내는 luminous
pich'uda 비추다 shine; flash; reflect; ***...e pich'uŏsŏ*** ...에 비추어서 in the light of
pich'uk'ada 비축하다 stockpile, hoard; ***muŏsŭl pich'uk'ada*** 무엇을 비축하다 keep sth in reserve
pida 비다 be empty
pidan 비단 silk
pidio 비디오 video
pidio k'amera 비디오 카메라 video camera
pidio k'aset'ŭ 비디오 카세트 video cassette
pidio nok'wa 비디오 녹화 video recording
pidio nok'wagi 비디오 녹화기 video recorder
pidioro ch'waryŏnghada 비디오로 촬영하다 video
pidio t'eip'ŭ 비디오 테이프 videotape
pidodŏktchŏgin 비도덕적인 unprincipled
pidŭm 비듬 dandruff
pidulgi 비둘기 dove; pigeon
piga oda 비가 오다 rain
piga onŭn 비가 오는 rainy, wet
pigida 비기다 draw SP
pigŏjuja 비거주자 non-resident
pigŏp 비겁 cowardice
pigŏp'an 비겁한 cowardly
pigongshigŭi 비공식의 informal
pigongshik 비공식 informality
pigongshiktchŏgin 비공식적인 unofficial
pigongshiktchŏgŭro 비공식적으로 unofficially
pigŭk 비극 tragedy
pigŭktchŏgin 비극적인 tragic
pigwanjŏgin 비관적인 pessimistic
pigwanjuŭi 비관주의 pessimism
pigwanjuŭija 비관주의자 pessimist
pigwansŭptchŏgin 비관습적인 unconventional
pigyŏl 비결 tip, piece of advice
pigyo 비교 comparison
pigyodoel su innŭn 비교될 수 있는 comparable
pigyogŭp 비교급 comparative GRAM
pigyohada 비교하다 compare; ***...wa / gwa pigyohaesŏ*** ...와 / 과 비교해서 compared with
pigyojŏgin 비교적인 comparative, relative
pigyojŏgŭro 비교적으로 comparatively
pihaeng 비행 flight; flying; ***pihaeng chung-ŭi*** 비행 중의 in-flight
pihaenggi 비행기 airplane; ***pihaenggiro*** 비행기로 by air; ***pihaenggiro toragada*** 비행기로 돌아가다 fly back
pihaengjang 비행장 airfield
pihaeng kyŏngno 비행 경로 flight path
pihal te ŏmnŭn 비할 데 없는 incomparable
pihamnijŏgin 비합리적인

unreasonable
pihŭbyŏnja 비흡연자 non-smoker
pihyŏnshiltchŏgin 비현실적인 impractical, unrealistic
pihyŏptchojŏgin 비협조적인 uncooperative
piin-ganjŏgin 비인간적인 inhuman
pija 비자 visa
pijagŭm 비자금 slush fund
pijŏngsangtchŏgin moyang-ŭi 비정상적인 모양의 misshapen
pijŏngsang-ŭi 비정상의 abnormal
pijobŭn 비좁은 cramped
pijŭnisŭ k'ŭllaesŭ 비즈니스 클래스 business class
pijŭnisŭ mit'ing 비즈니스 미팅 business meeting
pikkoda 비꼬다 twist; give an ironic twist to
pikkonŭn 비꼬는 dry; ironic
pik'ida 비키다 get out of the way; ***kirŭl pik'yŏjuda*** 길을 비켜주다 make way
pik'ini 비키니 bikini
pilda 빌다 beg; pray; implore
pillida 빌리다 borrow; lend
pillin 빌린 on loan
pillyŏjuda 빌려주다 lend; rent out
pimanhan 비만한 corpulent
pimil 비밀 confidence; secret; ***muŏsŭl pimillie hada*** 무엇을 비밀리에 하다 do sth in secret; ***pimillo*** 비밀로 in secret; ***nuguege pimirŭl t'ŏrŏnot'a*** 누구에게 비밀을 털어놓다 confide in s.o.
pimil chŏngbo kigwan 비밀 정보 기관 secret service
pimil kyŏngch'al 비밀 경찰 secret police
pimillie sumgyŏjin 비밀리에 숨겨진 undercover
pimil pŏnho 비밀 번호 PIN
pimirŭi 비밀의 secret; underground, covert
Pimujang Chidae 비무장 지대 Demilitarized Zone, DMZ
pimun 비문 epitaph
pimyŏng 비명 screech, shriek
pimyŏngŭl chirŭda 비명을 지르다 screech, shriek
pin 빈 empty, free
pinan 비난 blame; accusation; condemnation, reproach
pinanhada 비난하다 accuse; blame; condemn
pinanhanŭn 비난하는 reproachful
pinan padŭlmanhan 비난 받을만한 reprehensible
pinanŭi yŏjiga ŏptta 비난의 여지가 없다 be beyond reproach
pinbŏnhada 빈번하다 be frequent
pindungbindung chinaeda 빈둥빈둥 지내다 while away; bum around, be lazy
pindunggŏrida 빈둥거리다 laze around
pingbing tolda 빙빙 돌다 circle (*of plane*)
pingbing tollida 빙빙 돌리다 twirl
pingha 빙하 glacier
pin-gone tchidŭn 빈곤에 찌든 impoverished
pin-gonhan 빈곤한 destitute
pin-got 빈 곳 gap
pingsan 빙산 iceberg
pingtchŏm 빙점 freezing point
pin-gunghan 빈궁한 needy, poor
pinhyŏltchŭng 빈혈증 anemia
pinil pongji 비닐 봉지 plastic bag
pinjŏngdaeda 빈정대다 get at, criticize
pinjŏngdaenŭn 빈정대는 sarcastic
pin konggan 빈 공간 void
pinmin-ga 빈민가 ghetto, slum
pinnada 빛나다 shine; sparkle, twinkle
pinnagada 빗나가다 swerve; digress; misfire; ***yŏp killo pinnagada*** 옆길로 빗나가다 stray
pinnagan 빗나간 stray *bullet*
pinollijŏgin 비논리적인 illogical
pint'ŏlt'ŏri 빈털터리 down-and-out
pint'ŭm ŏmnŭn 빈틈 없는 alert, shrewd, on the ball; scrupulous
pinŭl 비늘 scale (*on fish*)
pinŭngnyultchŏgin 비능률적인 inefficient
pinu 비누 soap; ***pinu hanjang*** 비누 한 장 a bar of soap
pinyak'an 빈약한 flimsy, skimpy
piŏinnŭn 비어있는 unoccupied
piŏinnŭn shigan 비어있는 시간

(time) slot
piok 비옥 fertility (*of soil*)
piok'an 비옥한 fertile *soil*
pip'anjŏgin 비판적인 critical
pip'anjŏgŭro 비판적으로 critically
pip'anŭl pat-tta 비판을 받다 come in for criticism
pip'ongnyŏgŭi 비폭력의 non-violent
pip'ongnyŏk 비폭력 non-violence
pip'ŭbŏgŏ 비프버거 beefburger
pip'yŏng 비평 criticism, review
pip'yŏngga 비평가 critic
pip'yŏnghada 비평하다 criticize
pirŏmŏgŭl 빌어먹을! blast!
pirok ...-l / -ŭltchirado 비록 ...-ㄹ / -을지라도 although, even if
pirot-ttoeda 비롯되다 originate
pirot'ada 비롯하다 begin, start
piryehada 비례하다 be proportional to
piryehanŭn 비례하는 proportional, in proportion
piryo 비료 fertilizer, manure
pisaengsanjŏgin 비생산적인 unproductive
pisagyojŏgin 비사교적인 unsociable
pisang 비상 emergency
pisang ch'angnyuk 비상 착륙 emergency landing
pisangdŭng 비상등 hazard lights
pisanggu 비상구 emergency exit
pisangnyong hwalgangno 비상용 활강로 escape chute
pisangsat'ae 비상사태 state of emergency
pisangshi 비상시 time of emergency; ***pisangshie*** 비상시에 in an emergency
pisŏ 비서 secretary
pisŏk 비석 tombstone
pissada 비싸다 be expensive
pissan 비싼 expensive
pisŭdŭmhan 비스듬한 slanting
pisŭk'et 비스켓 biscuit
pisŭt'ada 비슷하다 be alike, be similar
pisŭt'an 비슷한 similar
pisugi 비수기 low season
pit 빗 comb
pit 빚 debt; ***piji it-tta*** 빚이 있다 be in debt
pit 빛 light; ray
pitchang 빗장 bar, bolt
pitcharu 빗자루 broom
pitchida 빚지다 owe
pitchirhada 빗질하다 brush
pitkkŭm 빗금 slash, oblique
pitppang-ul 빗방울 raindrop
pit-tta 빗다 comb
pitturŏjida 비뚤어지다 be warped
pitturŏjin 비뚤어진 crooked; warped
pit'amin 비타민 vitamin
pit'an 비탄 lament
pit'ong 비통 grief
pit'onghaehada 비통해하다 grieve
pit'onghan 비통한 heartrending; bitter
pit'ŭ 비트 bit COMPUT
pit'ŭlda 비틀다 contort; wrench
pit'ŭlgŏrida 비틀거리다 lurch, stagger; totter
pit'ŭlgŏrinŭn 비틀거리는 unsteady
pit'ŭmaep 비트맵 bitmap
piuda 비우다 empty; vacate; ***chip piuranŭn t'ongjirŭl pat-tta*** 집 비우라는 통지를 받다 get one's eviction notice
piunnŭn 비웃는 derisive
piusŭm 비웃음 derision; sneer
piut-tta 비웃다 laugh at, mock, deride; sneer
piwisaengjŏgin 비위생적인 unhygienic
piyŏrhan 비열한 petty; nasty; ***piyŏrhan ch'aengnyak*** 비열한 책략 dirty trick
piyong 비용 expense; ***Xege Yŭi piyong-ŭl kyŏnjŏk'ada*** X에게 Y의 비용을 견적하다 give X a quotation for Y; ***piyong-i ŏlmana tŭmnikka?*** 비용이 얼마나 듭니까? how much does it cost?
piyong myŏngse 비용 명세 expense account
piyong-ŭl kaptta 비용을 갚다 reimburse
piyujŏgin 비유적인 figurative
piyul 비율 proportion; percentage; rate
pŏban 법안 bill POL
pŏbin chojigŭi 법인 조직의 incorporated

pŏbin hoesa 법인 회사 incorporated, inc
pŏbwŏn 법원 courthouse
pŏbwŏn myŏngnyŏng 법원 명령 court order
pŏdŭlgaji 버들가지 wicker
pŏdŭnamu 버드나무 willow
pŏdunggŏrida 버둥거리다 squirm, wriggle
pŏgŭ 버그 bug COMPUT
pŏjŏn 버전 version
pŏk'ŭl 버클 buckle
pŏl 벌 bee; deck, pack; suit; pair; set; plain; punishment ◊ *countword for suit of clothes*; ***pŏrŭl momyŏnhada*** 벌을 모면하다 get off scot-free; ***pŏrŭl myŏnhada*** 벌을 면하다 get off (*not be punished*); ***pŏrŭl pat-tchi ank'o*** 벌을 받지 않고 with impunity
pŏlch'unghada 벌충하다 make up for, compensate for
pŏlda 벌다 earn
pŏlgŏbŏsŭn 벌거벗은 naked
pŏlgŭm 벌금 fine; penalty
pŏlk'ŏk sŏngnaeda 벌컥 성내다 fly into a rage
pŏlle 벌레 bug; worm
pŏlle mŏgŭn 벌레 먹은 worm-eaten
pŏllida 벌리다 open
pŏlmok 벌목 woodcut
pŏlssŏ 벌써 already
pŏltchip 벌집 beehive; honeycomb
pŏlttŏk 벌떡 suddenly; ***pŏlttŏk irŏnada*** 벌떡 일어나다 jump to one's feet
pŏm 범 tiger
Pŏma 버마 Burma ◊ Burmese
pŏmhada 범하다 commit
pŏmin 범인 culprit
pŏmin susaek 범인 수색 manhunt
pŏmjoe 범죄 crime; offense; guilt ◊ criminal
pŏmjoein indo 범죄인 인도 extradition
pŏmjoein indo hyŏptchŏng 범죄인 인도 협정 extradition treaty
pŏmjoeja 범죄자 criminal; offender
pŏmju 범주 category
pŏmnam 범람 flood; flooding
pŏmnamhada 범람하다 flood
pŏmnyŏng 법령 law, statute
pŏmppoptcha 범법자 offender
pŏmp'ŏ 범퍼 bumper
pŏmsŏn 범선 sailing ship
pŏmurida 버무리다 toss
pŏmwi 범위 extent, range; ***...ŭi pŏmwirŭl nŏmŏsŏ*** ...의 범위를 넘어서 beyond
pŏmyul 법률 legislation
pŏn 번 time, occasion; number; duty; ***han pŏn*** 한 번 once
pŏnch'ang 번창 prosperity
pŏnch'anghada 번창하다 prosper, flourish
pŏnch'anghanŭn 번창하는 prosperous, flourishing
pŏn-gae 번개 lightning
pŏn-gaech'ŏrŏm tallida 번개처럼 달리다 race; run like the wind; streak
pŏn-gaetppul 번갯불 bolt of lightning
pŏn-gara hanŭn 번갈아 하는 alternate
pŏng-ŏri 벙어리 mute; dumb
pŏng-ŏri changgap 벙어리 장갑 mitten
pŏn-gŏrŏun 번거러운 complex
pŏnho 번호 number
pŏnhop'an 번호판 license plate
pŏnhorŭl maegida 번호를 매기다 number, put a number on
pŏnhwahan 번화한 busy, lively, bustling
pŏnjida 번지다 run (*of paint, make-up etc*)
pŏnnamu 벚나무 cherry (tree)
pŏnshik 번식 breeding
pŏnshik'ada 번식하다 breed
pŏnshingnyŏgi ŏmnŭn 번식력이 없는 infertile
pŏntchŏk-kkŏrinŭn 번쩍거리는 flashing
pŏnttŭgida 번득이다 glint
pŏnyŏk 번역 translation
pŏnyŏkka 번역가 translator
pŏnyŏk'ada 번역하다 translate
pŏnyŏnghada 번영하다 bloom, flourish
pŏp 법 law; method; ***pŏbe ŏgŭnnanŭn*** 법에 어긋나는 against

the law
pŏp-ppok 법복 robe (*of judge*)
pŏptchŏgin 법적인 legal
pŏptchŏk choŏnja 법적 조언자 legal adviser
pŏptchŏng 법정 court; courtroom
pŏp'ak 법학 law (*as subject of study*)
pŏrida 버리다 abandon, leave; discard; dump
pŏrida 벌이다 stage *demo*; start *business*
pŏrigo ttŏnada 버리고 떠나다 abandon
pŏrŭdŏpsshi mandŭlda 버릇없이 만들다 spoil *child*
pŏrŭsŭl karŭch'ida 버릇을 가르치다 discipline
pŏrŭt ŏmnŭn 버릇 없는 impolite; spoilt
pŏryŏduda 버려두다 abandon; ***naenoŭn ch'ae pŏryŏduda*** 내놓은 채 버려두다 leave out, not put away
pŏryŏjin 버려진 derelict, neglected
pŏsŏnada 벗어나다 break away; elude; outgrow; ***...esŏ pŏsŏnada*** ...에서 벗어나다 depart from; deviate from
pŏsŏt 버섯 mushroom
pŏsŭ 버스 bus *also* COMPUT; ***pŏsŭro*** 버스로 by bus
pŏsŭ chŏngnyujang 버스 정류장 bus stop
pŏsŭ t'ŏminŏl 버스 터미널 bus terminal, bus station
pŏtkkida 벗기다 remove; rub away; strip; undress; unveil; shell; ***kkŏptchirŭl pŏtkkida*** 껍질을 벗기다 skin; peel, pare
pŏtkkyŏjida 벗겨지다 come off; peel off (*of paint*)
pŏt-tta 벗다 remove
pŏt'ida 버티다 hold out, survive; resist
pŏt'ŏ 버터 butter
pŏt'ŏrŭl parŭda 버터를 바르다 butter *bread*
pŏt'ŭn 버튼 button
poan 보안 security
poan-gyŏng 보안경 goggles
poan hwagin 보안 확인 security check
poankkwa 보안과 security (*department*)
poan kyŏnggye 보안 경계 security alert
poanŭl chungshihanŭn 보안을 중시하는 security-conscious
pobae 보배 jewel *fig*
pobok 보복 revenge
poboktchŏgin 보복적인 vindictive
pobok'ada 보복하다 take one's revenge
pobyŏng 보병 infantry soldier
pobyŏngdae 보병대 infantry
poch'ŏnggi 보청기 hearing aid
poch'o 보초 sentry
poch'ung 보충 compensation, reward
poch'unghada 보충하다 supplement
poda 보다 look; look at; eye; make out; see; watch ◊ than; ***...poda tŏ mani*** ...보다 더 많이; ***... ŭl / rŭl poji mot'anŭn*** ...을 / 를 보지 못하는 blind to; ***shihŏmŭl poda*** 시험을 보다 take an exam
poda chagŭn 보다 작은 minor, slight
poda chungnyohada 보다 중요하다 outweigh
...poda natkke ...보다 낮게 beneath (*in status, value*)
poda nat-tta 보다 낫다 be better than
poda naŭn 보다 나은 better
poda orae salda 보다 오래 살다 survive, outlive
podap'ada 보답하다 repay, return
poda suga mant'a 보다 수가 많다 outnumber
poda tŏ 보다 더 more than, over, above
poda tŏ charhada 보다 더 잘하다 outdo
poda tŏ orae salda 보다 더 오래 살다 outlive
poda ttwiŏnan 보다 뛰어난 superior, better
...poda wi ...보다 위 above, higher than
podisut'ŭ 보디수트 body (suit)
podo 보도 report, coverage
podohada 보도하다 report, cover

podŭ keim 보드 게임 board game
podŭk'a 보드카 vodka
poganghada 보강하다 follow up; reinforce
pogang hoeŭi 보강 회의 follow-up meeting
pogie 보기에 apparently
pogienŭn 보기에는 seemingly; ***naega pogienŭn*** 내가 보기에는 in my estimation; as far as I'm concerned
pogi hyunghan 보기 흉한 unsightly
pogiwanŭn tarŭn 보기와는 다른 deceptive
pogo 보고 account, report
pogohada 보고하다 report
pogosŏ 보고서 report, account
Pogŭm 복음 the Word REL; Gospels
pogŭm chŏndosa 복음 전도사 evangelist
pogŭmsŏ 복음서 Gospel
pogwan 보관 storage
pogwan changso 보관 장소 storage space
pogwanhada 보관하다 keep, store
pogwansoe matkkida 보관소에 맡기다 check (*in checkroom*)
pogwŏnhada 복원하다 reinstate
pogyŏl sŏnsu 보결 선수 substitute
pogyongnyang 복용량 dosage
pogyongppŏp 복용법 directions (*for medicine*)
pogyongshik'ida 복용시키다 administer, give *medicine*
pogyunja 보균자 carrier (*of disease*)
pohaenggi 보행기 walker (*for baby*)
pohaengja 보행자 pedestrian, walker
pohaengja chŏnyong kuyŏk 보행자 전용 구역 pedestrian precinct
pohamhada 포함하다 include, comprise
pohŏm 보험 insurance
pohŏm chŭngsŏ 보험 증서 insurance policy
pohŏme tŭlda 보험에 들다 insure
pohŏm hoesa 보험 회사 insurance company
poho 보호 protection
pohoch'aek 보호책 safeguard
pohohada 보호하다 protect, preserve
pohohanŭn 보호하는 protective
poho kamch'algwan 보호 감찰관 probation officer
poho kuyŏk 보호 구역 (wild animal) sanctuary
poida 보이다 be able to see; be visible; show; seem; ***poiji annŭn*** 보이지 않는 out of sight
poik'ot 보이콧 boycott
poik'ot'ada 보이콧하다 boycott
poillŏ 보일러 boiler
poinŭn 보이는 visible
poisŭk'aut 보이스카웃 boy scout
pojal kŏt omnŭn 보잘 것 없는 trivial; worthless
pojang 보장 security, guarantee (*for investment*)
pojanghada 보장하다 guarantee, assure
pojogae 보조개 dimple
pojogŭm 보조금 grant, subsidy; ***pojogŭmŭl chigŭp'ada*** 보조금을 지급하다 subsidize
pojojŏgin 보조적인 auxiliary, supplementary
pojo kyojae 보조 교재 teaching aid
pojon 보존 preservation, maintenance
pojonhada 보존하다 preserve, maintain; conserve
pojoŭi 보조의 auxiliary
pojŭng 보증 guarantee, warranty; assurance; ***pojŭng kigan chung-ida*** 보증 기간 중이다 be under warranty
pojŭnghada 보증하다 sponsor; guarantee; underwrite; vouch for
pojŭng-in 보증인 guarantor; sponsor
pojŭng kigan 보증 기간 guarantee period
pojŭngsŏ 보증서 letter of guarantee
pok-kku 복구 restoration
pok-kkuhada 복구하다 restore
pok-kkwihada 복귀하다 make a comeback; return; be restored
pokppu 복부 abdomen ◊ abdominal
pokssa 복사 copy
pokssadoen yŏlssoe 복사된 열쇠 duplicate key
pokssagi 복사기 photocopier
pokssahada 복사하다 copy; take a

photocopy of
pokssappyŏ 복사뼈 ankle bone
poksshik 복식 doubles (*in tennis*)
pokssŭp'ada 복습하다 brush up; review
pokssu 복수 retaliation, reprisal; vengeance
pokssuhada 복수하다 retaliate, take reprisals
pokssuhyŏng 복수형 plural
pokssung-a 복숭아 peach
poktchap'ada 복잡하다 be complicated
poktchap'an 복잡한 complicated; complex
poktche 복제 reproduction
poktchep'um 복제품 replica
poktchi 복지 welfare
poktchiksshik'ida 복직시키다 reinstate
poktchi kuk-kka 복지 국가 welfare state
poktchi saŏp 복지 사업 welfare work
poktchi saŏpkka 복지 사업가 welfare worker
poktchong 복종 obedience; submission
poktta 볶다 stir-fry
poktto 복도 corridor, passage
pokt'ong 복통 stomach-ache
pok'ŏl kŭrup 보컬 그룹 vocal group
pollae 본래 originally; naturally
polling 볼링 bowling
pollinghada 볼링하다 bowl
pollingjang 볼링장 bowling alley
polling kong 볼링 공 bowl
pollingp'in 볼링핀 pin
pol peŏring 볼 베어링 ball bearing
polp'en 볼펜 ballpoint (pen)
polp'umŏmnŭn 볼품없는 unattractive
polt'ŭ 볼트 bolt; volt
polt'ŭro choeda 볼트로 죄다 bolt
pom 봄 look, glance; spring
pomch'ŏl 봄철 springtime
pommaji taech'ŏngso 봄맞이 대청소 spring-cleaning
pomul 보물 treasure
ponaeda 보내다 pass (*of time*); spend *time*; send
ponbogi 본보기 model, pattern
ponbu 본부 base, center; headquarters
ponggoch'a 봉고차 van
ponggŭmnal 봉급날 payday
ponggŭp 봉급 pay check
ponggŭp pongt'u 봉급 봉투 pay envelope
ponggŭp sujun 봉급 수준 salary scale
ponghada 봉하다 seal *letter*
pong-in 봉인 seal
pongji 봉지 packet, sachet; seal
pongni 복리 well-being; compound interest
pongsahada 봉사하다 render a service, serve
pongswae 봉쇄 blockade
pongswaehada 봉쇄하다 blockade; seal off; freeze
pongt'u 봉투 envelope
ponin 본인 oneself; himself; herself; ***ponini chiktchŏp*** 본인이 직접 in person; ***ponin sajin*** 본인 사진 a photo of oneself
ponjiltchŏgin 본질적인 fundamental; substantial
ponjiltchŏgŭro 본질적으로 fundamentally, basically, mainly
ponmun 본문 text
ponnŭng 본능 instinct
ponnŭngjŏgin 본능적인 instinctive
ponŏsŭ 보너스 bonus
ponsa 본사 head office
ponttŭda 본뜨다 imitate, emulate
pont'o 본토 mainland
poonbyŏng 보온병 thermos flask
pop'yŏnjŏgin 보편적인 universal, general
pop'yŏnjŏgŭro 보편적으로 universally
porami innŭn 보람이 있는 worthwhile
poram ŏmnŭn 보람 없는 thankless
poratppit 보라빛 violet (*color*)
pori 보리 barley
porich'a 보리차 roasted barley tea
porŭmttal 보름달 full moon
poryŏnji 볼연지 blusher

poryuhada 보류하다 withhold
Posal 보살 Bodhisattva
posalp'ida 보살피다 look after
posalp'im 보살핌 care
posang 보상 reward; compensation; ***posangŭl hada*** 보상을 하다 make amends, compensate for
posanghada 보상하다 compensate for
poshint'ang 보신탕 dog meat soup
posŏk 보석 bail; jewel, gem; ***posŏgŭl patkke hada*** 보석을 받게 하다 bail out
posŏk-kkŭm 보석금 bail (*money*)
posŏkssang 보석상 jeweler
posŏngnyu 보석류 jewelry
posŭlbi 보슬비 drizzle
posu 보수 pay; reward, remuneration; conservativeness ◊ conservative
posuga ch'ungbunhan 보수가 충분한 remunerative
posuhada 보수하다 renovate, do up; repair
posujŏgin 보수적인 conservative; conventional
posurŭl chuda 보수를 주다 pay; reward
pot'ong 보통 usual; ordinary ◊ usually
pot'ong chŏngdoŭi 보통 정도의 average, mediocre
pot'ong saram 보통 사람 ordinary person
pot'ongsŏk 보통석 economy class
pot'ong ttaech'ŏrŏm 보통 때처럼 as usual
pot'ong-ŭi 보통의 normal, usual; ordinary; common; standard; mediocre
pot'ong-ŭro 보통으로 normally, usually
pot'ong yegŭm 보통 예금 savings account
pot'ŭ 보트 boat
powanhada 보완하다 complement
powanhanŭn 보완하는 complementary
poyangji 보양지 health resort
poyŏjida 보여지다 appear, seem; show; show up, be visible
poyŏjuda 보여주다 show; expose
poyugŭm 보유금 reserves
poyugwŏn 보육원 kindergarten
poyuja 보유자 holder (*of record*)
ppadŭt'an 빠듯한 full
ppaeat-tta 빼앗다 take by force; ***nugurobut'ŏ muŏsŭl ppaeat-tta*** 누구로부터 무엇을 빼앗다 take sth away from s.o. (by force), snatch sth from s.o.
ppaeda 빼다 drain off; omit; subtract; ***42 ppaegi 18ŭn 24ida*** 42 빼기 18은 24이다 42 minus 18 is 24; ***...man ppaego*** ...만 빼고 all but ..., except ...
ppaedalmŭn mosŭp 빼닮은 모습 image, exact likeness
ppaegi puho 빼기 부호 minus sign
ppaekppaek'age kkwak ch'an 빽빽하게 꽉 찬 jam-packed, crowded
ppaenaeda 빼내다 take out; eject; drain
ppaengsoni sago 뺑소니 사고 hit-and-run accident
ppaengsoni unjŏnsu 뺑소니 운전수 hit-and-run driver
ppajida 빠지다 drain away, ebb; sink in; fall in; fall out; pull out; be hooked on; miss; ***sarange ppajida*** 사랑에 빠지다 fall in love; ***muŏse ppajida*** 무엇에 빠지다 indulge in sth; give sth a miss
ppajyŏ nagada 빠져 나가다 slip out, go out; ebb away; ***sarami ppajyŏt-tta!*** 사람이 빠졌다! man overboard!
ppalda 빨다 wash; suck
ppalgaejida 빨개지다 flush, redden
ppalgan 빨간 red
ppalgan pul 빨간 불 red light
ppalgat'a 빨갛다 be red
ppallae 빨래 washing; ***ppallaerŭl hada*** 빨래를 하다 do the washing
ppallajida 빨라지다 accelerate
ppalli 빨리 quickly
ppalli chinagada 빨리 지나가다 speed by
ppalli hada 빨리 하다 speed up
ppalli hae! 빨리 해! be quick!
ppalli kada 빨리 가다 speed
ppang 빵 bread

ppangjip 빵집 bakery
ppang karu 빵 가루 breadcrumbs (*for cooking*)
ppang pusŭrŏgi 빵 부스러기 breadcrumbs (*for birds*)
ppanhi ch'yŏdaboda 빤히 쳐다보다 stare; stare at
pparadŭrida 빨아들이다 inhale; suck in; absorb
ppara mŏktta 빨아 먹다 suck
pparŭda 빠르다 be fast, be quick
pparŭge 빠르게 fast, quickly
pparŭn 빠른 fast, quick; speedy
ppatppat'an 빳빳한 stiff
ppattŭrida 빠뜨리다 skip, omit
ppida 삐다 sprain
ppigŏk-kkŏrida 삐걱거리다 creak, squeak
ppii hanŭn sori 삐이 하는 소리 bleep
ppŏdŏit-tta 뻗어있다 extend
ppŏdŏnagago innŭn 뻗어나가고 있는 sprawling
ppŏgŭnhan 뻐근한 stiff
ppŏnppŏnhada 뻔뻔하다 be shameless, be impudent
ppŏnppŏnham 뻔뻔함 impudence
ppŏnppŏnhan 뻔뻔한 impudent, fresh
ppŏnppŏnsŭrŏun 뻔뻔스러운 impudent, blatant, shameless
ppŏtch'ida 뻗치다 stretch, spread
ppŏtppŏt'aejida 뻣뻣해지다 stiffen
ppŏtppŏt'age hada 뻣뻣하게 하다 stiffen up
ppŏtppŏt'an 뻣뻣한 stiff, unyielding
ppoppo 뽀뽀 peck, kiss
ppoppohada 뽀뽀하다 give a peck, kiss
ppoptta 뽑다 pull out, extract; pluck; select
ppul 뿔 horn
ppult'e an-gyŏng 뿔테 안경 horn-rimmed spectacles
ppumŏjyŏ naoda 뿜어져 나오다 squirt, spurt
ppumŏnaeda 뿜어내다 squirt
ppun 뿐 nothing but, only; ***...l ppun*** ...ㄹ 뿐 nothing but; ***Xppunman anira Ydo ttohan*** X뿐만 아니라 Y도 또한 not only X but Y also
ppuri 뿌리 root
ppuribak'in 뿌리박힌 entrenched, deep-rooted
ppurida 뿌리다 scatter; sprinkle; slop; spray
ppuri kip'ŭn 뿌리 깊은 deep-rooted
ppurut'unghada 뿌루퉁하다 pout
ppyam 뺨 cheek
ppyŏ 뼈 bone
ppyŏdae 뼈대 frame
ppyojokt'ap 뾰족탑 spire, steeple
ppyojuk'an kkŭt 뾰족한 끝 spike
pp'im 삠 wrench (*injury*)
pu 부 copy (*of book*); ministry; wealth
pu- 부- vice-
pŭi ai p'i 브이 아이 피이 VIP
pŭi ssi al 브이 시이 알 VCR
pŭllaek pakssŭ 블랙 박스 black box, flight recorder
pŭllaekrisŭt'ŭe ollida 블랙리스트에 올리다 blacklist
pŭllaindŭ 블라인드 blind, shade
pŭllausŭ 블라우스 blouse
pŭllok 블록 block COMPUT
pŭllogŭl ssŭiuda 블록을 씌우다 highlight COMPUT
pŭraendi 브랜디 brandy
Pŭrajil 브라질 Brazil ◊ Brazilian
Pŭrajil saram 브라질 사람 Brazilian
pŭraujŏ 브라우저 browser COMPUT
pŭreik'ŭ 브레이크 brake
pŭreik'ŭ lait'ŭ 브레이크 라이트 brake light
pŭreik'ŭrŭl kŏlda 브레이크를 걸다 brake, put the brake(s) on
pŭrejiŏ 브레지어 brassière
pŭroch'i 브로치 brooch
pŭrogŭraem 프로그램 program
pŭrogŭraemŏ 프로그래머 programmer
pŭrogŭraem tchada 프로그램 짜다 program
pŭrok'olli 브로콜리 broccoli
pŭroshyŏ 브로셔 brochure
pubu 부부 couple
pubun 부분 part, proportion; portion; segment; slice
pubuntchŏgin 부분적인 segmented
pubuntchŏgŭro 부분적으로 partially, partly, part

puch'ae 부채 fan
puch'aejirhada 부채질하다 fan oneself
puch'ida 붙이다 attach, stick; pin up
puch'igi 붙이기 paste COMPUT
puch'ŏ 부처 Buddha; department
Puch'ŏnim Oshin Nal 부처님 오신 날 Buddha's Birthday
puch'u 부추 leek
puch'ugida 부추기다 encourage
pudae 부대 unit MIL
pudaep'yo 부대표 deputy leader
pudam 부담 burden; ***pudamŭl chuda*** 부담을 주다 strain *finances, budget*; ***nuguege pudamŭl chuda*** 누구에게 부담을 주다 impose oneself on s.o.
pudamhada 부담하다 bear *costs etc*
pudanghada 부당하다 be unjust
pudanghage 부당하게 wrongly, mistakenly
pudanghan 부당한 wrongful
pudich'ida 부딪히다 bump into; bump; ram
pudodŏk 부도덕 immorality
pudodŏk'an 부도덕한 immoral; unscrupulous
pudong-aek 부동액 antifreeze
pudongsan 부동산 real estate
pudongsan chunggaein 부동산 중개인 realtor
pudŭrŏpkke 부드럽게 softly
pudŭrŏpkke hada 부드럽게 하다 tone down, soften
pudŭrŏptta 부드럽다 be soft; be gentle
pudŭrŏun 부드러운 soft; gentle; mild; smooth
pudŭrŏwŏjida 부드러워지다 soften
pudu 부두 dock; port; wharf; ***pudue taeda*** 부두에 대다 dock, put in
pudu nodongja 부두 노동자 stevedore
pudut-kka 부둣가 quayside
pugajŏgin 부가적인 supplementary
pugamul 부가물 trappings; frills
puga yogŭm 부가 요금 surcharge
pugi 부기 swelling; book-keeping
pugŏm 부검 autopsy
pugo 부고 obituary
pugŭp'ada 보급하다 spread; disseminate
pugwahada 부과하다 impose; ***nuguege ch'aegimŭl pugwahada*** 누구에게 책임을 부과하다 set a task for s.o.
pugyeŭi 부계의 paternal
pugyŏng-yŏng-in 부경영인 assistant manager
pugyŏrhada 부결하다 throw out
pugyosu 부교수 associate professor
puha 부하 load ELEC
puhap'ada 부합하다 correspond with
puhwahada 부화하다 hatch out
puhwal 부활 revival; resurrection
Puhwaltchŏl 부활절 Easter
puhwarhada 부활하다 revive
puinhada 부인하다 contradict; deny
puja 부자 sage; father and son; rich man
pujae 부재 absence
pujagyong 부작용 side effect
pujang 부장 managing director; assistant director
pujayŏnsŭrŏun 부자연스러운 unnatural
pujibaein 부지배인 assistant manager
pujirŏmnŭn marŭl hada 부질없는 말을 하다 waffle
pujirŏnhan 부지런한 diligent
pujirŏnhi irhada 부지런히 일하다 work hard
pujŏgŭngja 부적응자 misfit
pujŏkkyŏgin 부적격인 (morally) unfit
pujŏktchŏrhan 부적절한 improper
pujŏkttanghada 부적당하다 be unsuitable; be unfit; be inadequate; ***mŏkkie / mashigie pujŏkttanghada*** 먹기에 / 마시기에 부적당하다 be unfit to eat / drink
pujŏkttanghan 부적당한 unsuitable, inappropriate; inadequate
pujŏng 부정 denial; injustice; infidelity
pujŏng haeng-wi 부정 행위 misconduct
pujŏnghal su ŏmnŭn 부정할 수 없는 undeniable
pujŏnghan 부정한 crooked, dishonest; unfaithful
pujŏnghwak'an 부정확한 inaccurate;

indeterminate
pujŏngjik 부정직 dishonesty
pujŏngjik'an 부정직한 dishonest
pujŏngjŏgin 부정적인 destructive; negative
pujŏngsa 부정사 infinitive
pujŏng-ŭi 부정의 negative
pujojongsa 부조종사 copilot
pujok 부족 shortage; shortfall; tribe; ***pujok'ami ŏptta*** 부족함이 없다 want for nothing
pujok'ada 부족하다 be lacking
pujuŭihan 부주의한 inattentive; slack; sloppy
puk 북 drum; north
pukch'ae 북채 drumstick
puk-kkŭk kom 북극 곰 polar bear
Puk-kkyŏng 북경 Beijing
Pukkŭk 북극 North Pole
Pukkŭkkwŏn 북극권 Arctic
pukkŭrŏptta 부끄럽다 be ashamed; be shy; ***...ege*** **pukkŭrŏpkke yŏgida** ...에게 부끄럽게 여기다 be ashamed of; ***pukkŭrŏptchido anni!*** 부끄럽지도 않니! shame on you!
pukkŭrŏun 부끄러운 shameful
pukppang-e 북방에 north of
Pukppet'ŭnam 북베트남 North Vietnam ◊ North Vietnamese
Pukppet'ŭnamin 북베트남인 North Vietnamese
pukppuŭi 북부의 northern
puksso 북서 northwest
puktchoge 북쪽에 to the north of
puktchogŭro 북쪽으로 northward
Pukttaesŏyang Choyak Kigu 북대서양 조약 기구 NATO
pukttoduda 북돋우다 bolster
Puk'an 북한 North Korea ◊ North Korean
Puk'an saram 북한 사람 North Korean (*person*)
puk'yang-ŭi 북향의 northerly
pul 불 fire; dollar; Buddha; France ◊ French; ***pul puch'ida*** 불 붙이다 light; ***pul kat'ŭn*** 불 같은 fiery
pul- 불- not; un-; in-; dis-; non-
pulboktchong 불복종 disobedience, insubordination
pulboktchonghanŭn 불복종하는 disobedient, insubordinate
pulch'ansŏng 불찬성 disapproval
pulch'ansŏnghada 불찬성하다 disapprove of
pulch'injŏrhada 불친절하다 be unkind
pulch'injŏrhan 불친절한 unfriendly; unkind; inhospitable
pulch'ippyŏng-ŭi 불치병의 terminally ill
pulch'ungbunhan 불충분한 meager; insufficient
pulch'ungsshil 불충실 disloyalty
pulch'ungsshirhan 불충실한 disloyal
pulda 불다 blow; inflate
puldoujŏ 불도우저 bulldozer
pulgabunŭi 불가분의 indivisible
pulgamtchŭng-ŭi 불감증의 frigid MED
pulgansŏp 불간섭 noninterference, nonintervention
pulganŭng 불가능 impossibility
pulganŭnghada 불가능하다 be impossible
pulganŭnghan 불가능한 impossible
pulgap'ihada 불가피하다 be unavoidable
pulgasari 불가사리 starfish
pulgasaŭi 불가사의 mystery
pulgasaŭihan 불가사의한 mysterious, inscrutable
pulgirhae poinŭn 불길해 보이는 sinister
pulgirhan 불길한 ominous
pulgirhan yegam 불길한 예감 foreboding
pulgŏjida 붉어지다 redden, blush
pulgogi 불고기 barbecued beef
pulgongjŏnghan 불공정한 unfair, unjust; unequal
pulgongp'yŏnghada 불공평하다 be unfair, be biased
pulgŭn 붉은 ruddy; red
pulguhago 불구하고 in spite of
pulgurŭi 불굴의 indomitable
pulguŭi 불구의 disabled
pulgyŏnggi 불경기 recession, slump
Pulgyo 불교 Buddhism ◊ Buddhist
Pulgyo Shinja 불교 신자 Buddhist
pulgyuch'iktchŏgin 불규칙적인 irregular
pulgyunhyŏng 불균형 disparity

pulgyunhyŏnghan 불균형한 disproportionate
pulkkil 불길 flames
pulkkonnori 불꽃놀이 fireworks
pulkkot 불꽃 flame; spark
pulk'wae 불쾌 displeasure
pulk'waehada 불쾌하다 put off, repel
pulk'waehage hada 불쾌하게 하다 displease
pulk'waehan 불쾌한 nasty, unpleasant; undesirable; offensive, repellent; rotten; sick
pulli 분리 division, separation; segregation
pullihada 분리하다 separate; isolate; segregate; partition; unfix
pullihada 불리하다 be prejudicial to
pullihal su innŭn 분리할 수 있는 detachable
pullihal su ŏmnŭn 분리할 수 없는 inseparable
pullihan 불리한 disadvantageous; ***pullihan chokkŏn*** 불리한 조건 handicap; ***pullihan iptchang-e it-tta*** 불리한 입장에 있다 be at a disadvantage
pullishik'ida 분리시키다 disconnect
pullŏ irŭk'ida 불러 일으키다 arouse; summon up; work up
pullŏogi 불러오기 open COMPUT
pullŏ tŭrida 불러 들이다 call in, summon
pulluk'ada 불룩하다 bulge
pullyangbae 불량배 hooligan
pullyang puch'ae 불량 부채 bad debt
pullyangp'um 불량품 inferior goods; reject
pullyŏnsŏng 불연성 non-combustibility ◊ incombustible; fireproof
pullyu 분류 classification
pullyuhada 분류하다 class; classify; sort; break down; itemize
pullyun 불륜 immorality
pullyunŭi kwangye 불륜의 관계 (love) affair
pulman 불만 discontent, dissatisfaction
pulmanida 불만이다 be unhappy with
pulmansŭrŏun 불만스러운 discontented
pulmo 불모 infertility ◊ barren
pulmoji 불모지 unproductive soil
pulmyŏl 불멸 immortality
pulmyŏnghwak'an 불명확한 uncertain
pulmyŏng-ye 불명예 dishonor; disgrace
pulmyŏng-yesŭrŏun 불명예스러운 dishonorable
pulmyŏntchŭng 불면증 insomnia
pulmyŏrŭi 불멸의 immortal
pulppŏp 불법 illegality ◊ illegal
pulppŏp haengwi 불법 행위 unlawful act
pulppŏp koyong 불법 고용 black economy
pulp'iryohan 불필요한 unnecessary
pulp'yŏnhage nŭkkida 불편하게 느끼다 feel ill at ease
pulp'yŏn 불편 inconvenience
pulp'yŏng 불평 complaint
pulp'yŏngdŭng 불평등 inequality
pulp'yŏnghada 불평하다 complain; complain about
pulp'yŏngkkŏri 불평거리 complaint, grievance
pulp'yŏng-ŭl nŭrŏnot-tta 불평을 늘어놓다 complain
pulp'yŏnhada 불편하다 be uncomfortable; be inconvenient
pulp'yŏnhan 불편한 uncomfortable; inconvenient
pulshich'ak 불시착 crash landing
pulssanghada 불쌍하다 be piteous, be wretched
pulssanghaejin 불쌍해진 wretched
pulssanghan 불쌍한 piteous, wretched
pulssanghi yŏgida 불쌍히 여기다 take pity on
pulsshie 불시에 unexpectedly, by surprise; ***Xŭl / rŭl pulsshie sŭpkkyŏk'ada*** X을 / 를 불시에 습격하다 catch X unawares
pulsshin 불신 mistrust, doubt
pulsshinhada 불신하다 mistrust
pulssonhan 불손한 insolent, arrogant

pulssuk marhada 불쑥 말하다 blurt out
pulssuk naoda 불쑥 나오다 stick out, protrude
pulssuk nat'anada 불쑥 나타나다 pop up, bob up
pulssuk saenggida 불쑥 생기다 shoot up (*of new suburb etc*)
pulssuk t'wiŏ naoda 불쑥 튀어 나오다 protrude
pulssunhan 불순한 impure
pult'anŭn 불타는 alight, burning
pult'aorŭnŭn 불타오르는 ablaze, blazing
pult'umyŏnghan 불투명한 opaque
pult'umyŏnghan yuri 불투명한 유리 frosted glass
pum 붐 boom
pumbida 붐비다 be busy, be crowded
pumbinŭn 붐비는 busy, crowded
pumo 부모 parent
pumok 부목 splint
pumo-ŭi 부모의 parental
pun 분 face powder; minute; flowerpot; anger; person (*respectful*) ◊ *countword for people* (*respectful*); ***pun tang hoejŏn*** 분 당 회전 revs per minute
punbae 분배 distribution
punbaehada 분배하다 share, allocate
punbal 분발 spurt
punbiaek 분비액 secretion
punbihada 분비하다 secrete
punbimul 분비물 secretion (*liquid secreted*)
punbyŏl innŭn 분별 있는 sound, prudent; level-headed; reasonable, sensible
punch'im 분침 minute hand
punch'ul 분출 torrent
punch'uldoeda 분출되다 spout
punch'ulgu 분출구 jet
punch'urhada 분출하다 erupt (*of volcano*)
pun-gae 분개 resentment; outrage
pun-gaehada 분개하다 resent
pun-gaehan 분개한 resentful; indignant
pun-ganhada 분간하다 distinguish
pungdae 붕대 bandage, dressing
pungdaerŭl kamtta 붕대를 감다 bandage, dress
punggoe 붕괴 fall, collapse
punggoedoeda 붕괴되다 disintegrate; crash
pun-gitchŏm 분기점 fork (*in road*)
Pungmi 북미 North America ◊ North American
Pungmiin 북미인 North American
Pungmiŭi 북미의 North American
punhaedoeda 분해되다 come apart
punhaehada 분해하다 take to pieces, dismantle
punhal maeip 분할매입 buying on an installment plan
punhongsaek 분홍색 pink
punhwa 분화 eruption
punhwagu 분화구 crater (*of volcano*)
punja 분자 molecule ◊ molecular
punjae 분재 bonsai
punjaeng 분쟁 dispute
punjaeng chiyŏk 분쟁 지역 hot spot
punjaeng chojŏngja 분쟁 조정자 troubleshooter, mediator
punjangshil 분장실 dressing room
punjuhi irhada 분주히 일하다 bustle about, be busy
punkkwa wiwŏnhoe 분과 위원회 subcommittee
punman 분만 delivery (*of baby*); labor; ***punman chung-ida*** 분만 중이다 be in labor
punmanhada 분만하다 give birth to
punmang 분망 scramble, rush
punmanshik'ida 분만시키다 deliver *baby*
punmanshil 분만실 labor ward
punmugi 분무기 atomizer; spraygun
punmyŏnghada 분명하다 be obvious; be clear
punmyŏnghage 분명하게 plainly, clearly
punmyŏnghan 분명한 clear, obvious
punmyŏnghi 분명히 clearly, evidently; explicitly
punno 분노 wrath
punnŭn 붙는 sticky *label*
pun parŭda 분 바르다 powder
punp'a 분파 sect; splinter group
punp'il 분필 chalk
punsagirŭl sayonghada 분사기를

사용하다 sandblast
punshilmul sent'ŏ 분실물 센터 lost-and-found
punsŏk 분석 analysis
punsŏk'ada 분석하다 analyze
punsu 분수 fraction; fountain
punsuryŏng 분수령 watershed
punswaegi 분쇄기 mill
punwigi 분위기 atmosphere; mood; tone
punya 분야 area, field
punyŏl 분열 division, split
punyŏlsshik'ida 분열시키다 split
punyŏlsshik'inŭn 분열시키는 disruptive
punyŏrhada 분열하다 be divided; be split
puŏk 부엌 kitchen
puŏngbuŏng ulda 부엉부엉 울다 hoot (*of owl*)
puŏ nŏt'a 부어 넣다 add *water*, *salt etc*
puŏrŭn 부어 오른 puffy, swollen
puŏp 부업 sideline, side job
pup'ae 부패 decay
pup'aehada 부패하다 decay
pup'aehan 부패한 rotten; corrupt
pup'aessŏng-ŭi 부패성의 septic
pup'e 부페 buffet
pup'iga k'ŭn 부피가 큰 bulky
pup'ullida 부풀리다 inflate; expand
pup'um 부품 part, piece; unit; spare part
pup'yo 부표 buoy
pural 불알 balls; testicles
puran 불안 alarm, unrest; ***puranhae hada*** 불안해 하다 feel uneasy about
purangja 부랑자 bum; street people
puranhada 불안하다 be uneasy
puranhaejida 불안해지다 get worked up, get nervous
puranhage hada 불안하게 하다 alarm, worry
puranhan 불안한 insecure, uneasy; unstable
puranjŏng 불안정 insecurity, instability
puranjŏnghage 불안정하게 precariously
puranjŏnghan 불안정한 precarious, unstable
purhaeng 불행 unhappiness; misfortune
purhaenghada 불행하다 be unhappy; be unlucky
puraenghan 불행한 poor, unfortunate; unhappy
purhaenghi 불행히 unfortunately
purhamnihan 불합리한 irrational
purhandang 불한당 ruffian
purhwa 불화 split; feud; discord
purhwaksshilssŏng 불확실성 uncertainty
purhwaksshirhada 불확실하다 be in doubt; be doubtful
purhwaksshirhan 불확실한 uncertain
purhwang-ida 불황이다 be in the doldrums
purhyŏp'waŭm 불협화음 discord, dissonance
puri 부리 beak
purilch'i 불일치 discrepancy; clash (*of personalities*)
purilch'ihada 불일치하다 clash; be inconsistent
purim 불임 infertility
purimk'ehada 불임케 하다 sterilize
purimŭi 불임의 infertile, sterile
purŏjida 부러지다 break; get broken
purŏjin 부러진 broken
purŏ nallida 불어 날리다 blow off
purŏttŭrida 부러뜨리다 break, snap
purŏumŭl sada 부러움을 사다 be envious of
purŏun 부러운 enviable
purŏwŏhada 부러워하다 be envious of
purŏwŏhanŭn 부러워하는 envious
purok 부록 appendix (*in book*)
purŭda 부르다 call; summon; ***...rago purŭda*** ...라고 부르다 address, call; describe as
purŭl puch'ida 불을 붙이다 ignite, light; set on fire
purŭrŏ ponaeda 부르러 보내다 send for
puruhan 불우한 deprived, underprivileged
purun 불운 bad luck; disaster
purunhan 불운한 ill-fated
purut'unghaejida 부루퉁해지다 sulk

purut'unghan 부루퉁한 sulky
purwanjŏnhan 불완전한 imperfect; incomplete
puryŏmŏktta 부려먹다 boss around
puryŏnsŏng-ŭi 불연성의 non(in)flammable
puryu 부류 class, category
pusa 부사 adverb
pusajang 부사장 vice president
Pusan 부산 Pusan
pusang 부상 injury; wound
pusangja 부상자 injured; wounded
pusanmul 부산물 by-product, spin-off
pushik 부식 corrosion
pushik'ada 부식하다 corrode
pusŏ 부서 department, division, unit; post
pusŏhada 부서하다 countersign
pusŏjida 부서지다 break, come apart; shatter, smash
pusŏjigi shwiun 부서지기 쉬운 brittle; fragile
pusŏjin 부서진 broken
pusŏng 부성 paternity ◊ paternal
pusŭrŏgi 부스러기 crumb; ***chandon pusŭrŏgi*** 잔돈 부스러기 loose change
pusŭrŏttŭrida 부스러뜨리다 crumble
pusŭrojida 부스러지다 crumble
pusuda 부수다 break, shatter; force
pusugo yŏlda 부수고 열다 break down *door*
puttchaptta 붙잡다 hold *prisoner etc*
put-tta 붙다 adhere, stick; ***shihŏme put-tta*** 시험에 붙다 pass (*in exam*)
put-tta 붓다 swell
put-ttŭlgo iyagihada 붙들고 이야기하다 buttonhole
put-ttŭrŏ tuda 붙들어 두다 keep; detain; keep in
put'ak'ada 부탁하다 ask; ask for; arrange for; ***mwŏ chom put'ak'aedo toemnikka?*** 뭐 좀 부탁해도 됩니까? can I ask you something?
Put'an 부탄 Bhutan ◊ Bhutanese
put'bagiŭi 붙박이의 built-in
put'ik'ŭ 부티크 boutique
put'ingdoeda 부팅되다 boot (up)
put'inghada 부팅하다 boot (up)
...put'ŏ ... kkaji ...부터 ... 까지 from ... to ...; ***...(esŏ)but'ŏ*** ... (에서)부터 from (*in time*); ***wŏryoilbut'ŏ suyoilkkaji*** 월요일부터 수요일까지 from Monday to Wednesday
pu-ŭn 부은 swollen
puyang 부양 support; boost
puyangbi 부양비 maintenance (*money*)
puyanghada 부양하다 support, maintain
puyang kajok 부양 가족 dependents
puyŏhada 부여하다 attach
puyŏjaptta 부여잡다 grab
puyŏnhada 부연하다 elaborate
puyuhada 부유하다 be rich
puyuhan 부유한 rich, wealthy
pyŏk 벽 wall
pyŏkppo 벽보 placard
pyŏktchi 벽지 wallpaper
pyŏkttol 벽돌 brick
pyŏkttolgong 벽돌공 bricklayer
pyŏk'wa 벽화 mural
pyŏl 별 star ◊ different; unusual; ***pyŏl il animnida*** 별 일 아닙니다 it's no problem
pyŏlgaero 별개로 independently of
pyŏlgaeŭi 별개의 different; separate
pyŏlgŏ 별거 separation
pyŏlgŏhada 별거하다 separate; live apart; be (legally) separated
pyŏlgŏhan 별거한 separated
pyŏlgŏ sudang 별거 수당 alimony
pyŏlgwan 별관 annex
pyŏllada 별나다 be eccentric; be strange
pyŏllan 별난 eccentric, quirky
pyŏllo 별로 nothing much
pyŏllon 변론 defense; justification
pyŏlloyeyo 별로예요 not really, not much
pyŏlmashi ŏmnŭn 별맛이 없는 bland
pyŏlmyŏng 별명 nickname
pyŏlp'yo 별표 asterisk
pyŏlsŭrŏn 별스런 whimsical
pyŏltchong 별종 freak
pyŏnanhada 편안하다 feel at ease
pyŏnapkki 변압기 transformer
pyŏnbi 변비 constipation
pyŏnbie kŏllin 변비에 걸린

constipated
pyŏnbiyak 변비약 laxative
pyŏndŏk 변덕 freak (*event*); whim
pyŏndŏkssŭrŏptta 변덕스럽다 be fickle
pyŏndŏkssŭrŏun 변덕스러운 temperamental; fickle; variable
pyŏndong 변동 variation, fluctuation
pyŏndonghada 변동하다 fluctuate
pyŏndong shisega toeda 변동 시세가 되다 float FIN
pyŏnduri 변두리 outskirts
pyŏng 병 bottle; flask; illness
pyŏng-ari 병아리 chick
pyŏngch'am ŏmmu 병참 업무 logistics
pyŏngch'unghae kwalli 병충해 관리 pest control
pyŏngdong 병동 ward, room (*in hospital*)
pyŏngdŭlda 병들다 fall ill, be taken ill
pyŏng-e kŏllida 병에 걸리다 catch an illness
pyŏngga 병가 sick leave
pyŏng-i chaebarhada 병이 재발하다 have a relapse
pyŏn-gie naeryŏbonaeda 변기에 내려보내다 flush down the toilet
pyŏng-i nat-tta 병이 낫다 get better (*in health*)
pyŏngja 병자 invalid (*person*)
pyŏngkkahada 평가하다 estimate
pyŏng magae 병 마개 stopper
pyŏngmok 병목 bottleneck
pyŏngnallo 벽난로 fireplace
pyŏngnihak 병리학 pathology
pyŏngnihaktcha 병리학자 pathologist
pyŏngnyŏk 병력 case history
pyŏngnyŏng 병영 quarters
pyŏngsang-e innŭn 병상에 있는 bedridden
pyŏngse 병세 case MED
pyŏngtchŏgin 병적인 morbid, pathological
pyŏngtchŏk hŭngbun 병적 흥분 hysterics; hysteria; ***pyŏngtchŏk hŭngbunsangt'aega toeda*** 병적 흥분상태가 되다 become hysterical
pyŏngtchok hŭngbun sangt'aeŭi 병적 흥분 상태의 hysterical
pyŏngttagae 병따개 bottle-opener
pyŏng-wŏn 병원 hospital
pyŏngyak'an 병약한 sickly
pyŏn-gyŏng 변경 alteration; shift
pyŏn-gyŏnghada 변경하다 be deflected from
pyŏnhada 변하다 change, shift
pyŏnhagi shwiun 변하기 쉬운 unsettled, changeable
pyŏnhohada 변호하다 defend
pyŏnhosa 변호사 attorney, counsel; counselor
pyŏnhosabi 변호사비 fee (*of lawyer*)
pyŏnhwa 변화 change, shift; variety
pyŏnhwahada 변화하다 change; convert
pyŏnhwan 변환 conversion
pyŏnhwashik'ida 변화시키다 change
pyŏnhyŏng 변형 transformation
pyŏnhyŏngshik'ida 변형시키다 transform; deform
pyŏnjang 변장 disguise
pyŏnjanghada 변장하다 dress up, wear a disguise; dress up as; disguise oneself as
pyŏnje 변제 repayment
pyŏnjehada 변제하다 pay back
pyŏnjildoeda 변질되다 degenerate into
pyŏnmyŏng 변명 excuse
pyŏnmyŏnghal su ŏmnŭn 변명할 수 없는 inexcusable
pyŏnsaeksshik'ida 변색시키다 discolor; tarnish
pyŏnsŏnghada 변성하다 break (*of boy's voice*)
pyŏnsokki 변속기 transmission
pyŏnssu 변수 variable
pyŏnt'ae 변태 perversion
pyŏnt'aejŏgin 변태적인 kinky, bizarre; perverted
pyŏrak ch'ulssehan nom 벼락 출세한 놈 upstart
pyŏril ŏmnŭn 별일 없는 uneventful
pyŏruk 벼룩 flea
pyŏt 볏 crest

P'

p'a 파 scallion; faction; par (*in golf*)
p'aak'agi himdŭn 파악하기 힘든 elusive *meaning*
p'ach'ungnyu 파충류 reptile
p'ada 파다 dig; mine
p'ado 파도 wave
p'aebae 패배 defeat
p'aebaejuŭijŏgin 패배주의적인 defeatist
p'aebaeshik'ida 패배시키다 defeat
p'aeda 패다 chop; beat
p'aegŏri 패거리 crowd, crew
p'aein kumŏng 패인 구멍 pothole
p'aeja 패자 loser SP
p'aejiŏ konggyŏk'ada 패지어 공격하다 gang up on
p'aek 팩 carton
p'aek'iji kwangwang 패키지 관광 package tour
p'aek'iji sangp'um 패키지 상품 package deal
p'aekssŭ 팩스 fax
p'aekssŭ munsŏ 팩스 문서 fax
p'aekssŭroponaeda 팩스로 보내다 fax; ***Xŭl / rŭl p'aekssŭro Yege ponaeda*** X을 / 를 팩스로 Y에게 보내다 fax X to Y
p'aen 팬 fan, supporter
p'aendŏ kom 팬더 곰 panda
p'aengch'ang 팽창 expansion
p'aengch'anghada 팽창하다 expand
p'aengi 팽이 spinning top
p'aengp'aenghan 팽팽한 taut
p'aengp'aenghan chul 팽팽한 줄 tightrope
p'aenji 팬지 pansy
p'aenk'eik'ŭ 팬케이크 pancake
p'aenŏl 패널 panel
p'aenŏlt'i 패널티 penalty
p'aenŏlt'i kuyŏk 패널티 구역 penalty area
p'aen pelt'ŭ 팬 벨트 fan belt
p'aent'i 팬티 panties, underpants
p'aent'i sŭt'ak'ing 팬티 스타킹 pantyhose
p'aesshyŏn 패션 fashion
p'aesshyŏn tijainŏ 패션 디자이너 fashion designer
p'aesŭ 패스 pass
p'aesŭhada 패스하다 pass
p'aesŭt'ŭp'udŭjŏm 패스트푸드점 fastfood restaurant
p'aet'ŏn 패턴 pattern
p'agidoenŭn 파기되는 doomed
p'agoe 파괴 destruction, demolition; ruin
p'agoehada 파괴하다 destroy, demolish; ruin
p'agoejŏgin 파괴적인 destructive
p'agŭp hyokkwa 파급 효과 repercussion
p'agyŏktchŏgin harin kagyŏk 파격적인 할인 가격 knockdown price
p'ahech'ida 파헤치다 dig up
p'ai 파이 pie
p'ail 파일 file COMPUT
p'aip'ŭ 파이프 pipe
p'ainaep'ŭl 파인애플 pineapple
p'aip'ŭrain 파이프라인 pipeline
p'ajang 파장 wavelength
p'ak'a 파카 parka
P'ak'isŭt'an 파키스탄 Pakistan ◊ Pakistani
p'al 팔 arm; eight
p'alda 팔다 sell
p'alkkumch'i 팔꿈치 elbow
p'al kup'yŏ p'yŏgi 팔 굽혀 펴기 push-up
p'allida 팔리다 fetch *price*, be sold for
P'almandaejanggyŏng 팔만대장경 Tripitaka Koreana
p'alsship 팔십 eighty
p'altchang-ŭl kkida 팔짱을 끼다 fold one's arms
p'altchi 팔찌 bracelet
p'ama 파마 perm

p'ama hada 파마 하다 perm
p'amp'ŭllet 팜플렛 pamphlet
p'amut-tta 파묻다 bury
p'amyŏl 파멸 destruction, doom
p'amyŏlshik'ida 파멸시키다 destroy; ruin
p'amyŏrhan 파멸한 ruined, in ruins
p'an 판 sheet (*of glass*, *metal*); tray; board; edition
p'anaeda 파내다 extract
p'andan 판단 opinion, judgment
p'andanhada 판단하다 judge; ***kŏnmosŭburo p'andanhada*** 겉모습으로 판단하다 judge by appearances, take at face value
p'andannyŏk 판단력 judgment, discernment
p'andok chŏnyong kiŏk changch'i 판독 전용 기억 장치 ROM, read-only memory
p'andok chŏnyong p'ail 판독 전용 파일 read-only file
p'andok'ada 판독하다 decipher
p'an-gyŏl 판결 ruling, sentence
p'an-gyŏrhada 판결하다 judge; ***nugurŭl mujoero / yujoero p'an-gyŏrhada*** 누구를 무죄로 / 유죄로 판결하다 find a person innocent / guilty; ***p'ansanŭn ...rago p'an-gyŏrhaet-tta*** 판사는 ...라고 판결했다 the judge ruled that ...
p'an-gyŏrŭl naerida 판결을 내리다 pass sentence; sentence
p'anhwa 판화 engraving
p'anja 판자 board
p'anjaro maktta 판자로 막다 board up
p'anji 판지 cardboard
p'anmae 판매 sale; selling; ***p'anmae chung-ida*** 판매 중이다 be on sale
p'anmaebusŏ 판매부서 sales (department)
p'anmae chŏmwŏn 판매 점원 sales clerk
p'anmae ch'oktchin 판매 촉진 promotion
p'anmaehada 판매하다 sell, market
p'anmaeja 판매자 seller
p'anmae kagyŏk 판매 가격 asking price
p'anmae kŭmaek 판매 금액 sales figures
p'anmae pujang 판매 부장 sales manager
p'anorama 파노라마 panorama
p'ansa 판사 judge
p'ansori 판소리 epic songs
p'antton 판돈 stake
p'aŏp 파업 strike
p'aŏptcha 파업자 striker
p'apk'on 팝콘 popcorn
p'apssong 팝송 pop song
p'ap'yŏn 파편 debris
p'aran 파란 blue
p'arangsaek 파랑색 blue
p'aranmanjanghan 파란만장한 checkered
p'arasol 파라솔 parasol, sunshade
p'arat'a 파랗다 be blue
p'ari 파리 fly (*insect*)
p'arwŏl 팔월 August
p'aryŏmch'ihan 파렴치한 shameless
p'asakp'asak'an 파삭파삭한 crisp
p'asan 파산 bankruptcy
p'asangp'ung 파상풍 tetanus
p'asanhada 파산하다 go bankrupt, go bust; be ruined
p'asanshik'ida 파산시키다 bankrupt; ruin
p'ason 파손 breakage
p'asshijŭm 파시즘 fascism
p'asshisŭt'ŭ 파시스트 fascist
p'asŭlli 파슬리 parsley
p'asŭt'el 파스텔 pastel
p'at'anhada 파탄하다 fail; go bankrupt
p'at'i 파티 party
p'at'ibok 파티 복 evening wear; evening dress; party dress
p'at'ŭ 파트 part MUS
p'awŏ sŭt'iŏring 파워 스티어링 power steering
p'awŏ yunit 파워 유닛 power unit
p'ayŏl 파열 rupture
p'ayŏldoeda 파열되다 rupture
p'edal 페달 pedal
p'edarŭl paltta 페달을 밟다 pedal
p'eiji 페이지 page
p'eint'ŭ 페인트 paint
p'eint'ŭ sol 페인트 솔 paintbrush
p'elt'ŭp'en 펠트펜 felt-tip (pen)
p'eminijŭm 페미니즘 feminism

p'eminisŭt'ŭ 페미니스트 feminist
p'endŏ 펜더 fender
p'enishillin 페니실린 penicillin
p'enp'al ch'in-gu 펜팔 친구 pen pal
p'enshing 펜싱 fencing SP
p'i 피 blood
p'ianisŭt'ŭ 피아니스트 pianist
p'iano 피아노 piano
p'ibu 피부 skin
p'ida 피다 open; unroll; blossom
p'igo 피고 the accused
p'igoch'ŭk 피고측 defense
p'igoch'ŭk chŭngin 피고측 증인 defense witness
p'igoch'ŭk pyŏnhosa 피고측 변호사 defense lawyer
p'igoin 피고인 defendant
p'igonhada 피곤하다 be tired
p'igonhaejida 피곤해지다 get tired
p'igonhan 피곤한 tired
p'igosŏk 피고석 dock LAW
p'igyŏ sŭk'eit'ing 피겨 스케이팅 figure skating
p'ihada 피하다 avoid; ward off; shelter
p'ihae 피해 damage
p'ihaega maksshimhan 피해가 막심한 disastrous
p'ihae mangsang 피해 망상 paranoia
p'ihaerŭl ip'ida 피해를 입히다 damage
p'ihal su innŭn 피할 수 있는 sheltered
p'ihal su ŏmnŭn 피할 수 없는 inevitable
p'ihal su ŏpsshi 피할 수 없이 inevitably
p'ihugyŏnin 피후견인 ward (*child*)
p'iim 피임 contraception
p'iimhada 피임하다 use contraception
p'iim kigu 피임 기구 contraceptive device
p'iimyak 피임약 (contraceptive) pill
p'iimyong p'esari 피임용 페사리 diaphragm
p'ija 피자 pizza
p'ijangp'ajang-i toeda 피장파장이 되다 be quits with
p'iksel 픽셀 pixel
p'ik'et 피켓 picket
p'ik'et lain 피켓 라인 picket line
p'ik'ŭl 피클 pickles
p'ildŭ kyŏnggi 필드 경기 field events
P'illandŭ 핀란드 Finland ◊ Finnish
P'illandŭŏ 핀란드어 Finnish (*language*)
P'illandŭ saram 핀란드 사람 Finn
p'ille sŭt'eik'ŭ 필레 스테이크 fillet steak
P'illip'in 필리핀 Philippines ◊ Filipino
p'illŭm 필름 film
p'ilmyŏng 필명 pen name
p'ilssabon 필사본 manuscript
p'ilssajŏgin 필사적인 desperate
p'ilssu chokkŏn 필수 조건 precondition
p'ilssujŏgin 필수적인 vital, essential
p'ilssup'um 필수품 necessity
p'ilssuŭi 필수의 indispensable
p'iltchŏk'ada 필적하다 match; parallel; equal
p'ilt'ŏ 필터 filter; filter tip
p'ilt'ŏ innŭn tambae 필터 있는 담배 filter-tipped (cigarettes)
p'imang 피망 pepper, pimiento
p'in 핀 pin ◊ open *flower*
p'inanch'ŏ 피난처 refuge, shelter; retreat
p'inanhada 피난하다 take refuge
p'inggye 핑계 excuse, pretext
p'ing tolda 핑 돌다 whirl
p'i pŭi sshi 피 브이 씨 PVC
p'iri 피리 Korean oboe
p'iro 피로 fatigue
p'iroech'im 피뢰침 lightning rod
p'iryo 필요 need; ***...l p'iryoga it-tta*** ...ㄹ 필요가 있다 it is necessary to ...
p'iryohada 필요하다 want; need, require, call for
p'iryohadamyŏn 필요하다면 if need be, as necessary
p'iryohan 필요한 necessary
p'iryoro hada 필요로 하다 need, require, take; entail, mean
p'iryossŏng 필요성 necessity
p'isaldanghada 피살당하다 be killed
p'isangjŏgin 피상적인 cursory
p'ishint'agin 피신탁인 trustee
p'isshi 피씨 PC, personal computer
p'isŭt'on 피스톤 piston

p'itchaguk 핏자국 bloodstain
p'it-ttŏng-ŏri 핏덩어리 (blood) clot
p'it'usŏng-iŭi 피투성이의 bloody
p'iuda 피우다 burn; smoke; give off *smell*; play *trick*
p'ŏbut-tta 퍼붓다 pour; pour on; ***chilmun kongserŭl p'ŏbut-tta*** 질문 공세를 퍼붓다 bombard with questions
p'ŏdakkŏrida 퍼덕거리다 flutter
p'ŏjida 퍼지다 spread
p'ŏjŭl 퍼즐 puzzle (*game*)
p'ŏllŏgida 펄럭이다 flap; flutter; wave
p'ŏlp'ŭ 펄프 pulp
p'ŏltchŏk ttwida 펄쩍 뛰다 jump
p'ŏmp'ŭ 펌프 pump
p'ŏng 펑 pop
p'ŏngk'ŭ 펑크 blow-out
p'ŏngp'ŏng sosanaoda 펑펑 솟아나오다 gush
p'ŏ ollida 퍼 올리다 scoop up
p'ŏreidŭ 퍼레이드 parade, procession
p'ŏsent'ŭ 퍼센트 percent
p'ŏtchi 버찌 cherry
p'ŏttŭrida 퍼뜨리다 spread; circulate *memo*
p'oak'ada 포악하다 be ruthless; be oppressive
p'oak'an 포악한 oppressive; ruthless
p'och'ak'ada 포착하다 capture, portray; seize
p'odae 포대 bag; sack
p'odaegi 포대기 baby quilt (*for carrying baby on mother's back*)
p'odo 포도 grape; ***p'odo han song-i*** 포도 한 송이 a bunch of grapes
p'odoju 포도주 wine
p'odoju menyu 포도주 메뉴 wine list
p'odoju pyŏng ttagae 포도주 병 따개 corkscrew
p'odonamu 포도나무 grapevine
p'odongp'odonghan 포동포동한 plump
p'odowŏn 포도원 vineyard
p'ogihada 포기하다 give up, renounce
p'ogŭmhada 폭음하다 drink too much
p'ogu 폭우 downpour
p'ogwaltchŏgin 포괄적인 comprehensive
p'ogyŏk 포격 gunfire
p'ogyŏk'ada 포격하다 shell
p'ohamhada 포함하다 include; add on
p'ohamhan 포함한 inclusive
p'ohamhayŏ 포함하여 including
p'ohwa 포화 shellfire
p'ojang 포장 packaging
p'ojang chaeryo 포장 재료 wrapping
p'ojanghada 포장하다 pack, package; giftwrap; ***haembŏgo p'ojanghaejuseyo*** 햄버거 포장해주세요 hamburger to go
p'ojangji 포장지 wrapper; wrapping paper; tissue paper
p'ojangnyong laep 포장용 랩 clingfilm
p'ojin 포진 herpes
p'ojŭ ch'wihada 포즈 취하다 pose
p'oju 포주 pimp
p'ok 폭 width, breadth; ***p'ok shimmit'ŏ*** 폭 10미터 10m across
p'ok-kkun 폭군 tyrant
p'ok-kkyŏk 폭격 bomb attack
p'ok-kkyŏk-kki 폭격기 bomber
p'okkunjŏgin 폭군적인 tyrannical, domineering
p'okŏ 포커 poker
p'okppal 폭발 explosion
p'okppalmul 폭발물 explosive
p'okppal sshik'ida 폭발시키다 detonate
p'okpparhada 폭발하다 explode, go off; blow up; erupt
p'okp'ahada 폭파하다 blow up, bomb
p'okp'ashik'ida 폭파시키다 blast
p'okp'o 폭포 waterfall
p'okp'ung 폭풍 storm
p'okp'ungju-ŭibo 폭풍주의보 storm warning
p'okp'ung-u 폭풍우 rainstorm
p'okp'ung-u-ga ch'inŭn 폭풍우가 치는 stormy
p'oksshik 폭식 gluttony
p'oksshik'ada 폭식하다 eat too much
p'okssorŭl t'ŏttŭrida 폭소를 터뜨리다 burst out laughing

p'okttong 폭동 riot, uprising
p'okttongja 폭동자 rioter
p'okttongŭl irŭk'ida 폭동을 일으키다 riot
p'okt'an 폭탄 bomb
p'ok'aeng 폭행 assault
p'ok'aenghada 폭행하다 assault
p'ok'etyong kyesan-gi 포켓용 계산기 pocket calculator
p'ok'ŭ 포크 fork
p'ok'ŭttaensŭ 포크댄스 folkdance
p'oldŏ 폴더 folder
P'ollandŭ 폴란드 Poland ◊ Polish
P'ollandŭŏ 폴란드어 Polish
p'olliesŭt'erŭ 폴리에스테르 polyester
p'olliet'illen 폴리에틸렌 polyethylene
p'ollisŭt'iren 폴리스티렌 polystyrene
p'omaet'ada 포맷하다 format
p'ongnak'ada 폭락하다 drop sharply (*of stock market*)
p'ongnirŭl ch'wihada 폭리를 취하다 rip off; profiteer
p'ong-nŏlbŭn 폭넓은 wide *experience*
p'ongno 폭로 revelation, disclosure
p'ongnohada 폭로하다 expose; ***uyŏnhi p'ongnohada*** 우연히 폭로하다 give oneself away
p'ongnyŏk 폭력 force, violence; outrage
p'ongnyŏktchŏgin 폭력적인 violent; outrageous
p'ongnyŏkttanwŏn 폭력단원 mobster
p'o-ong 포옹 cuddle; hug
p'o-onghada 포옹하다 cuddle; hug
p'oro 포로 captive; ***nugurŭl p'ororo chaptta*** 누구를 포로로 잡다 take s.o. prisoner
p'orŭno 포르노 pornography ◊ pornographic
p'orŭt 버릇 habit
P'orŭt'ugal 포르투갈 Portugal ◊ Portuguese
P'orŭt'ugarin 포르투갈인 Portuguese
P'orŭt'ugarŏ 포르투갈어 Portuguese (*language*)
p'oshik'ada 포식하다 overeat ***muŏsŭl p'oshik'ada*** 무엇을 포식하다 gorge oneself on sth
p'osŭt'ŏ 포스터 poster
p'ot'eit'o ch'ipssŭ 포테이토 칩스 potato chips
p'ot'ŏbŭl 포터블 portable COMPUT
p'ot'ŭ 포트 port COMPUT
p'owihada 포위하다 surround; close in
p'owi konggyŏk 포위 공격 siege
p'owi konggyŏk'ada 포위 공격하다 lay siege to
p'owŏdŭ 포워드 forward SP
p'oyu tongmul 포유 동물 mammal
p'ŭllaent'eishyŏn 플랜테이션 plantation
p'ŭllaeshwi 플래쉬 flash PHOT
p'ŭllaetp'om 플랫폼 platform
p'ŭllaja 플라자 plaza, shopping mall
p'ŭllasŭt'ik 플라스틱 plastic
p'ŭllŏgŭ 플러그 plug
p'ŭllŏgŭrŭl kkot-tta 플러그를 꽂다 plug in
p'ŭllŏgŭrŭl ppoptta 플러그를 뽑다 unplug
p'ŭllop'i tisŭk'ŭ 플로피 디스크 floppy (disk)
p'ŭllot'ŏ 플로터 plotter COMPUT
p'ŭllut'ŭ 플루트 flute
P'ŭrangssŭ 프랑스 France ◊ French
P'ŭrangssŭin 프랑스인 Frenchman; Frenchwoman
P'ŭrangssŭŏ 프랑스어 French (*language*)
p'ŭrik'ik 프리킥 free kick
p'ŭrima 프리마 creamer (*for coffee*)
p'ŭrimiŏm 프리미엄 premium
p'ŭrint'ŏ 프린터 printer (*machine*)
p'ŭro 프로 professional
p'ŭromp'ŭt'ŭ 프롬프트 prompt COMPUT
p'ŭront'ŭ 프론트 reception, check-in
p'ŭrop'ellŏ 프로펠러 propeller
p'ŭro sŏnsuro 프로 선수로 professionally SP
p'uda 푸다 scoop
p'uk chamdŭlda 푹 잠들다 be (fast) asleep
p'ukssinhan 푹신한 soft
p'ul 풀 glue; grass; ***p'urŭl ttŭdŏmŏktta*** 풀을 뜯어먹다 graze
p'ulda 풀다 undo; unpack; disentangle; solve; release *brake*; ***k'orŭl p'ulda*** 코를 풀다 blow one's nose

p'ullida 풀리다 unwind
p'ullin 풀린 frayed
p'ullo puch'ida 풀로 붙이다 glue
p'umhaeng-i tanjŏnghan 품행이 단정한 well-behaved
p'umjil 품질 quality
p'umjil kwalli 품질 관리 quality control
p'umjiri nappŭn 품질이 나쁜 poor quality, shoddy
p'umjong 품종 brand; breed
p'umkkyŏk 유행 style, fashion
p'umsa 품사 part of speech
p'umwi innŭn 품위 있는 gracious; dignified; classy
p'ungbu 풍부 abundance
p'ungbuhada 풍부하다 be abundant
p'ungbuhage hada 풍부하게 하다 enrich
p'ungbuhan 풍부한 abundant; lavish ◊ a wealth of
p'ungch'a 풍차 windmill
p'unggi sabŏm tansokppan 풍기 사범 단속반 vice squad
p'unggyŏng 풍경 scenery
p'unggyŏnghwa 풍경화 landscape (*painting*)
p'ungja 풍자 irony; sarcasm; satire
p'ungjagŭi 풍작의 bumper *crop*, *year*
p'ungjajŏgin 풍자적인 satirical
p'ungja manhwa 풍자 만화 caricature
p'ungmanhan 풍만한 buxom
p'ungmunŭro 풍문으로 by hearsay
p'ungnyoropkke hada 풍요롭게 하다 enrich
p'ungsŏn 풍선 balloon
p'ungsŏnghan 풍성한 hearty
p'ungsŏnkkŏm 풍선껌 bubble gum
p'ung-yo 풍요 plenty
p'ung-yoroun sahoe 풍요로운 사회 affluent society
p'unnaegi 풋내기 squirt; greenhorn
p'uri chugŭn 풀이 죽은 downhearted, downcast
p'uri ugŏjin 풀이 우거진 grassy
p'urŏjuda 풀어주다 untie
p'ŭromp'ŭt'ŭ 프롬프트 prompt COMPUT
p'urŏ naerida 풀어 내리다 let down
p'urŏ poda 풀어 보다 unwrap
p'ushwi maen 푸쉬맨 *person who pushes Seoul commuters into subway trains at rush hour*
p'ye 폐 lung
p'yeam 폐암 lung cancer
p'yegihada 폐기하다 discard, dump
p'yegimul 폐기물 waste, waste product
p'yegishik'ida 폐기시키다 scrap, drop, abandon
p'yegyŏnggi 폐경기 menopause
p'yehoeshik 폐회식 closing ceremony
p'yejihada 폐지하다 abolish
p'yejŏm 폐점 closure
p'yejŏmhada 폐점하다 close down
p'yejŏm shigan 폐점 시간 closing time
p'yemuri toen 폐물이 된 obsolete
p'yeŏp'ada 폐업하다 close down
p'yeryŏm 폐렴 pneumonia
p'yeswae 폐쇄 closure
p'yeswaehada 폐쇄하다 close; close up
p'yeswae hoero t'ellebijyŏn 폐쇄 회로 텔레비전 closed-circuit television
p'yŏda 펴다 unfold; smooth out
p'yŏlch'ida 펼치다 spread, lay
p'yŏlch'ŏjida 펼쳐지다 unfold
p'yŏlli 편리 convenience
p'yŏllihada 편리하다 be convenient
p'yŏllihan 편리한 convenient, handy
p'yŏn 편 side; faction; means; tendency; editing; volume; part, section; ***k'ŭn / chagŭn p'yŏn*** 큰 / 작은 편 on the big / small side; ***nuguŭi p'yŏni toeŏ chuda*** 누구의 편이 되어 주다 come to s.o.'s defense
p'yŏnanhada 편안하다 be comfortable
p'yŏnanhan 편안한 comfortable, easy, relaxed
p'yŏnanhi hada 편안히 하다 make oneself at home
p'yŏnch'in kajŏng 편친 가정 one-parent family
p'yŏndosŏn 편도선 tonsil
p'yŏndosŏnnyŏm 편도선염 tonsillitis

p'yŏndo sŭngch'akkwŏn 편도 승차권 one-way ticket
p'yŏndŭt'ong 편두통 migraine
p'yŏngbang mit'ŏ 평방 미터 square meter
p'yŏngbŏmhan 평범한 plain, regular; commonplace
p'yŏngdŭng 평등 equality
p'yŏngdŭngjuŭiŭi 평등주의의 egalitarian
p'yŏnggyŏl 평결 verdict
p'yŏnggyun 평균 average; ***p'yŏnggyŭn ...(ŭ)ro kyesandoeda*** 평균 ...(으)로 계산되다 average out at
p'yŏnggyunnaeda 평균내다 average out
p'yŏnggyunŭi 평균의 average
p'yŏnggyunŭro ... hada 평균으로 ... 하다 average
p'yŏnghaeng 평행 parallel (line)
p'yŏnghaenghanŭn 평행하는 parallel
p'yŏnghwa 평화 peace
p'yŏnghwajuŭi 평화주의 pacifism
p'yŏnghwajuŭija 평화주의자 pacifist; dove
P'yŏnghwa Pongsadan 평화 봉사단 Peace Corps
p'yŏnghwaropkke 평화롭게 peacefully
p'yŏnghwaroptta 평화롭다 be peaceful
p'yŏnghwaroun 평화로운 peaceful
p'yŏnghyŏng 평형 breaststroke
p'yŏng-il 평일 weekday; workday
p'yŏngkka 평가 evaluation; appreciation
p'yŏngkka chŏrha 평가 절하 devaluation
p'yŏngkka chŏrhashik'ida 평가 절하시키다 devalue
p'yŏngkkahada 평가하다 assess; appreciate; rate, rank, consider; rank among
p'yŏngkkajŏlssang 평가절상 revaluation
p'yŏngmyŏndo 평면도 ground plan
p'yŏngnon 평론 write-up, review
p'yŏngnon-ga 평론가 reviewer
P'yŏngnyang 평양 P'yongyang
p'yŏn-gok 편곡 arrangement MUS
p'yŏn-gok'ada 편곡하다 arrange MUS
p'yŏng-on 평온 calm
p'yŏng-onhada 평온하다 be tranquil
p'yŏng-onhan 평온한 serene, tranquil
p'yŏngp'an 평판 reputation
p'yŏngp'ani choŭn 평판이 좋은 reputable
p'yŏngp'ani nappŭn 평판이 나쁜 disreputable
p'yŏngp'yŏnghada 평평하다 be even, be flat
p'yŏngp'yŏnghage hada 평평하게 하다 flatten
p'yŏngp'yŏnghan 평평한 flat, level
p'yŏngsaeng 평생 lifetime; ***kŭnyŏ p'yŏngsaeng-e*** 그녀 평생에 all her life; ***nae p'yŏngsaeng-e*** 내 평생에 in my lifetime
p'yŏngsaeng-ŭi 평생의 lifelong
p'yŏngsangbok 평상복 casual wear
p'yŏngsangbok ch'arimŭi 평상복 차림의 informal
p'yŏngsangshich'ŏrŏm 평상시처럼 as usual
p'yŏngsang-ŭi 평상의 casual *shirt etc*
p'yŏng-ya 평야 plain; prairie
p'yŏn-gyŏn 편견 bias, prejudice; ***...e taehan p'yŏn-gyŏn*** ...에 대한 편견 bias against
p'yŏn-gyŏnŏmnŭn 편견없는 unbiased
p'yŏn-gyŏnŭl kajin 편견을 가진 biased, prejudiced
p'yŏnhan 편한 be comfortable; ***tangshini p'yŏnhan shigane*** 당신이 편한 시간에 at your convenience
p'yŏnhi shwida 편히 쉬다 relax
p'yŏnhyangshik'ida 편향시키다 deflect
p'yŏnida 편이다: ***...nŭn p'yŏnida*** ...는 편이다 tend to
p'yŏnji 편지 letter; letters, correspondence
p'yŏnjibin 편집인 editor
p'yŏnjihada 편지하다 mail
p'yŏnjiji 편지지 notepaper
p'yŏnjip 편집 editing ◊ editorial

p'yŏnjipkkwang 편집광 paranoia
p'yŏnjiptcha 편집자 editor
p'yŏnjiptchang 편집장 editor
p'yŏnjiptchŏgin 편집적인 paranoid
p'yŏnjip'ada 편집하다 edit, make corrections to; compile
p'yŏnjirŭl ponaeda 편지를 보내다 mail
p'yŏnjirŭl ssŭda 편지를 쓰다 write a letter
p'yŏnmo 편모 single mother
p'yŏnmul 편물 knitting
p'yŏnppŏp 편법 expedient
p'yŏnsŭnghada 편승하다 hitchhike
p'yŏnŭl tŭlda 편을 들다 take sides
p'yŏ parŭda 펴 바르다 apply *ointment etc*
p'yo 표 table (*of figures*); ticket
p'yobaek 표백 bleach
p'yobaek'ada 표백하다 bleach; whiten
p'yobŏm 표범 leopard
p'yobon 표본 sample, specimen
p'yo chadong p'anmaegi 표 자동 판매기 ticket machine
p'yogyŏrhada 표결하다 vote on
p'yohyŏn 표현 expression; display; wording
p'yohyŏnhada 표현하다 express
p'yohyŏnŭi p'ungbuhan 표현이 풍부한 expressive
p'yoje 표제 heading
p'yoji 표지 cover (*of book, magazine*)
p'yojip'an 표지판 (road) sign
p'yojŏk 표적 target
p'yojŏng 표정 appearance, expression, look
p'yojŏng-i p'ungbuhan 표정이 풍부한 expressive
p'yojŏrhada 표절하다 pirate *software etc*
p'yojun 표준 standard; ***p'yojune midarhada*** 표준에 미달하다 not be up to standard; ***p'yojune tarhada*** 표준에 달하다 be up to standard
p'yojune mat-tchi annŭn 표준에 맞지 않는 nonstandard
p'yojun midarŭi 표준 미달의 substandard
p'yojun shiganttae 표준 시간대 time zone
p'yo kŏmsawŏn 표 검사원 ticket inspector
p'yok'an 표칸 cell COMPUT
p'yomyŏn 표면 surface
p'yomyŏnghada 표명하다 voice *opinion*
p'yomyŏnjŏgin 표면적인 superficial; cosmetic
p'yop'i 표피 cuticle
p'yoryuhada 표류하다 drift
p'yoshi 표시 indication, sign; ***kamsaŭi p'yoshiro*** 감사의 표시로 as a token of my / our appreciation
p'yoshidŭng 표시등 indicator
p'yoshihada 표시하다 display, indicate; stand for; mark up
p'yujŭ 퓨즈 fuse
p'yujŭrŭl kkŭnt'a 퓨즈를 끊다 (blow a) fuse

...rago ...라고 that; ***chŏnŭn ...rago saenggak'amnida*** 저는 ...라고 생각합니다 I think that ...
...ranŭn ...라는 that; ***...ranŭn saenggagŭl kosuhada*** ...라는 생각을 고수하다 hold that, believe
...ro ...로 by; from, because of; of; into; in; with; to; toward
...robut'ŏ ...로부터 from
...rosŏ ...로서 as
...rŭl ...를 *object particle*
...ryŏgo hada ...려고 하다 try to do; intend to; be going to

S

sa 사 four
saak'an 사악한 wicked; sinister
saam 사암 sandstone
sabang 사방 all directions
sabip kwanggo 삽입 광고 insert (*in magazine etc*)
sabip'ada 삽입하다 insert
sabŏm 사범 (martial arts) instructor
sabŏp 사법 judicature ◊ judicial
sabŏpkkwŏn 사법권 jurisdiction
sabok 사복 plain clothes ◊ plain-clothes
sabon 사본 duplicate, copy; transcript
sabunŭi il 사분의 일 quarter
sabunŭi sam 사분의 삼 three quarters
sabun ŭmp'yo 사분 음표 quarter note
sabyŏng 사병 private MIL
sabyŏrhan 사별한 bereaved
sach'i 사치 luxury, extravagance
sach'inhoe 사친회 parent-teacher association
sach'isŭrŏptta 사치스럽다 be extravagant; be luxurious
sach'isŭrŏun 사치스러운 extravagant; luxurious
sach'on 사촌 cousin
sach'un-gi 사춘기 adolescence; puberty
sach'un-giŭi 사춘기의 adolescent
sada 사다 buy; pay for
sadari 사다리 ladder
sae 새 bird ◊ new
saebarŭi p'i 새발의 피 chickenfeed, peanuts
saebyŏk 새벽 dawn, daybreak
saech'igihada 새치기하다 shove in, cut in *line*
saeda 새다 leak, seep
saedanjanghada 새단장하다 freshen up
saegan-gyŏng 색안경 sunglasses
saegida 새기다 carve; engrave
saegin 색인 index
saegin k'adŭ 색인 카드 index card
Saehae 새해 New Year; ***Saehae Pok Mani Padŭseyo!*** 새해 복 많이 받으세요! Happy New Year!
Saehae Ch'ŏnnal 새해 첫날 New Year's Day
sae irŭmŭro (chŏjang hagi) 새이름으로 (저장하기) save as
saejang 새장 bird cage
saekch'aega p'ungbuhan 색채가 풍부한 colorful
saekch'aeŭi paehap 색채의 배합 color scheme
saekkaman 새까만 jet-black
saekki 새끼 cub, young animal; kid; brat
saekki koyang-i 새끼 고양이 kitten
saekkiyang 새끼양 lamb
saek-kkal 색깔 color
saek-kkal innŭn 색깔 있는 tinted
saekssŏp'on 색소폰 saxophone
saektchi 색지 tinted paper
saektchŏntchŭng 색전증 embolism
saektcho 색조 shade, tone
saek'omdalk'omhan 새콤달콤한 sweet and sour
saellŏdŭ 샐러드 salad
saem 샘 spring (*water*); envy; jealousy
saendŭl 샌들 sandal
saendŭwich'i 샌드위치 sandwich
saeng-ae 생애 career
saengbangsong 생방송 live broadcast
saengch'e konghak 생체 공학 biotechnology
saengdo 생도 cadet
saenggage chamgida 생각에 잠기다 muse, reflect
saenggage chamgin 생각에 잠긴 pensive

saenggagi kip'ŭn 생각이 깊은 thoughtful
saenggagŏmnŭn 생각없는 mindless, senseless
saenggak 생각 thought, idea; ***choŭn saenggagiya!*** 좋은 생각이야! good idea!
saenggak'ada 생각하다 think, consider; ***...rago saenggakttoenda*** ...라고 생각된다 it is considered to be ...
saenggak'aenaeda 생각해내다 come up with, hit on, think up
saenggak'al su choch'a ŏmnŭn 생각할 수 조차 없는 unthinkable; inconceivable
saenggak'al su innŭn 생각할 수 있는 conceivable
saenggang 생강 ginger
saenggangch'a 생강차 ginger tea
saenggi 생기 animation, liveliness
saenggida 생기다 occur; come into existence; ***musŭn iri saeng-gyŏssŏyo*** 무슨 일이 생겼어요 something has come up
saenggiga nada 생기가 나다 perk up, cheer up
saenggiinnŭn 생기있는 lively, fresh
saenggi tolge hada 생기 돌게 하다 cheer up
saenggye 생계 living, livelihood; ***kyŏu saenggyerŭl iŏnagada*** 겨우 생계를 이어나가다 eke out a living
saenghwal 생활 life, existence; living
saenghwalbi 생활비 cost of living; maintenance; budget; ***saenghwal-birŭl pŏlda*** 생활비를 벌다 earn one's living
saenghwal pangsshik 생활 방식 way of life, lifestyle
saenghwal pojo 생활 보조 welfare
saenghwal pojogŭm 생활 보조금 welfare check
saenghwalsa 생활사 life history
saenghwal sujun 생활 수준 standard of living
saeng-il 생일 birthday; ***saeng-il ch'uk'ahamnida!*** 생일 축하합니다! happy birthday!
saengjonhada 생존하다 exist; survive
saengjonhal ssu innŭn 생존할 수 있는 viable
saengjonja 생존자 survivor
saengjon kyŏngjaeng 생존 경쟁 struggle for survival
saeng k'ŭrim 생 크림 whipped cream
saengmaektchu 생맥주 draft (beer)
saengmaeng 색맹 color-blindness ◊ color-blind
saengmul 생물 organism, being ◊ bio-
saengmurhak 생물학 biology
saengmurhaktchŏgin 생물학적인 biological
saengmyŏng 생명 life
saengmyŏng ŏmnŭn 생명 없는 lifeless
saengmyŏng pohŏm 생명 보험 life assurance
saengmyŏng-ŭl wihyŏp'anŭn 생명을 위협하는 life-threatening
saengni 생리 menstruation; period
saengnidae 생리대 sanitary napkin
saengnihada 생리하다 menstruate
saengnyak'ada 생략하다 leave out, omit
saengnyŏnwŏril 생년월일 date of birth
saengp'ohada 생포하다 capture (alive)
saengsaenghada 생생하다 be vivid
saengsaenghan 생생한 vivid, graphic
saengsan 생산 production, output
saengsanbi 생산비 production costs
saengsanbirŭl kyŏnjŏk'ada 생산비를 견적하다 cost, calculate the cost of
saengsanhada 생산하다 produce, output
saengsanja 생산자 maker, producer
saengsanmul 생산물 product
saengsannyŏk 생산력 production capacity
saengsanssŏng 생산성 productivity
saengsanŭl kadonghada 생산을 가동하다 come into production; come on stream
saengshikki 생식기 genitals
saengshik nŭngnyŏk 생식 능력

virility
saengsŏn 생선 fish
saengsŏnppyŏ 생선뼈 fishbone
saengsu 생수 mineral water
saengt'aegye 생태계 ecosystem
saengt'aehak 생태학 ecology
saengt'aehaktcha 생태학자 naturalist, ecologist
saengt'aehaktchŏgin 생태학적인 ecological
saengt'aehaktchŏk kyunhyŏng 생태학적 균형 ecological balance
saenŭn 새는 leaky
saeŏ naoda 새어 나오다 leak out, seep out; filter through
saeppalgak'e tan 새빨갛게 단 red-hot
saeppalgan kŏjinmal 새빨간 거짓말 downright lie
saero koch'im 새로 고침 reload COMPUT
saeropkke nŭkkida 새롭게 느끼다 feel renewed
saeroptta 새롭다 be new
saeroun 새로운 fresh, new
sae tanjanghada 새 단장하다 redecorate
saeu 새우 shrimp
sagak'yŏng 사각형 square; quadrangle
sagi 사기 swindle, fraud, rip-off; con; morale, spirits ◊ fraudulent
sagi ch'ida 사기 치다 con, cheat
sagikkun 사기꾼 crook, con man
sagjik'ada 사직하다 resign
sago 사고 accident, mishap; thought; ***sagoro chuktta*** 사고로 죽다 be killed in an accident; ***sagorŭl tanghada*** 사고를 당하다 have an accident
sagwa 사과 apology; apple
sagwa chusŭ 사과 주스 apple juice
sagwahada 사과하다 apologize
sagwan saengdo 사관 생도 cadet
sagwasosŭ 사과소스 apple sauce
sagwida 사귀다 get acquainted, make friends; ***ch'in-gurŭl sagwida*** 친구를 사귀다 make friends; ***saramgwa sagwida*** 사람과 사귀다 socialize
sagyogye saramdŭl 사교계 사람들 glitterati
sagyojŏgin 사교적인 sociable; ***kŭnyŏnŭn sagyossŏng-i chot'a*** 그녀는 사교성이 좋다 she's a good mixer
sahaktcha 사학자 historian
sahoe 사회 society, community ◊ social
sahoehak 사회학 sociology
sahoeja 사회자 chairperson; chairwoman; host; master of ceremonies
sahoejuŭi 사회주의 socialism
sahoejuŭija 사회주의자 socialist
sahoejuŭijŏgin 사회주의적인 socialist
sahoe kyegŭp 사회 계급 (social) class
sahoe poda 사회 보다 preside
sahoe saŏp 사회 사업 social work
sahoe saŏpkka 사회 사업가 social worker
sahoe ssŭregi 사회 쓰레기 lowlife
sahyŏng chip'aeng 사형 집행 execution
sahyŏng chip'aenghada 사형 집행하다 execute
sahyŏng chip'aeng-in 사형 집행인 executioner
sahyŏng sŏn-gorŭl pat-tta 사형 선고를 받다 be sentenced to death
sai 사이 interval, space; relationship; ***kip'ŭn sai*** 깊은 사이 intimacy (*sexual*); ***kip'ŭn saiin*** 깊은 사이인 intimate (*sexually*)
saie 사이에 between
saiga chot'a 사이가 좋다 get on; be friendly with
saiga t'ŭrŏjida 사이가 틀어지다 fall out, argue
saijok'e chinaeda 사이좋게 지내다 get along
saim 사임 resignation
saimhada 사임하다 resign
sain 사인 killer; autograph
sairen 사이렌 siren
saja 사자 lion
sajang 사장 boss; president
sajik 사직 resignation; ***sajik'al kŏsŭl allida*** 사직할 것을 알리다 hand in one's notice

sajik'ada 사직하다 resign
sajin 사진 photo(graph); ***sajini chal pannŭn*** 사진이 잘 받는 photogenic
sajinaelbŏm 사진앨범 photo album
sajin ch'waryŏng 사진 촬영 photography
sajinsa 사진사 photographer
sajin tchiktta 사진 찍다 photograph
sajŏl 사절 delegation; envoy
sajŏn 사전 dictionary
sajŏng kŏri 사정 거리 range
sajŏng-ŏmnŭn 사정없는 relentless; ruthless
sajŏn kyŏnghŏm 사전 경험 foretaste
sajungju 사중주 quartet
sak-kkam 삭감 cut, cutback, reduction
sak-kkamhada 삭감하다 reduce, cut; slash
sakkŏn 사건 affair, matter, case; incident; ***sakkŏnŭi sunsŏ*** 사건의 순서 the sequence of events
sakpparhan 삭발한 shaven
saktche 삭제 deletion
saktchehada 삭제하다 delete
sak'arin 사카린 saccharin
sal 살 flesh, meat; years of age; arrow; spoke (*of wheel*)
salch'ungje 살충제 pesticide; insecticide
salda 살다 live
salgach'i kŏch'in 살갗이 거친 chapped
salgŭmŏni 살그머니 stealthily, furtively
salgŭmsalgŭm kŏt-tta 살금살금 걷다 creep
salgu 살구 apricot
salgyundoen 살균된 sterile MED
salgyunŭi 살균의 antiseptic
salk'ogi 살코기 lean meat
sallim kyŏngbiwŏn 산림 경비원 forest ranger
sallŏdŭ tŭreshing 샐러드 드레싱 salad dressing
sal ppaeda 살 빼다 slim
salp'yŏboda 살펴보다 see about, look into; check on; examine, look at; observe
salsal 살살 softly, lightly, gently
salssugi 살수기 sprinkler
sal su innŭn 살 수 있는 inhabitable
sal su ŏmnŭn 살 수 없는 uninhabitable
saltchak 살짝 furtively; easily; lightly
saltchak kkaemulda 살짝 깨물다 nibble
saltchak milch'ida 살짝 밀치다 jog *elbow etc*
saltchak sŭch'ida 살짝 스치다 brush, touch lightly
saltchida 살찌다 fill out, get fatter
sam 삼 three
samagwi 사마귀 wart
samak 사막 desert
samang 사망 death
samangjasu 사망자수 death toll
samangnyul 사망률 mortality, death rate
sambunŭi il 삼분의 일 one third
samch'on 삼촌 uncle (*father's brother, single*)
samgahada 삼가하다 refrain, desist
samgak 삼각 triangle ◊ triangular
samgak-kki 삼각기 pennant
samgak-kkŏn 삼각건 sling (*bandage*)
samgakttae 삼각대 tripod
samgak'yŏng 삼각형 triangle
Samguk 삼국 The Three Kingdoms
samgyet'ang 삼계탕 chicken boiled with ginseng
samgyŏpssal kui 삼겹살 구이 barbecued belly of pork
Samiltchŏl 삼일절 1 March Memorial Day
samja 삼자 third party
samjungju 삼중주 trio
samk'ida 삼키다 engulf, swallow
samnyu 삼류 third class ◊ third-rate
samohada 사모하다 adore
samonim 사모님 Madam, Mrs (*respectful*)
Samp'alssŏn 삼팔선 38th Parallel
samship 삼십 thirty
samtta 삶다 boil
samuguk 사무국 bureau, office
samugwan 사무관 clerk
samujang 사무장 steward
samujik sawŏn 사무직 사원 office worker, white-collar worker

samul 사물 thing
samushil 사무실 office (*room*)
samushillyong kŏnmul 사무실용 건물 office (*building*)
samushillyong koch'ŭng piltting 사무실용 고층 빌딩 office block
samwŏl 삼월 March
samyŏn 사면 amnesty, pardon; hill
samyŏng 사명 mission, vocation
samyŏnhada 사면하다 absolve, pardon
san 산 mountain; acid
sana chehan 산아 제한 birth control
sanaee(sŏ) 사내에(서) in-house
sanaeŭi 사내의 in-house
sanagin 산악인 mountaineer
sanapkke morach'ida 사납게 몰아치다 rage
sanaptta 사납다 be wild; be fierce; be unlucky
sanaun 사나운 rough, fierce
sanawajida 사나와지다 become abusive
sanbaltchŏgin 산발적인 sporadic; scattered; intermittent
sanbuinkkwa 산부인과 maternity hospital
sanbuinkkwa pyŏngdong 산부인과 병동 maternity ward
sanbuinkkwa ŭisa 산부인과 의사 gynecologist; obstetrician
sanch'aek 산책 ramble; rambling; stroll
sanch'aekshik'ida 산책시키다 walk *the dog*
sanch'aek'ada 산책하다 go for a walk; take a stroll; ramble
sanch'ul 산출 yield
sanch'urhada 산출하다 yield
sanch'urhae naeda 산출해 내다 calculate
sandaejŏgŭro 상대적으로 relatively
sandŏmi 산더미 mound, pile
sandŭlpparam 산들바람 breeze
sang 상 prize; icon (*cultural*); statue; table; mourning; ***sang chung-ida*** 상 중이다 be in mourning
sang-a 상아 ivory
sang-ajil 상아질 enamel (*on tooth*)
sangbandoen 상반된 opposite
sangbogŭl iptta 상복을 입다 wear mourning
sangbuŭi 상부의 top
sangbyŏng 상병 corporal
sangch'ŏ 상처 wound; sore; bruise
sangch'ŏ ibŭn 상처 입은 wounded, injured
sangch'ŏ ip'ida 상처 입히다 injure, wound
sangch'ŏnan 상처난 bruising, emotionally painful
sangch'ŏ ŏmnŭn 상처없는 uninjured
sangch'ŏ patkki shwiun 상처 받기 쉬운 vulnerable
sangch'ŏrŭl chuda 상처를 주다 bruise; hurt
sangch'ŏrŭl pat-tta 상처를 받다 get hurt
sangch'u 상추 lettuce
sangdae 상대 opponent; companion
sangdaejŏgin 상대적인 relative
sangdam 상담 consultancy; counseling; advice
sangdambi 상담비 (consultancy) fee
sangdamhada 상담하다 counsel
sangdamnyŏk 상담역 counselor, adviser
sangdanghada 상당하다 be appropriate; be considerable; be reasonable; be equivalent
sangdanghage 상당하게 substantially, considerably
sangdanghan 상당한 substantial, considerable, significant; equivalent
sangdanghi 상당히 reasonably, considerably, quite
sangdanghi choŭn 상당히 좋은 decent, reasonable
... sang-e ... 상에 on
sangga 상가 (shopping) mall
sanggam 상감 inlay
sanggapp'an 상갑판 upper deck
sanggihada 상기하다 recall, remember; relive
sanggishikida 상기시기다 remind
sanggo mŏri 상고 머리 crew cut
Sanggong Hoeŭiso 상공 회의소 Chamber of Commerce
sanggŭm 상금 winnings
sanggŭp 상급 senior rank; advanced level ◊ senior, superior

sanggwanŏmnŭn 상관없는 immaterial, irrelevant; ***chŏn, sanggwanŏpssŏyo*** 전, 상관없어요 it's all the same to me
sanggwanŏptta 상관없다 be irrelevant; not mind; ***chŏnŭn sanggwanopssŭmnida*** 저는 상관없습니다 I don't mind; ***kŭgŏsŭn sanggwanŏptta*** 그것은 상관없다 it doesn't matter
sanghada 상하다 go bad; be injured; be emaciated; ***muŏse kibun sanghada*** 무엇에 기분 상하다 get upset about sth
sanghage hada 상하게 하다 wound
sanghan 상한 sour
sangho chagyong 상호 작용 interaction
sangho chagyonghanŭn 상호 작용하는 interactive
sanghoganŭi 상호간의 mutual; reciprocal
sangho ŭijonhanŭn 상호 의존하는 interdependent
sanghwang 상황 situation, circumstances; ***ŏttŏn sanghwangesŏdo*** 어떤 상황에서도 under no circumstances
sanghwanhada 상환하다 redeem, pay off
sang-in 상인 merchant, dealer, trader
san-gisŭlk 산기슭 foot of a mountain
sangja 상자 case, box
sangjing 상징 symbol, emblem
sangjinghada 상징하다 symbolize
sangjingjŏgin 상징적인 symbolic
sangjingjuŭi 상징주의 symbolism
sangjŏm 상점 store, shop
sangk'waehada 상쾌하다 feel fresh
sangk'waehan 상쾌한 refreshing, invigorating; crisp
sangmak'ada 삭막하다 be bleak
sangmak'an 삭막한 stark, severe
sangnil 삯일 piecework
sangnokssu 상록수 evergreen
sangnyŏnghada 상영하다 show *movie*
sangnyu 상류 upper reaches; upper classes ◊ upper-class
sangnyuch'ŭng 상류층 upper classes
sangnyuch'ŭng-ŭi 상류층의 upper-class
sangnyuro 상류로 upstream
sangnyu sahoe 상류 사회 high society
sangnyu sahoeŭi saenghwal 상류 사회의 생활 high life
sangŏ 상어 shark
sang-ŏp 상업 commerce, trade ◊ commercial
sang-ŏpssang-ŭi 상업상의 commercial
sangp'um 상품 goods, merchandise, stock
sangp'umhwahada 상품화하다 commercialize
sangp'umkkwŏn 상품권 token
sangp'umŭi imiji 상품의 이미지 brand image
sangp'yo 상표 brand, make
sangp'yomyŏng 상표명 brand name
sangsa 상사 boss
sangsang 상상 imagination
sangsanghada 상상하다 imagine, conceive of, envisage
sangsanghal su innŭn 상상할 수 있는 imaginable
sangsanghal su ŏmnŭn 상상할 수 없는 unimaginable
sangsangnyŏgi ŏmnŭn 상상력이 없는 unimaginative
sangsangnyŏgi p'ungbuhan 상상력이 풍부한 imaginative
sangsang-ŭl ch'owŏrhanŭn 상상을 초월하는 exorbitant
sangsehada 상세하다 be detailed
sangsehage 상세하게 minutely, in detail
sangsehan 상세한 detailed, full
sangsehi 상세히 fully, in minute detail
sangshik 상식 sense, common sense
sangshil 상실 loss
sangshirhada 상실하다 forfeit, give up, lose
sangsogin 상속인 heir
sangsok 상속 inheritance
sangsok-kkwŏnŭl pakt'arhada 상속권을 박탈하다 disinherit
sangsok'ada 상속하다 inherit
sangsŭng 상승 rise ◊ rising

sangsŭnghada 상승하다 rise, ascend
sangsŭngse-ŭi 상승세의 buoyant
sangsŭptchŏgin 상습적인 habitual
sangsŭrŏptta 상스럽다 be crude, be vulgar
sangsŭrŏun 상스러운 crude, coarse, vulgar
sangsudo 상수도 waterworks
sangt'ae 상태 state, condition; circumstances
sang-ŭi 상의 top (*piece of clothing*); coat; consultation
sang-wŏn 상원 senate
sang-wŏnŭiwŏn 상원의원 senator
sanho 산호 coral
sanhwamul 산화물 oxide
sanjaehanŭn 산재하는 sparse
sanjŏk 산적 bandit; shish kebab
sankkil 산길 pass
sanmaek 산맥 (mountain) range
sanmanhada 산만하다 be loose; be vague
sanmanhage 산만하게 loosely
sanmanhan 산만한 loose, imprecise; vague; ***mŏriga sanmanhan*** 머리가 산만한 scatterbrained
sanmun 산문 prose
sannamul 산나물 wild greens
sanŏp 산업 industry ◊ industrial
sanŏpp'yegimul 산업폐기물 industrial waste
sanŏp'wahada 산업화하다 industrialize
sansanjogak naeda 산산조각 내다 smash to pieces
sansaram 산사람 hillbilly
sansat'ae 산사태 landslide
sanshin 산신 mountain spirit
sansŏngbi 산성비 acid rain
sanso 산소 oxygen; ancestral grave
sansul 산술 arithmetic
santtŏmi 산더미 heap, pile; ***santtŏmigach'i manŭn il*** 산더미같이 많은 일 a pile of work
santtŭngsŏng-i 산등성이 ridge
Sant'ak'ŭllosŭ 산타클로스 Santa Claus
sant'okki 산토끼 hare
sanyang 사냥 hunt; hunting
sanyanghada 사냥하다 hunt
sanyangkkun 사냥꾼 hunter
saŏp 사업 business; enterprise, undertaking; project; ***saŏpch'a*** 사업차 on business
saŏpkka 사업가 businessman
saŏp kwan-gye 사업 관계 business relations
sap 삽 shovel; scoop; spade
sapsshigane 삽시간에 in an instant; ***sapsshigane p'ŏjida*** 삽시간에 퍼지다 spread like wildfire
sap'aiŏ 사파이어 sapphire
sap'alnun 사팔눈 squint
sap'o 사포 sandpaper
sap'oro taktta 사포로 닦다 sandpaper
sap'oro tangnŭn changch'i 사포로 닦는 장치 sander
sap'wa 삽화 illustration
sap'waga 삽화가 illustrator
sap'warŭl kŭrida 삽화를 그리다 illustrate
saragada 살아가다 live; keep on living
sara innŭn 살아 있는 live, living
sara innŭn tŭt'an 살아 있는 듯한 lifelike
sarait-tta 살아있다 be alive
sarajida 사라지다 disappear; decline; die out
saram 사람 person; man; people; human ◊ *countword for people*
saramdaun 사람다운 humane
sarami salji annŭn 사람이 살지 않는 uninhabited
saramŭi shilssu 사람의 실수 human error
saranada 살아나다 revive; survive
sara nagada 살아 나가다 survive; carry on living
saranamtta 살아남다 survive
sarang 사랑 love
sarang-e ppajida 사랑에 빠지다 fall in love; fall in love with
saranghada 사랑하다 love
saranghanŭn 사랑하는 beloved
sarang-ni 사랑니 wisdom tooth
sarangsŭrŏun 사랑스러운 lovely; lovable, endearing
sarhae 살해 killing, slaying, murder
sarhaehada 살해하다 kill, slay, murder

sari 사리 coil; self-interest; Buddhist saint's relic; reason
sarin 살인 murder, homicide
sarinbŏm 살인범 homicide; murderer
sarinhada 살인하다 murder
sarinja 살인자 killer, murderer
sarisayok 사리사욕 self-interest
sarojaptta 사로잡다 capture
sarojap'ida 사로잡히다 be obsessed by
sarŭl enŭndŭshi 살을 에는듯이 bitterly *cold*
sarŭl enŭn tŭt'an 살을 에는 듯한 sharp, bitter *cold*
saryŏ kip'ŭn 사려 깊은 thoughtful, considerate
saryŏnggwan 사령관 commander
saryŏŏmnŭn 사려없는 inconsiderate
saryo 사료 fodder
saryun-gudong 사륜구동 four-wheel drive
sasaeng-a 사생아 illegitimate child, bastard
sasaenghwal 사생활 privacy
sasandoeda 사산되다 be stillborn
sasang 사상 thought, ideology; in history; death and injury
sasangja 사상자 casualty
sashil 사실 fact; truth
sashilssang 사실상 in fact, actually; virtually, more or less
sashilssang-ŭi 사실상의 actual; virtual
sashiltchuŭi 사실주의 realism
sashiltchuŭija 사실주의자 realist
saship 사십 forty
sashirŭl tŭrŏnaenŭn 사실을 드러내는 telltale *signs*
sashirŭn 사실은 in fact, as a matter of fact, actually
sashiŭi 사시의 cross-eyed
sasŏ 사서 librarian
sasŏham 사서함 PO Box
sasŏl 사설 editorial
sasŏng changgun 사성 장군 four-star general
sasohada 사소하다 be trivial
sasohan 사소한 trivial, minor
sasohan il 사소한 일 detail, trifle
sasohan kŏt 사소한 것 triviality
sasohan sahang 사소한 사항 technicality
sasŭl 사슬 chain
sasŭm 사슴 deer
sasŭm kogi 사슴 고기 venison
Sasunjŏl 사순절 Lent
satchŏgin 사적인 private
satssach'i twijida 샅샅이 뒤지다 comb; ransack
sat'aguni 사타구니 groin
Sat'an 사탄 Satan
sat'ang 사탕 candy
sat'angsusu 사탕 수수 sugar cane
sat'uri 사투리 dialect
Saudi Arabia 사우디 아라비아 Saudi Arabia ◊ Saudi
sauna 사우나 sauna
saundŭ k'adŭ 사운드 카드 sound card
sawi 사위 son-in-law
sawŏl 사월 April
sawŏn 사원 temple REL
sayanghada 사양하다 decline with thanks; ***sayangch'i mashigo kajiseyo*** 사양치 마시고 가지세요 please keep it, I insist
sayanghal su ŏmnŭn 사양할 수 없는 irresistible
sayŏrhada 사열하다 review *troops*
sayong 사용 use
sayonghada 사용하다 use, employ; exercise *control, restraint*; work
sayonghagi shwiun 사용하기 쉬운 user-friendly
sayongja 사용자 user
sayongppŏp 사용법 directions, instructions for use
sayong sŏlmyŏngsŏ 사용 설명서 instruction manual
sayuktcha 사육자 breeder
sebaero chŭnggahada 세배로 증가하다 treble
sebal chajŏn-gŏ 세발 자전거 tricycle
sebu chohang 세부 조항 small print
sebunhada 세분하다 subdivide
sebu sahang 세부 사항 detail
sech'ashik'ida 세차시키다 get the car washed
sech'a sŏbissŭ 세차 서비스 valet service

sech'igi 새치기 cutting in line
sech'ŏktche 세척제 detergent
seda 세다 count (up)
sedae 세대 generation
sedae ch'ai 세대 차이 generation gap
sedan 세단 sedan
sege ch'ida 세게 치다 punch; push, jolt
segehada 세게 하다 intensify
sege tchirŭda 세게 찌르다 thrust
segi 세기 century
segŭm 세금 tax
segŭm kiho 세금 기호 tax code
segŭm kongjega kanŭnghan 세금 공제가 가능한 tax deductible
segŭmŭl pugwahada 세금을 부과하다 tax
segŭmŭl p'ohamhan 세금을 포함한 pre-tax
segwan kŏmsa 세관 검사 customs inspection
segwan t'onggwa 세관 통과 customs clearance
segwanwŏn 세관원 customs officer
segye 세계 world
segyehwa 세계화 globalization
segyejŏgin 세계적인 worldwide
segyejŏgŭro 세계적으로 worldwide
segyejŏk kangdaeguk 세계적 강대국 world power
segye kyŏngje 세계 경제 global economy
segye onnanhwa 세계 온난화 global warming
Segye P'yojunshi 세계 표준시 GMT, Greenwich Mean Time
segye shijang 세계 시장 global market
segye taejŏn 세계 대전 world war
segyun 세균 germ
segyunjŏn 세균전 germ warfare
seil chung-ida 세일 중이다 be on sale (*at reduced prices*)
seiljŭmaen 세일즈맨 salesman; representative
seip 세입 revenue
sellŏri 셀러리 celery
sellop'an 셀로판 cellophane
selp'ŭ set'aksso 셀프세탁소 laundromat
selp'ŭssŏbisŭ shikttang 셀프서비스 식당 self-service restaurant
selp'ŭssŏbisŭŭi 셀프서비스의 self-service
sel su omnŭn 셀 수 없는 countless
sem 셈 count; intention, design; ***...ŭi semŭl ijŏbŏrida*** ...의 셈을 잊어버리다 lose count of; ***...ŭl / rŭl hal semŭro*** ...을 / 를 할 셈으로 with the intention of
semina 세미나 seminar
semirhi chosadoeda 세밀히 조사되다 come under scrutiny
semŭro ch'ida 셈으로 치다 count, qualify
semu chosagwan 세무 조사관 tax-inspector
semyŏndae 세면대 basin
semyŏndogu kabang 세면도구 가방 sponge bag
semyŏn-gi 세면기 washbasin, washbowl
semyŏnjang 세면장 bathroom
semyŏn t'awŏl 세면 타월 washcloth
semyŏn yongp'um 세면 용품 toiletries
senoe 세뇌 brainwashing
senoehada 세뇌하다 brainwash
sensseisyŏn 센세이션 sensation
sent'i(mit'ŏ) 센티(미터) centimeter
sent'ŏ 센터 center
sent'ŭ 센트 cent
se pŏntchae 세 번째 third
se pŏntchaeŭi 세 번째의 third
sep'o 세포 cell
seriju 세리주 sherry
seroro 세로로 portrait *print*
serye 세례 baptism
seryehada 세례하다 baptize, christen
seryemyŏng 세례명 Christian name
seryŏk 세력 power, leverage; influence
seryŏndoen 세련된 cultured, sophisticated
seryok-kkwŏn 세력권 sphere of influence
sesang 세상 world; ***sesang-e!*** 세상에! oh God!; ***sesang-e nae-not'a*** 세상에 내놓다 bring out; ***sesang multchŏng-e palgŭn*** 세상 물정에 밝은 worldly; streetwise;

sesang-ŭl ttŏdŭlssŏk'age hanŭn 세상을 떠들썩하게 하는 sensational; ***sesang-ŭl ttŭda*** 세상을 뜨다 depart this world, pass away
seshim 세심 carefulness; ***...ŭl / rŭl seshimhage poda*** ...을 / 를 세심하게 보다 keep a wary eye on ...
seshimhan 세심한 meticulous
sesogŭi 세속의 secular
sesoktchŏgin 세속적인 material, worldly
se ssangdung-i 세 쌍둥이 triplets
set 셋 three
set'agŭl matkkida 세탁을 맡기다 have laundered
set'ak-kki 세탁기 washing machine
set'ak sŏbissŭ 세탁 서비스 valet service
set'aksso 세탁소 laundry; dry cleaner
set'ak'ada 세탁하다 launder
set'ak'age hada 세탁하게 하다 get one's laundry done
set'angmul 세탁물 laundry (*clothes*)
set'inghada 세팅하다 set up
setŏp 셋업 set-up COMPUT
set'ŭ 세트 set
seuda 세우다 build; erect; establish, set up; turn up *collar*; stop *person in street*; ***ttokpparo seuda*** 똑바로 세우다 stand on end
shi 시 poetry, verse; poem; city; o'clock; ***tasŏt shie*** 다섯 시에 at five o'clock
shiabŏji 시아버지 father-in-law (*husband's father*)
shibi 십이 twelve
shibil 십일 eleven
shibiwŏl 십이월 December
shibirwŏl 십일월 November
shibo 십오 fifteen
shibobun 십오분 fifteen minutes, a quarter of an hour
shich'a 시차 time-lag
shich'al 시찰 inspection
shich'arhada 시찰하다 inspect
shich'e 시체 body, corpse, cadaver
shich'ŏng 시청 city hall; town hall
shich'ŏnggagŭi 시청각의 audiovisual
shich'ŏnghada 시청하다 view, tune in to
shich'ŏngja 시청자 audience; viewer; follower
shich'o 시초 beginning, dawn
shida 시다 be sour
shidae 시대 era, epoch; ***yojŭm shidaega kŭrŏssŭmnida*** 요즘 시대가 그렇습니다 it's a sign of the times
shidaee twittŏrŏjin 시대에 뒤떨어진 dated, old-fashioned
shidallida 시달리다 be harassed
shidallin 시달린 harassed; ***kŏktchŏng-e shidallin*** 걱정에 시달린 careworn
shido 시도 attempt, endeavor; ***saeroun shido*** 새로운 시도 new departure
shidohada 시도하다 try, attempt, endeavor
shidongdoeda 시동되다 start
shidonggi 시동기 starter MOT
shidongshik'ida 시동시키다 start
shidŭlda 시들다 droop, wilt, wither
shigaji 시가지 built-up area
shigak kyojae 시각 교재 visual aid
shigaktchŏgin 시각적인 visual
shigaktchŏgŭro 시각적으로 visually
shigaktchŏgŭro sonsangdoen 시각적으로 손상된 visually impaired
shigan 시간 time; hour
shigan chŏryak 시간 절약 timesaving
shiganjero 시간제로 part-time
shigan kan-gyŏk 시간 간격 interval
shiganmada 시간 마다 every hour
shigan ŏmsu 시간 엄수 punctuality
shiganp'yo 시간표 schedule, timetable
shiganŭl chik'inŭn 시간을 지키는 prompt, on time
shiganŭl hŏbihada 시간을 허비하다 dawdle
shiganŭl match'uda 시간을 맞추다 synchronize
shiganŭl match'uŏ 시간을 맞추어 in time
shiganŭl ŏmsuhanŭn 시간을 엄수하는 punctual
shigi 시기 phase, period, stage;

timescale
shigirŭl match'ugi 시기를 맞추기 timing
shigisangjoŭi 시기상조의 premature
shigi yoppŏp 식이 요법 diet (*as cure*)
shigol 시골 countryside; hick town; ***shigore*(*sŏ*)** 시골에(서) in the country
shigolkkil 시골길 country lane
shigoltchip 시골집 cottage
shigolttŭgi 시골뜨기 lout; hick
shigorŭi 시골의 rural
shigŭmch'i 시금치 spinach
shigurhada 시굴하다 prospect for
shigye 시계 clock; watch
shigye chejoin 시계 제조인 watchmaker
shigye panghyang-ŭro tora 시계 방향으로 돌아 clockwise
shigye panŭl 시계 바늘 hand (*of clock*)
shigyeradio 시계라디오 clock radio
shigye t'aeyŏp changch'i 시계 태엽 장치 clockwork (mechanism)
shigyogŭl todunŭn 식욕을 돋우는 appetizing
shigyok 식욕 appetite
shihan p'okt'an 시한 폭탄 time bomb
shihap 시합 tournament; event; match; bout (*in boxing*)
shihŏm 시험 exam; test, trial
shihŏmgwan 시험관 examiner; test tube
shihŏmgwan agi 시험관 아기 test-tube baby
shihŏmhada 시험하다 examine, test
shihŏmhae poda 시험해 보다 try out; have on trial
shihŏmji 시험지 examination paper
shihŏm kigan 시험 기간 trial period
shihŏm kongjang 시험 공장 pilot plant
shiin 시인 confession; poet
shiinhada 시인하다 admit, confess
shijak 시작 beginning, start; onset; ***choŭn / nappŭn shijagŭl hada*** 좋은 / 나쁜 시작을 하다 get off to a good / bad start
shijakdoeda 시작되다 begin, start; break out, start up; break (*of storm*)
shijak pŏt'ŭn 시작 버튼 start button; trigger; on switch
shijakttoeda 시작되다 begin, commence
shijak'ada 시작하다 begin, originate; institute; take up; get down to; log on; ***...ki shijak'ada ...*** 기 시작하다 start ...ing; ***irŭl shijak'ada*** 일을 시작하다 set to work
shijang 시장 market; marketplace; mayor; ***shijang-e*** 시장에 on the market; ***shijang-ŭl toktchŏmhada*** 시장을 독점하다 corner the market
shijangboda 시장보다 store, shop
shijang chŏmnyuyul 시장 점유율 market share
shijang chosa 시장 조사 market research
shijang kyŏngje 시장 경제 market economy
shijangnyŏk 시장력 market forces
shije 시제 tense GRAM
shijŏl 시절 season; time; ***kŭ shijŏrenŭn*** 그 시절에는 in those days
shijungdŭlda 시중들다 serve
shijung tŭnŭn saram 시중 드는 사람 valet
shijung-ŭl tŭlda 시중을 들다 wait on
shik 식 event; ceremony; eclipse
shikch'o 식초 vinegar
shikkŭrŏptta 시끄럽다 be loud; be noisy
shikkŭrŏun 시끄러운 loud, noisy
shikkŭrŏun sori 시끄러운 소리 din, noise
shikppyŏllyŏgi innŭn 식별력이 있는 discriminating, discerning
shikppyŏrhada 식별하다 spot, identify; discern; distinguish
shikp'umjŏm 식품점 grocery (store)
shikssa 식사 meal
shikssahada 식사하다 dine
shikssa shigan 식사 시간 mealtime; sitting
shikssŏng 식성 taste, preference (*in food*); ***shikssŏng-i kkadaroptta*** 식성이 까다롭다 be a fussy eater
shiktchahada 식자하다 typeset, set
shiktchungdok 식중독 food

poisoning
shiktta 식다 cool, cool down
shikttan 식단 menu
shikttang 식당 restaurant; dining room
shikttangch'a 식당차 restaurant car
shikttanp'yo 식단표 menu
shiktto 식도 gullet
shikt'ak 식탁 dining table
shikt'akppo 식탁보 tablecloth
shik'ida 식히다 cool down
shik'ida 시키다 (*causative*): ***shilmangshik'ida*** 실망시키다 disappoint; ***t'ŭrimŭl shik'ida*** 트림을 시키다 burp *baby*
shil 실 yarn, thread
shilch'ehwahada 실체화하다 materialize
shilk'ŏt mŏk-kki 실컷 먹기 blowout
shillae 실내 interior
shillae changshik-kka 실내 장식가 interior decorator
shillaee(sŏ) 실내에(서) indoors
shillae kyŏng-ŭmak 실내 경음악 piped music
shillalgat'ŭn hŭimang 실날같은 희망 glimmer of hope
shillang 신랑 groom, bridegroom
shillang tŭllŏri 신랑 들러리 best man
shillarhan 신랄한 cutting, stinging; bitter
shillijŏgin 실리적인 practical, pragmatic
shillijŏgŭro 실리적으로 practically, pragmatically
shillik'on 실리콘 silicon
shillik'on ch'ip 실리콘 칩 silicon chip
shilloe 신뢰 trust, confidence; faith
shilloegam kanŭn 신뢰감 가는 credible
shilloehada 신뢰하다 trust, believe in
shilloehal su innŭn 신뢰할 수 있는 trustworthy; trusted; reliable
shilloehanŭn 신뢰하는 trustful, trusting
shilloessŏng 신뢰성 reliability; credibility
shilluet 실루엣 silhouette
shillye 실례 illustration
shillyehamnida 실례합니다 excuse me
shilmang 실망 disappointment
shilmanghada 실망하다 disappoint
shilmanghan 실망한 disappointed
shilmangshik'ida 실망시키다 disappoint
shilmangsŭrŏun 실망스러운 disappointing
shilmari 실마리 clue
shilmul k'ŭgiŭi 실물 크기의 life-sized
shilp'ae 실패 failure; breakdown; reel, spool
shilp'aehada 실패하다 fail; break down; lose out; be out
shilp'aehan 실패한 unsuccessful
shilp'aeja 실패자 loser, failure
shilp'aejagida 실패작이다 flop, fail
shilp'aejak 실패작 flop, failure
shilp'aero kkŭnnada 실패로 끝나다 end in failure; fall through
shilsshidoeda 실시되다 come into effect
shilsshigan 실시간 real time
shilsshiganŭi 실시간의 real-time
shilsshihada 실시하다 carry out
shilssu 실수 mistake
shilssuhada 실수하다 make a mistake, go wrong
shilssuip 실수입 take-home pay
shilssuro 실수로 by mistake
shiltchaehaji annŭn 실재하지 않는 unreal
shiltche 실제 truth; fact; practice ◊ practical
shiltchejŏgin 실제적인 practical; down-to-earth
shiltcheŭi 실제의 actual, real
shiltchik'ada 실직하다 lose one's job; be unemployed
shiltchik'an 실직한 unemployed, out of work
shiltchiltchŏgin 실질적인 substantive
shiltchiltchŏgŭro 실질적으로 substantially
shiltchŏm 실점 lost points SP
shiltchong 실종 disappearance
shiltchŭng nada 싫증 나다 be tired of
shiltta 싣다 load; ***chimŭl shiltta*** 짐을 싣다 load
shilt'an 실탄 live ammunition

shilt'ohada 실토하다 confess
shim 심 pith
shimburŭm 심부름 errand
shimburŭmgada 심부름가다 run errands
shiment'ŭ 시멘트 cement; ***shiment'ŭro parŭda*** 시멘트로 바르다 cement
shimgak'ada 심각하다 be serious
shimgak'an 심각한 serious *illness*; deep *trouble*; heavy *loss*
shimgiga twit'ŭllin 심기가 뒤틀린 cranky, bad-tempered
shimgyehangjin 심계항진 palpitations
shimhada 심하다 be awful
shimhage 심하게 seriously; badly; severely
shimhage nappŭn 심하게 나쁜 atrocious
shimham 심함 severity
shimhan 심한 bad, awful; heavy; severe
shimin 시민 citizen
shimin-gun 시민군 militia
shiminkkwŏn 시민권 citizenship
shiminŭi 시민의 civil; civic
shimjang 심장 heart ◊ cardiac, coronary
shimjang chŏngji 심장 정지 cardiac arrest
shimjang ishik 심장 이식 heart transplant
shimjang mabi 심장 마비 heart attack, coronary
shimjang pakttong 심장 박동 heartbeat
shimji 심지 wick
shimjiga kujŭn 심지가 굳은 strong-minded, independent
shimmijŏgin 심미적인 esthetic
shimmun 심문 interrogation
shimmunhada 심문하다 interrogate
shimmunja 심문자 interrogator
shimnanhage hada 심란하게 하다 distract
shimnanhan 심란한 distracted, worried
shimni 심리 hearing LAW
shimnihak 심리학 psychology
shimnihaktcha 심리학자 psychologist
shimnijŏgin 심리적인 psychological
shimnijŏgŭro 심리적으로 psychologically
shimnya 심야 small hours
shimnyŏngjuŭi 심령주의 spiritualism
shimnyŏngjuŭija 심령주의자 spiritualist
shimnyŏng-ŭi 심령의 psychic
shimoham 심오함 depth (*of thought*)
shimohan 심오한 deep, profound
shimp'an 심판 referee; umpire
shimp'an wiwŏnhoe 심판 위원회 tribunal
shimsahada 심사하다 judge
shimsasuk-kko 심사숙고 reflection
shimsasuk-kkohan 심사숙고한 thoughtful
shimsa wiwŏn 심사 위원 judge
shimsa wiwŏndan 심사 위원단 jury; panel
shimsulgujŭn 심술궂은 sour; bitchy; bad-tempered
shimsulgut-tta 심술궂다 be bad-tempered
shimtta 심다 plant
shimŭi 심의 debate
shimuruk'an 시무룩한 glum
shimwŏnhan 심원한 deep
shimyuk 십육 sixteen
shin 신 deity; god ◊ sour
shinae t'onghwa 시내 통화 local call
shinang 신앙 belief, faith
shinangshim-i kip'ŭn 신앙심이 깊은 deeply religious
shinario 시나리오 scenario
shinbal 신발 footwear; shoe
shinbalkkage 신발가게 shoestore
shinbalkkŭn 신발끈 shoelace
shinbi 신비 mystery
shinbihada 신비하다 be mysterious
shinbihage 신비하게 mysteriously
shinbihan 신비한 mysterious
shinbingssŏng 신빙성 credibility; authenticity
shinbingssŏng-ŭl ttŏrŏttŭrida 신빙성을 떨어뜨리다 discredit
shinbiroun 신비로운 magical; delightful
shinbongja 신봉자 believer
shinbu 신부 bride; (Catholic) priest

shinbun 신분 rank
shinbun chŭngmyŏngsŏ 신분 증명서 identity card
shinbuntchŭng 신분증 (identity) papers
shinbunŭi sangjing 신분의 상징 status symbol
shinbu tŭllŏri 신부 들러리 bridesmaid
shinbyŏng 신병 recruit
shinchunghan 신중한 discreet
shinch'am 신참 newcomer
shinch'e chang-ae 신체 장애 physical handicap, physical disability
shinch'e chang-aeja 신체 장애자 the disabled; cripple
shinch'e chang-aeja innŭn 신체 장애가 있는 physically handicapped
shinch'e kŏmsa 신체 검사 medical
shinch'ŏng 신청 application
shinch'ŏnghada 신청하다 apply for; ***teit'ŭ shinch'ŏnghada*** 데이트 신청하다 ask out, ask for a date
shinch'ŏngsŏ 신청서 application form
shinch'ukssŏng 신축성 elasticity
shinch'ukssŏng innŭn 신축성 있는 stretchy, elastic
shinch'ukssŏng-ŭl kajin 신축성을 가진 elasticized
shindong 신동 child prodigy
shingandang 시간당 hourly rate
Shinggap'orŭ 싱가포르 Singapore ◊ Singaporean
shinggŭt usŭm 싱긋 웃음 grin
shinggŭt ut-tta 싱긋 웃다 grin
shin-giru 신기루 mirage
shingk'ŭ 싱크 sink
shingminji 식민지 colony
shingminjiŭi 식민지의 colonial
Shingmogil 식목일 Arbor Day
shingmul 식물 plant ◊ botanical
shingmurhak 식물학 botany
shingnyo chap'wajŏm 식료 잡화점 grocery store
shin-gohada 신고하다 register; declare; inform; turn in (*to police*)
shin-gwan 신관 fuse (*of bomb*)
shin-gwanŭl chegŏhada 신관을 제거하다 defuse
shin-gyŏng 신경 creed; beliefs; nerve; ***nuguŭi shin-gyŏng-ŭl kŏndŭrida*** 누구의 신경을 건드리다 get on s.o.'s nerves
shin-gyŏng enŏji 신경 에너지 nervous energy
shin-gyŏng-i kŏsŭllinŭn 신경이 거슬리는 annoyed
shin-gyŏng-i kwaminhan 신경이 과민한 nervous
shin-gyŏng-i ssŭida 신경이 쓰이다 bother; ***shin-gyŏng ssŭji maseyo!*** 신경 쓰지 마세요! don't bother!; ***shin-gyŏng ssŭl kŏt ŏpssŭmnida!*** 신경 쓸 것 없습니다! never mind!
shin-gyŏngjiltchŏgin 신경질적인 fussy
shin-gyŏngkkwa ŭisa 신경과 의사 neurologist
shin-gyŏng kwaminŭi 신경 과민의 jumpy, nervous; neurotic
shin-gyŏng soeyage kŏllida 신경 쇠약에 걸리다 crack up, have a nervous breakdown
shin-gyŏng soeyagida 신경 쇠약이다 be a nervous wreck
shin-gyŏng soeyak 신경 쇠약 nervous breakdown
shin-gyŏng soeyaktcha 신경 쇠약자 nervous wreck
shin-gyŏngssŭji annŭn 신경쓰지 않는 unconcerned
shin-gyŏngtchil 신경질 nervousness
shin-gyŏngtchilnage hada 신경질나게 하다 nettle, irritate
shin-gyŏngtchŭng 신경증 neurosis
Shin-gyodo 신교도 Protestant
Shin-gyodoŭi 신교도의 Protestant
shin-gyu mojip 신규 모집 recruitment
shin-gyu mojip k'aemp'ein 신규 모집 캠페인 recruitment drive
shinhak 신학 theology
shinho 신호 signal
shinhodŭng 신호등 traffic light
shinhohada 신호하다 signal
shinhon pubu 신혼 부부 newlyweds
shinhon yŏhaeng 신혼 여행 honeymoon
shinhwa 신화 myth
shinhwahak 신화학 mythology
shinhwaŭi 신화의 mythical

shinip 신입 newcomer
shinip sawŏn 신입 사원 recruit
shinip sawŏnŭl ppoptta 신입 사원을 뽑다 recruit
shinipssaeng 신입생 freshman
shinja 신자 believer
shinjakp'um 신작품 collection
shinjang 신장 kidney ANAT
shinjindaesa 신진대사 metabolism
Shinjŏng 신정 New Year
shinjo 신조 doctrine
shinju 신주 spirit tablet
shinjung 신중 prudence, caution; good sense
shinjunghada 신중하다 be careful; be wary
shinjunghage 신중하게 carefully
shinmang innŭn 신망 있는 serious
shinmun 신문 newspaper
shinmun kap'andae 신문 가판대 newsstand
shinmun p'anmaeso 신문 판매소 newsdealer
shinmun p'anmaewŏn 신문 판매원 newsvendor
shinnyŏm 신념 conviction, belief
shinsa 신사 gentleman
shinsabok 신사복 lounge suit
shinse 신세 debt of gratitude; ***nuguege shinserŭl chida*** 누구에게 신세를 지다 be indebted to s.o.
shinsŏndo 신선도 freshness
shinsŏng 신성 sanctity
shinsŏnghan 신성한 divine, sacred
shinsŏnhada 신선하다 be fresh
shinsŏnhan 신선한 fresh
shinssok 신속 rapidity
shinssok'ada 신속하다 be rapid
shinssok'an 신속한 rapid
shintta 신다 put on *shoes*
shinŭmhada 신음하다 groan, moan
shinŭm sori 신음 소리 groan, moan
shinui 시누이 sister-in-law (*husband's sister*)
shinwŏn 신원 identity
shinwŏn pojŭng-in 신원 보증인 referee (*for job*)
Shinyak Sŏngsŏ 구약 성서 New Testament
shinyong 신용 credit
shinyong-i ttŏrŏjigehada 신용이 떨어지게 하다 discredit
shinyonginnŭn 신용있는 creditworthy
shinyong k'adŭ 신용 카드 credit card
shinyong taebu 신용 대부 credit, loan
shinyong taebuŭi hando 신용 대부의 한도 credit limit
shinyongtchang 신용장 letter of credit
shinyung 시늉 act, pretense
shiŏmŏni 시어머니 mother-in-law (*wife's*)
shiŏmŏnim 시어머님 mother-in-law (*wife's*) (*polite*)
shioe pŏsŭ 시외 버스 bus (*long-distance*)
ship 십 ten
shipch'il 십칠 seventeen
shipkku 십구 nineteen
ship nyŏn 십 년 decade
ship ŏk 십억 billion
shipp'al 십팔 eighteen
shipssa 십사 fourteen
shipssam 십삼 thirteen
ship ssent'ŭ 십 센트 dime
ship tae 십 대 teens ◊ teenage; ***ship taega toeda*** 십 대가 되다 reach one's teens; ***ship tae sonyŏn / sonyŏ*** 십 대 소년 / 소녀 teenage boy / girl, teenager
ship taeida 십 대이다 be in one's teens
shiptchaga 십자가 cross; ***kasŭme shiptcharŭl kŭt-tta*** 가슴에 십자를 긋다 cross (oneself)
shiptchungp'algu 십중팔구 in all likelihood; nine times out of ten
shiptta 싶다 want; seem; ***...go ship'ŭn kibunida*** ...고 싶은 기분이다 be in the mood for; ***...ŭl / rŭl hago shipssŭmnikka?*** ...을 / 를 하고 싶습니까? would you like to ...?
ship'ŭt'ŭ k'i 시프트 키 shift key
shirhaeng 실행 fulfillment; execution (*of plan*); return COMPUT
shirhaenghada 실행하다 carry out; execute, put into effect; fulfill; run *software*

shirhaeng kanŭnghan 실행 가능한 feasible, workable
shirhŏm 실험 experiment
shirhŏm chaeryo 실험 재료 guinea pig *fig*
shirhŏmhada 실험하다 experiment, test
shirhŏmhaeboda 실험해보다 experiment with, try out
shirhŏmshil 실험실 lab, laboratory
shirhŏmshil kisultcha 실험실 기술자 laboratory technician
shirhŏmŭi 실험의 experimental
shirhwang-ŭi 실황의 actual
shirhyŏn 실현 realization (*of goal*)
shirhyŏndoeda 실현되다 come true
shiriŏl 시리얼 cereal
shirŏhada 싫어하다 dislike
shirŏjida 싫어지다 go off, stop liking
shirŏmnŭn 실없는 frivolous
shirŏn 실언 slip of the tongue
shirŏp 시럽 syrup
shirŏp 실업 unemployment
shirŏpkka 실업가 industrialist
shirŏptcha 실업자 the unemployed
shirŭl kkweda 실을 꿰다 thread
shirŭl ppoptta 실을 뽑다 take the stitches out
shirŭm 싫음 distaste
shirŭn 싫은 distasteful
shiryŏk 시력 eyesight, vision
shiryŏn 실연 demonstration
shiryŏn 시련 ordeal
shiryŏnhada 실연하다 demonstrate
shiryongjŏgin 실용적인 practical, functional
shiryongjuŭi 실용주의 pragmatism
shisa 시사 current affairs; preview
shisa p'ŭrograem 시사 프로그램 current affairs program
shisap'ungjagŭk 시사풍자극 revue
shishihada 시시하다 be trivial; be wishy-washy; be tame (*of joke etc*); be stupid
shisŏl 시설 establishment; facilities
shisŏn 시선 line of vision; ***nuguŭi shisŏnŭl kkŭlda*** 누구의 시선을 끌다 catch s.o.'s eye
shiso 시소 seesaw
shisok 시속: ***shisok 150mairŭi sokttoro*** 시속 150마일의 속도로 at a speed of 150 mph
shisŭt'em 시스템 system
shisŭt'em punsŏk-kka 시스템 분석가 systems analyst
shitta 싣다 embark, go on board ship
shittchŏgin 시적인 poetic
shit'ŭk'om 시트콤 sitcom
shiŭi 시의 municipal, civic
shi ŭihoe 시 의회 town council
shiŭihoe ŭiwŏn 시의회 의원 councilman
shi ŭiwŏn 시 의원 councilman
shiwi 시위 demonstration, protest
shiwi ch'amgaja 시위 참가자 demonstrator, protester
shiwihada 시위하다 demonstrate
shiwŏl 시월 October
shiwŏnhada 시원하다 be cool
shiya 시야 visibility
shiyŏn 시연 preview
shiyŏnhada 시연하다 rehearse, run through
shŏlttŭk'ae poda 설득해 보다 reason with
shwida 쉬다 rest; be off; not be at work; ***harurŭl / iltchuirŭl shwida*** 하루를 / 일주일을 쉬다 take a day / week off
shwim ŏpsshi 쉼 없이 without respite
shwimp'yo 쉼표 comma
shwin 쉰 fifty
shwin mokssori 쉰 목소리 croak
shwin mokssoriŭi 쉰 목소리의 husky
shwin pŏntchaeŭi 쉰 번째의 fiftieth
shwinŭn nal 쉬는 날 day off
shwinŭn shigan 쉬는 시간 recess EDU
shwipkke 쉽게 easily
shwipkke hŭngbunhanŭn 쉽게 흥분하는 excitable
shwiptta 쉽다 be easy; ***...gi shwiptta*** ...기 쉽다 be prone to ...
shwishwihaebŏrida 쉬쉬해버리다 hush up, conceal
shwit sorirŭl naeda 쉿 소리를 내다 hiss
shwiun 쉬운 easy, simple; ***...gi shwiun*** ...기 쉬운 be easy to ...
shyaemi kajuk 섀미 가죽 chamois

(leather)
shyaeshi 섀시 chassis
shyamp'ein 샴페인 champagne
shyamp'u 샴푸 shampoo
shyam ssangdung-i 샴 쌍둥이 Siamese twins
shyangdŭllie 샹들리에 chandelier
shyawŏ 샤워 shower
shyawŏhada 샤워하다 shower, take a shower
shyawŏ k'aep 샤워 캡 shower cap
shyawŏ k'ŏt'ŭn 샤워 커튼 shower curtain
shyeŏweŏ 셰어웨어 shareware
shyŏch'ŭ 셔츠 shirt
shyŏt'ŏ 셔터 shutter PHOT
shyŏt'ŭlppŏsŭ 셔틀버스 shuttlebus
shyŏt'ŭl sŏbissŭ 셔틀 서비스 shuttle service
shyo 쇼 show; vaudeville
shyok'ŭ 쇼크 shock ELEC
shyol 숄 shawl
shyo pijŭnisŭ 쇼 비즈니스 show business
shyop'ing 쇼핑 shopping
shyop'inghanŭn saram 쇼핑하는 사람 shopper
shyop'ingssent'ŏ 쇼핑센터 shopping center, shopping mall
shyo rum 쇼 룸 showroom
shyowindo 쇼윈도 store window
sidŭ 시드 seed (*in tennis*)
sik'ye 식혜 malted rice drink
Silla 신라 Silla (*Ancient Kingdom*)
siltchŭngnage hada 싫증나게 하다 bore
singgŭlp'an 싱글판 single MUS
singnyop'um chŏjangso 식료품 저장소 larder
sŏ 서 west
sŏbissŭ 서비스 service
sŏbissŭ chegonghoesa 서비스 제공회사 service provider
sŏbissŭhada 서비스하다 service *machine, car*
sŏbissŭryo 서비스료 service charge
sŏbissŭ sanŏp 서비스 산업 service industry
sŏbissŭ sanŏp pubun 서비스 산업 부분 service sector
sŏbŏ 서버 server COMPUT
sŏbŭ 서브 serve (*in tennnis*)
sŏbŭhada 서브하다 serve
sŏbu 서부 west
sŏbugŭk 서부극 western (*movie*)
sŏch'i 서치 search COMPUT
sŏchi'hada 서치하다 search, search for COMPUT
sŏda 서다 stand; stop
sŏdullŏ! 서둘러! come on! hurry up!
sŏdullŏ ttŏnada 서둘러 떠나다 dash off
sŏdurŭda 서두르다 hurry up, rush
sŏdurŭn 서두른 hurried
sŏgok 서곡 overture
sŏgŭlp'ŭn 서글픈 sad; lamentable
sŏgyŏnch'i anŭn 석연치 않은 dubious, suspect
sŏgyŏng 석영 quartz
sŏgyu 석유 oil; petroleum
sŏgyu hoesa 석유 회사 oil company
sŏgyu hwahak chep'um 석유 화학 제품 petrochemical
sŏgyu kulch'ak changch'i 석유 굴착 장치 oil rig
Sŏgyu Such'ulguk Kigu 석유 수출국 기구 OPEC, Organization of Petroleum Exporting Countries
Sŏhae 서해 West Sea, Yellow Sea
sŏjae 서재 study (*room*)
sŏjŏm 서점 bookstore
sŏkkarae 서까래 rafter
sŏkkida 섞이다 blend in
Sŏk-kkamoni 석가모니 Sakyamuni (*Buddha*)
sŏk-kkin 섞인 mixed
sŏk-kkosang 석고상 plaster cast
sŏkkŏ not'a 섞어 놓다 mix up, muddle up
sŏkkŭn kŏt 섞은 것 mix, mixture
sŏkppang 석방 release
sŏkppanghada 석방하다 free, release
sŏkp'an 석판 slab
sŏkssa(hagwi) 석사(학위) master's (degree)
sŏkssoe 석쇠 grill
sŏkssoero kuptta 석쇠로 굽다 grill
sŏkssu 석수 mason
sŏktcho 석조 stone (*material*)
sŏktta 섞다 mix, blend in; mingle
sŏkt'an 석탄 coal

sŏk'ŏsŭ 서커스 circus
sŏk'o 석호 lagoon
sŏk'oe 석회 lime (*substance*)
sŏk'oeam 석회암 chalk (*in soil*)
sŏlbi 설비 fixture
sŏlch'i 설치 installation
sŏlch'ihada 설치하다 install; ***chiro-erŭl sŏlch'ihada*** 지뢰를 설치하다 mine, lay mines in
sŏlch'in 설친 fitful
sŏlch'iryu 설치류 rodent
sŏldŭngnyŏk innŭn 설득력 있는 forceful
sŏlgŏji hada 설거지하다 wash the dishes
sŏlgŏji kigye 설거지 기계 dishwasher
sŏlgŏji mul 설겆이 물 dishwater
sŏlguwŏjin 설구워진 soggy
sŏlgyedo 설계도 design; plan
sŏlgyehada 설계하다 design; shape
sŏlgyeja 설계자 designer
sŏlgyesa 설계사 architect
sŏlgyesang-ŭi munjetchŏm 설계상의 문제점 design fault
sŏlgyo 설교 sermon
sŏlgyodan 설교단 pulpit
sŏlgyohada 설교하다 preach
sŏlgyoja 설교자 preacher
Sŏllal 설날 Lunar New Year
sŏlliptcha 설립자 founder
sŏllip'ada 설립하다 establish
sŏllo 선로 track; platform
sŏllye 선례 precedent; ***nuguŭi sŏllyerŭl ttarŭda*** 누구의 선례를 따르다 follow in s.o.'s footsteps
sŏlma! 설마! surely; come on! (*in disbelief*)
sŏlmyŏng 설명 explanation
sŏlmyŏnghada 설명하다 explain; account for; set out; ***Xege Ye tae-han kaeyorŭl sŏlmyŏnghada*** X에게 Y에 대한 개요를 설명하다 brief X on Y
sŏlmyŏnghal su ŏmnŭn 설명할 수 없는 inexplicable; unaccountable
sŏlmyŏng p'ail 설명파일 readme file
sŏlmyŏngsŏ 설명서 manual
sŏlssa 설사 diarrhea
sŏltchŏng 설정 institution, setting up
sŏlttŭk 설득 persuasion
sŏlttŭk'ada 설득하다 persuade
sŏlttŭngnyŏk innŭn 설득력 있는 convincing, persuasive
sŏlt'ang 설탕 sugar
sŏlt'ang-t'ong 설탕통 sugar bowl
sŏlt'ang-ŭl nŏt'a 설탕을 넣다 sugar; add sugar
sŏm 섬 island
sŏmgwang 섬광 flash
sŏmgwang chŏn-gu 섬광 전구 flashbulb
sŏmnyu 섬유 fiber
sŏmnyujil 섬유질 roughage
sŏmseham 섬세함 delicacy (*of fabric*)
sŏmsehan 섬세한 delicate, dainty; ***chinach'ige sŏmsehan*** 지나치게 섬세한 finicky
sŏmssaram 섬사람 islander
sŏmttŭk nollam 섬뜩 놀람 consternation
sŏmttŭk'an 섬뜩한 scary
sŏmun 서문 foreword, preface
sŏmyŏng 서명 signature
sŏmyŏnghada 서명하다 sign
sŏmyŏng-in 서명인 signatory
sŏmyŏnŭro 서면으로 in writing
sŏn 선 line; gland; (space) module; Zen; goodness
-sŏn -선 ship, vessel
sŏnbak 선박 boat, craft
sŏnbak soyuja 선박 소유자 shipowner
sŏnbal kwajŏng 선발 과정 selection process
sŏnban 선반 shelf; rack; lathe
sŏnbarhada 선발하다 choose, single out
sŏnbul 선불 advance (*money*) ◊ prepaid; ***sŏnbullo*** 선불로 cash in advance, cash up front
Sŏnbulgyo 선불교 Zen Buddhism
sŏnbul yogŭm 선불 요금 advance payment
sŏnburhada 선불하다 put down *deposit*
sŏnburŭi 선불의 prepaid
sŏnbyŏrhada 선별하다 screen (*for security reasons*)
sŏnch'e 선체 hull
sŏnch'ŏnjŏgin 선천적인 congenital,

hereditary
sŏnch'urhada 선출하다 vote in
sŏnch'wihada 선취하다 skim off
sŏndonghada 선동하다 stir up, arouse
sŏndongja 선동자 agitator
sŏndu 선두 lead (*in race*); ***sŏndue*(*sŏ*)** 선두에(서) in the lead, in front
sŏndu chuja 선두 주자 forerunner; pacemaker
sŏndue sŏda 선두에 서다 lead
sŏnduŭi 선두의 leading
sŏng 성 gender; surname; castle; ministry
sŏngbyŏk 성벽 rampart
sŏngbyŏrhoe 송별회 farewell party
Sŏng Chugan 성 주간 Holy Week
sŏngch'wi 성취 achievement
sŏngch'wihada 성취하다 accomplish, achieve
sŏngdae 성대 vocal cords
sŏngdang 성당 cathedral
sŏngdoch'ak 성도착 perversion
sŏngga 성가 hymn
sŏnggashige hada 성가시게 하다 annoy, provoke; bother
sŏnggashin 성가신 annoying; nagging; cumbersome
sŏngge 성게 sea urchin
sŏnggong 성공 success, hit
sŏnggonghada 성공하다 succeed, make it; prosper; ***...ŭl* / *rŭl hanŭn te sŏnggonghada*** ...을 / 를 하는 데 성공하다 succeed in doing
sŏnggonghaji mot'an 성공하지 못한 unsuccessful
sŏnggonghan 성공한 prosperous
sŏnggongtchŏgin 성공적인 successful
sŏnggongtchŏgŭro 성공적으로 successfully
sŏnggorham 성골함 shrine
sŏnggŭm 성금 donation, contribution
Sŏnggŭmnyoil 성금요일 Good Friday
sŏnggŭp'ada 성급하다 be impatient
sŏnggŭp'age 성급하게 impatiently
sŏnggŭp'am 성급함 impatience
sŏnggŭp'an 성급한 short-tempered, impatient; rash
sŏnggwan-gye 성관계 relationship (*sexual*)
sŏnggyŏgi choŭn 성격이 좋은 good-natured
Sŏnggyŏng 성경 Bible
sŏnggyo 성교 sexual intercourse, sex
sŏnggyohada 성교하다 have sex; ***sŏnggyorŭl hada*** 성교를 하다 have sex
sŏnghaeng 성행 epidemic
sŏngham 성함 name
sŏnghongnyŏl 성홍열 scarlet fever
sŏnghŭirong 성희롱 sexual harassment
sŏnghyang 성향 spirit; attitude; inclination, tendency; liking
sŏnghyŏng-oekkwa 성형외과 cosmetic surgery
sŏnghyŏng-oekkwa ŭisa 성형외과 의사 cosmetic surgeon, plastic surgeon
sŏnghyŏng susul 성형 수술 plastic surgery
sŏng-in 성인 adult (*over 20*) ◊ adult; saint
sŏng-i nada 성이 나다 get ruffled
sŏng-in kyoyuk 성인 교육 further education
sŏng-inŭi 성인의 adult (*over 20*)
sŏng-inyŏnghwa 성인영화 adult film
sŏngjang 성장 growth, development
sŏngjanghada 성장하다 grow (*of business*); dress up
sŏngjanghan tongmul 성장한 동물 adult animal
sŏngjiktcha 성직자 clergyman; priest; Reverend
sŏngjiktchadŭl 성직자들 clergy
sŏngjil 성질 characteristic, quality; (bad) temper
sŏngjiri koyak'an 성질이 고약한 vicious
sŏngjŏgŭl naeda 성적을 내다 grade, mark
sŏngjŏk 성적 grade, mark
sŏngjŏkp'yo 성적표 report card
sŏngjŏn 성전 sanctuary
Sŏngjogi 성조기 Stars and Stripes
sŏngkkal innŭn 성깔 있는 bad-tempered

sŏngkkwaga manŭn 성과가 많은 fruitful
sŏngkkyŏgŭl myosahada 성격을 묘사하다 characterize, describe
sŏngkkyŏk 성격 nature, character; personality; ***urinŭn sŏngkkyŏgi an mat-tta*** 우리는 성격이 안 맞다 we're not compatible; ***sŏngkkyŏgi nanp'ok'ada*** 성격이 난폭하다 have a violent temper
sŏng kwan-gyerŭl kajida 성 관계를 가지다 make love
sŏngk'ŭmsŏngk'ŭm kŏt-tta 성큼성큼 걷다 stride
sŏngmarŭn 성마른 petulant; prickly, irritable
sŏngmiga koyak'an 성미가 고약한 ill-natured
sŏngmi kŭp'an 성미 급한 bad-tempered, irritable
sŏngmyŏng 성명 declaration, statement; name (*on document*)
sŏngnada 성나다 be angry, be cross
sŏngnan 성난 angry, cross
sŏngnip'ada 성립하다 materialize; be formed; be concluded
sŏngnŭng 성능 capacity, performance
sŏngnŭng-i usuhan ch'a 성능이 우수한 차 performance car
sŏngnyang 성냥 match
sŏngnyangkkap 성냥갑 box of matches
sŏngnyŏn 성년 manhood, maturity
Sŏngnyŏng 성령 Holy Spirit
sŏn-gŏ 선거 election; the polls
sŏn-gŏil 선거일 election day
sŏn-gŏin 선거인 elector
sŏn-gŏ pangshik 선거 방식 electoral system
sŏn-gŏ undong 선거 운동 election campaign
sŏngppyŏng 성병 sexually transmitted disease
sŏng pullŭng 성 불능 impotence (*sexual*)
sŏngsaenghwal 성생활 sex life
sŏngshil 성실 sincerity
sŏngshirhada 성실하다 be sincere
sŏngshirhan 성실한 sincere
sŏngsŏ-ŭi 성서의 biblical
sŏngsŭrŏptta 성스럽다 be holy
sŏngsŭrŏun 성스러운 holy
sŏngsuk-kki 성숙기 maturity, adulthood
sŏngsuk'ada 성숙하다 be mature; ripen; reach maturity
sŏngsuk'am 성숙함 maturity
sŏngsuk'an 성숙한 mature, adult
sŏngtchŏgin 성적인 sexual
sŏngtchŏgŭro hŭironghada 성적으로 희롱하다 molest
sŏngtchŏgŭro hŭngbunhan 성적으로 흥분한 horny
sŏngtchŏgŭro hŭngbunshik'ida 성적으로 흥분시키다 turn on (*sexually*)
sŏngtchŏk hŭngmirŭl ilk'e hada 성적 흥미를 잃게 하다 turn off (*sexually*)
sŏngtchŏk maeryŏgi innŭn 성적 매력이 있는 sexually attractive
sŏngtchŏk yok-kku pulman 성적 욕구 불만 sexual frustration
Sŏngt'anjŏl 성탄절 Christmas; Christmas Day
sŏn-gŭm 선금 cash in advance
sŏn-guja 선구자 pioneer
sŏn-gujŏgin 선구적인 pioneering
sŏng-wŏn 성원 applause
sŏng-wŏnŭl ponaeda 성원을 보내다 applaud
sŏn-gyŏnjimyŏng 선견지명 foresight
sŏn-gyo 선교 bridge (*of ship*)
sŏn-gyosa 선교사 missionary
sŏnho 선호 preference
sŏnhohada 선호하다 prefer
sŏninjang 선인장 cactus
sŏnipkkyŏn 선입견 prejudice; preconception
sŏnjam 선잠 doze
sŏnjang 선장 captain, master, skipper
sŏnjin-guk 선진국 advanced country
sŏnjŏk 선적 shipping
sŏnjŏk hwamul 선적 화물 cargo
sŏnjŏk'ada 선적하다 ship
sŏnjŏn 선전 publicity; promotion; advertisement
sŏnjŏnhada 선전하다 publicize;

promote; advertise
sŏnjŏn hwalttong 선전 활동 propaganda
sŏnjŏn munkku 선전 문구 blurb
sŏnjŏnnyong 선전용 demo
sŏnjŏnnyong tisŭk'ŭ 선전용 디스크 demo disk
sŏnjŏn p'ogo 선전 포고 declaration of war
sŏnjŏn p'ogohada 선포 하다 declare war
sŏnmul 선물 gift, present
sŏnmul kyeyak 선물 계약 futures
sŏnmul shijang 선물 시장 futures market
sŏnmyŏngdo 선명도 resolution, sharpness
sŏnmyŏnghada 선명하다 be vivid
sŏnmyŏngham 선명함 brilliance; vividness
sŏnmyŏnghan 선명한 vivid
sŏnnyul 선율 melody
sŏnŏn 선언 declaration
sŏnŏnhada 선언하다 declare, proclaim
sŏnoe mot'ŏ 선외 모터 outboard motor
sŏnp'ung 선풍 whirlwind
sŏnp'unggi 선풍기 fan
sŏnp'ungŭl irŭk'ida 선풍을 이르키다 create a sensation
sŏnsaeng 선생 teacher
sŏnsaengnim 선생님 teacher; sir; Mr
sŏnsashidaeŭi 선사시대의 prehistoric
sŏnshil 선실 cabin
sŏnshim 선심 linesman
sŏnshimŭl ssŭnŭn tŭt'ada 선심을 쓰는 듯하다 patronize, be condescending toward
sŏnsŏ 선서 oath
sŏnsŏ chŭng-ŏn 선서 증언 deposition
sŏnsŏhada 선서하다 swear
sŏnsu 선수 athlete; player
sŏnsuch'ida 선수치다 outwit
sŏnsugwŏn 선수권 championship (*title*)
sŏnsugwŏn taehoe 선수권 대회 championship (*event*)
sŏnttŭt 선뜻 readily
sŏnt'aegŭi 선택의 optional, elective
sŏnt'aegŭi pŏmwi 선택의 범위 choice, selection
sŏnt'aek 선택 choice, selection
sŏnt'aek-kkwŏn 선택권 option
sŏnt'aekttoen 선택된 elected
sŏnt'aek'ada 선택하다 choose, select
sŏnŭiŭi 선의의 well-meaning; well-meant
sŏnŭl kŭt-tta 선을 긋다 mark out
sŏnŭrhaejida 서늘해지다 cool down
sŏnwŏn 선원 seaman
sŏnyŏl 선열 glandular fever
sŏpsshi 섭씨 Celsius; centigrade
sŏp'ing 서핑 surfing
sŏp'ing podŭ 서핑 보드 surfboard
sŏp'ung 서풍 west wind
sŏrap 서랍 drawer
sŏraptchang 서랍장 bureau, chest of drawers
sŏri 서리 frost
sŏriga naerinŭn 서리가 내리는 frosty
sŏrirŭl ŏpssaeda 서리를 없애다 defrost *freezer, windshield*
sŏro 서로 one another, each other
sŏro kwan-gyega innŭn 서로 관계가 있는 interrelated
sŏro mannŭn 서로 맞는 compatible
sŏro mannŭn chŏngdo 서로 맞는 정도 compatibility
sŏron 서론 introduction
sŏrŭn 서른 thirty
sŏrŭn pŏntchaeŭi 서른 번째의 thirtieth
sŏryu 서류 documentation, papers; document
sŏryu chŏlttan-gi 서류 절단기 shredder
sŏryuch'ŏl 서류철 file
sŏryuham 서류함 file cabinet
sŏryu kabang 서류 가방 briefcase
sŏshiktchi 서식지 habitat
sŏshin wangnae 서신 왕래 correspondence
sŏshin wangnaehada 서신 왕래하다 correspond
sŏsŏhi kkŭltta 서서히 끓다 simmer
sŏsŏhi kkŭnnada 서서히 끝나다 wind down, quieten down
sŏsŏhi sarajida 서서히 사라지다

melt away, vanish
sŏsŏngdaeda 서성대다 prowl
sŏsŭp'enshyŏn 서스펜션 suspension
sŏsŭp'ensŭ 서스펜스 suspense
sŏtchogesŏ punŭn 서쪽에서 부는 westerly *wind*
sŏtchogŭi 서쪽의 western; westerly
sŏtchogŭro 서쪽으로 west, westward
sŏtchok 서쪽 west; ***...e sŏtchoge*** ...의 서쪽에 west of
Sŏttal Kŭmŭmnal 섣달 그믐날 New Year's Eve
sŏt'un 서툰 rusty
sŏt'urŭda 서투르다 be bad at; be out of practice
sŏt'urŭge hada 서투르게 하다 fumble; make a mess of
sŏt'urŭge mandŭlda 서투르게 만들다 bungle
sŏt'urŭn 서투른 bad, poor; clumsy
Sŏul 서울 Seoul
sŏyak 서약 vow
Sŏyang 서양 the West ◊ Western
sŏyang changgi 서양 장기 checkers
sŏyang changgip'an 서양 장기판 checkerboard
sŏyanghwadoen 서양화된 westernized
Sŏyang saram 서양 사람 Westerner
sŏye 서예 calligraphy
so 소 cattle
soakkwa 소아과 pediatrics
soakkwa ŭisa 소아과 의사 pediatrician
soamabi 소아마비 polio
sobangch'a 소방차 fire truck
sobangsŏ 소방서 fire department
sobangsu 소방수 firefighter, fireman
sobi 소비 consumption
sobihada 소비하다 consume, expend, use
sobija 소비자 consumer, purchaser
sobija sahoe 소비자 사회 consumer society
sobip'um 소비품 consumer goods
sobyŏn 소변 urine
sobyŏnŭl poda 소변을 보다 urinate
soch'aektcha 소책자 booklet
soch'ong 소총 rifle
sodae 소대 platoon
sodok'ada 소독하다 sterilize, disinfect
sodong 소동 disturbance, uproar
sodongnyak 소독약 disinfectant, antiseptic
sodŭk 소득 income, earnings
sodŭksse 소득세 income tax
soe 쇠 iron
soech'angssal 쇠창살 grill, grille
soegogi 쇠고기 beef
soesalttae 쇠살대 grate
soesasŭl 쇠사슬 chain
soet'oe 쇠퇴 decay
soet'oehada 쇠퇴하다 decay; go downhill; slump
soet'oehanŭn 쇠퇴하는 decaying, dying
sogae 소개 introduction
sogaehada 소개하다 introduce, present
sogak'ae pŏrida 태워버리다 burn down
sogam 소감 opinion; sentiment
sogangno 소각로 incinerator
...soge ...속에 in
sogida 속이다 deceive, cheat; fiddle; rip off; ***namŭl soginŭn*** 남을 속이는 deceitful
sogim 속임 deception
sogimsu 속임수 deceit, cheat; hoax; trick; ***...ŭi sogimsue kŏllida*** ...의 속임수에 걸리다 fall for, be deceived by
sogimsuro yuhok'ada 속임수로 유혹하다 lure
sogimsurŭl ssŭda 속임수를 쓰다 cheat
sogi pich'inŭn 속이 비치는 transparent
sogi pin 속이 빈 hollow
sogi shiwŏnhajiyo! 속이 시원하지요! I hope you're satisfied!
sogŏ 속어 slang
sogogi kukppap 소고기 국밥 beef soup with rice
sogot 속옷 underwear; briefs
sogŭl ch'ae-uda 속을 채우다 stuff
sogŭl ch'aeunŭn chaeryo 속을 채우는 재료 stuffing
sogŭl ppaenaeda 속을 빼내다 core
sogŭm 소금 salt
sogŭm kŭrŭt 소금 그릇 saltcellar

sogŭp'anŭn 소급하는 retroactive
sogŭp'ayŏ chŏgyongshik'ida 소급하여 적용시키다 backdate
sogŭro ssaida 속으로 쌓이다 smolder *fig*
sohorhan 소홀한 negligent
sohwa 소화 digestion
sohwagi 소화기 fire extinguisher
sohwahada 소화하다 digest, assimilate; extinguish, put out
sohwahagi ŏryŏun 소화하기 어려운 indigestible
sohwajŏn 소화전 fire hydrant
sohwa kyet'ong 소화 계통 digestive system
sohwanhada 소환하다 call; summons, subpoena; recall
sohwantchang 소환장 subpoena, summons
sohwa pullyang 소화 불량 indigestion
sohyŏng 소형 small size
sohyŏng chadongch'a 소형 자동차 subcompact (car)
sohyŏngch'a 소형차 compact (car)
sohyŏnghwahada 소형화하다 downsize
sohyŏng pŏsŭ 소형 버스 minibus
soin 소인 postmark
sojangp'um 소장품 collection
sojil 소질 talent; temperament;
sojip'ada 소집하다 call, convene; summon
sojip'um 소지품 belongings
sojŏngŭi 소정의 prescribed; ***sojŏngŭi ch'aek*** 소정의 책 set book
soju 소주 distilled liquor
sojunghan saram 소중한 사람 treasure (*person*)
sojunghi hada 소중히 하다 take care of; cherish
sojunghi kanjik'ada 소중히 간직하다 cherish
sojunghi yŏgida 소중히 여기다 value
sok 속 core; filling; stuffing
sokch'ima 속치마 underskirt
sok-kkan shinmun 석간 신문 evening paper
sok-kki 속기 shorthand
sok-kki shwiun 속기 쉬운 gullible
sokkŏsŏ mandŭlda 섞어서 만들다 concoct
sokppo 속보 news flash
sokp'yŏn 속편 sequel
sokssagida 속삭이다 murmur; whisper
sokssagim 속삭임 murmur; whisper
sokssanghada 속상하다 be upsetting
sokssanghan 속상한 upsetting
sokssŏng 속성 attribute
sokssŏng taiŏt'ŭ 속성 다이어트 crash diet
sokttam 속담 proverb, saying
sokttanhada 속단하다 come to a hasty conclusion
soktto 속도 speed; pace, tempo; velocity
soktto chehan 속도 제한 speed limit
soktto chojŏl changch'i 속도 조절 장치 throttle
sokttogye 속도계 speedometer
soktto naeda 속도 내다 speed up
sok'et 소켓 socket
sol 솔 brush, scrubbing brush
solgi 솔기 seam
soljirhada 솔질하다 brush
solmyŏnghal su ŏmnŭn 설명할 수 없는 mystifying
solppang-ul 솔방울 cone
solssŏnhada 솔선하다 lead the way; ***muŏsŭl solssŏnhaesŏ hada*** 무엇을 솔선해서 하다 do sth on one's own initiative
soltchik'ada 솔직하다 be frank, be candid; be blunt; be straight; be outspoken; ***soltchik'i malhamyŏn*** 솔직히 말하면 to be frank
soltchik'age 솔직하게 bluntly, plainly; honestly
soltchik'i 솔직히 frankly
som 솜 absorbent cotton
somae 소매 sleeve
somaech'igi 소매치기 shoplifter; pickpocket
somaega ŏmnŭn 소매가 없는 sleeveless
somae kagyŏk 소매 가격 retail price
somaero 소매로 retail; ***...e somaero p'alda*** ...에 소매로 팔다 retail at
somaesang-in 소매상인 shopkeeper; retailer

somaetppuri 소맷부리 cuff
somo chingmul 소모 직물 worsted
somsat'ang 솜사탕 cotton candy
somsshi 솜씨 workmanship
somsshi choŭn 솜씨 좋은 deft
somsshi innŭn 솜씨 있는 workmanlike
somt'ŏlgat'ŭn 솜털같은 fluffy
somun 소문 rumor
somyŏl 소멸 disappearance; demise
somyŏrhada 소멸하다 die out
son 손 hand; ***soni tach'i annŭn kose*** 손이 닿지 않는 곳에 out of reach; ***soni tannŭn kose*** 손이 닿는 곳에 within reach; ***son tteseyo!*** 손 떼세요! hands off!; ***son tŭrŏ!*** 손 들어! hands up!
sonagi 소나기 shower (*of rain*)
sonamu 소나무 pine (tree)
sonaraet saram 손아랫 사람 junior, subordinate
sonaraeŭi 손아래의 junior, subordinate
sonbal 손발 limb
sondokki 손도끼 hatchet
sone chwida 손에 쥐다 purchase, grip
son-gabang 손가방 purse, pocketbook
song-aji 송아지 calf
songaji kogi 송아지 고기 veal
songbyŏrhoe 송별회 leaving party
songgŭmhada 송금하다 transfer
songgŭmhwan 송금환 transfer
song-i 송이 cluster ◊ *countword for flowers, bunches of grapes etc*
songmaŭmŭl t'ŏnot'a 속마음을 터놓다 open up (*of person*)
songmul 속물 snob
songmurŭi 속물의 snobbish
songnunssŏp 속눈썹 eyelash
songnyŏgŭl naeda 속력을 내다 lengthen one's stride
songnyŏgŭl nŭllyŏgada 속력을 늘려가다 gather speed
song-ŏ 송어 trout
son-gŏhada 선거하다 elect
songp'yŏn 송편 rice cake steamed with pine needles
songshin-gi 송신기 transmitter
songshinhada 송신하다 transmit, beam
songwanhada 송환하다 repatriate
sonhae 손해 harm; loss
sonhae paesanggŭm 손해 배상금 damages LAW
sonik pun-gijŏm 손익 분기점 break-even point
sonil 손일 manual labor
sonja 손자 grandson
sonjabi 손잡이 handle; knob; stem (*of glass*)
sonjirhada 손질하다 trim; groom; touch up
sonkkabang 손가방 pocketbook, purse
sonkkaragŭro karik'ida 손가락으로 가리키다 point; point to
sonkkarak 손가락 finger; ***kŭnyŏnŭn sonkkaraktto kkadak'aji annŭnda*** 그녀는 손가락도 까닥하지 않는다 she never lifts a finger
sonkkarak kkŭt 손가락 끝 fingertip
sonkkarak madi 손가락 마디 knuckle
sonmok 손목 wrist
sonmok shigye 손목 시계 wrist watch
sonnim 손님 guest; visitor; company
sonnimnyong ch'imshil 손님용 침실 guestroom
sonnyŏ 손녀 granddaughter
sonppadagŭro ch'alssak ttaerida 손바닥으로 찰싹 때리다 smack, spank
sonppadak 손바닥 palm (*of hand*)
sonppadangmanhan 손바닥만한 scanty
sonsang 손상 damage
sonsangdoeji anŭn 손상되지 않은 undamaged, intact
sonsangshik'ida 손상시키다 damage, prejudice
sonsangshik'inŭn 손상시키는 damaging
sonshil 손실 loss
sonshiri k'ŭn 손실이 큰 costly
sonsugŏn 손수건 handkerchief
sonsu mandŭlgi 손수 만들기 DIY, do-it-yourself
sontchisŭro marhada 손짓으로 말하다 gesticulate

sontchit 손짓 gesture
sontchit'ayŏ purŭda 손짓하여 부르다 beckon
sont'op 손톱 fingernail
sont'opkkak-kki 손톱깎이 nail clippers
sont'op kkangnŭn kawi 손톱 깎는 가위 nail scissors
sont'optchul 손톱줄 nail file
sonŭl hŭndŭlda 손을 흔들다 wave; wave to
sonŭl ppŏtch'ida 손을 뻗치다 reach out
sonŭl taeda 손을 대다 touch; feel up (*sexually*); ***chamkkan sonŭl taeda*** 잠깐 손을 대다 dabble in
sonŭl tteda 손을 떼다 back out
sonŭro 손으로 by hand
sonŭro hanŭn 손으로 하는 manual
sonŭro manjida 손으로 만지다 paw
sonŭro ssŭn 손으로 쓴 handwritten
sonŭro tŏdŭmtta 손으로 더듬다 grope
sonwiŭi 손위의 senior, older
sonyŏ 소녀 girl
sonyŏn 소년 juvenile; boy
sonyŏn-kat'ŭn 소년같은 boyish
sonyŏn pŏmjoe 소년 범죄 juvenile delinquency
sonyŏn pŏmjoeja 소년 범죄자 juvenile delinquent
sonyŏnŭi 소년의 juvenile
sonyŏ tanwŏn 소녀단원 girl guide
so-oegam 소외감 sense of alienation
so-oeja 소외자 outcast
sop'a 소파 couch, sofa
sop'a sett'ŭ 소파 셋트 (three-piece) suite
sop'ashik ch'imdae 소파식 침대 sofa bed
sop'o 소포 parcel, package
sop'ŭrano 소프라노 soprano
sop'ŭt'ŭweŏ 소프트웨어 software
sop'um 소품 (stage) prop
sop'ung 소풍 outing, trip; picnic
soran 소란 uproar, tumult, commotion; scene; ***soranŭl p'iuda*** 소란을 피우다 make a scene
soranhada 소란하다 be noisy
soranhan 소란한 loud, noisy
soransŭrŏun 소란스러운 tumultuous
sori 소리 sound, noise; ***k'ŭn soriro iltta*** 큰 소리로 읽다 read out loud; ***k'ŭn soriro marhada*** 큰 소리로 말하다 speak up, speak louder
sorich'ida 소리치다 shout; scream
sorich'yŏ purŭda 소리쳐 부르다 call, call out, shout
sorijirŭm 소리지름 shouting
sorinop'yŏ ut-tta 소리높여 웃다 howl (with laughter)
sori ŏmnŭn 소리 없는 silent
soriŏpsshi kŏt-tta 소리없이 걷다 pad, move quietly
soriptcha 소립자 (elementary) particle
sorirŭl naeŏ 소리를 내어 aloud
sorŭm 소름 gooseflesh; ***narŭl sorŭmkkich'ige handa*** 나를 소름끼치게 한다 it gives me gooseflesh
soryang 소량 dab, splash; ***soryang-ŭi...*** 소량의 ... a little ...
Soryŏn 소련 Soviet Union
soryŏng 소령 major MIL
sosaeng 소생 revival
sosaengshik'ida 소생시키다 revive, resuscitate
sosa orŭda 솟아 오르다 soar; lift off; rise
soshiji 소시지 sausage
soshik 소식 news; ***...(ŭ)ro put'ŏ soshigŭl tŭt-tta*** ...(으)로 부터 소식을 듣다 have news from, hear from
sosŏl 소설 novel; fiction
sosŏlga 소설가 novelist
sosong 소송 lawsuit
sosong sakkŏn 소송 사건 court case
sossŭ 소스 sauce; dressing (*for salad*)
sosŭrach'ige hada 소스라치게 하다 petrify, terrify
sosŭrach'in 소스라친 petrified
sosu 소수 decimal
sosu minjok 소수 민족 ethnic minority
sosup'a 소수파 minority
sosup'aida 소수파이다 be in the minority
sosutchŏm 소수점 decimal point
sot'anghada 소탕하다 mop up

sot'ongdoeda 소통되다 flow
sot'ŭ 소트 sort COMPUT
soŭm 소음 sound, noise
souju 소우주 microcosm
sowi 소위 so-called *pej* ◊ second lieutenant
sowŏn 소원 wish
sowŏnhada 소원하다 be estranged; petition
sowŏnhaejin 소원해진 estranged
sowŏnhan 소원한 distant, aloof
soyo 소요 disturbances, civil unrest
soyongdori 소용돌이 whirlpool
soyongŏmnŭn 소용없는 pointless, futile, useless; ***noryŏk'aedo soyong-ŏpssŏyo*** 노력해도 소용없어요 it's pointless trying
soyu 소유 possession, ownership
soyuhada 소유하다 have, own; possess
soyuja 소유자 owner; holder
soyukkwŏn 소유권 ownership
soyukkyŏk 소유격 possessive GRAM
soyumul 소유물 belongings, things; property; possession
soyuŭi 소유의 own
soyuyogi kanghan 소유욕이 강한 possessive
ssaaollida 쌓아올리다 stack, heap up; build up
ssaa ollin tŏmi 쌓아 올린 더미 heap
ssada 싸다 wrap; pack; envelop; be cheap; be fast; excrete
ssaguryŏmulgŏn 싸구려물건 cheap goods
ssain nundŏmi 쌓인 눈더미 snowdrift
ssak 싹 germ; bud
ssal 쌀 rice (*uncooked*)
ssalongch'a 쌀롱차 sedan MOT
ssalssarhada 쌀쌀하다 be chilly
ssalssarhan 쌀쌀한 chilly; fresh; icy; standoffish
ssamjit-tton 쌈짓돈 loose change
ssan 싼 inexpensive, cheap; low
ssang 쌍 pair; couple; ***namnyŏ han ssang*** 남녀 한 쌍 couple
ssang-an-gyŏng 쌍안경 binoculars
ssangdung-i 쌍둥이 twins
ssang-ŭro toen 쌍으로 된 double
ssan mulgŏn 싼 물건 cheap goods
ssaragi nun 싸라기 눈 sleet
ssat'a 쌓다 stack; run up *debts*
ssauda 싸우다 fight, battle; combat; ***...ŭl / rŭl wihae ssauda*** ...을 / 를 위해 싸우다 fight for
ssaum 싸움 fight, scrap, brawl; struggle; row
ssaumjirhada 싸움질하다 brawl
ssayŏjida 쌓여지다 accumulate, build up
sseda 세다 be strong; turn gray; count
ssekssihan 섹시한 sexy
ssekssŭ 섹스 sex
ssen 센 strong
sshi 씨 Mr; Ms; seed, pip, stone; ***Hong Kildongsshi*** 홍길동씨 Mr Kildong Hong; ***I Sunmisshi*** 이순미씨 Ms Sunmi Lee
sshibal! V 씨발! fuck!
sshidaek 씨댁 care of
sshidirom 씨디롬 CD-ROM
sshidirom tŭraibŭ 씨디롬 드라이브 CD-ROM drive
sshiep'ŭsshi 씨에프씨 CFC, chlorofluorocarbon
sshigŭn-gŏrida 씨근거리다 wheeze
sshijok 씨족 clan
sshing chinagada 씽 지나가다 whizz by
sshing pulda 씽 불다 whistle (*of wind*)
sshiptta 씹다 chew
sshiriŏl p'ot'ŭ 씨리얼 포트 serial port
sshirŭm 씨름 (Korean-style) wrestling
sshirŭmhada 씨름하다 tackle *problem*; grapple with; wrestle
sshirŭm kyŏnggi 씨름 경기 (Korean-style) wrestling match
sshirŭm sŏnsu 씨름 선수 (Korean-style) wrestler
sshit-tta 씻다 clean; wash
sshit'ŭ 시트 sheet
ssŏbŏrida 써버리다 use, consume
ssŏgŭn 썩은 rotten, bad, rancid
ssŏk-kki shwiun 썩기 쉬운 perishable
ssŏktta 썩다 rot; go bad
ssŏlda 썰다 chop

ssŏlmae 썰매 sled(ge), toboggan; sleigh
ssŏlmul 썰물 ebb tide; low tide
ssŏlmurida 썰물이다 the tide is out
ssŏn k'urim 썬 크림 sun cream
ssŏnt'en 썬텐 suntan
ssoa ttŏrŏttŭrida 쏘아 떨어뜨리다 shoot down, bring down
ssoda 쏘다 fire; shoot; sting; ***ch'ongŭl ssoda*** 총을 쏘다 fire a gun
ssoda put-tta 쏟아 붓다 pour
ssonsalgach'i chinagada 쏜살같이 지나가다 fly past, pass quickly (*of time*)
ssonsalgach'i naragada 쏜살같이 날아가다 dart
ssŭda 쓰다 use; spend; write; put on *glasses*; be bitter
ssŭdadŭmtta 쓰다듬다 stroke, caress; smooth *hair*
ssŭgi 쓰기 writing; use
ssŭiuda 씌우다 coat, cover; get on; crown *tooth*
ssŭium 씌움 coating, layer
ssŭlda 쓸다 sweep
ssŭlgae 쓸개 gall bladder
ssŭlmo 쓸모 usefulness
ssŭlmoinnŭn 쓸모있는 useful
ssŭlmoŏmnŭn 쓸모없는 useless, worthless; trashy; waste *land*, *material*
ssŭl su innŭn 쓸 수 있는 usable
ssŭltteŏmnŭn 쓸데없는 futile; idle *threat*
ssŭn 쓴 bitter
ssŭrarige hada 쓰라리게 하다 embitter
ssŭrebatkki 쓰레받기 dustpan
ssŭregi 쓰레기 garbage, litter; scum (*people*); crap
ssŭregi p'yegijang 쓰레기 폐기장 garbage dump
ssŭregi sujip 쓰레기 수집 garbage collection
ssŭregi tŏmi 쓰레기 더미 scrap heap
ssŭregi t'ong 쓰레기 통 garbage can, trashcan
ssŭregi t'ongno 쓰레기 통로 garbage chute
ssŭrŏjida 쓰러지다 fall, fall over; fall down; slump
ssŭrŏttŭrida 쓰러뜨리다 topple, bring down
ssukssuk charada 쑥쑥 자라다 shoot up (*of children*)
ssukttŭm 쑥뜸 moxibustion
ssurŏ moŭda 쓸어 모으다 sweep up
ssushida 쑤시다 prod, poke; have a stitch; hurt, smart
ssushyŏ nŏt'a 쑤셔 넣다 jam, ram
sswabŏrida 쏴버리다 blaze away (*with gun*)
sswaegi 쐐기 wedge
sŭch'idŭt chinagada 스치듯 지나가다 skim
sŭk'ach'i 스카치 Scotch
sŭk'aen 스캔 scan
sŭk'aendŭl 스캔들 scandal
sŭk'aenhada 스캔하다 scan; scan in
sŭk'aenŏ 스캐너 scanner
sŭk'airain 스카이라인 skyline
sŭk'ap'ŭ 스카프 scarf
sŭk'aut'ŭ 스카우트 (boy) scout
sŭk'ech'i 스케치 sketch
sŭk'ech'ibuk 스케치북 sketchbook
sŭk'ech'ihada 스케치하다 sketch
sŭk'eit'ŭ 스케이트 skate
sŭk'eit'ŭbodŭ 스케이트보드 skateboard
sŭk'eit'ŭjang 스케이트장 ice rink
sŭk'eit'ŭ t'ada 스케이트 타다 skate
sŭk'eit'ŭ t'agi 스케이트 타기 skating
sŭk'i 스키 ski
sŭk'i chip'ang-i 스키 지팡이 ski pole
sŭk'i hwaltchuro 스키 활주로 ski run
sŭk'i k'ŭrosŭk'ŏnt'ŭri 스키 크로스컨트리 cross-country skiing
sŭk'i lip'ŭt'ŭ 스키 리프트 ski lift
sŭk'in taibing 스킨 다이빙 skin diving
sŭk'i t'ada 스키 타다 ski
sŭk'i t'agi 스키 타기 skiing
sŭk'it'o 스키토 ski tow
Sŭk'ot'ŭllaendŭ 스코틀랜드 Scotland ◊ Scottish
sŭk'ŭraep puk 스크랩 북 scrapbook
sŭk'ŭrin 스크린 screen
sŭk'ŭrin t'esŭt'ŭ 스크린 테스트 screen test

sŭk'ubŏ taibing 스쿠버 다이빙 scuba diving
sŭk'ut'ŏ 스쿠터 motorscooter
sŭk'wŏshi 스쿼시 squash SP
sŭlgaegol 슬개골 kneecap
sŭlgŭmŏni 슬그머니 stealthily
sŭllaeshwi 슬래쉬 slash, oblique
sŭllaidŭ 슬라이드 slide, transparency
sŭlleit'ŭ 슬레이트 slate
sŭllip'ing paek 슬리핑 백 sleeping bag
sŭllip'ŏ 슬리퍼 slipper
sŭllogŏn 슬로건 slogan
sŭllot mŏshin 슬롯 머신 slot machine
sŭlloumoshŏn 슬로우모션 slow motion; action replay
sŭlp'ŏhada 슬퍼하다 lament, mourn; ***sŭlp'ŏhajima*** 슬퍼하지마 don't be sad
sŭlp'ŭda 슬프다 be sad
sŭlp'ŭge 슬프게 sadly
sŭlp'ŭm 슬픔 sadness
sŭlp'ŭme chamgin 슬픔에 잠긴 mournful
sŭlp'ŭn 슬픈 sad
sŭltchŏk kajida 슬쩍 가지다 pocket, take
sŭltchŏk kajyŏgada 슬쩍 가져가다 sneak, steal
sŭltchŏk nagada 슬쩍 나가다 make oneself scarce
sŭmaeshi 스매시 smash (*in tennis*)
sŭmiŏ shihŏm 스미어 시험 smear MED
sŭmogŭ 스모그 smog
sŭmul 스물 twenty
sŭmu pŏntchaeŭi 스무 번째의 twentieth
sŭmyŏnaoda 스며나오다 ooze
sŭnaep sajin 스냅 사진 snap, snapshot
sŭnggaek 승객 passenger; occupant
sŭnggaeksŏk 승객석 passenger seat
sŭngganggi 승강기 elevator
sŭng-in 승인 approval
sŭng-inhada 승인하다 approve; recognize; grant
sŭng-in patta 승인 받다 pass; gain approval
sŭngjin 승진 promotion
sŭngjinhada 승진하다 promote
sŭngma 승마 riding; horse, mount
sŭngmahada 승마하다 ride *horse*
sŭngmuwŏn 승무원 cabin crew, flight crew
sŭngmuwŏn chŏnwŏn 승무원 전원 crew
sŭngmuwŏnshil 승무원실 cabin
sŭngnak 승낙 approval, blessing
sŭngni 승리 win, victory; triumph; ***...e taehae sŭngnihada*** ...에 대해 승리하다 win a victory over
sŭngnihan 승리한 victorious
sŭngnija 승리자 victor
sŭnok'ŭl 스노클 snorkel
sŭnou ch'ein 스노우 체인 snow chains
sŭpkki 습기 humidity; moisture
sŭpkkich'an 습기찬 damp
sŭpkki innŭn 습기 있는 moist
sŭpkkwan 습관 practice, custom, habit; ***kŭŭi sŭpkkwanŭro*** 그의 습관으로 as was his custom; ***sŭpkkwani toeda*** 습관이 되다 become a habit; ***...nŭn sŭpkkwani tŭlda*** ...는 습관이 들다 take to ...ing, get into the habit of ...ing
sŭpkkwanjŏgin 습관적인 customary, habitual
sŭpkkyŏk 습격 assault, attack
sŭpp'o 습포 compress MED
sŭptchi 습지 marsh
sŭptchin 습진 eczema
sŭptchiŭi 습지의 marshy
sŭpttŭk'ada 습득하다 acquire
sŭp'ai 스파이 spy
sŭp'ai haeng-wi 스파이 행위 espionage
sŭp'aijisŭl hada 스파이짓을 하다 spy
sŭp'an 습한 humid
sŭp'eidŭ 스페이드 spades
Sŭp'ein 스페인 Spain ◊ Spanish
Sŭp'einŏ 스페인어 Spanish (*language*)
sŭp'eisŭ pa 스페이스 바 space bar
sŭp'iamint'ŭ 스피아민트 spearmint
sŭp'ik'ŏ 스피커 speaker
sŭp'och'ŭ 스포츠 sport
sŭp'och'ŭin 스포츠인 athlete
sŭp'och'ŭ kija 스포츠 기자 sports journalist

sŭp'och'ŭ k'a 스포츠 카 sportscar
sŭp'och'ŭ nyusŭ 스포츠 뉴스 sports news
sŭp'och'ŭran 스포츠란 sports page
sŭp'onji 스폰지 sponge
sŭp'onji komu 스폰지 고무 foam rubber
sŭp'onji k'eik'ŭ 스폰지 케이크 sponge cake
sŭp'otŭrait'ŭ 스포트라이트 spotlight
sŭp'ot'ihan 스포티한 sporty
sŭp'ŭredŭshit'ŭ 스프레드시트 spreadsheet
sŭp'ŭrei 스프레이 aerosol, spray
sŭrasoni 스라소니 lynx
sŭrillŏmul 스릴러물 thriller
sŭroin 스로인 throw-in
Sŭsŭng-ŭi nal 스승의 날 Teachers' Day
sŭsŭro 스스로 by oneself
sŭt'a 스타 star
sŭt'aillisŭt'ŭ 스타일리스트 (hair)stylist
sŭt'ak'ing 스타킹 stocking
sŭt'eik'ŭ 스테이크 steak
sŭt'eindŭ kŭllasŭ 스테인드 글라스 stained glass
sŭt'einlesŭ 스테인레스 stainless steel
sŭt'eip'ŭl kŏn 스테이플 건 staple gun
sŭt'ereo 스테레오 stereo
sŭt'eroidŭ 스테로이드 steroids
sŭt'ik'ŏ 스티커 sticker
sŭt'im tarimi 스팀 다리미 steam iron
sŭt'ŏnt'ŭmaen 스턴트맨 stuntman
sŭt'obŭ 스토브 stove
sŭt'ok'ŏ 스토커 stalker
sŭt'op lait'ŭ 스톱 라이트 stoplight
sŭt'op wŏch'i 스톱 워치 stopwatch
sŭt'ŭraik'ŏ 스트라이커 striker
sŭt'ŭraik'ŭ 스트라이크 strike
sŭt'ŭreit'ŭ 스트레이트 straight (up) *whiskey etc*
sŭt'ŭresŭ 스트레스 stress; ***sŭt'ŭresŭrŭl pat-tta*** 스트레스를 받다 be under stress; ***sŭt'ŭresŭga it-tta*** 스트레스가 있다 be under pressure
sŭt'ŭresŭ chojŏlppŏp 스트레스 조절법 stress management
sŭt'ŭresŭga shimhan 스트레스가 심한 stressful
sŭt'ŭresŭrŭl shimhage pannŭn 스트레스를 심하게 받는 stressed out
sŭt'ŭripssho 스트립쇼 strip show, striptease
sŭt'ŭrip'ŏ 스트리퍼 stripper
sŭt'ŭro 스트로 straw
sŭt'yu 스튜 stew
sŭt'yudio pakkŭi pangsong 스튜디오 밖의 방송 outside broadcast
sŭt'yuŏdissŭ 스튜어디스 air hostess, stewardess
Sŭweden 스웨덴 Sweden ◊ Swedish
Sŭweden mal 스웨덴 말 Swedish
Sŭweden saram 스웨덴 사람 Swede
Sŭwedenŭi 스웨덴의 Swedish
sŭweidŭ 스웨이드 suede
sŭwet'ŏ 스웨터 sweater
sŭwet'ŭ shyŏch'ŭ 스웨트 셔츠 sweatshirt
sŭwich'i 스위치 switch
Sŭwisŭ 스위스 Switzerland ◊ Swiss
sŭwit'ŭ 스위트 suite
su 수 number; figure; quantity; move (*in chess*) ◊ hydro...
su 수: ***...l su it-tta*** ...ㄹ 수 있다 can; ***...l su ŏptta*** ...ㄹ 수 없다 cannot
suabŭi 수압의 hydraulic
suaek 수액 sap
subak 수박 water melon
subanhada 수반하다 involve, mean
subi 수비 defense SP
subisu 수비수 defense player
subunkonggŭpp'aek 수분공급팩 moisturizing face mask
subyŏng 수병 sailor
such'aehwa 수채화 watercolor
such'aehwa mulkkam 수채화 물감 watercolor
such'iga toeda 수치가 되다 disgrace
such'ishim 수치심 shame; ***...e such'ishimŭl an-gyŏjuda*** ...에 수치심을 안겨주다 bring shame on
such'isŭrŏptta 수치스럽다 be disgraceful
such'isŭrŏun 수치스러운 disgraceful, scandalous
such'ŏk'an 수척한 emaciated; gaunt; haggard
su ch'ŏnŭi 수 천의 thousands of

such'uk p'ojang 수축 포장 shrink-wrapping
such'uk'ada 수축하다 contract, shrink
such'uk p'ojanghada 수축 포장하다 shrink-wrap
such'ul 수출 export, exporting
such'ulguk 수출국 exporter (*country*)
such'ul k'aemp'ein 수출 캠페인 export campaign
such'ulp'um 수출품 export
such'urhada 수출하다 export
such'urŏptcha 수출업자 exporter (*person*)
such'wiin 수취인 recipient, receiver; payee
suda 수다 chatter
sudajaeng-i 수다쟁이 chatterbox
sudal 수달 otter
sudan 수단 means, way
sudasŭrŏun 수다스러운 chatty
suda ttŏlda 수다 떨다 chatter, talk
sudo 수도 capital (*of country*); metropolis; waterworks
sudongjŏgin 수동적인 passive
sudong pŭreik'ŭ 수동 브레이크 parking brake
sudongt'ae 수동태 passive GRAM
sudosa 수도사 monk
sudosŭng kat'ŭn 수도승 같은 monastic
sudowŏn 수도원 monastery; convent; abbey
sudu 수두 chicken pox
sugaeng 수갱 shaft
sugamja 수감자 inmate
suganghada 수강하다 take a course
sugap 수갑 handcuffs
sugida 숙이다 bow, lower
sugŏjip 숙어집 phrasebook
sugŏn 수건 towel; washcloth
sugŏn kŏri 수건 걸이 towel rail
sugo 수고 effort, struggle; ***sugo-haseyo*** 수고하세요 keep up the good work (*when taking one's leave of s.o. who is working*)
sugong 수공 handiwork
sugong-ŏptcha 수공업자 artisan
sugongp'um 수공품 handiwork; handmade goods
sugong-ŭi 수공의 handmade
sugong-ye 수공예 handicraft
sugorŭl akkiji annŭn 수고를 아끼지 않는 painstaking
sugŭrŏdŭlda 수그러들다 die down
sugu 수구 water polo
suhaenghada 수행하다 conduct, carry out
suhage nŭnghan 수학에 능한 mathematical
suhagŭi 수학의 mathematical
suhak 수학 mathematics, math
suhaktcha 수학자 mathematician
suhamul pogwanso 수하물 보관소 (baggage) checkroom
suhoja 수호자 protector
suhwa 수화 sign language
suhwagi 수화기 receiver TELEC
suhwak 수확 crop
suhwak'ada 수확하다 reap
suhwamul 수화물 baggage; luggage; hand baggage
suhwamul k'ŭlleim 수화물 클레임 baggage reclaim
suhwamul pogwantchŭng 수화물 보관증 baggage check
suhwamul unbanch'a 수화물 운반차 baggage cart
suhwamul yŏlch'a 수화물 열차 baggage car
suhwa pŏt'ŭn 수화 버튼 hook TELEC
suhyŏl 수혈 blood transfusion
suigi choŭn 수익이 좋은 profitable
suibi ch'ungbunhan 수입이 충분한 financially comfortable
suik 수익 proceeds
suikssŏng 수익성 profitability
suimnyo 수임료 retainer
suip 수입 import; receipts FIN
suiptcha 수입자 importer
suip'ada 수입하다 import
sujang 수장 burial at sea
suji 수지 resin
sujiga mat-tta 수지가 맞다 be profitable, pay
sujigŭi 수직의 vertical; perpendicular
sujigŭro ttŏrŏjida 수직으로 떨어지다 plummet
sujip 수집 collection
sujipkka 수집가 collector
sujip'ada 수집하다 collect

sujŏ 수저 spoon and chopsticks
sujŏng 수정 amendment, modification, revision; crystal
sujŏng-aek 수정액 whiteout, correcting fluid
sujŏnghada 수정하다 amend, revise
sujŏngjuŭi 수정주의 revisionism
sujŏngshik'ida 수정시키다 fertilize
sujubŏhada 수줍어하다 be shy
sujubŏhanŭn 수줍어하는 shy; coy
sujubŭm 수줍음 shyness
sujun 수준 level
sujung hohŭpkki 수중 호흡기 air cylinder
sujung-iksŏn 수중익선 hydrofoil
sujung-ŭi 수중의 aquatic
sukch'ŏng 숙청 purge
sukch'ŏnghada 숙청하다 purge
sukch'wi 숙취 hangover
suk-kko 숙고 consideration, thought
suk-kkohada 숙고하다 contemplate, think about, deliberate; debate
sukppak shisŏl 숙박 시설 accommodations
sukssŏng 숙성 ripeness
sukssŏnghan 숙성한 ripe; mellow
suktche 숙제 assignment; homework
suk'ŏsŭi 수컷의 male
suk'ŏt 수컷 male (*of animal, bird, fish*); cock
suk'oyang-i 수코양이 tomcat
sul 술 liquor; fringe; tassel; tuft
sul chanch'i 술 잔치 drinking party
sul ch'wihan 술 취한 drunk; intoxicated
sulgorae 술고래 heavy drinker
sulkkun 술꾼 drunk
sullye 순례 pilgrimage
sullyeja 순례자 pilgrim
sulp'ŭm 슬픔 sorrow, sadness
sultchan 술잔 stemware
sultchip 술집 bar
sultchip yŏjong-ŏbwŏn 술집 여종업원 bartender
sum 숨 breath; ***sumŭl kip'i tŭrŏ mashida*** 숨을 깊이 들어 마시다 take a deep breath; ***sumi ch'ada*** 숨이 차다 be out of breath, pant; ***sumŭl chugida*** 숨을 죽이다 hold one's breath; gulp; ***sumŭl hŏlttŏgida*** 숨을 헐떡이다 gasp for breath; ***sumŭl naeshwida*** 숨을 내쉬다 breathe out; ***sumŭl tŭryŏ mashida*** 숨을 들여 마시다 breathe in
sumanŭn 수많은 a great many, a large number of
sumbakkoktchil 숨바꼭질 hide-and-seek
sumch'an 숨찬 breathless
sumgida 숨기다 hide, conceal; hold back
sumgimŏmnŭn 숨김없는 open, honest, frank
sumgimŏpsshi 숨김없이 openly, honestly, frankly
sumgyŏjin 숨겨진 hidden
summak'il chŏngdoŭi 숨막힐 정도의 breathtaking
sumnŭn kot 숨는 곳 hiding place
sumshwida 숨쉬다 breathe
sumtta 숨다 hide; go into hiding
sumt'ong 숨통 windpipe
sumyŏn 수면 surface; ***sumyŏni orŏbut-tta*** 수면이 얼어붙다 freeze over
sumyŏng 수명 life (*of machine*)
sumyŏnje 수면제 sleeping pill
sun 순 pure *silver*, *gold*; complete, total ◊ ten days; ten years
-sun -순 order; ***yŏllyŏngsunŭro*** 연령순으로 in order of age
sunch'al 순찰 patrol
sunch'alch'a 순찰차 patrol car
sunch'algwan 순찰관 patrolman
sunch'arhada 순찰하다 patrol; be on patrol
sun-gan 순간 moment, instant
sun-gan chŏngjishik'ida 순간 정지시키다 freeze *video*
sun-ganŭi 순간의 momentary
sungbae 숭배 worship
sungbaehada 숭배하다 worship; idolize
sungmo 숙모 aunt (*father's younger brother's wife*)
sungmyŏn 숙면 sound sleep
sungnyŏ 숙녀 lady
sungnyŏndoen 숙련된 skilled, expert
sungnyŏn-gong 숙련공 skilled worker

sun-gyŏrŭl ilt'a 순결을 잃다 lose one's virginity
sun-gyoja 순교자 martyr
sunhada 순하다 be gentle; be mild
sunhan 순한 mild; docile
sunhang 순항 cruise
sunhanghada 순항하다 cruise
sunhangsŏn 순항선 cruise liner
sunhan soktto 순항 속도 cruising speed
sunhwan 순환 cycle; circulation
suniik 순이익 net profit
sunjinhada 순진하다 be innocent, be pure
sunjinham 순진함 innocence
sunjinhan 순진한 innocent; naïve
sunjŏnhan 순전한 unadulterated, absolute
sunjong 순종 obedience
sunjonghada 순종하다 obey
sunjonghanŭn 순종하는 obedient
sunjongjŏgin 순종적인 submissive
sunjoroun 순조로운 smooth
sunmu 순무 turnip
sunnyang 숫양 ram
sunoe hoedam 수뇌 회담 summit POL
sunot'a 수놓다 embroider
sunp'ung 순풍 tail wind
sunshik-kkane 순식간에 in an instant, quickly
sunshik-kkanŭi 순식간의 instantaneous
sunsŏ 순서 sequence; system; ***ajik tangshin sunsŏga animnida*** 아직 당신 순서가 아닙니다 it's not your turn yet; ***sunsŏga pakkwin*** 순서가 바뀐 out of order, not in sequence
sunsŏdaero 순서대로 in sequence; ***sunsŏdaero chŏngnihada*** 순서대로 정리하다 order, put in sequence
sunsuhan 순수한 pure; natural; neat; net
sunsuibŭl ollida 순수입을 올리다 earn; clear, net
sunsuik 순수익 profit margin
sunŭnghada 순응하다 conform; ***...e sunŭnghayŏ*** ...에 순응하여 in line with
sunyŏ 수녀 nun
suŏbil 수업일 school days
suŏp 수업 tuition; lesson, class
sup 숲 forest; wood
suppŏp 수법 gimmick (*promotional*)
sup'ŏmak'et 수퍼마켓 supermarket
sup'ŭ 수프 soup
sup'ul 수풀 tuft
sup'yŏng kŏnnŏlmok 수평 건널목 grade crossing
sup'yŏngsŏn 수평선 horizon (*at sea*)
sup'yo 수표 check FIN
sup'yoch'aek 수표책 checkbook
surak 수락 *fml* acceptance
surak'ada 수락하다 *fml* take up, accept *offer*; undertake, take on *task*
suran 수란 poached egg
sure ch'wihada 술에 취하다 get drunk
surigong 수리공 repairman
surihada 수리하다 repair, recondition
suri kkaeda 술이 깨다 sober up
surishik'ida 수리시키다 get fixed
suro 수로 waterway, channel; watercourse
surŭl mashida 술을 마시다 drink *alcohol*
surŭl seda 수를 세다 count
suryŏk chŏn-gi 수력 전기 hydroelectricity ◊ hydroelectric
suryŏn 수련 water lily
suryŏng-in 수령인 recipient
suryŏngtchŭng 수령증 delivery note
suryut'an 수류탄 grenade
susa 수사 rhetoric
susaek 수색 search, hunt
susaekttae 수색대 search party
susaek yŏngtchang 수색 영장 search warrant
susaek'ada 수색하다 search for; trace
susaek'anŭn 수색하는 searching
susang 수상 premier
susang ch'angnyuk'ada 수상 착륙하다 splash down
susanghada 수상하다 win a prize; be suspicious
susanghan 수상한 suspicious, fishy
susangja 수상자 prizewinner; medalist
susangsŭk'i 수상스키 waterskiing

suseshik pyŏn-gi 수세식 변기 water closet, flush toilet
sushin 수신 reception (*for phone etc*); for the attention of
sushin-gi 수신기 receiver RAD
sushinin 수신인 addressee
sushinin pudamŭi chŏnhwa 수신인 부담의 전화 collect call
sushinin pudamŭro chŏnhwahada 수신인 부담으로 전화하다 call collect
sushinyŏburŭl allida 수신여부를 알리다 acknowledge
susŏk paiollinisŭt'ŭ 수석 바이올리니스트 concert master
susŏk weit'ŏ 수석 웨이터 head waiter
susŏn 수선 repair; alteration
susŏnhada 수선하다 mend, repair
suso 수소 hydrogen
susong 수송 transport; transportation; ***susong chung-in*** 수송 중인 in transit
susonghada 수송하다 transport
suso p'okt'an 수소 폭탄 hydrogen bomb
susuham 수수함 modesty
susuhan 수수한 modest; conservative
susukkekki 수수께끼 puzzle, mystery; riddle; enigma
susukkekkigat'ŭn 수수께끼같은 enigmatic
susul 수술 surgery; operation
susulshil 수술실 operating room
susurŭl hada 수술을 하다 operate
susurŭl pat-tta 수술을 받다 have an operation, undergo surgery
susurhada 수술하다 operate on
susuryo 수수료 commission
sut 숱 thickness; ***such'i manŭn mŏri*** 숱이 많은 머리 thick hair
sut 숯 charcoal
sutcha 숫자 numeral, digit, figure
sutchap'an 숫자판 numeric keys
sutch'onggak 숫총각 virgin (*male*)
sutkkarak 숟가락 spoon
sutppure kuwŏjin 숯불에 구워진 charbroiled
sut'ak 수탉 cock (*chicken*)
suŭisa 수의사 veterinarian
suŭn 수은 mercury, quicksilver
suwi 수위 janitor; water level
suwŏnji 수원지 source
suwŏrhada 수월하다 be easy
suwŏrhan 수월한 easy, simple
suyang pŏdŭl 수양 버들 weeping willow
suyŏhada 수여하다 award, confer
suyŏk 수역 body of water
suyŏm 수염 whiskers; bristles
suyŏng 수영 swimming; swim
suyŏngbok 수영복 swimsuit
suyŏnghada 수영하다 swim
suyŏngjang 수영장 swimming pool
suyŏngppŏp 수영법 stroke (*swimming*)
suyo 수요 demand COM; ***suyoga it-tta*** 수요가 있다 be in demand
suyoil 수요일 Wednesday
suyong inwŏn 수용 인원 intake (*of people*)
suyongnyŏk 수용력 capacity
suyongso 수용소 camp
swaebingsŏn 쇄빙선 icebreaker
swaedo 쇄도 deluge; stampede
swaedohada 쇄도하다 deluge
swaegol 쇄골 collarbone

T

ta 다 completely, fully; ***ta ssŏbŏrida*** 다 써버리다 run out of; use up
tabal 다발 wad (*of paper*); wisp (*of hair*)
tabang 다방 café
tabunhi 다분히 no doubt, probably
ta charan 다 자란 full-grown
tach'aeropkke hada 다채롭게 하다 jazz up
tach'aeroun 다채로운 colorful
tach'ida 닫히다 close
tach'ige hada 다치게 하다 hurt
tach'iji anŭn 다치지 않은 unhurt
tach'in 닫힌 shut, closed
tach'in te ŏmnŭn 다친 데 없는 unhurt, unscathed
tach'ŭl naerida 닻을 내리다 anchor
tach'ŭl ollida 닻을 올리다 weigh anchor
tadarŭda 다다르다 span
tado 다도 tea ceremony
tadŭmtta 다듬다 polish, perfect; trim *hair*; smooth out; ***k'allo tadŭmtta*** 칼로 다듬다 scrape
tae 대 great; huge ◊ versus ◊ stem ◊ *countword for vehicles, airplanes, machines, pipe tobacco, cigarettes*
taean 대안 alternative
taebon 대본 script
taebu 대부 loan; godfather
taebubun 대부분 most
taebubunŭi 대부분의 most
taebubunŭn 대부분은 mostly, mainly
taebumo 대부모 godparent
taebyŏnin 대변인 spokesperson; mouthpiece
taebyŏnja 대변자 representative
taech'adaejop'yo 대차대조표 balance sheet
taech'ebup'um 대체부품 replacement part
taech'ehal su ŏmnŭn 대체할 수 없는 irreplaceable
taech'e ŏdie 대체 어디에 wherever
taech'ep'um 대체품 replacement
taech'ero 대체로 on the whole, as a rule
taech'ing 대칭 symmetry
taech'ingjŏgin 대칭적인 symmetrical
taech'owŏn 대초원 prairie
taech'u 대추 date (*fruit*)
taech'ung hult'ŏboda 대충 훑어보다 look over
taeda 대다 pad (*with material*)
taedamhada 대담한 be bold
taedanhage 대단하게 enormously
taedanhan 대단한 enormous, tremendous; serious ◊ a great deal of; ***kŭnŭn taedanhan inmuriyeyo*** 그는 대단한 인물이예요 he's a real character; ***tangshinŭn taedanhagunyo*** 당신은 대단하군요 you're incredible
taedanhi 대단히 very, extremely, remarkably; ***taedanhi manŭn*** 대단히 많은 a great many
taedap 대답 answer, reply
taedap'ada 대답하다 answer, reply
taedasu 대다수 majority
taedoshi 대도시 metropolis
taedoshiŭi 대도시의 metropolitan
taedŭlbo 대들보 girder
taedŭnghada 대등하다 equalize
taegae 대개 principally, mainly, chiefly
taegakssŏnŭi 대각선의 diagonal
taegang 대강 general features ◊ roughly; cursorily
taegang hult'ŏboda 대강 훑어보다 flip through
taegang miruŏ poda 대강 미루어 보다 judge, estimate
taegang-ŭi 대강의 approximate, rough; sweeping *generalization*
taegi 대기 atmosphere
taegihada 대기하다 stand by, be ready
taegihago innŭn 대기하고 있는 on

standby
taegija myŏngdan 대기자 명단 waiting list
taegi oyŏm 대기 오염 atmospheric pollution
taegishil 대기실 waiting room
taegŏlle 대걸레 mop
taegŭm 대금 (large) flute
taegŭmŏptcha 대금업자 money-lender
taegŭm sanghwan 대금 상환 COD, collect on delivery
taegyŏl 대결 confrontation; clash; dispute
taegyumoŭi 대규모의 large scale
taehae(sŏ) 대해(서): ***...e taehae(sŏ)*** ...에 대해(서) about; regarding
taehagwŏn 대학원 graduate school
taehagwŏnsaeng 대학원생 graduate
taehak 대학 university, school
taehak-kkyo 대학교 university
taehak kyojŏng 대학 교정 university campus
taehakssaeng 대학생 university student
taehakssal 대학살 carnage, slaughter
taehak k'aemp'ŏsŭ 대학 캠퍼스 university campus
taehamul 대하물 epic
taehan 대한: ***...e taehan*** ...에 대한 about
Taehanjeguk 대한제국 Great Han Empire
Taehanmin-guk 대한민국 Republic of Korea, ROK
taehap chogae 대합 조개 clam
taehapsshil 대합실 departure lounge
taehayŏ 대하여: ***...e taehayŏ*** ...에 대하여 with respect to, with regard to
taehit'ŭ 대히트 smash hit
taehit'ŭjak 대히트작 blockbuster
taehoe 대회 convention, rally; contest
taehoe ch'amgaja 대회 참가자 conventioneer
taehollan 대혼란 chaos
taehongsu 대홍수 deluge
taehwa 대화 talk; conversation; dialog; ***taehwarŭl chungdanhada*** 대화를 중단하다 break off, stop talking
taehwasangja 대화상자 dialog box COMPUT
taehyŏng 대형 large size
taeja 대자 godchild; godson
taejesajang 대제사장 high priest
taejŏnhada 대전하다 meet (*in competition*)
taejŏp 대접 dish; bowl; beaker
taejŏp'ada 대접하다 entertain; treat
taejo 대조 contrast
taejohada 대조하다 contrast
taejojŏgin 대조적인 contrasting
taejop'yo 대조표 checklist
taejo p'yoshirŭl hada 대조 표시를 하다 check off
taejung 대중 the public, the masses ◊ popular, mass
taejunggayo 대중가요 pop MUS
taejung kyot'ong 대중 교통 public transportation
taejung maech'e 대중 매체 mass media
taejungtchŏgin 대중적인 popular, general, widespread; mass, downmarket
taema 대마 hemp
taemach'o 대마초 cannabis, hashish
Taeman 대만 Taiwan ◊ Taiwanese
Taemanin 대만인 Taiwanese (*person*)
Taemanŏ 대만어 Taiwanese (*dialect*)
taemŏriŭi 대머리의 bald
taemo 대모 godmother
taemosŭro paktta 대못으로 박다 rivet
taemot 대못 rivet; spike
taemŭro maktta 댐으로 막다 dam
taemun 대문 gate
taemuntcha 대문자 capital (letter)
taemyŏngsa 대명사 pronoun; ***...ŭi taemyŏngsaga toeda*** ...의 대명사가 되다 be a byword for, be synonymous with
taemyŏnhago 대면하고 face to face
taenaje 대낮에 in broad daylight
taenamu 대나무 bamboo
taenggŭranghanŭn sori 댕그랑하는 소리 chink (*sound*)
taensŭ p'ati 댄스 파티 dance
taenyŏ 대녀 god-daughter

taep'ae 대패 plane (*tool*)
taep'ihada 대피하다 evacuate, leave
taep'iho 대피호 shelter
taep'ishik'ida 대피시키다 evacuate
taep'iro 대피로 pull-in
taep'iso 대피소 shelter
taep'o 대포 artillery
taep'ok ollida 대폭 올리다 bump up
taep'yodan 대표단 delegation
taep'yohada 대표하다 represent, stand for
taep'yoja 대표자 representative, delegate
taep'yojŏgin myŏn 대표적인 면 cross-section
taep'yoro immyŏnghada 대표로 임명하다 delegate
taeri 대리 deputy
taerihada 대리하다 represent, act as
taeriin 대리인 agent, representative, proxy; substitute
taerikkwŏn 대리권 proxy, authority
taerimo 대리모 surrogate mother
taerip 대립 conflict, disagreement
taerisŏk 대리석 marble
taeryagŭi 대략의 approximate
taeryak 대략 approximately
taeryang 대량 large quantity
taeryang hakssal 대량 학살 massacre, slaughter
taeryang saengsan 대량 생산 mass production
taeryang saengsanhada 대량 생산하다 mass-produce
taeryang-ŭi 대량의 wholesale, indiscriminate
taeryang-ŭro 대량으로 in bulk
taeryŏng 대령 colonel
taeryugŭi 대륙의 continental
taeryuk 대륙 continent
taesa 대사 speech; ambassador
taesagwan 대사관 embassy
taesang 대상 object
taesangja myŏngdan 대상자 명단 hit list
taesangp'ojin 대상포진 shingles
taesarŭl illŏjuda 대사를 일러주다 prompt *actor*
taeshi 대시 dash
taeshikka 대식가 glutton
taeshilp'ae 대실패 fiasco
taeshin 대신 substitute; compensation ◊ instead of; ***taeshin kiyonghada*** 대신 기용하다 make a substitution SP
taeshine 대신에 instead; instead of
taeshinhada 대신하다 replace, stand in for; take over; substitute
taeshinhaesŏ hada 대신해서 하다 stand in for; ***narŭl / kŭrŭl taeshinhaesŏ*** 나를 / 그를 대신해서 on my / his behalf
taeshinhal 대신할 alternative
taesŏnggong 대성공 coup
taesŏnggong-ida 대성공이다 be a success
taesŏnggong-ŭl kŏduda 대성공을 거두다 hit the bull's-eye
Taesŏyang 대서양 Atlantic
Taesŏyang hoengdanŭi 대서양 횡단의 transatlantic
taesuroptchi anŭn 대수롭지 않은 peripheral
taet'ongnyŏng 대통령 president
taet'ongnyŏng imgi 대통령 임기 presidency (*term*)
taet'ongnyŏngjik 대통령직 presidency (*office*)
taeŭnghanŭn 대응하는 corresponding, equivalent
taeu 대우 treatment
taeuhada 대우하다 treat, behave toward
taeyŏk 대역 double (*person*)
taeyŏl 대열 file; ranks MIL
taeyong 대용 substitution
taeyongp'um 대용품 substitute
taeyuhaeng 대유행 all the rage, fashionable ◊ craze, fad; ***ch'oegŭnŭi taeyuhaeng*** 최근의 대유행 the latest craze
tagagada 다가가다 walk up to
tagak'wa 다각화 diversification
tagak'washik'ida 다각화시키다 diversify
tagaoda 다가오다 close in, move closer
tagaonŭn 다가오는 forthcoming
tagugŏŭi 다국어의 multilingual
taguktchŏk 다국적 multinational
taguktchŏk kiŏp 다국적 기업 multinational company

tagwa 다과 refreshments; tea and cookies
ta hada 다 하다 run out (*of time*); carry out, perform
tahaenghido 다행히도 thankfully, luckily
tahaengsŭrŏpkkedo 다행스럽게도 mercifully, thankfully
taiamondŭ 다이아몬드 diamond
taibing 다이빙 (high) diving
taibing tae 다이빙 대 diving board
taibŏ 다이버 diver
tainŏmait'ŭ 다이너마이트 dynamite
taiŏl 다이알 dial; ***taiŏrŭl tollida*** 다이얼을 돌리다 dial
taiŏri 다이어리 (appointments) diary
taiŏt'ŭ 다이어트 diet
taiŏt'ŭhada 다이어트하다 diet; be on a diet
tajaedanŭnghan 다재다능한 versatile
tajagŭi 다작의 prolific
tajŏngdagamhan 다정다감한 warm-hearted
tajŏnghada 다정하다 be affectionate; be friendly
tajŏnghan 다정한 affectionate, loving; genial; pleasant, friendly
tajung maech'e 다중 매체 multimedia
tak 닭 chicken
takkanaeda 닦아내다 wipe off
tak-kkogi 닭고기 chicken (*as food*)
taktta 닦다 wipe; clean; wash; mop up
takttari 닭다리 drumstick (*of poultry*)
tak'yument'ŏri 다큐멘터리 documentary (program)
tak'yument'ŏri tŭrama 다큐멘터리 드라마 docudrama
tal 달 month; moon ◊ lunar
talch'angnyukssŏn 달착륙선 lunar module
talda 달다 fit, install; attach; be sweet
talge hada 달게 하다 sweeten
talgyal 달걀 egg
talgyal kkŏptchil 달걀 껍질 eggshell
talgyal wansuk 달걀 완숙 hard-boiled egg
talgyarhyŏng 달걀형 oval
talk'e hada 닳게 하다 wear; wear away; damage
talk'omhada 달콤하다 be sweet
tallabut-tta 달라붙다 stick, jam; stick to, adhere to; cling
tallak 단락 passage; short circuit
tallanggŏrida 달랑거리다 dangle
tallida 달리다 hang; depend; be attached; run short; not be enough; run, rush; drive
talligi 달리기 run; running SP
tallŏ 달러 dollar
tallyŏdŭlda 달려들다 tackle
tallyŏk 달력 calendar
tallyŏnhada 단련하다 build up
tallyŏnshik'ida 단련시키다 exercise
talppich'i ŏrin 달빛이 어린 moonlit
talppit 달빛 moonlight
talp'aeng-i 달팽이 snail
taltta 닳다 run down
tam 담 wall
tambae 담배 tobacco; cigarette; ***tambaerŭl samgahae chushigi paramnida*** 담배를 삼가해 주시기 바랍니다 please refrain from smoking; ***tambae p'iuda*** 담배 피우다 smoke a cigarette
tambae kkongch'o 담배 꽁초 cigarette butt
tamdamhan 담담한 matter-of-fact, calm; unemotional
tamdang 담당 charge ◊ in charge
tamdanghada 담당하다 take charge of
tamdang-ida 담당이다 be in charge
tamgŭda 담그다 immerse, soak
tamhwangsaek 담황색 cream (*color*)
tamjaeng-i 담쟁이 ivy
tamkko it-tta 담고 있다 contain
tamnyo 담요 blanket
tamsŏk 담석 gallstone
tamtta 담다 hold, contain; resemble, take after; ***nuguwa tamtta*** 누구와 닮다 be like s.o.
tamyo 담요 rug
tan 단 column (*in newspaper*); rung; hit squad; tuck (*in dress*) ◊ sweet ◊ *countword for firewood, spinach etc*
tanbaektchil 단백질 protein
tanbal 단발 bob (*haircut*)

tanch'e 단체 society, organization
tanch'e chŏngshin 단체 정신 team spirit
tanch'e hyŏp'oe 단체 협회 association, organization
tanch'e kyosŏp 단체 교섭 collective bargaining
tanch'ŏl 단철 wrought iron
tan ch'ŏri 단처리 braid, trimming
tanch'ŭng 단층 rift (*in earth*)
tanch'u 단추 button
tanch'ukk'i 단축키 shortcut key COMPUT
tanch'u kumŏng 단추구멍 buttonhole
tanch'urŭl ch'aeuda 단추를 채우다 button (up)
tandanhada 단단하다 be solid; be firm; be tight
tandanhi 단단히 tight
tandanhi choida 단단히 조이다 tighten
tandanhi ch'unggyŏgŭl padŭn 단단히 충격을 받은 shattered, upset
tandanhi muktta 단단히 묶다 lash down (*with rope*)
tandanhi pak'in 단단히 박힌 stuck fast
tando 단도 dagger
tandogŭi 단독의 single-handed
tang 당 party; faction
tang- 당- this; that; the present; ***tangshi*** 당시 that time
-tang -당 per; ***irindang*** 일인당 per head, per person
tangbŏn 당번 rota
tangbun-gan 당분간 for the moment, for the time being
tangch'an 당찬 brisk
tangch'ŏmdoen 당첨된 winning
tangch'ŏmja 당첨자 winner
tangdanghan 당당한 regal
tanggida 당기다 pull
tanggŭn 당근 carrot
tanggu 당구 pool; snooker; billiards
tanggudae 당구대 pool table
tanggujang 당구장 pool hall
tangguk 당국 the authorities
tanghok 당혹 perplexity
tanghok'age hada 당혹하게 하다 perplex, puzzle
tanghok'an 당혹한 perplexed, puzzled
tanghwang 당황 alarm, panic
tanghwanghada 당황하다 be embarrassed; panic, get flustered
tanghwanghae hada 당황해 하다 be baffled
tanghwanghage hada 당황하게 하다 baffle; embarrass; disconcert
tanghwanghage hanŭn 당황하게 하는 embarrassing
tanghwanghan 당황한 embarrassed; disconcerted
tan-gigan 단기간 short-term
tan-gijŏgŭro 단기적으로 in the short term
tang-ilch'igi yŏhaeng 당일치기 여행 daytrip
tangjang 당장 right now, immediately
tangjigida 당직이다 be on duty
tangjwa yegŭm kujwa 당좌 예금 구좌 checking account
tangmil 당밀 molasses
tangnagwi 당나귀 donkey
tangnyŏnhada 당연하다 be natural, be right
tangnyŏnhan 당연한 natural, obvious; ***muŏsŭl tang-yŏnhan illo yŏgida*** 무엇을 당연한 일로 여기다 take sth for granted
tangnyŏnhi 당연히 naturally, of course; automatically
tangnyoppyŏng 당뇨병 diabetes ◊ diabetic
tan-gŏri yukssang kyŏnggi 단거리 육상 경기 sprint
tan-gŏri yukssang sŏnsu 단거리 육상 선수 sprinter
tan-gol 단골 custom; regular (*person*)
tan-gollo tanida 단골로 다니다 patronize, be a customer of
tangshin 당신 (*polite*) you
tangshin chashin 당신 자신 (*polite*) yourself
tangshindŭl chashin 당신들 자신 (*polite*) yourselves
tangshinŭi 당신의 (*polite*) your
tangsŏndoeda 당선되다 be elected; ***sŏn-gŏro tangsŏndoen*** 선거로

당선된 elected
tangsŏnja 당선자 winner
tan-gye 단계 stage, period, phase
tan-gyejŏgŭro chegŏhada 단계적으로 제거하다 phase out
tan-gyejŏgŭro t'uip'ada 단계적으로 투입하다 phase in
tan-gyŏl solidarity
tang-yŏnhae! 당연해! no wonder!
tang-yŏnhi 당연히 of course, naturally
tan hanaŭi 단 하나의 sole, only; single, solitary, lone
tanhohan 단호한 decisive, resolute, emphatic; purposeful, determined, relentless; stalwart
tanilssŏng 단일성 unity
tanja 단자 terminal ELEC
tanji 단지 only, just ◊ mere ◊ jar; container; urn; housing development
tanjŏl 단절 rupture
tanjŏnghada 단정하다 determine, establish; be neat; be decent
tanjŏnghan 단정한 tidy, neat; decent, upright
tanjŏnghi hada 단정히 하다 tidy oneself up
tanjŏngtchŏgin 단정적인 assertive
tanjoroptta 단조롭다 be monotonous; be boring
tanjoroum 단조로움 monotony
tankkwa taehak 단과 대학 college
tanmal changch'i 단말 장치 terminal COMPUT
tanmyŏnghan 단명한 short-lived
tannyŏm 단념 resignation
tannyŏmhada 단념하다 relinquish, abandon
tannyŏmshik'ida 단념시키다 deter; ***Xi/ga Yŭl/rŭl tannyŏmhage hada*** X이/가 Y을/를 단념하게 하다 put X off Y
tanŏ 단어 word
tanp'a 단파 short wave
tanp'ungnamu 단풍나무 maple
tanp'yŏn 단편 fragment, shred
tanp'yŏnsosŏl 단편소설 short story
tanp'yŏntchŏgin 단편적인 sketchy; piecemeal; fragmentary
tansang 단상 platform, stage
tanshigan 단시간 a short time
tanshik 단식 singles (*in tennis*)
tansŏ 단서 proviso, stipulation
tanso 단소 bamboo flute
tansok 단속 crackdown
tansok'ada 단속하다 crack down, clamp down
tansu 단수 singular GRAM
tansume 단숨에 at a stretch, non-stop; ***tansume ssŭda*** 단숨에 쓰다 dash off, write quickly; ***tansume tallyŏgada*** 단숨에 달려가다 dash; make a dash for
tansunhada 단순하다 be simple; be unsophisticated
tansunhwahada 단순화하다 simplify
tansuro 단수로 in the singular
tansuŭi 단수의 singular GRAM
tantchŏm 단점 disadvantage, drawback
tantcho 단조 minor MUS
tanŭl naerida 단을 내리다 let down *dress etc*
tanwi 단위 unit (of measurement)
tanwi wŏnkka 단위 원가 unit cost
tanyŏnhi 단연히 easily, by far
tap 답 answer
tapp'ahada 답파하다 cover, travel
tapssahada 답사하다 travel; explore
taptchang 답장 reply (*letter*)
taptchanghada 답장하다 reply (*to letter*)
tapttap'ada 답답하다 be gloomy; be stifling; be hidebound; be anxious
tapttap'an 답답한 stifling
tap'ada 답하다 answer
tarajida 닳아지다 wear; wear away, wear out
tarakppang 다락방 attic, loft
taramjwi 다람쥐 squirrel
taranada 달아나다 run away, rush off
taraorŭda 달아오르다 glow
tarappajin 닳아빠진 well-worn, worn-out
tara ttŏrŏjida 닳아 떨어지다 wear out
tari 다리 bridge; leg
tarimi 다리미 iron
tarimjil 다림질 ironing
tarimjilttae 다림질대 ironing board
tarimjirhada 다림질하다 iron; press; do the ironing

tarimjiri p'iryoŏmnŭn 다림질이 필요없는 non-iron
tarŭda 다르다 differ, be different
tarŭge 다르게 differently; ***...wa / kwanŭn tarŭge*** ...와 / 과는 다르게 as distinct from
tarŭn 닳은 threadbare; dead *battery*
tarŭn 다른 different; distinct; another; other
tarŭn kŏt 다른 것 another
tarŭn nugun-ga 다른 누군가 someone else
tarŭn ŏttŏn kŏt 다른 어떤 것 something else
taruda 다루다 handle; manage; treat
tarugi himdŭn 다루기 힘든 unruly; tricky
tarugi ŏryŏun 다루기 어려운 awkward *customer*; not user-friendly
tarugi shwiun 다루기 쉬운 manageable; docile
taryang 다량 mass
tasahan 다사한 eventful
tasan 다산 fertility
tasanŭi 다산의 fertile
tashi 다시 again; ***tashi han pŏn*** 다시 한 번 once more
tashi chada 다시 자다 go back to sleep
tashi ch'aeuda 다시 채우다 refill
tashi ch'irhada 다시 칠하다 repaint
tashi ch'usŭrida 다시 추스리다 reconstruct
tashi hwaginhada 다시 확인하다 doublecheck
tashi kamtta 다시 감다 rewind
tashi nat'anada 다시 나타나다 reappear
tashi padadŭrida 다시 받아들이다 take back, accept back
tashi pangmunhada 다시 방문하다 call back
tashi ssŭda 다시 쓰다 rewrite
tasŏt 다섯 five
tasŏt pŏntchaeŭi 다섯 번째의 fifth
taso 다소 rather, sort of, somewhat
tasŭrida 다스리다 govern, rule
tasuŭi 다수의 many
tat 닻 anchor
tatch'ida 닫히다 shut
tatki 닫기 close COMPUT
tatkki shwiun 닿기 쉬운 easy to reach, accessible
tat-tta 닫다 close; fasten; be closed
tat'a 닿다 reach
tat'ŭ 다트 dart
tat'uda 다투다 fight; quarrel; ***...ŭl / rŭl wihae tat'uda*** ...을 / 를 위해 다투다 contend for
tat'um 다툼 quarrel
taŭm 다음 next; ***taŭmŭi kŏt*** 다음의 것 the following
taŭme 다음에 after, next; ***taŭme kyesok*** 다음에 계속 to be continued; ***taŭmgwa kat'ŭn*** 다음과 같은 as follows; ***taŭm pun?*** 다음 분? who's next?
taŭmnal 다음날 the day after
Tau Chonsŭ P'yŏnggyun Chuga 다우 존스 평균 주가 Dow Jones Average
taunnodŭ 다운로드 download
taunnodinghada 다운로딩하다 download
tayanghada 다양하다 be diverse
tayanghage twisŏkkin 다양하게 뒤섞인 miscellaneous
tayanghan 다양한 diverse, varied; multiple
tayangssŏng 다양성 diversity, variety
tayongdoŭi 다용도의 all-purpose; adaptable
-tcha -자 (*suffix for persons*) → ***-ja*** -자
tchada 짜다 structure, plan; press, squeeze; weave; spin; wring; be salty
tchaenggŭrŏnghanŭn sori 쨍그렁하는 소리 clink
tchajangmyŏn 짜장면 noodles and black bean sauce
tchajŭngnadorok 짜증나도록 frustratingly
tchajŭngnage hada 짜증나게 하다 irritate
tchajŭngnage hanŭn 짜증나게 하는 irritating
tchajŭngnanŭn 짜증나는 irritating; frustrating; trying, annoying
tchajŭng-ŭl chal naenŭn 짜증을 잘 내는 irritable
tchak 짝 partner; mate (*of animal*)

tchakssuŭi 짝수의 even *number*
tchaktchit-tta 짝짓다 mate
tchalbŭn 짧은 short
tchalkke charŭda 짧게 자르다 cut shorter; crop
tchalkke hada 짧게 하다 shorten
tchalkke pomyŏn 짧게 보면 in the short run
tchallida 짤리다 ax *employee*
tchalptta 짧다 be short
tcham 짬 slot (*in schedule*)
tcha match'uda 짜 맞추다 piece together
tchan 짠 salty
tchaptcharhan 짭짤한 savory
tchatchŭng 짜증 tantrum
tchiburŏttŭrida 찌부러뜨리다 mangle, crush
tchida 찌다 steam
tchigŏ mŏktta 찍어 먹다 dip, dunk
tchigŏ naegi 찍어 내기 chop
tchigŭrŏttŭrida 찌그러뜨리다 crush; ***nullŏ tchigŭrŏttŭrida*** 눌러 찌그러뜨리다 squash, crush
tchijŏjida 찢어지다 split
tchijŏjige kananhan 찢어지게 가난한 poverty-stricken
tchijŏjigi shwiun 찢어지기 쉬운 flimsy
tchijŏjin 찢어진 ragged, tattered
tchijŏjin kot 찢어진 곳 slit; tear
tchijŏ yŏlda 찢어 열다 slit; rip open
tchikkŏgi 찌꺼기 dregs
tchiktchigi 찍찍이 Velcro®
tchiktchk-kkŏrida 찍찍거리다 squeak
tchimt'ong 찜통 steamer (*for cooking*)
tchinggŭrida 찡그리다 scowl; contort; screw up *eyes*
tchinggŭrin ŏlgul 찡그린 얼굴 scowl
tchinŭn tŭshi tŏun 찌는 듯이 더운 scorching hot
tchinŭn tŭt'an 찌는 듯한 sweltering
tchip'urida 찌푸리다 frown
tchip'urin 찌푸린 threatening
tchip'urin ŏlgul 찌푸린 얼굴 frown
tchirŭda 찌르다 plunge; thrust; prick; jab; stab; lunge at; ***k'allo tchirŭda*** 칼로 찌르다 knife, stab
tchirŭregi 찌르레기 blackbird; starling
tchit-tta 찢다 rip, tear; split
tchit'ŭn 짙은 thick, dense
tchoch'abŏrida 쫓아버리다 chase away; turn away, send away
tchoch'anaeda 쫓아내다 eject; expel; evict
tchoch'a ponaeda 쫓아 보내다 see off, chase away
tchoda 쪼다 peck
tchogaeda 쪼개다 split
tchogaejida 쪼개지다 split
tchok 쪽 page; slice
tchok pŏnho 쪽 번호 page number
tchotkkyŏnada 쫓겨나다 be expelled, be kicked out
-tchŭm -쯤 around, approximately; ***tushitchŭm*** 두시쯤 around two o'clock
tchugŭlgŏrige hada 쭈글거리게 하다 shrivel
tchuk ppŏt-tta 쭉 뻗다 stretch
tebyu 데뷰 début
teda 데다 get burnt; get scalded
teit'ŏ 데이터 data
teit'ŏ chŏjang 데이터 저장 data storage
teit'ŏ ch'ŏri 데이터 처리 data processing
teit'ŏ peisŭ 데이터 베이스 database
teit'ŏ poho 데이터 보호 data protection
teit'ŏ sujip 데이터 수집 data capture
teit'ŭ 데이트 date, meeting
teit'ŭ hada 데이트하다 date, go out with
teit'ŭ sangdae 데이트 상대 date (*person*)
tek'ŭnosedae 테크노세대 techno music fans
temo 데모 demo, demonstration, protest
temohada 데모하다 demonstrate, protest
temo haengjin 데모 행진 demo, demonstration, march
temo haengjinhada 데모 행진하다 march
temoja 데모자 demonstrator, protester
tenim 데님 denim

Tenishwi p'aesŭch'yuri 데니쉬 패스츄리 Danish pastry
Tenmak'ŭ 덴마크 Denmark ◊ Danish
Tenmak'ŭŏ 덴마크어 Danish
terigo kada 데리고 가다 take, accompany
terigo nagada 데리고 나가다 take out (*to dinner etc*)
terigo oda 데리고 오다 fetch *person, animal*
terirŏ kada 데리러 가다 call for, collect
terirŏ oda 데리러 오다 come for, collect
teryŏdajuda 데려다주다 take back
teryŏgada 데려가다 draw, lead
teryŏoda 데려오다 bring; pick up
teshibel 데시벨 decibel
tesŭk'ŭ 데스크 (reception) desk
teuda 데우다 heat up
teun 데운 heated
tewŏjida 데워지다 warm up
tidimp'an 디딤판 tread
tidimttol 디딤돌 stepping stone
tijain 디자인 design
tijainhada 디자인하다 design, plan
tijain hak-kkyo 디자인 학교 design school
tijainŏ 디자이너 designer
tijel 디젤 diesel
tijit'ŏl 디지털 digital
tillŏ 딜러 dealer (*in card game*)
tinŏ p'at'i 디너 파티 dinner party
tioksshiribo haekssan 디옥시리보 핵산 DNA, deoxyribonucleic acid
tip'olt'ŭkkap 디폴트값 default COMPUT
tisŭk'et 디스켓 disk
tisŭk'et tŭraibŭ 디스켓 드라이브 disk drive
tisŭk'o 디스코 disco
tisŭk'o t'ek 디스코 텍 discotheque
tisŭk'ŭ 디스크 disc
tisŭk'ŭ chak'i 디스크 자키 disc jockey
tisŭp'ŭllei 디스플레이 display COMPUT
tŏ 더 far, much; further; ***tŏ chagŭn*** 더 작은 fewer; ***tŏ chal*** 더 잘 better; ***chogŭmman tŏ*** 조금만 더 a little more
tŏbinghada 더빙하다 dub
tŏbŭl 더블 double
tŏbŭlbedŭ 더블베드 double bed
tŏbŭlbeisŭ 더블베이스 double-bass
tŏbŭl k'ŭllik 더블클릭 double click COMPUT
tŏch'e kŏllida 덫에 걸리다 be trapped
toch'ŏng 도청 provincial office
tŏch'ŭro chaptta 덫으로 잡다 trap
tŏdŏl ttŏlda 덜덜 떨다 quake, tremble
tŏdŭmgŏrim 더듬거림 impediment (*in speech*)
tŏdŭmgŏrimyŏ ch'at-tta 더듬거리며 찾다 fumble around
tŏdŭmi 더듬이 feeler, antenna
tŏdŭmtta 더듬다 stumble over *words*; ***marŭl tŏdŭmtta*** 말을 더듬다 stammer, stutter
tŏhada 더하다 add
tŏhagi 더하기 plus (sign)
tŏhayŏ 더하여 plus, in addition to
tŏ isang 더 이상 any more
tŏk 덕 goodness, virtue; ***...tŏkt'aege*** ...덕택에 thanks to ...; ***kŭ tŏkppune*** 그 덕분에 because of that
tŏl 덜 less; incompletely
tŏlda 덜다 ease, alleviate, relieve
tŏldŏl ttŏllida 덜덜 떨리다 chatter (*of teeth*)
tŏlgŏdŏk'anŭn sori 덜거덕하는 소리 clatter
tŏl ik'in 덜 익힌 rare, underdone
tŏlk'ŏk-kkŏrida 덜컥거리다 rattle; jolt
tŏm 덤 bonus; freebie
tŏ manŭn 더 많은 more
tŏmbida 덤비다 pounce
tŏmbul 덤불 clump, group; undergrowth
tŏmbyŏdŭlda 덤벼들다 go for, attack
tŏmi 더미 pile, heap
tŏ mŏlli 더 멀리 farther
tŏ mŏn 더 먼 further
tŏmp'ŭlling 덤플링 dumpling
tŏ naajida 더 나아지다 be better; be on the mend
tŏ nappajida 더 나빠지다 worsen
tŏ nappŭge 더 나쁘게 worse

tŏ nappŭn 더 나쁜 worse
tŏ natkke 더 낫게 better
tŏnggul shingmul 덩굴 식물 creeper
tŏnggulwŏlgyul 덩굴월귤 cranberry
tŏng-ŏri 덩어리 lump, block; loaf
tŏng-ŏrijida 덩어리지다 cake, solidify
tŏng-ŏri t'usŏng-iŭi 덩어리 투성이의 lumpy
tŏnjida 던지다 throw; ***Xege Yŭl / rŭl tŏnjida*** X에게 Y을 / 를 던지다 pelt X with Y
tŏnjigi 던지기 throw
tŏnmun 덧문 shutter
tŏ ŏmnŭn haengbok 더 없는 행복 bliss, no greater happiness
tŏpch'ida 덮치다 pounce; swoop on
tŏpch'iryŏ tŭlda 덮치려 들다 attack, go for
tŏpkkae 덮개 cover, hood; ***tŏpkkaerŭl pŏtkkida*** 덮개를 벗기다 uncover
tŏpssuruk'an 덥수룩한 shaggy
tŏptta 덥다 be hot (*of weather*); be warm (*of water*)
tŏptta 덮다 cover
tŏp'ida 덮히다 be buried under, be covered by
tŏp'in 덮힌: ***k'ŭrimŭro tŏp'in*** 크림으로 덮힌 topped with cream
tŏp'ŏ kkŭda 덮어 끄다 smother
tŏrhada 덜하다 ease
tŏrŏptta 더럽다 be dirty; be sordid
tŏrŏp'ida 더럽히다 soil, stain, dirty; smudge; blemish; smear *character*
tŏrŏwŏjida 더러워지다 stain
tŏt 덫 trap
tŏt-ch'angmun 덧창문 storm window
tŏtch'il 덧칠 coat (*of paint etc*)
tŏtppuch'ida 덧붙이다 add
tŏtppuch'yŏ marhada 덧붙여 말하다 add
tŏtssem 덧셈 addition
tŏŭk 더욱 more; ***tŏŭk chung-yohan*** 더욱 중요한 more important; ***tŏuk tŏ*** 더욱 더 more and more, even more
tŏugi 더욱이 moreover; in addition; plus
tŏun 더운 hot; warm
...to ...도 too, also
to 도 province, *do*; degree
toan 도안 engraving
toan-ga 도안가 draftsman
tobaehada 도배하다 paper *room, walls*
tobak 도박 gambling
tobak-kkun 도박꾼 gambler
tobak'ada 도박하다 gamble
tobaldoeji anŭn 도발되지 않은 unprovoked; spontaneous
tobalshik'ida 도발시키다 whip up, arouse
tobo yŏhaeng 도보 여행 walk; walking; hike; hiking; walking tour
tobo yŏhaenghada 도보 여행하다 walk, hike
toboyŏhaengja 도보여행자 hiker
toch'ak 도착 arrival
toch'ak yejŏng shigan 도착 예정 시간 ETA, estimated time of arrival
toch'ak'ada 도착하다 arrive, reach
toch'ak'anŭn 도착하는 incoming
toch'ŏe 도처에 throughout
toch'ŏnggi 도청기 bug (*electronic*)
toch'ŏnggirŭl sŏlch'ihada 도청기를 설치하다 bug, wire up
toch'ŏnghada 도청하다 bug, tap
todaech'e 도대체 on earth, the hell; ***todaech'e muŏsŭl hanŭn / wŏnhanŭn kŏmnikka?*** 도대체 무엇을 하는 / 원하는 겁니까? what the hell are you doing / do you want?
todarhada 도달하다 arrive at
todŏk kwannyŏm 도덕 관념 morals; scruples
todŏkssŏng 도덕성 morality
todŏktchŏgin 도덕적인 moral; scrupulous
toduda 돋우다 boost
toduktchil 도둑질 theft
toduktchirhada 도둑질하다 steal
toebadach'ida 되받아치다 hit back, retaliate
toech'ajŭm 되찾음 recovery
toech'at-tta 되찾다 recover, regain
toeda 되다 amount to; become, get; ***...ke / ge toeda*** ...게 되다 turn out so that ...; be arranged so that; ***ak'wadoeda*** 악화되다 get worse, become worse

toedollyŏjuda 되돌려주다 return, give back; take back
toedollyŏnot'a 되돌려놓다 replace, put back
toedoragada 되돌아가다 go back, return; retrace
toedoraoda 되돌아오다 come back, return
toedorok imyŏn 되도록 이면 preferably, if possible
toejŏra! 뒈져라! go to hell!
toel ssu innŭn han 될 수 있는 한 as possible; if possible
toen 된 stiff
toenjang 된장 fermented soya paste
toeŏ it-tta 되어 있다 be scheduled; ***taŭmttare kkŭnmach'igiro toeŏ issŏyo*** 다음달에 끝마치기로 되어 있어요 it's scheduled for completion next month; ***...giro toeŏ it-tta*** ...기로 되어 있다 be supposed to ...
toep'uridoenŭn 되풀이되는 repetitive
toep'urihada 되풀이하다 repeat; go over
toesallida 되살리다 revive; resuscitate; jog *memory*
toetch'atta 되찾다 retrieve
toetollida 되돌리다 reintroduce, bring back
toet'wida 되튀다 rebound
togani 도가니 melting pot
togi 도기 pottery
Togil 독일 Germany ◊ German
Togirin 독일인 German
Togirŏ 독일어 German (*language*)
togong 도공 potter
togŭl t'ada 독을 타다 poison
togu 도구 tool, device
Togyo 도교 Taoism
tohwasŏn 도화선 fuse wire
toip 도입 introduction; injection; input
toip'ada 도입하다 introduce; inject, contribute; input
tojagi 도자기 ceramics; porcelain
tojagiro toen 도자기로 된 ceramic
tojagiryu 도자기류 crockery
tojang 도장 paintwork; stamp, seal
tojang chaguk 도장 자국 stamp
tojang tchiktta 도장 찍다 stamp
tojŏhi 도저히 at all, by no means; ***tojŏhi ...l su ŏptta*** 도저히 ...ㄹ 수 없다 be completely unable to ...
tojŏn 도전 challenge
tojŏnhada 도전하다 challenge; dare
tojŏnja 도전자 challenger
toju ch'aryang 도주 차량 getaway car
tojung-e 도중에 on the way; ***kirŭl kŏnnŏnŭn tojung-e*** 길을 건너는 도중에 in crossing the road, while crossing the road
tojung-e tŭllŭda 도중에 들리다 stop off, break a journey
tok 독 poison; pot; dock
tokch'ang 독창 solo
tokch'angja 독창자 soloist
tokch'angjŏgin 독창적인 clever, ingenious
tokch'angnyŏk 독창력 ingenuity
tokch'angssŏng 독창성 originality
tokch'oktchang 독촉장 reminder COM
tokki 도끼 ax
tok-kkam 독감 flu, influenza
tokppaek 독백 monolog
tokppŏsŏt 독버섯 toadstool, poisonous mushroom
...tokppune ...덕분에 through, thanks to
tokssarhada 독살하다 poison
toksshinin 독신인 unattached, single
toksshinja 독신자 single (person)
toksshirhan 독실한 devout
toksso 독서 reading
toksso chang-ae 독서 장애 dyslexia
toksso chang-aeja 독서 장애자 dyslexic (*person*)
tokssŏga 독서가 reader (*person*)
tokssŏl 독설 sharp tongue
tokssŏnjŏgin 독선적인 dogmatic; self-righteous
tokssuri 독수리 eagle; vulture
toktchae chŏngkkwŏn 독재 정권 dictatorship
toktchaeja 독재자 dictator
toktchaejŏgin 독재적인 dictatorial
toktchajŏgin chosa podo 독자적인 조사 보도 investigative journalism
toktchŏm 독점 monopoly
toktchŏmhada 독점하다 monopolize

toktchŏmjŏgin 독점적인 exclusive, sole
toktchu 독주 solo
toktchuja 독주자 soloist
tokttanjŏgin 독단적인 arbitrary
tokt'ŭk'ada 독특하다 be unique
tokt'ŭk'an 독특한 unique
tok'ada 독하다 be poisonous; be strong (*of coffee etc*); be spiteful; be firm
tok'ingshik'ida 도킹시키다 dock
tol 돌 rock, stone; ***tori manŭn*** 돌이 많은 stony
tol 돐 first birthday
tolbal 돌발 outbreak
tolbarhada 돌발하다 flare up
tolboda 돌보다 look after
tolbom 돌봄 care
tolbwajuda 돌봐주다 watch, look after; ***agirŭl tolbwajuda*** 아기를 돌봐주다 baby-sit
tolch'ul 돌출 bulge
tolch'urhada 돌출하다 jut out
tolda 돌다 turn, turn around; circulate
toldol mungch'ida 돌돌 뭉치다 screw up *paper etc*
tolgi 돌기 turn
tolgyŏk'ada 돌격하다 charge, attack
tolkkorae 돌고래 dolphin
tollida 돌리다 turn, turn around; pass around; deal; direct
tollyŏbat-tta 돌려받다 have back, get back
tollyŏjuda 돌려주다 return, give back; pass on *costs, savings*
tollyŏnot'a 돌려놓다 return, put back
tollyŏ ponaeda 돌려 보내다 send back
tollyŏsŏ ŏn-gŭp'ada 돌려서 언급하다 allude to
tolp'ari 돌팔이 itinerant tradesman ◊ unqualified, quack
tolp'ung 돌풍 blast; gust, freak wind
tol segong 돌 세공 masonry
tomabaem 도마뱀 lizard
tomae 도매 wholesale
tomaekkapssŭro 도매값으로 wholesale
tomae-ŏptcha 도매업자 wholesaler
tomal p'yobon kŏmsa 도말 표본 검사 smear (test)
tomang 도망 escape
tomangch'ida 도망치다 escape; break away; flee
tomanggada 도망가다 escape; run away; scram
tomangja 도망자 fugitive
ton 돈 money; cash; currency
tonan kyŏngbogi 도난 경보기 burglar alarm
tong 동 sub-district, *dong*
...tong-an ... 동안 during ◊ while; ***...nŭn tong-ane*** ...는 동안에 while ...ing; ***...tong-an naenae*** ...동안 내내 throughout, during
tongbanhada 동반하다 accompany
tongbanja 동반자 escort
tongbong 동봉 inclosure ◊ inclosed
tongbonghada 동봉하다 attach, inclose
tongbongmul 동봉물 inclosure (*in letter etc*)
tongbuk 동북 north-east
tongch'e 동체 fuselage
tongdŭnghada 동등하다 be equal
tongdŭnghage 동등하게 equally
tongdŭnghan 동등한 equal, equivalent; ***tongdŭnghan kach'iga it-tta*** 동등한 가치가 있다 be equivalent to
tonggamhada 동감하다 empathize with
tonggi 동기 incentive, motive
tonggi puyŏ 동기 부여 motivation
tonggirŭl puyŏhada 동기를 부여하다 motivate
tonggisaeng 동기생 contemporary
tonggŏhada 동거하다 live with; cohabit
tonggŭpssaeng 동급생 classmate
tonggŭrami 동그라미 circle; ***tonggŭramirŭl ch'ida*** 동그라미를 치다 circle, draw a circle around
tonggul 동굴 cave
tonggyŏldoeda 동결되다 ice up
Tonggyŏng 동경 Tokyo
tonggyŏng-ŭi taesang 동경의 대상 heart-throb
tonggyŏrhada 동결하다 freeze
Tonghae 동해 East Sea, Sea of Japan
tonghwa 동화 fairy tale

tonghyŏng-iŭiŏ 동형이의어 homograph
tong-irhan 동일한 identical
tongjagŭro p'yohyŏnhada 동작으로 표현하다 mime
tongjak 동작 motion
tongji 동지 comrade
tongjŏn 동전 coin
tongjŏng 동정 pity; virginity; collar
tongjŏnghada 동정하다 pity; commiserate
tongjŏnghanŭn 동정하는 sympathetic, compassionate
tongjŏngshim 동정심 sympathy, pity, compassion
tongjŏngshimi manŭn 동정심이 많은 considerate
tongjoja 동조자 sympathizer
tongjongnyoppŏp 동종요법 homeopathy
tongjong pŏnshik 동종 번식 inbreeding
tongmaek 동맥 artery
tongmaeng 동맹 alliance
tongmaengguk 동맹국 ally (*country*)
tongmaeng p'aŏp 동맹 파업 strike; ***tongmaeng p'aŏp'ada*** 동맹 파업하다 go on strike; ***tongmaeng p'aŏp chung-ida*** 동맹 파업 중이다 be on strike
tongmedal 동메달 bronze medal
tongmu 동무 friend; comrade; companion
tongmul 동물 animal, creature
tongmurhak 동물학 zoology
tongmurhakssang-ŭi 동물학상의 zoological
tongmuro sagwigi 동무로 사귀기 companionship
tongmurwŏn 동물원 zoo
tongmyŏng-iin 동명이인 namesake
tongmyŏnhada 동면하다 hibernate
Tongnam Ashia 동남 아시아 Southeast Asia ◊ Southeast Asian
Tongnam Ashia Kuk-kka Yŏnhap 동남 아시아 국가 연합 ASEAN, Association of South East Asian Nations
tongnip 독립 independence ◊ independent
Tongnip Kinyŏmil 독립 기념일 Independence Day
tongnipkkuk 독립국 independent country
tongniptchŏgin 독립적인 independent, self-reliant
tongniptchŏgŭro 독립적으로 independently
tongnip'ada 독립하다 break away
tongnŏk 동력 movement; play
Tongnyang 동양 East Asia ◊ East Asian
Tongnyang saram 동양 사람 East Asian
tongnyŏgŭro chojonghanŭn 동력으로 조종하는 power-assisted
tongnyŏk 동력 power
tongnyo 동료 companion; colleague
tongnyo 동요 nursery rhyme; turbulence; ***chŏllyuŭi tongnyo*** 전류의 동요 surge ELEC
tongnyohanŭn 동요하는 turbulent
tongnyo kwan-gye 동료 관계 comradeship, friendship
tong-ŏp 동업 partnership
tong-ŏptcha 동업자 partner
tongp'o 동포 fellow citizen, fellow countryman
tongp'ung 동풍 easterly wind
tongsa 동사 verb
tongsamuso 동사무소 sub-district office
tongsang 동상 frostbite; chilblain
tongsang-e kŏllin 동상에 걸린 frostbitten
tongshi 동시 the same time ◊ simultaneous ◊ nursery rhyme
tongshie 동시에 at the same time, simultaneously
tongshie irŏnanŭn 동시에 일어나는 parallel, simultaneous
tongsŏ 동서 sister-in-law (*husband's younger / elder brother's wife*)
tongsŏng-ae hyŏmotchŭng 동성애 혐오증 homophobia
tongsŏng-aeja 동성애자 homosexual, gay
tongsŏng-aeŭi 동성애의 homosexual, gay
tongtchŏm 동점 draw, tie; ***tongtchŏmŭl mandŭlda*** 동점을 만들다 even the score; ***i tae iro***

tongtchŏmin 이 대 이로 동점인 two all
tongtchŏmi toeda 동점이 되다 draw, tie
tongtchogŭro 동쪽으로 east, eastward
tongtchok 동쪽 east
tongtŭnghan chonjae 동등한 존재 equal
tongt'ae chigae 동태 찌개 pollack chowder
tong-ŭi 동의 agreement, consent; arrangement; understanding
tong-ŭihada 동의하다 agree, consent; agree with, support
tong-ŭiŏ 동의어 synonym
tong-yo 동요 agitation
tong-yohan 동요한 agitated
tonŏt 도넛 donut
tonŭl kŏlda 돈을 걸다 back, put money on
tonŭl moktchŏgŭro hanŭn 돈을 목적으로 하는 mercenary
tonŭl naeda 돈을 내다 pay
tonŭl pŏlda 돈을 벌다 earn money
toŏ maen 도어 맨 doorman
toptta 돕다 help
top'yo 도표 diagram, graph
toragada 돌아가다 go back, return
torang 도랑 ditch; gutter
toraoda 돌아오다 come back, get back
toratanida 돌아다니다 move around; wander, roam
torie mannŭn 도리에 맞는 honorable
torie mat-tta 도리에 맞다 be in the right
torik'il su ŏmnŭn 돌이킬 수 없는 irretrievable
torip'ada 돌입하다 fall, plunge
torirŭl anŭn 도리를 아는 honorable
toro 도로 roadway
toro chido 도로 지도 road map
toro kongsa 도로 공사 road works
toro p'yojip'an 도로 표지판 roadsign
toroŭi chung-ang pullidae 도로의 중앙 분리대 median strip
toroŭi taep'isŏn 도로의 대피선 hard shoulder
torŭrae 도르래 pulley
toryŏnhan 돌연한 freak
tosal 도살 slaughter
tosarhada 도살하다 slaughter
toshi 도시 city; town ◊ urban
toshihwa 도시화 urbanization
toshim-ŭi 도심의 down-town
toshirak 도시락 lunch box
toshiŭi 도시의 city, urban
toshiŭi chungshim 도시의 중심 city center
toshiŭi chungshimbue(sŏ) 도시의 중심부에(서) down-town
tosŏgwan 도서관 library
tot 돛 sail
totkkuda 돋구다 work up, develop
totppogi 돋보기 magnifying glass
tot-ttae 돛대 mast
totuk 도둑 thief
toŭi 도의 (moral) principle; ***toŭisang*** 도의상 on principle, as a matter of principle
tourŏ moida 도우러 모이다 rally around
toum 도움 help, aid; ***toumŭi p'iryohan*** 도움이 필요한 in need
toumdatkki 도움닫기 run-up SP
toumi toenŭn 도움이 되는 helpful; conducive to
toummal hwamyŏn 도움말 화면 help screen
tourŏ tallyŏoda 도우러 달려오다 rally around
toyak 도약 leap; vault
toyak sŏnsu 도약 선수 jumper
toye 도예 pottery; ceramics
toyeji 도예지 pottery (*place*)
ttabunhan 따분한 boring
ttada 따다 win; pick; unstop, pop *cork*
ttadollida 따돌리다 leave out; ostracize
ttadollimŭl pat-tta 따돌림을 받다 be alienated; be excluded
ttae 때 occasion; grime; ***-l ttae*** -ㄹ 때 when; ***naega ŏryŏssŭl ttae*** 내가 어렸을 때 when I was a child; ***...se ttaee*** ...세 때에 at the age of ...; ***-l ttaemada*** -ㄹ 때마다 whenever; ***ttaerŭl chal match'un*** 때를 잘 맞춘 well-timed

ttae anin 때 아닌 untimely
ttaega toemyŏn 때가 되면 in due course, eventually
ttaekkaji 때까지 until; ***-l ttaekkaji*** -ㄹ 때까지 until
ttaelnamu 땔나무 firewood
ttaem 댐 dam
ttaemudŭn 때묻은 grimy
...ttaemune ...때문에 because ◊ because of; out of; ***...gi ttaemune*** ...기 때문에 since, because of; ***...ttaemune irŏnada*** ...때문에 일어나다 be due to, be caused by
...ttaemunŭro ...때문으로 because of
ttaerida 때리다 hit, beat (up)
ttaerigi 때리기 thrashing, beating
ttaettaero 때때로 sometimes, occasionally
ttagae 따개 tab
ttak 딱 punctually; exactly; just
ttakttak'ada 딱딱하다 be hard; be stiff
ttakkŭmgŏrida 따금거리다 sting; tingle
ttakkŭmgŏrinŭn 따끔거리는 prickly
ttak tallabut-tta 딱 달라붙다 adhere
ttaktchi 딱지 scab
ttaktchŏngbŏlle 딱정벌레 beetle
ttakttaguri 딱따구리 woodpecker
ttakttak-kkŏrida 딱딱거리다 snap
ttakttak sorirŭl naeda 딱딱 소리를 내다 crackle
ttakttak'an 딱딱한 hard; stiff, stilted
ttakttak'an kkŏptchil 딱딱한 껍질 crust
ttak'anŭn sori 딱하는 소리 snap
ttal 딸 daughter
ttalgi 딸기 strawberry
ttalkkuktchil 딸꾹질 hiccup
ttalkkuktchirhada 딸꾹질하다 have the hiccups
ttallanggŏrida 딸랑거리다 jingle
ttallangttallang 딸랑딸랑 tinkling, jingling
ttam 땀 sweat, perspiration
ttami paen 땀이 밴 sweaty
ttamnae nanŭn 땀내 나는 sweaty
ttamt'usŏng-iin 땀투성이인 covered in sweat
ttamŭl hŭllida 땀을 흘리다 sweat, perspire
ttang 땅 property, land; estate
ttangbŏlle 땅벌레 grub (*of insect*)
ttangk'ong 땅콩 groundnut, peanut
ttangk'ong pŏt'ŏ 땅콩 버터 peanut butter
ttangttalmak'an 땅딸막한 squat, stocky
ttanim 따님 daughter
ttan 딴 another; different; separate; irrelevant; ***ttan tero tollida*** 딴 데로 돌리다 divert; ***kŭgŏn ttan yaegi-yeyo*** 그건 딴 얘기예요 that's beside the point
ttara 따라 down, along
ttaragada 따라가다 follow, come too
ttarajaptta 따라잡다 catch; catch up; overtake
ttarasŏ 따라서 therefore; thus ◊ in accordance with; along
ttarasŏ irŏnan 따라서 일어난 subsequent, later
ttaro 따로 separately, apart ◊ extra, additional; ***kakki ttaro salda*** 각기 따로 살다 live apart
ttarŭda 따르다 abide by, follow, conform; go along with; pour out *liquid*; ***sanghwang-e ttara tarŭda*** 상황에 따라 다르다 that depends (on the circumstances)
ttarŭmyŏn 따르면 according to
ttattŭt'ada 따뜻하다 be warm
ttattŭt'aejida 따뜻해지다 warm up
ttattŭt'age 따뜻하게 warmly
ttattŭt'age iptta 따뜻하게 입다 wrap up
ttattŭt'age kamssada 따뜻하게 감싸다 muffle up
ttattŭt'an 따뜻한 warm
ttat'a 땋다 braid
ttaŭn mŏri 땋은 머리 braid, pigtail
tte 떼 crowd; mob; herd; flock; swarm; ***tte tonŭl pŏlda*** 떼 돈을 벌다 make a killing; ***tterŭl chiŏ moida*** 떼를 지어 모이다 huddle together; ***tterŭl chiŏ tallyŏdŭlda*** 떼를 지어 달려들다 mob; ***tterŭl chit-tta*** 떼를 짓다 swarm
ttemilgi 떼밀기 shove
ttemilgo tŭrŏgada 떼밀고 들어가다 squeeze into *room*
ttenmok 뗏목 raft

tteŏnaeda 떼어내다 detach; pull off; separate; ***t'ellebijŏnesŏ tteŏ not'a*** 텔레비전에서 떼어 놓다 drag oneself away from the TV
tti 띠 sash
ttŏdoradanida 떠돌아다니다 wander, roam
ttŏdori 떠돌이 hobo
ttŏdŭlssŏk'an 떠들썩한 boisterous
ttŏ innŭn 떠 있는 afloat
ttŏk 떡 rice cake
ttŏkch'iri toeda 떡칠이 되다 be plastered with
ttŏk-kkuk 떡국 rice cake soup
ttŏk pŏrŏjin 떡 벌어진 broad
ttŏkppok-kki 떡볶기 rice cake in hot sauce
ttŏlch'yŏbŏrida 떨쳐버리다 dismiss
ttŏlda 떨다 shake, tremble; shiver
ttŏllida 떨리다 quaver, tremble; shudder; throb
ttŏllim 떨림 shudder
ttŏllimŭm 떨림음 throb
ttŏllinŭn 떨리는 wobbly
ttŏmat-tta 떠맡다 take charge
ttŏnada 떠나다 leave, go away
ttŏnaganŭn 떠나가는 outgoing
ttŏnage hada 떠나게 하다 excuse, allow to leave
ttŏngmanduguk 떡만두국 rice cake and dumpling soup
ttŏorŭda 떠오르다 occur to; haunt (*of memory*); surface, come up, rise
ttŏrŏjida 떨어지다 fall, drop, decline; run out; run out of; come off (*of handle etc*); strike (*of disaster*); set (*of sun*); deteriorate; be apart; separate; be left behind; fail *exam*; miscarry; be evenly divisible; get finished; die; get over *illness*; ***imail ttŏrŏjyŏit-tta*** 2마일 떨어져있다 it's 2 miles away
ttŏrŏjyŏsŏ 떨어져서 apart; ***chudoroesŏ ttŏrŏjyŏ*** 주도로에서 떨어져 off the main road; ***...put'ŏ ttŏrŏjyŏ it-tta*** ...부터 떨어져 있다 stay away from; ***...esŏ ttŏrŏjyŏsŏ sŏda*** ...에서 떨어져서 서다 stand clear of
ttŏrŏttŭrida 떨어뜨리다 drop, lower; shed *leaves*; strip *leaves*; throw off
ttŏrŏttŭryŏ 떨어뜨려 aside
tto 또 again; also; ***tto poja!*** 또 보자! see you!
ttohan 또한 also, too; either; ***...to ttohan ...*** ...도 또한 ... (+ *negative verb*) nor
tto hana 또 하나 another, additional
ttokkatchi anŭn 똑같지 않은 unequal
ttokkatkkehada 똑같게하다 equalize
ttok-kkat-tta 똑같다 be exactly like; ***soriga ttok-kkat'ayo*** 소리가 똑같아요 sound the same
ttokpparo 똑바로 straight; straight ahead; upright; ***ttokpparo kada*** 똑바로 가다 carry straight on; ***ttokpparo antta*** 똑바로 앉다 sit up (straight)
ttokppparŭge hada 똑바르게 하다 straighten
ttokpparŭn 똑바른 straight
ttokttak-kkŏrida 똑딱거리다 tick
ttokttok ttŏrŏjida 똑똑 떨어지다 drip, trickle
ttokttok'ada 똑똑하다 be intelligent
ttokttok'an 똑똑한 intelligent, smart, clever
ttolttol kamtta 똘똘 감다 coil
ttong 똥 dung; shit; poop; excrement
ttongkkumŏng 똥구멍 anus, rectum; bottom; butt
ttongppae 똥배 paunch, belly
ttonŭn 또는 or
tto tarŭn 또 다른 further, additional; ***tto tarŭn kŏt*** 또 다른 것 another (one)
ttŭda 뜨다 float; scoop
ttŭgaejil 뜨개질 knitting
ttŭgaejirhada 뜨개질하다 knit
ttŭgŏptta 뜨겁다 be hot; be burning
ttŭgŏun 뜨거운 hot
ttŭiŏmttŭiŏm 띄엄띄엄 sparsely; intermittently; slowly; ***ttŭiŏmttŭiŏm iltta*** 띄엄띄엄 읽다 browse through a book
ttŭiuda 띄우다 sail
ttŭkppakkŭi il 뜻밖의 일 contingency
ttŭl 뜰 garden
ttŭnaegi 뜨내기 hobo
ttŭnaegi ilkkun 뜨내기 일꾼 hobo (*itinerant worker*)

ttŭn-gurum chapkki 뜬구름 잡기 wild-goose chase
ttŭsŭl palk'ida 뜻을 밝히다 define, specify
ttŭsŭl palk'im 뜻을 밝힘 definition
ttŭt 뜻 sense, meaning; intention; aim, purpose
ttŭtppakk 뜻밖 surprise
ttŭtppakke 뜻밖에 unexpectedly
ttŭtppakkŭi 뜻밖의 unexpected
ttŭtppakkŭi haeng-un 뜻밖의 행운 stroke of luck
ttŭt'aji anŭn chang-ae 뜻하지 않은 장애 snag, problem; twist (*in story*)
ttukkŏng 뚜껑 lid; top, cap; flap
ttukttuk ttŏrŏjida 뚝뚝 떨어지다 dribble
ttulkko nagada 뚫고 나가다 negotiate *obstacles*; weather *crisis*
ttult'a 뚫다 drill; pierce *ears*; unblock
ttungbo 뚱보 fatty
ttungttungbo 뚱뚱보 fatso
ttungttunghada 뚱뚱하다 be fat
ttungttunghan 뚱뚱한 fat
tturŏjige poda 뚫어지게 보다 peer at
tturyŏt'ada 뚜렷하다 be clear, distinct
tturyŏt'age 뚜렷하게 clearly, distinctly
tturyŏt'aji anŭn 뚜렷하지 않은 indistinct
tturyŏt'an 뚜렷한 clear; distinct; definite
ttwida 뛰다 pound, throb
ttwigi 뛰기 spring, jump
ttwiŏdanida 뛰어다니다 jump, bounce
ttwiŏdŭlda 뛰어들다 dive; ***pang anŭro ttwiŏdŭlda*** 방 안으로 뛰어들다 burst into the room
ttwiŏdŭlgi 뛰어들기 dive
ttwiŏdŭm 뛰어듦 plunge, fall
ttwiŏnada 뛰어나다 excel; excel at; be excellent; ***poda ttwiŏnada*** 보다 뛰어나다 outperform
ttwiŏ nagada 뛰어 나가다 fly out, rush out
ttwiŏnage 뛰어나게 extremely
ttwiŏnam 뛰어남 excellence
ttwiŏnan 뛰어난 excellent
ttwiŏnan somsshi 뛰어난 솜씨 prowess
ttwiŏ nŏmtta 뛰어 넘다 jump, vault
ttwiŏ orŭda 뛰어 오르다 jump
ttwiŏorŭgi 뛰어오르기 jump
ttwiŏ orŭm 뛰어 오름 jump
tŭk 득 profit, benefit; ***...nŭn kŏshi tŭgi toeji anayo*** ...는 것이 득이 되지 않아요 it doesn't pay to ...
tŭkp'yohada 득표하다 poll, obtain
tŭksshiri ŏpkke toeda 득실이 없게 되다 break even
tŭktchŏm 득점 score; goal; ***tŭktchŏm maganaegi*** 득점 막아내기 save SP
tŭktchŏmhada 득점하다 score; touch down
tŭktchŏmja 득점자 scorer
tŭlch'angmun 들창문 trapdoor
tŭlch'uŏnaeda 들추어내다 dredge up, unearth
tŭlda 들다 enter; join *club*; catch *cold*; contain; accommodate; get; begin; dye; be pleased, be satisfied; cost; put up *hand*; take out *insurance policy*; cut; grow older; hold *pen*; lift; cite *example*; eat; drink
tŭlgo kada 들고 가다 carry
tŭlkkae p'ohoegin 들개 포획인 dog catcher
tŭlkkŏt 들것 stretcher
tŭlkkŭlt'a 들끓다 be overrun with; smolder
tŭllida 들리다 hear; be audible; be rumored; be obsessed by; be lifted up
tŭllinŭn pŏmwi ane(sŏ) 들리는 범위 안에(서) within hearing
tŭllinŭn pŏmwi pakke(sŏ) 들리는 범위 밖에(서) out of hearing
tŭllŏbunnŭn 들러붙는 clingy
tŭllŭda 들르다 drop in, stop by
tŭlppo 들보 beam
tŭlp'an 들판 field
tŭlsso 들소 buffalo
tŭltchungnaltchuk'an 들쭉날쭉한 ragged, jagged
tŭmppuk 듬뿍 plenty, lots
tŭmulda 드물다 be rare
tŭmulge 드물게 rarely, seldom, unusually
tŭmun 드문 rare; infrequent; unusual

tŭndŭnhan 든든한 stalwart, steadfast
tŭng 등 back, spine (*of book*); light, lantern; ***nuguege tŭng-ŭl tollida*** 누구에게 등을 돌리다 turn one's back on s.o.
tŭngban 등반 climb
tŭngbanhada 등반하다 climb
tŭngch'yŏmŏktta 등쳐먹다 prey on
tŭngdae 등대 lighthouse
tŭnggamul 등가물 equivalent
tŭnggŭbŭl maegida 등급을 매기다 grade, rank
tŭnggŭp 등급 grade, quality
tŭng-i kuptta 등이 굽다 stoop
tŭngjang 등장 entrance THEAT
tŭngjanghada 등장하다 enter THEAT
tŭngjang inmul 등장 인물 characters, cast THEAT
tŭngjida 등지다 desert
tŭngkkiro puch'ida 등기로 부치다 register; ***pyŏnjirŭl tŭngkkiro ponaeda*** 편지를 등기로 보내다 send a letter registered
tŭngkki up'yŏn 등기 우편 registered letter
tŭngnogŭl hada 등록을 하다 register
tŭngnok 등록 entry; enrollment, registration
tŭngnok pŏnho 등록 번호 license number
tŭngnok sangp'yo 등록 상표 trademark
tŭngnok'ada 등록하다 register, enroll
tŭngppul 등불 lamp
tŭngsan 등산 mountaineering
tŭngsan-ga 등산가 mountaineer, climber
tŭngsanhwa 등산화 climbing boots
tŭngssu 등수 place, position
tŭngtcha 등자 stirrup
tŭngttaktchi 등딱지 shell (*of tortoise*)
tŭng-yu 등유 kerosene
tŭnŏlbŭn 드넓은 spacious
tŭraibŏ 드라이버 screwdriver; driver COMPUT
tŭraibŭ 드라이브 drive; outing
tŭraik'ŭllining 드라이클리닝 dry-cleaning
tŭraik'ŭlliningh ada 드라이클리닝하다 dry-clean
tŭraik'ŭllining set'aksso 드라이클리닝 세탁소 dry-cleaner
tŭraiŏro mŏrirŭl mallida 드라이어로 머리를 말리다 blow-dry
tŭrama 드라마 drama
tŭresŭ 드레스 dress
tŭribat-tta 들이받다 knock down; run into
tŭribŭrhada 드리블하다 dribble SP
tŭrida 드리다 give
tŭrimashida 들이마시다 suck in, gulp down; inhale
tŭrishwida 들이쉬다 breathe in; ***k'oro tŭrishwida*** 코로 들이쉬다 sniff
tŭrŏgada 들어가다 enter, go into; let in
tŭrŏ it-tta 들어 있다 be inside; ***nae k'ameraga tŭrŏ issŏt-tta*** 내 카메라가 들어 있었다 my camera was in it
tŭrŏjuda 들어주다 accommodate *requirement*; grant *wish*
tŭrŏm 드럼 drum
tŭrŏ mat-tta 들어 맞다 fit
tŭrŏmŏ 드러머 drummer
tŭrŏmt'ong 드럼통 drum (*container*)
tŭrŏnaeda 드러내다 reveal; take out; throw out; ***kamjŏng-ŭl tŭrŏnaeda*** 감정을 드러내다 be demonstrative
tŭrŏnuptta 드러눕다 lie down
tŭrŏoda 들어오다 come in, enter
tŭrŏ ollida 들어 올리다 lift; heave; hand
tŭrŏsŏda 들어서다 enter; ***tarŭn killo tŭrŏsŏda*** 다른 길로 들어서다 turn off
tŭryŏda ponŭn kumŏng 들여다 보는 구멍 peephole
tŭryŏnot'a 들여놓다 stock up on
tŭryŏ ponaeda 들여 보내다 send in
tŭt-tta 듣다 hear; listen; listen to; ***tŭrŭl su innŭn*** 들을 수 있는 audible
tu 두 two
tubu 두부 tofu
tu chari su 두 자리 수 in double figures
tudŭrida 두드리다 beat; knock; pound

tudŭrŏjin 두드러진 conspicuous
tudŭrŏjinŭn 두드러지는 striking, marked
tudunhada 두둔하다 cover up for
tugaegol 두개골 skull
tugoboda 두고보다 watch, keep watch; ***nŏ tugo poja!*** 너 두고 보자! just you wait!
tugo kada 두고 가다 leave behind
tugo marhada 두고 말하다 be meant for, be aimed at
tugŭndugŭn ttwida 두근두근 뛰다 thump
tugŭn-gŏrida 두근거리다 flutter
tujŏl 두절 disruption
tujŏlshik'ida 두절시키다 disrupt
tuk 둑 dike; embankment; weir
tuk-kkil 둑길 embankment
tukkŏbi 두꺼비 toad
tukkŏbijip 두꺼비집 fusebox
tukkŏun 두꺼운 thick
tukkŏuptta 두껍다 be thick
tu kyŏbŭi 두 겹의 double *layer*
tul 둘 two; ***kŭdŭl tul*** 그들 둘 the two of them; ***...wa / gwa ..., tul ta*** ...와 / 과 ..., 둘 다 both... and ...
tulle 둘레 around
tullŏboda 둘러보다 look around; survey; view
tullŏdaeda 둘러대다 beat about the bush; dodge
tullŏdaenŭn kŏjinmal 둘러대는 거짓말 whitewash
tullŏ ssada 둘러 싸다 enclose; surround; ***tullŏssaida*** 둘러싸이다 be surrounded by
tullŏ ssŭiuda 둘러 씌우다 drape
tul ta 둘 다 both; ***kŭdŭl tul ta*** 그들 둘 다 both of them
tultchaero 둘째로 secondly
tumal hal kŏt ŏpsshi 두말 할 것 없이 it goes without saying; ***tumal hal kŏt ŏpsshi ch'oegoimnida*** 두말 할 것 없이 최고입니다 it is simply the best
tumesankkol 두메산골 the sticks, the boonies
tumok haengsehanŭn 두목 행세하는 bossy
tunbu 둔부 haunch
tun-gamhan 둔감한 stolid
tunggŭlda 둥글다 be round
tunggŭlge hada 둥글게 하다 round off *edges*
tunggŭlge ogŭradŭlda 둥글게 오그라들다 curl
tunggŭn 둥근 round, circular
tunggŭn ch'ŏnjang 둥근 천장 dome; vault
tungji 둥지 nest
tunhan 둔한 dull; thick; stupid
tunoe 두뇌 brain
tunt'ak'an 둔탁한 dull
tu pae 두 배 double *amount*
tu paega toeda 두 배가 되다 double
tu paero 두 배로 double
tu paero hada 두 배로 하다 double
tu paeŭi 두 배의 double, twice as much
tu pŏn 두 번 twice
tu pŏntchae 두 번째 second
tu pŏntchaero 두 번째로 second; ***tu pŏntchaero chal hanŭn*** 두 번째로 잘 하는 second best
tu pŏntchaeŭi 두 번째의 second
tup'yoham 투표함 ballot box
turŏnada 들어나다 emerge
turŏ ollida 들어 올리다 take up *carpet etc*
turŭda 두르다 enclose
turumagi 두루마기 (traditional) long coat
turumari 두루마리 scroll, manuscript
turyŏptta 두렵다 be fearful
turyŏum 두려움 fear
turyŏum ŏmnŭn 두려움 없는 fearless
turyŏwŏhada 두려워하다 be afraid; be afraid of
tusŏnŏ kae 두서너 개 a couple of
tusŏnŏsŭi 두서넛의 a couple of (*people*)
tusŏŏmnŭn 두서없는 incoherent, rambling
tusŏŏpsshi iyagihada 두서없이 이야기하다 ramble
tut'ong 두통 headache
tu t'ong-ŭro 두 통으로 in duplicate
tuyu 두유 soy(a) milk
twaeji 돼지 hog, pig
twaeji chŏgŭmt'ong 돼지 저금통 piggybank

twaeji chokppal 돼지 족발 pig's trotters
twaejigogi 돼지고기 pork
twaeji kajuk 돼지 가죽 pigskin
twaejiuri 돼지우리 pigpen
twaessŏyo 됐어요 that's plenty; that's it
twaessŭmnida 됐습니다 there you are (*completing sth*)
twengbŏl 뒝벌 bumblebee
twesalligi 되살리기 undelete COMPUT
twi 뒤 back, rear; **(*ch'aŭi*) *twit chwasŏge*(*sŏ*)** (차의) 뒷 좌석에(서) in back (of the car); ***pŏsŭ twit chwasŏge*(*sŏ*)** 버스 뒷 좌석에(서) at the back of the bus
twibŏmbŏk 뒤범벅 jumble
twich'ŏgida 뒤척이다 stir, move
twich'ŏk-kkŏrida 뒤척거리다 toss and turn; turn over
twich'uk 뒤축 heel (*of shoe*)
twich'yŏjige hada 뒤쳐지게 하다 set back
twidoraboda 뒤돌아보다 look back
twie(sŏ) 뒤에(서) behind; at the back
twie namgida 뒤에 남기다 leave behind
twie namtta 뒤에 남다 stay behind
twiesŏ chidohada 뒤에서 지도하다 mastermind
twiiŭn 뒤이은 succeeding, following
twijibŏjida 뒤집어지다 turn over (*of vehicle*)
twijibŏsŏ 뒤집어서 inside out
twijibŭm 뒤집음 demolition (*of argument*)
twijida 뒤지다 poke around; search
twijiji ank'o ttaragada 뒤지지 않고 따라가다 keep up (*when walking etc*)
twijiptta 뒤집다 upset, overturn *drink*, *glass*; capsize; fold; back; demolish *argument*; turn inside out
twijip'ida 뒤집히다 overturn, capsize
twijukppaktchugin 뒤죽박죽인 topsy-turvy
twijyŏ ch'ajanaeda 뒤져 찾아내다 rummage around
twijyŏsŏ 뒤져서 behind (*in progress, order*)
twikkumch'i 뒤꿈치 heel (*of foot*)
twinggulda 뒹굴다 roll over
twinmadang 뒷마당 backyard
twinmun 뒷문 backdoor
twinmyŏn 뒷면 back, reverse; ***am-myŏn animyŏn twinmyŏn?*** 앞면 아니면 뒷면? heads or tails?
twinŭjŭn kkaedarŭm 뒤늦은 깨달음 hindsight
twiŏlk'in 뒤얽힌 intricate
twiŏptta 뒤엎다 overturn, tip over
twiro chŏp'ae it-tta 뒤로 접해 있다 back onto
twiro mungnŭn mŏri 뒤로 묶는 머리 ponytail
twiro tanggida 뒤로 당기다 draw back, pull back
twirŭl paltta 뒤를 밟다 stalk
twisŏk-kkida 뒤섞이다 be mixed up (*of figures, papers*)
twisŏktta 뒤섞다 shuffle; ***ilburŏ twisŏktta*** 일부러 뒤섞다 scramble *message*
twitchoch'a ch'ajanaeda 뒤쫓아 찾아내다 track down
twitchot-tta 뒤쫓다 chase
twitch'ŭnggye 뒷층계 backstairs
twitjwasŏk 뒷좌석 pillion
twitkkil 뒷길 back road
twitkŭlswe 뒷글쇠 backspace COMPUT
twitppatch'imhae chuda 뒷받침해 주다 back up *claim*, *argument*
twittchang 뒷장 back, reverse
twittchoge(sŏ) 뒷쪽에(서) behind (*in position*)
twittchoge innŭn 뒷쪽에 있는 back, at the back
twittchogŭi 뒷쪽의 backward; rear
twittchogŭro 뒷쪽으로 backward
twittchok 뒷쪽 back
twittchumŏni 뒷주머니 hip pocket
twittŏrŏjida 뒤떨어지다 lag behind
twit-ttŭl 뒷뜰 backyard
twittunggŏrimyŏ kŏt-tta 뒤뚱거리며 걷다 waddle
twiŭi 뒤의 rear
tyusŭ 듀스 deuce (*in tennis*)

T'

t'aak-kki 타악기 percussion; percussion instrument
t'abŏrida 타버리다 burn down
t'abŭlloidŭp'an shinmun 타블로이드판 신문 tabloid (newspaper)
t'ada 타다 get in (*to car*); board; catch *bus etc*; mount *horse*, *bicycle*; ride *horse*, *bicycle*; fly; burn; glow
t'adanghada 타당하다 be just; be valid
t'adanghan 타당한 just; valid
t'adangsŏng 타당성 validity
t'adangsŏng chosa 타당성 조사 feasibility study
t'aea 태아 embryo; fetus
t'aedo 태도 attitude, manner
T'aegugin 태국인 Thai
T'aegugŏ 태국어 Thai (*language*)
t'aegŭk-kki 태극기 (South Korean) national flag
T'aeguk 태국 Thailand ◊ Thai
T'aekkwŏndo 태권도 T'aekwondo
t'aeksshi 택시 taxi, cab
t'aeksshi sŭngch'ajang 택시 승차장 taxi rank, cab stand
t'aeksshi unjŏnsa 택시 운전사 taxi driver, cab driver
t'aek'ŭl 태클 tackle SP
t'aek'ŭrhada 태클하다 tackle SP
t'aemanhada 태만하다 neglect, omit
t'aenggo 탱고 tango
t'aengk'ŭ 탱크 tank
t'aeŏnada 태어나다 be born
t'aeŏp 태업 slowdown, go-slow
t'aep 탭 tab
t'aepttaensŭ 탭댄스 tap dance
t'aep'ung 태풍 hurricane, typhoon
T'aep'yŏng-yang 태평양 Pacific (Ocean)
T'aep'yŏng-yang yŏnan 태평양 연안 Pacific Rim
t'aetchul 탯줄 umbilical cord
t'aeuda 태우다 burn; give a ride; ***ch'a-e t'aeuda*** 차에 태우다 pick up (*in car*)
t'aeugi 태우기 ride (*in car*)
t'aewŏbŏrida 태워버리다 burn out, gut
t'aewŏ chuda 태워 주다 take, drive
t'aeyang 태양 sun
t'aeyang chŏnjip'an 태양 전지판 solar panel
t'aeyang enŏji 태양 에너지 solar energy
t'aeyŏnhan 태연한 nonchalant
t'agae 타개 breakthrough
t'agi shwiun 타기 쉬운 combustible
t'agonan 타고난 innate; natural
t'agonan chaenŭng 타고난 재능 gift, natural ability
t'agonan kŭmbal 타고난 금발 natural blonde
t'agwŏrhan 탁월한 prominent, significant
t'agyŏk 타격 knock, blow
t'ahyŏp 타협 compromise
t'ahyŏpsshik'ida 타협시키다 compromise
t'ahyŏp'ada 타협하다 compromise
t'ahyŏp'aji annŭn 타협하지 않는 uncompromising
t'ail 타일 tile
t'aim aut 타임 아웃 time out
t'aiming 타이밍 timing
t'aimŏ 타이머 timer
t'aim sŭwich'i 타임 스위치 time switch
t'aiŏ 타이어 tire
t'aip'isŭt'ŭ 타이피스트 typist
t'airŭda 타이르다 preach, moralize
t'aja 타자 batter SP
t'aja ch'ida 타자 치다 type
t'ajagi 타자기 typewriter
t'ajagiro ch'ida 타자기로 치다 type
t'ak-kku 탁구 ping-pong
t'alch'um 탈춤 mask dance
t'alch'urhada 탈출하다 escape; get

away; bail out
t'alch'urhan 탈출한 at large
t'alch'wi 탈취 hijack
t'alch'wibŏm 탈취범 hijacker
t'alch'wihada 탈취하다 hijack
t'alch'wije 탈취제 deodorant
t'algok'ada 탈곡하다 thresh *corn*
t'algushik'ida 탈구시키다 dislocate
t'allak 탈락 elimination
t'allak'ada 탈락하다 be eliminated
t'allo 탄로 exposure
t'allonada 탄로나다 be out (*of secret*)
t'allyŏginnŭn 탄력있는 elastic
t'alsse 탈세 tax evasion
t'alssŏndoeda 탈선되다 be derailed
t'alssudoen 탈수된 dehydrated
t'alssugi 탈수기 spin-dryer
t'alssuhada 탈수하다 spin-dry
t'altchang 탈장 hernia
t'altchimyŏn 탈지면 absorbent cotton
t'altchi uyu 탈지 우유 skimmed milk
t'alt'oehada 탈퇴하다 break away (*from organization*)
t'am 탐 ride
t'amdok'ada 탐독하다 devour
t'amgujŏgin 탐구적인 inquisitive
t'amhŏm 탐험 expedition, exploration
t'amhŏmdae 탐험대 expedition
t'amhŏmga 탐험가 explorer
t'amji 탐지 detection
t'amjigi 탐지기 detector
t'amjihada 탐지하다 detect
t'amjŏng sosŏl 탐정 소설 detective novel
t'amjodŭng 탐조등 searchlight
t'amnanŭn 탐나는 desirable, coveted
t'amnik 탐닉 indulgence
t'amnik'ada 탐닉하다 indulge
t'amp'on 탐폰 tampon
t'amsa 탐사 probe
t'amsaek 탐색 search
t'amsaek'ada 탐색하다 explore, look into, examine; seek, search for
t'amyokssŭrŏun 탐욕스러운 insatiable
t'ando misail 탄도 미사일 ballistic missile
t'andu 탄두 warhead
t'an-gwang 탄광 coal mine
t'annyak 탄약 ammunition
t'ansaeng 탄생 birth
t'ansansu 탄산수 soda (water)
t'ansanŭi 탄산의 carbonated
t'ansŏng-i innŭn 탄성이 있는 springy
t'ansuhwamul 탄수화물 carbohydrate
t'anyakt'ong 탄약통 cartridge
t'aorŭda 타오르다 blaze; flare up
t'ap 탑 pagoda; tower
t'apssŭnggu 탑승구 gate (*at airport*)
t'apssŭngkkwŏn 탑승권 boarding card
t'apssŭng susogŭl hada 탑승 수속을 하다 check in
t'apssŭng susok k'aunt'ŏ 탑승 수속 카운터 check-in (counter)
t'apssŭng susok shigan 탑승 수속 시간 check-in time
t'apssŭng taegija 탑승 대기자 standby passenger
t'arae 타래 lock (*of hair*)
t'arak 타락 corruption
t'araksshik'ida 타락시키다 corrupt
t'arak'ada 타락하다 degenerate; be corrupt
t'arak'an 타락한 corrupt, sleazy
t'arhwan 탈환 recapture
t'arok'ada 탈옥하다 break out, escape
t'arŭ 타르 tar
t'arŭishil 탈의실 cubicle; changing room
t'aryŏng 탈영 desertion
t'aryŏngbyŏng 탈영병 deserter
t'aryŏnghada 탈영하다 desert MIL
t'at 탓 fault, blame; result; effect; ***Xŭl / rŭl Yŭi t'asŭro tollida*** X을 / 를 Y의 탓으로 돌리다 put X down to Y
t'at'ada 탓하다 blame
t'awŏnhyŏng 타원형 ellipse
t'e 테 frame, rim; hoop
t'eduri 테두리 brim, rim
t'eibŭl 테이블 table
t'eibŭl po 테이블 보 table cloth
t'eip'ŭ 테이프 tape
t'eip'ŭ nogŭm 테이프 녹음 tape recording
t'eip'ŭro puch'ida 테이프로 붙이다 tape (*with sticky tape*)

t'eksŭt'ŭ p'ail 텍스트 파일 text file
t'ellebi 텔레비 TV
t'ellebijŏn 텔레비전 television
t'ellebijŏn p'ŭrogŭraem 텔레비전 프로그램 television program
t'ellebijŏn set'ŭ 텔레비전 세트 television (set)
t'ellebijŏn susanggi 텔레비전 수상기 television (set)
t'ema 테마 theme
t'ema kong-wŏn 테마 공원 theme park
t'ema ŭmak 테마 음악 theme tune; signature tune
t'enissŭ 테니스 tennis
t'enissŭ chang 테니스 장 tennis court
t'enissŭ kong 테니스 공 tennis ball
t'enissŭ lak'et 테니스 라켓 tennis racket
t'enissŭ sŏnsu 테니스 선수 tennis player
t'enŏ 테너 tenor
t'erŏbŏm 테러범 terrorist
t'erŏ chojik 테러 조직 terrorist organization
t'erŏrijŭm 테러리즘 terrorism
t'erŭl talda 테를 달다 edge
t'i 티 tee
T'ibet'ŭ 티베트 Tibet ◊ Tibetan
T'ibet'ŭin 티베트인 Tibetan (*person*)
T'ibet'ŭŏ 티베트어 Tibetan (*language*)
t'ibi 티비 TV
t'ik'ŭ namu 티크 나무 teak
t'im 팀 team; crew
t'imjang 팀장 team captain
t'ineijŏ 틴에이저 teenager
t'i ŏmnŭn 티 없는 immaculate
t'ip 팁 tip, gratuity
t'ishyŏch'ŭ 티셔츠 T-shirt
t'ŏbin 터빈 turbine
t'ŏch'i 터치 touch SP
t'ŏch'idaun 터치다운 touchdown
t'ŏch'irain 터치라인 touchline
t'ŏjida 터지다 burst
t'ŏjin 터진 burst
t'ŏk 턱 chin; jaw; ledge
t'ŏkppaji 턱받이 bib
t'ŏksshido 턱시도 tuxedo
t'ŏkssuyŏm 턱수염 beard
T'ŏk'i 터키 Turkey ◊ Turkish
T'ŏk'iin 터키인 Turk
T'ŏk'iŏ 터키어 Turkish (*language*)
t'ŏl 털 hair; fur; bristles
t'ŏlshillo ttŭda 털실로 뜨다 knit
t'ŏlssŏk naeryŏnot'a 털썩 내려놓다 slam down
t'ŏminŏl 터미널 terminal
t'ŏmuniŏmnŭn 터무니없는 outrageous, ridiculous
t'ŏng pin 텅 빈 bare, empty
t'ŏnŏl 터널 tunnel
t'ŏ noch'i annŭn 터 놓지 않는 secretive
t'ŏnot'a 터놓다 pour out, tell *troubles*; ***songmaŭmŭl t'ŏnot'a*** 속마음을 터놓다 speak one's mind
t'ŏnt'eibŭl 턴테이블 turntable
t'ŏpssuruk'an 텁수룩한 bushy
t'ŏri manŭn 털이 많은 woolly
t'ŏri ŏmnŭn 털이 없는 hairless
t'ŏri p'ungsŏnghan 털이 풍성한 furry
t'ŏrŏnaeda 털어내다 brush off *dust etc*
t'ŏrŏnot'a 털어놓다 confide
t'ŏttŭrida 터뜨리다 burst; give vent to
t'obŭro charŭda 톱으로 자르다 saw
t'obŭro k'yŏda 톱으로 켜다 saw off
t'odae 토대 support
t'oebohada 퇴보하다 go backward; degenerate
t'oebohanŭn 퇴보하는 backward *society*
t'oegŏ myŏngnyŏng 퇴거 명령 deportation order
t'oehak 퇴학 expulsion
t'oejanghada 퇴장하다 leave; exit (*of actor*); walk out
t'oejangshik'ida 퇴장시키다 expel from the game
t'oejikkŭm 퇴직금 golden handshake
t'oejik sudang 퇴직 수당 unemployment compensation
t'oejŏkshik'ida 퇴적시키다 deposit
t'oep'yejŏgin 퇴폐적인 decadent
t'oerak'ada 퇴락하다 go to seed, become shabby
t'oetcha 퇴짜 brush-off
t'oewihada 퇴위하다 abdicate

t'oewŏn 퇴원 discharge
t'oewŏnshik'ida 퇴원시키다 discharge
t'ogi 토기 earthenware
t'ohada 토하다 vomit
t'oji kaebarŏptcha 토지 개발업자 property developer
t'okki 토끼 rabbit
t'okt'ok tudŭrida 톡톡 두드리다 rap
t'ok'ŭn 토큰 token
t'omak 토막 fragment, chip
t'omakch'ida 토막치다 cut up
t'omat'o 토마토 tomato
t'omat'o k'ech'ap 토마토 케찹 tomato ketchup
t'omnibak'wi 톱니바퀴 cog
t'omni moyang-ŭi 톱니 모양의 jagged
t'omok kisa 토목 기사 civil engineer
t'on 톤 ton
t'ong 통 pack; tub; barrel; *t'ong, subdivision of a city* ◊ *countword for letters or documents*
t'ongch'al 통찰 insight
t'ongch'allyŏk innŭn 통찰력 있는 perceptive, shrewd
t'ongch'ihada 통치하다 rule (*of monarch*)
t'ongch'ija 통치자 ruler (*of state*)
t'ongdok'ada 통독하다 go through, read through
t'onggi 통기 ventilation
t'onggi kumŏng 통기 구멍 vent
t'onggŭnhada 통근하다 commute
t'onggŭnja 통근자 commuter
t'onggŭn kyot'ong 통근 교통 commuter traffic
t'onggŭn yŏlch'a 통근 열차 commuter train
t'onggwashik'ida 통과시키다 carry *proposal*, approve
t'onggwa yŏgaek 통과 여객 transit passenger
t'onggwa yŏgaek taehapsshil 통과 여객 대합실 transit lounge
t'onggye 통계 statistics, figures ◊ statistical
t'onggyehak 통계학 statistics
t'onggyejŏguro 통계적으로 statistically
t'onghada 통하다 flow; be understood; be versed in; go through; open onto
t'onghae chinagada 통해 지나가다 pass through
t'onghaengin 통행인 passer-by
t'onghaengkkwŏn 통행권 right of way
t'onghaengnyo 통행료 toll
t'onghaeng usŏnkkwŏn 통행 우선권 priority, right of way
t'onghap'ada 통합하다 integrate
t'onghwa 통화 currency; telephone call
t'onghwa chaep'aengch'ang 통화 재팽창 reflation
t'onghwa chung shinho 통화중 신호 busy signal TELEC
t'onghwahada 통화하다 get through TELEC
t'onghwajung-in 통화중인 busy TELEC
t'onghwajung shinhoŭm 통화중 신호음 busy tone TELEC
t'onghwa p'aengch'angshik'ida 통화 팽창시키다 inflate
t'onghwaryo 통화료 toll TELEC
t'ong-il 통일 unification; reunification
t'ong-irhada 통일하다 unify
t'ongjang 통장 bank book, pass book; head of a *t'ong, subdivision of a city*
t'ongjehada 통제하다 control, regulate; master; ***uriga t'ongjehal su ŏmnŭn sanghwang-ida*** **우리가 통제할 수 없는 상황이다** these are circumstances beyond our control
t'ongjeshil 통제실 control center
t'ongji 통지 notice (*to leave job, house*); ***nuguege chibŭl nagarago t'ongjihada*** **누구에게 집을 나가라고 통지하다** give s.o. his/her notice
t'ongjorim 통조림 can
t'ongjorimdoen 통조림된 canned
t'ongjorimhada 통조림 하다 can
t'ongmilppang 통밀빵 wholemeal bread
t'ongnamu 통나무 log
t'ongnamu odumaktchip 통나무 오두막집 log cabin
t'ongno 통로 aisle; passageway;

gangway
t'ongnye 통례 custom
t'ongnyeŭi 통례의 customary
t'ongnyŏrhan 통렬한 scathing
t'ongp'ung 통풍 draft
t'ongp'ung-i chal toenŭn 통풍이 잘 되는 drafty
t'ongshin 통신 communications; telecommunications
t'ongshin p'anmae ch'aektcha 통신 판매 책자 mail-order catalog
t'ongshin p'anmae hoesa 통신 판매 회사 mail-order firm
t'ongshinsa 통신사 news agency
t'ongshin wisŏng 통신 위성 communications satellite
t'ongsollyŏk 통솔력 leadership
t'ongsorhada 통솔하다 lead
t'ongtchaero kuptta 통째로 굽다 barbecue
t'ongt'onghada 통통하다 be chubby
t'ongt'onghan 통통한 chubby
t'ongyŏk 통역 interpretation
t'ongyŏk-kka 통역가 interpreter
t'ongyŏk'ada 통역하다 interpret
t'onik wŏt'ŏ 토닉 워터 tonic water
t'onŏ 토너 toner
t'op 톱 saw
t'opkkiŏ 톱기어 top (gear)
t'op-ppap 톱밥 sawdust
t'op'i 토피 toffee
t'op'ing 토핑 topping
t'op'ŭllisŭ 토플리스 topless
t'oron 토론 discussion, debate
t'osŭt'ŭ 토스트 toast
t'oyoil 토요일 Saturday
t'ŭda 트다 open *bank account*; sprout (*of seed*)
t'ŭgi ch'ejil 특이 체질 peculiarity
t'ŭgihan 특이한 peculiar to
t'ŭgiŏptcha 투기업자 speculator
t'ŭgyuŭi 특유의 distinctive
t'ŭkch'urhan 특출한 outstanding; high-powered
t'ŭk-kkwŏnŭl kajin 특권을 가진 privileged
t'ŭkppyŏl chosadan 특별 조사단 task force
t'ŭkppyŏl kwallamsŏk 특별 관람석 grandstand
t'ŭkppyŏl poryuji 특별 보류지 reservation (*special area*)
t'ŭkppyŏrhada 특별하다 be special
t'ŭkppyŏrhage 특별하게 particularly, especially
t'ŭkppyŏrhan 특별한 particular, special
t'ŭkppyŏrhan yeoeŭi 특별한 예외의 exceptional, special
t'ŭkppyŏrhi 특별히 especially, in particular, particularly
t'ŭkp'awŏn 특파원 (special) correspondent
t'ŭkssang-ŭi 특상의 choice, top quality
t'ŭkssŏng 특성 characteristic, trait; special quality
t'ŭkssŏng-ŭl nat'anaeda 특성을 나타내다 characterize, be typical of
t'ŭkssŏng-ŭl nat'anaenŭn 특성을 나타내는 characteristic, typical
t'ŭkssu kidongdae 특수 기동대 taskforce
t'ŭktchil 특질 idiosyncrasy
t'ŭktching 특징 character, feature; ***...ŭl / rŭl t'ŭktching-ŭro hada*** ...을 / 를 특징으로 하다 make a feature of; emphasize
t'ŭktching-ŏmnŭn 특징없는 nondescript
t'ŭktchŏn 특전 privilege; prerogative
t'ŭktchŏnghada 특정하다 specify
t'ŭktchŏnghan 특정한 particular, specific
t'ŭktchong 특종 scoop (*in journalism*)
t'ŭkttaehyŏng-ŭi 특대형의 outsize
t'ŭk'i 특히 especially; specifically
t'ŭk'i choahanŭn 특히 좋아하는 favorite
t'ŭk'ŏ 특허 patent
t'ŭk'ŏrŭl ŏt-tta 특허를 얻다 patent
t'ŭl 틀 frame; casing; mold
t'ŭlda 틀다 put on, turn on
t'ŭlli 틀니 false teeth
t'ŭllida 틀리다 be wrong; go wrong, make a mistake
t'ŭllige 틀리게 incorrectly
t'ŭllimŏmnŭn 틀림없는 correct; unmistakable
t'ŭllimŏptta 틀림없다 must be; ***6shiime t'ŭllimŏptta*** 6시임에

틀림없다 it must be about 6 o'clock; ***t'ŭllimŏpsshi ...l kŏshida*** 틀림없이 ...ㄹ 것이다 be bound to, be sure to
t'ŭllin 틀린 incorrect, wrong, mistaken
t'ŭllin koshi manŭn 틀린 곳이 많은 corrupt COMPUT
t'ŭllin parŭm 틀린 발음 mispronunciation
t'ŭllin parŭmŭl hada 틀린 발음을 하다 mispronounce
t'ŭm 틈 space; gap; opening; ***kip'ŭn t'ŭm*** 깊은 틈 gulf
t'ŭmsae 틈새 niche, slot
t'ŭnt'ŭnhada 튼튼하다 be robust, be healthy
t'ŭnt'ŭnhan 튼튼한 healthy, robust, solid
t'ŭraek 트랙 track
t'ŭraekt'ŏ 트랙터 tractor
t'ŭraemp'ollin 트램폴린 trampoline
t'ŭraenjisŭt'ŏ 트랜지스터 transistor
t'ŭraenjisŭt'ŏ ladio 트랜지스터 라디오 transistor radio
t'ŭraiaenggŭl 트라이앵글 triangle MUS
t'ŭredŭ 트레드 tread (*of tire*)
t'ŭreillŏ 트레일러 trailer
t'ŭre kkiuda 틀에 끼우다 frame
t'ŭre nŏŏ mandŭlda 틀에 넣어 만들다 mold
t'ŭrim 트림 belch
t'ŭrimhada 트림하다 belch
t'ŭrŏk 트럭 truck
t'ŭrŏk unjŏnsa 트럭 운전사 truck driver, teamster
t'ŭrŏ maktta 틀어 막다 plug *hole*
t'ŭrŏmbon 트럼본 trombone
t'ŭrŏmp'et 트럼펫 trumpet
t'ŭrŏngk'ŭ 트렁크 trunk
t'ŭrŏollin mŏri 틀어올린 머리 bun (*in hair*)
t'ŭrol ŏsŏn 트롤 어선 trawler
t'ŭwin pedŭ 트윈 베드 twin beds
t'udŏlgŏrida 투덜거리다 grumble
t'ugi 투기 speculation FIN; jealousy
t'ugihada 투기하다 speculate FIN
t'ugijŏk saŏp 투기적 사업 venture
t'uguhada 투구하다 pitch SP
t'ugwang chomyŏng 투광 조명 floodlight
t'uhahada 투하하다 jettison, throw overboard; drop *bomb*
t'uip chŏnyŏlgi 투입 전열기 immersion heater
t'uja 투자 stake, investment
t'ujaeng 투쟁 fight, conflict
t'ujaengtchŏgin 투쟁적인 militant
t'ujahada 투자하다 invest
t'ujaja 투자자 investor
t'uk t'wiŏ naon 툭 튀어 나온 prominent
t'umyŏnghan 투명한 transparent
t'ungmyŏngsŭrŏptta 퉁명스럽다 be curt, be blunt
t'ungmyŏngssŭrŏun 퉁명스러운 abrupt, curt
t'uok 투옥 imprisonment
t'uok'ada 투옥하다 imprison
t'up'isŭ 투피스 two-piece
t'up'yo 투표 vote; voting; ***t'up'yokkwŏnŭl kajida*** 투표권을 가지다 have the vote
t'up'yohada 투표하다 vote
t'up'yoro chŏnghada 투표로 정하다 ballot
t'usa 투사 militant
t'usu 투수 pitcher SP
t'usuk shigan 투숙 시간 check-in time (*at hotel*)
t'wida 튀다 bounce; splash
t'wige hada 튀게 하다 bounce
t'wigida 튀기다 splatter; deep-fry
t'wigim 튀김 (deep) fried food
t'winggida 튕기다 twang
t'wiŏ naoda 튀어나오다 bulge, project
t'yubŭ 튜브 tube
t'yubŭga ŏmnŭn 튜브가 없는 tubeless *tire*
t'yullip 튤립 tulip
t'yunŏ 튜너 tuner

Ŭ

ŭddŭm direkt'ori 으뜸 디렉토리 root directory
...ŭi ...의 of; ***kŭ ch'aŭi saek*** 그 차의 색 the color of the car
ŭi-ahage yŏgida 의아하게 여기다 wonder, think
ŭibok 의복 garment
ŭibudadŭl 의붓아들 stepson
ŭibut-tchamae 의붓자매 stepsister
ŭibut-ttal 의붓딸 stepdaughter
ŭibut'yŏngje 의붓형제 stepbrother
ŭibyŏng 의병 righteous army
ŭichimhaji annŭn 의심하지 않는 unsuspecting
ŭich'i 의치 dentures
ŭido 의도 intention
ŭidohada 의도하다 mean, intend; ***muŏsŭl ŭidohada*** 무엇을 의도하다 intend to do sth, do sth on purpose
ŭidojŏgin 의도적인 intentional
ŭigiyangyang 의기양양 elation
ŭigiyangyanghan 의기양양한 elated
ŭigushim 의구심 doubt, uncertainty; reservation
ŭigyŏn 의견 opinion; ***naŭi ŭigyŏnŭronŭn*** 나의 의견으로는 in my opinion
ŭigyŏn ch'ai 의견 차이 disagreement, misunderstanding
ŭigyŏni mat-tchi ant'a 의견이 맞지 않다 disagree with
ŭigyŏnŭl murŏboda 의견을 물어보다 canvass, seek opinion of
ŭigyŏnŭl mut-tta 의견을 묻다 consult, seek the advice of
ŭigyŏnŭl tallihada 의견을 달리하다 differ, dissent from, disagree
ŭihae 의해 by
ŭihak 의학 medicine (*science*) ◊ medical
ŭihak pakssa 의학 박사 MD, Doctor of Medicine
ŭihoe 의회 assembly; council; parliament
ŭihoeŭi 의회의 parliamentary
ŭija 의자 chair
ŭijang 의장 chairman, the chair
ŭijangjigŭl mat-tta 의장직을 맡다 chair; take the chair
ŭiji 의지 will, willpower
ŭijiga kanghan 의지가 강한 strong-willed
ŭijiga kudŭn 의지가 굳은 resolute
ŭijihada 의지하다 rely on, look to
ŭijiryŏk 의지력 willpower
ŭijŏrhada 의절하다 disown
ŭijonhada 의존하다 depend; ***muŏse ŭijonhada*** 무엇에 의존하다 depend on sth; ***nanŭn nŏhant'e ŭijonhago it-tta*** 난는 너한테 의존하고 있다 I depend on you
ŭijonhanŭn 의존하는 dependant
ŭimi 의미 sense, meaning
ŭimihada 의미하다 signify, mean
ŭimiinnŭn 의미있는 meaningful, constructive
ŭimu 의무 duty; obligation; responsibility
ŭimujŏgin 의무적인 compulsory, mandatory
ŭimu kyoyuk 의무 교육 compulsory education
ŭimun 의문 query
ŭimunsa 의문사 interrogative
ŭimunŭl chegihada 의문을 제기하다 query
ŭimurŭl chiuda 의무를 지우다 bind, oblige
ŭimuŭi 의무의 obligatory
ŭinonhada 의논하다 discuss, talk over, talk
ŭiroe 의뢰 commission (*job*)
ŭiroehada 의뢰하다 commission (*for a job*)
ŭiroein 의뢰인 client
ŭirye 의례 protocol, etiquette
ŭiryo pohŏm 의료 보험 medical insurance

ŭiryu 의류 clothing
ŭisa 의사 doctor
ŭisa chŏndal 의사 전달 communication
ŭisa kyŏltchŏngja 의사 결정자 decision-maker
ŭisang 의상 outfit, costume
ŭisa p'yoshi 의사 표시 gesture
ŭisarok 의사록 minutes (*of meeting*)
ŭisarŭl sot'onghada 의사를 소통하다 communicate
ŭishigi innŭn 의식이 있는 conscious
ŭishigŭi 의식의 ritual
ŭishigŭl hoebok'ada 의식을 회복하다 come to, regain consciousness
ŭishigŭl ilt'a 의식을 잃다 lose consciousness, black out
ŭishik 의식 ritual, ceremony; consciousness
ŭishik sangshil 의식 상실 blackout
ŭishiktchŏgin 의식적인 conscious, deliberate
ŭishim 의심 suspicion, doubt
ŭishimhada 의심하다 doubt, question, suspect; ***ŭishimhal yŏji ŏpsshi*** 의심할 여지 없이 undoubtedly, indisputably
ŭishimŏmnŭn 의심없는 unquestioning
ŭishimsŭrŏpkke 의심스럽게 doubtfully
ŭishimsŭrŏptta 의심스럽다 be doubtful (*of person*)
ŭishimsŭrŏun 의심스러운 dubious; suspicious; questionable
ŭishimtchŏgŭn 의심쩍은 doubtful; in question; shady
ŭishimtchŏk-kke saenggak'ada 의심쩍게 생각하다 doubt
ŭisŏk 의석 seat POL
ŭiwŏn 의원 councilor
ŭiyok 의욕 will, motivation; ***nanŭn pyŏllo ŭiyogi annanda*** 나는 별로 의욕이 안난다 I don't feel very motivated
ŭkkaeda 으깨다 mash
ŭkkaen kamja 으깬 감자 mashed potatoes
...ŭl ...을 *object particle*; *future particle*
-(ŭ)lsurok -(으)ㄹ수록 the more... the more ...; ***manŭlsurok chohayo*** 많을수록 좋아요 the more the better
ŭmak 음악 music
ŭmak hak-kkyo 음악 학교 music school, conservatory
ŭmakkat'ŭn 음악같은 musical, melodious
ŭmak-kka 음악가 musician
ŭmaktchŏgin 음악적인 musical *person*
ŭmaktchŏk sojiri ŏmnŭn 음악적 소질이 없는 unmusical
ŭmban 음반 album
ŭmch'imhan 음침한 bleak, dingy
ŭmgŭgŭi 음극의 negative ELEC
ŭmgye 음계 scale MUS
ŭmgyŏng 음경 penis
ŭmhŏmhan 음험한 underhand, devious; insidious
ŭmhyanghak 음향학 acoustics
ŭmjŏl 음절 syllable
ŭmjŏng-i mannŭn 음정이 맞는 in tune
ŭmjŏng-i t'ŭllin 음정이 틀린 out of tune
ŭmju 음주 drinking
ŭmju ch'ŭktchŏnggi 음주 측정기 Breathalyzer®, breath analyzer
ŭmjuja 음주자 drinker
ŭmju unjŏn 음주 운전 drink driving
ŭmmi 음미 taste, savor
ŭmmihada 음미하다 taste, savor
ŭmmo 음모 conspiracy, intrigue; pubic hair
ŭmmohada 음모하다 plot
ŭmmoja 음모자 conspirator
ŭmmorŭl kkumida 음모를 꾸미다 conspire
ŭmnanhada 음란하다 be obscene
ŭmnanhan 음란한 dirty; obscene; pornographic
ŭmnyang 음량 volume
ŭmnyang 음양 yin and yang
ŭmnyang chojŏlgi 음량 조절기 volume control
ŭmnyŏk 음역 range
ŭmnyŏk 음력 lunar calendar
ŭmnyŏk'ada 음역하다 transliterate
ŭmnyo 음료 beverage, drink
ŭmp'yo 음표 note MUS
ŭmsaek 음색 tone

ŭmsanhan 음산한 dismal
ŭmshik 음식 food
ŭmsŏng up'yŏn 음성 우편 voice mail
ŭn 은 silver
...ŭn ... 은 → ***nŭn*** 는
ŭnbang-ul kkot 은방울 꽃 lily of the valley
ŭnch'ong 은총 blessing
ŭndunja 은둔자 recluse, hermit
ŭndunsaenghwal 은둔생활 secluded life
ŭngch'uk 응축 condensation
ŭngch'uk'ada 응축하다 condense
ŭngdal 응달 shade; ***ŭngdare(sŏ)*** 응달에(서) in the shade
ŭngdap 응답 answer
ŭngdap'ada 응답하다 answer
ŭnggohada 응고하다 set, congeal; curdle
ŭnggoshik'ida 응고시키다 coagulate
ŭnggŭp ch'iryo 응급 치료 first aid
ŭnghada 응하다 comply; comply with; ***k'waehi ŭnghada*** 쾌히 응하다 jump at, take eagerly
ŭngmoja 응모자 applicant
ŭngmojak 응모작 entry (*for competition*)
ŭngmo sŏryu 응모 서류 entry form
ŭngnak 응낙 compliance
ŭn-goe 은괴 silver ingot
ŭngshi 응시 gaze
ŭngshihada 응시하다 gaze; gaze at; contemplate
ŭngshija 응시자 entrant, candidate
ŭn-gŭnhi 은근히 politely; secretly; ***...ranŭn ŭishimŭl ŭn-gŭnhi kajida*** ...라는 의심을 은근히 가지다 have a sneaking suspicion that
ŭng-wŏnhada 응원하다 cheer on
ŭngyong p'ŭrogŭraem 응용 프로그램 application (program)
ŭnhaeng 은행 bank
ŭnhaeng chan-go 은행 잔고 bank balance
ŭnhaengga 은행가 banker
ŭnhaeng t'ongjang 은행 통장 bank book
ŭnhaeng yungja 은행 융자 bank loan
ŭnhye 은혜 obligation, moral indebtedness; ***nuguege ŭnhyerŭl ipkko it-tta*** 누구에게 은혜를 입고 있다 be under an obligation to s.o.
ŭnhyerŭl pep'unŭn saram 은혜를 베푸는 사람 benefactor
...(ŭ)nji ...(으)ㄴ지 → ***...inji*** ...인지
ŭnjong-i 은종이 tinfoil
ŭnmirhi 은밀히 secretly
ŭnnik 은닉 secretion, concealment
ŭnnik'ada 은닉하다 conceal, hide; ***chiharo ŭnnik'ada*** 지하로 은닉하다 go underground
ŭnŏ 은어 slang
ŭnppich'ŭi 은빛의 silver
ŭnp'ye 은폐 cover-up
ŭnshinch'ŏ 은신처 hideaway
ŭnshinhada 은신하다 be in hiding
ŭn togŭmhan 은 도금한 silver-plated
ŭnt'oe 은퇴 retirement
ŭnt'oehada 은퇴하다 retire
ŭnt'oehan 은퇴한 retired
ŭp 읍 large township
...ŭro ...으로 by; from, because of; of; into; in; with; to; toward
...ŭrobut'ŏ ...으로부터 from
...ŭrosŏ ...으로서 as
ŭrŭrŏnggŏrida 으르렁거리다 growl, snarl

U

uahada 우아하다 be graceful; be elegant
uahan 우아한 graceful; elegant
ubak 우박 hail
ubi 우비 raincoat
Uchahyŏng k'ŏbŭ U자형 커브 hairpin curve
uch'ebu 우체부 mailman
uch'eguk 우체국 post office
uch'et'ong 우체통 mailbox
uch'ŭgŭi 우측의 starboard; right
uch'ŭk haendul unjŏn 우측 핸들 운전 right-hand drive
uch'ŭk konggyŏkssu 우측 공격수 right wing
udaehanŭn 우대하는 preferential
udumŏri 우두머리 head; boss; leader
udunhan 우둔한 dense, dim, stupid
ugŏjin 우거진 dense *foliage*
ugŭlgŏrida 우글거리다 swarm, crowd
uhoe 우회 detour, diversion
uhoehada 우회하다 bypass, circumvent
uhoero 우회로 bypass
uhoeshik'ida 우회시키다 divert
uhoeŭi 우회의 roundabout
uhojŏgin 우호적인 amicable
uigŭi 우익의 right-wing
uik 우익 right, right wing; ***uige*(*sŏ*)** 우익에(서) on the right
uik chijija 우익 지지자 right winger
ujŏkujŏk sshiptta 우적우적 씹다 munch
ujŏng 우정 friendship
uju 우주 space, outer space; universe
ujubok 우주복 spacesuit
uju chŏnggŏjang 우주 정거장 space station
ujuin 우주인 astronaut
uju pihaengsa 우주 비행사 cosmonaut
ujusŏn 우주선 spaceship, spacecraft
uju wangbokssŏn 우주 왕복선 space shuttle
ujuyŏhaeng 우주여행 voyage (*in space*)
ulbujit-tta 울부짖다 howl, wail
ulch'anghage charada 울창하게 자라다 thrive
ulda 울다 weep, cry; bawl, bellow
ullida 울리다 go off (*of alarm*); blow; ring; honk
ullim 울림 ring (*of bell*); roll (*of thunder*); echo
Ullŭngdo 울릉도 Ullung Island
ullyŏ p'ŏjida 울려 퍼지다 echo, reverberate; blare out
ultchŏk'ada 울적하다 be melancholy
ult'ari 울타리 fence; railings; hedge; barrier
ult'ariro tullŏ ssada 울타리로 둘러 싸다 fence in
ult'ungbult'unghada 울퉁불퉁하다 be bumpy
ult'ungbult'unghan 울퉁불퉁한 rough; bumpy; lumpy
umch'ŭrida 움츠리다 cower
umch'urida 움추리다 curl up
umjigida 움직이다 move, budge; dislodge; operate, run
umjigim 움직임 motion; move; movement; maneuver
umjiginŭn 움직이는 moving (*which can move*)
umk'yŏjaptta 움켜잡다 grasp
ummorŭl kkumida 음모를 꾸미다 frame, set up
ump'uk kkŏjida 움푹 꺼지다 cave in
ump'uk tŭrŏgage hada 움푹 들어가게 하다 dent
ump'uk tŭrŏgan 움푹 들어간 hollow
umtchirhada 움찔하다 flinch
umul 우물 well
un 운 luck, fortune; rhyme; ***une matkkigo haeboda*** 운에 맡기고 해보다 take a chance; ***uni chot'a*** 운이 좋다 be lucky, luck out; ***uni mat-tta*** 운이 맞다 rhyme with

unban 운반 haulage
unbanhada 운반하다 convey, carry
unbanin 운반인 porter
unban sudan 운반 수단 vehicle
un chok'e 운 좋게 luckily
un choŭn 운 좋은 lucky
undong 운동 campaign, drive; movement; exercise ◊ sporting, athletic
undongga 운동가 athlete; campaigner
undonggyŏnggi 운동경기 athletics
undonghada 운동하다 exercise, take exercise; work out; play SP
undonghwa 운동화 sneakers
undongjang 운동장 arena
undong pujogin 운동 부족인 unfit
undongshik'ida 운동시키다 exercise
undong-ŭl hada 운동을 하다 campaign
ungbyŏn-ga 웅변가 speaker, orator
ungdaehan 웅대한 epic; tremendous; impressive; majestic
ungdŏng-i 웅덩이 pool; puddle
ungjanghada 웅장하다 be grand
ungjangham 웅장함 grandeur
ungjanghan 웅장한 grand
ungk'ŭrida 웅크리다 stoop, bend down
unha 운하 canal
unhaengdoeda 운행되다 run (*of trains etc*)
unim mit pohŏm p'oham kagyŏk 운임 및 보험 포함 가격 CIF, cost insurance freight
unjŏn 운전 drive; driving
unjŏnhada 운전하다 drive
unjŏn hagwŏn 운전 학원 driving school
unjŏnja 운전자 driver; motorist
unjŏn kyoyuk 운전 교육 driving lesson
unjŏn kyoyuk kangsa 운전 교육 강사 driving instructor
unjŏn myŏnhŏ shihŏm 운전 면허 시험 driving test
unjŏn myŏnhŏtchŭng 운전 면허증 driver's license
unjŏntae 운전대 steering column
unmyŏng 운명 fate, destiny
unmyŏng chiuda 운명 지우다 condemn
unmyŏng yejŏngsŏl 운명 예정설 predestination
unŏmnŭn 운없는 unlucky, unfortunate
unŏpkke 운없게 unluckily
unsŏk 운석 meteorite
unsong hoesa 운송 회사 carrier, haulage company
unsuŏptcha 운수업자 forwarding agent
unttaega mannŭn 운때가 맞는 lucky
unyŏng 운영 operations
unyŏngdoeda 운영되다 operate
unyŏnghada 운영하다 run, manage
up'yŏn 우편 mail ◊ postal; ***muŏsŭl up'yŏnŭro ponaeda*** 무엇을 우편으로 보내다 put sth in the mail
up'yŏnham 우편함 mailbox
up'yŏnhwan 우편환 money order
up'yŏn pŏnho 우편 번호 zip code
up'yŏn yogŭm 우편 요금 postage
up'yo 우표 stamp
uranyum 우라늄 uranium
uri 우리 we; us ◊ cage; pen; pound
uri chashin 우리 자신 ourselves; ***uri chashinŭro*** 우리 자신으로 by ourselves; ***urikkiriŭi yaegiijiman*** 우리끼리의 얘기이지만 between you and me
urida 우리다 infuse
uriŭi 우리의 our; my
uriŭi kŏt 우리의 것 ours; mine
urŏnada 우러나다 well up; soak out; ***chinshimesŏ urŏnan*** 진심에서 우러난 heartfelt
urŭmŭl t'ŏttŭrida 울음을 터뜨리다 burst into tears
urŭrunggŏrida 우르릉거리다 roar
ururu taranada 우루루 달아나다 stampede
ururu taranam 우루루 달아남 stampede
uryang chushik 우량 주식 blue chip
uryangju 우량주 gilts
uryŏhada 우려하다 worry
usan 우산 umbrella
usang 우상 idol
use 우세 domination, superiority
usehan 우세한 prevailing
usŏn 우선 firstly

usŏng-ŭi 우성의 dominant
usŏn-gwŏnŭl chuda 우선권을 주다 give preference to
usŏnhada 우선하다 take precedence; take precedence over
usŏnkkwŏni it-tta 우선권이 있다 have priority
usŏnkkwŏnŭl chuda 우선권을 주다 prioritize, give priority to
usŏn sunwirŭl maegida 우선 순위를 매기다 prioritize, put in order of priority
usŏnŭn 우선은 first of all
usosŭl pŏtkko 웃옷을 벗고 in his shirt sleeves
usŭgae sori 우스개 소리 joke
usŭkkwangsŭrŏun 우스꽝스러운 comical
usŭl iri anida 웃을 일이 아니다 it's no joke
usŭm 웃음 laugh; laughter
usŭmkkŏriga toeda 웃음거리가 되다 make a fool of oneself, become a laughing stock
usŭmŭl chaanaenŭn 웃음을 자아내는 hilarious
usŭngja 우승자 winner
usŭngk'ŏp 우승컵 trophy, cup
usŭngp'ae 우승패 shield, trophy
usŭpkkedo 우습게도 funnily enough
usŭpkke yŏgida 우습게 여기다 jeer at
usŭptta 우습다 be funny
usŭun 우스운 funny, humorous
utchuldaenŭn 우쭐대는 big-headed
utkkida 웃기다 amuse
utkkige 웃기게 comically
utkkinŭn chit 웃기는 짓 farce
utkkinŭn nom 웃기는 놈 joker, comedian, clown *pej*
uttchuldaeda 우쭐대다 show off *pej*
ut-tta 웃다 laugh
uul 우울 gloom
uultchŭng 우울증 depression
uultchŭng hwanja 우울증 환자 hypochondriac
uurhada 우울하다 be gloomy
uurhaehada 우울해하다 depress, get down; mope
uurhagehada 우울하게하다 depress, get down
uurhagehanŭn 우울하게하는 depressing; oppressive
uurhan 우울한 depressed; gloomy; morose
uusorirŭl naeda 우우소리를 내다 hoot
uyŏn 우연 chance, luck
uyŏnhada 우연하다 be accidental
uyŏnhan 우연한 casual; accidental; chance
uyŏnhan mannam 우연한 만남 chance encounter
uyŏnhan sakkŏn 우연한 사건 accident
uyŏnhi 우연히 by accident, by chance
uyŏnhi irŏnanŭn 우연히 일어나는 incidental
uyŏnhi majuch'ida 우연히 마주치다 meet by chance
uyŏnhi mannada 우연히 만나다 bump into, meet by chance, run across
uyŏnhi palgyŏnhada 우연히 발견하다 happen across, find by chance
uyŏnhi tŭt-tta 우연히 듣다 overhear
uyŏnŭi ilch'i 우연의 일치 coincidence
uyu 우유 milk
uyubudan 우유부단 indecisiveness
uyubyŏng 우유병 bottle (*for baby*)

W

...wa ...와 and
wa! 와! wow!
wae 왜 why, what for; what is it?; ***wae andwae?*** 왜 안돼? why not?
waegari 왜가리 heron
waegŏn 왜건 station wagon
waegokttoen shigandae 왜곡된 시간대 timewarp
waegok'ada 왜곡하다 distort
Waegu 왜구 Japanese marauders
waenyahamyŏn ...ki ttaemunida 왜냐하면 ...기 때문이다 as, because
waip'ŏ 와이퍼 windshield wiper
waip'ŭ 와이프 wife
wajak-wajak soriga nada 와작와작 소리가 나다 crunch
wakssŭ 왁스 wax
walch'ŭ 왈츠 waltz
wallyohyŏng 완료형 perfect GRAM
wanbyŏk 완벽 perfection
wanbyŏkjuŭija 완벽주의자 perfectionist
wanbyŏk'ada 완벽하다 be perfect
wanbyŏk'age 완벽하게 perfectly; impeccably; soundly *beaten*; ***muŏsŭl wanbyŏk'age alda*** 무엇을 완벽하게 알다 know sth inside out
wanbyŏk'an 완벽한 perfect; impeccable
wanbyŏk'i 완벽히 perfectly
wanch'ung changch'i 완충 장치 buffer
wanch'unggi 완충기 shock absorber
wanch'ung kiŏk changch'i 완충 기억 장치 memory buffer
wanch'ungnyŏk 완충역 buffer
wanduk'ong 완두콩 pea
wang 왕 king
wan-ganghada 완강하다 be stubborn, be dogged
wan-ganghan 완강한 determined, tenacious; stubborn
wangbok pihaenggi 왕복 비행기 return flight
wangbok yŏhaeng 왕복 여행 round trip
wangbok yŏhaengp'yo 왕복 여행표 round trip ticket
wangbok'ada 왕복하다 shuttle
wangguk 왕국 kingdom
wanggwan 왕관 crown
wangja 왕자 prince
wangjo 왕조 dynasty
wangjok 왕족 royalty
wangjwa 왕좌 throne
wan-gogŏ 완곡어 euphemism
wan-gohan 완고한 inflexible, rigid; headstrong; pigheaded
wangsŏnghada 왕성하다 be hearty
wangsŏnghan 왕성한 hearty; voracious
wang-wie ollida 왕위에 올리다 crown
wanhwahada 완화하다 soften, cushion
wanhwashik'ida 완화시키다 relax
wanje 완제 wipe out
wanjep'um 완제품 end product
wanjŏnhada 완전하다 be perfect, be complete
wanjŏnhage 완전하게 perfectly, totally
wanjŏnhan 완전한 complete, thorough; pure; outright
wanjŏnhi 완전히 purely, nothing but; absolutely, completely; entirely fully; outright *win*
wanjŏnhi chami kkaen 완전히 잠이 깬 wide awake
wanjŏnhi kkŭnnaeda 완전히 끝내다 terminate
wanjŏnhi mach'ida 완전히 마치다 complete
wanjŏnhi mich'in 완전히 미친 raving mad
wanjŏnhi pusuda 완전히 부수다 completely destroy, wipe out
wanjŏnhi p'agoehada 완전히

파괴하다 obliterate
wank'waehada 완쾌하다 make a complete recovery
wanmanhan 완만한 sluggish
wanp'aeshik'ida 완패시키다 bomb
wansŏng 완성 completion
wansŏngdoen 완성된 complete, finished
wansŏnghada 완성하다 complete
wap'ŭl 와플 waffle
washyŏ 와셔 washer
watta katta hada 왔다 갔다 하다 pace up and down
wat'ŭ 와트 watt
webbŭraujŏ 웹브라우저 web browser
weding k'eik'ŭ 웨딩 케이크 wedding cake
weding tŭresŭ 웨딩 드레스 wedding dress
Weiljŭ 웨일즈 Wales ◊ Welsh
weip'ŏ 웨이퍼 wafer
weit'ŏ 웨이터 waiter
weit'ŭrisŭ 웨이트리스 waitress
wep 웹 the Web
wep p'eiji 웹 페이지 web page
wep sa-it'ŭ 웹 사이트 web site
wi 위 upper side; top; superiority; rank; position; stomach ◊ gastric ◊ over, above
wian 위안 comfort, consolation
wianhada 위안하다 comfort, console
wiban 위반 violation, breach
wibanhada 위반하다 break, violate, contravene
wibŏp 위법 offense ◊ illicit
wich'i 위치 position, location, setting; situation
wich'ihada 위치하다 lie, be situated, be located; stand
wich'irŭl aranaeda 위치를 알아내다 locate
wich'irŭl chŏnghada 위치를 정하다 locate, site
wich'i sŏnjŏng 위치 선정 location, siting
wich'ŭng-e 위층에 upstairs, on the floor above
wich'ŭng-ŭi 위층의 upstairs
widaehada 위대하다 be great
widaeham 위대함 greatness
widaehan 위대한 grand
wido 위도 latitude; parallel
widok'ada 위독하다 be critically ill
widok'an 위독한 critical; critically ill
wie 위에 up; above; on top of; ***hanŭl / chibung wie*** 하늘 / 지붕 위에 up in the sky / up on the roof
wigi 위기 crisis; ***...a(ŏ, yŏ)ya hal wigie mollyŏ it-tta*** ...아(어, 여)야 할 위기에 몰려있다 be under pressure to ...
wigie ch'ŏhada 위기에 처하다 be at stake, be at risk
wigijŏgin 위기적인 critical, serious
wihae 위해 for; ***...gi wihae*** ...기 위해 to, in order to; ***...gi wihayŏ*** ...기 위하여 in order to; ***...ŭl / rŭl wihaesŏ*** ...을 / 를 위해서 for the sake of ...
wihan 위한 for; ***igŏsŭn nŏrŭl wihan kŏshida*** 이것은 너를 위한 것이다 this is for you
wihayŏ 위하여 on behalf of; for the sake of; in favor of
wihŏm 위험 risk, chance; danger, peril; ***wihŏmŭl murŭpssŭda*** 위험을 무릅쓰다 take a risk; ***wihŏme ppajige hada*** 위험에 빠지게 하다 endanger
wihŏmhada 위험하다 be dangerous
wihŏmhan 위험한 risky, dangerous; hazardous; treacherous
wihŏm inmul 위험 인물 menace; security risk (*person*)
wihŏmjidae 위험 지대 minefield
wihŏm yoso 위험 요소 hazard
wihyŏp 위협 threat, menace
wihyŏp'ada 위협하다 threaten, menace, terrorize
wihyŏp'anŭn 위협하는 threatening, menacing
wiim 위임 delegation
wiimhada 위임하다 delegate
wiimkkwŏn 위임권 power of attorney
wijak 위작 forgery (*painting*)
wijang 위장 disguise, camouflage; insides
wijanghada 위장하다 disguise, camouflage; impersonate
wijaryo 위자료 alimony
wijo 위조 forgery

wijo chip'ye 위조 지폐 forged bill, dud
wijodoen sŏryu 위조된 서류 forgery
wijohada 위조하다 falsify; forge, counterfeit
wijoja 위조자 forger
wijop'um 위조품 forgery
wijoŭi 위조의 counterfeit
wijŭng 위증 perjury
wijŭnghada 위증하다 perjure oneself
windou 윈도우 window COMPUT
windŭsŏp'ing 윈드서핑 windsurfing, sailboarding
windŭsŏp'ing podŭ 윈드서핑 보드 windsurfer, sailboard
wingk'ŭ 윙크 wink
wingk'ŭhada 윙크하다 wink
wing-winggŏrida 윙윙거리다 hum
wing-winghanŭn sori 윙윙하는 소리 buzz, drone
wingwing sorirŭl naeda 윙윙 소리를 내다 buzz
wingwing tolda 윙윙 돌다 whirr
wiŏmminnŭn 위엄있는 dignified, majestic
wiŏp 위업 exploit, feat
wiro 위로 up, upward ◊ consolation
wirohada 위로하다 console
wirohal kil ŏmnŭn 위로할 길 없는 inconsolable
wiro ollida 위로 올리다 scroll up
wiro tŏnjida 위로 던지다 throw up *ball*
wiro unbanhada 위로 운반하다 take up, carry up
wisaeng 위생 hygiene ◊ sanitary
wisaengch'ŏri 위생처리 sanitation
wisaengjŏgin 위생적인 sanitary
wisaengsang-ŭi 위생상의 hygienic
wisaengsŏlbi 위생설비 sanitation, sanitary installation
wishŏme ppattŭrida 위험에 빠뜨리다 risk
wisŏn 위선 hypocrisy
wisŏng t'ibŭi 위성 티브이 satellite TV
wisŏnja 위선자 hypocrite
wisŏnjŏgin 위선적인 hypocritical
wisŭk'i 위스키 whiskey
wit'aeroptta 위태롭다 be in jeopardy
wit'aeroun 위태로운 dangerous
wit'ak 위탁 consignment; trust FIN
witchoge 위쪽에 at the top of
wi tchogŭi 위 쪽의 upper
witppubun 윗부분 top
witssaram 윗사람 superior
wittchari 윗자리 superior position; ***Xboda wittcharie innŭn*** X보다 윗자리에 있는 be senior to X
wiŭi 위의 upper
wiwŏndan 위원단 panel, committee
wiwŏnhoe 위원회 committee, commission
wŏdŭ p'ŭrosesŏ 워드 프로세서 word processor
wŏdŭ p'ŭrosesŭrŭl sayong 워드 프로세스를 사용 word processing
wŏk'ŭmaen 워크맨 Walkman®
wŏk'ŭshyop 워크숍 workshop
wŏl 월 month; moon
wŏlbu 월부 monthly installment
Wŏldŭwaidŭwep 월드와이드웹 World Wide Web
wŏlganji 월간지 monthly (magazine)
wŏlgŭp 월급 wage; salary
wŏlgŭp pongt'u 월급 봉투 wage packet
wŏlgyesu 월계수 laurel
wŏlgyŏng 월경 menstruation
wŏlgyŏnghada 월경하다 menstruate
wŏllae 원래 originally
wŏllyo 원료 raw materials
Wŏlnam 월남 Vietnam ◊ Vietnamese
Wŏlnamin 월남인 Vietnamese
Wŏlnamŏ 월남어 Vietnamese (*language*)
wŏlsshik 월식 eclipse of the moon
Wŏl Sŭt'ŭrit'ŭ 월 스트리트 Wall Street
wŏn 원 circle; won FIN
wŏnban 원반 discus (*object*)
wŏnbanhyŏng 원반형 disk (*shape*)
wŏnban tŏnjigi 원반 던지기 discus (*event*)
wŏnbon 원본 original manuscript
Wŏnbulgyo 원불교 Won Buddhism
wŏnch'ik 원칙 principle, rule; ***wŏnch'iktchŏgŭro*** 원칙적으로 in principle, in theory
wŏnch'ŏn 원천 source
wŏndongnyŏk 원동력 dynamism
wŏn-giwangsŏnghan 원기왕성한

lively, sprightly; forceful
wŏn-gŏri 원거리 long-range
wŏn-go 원고 claimant, plaintiff; manuscript
wŏn-gwang 원광 halo
wŏnhada 원하다 want, desire; ***...ŭl / rŭl wŏnhamnikka?*** ...을 / 를 원합니까? would you like ...?
wŏnhan 원한 rancor; ***nuguege ssain wŏnhanŭl p'ulda*** 누구에게 쌓인 원한을 풀다 have a score to settle with s.o.
wŏnhyŏng 원형 circle, ring; prototype
wŏnin 원인 cause; ***...ŭihan wŏnini toeda*** ...의한 원인이 되다 contribute to
wŏnin kyumyŏng 원인 규명 inquest
wŏnja 원자 atom ◊ atomic
wŏnjak 원작 original *painting etc*
wŏnja p'okt'an 원자 폭탄 atom bomb
wŏnjaro 원자로 nuclear reactor
wŏnjaryŏk 원자력 nuclear power, atomic energy
wŏnjaryŏk paltchŏnso 원자력 발전소 nuclear power station
wŏnjŏng shihap 원정 시합 away game
wŏnjohada 원조하다 assist; ***kyŏngjejŏgŭro wŏnjohada*** 경제적으로 원조하다 stake, help financially
wŏnju 원주 circumference
wŏnjumin 원주민 native
wŏnkka 원가 cost, cost price
wŏnkkŭbŭi 원급의 positive GRAM
wŏnkkyŏk chŏpkkŭn 원격 접근 remote access
wŏnkkyŏk chojong 원격 조종 remote control
wŏnmang 원망 resentment
wŏnmanghada 원망하다 resent; bear a grudge; ***Xttaemune Yŭl / rŭl wŏnmanghada*** X때문에 Y을 / 를 원망하다 hold X against Y
wŏnmanhage haegyŏrhada 원만하게 해결하다 smooth things over
wŏnŏmin 원어민 native speaker
wŏnppul 원뿔 cone
wŏnshijŏgin 원시적인 primitive
wŏnshiŭi 원시의 primitive; far-sighted
wŏnso 원소 element
wŏnsu 원수 enemy
wŏnsuk'ada 원숙하다 mellow
wŏnsuk'an 원숙한 mellow
wŏnsung-i 원숭이 monkey
wŏntchang 원장 ledger
wŏntchŏm 원점 original point, square one; ***urinŭn wŏntchŏmŭro torawat-tta*** 우리는 원점으로 돌아왔다 we're back to square one
wŏnyang 원양 deep-sea, ocean ◊ ocean-going
wŏnye 원예 gardening; horticulture
wŏnyu 원유 crude (oil)
wŏnt'ong 원통 cylinder
wŏnt'ong moyang-ŭi 원통 모양의 cylindrical
wŏryoil 월요일 Monday
Wŏshingt'ŏn 워싱턴 Washington

XY

Xsŏn X선 X-ray (*picture*)
Xsŏn ch'waryŏng-ŭl hada X선 촬영을 하다 X-ray *patient*

yabihan nom 야비한 놈 jerk
yach'ae 야채 vegetable
yadanbŏpsŏgŭl p'iuda 야단법석을 피우다 play up (*of child*)
yadang 야당 opposition
yadŭ 야드 yard
yagan hak-kkyo 야간 학교 night school
yagan kŭnmu 야간 근무 night shift
yagan kŭnmuida 야간 근무이다 work nights
yagan oech'ul kŭmji 야간 외출 금지 curfew
yagan suŏp 야간 수업 evening classes
yagihada 야기하다 create, bring about, produce, generate
yagishik'ida 야기시키다 precipitate, cause to happen
yagŭn poi 야근 보이 night porter
yagu 야구 ball game, baseball
yagugong 야구공 baseball (*ball*)
yagujang 야구장 ballpark
yagu kŭllŏbŭ 야구 글러브 baseball glove
yagu moja 야구 모자 baseball cap
yagu pangmang-i 야구 방망이 baseball bat
yagu sŏnsu 야구 선수 baseball player
yagyŏngkkun 야경군 watchman
yagyong-ŭi 약용의 medicated
yahan 야한 gaudy; vulgar
yahoebok 야회복 evening dress; suit
yajanamu 야자나무 palm (tree)
yak 약 medicine; medication; drug ◊ in the region of, around; ***yak 5,000 tallŏ*** 약 5,000 달러 in the region of $5,000; ***yak ...tchŭm*** 약 ...쯤 around (*with expressions of time*); ***yagŭl mŏgida*** 약을 먹이다 give medicine
yakkan 약간 drop, dash, touch ◊ slightly, vaguely
yakkanŭi 약간의 slight, small
yak-kkuk 약국 pharmacy
yak-kkwan 약관 (insurance) policy
yakssa 약사 druggist, pharmacist
yaksshigŭi 약식의 informal
yaksshik 약식 informality
yaksshik ch'ayong chŭngsŏ 약식 차용 증서 IOU
yaksshik yahoebok 약식 야회복 dinner jacket, tuxedo
yakssok 약속 promise, undertaking; engagement, appointment
yakssok changso 약속 장소 meeting place
yakssok'ada 약속하다 promise, pledge; ***naega yakssok'agessumnida*** 내가 약속하겠습니다 you have my word
yaktcha 약자 weakling; underdog; monogram; abbreviation
yaktchaga saegyŏjin 약자가 새겨진 monogrammed
yaktchang 약장 medicine cabinet
yaktchin 약진 tremor
yaktchŏm 약점 weakness, weak point
yakt'alp'um 약탈품 loot
yakt'altcha 약탈자 looter
yakt'arhada 약탈하다 loot
yak'ada 약하다 be weak; have a weakness for; abridge; omit
yak'aejida 약해지다 weaken
yak'aejinŭn 약해지는 ailing
yak'agehada 약하게 하다 weaken
yak'an 약한 weak, frail; flimsy; muted
yak'on 약혼 engagement
yak'onhada 약혼하다 get engaged
yak'onhan 약혼한 engaged
yak'onja 약혼자 fiancé
yak'onnyŏ 약혼녀 fiancée

yak'on panji 약혼 반지 engagement ring
yak'wadoeda 악화되다 go downhill (*of health*); slacken off
yak'washik'ida 악화시키다 sap
yalbda 얇다 be thin
yalbŭn 얇은 thin, flimsy
yalbŭn p'anyuri 얇은 판유리 laminated glass
yalkke charŭda 얇게 자르다 slice
yamang 야망 ambition
yamjŏnhada 얌전하다 be meek; be gentle; be nice
yamjŏnhan 얌전한 meek; gentle; nice
yang 양 Ms; quantity, amount, level; sheep; tripe; ***Kim yang*** 김 양 Miss Kim
yangbaech'u 양배추 cabbage
yangban 양반 aristocrat
yangbanghyang t'onghaengno 양방향 통행로 two-way traffic
yangbo 양보 concession, giving in
yangbohada 양보하다 give way, yield; back down, climb down; concede
yangbok 양복 suit (*man's*)
yangbok chokki 양복 조끼 vest
yangbumo 양부모 foster parents
yangbunhwahada 양분화하다 polarize
yangch'iaek 양치액 mouthwash
yangch'ijirhada 양치질하다 brush *teeth*
yangch'iryu 양치류 fern
yangch'o 양초 candle
yangdohada 양도하다 transfer
yangdong-i 양동이 bucket, pail
yanggagŭro 양각으로 in relief
yanggajuk 양가죽 sheepskin
yanggogi 양고기 lamb
yanggŭgŭi 양극의 positive
yanggwibi 양귀비 poppy
yanghoshil 양호실 infirmary
yangjaesa 양재사 dressmaker
yangjohada 양조하다 brew
yangjojang 양조장 brewery
yangjoŏptcha 양조업자 brewer
yangmal 양말 sock
yangmo 양모 wool
yangnip'ada 양립하다 coexist; be compatible
yangnowŏn 양로원 nursing home
yangnyŏm 양념 spice, seasoning; relish; sauce
yangnyŏmtchang 양념장 dip
yangnyŏp'e kŏnŭrida 양옆에 거느리다 be flanked by
yangnyŏp'e tuda 양옆에 두다 be flanked by
yangnyuk-kkwŏn 양육권 custody
yangnyuk'ada 양육하다 bring up *child*
yangp'a 양파 onion
yangshik 양식 form, document; pattern (*in behavior*); style; Western-style food; food ◊ Western-style
yangshik'wahada 양식화하다 format, lay out
yangshim 양심 conscience; ***...e taehae yangshimŭi kach'aegŭl pat-tchi ant'a*** ...에 대해 양심의 가책을 받지 않다 have no qualms about ...
yangshimjŏgin 양심적인 conscientious
yangshimjŏgŭro 양심적으로 religiously, conscientiously
yangshimtchŏk pyŏngnyŏk kŏbuja 양심적 병역 거부자 conscientious objector
yangshimŭi kach'aek 양심의 가책 qualm; guilty conscience
yangsŏng-aeja 양성애자 bisexual
yangsŏng-ŭi 양성의 positive; benign; bisexual
yangtchok 양쪽 both; both sides
yang-ŭl chaeda 양을 재다 quantify
yaoe 야외 the open air ◊ outdoor, open-air; ***yaoe ch'waryŏngjung*** 야외 촬영중 on location
yaoeesŏ 야외에서 outdoors, in the open air
yaong 야옹 miaow
yasaeng 야생 wild
yasaeng tongmul 야생 동물 wildlife
yashiminnŭn 야심있는 ambitious
yat-tta 얕다 be shallow; be superficial; be low
yatchababonŭn 얕잡아보는 contemptuous

yat'ŭn 얕은 shallow, superficial
yawida 야위다 waste away
yayŏngji 야영지 campsite, camp ground
yayu 야유 jeer
yayuhada 야유하다 jeer; heckle; boo
yayurŭl ponaeda 야유를 보내다 hiss
ye 예 example, instance; old times; ceremony; courtesy; salute; bow ◊ yes; ***choŭn / nappŭn yega toeda*** 좋은 / 나쁜 예가 되다 set a good / bad example
yebaedang 예배당 chapel
yebang 예방 prevention; precaution
yebang chŏptchong 예방 접종 vaccination, inoculation; ***... yebang chŏptchong chusarŭl mat-tta*** ... 예방 접종 주사를 맞다 be vaccinated against
yebang chŏptchonghada 예방 접종하다 vaccinate, inoculate
yebanghada 예방하다 ward off
yebang-ŭi 예방의 preventive, precautionary
yebihada 예비하다 anticipate
yebi kyehoek 예비 계획 pilot scheme
yebi pak'wi 예비 바퀴 spare wheel
yebip'um 예비품 spare (part)
yebisŏn-gŏ 예비선거 primary POL
yebi t'aiŏ 예비 타이어 spare tire
yebiŭi 예비의 preliminary; spare
yebok 예복 robe (*of priest*)
yech'ŭk'al su ŏmnŭn 예측할 수 없는 unpredictable
yegam 예감 premonition; hunch; idea
yegihada 예기하다 expect, anticipate
yegop'yŏn 예고편 trailer (*of movie*)
yegŭm 예금 savings; deposit; ***yegŭmi it-tta*** 예금이 있다 be in credit
yegŭmaek 예금액 credit (*payment received*)
yegŭmhada 예금하다 bank, deposit; ***kyejwae yegŭmhada*** 계좌에 예금하다 credit an amount to an account
yegyŏn 예견 prediction
yegyŏnhada 예견하다 predict, foresee, visualize
yeinsŏn 예인선 tug NAUT
yeji 예지 prognosis
yejŏn 예전 former times
yejŏne 예전에 way back
yejŏng 예정 schedule; ***yejŏngboda nŭt-tta*** 예정보다 늦다 be behind schedule; ***yejŏngdaero*** 예정대로 as scheduled, duly, as expected; ***...l yejŏng-ida*** ...ㄹ 예정이다 be due to
yejŏnghada 예정하다 schedule
yennal 옛날 old days; ***yennal saenggagi nage handa*** 옛날 생각이 나게 한다 that takes me back; ***yennal yettchŏge ...i issŏt-tta*** 옛날 옛적에 ...이 있었다 once upon a time there was ...
yeŏn 예언 prophecy
yeŏnhada 예언하다 foretell, prophesy
yeoe 예외 exception
yeppŭda 예쁘다 be pretty
yeppŭjanghada 예쁘장하다 be lovely
yeppŭjanghan 예쁘장한 pretty
yeppŭn 예쁜 pretty
yerihada 예리하다 be sharp
yerihan 예리한 sharp; acute
yerŭl tŭlmyŏn 예를 들면 e.g.
yerŭl tŭrŏ 예를 들어 for instance
yerŭl tŭrŏsŏ 예를 들어서 for example
yesan 예산 budget; projection, forecast
yesane nŏt'a 예산에 넣다 budget for
yesang 예상 anticipation; forecast; prospect
yesanghada 예상하다 expect; forecast; anticipate; bargain for
yesang pakke 예상 밖에 unexpectedly
yesang sumyŏng 예상 수명 life expectancy
yesanhada 예산하다 project, work out in advance
yesanŭl seuda 예산을 세우다 budget
yeshihada 예시하다 illustrate (*with examples*)
yeshiktchang 예식장 wedding hall
yesŏnŭl t'onggwahada 예선을 통과하다 qualify
Yesu(**nim**) 예수(님) Jesus
yesul 예술 art
yesulga 예술가 artist

yesulp'um 예술품 art; work of art
yesultchŏgin 예술적인 artistic
yesun 예순 sixty
yesun pŏntchaeŭi 예순 번째의 sixtieth
yeŭi 예의 politeness; manners
yeŭiga ŏptta 예의가 없다 have no manners
yeŭi parŭge haengdonghada 예의 바르게 행동하다 behave (oneself)
yeŭi parŭn 예의 바른 polite, well-mannered
yeuhada 예우하다 honor
yeyagi kkwak ch'ada 예약이 꽉 차다 booked up
yeyak 예약 reservation
yeyak-kkŭm 예약금 deposit
yeyaktoen 예약된 reserved
yeyak'ada 예약하다 book, reserve; arrange
yŏbaek 여백 margin
yŏbo 여보 honey (*form of address to husband*)
yŏboge! 여보게! buddy! (*form of address*)
yŏboseyo 여보세요 hello TELEC
yŏbuni nama innŭn hando naeesŏ 여분이 남아 있는 한도 내에서 subject to availability
yŏdŏl 여덟 eight
yŏdŏl pŏntchaeŭi 여덟 번째의 eighth
yŏdŭn 여든 eighty
yŏdŭn pŏntchaeŭi 여든 번째의 eightieth
yŏdŭrŭm 여드름 spot; pimple
yŏdŭrŭmi nan 여드름이 난 spotty
yŏga 여가 leisure
yŏgajang 여가장 matriarch
yŏga shigan 여가 시간 leisure time
yŏgi 여기 here; ***yŏgi issŭmnida*** 여기 있습니다 here you are, there you are; ***yŏgi itkkuna*** 여기 있구나 here we are (*finding sth*)
yŏgida 여기다 consider, regard; ***charangsŭrŏpkke yŏgida*** 자랑스럽게 여기다 pride oneself on
yŏgie(sŏ) 여기에(서) here; in here
yŏgijŏgi 여기저기 here and there
yŏgijŏgi toradanida 여기저기 돌아다니다 wander around
yŏgijŏgi yŏhaenghada 여기저기 여행하다 get about, travel around
yŏgwagi 여과기 filter
yŏgwan 여관 guesthouse; inn; hostel
yŏgyŏng 여경 policewoman
yŏgyojang 여교장 principal, headmistress
yŏhaeng 여행 trip, journey; ride; travel; travels
yŏhaenggaek 여행객 traveler
yŏhaenghada 여행하다 travel
yŏhaengja sup'yo 여행자 수표 traveler's check
yŏhaeng kabang 여행 가방 travel bag; suitcase
yŏhaeng piyong 여행 비용 travel expenses
yŏhaeng pohŏm 여행 보험 travel insurance
yŏhaengsa 여행사 travel agency
yŏhaeng shigan 여행 시간 journey time; flight time
yŏhakssaeng 여학생 schoolgirl
Yŏhowaŭi Chŭng-in 여호와의 증인 Jehovah's Witness
yŏja 여자 woman
yŏja ch'in-gu 여자 친구 girl friend
yŏjadaun 여자다운 womanly
yŏjagat'ŭn 여자같은 effeminate
yŏja hwajangshil 여자 화장실 ladies' room
yŏja hyŏngje 여자 형제 sister
yŏjangbu 여장부 heroine
yŏjang-ŭl hago 여장을 하고 disguised as a woman; in drag
yŏja paeu 여자 배우 actress
yŏja sone chwiyŏ sanŭn 여자 손에 쥐여 사는 henpecked
yŏja undongga 여자 운동가 sportswoman
yŏje 여제 empress
yŏji 여지 scope, latitude
...yŏjida ...여지다 become ..., get ..., go ...
yŏjŏng 여정 itinerary; stage (*of journey*)
yŏjŏnhi 여전히 yet; still; as ever
yŏjong-ŏbwŏn 여종업원 hostess
yŏjuin 여주인 landlady; mistress
yŏk 역 station; part, role; ***Haemlit yŏgŭro*** 햄릿 역으로 in the role of

Hamlet, as Hamlet
yŏk-kkyŏpkke hada 역겹게 하다 nauseate, disgust
yŏk-kkyŏptta 역겹다 be nauseating; be nauseated; feel nauseous
yŏk-kkyŏun 역겨운 nauseating
yŏk-kkyŏwŏ hada 역겨워 하다 sicken, disgust
yŏkkŏnaeda 엮어내다 concoct
yŏkkwŏn 여권 passport
yŏkkwŏnjuŭi 여권주의 feminism
yŏkkwŏnjuŭija 여권주의자 feminist
yŏkkwŏnjuŭijaŭi 여권주의자의 feminist
yŏkkwŏnjuŭiŭi 여권주의의 feminist
yŏkkwŏn kwalli 여권 관리 passport control
yŏkkyŏun 역겨운 foul
yŏkssa 역사 history
yŏkssajŏgin 역사적인 historical
yŏkssasang-ŭro chungnyohan 역사상으로 중요한 historic
yŏksshi 역시 too, also; still; after all; but, nevertheless; ***yŏksshi isanghagedo*** 역시 이상하게도 strangely enough
yŏkssŏl 역설 paradox
yŏkssŏltchŏgin 역설적인 paradoxical
yŏkssŭp 역습 counter-attack
yŏkssŭp'ada 역습하다 counter-attack
yŏktto 역도 weightlifting
yŏktto sŏnsu 역도 선수 weightlifter
yŏk'al 역할 role
yŏk'yokkwaga nada 역효과가 나다 backfire, rebound
yŏk'yokkwaŭi 역효과의 counter-productive
yŏl 열 ten; row, line; tier; heat; fever; temperature
yŏlbyŏngshik 열병식 review
yŏlda 열다 open; be off (*of lid, top*); inaugurate; throw *party*
yŏldasŏt 열 다섯 fifteen
yŏldasŏt pŏntchaeŭi 열 다섯 번째의 fifteenth
yŏldu kae 열두 개 dozen
yŏldul 열 둘 twelve
yŏldu pŏntchaeŭi 열두 번째의 twelfth
yŏlgi 열기 open
yŏlgŏhada 열거하다 recite
yŏlgwang 열광 fascination;
yŏlgwanghada 열광하다 be crazy about; go wild
yŏlgwanghan 열광한 delirious, ecstatic
yŏlgwangtchŏgin 열광적인 wild, rapturous; feverish; avid
yŏllagi it-tta 연락이 있다 communicate; ***nuguwa yŏllagi kkŭnkkida*** 누구와 연락이 끊기다 lose touch with s.o.
yŏllak 연락 contact, liaison, communication; ***...wa / gwa yŏllagŭl chugo pat-tta*** ...와 / 과 연락을 주고 받다 keep in contact with; ***yŏllagŭl ch'wihada*** 연락을 취하다 liaise with
yŏllakch'ŏ 연락처 contact number
yŏllak'ada 연락하다 apply to; contact, get in touch with; ***nuguwa kyesok yŏllak'ada*** 누구와 계속 연락하다 keep in touch with s.o.
yŏllet 열 넷 fourteen
yŏllida 열리다 open; take place
yŏllin 열린 open
yŏllip chut'aek 연립 주택 row house
yŏllu 연루 involvement; ***nugurŭl muŏse yŏllu shik'ida*** 누구를 무엇에 연루 시키다 involve s.o. in sth
yŏlludoeda 연루되다 be a party to, be involved in; ***muŏse yŏlludoeda*** 무엇에 연루되다 get involved with sth
yŏllyŏ innŭn 열려 있는 open
yŏllyŏrhan 열렬한 enthusiastic; ardent, fervent; glowing
yŏllyo 연료 fuel
yŏllyorŭl konggŭp'ada 연료를 공급하다 refuel
yŏllyorŭl pogŭp pat-tta 연료를 보급 받다 refuel
yŏlne pŏntchaeŭi 열 네 번째의 fourteenth
yŏl pat-tta 열 받다 be steamed up
yŏl pŏntchaeŭi 열 번째의 tenth
yŏlp'a 열파 heatwave
yŏlshi pan 열시 반 half past ten, half after ten

yŏlsoe 열쇠 key
yŏlsoe kori 열쇠 고리 keyring
yŏlsoe kumŏng 열쇠 구멍 keyhole
yŏlsoe mungch'i 열쇠 뭉치 bunch of keys
yŏlssabyŏng 열사병 heatstroke
yŏlsse pŏntchaeŭi 열 세 번째의 thirteenth
yŏlsset 열 셋 thirteen
yŏlsshim 열심 zeal, enthusiasm
yŏlsshimhi 열심히 enthusiastically, eagerly
yŏlsshimhi irhanŭn 열심히 일하는 hard-working
yŏlsshimin 열심인 enthusiastic
yŏlssŏltchŏgŭro 역설적으로 paradoxically
yŏltchŏng 열정 enthusiasm; zest; passion
yŏltchŏngjŏgin 열정적인 passionate; fervent; impassioned
yŏltchunghada 열중하다 be enthusiastic about; be absorbed in; ***muŏsŭl hanŭnde yŏltchunghada*** 무엇을 하는데 열중하다 concentrate on doing sth
yŏlttae chibang 열대 지방 tropics
yŏlttaeŭi 열대의 tropical
yŏlttae urim 열대 우림 tropical rain forest
yŏlttŭng ŭishik 열등 의식 inferiority complex
yŏlyŏdŏl 열 여덟 eighteen
yŏlyŏdŏl pŏntchaeŭi 열 여덟 번째의 eighteenth
yŏlyŏsŏt 열 여섯 sixteen
yŏlyŏsŏt pŏntchaeŭi 열 여섯 번째의 sixteenth
yŏm mosŭp 옆 모습 profile (*of face*)
yŏmmyŏn 옆면 side
yŏmnyŏ 염려 concern, anxiety; misgiving
yŏmnyŏhada 염려하다 be anxious
yŏmnyŏhanŭn 염려하는 concerned, anxious
yŏmnyo 염료 dye
yŏmsaek 염색 tint
yŏmsaek'ada 염색하다 color; tint; dye
yŏmso 염소 goat; chlorine
yŏmtchŭng 염증 inflammation
yŏn 연 kite
yŏnae 연애 romance
yŏnae kyŏrhon 연애 결혼 love marriage, love match
yŏnae p'yŏnji 연애 편지 love letter
yŏnae sakkŏn 연애 사건 love affair
yŏnan 연안 coast; ***yŏnane(sŏ)*** 연안에(서) at the coast
yŏnan kyŏngbidae 연안 경비대 coastguard (*organization*)
yŏnan kyŏngbiwŏn 연안 경비원 coastguard (*person*)
yŏnanŭi 연안의 coastal
yŏnbal 연발 torrent (*of words, abuse*)
yŏnbang chŏngbu 연방 정부 federal government
yŏnbang chŏngbuŭi 연방 정부의 federal
Yŏnbang Susaguk 연방 수사국 FBI, Federal Bureau of Investigation
yŏnbong 연봉 annual salary
yŏnbun 연분 bond
yŏnch'ach'onghoe 연차총회 annual general meeting
yŏnch'ak'ada 연착하다 be delayed
yŏnch'ul 연출 direction
yŏnch'ultcha 연출자 director
yŏnch'urhada 연출하다 direct
yŏndae 연대 regiment; chronology; era
yŏndaesunŭi 연대순의 chronological; ***yŏndaesunŭro*** 연대순으로 in chronological order
yŏndan 연단 podium, dais; rostrum
yŏng 영 zero
yŏng-anshil 영안실 morgue, mortuary
yŏng-anso 영안소 funeral home
yŏnggam 영감 inspiration; old man; husband (*used by elderly persons*); sir; ***nuguege / muŏse yŏnggamŭl pat-tta*** 누구에게 / 무엇에 영감을 받다 be inspired by s.o. / sth
yŏnggong 영공 airspace
yŏngguch'a 영구차 hearse
Yŏnggugin 영국인 the British; the English
yŏngguhi 영구히 permanently
yŏnggujŏgin 영구적인 permanent
Yŏngguk 영국 Britain; United Kingdom; England ◊ British;

English
Yŏngguk saram 영국 사람 Briton
yŏnggwang 영광 glory; privilege, honor
yŏnggwangsŭrŏptta 영광스럽다 be glorious
yŏnggwangsŭrŏun 영광스러운 glorious; privileged, honored
yŏngha 10to 영하 10도 10 below zero
yŏnghae 영해 waters; territorial waters
yŏngha-ŭi 영하의 subzero
yŏnghon 영혼 soul, spirit
yŏnghwa 영화 movie, film
yŏnghwa chejaktcha 영화 제작자 film-maker
yŏnghwa ch'waryŏngso 영화 촬영소 film studio
yŏnghwagwan 영화관 movie theater
yŏnghwa sanŏp 영화 산업 cinema, movie industry
yŏnghwa sŭt'a 영화 스타 movie star
yŏnghyang 영향 effect, impact; influence; ***yŏnghyang-ŭl mich'ida*** 영향을 미치다 affect; have an effect; influence; ***yŏnghyang-ŭl namgida*** 영향을 남기다 leave one's mark
yŏnghyang chuda 영향 주다 influence
yŏnghyang kkich'ida 영향 끼치다 influence
yŏnghyangnyŏk 영향력 impact; influence
yŏnghyangnyŏk innŭn 영향력 있는 influential
yŏn-gi 연기 action; acting (*profession*); portrayal; smoke; delay, postponement
yŏn-gich'ŏrŏm sarajida 연기처럼 사라지다 evaporate; vanish
yŏn-gidoen 연기된 belated
yŏn-giga chauk'an 연기가 자욱한 smoky
yŏn-giga nada 연기가 나다 smoke
yŏn-gihada 연기하다 act; portray; delay, postpone; put off
yŏn-gija 연기자 act; actor
yŏn-giman p'iuda 연기만 피우다 smolder
yŏngmae 영매 medium, spiritualist
yŏngmun morŭl 영문 모를 puzzling
yŏngmunŭl morŭge hada 영문을 모르게 하다 puzzle
yŏngnihada 영리하다 be smart, be clever
yŏngnihan 영리한 smart, clever
yŏngnyang 영양 nutrition
yŏngnyangbujogŭi 영양부족의 underfed
yŏngnyangbun 영양분 nourishment, goodness; nutrient
yŏngnyang-innŭn 영양있는 nourishing, nutritious
yŏngnyang shiltcho 영양 실조 malnutrition
yŏngnyŏk 영역 sector
yŏngnyŏk'ada 역력하다 be clear; ***kunŭn kamdong padŭn kŏshi yŏngnyŏk'aet-tta*** 그는 감동 받은 것이 역력했다 he was visibly moved
Yŏng-ŏ 영어 English (*language*)
yŏn-go 연고 ointment
yŏn-goja 연고자 relative
yŏn-gol 연골 gristle
yŏngsa 영사 consul
yŏngsagi 영사기 projector
yŏngsagwan 영사관 consulate
yŏngsahada 영사하다 project
yŏngsang p'yoshi changch'i 영상 표시 장치 visual display unit
yŏngsujŭng 영수증 receipt; bill of sale
yŏngtchang 영장 warrant, writ
yŏngt'o 영토 territory ◊ territorial
yŏn-gŭk 연극 theater; play ◊ theatrical
yŏn-gŭm 연금 pension
yŏn-gŭm chedo 연금 제도 pension scheme
yŏn-gu 연구 research, study; ***...e taehan yŏn-gu*** ...에 대한 연구 research into
yŏn-guhada 연구하다 research
yŏn-gu kaebal 연구 개발 R & D, research and development
yŏn-gu kyehoek 연구 계획 research plan
yŏng-ung 영웅 hero
yŏng-ungjŏgin 영웅적인 heroic
yŏn-gu pojowŏn 연구 보조원 research assistant

yŏn-guso 연구소 research institute
yŏn-guwŏn 연구원 researcher
yŏn-gwan 연관 link, connection
yŏn-gwanjit-tta 연관짓다 link
yŏngwŏn 영원 eternity
yŏngwŏnhada 영원하다 be eternal
yŏng-wŏnhage hada 영원하게 하다 perpetuate
yŏngwŏnhan 영원한 eternal, everlasting
yŏng-wŏnhi 영원히 forever, eternally
yŏng-ye 영예 kudos
yŏngyŏk 영역 preserve, domain
yŏn-gyŏl 연결 connection; ***yŏn-gyŏldwaessŭmnida*** 연결됐습니다 you're through TELEC
yŏn-gyŏlp'yŏn 연결편 connecting flight, connection
yŏn-gyŏrhada 연결하다 connect, join, link
yŏnhabŭi 연합의 federal
yŏnhada 연하다 be tender; be soft
yŏnhan 연한 weak; tender *steak*
yŏnhan hŏrisal 연한 허리살 fillet
yŏnhan saektcho 연한 색조 tint
yŏnhap 연합 union, confederation; coalition; federation
yŏnhapttoen 연합된 united
yŏnhoe 연회 banquet
yŏniŏsŏ 연이어서 consecutively, in a row
yŏniyul 연이율 APR, annual percentage rate
yŏnjaeŭi il hoebun 연재의 일 회분 installment, episode
yŏnjang 연장 extension
yŏnjanghada 연장하다 extend, prolong
yŏnjang k'eibŭl 연장 케이블 extension cable
yŏnjangshik'ida 연장시키다 extend; ***kiganŭl yŏnjangshik'ida*** 기간을 연장시키다 roll over, renew
yŏnju 연주 rendering
yŏnjuhada 연주하다 play (*of musician*)
yŏnjuhoe 연주회 concert
yŏnjuja 연주자 player, musician
yŏnjung 연중 throughout the year ◊ annual
yŏnjung haengsa 연중 행사 annual event
yŏnjung-ŭi 연중의 annual
yŏnmaeng 연맹 league
yŏnmahada 연마하다 sharpen *skills*
yŏnminŭl cha-anaenŭn 연민을 자아내는 pitiful
yŏnmot 연못 pond
yŏnnalligi 연날리기 kite flying
yŏnŏ 연어 salmon
yŏnp'il 연필 pencil
yŏnp'il kkak-kki 연필 깍기 pencil sharpener
yŏnsang 연상 elder
yŏnsanghada 연상하다 associate
yŏnsangshik'ida 연상시키다 be reminiscent of
yŏnsang-ŭi 연상의 elder
yŏnse 연세 age
yŏnsŏl 연설 speech, address
yŏnsŏlga 연설가 orator
yŏnsŏlmun chakssŏngja 연설문 작성자 speech writer
yŏnsŏltcha 연설자 speaker
yŏnsŏrhada 연설하다 speak; address; make a speech
yŏnso 연소 combustion
yŏnsohada 연소하다 burn, consume *fuel*
yŏnsok 연속 series; succession; sequence
yŏnsok kong-yŏn 연속 공연 run (*of play*)
yŏnsok kong-yŏndoeda 연속 공연되다 run (*of play*)
yŏnsok pangyŏnghada 연속 방영하다 serialize
yŏnsok sarhaebŏm 연속 살해범 serial killer
yŏnsokssŏng 연속성 continuity
yŏnsoktchŏgin 연속적인 consecutive
yŏnsok tŭrama 연속 드라마 soap (opera)
yŏnsongmul 연속물 serial
yŏnssŭp 연습 exercise; drill; practice; workout
yŏnsŭptchang 연습장 exercise book
yŏnssŭp'ada 연습하다 practice; exercise; train
yŏnsuip 연수입 annual income
yŏnswae ch'ungdol 연쇄 충돌 pile-

up, crash
yŏnswaejŏm 연쇄점 chain store
yŏnswae panŭng 연쇄 반응 chain reaction
yŏntchul 연줄 connection, personal contact; ***choŭn yŏntchuri innŭn*** 좋은 연줄이 있는 be well-connected
yŏnyak'an 연약한 feeble
yŏnyein 연예인 entertainer
yŏnyu 연유 condensed milk
yŏpch'ong 엽총 shotgun
yŏpkkuri 옆구리 side, flank
yŏp saram 옆 사람 neighbor
yŏpssŏ 엽서 (post)card
yŏptchip 옆집 next door
yŏp'a 여파 hangover
yŏp'e 옆에 next to, beside
yŏp'ŭi 옆의 adjoining
yŏp'ŭro 옆으로 sideways
yŏrahop 열 아홉 nineteen
yŏrahop pŏntchaeŭi 열 아홉 번째의 nineteenth
yŏrhana 열 하나 eleven
yŏrhan pŏntchaeŭi 열 한 번째의 eleventh
yŏri innŭn 열이 있는 feverish
yŏri it-tta 열이 있다 have a temperature
yŏrilgop 열 일곱 seventeen
yŏrilgop pŏntchaeŭi 열 일곱 번째의 seventeenth
yŏrŏ 여러 various; several; ***yŏrŏ hae tong-an*** 여러 해 동안 for several years; ***yŏrŏmoro kŏmt'ohada*** 여러모로 검토하다 examine from various angles
yŏrŏbun 여러분 everyone; ladies and gentlemen
yŏrŏgaeŭi sŏnban 여러개의 선반 shelves
yŏrŏgaji 여러가지 all sorts of, various kinds of, various
yŏrŏ myŏnesŏ 여러 면에서 in many respects
yŏrŏ pŏn 여러 번 many times
yŏrŏ puryuŭi saram 여러 부류의 사람 assortment of people
yŏron chosa 여론 조사 poll, survey
yŏron chosawŏn 여론 조사원 pollster
yŏronŭl mut-tta 여론을 묻다 poll
yŏrŭi 열의 enthusiasm
yŏrŭm 여름 summer; ***yŏrŭme*** 여름에 in the summer
yŏsa 여사 Mrs (*honoring term generally used for famous or accomplished women*)
yŏse 여세 impetus
yŏshin 여신 goddess
yŏsŏng 여성 female (*person*); women; feminine
yŏsŏng haebang undong 여성 해방 운동 women's lib
yŏsŏng haebang undongga 여성 해방 운동가 women's libber
yŏsŏngjŏgin 여성적인 feminine
yŏsŏng kyŏngnyŏng-in 여성 경영인 proprietress
yŏsŏng saŏpkka 여성 사업가 businesswoman
yŏsŏng-ŭi 여성의 female, feminine GRAM
yŏsŏnsaengnim 여선생님 woman teacher
yŏsŏt 여섯 six
yŏsŏt pŏntchaeŭi 여섯 번째의 sixth
yŏsong-yŏn 여송연 cigar
yŏttŭt-tta 엿듣다 intercept *message*; listen in, eavesdrop
yŏt'ŭn 엷은 pale; ***yŏt'ŭn punhong-saek*** 엷은 분홍색 pale pink
yŏt'ŭn saektcho 엷은 색조 tinge
yŏŭisa 여의사 woman doctor
yŏu 여우 fox
yŏwang 여왕 queen
yŏwangbŏl 여왕벌 queen bee
...yŏya handa ...여야 한다 have to, must; be bound to
...yŏyaman hada ...여야만 하다 have (got) to; should, must
yŏyuga it-tta 여유가 있다 afford
yŏyuitkke hada 여유있게 하다 take things easy
yŏyuroun 여유로운 free and easy
yo 요 Korean-style mattress (*for sleeping on the floor*)
yoch'ŏng 요청 request; ***yoch'ŏnge ttara*** 요청에 따라 on request
yoch'ŏnghada 요청하다 request, put in for
yoga 요가 yoga

yogŭl hada 욕을 하다 swear; swear at
yogŭm 요금 fare; fee; charge; rate
yogŭm chingsuso 요금 징수소 toll booth
yogŭm kyesan-gi 요금 계산기 meter
yogŭmp'yo 요금표 tariff, price
yogu 요구 demand, requirement
yoguga shimhan 요구가 심한 demanding
yoguhada 요구하다 demand, call for, require; urge
yoguja 요구자 claimant
yogurŭt'ŭ 요구르트 yoghurt
yogyŏk'ada 요격하다 intercept
yohaengsu 요행수: ***yohaengsurŭl paraji anssŭmnida*** 요행수를 바라지 않습니다 I'm not taking any chances
yoin 요인 factor
yojŏl 요절 premature death
yojŏng 요정 fairy
yojŭŭm 요즈음 nowadays
yok 욕 abuse; abusive language; swearword
yokku 욕구 appetite
yoksshil 욕실 bathroom
yoksshim 욕심 greed
yoksshimi ŏmnŭn 욕심이 없는 selfless
yoksshim manŭn 욕심 많은 greedy
yokssŏl 욕설 bad language; curse, oath; derogatory remark
yoktchŏng 욕정 passion, sexual desire
yoktcho 욕조 tub, bathtub
yok'ada 욕하다 abuse; curse; call names
yomojomo saenggak'ae poda 요모조모 생각해 보다 think through
yong 용 dragon
yongbyŏnboda 용변보다 relieve oneself
yongbyŏng 용병 mercenary MIL
yonggamhada 용감하다 be brave
yonggamham 용감함 bravery
yonggamhan 용감한 brave, valiant
yonggi 용기 container; courage; spirit
yonggi innŭn 용기 있는 courageous
yonggirŭl chunŭn 용기를 주는 encouraging
yonggirŭl naeda 용기를 내다 pluck up courage
yonggol 용골 keel
yonggu 용구 equipment, gear; utensil
yonggwangno 용광로 furnace; blast furnace
yonghaedoeji annŭn 용해되지 않는 insoluble
yong-i 용이 ease, simplicity
yongjŏk 용적 proportions; dimensions; capacity
yongjŏpkkong 용접공 welder
yongjŏp'ada 용접하다 weld
yongk'e haenaeda 용케 해내다 contrive
yongk'e kuhada 용케 구하다 wangle
yongmang 욕망 desire, lust; ambition
yongmo 용모 looks, beauty
yongnap'ada 용납하다 approve; countenance
yongnyang 용량 capacity; memory
yong-ŏ 용어 term, word
yong-ŏ p'uri 용어 풀이 glossary
yongsŏ 용서 forgiveness
yongsŏhada 용서하다 forgive; excuse; let off; condone
yongsŏhal su ŏmnŭn 용서할 수 없는 unforgivable
yongsuch'ŏl 용수철 spring (*device*)
yongtton 용돈 allowance
yoodŭ 요오드 iodine
yoram 요람 cradle
yoranhada 요란하다 be loud
yoranhage ullida 요란하게 울리다 blare out
yori 요리 cooking; dish; food
yorich'aek 요리책 cookbook
yorihada 요리하다 cook
yorippŏp 요리법 cookery
yorisa 요리사 cook
yoriŭi 요리의 culinary
yoriyong ch'ŏlp'an 요리용 철판 burner
yoriyong konno 요리용 곤로 stove
yoryŏng 요령 knack
yosae 요새 fort, fortress
yoso 요소 ingredient
yosul 요술 magic; magic trick
yosulgach'i 요술같이 like magic
yosuljaeng-i 요술쟁이 magician

yosurŭl purida 요술을 부리다 juggle
yotchŏm 요점 point (*in argument*); gist; ***yotchŏmŭl marhada*** 요점을 말하다 get to the point; ***yotchŏmŭl pŏsŏnan*** 요점을 벗어난 beside the point, irrelevant
yot'ong 요통 lumbago
yot'ŭ 요트 sailboat, yacht
yot'ŭ chojongja 요트 조종자 yachtsman
yot'ŭ kyeryujang 요트 계류장 marina
yot'ŭ kyŏnggi 요트 경기 sailing
yot'ŭ kyŏnggija 요트 경기자 sailor
yot'ŭ t'agi 요트 타기 yachting
yoyak 요약 summary; précis; round-up
yoyak'ada 요약하다 summarize; sum up; abridge; compress
yoyak'amyŏn 요약하면 in short
yoyangso 요양소 rest home; hospice; sanatorium
yua 유아 infant
yuabŭi 유압의 hydraulic (*using oil*)
yuagi 유아기 infancy
yuayong pyŏn-gi 유아용 변기 potty
yubalshik'ida 유발시키다 cause; prompt
yubal yoin 유발 요인 trigger
yubang 유방 breast
yubarhada 유발하다 provoke, trigger
yuboktcha 유복자 posthumous child
yubok'an 유복한 fortunate
yubunam 유부남 married man
yubyŏlnan kŏt 유별난 것 the odd one out (*thing*)
yubyŏlnan saram 유별난 사람 the odd one out (*person*)
yuch'anghada 유창하다 be fluent
yuch'anghage 유창하게 eloquently, fluently
yuch'anghan 유창한 eloquent, fluent
yuch'anghan hwasul 유창한 화술 eloquence
yuch'ihada 유치하다 be childish
yuch'ihan 유치한 childish, infantile
yuch'iwŏn 유치원 kindergarten
yuch'ung 유충 larva; caterpillar
Yudaegyoŭi 유대교의 Jewish
Yudaein 유대인 Jew ◊ Jewish
yudae kwan-gye 유대 관계 link
yudo 유도 judo
yudok'an 유독한 virulent *disease*; poisonous
yudong-aek 유동액 fluid
yudong chasan 유동 자산 liquidity FIN
yudot'an 유도탄 guided missile
yudu 유두 nipple
Yuen 유엔 UN, United Nations
Yuen-gigu 유엔기구 United Nations
yugam 유감 regret; grudge; ***Sŏurŭl ttŏnani yugamimnida*** 서울을 떠나니 유감입니다 I will be sorry to leave Seoul; ***yugamŭl kajida*** 유감을 가지다 bear a grudge
yugamsŭrŏn 유감스런 criminal, shameful
yugamsŭrŏn il 유감스런 일 crime, shameful thing to do
yugamsŭrŏpkkedo 유감스럽게도 regrettably
yugamsŭrŏptta 유감스럽다 be regrettable
yugamsŭrŏun 유감스러운 regrettable
yuganŭronŭn 육안으로는 to the naked eye
yugashil 육아실 nursery
yugi nongppŏbŭi 유기 농법의 organic
Yugio Tongnan 육이오 동란 Korean War
yugiŭi 유기의 organic
yugoe 유괴 kidnapping
yugoebŏm 유괴범 kidnapper
yugoehada 유괴하다 kidnap
yugŭp koyong 유급 고용 paid employment
Yugyo 유교 Confucianism
yuhae 유해 remains
yuhaehada 유해하다 be harmful
yuhaehan kŏt 유해한 것 hazard
yuhaeng 유행 fashion, vogue; ***yuhaeng chung-ida*** 유행 중이다 be in fashion; ***yuhaeng-e twijida*** 유행에 뒤지다 be out of fashion; ***yuhaeng-e min-gamhan*** 유행에 민감한 fashion-conscious; ***yuhaeng-i chinada*** 유행이 지나다 go out of fashion; ***yuhaeng-i chinan*** 유행이 지난 old-fashioned, out of fashion

yuhaenghago innŭn 유행하고 있는 in, fashionable, popular
yuhaenghanŭn 유행하는 in fashion
yuhaeng-ida 유행이다 be around (*of illness*)
yuhaengppyŏng 유행병 epidemic
yuhaeng-ŭi kyŏnghyang 유행의 경향 fashion, trend
yuhaeng-ŭl ttarŭnŭn 유행을 따르는 fashionable, trendy
yuhok 유혹 temptation; seduction; ***yuhoge kulbok'ada*** 유혹에 굴복하다 succumb to temptation
yuhoktchŏgin 유혹적인 tempting; seductive; alluring
yuhok'ada 유혹하다 tempt, entice; seduce; make advances to
yuhwa 유화 oil painting
yuhwang 유황 sulfur
yuhyŏl 유혈 bloodshed
yuhyŏng 유형 type, sort
yuhyŏrŭi 유혈의 bloody
yuhyohaejida 유효해지다 come into force
yuhyohage hada 유효하게 하다 validate
yuhyohan 유효한 valid
yuhyo mallyoil 유효 만료일 expiry date
yuik'ada 유익하다 be beneficial
yuik'an 유익한 beneficial, salutary
yuinyong 유인용 decoy
yuirhada 유일하다 be unique
yuirhan 유일한 only, sole; unique
yujep'um 유제품 dairy products
yuji 유지 upkeep, maintenance; grease
yujihada 유지하다 hold; stay; keep; keep up; uphold, maintain; ***kŏn-gang-ŭl yujihada*** 건강을 유지하다 keep fit
yujŏk 유적 ruins, vestige
yujŏn 유전 inheritance (*characteristics*); oil field
yujŏndoenŭn 유전되는 hereditary
yujŏng 유정 oil well
yujŏnhak 유전학 genetics
yujŏnhaktcha 유전학자 geneticist
yujŏnja 유전자 gene
yujŏnja chimun 유전자 지문 genetic fingerprint
yujŏnjŏgin 유전적인 genetic
yujŏnjŏgŭro 유전적으로 genetically
yujŏn konghak 유전 공학 genetic engineering
yujoch'a 유조차 tanker, truck
yujoerŭl sŏn-gohada 유죄를 선고하다 convict
yujoeŭi 유죄의 guilty
yujoeŭi p'an-gyŏl 유죄의 판결 conviction
yujok 유족 bereaved family
yujosŏn 유조선 oil tanker
yuk 육 six
yukch'e 육체 flesh ◊ physical
yukch'ejŏgŭro 육체적으로 physically
yukch'e nodongja 육체 노동자 manual worker, blue-collar worker
yukch'in 육친 blood relative
yukka chŭngkkwŏn 유가 증권 securities
yukka chŭngkkwŏn shijang 유가 증권 시장 securities market
yuk-kkamjŏgin 육감적인 voluptuous
yuk-kkun 육군 army
yuk-kkun hasagwan 육군 하사관 noncommissioned officer
yuk-kkun sagwan hak-kkyo 육군 사관 학교 military academy
yukkwŏnja 유권자 voter; electorate
yukkyo 육교 footbridge, overpass
yukp'il 육필 handwriting
yukssang-e(sŏ) 육상에(서) on shore
yukssang up'yŏnmul 육상 우편물 surface mail
yuksshik tongmul 육식 동물 predator
yuksship 육십 sixty
yuktchi 육지 land, shore; ***yuk-tchie(sŏ)*** 육지에(서) on land
yuktchi tchogŭi 육지 쪽의 inland
yuktchŭp 육즙 gravy; juice
yukt'anjŏn 육탄전 unarmed combat
yuk'waehada 유쾌하다 be pleasant
yuk'waehan 유쾌한 pleasant, delightful
yulli 윤리 ethics
yullijŏgin 윤리적인 ethical, moral
yumanghan 유망한 rosy *future*
yumŏ kamgak 유머 감각 sense of humor

yumo 유모 nanny
yumoch'a 유모차 buggy, stroller; baby carriage
yulmuch'a 율무차 Job's tears tea
yumul 유물 remnant, relic
yumullon 유물론 materialism
yumullonja 유물론자 materialist
yumullonjŏgin 유물론적인 materialistic
yumyŏng 유명 fame
yumyŏnghada 유명하다 be famous; be famous for
yumyŏnghaejida 유명해지다 make a name for oneself
yumyŏnghan 유명한 famous, renowned
yumyŏng-in 유명인 personality, celebrity
yumyŏng insa 유명 인사 celebrity
yun 윤 gloss, shine
yunggi 융기 bump
yunghap 융합 fusion
yungja 융자 financing; loan
yungnoro 육로로 by land, overland
yungt'ongssŏng innŭn 융통성 있는 flexible
yun-gwagŭl chaptta 윤곽을 잡다 outline
yun-gwak 윤곽 outline, contour
yunhwaltche 윤활제 lubricant
yunhwalyu 윤활유 grease
yunip'om 유니폼 uniform, strip
yun naeda 윤 내다 rub, polish
yunnyŏn 윤년 leap year
yunyŏm 유념 regard, attention
yunyŏmhada 유념하다 pay heed to
yuraehada 유래하다 stem from
yuri 유리 glass
yuri chŏp'aptche 유리 접합제 putty
yurihada 유리하다 be profitable; be advantageous; ***kŭgŏshi nŏege yurihada*** 그것이 너에게 유리하다 it's to your advantage
yurihan 유리한 advantageous
yurihan chŏm 유리한 점 advantage
yuriŏptcha 유리업자 glazier
yuri sujokkwan 유리 수족관 aquarium
Yurŏbin 유럽인 European
Yurŏp 유럽 Europe ◊ European
yuryŏhage 유려하게 fluently
yuryŏhan 유려한 fluent
yuryŏk'an 유력한 strong, dominant
yuryŏng 유령 ghost; ***igosŭn yuryŏng-i nat'ananŭn koshida*** 이곳은 유령이 나타나는 곳이다 this place is haunted
yuryo kosokttoro 유료 고속도로 turnpike
yuryo toro 유료 도로 toll road
yusa 유사 similarity, resemblance; analogy; quicksand
yusahan 유사한 close, similar; comparable
yusan 유산 heritage; estate, legacy; miscarriage MED
yusanŭro namgida 유산으로 남기다 bequeath
yusashie 유사시에 in an emergency
yusassŏng 유사성 affinity
yusattchŏm 유사점 parallel
yusehada 유세하다 canvass POL
yusŏ 유서 will
yusŏng 유성 meteor, falling star
yusŏnggat'ŭn 유성같은 meteoric
yusŏng-ŭi 유성의 oily
yusŏnhyŏng 유선형 streamlined shape ◊ streamlined
yusŭ hosŭt'el 유스 호스텔 youth hostel
yusu 유수 running water
yut 윷 Four-Stick Game
yut'an 유탄 shell MIL
yut'illit'i 유틸리티 utility COMPUT
yut'ŏn U턴 U-turn
yut'ong 유통 distribution
yut'onghada 유통하다 distribute
yut'ong hyŏptchŏng 유통 협정 distribution arrangement
yuwŏl 유월 June
yuwŏnji 유원지 amusement park; recreation ground
yuyak 유약 enamel; glaze
yuyŏnhan 유연한 supple
yuyonghage hada 유용하게 하다 utilize
yuyongssŏng 유용성 utility, usefulness

A

a, **an** ◊ (*no equivalent in Korean*): ***a book about Korea*** Han-guge kwanhan ch'aek 한국에 관한 책; ***he bought a car*** kŭnŭn ch'arŭl sassŏyo 그는 차를 샀어요 ◊ (*with a countword*) hanaŭi 하나의, han 한; ***a cup of coffee*** k'ŏp'i han chan 커피 한 잔; ***five men and a woman*** tasŏt namjawa han yŏja 다섯 남자와 한 여자 ◊ (*per*) han 한; ***$50 a ride*** han pŏne 50tallŏ 한 번에 50달러; ***$15 a head*** han saram tang 15tallŏ 한 사람 당 15달러

abandon *object* pŏryŏduda 버려두다; *person* pŏrigo ttŏnada 버리고 떠나다; *plan* p'ogihada 포기하다

abbreviate churyŏssŭda 줄여쓰다

abbreviation yaktcha 약자

abdomen pokppu 복부

abdominal pokppuŭi 복부의

abduct napch'ihada 납치하다

♦**abide by** ttarŭda 따르다

ability nŭngnyŏk 능력

ablaze: ***be ~*** pult'aorŭ it-tta 불타오르고 있다

able (*skillful*) nŭngnyŏginnŭn 능력있는; ***be ~ to ...*** …hal su it-tta …할 수 있다; ***I wasn't ~ to see/hear*** nanŭn pol/tŭrŭl su ŏpssŏt-tta 나는 볼/들을 수 없었다

abnormal pijŏngsang-ŭi 비정상의

aboard 1 *prep* …e t'ago …에 타고 **2** *adv*: ***be ~*** t'ago it-tta 타고 있다; ***go ~*** t'ada 타다

abolish p'yejihada 폐지하다

abort *v/t mission*, *rocket launch*, COMPUT chungjihada 중지하다

abortion nakt'ae 낙태; ***have an ~*** nakt'aehada 낙태하다

about 1 *prep* (*concerning*) ...e kwanhan ...에 관한, ...e taehan ...에 대한; ***what's it ~?*** (*book*, *movie*) muŏse kwanhan kŏshimnikka? 무엇에 관한 것입니까? **2** *adv* (*roughly*) yak 약; (*in the area*) chuwie 주위에; ***~ 20 books*** yak 20kwŏn 약 20권; ***be ~ to ...*** mak ...haryŏgo hada 막 ...하려고 하다; ***I was just ~ to leave*** nanŭn mak ...ttŏnaryŏgo haessŏyo 나는 막 떠나려고 했어요; ***how ~ ...?*** ...i/ga ŏttaeyo? ...이/가 어때요?; ***how ~ going to the movies?*** yŏnghwagwane kanŭn kŏshi ŏttaeyo? 영화관에 가는 것이 어때요?

above 1 *prep* (*higher than*) … poda wi … 보다 위; (*more than*) … poda tŏ … 보다 더; ***~ all*** muŏtppodado 무엇보다도 **2** *adv* wie 위에; ***on the floor ~*** wich'ŭng-e 위층에

above-mentioned sanggihan 상기한

abrasion pŏtkkyŏjin kot 벗겨진 곳

abrasive *personality* kŏsŭllinŭn 거슬리는

abridge yoyak'ada 요약하다

abroad *live* haeoeesŏ 해외에서; *go* haeoero 해외로

abrupt *departure* kaptchakssŭrŏn 갑작스런; *manner* t'ungmyŏngssŭrŏun 퉁명스러운

abscess nong-yang 농양

absence (*of person*) pujae 부재; (*from school*) kyŏlssŏk 결석; (*from work*) kyŏlgŭn 결근; (*lack*) kyŏlp'ip 결핍

absent *adj* (*from school*) kyŏlssŏk'an 결석한; (*from work*) kyŏlgŭnhan 결근한

absent-minded mŏnghan 멍한

absolute *power* chŏlttaejŏgin 절대적인; *idiot* wanjŏnhan 완전한

absolutely (*completely*) wanjŏnhi 완전히; ***~ not!*** chŏlttae andoemnida! 절대 안됩니다!; ***do you agree? – ~*** tong-ŭihaseyo? – kŭya mullonimnida 동의하세요? – 그야 물론입니다

absolve samyŏnhada 사면하다
absorb *liquid, shock, group* hŭpssuhada 흡수하다; *changes, information* padadŭrida 받아들이다; **~ed in** ...e molttuhan ...에 몰두한
absorbent hŭpssussŏng-ŭi 흡수성의
absorbent cotton t'altchimyŏn 탈지면, som 솜
abstain (*from voting*) kikkwŏnhada 기권하다
abstention (*in voting*) kikkwŏn 기권
abstract *adj* ch'usangjŏgin 추상적인
absurd ŏrisŏgŭn 어리석은
absurdity ŏrisŏgŭm 어리석음
abundance p'ungbu 풍부
abundant p'ungbuhan 풍부한
abuse[1] *n* (*insults*) yok 욕; (*of child*) hakttae 학대; (*of machine etc*) namyong 남용
abuse[2] *v/t* (*physically, sexually*) hakttaehada 학대하다; (*verbally*) yok'ada 욕하다
abusive: **~ *language*** yok 욕; ***become* ~** sanawajida 사나와지다
abysmal (*very bad*) hyŏngp'yŏnŏmnŭn 형편없는
abyss kurŏngt'ŏng-i 구렁텅이
academic 1 *n* kyosa 교사 **2** *adj* kodŭnggyoyugŭi 고등교육의; *person* hak-kkujŏgin 학구적인; **~ *year*** hangnyŏn 학년
academy hagwŏn 학원
accelerate 1 *v/i* ppallajida 빨라지다 **2** *v/t production* kasokshik'ida 가속시키다
acceleration (*of car*) kasoktto 가속도
accelerator aeksellŏreit'ŏ 액셀러레이터
accent (*when speaking*) akssent'ŭ 악센트; (*emphasis*) kangjo 강조
accentuate kangjohada 강조하다
accept 1 *v/t offer, present* padadŭrida 받아들이다; *behavior, conditions* kyŏndida 견디다 **2** *v/i* padadŭrida 받아들이다
acceptable padadŭril su innŭn 받아들일 수 있는
acceptance padadŭrim 받아들임
access 1 *n* (*to secrets, one's children*) chŏpkkŭn 접근; (*to a building*) ch'urip 출입; ***have* ~ *to*** *computer* ...e chŏpkkŭnhal su it-tta ...에 접근할 수 있다; *child* ...ŭl / rŭl mannal kwŏllirŭl kat-tta ...을 / 를 만날 권리를 갖다 **2** *v/t* chŏpkkŭnhada 접근하다; COMPUT ipch'ullyŏk'ada 입출력하다
access code COMPUT ipch'ullyŏk k'odŭ 입출력 코드
accessible (*easy to reach*) tatkki shwiun 닿기 쉬운; *house* kagi shwiun 가기 쉬운; *information* ipssuhagi shwiun 입수하기 쉬운
accessory (*for wearing*) changshingu 장신구; LAW chongbŏm 종범
access road chinimno 진입로
access time COMPUT hoch'ul shigan 호출 시간
accident uyŏnhan sakkŏn 우연한 사건; (*crash etc*) sago 사고; ***by* ~** uyŏnhi 우연히
accidental uyŏnhan 우연한
acclimate, acclimatize *v/t* chŏgŭnghada 적응하다
accommodate chinael kosŭl chegonghada 지낼 곳을 제공하다; *special requirements* tŭrŏjuda 들어주다
accommodations sukppak shisŏl 숙박 시설; ***have you found* ~?** chinael kosŭn ch'ajŭsyŏssŏyo? 지낼 곳은 찾으셨어요?
accompaniment MUS panju 반주
accompany tongbanhada 동반하다; MUS panjurŭl hada 반주를 하다
accomplice kongbŏm 공범
accomplish *task* sŏngch'wihada 성취하다
accomplished (*person*) ttwiŏnan 뛰어난
accord: ***of one's own* ~** chabaltchŏgŭro 자발적으로
accordance: ***in* ~ *with*** ...e ttarasŏ ...에 따라서
according: **~ *to*** ...e ttarŭmyŏn ...에 따르면
accordingly (*consequently*) kŭrŏmŭro 그러므로; (*appropriately*) kŭe match'uŏ 그에 맞추어
account *n* (*financial*) kujwa 구좌; (*report, description*) pogo 보고; ***give an* ~ *of*** ...ŭi iyagirŭl hada ...의

이야기를 하다; ***on no ~ must you tell anybody*** chŏlttaero amuegedo iyagihaesŏnŭn andoemnida 절대로 아무에게도 이야기해서는 안됩니다; ***on ~ of*** …ttaemune …때문에; ***take … into ~, take ~ of*** …ŭl / rŭl koryŏhada …을 / 를 고려하다
♦**account for** (*explain*) sŏlmyŏnghada 설명하다; (*make up, constitute*) pijung-ŭl ch'ajihada 비중을 차지하다
accountability ch'aegim 책임
accountable: ***be held ~*** ch'aegimŭl chida 책임을 지다
accountant hoegyesa 회계사
account number kujwa pŏnho 구좌 번호
accounts hoegye 회계
accumulate 1 *v/t* moŭda 모으다 **2** *v/i* moida 모이다
accuracy chŏnghwak 정확
accurate chŏnghwak'an 정확한
accusation pinan 비난
accuse pinanhada 비난하다; ***he ~d me of lying*** kŭnŭn naega kŏjinmarŭl haet-ttago pinanhaet-tta 그는 내가 거짓말을 했다고 비난했다; ***be ~d of*** LAW …(ŭ)ro kobaldoeda …(으)로 고발되다
accused: ***the ~*** LAW p'igo 피고
accustom: ***get ~ed to*** …e ikssuk'aejida …에 익숙해지다; ***be ~ed to*** …nŭn supkkwani it-tta …는 습관이 있다
ace (*in cards, tennis: shot*) eisŭ 에이스
ache 1 *n* ap'ŭm 아픔 **2** *v/i* ap'ŭda 아프다
achieve sŏngch'wihada 성취하다
achievement (*of ambition*) sŏngch'wi 성취; (*thing achieved*) ŏptchŏk 업적
acid *n* san 산
acid rain sansŏngbi 산성비
acid test *fig* kyŏltchŏngjŏgin kŏmt'o 결정적인 검토
acknowledge injŏnghada 인정하다; *receipt* sushinyŏburŭl allida 수신여부를 알리다
acknowledg(e)ment injŏng 인정; (*of a letter*) sushinyŏburŭl allinŭn kŏt 수신여부를 알리는 것
acoustics ŭmhyanghak 음향학
acquaint: ***be ~ed with*** (*with person*) …wa / kwa mannan chŏgi it-tta …와 / 과 만난 적이 있다; (*with things, poem*) …ŭl / rŭl algo it-tta …을 / 를 알고 있다
acquaintance (*person*) anŭn saram 아는 사람
acquire *skill, knowledge* sŭpttŭk'ada 습득하다; *property* hoekttŭk'ada 획득하다
acquisitive ŏtkkoja hanŭn 얻고자 하는
acquit LAW mujoeimŭl sŏnŏnhada 무죄임을 선언하다
acre eik'ŏ 에이커
acrobat kogyesa 곡예사
acrobatics kogye 곡예
across 1 *prep* ◊ (*on the other side of*) ...ŭi majŭn p'yŏne(sŏ) ...의 맞은 편에(서); ***the person sitting ~ the table from me*** shikt'agŭi majŭn p'yŏne anjŭn saram 식탁의 맞은 편에 앉은 사람; ***~ the street*** kŏriŭi majŭn p'yŏne(sŏ) 거리의 맞은 편에(서) ◊ (*to the other side of*) ...ŭi majŭn p'yŏnŭro ...의 맞은 편으로; ***walk ~ the street*** kirŭl kŏnnŏda 길을 건너다; ***sail ~ the Pacific*** T'aep'yŏng-yang-ŭi majŭn p'yŏnŭro hanghaehada 태평양의 맞은 편으로 항해하다 **2** *adv* (*to the other side*) kŏnnosŏ 건너서; ***10 meters ~*** p'ok 10mit'ŏ 폭 10미터
act 1 *v/i* THEA yŏn-gihada 연기하다; (*pretend*) kajanghada 가장하다; (*take action*) haengdonghada 행동하다; ***~ as*** …ŭl / rŭl taerihada …을 / 를 대리하다 **2** *n* (*deed*) haengdong 행동; (*of play*) mak 막; (*in vaudeville*) yŏn-gija 연기자; (*pretense*) shinyung 시늉; (*law*) pŏmnyŏng 법령
acting 1 *n* yŏn-gi 연기 **2** *adj* (*temporary*) imshiŭi 임시의
action haengwi 행위; ***out of ~*** (*not functioning*) chakttong-i andoenŭn 작동이 안되는; ***take ~*** choch'wirŭl ch'wihada 조취를 취하다; ***bring an ~ against*** LAW kobarhada 고발하다
action replay TV kyŏnggi chaeyŏn

경기 재연; (*in slow motion*) sŭlloumoshŏn 슬로우모션
active hwalttongjŏgin 활동적인; GRAM nŭngdongt'aeŭi 능동태의
activist POL hwalttongga 활동가
activity (*being busy*) hwalbarhan umjigim 활발한 움직임; (*pastime*) hwalttong 활동
actor namja paeu 남자 배우
actress yŏja paeu 여자 배우
actual (*real*) shiltcheŭi 실제의
actually (*in fact, to tell the truth*) sashirŭn 사실은; (*surprised*) chŏngmallo 정말로; **~ *I do know him*** (*stressing converse*) nanŭn chŏngmallo kŭrŭl arayo 나는 정말로 그를 알아요
acupressure massage chiap 지압
acupuncture ch'imsul 침술
acute *pain* kŭksshimhan 극심한; *sense of smell* min-gamhan 민감한; *analysis, mind* yerihan 예리한
ad kwanggo 광고, (*on TV*) sŏnjŏn 선전
adapt 1 *v/t* chŏk'ap'age hada 적합하게 하다 **2** *v/i* chŏgŭnghada 적응하다
adaptable *person, plant* chŏgŭngnyŏgi innŭn 적응력이 있는; *vehicle etc* tayongdoŭi 다용도의
adaptation (*of play etc*) kakssaek 각색
adapter ELEC ŏdaept'ŏ 어댑터
add 1 *v/t* MATH tŏhada 더하다; (*say*) tŏtppuch'yŏ marhada 덧붙여 말하다; *comment* tŏtppuch'ida 덧붙이다; *sugar, salt etc* puŏ nŏt'a 부어 넣다 **2** *v/i* (*of person*) tŏhada 더하다
♦**add on** *15% etc* p'ohamhada 포함하다
♦**add up 1** *v/t* hapkkyehada 합계하다 **2** *v/i fig* ihaedoeda 이해되다
addict chungdoktcha 중독자
addicted: ***be ~ to*** …e chungdogida …에 중독이다
addiction (*to drugs, TV etc*) chungdok 중독
addictive: ***be ~*** chungdokssŏng-ida 중독성이다
addition MATH tŏtssem 덧셈; (*to list, company etc*) ch'uga 추가; ***in ~*** ch'ugaro 추가로; ***in ~ to*** …e tŏhayŏ …에 더하여
additional ch'ugaŭi 추가의
additive (*in food*) ch'ŏmgaje 첨가제
add-on ch'uga hangmok 추가 항목
address 1 *n* chuso 주소; ***form of ~*** ch'ingho 칭호 **2** *v/t letter* chusorŭl ssŭda 주소를 쓰다; *audience* yŏnsŏrhada 연설하다; *person* …rago purŭda …라고 부르다
address book chusorok 주소록
addressee sushinin 수신인
adequate chŏkttanghan 적당한; (*satisfactory*) manjokssŭrŏun 만족스러운
adhere ttak tallabut-tta 딱 달라붙다
♦**adhere to** *surface* …e tallabut-tta …에 달라붙다; *rules* …ŭl/rŭl chik'ida …을/를 지키다; *opinion* …ŭl/rŭl kosuhada …을/를 고수하다
adhesive *n* chŏpch'aktche 접착제
adhesive plaster panch'anggo 반창고
adhesive tape panch'anggo 반창고
adjacent injŏp'an 인접한
adjective hyŏng-yongsa 형용사
adjoining yŏp'ŭi 옆의
adjourn *v/i* (*of court*) hyujŏngdoeda 휴정되다; (*of meeting*) chungdandoeda 중단되다
adjust *v/t* match'uda 맞추다
adjustable chojŏnghal su innŭn 조정할 수 있는
administer *medicine* pogyongshik'ida 복용시키다; *company* kwallihada 관리하다; *country* tasŭrida 다스리다
administration (*of company etc*) kwalli 관리; (*of country*) haengjŏng 행정; (*government*) chŏngbu 정부
administrative haengjŏng-ŭi 행정의
administrator kwalliin 관리인; (*of company*) kwallija 관리자; (*in government*) haengjŏnggwan 행정관
admirable hullyunghan 훌륭한
admiral haegun changsŏng 해군 장성
admiration kamt'an 감탄
admire kamt'anhada 감탄하다
admirer ch'anmija 찬미자
admissible padadŭril su innŭn 받아들일 수 있는
admission (*confession*) shiin 시인; (*to building*) iptchang hŏga 입장 허가;

(*to country*) ipkkuk hŏga 입국 허가; (*to organization*) ip'oe hŏga 입회 허가; (*fee*) iptchangnyo 입장료; **~ *free*** muryo iptchang 무료 입장
admit injŏnghada 인정하다; (*allow in*) tŭrŏonŭn kŏsŭl hŏgahada 들어오는 것을 허가하다; (*confess*) shiinhada 시인하다; (*accept*) padadŭrida 받아들이다; ***he was ~ted to the hospital*** kŭnŭn pyŏng-wŏne ibwŏnhaet-tta 그는 병원에 입원했다
admittance: ***no ~*** iptchang kŭmji 입장 금지
adolescence sach'un-gi 사춘기
adolescent 1 *n* sach'un-giŭi namnyŏ 사춘기의 남녀 **2** *adj* sach'un-giŭi 사춘기의
adopt *child* ibyanghada 입양하다; *plan* ch'aet'aek'hada 채택하다
adoption (*of child*) ibyang 입양; (*of plan*) ch'aet'aek 채택
adorable panhal manhan 반할 만한
adore samohada 사모하다
adult 1 *n* ŏrŭn 어른; (*over 20*) sŏng-in 성인; (*animal*) sŏngjanghan tongmul 성장한 동물 **2** *adj* sŏngsuk'an 성숙한; *person* ŏrŭnŭi 어른의; (*over 20*) sŏng-inŭi 성인의; **~ *movie*** sŏng-inyŏnghwa 성인영화
adultery kant'ŏng kwan-gye 간통 관계
advance 1 *n* (*money*) sŏnbul 선불; (*in science etc*) chinbo 진보; MIL chŏnjin 전진; ***in ~*** miri 미리; *get money* sŏnbullo 선불로; ***48 hours in ~*** sashipp'alshigan chŏne 48시간 전에; ***make ~s*** (*progress*) chinbohada 진보하다; (*sexually*) yuhok'ada 유혹하다 **2** *v/i* MIL chŏnjinhada 전진하다; (*make progress*) chinbohada 진보하다 **3** *v/t theory* cheanhada 제안하다; *sum of money* miri naeda 미리 내다; *human knowledge, a cause* paltchŏnhada 발전하다
advance booking yeyak 예약
advanced ap sŏn 앞 선; **~ *country*** sŏnjin-guk 선진국; **~ *learner*** sanggŭptcha 상급자; **~ *level*** sanggŭp 상급
advance payment sŏnbul yogŭm 선불 요금
advantage yurihan chŏm 유리한 점; ***it's to your ~*** kŭgŏshi nŏege yurihada 그것이 너에게 유리하다; ***take ~ of sth*** *of opportunity* muŏsŭl iyonghada 무엇을 이용하다
advantageous yurihan 유리한
adventure mohŏm 모험
adventurous mohŏmjŏk 모험적; *person* mohŏmŭl chŭlginŭn 모험을 즐기는
adverb pusa 부사
adversary chŏk 적
advertise *v/t* & *v/i* kwanggohada 광고하다
advertisement kwanggo 광고
advertiser kwanggoju 광고주
advertising kwanggo 광고; (*industry*) kwanggo-ŏp 광고업
advertising agency kwanggo taehaengsa 광고 대행사
advice choŏn 조언; ***take s.o.'s ~*** nuguŭi choŏnŭl padadŭrida 누구의 조언을 받아들이다
advisable hyŏnmyŏnghan 현명한
advise *person* choŏnhada 조언하다; *caution etc* ch'unggohada 충고하다; **~ *s.o. to …*** nuguege …rago cho-ŏnhada 누구에게 …라고 조언하다
adviser komun 고문
aerial 1 *n* ant'ena 안테나 **2** *adj* kongjung-ŭi 공중의
aerial photograph hanggongsajin 항공사진
aerobics eŏrobik 에어로빅
aerodynamic konggi yŏk'agŭi 공기 역학의
aeronautical hanggonghagŭi 항공학의
aerosol sŭp'ŭrei 스프레이
aerospace industry hanggong-ujugonghak 항공우주공학
affair (*matter*) il 일; (*business*) ŏmmu 업무; (*love*) pullyun 불륜; ***foreign ~s*** oemuŏmmu 외무업무; ***have an ~ with*** …wa / kwa param p'iuda …와 / 과 바람피우다; ***that's my ~*** kŭgŏsŭn che ŏmmuimnida 그것은 제 업무입니다
affect MED palbyŏnghada 발병하다; (*influence*) yŏnghyang-ŭl mich'ida

영향을 미치다; (*concern*) kŏktchŏng-ŭl kkich'ida 걱정을 끼치다
affection aejŏng 애정
affectionate tajŏnghan 다정한
affinity yusassŏng 유사성
affirmative: ***answer in the ~*** yerago tap'ada 예라고 답하다
affluent puyuhan 부유한; ***~ society*** p'ung-yoroun sahoe 풍요로운 사회
afford (*financially*) yŏyuga it-tta 여유가 있다
Afghan 1 *adj* Ap'ŭganisŭt'anŭi 아프가니스탄의 **2** *n* (*person*) Ap'ŭganisŭt'anin 아프가니스탄인
Afghanistan Ap'ŭganisŭt'an 아프가니스탄
afloat *boat* ttŏ innŭn 떠 있는
afraid: ***be ~*** turyŏwŏhada 두려워하다; ***be ~ of*** …ŭl / rŭl musŏwŏhada …을 / 를 무서워하다; *of upsetting s.o.* …ŭl / rŭl turyŏwŏhada …을 / 를 두려워하다; ***I'm ~ …*** (*expressing regret*) choesonghajiman … 죄송하지만 …; ***I'm ~ he will lose his job*** kŭga iltcharirŭl irŭlkkabwa kŏktchŏng imnida 그가 일자리를 잃을까봐 걱정입니다; ***I'm ~ so*** choesonghajiman, kŭrŏn kŏt kat'ayo 죄송하지만, 그런 것 같아요; ***I'm ~ not*** choesonghajiman, andoelgŏt kat'ayo 죄송하지만, 안될 것 같아요
Africa Ap'ŭrik'a 아프리카
African 1 *adj* Ap'ŭrik'aŭi 아프리카의 **2** *n* Ap'ŭrik'a saram 아프리카 사람
after 1 *prep* (*in order, time*) hue 후에; (*in position*) taŭme 다음에; ***~ all*** kyŏlguk 결국; ***~ that*** kŭ ihue 그 이후에; ***it's ten ~ two*** tushi shippunimnida 두시 십분입니다 **2** *adv* (*afterward*) taŭme 다음에, hue 후에; ***the day ~*** taŭmnal 다음날
afternoon ohu 오후; ***in the ~*** ohue 오후에; ***this ~*** onŭl ohue 오늘 오후에; ***good ~*** annyŏnghaseyo 안녕하세요
after sales service aep'ŭt'ŏ sŏbisŭ 애프터 서비스; **aftershave** aep'ŭt'ŏ shyeibŭ loshyŏn 애프터 셰이브 로션; **aftertaste** kkŭnmat 끝맛
afterward najung-e 나중에
again tashi 다시
against (*opposed to*) …e pandaehayŏ …에 반대하여; (*leaning on*) …e kidaeŏ …에 기대어; ***America ~ Brazil*** SP Miguk tae Pŭrajil 미국 대 브라질; ***I'm ~ the idea*** nanŭn kŭ ŭigyŏne pandaehamnida 나는 그 의견에 반대합니다; ***what do you have ~ him?*** wae kŭrŭl pandaehanŭn kŏyeyo? 왜 그를 반대하는 거예요?; ***be ~ the law*** pŏbe ŏgŭnnada 법에 어긋나다
age 1 *n* (*of person, object*) nai 나이; (*respectful: of older person*) yŏnse 연세; (*era*) ki 기; ***at the ~ of*** …se ttaee …세 때에; ***under ~*** misŏngnyŏnŭi 미성년의; ***she's five years of ~*** kŭnyŏnŭn tasŏt sarimnida 그녀는 다섯 살입니다 **2** *v/i* nai tŭlda 나이 들다
agency chunggaeŏp 중개업
agenda iltchŏng 일정; ***on the ~*** iltchŏngsang 일정상
agent taeriin 대리인
aggravate ak'washik'ida 악화시키다
aggression konggyŏk 공격
aggressive konggyŏktchŏgin 공격적인; (*dynamic*) chinch'wijŏgin 진취적인
agile chaepparŭn 재빠른
agitated tong-yohan 동요한
agitation tong-yo 동요
agitator sŏndongja 선동자
ago: ***3 days ~*** samil chŏne 3일 전에; ***long ~*** orae chŏne 오래 전에; ***how long ~?*** ŏlmana chŏne? 얼마나 전에?
agonizing kot'ongsŭrŏun 고통스러운
agony kot'ong 고통
agree 1 *v/i* tong-ŭihada 동의하다; (*of figures, accounts*) ilch'ihada 일치하다; (*reach agreement*) habŭihada 합의하다; ***I ~*** nanŭn tong-ŭihanda 나는 동의한다; ***I don't ~*** nanŭn tong-ŭihaji annŭnda 나는 동의하지 않는다; ***it doesn't ~ with me*** (*of food*) nanŭn i ŭmshigi patchi annŭnda 나는 이 음식이 받지 않는다 **2** *v/t price* ilch'ishik'ida 일치시키다; ***~ that something should be done*** muŏsŭl haeyahamŭl tong-ŭihada 무엇을

해야함을 동의하다
agreeable (*pleasant*) kibunjoŭn 기분좋은; (*in agreement*) tong-ŭihal manhan 동의할 만한
agreement (*consent*) tong-ŭi 동의; (*contract*) kyeyak 계약; ***reach ~ on*** ...e habŭihada ...에 합의하다
agricultural nong-ŏbŭi 농업의
agriculture nong-ŏp 농업
ahead: ***be ~ of*** ...ŭi ap'e ...의 앞에; ***plan / think ~*** miraeeŭi kyehoek / saenggak 미래에의 계획 / 생각
aid 1 *n* toum 도움 **2** *v/t* toptta 돕다
Aids eijŭ 에이즈, huch'ŏnssŏng myŏnnyŏk kyŏlp'iptchŭng 후천성 면역 결핍증
ailing *economy* yak'aejinŭn 약해지는
aim 1 *n* (*in shooting*) kyŏnyang 겨냥; (*objective*) moktchŏk 목적 **2** *v/i* (*in shooting*) kyŏnyanghada 겨냥하다; ***~ at doing sth***, ***~ to do sth*** muŏsŭl hanŭn kŏsŭl mokp'yoro samtta 무엇을 하는 것을 목표로 삼다 **3** *v/t*: ***be ~ed at*** (*of remark etc*) ...ŭl / rŭl kyŏnun kŏshida ...을 / 를 겨눈 것이다; (*of guns*) ...ŭl / rŭl kyŏnyanghada ...을 / 를 겨냥하다
air 1 *n* kongjung 공중; (*what we breathe*) konggi 공기; ***by ~*** *travel* pihaenggiro 비행기로; *send mail* hanggongp'yŏnŭro 항공편으로; ***in the open ~*** yaoeesŏ 야외에서; ***on the ~*** RAD, TV pangsong chung-e 방송 중에 **2** *v/t room* hwan-gishik'ida 환기시키다; *fig*: *views* palk'ida 밝히다
airbase konggun kiji 공군 기지; **air-conditioned** naengbangjung 냉방중; **air-conditioning** naengbang 냉방, eŏk'on 에어콘; **aircraft** hanggonggi 항공기; **aircraft carrier** hanggongmoham 항공모함; **air cylinder** sujung hohŭpkki 수중 호흡기; **airfield** pihaengjang 비행장; **air force** konggun 공군; **air hostess** sŭt'yuŏdissŭ 스튜어디스; **air letter** hanggongbonghamnyŏpssŏ 항공봉함엽서; **airline** hanggongsa 항공사; **airmail**: ***by ~*** hanggong-up'yŏnŭro 항공우편으로; **airplane** pihaenggi 비행기; **air pollution** taegioyŏm 대기오염; **airport** konghang 공항; **airsick**: ***get ~*** pihaenggi mŏlmirŭl hada 비행기 멀미를 하다; **airspace** yŏnggong 영공; **air terminal** konghang t'ŏminŏl 공항 터미널; **airtight** *container* konggiga ant'onghanŭn 공기가 안통하는; **air traffic** hanggong kyot'ong 항공 교통; **air-traffic control** hanggong kyot'ong kwanje 항공 교통 관제; **air-traffic controller** hanggong kyot'ong kwanjewŏn 항공 교통 관제원
airy *room* konggiga shinsŏnhan 공기가 신선한; *attitude* kabyŏun 가벼운
aisle t'ongno 통로
aisle seat t'ongno tchok chari 통로 쪽 자리
alarm 1 *n* (*feeling*) puran 불안; (*warning*) kyŏnggo 경고; (*device*) kyŏngbogi 경보기; ***raise the ~*** kyŏnggohada 경고하다 **2** *v/t* puranhage hada 불안하게 하다
alarm clock chamyŏngjong shigye 자명종 시계
album (*for photographs*) aelbŏm 앨범; (*record*) ŭmban 음반
alcohol alk'o-ol 알코올
alcoholic 1 *n* alk'o-ol chungdoktcha 알코올 중독자 **2** *adj* alk'o-olssŏng-ŭi 알코올성의
alert 1 *n* (*signal*) kyŏngboŭm 경보음; ***be on the ~*** kyŏnggyehada 경계하다 **2** *v/t* kyŏnggohada 경고하다 **3** *adj* kyŏnggyehanŭn 경계하는
alibi allibai 알리바이
alien 1 *n* (*foreigner*) oegugin 외국인; (*from space*) oegyein 외계인 **2** *adj* ijiltchŏgin 이질적인; ***be ~ to*** ...wa / kwa mat-tchi ant'a ..와 / 과 맞지 않다
alienate sowŏnhage hada 소원하게 하다; ***be ~d*** ttadollimŭl pat-tta 따돌림을 받다
alight *adj*: ***be ~*** pult'aorŭda 불타오르다
alike 1 *adj*: ***be ~*** pisŭt'ada 비슷하다 **2** *adv*: ***old and young ~*** nŭlgŭnina chŏlmŭnina ttokkach'i 늙은이나

젊은이나 똑같이
alimony wijaryo 위자료
alive: ***be ~*** sarait-tta 살아있다
all 1 *adj* modŭn 모든; ***~ the cars*** modŭn ch'a 모든 차; ***~ the time*** hangsang 항상 **2** *pron* modu 모두; ***~ of us / them*** uridŭl / kŭdŭl modu 우리들 / 그들 모두; ***he ate ~ of it*** kŭga modu ta mŏgŏssŏyo 그가 모두 다 먹었어요; ***that's ~, thanks*** twaessŭmnida, kamsahamnida 됐습니다, 감사합니다; ***for ~ I care*** naega al pa aniyeyo 내가 알 바 아니예요; ***for ~ I know*** naega anŭn paronŭn 내가 아는 바로는; ***~ but ...*** (*except*) ...man ppaego ...만 빼고; ***~ but John agreed*** Chonman ppaego modu tong-ŭihaessŏyo 존만 빼고 모두 동의했어요 **3** *adv*: ***~ at once*** (*suddenly*) kaptchagi 갑자기; ***~ but*** (*nearly*) kŏŭi ta 거의 다; ***~ right*** choayo 좋아요; ***be ~ the better*** ohiryŏ tŏ nat-tta 오히려 더 낫다; ***it is ~ the better for having been cleaned*** ch'ongsoga ta toeŏsŏ ohiryŏ tŏ natkkunnyo 청소가 다 되어서 오히려 더 낫군요; ***they're not at ~ alike*** kŭdŭrŭn chŏnhyŏ tamtchi anassŏyo 그들은 전혀 닮지 않았어요; ***not at ~!*** (*please do*) chŏnmaneyo! 천만에요!; ***two ~*** (*in score*) i tae iro tongtchŏm 이 대 이로 동점
allegation chujang 주장
alleged chujangdoen 주장된
allergic: ***be ~ to*** ...e allerŭgi panŭng-i it-tta ...에 알레르기 반응이 있다
allergy allerŭgi 알레르기
alleviate *pain*, *suffering* tŏlda 덜다
alley (*between buildings*) kolmok 골목; (*in a garden*) osolkkil 오솔길
alliance tongmaeng 동맹
alligator agŏ 악어
allocate punbaehada 분배하다
allot paebunhada 배분하다
allow (*permit*) hŏrak'ada 허락하다; *money*, *time* chuda 주다; ***it's not ~ed*** kŭgŏsŭn kŭmjisahang-imnida 그것은 금지사항입니다; ***~ s.o. to ...*** nuguege ...ŭl / rŭl hŏrak'ada 누구에게 ...을 / 를 허락하다
♦**allow for** ...ŭl / rŭl koryŏhada ...을 / 를 고려하다
allowance (*money*) kŭbyŏ 급여; (*pocket money*) yongtton 용돈; ***make ~s*** (*for thing*, *weather etc*) koryŏhada 고려하다; (*for person*) kamanhaejuda 감안해주다
alloy hapkkŭm 합금
all-purpose tayongdoŭi 다용도의; **all-round** mannŭng-ŭi 만능의; **all-time**: ***be at an ~ low*** chŏllyeŏpsshi chŏgŭn 전례없이 적은
♦**allude to** tollyŏsŏ ŏn-gŭp'ada 돌려서 언급하다
alluring yuhoktchŏgin 유혹적인
all-wheel drive saryun-gudong 사륜구동
ally *n* (*country*) tongmaengguk 동맹국; (*person*) hyŏmnyŏktcha 협력자
almond amondŭ 아몬드
almost kŏŭi 거의
alone honja 혼자
along 1 *prep* ...ŭl / rŭl ttarasŏ ...을 / 를 따라서 **2** *adv* hamkke 함께; ***~ with*** ...wa / kwa hamkke ...와 / 과 함께; ***all ~*** (*all the time*) naenae 내내
aloud sorirŭl naeŏ 소리를 내어; *think* chung-ŏl kŏrimyŏ 중얼 거리며
alphabet alp'abet 알파벳
alphabetical alp'abesŭi 알파벳의
already pŏlssŏ 벌써, imi 이미
alright: ***that's ~*** (*doesn't matter*) kwaench'anayo 괜찮아요; (*when s.o. says thank you*) ch'ŏnmaneyo 천만에요; (*is quite good*) choŭndeyo 좋은데요; ***I'm ~*** (*not hurt*) chŏn, kwaench'anayo 전, 괜찮아요; (*have got enough*) chŏn, kŭman twaessŭmnida 전, 그만 됐습니다; ***~, that's enough!*** kŭgŏllo twaessŏyo 그걸로 됐어요
also ttohan 또한
altar chedan 제단
alter *v/t* pakkuda 바꾸다
alteration pyŏn-gyŏng 변경; (*to clothes*) susŏn 수선
alternate 1 *v/i* kyoch'ehada 교체하다 **2** *adj* pŏn-gara hanŭn 번갈아 하는; ***on ~ days*** kyŏgillo 격일로
alternating current kyoryu 교류

alternative 1 *n* taean 대안 **2** *adj* taeshinhal 대신할
alternatively taeshin 대신
although pirok ... haljirado 비록 ...할지라도; **~ *I don't like it*** pirok naega choahaji anŭltchirado 비록 내가 좋아하지 않을지라도
altitude haebalgodo 해발고도; (*of plane*) kodo 고도
altogether (*completely*) wanjŏnhi 완전히; (*in all*) chŏnbu 전부
altruistic aet'ajŏgin 애타적인
aluminum alluminyum 알루미늄
always hangsang 항상, ŏnjena 언제나, nŭl 늘
a.m. ojŏn 오전
amalgamate *v/i* (*of companies*) happpyŏnghada 합병하다
amateur *n* amach'uŏ 아마추어
amaze kkamtchak nollage hada 깜짝 놀라게 하다
amazement kkamtchak nollam 깜짝 놀람
amazing (*surprising*) aju nollaun 아주 놀라운; (*very good*) aju choŭn 아주 좋은
ambassador taesa 대사
amber: ***at* ~** hwangsaek shinho-e 황색 신호에
ambiguous aemaemohohan 애매모호한
ambition yamang 야망; (*something desired*) kkum 꿈; *pej* yongmang 욕망
ambitious *person*, *plan* yashiminnŭn 야심있는
ambulance kugŭpch'a 구급차
ambush 1 *n* maebok 매복 **2** *v/t* maepok'ayŏ sŭpkkyŏk'ada 매복하여 습격하다
amend sujŏnghada 수정하다
amendment sujŏng 수정
amends: ***make* ~** posangŭl hada 보상을 하다
amenities (*leisure facilities*) oraksshishŏl 오락시설
America Miguk 미국
American 1 *adj* Migugŭi 미국의 **2** *n* Miguk saram 미국 사람
amiable hogamŭl chunŭn 호감을 주는
amicable uhojŏgin 우호적인
Amitabha Buddha Amit'abul 아미타불
ammunition t'annyak 탄약; *fig* mugi 무기
amnesty *n* samyŏn 사면
among(st) kaunde 가운데
amount yang 양; (*sum of money*) kŭmaek 금액
♦**amount to** ...i / ka toeda ...이 / 가 되다
ample ch'ungbunhan 충분한
amplifier aemp'ŭ 앰프
amplify *sound* chŭngp'ok'ada 증폭하다
amputate chŏlttanhada 절단하다
amuse (*make laugh etc*) utkkida 웃기다; (*entertain*) chŭlgŏpkkehada 즐겁게하다
amusement (*merriment*) chaemi 재미; (*entertainment*) chŭlgŏum 즐거움; **~*s*** (*games*) orangmul 오락물; ***to our great* ~** usŭpkkedo 우습게도
amusement park yuwŏnji 유원지
amusing chaemiinnŭn 재미있는
anabolic steroid kŭnyuk chŭnggangje 근육 증강제
analog COMPUT anallogŭ 아날로그
analogy yusa 유사
analysis punsŏk 분석; PSYCH chŏngshinbunsŏk 정신분석
analyze punsŏk'ada 분석하다
anarchy mujŏngbu sangt'ae 무정부 상태
anatomy haebuhak 해부학
ancestor chosang 조상; **~ *worship*** chosang sungbae 조상 숭배
ancestral grave sanso 산소
ancestral rite chesa 제사
anchor NAUT **1** *n* tat 닻 **2** *v/i* tach'ŭl naerida 닻을 내리다
anchor man TV aengk'ŏ 앵커
anchovies myŏlch'i 멸치
ancient *adj* kodaeŭi 고대의
and ◊ (*joining nouns*) wa / kwa 와 / 과; ***you* ~ *me*** tangshin-gwa na 당신과 나 ◊ (*joining adjectives*) ...go ...고 ; ***tall* ~ *thin*** k'iga k'ŭgo marŭn 키가 크고 마른 ◊ (*joining verbs*) ...hago ...하고; ***I did some exercises* ~ *had a shower*** nanŭn undong-ŭl hago

shyawŏrŭl haet-tta 나는 운동을 하고 샤워를 했다; ***they were eating ~ drinking*** kŭdŭrŭn mŏk-kko mashigo issŏssŏyo 그들은 먹고 마시고 있었어요 ◊ (*starting a new sentence*) kŭrigo 그리고; ***And it was expensive*** kŭrigo pissassŏyo 그리고 비쌌어요 ◊ (*expressing a result*) ...haesŏ ...해서; ***he fell ~ broke his leg*** kŭnŭn nŏmŏjyŏsŏ tariga purŏjyŏt-tta 그는 넘어져서 다리가 부러졌다 ◊: ***it's getting hotter ~ hotter*** chŏmjŏm tŏ tŏwŏjinda 점점 더 더워진다
anemia pinhyŏltchŭng 빈혈증
anemic: ***be ~*** MED pinhyŏltchŭng-ida 빈혈증이다
anesthetic mach'wije 마취제
anesthetist mach'wisa 마취사
anger 1 *n* noyŏum 노여움 **2** *v/t* hwanaege hada 화내게 하다
angina hyopsshimtchŭng 협심증
angle *n* kak 각
angry hwaga nan 화가 난; ***be ~ with s.o.*** nuguege hwaga nada 누구에게 화가 나다
anguish k'ŭn kot'ong 큰 고통
animal tongmul 동물
animated hwalbarhan 활발한
animated cartoon manhwa yŏnghwa 만화 영화
animation (*liveliness*) saenggi 생기; (*cinematic*) aenimeishyŏn 애니메이션
animosity chŭng-o 증오
ankle palmok 발목
annex 1 *n* (*building*) pyŏlgwan 별관 **2** *v/t state* hap-ppyŏnghada 합병하다
anniversary (*wedding ~*) kinyŏmil 기념일
announce kongshiktchŏgŭro allida 공식적으로 알리다
announcement allim 알림; (*official*) konggo 공고
announcer TV, RAD anaunsŏ 아나운서
annoy sŏnggashigehada 성가시게 하다; ***be ~ed*** hwanada 화나다
annoyance (*anger*) hwa 화; (*nuisance*) sŏnggashim 성가심
annoying sŏnggashin 성가신
annual *adj* (*once a year*) illyŏne han ponŭi 일년에 한 번의; (*of a year*) yŏnjung-ŭi 연중의; ***~ salary*** yŏnbong 연봉; ***an ~ income*** yŏnsuip 연수입; ***an ~ event*** yŏnjung haengsa 연중 행사
annul *marriage* muhyorohada 무효로 하다
anonymous ingmyŏng-ŭi 익명의
anorexia kŏshiktchŭng 거식증
anorexic: ***be ~*** kŏshiktchŭng-ŭl alt'a 거식증을 앓다
another 1 *adj* (*different*) tarŭn 다른; (*additional*) tto hana 또 하나 **2** *pron* (*different one*) tarŭn kŏt 다른 것; (*additional one*) tto tarŭn kŏt 또 다른 것; ***one ~*** sŏro 서로
answer 1 *n* tap 답; (*to problem*) haedap 해답 **2** *v/t* tap'ada 답하다; ***~ the door*** munŭl yŏllŏ kada 문을 열러 가다; ***~ the telephone*** chŏnhwarŭl pat-tta 전화를 받다
♦**answer back 1** *v/t person* ...ege maldaekkuhada ...에게 말대꾸하다 **2** *v/i* maldaekkuhada 말대꾸하다
♦**answer for** ch'aegimŭl chida 책임을 지다
answerphone chadong-ŭngdapkki 자동응답기
ant kaemi 개미
antagonism chŏktaeshim 적대심
Antarctic *n* Namgŭk-kkwŏn 남극권
antenatal ch'ulssan chŏnŭi 출산 전의
antenna (*of insect*) tŏdŭmi 더듬이; (*for TV*) ant'ena 안테나
antibiotic *n* hangsaeng multchil 항생 물질
antibody hangch'e 항체
anticipate (*expect*) yesanghada 예상하다
anticipation yesang 예상
anti-Communism pan-gongjuŭi 반공주의
antidote haedoktche 해독제
antifreeze pudong-aek 부동액
antipathy pan-gam 반감
antiquated kushigŭi 구식의
antique *n* kolttongp'um 골동품
antique dealer kolttongp'um sang-in 골동품 상인
antiseptic 1 *adj* salgyunŭi 살균의 **2** *n*

sodongnyak 소독약
antisocial pisagyojŏgin 비사교적인; ***I'm feeling very ~*** nanŭn pyŏllo nugurŭl mannal kibuni anida 나는 별로 누구를 만날 기분이 아니다
antivirus program COMPUT pairŏsŭ paeksshin p'ŭrogŭraem 바이러스 백신 프로그램
anxiety kŏktchŏng
anxious kŏktchŏnghanŭn 걱정하는; (*eager*) maeu paranŭn 매우 바라는; ***be ~ for*** (*for news etc*) ...ŭl/rŭl kodaehada ...을/를 고대하다
any 1 *adj* ◊ (*no translation*): ***are there ~ diskettes/glasses?*** tisŭk'eshi/ chani issŏyo? 디스켓이/잔이 있어?; ***is there ~ bread/improvement?*** ppang-i/hyangsang-i issŭmnikka? 빵이/향상이 있습니까? ◊ (*in negatives*) amu 아무; ***there aren't ~ diskettes/glasses*** amu tisŭk'et-tto/chando ŏpssŏyo 아무 디스켓도/잔도 없어요; ***there isn't ~ bread/improvement*** amu ppangdo/hyangsangdo ŏpssŭmnida 아무 빵도/향상도 없습니다; ***take ~ one you like*** choahanŭn kŏsŭn muŏidŭn kajiseyo 좋아하는 것은 무엇이든 가지세요 ◊ (*emphatic*) ŏttŏn 어떤; ***have you ~ idea at all?*** ŏttŏn saenggagi issŭmnikka? 어떤 생각이 있습니까? **2** *pron* (*thing*) amu kŏt 아무 것; (*person*) nugudo 누구도; ***don't you have ~?*** amu kŏtto ŏpssŭseyo? 아무 것도 없으세요?; ***there isn't/aren't ~ left*** namŭn kŏshi ŏptta 남은 것이 없다; ***~ of them could be guilty*** kŭtŭl chung nuguegedo choega issŭl su issŏyo 그들 중 누구에게도 죄가 있을 수 있어요 **3** *adv* chogŭm 조금; ***is that ~ better/easier?*** chogŭmirado tŏ nassŭmnikka/ shwissŭmnikka? 조금이라도 더 낫습니까/쉽습니까?; ***I don't like it ~ more*** nanŭn tŏ isang kŭgŏsŭl choahaji annŭnda 나는 더이상 그것을 좋아하지 않는다
anybody nugun-ga 누군가; ***was ~ at home?*** nugun-ga chibe issŏssŏyo? 누군가 집에 있었어요? ◊ (*with negatives*) amudo ... (+ *negative verb*) 아무도 ...; ***there wasn't ~ there*** amudo kŏgi ŏpssŏssŏyo 아무도 거기 없었어요; ***wasn't ~ at home?*** amudo chibe ŏpssŏssŏyo? 아무도 집에 없었어요? ◊ (*emphatic*) nugurado 누구라도; ***~ can do that*** kŭgŏsŭn nugurado hal su issŏyo 그것은 누구라도 할 수 있어요
anyhow ŏtchaet-ttŭn 어쨌든
anyone → ***anybody***
anything muŏt 무엇; (*with negatives*) amu kŏt-tto 아무 것도; ***I didn't hear ~*** nanŭn amu kŏt-tto tŭt-tchi anat-tta 나는 아무 것도 듣지 않았다; ***~ but ...*** chŏnhyŏ ...haji ant'a 전혀 ...하지 않다; ***she was ~ but helpful*** kŭnyŏnŭn chŏnhyŏ toumi toeji anassŏyo 그녀는 전혀 도움이 되지 않았어요; ***~ else?*** tarŭn kŏsŭnyo? 다른 것은요?
anyway → ***anyhow***
anywhere ŏdidŭnji 어디든지; ***if you see one ~, buy it*** ŏdidŭnji kŭgŏsŭl pomyŏn saseyo 어디든지 그것을 보면 사세요 ◊ (*with negatives*) amudedo 아무데도; ***he won't go ~ without me*** kŭnŭn naŏpsshinŭn amudedo kaji anŭl kŏyeyo 그는 나 없이는 아무데도 가지 않을 거예요
apart (*in distance*) ttŏrŏjyŏsŏ 떨어져서; ***live ~*** (*of people*) kakki ttaro salda 각기 따로 살다; ***~ from*** (*excepting*) cheoehago 제외하고; (*in addition to*) ...edaga tŏ ...에다가 더
apartment ap'at'ŭ 아파트
apartment block ap'at'ŭ tanji 아파트 단지
apathetic mukwanshimhan 무관심한
ape *n* k'ŭn wŏnsung-iryu 큰 원숭이류
aperture PHOT kugyŏng 구경
apologize sagwahada 사과하다
apology sagwa 사과
apostrophe GRAM ŏp'asŭt'ŭrop'i 어파스트로피
appall chilgŏp'age hada 질겁하게 하다
appalling musŏun 무서운; *language* chijŏbunhan 지저분한
apparatus changch'i 장치

apparent myŏngbaek'an 명백한; ***become ~ that*** ... ranŭn kŏshi punmyŏnghaejida ...라는 것이 분명해지다

apparently pogie 보기에; ***~ they are married*** pogie kŭdŭrŭn kyŏrhonhan kŏt kat'ayo 보기에 그들은 결혼한 것 같아요

appeal 1 *n* (*charm*) maeryŏk 매력; (*for funds etc*) kanch'ŏng 간청; LAW hangso 항소 **2** *v/i* LAW hangsohada 항소하다

♦**appeal to** (*be attractive to*) ...ŭl/rŭl kkŭlda ...을/를 끌다

♦**appeal for** ...ŭl/rŭl hosohada ...을/를 호소하다

appear nat'anada 나타나다; (*in movie*) ch'uryŏnhada 출연하다; (*of new product*) ch'ulsshihada 출시하다; (*in court*) ch'ulttuhada 출두하다; ***he ~s calm*** kŭnŭn choyonghae poinda 그는 조용해 보인다; ***it ~s that*** ...in kŏt kat-tta ...인 것 같다

appearance (*arrival*) ch'urhyŏn 출현; (*in movie etc*) ch'uryŏn 출연; (*in court*) ch'ulttu 출두; (*look*) p'yojŏng 표정; ***put in an ~*** chamkkan ch'amsŏk'ada 잠깐 참석하다

appendicitis maengjangnyŏm 맹장염, ch'ungsuyŏm 충수염

appendix MED maengjang 맹장, ch'ungsu 충수; (*of book etc*) purok 부록

appetite shigyok 식욕; *fig* yokku 욕구

appetizer (*food*) chŏnch'ae 전채; (*drink*) shiktchŏnŭi ŭmnyo 식전의 음료

appetizing shigyogŭl todunŭn 식욕을 돋우는

applaud 1 *v/i* sŏng-wŏnŭl ponaeda 성원을 보내다 **2** *v/t* ...ege pakssurŭl ponaeda ...에게 박수를 보내다; *fig* ch'ingsonghada 칭송하다

applause sŏng-wŏn 성원; (*praise*) ch'ingsong 칭송

apple sagwa 사과

apple pie sagwa p'ai 사과 파이

apple sauce sagwasosŭ 사과소스

appliance kigye 기계; (*household*) kajŏnjep'um 가전제품; ***electrical ~*** chŏnja chep'um 전자 제품

applicable chŏgyonghal su innŭn 적용할 수 있는

applicant ŭngmoja 응모자

application (*for job, university etc*) chiwŏn 지원; (*for passport, visa*) shinch'ŏng 신청

application form chiwŏnsŏ 지원서; (*for passport, visa*) shinch'ŏngsŏ 신청서; (*for university*) ip'ak wŏnsŏ 입학 원서

apply 1 *v/t* chŏgyonghada 적용하다; *ointment* p'yŏ parŭda 펴 바르다 **2** *v/i* (*of rule, law*) chŏgyongdoeda 적용되다

♦**apply for** *job, university* chiwŏnhada 지원하다; *passport* shinch'ŏnghada 신청하다

♦**apply to** *address, department etc* ...(ŭ)ro yŏllak'ada ...(으)로 연락하다; *person* ...ege yŏllak'ada ...에게 연락하다; (*affect*) ...e chŏgyongdoeda ...에 적용되다

appoint (*to position*) immyŏnghada 임명하다

appointment (*to position*) immyŏng 임명; (*meeting*) yakssok 약속

appointments diary taiŏri 다이어리

appreciate 1 *v/t* (*value*) p'yŏngkkahada 평가하다; (*be grateful for*) kamsahada 감사하다; (*acknowledge*) alda 알다; ***thanks, I ~ it*** ch'injŏre kamsadŭrimnida 친절에 감사드립니다 **2** *v/i* FIN kagyŏgi orŭda 가격이 오르다

appreciation (*of kindness etc*) kamsa 감사; (*of music etc*) p'yŏngkka 평가; ***as a token of our ~*** kamsaŭi p'yoshiro 감사의 표시로

apprehensive puranhan 불안한

apprentice kyŏnsŭpsaeng 견습생

approach 1 *n* chean 제안; (*offer etc*) kyosŏp 교섭; (*to problem*) chŏpkkŭn pangbŏp 접근 방법 **2** *v/t* (*get near to*) kakkai tagagada 가까이 다가가다; (*contact*) chŏpch'ok'ada 접촉하다; *problem* taruda 다루다

approachable *person* kakkai hagi shwiun 가까이 하기 쉬운

appropriate *adj* chŏktchŏrhan 적절한

approval sŭng-in 승인

approve 1 *v/i* ch'ansŏnghada 찬성하다 **2** *v/t* sŭng-inhada 승인하다
♦**approve of** injŏnghada 인정하다
approximate *adj* taeryagŭi 대략의
approximately taeryak 대략
APR (= ***annual percentage rate***) yŏniyul 연이율
apricot salgu 살구
April sawŏl 사월
apt *pupil* chaenŭng-innŭn 재능있는; *remark* chŏkttanghan 적당한; ***be ~ to*** (*likely*) …hanŭn kyŏnghyang-i it-tta …하는 경향이 있다
aptitude chŏkssŏng 적성
aquarium yuri sujokkwan 유리 수족관
aquatic sujung-ŭi 수중의
Arab 1 *adj* Arabŭi 아랍의 **2** *n* Arabin 아랍인
Arabic 1 *adj* Arabŭi 아랍의; ***~ numerals*** Arabia suttcha 아라비아 숫자 **2** *n* Arabŏ 아랍어
arable nonggyŏng-e almajŭn 농경에 알맞은
arbitrary *decision, remark* tokttanjŏgin 독단적인; *attack* mujagwihan 무작위한
arbitrate *v/i* chungjaehada 중재하다
arbitration chungjae 중재
arch *n* ach'i 아치
archeologist kogohaktcha 고고학자
archeology kogohak 고고학
archer kungsu 궁수
architect sŏlgyesa 설계사
architecture (*subject*) kŏnch'uk'ak 건축학; (*style*) kŏnch'ungnyangshik 건축양식
archives kirok 기록
archway ach'i mich'ŭi t'ongno 아치 밑의 통로
Arctic *n* Pukkŭkkwŏn 북극권
ardent yŏllyŏrhan 열렬한
area (*region*) chiyŏk 지역; (*of activity, study etc*) punya 분야; (*square meters etc*) myŏnjŏk 면적
area code TELEC chiyŏk pŏnho 지역 번호
arena SP undongjang 운동장
Argentina Arŭhent'ina 아르헨티나
Argentinian 1 *adj* Arŭhent'inaŭi 아르헨티나의 **2** *n* Arŭhent'inain 아르헨티나인
arguably ama t'ŭllimŏpsshi 아마 틀림없이
argue 1 *v/i* (*quarrel*) maldat'umhada 말다툼하다; (*reason*) nonhada 논하다 **2** *v/t*: ***~ that*** …rago chujanghada …라고 주장하다
argument (*quarrel*) nonjaeng 논쟁; (*reasoning*) nolli 논리
argumentative nonjaeng-ŭl choahanŭn 논쟁을 좋아하는
arid *land* kŏnjohan 건조한
arise (*of situation, problem*) irŏnada 일어나다
aristocrat kwijok 귀족
arithmetic sansul 산술
arm[1] *n* (*of person*) p'al 팔; (*of chair*) p'algŏri 팔걸이
arm[2] *v/t* mujangshik'ida 무장시키다
armaments kunbi 군비
armchair allak ŭija 안락 의자
armed mujanghan 무장한
armed forces kukkun 국군
armed robbery mujang kangdo 무장 강도
armor pangt'an chokki 방탄 조끼
armored vehicle changgapch'a 장갑차
armpit kyŏdŭrang-i 겨드랑이
arms (*weapons*) kunbi 군비
army yuk-kkun 육군
aroma hyanggi 향기
around 1 *prep* (*in circle*) …ŭi chuwi …의 주위, …ŭi tulle …의 둘레; (*roughly*) taeryak … 대략 …; (*with expressions of time*) yak … tchŭm 약 … 쯤; ***it's ~ the corner*** igŏsŭn chŏ kusŏktchŭme it-tta 이것은 저 구석 쯤에 있다 **2** *adv* (*in the area*) kŭnch'ŏe 근처에; (*encircling*) tullee 둘레에; ***be ~*** (*somewhere near*) kŭnch'ŏe it-tta 근처에 있다; ***he's ~ somewhere*** kŭnŭn ŏdi kŭnch'ŏe issŏyo 그는 어디 근처에 있어요; ***there are a lot of people ~*** sabang-e manŭn saramdŭri issŏyo 사방에 많은 사람들이 있어요; ***there's a nasty flu ~*** tok-kkami yuhaeng-ida 독감이 유행이다; ***he lives ~ here*** kŭnŭn i kŭnch'ŏe sanda 그는 이 근처에 산다; ***walk ~*** kŏrŏdanida

걸어다니다; ***she has been ~*** (*has traveled, is experienced*) kŭnyŏnŭn insaenggyŏnghŏmi mant'a 그녀는 인생경험이 많다
arouse *interest, feelings* pullŏ irŭk'ida 불러 일으키다; (*sexually*) chagŭk'ada 자극하다
arrange (*put in order*) paeyŏrhada 배열하다; *furniture* paech'ihada 배치하다; *flowers, books* kajirŏnhi kkot-tta 가지런히 꽂다; *music* p'yŏn-gok'ada 편곡하다; *meeting, party etc* chunbihada 준비하다; *time and place* yeyak'ada 예약하다; ***I've ~d to meet him*** nanŭn kŭwa mannagiro haet-tta 나는 그와 만나기로 했다
♦**arrange for** …ege put'ak'ada …에게 부탁하다
arranged marriage chungmae kyŏrhon 중매 결혼
arrangement (*plan*) kyehoek 계획; (*agreement*) tong-ŭi 동의; (*of furniture etc*) paech'i 배치; (*of flowers*) kkotkkoji 꽃꽂이; (*of music*) p'yŏn-gok 편곡
arrears minapkkŭm 미납금; ***be in ~*** (*of person*) minap'ada 미납하다; ***I'm paid in ~*** nanŭn hubullo chigŭppannŭnda 나는 후불로 지급받는다
arrest 1 *n* ch'ep'o 체포; ***be under ~*** kugŭm sangt'aee it-tta 구금 상태에 있다 **2** *v/t criminal* ch'ep'ohada 체포하다
arrival toch'ak 도착; **~s** (*at airport*) ipkkuk 입국
arrive toch'ak'ada 도착하다
♦**arrive at** *place* …e toch'ak'ada …에 도착하다; *decision etc* …e todarhada …에 도달하다
arrogance kŏman 거만
arrogant kŏmanhan 거만한
arrow hwasal 화살
arrow key COMPUT hwasalp'yo kŭlsoe 화살표 글쇠
arson panghwa 방화
art yesul 예술; (*things produced*) yesulp'um 예술품; (*skill*) kisul 기술; ***the ~s*** munhwayesul 문화예술; ***~s degree*** munhakssa 문학사
arterial road kansŏndoro 간선도로
artery MED tongmaek 동맥
art gallery misulgwan 미술관
arthritis kwanjŏllyŏm 관절염
article (*item*) han p'ummok 한 품목; (*in newspaper*) kisa 기사; (*section*) chohang 조항; GRAM kwansa 관사
articulate *adj* myŏnghwak'an 명확한
artificial in-gongjŏgin 인공적인; *pearls, leather, flowers* injoŭi 인조의; (*not sincere*) inwijŏgin 인위적인
artificial intelligence in-gongjinŭng 인공지능
artillery taep'o 대포
artisan sugong-ŏptcha 수공업자
artist (*painter*) misulga 미술가; (*artistic person*) yesulga 예술가
artistic yesultchŏgin 예술적인
as 1 *conj* ◊ (*while, when*) ...hal ttae ...할 때; ***he came in ~ I was going out*** naega nagaryŏgo hal ttae kŭga tŭrŏwassŏyo 내가 나가려고 할 때 그가 들어왔어요 ◊ (*because*) waenyahamyŏn ...(i)ki ttaemunida 왜냐하면 ...(이)기 때문이다; ***~ it's so rainy today*** waenyahamyŏn onŭl piga nŏmu ogi ttaemuniyeyo 왜냐하면 오늘 비가 너무 오기 때문이예요 ◊ (*like*) ...ch'ŏrŏm ...처럼; ***she married a miner, ~ her sister had done*** kŭnyŏnŭn ŏnnich'ŏrŏm kwangbuwa kyŏrhonhaet-tta 그녀는 언니처럼 광부와 결혼했다; ***~ if ...*** ...in-gŏt ch'ŏrŏm ...인것 처럼; ***don't treat me ~ if I was a child*** narŭl aiin-gotch'ŏrŏm ch'igŭp'aji maseyo 나를 아이인것 처럼 취급하지 마세요; ***~ usual*** p'yŏngsoch'ŏrŏm 평소처럼; ***~ necessary*** p'iryohadamyŏn 필요하다면 **2** *adv* mank'ŭm 만큼; ***~ high / pretty ~ ...*** ...mank'ŭm nop'ŭn / yeppŭn ...만큼 높은 / 예쁜; ***~ much ~ that?*** kŭrŏke mani? 그렇게 많습니까? **3** *prep* ...(ŭ)rosŏ ...(으)로서; ***~ a child*** ŏryŏssŭl ttae 어렸을 때; ***work ~ a teacher / translator*** sŏnsaengnimŭro / pŏnyŏkkaro irhada 선생님으로 / 번역가로 일하다; ***~ for you*** nŏnŭn 너는; ***~ Hamlet*** haemlit yŏgŭro 햄릿 역으로
asap (= ***as soon as possible***)

kanŭnghanhan ppalli 가능한한 빨리

ASEAN (= ***Association of South East Asian Nations***) Tongnam Ashia Kuk-kka Yŏnhap 동남 아시아 국가 연합

ash chae 재; ***~es*** chae 재

ashamed: ***be ~*** pukkŭrŏwŏhada 부끄러워하다; ***be ~ of*** ...ege pukkŭrŏpkke yŏgida ...에게 부끄럽게 여기다; ***you should be ~ of yourself*** tangshinŭn chashinege pukkŭrŏun churŭl arayadoeyo 당신은 자신에게 부끄러운 줄을 알아야되요

ash can ssŭregi t'ong 쓰레기 통

ashore mut'e 뭍에; ***go ~*** mut'e orŭda 뭍에 오르다

ashtray chaettŏri 재떨이

Asia Ashia 아시아

Asian 1 *adj* Ashiaŭi 아시아의 **2** *n* Ashiain 아시아인

aside ttŏrŏttŭryŏ 떨어뜨려; ***~ from*** ...ŭl/rŭl cheoehago ...을/를 제외하고; (*in addition to*) ...edaga tŏ ...에다가 더

ask 1 *v/t* (*put a question to*) ...ege mut-tta ...에게 묻다; (*invite*) ch'odaehada 초대하다; *question* chilmunhada 질문하다; *favor* put'ak'ada 부탁하다; ***can I ~ you something?*** mwŏ chom put'ak'aedo toemnikka? 뭐 좀 부탁해도 됩니까?; ***~ s.o. about sth*** nuguege muŏse kwanhayŏ mut-tta 누구에게 무엇에 관하여 묻다; ***~ s.o. for*** nuguege ...ŭl/rŭl put'ak'ada 누구에게 ...을/를 부탁하다; ***~ s.o. to*** nuguege ... haedallago hada 누구에게 ... 해달라고 하다 **2** *v/i* mut-tta 묻다

♦**ask after** *person* ..ŭi kŭnhwang-ŭl mut-tta ...의 근황을 묻다

♦**ask for** ...ŭl/rŭl put'ak'ada ...을/를 부탁하다; *person* ...ŭl/rŭl ch'at-tta ...을/를 찾다

♦**ask out** teit'ŭ shinch'ŏnghada 데이트 신청하다

asking price p'anmae kagyŏk 판매 가격

asleep: ***be*** (***fast***) ***~*** p'uk chamdŭlda 푹 잠들다; ***fall ~*** chamdŭlda 잠들다

asparagus asŭp'aragŏsŭ 아스파라거스

aspect myŏn 면

aspirin asŭp'irin 아스피린

ass[1] (*idiot*) pabo 바보

ass[2] V (*backside*) ŏngdŏng-i 엉덩이; (*sex*) sekssŭ 섹스

assassin amsalbŏm 암살범

assassinate amsarhada 암살하다

assassination amsal 암살

assault 1 *n* p'ok'aeng 폭행 **2** *v/t* p'ok'aenghada 폭행하다

assemble 1 *v/t parts* chorip'ada 조립하다 **2** *v/i* (*of people*) moida 모이다

assembly (*of parts*) chorip 조립; POL ŭihoe 의회

assembly line ilgwanjagŏp yŏl 일관작업 열

assembly plant chorip kongjang 조립 공장

assent *v/i* tong-ŭihada 동의하다

assert: ***~ oneself*** chagirŭl chujanghada 자기를 주장하다

assertive *person* tanjŏngtchŏgin 단정적인

assess *situation, value* p'yŏngkkahada 평가하다

asset FIN, *fig* chasan 자산

asshole V ttongkkumŏng 똥구멍; (*idiot*) kaesaekki 개새끼

assign *task* chuda 주다; *room* halttanghada 할당하다

assignment (*task*) immu 임무; EDU suktche 숙제

assimilate *v/t facts* sohwahada 소화하다; *person into group* padadŭrida 받아들이다

assist toptta 돕다

assistance toum 도움

assistant chosu 조수

assistant director pujang 부장; (*for movie*) chogamdok 조감독

assistant manager pugyŏng-yŏng-in 부경영인; (*of hotel, restaurant, store*) pujibaein 부지배인

associate 1 *v/t* kwallyŏnshik'ida 관련시키다; (*in one's mind*) yŏnsanghada 연상하다 **2** *v/i*: ***~ with*** kyojehada 교제하다 **3** *n* tongnyo 동료

associate professor pugyosu 부교수
association tanch'e hyŏp'oe 단체 협회; ***in ~ with*** ...wa / kwa hyŏmnyŏk'ayŏ ...와 / 과 협력하여
assortment kajigakssaek 가지각색
assume (*suppose*) kajŏnghada 가정하다
assumption kajŏng 가정
assurance pojŭng 보증; (*confidence*) chashin 자신
assure (*reassure*) pojanghada 보장하다
assured (*confident*) hwaksshine ch'an 확신에 찬
asterisk pyŏlp'yo 별표
asthma ch'ŏnshik 천식
astonish kkamtchak nollagehada 깜짝 놀라게하다; ***be ~ed*** kkamtchak nollada 깜짝 놀라다
astonishing maeu nollaun 매우 놀라운
astonishment kkamtchak nollam 깜짝 놀람
astrologer chŏmsŏngga 점성가
astrology chŏmsŏngsul 점성술
astronaut ujuin 우주인
astronomer ch'ŏnmunhaktcha 천문학자
astronomical ch'ŏnmunhaktchŏgin 천문학적인; *price* ŏmch'ŏngnage nop'ŭn 엄청나게 높은
astronomy ch'ŏnmunhak 천문학
asylum (*mental*) chŏngshinppyŏng-wŏn 정신병원; (*political*) mangmyŏng 망명; ***seek political ~*** chŏngch'ijŏk mangmyŏng-ŭl shinch'ŏnghada 정치적 망명을 신청하다
at (*with places*) ...e(sŏ) ...에(서); ***~ the cleaner's*** set'akssoe(sŏ) 세탁소에(서); ***~ Joe's*** cho nechibesŏ(sŏ) 조 네집에(서); ***~ the door*** mune 문에; ***~ 10 dollars*** 10tallŏro 10달러로; ***~ the age of 18*** yoryŏdŏl sal ttaee 열여덟 살 때에; ***~ 5 o'clock*** 5shie 5시에; ***~ 150 km / h*** shisok 150k'illomit'ŏro 시속 150 킬로미터로; ***be good / bad ~ sth*** muŏse nŭngsuk'ada / nŭngsuk'aji mot'ada 무엇에 능숙하다 / 능숙하지 못하다
atheist mushillonja 무신론자
athlete undongga 운동가, sŭp'och'ŭin 스포츠인
athletic undong-ŭi 운동의; *person* ch'eryŏginnŭn 체력있는
athletics undonggyŏnggi 운동경기
Atlantic *n* Taesŏyang 대서양
atlas chidoch'aek 지도책
ATM (= ***automated teller machine***) hyŏn-gŭm inch'ulgi 현금 인출기
atmosphere (*of earth*) taegi 대기; (*ambiance*) punwigi 분위기
atmospheric pollution taegi oyŏm 대기 오염
atom wŏnja 원자
atom bomb wŏnja p'okt'an 원자 폭탄
atomic wŏnjaŭi 원자의
atomic energy wŏnjaryŏk 원자력
atomic waste haekssŭregi 핵쓰레기
atomizer punmugi 분무기
atrocious shimhage nappŭn 심하게 나쁜
atrocity hyung-ak 흉악
attach puch'ida 붙이다; *importance* puyŏhada 부여하다; (*to letter*) tongbonghada 동봉하다; ***be ~ed to*** (*fond of*) ...e(ge) maŭmi kkŭllida ...에(게) 마음이 끌리다
attachment (*with e-mail*) ch'ŏmga 첨가
attack 1 *n* konggyŏk 공격 **2** *v/t* konggyŏk'ada 공격하다
attempt 1 *n* shido 시도 **2** *v/t* shidohada 시도하다
attend ch'amsŏk'ada 참석하다
♦**attend to** ch'ŏrihada 처리하다; *customer* moshida 모시다; (*pay attention to*) chuŭihada 주의하다
attendance ch'amsŏk 참석; (*at school*) ch'ulssŏk 출석
attendant (*in museum*) chigwŏn 직원
attention chuŭi 주의; ***bring X to the ~ of Y*** Xe taehan chuŭirŭl Yege hwan-gishik'ida X에 대한 주의를 Y에게 환기시키다; ***your ~ please*** chumok'ae chushipsshio 주목해 주십시오; ***pay ~*** chuŭihada 주의하다
attentive *listener* chuŭigip'ŭn 주의깊은
attic tarakppang 다락방

attitude t'aedo 태도
attn (= ***for the attention of***) sushin 수신
attorney pyŏnhosa 변호사; ***power of ~*** wiimkkwŏn 위임권
attract *person, attention* kkŭlda 끌다; ***be ~ed to s.o.*** nuguege maŭmi kkŭllida 누구에게 마음이 끌리다
attraction (*also romantic*) maeryŏk 매력
attractive maeryŏginnŭn 매력있는
attribute[1] *v/t*: ***~ sth to*** muŏshi ... ttaemunŭro ch'ujŏngdoeda 무엇이 ... 때문으로 추정되다; *painting, poem* muŏsŭl ...ŭi chakp'umŭro ch'ujŏnghada 무엇을 ...의 작품으로 추정하다
attribute[2] *n* sokssŏng 속성
auction 1 *n* kyŏngmae 경매 **2** *v/t* kyŏngmaehada 경매하다
♦**auction off** kyŏngmaehada 경매하다
audacious *plan* taedamhan 대담한
audacity taedamhan haengdong 대담한 행동
audible tŭrŭl su innŭn 들을 수 있는
audience ch'ŏngjung 청중; (*in theater, at show*) kwanjung 관중; TV shich'ŏngja 시청자; (*of radio program*) ch'ŏngch'wija 청취자
audio *adj* odioŭi 오디오의
audiovisual shich'ŏnggagŭi 시청각의
audit 1 *n* kamsa 감사 **2** *v/t* kamsahada 감사하다; *course* ch'ŏngganghada 청강하다
audition 1 *n* odishyŏn 오디션 **2** *v/i* odishyŏnŭl pat-tta 오디션을 받다
auditor FIN kamsagwan 감사관; (*of course*) ch'ŏnggangsaeng 청강생
auditorium (*of theater etc*) kwanjungsŏk 관중석
August p'arwŏl 팔월
aunt (*own, sister of father*) komo 고모; (*own, sister of mother*) imo 이모; (*own, wife of uncle on father's side*) sungmo 숙모; (*own, wife of uncle on mother's side*) oesungmo 외숙모; (*somebody else's*) ajumma 아줌마
austere *interior, style* kkumijianŭn 꾸미지 않은; *person, face* chunŏmhan 준엄한; *life* kŭmyoktchŏgin 금욕적인
austerity (*economic*) naep'ip 내핍
Australasia Oseania 오세아니아
Australia Hoju 호주
Australian 1 *adj* Hojuŭi 호주의 **2** *n* Hojuin 호주인
Austria Osŭt'ŭria 오스트리아
Austrian 1 *adj* Osŭt'ŭriaŭi 오스트리아의 **2** *n* Osŭt'ŭriain 오스트리아인
authentic chintchaŭi 진짜의
authenticity shinbingssŏng 신빙성
author chakka 작가; (*of report etc*) chipp'iltcha 집필자
authoritative kwŏnwiinnŭn 권위있는
authority kwŏnwi 권위; (*permission*) hŏga 허가; ***be an ~ on*** ...ŭi kwŏnwijaida ...의 권위자이다; ***the authorities*** tangguk 당국
authorize kwŏnhanŭl chuda 권한을 주다; ***be ~d to ...*** ...l / ŭl hŏga pat-tta ...ㄹ / 을 허가 받다
autistic chap'yetchŭng-ŭi 자폐증의
auto *n* chadongch'a 자동차
autobiography chasŏjŏn 자서전
autograph *n* sain 사인
automate chadonghwahada 자동화하다
automatic 1 *adj* chadong-ŭi 자동의 **2** *n* (*car, gun etc*) chadongkigye 자동기계
automatically chadong-ŭro 자동으로
automation chadonghwa 자동화
automobile chadongch'a 자동차
automobile industry chadongch'a sanŏp 자동차 산업
autonomy chach'i 자치
autopilot chadong chojong changch'i 자동 조종 장치
autopsy pugŏm 부검
auxiliary *adj* pojoŭi 보조의
available *facility, service* ŏdŭl su innŭn 얻을 수 있는; *book, information* ch'ajŭl su innŭn 찾을 수 있는; *person* shiganinnŭn 시간있는
avalanche nunsat'ae 눈사태
avenue *also fig* kil 길
average 1 *adj* p'yŏnggyunŭi 평균의; (*ordinary*) pot'ong-ŭi 보통의; (*mediocre*) pot'ong chŏngdoŭi 보통

정도의 **2** *n* p'yŏnggyun 평균; ***above / below ~*** p'yŏnggyun wiŭi / araeŭi 평균 위의 / 아래의; ***on ~*** pot'ong 보통 **3** *v/t* p'yŏnggyunŭro … hada 평균으로 … 하다; ***I ~ six hours sleep a night*** nanŭn harue p'yŏnggyŭn yŏsŏt shiganŭl chanda 나는 하루에 평균 여섯 시간을 잔다

♦ **average out** *v/t* p'yŏnggyunnaeda 평균내다

♦ **average out at** p'yŏnggyŭn …(ŭ)ro kyesandoeda 평균 …(으)로 계산되다

aversion: ***have an ~ to*** …ŭl / rŭl aju shirŏhada …을 / 를 아주 싫어하다

avert *one's eyes* p'ihada 피하다; *crisis* maktta 막다

aviary k'ŭn saejang 큰 새장

aviation hanggong 항공

avid yŏlgwangtchŏgin 열광적인

avoid p'ihada 피하다

awake *adj* kkaeŏinnŭn 깨어있는; ***it's keeping me ~*** kŭgŏshi chamŭl sŏlch'ige haet-tta 그것이 잠을 설치게 했다

award 1 *n* (*prize*) sang 상 **2** *v/t* suyŏhada 수여하다; ***he was ~ed $10,000 in damages*** kŭnŭn mandallŏŭi sonhae paesang-ŭl padat-tta 그는 10,000달러의 손해 배상을 받았다

aware: ***be ~ of sth*** muŏsŭl alda 무엇을 알다; ***become ~ of sth*** muŏsŭl arach'arida 무엇을 알아차리다

awareness inshik 인식

away: ***be ~*** (*traveling, sick etc*) ŏptta 없다; ***I'll be ~ until next Friday*** nanŭn taŭm chu kŭmnyoilkkaji ŏpssŭl kŏyeyo 나는 다음 주 금요일까지 없을 거예요; ***walk / run ~*** kŏrŏgada / tomanggada 걸어가다 / 도망가다; ***look ~*** nunkkirŭl tollida 눈길을 돌리다; ***it's 2 miles ~*** 2mail ttŏrŏjyŏit-tta 2마일 떨어져있다; ***Christmas is still six weeks ~*** Sŏngt'anjŏlkkajinŭn yŏjŏnhi yuk chuna nama issŏyo 성탄절까지는 여전히 육 주나 남아 있어요; ***take sth ~ from s.o.*** nugurobut'ŏ muŏsŭl ppaeat-tta 누구로부터 무엇을 빼앗다; ***put sth ~*** muŏsŭl ch'iuda 무엇을 치우다

away game SP wŏnjŏng shihap 원정 시합

awesome F (*terrific*) koengjanghan 굉장한

awful shimhan 심한

awkward (*clumsy*) sŏt'urŭn 서투른; (*difficult*) himdŭn 힘든; (*embarrassing*) kŏbuk'an 거북한; ***feel ~*** kŏbuk'aehada 거북해하다

awning ch'ayang 차양

ax 1 *n* tokki 도끼 **2** *v/t job etc* tchallida 짤리다; *budget* sakkkamhada 삭감하다

axle ch'ach'uk 차축

B

BA (= ***Bachelor of Arts***) hakssa hagwi 학사 학위
baboon kaek'owŏnsung-i 개코원숭이
baby *n* agi 아기
baby carriage yumoch'a 유모차; **baby quilt** (*for carrying baby*) p'odaegi 포대기; **baby-sit** agirŭl tolbwajuda 아기를 돌봐주다; **baby-sitter** agirŭl tolbwajunŭn saram 아기를 돌봐주는 사람
bachelor ch'onggak 총각
back 1 *n* (*of person, book, knife, chair*) tŭng 등; (*of car, bus, paper*) twinmyŏn 뒷면; (*of house*) twittchok 뒷쪽; SP huwi 후위; ***in ~*** antchoge(sŏ) 안쪽에(서); ***in ~*** (***of the car***) (ch'aŭi) twit chwasŏge(sŏ) (차의) 뒷좌석에(서); ***at the ~ of the bus*** pŏsŭ twit chwasŏge(sŏ) 버스 뒷좌석에(서); ***~ to front*** kŏkkuro 거꾸로; ***at the ~ of beyond*** mopsshi oejin kose(sŏ) 몹시 외진 곳에(서) **2** *adj* twittchoge innŭn 뒷쪽에 있는; ***~ road*** twitkkil 뒷길 **3** *adv*: ***please move / stand ~*** twiro mullŏna chushipsshiyo / twie sŏ chushipsshiyo 뒤로 물러나 주십시요 / 뒤에 서 주십시요; ***2 meters ~ from the edge*** kajangjariesŏ 2mit'ŏ tŭrŏgasŏ 가장자리에서 2미터 들어가서; ***~ in 1935*** 1935nyŏnŭro kŏsŭllŏ ollagasŏ 1935년으로 거슬러 올라가서; ***give X ~ to Y*** Xŭl / rŭl Yege toedollyŏjuda X을 / 를 Y에게 되돌려주다; ***she'll be ~ tomorrow*** kŭnyŏnŭn naeil toraol kŏshimnida 그녀는 내일 돌아올 것입니다; ***when are you coming ~?*** ŏnje tora-ol kŏmnikka? 언제 돌아올 겁니까?; ***take X ~ to the store*** (*because unsatisfactory*) Xŭl / rŭl kagee murŭda X을 / 를 가게에 무르다; ***they wrote / phoned ~*** kŭdŭrŭn hoeshin haet-tta / hoedap haet-tta 그들은 회신 했다 / 회답 했다; ***he hit me ~*** kŭnŭn narŭl toettaeryŏt-tta 그는 나를 되때렸다 **4** *v/t* (*support*) huwŏnhada 후원하다; *car* hujinshik'ida 후진시키다; *horse* tonŭl kŏlda 돈을 걸다 **5** *v/i* (*of car*) hujinhada 후진하다, ida 이다
♦**back away** mullŏsŏda 물러서다
♦**back down** yangbohada 양보하다
♦**back off** twiro mullŏnada 뒤로 물러나다; (*from danger*) …esŏ mullŏnada …에서 물러나다
♦**back onto** …wa / kwa twiro chŏp'ae it-tta …와 / 과 뒤로 접해 있다
♦**back out** (*of commitment*) sonŭl tteda 손을 떼다
♦**back up 1** *v/t* (*support*) huwŏnhada 후원하다; *claim, argument* twitppatch'imhae chuda 뒷받침해 주다; *file* paegŏp'ada 백업하다; ***be backed up*** (*of traffic*) millyŏ it-tta 밀려 있다 **2** *v/i* (*in car*) hujinhada 후진하다
back burner: ***put sth on the ~*** muŏsŭl yŏn-gihada 무엇을 연기하다; **backdate** sogŭp'ayŏ chŏgyongshik'ida 소급하여 적용시키다; **backdoor** twinmun 뒷문
backer huwŏnja 후원자
backfire *v/i fig* yŏk'yokkwaga nada 역효과가 나다; **background** paegyŏng 배경; (*of person*) ch'ulsshin sŏngbun 출신 성분; (*of situation*) paehu 배후; ***she prefers to stay in the ~*** kŭnyŏnŭn ohiryŏ nasŏji ankirŭl choahanda 그녀는 오히려 나서지 않기를 좋아한다; **backhand** *n* (*in tennis*) paek haendŭ 백 핸드
backing (*support*) chiji 지지; MUS panju 반주
backing group MUS panjudan 반주단
backlash panbal 반발; **backlog**

mich'ŏribun 미처리분; **backpack 1** *n* paenang 배낭 **2** *v/i* paenang maego yŏhaenghada 배낭 매고 여행하다; **backpacker** paenang yŏhaengja 배낭 여행자; **backpedal** *fig* ch'ŏrhoehada 철회하다; **backslash** COMPUT yŏksŭllaeshi 역슬래시; **backspace (key)** COMPUT paekssŭp'eisŭ k'i 백스페이스 키; **backstairs** twitch'ŭnggye 뒷층계; **backstroke** SP paeyŏng 배영; **backup** (*support*) chiwŏn 지원; COMPUT paegŏp 백업; ***take a ~*** COMPUT paegŏbŭl hada 백업을 하다; **backup disk** COMPUT paegŏp tisŭk'ŭ 백업 디스크
backward 1 *adj child* twittŏrŏjin 뒤떨어진; *society* t'oebohanŭn 퇴보하는; *glance* twittchogŭi 뒷쪽의 **2** *adv* twittchogŭro 뒷쪽으로
backyard twit-ttŭl 뒷뜰; *fig* kŭnch'ŏ 근처
bacon peik'ŏn 베이컨
bacteria pakt'eria 박테리아
bad nappŭn 나쁜; *spelling* sŏt'urŭn 서투른; *cold, headache etc* shimhan 심한; (*rotten*) ssŏgŭn 썩은; ***it's not ~*** kwaench'anayo 괜찮아요; ***that's really too ~*** (*shame*) nŏmu andwaessŏyo 너무 안됐어요; ***feel ~ about*** …e taehae choech'aek-kkamŭl nŭkkida …에 대해 죄책감을 느끼다; ***be ~ at*** …e sŏt'urŭda …에 서투르다; ***Friday's ~, how about Thursday?*** kŭmnyoirŭn andoenŭnde, mogyoirŭn ŏttaeyo? 금요일은 안되는데, 목요일은 어때요?
bad debt pullyang puch'ae 불량 부채
badge paeji 배지
badger *v/t* chorŭda 조르다
bad language yokssŏl 욕설
badly nappŭge 나쁘게; (*making mistakes, errors*) chalmot 잘못; *injured, damaged* shimhage 심하게; ***he ~ needs a haircut / rest*** kŭnŭn chŏngmal mŏrirŭl challayagessŏyo / shwiŏyagessŏyo 그는 정말 머리를 잘라야겠어 요 / 쉬어야겠어요; ***he is ~ off*** (*poor*) kŭnŭn kananhada 그는 가난하다
badminton paedŭmint'ŏn 배드민턴
baffle tanghwanghage hada 당황하게 하다; ***be ~d*** tanghwanghae hada 당황해 하다
baffling ihaehal su ŏmnŭn 이해할 수 없는
bag (*travel ~*) yŏhaeng kabang 여행 가방; (*plastic, paper*) kabang 가방; (*for school*) ch'aek-kkabang 책가방; (*pocketbook*) haendŭbaek 핸드백
baggage suhwamul 수화물
baggage car RAIL suhwamul yŏlch'a 수화물 열차; **baggage cart** suhwamul unbanch'a 수화물 운반차; **baggage check** suhwamul pogwantchŭng 수화물 보관증; **baggage reclaim** suhwamul k'ŭlleim 수화물 클레임
baggy hŏllŏnghan 헐렁한
bail *n* LAW posŏk 보석; (*money*) posŏk-kkŭm 보석금; ***on ~*** posŏk-kkŭmŭl naego 보석금을 내고
♦**bail out 1** *v/t* LAW posŏgŭl patkke hada 보석을 받게 하다; *fig* kon-gyŏng-esŏ …ŭl / rŭl kuhaenaeda 곤경에서 …을 / 를 구해내다 **2** *v/i* (*from airplane*) nak'asanŭro t'alch'urhada 낙하산으로 탈출하다
bait *n* mikki 미끼
bake *v/t* kuptta 굽다
baked potato kuŭn kamja yori 구운 감자 요리
baker cheppang-ŏptcha 제빵업자
bakery ppangjip 빵집
balance 1 *n* kyunhyŏng 균형; (*remainder*) chanyŏgŭm 잔여금; (*of bank account*) chan-go 잔고 **2** *v/t* …ŭi kyunhyŏng-ŭl chaptta ..의 균형을 잡다; ***~ the books*** hoegye kyŏlssanhada 회계 결산하다 **3** *v/i* kyunhyŏng chaptta 균형 잡다; (*of accounts*) kyŏlssandoeda 결산되다
balanced (*fair*) kongjŏnghan 공정한; *diet* kyunhyŏng chap'in 균형 잡힌; *personality* anjŏngdoen 안정된
balance of payments kuktche suji 국제 수지; **balance of trade** muyŏk suji 무역 수지; **balance sheet** taech'adaejop'yo 대차대조표
balcony (*of house*) peranda 베란다; (*in theater*) ich'ŭng chwasŏk 이층

좌석
bald *man* taemŏriŭi 대머리의; ***he's going ~*** kŭnŭn taemŏriga toeŏ kanda 그는 대머리가 되어 간다
ball kong 공; ***on the ~*** *fig* pint'ŭm ŏmnŭn 빈틈 없는; ***play ~*** *fig* hyŏmnyŏk'ada 협력하다; ***the ~'s in his court*** *fig* taŭmŭn kŭŭi ch'aryeida 다음은 그의 차례이다
ball bearing pol peŏring 볼 베어링
ballerina pallerina 발레리나
ballet palle 발레
ballet dancer palle muyongga 발레 무용가
ball game (*baseball game*) yagu 야구; ***that's a different ~*** kŭgŏn tarŭn chongnyuŭi munjeimnida 그건 다른 종류의 문제입니다
ballistic missile t'ando misail 탄도 미사일
balloon (*child's*) p'ungsŏn 풍선; (*for flight*) kigu 기구
ballot 1 *n* t'up'yo 투표 **2** *v/t members* t'up'yoro chŏnghada 투표로 정하다
ballot box tup'yoham 투표함
ballpark (*baseball*) yagujang 야구장; ***be in the right ~*** *fig* kŏŭi mat-tta 거의 맞다; ***~ figure*** taegang-ŭi ŏrim 대강의 어림
ballpoint (pen) polp'en 볼펜
balls V pural 불알; (*courage*) paetchang 배짱
bamboo taenamu 대나무
ban 1 *n* kŭmji 금지 **2** *v/t* kŭmjihada 금지하다
banana panana 바나나
band akdan 악단; (*pop*) paendŭ 밴드; (*of material*) kkŭn 끈
bandage 1 *n* pungdae 붕대 **2** *v/t* pungdaerŭl kamtta 붕대를 감다
Band-Aid® panch'anggo 반창고
bandit sanjŏk 산적
bandwagon: ***jump on the ~*** shiryurŭl t'ada 시류를 타다
bandy *legs* hwin 휜
bang 1 *n* (*noise*) k'wang hanŭn sori 쾅 하는 소리; (*blow*) k'wang pudich'im 쾅 부딪힘 **2** *v/t door* k'wang tat-tta 쾅 닫다; (*hit*) k'wang pudich'ida 쾅 부딪히다 **3** *v/i* (*of door*) k'wang tach'ida 쾅 닫히다
Bangladesh Panggŭlladeshi 방글라데시
Bangladeshi 1 *adj* Panggŭlladeshiŭi 방글라데시의 **2** *n* Panggŭlladeshiin 방글라데시인
banjo paenjo 밴조
bank[1] (*of river*) chebang 제방
bank[2] **1** *n* FIN ŭnhaeng 은행 **2** *v/i*: ***~ with*** ...wa / kwa kŏraehada ...와 / 과 거래하다 **3** *v/t money* yegŭmhada 예금하다
♦**bank on** ...ŭl / rŭl kidaehada ...을 / 를 기대하다; ***don't ~ it*** nŏmu hwaksshinhaji mara 너무 확신하지 마라
bank account ŭnhaeng kujwa 은행 구좌; **bank balance** ŭnhaeng chan-go 은행 잔고; **bank bill** chip'ye 지폐
banker ŭnhaengga 은행가
banker's card ŭnhaeng shinyong k'adŭ 은행 신용 카드
banker's order chadong taech'e 자동 대체
bank loan ŭnhaeng yungja 은행 융자; **bank manager** ŭnhaeng chijŏmjang 은행 지점장; **bank rate** (chung-ang ŭnhaengŭi) ijayul (중앙 은행의) 이자율; **bankroll** *v/t* chagŭmŭl taeda 자금을 대다
bankrupt 1 *adj* (*person, company*) p'asanhan 파산한; ***go ~*** p'asanhada 파산하다 **2** *v/t* p'asanshik'ida 파산시키다
bankruptcy p'asan 파산
bank statement chan-go chohoe 잔고 조회
banner ki 기
banns kyŏrhon yego 결혼 예고
banquet yŏnhoe 연회
banter *n* kabyŏun nongdam 가벼운 농담
baptism serye 세례
baptize seryehada 세례하다
bar[1] (*iron*) pitchang 빗장; (*of chocolate*) makttaegi 막대기; (*for drinks*) sultchip 술집; (*counter*) kyesandae 계산대; ***a ~ of soap*** pinu hanjang 비누 한 장; ***be behind ~s*** kamoge it-tta 감옥에 있다
bar[2] *v/t* kŭmhada 금하다
bar[3] *prep* (*except*) ...ŭl / rŭl cheoehago

…을/를 제외하고
barbecue 1 *n* pabek'yu 바베큐; (*equipment*) pabek'yuyong ch'ŏlp'an 바베큐용 철판 **2** *v/t* t'ongtchaero kuptta 통째로 굽다
barbecued beef pulgogi 불고기
barbed wire kashi ch'ŏlssa 가시 철사
barber ibalssa 이발사
bar code pak'odŭ 바코드
bare *adj* (*naked*) palgabŏsŭn 발가벗은; *room* t'ŏng pin 텅 빈; ~ ***floor*** maenmaru 맨마루
barefoot: ***be*** ~ maenbarida 맨발이다
bare-headed mojarŭl ssŭji anŭn 모자를 쓰지 않은
barely kanshinhi 간신히
bargain 1 *n* (*deal*) yakssok 약속; (*good buy*) ssan mulgŏn 싼 물건; ***it's a ~!*** (*deal*) kyŏltchŏngnassŏyo! 결정났어요! **2** *v/i* hŭngjŏnghada 흥정하다
♦**bargain for** (*expect*) yesanghada 예상하다
barge *n* NAUT kŏrutppae 거룻배
bark[1] **1** *n* (*of dog*) kae chinnŭn sori 개 짖는 소리 **2** *v/i* chit-tta 짖다
bark[2] (*of tree*) kkŏptchil 껍질
barley pori 보리
barn hŏtkkan 헛간
barometer kiapkkye 기압계; *fig* chip'yo 지표
barracks MIL makssa 막사
barrel (*container*) t'ong 통
barren *land* pulmoŭi 불모의
barrette mŏrip'in 머리핀
barricade *n* parik'eidŭ 바리케이드
barrier ult'ari 울타리; (*cultural*) chang-ae 장애; ***language*** ~ ŏnŏ chang-ae 언어 장애
bar tender pat'endŏ 바텐더
barter 1 *n* mulmul kyohwan 물물 교환 **2** *v/t* mulmul kyohwanhada 물물 교환하다
base 1 *n* (*bottom*) mit 밑; (*center*) ponbu 본부; MIL chaktchŏn kiji 작전 기지 **2** *v/t*: ~ ***on*** …e pat'angŭl tuda …에 바탕을 두다; ~ ***X on Y*** Xŭi pat'angŭl Y(ŭ)ro hada X의 바탕을 Y(으)로 하다; ***be ~d in*** (*in city, country*) …e kŭn-gŏjirŭl tugo it-tta …에 근거지를 두고 있다
baseball (*ball*) yagugong 야구공; (*game*) yagu 야구
baseball bat yagu pangmang-i 야구 방망이; **baseball cap** yagu moja 야구 모자; **baseball player** yagu sŏnsu 야구 선수
base camp peisŭ k'emp'ŭ 베이스 캠프
basement (*of house*) chihashil 지하실; (*of store*) chihach'ŭng 지하층
base rate FIN chung-ang ŭnhaeng-ŭi kibon kŭmni 중앙 은행의 기본 금리
basic (*rudimentary*) kibonjŏgin 기본적인; (*fundamental*) kŭnbonjŏgin 근본적인; *level* kich'ojŏgin 기초적인; ***a ~ hotel*** susuhan hot'el 수수한 호텔
basically kibonjŏgŭro 기본적으로
basics: ***the*** ~ kich'o 기초; ***get down to*** ~ kich'obut'ŏ hada 기초부터 하다
basin (*for washing*) semyŏndae 세면대
basis kich'o 기초; (*of argument*) kŭngŏ 근거
bask haetppyŏch'ŭl tchoeda 햇볕을 쬐다
basket paguni 바구니; (*in basketball*) pasŭk'et 바스켓
basketball nonggu 농구
bass 1 *n* (*part, singer*) peisŭ 베이스; (*instrument*) pasŭ 바스 **2** *adj* chŏŭmŭi 저음의; ~ ***clef*** najŭn ŭmjarip'yo 낮은 음자리표
bastard sasaeng-a 사생아; F kaesaekki 개새끼; ***poor/stupid*** ~ pulssanghan/pabokat'ŭn nyŏsŏk 불쌍한/바보같은 녀석
bat[1] **1** *n* (*for baseball*) pangmang-i 방망이; (*for table tennis*) ch'ae 채 **2** *v/i* (*in baseball*) pangmang-iro ch'ida 방망이로 치다
bat[2]: ***he didn't ~ an eyelid*** kŭnŭn nun hana kkamtchak'aji anat-tta 그는 눈 하나 깜짝하지 않았다
bat[3] (*animal*) paktchwi 박쥐
batch *n* (*of students*) ilttan 일단; (*of data*) paech'i 배치; (*of goods produced*) han mukkŭm 한 묶음; (*of bread*) han kama 한 가마
bath mogyok 목욕; ***have a ~, take a*** ~ mogyok'ada 목욕하다

bathe *v/i* (*have a bath*) mogyok'ada 목욕하다

bath mat mogyokt'ang kkalgae 목욕탕 깔개; **bathrobe** mogyok kaun 목욕 가운; **bathroom** (*for bath*) yoksshil 욕실; (*for washing hands*) semyŏnjang 세면장; (*toilet*) hwajangshil 화장실; **bath towel** mogyok sugŏn 목욕 수건; **bathtub** yoktcho 욕조

batter[1] *n* (*in cooking*) milkkaru panjuk 밀가루 반죽

batter[2] (*in baseball*) t'aja 타자

battery chŏnji 전지; MOT paet'ŏri 배터리

battle *n* chŏnt'u 전투; *fig* t'ujaeng 투쟁

♦**battle against** *illness etc* …wa / kwa ssauda …와 / 과 싸우다

battlefield, **battleground** chŏnjaengt'ŏ 전쟁터

bawdy oesŏlssŭrŏun 외설스러운

bawl (*shout*) kohamch'ida 고함치다; (*weep*) ulda 울다

♦**bawl out** *v/t* F hot'ong-ŭl ch'ida 호통을 치다

bay (*inlet*) man 만

bay window naeminch'ang 내민창

BBS (= ***Buddhist Broadcasting System***) Pulgyo Pangsong 불교 방송

be ◊ ida 이다; (*exist*) it-tta 있다; ***I am a student*** nanŭn hakssaeng-iyeyo 나는 학생이예요; ***was she there?*** kŏgi kŭ yŏjaga itssŏssŏyo? 거기 그 여자가 있었어요?; ***it's me*** chŏyeyo 저예요; ***how much is / are ...?*** …ŭn / nŭn ŏlmaimnikka? …은 / 는 얼마입니까?; ***there is***, ***there are*** ...i / ga it-tta …이 / 가 있다; ***there are some books in my bag*** nae kabang soge ch'aegi it-tta 내 가방 속에 책이 있다 ◊ (*with adjectives*) ...ta ...다; ***she is pretty*** kŭnyŏnŭn yeppŭda 그녀는 예쁘다; ***I am tired*** nanŭn p'igonhada 나는 피곤하다; ***~ careful*** choshimhaseyo 조심하세요; ***don't ~ sad*** sŭlp'ŏhajima 슬퍼하지마 ◊: ***has the mailman been?*** uch'ebuga tŭllŏt-tta kassŏyo? 우체부가 들렀다 갔어요?; ***I've never been to Korea*** nanŭn Han-guge kabon chŏgi ŏptta 나는 한국에 가본 적이 없다; ***I've been here for hours*** nanŭn yŏgi myŏt shiganina kyesok issŏt-tta 나는 여기 몇 시간이나 계속 있었다 ◊ (*tag questions*) ...jiyo? ...지요?; ***that's right, isn't it?*** mat-tchiyo? 맞지요?; ***she's Korean, isn't she?*** kŭ yŏjanŭn Han-guk saram ijiyo? 그 여자는 한국 사람 이지요? ◊ (*auxiliary*) … hago it-tta … 하고 있다; ***I am thinking*** nanŭn saenggak'ago issŏyo 나는 생각하고 있어요; ***he was running*** kŭnŭn ttwigo issŏt-tta 그는 뛰고 있었다; ***you're ~ing silly*** nŏnŭn pabosŭrŏun chisŭl hago issŏ 너는 바보스러운 짓을 하고 있어 ◊ (*obligation*) … haeya handa … 해야 한다; ***you are to do what I tell you*** nŏnŭn naega marhanŭn taero haeya handa 너는 내가 말하는 대로 해야 한다; ***I was to tell you this*** nanŭn nŏege igŏsŭl marhaessŏya haessŏ 나는 너에게 이것을 말했어야 했어; ***you are not to tell anyone*** amuegedo marhaesŏn andwae 아무에게도 말해선 안돼 ◊ (*passive*): ***he was killed*** kŭnŭn p'isaldanghaet-tta 그는 피살당했다; ***they have been sold*** kŭgŏt-ttŭrŭn p'allyŏt-tta 그것들은 팔렸다; ***it was discovered*** kugŏsŭn palgyŏndoeŏt-tta 그것은 발견되었다

♦**be in for** …ŭl / rŭl yesanghago it-tta …을 / 를 예상하고 있다

beach haebyŏn 해변

beachwear pich'iweŏ 비치웨어

beads kusŭl 구슬

beak puri 부리

beaker taejŏp 대접

be-all: ***the ~ and end-all*** kajang chungnyohan kŏt 가장 중요한 것

beam 1 *n* (*in ceiling etc*) tŭlppo 들보 **2** *v/i* (*smile*) hwaltchak ut-tta 활짝 웃다 **3** *v/t* (*transmit*) songshinhada 송신하다

beans k'ong 콩; ***be full of ~*** kiuni nŏmch'yŏ nanŭn 기운이 넘쳐 나는

bear[1] (*animal*) kom 곰

bear[2] **1** *v/t weight* chit'aenghada 지탱하다; *costs* pudamhada 부담하다;

(*tolerate*) kyŏndida 견디다; *child* ch'ulssanhada 출산하다 **2** *v/i*: ***bring pressure to ~ on*** ...e amnyŏgŭl kahada ...에 압력을 가하다
♦**bear out** (*confirm*) chijihada 지지하다
bearable kyŏndil su innŭn 견딜 수 있는
beard t'ŏkssuyŏm 턱수염
bearing (*in machine*) peŏring 베어링; ***that has no ~ on the case*** kŭ ilgwanŭn amurŏn kwallyŏni ŏptta 그 일과는 아무런 관련이 없다
bear market FIN hahyang shiseŭi shijang 하향 시세의 시장
beast (*animal*) chimsŭng 짐승
beat 1 *n* (*of heart*) kodong 고동; (*of music*) paktcha 박자 **2** *v/i* (*of heart*) kodongch'ida 고동치다; (*of rain*) t'ungt'ung tudŭrida 퉁퉁 두드리다; ~ ***around the bush*** tullŏdaeda 둘러대다 **3** *v/t* (*in competition*) igida 이기다; (*hit*) ttaerida 때리다; (*pound*) tudŭrida 두드리다; ~ ***it!*** F kkŏjyŏ pŏryŏ! 꺼져 버려!; ***it ~s me*** F nanŭn todaech'e ihae hal su ŏptta 나는 도대체 이해할 수 없다
♦**beat up** kut'ahada 구타하다
beaten: ***off the ~ track*** sandorŭl pŏsŏnan 상도를 벗어난
beating (*physical*) kut'a 구타
beat-up F nalgŭn 낡은
beautician miyongsa 미용사
beautiful arŭmdaun 아름다운; *day* mŏtchin 멋진; *weather* hwach'anghan 화창한; ***thanks, that's just ~!*** komawŏyo, nŏmu mashissŭmnida 고마워요, 너무 맛있습니다
beautifully *cooked*, *done* hullunghage 훌륭하게; *simple* koengjanghi 굉장히
beauty arŭmdaum 아름다움
beauty parlor miyongshil 미용실
♦**beaver away** pujirŏnhi irhada 부지런히 일하다
because ... ttaemune ... 때문에; ~ ***it was too expensive*** kŭgŏshi nŏmu pissatkki ttaemunida 그것이 너무 비쌌기 때문이다; ~ ***of*** ... ttaemune ... 때문에; ~ ***of the weather*** nalsshi ttaemune 날씨 때문에
beckon *v/i* sontchit'ayŏ purŭda 손짓하여 부르다
become ◊ (+ *adj*) ... haejida ... 해지다; ***the weather became colder*** nalsshiga ch'uwŏjyŏt-tta 날씨가 추워졌다 ◊ (+ *noun*) ...i/ga toeda ...이/가 되다; ***he became a priest*** kŭnŭn shibuga toeŏt-tta 그는 신부가 되었다; ***what's ~ of her?*** kŭ yŏjanŭn ŏttŏk'e toeottchiyo? 그 여자는 어떻게 되었지요?
bed ch'imdae 침대; (*of flowers*) hwadan 화단; (*of sea, river*) mitppadak 밑바닥; ***go to ~*** chamjarie tŭlda 잠자리에 들다; ***he's still in ~*** kŭnŭn ajiktto chago it-tta 그는 아직도 자고 있다; ***go to ~ with*** ...wa/kwa kach'i chada ...와/과 같이 자다
bedclothes ch'imgu 침구
bedding ch'imgu 침구
bedridden pyŏngsang-e innŭn 병상에 있는; **bedroom** ch'imshil 침실; **bedspread** ch'imdaebo 침대보; **bedtime** ch'wich'im shigan 취침 시간
bee pŏl 벌
beech nŏdobamnamu 너도밤나무
beef 1 *n* soegogi 쇠고기; F (*complaint*) pulp'yŏng 불평 **2** *v/i* F (*complain*) pulp'yŏnghada 불평하다
♦**beef up** poganghada 보강하다
beefburger pip'ŭbŏgŏ 비프버거
beehive pŏltchip 벌집
beeline: ***make a ~ for*** ...(ŭ)ro kottchang tallyŏgada ...(으)로 곧장 달려가다
beep 1 *n* shinhoŭm 신호음 **2** *v/i* shimhoŭmi ullida 신호음이 울리다 **3** *v/t* (*call on pager*) hoch'urhada 호출하다
beeper hoch'ulgi 호출기
beer maektchu 맥주
beetle ttaktchŏngbŏlle 딱정벌레
before 1 *prep* (*in time, order*) ... chŏne ... 전에; ~ ***8 o'clock*** 8shi chŏne 8시 전에 **2** *adv* ijŏne 이전에; ***you should have let me know ~*** ijŏne na-ege allyŏjuŏssŏya haessŏ 이전에 내게 알려주었어 야 했어; ***the week/day ~*** kŭ chŏnjue/chŏnnare

그 전주에 / 전날에 **3** *conj* ...hagi chŏne ...하기 전에; ~ ***he leaves*** kŭga ttŏnagi chŏne 그가 떠나기 전에
beforehand miri 미리
beg 1 *v/i* kugŏrhada 구걸하다 **2** *v/t*: ~ ***s.o. to ...*** nuguege ...hae tallago kanch'ŏnghada 누구에게 ... 해 달라고 간청하다
beggar kŏji 거지
begin 1 *v/i* shijakttoeda 시작되다; ***to ~ with*** (*at first*) ch'ŏumenŭn 처음에는; (*in the first place*) ch'ŏt-tchaero 첫째로 **2** *v/t* shijak'ada 시작하다
beginner ch'oboja 초보자
beginner driver unjŏnŭl paeunŭn saram 운전을 배우는 사람
beginning shijak 시작; (*origin*) shich'o 시초
behalf: ***on*** *or* ***in ~ of*** ...ŭl / rŭl wihayŏ ...을 / 를 위하여; ***on my*** / ***his ~*** narŭl / kŭrŭl taeshinhaesŏ 나를 / 그를 대신해서
behave *v/i* haengdonghada 행동하다; ~ (***oneself***) yeŭi parŭge haengdonghada 예의 바르게 행동하다; ~ (***yourself***)***!*** yeŭi parŭge haengdonghaera 예의바르게 행동해라
behavior haengdong 행동
behind 1 *prep* (*in position*) ... twittchoge(sŏ) ... 뒷쪽에(서); (*in progress, order*) ...e twijyŏsŏ ...에 뒤져서; ***be ~ ...*** (*responsible for*) ...e ch'aegimi it-tta ...에 책임이 있다; (*support*) chijihada 지지하다 **2** *adv* (*at the back*) twie(sŏ) 뒤에(서); ***be ~ with*** ...i / ga millyŏ it-tta ...이 / 가 밀려있다
Beijing Puk-kkyŏng 북경
being (*existence*) chonjae 존재; (*creature*) saengmul 생물
belated yŏn-gidoen 연기된
belch 1 *n* t'ŭrim 트림 **2** *v/i* t'ŭrimhada 트림하다
Belgian 1 *adj* Pelgieŭi 벨기에의 **2** *n* Pelgiein 벨기에인
Belgium Pelgie 벨기에
belief midŭm 믿음; (*religious*) shinang 신앙
believe mit-tta 믿다
♦**believe in** ...ŭl / rŭl mit-tta ...을 / 를 믿다; *ghosts* ...ŭi chonjaerŭl mit-tta ...의 존재를 믿다; *a person* shilloehada 신뢰하다
believer shinja 신자; *fig* shinbongja 신봉자
bell chong 종
bellhop pelboi 벨보이
belligerent *adj* hojŏnjŏgin 호전적인
bellow 1 *n* koham 고함; (*of bull*) soga unŭn sori 소가 우는 소리 **2** *v/i* kohamch'ida 고함치다; (*of bull*) ulda 울다
belly (*of person*) pae 배; (*fat stomach*) ttongppae 똥배; (*of animal*) wi 위
bellyache *v/i* F pulp'yŏng-ŭl nŭrŏnot-tta 불평을 늘어놓다
belong *v/i*: ***where does this ~?*** ŏdie noŭlkkayo? 어디에 놓을까요?; ***I don't ~ here*** nanŭn yŏgie mat-tchi anayo 나는 여기에 맞지 않아요
♦**belong to** ...ŭi kŏshida ...의 것이다; *club, organization* ...ŭi irwŏnida ..의 일원이다
belongings sojip'um 소지품
beloved *adj* saranghanŭn 사랑하는
below 1 *prep* ... araee(sŏ) ... 아래에(서); (*in amount, rate, level*) ... iharo ... 이하로 **2** *adv* araet-tchoge(sŏ) 아랫쪽에(서); (*in text*) araee(sŏ) 아래에(서); ***see*** ~ araet-tchogŭl poseyo 아랫쪽을 보세요; ***10 degrees*** ~ yŏngha shiptto 영하 십도
belt hŏritti 허리띠; ***tighten one's ~*** *fig* hŏrittirŭl chollamaeda 허리띠를 졸라매다
bench (*seat*) pench'i 벤치; (*work~*) chagŏpttae 작업대
benchmark kijun 기준
bend 1 *n* man-gok 만곡 **2** *v/t* kuburida 구부리다 **3** *v/i* hwida 휘다; (*of person*) kuburida 구부리다
♦**bend down** kuburida 구부리다
bender F sul mashigo hŭngch'ŏnggŏrim 흥청거림; ***go on a ~*** chint'ang surŭl mashida 진탕 술을 마시다
beneath 1 *prep* ...ŭi araee(sŏ) ...의 아래에(서); (*in status, value*) ... poda natkke ... 보다 낮게 **2** *adv* araee(sŏ) 아래에(서)

benefactor ŭnhyerŭl pep'unŭn saram 은혜를 베푸는 사람
beneficial yuik'an 유익한
benefit 1 *n* iik 이익 **2** *v/t* ...ŭi iigi toeda ...의 이익이 되다 **3** *v/i* iigŭl ŏt-tta 이익을 얻다
benevolent injŏng manŭn 인정 많은
benign onhwahan 온화한; MED yangsŏng-ŭi 양성의
bequeath yusanŭro namgida 유산으로 남기다; *fig* chŏnhada 전하다
bereaved 1 *adj* sabyŏrhan 사별한; ***the ~ family*** yujok 유족 **2** *n*: ***the ~*** sabyŏrhan saramdŭl 사별한 사람들
berry ttalgiryuŭi yŏlmae 딸기류의 열매
berserk: ***go ~*** kwangp'ok'aejida 광폭해지다
berth (*for sleeping*) ch'imdaek'an 침대칸; (*for ship*) chŏngbaktchang 정박장; ***give a wide ~ to*** ...ŭl/rŭl p'ihada ...을/를 피하다
beside ...ŭi kyŏt'e(sŏ) ...의 곁에(서); ***be ~ oneself*** chejŏngshinŭl ilt'a 제정신을 잃다; ***that's ~ the point*** kŭgŏn ttan yaegiyeyo 그건 딴 얘기예요
besides 1 *adv* kedaga 게다가 **2** *prep* (*apart from*) ... ioe-e ... 이외에
best 1 *adj* kajang choŭn 가장 좋은, ch'oegoŭi 최고의 **2** *adv* kajang chal 가장 잘, cheil 제일; ***it would be ~ if*** ... hanŭn kŏshi kajang choŭl tŭt'ada ... 하는 것이 가장 좋을 듯하다; ***I like her ~*** nanŭn kŭnyŏrŭl cheil choahanda 나는 그녀를 제일 좋아한다 **3** *n*: ***do one's ~*** ch'oesŏnŭl tahada 최선을 다하다; ***the ~*** (*thing*) ch'oego 최고; (*person*) ch'oegoro chal hanŭn saram 최고로 잘 하는 사람; ***make the ~ of*** ...ŭl/rŭl ch'oedaehanŭro iyonghada ...을/를 최대한으로 이용하다; ***all the ~!*** haeng-uni itkkirŭl! 행운이 있기를!
best before date ch'oego p'umjil pojŭng kigan 최고 품질 보증 기간;
best man (*at wedding*) shillang tŭllŏri 신랑 들러리; **best-seller** pesŭt'ŭsellŏ 베스트셀러
bet 1 *n* naegi 내기 **2** *v/i* naegirŭl kŏlda 내기를 걸다; ***you ~!*** mullonijyo! 물론이죠! **3** *v/t* (*reckon*) t'ŭllimŏpsshi ...hal kŏshirago saenggak'ada 틀림없이 ...할 것이라고 생각하다
betray paebanhada 배반하다
betrayal paeban 배반
better 1 *adj* poda naŭn 보다 나은; ***get ~*** (*skills*) hyangsangdoeda 향상되다; (*in health*) pyŏng-i nat-tta 병이 낫다; ***he's ~*** (*in health*) kŭŭi kŏn-gang-i choajyŏt-tta 그의 건강이 좋아졌다 **2** *adv* tŏ chal 더 잘, tŏ natkke 더 낫게; ***she sings ~ than I do*** kŭnyŏnŭn naboda noraerŭl tŏ chal handa 그녀는 나보다 노래를 더 잘 한다; ***you look ~ today*** onŭl tŏ naa poinda 오늘 더 나아 보인다; ***you'd ~ ask permission*** tangshin-ŭn hŏragŭl pannŭn kŏshi natkkessŏyo 당신은 허락을 받는 것이 낫겠어요; ***I'd really ~ not*** nanŭn haji annŭn p'yŏni natkkessŏyo 나는 하지 않는 편이 낫겠어요; ***all the ~ for us*** urihant'enŭn tŏ chaldoen irimnida 우리한테는 더 잘된 일입니다; ***I like her ~*** nanŭn kŭnyrŭl tŏ choahamnida 나는 그녀를 더 좋아합니다
better-off yubok'an 유복한
between *prep* saie 사이에; ***~ you and me*** urikkiriŭi yaegiijiman 우리끼리의 얘기이지만
beverage *fml* ŭmnyo 음료
beware: ***~ of*** ...ŭl/rŭl choshimhada ...을/를 조심하다
bewilder tanghwanghage hada 당황하게 하다
beyond 1 *prep* (*in time*) ...ŭl/rŭl chinasŏ ...을/를 지나서; (*in space*) ...ŭl/rŭl nŏmŏsŏ ...을/를 넘어서; (*in degree*) ...ŭi pŏmwirŭl nŏmŏsŏ ...의 범위를 넘어서; ***it's ~ me*** (*don't understand*) narosŏn al su ŏmnŭn irida 나로선 알 수 없는 일이다; (*can't do it*) nae nŭngnyŏk pakkŭi irida 내 능력 밖의 일이다 **2** *adv* chŏp'yŏnŭro 저편으로
Bhutan Put'an 부탄
Bhutanese 1 *adj* Put'anŭi 부탄의 **2** *n* (*person*) Put'anin 부탄인
bias *n* p'yŏn-gyŏn 편견

bias(s)ed p'yŏn-gyŏnŭl kajin 편견을 가진
bib (*for baby*) t'ŏkppaji 턱받이
Bible Sŏnggyŏng 성경
bibliography munhŏn mongnok 문헌 목록
biceps p'arŭi alt'ong 팔의 알통
bicker *v/i* maldat'umhada 말다툼하다
bicycle *n* chajŏn-gŏ 자전거
bid 1 *n* (*at auction*) ipch'al 입찰; (*attempt*) shido 시도 **2** *v/i* (*at auction*) ipch'arhada 입찰하다
biennial *adj* kyŏng-nyŏnŭi 격년의
big 1 *adj* k'ŭn 큰; ***my ~ brother / sister*** (*man's*) naŭi k'ŭn hyŏng / nuna 나의 큰 형 / 누나; (*woman's*) naŭi k'ŭn oppa / ŏnni 나의 큰 오빠 / 언니; ***~ name*** yumyŏnghan irŭm 유명한 이름 **2** *adv*: ***talk ~*** hŏp'ung ttŏlda 허풍 떨다
bigamy chunghon 중혼
big-headed utchuldaenŭn 우쭐대는
bike 1 *n* chajŏn-gŏ 자전거 **2** *v/i* chajŏn-gŏrŭl t'ada 자전거를 타다
bikini pik'ini 비키니
bilingual tu nara marŭl hanŭn 두 나라 말을 하는
bill 1 *n* (*money*) chip'ye 지폐; (*for gas, electricity*) ch'ŏngguso 청구서; (*in hotel, restaurant etc*) kyesansŏ 계산서; POL pŏban 법안; (*poster*) kwanggo p'osŭt'ŏ 광고 포스터 **2** *v/t* (*invoice*) kyesansŏro ch'ŏngguhada 계산서로 청구하다
billboard kwanggop'an 광고판
billfold chigap 지갑
billiards tanggu 당구
billion ship ŏk 십억
bill of exchange hwanŏŭm 환어음
bill of sale yŏngsujŭng 영수증
bin (*for storage*) chŏjangt'ong 저장통
binary ijinppŏbŭi 이진법의
bind *v/t* (*connect*) yŏn-gyŏrhada 연결하다; (*tie*) muktta 묶다; (LAW: *oblige*) …ŭi ŭimurŭl chiuda …의 의무를 지우다
binder (*for papers*) paindŏ 바인더
binding 1 *adj agreement, promise* kusongnyŏgi innŭn 구속력이 있는 **2** *n* (*of book*) changjŏng 장정
binoculars ssang-an-gyŏng 쌍안경
biodegradable misaengmure ŭihae punhaega toenŭn 미생물에 의해 분해가 되는
biography chŏn-gi 전기
biological saengmurhagŭi 생물학의; ***~ parents*** ch'inbumo 친부모; ***~ detergent*** ch'inhwan-gyŏng sech'ŏktche 친환경 세척제
biology saengmurhak 생물학
biotechnology saengch'e konghak 생체 공학
bird sae 새
bird of prey sanaun naljimsŭng 사나운 날짐승
bird sanctuary choryu poho kuyŏk 조류 보호 구역
birth (*of child*) t'ansaeng 탄생; (*labor*) ch'ulssan 출산; (*of country*) kiwŏn 기원; ***give ~ to*** *child* airŭl nat'a 아이를 낳다; ***date of ~*** saengnyŏnwŏril 생년월일; ***place of ~*** ch'ulssaengji 출생지
birth certificate ch'ulssaeng chŭngmyŏngsŏ 출생 증명서; **birth control** sana chehan 산아 제한; **birthday** saeng-il 생일; ***happy ~!*** saeng-il ch'uk'ahamnida! 생일 축하합니다!; **birthplace** ch'ulssaengji 출생지; **birthrate** ch'ulssaengnyul 출생률
biscuit pisŭk'et 비스켓
bisexual 1 *adj* yangsŏng-ŭi 양성의 **2** *n* yangsŏng-aeja 양성애자
bishop chugyo 주교
bit *n* (*piece*) chogak 조각; (*part of a whole*) pubun 부분; COMPUT pit'ŭ 비트; ***a ~*** (*a little*) chogŭm 조금; (*a while*) chamkkan 잠깐; ***a ~ of*** (*a little*) chogŭm 조금; ***a ~ of news / advice*** yakkanŭi soshik / ch'unggo 약간의 소식 / 충고; ***~ by ~*** chogŭmsshik 조금씩; ***I'll be there in a ~*** nanŭn chamshi hue kŏgi toch'ak'al kŏmnida 나는 잠시 후에 거기 도착할 겁니다
bitch 1 *n* (*dog*) amk'ae 암캐; F (*woman*) nappŭn nyŏn 나쁜 년 **2** *v/i* F (*complain*) pulp'yŏnghada 불평하다
bitchy F *person, remark* shimsulgujŭn

심술궂은

bite 1 *n* mum 묾; (*of food*) han ip 한 입; ***get a ~*** (*of angler*) mikkirŭl mulda 미끼를 물다; ***let's have a ~*** (***to eat***) shikssahapsshida 식사합시다 **2** *v/t* mulda 물다 **3** *v/i* mulda 물다; (*of fish*) mikkirŭl mulda 미끼를 물다

bitmap COMPUT pit'ŭmaep 비트맵

bitmap font COMPUT chŏm kŭlkkol 점 글꼴

bitter *taste* ssŭn 쓴; *person* pit'onghan 비통한; *weather* hokttok'an 혹독한; *argument* shillarhan 신랄한

bitterly *cold* sarŭl enŭndŭshi 살을 에는듯이

black 1 *adj* kŏmŭn 검은; *music, history* hŭginŭi 흑인의; *coffee* pŭllaek 블랙; *fig* amdamhan 암담한 **2** *n* (*color*) kŏmjŏngsaek 검정색; (*person*) hŭgin 흑인; ***in the ~*** FIN hŭktcharo 흑자로

♦**black out** *v/i* ŭishigŭl ilt'a 의식을 잃다

blackberry pŭllaekpperi 블랙베리; **blackbird** tchirŭregi 찌르레기; **blackboard** ch'ilp'an 칠판; **black box** pŭllaek pakssŭ 블랙 박스; **black economy** pulppŏp koyong 불법 고용

blacken *person's name* omyŏng-ŭl ssŭiuda 오명을 씌우다

black eye mŏngdŭn nun 멍든 눈; **black ice** pŭllaek aisŭ 블랙 아이스, *toro wiŭi kŏmkke poinŭn pingp'an* 도로 위의 검게 보이는 빙판; **blacklist 1** *n* pŭllaekrisŭt'ŭ 블랙리스트 **2** *v/t* pŭllaekrisŭt'ŭe ollida 블랙리스트 에 올리다; **blackmail 1** *n* konggal 공갈; ***emotional ~*** shimtchŏk konggal 심적 공갈 **2** *v/t* konggal ch'ida 공갈 치다; **blackmailer** konggal ch'inŭn saram 공갈 치는 사람; **black market** amshijang 암시장

blackness amhŭk 암흑

blackout ELEC chŏngjŏn 정전; MED ŭishik sangshil 의식 상실; **blacksmith** taejangjang-i 대장장이; **black tea** hongch'a 홍차

bladder panggwang 방광

blade (*of knife*) k'allal 칼날; (*of helicopter*) nalgae 날개; (*of grass*) ip 잎

blame 1 *n* pinan 비난; (*responsibility*) ch'aegim 책임 **2** *v/t* pinanhada 비난하다; ***~ X for Y*** Xŭi ch'aegimi Yege it-ttago pinanhada Y의 책임이 X에게 있다고 비난하다

bland *smile, answer* kimppajin 김빠진; *food* pyŏlmashi ŏmnŭn 별맛이 없는

blank 1 *adj* (*not written on*) kongbaegŭi 공백의; *look* mŏnghan 멍한; ***~ tape*** kongt'eip'ŭ 공테이프 **2** *n* (*empty space*) kongbaek 공백; ***my mind's a ~*** chŏngshini mŏnghada 정신이 멍하다

blank check paektchi sup'yo 백지 수표

blanket *n* tamnyo 담요; ***a ~ of*** *fig* ...(ŭ)ro ont'ong tŏp'in ...(으)로 온통 덮인; ***a ~ of snow*** onnurirŭl tŏp'ŭn nun 온누리를 덮은 눈

blare *v/i* yoranhage ullida 요란하게 울리다

♦**blare out 1** *v/i* ullyŏp'ŏjida 울려퍼지다 **2** *v/t* yoranhage ullida 요란하게 울리다

blaspheme *v/i* modok'ada 모독하다

blast 1 *n* (*explosion*) p'okppal 폭발; (*gust*) tolp'ung 돌풍 **2** *v/t* p'okp'ashik'ida 폭파시키다; ***~!*** pirŏmŏgŭl 빌어먹을!

♦**blast off** (*of rocket*) palssashik'ida 발사시키다

blast furnace yonggwangno 용광로

blast-off palssa 발사

blatant ppŏnppŏnsŭrŏun 뻔뻔스러운

blaze 1 *n* (*fire*) hwajae 화재; ***a ~ of color*** manbarhan saek ch'ae 만발한 색채 **2** *v/i* (*of fire*) t'aorŭda 타오르다

♦**blaze away** (*with gun*) sswabŏrida 쏴버리다

blazer pŭlleijyŏ chak'et 블레이저 자켓

bleach 1 *n* p'yobaek 표백; (*for hair*) kŭmballo yŏmsaek 금발로 염색 **2** *v/t* p'yobaek'ada 표백하다; *hair* kŭmballo yŏmsaek'ada 금발로 염색하다

bleak *countryside* hwangnyanghan 황량한; *weather* ŭmch'imhan 음침한;

future ŏduun 어두운
bleary-eyed nuni ch'imch'imhan 눈이 침침한
bleat *v/i* (*of sheep*) maeaehago ulda 매애하고 울다
bleed 1 *v/i* ch'urhyŏrhada 출혈하다; ***my nose is ~ing*** nanŭn k'op'iga nanda 나는 코피가 난다 **2** *v/t fig* tonŭl ch'akch'wihada 돈을 착취하다
bleeding *n* ch'urhyŏl 출혈
bleep 1 *n* ppii hanŭn sori 삐이 하는 소리 **2** *v/i* ppii hanŭn soriga nada 삐이 하는 소리가 나다
bleeper hoch'ulgi 호출기
blemish 1 *n* hŭm 흠 **2** *v/t* hŭmnaeda 흠내다; *reputation* tŏrŏp'ida 더럽히다
blend 1 *n* honhap 혼합 **2** *v/t* honhap'ada 혼합하다
♦**blend in 1** *v/i* sŏkkida 섞이다 **2** *v/t* (*in cooking*) sŏktta 섞다
blender mikssŏgi 믹서기
bless ch'ukppok'ada 축복하다; ***~ you!*** (*when s.o. sneezes*) chŏrŏn! 저런!; ***be ~ed with*** …(ŭ)ro ch'ukppok pat-tta …(으)로 축복 받다
blessing REL ŭnch'ong 은총; *fig* (*approval*) sŭngnak 승낙
blind 1 *adj* nun mŏn 눈 먼; *corner* ap'i poiji annŭn 앞이 보이지 않는; ***~ to*** …ŭl/rŭl poji mot'anŭn …을/를 보지 못하는 **2** *n*: ***the ~*** maeng-in 맹인; **3** *v/t* nun mŏlge hada 눈 멀게 하다; *fig* poji mot'age hada 보지 못하게 하다
blind alley makttarŭn kolmok 막다른 골목; **blind date** pŭllaindŭ teit'ŭ 블라인드 데이트, mit'ing 미팅; **blindfold 1** *n* nun karigae 눈 가리개 **2** *v/t* nunŭl karida 눈을 가리다 **3** *adv* nunŭl karigo 눈을 가리고
blinding *light* nun pushige hanŭn 눈 부시게 하는; *headache* nuni mŏl chŏngdoŭi 눈이 멀 정도의
blind spot (*in road*) chadongch'a unjŏnjaŭi sagak 자동차 운전자의 사각; *fig* maengtchŏm 맹점
blink *v/i* (*of person, light*) kkamppakkŏrida 깜박거리다
blip (*on radar screen*) leida yŏngsang 레이더 영상; *fig* ilsshijŏk pyŏndong 일시적 변동
bliss tŏ ŏmnŭn haengbok 더 없는 행복
blister 1 *n* multchip 물집 **2** *v/i* multchibi saenggida 물집이 생기다; (*of paint*) kip'oga saenggida 기포가 생기다
blizzard shimhan nunbora 심한 눈보라
bloated puŭn 부은
blob (*of liquid*) han pang-ul 한 방울
bloc POL kwŏn 권
block 1 *n* tŏng-ŏri 덩어리; (*in town*) kuhoek 구획; (*of shares*) han cho 한 조; (*blockage*) chang-aemul 장애물 **2** *v/t* maktta 막다
♦**block in** (*with vehicle*) pongswaehada 봉쇄하다
♦**block out** *light* ch'adanhada 차단하다
♦**block up** *sink etc* maktta 막다
blockade 1 *n* pongswae 봉쇄 **2** *v/t* pongswaehada 봉쇄하다
blockage mak'yŏ innŭn kŏt 막혀있는 것
blockbuster taehit'ŭjak 대히트작
block letters taemuntcha 대문자
blond *adj* kŭmbarŭi 금발의
blonde *n* (*woman*) kŭmbal mŏri yŏja 금발 머리 여자
blood p'i 피; ***in cold ~*** naenghok'age 냉혹하게
blood bank hyŏraek ŭnhaeng 혈액 은행; **blood donor** hŏnhyŏltcha 헌혈자; **blood group** hyŏraek'yŏng 혈액형
bloodless *coup* muhyŏrŭi 무혈의
blood poisoning p'yehyŏltchŭng 폐혈증; **blood pressure** hyŏrap 혈압; **blood relation**, **blood relative** yukch'in 육친; **blood sample** hyŏraek saemp'ŭl 혈액 샘플; **bloodshed** yuhyŏl 유혈; **bloodshot** ch'unghyŏldoen 충혈된; **bloodstain** p'itchaguk 핏자국; **bloodstream** hyŏllyu 혈류; **blood test** hyŏraek kŏmsa 혈액 검사; **blood transfusion** suhyŏl 수혈; **blood vessel** hyŏlgwan 혈관
bloody *hands etc* p'it'usŏng-iŭi 피투성이의; *battle* yuhyŏrŭi 유혈의
bloody mary pŭllŏdi maeri 블러디

매리
bloom 1 *n* kkot 꽃; ***in full ~*** hwaltchak p'in 활짝 핀 **2** *v/i* kkoch'i p'ida 꽃이 피다; *fig* pŏnyŏnghada 번영하다
blossom 1 *n* kkot 꽃 **2** *v/i* p'ida 피다; *fig* k'waehwarhaejida 쾌활해지다
blot 1 *n* ŏlluk 얼룩; *fig* hŭm 흠 **2** *v/t* (*dry*) mulkkirŭl tudŭryŏ chiuda 물기를 두드려 지우다
♦**blot out** *memory* chiuda 지우다; *view* kamch'uda 감추다; *sun* karida 가리다
blotch panjŏm 반점
blotchy ŏllukt'usŏng-iŭi 얼룩투성이의
blouse pŭllausŭ 블라우스
blow[1] kangt'a 강타; (*shock*) ch'unggyŏk 충격
blow[2] **1** *v/t* (*of wind, whistle*) pulda 불다; *smoke* naeppumtta 내뿜다; F (*spend*) nallida 날리다; F *opportunity* nallyŏ pŏrida 날려 버리다; ***~ one's nose*** k'orŭl p'ulda 코를 풀다 **2** *v/i* (*of wind*) pulda 불다; (*of whistle*) ullida 울리다; (*breathe out*) ipkkimŭl pulda 입김을 불다; (*of fuse*) kkŭnŏjida 끊어지다; (*of tire*) t'ŏjida 터지다
♦**blow off 1** *v/t* purŏ nallida 불어 날리다 **2** *v/i* parame nallida 바람에 날리다
♦**blow out 1** *v/t candle* kkŭda 끄다 **2** *v/i* (*of candle*) kkŏjida 꺼지다
♦**blow over 1** *v/t* purŏ nŏmŏttŭrida 불어 넘어뜨리다 **2** *v/i* karaantta 가라앉다; (*of argument*) musahi chinagada 무사히 지나가다
♦**blow up 1** *v/t* (*with explosives*) p'okp'ahada 폭파하다; *balloon* pulda 불다; *photograph* hwakttaehada 확대하다 **2** *v/i* p'okpparhada 폭발하다; F (*get angry*) hwanaeda 화내다
blow-dry *v/t* tŭraiŏro mŏrirŭl mallida 드라이어로 머리를 말리다; **blow job** V p'ellach'io 펠라치오; **blow-out** (*of tire*) p'ŏngk'ŭ 펑크; F (*big meal*) shilk'ŏt mŏk-kki 실컷 먹기; **blow-up** (*of photo*) hwakttae 확대
blue 1 *adj* p'aran 파란; *movie* p'orŭno 포르노 **2** *n* p'arangsaek 파랑색
blueberry pŭlluberi 블루베리; **blue chip** uryang chushik 우량 주식; **blue-collar worker** yukch'e nodongja 육체 노동자; **Blue House** Ch'ŏng-wadae 청와대; **blueprint** ch'ŏngsajin 청사진; *fig* (*plan*) sangsehan kyehoek 상세한 계획
blues MUS pŭllusŭ 블루스; ***have the ~*** ultchŏk'ada 울적하다
blues singer pŭllusŭ kasu 블루스 가수
bluff 1 *n* (*deception*) ŏmp'o 엄포 **2** *v/i* ŏmp'orŭl not'a 엄포를 놓다
blunder 1 *n* k'ŭn shilssu 큰 실수 **2** *v/i* k'ŭn shilssurŭl hada 큰 실수를 하다
blunt *adj* mudin 무딘; *person* soltchik'an 솔직한
bluntly *speak* soltchik'age 솔직하게
blur 1 *n* hŭrim 흐림 **2** *v/t* hŭrige hada 흐리게 하다
blurb (*on book*) sŏnjŏn munkku 선전 문구
♦**blurt out** pulssuk marhada 불쑥 말하다
blush 1 *n* hongjo 홍조 **2** *v/i* ŏlgurŭl pulk'ida 얼굴을 붉히다
blusher (*cosmetic*) poryŏnji 볼연지
BO (= ***body odor***) amnae 암내
board 1 *n* p'anja 판자; (*for game*) p'an 판; (*for notices*) keship'an 게시판; **~ (*of directors*)** isahoe 이사회; ***on ~*** (*on plane*) pihaenggi ane 비행기 안에; (*on train*) kich'a ane 기차 안에; (*on boat*) pae ane 배 안에; ***take on ~*** *comments etc* koryŏhada 고려하다; (*fully realize truth of*) hwaksshirhi ihaehada 확실히 이해하다; ***across the ~*** chŏnmyŏnjŏgŭro 전면적으로 **2** *v/t airplane etc* t'ada 타다 **3** *v/i* t'ada 타다
♦**board up** p'anjaro maktta 판자로 막다
♦**board with** …e hasuk'ada …에 하숙하다
board and lodging hasuk 하숙
boarder hasugin 하숙인; EDU hasukssaeng 하숙생
board game podŭ keim 보드 게임
boarding card t'apssŭngkkwŏn 탑승권; **boarding house** hasuktchip

하숙집; **boarding pass** t'apssŭngkkwŏn 탑승권; **boarding school** kisuk hak-kkyo 기숙 학교
board meeting isa hoeŭi 이사 회의; **board room** isa hoeŭishil 이사 회의실; **boardwalk** *p'anjarŭl kkan podo* 판자를 깐 보도
boast 1 *n* charang kŏri 자랑 거리 **2** *v/i* charanghada 자랑하다
boat pae 배; (*small, for leisure*) pot'ŭ 보트; ***go by ~*** paero kada 배로 가다
bob[1] (*haircut*) tanbal 단발
bob[2] *v/i* (*of boat etc*) wi araero kabyŏpkke umjigida 위 아래로 가볍게 움직이다
♦**bob up** pulssuk nat'anada 불쑥 나타나다
bobsleigh, **bobsled** popsŭllei 봅슬레이
bodhisattva posal 보살
bodily 1 *adj* momŭi 몸의 **2** *adv eject* momŭro 몸으로
body mom 몸; (*dead*) shich'e 시체; ***~ of water*** suyŏk 수역; ~ (***suit***) (*undergarment*) podisut'ŭ 보디수트
bodyguard kyŏnghowŏn 경호원; **body language** momtchit ŏnŏ 몸짓 언어; **body odor** amnae 암내; **body shop** MOT ch'ach'e kongjang 차체 공장; **bodywork** MOT ch'ach'e 차체
boggle: ***it ~s the mind!*** sangsangdo hal su ŏmnŭn irida! 상상도 할 수 없는 일이다!
bogus katchaŭi 가짜의
boil[1] *n* (*swelling*) chonggi 종기
boil[2] **1** *v/t liquid* kkŭrida 끓이다; *egg, vegetables* samtta 삶다 **2** *v/i* kkŭlt'a 끓다
♦**boil down to** kyŏlguk …(ŭ)ro toeda 결국 …(으) 로 되다
♦**boil over** (*of milk etc*) kkŭrŏ nŏmch'ida 끓어 넘치다
boiler poillŏ 보일러
boisterous ttŏdŭlssŏk'an 떠들썩한
bold 1 *adj* taedamhan 대담한 **2** *n* (*print*) kulgŭn kŭlsshich'e 굵은 글씨체; ***in ~*** kulgŭn kŭlsshich'ero 굵은 글씨체로
bolster *v/t confidence* pukttoduda 북돋우다
bolt 1 *n* polt'ŭ 볼트; (*on door*) chamulssoe 자물쇠; (*of lightning*) pŏn-gae 번개; ***like a ~ from the blue*** ch'ŏngch'ŏnbyŏngnyŏk-kkwa kach'i 청천벽력과 같이 **2** *adv*: ***~ upright*** ttokpparo 똑바로 **3** *v/t* (*fix with bolts*) polt'ŭro choeda 볼트로 죄다; (*close*) chamulssoero chamgŭda 자물쇠로 잠그다 **4** *v/i* (*run off*) tomangch'ida 도망치다
bomb 1 *n* p'okt'an 폭탄 **2** *v/t* p'okp'ahada 폭파하다
bombard: ***~ with questions*** chilmun kongserŭl p'ŏbut-tta 질문 공세를 퍼붓다
bomb attack p'ok-kkyŏk 폭격
bomber (*airplane*) p'ok-kkyŏk-kki 폭격기; (*terrorist*) p'okp'abŏm 폭파범
bomber jacket kunnyong chamba 군용 잠바
bomb scare p'okt'anŭi uryŏ 폭탄의 우려
bond 1 *n* (*tie*) kkŭn 끈; (*of matrimony*) yŏnbun 연분; FIN ch'aekkwŏn 채권 **2** *v/i* (*of glue*) chŏpch'ak'ada 접착하다
bone 1 *n* ppyŏ 뼈 **2** *v/t meat, fish* ppyŏrŭl pallanaeda 뼈를 발라내다
bonfire modakppul 모닥불
bonsai punjae 분재
bonus (*money*) ponŏsŭ 보너스; (*something extra*) tŏm 덤
boo 1 *n* yayuhanŭn sori 야유하는 소리 **2** *v/t & v/i* yayuhada 야유하다
book 1 *n* ch'aek 책; ***~ of matches*** sŏngnyangkkap 성냥갑 **2** *v/t* (*reserve*) yeyak'ada 예약하다; (*for crime*) pŏlgŭm changbue ollida 벌금 장부에 올리다 **3** *v/i* (*reserve*) yeyak'ada 예약하다
bookcase ch'aektchang 책장
booked up *hotel, flight* yeyagi kkwak ch'ada 예약이 꽉 차다; *person* iltchŏng-i kkwak ch'ada 일정이 꽉 차다
bookie F makkwŏnŏptcha 마권업자
booking (*reservation*) yeyak 예약
booking clerk maep'yogyewŏn 매표계원
bookkeeper hoegyejangburŭl chŏngnihanŭn saram 회계장부를

정리하는 사람
bookkeeping pugi 부기
booklet soch'aektcha 소책자
bookmaker magwŏnŏptcha 마권업자
books (*accounts*) hoegyejangbu 회계장부; ***do the ~*** hoegyejangburŭl chŏngnihada 회계장부를 정리하다
bookseller ch'aek changsa 책 장사; **bookstall** maejŏm 매점; **bookstore** sŏjŏm 서점
boom[1] **1** *n* (*economic*) kyŏnggi p'okttŭng 경기 폭등, pum 붐 **2** *v/i* (*of business*) kyŏnggiga p'okttŭnghada 경기가 폭등하다
boom[2] *n* (*noise*) koeng-ŭm 굉음
boonies: ***out in the ~*** F ojie(sŏ) 오지에(서)
boost 1 *n* (*to sales*) ch'oktchin 촉진; (*to confidence*) kyŏngnyŏ 격려; (*to economy*) puyang 부양 **2** *v/t production*, *sales* ch'oktchinshik'ida 촉진시키다; *prices* kkŭrŏ ollida 끌어올리다; *confidence*, *morale* toduda 돋우다
boot *n* changhwa 장화; ***climbing ~s*** tŭngsanhwa 등산화
♦**boot out** F naetchot-tta 내쫓다
♦**boot up 1** *v/t* COMPUT put'inghada 부팅하다 **2** *v/i* COMPUT put'ingdoeda 부팅되다
booth (*at market*, *fair*) chŏmp'o 점포; (*in restaurant*) k'anmagihan chwasŏk 칸막이한 좌석; (*at exhibition*) kwallamsŏk 관람석
booze *n* F sul 술
booze-up *Br* F sul chanch'i 술 잔치
border 1 *n* (*between countries*) kukkkyŏng 국경; (*edge*) kajangjari 가장자리 **2** *v/t country*, *river* …e chŏp'ae it-tta …에 접해 있다
♦**border on** *country* …e iut'ada …에 이웃하다; (*be almost*) kŏŭi …ida 거의 …이다
borderline: ***a ~ case*** idojŏdo anin kyŏng-u 이도저도 아닌 경우
bore[1] *v/t hole* ttult'a 뚫다
bore[2] **1** *n* (*person*) ttabunhan saram 따분한 사람 **2** *v/t* siltchŭngnage hada 싫증나게 하다; ***be ~d*** chiruhaejida 지루해지다
boredom kwŏnt'ae 권태
boring ttabunhan 따분한
born: ***be ~*** t'aeŏnada 태어나다; ***where were you ~?*** kohyang-i ŏdiimnikka? 고향이 어디입니까?; ***be a ~ …*** t'agonan … ida 타고난 … 이다
borrow pilda 빌다
bosom (*of woman*) chŏtkkasŭm 젖가슴
boss (*one's own*) sangsa 상사; (*of company*) sajang 사장
♦**boss around** puryŏmŏktta 부려먹다
bossy tumok haengsehanŭn 두목 행세하는
botanical shingmulŭi 식물의
botany shingmurhak 식물학
botch *v/t* sŏt'urŭge haesŏ mangch'yŏbŏrida 서투르게 해서 망쳐버리다
both 1 *adj* yangtchogŭi 양쪽의 **2** *pron* tul ta 둘 다; ***I know ~ of the brothers*** nanŭn kŭ hyŏngjerŭl tul ta algo issŏyo 나는 그 형제를 둘 다 알고 있어요; ***~ of the brothers were there*** tu hyŏngjega ta kŏgie issŏssŏyo 두 형제가 다 거기에 있었어요; ***~ of them*** (*things*) kŭgŏt tul ta 그것 둘 다; (*people*) kŭdŭl tul ta 그들 둘 다 **3** *adv*: ***~ … and …*** (*with nouns*) …wa / kwa …, tul ta … 와 / 과 …, 둘 다; (*with adjs*) … go …ta … 고 … 다; ***~ my sister and I*** ŏnni wa na, tul ta 언니와 나, 둘 다; ***it's ~ easy and interesting*** kŭgŏsŭn shwipkko chaemiit-tta 그것은 쉽고 재미있다; ***is it business or pleasure? – ~*** illo hanŭn kŏmnikka, animyŏn chaemiro hanŭn kŏmnikka? - tul tayeyo 일로 하는 겁니까, 아니면 재미로 하는 겁니까? - 둘 다예요
bother 1 *n* kolch'itkkŏri 골칫거리; ***it's no ~*** pyŏl il animnida 별 일 아닙니다 **2** *v/t* (*disturb*) kwich'ank'e hada 귀찮게 하다; *person working* sŏnggashige hada 성가시게 하다; (*worry*) kŏktchŏngdoege hada 걱정되게 하다 **3** *v/i* shin-gyŏng-i ssŭida 신경이 쓰이다; ***don't ~!*** shin-gyŏng ssŭji maseyo! 신경 쓰지

마세요!; ***you needn't have ~ed*** shin-gyŏng ssŭl p'iryo ŏpssŏssŏyo 신경 쓸 필요 없었어요
bottle 1 *n* pyŏng 병; (*for baby*) uyubyŏng 우유병 **2** *v/t* pyŏng-e tamtta 병에 담다
♦**bottle up** *feelings* ŏngnurŭda 억누르다
bottle bank chaehwaryongppyŏng sujipsso 재활용병 수집소
bottled water p'anŭn mul 파는 물
bottleneck *n* (*in road*) pyŏngmok 병목; (*in production*) aero sahang 애로 사항
bottle-opener pyŏngttagae 병따개
bottom 1 *adj* maen mitppadagŭi 맨 밑바닥의 **2** *n* (*on the inside*) antchok ppadak 안쪽 바닥; (*underside*) mitppadak 밑바닥; (*of hill*) ŭi kajang araetppubun 가장 아랫부분; (*of pile*) maen araetchok 맨 아래쪽; (*of street*) kkŭt 끝; (*of garden*) maen katchok 맨 가쪽; (*buttocks*) ŏngdŏng-i 엉덩이; ***at the ~ of the screen*** hwamyŏnŭi hadane 화면의 하단에
♦**bottom out** padagŭl pŏsŏnada 바닥을 벗어나다
bottom line *fig* (*financial outcome*) ch'ongkyŏlssan 총결산; (*the real issue*) kajang chungnyohan sahang 가장 중요한 사항
boulder k'ŭn chagal 큰 자갈
bounce 1 *v/t ball* t'wige hada 튀게 하다 **2** *v/i* (*of ball, rain etc*) t'wida 튀다; (*on sofa etc*) ttwiŏdanida 뛰어다니다; (*of check*) pudoga toeŏ toedoraoda 부도가 되어 되돌아오다
bouncer kyŏngbiwŏn 경비원
bound[1]: ***be ~ to …*** (*sure to*) t'ŭllimŏpsshi …hal kŏshida 틀림없이 …할 것이다; (*obliged to*) … haeya handa … 해야 한다
bound[2]: ***be ~ for*** (*of ship*) … haeng … 행; ***a plane ~ for Seoul*** Sŏurhaeng pihaenggi 서울행 비행기
bound[3] **1** *n* (*jump*) ttwiŏorŭgi 뛰어오르기 **2** *v/i* ttwiŏdanida 뛰어다니다
boundary kyŏnggye 경계
boundless muhanŭi 무한의
bouquet (*flowers*) kkot-ttabal 꽃다발; (*of wine*) hyanggi 향기
bourbon pŏbon wisŭk'i 버본 위스키
bout MED palppyŏng 발병; (*in boxing*) shihap 시합
boutique put'ik'ŭ 부티크
bow[1] **1** *n* (*as greeting*) chŏl 절 **2** *v/i* insahada 인사하다 **3** *v/t head* sugida 숙이다
bow[2] (*knot*) maedŭp 매듭; MUS, (*weapon*) hwal 활
bow[3] (*of ship*) paenmŏri 뱃머리
bowels ch'angja 창자
bowl[1] (*container*) kŭrŭt 그릇; (*for rice*) konggi 공기; (*for soup*) taejŏp 대접; (*for cooking, salad*) k'ŭn kŭrŭt 큰 그릇
bowl[2] *v/i* (*in bowling*) pollinghada 볼링하다
♦**bowl over** *fig* …ŭl / rŭl kkamtchak nollage hada …을 / 를 깜짝 놀라게 하다
bowling polling 볼링
bowling alley pollingjang 볼링장
bow tie nabi nekt'ai 나비 넥타이
box[1] *n* (*container*) sangja 상자; (*on form*) pin k'an 빈 칸
box[2] *v/i* kwŏnt'uhada 권투하다
boxer kwŏnt'u sŏnsu 권투 선수
boxing kwŏnt'u 권투
boxing match kwŏnt'u shihap 권투 시합
box office maep'yoso 매표소
boy sonyŏn 소년; (*son*) adŭl 아들
boycott 1 *n* poik'ot 보이콧 **2** *v/t* poik'ot'ada 보이콧하다
boyfriend namja ch'in-gu 남자 친구; (*lover*) aein 애인
boyish sonyŏn-kat'ŭn 소년같은
boyscout poisŭk'aut 보이스카웃
bra pŭrejiŏ 브레지어
brace (*on teeth*) ch'iyŏl kyojŏnggi 치열 교정기
bracelet p'altchi 팔찌
bracket (*for shelf*) kkach'ibal 까치발; (*in text*) kwarho 괄호
brag *v/i* charanghada 자랑하다
braid *n* (*in hair*) ttaŭn mŏri 땋은 머리; (*trimming*) tan ch'ŏri 단처리
braille chŏmtcha 점자
brain tunoe 두뇌

brainless F mŏriga nappŭn 머리가 나쁜
brains (*intelligence*) chinŭng 지능
brainstorm → ***brainwave***; **brainstorming** pŭreinsŭt'oming 브레인스토밍; **brain surgeon** noe chŏnmun oekkwa ŭisa 뇌 전문 외과 의사; **brainwash** senoehada 세뇌하다; **brainwashing** senoe 세뇌; **brainwave** (*brilliant idea*) myoan 묘안
brainy F ch'ongmyŏnghan 총명한
brake 1 *n* pŭreik'ŭ 브레이크; *fig* kyŏnje 견제 **2** *v/i* pŭreik'ŭrŭl kŏlda 브레이크를 걸다
brake light pŭreik'ŭ lait'ŭ 브레이크 라이트
brake pedal pŭreik'ŭ p'edal 브레이크 페달
branch *n* (*of tree*) kaji 가지; (*of bank, company*) chijŏm 지점
♦**branch off** (*of road*) kallajida 갈라지다
♦**branch out** saŏbŭl hwaktchanghada 사업을 확장하다
brand 1 *n* (*of product*) sangp'yo 상표 **2** *v/t*: **~ *s.o. a liar*** nuguege kŏjitmaltchang-iŭi numyŏng-ŭl ssŭiuda 누구에게 거짓말장이의 누명을 씌우다
brand image sangp'umŭi imiji 상품의 이미지
brandish hwidurŭda 휘두르다
brand leader kajang chal naganŭn sangp'yo 가장 잘 나가는 상표; **brand loyalty** pŭraendŭ loyŏlt'i 브랜드 로열티; **brand name** sangp'yomyŏng 상표명
brand-new shinp'umŭi 신품의
brandy pŭraendi 브랜디
brass (*alloy*) notssoe 놋쇠
brass band ch'wiji akttan 취주 악단
brassière pŭrejiŏ 브레지어
brat *pej* saekki 새끼
bravado hŏse 허세
brave *adj* yonggamhan 용감한
bravery yonggamham 용감함
brawl 1 *n* ssaum 싸움 **2** *v/i* ssaumjirhada 싸움질하다
brawny kŏnjanghan 건장한
Brazil Pŭrajil 브라질
Brazilian 1 *adj* Pŭrajirŭi 브라질의 **2** *n* Pŭrajil saram 브라질 사람
breach (*violation*) wiban 위반; (*in party*) purhwa 불화
breach of contract LAW kyeyak wiban 계약 위반
bread *n* ppang 빵
breadcrumbs (*for cooking*) ppang karu 빵 가루; (*for birds*) ppang pusŭrŏgi 빵 부스러기
breadth p'ok 폭
breadwinner chibanŭi pŏrihanŭn saram 집안의 벌이하는 사람
break 1 *n* (*in bone etc*) kŭm 금; (*rest*) hyushik 휴식; (*in relationship*) hyushik-kki 휴식기; ***give ... a ~*** (*opportunity*) ...ege kihoerŭl chuda ...에게 기회를 주다; ***take a ~*** chamshi chungdanhada 잠시 중단하다; ***without a ~*** *work, travel* shwiji ank'o 쉬지 않고 **2** *v/t machine, device, toy* pusuda 부수다; *stick, arm, leg* purŏttŭrida 부러뜨리다; *china, glass, egg* kkaettŭrida 깨뜨리다; *rules, law, promise* wibanhada 위반하다; *news* chŏnhada 전하다; *record* kkaeda 깨다 **3** *v/i* (*of machine, device, toy*) pusŏjida 부서지다; (*of china, glass, egg*) kkaejida 깨지다; (*of stick*) purŏjida 부러지다; (*of news*) allyŏjida 알려지다; (*of storm*) shijakdoeda 시작되다; (*of boy's voice*) pyŏnsŏnghada 변성하다
♦**break away** *v/i* (*escape*) tomangch'ida 도망치다; (*from family*) tongnip'ada 독립하다; (*from organization*) t'alt'oehada 탈퇴하다; (*from tradition*) pŏsŏnada 벗어나다
♦**break down 1** *v/i* (*of vehicle, machine*) kojangnada 고장나다; (*of talks*) shilp'aehada 실패하다; (*in tears*) urŭmŭl t'ŏttŭrida 울음을 터뜨리다; (*mentally*) shin-gyŏng-i soeyak'aejida 신경이 쇠약해지다 **2** *v/t door* pusugo yŏlda 부수고 열다; *figures* pullyuhada 분류하다
♦**break even** COM tŭksshiri ŏpkke toeda 득실이 없게 되다
♦**break in** (*interrupt*) pyŏran-gan malch'amgyŏnhada 별안간

말참견하다; (*of burglar*) ch'imip'ada 침입하다
♦**break off 1** *v/t* kkŏkkŏnaeda 꺾어내다; *branch* kkŏktta 꺾다; *relationship* kkaettŭrida 깨뜨리다; ***they've broken it off*** kŭdŭl saiga kkaeŏjyŏt-tta 그들 사이가 깨어졌다 **2** *v/i* (*stop talking*) taehwarŭl chungdanhada 대화를 중단하다
♦**break out** (*start up*) shijakdoeda 시작되다; (*of disease*) palppyŏnghada 발병하다; (*of prisoners*) t'arok'ada 탈옥하다; ***he broke out in a rash*** kŭnŭn kaptchagi paltchini nat-tta 그는 갑자기 발진이 났다
♦**break up 1** *v/t* (*into component parts*) haech'ehada 해체하다; *fight* mallida 말리다 **2** *v/i* (*of ice*) kkaeŏjida 깨어지다; (*of couple*) heŏjida 헤어지다; (*of band, meeting*) haech'ehada 해체하다
breakable kkaeŏjigi shiun 깨어지기 쉬운
breakage p'ason 파손
breakdown (*of vehicle, machine*) kojang 고장; (*of talks*) shilp'ae 실패; (*nervous ~*) shin-gyŏng soeyak 신경 쇠약; (*of figures*) punsŏk 분석
break-even point sonik pun-gitchŏm 손익 분기점
breakfast *n* ach'im 아침; ***have ~*** ach'imŭl mŏktta 아침을 먹다
break-in ch'imip 침입
breakthrough (*in talks*) t'agae 타개; (*in science, technology*) k'ŭn paltchŏn 큰 발전
breakup (*of partnership etc*) purhwa 불화
breast (*of woman*) yubang 유방
breastfeed *v/t* moyurŭl mŏgida 모유를 먹이다
breaststroke p'yŏnghyŏng 평형
breath sum 숨; ***be out of ~*** sumi ch'ada 숨이 차다; ***take a deep ~*** sumŭl kip'i tŭrŏ mashida 숨을 깊이 들어 마시다
Breathalyzer®, breath analyzer ŭmju ch'ŭktchŏnggi 음주 측정기
breathe 1 *v/i* sumshwida 숨쉬다 **2** *v/t* (*inhale*) tŭri mashida 들이 마시다; (*exhale*) naeshwida 내쉬다
♦**breathe in 1** *v/i* sumŭl tŭryŏ mashida 숨을 들여 마시다 **2** *v/t* tŭrishwida 들이쉬다
♦**breathe out** *v/i* sumŭl naeshwida 숨을 내쉬다
breathing hohŭp 호흡
breathless sumch'an 숨찬
breathlessness hohŭp kollan 호흡 곤란
breathtaking summak'il chŏngdoŭi 숨막힐 정도의
breed 1 *n* p'umjong 품종 **2** *v/t* kirŭda 기르다; *fig* irŭk'ida 일으키다 **3** *v/i* (*of animals*) pŏnshik'ada 번식하다
breeding (*of animals*) pŏnshik 번식
breeding ground *fig* onsang 온상
breeze sandŭlpparam 산들바람
brew 1 *v/t beer* yangjohada 양조하다; *tea* kkŭrida 끓이다 **2** *v/i* (*of storm*) ilda 일다; (*of trouble*) irŏnaryŏgo hada 일어나려고 하다
brewer yangjoŏptcha 양조업자
brewery yangjojang 양조장
bribe 1 *n* noemul 뇌물 **2** *v/t* maesuhada 매수하다
bribery noemul susu 뇌물 수수
brick pyŏkttol 벽돌
bricklayer pyŏkttolgong 벽돌공
bride shinbu 신부
bridegroom shillang 신랑
bridesmaid shinbu tŭllŏri 신부 들러리
bridge[1] **1** *n* tari 다리; (*of nose*) k'onmaru 콧마루; (*of ship*) sŏn-gyo 선교 **2** *v/t gap* chunggae yŏk'arŭl hada 중개 역할을 하다
bridge[2] (*card game*) pŭritchi 브릿지
brief[1] *adj* kan-gyŏrhan 간결한; *time* tanshiganŭi 단시간의
brief[2] **1** *n* (*mission*) immu 임무 **2** *v/t*: ***~ X on Y*** Xege Ye taehan kaeyorŭl sŏlmyŏnghada X에게 Y에 대한 개요를 설명하다
briefcase sŏryu kabang 서류 가방
briefing pŭrip'ing 브리핑
briefly (*for a short period of time*) chamshidong-an 잠시동안; (*in a few words*) kan-gyŏrhage 간결하게; (*to sum up*) yoyak'ajamyŏn 요약하자면
briefs p'aench'ŭ 팬츠

bright *color, future, room* palgŭn 밝은; *smile* hwanhan 환한; (*sunny*) hwach'anghan 화창한; (*intelligent*) ttokttok'an 똑똑한
♦**brighten up 1** *v/t* hwanhage hada 환하게 하다 **2** *v/i* (*of weather*) malgajida 맑아지다
brighten (*of face, person*) palgajida 밝아지다
brightly hwanhage 환하게
brightness (*of weather*) malgŭm 맑음; (*of smile*) hwanham 환함; (*intelligence*) ch'ongmyŏngham 총명함
brilliance (*of person*) chitchŏgin t'agwŏrham 지적인 탁월함; (*of color*) sŏnmyŏngham 선명함
brilliant *sunshine etc* palgŭn 밝은; (*very good*) hullyunghan 훌륭한; (*very intelligent*) much'ŏk ttokttok'an 무척 똑똑한; *idea* aju hullyunghan 아주 훌륭한
brim (*of container*) kajangjari 가장자리; (*of hat*) t'eduri 테두리
brimful nŏmch'ildŭt'an 넘칠듯한
bring *object* kajyŏoda 가져오다; *person* teryŏoda 데려오다; *peace, happiness* ch'oraehada 초래하다; **~ *it here, will you?*** iriro kŭgŏsŭl kajyŏda chullaeyo? 이리로 그것을 가져다 줄래요?; ***can I ~ a friend?*** ch'in-gurŭl terigo kado twaeyo? 친구를 데리고 가도 돼요?
♦**bring about** yagihada 야기하다
♦**bring around** *from a faint* chŏnshin ch'arigehada 정신 차리게 하다; (*persuade*) sŏlttŭk'ada 설득하다
♦**bring back** (*return*) tollyŏjuda 돌려주다; (*re-introduce*) toetollida 되돌리다; *memories* saenggangnage hada 생각나게 하다
♦**bring down** *fence, tree* ssŭrŏjige hada 쓰러지게 하다; *government* chŏnbokshik'ida 전복시키다; *bird, airplane* ssoa ttŏrŏttŭrida 쏘아 떨어뜨리다; *rates, inflation, price* naerige hada 내리게 하다
♦**bring in** *interest, income* kajyŏoda 가져오다; *legislation* chech'urhada 제출하다; *verdict* naerida 내리다; (*involve*) kwallyŏnshik'ida 관련시키다
♦**bring out** sesang-e naenot'a 세상에 내놓다; *book* ch'ulp'anhada 출판하다; *video, CD* ch'ulsshihada 출시하다; *new product* palmaehada 발매하다
♦**bring to** (*from a faint*) chŏnshin ch'arigehada 정신 차리게 하다
♦**bring up** *child* yangnyuk'ada 양육하다; *subject* marŭl kkŏnaeda 말을 꺼내다; (*vomit*) t'ohada 토하다
brink kajangjari 가장자리; *fig* kyŏltchŏngjŏk shigi 결정적 시기
brisk *person, voice, walk* tangch'an 당찬; *trade* hwalbarhan 활발한
bristles (*on chin*) suyŏm 수염; (*of brush*) t'ŏl 털
bristling: ***be ~ with*** …(ŭ)ro kadŭk ch'ait-tta …(으)로 가득 차있다
Britain Yŏngguk 영국
British 1 *adj* Yonggugŭi 영국의 **2** *n*: ***the ~*** Yŏnggugin 영국인, Yŏngguginŭi 영국인의
Briton Yŏngguk saram 영국 사람
brittle *adj* pusŏjigi shwiun 부서지기 쉬운
broach *subject* marŭl kkŏnaeda 말을 꺼내다
broad 1 *adj street, hips* p'ok nŏlbŭn 폭 넓은; *shoulders* ttŏk pŏrŏjin 떡 벌어진; *smile* hwanhan 환한; (*general*) ilbanjŏgin 일반적인; ***in ~ daylight*** taenaje 대낮에 **2** *n* F (*woman*) yŏja 여자
broadcast 1 *n* pangsong 방송 **2** *v/t* pangsonghada 방송하다
broadcaster pangsong-in 방송인
broadcasting pangsong 방송
broaden 1 *v/i* nŏlbŏjida 넓어지다 **2** *v/t* nŏlp'ida 넓히다
broadjump nŏlbi ttwigi 넓이 뛰기;
broadly: **~ *speaking*** ilbanjŏgŭro marhajamyŏn 일반적으로 말하자면
broadminded kwandaehan 관대한
broccoli pŭrok'olli 브로콜리
brochure pŭroshyŏ 브로셔
broil *v/t* kuptta 굽다
broiler *n* (*on stove*) kumnŭn kigu 굽는 기구; (*chicken*) kuiyong yŏnggye 구이용 영계
broke F muilp'unŭi 무일푼의;

(*bankrupt*) p'asanhan 파산한; ***go ~*** p'asanhada 파산하다
broken *adj* pusŏjin 부서진; *window, promise* kkaejin 깨진; *neck, arm* purŏjin 부러진; *home* kyŏlssonŭi 결손의; *English etc* ŏngt'ŏriŭi 엉터리의
broken-hearted maŭmŭi sangch'ŏrŭl ibŭn 마음의 상처를 입은
broker chunggaeŏptcha 중개업자
bronchitis kigwanjiyŏm 기관지염
bronze *n* (*metal*) ch'ŏngdong 청동; (*color*) ch'ŏngdongsaek 청동색; ***~ medal*** tongmedal 동메달
brooch pŭroch'i 브로치
brood *v/i* (*of person*) komgomhi saenggak'ada 곰곰히 생각하다
broom pitcharu 빗자루
broth (*soup*) mulgŭn sup'ŭ 묽은 수프; (*stock*) kungmul 국물
brothel maech'un-gul 매춘굴
brother (*man's elder*) hyŏng 형; (*woman's elder*) oppa 오빠; (*younger*) namdongsaeng 남동생; ***they're ~s*** kŭdŭrŭn hyŏngjeyeyo 그들은 형제예요; ***~s and sisters*** hyŏngje chamae 형제 자매
brother-in-law (*woman's elder sister's husband*) hyŏngbu 형부; (*wife's younger brother*) ch'ŏ-nam 처남; (*man's elder sister's husband*) maehyŏng 매형
brotherly hyŏngjeŭi 형제의
browbeat mallo wihyŏp'ada 말로 위협하다
brow (*forehead*) ima 이마; (*of hill*) maru 마루
brown 1 *n* kalsaek 갈색 **2** *adj* kalsaegŭi 갈색의; (*tanned*) haetppyŏch'e t'an 햇볕에 탄 **3** *v/t* (*in cooking*) norŭnnorŭt'age kuptta 노릇노릇하 게굽다 **4** *v/i* (*in cooking*) norŭnnorŭt'age toeda 노릇노릇하 게되다
brownbag: ***~ it*** toshiragŭl ssaoda 도시락을 싸오다
brownie kŏlsŭk'aut'ŭŭi yunyŏn tanwŏn 걸스카우트의 유년 단원; (*cake*) ch'ok'ollit k'eik 초콜릿 케익
brownie points: ***earn ~*** ach'ŏmŭro ŏdŭn shinyong 아첨으로 얻은 신용
brown-nose *v/t* F …ege ach'ŏmhada …에게 아첨하다
browse (*in store*) kugyŏngman hago tanida 구경만 하고 다니다; ***~ through a book*** ttŭiŏmttŭiŏm iltta 띄엄띄엄 읽다
browser COMPUT pŭraujŏ 브라우저
bruise 1 *n* mŏng 멍; (*emotional*) sangch'ŏ 상처 **2** *v/t person, fruit* mŏngdŭlge hada 멍들게 하다 **3** *v/i* (*of person*) mŏngdŭlda 멍들다; (*of fruit*) hŭmi saenggida 흠이 생기다
bruising *adj fig* sangch'ŏnan 상처난
brunch ach'im kyŏm chŏmshim 아침 겸 점심
brunette kalssaek mŏriŭi yŏja 갈색 머리의 여자
brunt: ***bear the ~ of*** …(ŭ)ro cheil shimhage kot'ongbat-tta …(으)로 제일 심하게 고통받다
brush 1 *n* sol 솔; (*conflict*) yakkanŭi ch'ungdol 약간의 충돌 **2** *v/t hair, floor* pitchirhada 빗질하다; *teeth* yangch'ijirhada 양치질하다; *jacket* soljirhada 솔질하다; (*touch lightly*) saltchak sŭch'ida 살짝 스치다; (*remove*) ch'iuda 치우다
♦**brush against** saltchak sŭch'imyŏnsŏ chinagada 살짝 스치면서 지나가다
♦**brush aside** mushihada 무시하다
♦**brush off** t'ŏrŏnaeda 털어내다; *criticism* mushihada 무시하다
♦**brush up** pokssŭp'ada 복습하다
brushoff F t'oetcha 퇴짜; ***get the ~*** t'oetacharŭl mat-tta 퇴짜를 맞다
brusque muttukttuk'an 무뚝뚝한
Brussels sprouts yangbaech'uŭi iltchong 양배추의 일종
brutal *person* chaninhan 잔인한; *treatment* hokttok'an 혹독한; *honesty* naeng-ŏmhan 냉엄한
brutality chaninham 잔인함
brutally chaninhage 잔인하게; ***be ~ frank*** chinach'ige soltchik'ada 지나치게 솔직하다
brute chimsŭng kat'ŭn saram 짐승 같은 사람
brute force p'ongnyŏk 폭력
bubble *n* kŏp'um 거품
bubble gum p'ungsŏnkkŏm 풍선껌

buck[1] *n* F (*dollar*) tallŏ 달러
buck[2] *v/i* (*of horse*) p'ŏltchŏk ttwida 펄쩍 뛰다
buck[3]: ***pass the*** ~ ch'aegimŭl chŏngahada 책임을 전가하다
bucket *n* yangdong-i 양동이
buckle[1] **1** *n* pŏk'ŭl 버클 **2** *v/t belt* pelt'ŭrŭl maeda 벨트를 매다
buckle[2] *v/i* (*of wood*, *metal*) kuburŏjida 구부러지다
bud *n* BOT ssak 싹
Buddha Puch'ŏ 부처
Buddha's Birthday Puch'ŏnim Oshin Nal 부처님 오신 날
Buddhism Pulgyo 불교
Buddhist 1 *n* pulgyo shinja 불교 신자 **2** *adj* pulgyoŭi 불교의
Buddhist Broadcasting System Pulgyo Pangsong 불교 방송
buddy F ch'in-gu 친구; (*form of address*) yŏboge 여보게
budge 1 *v/t* umjigida 움직이다; (*make reconsider*) maŭmŭl pakkuge hada 마음을 바꾸게 하다 **2** *v/i* umjigida 움직이다; (*change one's mind*) maŭmŭl pakkuda 마음을 바꾸다
budgerigar ingkko 잉꼬
budget 1 *n* yesan 예산; (*of a family*) saenghwalbi 생활비; ***be on a*** ~ kyŏlp'ip saenghwarŭl hada 결핍 생활을 하다 **2** *v/i* yesanŭl seuda 예산을 세우다
♦**budget for** yesane nŏt'a 예산에 넣다
buff[1] *adj color* hwanggalssaek 황갈색
buff[2]: ***a movie / jazz*** ~ yŏnghwagwang / chaejŭgwang 영화광 / 재즈광
buffalo tŭlsso 들소
buffer RAIL wanch'ung changch'i 완충 장치; *fig* wanch'ungnyŏk 완충역; ***memory*** ~ COMPUT wanch'ung kiŏk changch'i 완충 기억 장치
buffet[1] *n* (*meal*) pup'e 부페
buffet[2] *v/t* (*of wind*) ch'ida 치다
bug 1 *n* (*insect*) pŏlle 벌레; (*virus*) pairŏsŭ 바이러스; (*spying device*) toch'ŏnggi 도청기; COMPUT pŏgŭ 버그 **2** *v/t room* toch'ŏnggirŭl sŏlch'ihada 도청기를 설치하다; *telephones* toch'ŏnghada 도청하다; F (*annoy*) koerop'ida 괴롭히다
buggy (*for baby*) yumoch'a 유모차
build 1 *n* (*of person*) ch'egyŏk 체격 **2** *v/t* seuda 세우다
♦**build up 1** *v/t strength* tallyŏnhada 단련하다; *relationship* ssaa ollida 쌓아 올리다; *collection* moŭda 모으다 **2** *v/i* ssayŏjida 쌓여지다
builder (*company*) kŏnch'ugŏp 건축업; (*person*) kŏnch'ugŏptcha 건축업자
building kŏnmul 건물; (*activity*) kŏnch'uk 건축
building site kongsajang 공사장
building trade kŏnch'ugŏp 건축업
build-up (*accumulation*) ssayŏjim 쌓여짐; (*publicity*) sŏnjŏn 선전
built-in put'bagiŭi 붙박이의; *flash* naejangdoeŏ innŭn 내장되어 있는
built-up area shigaji 시가지
bulb BOT kugŭn 구근; (*light* ~) chŏngu 전구
bulge 1 *n* tolch'ul 돌출; (*in number*, *quantity*) ilsshijŏk chŭngga 일시적 증가 **2** *v/i* (*of pocket*) pulluk'ada 불룩하다; (*of wall*, *eyes*) t'wiŏ naoda 튀어 나오다
bulk taebubun 대부분; ***in*** ~ taeryangŭro 대량으로
bulky pup'iga k'ŭn 부피가 큰
bull hwangso 황소
bulldoze (*demolish*) puldoujŏro chegŏhada 불도우저로 제거하다; ~ ***X into Y*** *fig* Xŭl / rŭl kangjero Yhadorok mandŭlda X을 / 를 강제로 Y하도록 만들다
bulldozer puldoujŏ 불도우저
bullet ch'ong-al 총알
bulletin keshi 게시
bulletin board (*on wall*) keship'an 게시판; COMPUT chŏnja keship'an 전자 게시판
bullet-proof pangt'anŭi 방탄의
bull market FIN kangse chusik shijang 강세 주식 시장
bull's-eye kwanyŏgŭi hanbokp'an 과녁의 한복판; ***hit the*** ~ kwanyŏgŭl match'uda 과녁을 맞추다; *fig* taesŏnggong-ŭl kŏduda 대성공을 거두다
bullshit V **1** *n* hŏp'ung 허풍 **2** *v/i*

hŏp'ung-ŭl ttŏlda 허풍을 떨다
bully 1 *n* kkangp'ae 깡패 **2** *v/t* mot salge kulda 못 살게 굴다
bum 1 *n* F (*tramp*) purangja 부랑자; (*worthless person*) mangnani 망나니 **2** *adj* (*useless*) ssŭlmoŏmnŭn 쓸모없는 **3** *v/t cigarette etc* kŏjŏ ŏt-tta 거저 얻다
♦**bum around** F (*travel*) pangnanghada 방랑하다; (*be lazy*) pindungbindung chinaeda 빈둥빈둥 지내다
bumblebee twengbŏl 뒝벌
bump 1 *n* (*swelling*) hok 혹; (*in road*) yunggi 융기; ***get a ~ on the head*** mŏrirŭl handae mat-tta 머리를 한대 맞다 **2** *v/t* puditch'ida 부딪히다
♦**bump into** …e puditch'ida …에 부딪히다; (*meet*) …wa / kwa uyŏnhi mannada …와 / 과 우연히 만나다
♦**bump off** F (*murder*) chugida 죽이다
♦**bump up** F *prices* taep'ok ollida 대폭 올리다
bumper *n* MOT pŏmp'ŏ 범퍼
bumpy *flight* tŏlk'ŏk-kkŏrinŭn 덜컥거리는; *road* ult'ungbult'unghan 울퉁불퉁한
bun (*hairstyle*) t'ŭrŏollin mŏri 틀어올린 머리; (*for eating*) chagŭn lolppang 작은 롤빵
bunch (*of people*) muri 무리; ***a ~ of keys*** yŏlsoe mungch'i 열쇠 뭉치; ***a ~ of flowers*** kkot hantabal 꽃 한 다발; ***a ~ of grapes*** p'odo han song-i 포도 한 송이; ***thanks a ~*** (*ironic*) nunmulnage komapkkunyo 눈물나게 고맙군요
bundle (*of clothes*) kkurŏmi 꾸러미; (*of wood*) mungch'i 뭉치
♦**bundle up** kkurida 꾸리다; (*dress warmly*) ttattŭt'a-ge ip'ida 따뜻하게 입히다
bungle *v/t* sŏt'urŭge mandŭlda 서투르게 만들다
bunk sŏnban moyang-ŭi ch'imdae 선반 모양의 침대
bunk beds ich'ŭng ch'imdae 이층 침대
buoy *n* pup'yo 부표
buoyant hwallyŏgi innŭn 활력이 있는; *fig* sangsŭngse-ŭi 상승세의
burden 1 *n* chim 짐; *fig* pudam 부담 **2** *v/t*: ***~ X with Y*** Xŭl / rŭl Y(ŭ)ro pudam chiuda X을 / 를 Y(으)로 부담 지우다
bureau (*chest of drawers*) sŏraptchang 서랍장; (*office*) samuguk 사무국
bureaucracy (*red tape*) pŏn-gŏrŏun haengjŏng chŏlch'a 번거러운 행정 절차; (*system*) kwallyoje 관료제
bureaucrat kwallyo 관료
bureaucratic kwallyojŏgin 관료적인
burger haembŏgŏ 햄버거
burglar kangdo 강도
burglar alarm tonan kyŏngbogi 도난 경보기
burglarize kangdojirhada 강도질하다
burglary kangdo 강도
burial maejang 매장; ***~ at sea*** sujang 수장
burly kŏnjanghan 건장한
Burma Pŏma 버마
Burmese 1 *adj* Pŏmaŭi 버마의 **2** *n* (*person*) Pŏmain 버마인; (*language*) Pŏmaŏ 버마어
burn 1 *n* hwasang 화상 **2** *v/t* t'aeuda 태우다; *fuel* yŏnsohada 연소하다 **3** *v/i* t'ada 타다
♦**burn down 1** *v/t* t'aewŏbŏrida 태워버리다 **2** *v/i* t'abŏrida 타버리다
♦**burn out** *v/t*: ***burn oneself out*** chŏngnyŏgŭl tahada 정력을 다하다; ***a burned-out car*** pult'abŏrin ch'a 불타버린 차
burner (*on cooker*) naembirŭl ollyŏdunŭn tae 냄비를 올려두는 대
burp 1 *n* t'ŭrim 트림 **2** *v/i* t'ŭrimhada 트림하다 **3** *v/t baby* t'ŭrimŭl shik'ida 트림을 시키다
burst 1 *n* (*in water pipe*) p'ayŏl 파열; (*of gunfire*) chiptchung sagyŏk 집중 사격; ***in a ~ of energy*** kiuni p'ŏlp'ŏl nŏmch'yŏnasŏ 기운이 펄펄 넘쳐나서 **2** *adj tire* t'ŏjin 터진 **3** *v/t balloon* t'ŏttŭrida 터뜨리다 **4** *v/i* (*of balloon, tire*) t'ŏjida 터지다; ***~ into a room*** pang anŭro ttwiŏdŭlda 방 안으로 뛰어들다; ***~ into tears*** urŭmŭl t'ŏttŭrida 울음을 터뜨리다; ***~ out laughing*** p'okssorŭl t'ŏttŭrida

폭소를 터뜨리다

bury *person, animal* p'amut-tta 파묻다; (*conceal*) sumgida 숨기다; ***be buried under*** (*covered by*) ...(ŭ)ro tŏp'ida ...(으)로 덮히다; ***~ oneself in one's work*** ire molttuhada 일에 몰두하다

bus[1] **1** *n* (*local*) pŏsŭ 버스; (*long distance*) shioe pŏsŭ 시외 버스 **2** *v/t* pŏsŭro idonghada 버스로 이동하다

bus[2] COMPUT pŏsŭ 버스

busboy weit'ŏŭi chosu 웨이터의 조수

bush (*plant*) kwanmok 관목; (*terrain*) oji 오지

bushed F (*tired*) p'igonhan 피곤한

bushy *beard* t'ŏpssuruk'an 텁수룩한

business (*trade*) muyŏk 무역; (*company*) hoesa 회사; (*work*) il 일; (*sector*) saŏbŭi chongnyu 사업의 종류; (*affair, matter*) sakkŏn 사건; (*as subject of study*) kyŏngnyŏnghak 경영학; ***on ~*** saŏpch'a 사업차; ***that's none of your ~!*** nega sanggwan hal paga anida! 네가 상관 할 바가 아니다!; ***mind your own ~!*** ne irina haera! 네 일이나 해라!

business card myŏngham 명함; **business class** pijŭnisŭ k'ŭllaesŭ 비즈니스 클래스; **business hours** ŏmmu shigan 업무 시간; **businesslike** nŭngnyultchŏgin 능률적인; **business lunch** saŏpch'a hanŭn shikssa 사업차 하는 식사; **businessman** saŏpkka 사업가; **business meeting** pijŭnisŭ mit'ing 비즈니스 미팅; **business school** kyŏngnyŏng taehagwŏn 경영 대학원; **business studies** kyŏngnyŏnghak 경영학; **business trip** ch'ultchang 출장; **businesswoman** yŏsŏng saŏpkka 여성 사업가

bus station pŏsŭ t'ŏminŏl 버스 터미널

bus stop pŏsŭ chŏngnyujang 버스 정류장

bust[1] *n* (*of woman*) kasŭm 가슴

bust[2] **1** *adj* F (*broken*) pusŏjin 부서진; ***go ~*** (*bankrupt*) p'asanhada 파산하다 **2** *v/t* pusuda 부수다

♦**bustle around** punjuhi irhada 분주히 일하다

bust-up F kyŏlbyŏl 결별

busty kasŭmi p'ungmanhan 가슴이 풍만한

busy 1 *adj* pappŭn 바쁜; *street* pŏnhwahan 번화한; (*making money*) pumbinŭn 붐비는; (*full of people*) saramdŭri puktchŏkttaenŭn 사람들이 북적대는; TELEC t'onghwajung-in 통화중인; ***be ~ doing ...*** ...ŭl/rŭl hanŭra pappŭda ...을/를 하느라 바쁘다 **2** *v/t*: ***~ oneself with*** ...(ŭ)ro pappŭda ...(으)로 바쁘다

busybody ch'am-gyŏn chal hanŭn saram 참견 잘 하는 사람

busy signal TELEC t'onghwa chung shinho 통화중 신호

but 1 *conj* ...hajiman ...하지만; ***I tried to tell him ~ he wouldn't listen*** kŭege marharyŏgo haet-tchiman tŭt-tchi anassŏyo 그에게 말하려고 했지만 듣지 않았어요; ***it's not me ~ my father you want*** tangshini wŏnhan saramŭn naega anira nae abŏjigunyo 당신이 원한 사람은 내가 아니라 내 아버지군요; ***~ then*** (***again***) kŭrŏt'a hadŏrado 그렇다 하더라도; ***~ that's not fair*** hajiman kŭgŏn kongp'yŏnghaji anayo 하지만 그건 공평하지 않아요 **2** *prep*: ***all ~ him*** kŭ saramŭl cheoehago modŭ ta 그 사람을 제외하고 모두 다; ***the last ~ one*** hana ppaego maen majimak 하나 빼고 맨 마지막; ***the next ~ one*** hana kŏnnŏ ap'e 하나 건너 앞에; ***~ for you*** nega ŏpssŭmyŏn 네가 없으면; ***nothing ~ the best*** ojik ch'oegoman 오직 최고만

butcher chŏngnyuktchŏm chuin 정육점 주인; (*murderer*) hakssaltcha 학살자

butt 1 *n* (*of cigarette*) tambae kkongch'o 담배 꽁초; (*of joke*) nongdamŭi p'yojŏk 농담의 표적; F (*buttocks*) ŏngdŏng-i 엉덩이 **2** *v/t* mŏriro pat-tta 머리로 받다; (*of goat, bull*) pat-tta 받다

♦**butt in** panghaehada 방해하다

butter 1 *n* pŏt'ŏ 버터 **2** *v/t* pŏt'ŏrŭl

parŭda 버터를 바르다
♦**butter up** F ach'ŏmhada 아첨하다
butterfly (*insect*) nabi 나비
buttocks ŏngdŏng-i 엉덩이
button 1 *n* tanch'u 단추; (*on machine*) pŏt'ŭn 버튼; (*badge*) paeji 배지 **2** *v/t* tanch'urŭl ch'aeuda 단추를 채우다
♦**button up** → ***button***
buttonhole 1 *n* (*in suit*) tanch'u kumŏng 단추구멍 **2** *v/t* put-ttŭlgo iyagihada 붙들고 이야기하다
buxom p'ungmanhan 풍만한
buy 1 *n* san mulgŏn 산 물건 **2** *v/t* sada 사다; ***can I ~ you a drink?*** chega han chan sado toelkkayo? 제가 한 잔 사도 될까요?; ***$50 doesn't ~ much*** 50tallŏronŭn pyŏllo sal kŏshi ŏptta 50달러로는 별로 살 것이 없다
♦**buy off** (*bribe*) maesuhada 매수하다
♦**buy out** COM hoesa chibunŭl sadŭrida 회사 지분을 사들이다
♦**buy up** maejŏmhada 매점하다
buyer kumaeja 구매자; (*for a company*) paiŏ 바이어
buzz 1 *n* wing-winghanŭn sori 윙윙하는 소리; F (*thrill*) sŭril 스릴 **2** *v/i* (*of insect*) wingwing sorirŭl naeda 윙윙 소리를 내다; (*with buzzer*) pujŏrŭl ullida 부저를 울리다 **3** *v/t* (*with buzzer*) pujŏro purŭda 부저로 부르다
♦**buzz off** F kkŏjyŏ pŏrida 꺼져 버리다; ***~!*** kkŏjyŏ pŏryŏ! 꺼져 버려!
buzzer pujŏ 부저
by 1 *prep* ◊ (*agency*) …e ŭihae …에 의해; ***she was murdered ~ her husband*** kŭnyŏnŭn namp'yŏne ŭihae sarhaedanghaet-tta 그녀는 남편에 의해 살해당했다; ***a play ~ …*** …i/ga ssŭn yŏn-gŭk …이/가 쓴 연극 ◊ (*near, next to*) …yŏp'e …옆에; ***a seat ~ the window*** ch'angmun yŏp'e innŭn chari 창문 옆에 있는 자리; ***side ~ side*** naranhi 나란히 ◊ (*no later than*) …kkaji …까지; ***~ midnight*** chajŏngkkaji 자정까지; ***~ this time tomorrow*** naeil i shigankkaji 내일 이 시간까지 ◊ (*past*) …ŭl/rŭl chinasŏ …을/를 지나서; ***as we walked ~ the church*** uriga kyohoerŭl china kŏrŏgassŭl ttae 우리가 교회를 지나 걸어갔을 때 ◊ (*mode of transport*) …(ŭ)ro …(으)로; ***~ bus/train*** pŏsŭro/kich'aro 버스로/기차로; ***~ day/night*** naje/pame 낮에/밤에 ◊ (*measuring*): ***~ the hour/ton*** shigandang/t'ondang 시간당/톤당; ***~ a couple of minutes*** myŏt pun ch'airo 몇 분 차이로; ***2 ~ 4*** p'ogi 2, kiriga 4in nŏlbi 폭이 2, 길이가 4인 넓이; ***~ my watch*** nae shigyero 내 시계로 ◊: ***~ oneself*** honjasŏ 혼자서 **2** *adv*: ***~ and ~*** (*soon*) kot 곧
bye(-bye) annyŏng 안녕
bygone: ***let ~s be ~s*** chinan irŭn kŭnyang chŏbŏduja 지난 일은 그냥 접어두자
bypass 1 *n* (*road*) uhoero 우회로; MED hyŏlgwan ishik 혈관 이식 **2** *v/t* uhoehada 우회하다
by-product pusanmul 부산물
bystander panggwanja 방관자
byte COMPUT pait'ŭ 바이트
byword: ***be a ~ for*** …ŭi taemyŏngsaga toeda …의 대명사가 되다

C

cab (*taxi*) t'aeksshi 택시; (*of truck*) unjŏnsŏk 운전석
cabaret k'yabare 캬바레
cabbage yangbaech'u 양배추
cab driver t'aeksshi unjŏnsa 택시 운전사
cabin (*of plane, for crew*) sŭngmuwŏnshil 승무원실; (*of plane, for passengers*) kaeksshil 객실; (*on ship*) sŏnshil 선실
cabin crew sŭngmuwŏn 승무원
cabinet changshiktchang 장식장; POL naegak 내각; ***medicine ~*** yaktchang 약장
cable (*of electrical appliance, telephone etc*) k'eibŭl 케이블; ~ (***TV***) yusŏn pangsong 유선 (방송)
cable car k'eibŭlk'a 케이블카
cable television yusŏn pangsong 유선 방송
cab stand t'aeksshi t'anŭn kot 택시 타는 곳
cactus sŏninjang 선인장
cadaver shich'e 시체
CAD-CAM k'aedŭ / k'aem 캐드 / 캠
caddie 1 *n* (*in golf*) k'aedi 캐디 **2** *v/i*: ***~ for*** …ŭl / rŭl wihan k'aediro irhada …을 / 를 위한 캐디로 일하다
cadet (*in police etc*) saengdo 생도; MIL sagwan saengdo 사관 생도
cadet corps hakssaeng kunsa kyoryŏndan 학생 군사 교련단
cadge: ***~ X from Y*** Y(ŭ)robut'ŏ Xŭl / rŭl kugŏrhada Y(으)로부터 X을 / 를 구걸하다
café tabang 다방
cafeteria k'ap'et'eria 카페테리아
caffeine k'ap'ein 카페인
cage (*for bird*) saejang 새장; (*for lion*) uri 우리
cagey t'ŏnoŭryŏ haji annŭn 터놓으려 하지 않는
cahoots: ***be in ~ with*** …wa / kwa kongmohada …와 / 과 공모하다
cake 1 *n* k'eik'ŭ 케이크; ***be a piece of ~*** *fig* maeu shwiun irida 매우 쉬운 일이다 **2** *v/i* tŏng-ŏrijida 덩어리지다
calcium k'alshyum 칼슘
calculate (*work out*) sanch'urhae naeda 산출해 내다; (*in arithmetic*) kyesanhada 계산하다
calculating *adj* kyesanjŏgin 계산적인
calculation kyesan 계산
calculator kyesan-gi 계산기
calendar tallyŏk 달력
calf[1] (*young cow*) song-aji 송아지
calf[2] ANAT chong-ari 종아리
caliber (*of gun*) kugyŏng 구경; ***a man of his ~*** suwan choŭn saram 수완 좋은 사람
call 1 *n* TELEC chŏnhwa 전화; (*shout*) oech'im 외침; (*demand*) yogu 요구; ***there's a ~ for you*** tangshinhant'e chŏnhwaga wassŏyo 당신한테 전화가 왔어요 **2** *v/t* TELEC chŏnhwarŭl kŏlda 전화를 걸다; (*summon*) purŭda 부르다; *meeting* sojip'ada 소집하다; (*summons*) sohwanhada 소환하다; (*describe as*) …rago purŭda …라고 부르다; (*shout*) sorich'yŏ purŭda 소리쳐 부르다; ***what have they ~ed the baby?*** kŭdŭrŭn agi irŭmŭl mwŏrago chiŏt-tchiyo? 그들은 아기 이름을 뭐라고 지었지요?; ***but we ~ him Tom*** kŭrŏch'iman urinŭn kŭrŭl T'omirago pullŏyo 그렇지만 우리는 그를 톰이라고 불러요; ***~ s.o. names*** nugurŭl yok'ada 누구를 욕하다 **3** *v/i* TELEC chŏnhwahada 전화하다; (*shout*) sorich'yŏ purŭda 소리쳐 부르다; (*visit*) pangmunhada 방문하다
♦**call at** (*stop at*) …e tŭllida …에 들리다; (*of train*) …e chŏngch'ahada …에 정차하다
♦**call back 1** *v/t* TELEC najung-e tashi chŏnhwahada 나중에 다시 전화하다;

(*summon*) pullŏsŏ toedoraoge hada 불러서 되돌아오게 하다 **2** *v/i* TELEC najung-e tashi chŏnhwahada 나중에 다시 전화하다; (*visit*) tashi pangmunhada 다시 방문하다

♦**call for** (*collect*) …ŭl / rŭl kajirŏ kada …을 / 를 가지러 가다; *person* …ŭl / rŭl terirŏ kada …을 / 를 데리러 가다; (*demand*) yoguhada 요구하다; (*require*) …i / ga p'iryohada …이 / 가 필요하다

♦**call in 1** *v/t* (*summon*) pullŏ tŭrida 불러 들이다 **2** *v/i* TELEC chŏnhwaro allida 전화로 알리다

♦**call off** (*cancel*) ch'wisohada 취소하다

♦**call on** (*urge*) yoguhada 요구하다; (*visit*) pangmunhada 방문하다

♦**call out** sorich'yŏ purŭda 소리쳐 부르다; (*summon*) ch'ulttongshik'ida 출동시키다

♦**call up** *v/t* TELEC chŏnhwahada 전화하다; COMPUT yŏlda 열다

caller TELEC chŏnhwa kŏn saram 전화 건 사람; (*visitor*) sonnim 손님

call girl maech'unbu 매춘부

calligraphy sŏye 서예

callous mugamgak'an 무감각한

calm 1 *adj sea*, *weather* koyohan 고요한; *person* ch'imch'ak'an 침착한 **2** *n* (*of the countryside etc*) p'yŏng-on 평온; (*of person*) ch'imch'ak 침착

♦**calm down 1** *v/t* karaanch'ida 가라앉히다 **2** *v/i* (*of sea*, *weather*) koyohaejida 고요해지다; (*of person*) ch'imch'ak'aejida 침착해지다

calorie k'allori 칼로리

Cambodia K'ambodia 캄보디아

Cambodian 1 *adj* K'ambodiaŭi 캄보디아의 **2** *n* (*person*) K'ambodia saram 캄보디아 사람

camcorder k'aemk'odŏ 캠코더

camera k'amera 카메라

cameraman ch'waryŏng kisa 촬영 기사

camouflage 1 *n* wijang 위장 **2** *v/t* wijanghada 위장하다

camp 1 *n* k'aemp'ŭ 캠프; (*for prisoners*, *refugees*) suyongso 수용소 **2** *v/i* ch'ŏnmagŭl ch'ida 천막을 치다

campaign 1 *n* undong 운동 **2** *v/i* undong-ŭl hada 운동을 하다

campaigner undongga 운동가

camper (*person*) k'aemp'inghanŭn saram 캠핑하는 사람; (*vehicle*) k'aemp'ŭyong t'ŭreillŏ 캠프용 트레일러

camp ground yayŏngji 야영지

camping k'aemp'ing 캠핑

campsite yayŏngji 야영지

campus: ***university ~*** taehak kyojŏng 대학 교정, taehak k'aemp'ŏsŭ 대학 캠퍼스

can[1] ◊ (*ability*) ...hal su it-tta ...할 수 있다; ***~ you hear me?*** nae marŭl tŭrŭl su issŏyo? 내 말을 들을 수 있어요?; ***~ you speak French?*** Puŏrŭl marhal su issŏyo? 불어를 말할 수 있어요?; ***~ you help me?*** towajul su issŏyo? 도와줄 수 있어요?; ***~ he call me back?*** kŭnŭn na-ege najung-e chŏnhwahae chul su issŏyo? 그는 내게 나중에 전화해 줄 수 있어요?; ***I ~ do it by tomorrow*** naeil kkaji hal su issŏyo 내일까지 할 수 있어요 ◊ (*in negative*) ...hal su ŏptta ...할 수 없다; ***I ~'t see*** pol su ŏpssŏyo 볼 수 없어요; ***you ~'t give up now*** tangshinŭn chigŭm p'ogihal su ŏpssŏyo 당신은 지금 포기할 수 없어요; ***that ~'t be right*** majŭl li ŏpssŏ 맞을 리 없어 ◊ (*permission*) ...hayŏdo chot'a ...하여도 좋다; ***~ I use the phone?*** chŏnhwarŭl ssŏdo toemnikka? 전화를 써도 됩니까?; ***~ I help you?*** towadŭrilkkayo? 도와드릴까요?; ***~ I have a beer / coffee?*** maektchuga / k'ŏp'iga issŏyo? 맥주가 / 커피가 있어요?

can[2] **1** *n* (*for drinks etc*) kkangt'ong 깡통; (*of preserved food*) t'ongjorim 통조림 **2** *v/t* t'ongjorimhada 통조림하다

Canada K'aenada 캐나다

Canadian 1 *adj* K'aenadaŭi 캐나다의 **2** *n* K'aenada saram 캐나다 사람

canal (*waterway*) unha 운하

canary k'anaria 카나리아

cancel ch'wisohada 취소하다

cancellation ch'wiso 취소

cancer am 암

c & f (= ***cost and freight***) unim p'oham kagyŏk 운임 포함 가격
candid soltchik'an 솔직한
candidacy ip'ubo 입후보
candidate (*for position*) huboja 후보자; (*in exam*) ŭngshija 응시자
candle yangch'o 양초
candlestick ch'ot-ttae 촛대
candor hŏshim t'anhoe 허심 탄회
candy sat'ang 사탕
cannabis taemach'o 대마초
canned *fruit etc* t'ongjorimdoen 통조림된; (*recorded*) nogŭmdoen 녹음된
cannot → ***can***[1]
canoe k'anu 카누
can opener kkangt'ong ttagae 깡통 따개
can't → ***can***[1]
canteen (*in factory*) kunae shikttang 구내 식당
canvas (*for painting*) kaenbŏsŭ 캔버스; (*material*) chŭk'ŭ 즈크
canvass 1 *v/t* (*seek opinion of*) …ŭi ŭigyŏnŭl murŏboda …의 의견을 물어보다 **2** *v/i* POL yusehada 유세하다
canyon kip'ŭn hyŏpkkok 깊은 협곡
cap (*hat*) k'aep 캡; (*of bottle*, *pen*, *lens etc*) ttukkŏng 뚜껑
capability (*of person*) nŭngnyŏk 능력; (*of military*) kunsaryŏk 군사력
capable (*efficient*) nŭngnyŏk innŭn 능력 있는; ***be ~ of*** …hal nŭngnyŏgi it-tta …할 능력이 있다
capacity (*of container*, *engine*) yongnyang 용량; (*of building*) yongjŏk 용적; (*of elevator*) suyongnyŏk 수용력; (*of factory*) ch'oedae saengsannyŏk 최대 생산력; (*ability*) nŭngnyŏng 능력; ***in my ~ as*** nanŭn …(ŭ)rosŏ 나는 …(으)로서
capital *n* (*of country*) sudo 수도; (*letter*) taemuntcha 대문자; (*money*) chabon 자본
capital expenditure ch'ongbiyong 총비용; **capital gains tax** chasan sodŭksse 자산 소득세; **capital growth** chabon chŭngga 자본 증가
capitalism chabonjuŭi 자본주의
capitalist 1 *adj* chabonjuŭijŏk 자본주의적 **2** *n* chabonjuŭija 자본주의자; (*businessman*) chabonga 자본가
capital letter taemuntcha 대문자
capital punishment kŭk'yŏng 극형
capitulate hangbok'ada 항복하다
capsize 1 *v/i* twijip'ida 뒤집히다 **2** *v/t* twijiptta 뒤집다
capsule MED, (*in space*) k'aepsshyul 캡슐
captain *n* (*of ship*) sŏnjang 선장; (*of aircraft*) kijang 기장; (*of team*) t'imjang 팀장
caption *n* k'aepsshyŏn 캡션
captivate maŭmŭl sarojaptta 마음을 사로잡다
captive (*of war*) p'oro 포로
captivity kamgŭm 감금
capture 1 *n* (*of city*) chŏmnyŏng 점령; (*of criminal*) saengp'o 생포; (*of animal*) p'ohoek 포획 **2** *v/t person*, *animal* sarojaptta 사로잡다; *city*, *building* chŏmnyŏnghada 점령하다; *market share etc* hoekttŭk'ada 획득하다; (*portray*) p'och'ak'ada 포착하다
car chadongch'a 자동차; (*of train*) ch'aryang 차량; ***by ~*** chadongch'aro 자동차로
carafe pyŏng 병
carat k'aerŏt 캐럿
carbohydrate t'ansuhwamul 탄수화물
carbonated *drink* t'ansanŭi 탄산의
carbon monoxide ilssanhwat'anso 일산화탄소
carbureter, **carburetor** k'aburet'ŏ 카부레터
carcinogen param multchil 발암 물질
carcinogenic paramsŏng-ŭi 발암성의
card k'adŭ 카드; (*post~*) yŏpssŏ 엽서; (*business ~*) myŏngham 명함
cardboard p'anji 판지
cardiac shimjang-ŭi 심장의
cardiac arrest shimjang chŏngji 심장 정지
cardigan k'adigŏn 카디건
card index k'adŭshik saegin 카드식 색인

card key k'adŭro toen yŏlssoe 카드로 된 열쇠
care 1 *n* (*of baby*, *pet*) tolbom 돌봄; (*of the elderly*) posalp'im 보살핌; (*of sick person*) kanho 간호; (*medical ~*) ch'iryo 치료; (*worry*) kŏktchŏng 걱정; **~ *of*** → ***c / o***; ***take ~*** (*be cautious*) choshimhada 조심하다; ***take ~*** (***of yourself***)***!*** (*goodbye*) choshimhaesŏ kaseyo! 조심해서 가세요!; ***take ~ of*** *baby*, *dog* tolboda 돌보다; *tool*, *house*, *garden* sojunghi hada 소중히 하다; (*deal with*) ch'ŏrihada 처리하다; (***handle***) ***with ~!*** (*on label*) ch'wigŭp chuŭi 취급 주의 **2** *v/i* kwanshimŭl kajida 관심을 가지다; ***I don't ~!*** sanggwan ŏpssŏ! 상관 없어!; ***I couldn't ~ less*** chŏnhyŏ kwanshimi ŏpssŏ 전혀 관심이 없어
♦**care about** …e kwanshimŭl kajida …에 관심을 가지다
♦**care for** (*look after*) tolboda 돌보다; (*like*, *be fond of*) choahada 좋아하다; ***would you ~ …?*** …ŭl / rŭl chom tŭshigessŏyo? …을 / 를 좀 드시겠어요?
career (*profession*) kyŏngnyŏk 경력; (*path through life*) saeng-ae 생애
carefree amu kŏktchŏng ŏmnŭn 아무 걱정 없는
careful (*cautious*) choshimsŏng innŭn 조심성 있는; (*thorough*) shinjunghan 신중한; (***be***) ***~!*** choshimhae! 조심해!
carefully (*with caution*) choshimsŭrŏpkke 조심스럽게; *worded etc* shinjunghage 신중하게
careless choshimsŏng ŏmnŭn 조심성 없는; ***you are so ~!*** nŏnŭn nŏmu choshimsŏng-i ŏpkkuna! 너는 너무 조심성이 없구나!
caress 1 *n* aemu 애무 **2** *v/t* aemuhada 애무하다
caretaker kwalliin 관리인
careworn kŏktchŏng-e shidallin 걱정에 시달린
cargo sŏnjŏk hwamul 선적 화물
caricature *n* p'ungja manhwa 풍자 만화
caring *adj* chal tolbonŭn 잘 돌보는
carnage taehakssal 대학살
carnation k'aneishyŏn 카네이션
carnival ch'uktche 축제; (*amusement park*) yuwŏnji 유원지
carol *n* ch'uk-kka 축가
carousel (*at airport*) hoejŏnshik k'onbeiŏ 회전식 콘베이어; (*for slide projector*) hwandŭnggi p'illŭm k'arusel 환등기 필름 카루셀; (*merry-go-round*) hoejŏn mongma 회전 목마
carpenter mokssu 목수
carpet k'ap'et 카펫
carpool 1 *n* chagayong-ŭi hapssŭng iyong 자가용의 합승 이용 **2** *v/i* chagayong-ŭl hapssŭng-ŭro iyonghada 자가용을 합승으로 이용하다
car port kani ch'ago 간이 차고
carrier (*company*) unsong hoesa 운송 회사; (*of disease*) pogyunja 보균자
carrot tanggŭn 당근
carry 1 *v/t* (*in hand*) tŭlgo kada 들고 가다; (*from one place to another*) narŭda 나르다; (*have on one's person*) chinigo tanida 지니고 다니다; (*of pregnant woman*) paego it-tta 배고 있다; *disease* omgida 옮기다; (*of ship*, *plane*, *bus etc*) narŭda 나르다; *proposal* t'onggwashik'ida 통과시키다; ***get carried away*** nŏkssŭl ilt'a 넋을 잃다 **2** *v/i* (*of sound*) irŭda 이르다
♦**carry on 1** *v/i* (*continue*) kyesok'ada 계속하다; (*make a fuss*) soranŭl p'iuda 소란을 피우다; (*have an affair*) paramŭl p'iuda 바람을 피우다 **2** *v/t* (*conduct*) haenagada 해나가다
♦**carry out** *survey etc* shilsshihada 실시하다; *orders etc* shirhaenghada 실행하다
car seat (*for child*) ŏriniyong chwasŏk 어린이용 좌석
cart chimmach'a 짐마차
cartel k'arŭt'el 카르텔
carton (*for storage*, *transport*) pakssŭ 박스; (*for eggs*) kwak 곽; (*for milk etc*) p'aek 팩; (*of cigarettes*) kap 갑
cartoon (*in newspaper*, *magazine*) manhwa 만화; (*on TV*, *movie*) manhwa yŏnghwa 만화 영화

cartridge (*for gun*) t'anyakt'ong 탄약통
carve *meat* charŭda 자르다; *wood* saegida 새기다
carving (*figure*) chogak 조각
car wash ch'a sech'ŏk 차 세척
case[1] (*container*) k'eisŭ 케이스; (*of Scotch, wine*) sangja 상자; *Br* (*suitcase*) otkkabang 옷가방
case[2] *n* (*instance*) kyŏng-u 경우; (*argument*) chujang 주장; (*for investigation*) sakkŏn 사건; MED pyŏngse 병세; LAW sosong sakkŏn 소송 사건; ***in ~ …*** manil … hal kyŏng-urŭl saenggak'ayŏ 만일 … 할 경우를 생각하여; ***in ~ it rains*** manil piga ol kyŏng-urŭl saenggak'ayŏ 만일 비가 올 경우를 생각하여; ***in any ~*** ŏtchaettŭn 어쨋든; ***in that ~*** kŭrŏn kyŏng-ue 그런 경우에
case history MED pyŏngnyŏk 병력
cash 1 *n* hyŏn-gŭm 현금; ***~ down*** kŭ charieso hyŏn-gŭmŭro 그 자리에서 현금으로; ***pay*** (***in***) ~ hyŏn-gŭmŭro naeda 현금으로 내다; ***~ in advance*** sŏn-gŭm 선금 **2** *v/t check* hyŏn-gŭmŭro pakkuda 현금으로 바꾸다
♦**cash in on** …(ŭ)ro tonŭl pŏlda …(으)로 돈을 벌다
cash cow kiŏbŭi hŭktcha hoesa 기업의 흑자 회사; **cash desk** kyesandae 계산대; **cash discount** hyŏn-gŭm harin 현금 할인; **cash flow** hyŏn-gŭm yuch'urip 현금 유출입
cashier *n* (*in store etc*) ch'ullabwŏn 출납원
cash machine hyŏn-gŭm inch'ulgi 현금 인출기
cashmere *adj* k'aeshimiŏ 캐시미어
cash register kŭmjŏn tŭngnok-kki 금전 등록기
casino k'ajino 카지노
casket (*coffin*) kwan 관
cassette nogŭm t'eip'ŭ 녹음 테이프
cassette player nogŭmgi 녹음기
cassette recorder nogŭmgi 녹음기
cast 1 *n* (*of play*) ch'uryŏnjin 출연진; (*mold*) chuhyŏng 주형 **2** *v/t doubt, suspicion* irŭk'ida 일으키다; *metal* chujohada 주조하다; *play* paeurŭl chŏnghada 배우를 정하다; *actor* paeyŏgŭl chŏnghada 배역을 정하다
♦**cast off** *v/i* (*of ship*) pattchurŭl p'ulda 밧줄을 풀다
caste k'asŭt'ŭ chedo 카스트 제도
caster (*on chair etc*) tari pak'wi 다리 바퀴
cast iron *n* musoe 무쇠
cast-iron *adj* musoero mandŭn 무쇠로 만든
castle sŏng 성
castrate kŏsehada 거세하다
casual (*chance*) uyŏnhan 우연한; (*offhand*) mugwanshimhan 무관심한; (*not formal*) p'yŏngsang-ŭi 평상의; (*not permanent*) ilsshijŏgin 일시적인
casualty sasangja 사상자
casual wear p'yŏngsangbok 평상복
cat koyang-i 고양이
catalog *n* mongnok 목록
catalyst *fig* ch'oktchinje 촉진제
catalytic converter ch'ongmae k'ŏnbŏt'ŏ 촉매 컨버터
catastrophe ch'ŏnjaejibyŏn 천재지변
catch 1 *n* chapkki 잡기; (*of fish*) nakkŭn kŏt 낚은 것; (*locking device*) kori 고리; (*problem*) munje 문제 **2** *v/t ball, escaped prisoner, fish* chaptta 잡다; (*bus, train*) chaba t'ada 잡아 타다; (*in order to speak to*) ttarajaptta 따라잡다; (*hear*) ara tŭt-tta 알아 듣다; *illness* …e kŏllida …에 걸리다; ~ (***a***) ***cold*** kamgie kŏllida 감기에 걸리다; ***~ s.o.'s eye*** (*of person, object*) nuguŭi shisŏnŭl kkŭlda 누구의 시선을 끌다; ***~ sight of*** …ŭl / rŭl hŭlkkŭt poda …을 / 를 흘끗 보다; ***~ X doing Y*** Xi / ga Yhago innŭn changmyŏnŭl puttchaptta X이 / 가 Y하고 있는 장면을 붙잡다
♦**catch on** (*become popular*) in-girŭl ŏt-tta 인기를 얻다; (*understand*) ihaehada 이해하다
♦**catch up** *v/i* ttarajaptta 따라잡다
♦**catch up on** ...ŭl/rŭl poch'unghada ...을/를 보충하다
catch-22: ***it's a ~ situation*** pujorihan sanghwang-ida 부조리한 상황이다

catcher (*in baseball*) k'aech'ŏ 캐처
catching *disease* chŏnyŏmsŏng-ŭi 전염성의; *fear*, *panic* ŏmssŭp'anŭn 엄습하는
catchy *tune* kŭmbang shwipkke oewŏjinŭn 금방 쉽게 외워지는
category pŏmju 범주
♦**cater for** (*meet the needs of*) …ŭi kumie mat-tta …의 구미에 맞다; (*provide food for*) …ŭl/rŭl wihan yorirŭl chegonghada …을/를 위한 요리를 제공하다
caterer yori chodaltcha 요리 조달자
caterpillar yuch'ung 유충
cathedral sŏngdang 성당
Catholic 1 *adj* Ch'ŏnjugyoŭi 천주교의 **2** *n* Ch'ŏnjugyo shinja 천주교 신자
catsup k'ech'ŏp 케첩
cattle so 소
catty pianyanggŏrinŭn 비아냥거리는
cauliflower k'ollip'ŭllawŏ 콜리플라워
cause 1 *n* wŏnin 원인; (*grounds*) iyu 이유; (*aim of movement*) moktchŏk 목적 **2** *v/t* irŭk'ida 일으키다
caution 1 *n* (*care*) choshim 조심; ***~ is advised*** choshimhaeya hamnida 조심해야 합니다 **2** *v/t* (*warn*) chuŭishik'ida 주의시키다
cautious choshimsŭrŏun 조심스러운
cave tonggul 동굴
♦**cave in** (*of roof*) ump'uk kkŏjida 움푹 꺼지다
caviar ch'ŏlgap sang-ŏ aljŏt 철갑 상어 알젓
cavity ch'ungch'i 충치
CBS (= ***Christian Broadcasting System***) Kidok-kkyo Pangsong 기독교 방송
cc 1 *n* saboni ponaejim 사본이 보내짐 **2** *v/t* sabonŭl ponaeda 사본을 보내다
CD (= ***compact disc***) k'omp'aekt'ŭ tisŭk'ŭ 콤팩트 디스크
CD player CD p'ŭlleiŏ CD 플레이어
CD-ROM sshidirom 씨디롬
CD-ROM drive sshidirom tŭraibŭ 씨디롬 드라이브
cease 1 *v/i* chungdanhada 중단하다 **2** *v/t* chungdanshik'ida 중단시키다
ceasefire hyujŏn 휴전
ceiling (*of room*) ch'ŏnjang 천장; (*limit*) ch'oego hando 최고 한도
celadon ware ch'ŏngja 청자
celebrate 1 *v/i* ch'uk'ahada 축하하다 **2** *v/t* ch'uk'ahada 축하하다; (*observe*) chinaeda 지내다
celebrated yumyŏnghan 유명한; ***be ~ for*** …(ŭ)ro yumyŏnghada ..(으)로 유명하다
celebration ch'uk'ayŏn 축하연
celebrity yumyŏng insa 유명 인사
celery sellŏri 셀러리
cell (*for prisoner*) kambang 감방; BIO sep'o 세포; COMPUT p'yok'an 표칸
cellar chihashil 지하실
cello ch'ello 첼로
cellophane sellop'an 셀로판
cell(ular) phone haendŭp'on 핸드폰, idong chŏnhwa 이동 전화
Celsius sŏpsshi 섭씨
cement 1 *n* shiment'ŭ 시멘트 **2** *v/t* shiment'ŭro parŭda 시멘트로 바르다; *friendship* kuch'ida 굳히다
cemetery myoji 묘지
censor *v/t* kŏmyŏrhada 검열하다
censorship kŏmyŏl chedo 검열 제도
cent sent'ŭ 센트
centennial paek chunyŏn 백 주년
center 1 *n* (*middle*) han-gaunde 한가운데; (*building*) sent'ŏ 센터; (*region*) chungshimji 중심지; POL chungdop'a 중도파; ***in the ~ of*** …ŭi han-gaundee(sŏ) …의 한가운데에(서) **2** *v/t* han-gaundero tuda 한가운데로 두다
♦**center on** …e chungshimŭl tuda …에 중심을 두다
centigrade sŏpsshi 섭씨; ***10 degrees ~*** sŏpsshi 10to 섭씨 10도
centimeter sent'i(mit'ŏ) 센티(미터)
central chungshimŭi 중심의; *location*, *apartment* chungshimbue innŭn 중심부에 있는; (*main*) chuyohan 주요한; ***~ France*** P'ŭrangsŭ chungbu 프랑스 중부; ***be ~ to sth*** muŏse chungshimjŏgida 무엇에 중심적이다
central heating chung-ang chamgŭm changch'i 중앙 잠금 장치
centralize chiptchung kyŏrŭihada 집중 결의하다
central locking MOT chung-ang anjŏn changch'i 중앙 안전 장치

central processing unit → ***CPU***
century segi 세기
CEO (= ***Chief Executive Officer***) ch'oego kyŏngnyŏngja 최고 경영자
ceramic tojagiro toen 도자기로 된
ceramics (*objects*) tojagi 도자기; (*art*) toye 도예
cereal (*grain*) kongmul 곡물; ***breakfast ~*** shiriŏl 시리얼
ceremonial 1 *adj* ŭishigŭl wihan 의식을 위한 **2** *n* ŭishik 의식
ceremony (*event*) shik 식; (*ritual*) ŭishik 의식; ***the Oscars ~*** Osŭk'a shisangshik 오스카 시상식; ***opening ~ / closing ~*** kaehoeshik / p'yehoeshik 개회식 / 폐회식
certain (*sure*) hwaksshinhanŭn 확신하는; (*particular*) ottŏn 어떤; (*specific*) iltchŏnghan 일정한; ***it's ~ that*** ...ranŭn kŏsŭn hwaksshirada ... 라는 것은 확실하다; ***a ~ Mr Park*** Pak mosshi 박 모씨; ***make ~*** hwaginhada 확인하다; ***know / say for ~*** hwaksshirhi alda / marhada 확실히 알다 /말하다
certainly (*definitely*) hwaksshirhi 확실히; (*of course*) mullon 물론; ***~ not!*** mullon andwaeji! 물론 안돼지!
certainty (*confidence*) hwaksshin 확신; (*inevitability*) hwaksshilssŏng 확실성; ***it's / he's a ~*** kŭgŏsŭn / kŭnŭn hwaksshirhada 그것은 / 그는 확실하다
certificate (*qualification*) chagyŏktchŭng 자격증; (*official paper*) chŭngmyŏngsŏ 증명서
certified public accountant kong-in hoegyesa 공인 회계사
certify pojŭnghada 보증하다
Cesarean *n* chewang chŏlgae 제왕 절개
cessation chungji 중지; ***~ of hostilities*** hyujŏn 휴전
CFC (= ***chlorofluorocarbon***) sshiep'ŭsshi 씨에프씨
chain 1 *n* (*for animal, anchor*) soesasŭl 쇠사슬; (*jewelry*) mokkkŏrijul 목걸이줄; (*for bicycle, tire*) ch'ein 체인; (*of stores, hotels*) ch'einjom 체인점 **2** *v/t*: ***~ X to Y*** Xŭl / rŭl Ye sasŭllo muktta X을 / 를 Y에 사슬로 묶다
chain reaction yŏnswae panŭng 연쇄 반응; **chain smoke** chuldambaerŭl p'iuda 줄담배를 피우다; **chain smoker** chuldambaerŭl p'iunŭn saram 줄담배를 피우는 사람; **chain store** yŏnswaejŏm 연쇄점
chair 1 *n* ŭija 의자; (*arm~*) allak ŭija 안락 의자; (*at university*) chŏnggyosujik 정교수직; ***the ~*** (*electric*) chŏn-gi ŭija 전기 의자; (*at meeting*) ŭijang 의장; ***take the ~*** ŭijangjigŭl mat-tta 의장직을 맡다 **2** *v/t meeting* ŭijangjigŭl mat-tta 의장직을 맡다
chair lift ch'eŏ lip'ŭt'ŭ 체어 리프트; **chairman** ŭijang 의장; **chairperson** sahoeja 사회자; **chairwoman** sahoeja 사회자
chalk (*for writing*) punp'il 분필; (*in soil*) sŏk'oeam 석회암
challenge 1 *n* (*difficult task*) haebol manhan il 해볼 만한 일; (*in race, competition*) tojŏn 도전 **2** *v/t* (*to race, debate*) tojŏnhada 도전하다; (*call into question*) hwan-gishik'ida 환기시키다
challenger tojŏnja 도전자
challenging nŭngnyŏgŭl shihŏmhaebonŭn 능력을 시험해보는
chambermaid kaekshil tamdang yŏjong-ŏbwŏn 객실 담당 여종업원
Chamber of Commerce Sanggong hoeŭiso 상공 회의소
chamois (leather) shyaemi kajuk 섀미 가죽
champagne shyamp'ein 샴페인
champion 1 *n* SP ch'aemp'iŏn 챔피언; (*of cause*) onghoja 옹호자 **2** *v/t* (*cause*) onghohada 옹호하다
championship (*event*) sŏnsugwŏn taehoe 선수권 대회; (*title*) sŏnsugwŏn 선수권
chance (*possibility*) kamang 가망; (*opportunity*) kihoe 기회; (*risk*) wihŏm 위험; (*luck*) uyŏn 우연; ***by ~*** uyŏnhi 우연히; ***take a ~*** une matkkigo haeboda 운에 맡기고 해보다; ***I'm not taking any ~s*** yohaengsurŭl paraji anssŭmnida 요행수를 바라지 않습니다

chandelier shyangdŭllie 샹들리에
change 1 *n* (*to plan, idea etc*) pyŏnhwa 변화; (*small coins, from purchase*) chandon 잔돈; (*different situation etc*) kibun chŏnhwan 기분 전환; ***for a ~*** kibun chŏnhwanŭro 기분 전환으로; ***a ~ of clothes*** karaibŭl ot 가라입을 옷 **2** *v/t* (*alter*) pakkuda 바꾸다; *world, society* pyŏnhwashik'ida 변화시키다; *bankbill* pakkuŏ chuda 바꾸어 주다; (*replace*) kalda 갈다; *trains, planes* karat'ada 갈아타다; *one's clothes* pakkuŏ iptta 바꾸어 입다 **3** *v/i* pakkuŏjida 바뀌어지다; (*of world, society*) pyŏnhwahada 변화하다; (*put on different clothes*) pakkuŏ iptta 바꾸어 입다; (*take different train etc*) karat'ada 갈아타다
channel (*on TV, radio*) ch'aenŏl 채널; (*waterway*) suro 수로
chant 1 *n* norae 노래 **2** *v/i* noraehada 노래하다
chaos taehollan 대혼란
chaotic hollansŭrŏun 혼란스러운
chapel yebaedang 예배당
chapped salgach'i t'ŭn 살갗이 튼
chapter (*of book*) chang 장; (*of organization*) chibu 지부
character (*nature*) sŏngkkyŏk 성격; (*person*) inmul 인물; (*in book, play*) tŭngjang inmul 등장 인물; (*special aura*) t'ŭktching 특징; (*letter*) muntcha 문자; ***he's a real ~*** kŭnŭn taedanhan inmuriyeyo 그는 대단한 인물이에요
characteristic 1 *n* t'ŭkssŏng 특성 **2** *adj* t'ŭkssŏng-ŭl nat'anaenŭn 특성을 나타내는
characterize (*be typical of*) …ŭi t'ŭkssŏng-ŭl nat'anaeda …의 특성을 나타내다; (*describe*) sŏngkkyŏgŭl myosahada 성격을 묘사하다
character set COMPUT munjap'yo 문자표
charbroiled sutppure kuwŏjin 숯불에 구워진
charcoal (*for barbecue*) sut 숯; (*for drawing*) mokt'an 목탄
charge 1 *n* (*fee*) yogŭm 요금; LAW hyŏmŭi 혐의; ***free of ~*** muryoro 무료로; ***will that be cash or ~?*** hyŏn-gŭmimnikka, oesang-imnikka? 현금입니까, 외상입니까?; ***be in ~*** tamdang-ida 담당이다; ***take ~*** ttŏmat-tta 떠맡다 **2** *v/t sum of money* ch'ŏngguhada 청구하다; (*put on account*) ap'ŭro taranot'a 앞으로 달아놓다; LAW kobarhada 고발하다; *battery* ch'ungjŏnshik'ida 충전시키다 **3** *v/i* (*attack*) tolgyŏk'ada 돌격하다
charge account oesang kŏrae 외상 거래
charge card shinyong k'adŭ 신용 카드
charisma k'arisŭma 카리스마
charitable *institution, donation* chasŏnŭi 자선의; *person* chasŏnshimi manŭn 자선심이 많은
charity (*assistance*) chasŏn 자선; (*organization*) chasŏn tanch'e 자선 단체
charm 1 *n* (*appealing quality*) maeryŏk 매력 **2** *v/t* (*delight*) maehok'ada 매혹하다
charming maehoktchŏgin 매혹적인
charred kŭsŭllin 그슬린
chart (*diagram*) top'yo 도표; NAUT haedo 해도; (*for airplane*) ch'yat'ŭ 챠트; ***the ~s*** MUS hit'ŭgok sunwi 히트곡 순위
charter *v/t* chŏnse naeda 전세 내다
charter flight chŏnsegi 전세기
chase 1 *n* ch'ugyŏk 추격 **2** *v/t* twitchot-tta 뒤쫓다
♦**chase away** tchoch'abŏrida 쫓아버리다
chaser (*drink*) ch'eisŏ 체이서
chassis (*of car*) shyaeshi 섀시
chat 1 *n* chapttam 잡담 **2** *v/i* chapttamhada 잡담하다
chatter 1 *n* suda 수다 **2** *v/i* (*talk*) suda ttŏlda 수다 떨다; (*of teeth*) tŏldŏl ttŏllida 덜덜 떨리다
chatterbox sudajaeng-i 수다쟁이
chatty *person* sudasŭrŏun 수다스러운; *letter* hŏmurŏmnŭn 허물없는
chauffeur *n* chagayong unjŏnsa 자가용 운전사
chauvinist (*male ~*) namsŏng uwŏltchuŭija 남성 우월주의자
cheap *adj* (*inexpensive*) ssan 싼;

(*nasty*) piyŏrhan 비열한; (*mean*) insaek'an 인색한

cheat 1 *n* (*person*) sogimsu 속임수 **2** *v/t* sogida 속이다; **~ X out of Y** Yŭl/rŭl sogyŏsŏ Xŭl/rŭl ppaeat-tta Y을/를 속여서 X을/를 빼앗다 **3** *v/i* (*in exam, cards etc*) sogimsurŭl ssŭda 속임수를 쓰다; **~ on one's wife** anae mollae param p'iuda 아내 몰래 바람 피우다

check[1] **1** *adj shirt* ch'ek'ŭ munŭiŭi 체크 무늬의 **2** *n* ch'ek'ŭ munŭi 체크 무늬

check[2] FIN sup'yo 수표; (*in restaurant etc*) kyesansŏ 계산서; **~ please** kyesanhae chuseyo 계산해 주세요

check[3] **1** *n* (*to verify sth*) hwagin 확인; **keep in ~, hold in ~** ŏktchehada 억제하다; **keep a ~ on** hwaginhae tuda 확인해 두다 **2** *v/t* (*verify*) hwaginhada 확인하다; (*inspect*) chŏmgŏmhada 점검하다; (*restrain*) ŏktchehada 억제하다; (*stop*) maktta 막다; (*with a ~mark*) ch'ekk'ŭ p'yoshirŭl hada 첵크 표시를 하다; *coat, package etc* pogwansoe matkkida 보관소에 맡기다 **3** *v/i* hwaginhae chuda 확인해 주다; **~ for** hwaginhada 확인하다

♦**check in** (*at airport*) t'apssŭng susogŭl hada 탑승 수속을 하다; (*at hotel*) ch'ek'ŭinhada 체크인하다

♦**check off** taejo p'yoshirŭl hada 대조 표시를 하다

♦**check on** salp'yŏboda 살펴보다

♦**check out 1** *v/i* (*of hotel*) ch'ek'ŭaut'ada 체크아웃하다 **2** *v/t* (*look into*) chosahada 조사하다; *club, restaurant etc* tŭllyŏboda 들려보다

♦**check up on** ... ŭl/rŭl naeryŏgŭl chosahada ...을/를 내력을 조사하다

♦**check with** (*of person*) ...wa/kwa mŏnjŏ araboda ... 와/과 먼저 알아보다; (*of information*) ...wa/kwa ilch'ihada ...와/과 일치하다

checkbook sup'yoch'aek 수표책

checked *material* ch'ek'ŭ munŭiŭi 체크 무늬의

checkerboard sŏyang changgip'an 서양 장기판

checkered *pattern* ch'ek'ŭ munŭiŭi 체크 무늬의; *career* p'aranmanjanghan 파란만장한

checkers sŏyang changgi 서양 장기

check-in (counter) t'apssŭng susok k'aunt'ŏ 탑승 수속 카운터

checking account tangjwa yegŭm kujwa 당좌 예금 구좌

check-in time (*in hotel*) t'usuk shigan 투숙 시간; (*at airport*) t'apssŭng susok shigan 탑승 수속 시간; **checklist** taejop'yo 대조표; **checkmark** ch'ek'ŭ p'yoshi 체크 표시; **checkmate** *n* changgun 장군; **checkout** kyesandae 계산대; **checkout time** pang-ŭl naeŏjul shigan 방을 내어줄 시간; **checkpoint** MIL kŏmmunso 검문소; (*in race etc*) ch'ek'ŭp'oint'ŭ 체크포인트; **checkroom** (*for coats*) hyudaep'um pogwanso 휴대품 보관소; (*for baggage*) suhamul pogwanso 수하물 보관소; **checkup** MED kŏn-gang chindan 건강 진단; (*dental*) ch'ia kŏmsa 치아 검사

cheek (*of face*) ppyam 뺨

cheekbone kwangdaeppyŏ 광대뼈

cheer 1 *n* hwanho 환호; **~s!** (*toast*) kŏnbae! 건배! **2** *v/t & v/i* hwanhohada 환호하다

♦**cheer on** ŭng-wŏnhada 응원하다

♦**cheer up 1** *v/i* kiuni nada 기운이 나다; **~!** kiun nae! 기운 내! **2** *v/t* kiunŭl na-ege hada 기운을 내게 하다

cheerful myŏngnanghan 명랑한

cheering hwanho 환호

cheerleader ch'iŏridŏ 치어리더

cheese ch'ijŭ 치즈

cheeseburger ch'ijŭbŏgŏ 치즈버거

cheesecake ch'ijŭk'eik 치즈케익

chef chubangjang 주방장

Cheju Island Chejudo 제주도

chemical 1 *adj* hwahagŭi 화학의 **2** *n* hwahak chep'um 화학 제품

chemical warfare hwahaktchŏn 화학전

chemist hwahaktcha 화학자

chemistry hwahak 화학; *fig* sŏnggyŏgi mannŭn yŏbu 성격이 맞는 여부

chemotherapy hwahak yoppŏp 화학 요법
cherish sojunghi hada 소중히 하다; *memory*, *hope* sojunghi kanjik'ada 소중히 간직하다
cherry (*fruit*) p'ŏtchi 버찌; (*tree*) pŏnnamu 벚나무
chess ch'esŭ 체스
chessboard ch'esŭp'an 체스판
chest (*of person*) kasŭm 가슴; (*box*) changnong 장롱
chestnut pam 밤; (*tree*) pamnanu 밤나무
chest of drawers sŏraptchang 서랍장
chew *v/t* sshiptta 씹다
♦**chew out** F hodoege kkujit-tta 호되게 꾸짖다
chewing gum kkŏm 껌
chick pyŏng-ari 병아리; F (*girl*) kyejibae 계집애
chicken 1 *n* tak 닭; (*food*) tak-kkogi 닭고기; F kŏptchaeng-i 겁쟁이 **2** *adj* F (*cowardly*) kŏbŭl mŏgŭn 겁을 먹은
♦**chicken out** kŏbŭl mŏk-kko mullŏsŏda 겁을 먹고 물러서다
chickenfeed F saebarŭi p'i 새발의 피
chicken pox sudu 수두
chief 1 *n* (*head*) chang 장; (*of tribe*) choktchang 족장 **2** *adj* chuyohan 주요한
chiefly churo 주로
chilblain tongsang 동상
child ai 아이; *pej* yuch'ihan saram 유치한 사람
childbirth haesan 해산
childhood ŏrinshijŏl 어린시절
childish *pej* yuch'ihan 유치한
childless ai ŏmnŭn 아이 없는
childlike ch'ŏnjinhan 천진한
Children's Day Ŏrininal 어린이날
chill 1 *n* (*in air*) han-gi 한기; (*illness*) kamgi 감기 **2** *v/t* (*wine*) ch'age hada 차게 하다
chilli (pepper) koch'u 고추
chilli (pepper) powder koch'ugaru 고추가루
chilly *weather* ssalssarhan 쌀쌀한; *welcome* naengdamhan 냉담한; ***I'm ~*** ssalssarhaneyo 쌀쌀하네요
chime *v/i* chong-i ullida 종이 울리다
chimney kulttuk 굴뚝
chimpanzee ch'imp'anji 침판지
chin t'ŏk 턱
China Chungguk 중국
china chagi 자기; (*material*) chagi kŭrŭt 자기 그릇
Chinese 1 *adj* Chungguguĭ 중국의 **2** *n* (*language*) Chunggugŏ 중국어; (*person*) Chungguk saram 중국 사람
Chinese cabbage paech'u 배추; **Chinese character** hantcha 한자; **Chinese character dictionary** okp'yŏn 옥편; **Chinese herbal medicine** hanyak 한약; **Chinese medicine clinic** hanŭiwŏn 한의원
Chin Island Chindo 진도
chink (*gap*) t'ŭm 틈; (*sound*) taenggŭranghanŭn sori 댕그랑하는 소리
chip 1 *n* (*fragment*) t'omak 토막; (*damage*) i ppajin chaguk 이 빠진 자국; (*in gambling*), COMPUT ch'ip 칩; ***~s*** p'ot'eit'o ch'ipssŭ 포테이토 칩스 **2** *v/t* (*damage*) iga ppajida 이가 빠지다
♦**chip in** (*interrupt*) malch'amgyŏnhada 말참견하다; (*with money*) chogŭmsshik tonŭl naeda 조금씩 돈을 내다
chipset COMPUT ch'ipset 칩셋
chiropractor ch'ŏkch'u chiapssa 척추 지압사
chirp *v/i* chijŏgwida 지저귀다
chisel *n* kkŭl 끌
chivalrous kisadojŏgin 기사도적인
chives kolp'aŭi ip 골파의 잎
chlorine yŏmso 염소
chockfull kkwak tŭrŏch'an 꽉 들어찬
chocolate ch'ok'ollit 초콜릿; ***hot ~*** hat ch'ok'ollit 핫 초콜릿
chocolate cake ch'ok'ollit k'eik 초콜릿 케익
choice 1 *n* sŏnt'aek 선택; (*selection*) sŏnt'aegŭi pŏmwi 선택의 범위; ***I had no ~*** sŏnt'aegŭi yŏjiga ŏpssŏt-tta 선택의 여지가 없었다 **2** *adj* (*top quality*) t'ŭkssang-ŭi 특상의
choir hapch'angdan 합창단
choke 1 *n* MOT ch'ok'ŭ 초크 **2** *v/i* mogi maeida 목이 매이다; ***he ~d on a bone*** kŭnŭn kashiga kŏllyŏ mogi

maeyŏt-tta 그는 가시가 걸려 목이 매였다 **3** *v/t* mogŭl chorŭda 목을 조르다
cholesterol k'ollesŭt'erol 콜레스테롤
choose *v/t & v/i* sŏnt'aek'ada 선택하다
choosey F kkadaroun 까다로운
chop 1 *n* tchigŏ naegi 찍어 내기; (*meat*) tukkŏpkke charŭn kogittchŏm 두껍게 자른 고깃점 **2** *v/t wood* p'aeda 패다; *meat, vegetables* ssŏlda 썰다
♦**chop down** *tree* p'aenŏmgida 패넘기다
chopper (*tool*) tokki 도끼; F (*helicopter*) hellik'opt'ŏ 헬리콥터
chopsticks chŏtkkarak 젓가락
chord MUS hyŏn 현
chore chiban il 집안 일
choreographer anmuga 안무가
choreography anmu 안무
chorus (*singers*) hapch'angdan 합창단; (*of song*) hapch'ang 합창
Choson Chosŏn 조선
Christ Kŭrisŭdo 그리스도; *~!* chegirŏl! 제기럴!
christen seryehada 세례하다
Christian 1 *n* Kidok-kkyo shinja 기독교 신자 **2** *adj* Kidok-kkyoŭi 기독교의; *attitude* in-ganjŏgin 인간적인
Christian Broadcasting System Kidok-kkyo Pangsong 기독교 방송
Christianity Kidok-kkyo 기독교
Christian name seryemyŏng 세례명
Christmas Sŏngt'anjŏl 성탄절; ***at ~*** Sŏngt'anjŏre 성탄절에; ***Merry ~!*** meri K'ŭrisŭmasŭ! 메리 크리스마스!
Christmas card K'ŭrisŭmasŭ k'adŭ 크리스마스 카드; **Christmas Day** Sŏngt'anjŏl 성탄절; **Christmas Eve** K'ŭrisŭmasŭ ibŭ 크리스마스 이브; **Christmas present** K'ŭrisŭmasŭ sŏnmul 크리스마스 선물; **Christmas tree** K'ŭrisŭmasŭ t'ŭri 크리스마스 트리
chrome, chromium k'ŭrom 크롬
chronic mansŏng-ŭi 만성의
chronological yŏndaesunŭi 연대순의; ***in ~ order*** yŏndaesunŭro 연대순으로
chrysanthemum kuk'wa 국화
chubby t'ongt'onghan 통통한
chuck *v/t* F naedŏnjida 내던지다
♦**chuck out** *object* naebŏrida 내버리다; *person* naetchot-tta 내쫓다
chuckle 1 *n* k'ilk'il usŭm 킬킬 웃음 **2** *v/i* k'ilk'il ut-tta 킬킬 웃다
chunk k'ŭn tŏng-ŏri 큰 덩어리
church kyohoe 교회
chute hwalgangno 활강로; (*for garbage*) ssŭregi t'ongno 쓰레기 통로
CIA (= ***Central Intelligence Agency***) Miguk chung-ang chŏngbobu 미국 중앙 정보부
cider sagwa chusŭ 사과 주스
CIF (= ***cost insurance freight***) unim mit pohŏm p'oham kagyŏk 운임 및 보험 포함 가격
cigar yŏsong-yŏn 여송연
cigarette tambae 담배
cinema (*industry*) yŏnghwa sanŏp 영화 산업; *Br* (*building*) yŏnghwagwan 영화관
cinnamon kyep'i 계피
circle 1 *n* wŏn 원; (*group*) chipttan 집단 **2** *v/t* (*draw circle around*) tonggŭramirŭl ch'ida 동그라미를 치다 **3** *v/i* (*of plane, bird*) pingbing tolda 빙빙 돌다
circuit hoero 회로
circuit board hoero kyegip'an 회로 계기판
circuit breaker hoero ch'adan-gi 회로 차단기
circular 1 *n* (*giving information*) hoeram 회람 **2** *adj* tunggŭn 둥근
circulate 1 *v/i* tolda 돌다 **2** *v/t* (*memo*) p'ŏttŭrida 퍼뜨리다
circulation BIO sunhwan 순환; (*of newspaper, magazine*) parhaeng pusu 발행 부수
circumference wŏnju 원주
circumstances sanghwang 상황; (*financial*) sangt'ae 상태; ***under no ~*** ŏttŏn sanghwang-esŏdo (+ *negative verb*) 어떤 상황에서도; ***under the ~*** kŭrŏn sanghwang-esŏnŭn 그런 상황에서는
circus sŏk'ŏsŭ 서커스
cistern mul t'aengk'ŭ 물 탱크
citizen shimin 시민

citizenship shiminkkwŏn 시민권
city toshi 도시; ~ ***center*** toshiŭi chungshim 도시의 중심; ~ ***hall*** shich'ŏng 시청
civic *adj* shiŭi 시의; *pride, responsibilities* shiminŭi 시민의
civil (*not military*) min-ganŭi 민간의; *disobedience etc* shiminŭi 시민의; (*polite*) yeŭi parŭn 예의 바른
civil defense minbang-wi 민방위
civil engineer t'omok kisa 토목 기사
civilian 1 *n* min-ganin 민간인 **2** *adj clothes* ilbaninŭi 일반인의
civilization munmyŏng 문명
civilize *person* kaehwahada 개화하다
civil rights kongmin p'yŏngdŭngkkwŏn 공민 평등권; **civil servant** kongmuwŏn 공무원; **civil service** haengjŏng samu 행정 사무; **civil war** naejŏn 내전
claim 1 *n* (*for damages*) ch'ŏnggu 청구; (*right*) kwŏlli 권리; (*assertion*) chujang 주장 **2** *v/t* (*ask for as a right*) ch'ŏngguhada 청구하다; (*assert*), *property* chujanghada 주장하다; ***they have ~ed responsibility for the attack*** kŭdŭrŭn konggyŏge taehan ch'aegimŭl yoguhaet-tta 그들은 공격에 대한 책임을 요구했다
claimant yoguja 요구자; LAW wŏn-go 원고
clam taehap chogae 대합 조개
♦**clam up** F ibŭl tamulda 입을 다물다
clammy ch'ago kkŭnjŏk-kkŭnjŏk'an 차고 끈적끈적한
clamor (*noise*) ttŏdŭlssŏk'am 떠들썩함; (*outcry*) ausŏng 아우성
♦**clamor for** shikkŭrŏpkke yoguhada 시끄럽게 요구하다
clamp 1 *n* (*fastener*) choemsoe 죔쇠 **2** *v/t* (*fasten*) choemsoero choeda 죔쇠로 죄다
♦**clamp down** tansok'ada 단속하다
♦**clamp down on** kangnyŏk'i tansok'ada 강력히 단속하다
clan sshijok 씨족
clandestine pimirŭi 비밀의
clang 1 *n* ch'ŏlk'ŏdŏnghanŭn sori 철커덩하는 소리 **2** *v/i* ch'ŏlk'ŏdŏnghanŭn soriga nada 철커덩하는 소리가 나다
clap 1 *v/i* (*applaud*) pakssurŭl ch'ida 박수를 치다 **2** *v/t* pakssu ch'ida 박수 치다
clarify myŏnghwak'age hada 명확하게 하다
clarinet k'ŭllarinet 클라리넷
clarity myŏnghwak'am 명확함
clash 1 *n* ch'ungdol 충돌; (*of personalities*) purilch'i 불일치 **2** *v/i* ch'ungdorhada 충돌하다; (*of opinions*) purilch'ihada 불일치하다; (*of colors*) ŏulliji ant'a 어울리지 않다; (*of events*) kyŏpch'ida 겹치다
clasp 1 *n* kŏlssoe 걸쇠 **2** *v/t* (*in hand*) kkwak chwida 꽉 쥐다; (*to self*) kkyŏantta 껴안다
class 1 *n* (*lesson*) suŏp 수업; (*students in a ~*) hak-kkŭp 학급; (*social*) kyegŭp 계급; (*category*) puryu 부류 **2** *v/t* pullyuhada 분류하다
classic 1 *adj* (*typical*) chŏnhyŏngjŏgin 전형적인; (*definitive*) kwŏnwi innŭn 권위 있는 **2** *n* kojŏn 고전
classical *music* k'ŭllaeshik 클래식
classification (*activity*) tŭnggŭbŭl maegim 등급을 매김; (*category*) pullyu 분류
classified *information* kimirŭi 기밀의
classified ad(vertisement) hangmokppyŏl kwanggo 항목별 광고
classify (*categorize*) pullyuhada 분류하다
classmate tonggŭpssaeng 동급생; **classroom** kyoshil 교실; **class warfare** kyegŭp t'ujaeng 계급 투쟁
classy F kogŭbin 고급인; *person* p'umwi innŭn 품위 있는
clatter 1 *n* tŏlgŏdŏk'anŭn sori 덜거덕하는 소리 **2** *v/i* soransŭrŏn sorirŭl naemyŏ ppalli umjigida 소란스런 소리를 내며 빨리 움직이다
clause (*in agreement*) chohang 조항; GRAM chŏl 절
claustrophobia milsshil kongp'otchŭng 밀실 공포증
claw 1 *n* palt'op 발톱; *fig* ansanghage marŭn son-garak 앙상하게 마른 손가락 **2** *v/t* (*scratch*) halk'wida 할퀴다

clay chinhŭk 진흙
clean 1 *adj* kkaekkŭt'an 깨끗한 **2** *adv* F (*completely*) kkaekkŭshi 깨끗이 **3** *v/t* kkaekkŭt'age hada 깨끗하게 하다; *teeth, shoes* taktta 닦다; *house, room* ch'ŏngsohada 청소하다; *car, hands, face* sshit-tta 씻다; *clothes* ppalda 빨다; ***have sth ~ed*** muŏsŭl set'age matkkida 무엇을 세탁에 맡기다
♦**clean out** *room, cupboard* kkaekkŭt'age ch'ŏngsohada 깨끗하게 청소하다; *fig* pint'ŏlt'ŏriro mandŭlda 빈털털이로 만들다
♦**clean up 1** *v/t* ch'ŏngsohada 청소하다; *fig* ilssohada 일소하다 **2** *v/i* ch'ŏngsohada 청소하다; (*wash*) malssuk'aejida 말쑥해지다; (*on stock market etc*) k'ŭn tonŭl pŏlda 큰 돈을 벌다
cleaner ch'ŏngsobu 청소부; ***dry ~*** tŭraik'ŭllining set'aksso 드라이클리닝 세탁소
cleaning woman ch'ŏngsohanŭn ajumma 청소하는 아줌마
cleanse (*skin*) kkaekkŭt'age sshit-tta 깨끗하게 씻다
cleanser (*for skin*) k'ŭllenjŏ 클렌저
clear 1 *adj voice, weather, water, skin* malgŭn 맑은; (*bright*) palgŭn 밝은; *photograph, vision* tturyŏt'an 뚜렷한; (*easy to understand*) punmyŏnghan 분명한; (*obvious*) myŏngbaek'an 명백한; *thinker* myŏngsŏk'an 명석한; ***I'm not ~ about it*** musŭn irinji punmyŏnghaji anayo 무슨 일인지 분명하지 않아요; ***I didn't make myself ~*** nae shimjung-ŭl tturyŏt'age marhaji anassŏ 내 심중을 뚜렷하게 말하지 않았어 **2** *adv*: ***stand ~ of*** ...esŏ ttŏrŏjyŏsŏ sŏda ...에서 떨어져서 서다; ***steer ~ of*** ...e chŏpkkŭnhaji ant'a ...에 접근하지 않다 **3** *v/t roads etc* ch'iuda 치우다; (*acquit*) mujoero hada 무죄로 하다; (*authorize*) hŏgahada 허가하다; (*earn*) ...ŭi sunsuibŭl ollida ...의 순수입을 올리다; ***~ one's throat*** hŏtkkich'imhada 헛기침하다 **4** *v/i* (*of sky, mist*) kaeda 개다; (*of face*) palgajida 밝아지다
♦**clear away** *v/t* ch'iuda 치우다
♦**clear off** *v/i* sarajida 사라지다
♦**clear out 1** *v/t closet* piuda 비우다 **2** *v/i* kabŏrida 가버리다
♦**clear up 1** *v/i* chŏngdonhada 정돈하다; (*of weather*) kaeda 개다; (*of illness, rash*) nat-tta 낫다 **2** *v/t* (*tidy*) chŏngdonhada 정돈하다; *mystery, problem* p'ulda 풀다
clearance (*space*) t'ŭm 틈; (*authorization*) hŏga 허가
clearance sale chaego chŏngni seil 재고 정리 세일
clearly (*with clarity*) tturyŏt'age 뚜렷하게; (*evidently*) punmyŏnghi 분명히
clemency kwannyong 관용
clench *teeth* angmulda 악물다; *fist* kkwak chwida 꽉 쥐다
clergy sŏngjiktchadŭl 성직자들
clergyman sŏngjiktcha 성직자
clerk (*administrative*) samugwan 사무관; (*in store*) chŏmwŏn 점원
clever *person, animal* ttokttok'an 똑똑한; *idea* hyŏnmyŏnghan 현명한; *gadget* tokch'angjŏgin 독창적인
click 1 *n* COMPUT k'ŭllik 클릭 **2** *v/i* (*make noise*) ch'alk'ak'anŭn soriga nada 찰칵하는 소리가 나다
♦**click on** COMPUT k'ŭllik'ada 클릭하다
client (*of lawyer etc*) ŭiroein 의뢰인; (*customer*) kogaek 고객
cliff chŏlbyŏk 절벽
climate kihu 기후
climax *n* chŏltchŏng 절정
climb 1 *n* (*up mountain*) tŭngban 등반 **2** *v/t* orŭda 오르다 **3** *v/i* orŭda 오르다; *mountain* tŭngbanhada 등반하다; *fig* (*of inflation etc*) chŭnggahada 증가하다
♦**climb down** naerida 내리다; *fig* yangbohada 양보하다
climber (*person*) tŭngsan-ga 등산가
clinch: ***~ a deal*** kŏraerŭl maedŭp chit-tta 거래를 매듭 짓다
cling (*of clothes*) tallabut-tta 달라붙다
♦**cling to** (*of child*) ...e maedallida ...에 매달리다; *ideas, tradition* ...e chipch'ak'ada ...에 집착하다
clingfilm p'ojangnyong laep 포장용

랩
clingy *child*, *boyfriend* tŭllŏbunnŭn 들러붙는
clinic chillyoso 진료소
clinical imsang-ŭi 임상의
clink 1 *n* (*noise*) tchaenggŭrŏnghanŭn sori 쨍그렁하는 소리 **2** *v/i* tchaenggŭrŏnghanŭn soriga nada 쨍그렁하는 소리가 나다
clip[1] **1** *n* (*fastener*) k'ŭllip 클립 **2** *v/t* k'ŭllibŭro kojŏngshik'ida 클립으로 고정시키다; **~ *X* to *Y*** Xŭl / rŭl Ye k'ŭllibŭro kojŏngshik'ida X을 / 를 Y에 클립으로 고정시키다
clip[2] **1** *n* (*extract*) palch'we 발췌 **2** *v/t hair*, *hedge*, *grass* kawiro charŭda 가위로 자르다
clipboard k'ŭllip-ppodŭ 클립보드
clippers (*for hair*) parik'ang 바리캉; (*for nails*) sont'op kkak-kki 손톱 깍기; (*for gardening*) chŏng-wŏnnyong kawi 정원용 가위
clipping (*from newspaper etc*) oryŏnaen kŏt 오려낸 것
clock shigye 시계
clock radio shigyega innŭn ladio 시계가 있는 라디오
clockwise shigye panghyang-ŭro tora 시계 방향으로 돌아
clockwork shigye t'aeyŏp changch'i 시계 태엽 장치; ***it went like ~*** mansaga chal chinhaengdoeŏt-tta 만사가 잘 진행되었다
♦**clog up 1** *v/i* mak'ida 막히다 **2** *v/t* mak'ige hada 막히게 하다
close[1] **1** *adj family* kakkaun 가까운; *friend* ch'inhan 친한; *resemblance* yusahan 유사한 **2** *adv* kakkapkke 가깝게; **~ *at hand*** paro kakkaie 바로 가까이에; **~ *by*** paro kyŏt'e 바로 곁에; ***be ~ to*** (*emotionally*) ...wa / kwa ch'inhada ...와 / 과 친하다
close[2] **1** *v/t* tat-tta 닫다; *eyes* kamtta 감다; *factory* p'yeswaehada 폐쇄하다; (*permanently*) p'yeŏp'ada 폐업하다 **2** *v/i* (*of door*, *store*) tach'ida 닫히다; (*of eyes*) kamgida 감기다; (*of store: permanently*) p'yeŏp'ada 폐업하다
♦**close down 1** *v/t* p'yeŏpsshik'ida 폐업시키다 **2** *v/i* (*permanently*) p'yeŏp'ada 폐업하다
♦**close in** *v/i* (*of fog*) tagaoda 다가오다; (*of troops*) p'owihada 포위하다
♦**close up 1** *v/t building* p'yeswaehada 폐쇄하다 **2** *v/i* (*move closer*) tagaoda 다가오다
closed *store* tach'in 닫힌; *eyes* kamgin 감긴
closed-circuit television p'yeswae hoero t'ellebijyŏn 폐쇄 회로 텔레비전
closely *listen*, *watch* yŏlsshimhi 열심히; *cooperate* ŏmmirhi 엄밀히
closet ot-tchang 옷장
close-up k'ŭllojŭŏp 클로즈업
closing time (*of store*) p'yejŏm shigan 폐점 시간; (*of museum*, *library*) p'yegwan shigan 폐관 시간
closure *permanent* p'yeswae 폐쇄; (*of shop*) p'yejŏm 폐점
clot 1 *n* (*of blood*) p'it-ttŏng-ŏri 핏덩어리 **2** *v/i* (*of blood*) ŏnggida 엉기다
cloth (*fabric*) ch'ŏn 천; (*for kitchen*) haengju 행주; (*for cleaning*) kŏlle 걸레
clothes ot 옷
clothes brush ott'ŏri 옷털이
clothes hanger otkkŏri 옷걸이
clothing ŭiryu 의류
cloud *n* kurŭm 구름; ***a ~ of smoke / dust*** sabang-e kkin yŏn-gi / mŏnji 사방에 낀 연기 / 먼지
♦**cloud over** ont'ong hŭryŏjida 온통 흐려지다
cloudburst p'ogu 폭우
cloudy hŭrin 흐린
clout *fig* (*influence*) yŏnghyangnyŏk 영향력
clown (*in circus*) ŏritkkwangdae 어릿광대; (*joker*) chaemiinnŭn saram 재미있는 사람; *pej* utkkinŭn nom 웃기는 놈
club *n* (*weapon*) konbong 곤봉; (*golf iron*, *organization*) k'ullŏp 클럽; **~s** (*in cards*) k'ŭllŏp 클럽
clue shilmari 실마리; ***I haven't a ~*** orimujung-iya 오리무중이야
clued-up F ...e taehae chal algo it-tta ...에 대해 잘 알고 있다

clump *n* (*of earth*) hŭkttŏng-ŏri 흙덩어리; (*group*) tŏmbul 덤불
clumsiness kkolsanaum 꼴사나움; (*lack of tact*) sŏt'urŭm 서투름
clumsy *person* haengdong-i ŏsusŏnhan 행동이 어수선한; (*tactless*) nunch'i ŏmnŭn 눈치 없는
cluster 1 *n* (*of people*) muri 무리; (*of houses*) miltchip chiyŏk 밀집 지역 **2** *v/i* (*of people*) muri chit-tta 무리 짓다; (*of houses*) moyŏ it-tta 모여 있다
clutch 1 *n* MOT k'ŭllŏch'i 클러치 **2** *v/t* kkwak chaptta 꽉 잡다
♦ **clutch at** chabŭryŏ tŭlda 잡으려 들다
Co. (= ***Company***) hoesa 회사
c/o (= ***care of***) ...sshidaek ...씨댁
coach 1 *n* (*trainer*) k'och'i 코치 **2** *v/t* karŭch'ida 가르치다
coagulate (*of blood*) ŭnggoshik'ida 응고시키다
coal sŏkt'an 석탄
coalition yŏnhap 연합
coalmine t'an-gwang 탄광
coarse kŏch'in 거친
coast *n* yŏnan 연안; ***at the ~*** yŏnane(sŏ) 연안에(서)
coastal yŏnanŭi 연안의
coastguard yŏnan kyŏngbidae 연안 경비대; (*person*) yŏnan kyŏngbiwŏn 연안 경비원
coastline haeansŏn 해안선
coat 1 *n* sang-ŭi 상의; (*over~*) oet'u 외투; (*of animal*) oep'i 외피; (*of paint etc*) tŏtch'il 덧칠 **2** *v/t* (*cover*) ssŭiuda 씌우다; (*of paint*) ch'irhada 칠하다
coathanger otkkŏri 옷걸이
coating ssŭium 씌움
coax kusŭllida 구슬리다
cobweb kŏmijul 거미줄
cocaine k'ok'ain 코카인
cock *n* (*chicken*) sut'ak 수탉; (*any male bird*) suk'ŏt 수컷
cockeyed *idea etc* ŏch'ŏguniŏmnŭn 어처구니없는
cockpit (*of plane*) chojongshil 조종실
cockroach pak'wi pŏlle 바퀴 벌레
cocktail k'akt'eil 칵테일
cocoa (*plant, drink*) k'ok'oa 코코아
coconut k'ok'oyaja yŏlmae 코코야자 열매
coconut palm k'ok'oyaja namu 코코야자 나무
COD (= ***collect on delivery***) taegŭm sanghwan 대금 상환
coddle *sick person* momjorishik'ida 몸조리시키다; *child* kwaing pohohada 과잉 보호하다
code *n* k'odŭ 코드
coeducational namnyŏ konghagŭi 남녀 공학의
coerce kangyohada 강요하다
coexist kongjonhada 공존하다
coexistence kongjon 공존
coffee k'ŏp'i 커피; ***two ~s please*** k'ŏp'i tu jan chuseyo 커피 두 잔 주세요
coffee break kabyŏun hyushik shigan 가벼운 휴식 시간; **coffee maker** k'ŏp'i kkŭrinŭn kigu 커피 끓이는 기구; **coffee pot** k'ŏp'i p'ot'ŭ 커피 포트; **coffee shop** k'ŏp'i shyop 커피 숍; **coffee table** k'ŏp'iyong chagŭn t'aktcha 커피용 작은 탁자
coffin kwan 관
cog t'omnibak'wi 톱니바퀴
cognac k'onyak 코냑
cogwheel manmullinŭn t'omnibak'wi 맞물리는 톱니바퀴
cohabit tonggŏhada 동거하다
coherent chŏnghaptchŏgin 정합적인; (*in speech*) choriga sŏnŭn 조리가 서는
coil 1 *n* (*of rope*) sari 사리 **2** *v/t* kamtta 감다
coin *n* tongjŏn 동전
coincide tongshie irŏnada 동시에 일어나다
coincidence uyŏnŭi ilch'i 우연의 일치
coke F (*cocaine*) k'ok'ain 코카인
Coke® k'ok'a k'olla 코카 콜라
cold 1 *adj weather, day, room* ch'uun 추운; *air, water, character* ch'agaun 차가운; ***I'm (feeling) ~*** ch'uwŏyo 추워요; ***it's ~*** ch'uptta 춥다; ***in ~ blood*** naenghyŏrhage 냉혈하게; ***get ~ feet*** *fig* kŏmmŏktta 겁먹다 **2** *n* ch'uwi 추위; ***I have a ~*** kamgi kŏllyŏt-tta 감기 걸렸다

cold-blooded naenghyŏrŭi 냉혈의; *fig* naenghyŏrhan 냉혈한; **cold cuts** naeng-yuk 냉육; **cold sore** ipkkaŭi paltchin 입가의 발진
coleslaw k'osŭllo 코슬로
collaborate kongdong-ŭro irhada 공동으로 일하다; (*with enemy*) hyŏmnyŏk'ada 협력하다; (*in research*) kongdong yŏn-guhada 공동 연구하다; (*on book etc*) kongdong-ŭro chŏjak'ada 공동으로 저작하다
collaboration hyŏpttong 협동; (*on book etc*) kongjŏ 공저
collaborator hyŏmnyŏktcha 협력자; (*with enemy*) ijŏk haeng-wija 이적 행위자; (*in writing book etc*) kongdong chŏja 공동 저자
collapse munŏjida 무너지다; (*of person*) chwajŏrhada 좌절하다
collapsible chŏbŭl su innŭn 접을 수 있는
collar kit 깃; (*for dog*) kae mok-kkŏri 개 목걸이
collarbone swaegol 쇄골
colleague tongnyo 동료
collect 1 *v/t person* terirŏ kada 데리러 가다; *tickets, cleaning etc* kajirŏ kada 가지러 가다; (*as hobby*) sujip'ada 수집하다; (*gather*) moŭda 모으다 **2** *v/i* (*gather together*) moida 모이다 **3** *adv*: ***call ~*** sushinin pudamŭro chŏnhwahada 수신인 부담으로 전화하다
collect call sushinin pudamŭi chŏnhwa 수신인 부담의 전화
collected moŭn 모은; *person* ch'imch'ak'an 침착한; ***~ works*** chŏnjip 전집
collection sujip 수집; (*in church*) kibugŭm mojip 기부금 모집; (*in art*) sojangp'um 소장품; (*in fashion*) shinjakp'um 신작품
collective chipttanjŏgin 집단적인
collective bargaining tanch'e kyosŏp 단체 교섭
collector sujipkka 수집가
college tankkwa taehak 단과 대학
collide ch'ungdorhada 충돌하다
collision ch'ungdol 충돌
colloquial ilssang hoehwaŭi 일상 회화의
colon (*punctuation*) k'ollon 콜론; ANAT kyŏltchang 결장
colonel taeryŏng 대령
colonial *adj* shingminjiŭi 식민지의
colonize shingminjiro mandŭlda 식민지로 만들다
colony shingminji 식민지
color 1 *n* saek-kkal 색깔; (*in cheeks*) ansaek 안색; ***in ~ movie*** k'allaro toen 칼라로 된; ***~s*** MIL kun-gi 군기 **2** *v/t hair* yŏmsaek'ada 염색하다
color-blind saengmaeng-ŭi 색맹의
colored *adj person* hŭginŭi 흑인의
color fast paraeji annŭn 바래지 않는
colorful saekch'aega p'ungbuhan 색채가 풍부한; *fig* tach'aeroun 다채로운
coloring ansaek 안색
color photograph k'alla sajin 칼라 사진; **color scheme** saekch'aeŭi paehap 색채의 배합; **color TV** k'alla t'ellebijŏn 칼라 텔레비젼
colt mang-aji 망아지
column (*of figures, people*) chul 줄; (*architectural*) kidung 기둥; (*of text*) tan 단; (*newspaper feature*) nan 난
columnist kigoga 기고가
coma honsu sangt'ae 혼수 상태
comb 1 *n* pit 빗 **2** *v/t* pit-tta 빗다; *area* satssach'i twijida 샅샅이 뒤지다
combat 1 *n* chŏnt'u 전투 **2** *v/t* ssauda 싸우다
combination kyŏrhap 결합; (*of safe*) chamulssoeŭi pŏnho 자물쇠의 번호
combine 1 *v/t* kyŏrhap'ada 결합하다; *ingredients* hapch'ida 합치다 **2** *v/i* (*of chemical elements*) kyŏrhap'ada 결합하다
combine harvester k'ombain 콤바인
combustible t'agi shwiun 타기 쉬운
combustion yŏnso 연소
come (*toward speaker*) oda 오다; (*toward listener*) kada 가다; ***you'll ~ to like it*** choahage toel kŏyeyo 좋아하게 될 거예요; ***how ~?*** F ŏtchidoen iriya? 어찌된 일이야?
♦**come about** (*happen*) irŏnada 일어나다
♦**come across 1** *v/t* (*find*) palgyŏnhada 발견하다 **2** *v/i* (*of idea,*

humor) ihaedoeda 이해되다; ***she comes across as ...*** kŭnyŏnŭn ... chŏrŏm poinda 그녀는 ... 처럼 보인다
♦**come along** (*come too*) kach'i oda 같이 오다; (*turn up*) nat'anada 나타나다; (*progress*) chinhaengdoeda 진행되다
♦**come apart** punhaedoeda 분해되다; (*break*) pusŏjida 부서지다
♦**come around** (*to s.o.'s home*) tŭllida 들리다; (*regain consciousness*) ŭishigŭl hoebok'ada 의식을 회복하다
♦**come away** (*leave*) ttŏnada 떠나다; (*of button etc*) ttŏrŏjida 떨어지다
♦**come back** toraoda 돌아오다; ***it came back to me*** tashi saenggangnassŏ 다시 생각났어
♦**come by 1** *v/i* tŭllida 들리다 **2** *v/t* (*acquire*) ŏt-tta 얻다; (*find*) kuhada 구하다
♦**come down** *v/i* naeryŏoda 내려오다; (*in price, amount etc*) ttŏrŏjida 떨어지다; (*of rain, snow*) naerida 내리다; ***he came down the stairs*** kŭnŭn kyedanŭl naeryŏwat-tta 그는 계단을 내려왔다
♦**come for** (*collect*) kajirŏ oda 가지러 오다; *person* terirŏ oda 데리러 오다; (*attack*) tŏpch'iryŏ tŭlda 덮치려 들다
♦**come forward** (*present oneself*) ap'ŭro nasŏda 앞으로 나서다
♦**come from** ...esŏ oda ...에서 오다
♦**come in** tŭrŏoda 들어오다; ***~!*** tŭrŏoseyo! 들어오세요!
♦**come in for**: ***~ criticism*** pip'anŭl pat-tta 비판을 받다
♦**come in on**: ***~ a deal*** kŏraee ch'amgahada 거래에 참가하다
♦**come off** (*of handle etc*) ttŏrŏjida 떨어지다
♦**come on** (*progress*) chinhaengdoeda 진행되다; ***~!*** sŏdullŏ! 서둘러!; (*in disbelief*) sŏlma! 설마!
♦**come out** (*of person, sun, results, new product*) naoda 나오다; (*of stain*) ppajida 빠지다
♦**come to 1** *v/t place* ...e irŭda ...에 이르다; (*of hair, dress, water*) ...kkaji irŭda ...까지이르다; ***that comes to $70*** chŏgŏsŭn 70tallŏe irŭnda 저것은 70달러에 이른다 **2** *v/i* (*regain consciousness*) ŭishigŭl hoebok'ada 의식을 회복하다
♦**come up** ollaoda 올라오다; (*of sun*) ttŏorŭda 떠오르다; ***something has come up*** musŭn iri saenggyŏssŏyo 무슨 일이 생겼어요
♦**come up with** *new idea etc* saenggak'aenaeda 생각해내다
comeback: ***make a ~*** pok-kkwihada 복귀하다
comedian k'omidiŏn 코미디언; *pej* utkkinŭn nyŏsŏk 웃기는 녀석
comedown mollak 몰락
comedy hŭigŭk 희극
comet hyesŏng 혜성
comeuppance: ***he'll get his ~*** kŭnŭn ŭngborŭl padŭl kŏshida 그는 응보를 받을 것이다
comfort 1 *n* allak 안락; (*consolation*) wian 위안 **2** *v/t* wianhada 위안하다
comfortable *chair* p'yŏnanhan 편안한; *house, room* allak'an 안락한; ***be ~*** (*of person*) p'yŏnhan 편한; (*financially*) suibi ch'ungbunhan 수입이 충분한
comic 1 *n* (*magazine*) manhwa chaptchi 만화 잡지 **2** *adj* hŭigŭgŭi 희극의
comical usŭkkwangsŭrŏun 우스꽝스러운
comic book manhwa ch'aek 만화 책
comics manhwaran 만화란
comma shwimp'yo 쉼표
command 1 *n* myŏngnyŏng 명령 **2** *v/t* myŏngnyŏnghada 명령하다
commander saryŏnggwan 사령관
commander-in-chief ch'oego saryŏnggwan 최고 사령관
commemorate kinyŏmhada 기념하다
commemoration: ***in ~ of*** ...ŭi kinyŏmŭro ...의 기념으로
commence 1 *v/i* shijakttoeda 시작되다 **2** *v/t* shijak'ada 시작하다
comment 1 *n* ŏn-gŭp 언급; ***no ~*** hal mal ŏpssŭmnida 할 말 없습니다 **2** *v/i* ŏn-gŭp'ada 언급하다
commentary haesŏl 해설
commentator haesŏltcha 해설자

commerce sang-ŏp 상업
commercial 1 *adj* sang-ŏbŭi 상업의; *success, failure* sang-ŏpssang-ŭi 상업상의 **2** *n* (*advert*) kwanggo 광고
commercial break kwanggo pangsong 광고 방송
commercialize *v/t* sangp'umhwahada 상품화하다
commercial traveler oep'anwŏn 외판원
commiserate tongjŏnghada 동정하다
commission 1 *n* (*payment*) susuryo 수수료; (*job*) ŭiroe 의뢰; (*committee*) wiwŏnhoe 위원회 **2** *v/t* (*for a job*) ŭiroehada 의뢰하다
commit *crime* pŏmhada 범하다; *money* halttanghada 할당하다; **~ *oneself*** ŏnjirŭl chuda 언질을 주다
commitment (*in professional relationship*) chŏllyŏm 전렴; (*in personal relationship*) hŏnshin 헌신; (*responsibility*) ch'aegim 책임
committee wiwŏnhoe 위원회
commodity iryongp'um 일용품
common (*not rare*) pot'ong-ŭi 보통의; (*shared*) kongt'ong-ŭi 공통의; ***in ~*** kongt'ong-ŭro 공통으로; ***have sth in ~ with s.o.*** muŏsŭl nuguwa kongt'ong-ŭro kajigo it-tta 무엇을 누구와 공통으로 가지고 있다
common law wife naeyŏnŭi ch'ŏ 내연의 처; **commonplace** *adj* p'yŏngbŏmhan 평범한; **common sense** sangshik 상식
commotion soran 소란
communal kongdong-ŭi 공동의
communicate 1 *v/i* (*be in contact*) yŏllagi it-tta 연락이 있다; (*make self understood*) ŭisarŭl sot'onghada 의사를 소통하다 **2** *v/t* chŏndarhada 전달하다
communication ŭisa chŏndal 의사 전달
communications t'ongshin 통신
communications satellite t'ongshin wisŏng 통신 위성
communicative *person* marhagi choahanŭn 말하기 좋아하는
Communism Kongsanjuŭi 공산주의
Communist 1 *adj* Kongsanjuŭiŭi 공산주의의; (*of Communist party*) Kongsandang-ŭi 공산당의 **2** *n* Kongsanjuŭija 공산주의자
Communist Party Kongsandang 공산당
community kongdongch'e 공동체; (*social group*) sahoe 사회
commute 1 *v/i* t'onggŭnhada 통근하다 **2** *v/t* LAW kamhyŏnghada 감형하다
commuter t'onggŭnja 통근자
commuter traffic t'onggŭn kyot'ong 통근 교통
commuter train t'onggŭn yŏlch'a 통근 열차
compact 1 *adj* apch'ukttoen 압축된; *house* adamhan 아담한; MOT sohyŏng-ŭi 소형의 **2** *n* MOT sohyŏngch'a 소형차
compact disc k'omp'aekt'ŭ tisŭk'ŭ 콤팩트 디스크
companion tongnyo 동료
companionship tongmuro sagwigi 동무로 사귀기
company COM hoesa 회사; (*companionship*) tongmuro sagwigi 동무로 사귀기; (*guests*) sonnim 손님; ***keep ... ~*** ...wa / kwa kyojehada ...와 / 과 교제하다
company car hoesa ch'a 회사 차
company law hoesapŏp 회사법
comparable (*can be compared*) pigyodoel su innŭn 비교될 수 있는; (*similar*) yusahan 유사한
comparative 1 *adj* (*relative*) pigyojŏgin 비교적인; *study* pigyoŭi 비교의; GRAM pigyogŭbŭi 비교급의 **2** *n* GRAM pigyogŭp 비교급
comparatively pigyojŏgŭro 비교적으로
compare 1 *v/t* pigyohada 비교하다; **~ *X with Y*** Xŭl / rŭl Ywa / gwa pigyohada X을 / 를 Y와 / 과 비교하다; ***~d with*** ...wa / kwa pigyohaesŏ ...와 / 과 비교해서 **2** *v/i* pigyodoeda 비교되다
comparison pigyo 비교; ***there's no ~*** pigyohal su ŏpssŏyo 비교할 수 없어요
compartment k'an 칸
compass nach'imban 나침반; (*for geometry*) k'ŏmp'ŏsŭ 컴퍼스

compassion tongjŏngshim 동정심
compassionate tongjŏnghanŭn 동정하는
compatibility sŏro mannŭn chŏngdo 서로 맞는 정도; (*of systems*) chŏk'apssŏng 적합성; (*of software*) hohwansŏng 호환성; (*of blood types*) ilch'i yŏbu 일치 여부
compatible *people* sŏro mannŭn 서로 맞는; *blood types, lifestyles* ilch'ihanŭn 일치하는; COMPUT hohwanhal su innŭn 호환할 수 있는; ***we're not ~*** urinŭn sŏngkkyŏgi an mat-tta 우리는 성격이 안 맞다
compel ŏktchiro …shik'ida 억지로 …시키다; ***be ~led to*** hal su ŏpsshi … hada 할 수 없이 … 하다
compelling *argument* sŏlttŭngnyŏk innŭn 설득력 있는; *movie, book* hŭngmirŭl todunŭn 흥미를 돋우는
compensate 1 *v/t* (*with money*) paesanghada 배상하다 **2** *v/i*: ***~ for*** …ŭl / rŭl posanghada …을 / 를 보상하다
compensation (*money*) paesang 배상; (*reward*) poch'ung 보충; (*comfort*) posang 보상
compete kyŏngjaenghada 경쟁하다; (*take part*) ch'ultchŏnhada 출전하다; ***~ for*** …ŭl / rŭl wihae kyŏngjaenghada …을 / 를 위해 경쟁하다
competence, competency nŭngnyŏk 능력
competent *person* nŭngnyŏk innŭn 능력 있는; *work* chungbunhan 충분한; ***I'm not ~ to judge*** nanŭn p'andanhal chagyŏgi ŏptta 나는 판단할 자격이 없다
competition kyŏngjaeng 경쟁; (*competitors*) kyŏngjaengja 경쟁자; ***the government wants to encourage ~*** chŏngbunŭn kyŏngjaeng-ŭl puch'uk'igo ship'ŏhanda 정부는 경쟁을 부추키고 싶어한다
competitive kyŏngjaengjŏgin 경쟁적인; *price, offer* kyŏngjaengnyŏk innŭn 경쟁력 있는
competitor (*in contest*) kyŏngjaengja 경쟁자; COM kyŏngjaeng sangdae 경쟁 상대
compile p'yŏnjip'ada 편집하다
complacency chagi manjok 자기 만족
complacent chagi manjoktchŏgin 자기 만족적인
complain *v/i* pulp'yŏnghada 불평하다; ***~ of*** MED …ŭl / rŭl hosohada …을 / 를 호소하다
complaint pulp'yŏng 불평; MED pyŏng 병
complement *v/t* powanhada 보완하다; ***they ~ each other*** kŭdŭrŭn sŏro powanhanda 그들은 서로 보완한다
complementary powanhanŭn 보완하는
complete 1 *adj* (*utter*) wanjŏnhan 완전한; (*whole, entire*) chŏnbuŭi 전부의; (*finished*) wansŏngdoen 완성된 **2** *v/t task, building etc* wansŏnghada 완성하다; *course* wanjŏnhi mach'ida 완전히 마치다; *form* ch'aeuda 채우다
completely wanjŏnhi 완전히
completion wansŏng 완성
complex 1 *adj* poktchap'an 복잡한 **2** *n* PSYCH k'omp'ŭllekssŭ 콤플렉스; (*of buildings*) chip'apch'e 집합체
complexion (*facial*) ansaek 안색
compliance ŭngnak 응낙
complicate poktchap'age hada 복잡하게 하다
complicated poktchap'an 복잡한
complication poktchap'age hanŭn kŏt 복잡하게 하는 것; ***~s*** MED hap-ppyŏngtchŭng 합병증
compliment 1 *n* ch'ansa 찬사 **2** *v/t* ch'ansahada 찬사하다
complimentary ch'ansahanŭn 찬사하는; (*free*) muryoŭi 무료의
compliments slip kŭnjŏng tchoktchi 근정 쪽지
comply ŭnghada 응하다; ***~ with*** …e ŭnghada …에 응하다
component (*constituent part*) kusŏng yoso 구성 요소; (*of machine etc*) pup'um 부품
compose *v/t* kusŏnghada 구성하다; MUS chak-kkok'ada 작곡하다; ***be ~d of*** …(ŭ)ro kusŏngdoeŏ it-tta

...(으)로 구성되어 있다; ~ ***oneself*** maŭmŭl karaanch'ida 마음을 가라앉히다
composed (*calm*) ch'imch'ak'an 침착한
composer MUS chak-kkok-kka 작곡가
composition (*make-up*) kusŏng 구성; MUS chak-kkok 작곡; (*essay*) changmun 작문
composure ch'imch'ak 침착
compound *n* CHEM hapssŏngmul 합성물
compound interest pongni 복리
comprehend (*understand*) ihaehada 이해하다
comprehension ihae 이해
comprehensive p'ogwaltchŏgin 포괄적인
comprehensive insurance chonghap pohŏm 종합 보험
compress 1 *n* MED sŭpp'o 습포 **2** *v/t air, gas, file* apch'uk'ada 압축하다; *information* yoyak'ada 요약하다
comprise kusŏngdoeda 구성되다; ***be ~d of*** ...(ŭ)ro kusŏngdoeŏ it-tta ...(으)로 구성되어 있다
compromise 1 *n* t'ahyŏp 타협 **2** *v/i* t'ahyŏp'ada 타협하다 **3** *v/t principles* t'ahyŏpsshik'ida 타협시키다; (*damage*: *reputation etc*) sonsangshik'ida 손상시키다; ~ ***oneself*** chagiŭi ch'emyŏnŭl sonsangshik'ida 자기의 체면을 손상시키다
compulsion PSYCH kangbak kwannyŏm 강박 관념
compulsive *behavior* kangbak kwannyŏme sarojap'in 강박 관념에 사로잡힌; *reading* murihanŭn 무리하는
compulsory ŭimujŏgin 의무적인; ~ ***education*** ŭimu kyoyuk 의무 교육
computer k'ŏmp'yut'ŏ 컴퓨터; ***put sth on ~*** muŏsŭl k'ŏmp'yut'ŏe imnyŏksshik'yŏ not'a 무엇을 컴퓨터에 입력시켜 놓다
computer-controlled k'ŏmp'yut'ŏro t'ongjedoenŭn 컴퓨터로 통제되는
computer game k'ŏmp'yut'ŏ keim 컴퓨터 게임
computerize chŏnsanhwahada 전산화하다
computer literate k'ŏmp'yut'ŏrŭl tarul chul anŭn 컴퓨터를 다룰 줄 아는; **computer science** k'ŏmp'yut'ŏ kwahak 컴퓨터 과학; **computer scientist** k'ŏmp'yut'ŏ kwahaktcha 컴퓨터 과학자
computing k'ŏmp'yut'ŏ sayong 컴퓨터 사용
comrade (*friend*) tongnyo 동료; POL tongji 동지
comradeship tongnyo kwan-gye 동료 관계
con F **1** *n* (*trick*) sagi 사기 **2** *v/t* sagi ch'ida 사기 치다
conceal kamch'uda 감추다
concede *v/t* (*admit*) injŏnghada 인정하다
conceit chaman 자만
conceited chamanhanŭn 자만하는
conceivable saenggak'al su innŭn 생각할 수 있는
conceive *v/i* (*of woman*) imshinhada 임신하다; ~ ***of*** (*imagine*) ...ŭl / rŭl sangsanghada ...을 / 를 상상하다
concentrate 1 *v/i* chiptchunghada 집중하다; (*on task*) chŏnnyŏmhada 전념하다 **2** *v/t one's attention, energies* chiptchungshik'ida 집중시키다
concentrated *juice etc* nongch'ukttoen 농축된
concentration chiptchung 집중
concept kaenyŏm 개념
conception (*of child*) imshin 임신
concern 1 *n* (*anxiety*) kŏktchŏng 걱정; (*care*) yŏmnyŏ 염려; (*business*) kwanshimsa 관심사; (*company*) hoesa 회사 **2** *v/t* (*involve*) ...e kwan-gyehada ...에 관계하다; (*worry*) kŏktchŏnghada 걱정하다; ~ ***oneself with*** ...e kwanyŏhada ...에 관여하다
concerned (*anxious*) kŏktchŏnghanŭn 걱정하는; (*caring*) yŏmnyŏhanŭn 염려하는; (*involved*) kwan-gyedoenŭn 관계되는; ***as far as I'm ~*** naega pogienŭn 내가 보기에는
concerning *prep* ...e kwanhayŏ ...에 관하여

concert yŏnjuhoe 연주회
concerted (*joint*) habŭidoen 합의된
concertmaster susŏk paiollinisŭt'ŭ 수석 바이올리니스트
concerto hyŏptchugok 협주곡
concession (*giving in*) yangbo 양보
conciliatory hoeyujŏgin 회유적인
concise kan-gyŏrhan 간결한
conclude 1 *v/t* (*deduce*) kyŏllonŭl naerida 결론을 내리다; (*end*) kkŭnnaeda 끝내다; ~ ***X from Y*** Y(ŭ)robut'ŏ Xranŭn kyŏllonŭl naerida Y(으)로부터 X라는 결론을 내리다 **2** *v/i* kkŭnnada 끝나다
conclusion (*deduction*) kyŏllon 결론; (*end*) kyŏlmal 결말; ***in*** ~ kkŭt'ŭro 끝으로
conclusive kyŏltchŏngjŏgin 결정적인
concoct *meal*, *drink* sokkŏsŏ mandŭlda 섞어서 만들다; *excuse*, *story* yŏkkŏnaeda 엮어내다
concoction (*food*, *drink*) honhammul 혼합물
concrete[1] *adj* (*not abstract*) kuch'ejŏgin 구체적인
concrete[2] *n* k'onk'ŭrit'ŭ 콘크리트
concur *v/i* tong-ŭihada 동의하다
concussion noejint'ang 뇌진탕
condemn *action* pinanhada 비난하다; *building* p'yegi ch'ŏbunŭl sŏn-gohada 폐기 처분을 선고하다; (*fate*) unmyŏng chiuda 운명 지우다
condemnation (*of action*) pinan 비난
condensation ŭngch'uk 응축
condense 1 *v/t* (*shorten*) apch'uk'ada 압축하다 **2** *v/i* (*of steam*) ŭngch'uk'ada 응축하다
condensed milk yŏnyu 연유
condescend: ***he ~ed to speak to me*** kŭnŭn hwangsonghagedo na-ege marŭl kŏrŏssŏ 그가 황송하게도 내게 말을 걸었어
condescending kyŏmsonhan ch'ŏk'anŭn 겸손한 척하는
condition 1 *n* (*state*) sangt'ae 상태; (*of health*) kŏn-gang sangt'ae 건강 상태; MED chirhwan 질환; (*requirement*, *term*) chokkŏn 조건; **~*s*** (*circumstances*) hwan-gyŏng 환경; ***on ~ that*** …ranŭn chokkŏnŭro …라는 조건으로 **2** *v/t* PSYCH chokkŏn pansarŭl irŭk'ige hada 조건 반사를 일으키게 하다
conditional 1 *adj acceptance* chokkŏnbuŭi 조건부의 **2** *n* GRAM chokkŏnppŏp 조건법
conditioner (*for hair*, *fabric*) k'ondishyŏnŏ 콘디셔너
conditioning PSYCH chŏgŭngshik'igi 적응시키기
condo k'ondo 콘도
condolences aedo 애도
condom k'ondom 콘돔
condominium k'ondominium 콘도미니움
condone *actions* yongsŏhada 용서하다
conducive: ~ ***to*** …e toumi toenŭn …에 도움이 되는
conduct 1 *n* (*behavior*) haeng-wi 행위 **2** *v/t* (*carry out*) suhaenghada 수행하다; ELEC chŏndohada 전도하다; MUS chihwihada 지휘하다; ~ ***oneself*** ch'ŏshinhada 처신하다
conducted tour kwan-gwang annae 관광 안내
conductor MUS chihwija 지휘자; (*on train*) ch'ajang 차장
cone (*in geometry*) wŏnppul 원뿔; (*for ice cream*) k'on 콘; (*of pine tree*) solppang-ul 솔방울; (*on highway*) wŏnppul 원뿔
confectioner (*shop*) chegwajŏm 제과점
confectioners' sugar chŏngje sŏlt'ang 정제 설탕
confectionery (*candy*) kwajaryu 과자류
confederation yŏnhap 연합
confer 1 *v/t* (*bestow*) suyŏhada 수여하다 **2** *v/i* (*discuss*) hyŏbŭihada 협의하다
conference hoeŭi 회의
conference room hoeŭishil 회의실
confess 1 *v/t sin*, *guilt* kobaek'ada 고백하다; (*to police*) chabaek'ada 자백하다; REL kohaehada 고해하다; ***I ~ I don't know*** morŭndanŭn kŏsŭl kobaek'amnida 모른다는 것을 고백합니다 **2** *v/i* kobaek'ada 고백하다; (*to police*) chabaek'ada 자백하다; REL kohaehada 고해하다;

~ ***to a weakness for sth*** muŏse yak'adanŭn kŏsŭl shilt'ohada 무엇에 약하다는 것을 실토하다
confession kobaek 고백; (*to police*) chabaek 자백; REL kohae 고해
confessional REL kohaeshil 고해실
confessor REL kohae shinbu 고해 신부
confide 1 *v/t* t'ŏrŏnot'a 털어놓다 **2** *v/i*: ~ ***in s.o.*** nuguege pimirŭl t'ŏrŏnot'a 누구에게 비밀을 털어놓다
confidence (*assurance*) hwaksshin 확신; (*trust*) shilloe 신뢰; (*secret*) pimil 비밀; ***in*** ~ pimillo 비밀로
confident (*self-assured*) chashinhanŭn 자신하는; (*convinced*) hwaksshinhanŭn 확신하는
confidential kŭkppiŭi 극비의
confine (*imprison*) kamgŭmhada 감금하다; (*restrict*) chehanhada 제한하다; ***be ~d to one's bed*** ara nuwŏ it-tta 앓아 누워 있다
confined *space* chehandoen 제한된
confinement (*imprisonment*) kamgŭm 감금; MED haesan 해산
confirm *v/t* hwaginhada 확인하다; *theory*, *statement*, *fears* hwaktchŭnghada 확증하다
confirmation hwagin 확인; (*of theory*, *statement*, *fears*) hwaktchŭng 확증
confirmed (*inveterate*) kudŏbŏrin 굳어버린
confiscate apssuhada 압수하다
conflict 1 *n* (*disagreement*) taerip 대립; (*clash*) ch'ungdol 충돌; (*war*) t'ujaeng 투쟁 **2** *v/i* (*clash*) ch'ungdorhada 충돌하다
conform sunŭnghada 순응하다; (*of product*) ttarŭda 따르다; ~ ***to government standards*** chŏngbu kyugyŏge ttarŭda 정부 규격에 따르다
conformist *n* chunsuja 준수자
confront (*face*) majuhada 마주하다; (*tackle*) matssŏda 맞서다
confrontation taegyŏl 대결
Confucianism Yugyo 유교
Confucius Kongja 공자
confuse (*muddle*) hollanshik'ida 혼란시키다; (*one thing with another*) hondonghada 혼동하다; ~ ***X with Y*** Xŭl / rŭl Ywa / gwa hondonghada X을 / 를 Y와 / 과 혼동하다
confused hollansŭrŏun 혼란스러운
confusing hollanshik'inŭn 혼란시키는
confusion hollan 혼란
congeal ŭnggohada 응고하다
congenial maŭme mannŭn 마음에 맞는
congenital MED sŏnch'ŏnjŏgin 선천적인
congested *roads* honjap'an 혼잡한
congestion (*on roads*) honjap 혼잡; (*in chest*) mak'im 막힘; ***traffic*** ~ kyot'ong honjap 교통 혼잡
conglomerate chaebŏl 재벌
congratulate ch'uk'ahada 축하하다
congratulations ch'uk'a 축하; ~ ***on*** …ŭl / rŭl ch'uk'ahamnida …을 / 를 축하합니다
congregate (*gather*) moida 모이다
congregation REL chip'oe 집회
congress (*conference*) hoeŭi 회의; ***Congress*** (*of US*) Kuk'oe 국회
congressional kuk'oeŭi 국회의
congressman kuk'oe ŭiwŏn 국회 위원
congresswoman yŏja kuk'oe ŭiwŏn 여자 국회 의원
conifer ch'imnyŏpssu 침엽수
conjecture *n* (*speculation*) ch'uch'ŭk 추측
conjugate *v/t* GRAM hwaryongshik'ida 활용시키다
conjunction GRAM chŏpssokssa 접속사; ***in ~ with*** …wa / kwa hamkke …와 / 과 함께
conjunctivitis kyŏlmangnyŏm 결막염
♦**conjure up** (*produce*) nun kkamtchak'al saie mandŭlda 눈 깜짝할 사이에 만들다; (*evoke*) pullŏ irŭk'ida 불러 일으키다
conjurer, **conjuror** masulsa 마술사
conjuring tricks masul 마술
con man sagikkun 사기꾼
connect (*join*), TELEC yŏn-gyŏrhada 연결하다; (*link*) kwallyŏnshik'ida 관련시키다; (*to power supply*) chŏpssoksshik'ida 접속시키다
connected: ***be well-~*** choŭn yŏntchuri innŭn 좋은 연줄이 있는; ***be ~ with*** …wa / kwa

kwallyŏndoeda …와 / 과 관련되다
connecting flight yŏn-gyŏlp'yŏn 연결편
connection (*in wiring*) yŏn-gyŏl 연결; (*link*) kwallyŏn 관련; (*when traveling*) yŏn-gyŏlp'yŏn 연결편; (*personal contact*) yŏntchul 연줄; ***in ~ with*** …wa / kwa kwallyŏnhayŏ …와 / 과 관련하여
connoisseur kamjŏngga 감정가
conquer chŏngbok'ada 정복하다; *fear etc* kŭkppok'ada 극복하다
conqueror chŏngboktcha 정복자
conquest (*of territory*) chŏngbok 정복
conscience yangshim 양심; ***a guilty ~*** yangshimŭi kach'aek 양심의 가책; ***it has been on my ~*** kŭgŏshi maŭme kŏllyŏssŏyo 그것이 마음에 걸렸어요
conscientious yangshimjŏgin 양심적인
conscientious objector yangshimtchŏk pyŏngnyŏk kŏbuja 양심적 병역 거부자
conscious *adj* (*aware*) chigagi innŭn 지각이 있는; (*deliberate*) ŭishiktchŏgin 의식적인; MED ŭishigi innŭn 의식이 있는; ***be ~ of*** …ŭl / rŭl algo it-tta …을 / 를 알고 있다
consciousness (*awareness*) chigak 지각; MED ŭishik 의식; ***lose / regain ~*** ŭishigŭl ilt'a / hoebok'ada 의식을 잃다 / 회복하다
consecutive yŏnsoktchŏgin 연속적인
consensus ilch'i 일치
consent 1 *n* tong-ŭi 동의 **2** *v/i* tong-ŭihada 동의하다
consequence (*result*) kyŏlkwa 결과
consequently (*therefore*) ttarasŏ 따라서
conservation (*preservation*) pojon 보존
conservationist *n* chawŏn pohoronja 자원 보호론자
conservative *adj* (*conventional*) posujŏgin 보수적인; *clothes* susuhan 수수한; *estimate* chuljabŭn 줄잡은
conservatory (*for plants*) onshil 온실; MUS ŭmak hak-kkyo 음악 학교
conserve 1 *n* (*jam*) chaem 잼 **2** *v/t energy, strength* pojonhada 보존하다
consider (*regard*) yŏgida 여기다; (*show regard for*) koryŏhada 고려하다; (*think about*) saenggak'ada 생각하다; ***it is ~ed to be*** …rago saenggakttoenda …라고 생각된다
considerable sangdanghan 상당한
considerably sangdanghi 상당히
considerate tongjŏngshimi manŭn 동정심이 많은
consideration (*thought*) suk-kko 숙고; (*thoughtfulness, concern*) koryŏ 고려; (*factor*) koryŏhal sahang 고려할 사항; ***take X into ~*** Xŭl / rŭl koryŏhada X을 / 를 고려하다
consignment COM wit'ak 위탁
♦**consist of** …(ŭ)ro iruŏjyŏ it-tta …(으)로 이루어져 있다
consistency (*texture*) nongdo 농도; (*of attitude, behavior*) ilgwansŏng 일관성
consistent *attitude, behavior* ilgwansŏng innŭn 일관성 있는
consolation wiro 위로
console *v/t* wirohada 위로하다
consonant *n* GRAM chaŭm 자음
consortium ch'agwandan 차관단
conspicuous tudŭrŏjin 두드러진
conspiracy ŭmmo 음모
conspire ŭmmorŭl kkumida 음모를 꾸미다
constant (*continuous*) kyesokttoenŭn 계속되는
consternation sŏmttŭk nollam 섬뜩 놀람
constipated pyŏnbie kŏllin 변비에 걸린
constipation pyŏnbi 변비
constituent *n* (*component*) kusŏng yoso 구성 요소
constitute (*account for*) kusŏnghada 구성하다; (*represent*) nat'anaeda 나타내다
constitution POL hŏnppŏp 헌법; (*of person*) ch'ejil 체질
constitutional *adj* POL hŏnppŏpssang-ŭi 헌법상의
Constitution Day Chaehŏnjŏl 재헌절
constraint (*restriction*) ŏktche 억제
construct *v/t building etc* seuda

세우다
construction (*of building etc*) kŏnsŏl 건설; (*building etc*) kŏnch'ungmul 건축물; (*trade*) kŏnsŏrŏp 건설업; ***under ~*** kongsa chung 공사 중
construction industry kŏnsŏrŏp 건설업; **construction site** kongsajang 공사장; **construction worker** kongsajang inbu 공사장 인부
constructive kŏnsŏltchŏgin 건설적인
consul yŏngsa 영사
consulate yŏngsagwan 영사관
consult (*seek the advice of*) …ŭi ŭigyŏnŭl mut-tta …의 의견을 묻다; *dictionary* ch'amgohada 참고하다
consultancy (*company*) k'ŏnssŏlt'ŏnt'ŭŏp 컨설턴트업; (*advice*) sangdam 상담
consultant (*adviser*) k'ŏnssŏlt'ŏnt'ŭ 컨설턴트
consultation sang-ŭi 상의
consume (*eat*) mŏgŏbŏrida 먹어버리다; (*drink*) mashyŏbŏrida 마셔버리다; (*use*) ssŏbŏrida 써버리다
consumer (*purchaser*) sobija 소비자
consumer confidence kumae ŭiji 구매 의지; **consumer goods** sobip'um 소비품; **consumer society** sobija sahoe 소비자 사회
consumption sobi 소비
contact 1 *n* (*person*) chunggyein 중계인; (*communication*) yŏllak 연락; (*social*) kyoje 교제; (*by radio*) kyoshin 교신; (*physical*) chŏpch'ok 접촉; ***keep in ~ with X*** Xwa / gwa yŏllagŭl chugo pat-tta X와 / 과 연락을 주고 받다 **2** *v/t* yŏllak'ada 연락하다; (*by radio*) kyoshinhada 교신하다
contact lens k'ont'aekt'ŭrenjŭ 콘택트렌즈
contact number yŏllakch'ŏ 연락처
contagious *illness, laughter* chŏnyŏmdoenŭn 전염되는
contain tamkko it-tta 담고 있다; *tears, laughter* ch'amtta 참다; *flood* maktta 막다; ***it ~ed my camera*** nae k'ameraga tŭrŏ issŏt-tta 내 카메라가 들어 있었다; ***~ oneself*** ch'amtta 참다
container (*recipient*) yonggi 용기; COM k'ŏnt'einŏ 컨테이너
container ship k'ŏnt'einŏsŏn 컨테이너선
contaminate oyŏmshik'ida 오염시키다
contamination oyŏm 오염
contemplate *v/t* (*look at*) ŭngshihada 응시하다; (*think about*) suk-kkohada 숙고하다
contemporary 1 *adj* hyŏndaeŭi 현대의 **2** *n* tongnyŏnbaeŭi saram 동년배의 사람; (*at school*) tonggisaeng 동기생
contempt kyŏngmyŏl 경멸; ***be beneath ~*** kyŏngmyŏrhal kach'ijoch'a ŏmnŭn 경멸할 가치조차 없는
contemptible kyŏngmyŏrhal manhan 경멸할 만한
contemptuous yatchababonŭn 얕잡아보는
contend: ***~ for*** …ŭl / rŭl wihae tat'uda …을 / 를 위해 다투다; ***~ with*** ch'ŏrihada 처리하다
contender (*in sport, competition*) kyŏngjaengja 경쟁자; (*against champion*) tojŏnja 도전자
content[1] *n* naeyong 내용
content[2] **1** *adj* manjok'anŭn 만족하는 **2** *v/t*: ***~ oneself with*** …(ŭ)ro manjok'ada …(으)로 만족하다
contented majok'ago innŭn 만족하고 있는
contention (*assertion*) chujang 주장; ***be in ~ for*** …ŭl / rŭl wihae kyŏngjaenghada …을 / 를 위해 경쟁하다
contentment manjok 만족
contents naeyong 내용
contest[1] (*competition*) taehoe 대회; (*struggle, for power*) kyŏngjaeng 경쟁
contest[2] *leadership etc* kyŏruda 겨루다; (*oppose*) pandaehada 반대하다
contestant kyŏngjaengja 경쟁자
context munmaek 문맥; ***look at X in ~ / out of ~*** Xŭl / rŭl munmaege match'wŏ / munmaegŭl pŏsŏna poda X을 / 를 문맥에 맞춰 / 문맥을 벗어나 보다
continent *n* taeryuk 대륙

continental taeryugŭi 대륙의
contingency ttŭkppakkŭi il 뜻밖의 일
continual kyesoktchŏgin 계속적인
continuation kyesok 계속
continue 1 *v/t* kyesok'ada 계속하다; ***to be ~d*** taŭme kyesok 다음에 계속 **2** *v/i* kyesokttoeda 계속되다
continuity yŏnsokssŏng 연속성
continuous kkŭnimŏmnŭn 끊임없는
contort *face* tchinggŭrida 찡그리다; *body* pit'ŭlda 비틀다
contour yun-gwak 윤곽
contraception p'iim 피임
contraceptive *n* (*device*) p'iim kigu 피임 기구; (*pill*) p'iimyak 피임약
contract[1] *n* kyeyak 계약
contract[2] **1** *v/i* (*shrink*) such'uk'ada 수축하다 **2** *v/t illness* …e kŏllida …에 걸리다
contractor kyeyaktcha 계약자
contractual kyeyakssang-ŭi 계약상의
contradict *statement* puinhada 부인하다; *person* panbak'ada 반박하다
contradiction mosun 모순
contradictory *account* mosundoen 모순된
contraption F sae koanmul 새 고안물
contrary[1] **1** *adj* pandaeŭi 반대의; ***~ to*** …e panhayŏ …에 반하여 **2** *n*: ***on the ~*** pandaero 반대로
contrary[2] (*perverse*) pandaeroman hanŭn 반대로만 하는
contrast 1 *n* taejo 대조 **2** *v/t* taejohada 대조하다 **3** *v/i* taejodoeda 대조되다
contrasting taejojŏgin 대조적인
contravene wibanhada 위반하다
contribute 1 *v/i* (*with money, material*) kibuhada 기부하다; (*with time*) konghŏnhada 공헌하다; (*to magazine, paper*) kigohada 기고하다; (*to discussion*) kiyŏhada 기여하다; ***~ to*** (*help to cause*) …ŭihan wŏnini toeda …의한 원인이 되다 **2** *v/t money* kibuhada 기부하다
contribution (*money*) kibu 기부; (*of time, effort*) konghŏn 공헌; (*to discussion*) kiyŏ 기여; (*to magazine*) kigo 기고
contributor (*of money*) kibuja 기부자; (*to magazine*) kigoga 기고가
contrive yongk'e haenaeda 용케 해내다
control 1 *n* (*of country, organization*) chibae 지배; (*of emotions*) cheŏ 제어; (*of ball*) cheguryŏk 제구력; ***be in ~ of*** …ŭl / rŭl chibaehada …을 / 를 지배하다; ***bring X under ~*** Xŭl / rŭl cheŏhada X을 / 를 제어하다; ***get out of ~*** cheŏhal su ŏpkke toeda 제어할 수 없게 되다; ***lose ~ of*** …ŭl / rŭl cheŏhal su ŏpkke toeda …을 / 를 제어할 수 없게 되다; ***lose ~ of oneself*** chashinŭl ŏktchehal su ŏpkke toeda 자신을 억제할 수 없게 되다; ***the situation is under ~*** sanghwang-ŭn t'ongjedoeŏt-tta 상황은 통제되었다; ***circumstances beyond our ~*** uriga t'ongjehal su ŏmnŭn sanghwang-ida 우리가 통제할 수 없는 상황이다; ***~s*** (*of aircraft, vehicle*) chojong changch'i 조종 장치; (*restrictions*) chehan 제한 **2** *v/t* (*govern*) chibaehada 지배하다; (*restrict*) chehanhada 제한하다; (*regulate*) t'ongjehada 통제하다; ***~ oneself*** chajehada 자제하다
control center t'ongjeshil 통제실
control freak F kwŏllyŏk chungdoktcha 권력 중독자
controlled substance kyuje yangmul 규제 약물
controlling interest FIN chibaejŏk ikkwŏn 지배적 이권
control panel cheŏban 제어반
control tower kwanjet'ap 관제탑
controversial nonjaeng-ŭl irŭk'inŭn 논쟁을 일으키는
controversy nonjaeng 논쟁
convalesce kŏn-gang-ŭl hoebok'ada 건강을 회복하다
convalescence hoebok-kki 회복기
convene *v/t* sojip'ada 소집하다
convenience (*of location, time*) p'yŏlli 편리; ***at your / my ~*** tangshini / naega p'yŏllihan ttaee 당신이 / 내가 편리한 때에; ***all (modern) ~s*** modŭn hyŏndaejŏgin p'yŏnŭi shisŏl 모든 현대적인 편의 시설

convenience food insŭt'ŏnt'ŭ shikp'um 인스턴트 식품
convenience store iryong chap'wa shikp'umjŏm 일용 잡화 식품점
convenient p'yŏllihan 편리한
convent sudowŏn 수도원
convention (*tradition*) kwansŭp 관습; (*conference*) taehoe 대회
conventional chŏnt'ongjŏgin 전통적인
convention center k'ŏnbenshyŏn sent'ŏ 컨벤션 센터
conventioneer taehoe ch'amgaja 대회 참가자
conversant: ***be ~ with*** ...ŭl/rŭl chal anŭn ...을/를 잘 아는
conversation taehwa 대화
conversational hoehwaŭi 회화의
converse *n* (*opposite*) pandae 반대
conversely pandaero 반대로
conversion chŏnhwan 전환; (*of unit of measurement*) hwansan 환산; (*of building*) kaejo 개조
conversion table hwansanp'yo 환산표
convert 1 *n* chŏnhyang 전향 **2** *v/t* pyŏnhage hada 변하게 하다; *unit of measurement* hwansanhada 환산하다; *building* kaejohada 개조하다; *person* chŏnhyangshik'ida 전향시키다
convertible *n* (*car*) kŏnbŏt'ŏbŭl 컨버터블
convey (*transmit*) chŏndarhada 전달하다; (*carry*) unbanhada 운반하다
conveyor belt k'ŏnbeiŏ pelt'ŭ 컨베이어 벨트
convict 1 *n* kigyŏlssu 기결수 **2** *v/t* LAW yujoerŭl sŏn-gohada 유죄를 선고하다; ***~ X of Y*** Xege Yŭi p'an-gyŏrŭl naerida X에게 Y의 판결을 내리다
conviction LAW yujoeŭi p'an-gyŏl 유죄의 판결; (*belief*) shinnyŏm 신념
convince hwaksshinshik'ida 확신시키다
convincing sŏlttŭngnyŏk innŭn 설득력 있는
convivial (*friendly*) k'waehwarhan 쾌활한
convoy (*of ships*) hosonghada 호송하다; (*of vehicles*) howihada 호위하다
convulsion MED kyŏngnyŏn 경련
cook 1 *n* yorisa 요리사 **2** *v/t* yorihada 요리하다; ***a ~ed meal*** yoridoen shikssa 요리된 식사 **3** *v/i* yorihada 요리하다
cookbook yorich'aek 요리책
cookery yorippŏp 요리법
cookie k'uk'i 쿠키
cooking (*food*) yori 요리
cool 1 *n* F ***keep one's ~*** ch'imch'ak'ada 침착하다; ***lose one's ~*** hŭngbunhada 흥분하다 **2** *adj weather, breeze* shiwŏnhan 시원한; *drink* ch'agaun 차가운; (*calm*) naengjŏnghan 냉정한; (*unfriendly*) naengdamhan 냉담한; F (*great*) kimak'ige kŭnsahan 기막히게 근사한 **3** *v/i* (*of food*) shiktta 식다; (*of tempers, interest*) karaantta 가라앉다 **4** *v/t* F: ***~ it*** ch'imch'ak'aseyo 침착하세요
♦**cool down 1** *v/i* (*of food, person*) shiktta 식다; (*of weather*) sŏnŭrhaejida 서늘해지다; (*of tempers*) karaantta 가라앉다 **2** *v/t food* shik'ida 식히다; *fig* karaanch'ida 가라앉히다
cooperate hyŏmnyŏk'ada 협력하다
cooperation hyŏmnyŏk 협력
cooperative 1 *n* COM hyŏpttong chohap 협동 조합 **2** *adj* COM hyŏpttong-ŭi 협동의; (*helpful*) hyŏmnyŏktchŏgin 협력적인
coordinate *activities* chojŏng chohwashik'ida 조정 조화시키다
coordination (*of activities*) chojŏng chohwa 조정 조화; (*of body*) undong shingyŏng 운동 신경
cop F kyŏngch'al 경찰
cope ch'ŏrihada 처리하다; ***~ with*** ...ŭl/rŭl ch'ŏrihada ...을/를 처리하다
copier (*machine*) pokssagi 복사기
copilot pujojongsa 부조종사
copious *amount* p'ungbuhan 풍부한; *notes* chasehan 자세한
copper *n* (*metal*) kuri 구리
copy 1 *n* (*duplicate, photocopy*)

pokssa 복사; (*imitation*) mobang 모방; (*of book*) pu 부; (*of record, CD*) chang 장; (*written material*) kisa kŏri 기사 거리; (*in advertisement*) kwanggo munan 광고 문안; ***make a ~ of a file*** COMPUT p'airŭl pokssahada 파일을 복사하다 **2** *v/t* (*imitate*) mobanghada 모방하다; (*duplicate, photocopy*) pokssahada 복사하다; (*in writing*) pekkyŏ ssŭda 베껴 쓰다; (*in order to cheat*) mollae pekkida 몰래 베끼다

copy cat F mobanghanŭn saram 모방하는 사람; **copycat crime** mobang pŏmjoe 모방 범죄; **copyright** *n* chŏjak-kkwŏn 저작권; **copywriter** k'ap'irait'ŏ 카피라이터

coral (*on seabed*) sanho 산호

cord (*string*) nokkŭn 노끈; (*cable*) chŏnsŏn 전선

cordial *adj* ch'ungshimŭrobut'ŏŭi 충심으로부터의

cordless phone musŏn chŏnhwagi 무선 전화기

cordon pisang kyŏnggyesŏn 비상 경계선

♦**cordon off** pisang kyŏnggyesŏnŭl ch'ida 비상 경계선을 치다

cords (*pants*) kolden paji 골덴 바지

corduroy kolden 골덴

core 1 *n* (*of fruit*) sok 속; (*of problem*) koltcha 골자; (*of organization, party*) haeksshim 핵심 **2** *adj issue* haeksshimjŏgin 핵심적인

cork (*in bottle*) k'orŭk'ŭ magae 코르크 마개; (*material*) k'orŭk'ŭ 코르크

corkscrew p'odoju pyŏng ttagae 포도주 병 따개

corn okssusu 옥수수

corner 1 *n* (*of page, room*) kusŏk 구석; (*of table, street*) mot'ung-i 모퉁이; (*bend: on road*) kilmot'ung-i 길모퉁이; (*in soccer*) k'onŏk'ik 코너킥; ***in the ~*** kusŏge(sŏ) 구석에(서); ***on the ~*** (*of street*) mot'ung-ie(sŏ) 모퉁이에(서) **2** *v/t person* kusŏgŭro molda 구석으로 몰다; ***~ the market*** shijang-ŭl toktchŏmhada 시장을 독점하다 **3** *v/i* (*of driver, car*) mot'ung-irŭl tolda 모퉁이를 돌다

corner kick k'onŏk'ik 코너킥

cornstarch nongmal 녹말

corny F (*trite*) chinbuhan 진부한; (*sentimental*) kamsangjŏgin 감상적인

coronary 1 *adj* shimjang-ŭi 심장의 **2** *n* shimjang mabi 심장 마비

coroner kŏmshigwan 검시관

corporal *n* sangbyŏng 상병

corporal punishment ch'ehyŏng 체형

corporate COM pŏbinŭi 법인의; ***~ image*** kiŏp imiji 기업 이미지; ***sense of ~ loyalty*** kiŏbe taehan ch'ungsŏngshim 기업에 대한 충성심

corporation (*business*) chushik hoesa 주식 회사

corps kundan 군단

corpse shich'e 시체

corpulent pimanhan 비만한

corpuscle hyŏlgu 혈구

corral *n* kach'uk uri 가축 우리

correct 1 *adj* orŭn 옳은; *time* chŏnghwak'an 정확한 **2** *v/t* koch'ida 고치다; *proofs* kyojŏnghada 교정하다

correction koch'in kŏt 고친 것

correspond (*match*) ilch'ihada 일치하다; (*write letters*) sŏshin wangnaehada 서신 왕래하다; ***~ to*** ...e haedanghada ...에 해당하다; ***~ with*** ...wa / kwa puhap'ada ...와 / 과 부합하다

correspondence (*match*) ilch'i 일치; (*letters*) p'yŏnji 편지; (*exchange of letters*) sŏshin wangnae 서신 왕래

correspondent (*letter writer*) p'yŏnjirŭl ssŭnŭn saram 편지를 쓰는 사람; (*reporter*) t'ŭkp'awŏn 특파원

corresponding *adj* taeŭnghanŭn 대응하는

corridor (*in building*) poktto 복도

corroborate hwaksshirhage hada 확실하게 하다

corrode *v/t & v/i* pushik'ada 부식하다

corrosion pushik 부식

corrugated cardboard kolp'anji 골판지

corrugated iron korhamsŏk 골함석

corrupt 1 *adj* t'arak'an 타락한; COMPUT t'ŭllin koshi manŭn 틀린 곳이 많은 **2** *v/t* t'araksshik'ida

타락시키다; (*bribe*) maesuhada 매수하다
corruption t'arak 타락
cosmetic *adj* hwajangnyŏng-ŭi 화장용의; *fig* p'yomyŏnjŏgin 표면적인
cosmetics hwajangp'um 화장품
cosmetic surgeon sŏnghyŏng-oekkwa ŭisa 성형외과 의사
cosmetic surgery sŏnghyŏng-oekkwa 성형외과
cosmonaut uju pihaengsa 우주 비행사
cosmopolitan *city* taguktchogŭi 다국적의
cost 1 *n* kagyŏk 가격; (*~ price, in manufacturing*) wŏnkka 원가; *fig* hŭisaeng 희생; **~s** piyong 비용 **2** *v/t money, time* tŭlda 들다; FIN *project* saengsanbirŭl kyŏnjŏk'ada 생산비를 견적하다; ***how much does it ~?*** piyong-i ŏlmana tŭmnikka? 비용이 얼마나 듭니까?; ***it ~ me my health*** kŭgot-ttaemune kŏn-gang-ŭl irŏt-tta 그것때문에 건강을 잃었다
cost and freight COM unim p'oham kagyŏk 운임 포함 가격; **cost-conscious** kyŏngbirŭl chŏlgamhanŭn 경비를 절감하는; **cost-effective** piyong hyokkwajŏgin 비용 효과적인; **cost, insurance and freight** COM pohŏm mit unim p'oham kagyŏk 보험 및 운임 포함 가격
costly *error* sonshiri k'ŭn 손실이 큰
cost of living saenghwalbi 생활비
cost price wŏnkka 원가
costume (*for actor*) ŭisang 의상
costume jewelry mojo posŏngnyu 모조 보석류
cot (*camp-bed*) kani ch'imdae 간이 침대
cottage shigoltchip 시골집
cotton 1 *n* myŏn 면 **2** *adj* myŏnŭro mandŭn 면으로 만든
♦**cotton on** F ihaehada 이해하다
♦**cotton on to** F …ŭl / rŭl kkaedatkke toeda …을 / 를 깨닫게 되다
♦**cotton to** F …ege hogamŭl kajida …에게 호감을 가지다
cotton candy somsat'ang 솜사탕
couch *n* sop'a 소파
couch potato F t'edori 테돌이
couchette chimdaech'atkkan 침대찻간
cough 1 *n* kich'im 기침; (*to get attention*) kich'im sori 기침 소리 **2** *v/i* kich'imhada 기침하다; (*to get attention*) kich'im sorirŭl naeda 기침 소리를 내다
♦**cough up 1** *v/t blood etc* kich'imhayŏ naebaet-tta 기침하여 내뱉다; F *money* maji mot'ae naejuda 마지 못해 내주다 **2** *v/i* F (*pay*) maji mot'ae naeda 마지 못해 내다
cough medicine, cough syrup kich'im yak / shirŏp 기침 약 / 시럽
could: ***~ I have my key?*** che yŏlsoerŭl chushigessŏyo? 제 열쇠를 주시겠어요?; ***~ you help me?*** chŏl towajushil su issŏyo? 절 도와주실 수 있어요?; ***this ~ be our bus*** uri pŏsŭinjido morŭnda 우리 버스인지도 모른다; ***you ~ be right*** nega majŭl sudo issŏ 네가 맞을 수도 있어; ***I ~n't say for sure*** hwaksshirhadago marhal sunŭn ŏpssŏyo 확실하다고말할 수는 없어요; ***he ~ have got lost*** kŭnŭn kirŭl irŏbŏryŏssŭltchido morŭnda 그는 길을 잃어버렸을지도 모른다; ***you ~ have warned me!*** nahant'e miri yaegirŭl haessŏyaji! 나한테 미리 얘기를 했어야지!
council (*assembly*) hoeŭi 회의; POL ŭihoe 의회
councilman shiŭihoe ŭiwŏn 시의회 의원
councilor ŭiwŏn 의원
counsel 1 *n* (*advice*) choŏn 조언; (*lawyer*) pyŏnhosa 변호사 **2** *v/t* (*advise*) choŏnhada 조언하다; (*because of problems*) …wa / kwa sangdamhada …와 / 과 상담하다
counseling sangdam 상담
counselor (*adviser*) sangdamnyŏk 상담역; LAW pyŏnhosa 변호사
count 1 *n* (*number arrived at*) ch'onggye 총계; (*counting*) sem 셈; (*in baseball, boxing*) k'aunt'ŭ

카운트; ***keep ~ of*** ...ŭl / rŭl kyesok seda ...을 / 를 계속 세다; ***lose ~ of*** ...ŭi semŭl ijŏbŏrida ...의 셈을 잊어버리다; ***at the last ~*** ch'oejongsuro 최종수로 **2** *v/i* (*to ten etc*) surŭl seda 수를 세다; (*calculate*) kyesanhada 계산하다; (*be important*) kach'iga it-tta 가치가 있다; (*qualify*) semŭro ch'ida 셈으로 치다 **3** *v/t* (*~ up*) seda 세다; (*calculate*) kyesanhada 계산하다; (*include*) ch'ida 치다

♦**count on** ...ege kidaeda ...에게 기대다

countdown ch'o ilkki 초 읽기

countenance *v/t* yongnap'ada 용납하다

counter[1] (*in shop, café*) k'aunt'ŏ 카운터; (*in game*) san-gaji 산가지

counter[2] **1** *v/t* ...ŭi hyokkwarŭl churida ..의 효과를 줄이다 **2** *v/i* (*retaliate*) matssŏda 맞서다

counter[3]: ***run ~ to*** ...e pandaedoeda ...에 반대되다

counteract chunghwahada 중화하다; **counter-attack 1** *n* yŏkssŭp 역습 **2** *v/i* yŏkssŭp'ada 역습하다; **counterclockwise** panshigye panghyang 반시계 방향; **counterespionage** pangch'ŏp 방첩

counterfeit 1 *v/t* wijohada 위조하다 **2** *adj* wijoŭi 위조의

counterpart (*person*) *kat'ŭn chiwiŭi saram* 같은 지위의 사람; **counterproductive** yŏk'yokkwaŭi 역효과의; **countersign** *v/t* pusŏhada 부서하다

countless sel su omnŭn 셀 수 없는

country nara 나라; (*not town*) shigol 시골; ***in the ~*** shigore(sŏ) 시골에(서)

country and western MUS k'ŏnt'ŭri myujik 컨트리 뮤직

countryman (*fellow ~*) kat'ŭn nara saram 같은 나라 사람

countryside shigol 시골

county kun 군

coup POL k'udet'a 쿠데타; *fig* taesŏnggong 대성공

couple (*married*) pubu 부부; (*man & woman*) namnyŏ han ssang 남녀 한 쌍; (*two people*) han ssang 한 쌍; ***just a ~*** chogŭm 조금; ***a ~ of*** (*people*) tusŏnŏsŭi 두서넛의; (*things*) tusŏnŏ kae 두서너 개; ***a ~ of days*** isahŭl 이사흘

coupon (*form*) shinch'ŏngkkwŏn 신청권; (*voucher*) k'up'on 쿠폰

courage yonggi 용기

courageous yonggi innŭn 용기 있는

courier (*messenger*) paedal 배달; (*with tourist party*) annaewŏn 안내원

course *n* (*series of lessons*) kyokkwa kwajŏng 교과 과정; (*part of meal, for race*) k'osŭ 코스; (*of ship, plane*) haengno 행로; ***of ~*** (*certainly*) mullon 물론; (*naturally*) tang-yŏnhi 당연히; ***of ~ not*** mullon anijyo 물론 아니죠; ***~ of action*** haengdong pangch'im 행동 방침; ***~ of treatment*** chillyo kwajŏng 진료 과정; ***in the ~ of*** ... tong-ane ... 동안에

court *n* LAW pŏptchŏng 법정; (*courthouse*) pŏbwŏn 법원; SP k'ot'ŭ 코트; ***take X to ~*** Xŭl / rŭl chaep'ane kŏlda X을 / 를 재판에 걸다

court case sosong sakkŏn 소송 사건

courteous chŏngjunghan 정중한

courtesy chŏngjungham 정중함

courthouse pŏbwŏn 법원; **court martial 1** *n* kunppŏp hoeŭi 군법 회의 **2** *v/t* kunppŏp hoeŭie hoebuhada 군법 회의에 회부하다; **court music** aak 아악; **court order** pŏbwŏn myŏngnyŏng 법원 명령; **courtroom** pŏptchŏng 법정; **courtyard** anmadang 안마당

cousin sach'on 사촌

cove (*bay*) humijin kot 후미진 곳

cover 1 *n* (*protective*) tŏpkkae 덮개; (*of book, magazine*) p'yoji 표지; (*for bed*) ch'imdaeppo 침대보; (*shelter*) ŏmhomul 엄호물; (*shelter from rain etc*) p'inanch'ŏ 피난처; (*insurance*) pohŏm 보험 **2** *v/t* tŏptta 덮다; (*in blood, mud etc*) ssŭiuda 씌우다; (*hide*) sumgida 숨기다; (*of insurance policy*) pohŏme kŏlda 보험에 걸다; *distance* tapp'ahada 답파하다; (*of journalist*) podohada 보도하다

♦**cover up 1** *v/t* tŏptta 덮다; *fig* kamch'uda 감추다 **2** *v/i fig* kamch'uda 감추다; ***~ for X*** Xŭl / rŭl tudunhada X을 / 를 두둔하다

coverage (*by media*) podo 보도
covering letter ch'ŏmbusŏ 첨부서
covert pimirŭi 비밀의
coverup (*of crime*) ŭnp'ye 은폐
cow *n* amso 암소
coward kŏptchaeng-i 겁쟁이
cowardice pigŏp 비겁
cowardly pigŏp'an 비겁한
cowboy k'auboi 카우보이
cower umch'ŭrida 움츠리다
coy (*evasive*) hoep'ihanŭn 회피하는; (*flirtatious*) sujubŏhanŭn 수줍어하는
cozy anŭk'an 아늑한
CPU (= ***central processing unit***) chung-ang ch'ŏri changch'i 중앙 처리 장치
crab *n* ke 게
crack 1 *n* kallajin kŭm 갈라진 금; (*joke*) pikkonŭn nongdam 비꼬는 농담 **2** *v/t cup*, *glass* kŭmgage hada 금가게 하다; *nut* kkaeda 깨다; *code* p'ulda 풀다; F (*solve*) haegyŏrhada 해결하다; ~ ***a joke*** nongdamhada 농담하다 **3** *v/i* kŭmi kada 금이 가다; ***get ~ing*** F irŭl shijak'ada 일을 시작하다
♦**crack down on** ...ŭl / rŭl ŏmhage tasŭrida ...을 / 를 엄하게 다스리다
♦**crack up** *v/i* (*have breakdown*) shin-gyŏng soeyage kŏllida 신경 쇠약에 걸리다; F (*laugh*) kaptchagi utkki shijak'ada 갑자기 웃기 시작하다
crackdown tansok 단속
cracked *cup*, *glass* kŭmi kan 금이 간
cracker (*to eat*) k'ŭraek'ŏ 크래커
crackle *v/i* (*of fire*) ttakttak sorirŭl naeda 딱딱 소리를 내다
cradle *n* (*for baby*) yoram 요람
craft[1] NAUT sŏnbak 선박
craft[2] (*art*) kong-ye 공예; (*skill*) kinŭng 기능
craftsman chang-in 장인
crafty kyohwarhan 교활한
crag (*rock*) hŏmhan pawi 험한 바위
cram *v/t* mirŏ nŏt'a 밀어 넣다
cramped *room* pijobŭn 비좁은
cramps kŭpkkyŏk'an pokt'ong 급격한 복통
cranberry tŏnggulwŏlgyul 덩굴월귤
crane 1 *n* (*machine*) kijunggi 기중기; (*bird*) hak 학 **2** *v/t*: ~ ***one's neck*** mogŭl kilge ppaeda 목을 길게 빼다
crank *n* (*strange person*) koetcha 괴짜
crankshaft kŭraengk'ŭch'uk 크랭크축
cranky (*bad-tempered*) shimgiga twit'ŭllin 심기가 뒤틀린
crap F (*garbage*) ssŭregi 쓰레기
crash 1 *n* (*noise*) k'wang hanŭn sori 쾅 하는 소리; (*accident*) ch'ungdol 충돌; (*plane* ~) ch'urak 추락; COM munŏjim 무너짐; COMPUT kojang 고장 **2** *v/i* (*make noise*) k'wang hanŭn sorirŭl naeda 쾅 하는 소리를 내다; (*of thunder*) ch'ida 치다; (*of car*) ch'ungdorhada 충돌하다; (*of airplane*) ch'urak'ada 추락하다; (COM: *of market*) punggoehada 붕괴하다; COMPUT kojangnada 고장나다; F (*sleep*) chada 자다 **3** *v/t car* ch'ungdolshik'ida 충돌시키다
♦**crash out** F (*fall asleep*) kora ttŏrŏjida 곯아 떨어지다
crash course chiptchung kangjwa 집중 강좌; **crash diet** sokssŏng taiŏt'ŭ 속성 다이어트; **crash helmet** anjŏn helmet 안전 헬멧; **crash landing** pulshich'ak 불시착
crate namu sangja 나무 상자
crater (*of volcano*) punhwagu 분화구
crave kalmanghada 갈망하다
craving kalmang 갈망
crawl 1 *n* (*stroke*) kŭrol suyŏng 크롤 수영; ***at a*** ~ (*slowly*) nŭrinnŭrit'age 느릿느릿하게 **2** *v/i* (*on floor*) kida 기다; (*move slowly*) nŭrinnŭrit kada 느릿느릿 가다
♦**crawl with** ...(ŭ)ro ugŭlgŏrida ...(으)로 우글거리다
crayon k'ŭreyong 크레용
craze ilsshijŏk taeyuhaeng 일시적 대유행; ***the latest*** ~ ch'oegŭnŭi taeyuhaeng 최근의 대유행
crazy *adj* mich'in 미친; ***be ~ about*** ...e yŏlgwanghada ...에 열광하다
creak 1 *n* ppigŏk-kkŏrinŭn sori 삐걱거리는 소리 **2** *v/i* ppigŏk-kkŏrida 삐걱거리다
cream 1 *n* (*for skin*, *coffee*, *cake*) k'ŭrim 크림; (*color*) tamhwangsaek 담황색 **2** *adj* tamhwangsaegŭi

담황색의

cream cheese k'ŭrim ch'ijŭ 크림 치즈

creamer (*pitcher*) k'ŭrim kŭrŭt 크림 그릇; (*for coffee*) p'ŭrima 프리마

creamy (*with lots of cream*) k'ŭrimi mani tŭrŏgan 크림이 많이 들어간

crease 1 *n* (*accidental*) kugimsal 구김살; (*deliberate*) churŭm 주름 **2** *v/t* (*accidentally*) kugida 구기다

create 1 *v/t* ch'angjohada 창조하다; *uncertainty*, *problem* yagihada 야기하다 **2** *v/i* ch'angjohada 창조하다

creation ch'angjo 창조; (*sth created*) ch'angjomul 창조물; ***the Creation*** REL Ch'ŏnji ch'angjo 천지 창조

creative ch'angjojŏgin 창조적인

creator ch'angjoja 창조자; (*author*) ch'angjaktcha 창작자; (*founder*) ch'angsŏltcha 창설자; ***the Creator*** REL Chomultchu 조물주

creature (*animal*) tongmul 동물; (*person*) saram 사람

credibility (*of person*) shilloesŏng 신뢰성; (*of story*) shinbingsŏng 신빙성

credible (*believable*) midŭl manhan 믿을 만한; *candidate etc* shilloegam kanŭn 신뢰감 가는

credit 1 *n* FIN oesang 외상; (*loan*) shinyong taebu 신용 대부; (*honor*) kongno 공로; (*payment received*) yegŭmaek 예금액; ***be in ~*** yegŭmi it-tta 예금이 있다; ***get the ~ for X*** Xe taehan kongnorŭl injŏngpat-tta X에 대한 공로를 인정받다 **2** *v/t* (*believe*) mit-tta 믿다; ***~ an amount to an account*** kyejwae yegŭmhada 계좌에 예금하다

creditable ch'ingch'anhal manhan 칭찬할 만한

credit card shinyong k'adŭ 신용 카드

credit limit (*of credit card*) shinyong taebuŭi hando 신용 대부의 한도

creditor ch'aegwŏnja 채권자

creditworthy shinyonginnŭn 신용있는

credulous chal minnŭn 잘 믿는

creed (*beliefs*) shin-gyŏng 신경

creek (*stream*) chagŭn nae 작은 내

creep 1 *n pej* anikkoun saram 아니꼬운 사람 **2** *v/i* salgŭmsalgŭm kŏt-tta 살금살금 걷다

creeper BOT tŏnggul shingmul 덩굴 식물

creeps: ***the house / he gives me the ~*** kŭ chibi / kŭga narŭl sŏmttŭk'age handa 그 집이 / 그가 나를 섬뜩하게 한다

creepy sŏmttŭk'an 섬뜩한

cremate hwajanghada 화장하다

cremation hwajang 화장

crematorium hwajangjang 화장장

crescent ch'osŭngttal moyang 초승달 모양

crest (*of hill*) kkokttaegi 꼭대기; (*of bird*) pyŏt 볏

crestfallen p'uri chugŭn 풀이 죽은

crevice kallajin t'ŭm 갈라진 틈

crew *n* (*of ship*, *airplane*) sŭngmuwŏn chŏnwŏn 승무원 전원; (*of repairmen etc*) t'im 팀; (*group*) p'aegŏri 패거리

crew cut sanggo mŏri 상고 머리

crew neck swet'aŭi tunggŭn mok 쉐타의 둥근 목

crib *n* (*for baby*) yuayong ch'imdae 유아용 침대

crick: ***~ in the neck*** mogŭl ppida 목을 삐다

cricket (*insect*) kwitturami 귀뚜라미

crime pŏmjoe 범죄; (*shameful act*) yugamsŭrŏn il 유감스런 일

criminal 1 *n* pŏmjoeja 범죄자 **2** *adj* pŏmjoeŭi 범죄의; (LAW: *not civil*) hyŏngsasang-ŭi 형사상의; (*shameful*) yugamsŭrŏn 유감스런

crimson *adj* chinhongsaegŭi 진홍색의

cringe momŭl umsshirhada 몸을 움찔하다

cripple 1 *n* (*disabled person*) shinch'e chang-aeja 신체 장애자 **2** *v/t person* pulguga toege hada 불구가 되게 하다; *fig* munŭnghage hada 무능하게 하다

crisis wigi 위기

crisp *adj weather*, *air* sangk'waehan 상쾌한; *apple*, *bacon* p'asakp'asak'an 파삭파삭한; *new shirt*, *bills* ppatppat'an 빳빳한

criterion (*standard*) kijun 기준

critic pip'yŏngga 비평가

critical (*making criticisms*) pip'anjŏgin 비판적인; (*serious*) wigijŏgin 위기적인; *moment etc* kyŏltchŏngjŏgin 결정적인; MED widok'an 위독한
critically *speak etc* pip'anjŏgŭro 비판적으로; ~ ***ill*** widok'an 위독한
criticism pip'yŏng 비평
criticize *v/t* pip'yŏnghada 비평하다
croak *v/i* (*of frog*) kaegulgaegul ulda 개굴개굴 울다; (*of person*) shwin mokssorirŭl naeda 쉰 목소리를 내다
crockery tojagiryu 도자기류
crocodile agŏ 악어
crony F ch'in-gu 친구
crook *n* (*dishonest*) sagikkun 사기꾼
crooked (*twisting*) kuburŏjin 구부러진; *necktie, picture* pitturŏjin 비뚤어진; (*dishonest*) pujŏnghan 부정한
crop 1 *n* nongjangmul 농작물; *fig* suhwak 수확 **2** *v/t hair, photo* tchalkke charŭda 짧게 자르다
♦**crop up** kaptchagi saenggida 갑자기 생기다
cross 1 *adj* (*angry*) sŏngnan 성난 **2** *n* (*X*) kopp'yo 곱표; (*Christian symbol*) shiptchaga 십자가 **3** *v/t* (*go across*) kŏnnŏgada 건너가다; ~ ***oneself*** REL kasŭme shiptcharŭl kŭt-tta 가슴에 십자를 긋다; ~ ***one's legs*** tarirŭl kkoda 다리를 꼬다; ***keep one's fingers ~ed*** haeng-unŭl pilda 행운을 빌다; ***it never ~ed my mind*** kŭ saenggagŭn na-ege ttŏorŭji anat-tta 그 생각은 내게 떠오르지 않았다 **4** *v/i* (*go across*) kŏnnŏgada 건너가다; (*of lines*) kyoch'ahada 교차하다
♦**cross off, cross out** chiuda 지우다
crossbar (*of goal*) kolttae 골대; (*of bicycle*) chungshimdae 중심대; (*in high jump*) pa 바
cross-country (**skiing**) sŭk'i k'ŭrosŭk'ŏnt'ŭri 스키 크로스컨트리
crossed check hoengsŏn sup'yo 횡선 수표
cross-examine LAW pandae shimmunhada 반대 심문하다
cross-eyed sashiŭi 사시의
crossing NAUT hoengdan 횡단
crossroads kyoch'aro 교차로; **cross-section** (*of people*) taep'yojŏgin myŏn 대표적인 면; **crosswalk** hoengdan podo 횡단 보도; **crossword** (**puzzle**) kŭltcha match'ugi nori 글자 맞추기 놀이
crouch *v/i* momŭl kuburida 몸을 구부리다
crow *n* (*bird*) kkamagwi 까마귀; ***as the ~ flies*** iljikssŏnŭro 일직선으로
crowd *n* kunjung 군중; (*at sports event*) kwanjung 관중
crowded pumbinŭn 붐비는
crown 1 *n* wanggwan 왕관; (*on tooth*) ch'igwan 치관 **2** *v/t* wang-wie ollida 왕위에 올리다; *tooth* ssŭiuda 씌우다
crucial kyŏltchŏngjŏgin 결정적인
crude 1 *adj* (*vulgar*) sangsŭrŏun 상스러운; (*unsophisticated*) chojap'an 조잡한 **2** *n*: ~ (***oil***) wŏnyu 원유
cruel chaninhan 잔인한
cruelty chaninham 잔인함
cruise 1 *n* sunhang 순항 **2** *v/i* (*in ship*) sunhanghada 순항하다; (*of car*) kyŏngje sokttoro kada 경제 속도로 가다; (*of plane*) sunhang sokttoro nalda 순항 속도로 날다
cruise liner sunhangsŏn 순항선
cruising speed sunhan soktto 순항 속도; (*of project*) sunjoroun soktto 순조로운 속도
crumb pusŭrŏgi 부스러기
crumble 1 *v/t* pusŭrŏttŭrida 부스러뜨리다 **2** *v/i* (*of bread, stone*) pusŭrojida 부스러지다; *fig* (*of opposition etc*) munŏjida 무너지다
crumple 1 *v/t* (*crease*) kugida 구기다 **2** *v/i* (*collapse*) munŏjida 무너지다
crunch 1 *n*: ***when it comes to the ~*** F kyŏltchŏngjŏgin shigiga omyŏn 결정적인 시기가 오면 **2** *v/i* (*of snow, gravel*) wajak-wajak soriga nada 와작와작 소리가 나다
crusade *n fig* kaehyŏk undong 개혁 운동
crush 1 *n* (*crowd*) kunjung 군중; ***have a ~ on*** …ege holttak panhada …에게 홀딱 반하다 **2** *v/t* pakssarŭl naeda 박살을 내다; (*crease*) kugida 구기다; ***they were ~ed to death***

kŭdŭrŭn pakssalla chugŏt-tta 그들은 박살나 죽었다 **3** *v/i* (*crease*) kugyŏjida 구겨지다
crust (*on bread*) ttakttak'an kkŏptchil 딱딱한 껍질
crutch (*for walking*) mokttari 목다리
cry 1 *n* (*call*) oech'im 외침; ***have a ~*** ulda 울다 **2** *v/t* (*call*) oech'ida 외치다 **3** *v/i* (*weep*) ulda 울다
♦**cry out 1** *v/t* oech'yŏ purŭda 외쳐 부르다 **2** *v/i* koham chirŭda 고함 지르다
♦**cry out for** (*need*) ...ŭl / rŭl p'iryoro hada ...을 / 를 필요로 하다
crystal (*mineral*) sujŏng 수정; (*glass*) k'urisŭt'ŏl 크리스털
crystallize *v/t & v/i* kuch'ehwahada 구체화하다
cub saekki 새끼
cube (*shape*) ip-ppangch'e 입방체
cubic ip-ppang-ŭi 입방의
cubic capacity TECH ip-ppang yongnyang 입방 용량
cubicle (*changing room*) t'arŭishil 탈의실
cucumber oi 오이
cuddle 1 *n* p'oong 포옹 **2** *v/t* kkok kkyŏantta 꼭 껴안다
cuddly *kitten etc* kkyŏankko ship'ŭn 껴안고 싶은; (*liking cuddles*) kkyŏankko ship'ŏhanŭn 껴안고 싶어하는
cue *n* (*for actor, pool etc*) k'yu 큐
cuff 1 *n* (*of shirt*) somaetppuri 소맷부리; (*of pants*) pajittan 바지단; (*blow*) ch'alssak ttaerim 찰싹 때림; ***off the ~*** chŭkssŏgŭi 즉석의 **2** *v/t* (*hit*) ch'alssak ttaerida 찰싹 때리다
cuff link k'ŏp'ŭsŭ tanch'u 커프스 단추
culinary yoriŭi 요리의
culminate: ***~ in*** ...(ŭ)ro chŏltchŏng-e tarhada ...(으)로 절정에 달하다
culmination chŏltchŏng 절정
culprit pŏmin 범인
cult (*sect*) sagyo chipttan 사교 집단
cultivate *land* kyŏngjak'ada 경작하다; *person* chal sagwida 잘 사귀다
cultivated *person* seryŏndoen 세련된
cultivation (*of land*) kyŏngjak 경작
cultural munhwajŏgin 문화적인
culture *n* munhwa 문화
cultured (*cultivated*) seryŏndoen 세련된
culture shock munhwajŏk ch'unggyŏk 문화적 충격
cumbersome sŏnggashin 성가신
cunning 1 *n* kyohwarham 교활함 **2** *adj* kyohwarhan 교활한
cup *n* chan 잔; (*trophy*) usŭngk'ŏp 우승컵; ***a ~ of tea*** ch'a han chan 차 한 잔
cupboard ch'antchang 찬장
curable ch'iryohal su innŭn 치료할 수 있는
curator k'yureit'ŏ 큐레이터
curb 1 *n* (*of street*) yŏnsŏk 연석; (*on powers etc*) ŏktche 억제 **2** *v/t* ŏktchehada 억제하다
curdle *v/i* (*of milk*) ŭnggohada 응고하다
cure 1 *n* MED ch'iryo 치료 **2** *v/t* MED ch'iryohada 치료하다; *meat, fish* pojon ch'ŏrihada 보존 처리하다
curfew yagan oech'ul kŭmji 야간 외출 금지
curiosity (*inquisitiveness*) hogishim 호기심
curious (*inquisitive*) hogishim manŭn 호기심 많은; (*strange*) isanghan 이상한
curiously (*inquisitively*) hogishimesŏ 호기심에서; (*strangely*) isanghage 이상하게; ***~ enough*** isanghagedo 이상하게도
curl 1 *n* (*in hair*) kopssŭlgŏrim 곱슬거림; (*of smoke*) maemdom 맴돔 **2** *v/t hair* kopssŭlgŏrige hada 곱슬거리게 하다; (*wind*) kamtta 감다 **3** *v/i* (*of hair*) kopssŭlgŏrida 곱슬거리다; (*of paper etc*) tunggŭlge ogŭradŭlda 둥글게 오그라들다
♦**curl up** umch'urida 움추리다
curly *hair* kopssŭlgŏrinŭn 곱슬거리는; *tail* kkobulgŏrinŭn 꼬불거리는
currant (*dried fruit*) kŏnp'odo 건포도
currency (*money*) t'onghwa 통화; ***foreign ~*** oehwa 외화
current 1 *n* hŭrŭm 흐름; (*tidal*) choryu 조류; ELEC chŏllyu 전류 **2** *adj* (*present*) chigŭmŭi 지금의
current affairs shisa 시사
current affairs program shisa

p'ŭrograem 시사 프로그램
currently chigŭm 지금
curriculum kyokkwa kwajŏng 교과 과정
curse 1 *n* (*spell*) chŏju 저주; (*swear-word*) yokssŏl 욕설 **2** *v/t* chŏjuhada 저주하다; (*swear at*) yok'ada 욕하다 **3** *v/i* (*swear*) yok'ada 욕하다
cursor COMPUT k'ŏsŏ 커서
cursory p'isangjŏgin 피상적인
curt t'ungmyŏngsŭrŏun 퉁명스러운
curtail churida 줄이다
curtain k'ŏt'ŭn 커튼; THEA mak 막
curve 1 *n* kokssŏn 곡선 **2** *v/i* (*bend*) kuburŏjida 구부러지다
cushion 1 *n* (*for couch etc*) k'ushyŏn 쿠션 **2** *v/t fall* wanhwahada 완화하다
custard k'ŏsŭt'ŏdŭ 커스터드
custody (*of children*) yangnyuk-kkwŏn 양육권; ***in ~*** LAW kuryu chung 구류 중
custom (*tradition*) kwansŭp 관습; COM tan-gol 단골; ***as was his ~*** kŭŭi sŭpkkwanŭro 그의 습관으로
customary sŭpkkwanjŏgin 습관적인; (*socially*) t'ongnyeŭi 통례의; ***it is ~ to ...*** ... hanŭn kŏshi t'ongnyeida ... 하는 것이 통례이다
customer kogaek 고객
customer relations kogaek kwalli 고객 관리
customs kwanse 관세
customs clearance segwan t'onggwa 세관 통과; **customs inspection** segwan kŏmsa 세관 검사; **customs officer** segwanwŏn 세관원
cut 1 *n* (*with knife*) pegi 베기; (*with scissors*) charŭgi 자르기; (*injury*) pen sangch'ŏ 벤 상처; (*of garment, hair*) marŭmjil 마름질; (*reduction*) sak-kkam 삭감; ***my hair needs a ~*** nanŭn mŏrirŭl challayagessŏyo 나는 머리를 잘라야겠어요 **2** *v/t* (*with knife*) peda 베다; (*with scissors*) charŭda 자르다; (*reduce*) sak-kkamhada 삭감하다; ***get one's hair ~*** mŏrirŭl charŭda 머리를 자르다
♦**cut back 1** *v/i* (*in costs*) ch'ukssohada 축소하다 **2** *v/t employees* sak-kkamhada 삭감하다
♦**cut down 1** *v/t* peŏ nŏmŏttŭrida 베어 넘어뜨리다 **2** *v/i* (*in smoking etc*) churida 줄이다
♦**cut down on** *smoking etc* ...ŭl / rŭl churida ...을 / 를 줄이다
♦**cut off** (*with knife etc*) peŏnaeda 베어내다; (*with scissors*) challanaeda 잘라내다; (*isolate*) koripsshik'ida 고립시키다; TELEC kkŭnt'a 끊다; ***we were ~*** chŏnhwaga kkŭnk'yŏssŏyo 전화가 끊겼어요
♦**cut out** (*with scissors*) oryŏnaeda 오려내다; (*eliminate*) chungdanhada 중단하다; (*exclude*) ch'adanhada 차단하다; ***cut that out!*** F kŭman twŏ! 그만 둬!; ***be ~ for X*** Xe ttak chŏk'ap'ada X에 딱 적합하다
♦**cut up** *v/t meat etc* t'omakch'ida 토막치다
cutback sak-kkam 삭감
cute (*pretty*) kwiyŏun 귀여운; (*sexually*) maeryŏktchŏgin 매력적인; (*clever*) yŏngnihan 영리한
cuticle p'yop'i 표피
cut-price harinkkaŭi 할인가의
cut-throat *competition* ch'iyŏrhan 치열한
cutting 1 *n* (*from newspaper*) oryŏnaen kŏt 오려낸 것 **2** *adj remark* shillarhan 신랄한
cyberspace kasang konggan 가상 공간
cycle 1 *n* (*bicycle*) chajŏn-gŏ 자전거; (*series of events*) sunhwan 순환 **2** *v/i* chajŏn-gŏro kada 자전거로 가다
cycling chajŏn-gŏ t'agi 자전거 타기
cyclist chajŏn-gŏ t'anŭn saram 자전거 타는 사람
cylinder (*container*) wŏnt'ong 원통; (*in engine*) kit'ong 기통
cylindrical wŏnt'ong moyang-ŭi 원통 모양의
cynic pikkonŭn saram 비꼬는 사람
cynical naengsojŏgin 냉소적인
cynicism naengso 냉소
cyst p'onang 포낭
Czech 1 *adj* Ch'ek'oŭi 체코의; ***the ~ Republic*** Ch'ek'o konghwaguk 체코 공화국 **2** *n* (*person*) Ch'ek'o saram 체코 사람; (*language*) Ch'ek'oŏ 체코어

D

DA (= ***district attorney***) chibang kŏmsa 지방 검사
dab 1 *n* (*small amount*) soryang 소량 **2** *v/t* (*remove*) saltchak takkanaeda 살짝 닦아내다; (*apply*) kabyŏpkke parŭda 가볍게 바르다
♦**dabble in** chamkkan sonŭl taeda 잠깐 손을 대다
dad appa 아빠
dagger tando 단도
daily 1 *n* (*paper*) shinmun 신문 **2** *adj* maeirŭi 매일의; ~ ***newspaper*** ilgan shinmun 일간 신문
dainty sŏmsehan 섬세한
dairy products yujep'um 유제품
dais yŏndan 연단
dam 1 *n* (*for water*) ttaem 댐 **2** *v/t river* taemŭro maktta 댐으로 막다
damage 1 *n* p'ihae 피해; *fig* (*to reputation etc*) sonsang 손상 **2** *v/t* p'ihaerŭl ip'ida 피해를 입히다; *fig: reputation etc* sonsangshik'ida 손상시키다
damages LAW sonhae paesanggŭm 손해 배상금
damaging sonsangshik'inŭn 손상시키는
dame F (*woman*) yŏja 여자
damn 1 *interj* F chegirŏl 제기랄 **2** *n* F: ***I don't give a ~!*** naega alkke mwŏya! 내가 알게 뭐야! **3** *adj* F pirŏmŏgŭl 빌어먹을 **4** *adv* F pirŏmŏk-kke 빌어먹게 **5** *v/t* (*condemn*) hŏlttŭt-tta 헐뜯다; ~ ***it!*** F chenjanghal! 젠장할!; ***I'm ~ed if*** F nanŭn chŏlttaero … haji ank'et-tta 나는 절대로 … 하지 않겠다
damned → ***damn*** *adj & adv*
damp *cloth* ch'ukch'uk'an 축축한; *building, room* sŭpkkich'an 습기찬
dampen ch'ukch'uk'age hada 축축하게 하다
dance 1 *n* ch'um 춤; (*social event*) taensŭ p'ati 댄스 파티 **2** *v/i* ch'umch'uda 춤추다; ***would you like to ~?*** ch'um ch'ushigessŏyo? 춤 추시겠어요?
dancer ch'umch'unŭn saram 춤추는 사람; (*performer*) muyongga 무용가
dancing muyong 무용
dandruff pidŭm 비듬
Dane Tenmak'ŭ saram 덴마크 사람
danger wihŏm 위험; ***out of ~*** (*of patient*) chungt'ae-esŏ pŏsŏnan 중태에서 벗어난
dangerous wihŏmhan 위험한; *assumption* wit'aeroun 위태로운
dangle *v/t & v/i* tallanggŏrida 달랑거리다
Danish 1 *adj* Tenmak'ŭŭi 덴마크의 **2** *n* (*language*) Tenmak'ŭŏ 덴마크어
Danish (**pastry**) tenishwi p'aesŭch'yuri 데니쉬 패스츄리
dare 1 *v/i*: ***he didn't ~*** kŭnŭn kamhi hal su ŏpssŏssŏyo 그는 감히 할 수 없었어요; ***how ~ you!*** nega kamhi ŏttŏk'e! 네가 감히 어떻게! **2** *v/t*: ~ ***X to do Y*** Xege Yŭl / rŭl tojŏnhae porago hada X에게 Y을 / 를 도전해 보라고 하다
daring *adj* taedamhan 대담한
dark 1 *n* ŏdum 어둠; ***after ~*** haejin hue 해진 후에; ***keep s.o. in the ~*** *fig* nuguege morŭge hada 누구에게 모르게 하다 **2** *adj room, night* ŏduun 어두운; *hair, eyes* kŏmusŭrŭmhan 거무스름한; *color* chinhan 진한; *clothes* ŏduun pitkkarŭi 어두운 빛깔의; ~ ***green / blue*** chinhan ch'orokssaek / p'aransaek 진한 초록색 / 파란색
darken (*of sky*) ŏduwŏjida 어두워지다
dark glasses saegan-gyŏng 색안경
darkness amhŭk 암흑
darling 1 *n* kajang sarangsŭrŏn saram 가장 사랑스런 사람; ~***!*** chagiya!

자기야! **2** *adj* kajang saranghanŭn 가장 사랑하는
darn[1] **1** *n* (*mend*) kkwemaen chari 꿰맨 자리 **2** *v/t* (*mend*) kkwemaeda 꿰매다
darn[2], **darned** → ***damn***
dart 1 *n* (*for throwing*) tat'ŭ 다트 **2** *v/i* ssonsalgach'i naragada 쏜살같이 날아가다
dash 1 *n* (*punctuation*) taeshi 대시; (*small amount*) yakkan 약간; (MOT: *dashboard*) kyegip'an 계기판; ***a ~ of brandy*** yakkanŭi pŭraendi 약간의 브랜디; ***make a ~ for*** ...(ŭ)ro tansume tallyŏgada ...(으)로 단숨에 달려가다 **2** *v/i* tansume tallyŏgada 단숨에 달려가다 **3** *v/t hopes* kkŏktta 꺾다
♦**dash off 1** *v/i* sŏdullŏ ttŏnada 서둘러 떠나다 **2** *v/t* (*write quickly*) tansume ssŭda 단숨에 쓰다
dashboard kyegip'an 계기판
data charyo 자료, teit'ŏ 데이터; (*information*) chŏngbo 정보
database teit'ŏ peisŭ 데이터 베이스; **data capture** teit'ŏ sujip 데이터 수집; **data processing** teit'ŏ ch'ŏri 데이터 처리; **data protection** teit'ŏ poho 데이터 보호; **data storage** teit'ŏ chŏjang 데이터 저장
date[1] (*fruit*) taech'u 대추
date[2] **1** *n* naltcha 날짜; (*meeting*) teit'ŭ 데이트; (*person*) teit'ŭ sangdae 데이트 상대; ***what's the ~ today?*** onŭl myŏch'irijyo? 오늘 몇일이죠?; ***out of ~*** *clothes* yuhaeng-i chinan 유행이 지난; *passport* naltchaga chinan 날짜가 지난; ***up to ~*** ch'oeshinŭi 최신의 **2** *v/t letter*, *check* naltcharŭl chŏktta 날짜를 적다; (*go out with*) ...wa / kwa teit'ŭ hada ...와 / 과 데이트하다; ***that ~s you*** kŭgŏsŭro nŏŭi nairŭl kanŭmhal su it-tta 그것으로 너의 나이를 가늠할 수 있다
dated shidaee twittŏrŏjin 시대에 뒤떨어진
daub *v/t* sŏt'urŭge ch'irhada 서투르게 칠하다; ***~ paint on a wall*** pyŏge sŏt'urŭge p'eint'ŭ ch'irŭl hada 벽에 서투르게 페인트 칠을 하다
daughter ttal 딸; (*somebody else's*) ttanim 따님
daughter-in-law myŏnŭri 며느리; (*somebody else's*) myŏnŭnim 며느님
daunt *v/t* kirŭl kkŏktta 기를 꺾다
dawdle (*waste time*) shiganŭl hŏbihada 시간을 허비하다; (*move slowly*) kkumulgŏrida 꾸물거리다; ***~ over*** nŭgŭt'age … hada 느긋하게 … 하다
dawn 1 *n* saebyŏk 새벽; *fig* (*of new age*) shich'o 시초 **2** *v/i*: ***it ~ed on me that*** ...ranŭn kŏsŭl nanŭn kkaedatkki shijak'aet-tta ...라는 것을 나는 깨닫기 시작했다
day nal 날; ***all ~*** haru chong-il 하루 종일; ***what ~ is it today?*** onŭrŭn musŭn yoiriyeyo? 오늘은 무슨 요일이예요?; ***~ off*** shwinŭn nal 쉬는 날; ***by ~*** naje 낮에; ***~ by ~*** nanari 나날이; ***the ~ after*** kŭ taŭmnal 그 다음날; ***the ~ after tomorrow*** more 모레; ***the ~ before*** kŭ chŏnnal 그 전날; ***the ~ before yesterday*** kŭjŏkke 그저께; ***~ in ~ out*** maeilmaeil kyesok'aesŏ 매일 매일 계속해서; ***in those ~s*** kŭ shijŏrenŭn 그 시절에는; ***one ~*** ŏnjen-ganŭn 언젠가는; ***the other ~*** (*recently*) iltchŏne 일전에; ***let's call it a ~!*** kŭman kkŭnnaepsshida! 그만 끝냅시다!
daybreak saebyŏk 새벽; **daydream 1** *n* paegilmong 백일몽 **2** *v/i* kongsang-e chamgida 공상에 잠기다; **daylight** nat 낮; **daytime**: ***in the ~*** naje 낮에; **daytrip** tang-ilch'igi yŏhaeng 당일치기 여행
dazed (*by news*) ŏridungjŏrhaejin 어리둥절해진; (*by a blow*) chŏngshini mŏnghan 정신이 멍한
dazzle *v/t* nunbushige hada 눈부시게 하다; *fig* apttodanghada 압도당하다
dead 1 *adj person*, *plant* chugŭn 죽은; *battery* tarŭn 닳은; *phone* kkŭnŏjin 끊어진; *flashlight*, *engine* kkŏjin 꺼진; *bulb* nagan 나간; F (*boring*: *place*) hwalgi ŏmnŭn 활기 없는 **2** *adv* F (*very*) ŏmch'ŏngnage 엄청나게; ***~ beat***, ***~ tired*** nokch'oga toeŏ 녹초가 되어; ***that's ~ right*** chŏntchŏgŭro

matsŭmnida 전적으로 맞습니다 **3** *n*: ***the ~*** koin 고인; ***in the ~ of night*** han pamtchung-e 한 밤중에
deaden *pain, sound* chugida 죽이다
dead end (*street*) makttarŭn 막다른; **dead-end job** changnaesŏng ŏmnŭn chigŏp 장래성 없는 직업; **dead heat** musŭngbu 무승부; **deadline** (*day*) magamil 마감일; (*hour*) magamshigan 마감시간; **deadlock** *n* (*in talks*) kyoch'ak sangt'ae 교착 상태
deadly *adj* (*fatal*) ch'imyŏngjŏgin 치명적인; F (*boring*) chiruhaesŏ mich'ilkkŏt kat'ŭn 지루해서 미칠것 같은
deaf kwimŏgŭn 귀먹은
deaf-and-dumb nong-aŭi 농아의
deafen kwimŏk-kke hada 귀먹게 하다
deafening kwich'ŏng-i ttŏrŏjil ttŭt'an 귀청이 떨어질 듯한
deafness ch'ŏnggak chang-ae 청각 장애
deal 1 *n* (*contract*) kyeyak 계약; (*in business*) kŏrae 거래; ***it's a ~!*** (*agreed*) habŭidoen kŏmnida! 합의된 겁니다!; (*it's a promise*) yakssok'an kŏmnida! 약속한 겁니다!; ***a good ~*** (*bargain*) charhan hŭngjŏng 잘한 흥정; (*a lot*) mani 많이; ***a great ~ of*** (*lots*) manŭn 많은 **2** *v/t cards* tollida 돌리다; ***~ a blow to*** ...ege t'agyŏgŭl chuda ...에게 타격을 주다
♦**deal in** (*trade in*) kŏraehada 거래하다
♦**deal out** *cards* nanuŏ chuda 나누어 주다
♦**deal with** (*handle*) ch'ŏrihada 처리하다; (*do business with*) kŏraehada 거래하다
dealer (*merchant*) sang-in 상인; (*drug ~*) mayak tillŏ 마약 딜러; (*in cards*) tillŏ 딜러
dealing (*drug ~*) mayak kŏrae 마약 거래
dealings (*business*) kŏrae 거래
dean (*of college*) haktchang 학장
dear *adj* ch'inaehanŭn 친애하는; (*expensive*) kagyŏgi pissan 가격이 비싼; ***Dear Sir*** chon-gyŏnghanŭn sŏnsaengnimkke 존경하는 선생님께; ***Dear Richard / Margaret*** saranghanŭn Rich'adŭ / Magaret 사랑하는 리차드 / 마가 렛; (***oh***) ***~!, ~ me!*** irŏn, sesange! 이런, 세상에!
dearly *love* kkŭmtchigi 끔찍이
death chugŭm 죽음; **~s** (*fatalities*) samangja 사망자; ***be sentenced to ~*** sahyŏng sŏn-gorŭl pat-tta 사형 선고를 받다
death penalty sahyŏng 사형
death toll samangjasu 사망자수
debatable nonjaeng-ŭi yŏjiga innŭn 논쟁의 여지가 있는
debate 1 *n* nonjaeng 논쟁; POL shimŭi 심의 **2** *v/i* suk-kkohada 숙고하다 **3** *v/t* nonjaenghada 논쟁하다
debauchery pangt'ang 방탕
debit 1 *n* chan-goran 잔고란 **2** *v/t account, amount* chan-gorane kiip'ada 잔고란에 기입하다
debris p'ap'yŏn 파편
debt pit 빚; ***be in ~*** piji it-tta 빚이 있다
debtor ch'aemuja 채무자
debug *room* toch'ŏng changch'irŭl chegŏhada 도청 장치를 제거하다; COMPUT kyŏrhamŭl koch'ida 결함을 고치다
début *n* tebyu 데뷰
decade ship nyŏn 십 년
decadent t'oep'yejŏgin 퇴폐적인
decaffeinated k'ap'eini chegŏdoen 카페인이 제거된
decapitate mogŭl charŭda 목을 자르다
decay 1 *n* (*process*) pup'ae 부패; (*of civilization*) soet'oe 쇠퇴; (*decayed matter*) ssŏgŭm 썩음 **2** *v/i* pup'aehada 부패하다; (*of civilization*) soet'oehada 쇠퇴하다; (*of teeth*) ch'ungch'iga saenggida 충치가 생기다
deceased: ***the ~*** chugŭn saram 죽은 사람
deceit sogimsu 속임수
deceitful namŭl soginŭn 남을 속이는
deceive sogida 속이다
December shibiwŏl 십이월
decency yeŭi parŭm 예의 바름; ***he had the ~ to ...*** kŭnŭn ... hal

chŏngdoŭi yeŭinŭn issŏt-tta 그는 … 할 정도의 예의는 있었다

decent *person* nŏgŭrŏun 너그러운; (*acceptable*) kwaench'anŭn chŏngdoŭi 괜찮은 정도의; (*reasonable*) sangdanghi choŭn 상당히 좋은; (*meal*, *sleep*) chŏkttanghan 적당한

decentralize *administration* chibang punkkwŏnhwa hada 지방 분권화 하다

deception sogim 속임

deceptive (*in appearance*) pogiwanŭn tarŭn 보기와는 다른

deceptively: ***it looks ~ simple*** pogiwanŭn taruge kandanhaji ant'a 보기와는 다르게 간단하지 않다

decibel teshibel 데시벨

decide 1 *v/t* (*make up one's mind*) kyŏlsshimhada 결심하다; (*conclude*) kyŏltchŏnghada 결정하다; (*settle*) kyŏltchŏng-ŭl naerida 결정을 내리다 **2** *v/i* kyŏltchŏnghada 결정하다; ***you ~*** nega kyŏltchŏnghae 네가 결정해

decided (*definite*) tturyŏt'an 뚜렷한

decider (*match etc*) kyŏlssŭngjŏn 결승전

decimal *n* sosu 소수

decimal point sosutchŏm 소수점

decimate manŭn surŭl chugida 많은 수를 죽이다

decipher p'andok'ada 판독하다

decision kyŏltchŏng 결정; (*conclusion*) kyŏllon 결론; ***come to a ~*** kyŏllone irŭda 결론에 이르다

decision-maker ŭisa kyŏltchŏngja 의사 결정자

decisive (*resolute*) tanhohan 단호한; (*crucial*) kyŏltchŏngjŏgin 결정적인

deck (*of ship*) kapp'an 갑판; (*of bus*) ch'ŭng 층; (*of cards*) han pŏl 한 벌

deckchair hyudaeyong ŭija 휴대용 의자

declaration (*statement*) sŏngmyŏng 성명; (*of independence*) sŏnŏn 선언; ***~ of war*** sŏnjŏn p'ogo 선전 포고

declare (*state*) kongp'yohada 공표하다; *independence* sŏnŏnhada 선언하다; (*at customs*) shin-gohada 신고하다; ***~ war*** sŏnjŏn p'ogohada 선전 포고하다

decline 1 *n* (*fall*) kamso 감소; (*in standards*) harak 하락; (*in health*) ak'wa 악화 **2** *v/t invitation* kŏjŏrhada 거절하다; ***~ to comment*** ŏn-gŭbŭl kŏbuhada 언급을 거부하다; ***~ to accept*** padadŭriji ant'a 받아들이지 않다 **3** *v/i* (*refuse*) kŏjŏrhada 거절하다; (*decrease*) kamsohada 감소하다; (*of health*) ak'wadoeda 악화되다

declutch k'ŭllŏch'irŭl p'ulda 클러치를 풀다

decode haedok'ada 해독하다

decompose pup'aehada 부패하다

décor changsshik 장식

decorate (*with paint*, *paper*) changsshik'ada 장식하다; (*adorn*) kkumida 꾸미다; *soldier* hunjang-ŭl suyŏhada 훈장을 수여하다

decoration (*paint*, *paper*, *ornament*) changshik 장식

decorative changshingnyong-ŭi 장식용의

decorator (*interior ~*) shillae changshik-kka 실내 장식가

decoy *n* yuinyong 유인용

decrease 1 *n* kamso 감소 **2** *v/t* churida 줄이다 **3** *v/i* chulda 줄다

dedicate *book etc* pach'ida 바치다; ***~ oneself to*** …e chŏnnyŏmhada …에 전념하다

dedication (*in book*) hŏnjŏngsa 헌정사; (*to cause*, *work*) chŏnnyŏm 전념

deduce ch'uronhada 추론하다

deduct: ***~ X from Y*** Yesŏ Xŭl / rŭl ppaeda Y에서 X을 / 를 빼다

deduction (*from salary*) kongje 공제; (*conclusion*) ch'uron 추론

deed *n* (*act*) haeng-wi 행위; LAW kimyŏng narinhan chŭngsŏ 기명 날인한 증서

deep *hole*, *water*, *sleep* kip'ŭn 깊은; *trouble* shimgak'an 심각한; *voice* chŏŭmŭi 저음의; *color* chinhan 진한; *thinker* shimwŏnhan 심원한

deepen 1 *v/t* kipkke hada 깊게 하다 **2** *v/i* kip'ŏjida 깊어지다; (*of crisis*, *mystery*) shimgak'aejida 심각해지다

deep freeze *n* kŭpssok naengdong naengjanggo 급속 냉동 냉장고;

deep-frozen food naengdong shikp'um 냉동 식품; **deep-fry** tŭmppuk t'wigida 듬뿍 튀기다
deer sasŭm 사슴
deface woegwanŭl sonsangshik'ida 외관을 손상시키다
defamation pibang 비방
defamatory pibanghanŭn 비방하는
default *adj* COMPUT miri sŏltchŏngdoen 미리 설정된; ***~ value*** tip'olt'ŭkkap 디폴트값
defeat 1 *n* p'aebae 패배 **2** *v/t* p'aebaeshik'ida 패배시키다; (*of task*) chwajŏlsshik'ida 좌절시키다
defeatist *adj attitude* p'aebaejuŭijŏgin 패배주의적인
defect *n* kyŏltchŏm 결점
defective kyŏltchŏmi innŭn 결점이 있는
defend chik'ida 지키다; (*back up*) onghohada 옹호하다; (*justify*) chŏngdanghwahada 정당화하다; LAW pyŏnhohada 변호하다
defendant (*in criminal case*) p'igoin 피고인
defense *n* (*protection*) pang-ŏ 방어; MIL, POL pang-wi 방위; SP subi 수비; LAW p'igoch'ŭk 피고측; (*justification*) pyŏllon 변론; (*of cause, support*) ongho 옹호; ***come to s.o.'s ~*** nuguŭi p'yŏni toeŏ chuda 누구의 편이 되어 주다
defense budget POL kukppangbi yesan 국방비 예산
defense lawyer p'igoch'ŭk pyŏnhosa 피고측 변호사
defenseless mubangbiŭi 무방비의
defense player SP subisu 수비수; **Defense Secretary** POL Kukppangbuhanggwan 국방부 장관; **defense witness** LAW p'igoch'ŭk chŭng-in 피고측 증인
defensive 1 *n*: ***on the ~*** pang-ŏhanŭn chasero 방어하는 자세로; ***go on the ~*** pangŏjŏgin chaserŭl ch'wihada 방어적인 자세를 취하다 **2** *adj weaponry* pang-ŏyong-ŭi 방어용의; *person* pang-ŏjŏgin 방어적인
defer *v/t* yŏn-gihada 연기하다
deference chon-gyŏng 존경
deferential chŏngjunghan 정중한
defiance panhang 반항; ***in ~ of*** ...ŭl/rŭl mushihago ...을/를 무시하고
defiant panhangjŏgin 반항적인
deficiency (*lack*) kyŏlp'ip 결핍
deficient: ***be ~ in*** ...i/ga kyŏlp'ipttoeda ...이/가 결핍되다
deficit chŏktcha 적자
define *word* chŏng-ŭirŭl naerida 정의를 내리다; *objective* ttŭsŭl palk'ida 뜻을 밝히다
definite *date, time* chŏnghwak'an 정확한; *answer, improvement* myŏnghwak'an 명확한; (*certain*) hwaksshinhanŭn 확신하는; ***are you ~ about that?*** hwaksshinhamnikka? 확신합니까?; ***nothing ~ has been arranged*** hwaktchŏngdoen kŏn, amu kŏtto ŏpssŭmnida 확정된 건, 아무 것도 없습니다
definite article chŏnggwansa 정관사
definitely hwaksshirhi 확실히
definition (*of word*) chŏng-ŭi 정의; (*of objective*) ttŭsŭl palk'im 뜻을 밝힘
definitive kyŏltchŏngjŏgin 결정적인
deflect *ball, blow* pinnagage hada 빗나가게 하다; *criticism* p'yŏnhyangshik'ida 편향시키다; (*from course of action*) pŏsŏnage hada 벗어나게 하다; ***be ~ed from*** ...ŭl/rŭl pyŏngyŏnghada ...을/를 변경하다
deform pyŏnhyŏngshik'ida 변형시키다
deformity kihyŏng 기형
defraud sach'wihada 사취하다
defrost *v/t food* nogida 녹이다; *fridge* sŏrirŭl ŏpssaeda 서리를 없애다
deft *person* somsshi choŭn 솜씨 좋은; *fingers* nŭngsuk'an 능숙한
defuse *bomb* shin-gwanŭl chegŏhada 신관을 제거하다; *situation* chinjŏngshik'ida 진정시키다
defy panhanghada 반항하다
degenerate *v/i* t'arak'ada 타락하다; ***~ into*** ...(ŭ)ro pyŏnjildoeda ...(으)로 변질되다
degrade ch'emyŏnŭl sonsangshik'ida 체면을 손상시키다
degrading *position, work* ch'emyŏnŭl sonsangshik'inŭn 체면을 손상시키는

degree (*from university*) hagwi 학위; (*of temperature, angle, latitude*) to 도; (*amount*) chŏngdo 정도; ***by ~s*** ch'ach'a 차차; ***get one's ~*** hagwirŭl ttada 학위를 따다
dehydrated t'alssudoen 탈수된
de-ice *windshield* chebinghada 제빙하다; *airplane wings* pangbinghada 방빙하다
de-icer (*spray*) chebingje 제빙제
deign: ***~ to*** komapkkedo … hae chushida 고맙게도 … 해 주시다
deity shin 신
dejected nakttamhan 낙담한
delay 1 *n* yŏn-gi 연기 **2** *v/t* yŏn-gihada 연기하다; ***be ~ed*** (*of person*) chigak'ada 지각하다; (*of train, plane*) yŏnch'ak'ada 연착하다 **3** *v/i* chich'ehada 지체하다
delegate 1 *n* taep'yoja 대표자 **2** *v/t task* wiimhada 위임하다; *person* taep'yoro immyŏnghada 대표로 임명하다
delegation (*of task*) wiim 위임; (*people*) taep'yodan 대표단
delete saktchehada 삭제하다; (*cross out*) chiuda 지우다
deletion (*act*) malsso 말소; (*that deleted*) saktche 삭제
deli shikp'umjŏm 식품점
deliberate 1 *adj* koŭijŏgin 고의적인 **2** *v/i* suk-kkohada 숙고하다
deliberately ilburŏ 일부러
delicacy (*of fabric*) sŏmseham 섬세함; (*of problem*) mimyoham 미묘함; (*of health*) hŏyak'am 허약함; (*tact*) paeryŏ 배려; (*food*) chinmi 진미
delicate *fabric* sŏmsehan 섬세한; *problem* mimyohan 미묘한; *health* hŏyak'an 허약한
delicatessen shikp'umjŏm 식품점
delicious mashinnŭn 맛있는; ***that was ~*** mashissŏssŏyo 맛있었어요
delight *n* kippŭm 기쁨
delighted kippŏhanŭn 기뻐하는
delightful *evening* chŭlgŏun 즐거운; *person* yuk'waehan 유쾌한; *house* k'waejŏk'an 쾌적한
delimit han-gyerŭl chŏnghada 한계를 정하다
delirious MED ilsshijŏk chŏngshin ch'angnanŭi 일시적 정신 착란의; (*ecstatic*) yŏlgwanghan 열광한
deliver paedarhada 배달하다; *message* chŏndarhada 전달하다; *baby* punmanshik'ida 분만시키다; ***~ a speech*** yŏnsŏrŭl hada 연설을 하다
delivery (*of goods, mail*) paedal 배달; (*of baby*) punman 분만
delivery date paedal naltcha 배달 날짜; **delivery note** suryŏngtchŭng 수령증; **delivery van** paedalch'a 배달차
delude sogida 속이다; ***you're deluding yourself*** tangshin sŭsŭro ch'ak-kkak'ago innŭn kŏyeyo 당신 스스로 착각하고 있는 거예요
deluge 1 *n* taehongsu 대홍수; *fig* swaedo 쇄도 **2** *v/t fig* swaedohada 쇄도하다
delusion ch'ak-kkak 착각
de luxe hohwaroun 호화로운
demand 1 *n* yogu 요구; COM suyo 수요; ***be in ~*** suyoga it-tta 수요가 있다 **2** *v/t* yoguhada 요구하다; (*require*) yoguhada 요구하다
demanding *job* sangdanghan noryŏgi yogudoenŭn 상당한 노력이 요구되는; *person* yoguga shimhan 요구가 심한
demented chŏngshin ch'angnane kŏllin 정신 착란에 걸린
Demilitarized Zone Pimujang Chidae 비무장 지대
demise samang 사망; *fig* somyŏl 소멸
demitasse chagŭn k'ŏp'itchan 작은 커피잔
demo (*protest*) temo 데모; (*of video etc*) sŏnjŏnnyong 선전용
democracy minjujuŭi 민주주의
democrat minjujuŭija 민주주의자; ***Democrat*** POL Minjudang-wŏn 민주당원; (*supporter*) Minjudang chijija 민주당 지지자
democratic minjujuŭiŭi 민주주의의
Democratic People's Republic of Korea Chosŏn Minjujuŭi Inmin Konghwaguk 조선 민주주의 인민 공화국
demo disk sŏnjŏnnyong tisŭk'ŭ 선전용 디스크

demolish *building* p'agoehada 파괴하다; *argument* twijiptta 뒤집다
demolition (*of building*) p'agoe 파괴; (*of argument*) twijibŭm 뒤집음
demon angma 악마
demonstrate 1 *v/t* (*prove*) iptchŭnghada 입증하다; *machine* shiryŏnhada 실연하다 **2** *v/i* (*politically*) shiwihada 시위하다
demonstration (*display*) kwashi 과시; (*protest*) shiwi 시위; (*of machine*) shiryŏn 실연
demonstrative: ***be ~*** kamjŏng-ŭl tŭrŏnaeda 감정을 드러내다
demonstrator (*protester*) shiwi ch'amgaja 시위 참가자
demoralized kiga kkŏkkin 기가 꺾인
demoralizing kirŭl kkŏngnŭn 기를 꺾는
den (*study*) sŏjae 서재
denial (*of rumor, accusation*) pujŏng 부정; (*of request*) kŏjŏl 거절
denim tenim 데님
denims (*jeans*) ch'ŏngbaji 청바지
Denmark Tenmak'ŭ 덴마크
denomination (*of money*) aengmyŏn kŭmaek 액면 금액; (*religious*) chongp'a 종파
dense tchit'ŭn 짙은; *foliage* ugŏjin 우거진; *crowd* miltchip'an 밀집한; (*stupid*) udunhan 우둔한
densely: ***~ populated*** in-guga chomirhan 인구가 조밀한
density (*of population*) in-gu miltto 인구 밀도
dent 1 *n* ump'uk p'aein kot 움푹 패인 곳 **2** *v/t* ump'uk tŭrŏgage hada 움푹 들어가게 하다
dental *treatment* ch'iaŭi 치아의; *school etc* ch'ikkwa 치과; ***~ clinic*** ch'ikkwa 치과
dentist ch'ikkwa ŭisa 치과 의사
dentures ŭich'i 의치
deny *charge, rumor* puinhada 부인하다; *right, request* kŏjŏrhada 거절하다
deodorant t'alch'wije 탈취제
depart ch'ulbarhada 출발하다: ***~ from*** (*deviate*) …esŏ pŏsŏnada …에서 벗어나다
department (*of company*) pusŏ 부서; (*of university*) hak-kkwa 학과; (*of government*) puch'ŏ 부처; (*of store*) maejang 매장; ***Department of Defense*** Kukppangbu 국방부; ***Department of the Interior*** Hwan-gyŏngch'ŏ 환경처; ***Department of State*** (Mi)Kungmusŏng (미)국무성
department store paek'wajŏm 백화점
departure (*of train, bus etc*) ch'ulbal 출발; (*of person from job*) kŭmandum 그만둠; (*deviation*) it'al 이탈; ***a new ~*** (*for goverment, organization*) sae ch'ulbŏm 새 출범; (*for company*) sae ch'ulbal 새 출발; (*for actor, artist, writer*) saeroun shido 새로운 시도
departure lounge taehapsshil 대합실
departure time ch'ulbal shigak 출발 시각
depend ŭijonhada 의존하다; ***that ~s*** sanghwang-e ttara tarŭda 상황에 따라 다르다; ***it ~s on the weather*** nalsshie tallyŏit-tta 날씨에 달려있다; ***~ on sth*** (*need*) muŏse ŭijonhada 무엇에 의존하다; ***I ~ on you*** nanŭn nŏhant'e ŭijonhago it-tta 나는 너한테 의존하고 있다
dependable ŭijonhal su innŭn 의존할 수 있는
dependence, dependency ŭijon 의존
dependent 1 *n* puyang kajok 부양 가족 **2** *adj* ŭijonhanŭn 의존하는
depict myosahada 묘사하다
deplorable hant'anhal 한탄할
deplore hant'anhada 한탄하다
deport kugoero ch'ubanghada 국외로 추방하다
deportation kugoe ch'ubang 국외 추방
deportation order t'oegŏ myŏngnyŏng 퇴거 명령
deposit 1 *n* (*in bank*) yegŭm 예금; (*of mineral*) maejangmul 매장물; (*on purchase*) yeyak-kkŭm 예약금; (*for the lease on an apartment*) chŏnsegŭm 전세금 **2** *v/t money* yegŭmhada 예금하다; (*put down*) not'a 놓다; *silt, mud* t'oejŏkshik'ida

퇴적시키다
deposition LAW sŏnsŏ chŭng-ŏn 선서 증언
depot (*train station*) chŏnggŏjang 정거장; (*bus station*) chŏngnyujang 정류장; (*for storage*) ch'anggo 창고
depreciate *v/i* FIN kach'iga ttŏrŏjida 가치가 떨어지다
depreciation FIN kach'i harak 가치 하락
depress *person* uurhagehada 우울하게하다
depressed *person* uurhan 우울한
depressing uurhagehanŭn 우울하게하는
depression MED uultchŭng 우울증; (*economic*) pulgyŏnggi 불경기; (*meteorological*) chŏgiap 저기압
deprive: ~ ***X of Y*** Xegesŏ Yŭl / rŭl ppaeat-tta X에게서 Y을 / 를 빼앗다
deprived *child* puruhan 불우한; *area* kananhan 가난한
depth kip'i 깊이; (*of shelf*) kip'ŭm 깊음; (*of color*) chit'ŭm 짙음; (*of thought*) shimoham 심오함; ***in ~*** ch'ŏltchŏhage 철저하게; ***in the ~s of winter*** han kyŏure 한 겨울에; ***he was out of his ~*** (*in water*) kŭŭi k'irŭl nŏmnŭn kip'iyŏt-tta 그의 키를 넘는 깊이였다; (*in discussion*) kŭŭi ihaega mich'iji anat-tta 그의 이해가 미치지 않았다
deputation taep'yodan 대표단
♦**deputize for** …ŭl / rŭl taerihada …을 / 를 대리하다
deputy taeri 대리
deputy leader pudaep'yo 부대표
derail: ***be ~ed*** (*of train*) t'alssŏndoeda 탈선되다
deranged hollandoen 혼란된
derelict *adj building* pŏryŏjin 버려진
deride piut-tta 비웃다
derision piusŭm 비웃음
derisive *remarks*, *laughter* piunnŭn 비웃는
derisory *amount* chwikkorimanhan 쥐꼬리만한
derivative (*not original*) tokch'angjŏgi anin 독창적이 아닌
derive *v/t* ŏt-tta 얻다; ***be ~d from*** (*of word*) …esŏ yuraedoeda …에서 유래되다
derogatory kyŏngmyŏrhanŭn 경멸하는; ~ ***remark*** yokssŏl 욕설
descend 1 *v/t* naeryŏgada 내려가다; ***she ~ed the staircase*** kŭnyŏnŭn kyedanŭl naeryŏgat-tta 그녀는 계단을 내려갔다; ***be ~ed from*** …ŭi chasonida …의 자손이다 **2** *v/i* (*of airplane*) haganghada 하강하다; (*of climber*) naeryŏgada 내려가다; (*of road*) kyŏngsajida 경사지다; (*of darkness*) naeryŏantta 내려앉다
descendant chason 자손
descent (*from mountain*) hasan 하산; (*of airplane*) hagang 하강; (*ancestry*) kagye 가계; ***of Korean ~*** Han-gukkkyeŭi 한국계의
describe myosahada 묘사하다; ~ ***X as Y*** Xŭl / rŭl Y(ŭ)ro myosahada X을 / 를 Y(으)로 묘사하다
description myosa 묘사
desegregate injong ch'abyŏl p'yeji 인종 차별 폐지
desert[1] *n* samak 사막; *fig* hwangmuji 황무지
desert[2] **1** *v/t* (*abandon*) pŏrida 버리다; *friends* tŭngjida 등지다 **2** *v/i* (*of soldier*) t'aryŏnghada 탈영하다
deserted injŏgi kkŭnk'in 인적이 끊긴
deserter MIL t'aryŏngbyŏng 탈영병
desertion (*abandoning*) pŏrim 버림; MIL t'aryŏng 탈영
deserve padŭl manhada 받을 만하다; ~ ***to …*** … hal manhada … 할 만하다
design 1 *n* tijain 디자인; (*drawing*) mitkkŭrim 밑그림; (*for building*, *car etc*) sŏlgyedo 설계도; (*pattern*) munŭi 무늬 **2** *v/t* tijainhada 디자인하다; *building*, *car*, *machine* sŏlgyehada 설계하다; ***not ~ed for use in the home*** kajŏngnyŏng-i anin 가정용이 아닌
designate *v/t person* immyŏnghada 임명하다; *area etc* chijŏnghada 지정하다
designer tijainŏ 디자이너; (*of car*, *building*) sŏlgyeja 설계자
designer clothes yumyŏng tijainŏŭi ot 유명 디자이너의 옷
design fault sŏlgyesang-ŭi

munjetchŏm 설계상의 문제점
design school tijain hak-kkyo 디자인 학교
desirable (*advisable*) paramjik'an 바람직한; (*coveted*) t'amnanŭn 탐나는
desire *n* param 바람; (*sexual*) yongmang 욕망
desk ch'aekssang 책상; (*in hotel*) tesŭk'ŭ 데스크
desk clerk chŏpssu kyewŏn 접수 계원
desktop publishing kŏmp'yut'ŏ ch'ulp'an 컴퓨터 출판
desolate *adj place* hwangnyanghan 황량한
despair 1 *n* chŏlmang 절망; ***in ~*** chŏlmanghayŏ 절망하여 **2** *v/i* chŏlmanghada 절망하다; ***~ of*** ...e taehae chŏlmanghada ...에 대해 절망하다
desperate *person*, *action* p'ilssajŏgin 필사적인; *situation* chŏlmangjŏgin 절망적인; ***be ~ for a drink / cigarette*** surŭl mashigo / tambaerŭl p'iugo ship'ŏ chugŭl chigyŏng-ida 술을 마시고 / 담배를 피우고 싶어 죽을 지경이다
desperation p'ilssajŏgim 필사적임; ***an act of ~*** chap'ojagishig-ŭi haengdong 자포자기식의 행동
despise kyŏngmyŏrhada 경멸하다
despite ...edo pulguhago ...에도 불구하고
despondent nakttamhan 낙담한
despot p'ok-kkun 폭군
dessert hushik 후식
destination moktchŏktchi 목적지
destiny unmyŏng 운명
destitute pin-gonhan 빈곤한
destroy p'agoehada 파괴하다; *fig* p'amyŏlshik'ida 파멸시키다; *trust*, *friendship*, *marriage* mangch'ida 망치다
destroyer NAUT kuch'uk'am 구축함
destruction p'agoe 파괴; *fig* p'amyŏl 파멸
destructive *power* p'agoejŏgin 파괴적인; *criticism* pujŏngjŏgin 부정적인
detach tteŏnaeda 떼어내다
detachable pullihal su innŭn 분리할 수 있는
detached (*objective*) kongp'yŏnghan 공평한
detachment (*objectivity*) kongp'yŏngham 공평함
detail *n* (*small point*) sebu sahang 세부 사항; (*piece of information*) chasehan naeyong 자세한 내용; (*trifle*) sasohan il 사소한 일; ***in ~*** chasehage 자세하게
detailed sangsehan 상세한
detain chich'eshik'ida 지체시키다; (*as prisoner*) kamgŭmhada 감금하다
detainee ŏngnyuja 억류자
detect arach'aeda 알아채다; (*of device*) t'amjihada 탐지하다
detection (*of criminal*) palgyŏn 발견; (*of crime*) palgak 발각; (*of smoke*) t'amji 탐지
detective (*policeman*) hyŏngsa 형사
detective novel t'amjŏng sosŏl 탐정 소설
detector t'amjigi 탐지기
détente POL kinjang wanhwa 긴장 완화
detention (*imprisonment*) kamgŭm 감금
deter tannyŏmshik'ida 단념시키다; ***~ X from doing Y*** Xi / ga Yhanŭn kŏsŭl mot'age hada X이 / 가 Y하는 것을 못하게 하다
detergent sech'ŏktche 세척제
deteriorate ak'wadoeda 악화되다
determination (*resolution*) kyŏlsshim 결심
determine (*decide*) kyŏltchŏnghada 결정하다; (*establish*) tanjŏnghada 단정하다
determined kyŏlsshimhan 결심한; *effort* hwakkohan 확고한
deterrent *n* panghaemul 방해물
detest hyŏmohada 혐오하다
detonate 1 *v/t* p'okppal sshik'ida 폭발시키다 **2** *v/i* p'okpparhada 폭발하다
detour *n* uhoe 우회; (*diversion*) tarŭn kil 다른 길
detract: ***~ from*** ...ŭi kach'irŭl ttŏrŏttŭrida ...의 가치를 떨어뜨리다
detriment: ***to the ~ of*** ...e haerŭl

ip'igo ...에 해를 입히고
detrimental haeroun 해로운
deuce (*in tennis*) tyusŭ 듀스
devaluation FIN p'yŏngkka chŏrha 평가 절하
devalue *currency* p'yŏngkka chŏrhashik'ida 평가 절하시키다
devastate p'agoehada 파괴하다; *fig*: *person* nŏkssŭl ilk'e hada 넋을 잃게 하다
devastating apttohanŭn 압도하는
develop 1 *v/t land*, (*invent*) kaebarhada 개발하다; *activity*, *business* paltchŏnshik'ida 발전시키다; *film* hyŏnsanghada 현상하다; (*progress*) palttalshik'ida 발달시키다; *illness*, *cold* ...e kŏllida ...에 걸리다 **2** *v/i* (*grow*) paltchŏnhada 발전하다; (*of country*, *business*) kaebarhada 개발하다
developer (*of property*) kaebaltcha 개발자
developing country kaebaldosangguk 개발도상국
development (*of land*) kaebal 개발; (*of business*, *country*) sŏngjang 성장; (*event*) nyussŭ 뉴스; (*of film*) hyŏnsang 현상; (*progression*) paltchŏn 발전
device changch'i 장치; (*tool*) togu 도구
devil angma 악마
devious (*sly*) kyohwarhan 교활한
devise koanhada 고안하다
devoid: ~ ***of*** ...i / ga chŏnhyŏ ŏmnŭn ...이/가 전혀 없는
devote *time*, *money*, *life* pach'ida 바치다; *effort* kiurida 기울이다
devoted *son etc* hŏnshinjŏgin 헌신적인; ***be ~ to s.o.*** nuguege hŏnshinjŏgida 누구에게 헌신적이다
devotion (*to a person*) hŏnshin 헌신; (*to one's job*) chŏnnyŏm 전념
devour *food* kegŏlssŭrŏpkke mŏktta 게걸스럽게 먹다; *book* t'amdok'ada 탐독하다
devout toksshirhan 독실한
dew isŭl 이슬
dexterity somsshi choŭm 솜씨 좋음
diabetes tangnyoppyŏng 당뇨병
diabetic 1 *n* tangnyoppŏng hwanja 당뇨병 환자 **2** *adj* tangnyoppyŏng-ŭi 당뇨병의
diagonal *adj* taegakssŏnŭi 대각선의
diagram top'yo 도표
dial 1 *n* (*of clock*) chap'an 자판; (*of meter*) nun-gŭmp'an 눈금판 **2** *v/i* TELEC chŏnhwarŭl kŏlda 전화를 걸다 **3** *v/t* TELEC: *number* taiŏrŭl tollida 다이얼을 돌리다
dialect sat'uri 사투리
dialog taehwa 대화
dial tone palsshinŭm 발신음
diameter chik-kkyŏng 직경
diametrically: ***~ opposed*** chŏngbandaeŭi 정반대의
diamond (*jewel*, *in cards*) taiamondŭ 다이아몬드; (*shape*) taiamondŭ moyang 다이아몬드 모양
Diamond Sutra Kŭmganggyŏng 금강경
diaper kijŏgwi 기저귀
diaphragm ANAT hoenggyŏngmak 횡격막; (*contraceptive*) p'iimyong p'esari 피임용 페사리
diarrhea sŏlssa 설사
diary (*for thoughts*) ilgi 일기; (*for appointments*) iltchi 일지
dice 1 *n* chusawi 주사위 **2** *v/t* (*cut*) kkakttugi moyang-ŭro ssŏlda 깍두기 모양으로 썰다
dichotomy ibunppŏp 이분법
dictate *v/t letter*, *novel* kusurhada 구술하다
dictation padassŭgi 받아쓰기
dictator POL toktchaeja 독재자
dictatorial *tone of voice* myŏngnyŏngjŏgin 명령적인; *person* toktchaejŏgin 독재적인; *powers* hoengp'orŭl purinŭn 횡포를 부리는
dictatorship toktchae chŏngkkwŏn 독재 정권
dictionary sajŏn 사전
die chuktta 죽다; ***~ of cancer / aids*** amŭro / eijŭro chuktta 암으로 / 에이즈로 죽다; ***I'm dying to know / leave*** algo / ttŏnago ship'ŏ chuk-kket-tta 알고 / 떠나고 싶어 죽겠다
♦**die away** (*of noise*) chŏmjŏm sarajida 점점 사라지다
♦**die down** (*of noise*) churŏdŭlda

줄어들다; (*of storm, fire*) sugŭrŏdŭlda 수그러들다; (*of excitement*) chŏmjŏm sarajida 점점 사라지다
♦**die out** (*of custom*) sarajida 사라지다; (*of species*) somyŏrhada 소멸하다
diesel (*fuel*) tijel 디젤
diet 1 *n* (*regular food*) shikttan 식단; (*for losing weight*) taiŏt'ŭ 다이어트; (*for health reasons*) shigi yoppŏp 식이 요법 **2** *v/i* (*to lose weight*) taiŏt'ŭhada 다이어트하다
differ (*be different*) tarŭda 다르다; (*disagree*) ŭigyŏnŭl tallihada 의견을 달리하다
difference ch'ai 차이; (*disagreement*) igyŏn 이견; ***it doesn't make any ~*** (*doesn't change anything*) amurŏn ch'aiga ŏptta 아무런 차이가 없다; (*doesn't matter*) sanggwan ŏpssŏyo 상관 없어요
different tarŭn 다른, pyŏlgaeŭi 별개의
differentiate: ~ ***between*** *between people* ch'abyŏrhada 차별하다; ~ ***between X and Y*** Xwa / kwa Yŭl / rŭl kubyŏrhada X와 / 과 Y을 / 를 구별하다
differently tarŭge 다르게
difficult himdŭn 힘든
difficulty ŏryŏum 어려움; ***with ~*** ŏryŏpkke 어렵게
dig 1 *v/t* p'ada 파다 **2** *v/i*: ***it was ~ging into me*** narŭl k'ukk'uk tchillŏt-tta 나를 쿡쿡 찔렀다
♦**dig out** (*find*) ch'ajanaeda 찾아내다
♦**dig up** p'ahech'ida 파헤치다; *information* ch'ajanaeda 찾아내다
digest *v/t* sohwahada 소화하다
digestible *food* sohwaga chal toenŭn 소화가 잘 되는
digestion sohwa 소화
digit (*number*) arabia suttcha 아라비아 숫자; ***a four ~ number*** arabia suttcha negae 아라비아 숫자 네개
digital tijit'ŏl 디지털; ~ ***camera*** tijit'ŏl k'amera 디지털 카메라
dignified wiŏm innŭn 위엄 있는
dignitary kowi insa 고위 인사
dignity chonŏm 존엄
digress pinnagada 빗나가다
digression pinnagam 빗나감
dike (*wall*) tuk 둑
dilapidated *house* hŏmurŏjin 허물어진; *car, sofa* hŏrŏppajin 헐어빠진
dilate (*of pupils*) nŏlp'ida 넓히다
dilemma chint'oeyangnan 진퇴양난; ***be in a*** ~ chint'oeyangnane ch'ŏhada 진퇴양난에 처하다
diligent pujirŏnhan 부지런한
dilute *v/t* muk-kke hada 묽게 하다
dim 1 *adj room, light* ŏdumch'imch'imhan 어둠침침한; *outline* hŭrit'an 흐릿한; (*stupid*) udunhan 우둔한; *prospects* irŏnal kŏt kattchi anŭn 일어날 것 같지 않은 **2** *v/t*: ~ ***the headlights*** hedŭrait'ŭrŭl kŭn-gŏriyong-ŭro pakkuda 헤드라이트를 근거리용으로 바꾸다 **3** *v/i* (*of lights*) hŭrige hada 흐리게 하다
dime ship ssent'ŭ 십 센트
dimension (*measurement*) ch'isu 치수
diminish 1 *v/t* churida 줄이다 **2** *v/i* chulda 줄다
diminutive 1 *n* churin irŭm 줄인 이름 **2** *adj* chagŭmahan 자그마한
dimple pojogae 보조개
din *n* shikkŭrŏun sori 시끄러운 소리
dine shikssahada 식사하다
diner (*person*) shikssahanŭn saram 식사하는 사람
dinghy chagŭn pae 작은 배
dingy (*gloomy*) ŭmch'imhan 음침한; (*dirty*) tŏrŏun 더러운; ***a rather ~ white*** taso ch'ikch'ik'an hayanssaek 다소 칙칙한 하얀색
dining car shikttangch'a 식당차; **dining room** shikttang 식당; **dining table** shikt'ak 식탁
dinner (*in the evening*) manch'an 만찬; (*at midday*) och'an 오찬; (*gathering*) hyang-yŏn 향연
dinner guest manch'an sonnim 만찬 손님; **dinner jacket** yaksshik yahoebok 약식 야회복; **dinner party** tinŏ p'at'i 디너 파티
dinosaur kongnyong 공룡
dip 1 *n* (*swim*) mure ttwiŏdŭm 물에 뛰어듦; (*for food*) yangnyŏmtchang

양념장; (*in road*) kyŏngsajin kot 경사진 곳 **2** *v/t* (*in liquid etc*) saltchak tamgŭda 살짝 담그다; ~ ***the headlights*** hedŭrait'ŭrŭl kŭngŏriyong-ŭro pakkuda 헤드라이트를 근거리용으로 바꾸다 **3** *v/i* (*of road*) kyŏngsaga chida 경사가 지다

diploma chŭngsŏ 증서

diplomacy oegyo 외교; (*tact*) oegyosul 외교술

diplomat oegyogwan 외교관

diplomatic oegyoŭi 외교의; (*tactful*) suwani choŭn 수완이 좋은

dire (*appalling*) hyŏngp'yŏnŏmnŭn 형편없는; (*extreme*) kŭkttanjŏgin 극단적인

direct 1 *adj* chiktchŏptchŏgin 직접적인; *flight*, *train* chik'aeng-ŭi 직행의; *person* nogoltchŏgin 노골적인; ***a ~ descendant of ...*** ...ŭi chik-kkye chason ...의 직계 자손 **2** *v/t* (*to a place*) annaehada 안내하다; *play* yŏnch'urhada 연출하다; *movie* kamdok'ada 감독하다; *attention* tollida 돌리다

direct current ELEC chingnyu 직류

direction panghyang 방향; (*of movie*) kamdok 감독; (*of play*) yŏnch'ul 연출; **~s** (*instructions*) annae 안내; (*to a place*) panghyang 방향; (*for use*) sayongppŏp 사용법; (*for medicine*) pogyongppŏp 복용법

direction indicator MOT panghyang p'yoshidŭng 방향 표시등

directly 1 *adv* (*straight*) paro 바로; (*soon*) kot 곧; (*immediately*) kŭmbang 금방 **2** *conj* ...hajamaja ...하자마자; ~ ***I've finished*** naega kkŭnnaejamaja 내가 끝내자마자

director (*of company*) isa 이사; (*of play*) yŏnch'ultcha 연출자; (*of movie*) kamdok 감독

directory chuso sŏngmyŏngnok 주소 성명록; TELEC chŏnhwa pŏnhobu 전화 번호부; COMPUT tirekt'ori 디렉토리

dirt mŏnji 먼지

dirt cheap aju hŏlkkapssŭi 아주 헐값의

dirty 1 *adj* tŏrŏun 더러운; (*pornographic*) ŭmnanhan 음란한 **2** *v/t* ...ŭl / rŭl tŏrŏp'ida ...을 / 를 더럽히다

dirty trick piyŏrhan ch'aengnyak 비열한 책략

disability shinch'e chang-ae 신체 장애

disabled 1 *n*: ***the ~*** shinch'e chang-aeja 신체 장애자 **2** *adj* pulguŭi 불구의

disadvantage (*drawback*) tantchŏm 단점; ***be at a ~*** pullihan iptchang-e it-tta 불리한 입장에 있다

disadvantaged hyet'aekppat-tchi mot'an 혜택받지 못한

disadvantageous pullihan 불리한

disagree ŭigyŏni tarŭda 의견이 다르다

♦**disagree with** ...wa / gwa ŭigyŏni mat-tchi ant'a ...와 / 과 의견이 맞지 않다; (*of food*) ...ŭi soge mat-tchi ant'a ...누 구의 속에 맞지 않다

disagreeable pulk'waehan 불쾌한

disagreement ŭigyŏn ch'ai 의견 차이; (*argument*) maldat'um 말다툼

disappear sarajida 사라지다; (*run away*) chach'wi-rŭl kamch'uda 자취를 감추다

disappearance (*of thing*) somyŏl 소멸; (*of person*) shiltchong 실종

disappoint shilmangshik'ida 실망시키다

disappointed shilmanghan 실망한

disappointing shilmangsŭrŏun 실망스러운

disappointment shilmang 실망

disapproval pulch'ansŏng 불찬성

disapprove pulch'ansŏnghada 불찬성하다; ~ ***of*** ...e pulch'ansŏnghada ...에 불찬성하다

disarm 1 *v/t robber* mugirŭl ppaeat-tta 무기를 빼앗다; *militia* mujang haejeshik'ida 무장 해제시키다 **2** *v/i* mujang-ŭl haejehada 무장을 해제하다

disarmament mujang haeje 무장 해제

disarming ch'ŏnjinhan 천진한

disaster (*natural*) ch'ŏnjaejibyŏn 천재지변; (*fiasco*) shilp'ae 실패

disaster area chaehae chiyŏk 재해 지역; *fig* (*person*) kujebullŭng-in

saram 구제불능인 사람
disastrous p'ihaega maksshimhan 피해가 막심한
disbelief: ***in*** ~ mitkkiji annŭn mosŭbŭro 믿기지 않는 모습으로
disc tisŭk'ŭ 디스크
discard *old clothes* pŏrida 버리다; *boyfriend* ch'abŏrida 차버리다; *theory*, *habits* p'yegihada 폐기하다
discern (*see*) shikppyŏrhada 식별하다
discernible arabol su innŭn 알아볼 수 있는
discerning anmogi nop'ŭn 안목이 높은
discharge 1 *n* (*from hospital*) t'oewŏn 퇴원; (*from army*) chedae 제대 **2** *v/t* (*from hospital*) t'oewŏnshik'ida 퇴원시키다; (*from army*) chedaeshik'ida 제대시키다; (*from job*) haegoshik'ida 해고시키다
disciple (*religious*) cheja 제자
disciplinary chinggyeŭi 징계의
discipline 1 *n* kyuyul 규율 **2** *v/t* pŏrŭsŭl karŭch'ida 버릇을 가르치다; *employee* chinggyehada 징계하다
disc jockey tisŭk'ŭ chak'i 디스크 자키
disclaim puinhada 부인하다
disclose tŭrŏnaeda 드러내다
disclosure (*of information*) nusŏl 누설; (*about scandal*) p'ongno 폭로
disco tisŭk'o 디스코
discolor pyŏnsaeksshik'ida 변색시키다
discomfort (*pain*) ap'ŭm 아픔; (*embarrassment*) ŏsaek'am 어색함
disconcert tanghwanghage hada 당황하게 하다
disconcerted tanghwanghan 당황한
disconnect pullishik'ida 분리시키다; (*supply*) chungdanshik'ida 중단시키다; *telephone* kkŭnt'a 끊다
disconsolate sŏgŭlp'ŭn 서글픈
discontent pulman 불만
discontented pulmansŭrŏun 불만스러운
discontinue chungjihada 중지하다
discord MUS purhyŏp'waŭm 불협화음; (*in relations*) purhwa 불화
discotheque tisŭk'o t'ek 디스코 텍
discount 1 *n* harin 할인 **2** *v/t goods* harinhada 할인하다; *theory* mushihada 무시하다
discourage (*dissuade*) mot'age hada 못하게 하다; (*dishearten*) nakttamshik'ida 낙담시키다
discover palgyŏnhada 발견하다; *talent* palgurhada 발굴하다
discoverer palgyŏnhan saram 발견한 사람
discovery palgyŏn 발견
discredit *v/t person* ...ŭi shinyong-i ttŏrŏjigehada ...의 신용이 떨어지게 하다; *theory* ...ŭi shinbingssŏng-ŭl ttŏrŏttŭrida ...의 신빙성을 떨어뜨리다
discreet *person* shinjunghan 신중한
discrepancy (*in story*) mosun 모순; (*in accounts etc*) purilch'i 불일치
discretion shinjungham 신중함; ***at your*** ~ tangshinŭi chaeryang-ŭro 당신의 재량으로
discriminate: ~ ***against*** ...ŭl / rŭl ch'abyŏrhada ...을 / 를 차별하다; ~ ***between X and Y*** (*distinguish*) Xwa / gwa Yŭl / rŭl kubyŏrhada X와 / 과 Y을 / 를 구별하다
discriminating shikppyŏllyŏgi innŭn 식별력이 있는
discrimination (*sexual*, *racial etc*) ch'abyŏl 차별
discus (*object*) wŏnban 원반; (*event*) wŏnban tŏnjigi 원반 던지기
discuss (*talk about*) hwaje sama yaegihada 화제 삼아 얘기하다; (*of article*) nonŭihada 논의하다; (*in negotiations*) ŭinonhada 의논하다
discussion (*debate*) t'oron 토론; ***have a ~ with s.o.*** nuguwa ŭinonhada 누구와 의논하다; ***it's still under*** ~ ajik nonŭijung-ida 아직 논의중이다
disease chilbyŏng 질병
disembark *v/i* naerida 내리다
disenchanted: ~ ***with*** ...e tŏ isang maeryŏgŭl nŭkkiji mot'anŭn ...에 더 이상 매력을 느끼지 못하는
disengage noajuda 놓아주다
disentangle p'ulda 풀다
disfigure *person* oemorŭl ch'uhage mandŭlda 외모를 추하게 만들다; *thing* oegwanŭl sonsangshik'ida

외관을 손상시키다
disgrace 1 *n* pulmyŏng-ye 불명예; ***a ~*** (*person*) ch'iyok 치욕; ***it's a ~*** ch'iyoktchŏgin iriyeyo 치욕적인 일이예요; ***in ~*** pulmyŏng-yesŭrŏpkke myŏnmogŭl irŭn 불명예스럽게 면목을 잃은, ch'emyŏnŭl irŭn 체면을 잃은 **2** *v/t* …ŭi such'iga toeda …의 수치가 되다
disgraceful such'isŭrŏun 수치스러운
disgruntled pulmansŭrŏun 불만스러운
disguise 1 *n* wijang 위장; (*costume, make-up*) pyŏn-jang 변장 **2** *v/t* wijanghada 위장하다; *fear, anxiety* naesaek'aji ant'a 내색하지 않다; ***~ oneself as*** …(ŭ)ro pyŏnjanghada …(으)로 변장하다; ***he was ~d as*** kŭnŭn …(ŭ)ro wijanghaet-tta 그는 …(으)로 위장했다
disgust 1 *n* hyŏmo 혐오 **2** *v/t* hyŏmogamŭl irŭk'ida 혐오감을 일으키다
disgusting *habit* hyŏmosŭrŏun 혐오스러운; *smell, food* kuyŏktchil nanŭn 구역질 나는; ***it is ~ that …*** …ranŭn kŏsŭn hyŏmosŭrŏptta …라는 것은 혐오스럽다
dish (*part of meal*) yori 요리; (*container*) kŭrŭt 그릇; (*for rice*) konggi 공기; (*for soup*) taejŏp 대접
dishcloth haengju 행주
disheartened nakttamhan 낙담한
disheartening nakttam shik'inŭn 낙담시키는
disheveled *hair* hŏngk'ŭrŏjin 헝클어진; *clothes* tanjŏngch'i mot'an 단정치 못한; *person* hŭt'ŭrŏjin 흐트러진
dishonest pujŏngjik'an 부정직한
dishonesty pujŏngjik 부정직
dishonor *n* pulmyŏng-ye 불명예; ***bring ~ on*** …ŭl / rŭl mangshinshik'ida …을 / 를 망신시키다
dishonorable pulmyŏng-yesŭrŏun 불명예스러운
dishwasher (*person*) sŏlgŏjihanŭn saram 설거지하는 사람; (*machine*) sŏlgŏji kigye 설거지 기계
dishwashing liquid chubangyong seje 주방용 세제
dishwater sŏlgŏji mul 설겆이 물
disillusion *v/t* hwansang-ŭl pŏrige hada 환상을 버리게 하다
disillusionment hwanmyŏl 환멸
disinclined maŭmi naek'iji annŭn 마음이 내키지 않는
disinfect sodok'ada 소독하다
disinfectant sodongnyak 소독약
disinherit sangsok-kkwŏnŭl pakt'arhada 상속권을 박탈하다
disintegrate hŏmurŏjida 허물어지다; (*of marriage, building*) punggoedoeda 붕괴되다
disinterested (*unbiased*) kongp'yŏnghan 공평한
disjointed chal yŏn-gyŏri toeji anŭn 잘 연결이 되지 않은
disk (*shape*) wŏnbanhyŏng 원반형; COMPUT tisŭk'et 디스켓; ***on ~*** tisŭk'ese chŏjangdoen 디스켓에 저장된
disk drive COMPUT tisŭk'et tŭraibŭ 디스켓 드라이브
diskette tisŭk'et 디스켓
dislike 1 *n* shirŏham 싫어함 **2** *v/t* shirŏhada 싫어하다
dislocate t'algushik'ida 탈구시키다
dislodge umjigida 움직이다
disloyal pulch'ungsshirhan 불충실한
disloyalty pulch'ungsshil 불충실
dismal *weather* ŭmsanhan 음산한; *news, prospect* ch'imurhan 침울한; (*depressed*) uurhan 우울한; (*pessimistic*) pujŏngjŏgin 부정적인; *failure* hyŏngp'yŏnŏmnŭn 형편없는
dismantle haech'ehada 해체하다
dismay 1 *n* (*alarm*) tanghwang 당황; (*disappointment*) nakttam 낙담 **2** *v/t* tanghwanghage hada 당황하게 하다
dismiss *employee* haegoshik'ida 해고시키다; *suggestion* kŏjŏrhada 거절하다; *idea, thought* ttŏlch'yŏbŏrida 떨쳐버리다; *possibility* mushihada 무시하다
dismissal (*of employee*) haego 해고
disobedience pulboktchong 불복종
disobedient marŭl tŭt-tchi annŭn 말을 듣지 않는
disobey kŏyŏk'ada 거역하다
disorder (*untidiness*) chijŏbunham

지저분함; (*unrest*) hollan 혼란; MED chang-ae 장애

disorderly *room*, *desk* ŏjillŏ noŭn 어질러 놓은; (*unruly*) mubŏbŭi 무법의

disorganized mujilssŏhan 무질서한

disoriented panghyang kamgagŭl irŏbŏrin 방향 감각을 잃어버린

disown ŭijŏrhada 의절하다

disparaging hŏlttŭnnŭn 헐뜯는

disparity pulgyunhyŏng 불균형

dispassionate naengjŏnghan 냉정한

dispatch *v/t* (*send*) palssonghada 발송하다

dispensary (*in pharmacy*) chojeshil 조제실

dispense: **~ *with*** … ŏpsshi hada … 없이 하다

disperse 1 *v/t* hŭt'ŏjige hada 흩어지게 하다 **2** *v/i* (*of crowd*) hŭt'ŏjida 흩어지다; (*of mist*) hŭt'ŏ ŏpssŏjida 흩어 없어지다

displace (*supplant*) pakkuŏ not'a 바꾸어 놓다

display 1 *n* chŏnshi 전시; (*in store window*) chinyŏl 진열; COMPUT tisŭp'ŭllei 디스플레이; ***be on ~*** (*at exhibition*) chŏnshi chung-ida 전시 중이다; (*in store*) chinyŏl chung-ida 진열 중이다 **2** *v/t emotion* p'yoshihada 표시하다; (*at exhibition*) chŏnshihada 전시하다; (*in store*) chinyŏrhada 진열하다; COMPUT hwamyŏne p'yoshihada 화면에 표시하다

display cabinet chinyŏltchang 진열장

displease pulk'waehage hada 불쾌하게 하다

displeasure pulk'wae 불쾌

disposable ssŭgo pŏril su innŭn 쓰고 버릴 수 있는; **~ *income*** kach'ŏbun sodŭk 가처분 소득

disposal ch'ŏbun 처분; (*of pollutants*, *nuclear waste*) p'yegi 폐기; ***I am at your ~*** ŏnjedŭn malman haseyo 언제든 말만 하세요; ***put X at Y's ~*** Xŭl/rŭl Yŭi maŭmdaero ssŭge hada X을/를 Y의 마음대로 쓰게 하다

dispose: **~ *of*** …ŭl/rŭl ch'ŏbunhada …을/를 처분하다

disposed: ***be ~ to do …*** (*willing*) … hagop'ŭ maŭmi nada … 하고픈 마음이 나다; ***be well ~ toward*** …ege hogamŭl kajida …에게 호감을 가지다

disposition (*nature*) kijil 기질

disproportionate pulgyunhyŏnghan 불균형한

disprove panjŭnghada 반증하다

dispute 1 *n* nonjaeng 논쟁; (*between countries*) punjaeng 분쟁; (*industrial*) chaeng-ŭi 쟁의 **2** *v/t* (*disagree with*) pallonhada 반론하다; (*fight over*) …ŭl/rŭl ŏdŭryŏgo ssauda …을/를 얻으려고 싸우다

disqualify chagyŏgŭl pakt'arhada 자격을 박탈하다

disregard 1 *n* mushi 무시 **2** *v/t* mushihada 무시하다

disrepair: ***in a state of ~*** hwangp'yehan sangt'aee 황폐한 상태에

disreputable *person* hyŏngp'yŏnŏmnŭn 형편없는; *area* p'yŏngp'ani nappŭn 평판이 나쁜

disrespect murye 무례

disrespectful muryehan 무례한

disrupt *train service* tujŏlshik'ida 두절시키다; *meeting*, *class* chungdanshik'ida 중단시키다

disruption (*of train service*) tujŏl 두절; (*of meeting*, *class*) chungdan 중단

disruptive punyŏlsshik'inŭn 분열시키는

dissatisfaction pulman 불만

dissatisfied pulmansŭrŏun 불만스러운

dissension ŭigyŏnŭi ch'ai 의견의 차이

dissent 1 *n* pandae ŭigyŏn 반대 의견 **2** *v/i*: **~ *from*** ...e pandaehada ...에 반대하다

dissident *n* pandaeja 반대자

dissimilar tarŭn 다른

dissociate: **~ *oneself from*** …wa/kwa kwan-gyerŭl kkŭnt'a ..와/과 관계를 끊다

dissolute pangt'anghan 방탕한

dissolve 1 *v/t substance* nogida 녹이다 **2** *v/i* (*of substance*) noktta 녹다

dissuade mallida 말리다; **~ *X from Y***

Xi / ga Yhanŭn kŏsŭl mallida X이 / 가 Y하는 것을 말리다
distance 1 *n* kŏri 거리; ***in the ~*** mŏn kose(sŏ) 먼 곳에(서) **2** *v/t*: ***~ oneself from*** ...(ŭ)robut'ŏ kŏrirŭl tuda ...(으) 로부터 거리를 두다
distant *place*, *time* mŏn 먼; *fig* (*aloof*) sowŏnhan 소원한
distaste shirŭm 싫음
distasteful shirŭn 싫은
distilled liquor soju 소주
distilled rice wine chŏngjong 정종
distinct (*clear*) tturyŏt'an 뚜렷한; (*different*) tarŭn 다른; ***as ~ from*** ...wa / kwanŭn tarŭge ...와 / 과는 다르게
distinction (*differentiation*) kubyŏl 구별; ***hotel / product of ~*** t'agwŏrhan hot'el / sangp'um 탁월한 호텔 / 상품
distinctive t'ŭgyuŭi 특유의
distinctly tturyŏt'age 뚜렷하게; (*decidedly*) hwaksshirhi 확실히
distinguish (*see*) pun-ganhada 분간하다; ***~ between X and Y*** Xwa / gwa Yŭl / rŭl shikppyŏrhada X와 / 과 Y을 / 를 식별하다
distinguished (*famous*) chŏmyŏnghan 저명한; (*dignified*) kip'um innŭn 기품 있는
distort waegok'ada 왜곡하다
distract *person* shimnanhage hada 심란하게 하다; *attention* ttan tero tollige hada 딴 데로 돌리게 하다
distracted (*worried*) shimnanhan 심란한
distraction (*of attention*) ttan tero tollim 딴 데로 돌림; (*amusement*) kibun chŏnhwan 기분 전환; ***drive s.o. to ~*** nugurŭl mich'ige mandŭlda 누구를 미치게 만들다
distraught mich'il tŭt'an 미칠 듯한
distress 1 *n* (*mental*) komin 고민; (*physical pain*) kot'ong 고통; ***in ~*** *ship*, *aircraft* chonan sangt'aeŭi 조난 상태의 **2** *v/t* (*upset*) koerop'ida 괴롭히다
distress signal chonan shinho 조난 신호
distribute nanuda 나누다; *wealth* punbaehada 분배하다; COM yut'onghada 유통하다
distribution (*handing out*) nanuŏ chum 나누어 줌; (*of wealth*) punbae 분배; COM yut'ong 유통
distribution arrangement COM yut'ong hyŏptchŏng 유통 협정
distributor COM paegŭbŏptcha 배급업자
district chiyŏk 지역; (*of city*) ku 구
district attorney chibang kŏmsa 지방 검사
district office kuch'ŏng 구청
distrust 1 *n* pulsshin 불신 **2** *v/t* pulsshinhada 불신하다
disturb (*interrupt*) panghaehada 방해하다; (*upset*) ...ŭi maŭmŭl ŏjirŏp'ida ...의 마음을 어지럽히다; ***do not ~*** panghaehaji mashio 방해하지 마시오
disturbance (*interruption*) panghae 방해; ***~s*** soyo 소요
disturbed (*concerned*, *worried*) maŭmi ŏjirŏun 마음이 어지러운; (*mentally*) chŏngshin isang-ŭi 정신 이상의
disturbing maŭmŭl ŏjirŏp'inŭn 마음을 어지럽히는
disused sayongdoeji annŭn 사용되지 않는
ditch 1 *n* torang 도랑 **2** *v/t* F (*get rid of*) pŏrida 버리다; (*drop*) kŭmanduda 그만두다
dive 1 *n* ttwiŏdŭlgi 뛰어들기; (*underwater*) chamsu 잠수; (*of plane*) kŭpkkangha 급강하; F (*bar*) ssaguryŏ sultchip 싸구려 술집; ***take a ~*** (*of dollar etc*) p'ongnak'ada 폭락하다 **2** *v/i* ttwiŏdŭlda 뛰어들다; (*underwater*) chamsuhada 잠수하다; (*of plane*) kŭpkkanghahada 급강하하다
diver (*off board*) taibŏ 다이버; (*underwater*) chamsubu 잠수부
diverge kallajida 갈라지다
diverse tayanghan 다양한
diversification COM saŏbŭi tagak'wa 사업의 다각화
diversify *v/i* COM saŏbŭl tagak'washik'ida 사업을 다각화시키다
diversion (*for traffic*) uhoe 우회; (*to

distract attention) chuŭirŭl ttan tero tollim 주의를 딴 데로 돌림
diversity tayangssŏng 다양성
divert *traffic* uhoeshik'ida 우회시키다; *attention* ttan tero tollida 딴 데로 돌리다
divest: **~ *X of Y*** Xegesŏ Yŭl / rŭl ppaeat-tta X에게서 Y을 / 를 빼앗다
divide nanuda 나누다
dividend FIN paedanggŭm 배당금; ***pay ~s*** *fig* idŭgi toeda 이득이 되다
divine REL shinsŏnghan 신성한; F aju mŏtchin 아주 멋진
diving (*from board*) taibing 다이빙; (*scuba ~*) sŭk'ubŏ taibing 스쿠버 다이빙
diving board taibing tae 다이빙 대
divisible nanul su innŭn 나눌 수 있는
division MATH nanutssem 나눗셈; (*in party etc*) punyŏl 분열; (*splitting into parts*) pulli 분리; (*of company*) pusŏ 부서
divorce 1 *n* ihon 이혼; ***get a ~*** ihonhada 이혼하다 **2** *v/t* …wa / kwa ihonhada …와 / 과 이혼하다 **3** *v/i* ihonhada 이혼하다
divorced ihonhan 이혼한; ***get ~d*** ihonhada 이혼하다
divorcee (*man*) ihonnam 이혼남; (*woman*) ihonnyŏ 이혼녀
divulge nusŏrhada 누설하다; *secret* palk'ida 밝히다
DIY (= ***do-it-yourself***) sonsu mandŭlgi 손수 만들기
DIY store tiaiwai kage 디아이와이 가게
dizzy: ***feel ~*** hyŏn-gitchŭng-i nada 현기증이 나다
DMZ (= ***Demilitarized Zone***) Pimujang Chidae 비무장 지대
DNA (= ***deoxyribonucleic acid***) tioksshiribo haekssan 디옥시리보 핵산
do 1 *v/t* hada 하다; *one's hair* sonjirhada 손질하다; *French, chemistry* kongbuhada 공부하다; *100mph etc* ...ŭi sokttorŭl naeda ...의 속도를 내다; ***what are you ~ing tonight?*** onŭl chŏnyŏk mwŏ halkkŏyeyo? 오늘 저녁에 뭐 할꺼예요?; ***I don't know what to ~*** ŏttŏk-kke haeya haltchi morŭgessŏyo 어떻게 해야 할지 모르겠어요; ***no, I'll ~ it*** aniyo, chega hagessŭmnida 아니요, 제가 하겠습니다; ***~ it right now!*** chigŭm tangjang hae! 지금 당장 해!; ***have you done this before?*** chŏne hae pon chŏgi issŏyo? 전에 해 본 적이 있어요?; ***have one's hair done*** mŏrirŭl sonjirhada 머리를 손질하다 **2** *v/i* (*be suitable, enough*) kwaench'ant'a 괜찮다; ***that will ~!*** kŭ chŏngdomyŏn twaessŏ! 그 정도면 됐어!; **~ *well*** (*of person*) chal haenaeda 잘 해내다; (*of business*) saŏbi chal toeda 사업이 잘 되다; ***well done!*** (*congratulations!*) chal haessŏyo! 잘 했어요!; ***how ~ you ~*** chŏŭm poepkkessŭmnida 처음 뵙겠습니다 **3** (*auxiliary*): ***~ you know him?*** kŭ saramŭl algo issŭmnikka? 그 사람을 알고 있습니까?; ***I don't know*** morŭgessŏyo 모르겠어요; ***~ you like Seoul? - yes I ~*** Sŏurŭl choahaeyo? - ne, choahaeyo 서울을 좋아해요? - 네, 좋아해요; ***he works hard, doesn't he?*** kŭnŭn chŏngmal yŏlsshimhiirhajyo? 그는 정말 열심히 일하죠?; ***don't you believe me?*** narŭl mittchi annayo? 나를 믿지 않아요?; ***you ~ believe me, don't you?*** narŭl mittchyo? 나를 믿죠?
♦ **do away with** p'yejihada 폐지하다
♦ **do in**: ***I'm done in*** F nanŭn nokch'oga toeŏt-tta 나는 녹초가 되었다
♦ **do out of**: ***do X out of Y*** Xŭl / rŭl sogyŏ Yŭl / rŭl ppaeat-tta X을 / 를 속여 Y을 / 를 빼앗다
♦ **do over** (*do again*) toep'urihada 되풀이하다
♦ **do up** (*renovate*) posuhada 보수하다; (*fasten*) chamgŭda 잠그다; *buttons* ch'aeuda 채우다; *laces* muktta 묶다
♦ **do with**: ***I could ~ …*** nanŭn …i / ga p'iryohada 나는 …이 / 가 필요하다; ***he won't have anything to ~ it*** kŭnŭn kŭ ilgwa mugwanhada 그는 그 일과 무관하다

♦**do without 1** *v/i* kyŏndida 견디다 **2** *v/t* … ŏpsshi chinaeda … 없이 지내다
docile *person* sunhan 순한; *animal* tarugi shwiun 다루기 쉬운
dock[1] **1** *n* NAUT pudu 부두 **2** *v/i* (*of ship*) pudue taeda 부두에 대다; (*of spaceship*) tok'ingshik'ida 도킹시키다
dock[2] LAW p'igosŏk 피고석
dockyard chosŏnso 조선소
doctor *n* MED ŭisa 의사; (*form of address*) ŭisa sŏnsaengnim 의사 선생님
doctorate pakssa hagwi 박사 학위
doctrine shinjo 신조
docudrama tak'yument'ŏri tŭrama 다큐멘터리 드라마
document *n* sŏryu 서류
documentary (*program*) tak'yument'ŏri 다큐멘터리
documentation (*documents*) sŏryu 서류
dodge *v/t blow* p'ihada 피하다; *person*, *issue* kyomyohi hoep'ihada 교묘히 회피하다; *question* tullŏdaeda 둘러대다
doe (*deer*) amssasŭm 암사슴
dog 1 *n* kae 개 **2** *v/t* (*follow*) mihaenghada 미행하다; (*of bad luck*) kyesok'aesŏ irŏnada 계속해서 일어나다
dog catcher tŭlkkae p'ohoegin 들개 포획인
dogged kkŭnjilgin 끈질긴
doggie mŏngmŏng-i 멍멍이
doggy bag *namŭn ŭmshigŭl ssajunŭn kŏt* 남은 음식을 싸주는 것
doghouse: ***be in the ~*** ch'emyŏnŭl ilt'a 체면을 잃다
dogma kyori 교리
dogmatic tokssŏnjŏgin 독선적인
do-gooder kongsangjŏk sahoe kaeryangga 공상적 사회 개량가
dog tag MIL kuninŭi insshikp'yo 군인의 인식표
dog-tired kijinmaektchinhan 기진맥진한
do-it-yourself sonsu mandŭlgi 손수 만들기
doldrums: ***be in the ~*** (*of economy*) purhwang-ida 불황이다; (*of person*) ch'imurhae it-tta 침울해 있다
♦**dole out** paebunhada 배분하다
doll (*toy*) inhyŏng 인형; F (*woman*) maeryŏktchŏgin yŏja 매력적인 여자
♦**doll up**: ***get dolled up*** mŏttchige ch'aryŏ iptta 멋지게 차려 입다
dollar tallŏ 달러
dollop *n* tŏng-ŏri 덩어리
dolmen koindol 고인돌
dolphin tolkkorae 돌고래
dome (*of building*) tunggŭn ch'ŏnjang 둥근 천장
domestic *adj chores* kasaŭi 가사의; *news*, *policy* kungnaeŭi 국내의
domestic animal (*for agriculture*) kach'uk 가축
domesticate *animal* kiltŭrida 길들이다; ***be ~d*** (*of person*) kasa irŭl hada 가사 일을 하다
domestic flight kungnaesŏn pihaenggi 국내선 비행기
dominant chuyohan 주요한; (*influential*) yuryŏk'an 유력한; BIO usŏng-ŭi 우성의
dominate chibaehada 지배하다; *landscape* apttohada 압도하다
domination (*control*) chibae 지배; (*superiority*) use 우세
domineering chibaejŏgin 지배적인; *husband* p'okkunjŏgin 폭군적인
donate *money* kibuhada 기부하다; *time* pach'ida 바치다; *toys*, *books* hŭisahada 희사하다; MED kijŭnghada 기증하다
donation (*of money*) kibuhada 기부; (*of time*) hŏnsshin 헌신; (*of toys*, *books*) hŭisa 희사; MED kijŭng 기증
donkey tangnagwi 당나귀
donor (*of money*) kibuja 기부자; MED kijŭngja 기증자
donut tonŏt 도넛
doom *n* (*fate*) agun 악운; (*ruin*) p'amyŏl 파멸
doomed *project* p'agidoenŭn 파기되는; ***we are ~*** (*bound to fail*) urinŭn shilp'aehage toeŏit-tta 우리는 실패하게 되어있다; (*going to die*) urinŭn chukke toeŏit-tta 우리는 죽게 되어있다; ***the ~ ship*** nanp'ahal

unmyŏng-ŭi pae 난파할 운명의 배
door mun 문; (*entrance, exit*) ch'urimmun 출입문; ***there's someone at the*** ~ nugun-ga mune it-tta 누군가 문에 있다
doorbell ch'oinjong 초인종; **doorknob** munjabi 문잡이; **doorman** toŏ maen 도어 맨; **doormat** hyŏngwane innŭn kudu tak-kkae 현관에 있는 구두 닦개; **doorstep** muntchibang 문지방; **doorway** ch'uripkku 출입구
dope 1 *n* (*drugs*) mayak 마약; F (*idiot*) mŏngch'ŏng-i 멍청이; F (*information*) pimil chŏngbo 비밀 정보 **2** *v/t* yagŭl mŏgida 약을 먹이다
dormant *plant* paryuk chŏngji chung-in 발육 정지 중인; ~ ***volcano*** hyuhwasan 휴화산
dormitory kisukssa 기숙사
dosage pogyongnyang 복용량
dose *n* irhoe pogyongnyang 일회 복용량
dot *n* (*also in e-mail address*) chŏm 점; ***on the*** ~ chŏnghwak'i 정확히
♦**dote on** ...e holttak ppajida ...에 홀딱 빠지다
dotted line chŏmsŏn 점선
double 1 *n* (*amount*) tu pae 두 배; (*person*) kkok talmŭn saram 꼭 닮은 사람; (*of movie star*) taeyŏk 대역; (*room*) iinyong pang 이인용 방 **2** *adj* (*twice as much*) tu paeŭi 두 배의; *whiskey* tŏbŭl 더블; *sink, oven* ssangŭro toen 쌍으로 된; *doors* yangtchogŭro yŏnŭn mun 양쪽으로 여는 문; *layer* tu kyŏbŭi 두 겹의; ***in ~ figures*** tu chari su 두 자리 수 **3** *adv* tu paero 두 배로 **4** *v/t* tu paero hada 두 배로 하다; (*fold*) panŭro chŏptta 반으로 접다 **5** *v/i* tu paega toeda 두 배가 되다
♦**double back** *v/i* (*go back*) toedoragada 되돌아가다
♦**double up** (*in pain*) ap'asŏ momŭl kuburida 아파서 몸을 구부리다; (*share a room*) pang-ŭl nanuŏ ssŭda 방을 나누어 쓰다
double-bass tŏbŭlbeisŭ 더블베이스; **double bed** tŏbŭlbedŭ 더블베드; **double-breasted** tanch'uga yangtchogŭro tallin 단추가 양쪽으로 달린; **doublecheck** *v/t & v/i* tashi hwaginhada 다시 확인하다; **double chin** ijungt'ŏk 이중턱; **double click** *n* tŏbŭl k'ŭllik 더블클릭; **double-cross** *v/t* paebanhada 배반하다; **double glazing** ijung yuri 이중 유리; **doublepark** *v/i* ijung chuch'ashik'ida 이중 주차시키다; **double-quick**: ***in ~ time*** hwanggŭp'i 황급히; **double room** iinyong pang 이인용 방
doubles (*in tennis*) poksshik 복식
doubt 1 *n* (*suspicion*) ŭishim 의심; (*mistrust*) pulsshin 불신; (*uncertainty*) ŭigushim 의구심; ***be in*** ~ purhwaksshirhada 불확실하다; ***no*** ~ (*probably*) tabunhi 다분히 **2** *v/t* ŭishimhada 의심하다
doubtful *remark, look* ŭishimtchŏgŭn 의심쩍은; ***be*** ~ (*of person*) ŭishimsŭrŏptta 의심스럽다; ***it is ~ whether*** ... halji purhwaksshirhada ... 할지 불확실하다
doubtfully ŭishimsŭrŏpkke 의심스럽게
doubtless hwaksshirhi 확실히
dough milkkaru panjuk 밀가루 반죽; F (*money*) ton 돈
dove pidulgi 비둘기; *fig* p'yŏnghwajuŭija 평화주의자
dowdy ch'onsŭrŏun 촌스러운
Dow Jones Average Tau Chonsŭ p'yŏnggyun chuga 다우 존스 평균 주가
down[1] *n* (*feathers*) kitt'ŏl 깃털
down[2] **1** *adv* (*downward*) najŭn tchogŭro 낮은 쪽으로; (*onto the ground*) araetchogŭro 아래쪽으로; ~ ***there*** chŏgi araetchoge 저기 아래쪽에; ***fall*** ~ ttŏrŏjida 떨어지다; ***look*** ~ naeryŏda poda 내려다 보다; ***$200*** ~ (*as deposit*) kyeyak-kkŭm 200tallŏ 계약금 200달러; ***go ~ south*** namtchogŭro naeryŏgada 남쪽으로 내려가다; ***be*** ~ (*of price, rate*) naerida 내리다; (*of numbers, amount*) churŏdŭrŏ it-tta 줄어들어 있다; (*not working*) kojangna it-tta 고장나 있다; (*depressed*) ultchŏk'ae hada 울적해 하다 **2** *prep* ...ŭi

araetchogŭro ...의 아래쪽으로; (*along*) ...ŭl / rŭl ttara ...을 / 를 따라; ***run ~ the stairs*** kyedanŭi araetchogŭro tallyŏ naeryŏgada 계단의 아래쪽으로 달려 내려가다; ***walk ~ the road*** kirŭl ttara kŏt-tta 길을 따라 걷다 **3** *v/t* (*swallow*) mashida 마시다; (*destroy*) ssoa nŏmŏttŭrida 쏘아 넘어뜨리다

down-and-out *n* pint'ŏlt'ŏri 빈털터리; **downcast** (*dejected*) p'uri chugŭn 풀이 죽은; **downfall** *n* mollak 몰락; (*cause of ruin*) shilp'aeŭi wŏnin 실패의 원인; **downgrade** *v/t person* kangdŭngshik'ida 강등시키다; *document, forecast* chŏngdorŭl ttŏrŏttŭrida 정도를 떨어뜨리다; **downhearted** p'uri chugŭn 풀이 죽은; **downhill** *adv*: ***go ~*** (*of road*) naerimak-kkiri toeda 내리막길이 되다; (*of quality of work*) ttŏrŏjida 떨어지다; (*of health*) yak'wadoeda 약화되다; (*of country*) soet'oehada 쇠퇴하다; **downhill skiing** hwalgang sŭk'i 활강 스키; **download** COMPUT taunrodinghada 다운로딩하다; **downmarket** *adj* taejungtchŏgin 대중적인; **down payment** kyeyak-kkŭm 계약금; **downplay** kyŏngshihada 경시하다; **downpour** p'ogu 폭우; **downright 1** *adj idiot* wanjŏnhan 완전한; **~ *lie*** saeppalgan kŏjinmal 새빨간 거짓말 **2** *adv dangerous, stupid etc* aju 아주; **downside** (*disadvantage*) tantchŏm 단점; **downsize 1** *v/t car* sohyŏnghwahada 소형화하다; *company* kyumorŭl churida 규모를 줄이다 **2** *v/i* (*of company*) kyumoga chulda 규모가 줄다; **downstairs 1** *adj* araech'ŭng-ŭi 아래층의 **2** *adv* araech'ung-e(sŏ) 아래층에(서); **down-to-earth** *approach* shiltchejŏgin 실제적인; *person* hyŏnshiljŏgin 현실적인; **down-town 1** *adj* toshim-ŭi 도심의 **2** *adv* toshiŭi chungshimbue(sŏ) 도시의 중심부에(서); **downturn** (*economic*) kyŏnggi ch'imch'e 경기 침체

downward 1 *adj* araetchogŭroŭi 아래쪽으로의 **2** *adv* araetchogŭro 아래쪽으로

doze 1 *n* sŏnjam 선잠 **2** *v/i* cholda 졸다

♦**doze off** kkubŏk-kkubŏk cholda 꾸벅꾸벅 졸다

dozen yŏldu kae 열두 개; **~*s of*** aju manŭn 아주 많은

DPRK (= ***Democratic People's Republic of Korea***) Chosŏn Minjujuŭi Inmin Konghwaguk 조선 민주주의 인민 공화국

drab tanjoroun 단조로운

draft 1 *n* (*of air*) t'ongp'ung 통풍; (*of document*) ch'ogo 초고; MIL chingbyŏng 징병; **~ (*beer*)** saengmaektchu 생맥주 **2** *v/t document* ch'ogorŭl chakssŏnghada 초고를 작성하다; MIL chingbyŏnghada 징병하다

draft dodger chingbyŏng kip'ija 징병 기피자

draftee chingjip-ppyŏng 징집병

draftsman (*of technical drawing*) toan-ga 도안가; (*of plan*) ibanja 입안자

drafty t'ongp'ung-i chal toenŭn 통풍이 잘 되는

drag 1 *n*: ***it's a ~ having to ...*** ... haeya hanŭn kŏshi sŏnggashida ... 해야 하는 것이 성가시다; ***he's a ~*** kŭnŭn ttabunhan saramida 그는 따분한 사람이다; ***the main ~*** han-gil 한길; ***in ~*** yŏjang-ŭl hago 여장을 하고 **2** *v/t* (*pull*) kkŭrŏ tanggida 끌어 당기다; *person, oneself* kkŭrŏ tŭrida 끌어 들이다; (*search*) hultta 훑다; **~ *X into Y*** (*involve*) Xŭl / rŭl Y(ŭ)ro kkŭrŏ tŭrida X을 / 를 Y(으)로 끌어 들이다; **~ *X out of Y*** (*get information from*) Y(ŭ)robut'ŏ Xŭl / rŭl kanshinhi ppaenaeda Y(으)로부터 X을 / 를 간신히 빼내다 **3** *v/i* (*of time*) kkŭlda 끌다; (*of show, movie*) chiruhada 지루하다

♦**drag away**: ***drag oneself away from the TV*** t'ellebijŏnesŏ tteŏ not'a 텔레비전에서 떼어 놓다

♦**drag in** (*into conversation*) ...e taehan marŭl kkŏnaeda ...에 대한 말을 꺼내다

♦**drag on** chiljil kkŭlda 질질 끌다
♦**drag out** (*prolong*) kkŭlda 끌다
♦**drag up** (*mention*) kkŭjibŏ naeda 끄집어 내다
dragon yong 용; *fig* ŏmkkyŏk'an saram 엄격한 사람
drain 1 *n* (*pipe*) paesuro 배수로; (*under street*) hasugu 하수구; ***a ~ on resources*** chawŏn kogal 자원 고갈 **2** *v/t water* ppaenaeda 빼내다; *engine oil* paech'ulshik'ida 배출시키다; *vegetables* mulkkirŭl ppaeda 물기를 빼다; *land* paesu shisŏrŭl hada 배수 시설을 하다; *glass, tank* piuda 비우다; (*exhaust: person*) chich'ige hada 지치게 하다 **3** *v/i* (*of dishes*) mulkkiga marŭda 물기가 마르다
♦**drain away** (*of liquid*) ppajida 빠지다
♦**drain off** *water* ppaeda 빼다
drainage (*drains*) paesu 배수; (*of water from soil*) ppajim 빠짐
drainpipe paesugwan 배수관
drama (*art form*) hŭigok 희곡; (*excitement*) kŭktchŏgin sanghwang 극적인 상황; (*play: on TV*) tŭrama 드라마
dramatic yŏn-gŭgŭi 연극의; (*exciting*) kŭktchŏgin 극적인; *gesture* kwajangdoen 과장된
dramatist kŭktchak-kka 극작가
dramatization (*play*) kŭk'wa 극화
dramatize *story* kŭk'wahada 극화하다; *fig* kwajanghayŏ p'yohyŏnhada 과장하여 표현하다
drape *v/t cloth, coat* tullŏ ssŭiuda 둘러 씌우다; ***~d in*** (*covered with*) ...(ŭ)ro tullŏ ssayŏjin ...(으)로 둘러 싸여진
drapery hwijang 휘장
drapes k'ŏt'ŭn 커튼
drastic (*extreme*) chinach'in 지나친; *measures* kwagamhan 과감한; *change* kyŏngnyŏrhan 격렬한
draw 1 *n* (*in match, competition*) tongtchŏm 동점; (*in lottery*) chebi ppopkki 제비 뽑기; (*attraction*) inkkiinnŭn kŏt 인기있는 것 **2** *v/t picture, map* kŭrida 그리다; *cart* kkŭrŏ tanggida 끌어 당기다; *curtain* ch'ida 치다; *gun, knife* ppaeda 빼다; (*attract*) ...ŭi chuŭirŭl kkŭlda ...의 주의를 끌다; (*lead*) teryŏgada 데려가다; (*from bank account*) inch'urhada 인출하다 **3** *v/i* kŭrimŭl kŭrida 그림을 그리다; (*in match, competition*) pigida 비기다; ***~ near*** kakkai tagagada 가까이 다가가다; (*of time*) kakkai tagaoda 가까이 다가오다
♦**draw back 1** *v/i* (*recoil*) twiro mullŏnada 뒤로 물러나다 **2** *v/t* (*pull back*) twiro tanggida 뒤로 당기다
♦**draw on 1** *v/i* (*advance*) kip'ŏgada 깊어가다 **2** *v/t* (*make use of*) iyonghada 이용하다
♦**draw out** *v/t pocketbook* kkŏnaeda 꺼내다; *money from bank* inch'urhada 인출하다
♦**draw up 1** *v/t document* chakssŏnghada 작성하다; *chair* nŭrŏnot'a 늘어놓다 **2** *v/i* (*of vehicle*) mŏmch'uda 멈추다
drawback kyŏltchŏm 결점
drawer[1] (*of desk etc*) sŏrap 서랍
drawer[2] (*person*) hwaga 화가
drawing kŭrim 그림
drawing board chedop'an 제도판; ***go back to the ~*** ch'ŏŭmbut'ŏ tashi shijak'ada 처음부터 다시 시작하다
drawl *n* nŭrin malt'u 느린 말투
dread *v/t* turyŏwŏhada 두려워하다
dreadful *movie, book* mushimushihan 무시무시한; *weather, pity* chidok'an 지독한
dreadfully (*extremely*) mopsshi 몹시; *behave* hyŏngp'yŏnŏpsshi 형편없이
dream 1 *n* kkum 꿈 **2** *adj house etc* kkumgat'ŭn 꿈같은 **3** *v/t* kkumkkuda 꿈꾸다; (*day~*) mongsanghada 몽상하다 **4** *v/i* kkumŭl kkuda 꿈을 꾸다; (*day~*) mongsanghada 몽상하다
♦**dream up** ŏngttunghan saenggagŭl haenaeda 엉뚱한 생각을 해내다
dreamer (*day~*) mongsangga 몽상가
dreamy *voice, look* kkumkkyŏlgat'ŭn 꿈결같은
dreary chiruhan 지루한
dredge *harbor, canal* chunsŏrhada 준설하다
♦**dredge up** *fig* tŭlch'uŏnaeda 들추어내다

dregs (*of coffee*) tchikkŏgi 찌꺼기; ***the ~ of society*** sahoe ssŭregi 사회 쓰레기
drench *v/t* hŭmppŏk chŏksshida 흠뻑 적시다; ***get ~ed*** hŭmppŏk chŏt-tta 흠뻑 젖다
dress 1 *n* (*for woman*) tŭresŭ 드레스; (*clothing*) ot 옷 **2** *v/t person* osŭl ip'ida 옷을 입히다; *wound* pungdaerŭl kamtta 붕대를 감다; ***get ~ed*** osŭl iptta 옷을 입다 **3** *v/i* (*get ~ed*) ot iptta 옷 입다; ***~ in black / conservatively*** kkaman saegŭro / posujŏgŭro osŭl iptta 까만 색으로 / 보수적으로 옷을 입다; ***~ well*** osŭl chal iptta 옷을 잘 입다
♦**dress up** *v/i* sŏngjanghada 성장하다; (*wear a disguise*) pyŏnjanghada 변장하다; ***~ as*** …(ŭ)ro pyŏnjanghada …(으)로 변장하다
dress circle kŭktchang-ŭi t'ŭkppyŏlssŏk 극장의 특별석
dresser (*dressing table*) hwajangdae 화장대; (*in kitchen*) ch'antchang 찬장
dressing (*for salad*) sosŭ 소스; (*for wound*) pungdae 붕대
dressing room THEA punjangshil 분장실
dressing table hwajangdae 화장대
dressmaker yangjaesa 양재사
dress rehearsal ŭisang lihŏsŏl 의상 리허설
dressy uahan 우아한
dribble *v/i* (*of person, baby*) ch'imŭl hŭllida 침을 흘리다; (*of liquid*) ttukttuk ttŏrŏjida 뚝뚝 떨어지다; SP tŭribŭrhada 드리블하다
dried *fruit etc* mallin 말린
drier kŏnjogi 건조기
drift 1 *n* (*of snow*) nundŏmi 눈더미 **2** *v/i* (*of snow*) parame nallyŏ ssaida 바람에 날려 쌓이다; (*of ship*) p'yoryuhada 표류하다; (*go off course*) hangnoesŏ pŏsŏnada 항로에서 벗어나다; (*of person*) chŏngch'ŏŏpsshi pangnanghada 정처없이 방랑하다
♦**drift apart** (*of couple*) maŭmi mŏrŏjida 마음이 멀어지다
drifter pangnangja 방랑자
drill 1 *n* (*tool*) ch'ŏn-gonggi 천공기; (*exercise*) yŏnssŭp 연습; MIL hullyŏn 훈련 **2** *v/t hole* ttult'a 뚫다 **3** *v/i* (*for oil*) kumŏng naeda 구멍 내다; MIL hullyŏnhada 훈련하다
drilling rig (*platform*) chŏn-gongdae 천공대
drily *remark* pikkoasŏ 비꼬아서
drink 1 *n* mashil kŏt 마실 것; ***a ~ of*** … han chan … 한 잔; ***a ~ of water*** mul han chan 물 한 잔; ***go for a ~*** han chan harŏ kada 한 잔 하러 가다 **2** *v/t* mashida 마시다 **3** *v/i* mashida 마시다; (*consume alcohol*) surŭl mashida 술을 마시다; ***I don't ~*** nanŭn surŭl ibe taeji anssŭmnida 나는 술을 입에 대지 않습니다
♦**drink up** *v/t & v/i* ta mashida 다 마시다
drinkable mashil su innŭn 마실 수 있는
drinker ŭmjuja 음주자
drinking (*of alcohol*) ŭmju 음주
drinking water mashinŭn mul 마시는 물
drip 1 *n* pang-ul 방울; MED chŏmjŏk 점적 **2** *v/i* ttokttok ttŏrŏjida 똑똑 떨어지다
dripdry nŏrŏsŏ mallida 널어서 말리다
dripping: ~ (***wet***) hŭmppŏk chŏjŭn 흠뻑 젖은
drive 1 *n* unjŏn 운전; (*outing*) tŭraibŭ 드라이브; (*energy*) hwallyŏk 활력; COMPUT tŭraibŭ 드라이브; (*campaign*) undong 운동; ***it's a long ~ to the station from here*** yŏgisŏ yŏk-kkajinŭn ch'aro orae kayo 여기서 역까지는 차로 오래 가요; ***left- / right-hand ~*** MOT oenson / orŭnson chabi unjŏn 왼손 / 오른손 잡이 운전 **2** *v/t vehicle* molda 몰다; (*take in car*) ch'aro teryŏda chuda 차로 데려다 주다; TECH chakttongshik'ida 작동시키다; ***that noise / he is driving me mad*** chŏ soŭmi / kŭga narŭl mich'ige mandŭrŏyo 저 소음이 / 그가 나를 미치게 만들어요 **3** *v/i* unjŏnhada 운전하다
♦**drive at**: ***what are you driving at?*** musŭn marŭl haryŏnŭn kŏyeyo?

무슨 말을 하려는 거예요?
♦**drive away 1** *v/t* ch'ae t'aeugo kabŏrida 차에 태우고 가버리다; (*chase off*) tchoch'abŏrida 쫓아버리다 **2** *v/i* ch'arŭl t'ago kabŏrida 차를 타고 가버리다
♦**drive in** *v/t nail* paktta 박다
♦**drive off** → ***drive away***
drive-in *n* (*movie theater*) tŭraibŭin kŭktchang 드라이브인 극장
driver unjŏnja 운전자; COMPUT tŭraibŏ 드라이버
driver's license unjŏn myŏnhŏtchŭng 운전 면허증
driveway ch'ado 차도
driving 1 *n* unjŏn 운전 **2** *adj rain* ŏkssugat'ŭn 억수같은
driving force ch'ujinnyŏk 추진력; **driving instructor** unjŏn kyoyuk kangsa 운전 교육 강사; **driving lesson** unjŏn kyoyuk 운전 교육; **driving school** unjŏn hagwŏn 운전 학원; **driving test** unjŏn myŏnhŏ shihŏm 운전 면허 시험
drizzle 1 *n* isŭlbi 이슬비 **2** *v/i* isŭlbiga naerida 이슬비가 내리다
drone *n* (*noise*) wingwinghanŭn sori 윙윙하는 소리
droop *v/i* ch'uk nŭrŏjida 축 늘어지다; (*of plant*) shidŭlda 시들다
drop 1 *n* (*of rain*) pang-ul 방울; (*small amount*) yakkan 약간; (*in price, temperature*) harak 하락; (*in number*) kamso 감소 **2** *v/t object* ttŏrŏttŭrida 떨어뜨리다; *person from car* naeryŏjuda 내려주다; *person from team* chemyŏngshik'ida 제명시키다; (*stop seeing*) ...wa / kwa chŏlgyohada ...와 / 과 절교하다; (*give up*) kŭmanduda 그만두다; *charges, demand etc* ch'wisohada 취소하다; ~ ***a line to*** ...ege kallyak'i p'yŏnjirŭl ssŭda ...에게 간략히 편지를 쓰다 **3** *v/i* ttŏrŏjida 떨어지다; (*of prices, inflation*) harak'ada 하락하다; (*of wind*) chada 자다
♦**drop in** (*visit*) tŭllŭda 들르다
♦**drop off 1** *v/t person* ch'a-esŏ naeryŏjuda 차에서 내려주다; (*deliver*) chŏndarhada 전달하다 **2** *v/i* (*fall asleep*) chami tŭlda 잠이 들다; (*decline*) sarajida 사라지다
♦**drop out** (*withdraw*) kŭmanduda 그만두다; (*of school*) chungt'oehada 중퇴하다
dropout (*from school*) chungt'oeja 중퇴자; (*from society*) nagoja 낙오자
drops (*for eyes*) chŏmanje 점안제
drought kamum 가뭄
drown 1 *v/i* ikssahada 익사하다 **2** *v/t person* ikssashik'ida 익사시키다; *sound* tŭlliji ank'e hada 들리지 않게 하다; ***be ~ed*** ikssahada 익사하다
drowsy narŭnhan 나른한
drudgery tanjoroun il 단조로운 일
drug 1 *n* MED yak 약; (*illegal*) mayak 마약; ***be on ~s*** mayagŭl hada 마약을 하다 **2** *v/t* mach'wihada 마취하다
drug addict mayak sang-yongja 마약 상용자
drug dealer mayak p'anmaeja 마약 판매자
druggist yakssa 약사
drugstore *yak-kkugi ttallin chap'wajŏm* 약국이 딸린 잡화점
drug trafficking mayak kŏrae 마약 거래
drum 1 *n* MUS puk 북; (*in western music*) tŭrŏm 드럼; (*container*) tŭrŏmt'ong 드럼통
♦**drum into**: ***drum X into Y*** Xŭl / rŭl Yege panbok'ayŏ karŭch'ida X을 / 를 Y에게 반복하여 가르치다
♦**drum up**: ~ ***support*** chijirŭl kwŏnyuhada 지지를 권유하다
drummer pugŭl ch'inŭn saram 북을 치는 사람; (*western or ethnic music*) tŭrŏmŏ 드러머; (*Korean music*) kosu 고수
drumstick MUS pukch'ae 북채; (*of poultry*) takttari 닭다리
drunk 1 *n* (*habitually*) sulkkun 술꾼; (*on one occasion*) sul ch'wihan saram 술 취한 사람 **2** *adj* sul ch'wihan 술 취한; ***get*** ~ sure ch'wihada 술에 취하다
drunk driving ŭmju unjŏn 음주 운전
drunken *voices, laughter* ch'wijung-ŭi 취중의; *party* manch'wihan 만취한
dry 1 *adj clothes* marŭn 마른; *skin, mouth, ground* kŏnjohan 건조한; *wine* talji anŭn 달지 않은; (*ironic*)

pikkonŭn 비꼬는; (*where alcohol is banned*) kŭmjuŭi 금주의 **2** *v/t clothes* mallida 말리다; *dishes* mallida 말리다; ~ ***one's eyes*** nunmurŭl taktta 눈물을 닦다 **3** *v/i* marŭda 마르다

♦**dry out** (*of alcoholic*) alk'ool chungdok ch'iryŏrŭl pat-tta 알코올 중독 치료를 받다

♦**dry up** (*of river*) passak marŭda 바싹 마르다; (*be quiet*) choyonghi hada 조용히 하다

dry-clean *v/t* tŭraik'ŭllininghada 드라이클리닝하다

dry-cleaner set'aksso 세탁소

dry-cleaning (*clothes*) tŭraik'ŭllining 드라이클리닝

dryer (*machine*) kŏnjogi 건조기

dry field pat 밭

DTP (= ***desktop publishing***) k'ŏmp'yut'ŏ ch'ulp'an 컴퓨터 출판

dual ijung-ŭi 이중의; ***have ~ nationality*** ijung kuktchŏgŭl kajida 이중 국적을 가지다

dub *movie* tŏbinghada 더빙하다

dubious (*suspect*) sŏgyŏnch'i anŭn 석연치 않은; (*having doubts*) ŭishimsŭrŏun 의심스러운

duck 1 *n* ori 오리 **2** *v/i* mŏrirŭl hwaek sugida 머리를 홱 숙이다 **3** *v/t head* hwaek sugŭrida 홱 수그리다; *question* p'ihada 피하다

dud *n* (*false bill*) wijo chip'ye 위조 지폐

due (*owed*) chiburhagiro toeŏ innŭn 지불하기로 되어 있는; (*proper*) mattanghan 마땅한; ***be ~*** (*of train, baby etc*) … hal yejŏng-ida … 할 예정이다; ***when is your husband ~?*** namp'yŏnŭn ŏnje ol yejŏng-iyeyo? 남편은 언제 올 예정이에요?; ***when is the baby ~?*** ainŭn ŏnje t'aeŏnal yejŏng-in-gayo? 아이는 언제 태어날 예정인가요?; ~ ***to*** (*because of*) … ttaemune … 때문에; ***be ~ to*** (*be caused by*) … ttaemune irŏnada … 때문에 일어나다; ***in ~ course*** ttaega toemyŏn 때가 되면

dull *weather* hŭrin 흐린; *sound* tunt'ak'an 둔탁한; *pain* tunhan 둔한; (*boring*) chiruhan 지루한

duly (*as expected*) yejŏngdaero 예정대로; (*properly*) ch'ungbunhi 충분히

dumb (*mute*) pŏng-ŏriŭi 벙어리의; (*stupid*) ŏrisŏgŭn 어리석은

dummy (*for clothes*) manek'ing 마네킹

dump 1 *n* (*for garbage*) ssŭregi pŏrinŭn kot 쓰레기 버리는 곳; (*unpleasant place*) chijŏbunhan changso 지저분한 장소 **2** *v/t* (*throw away*) naebŏrida 내버리다; (*dispose of*) pŏrida 버리다; *toxic waste, nuclear waste* p'yegihada 폐기하다

dumpling tŏmp'ŭlling 덤플링

dune morae ŏndŏk 모래 언덕

dung ttong 똥

dungarees melppang paji 멜빵 바지

dunk *biscuit* tchigŏ mŏktta 찍어 먹다

duo (*singers*) ijungch'ang 이중창; (*instrumentalists*) ijungju 이중주

duplex (apartment) chungch'ŭnghyŏng-ŭi ap'at'ŭ 중층형의 아파트

duplicate 1 *n* sabon 사본; ***in ~*** tu t'ong-ŭro 두 통으로 **2** *v/t* (*copy*) pokssahada 복사하다; (*repeat*) toep'urihada 되풀이하다

duplicate key pokssadoen yŏlssoe 복사된 열쇠

durable *material* naegusŏng-i innŭn 내구성이 있는; *relationship* orae kanŭn 오래 가는

duration chisok kigan 지속 기간

duress: ***under ~*** hyŏp-ppagŭl pada 협박을 받아

during … tong-an … 동안; ~ ***the week*** chu tong-an 주 동안

dusk haejil muryŏp 해질 무렵

dust 1 *n* mŏnji 먼지 **2** *v/t* mŏnjirŭl t'ŏlda 먼지를 털다; ~ ***X with Y*** (*sprinkle*) Yŭl / rŭl Xe ppurida Y을 / 를 X에 뿌리다

dust cover (*for furniture*) mŏnji magi tŏpkkae 먼지 막이 덮개

duster (*cloth*) mŏnji tangnŭn hŏnggŏp 먼지 닦는 헝겊

dust jacket (*of book*) ch'aek k'ŏbŏ 책 커버

dustpan ssŭrebatkki 쓰레받기

dusty mŏnjit'usŏng-iŭi 먼지투성이의

Dutch 1 *adj* Nedŏllandŭŭi 네덜란드의; ***go*** ~ kaktcha tonŭl naeda 각자 돈을 내다 **2** *n* (*language*) Nedŏllandŭŏ 네덜란드어; ***the*** ~ Nedŏllandŭin 네덜란드인

duty ŭimu 의무; (*task*) immu 임무; (*on goods*) kwanse 관세; ***be on*** ~ tangjigida 당직이다; ***be off*** ~ pibŏnida 비번이다

duty-free 1 *adj* myŏnseŭi 면세의 **2** *n* myŏnsep'um 면세품

duty-free shop myŏnsejŏm 면세점

dwarf 1 *n* nanjaeng-i 난쟁이 **2** *v/t* chaga poige hada 작아 보이게 하다

♦**dwell on** ...e taehae komgomhi saenggak'ada ...에 대해 곰곰히 생각하다

dwindle chŏmjŏm chagajida 점점 작아지다

dye 1 *n* yŏmnyo 염료 **2** *v/t* yŏmsaek'ada 염색하다

dying *person* chugŏganŭn 죽어가는; *industry, tradition* soet'oehanŭn 쇠퇴하는

dynamic *person* hwalttongjŏgin 활동적인

dynamism wŏndongnyŏk 원동력

dynamite *n* tainŏmait'ŭ 다이너마이트

dynamo TECH paltchŏn-gi 발전기

dynasty wangjo 왕조

dyslexia tokssŏ chang-ae 독서 장애

dyslexic 1 *adj* tokssŏ chang-aeŭi 독서 장애의 **2** *n* tokssŏ chang-aeja 독서 장애자

E

each 1 *adj* kak-kkagŭi 각각의 **2** *adv* kak-kkak 각각; ***they're $1.50 ~*** kŭgŏttŭrŭn kak-kkak hana-e 1.50 tallŏida 그것들은 각각 하나에 1.50 달러이다 **3** *pron* kak-kkak 각각; ***~ other*** sŏro 서로; ***we don't like ~ other*** urinŭn sŏro joahaji annŭnda 우리는 서로 좋아하지 않는다
eager kanjŏrhan 간절한; ***be ~ to do X*** Xhanŭn kŏse yŏlsshimida X하는 것에 열심이다
eager beaver ilbŏlle 일벌레
eagerly kanjŏrhi 간절히
eagerness kalmang 갈망
eagle tokssuri 독수리
ear[1] (*of person, animal*) kwi 귀
ear[2] (*of corn*) isak 이삭
earache kwiari 귀앓이
eardrum komak 고막
early 1 *adj* (*not late*) iltchigin 일찍인; (*ahead of time*) irŭn 이른; (*farther back in time*) ch'ogiŭi 초기의; (*in the near future*) pparŭn 빠른; ***in the ~ hours of the morning*** ojŏn irŭn shigane 오전 이른 시간에; ***in ~ March/June*** samwŏl/yuwŏl ch'oe 삼월/유월 초에 **2** *adv* (*not late*) iltchik 일찍; (*ahead of time*) irŭge 이르게
early bird (*in the morning*) iltchik irŏnanŭn saram 일찍 일어나는 사람; (*who arrives early*) iltchik onŭn saram 일찍 오는 사람
earmark: ***~ X for Y*** Xŭl/rŭl Yro paedanghada X을/를 Y로 배당하다
earn pŏlda 벌다; *holiday, drink etc* ŏt-tta 얻다; *respect* pat-tta 받다
earnest chinjihan 진지한; ***in ~*** chinjihage 진지하게
earnings sodŭk 소득
earphones hedŭp'on 헤드폰; (*inside ear*) iŏp'on 이어폰; **ear-piercing** *adj* kwich'ŏng-i ttŏrŏjil tŭt'an 귀청이 떨어질 듯한; **earring** kwigori 귀고리;
earshot: ***within ~*** kach'ŏng chiyŏgesŏ 가청 지역에서; ***out of ~*** nanch'ŏng chiyŏgesŏ 난청 지역에서
earth (*soil*) hŭk 흙; (*world, planet*) chigu 지구; ***where on ~ have you been?*** todaech'e ŏdie issŏssŏyo? 도대체 어디에 있었어요?
earthenware *n* t'ogi 토기
earthly chisang-ŭi 지상의; ***it's no ~ use ...*** ...ŭn/nŭn chŏnhyŏ ssŭlmoŏmnŭn irida ...은/는 전혀 쓸모없는 일이다
earthquake chijin 지진
earth-shattering ch'unggyŏktchŏgin 충격적인
ease 1 *n* (*comfort*) p'yŏnanham 편안함; (*simplicity*) yong-i 용이; ***feel at ~*** pyŏnanhada 편안하다; ***feel ill at ~*** maŭmŭl p'yŏnhi noch'i mot'ada 마음을 편히 놓지 못하다 **2** *v/t* (*relieve*) tŏlda 덜다 **3** *v/i* (*of pain*) tŏrhada 덜하다
♦**ease off 1** *v/t* (*remove*) salsal pŏtkkida 살살 벗기다 **2** *v/i* (*of pain, rain*) nugŭrŏjida 누그러지다
easel ijel 이젤
easily (*with ease*) shwipkke 쉽게; (*by far*) tanyŏnhi 단연히
east 1 *n* tongtchok 동쪽 **2** *adj* tongtchogŭi 동쪽의 **3** *adv travel* tongtchogŭro 동쪽으로
East Asia Tongnyang 동양
East Asian 1 *adj* Tongnyang 동양 **2** *n* Tongnyang saram 동양 사람
Easter Puhwaltchŏl 부활절
easterly tongtchogŭrobut'ŏŭi 동쪽으로부터의; ***an ~ wind*** tongp'ung 동풍
eastern tongbuŭi 동부의; (*Oriental*) tongnyang-ŭi 동양의
easterner tongbu saram 동부 사람
East Sea Tonghae 동해
eastward(s) tongtchogŭro 동쪽으로
easy (*not difficult*) shwiun 쉬운;

(*relaxed*) p'yŏnanhan 편안한; ***take things ~*** (*slow down*) yŏyuitkke hada 여유있게 하다; ***take it ~!*** (*calm down*) nŏmu hŭngbunhaji maseyo! 너무 흥분하지 마세요!
easy chair allak ŭija 안락 의자
easy-going nŭgŭt'an 느긋한
eat *v/t & v/i* mŏktta 먹다
♦**eat out** oeshik'ada 외식하다
♦**eat up** *food* ta mŏgŏ pŏrida 다 먹어 버리다; *fig* ta ssŭge hada 다 쓰게 하다
eatable mŏgŭl su innŭn 먹을 수 있는
eaves ch'ŏma 처마
eavesdrop yŏt-ttŭt-tta 엿듣다
ebb *v/i* (*of tide*) ppajida 빠지다
♦**ebb away** *fig* ppajyŏ yŏttŭt-tta 빠져 나가다
ebb tide ssŏlmul 썰물
eccentric 1 *adj* pyŏllan 별난 **2** *n* koetcha 괴짜
echo 1 *n* ullim 울림; (*in mountains*) meari 메아리 **2** *v/i* ullyŏ p'ŏjida 울려 퍼지다 **3** *v/t words* toep'uri hada 되풀이 하다; *views* tong-ŭihada 동의하다
eclipse 1 *n* shik 식; ***~ of the sun*** ilsshik 일식; ***~ of the moon*** wŏlsshik 월식 **2** *v/t fig* kŭnŭljige hada 그늘지게 하다
ecological saengt'aehaktchŏgin 생태학적인
ecological balance saengt'aehaktchŏk kyunhyŏng 생태학적 균형
ecologically friendly ch'inhwan-gyŏngjŏgin 친환경적인
ecologist saengt'aehaktcha 생태학자
ecology saengt'aehak 생태학
economic kyŏngjeŭi 경제의
economical (*cheap*) kyŏngjejŏgin 경제적인; (*thrifty*) chŏryak'anŭn 절약하는
economically (*in terms of economics*) kyŏngjejŏgŭro 경제적으로; (*thriftily*) chŏryak'ayŏ 절약하여
economics (*science*) kyŏngjehak 경제학; (*financial aspects*) kyŏngjejŏk ch'ŭngmyŏn 경제적 측면
economist kyŏngjehaktcha 경제학자
economize chŏryak'ada 절약하다
♦**economize on** ...ŭl / rŭl chŏryak'ada ...을 / 를 절약하다
economy (*of a country*) kyŏngje 경제; (*saving*) chŏryak 절약
economy class pot'ongsŏk 보통석; **economy drive** chŏryak undong 절약 운동; **economy size** chŏryak'yŏng 절약형
ecosystem saengt'aegye 생태계
ecstasy hwanghol 황홀
ecstatic hwanghorhan 황홀한
eczema sŭptchin 습진
edge 1 *n* (*of knife*) nal 날; (*of table, seat*) mosŏri 모서리; (*of lawn, road*) kajang chari 가장 자리; (*of cliff*) kkŭt 끝; (*in voice*) nalk'aroum 날카로움; ***on ~*** ch'ojohan 초조한 **2** *v/t* ...e t'erŭl talda ...에 테를 달다 **3** *v/i* (*move slowly*) ch'ŏnch'ŏnhi umjigida 천천히 움직이다
edgewise: ***I couldn't get a word in ~*** nanŭn mal han madi hal su ŏpssŏssŏyo 나는 말 한 마디 할 수 없었어요
edgy ch'ojohan 초조한
edible mŏgŭl su innŭn 먹을 수 있는
edit p'yŏnjip'ada 편집하다
edition p'an 판
editor p'yŏnjiptcha 편집자; (*of newspaper*) p'yŏnjiptchang 편집장; ***sports / political ~*** sŭp'och'ŭran / chŏngch'iran p'yŏnjibwiwŏn 스포츠란 / 정치란 편집위원
editorial 1 *adj* p'yŏnjibŭi 편집의 **2** *n* sasŏl 사설
EDP (= ***electronic data processing***) chŏnja chŏngbo ch'ŏri 전자 정보 처리
educate *children, consumers* kyoyuk'ada 교육하다
educated *person* kyoyukppadŭn 교육받은
education kyoyuk 교육
educational kyoyuge kwanhan 교육에 관한; (*informative*) kyoyuktchŏgin 교육적인
eel chang-ŏ 장어
eerie ossak'an 오싹한
effect *n* yŏnghyang 영향; ***take ~*** (*of medicine, drug*) hyoryŏgŭl nat'anaeda 효력을 나타내다; ***come***

into ~ (*of law*) shilsshidoeda 실시되다
effective (*efficient*) hyokkwajŏgin 효과적인; (*striking*) insangjŏgin 인상적인; ***~ May 1*** owŏl irilbut'ŏ yuhyohan 오월 일일부터 유효한
effeminate yŏjagat'ŭn 여자같은
effervescent kŏp'umnanŭn 거품나는; *personality* hwalgich'an 활기찬
efficiency (*of person*) nŭngnyul 능률; (*of machine, method*) hyoyul 효율
efficient *person* nŭngnyultchŏgin 능률적인; *machine, method* hyoyultchŏgin 효율적인
efficiently nŭngnyultchŏgŭro 능률적으로
effort (*struggle*) sugo 수고; (*attempt*) noryŏk 노력; ***make an ~ to ...*** ...ŭl / rŭl hagi wihae noryŏk'ada ...을 / 를 하기 위해 노력하다
effortless suwŏrhan 수월한
effrontery ppŏnppŏnham 뻔뻔함
effusive kamjŏng-i nŏmch'inŭn 감정이 넘치는
e.g. yerŭl tŭlmyŏn 예를 들면
egalitarian *adj* p'yŏngdŭngjuŭiŭi 평등주의의
egg al 알; (*of chicken*) talgyal 달걀, kyeran 계란
♦**egg on** puch'ugida 부추기다
eggcup *salmŭn talgyarŭl nonnŭn k'ŏp* 삶은 달걀을 놓는 컵; **egghead** F int'elli 인텔리; **eggplant** kaji 가지; **eggshell** talgyal kkŏptchil 달걀 껍질
ego PSYCH chaa 자아; (*self-esteem*) chabushim 자부심
egocentric chagi chungshimŭi 자기 중심의
Egypt Ijipt'ŭ 이집트
Egyptian 1 *adj* Ijipt'ŭŭi 이집트의 **2** *n* Ijipt'ŭ saram 이집트 사람
eiderdown (*quilt*) orit'ŏl ibul 오리털 이불
eight yŏdŏl 여덟, p'al 팔
eighteen yŏlyŏdŏl 열 여덟, shipp'al 십팔
eighteenth yŏlyŏdŏl pŏntchaeŭi 열 여덟 번째의
eighth yŏdŏl pŏntchaeŭi 여덟 번째의
eightieth yŏdŭn pŏntchaeŭi 여든 번째의
eighty yŏdŭn 여든, p'alsship 팔십
either 1 *adj* ŏnŭ han tchogŭi 어느 한 쪽의; (*both*) yangtchogŭi 양쪽의; ***which one do you want? - ~ one*** ŏnŭ kŏsŭl hashigessŏyo? - ŏnŭ tchoidŭn kwaench'anayo 어느 것을 하시겠어요? - 어느 쪽이든 괜찮아요 **2** *pron* ŏnŭ tchogina 어느 쪽이나; ***~ can do it*** ŏnŭ tchogina kŭirŭl hal su it-tta 어느 쪽이나 그 일을 할 수 있다 **3** *adv* ttohan 또한; ***I won't go ~*** na ttohan kaji ank'essŏyo 나 또한 가지 않겠어요 **4** *conj*: ***~ X or Y*** Xna Y X나 Y; ***~ my mother or my sister will come*** uri ŏmŏnina nae tongsaeng-i olgŏyeyo 우리 어머니나 내 동생이 올 거예요
eject 1 *v/t demonstrators* tchoch'anaeda 쫓아내다; *cartridge, diskette* ppaenaeda 빼내다 **2** *v/i* (*from plane*) t'alch'urhada 탈출하다
♦**eke out** ...ŭi pujogŭl meuda ...의 부족을 메우다; ***~ a living*** kyŏu saenggyerŭl iŏnagada 겨우 생계를 이어나가다
el → ***elevated railroad***
elaborate 1 *adj* kongdŭrin 공들인 **2** *v/i* puyŏnhada 부연하다
elapse kyŏnggwahada 경과하다
elastic 1 *adj* t'allyŏginnŭn 탄력있는 **2** *n* komujul 고무줄
elastic band komu paendŭ 고무 밴드
elasticity shinch'ukssŏng 신축성
elasticized shinch'ukssŏng-ŭl kajin 신축성을 가진
elated ŭigiyangyanghan 의기양양한
elation ŭigiyangnyang 의기양양
elbow 1 *n* p'alkkumch'i 팔꿈치 **2** *v/t*: ***~ s.o. out of the way*** nugurŭl p'alkkumch'iro mirŏjech'ida 누구를 팔꿈치로 밀어제치다
elder 1 *adj* yŏnsang-ŭi 연상의 **2** *n* yŏnsang 연상
elderly nai chigŭt'an 나이 지긋한
eldest 1 *adj* naiga kajang manŭn 나이가 가장 많은 **2** *n*: ***the ~*** (*in family*) maji 맏이
elect *v/t* son-gŏhada 선거하다; ***~ to ...*** ...ŭl / rŭl sŏnt'aek'ada ...을 / 를 선택하다
elected sŏn-gŏro tangsŏndoen 선거로

당선된
election sŏn-gŏ 선거
election campaign sŏn-gŏ undong 선거 운동
election day sŏn-gŏil 선거일
elective sŏnt'aegŭi 선택의
elector sŏn-gŏin 선거인
electoral system sŏn-gŏ pangshik 선거 방식
electorate yukkwŏnja 유권자
electric chŏn-giŭi 전기의; *fig* chagŭktchŏgin 자극적인
electrical chŏn-giŭi 전기의
electric blanket chŏn-gi tamnyo 전기 담요
electric chair chŏn-gi ŭija 전기 의자
electrician chŏn-gi kisa 전기 기사
electricity chŏn-gi 전기
electrify chŏn-girŭl t'onghage hada 전기를 통하게 하다; *fig* hŭngbunshik'ida 흥분시키다
electrocute kamjŏnsashik'ida 감전사시키다
electrode chŏn-gŭk 전극
electron chŏnja 전자
electronic chŏnjaŭi 전자의
electronic data processing chŏnja chŏngbo ch'ŏri 전자 정보 처리
electronic mail chŏnja up'yŏn 전자 우편
electronics chŏnja konghak 전자 공학
electronics industry chŏnja sanŏp 전자 산업
elegance kosang 고상
elegant kosanghan 고상한
element CHEM wŏnso 원소
elementary (*rudimentary*) kibonŭi 기본의
elementary school ch'odŭnghak-kkyo 초등학교
elementary teacher ch'odŭnghak-kkyo kyosa 초등학교 교사
elephant k'okkiri 코끼리
elevate nop'ida 높이다
elevated railroad koga ch'ŏltto 고가 철도
elevation (*altitude*) nop'i 높이
elevator sŭngganggi 승강기, ellibeit'ŏ 엘리베이터
eleven yŏrhana 열 하나, shibil 십일
eleventh yŏrhan pŏntchaeŭi 열 한 번째의; ***at the ~ hour*** majimak sungane 마지막 순간에
eligible chagyŏgi innŭn 자격이 있는
eligible bachelor mattanghan shillangkkam 마땅한 신랑감
eliminate (*get rid of*) chegŏhada 제거하다; (*rule out*) cheoehada 제외하다; (*kill*) chugyŏ ŏpssaeda 죽여 없애다; ***be ~d*** (*from competition etc*) t'allak'ada 탈락하다
elimination (*from competition*) t'allak 탈락; (*of poverty*) chegŏ 제거; (*murder*) sarin ch'ŏngbu 살인 청부
elite 1 *n* chŏng-ye 정예 **2** *adj* chŏng-yeŭi 정예의
elk k'ŭn sasŭm 큰 사슴
ellipse t'awŏnhyŏng 타원형
elm nŭrŭmnamu 느릅나무
elope nun maja taranada 눈 맞아 달아나다
eloquence yuch'anghan hwasul 유창한 화술
eloquent yuch'anghan 유창한
eloquently yuch'anghage 유창하게
else: ***anything ~?*** kŭbakkŭi tarŭn kŏsŭn? 그밖의 다른 것은?; ***if you have nothing ~ to do*** manyak tarŭn hal iri ŏpttamyŏn 만약 다른 할 일이 없다면; ***no one ~ spoke / came*** tarŭn nugudo marhaji / oji anat-tta 다른 누구도 말하지 / 오지 않았다; ***everyone ~ is going*** kŭbakke moduga kanda 그밖에 모두가 간다; ***who ~ was there?*** kŭgose ttonuga issŏssŏyo? 그곳에 또누가 있었어요?; ***someone ~*** tarŭn nugun-ga 다른 누군가; ***something ~*** tarŭn ŏttŏn kŏt 다른 어떤 것; ***let's go somewhere ~*** ŏdi tarŭn kosŭro kapsshida 어디 다른 곳으로 갑시다; ***or ~*** kurŏch'i anŭmyŏn 그렇지 않으면
elsewhere (*position*) ŏttŏn tarŭn kosesŏ 어떤 다른 곳에서; (*motion toward*) ŏttŏn tarŭn kosŭro 어떤 다른 곳으로
elude (*escape from*) pŏsŏnada 벗어나다; (*avoid*) p'ihada 피하다; ***her name ~s me*** kŭnyŏŭi irŭmi saenggangnaji anat-tta 그녀의

이름이 생각나지 않았다
elusive (*hard to define*) p'aak'agi himdŭn 파악하기 힘든; *person* ch'atkki himdŭn 찾기 힘든
emaciated such'ŏk'an 수척한
e-mail 1 *n* imeil 이메일 **2** *v/t person* …ege imeirŭl ponaeda …에게 이메일을 보내다; *text* imeillo ponaeda 이메일로 보내다
e-mail address imeil chuso 이메일 주소
emancipated haebangdoen 해방된; *woman* chayurowajin 자유로와진
emancipation haebang 해방
embalm pangbu ch'ŏrihada 방부 처리하다
embankment *of river* tuk 둑; RAIL tuk-kkil 둑길
embargo *n* ch'urip'ang kŭmji 출입항 금지
embark shitta 싣다
♦**embark on** shijak'ada 시작하다
embarrass tanghwanghage hada 당황하게 하다
embarrassed tanghwanghan 당황한
embarrassing tanghwanghage hanŭn 당황하게 하는
embarrassment tanghwangham 당황함
embassy taesagwan 대사관
embellish changshik'ada 장식하다; *story* kkumida 꾸미다
embers kkambugibul 깜부기불
embezzle hoengnyŏnghada 횡령하다
embezzlement hoengnyŏng 횡령
embitter ssŭrarige hada 쓰라리게 하다
emblem sangjing 상징
embodiment hwashin 화신
embody kuch'ehwahada 구체화하다
embolism MED saektchŏntchŭng 색전증
emboss *metal, paper, fabric* todŭrajinŭn saegimŭl hada 도드라지는 새김을 하다
embrace 1 *n* po-ong 포옹 **2** *v/t* (*hug*) p'o-onghada 포옹하다; (*take in*) p'ohamhada 포함하다 **3** *v/i* (*of two people*) p'o-onghada 포옹하다
embroider sunot'a 수놓다; *fig* kkumida 꾸미다
embroidery chasu 자수
embryo pae 배; (*of human*) t'aea 태아
emerald (*precious stone*) emeraldŭ 에메랄드; (*color*) palgŭn ch'orokssaek 밝은 초록색
emerge (*appear*) nat'anada 나타나다; ***it has ~d that*** …ranŭn kŏshi turŏnat-tta …라는 것이 들어났다
emergency pisang 비상; ***in an ~*** pisangshie 비상시에
emergency exit pisanggu 비상구
emergency landing pisang ch'angnyuk 비상 착륙
emigrant *n* imin 이민
emigrate iminhada 이민하다
emigration iju 이주
eminent chŏmyŏnghan 저명한
eminently (*extremely*) ttwiŏnage 뛰어나게
emission (*of gases*) palssan 발산
emotion kamjŏng 감정
emotional *problems, development* kamjŏngjŏgin 감정적인; (*full of emotion*) kamdongjŏgin 감동적인
empathize: ***~ with*** …ŭl / rŭl tonggamhada …을 / 를 동감하다
emperor hwangje 황제
emphasis kangjo 강조
emphasize kangjohada 강조하다
emphatic tanhohan 단호한
empire *also fig* cheguk 제국
employ koyonghada 고용하다; (*use*) sayonghada 사용하다; ***he's ~ed as a …*** kŭnŭn …(ŭ)ro koyongdoeŏ it-tta 그는 …(으)로 고용되어 있다
employee koyong-in 고용인
employer koyongju 고용주
employment chigŏp 직업; (*work*) il 일; ***be seeking ~*** kujik'ada 구직하다
employment agency chigŏp annaeso 직업 안내소
empress yŏje 여제
emptiness konghŏham 공허함
empty 1 *adj* pin 빈; *promises* muŭimihan 무의미한 **2** *v/t drawer, pockets, glass* piuda 비우다; **3** *v/i* (*of room, street*) pida 비다
emulate ponttŭda 본뜨다
enable kanŭnghage hada 가능하게 하다
enact *law* chejŏnghada 제정하다; THEA kongnyŏnhada 공연하다

enamel *n* enamel 에나멜; (*on tooth*) sang-ajil 상아질; (*paint*) yuyak 유약
enchanting maehoktchŏgin 매혹적인
encircle ewŏssada 에워싸다
encl (= ***enclosure*(*s*)**) tongbong 동봉
enclose (*in letter*) tongbonghada 동봉하다; *area* turŭda 두르다; ***please find ~d ...*** tongbonghan ...ŭl / rŭl poseyo 동봉한 ...을 / 를 보세요
enclosure (*with letter*) tongbongmul 동봉물
encore *n* angk'orŭ 앙코르, chaech'ŏng 재청
encounter 1 *n* uyŏnhan mannam 우연한 만남 **2** *v/t person* uyŏnhi mannada 우연히 만나다; *problem* mat-ttakttŭrida 맞닥뜨리다
encourage kyŏngnyŏhada 격려하다
encouragement kyŏngnyŏ 격려
encouraging yonggirŭl chunŭn 용기를 주는
♦**encroach on** *land* ch'imip'ada 침입하다; *rights* ch'imhaehada 침해하다; *time* ppaeat-tta 빼앗다
encyclopedia paek-kkwa sajŏn 백과 사전
end 1 *n* (*extremity*, *conclusion*) kkŭt 끝; (*of month*, *year*) mal 말; (*purpose*) moktchŏk 목적; ***at the ~ of this month*** idal mare 이달 말에; ***in the ~*** mach'imnae 마침내; ***for hours on ~*** kyesok myŏt shigan tong-an 계속 몇 시간 동안; ***stand X on ~*** Xŭl / rŭl ttokpparo seuda X을 / 를 똑바로 세우다; ***at the ~ of July*** ch'irwŏl mal 칠월 말; ***put an ~ to*** ...ŭl / rŭl kkŭttchangnaeda ...을 / 를 끝장내다 **2** *v/t* kkŭnnaeda 끝내다 **3** *v/i* kkŭnnada 끝나다
♦**end up**: ***you'll ~ in the hospital*** tangshinŭn pyŏng-wŏnesŏ insaeng-ŭl mach'ige toelkkŏyeyo 당신은 병원에서 인생을 마치게 될거예요; ***we ended up going to his place*** urinŭn kyŏlguk kŭi chibe kage toego marat-tta 우리는 결국 그의 집에 가게 되고 말았다
endanger wihŏme ppajigehada 위험에 빠지게 하다
endangered species myŏltchong wigiŭi p'umjong 멸종 위기의 품종
endearing sarangsŭrŏun 사랑스러운
endeavor 1 *n* shido 시도 **2** *v/t* shidohada 시도하다; ***~ to be early*** ppalli odorok hada 빨리 오도록 하다
ending kyŏlmal 결말; GRAM ŏmi 어미
endless kkŭdŏmnŭn 끝없는
endorse *check* isŏhada 이서하다; *candidacy* chijihada 지지하다; *product* ch'uch'ŏnhada 추천하다
endorsement (*of check*) isŏ 이서; (*of candidacy*) chiji 지지; (*of product*) ch'uch'ŏn 추천
end product wanjep'um 완제품
end result ch'oejong kyŏlgwa 최종 결과
endurance chiguryŏk 지구력
endure 1 *v/t* kyŏndida 견디다 **2** *v/i* (*last*) chisok'ada 지속하다
enduring chisoktchŏgin 지속적인
end-user ch'oejong sayongja 최종 사용자
enemy chŏk 적
energetic hwalttongjŏgin 활동적인; *fig*: *measures* kangnyŏk'an 강력한
energy (*gas*, *electricity etc*) enŏji 에너지; (*of person*) him 힘
energy-saving *device* enŏjirŭl chŏryak'anŭn 에너지를 절약하는
enforce kangnyŏk shilsshihada 강력 실시하다
engage 1 *v/t* (*hire*) koyonghada 고용하다 **2** *v/i* TECH chakttonghada 작동하다
♦**engage in** ...e kwallyŏndoeda ...에 관련되다
engaged (*to be married*) yak'onhan 약혼한; ***get ~*** yak'onhada 약혼하다
engagement (*appointment*) yakssok 약속; (*to be married*) yak'on 약혼; MIL kyojŏn 교전
engagement ring yak'on panji 약혼 반지
engaging maeryŏktchŏgin 매력적인
engine enjin 엔진
engineer 1 *n* kisa 기사; NAUT, RAIL kigwansa 기관사 **2** *v/t coup*, *meeting* kkoehada 꾀하다
engineering konghak 공학
England Yŏngguk 영국
English 1 *adj* Yŏnggugŭi 영국의 **2** *n* (*language*) Yŏng-ŏ 영어; ***the ~***

Yŏnggugin 영국인
Englishman Yŏngguk namja 영국 남자
Englishwoman Yŏngguk yŏja 영국 여자
engrave saegida 새기다
engraving (*drawing*) p'anhwa 판화; (*design*) toan 도안
engrossed: *~ in* …e molttudoen …에 몰두된
engulf samk'ida 삼키다
enhance nop'ida 높이다
enigma susukkekki 수수께끼
enigmatic susukkekkigat'ŭn 수수께끼같은
enjoy chŭlgida 즐기다; *~ oneself* chŭlgŏpkke chinaeda 즐겁게 지내다; *~!* (*said to s.o. eating*) mashitkke tŭseyo! 맛있게 드세요!
enjoyable chŭlgŏun 즐거운
enjoyment chŭlgŏum 즐거움
enlarge k'ŭge hada 크게 하다
enlargement hwakttae 확대
enlighten kyemonghada 계몽하다
enlightened (*liberal*) kyemongdoen 계몽된
enlist 1 *v/i* MIL chawŏn ipttaehada 자원 입대하다 **2** *v/t*: *~ the help of* …ŭi toumŭl ŏt-tta …의 도움을 얻다
enliven hwalgirŭl purŏnŏt'a 활기를 불어넣다
enormity (*of crime*) hyung-akssŏng 흉악성; (*of task*) kŏdaeham 거대함
enormous kŏdaehan 거대한; *satisfaction, patience* taedanhan 대단한
enormously taedanhage 대단하게
enough 1 *adj* ch'ungbunhan 충분한 **2** *pron* ch'ungbunhan yang 충분한 양; *will $50 be ~?* 50tallŏmyŏn ch'ungbunhamnikka? 50달러면 충분합니까?; *I've had ~!* ije kŭmanhae! 이제 그만해!; *that's ~, calm down!* ije twaessŭnikka kŭmanhae! 이제 됐으니까 그만해! **3** *adv* ch'ungbunhi 충분히; *big / old ~* ch'ungbunhi k'ŭn / naidŭn 충분히 큰 / 나이든; *strangely ~* yŏksshi isanghagedo 역시 이상하게도
enquire, **enquiry** → ***inquire***, ***inquiry***
enraged hwaga nan 화가 난
enrich *vocabulary* p'ungbuhage hada 풍부하게 하다; *s.o.'s life* p'ungnyoropkke hada 풍요롭게 하다
enroll *v/i* tŭngnok'ada 등록하다
enrollment tŭngnok 등록
ensure hwaksshirhage hada 확실하게 하다
entail p'iryoro hada 필요로 하다
entangle: *become ~d in* (*in rope*) …wa / kwa ŏlk'ida …와 / 과 얽히다; (*in love affair*) …e kkomtchagŏpsshi yŏlludoeda …에 꼼짝없이 연루되다
enter 1 *v/t* (*go into*) …e tŭrŏgada …에 들어가다; (*come into*) …(ŭ)ro tŭrŏoda …(으)로 들어오다; *competition* …e ch'amgahada …에 참가하다; *person, horse in race* ch'amgashik'ida 참가시키다; (*write down*) kiip'ada 기입하다; COMPUT imnyŏkshik'ida 입력시키다 **2** *v/i* (*go in*) tŭrŏgada 들어가다; (*come in*) tŭrŏoda 들어오다; THEA tŭngjanghada 등장하다; (*in competition*) ch'amgahada 참가하다 **3** *n* COMPUT imnyŏk 입력
enterprise (*initiative*) chinch'wijŏk kisang 진취적 기상; (*venture*) saŏp 사업
enterprising chinch'wijŏgin 진취적인
entertain 1 *v/t* (*amuse*) chŭlgŏpkke hada 즐겁게 하다; *idea* saenggak'ada 생각하다 **2** *v/i* (*have guests*) taejŏp'ada 대접하다
entertainer yŏnyein 연예인
entertaining *adj* chaemiinnŭn 재미있는
entertainment orak 오락
enthrall …ŭi maŭmŭl sarojaptta …의 마음을 사로잡다
enthusiasm yŏltchŏng 열정
enthusiast: *... ~* ...kwang ...광; *jazz ~* chaejŭgwang 재즈광
enthusiastic yŏllyŏrhan 열렬한
entice yuhok'ada 유혹하다; (*persuade*) kkoeda 꾀다
entire chŏnch'eŭi 전체의
entirely wanjŏnhi 완전히
entitle chagyŏgŭl chuda 자격을 주다
entitled *book* …(i)ranŭn chemogŭi …(이)라는 제목의
entrance *n* ipkku 입구; (*entering, admission*) iptchang 입장; THEA

tŭngjang 등장
entranced maeryodoen 매료된
entrance fee iptchangnyo 입장료
entrant (*in competition*) ch'amgaja 참가자; (*for exam*) ŭngshija 응시자
entrenched *attitudes* ppuribak'in 뿌리박힌
entrepreneur kiŏpkka 기업가
entrepreneurial kiŏpkkaŭi 기업의
entrust: ~ ***X with Y***, ~ ***Y to X*** Xege Yŭl / rŭl matkkida X에게 Y을 / 를 맡기다
entry (*way in*) ipkku 입구; (*act of entering*) iptchang 입장; (*to country*) ipkkuk 입국; (*for competition: person*) ch'amgaja 참가자; (*for competition: item submitted*) ŭngmojak 응모작; (*in diary, accounts*) tŭngnok 등록
entry form ŭngmo sŏryu 응모 서류
entry visa ipkkukpija 입국비자
envelop ssada 싸다
envelope pongt'u 봉투
enviable purŏun 부러운
envious purŏwŏhanŭn 부러워하는; ***be ~ of s.o.*** nugurŭl purŏwŏhada 누구를 부러워하다
environment hwan-gyŏng 환경
environmental hwan-gyŏng-ŭi 환경의
environmentalist hwan-gyŏngbohoronja 환경보호론자
environmentally friendly ch'inhwan-gyŏngjŏgin 친환경적인
environmental pollution hwan-gyŏng-oyŏm 환경오염
environmental protection hwan-gyŏngboho 환경보호
environs kŭn-gyo 근교
envisage sangsanghada 상상하다
envoy sajŏl 사절
envy 1 *n* saem 샘; ***be the ~ of*** …ŭi purŏumŭl sada …의 부러움을 사다 **2** *v/t*: ~ ***s.o. sth*** nuguŭi muŏsŭl purŏwŏhada 누구의 무엇을 부러워하다
epic 1 *n* taehamul 대하물 **2** *adj voyage, deed* ungdaehan 웅대한; ***~ journey*** changjŏng 장정; ***~ songs*** p'ansori 판소리; ***a task of ~ proportions*** ŏmch'ongnan halttangnyang-ŭi il 엄청난 할당량의 일
epicenter chinwŏnji 진원지
epidemic *n* (*of flu, measles*) yuhaengppyŏng 유행병; *fig* sŏnghaeng 성행
epilepsy kanjilppyŏng 간질병
epileptic *n* kanjilppyŏng hwanja 간질병 환자
epileptic fit kanjirŭi paltchak 간질의 발작
epilog hugi 후기
episode (*of story, soap opera*) sap'wa 삽화; (*happening*) ep'isodŭ 에피소드
epitaph pimun 비문
epoch shidae 시대
epoch-making hoek-kkijŏgin 획기적인
equal 1 *adj* kat'ŭn 같은; *standing, rank* tongdŭnghan 동등한; ***be ~ to*** *task* …ŭl / rŭl ch'ungbunhi hal su it-tta …을 / 를 충분히 할 수 있다 **2** *n* tongtŭnghan chonjae 동등한 존재 **3** *v/t* MATH …wa / kwa kat-tta …와 / 과 같다; (*be as good as*) p'iltchŏk'ada 필적하다; ***four plus five ~s nine*** sa toehagi onŭn kuda 4 더하기 5는 9이다
equality p'yŏngdŭng 평등
equalize 1 *v/t* ttokkatkkehada 똑같게하다 **2** *v/i* SP taedŭnghada 대등하다
equally kyundŭnghage 균등하게; ***~, …*** tongdŭnghage, … 동등하게, …
equate: ~ ***X with Y*** Xŭl / rŭl Ywa / kwa kat-ttago saenggak'ada X을 / 를 Y와 / 과 같다고 생각하다
equation MATH pangjŏngshik 방정식
equator chŏktto 적도
equilibrium kyunhyŏng 균형
equinox chuya p'yŏngbunshi 주야 평분시; ***the autumnal ~*** ch'ubun 추분; ***the spring ~*** ch'unbun 춘분
equip *v/t* katch'uŏ chuda 갖추어 주다; ***he's not ~ped to handle it*** *fig* kŭnŭn kŭirŭl halmanhan yŏngnyang-i katch'uŏjyŏ it-tchi an-tta 그는 그일을 할만한 역량이 갖추어져 있지 않다
equipment changbi 장비
equity capital FIN chagi chabon 자기 자본

equivalent 1 *adj* tongdŭnghan 동등한; ***be ~ to*** …wa / kwa tongdŭnghan kach'iga it-tta …와 / 과 동등한 가치가 있다 **2** *n* tŭnggamul 등가물
era shidae 시대
eradicate pangmyŏrhada 박멸하다
erase chiuda 지우다
eraser chiugae 지우개
erect 1 *adj* kotpparo sŏn 곧바로 선 **2** *v/t* paro seuda 바로 세우다
erection (*of building etc*) paro seugi 바로 세우기; (*of penis*) palgi 발기
erode ch'imshik'ada 침식하다; *rights, power* chommŏktta 좀먹다
erosion ch'imshik 침식; *fig* chommŏgŭm 좀먹음
erotic kwannŭngjŏgin 관능적인
eroticism kwannŭngjuŭi 관능주의
errand shimburŭm 심부름; ***run ~s*** shimburŭmgada 심부름가다
erratic *driving* chigŭjaegŭshigŭi 지그재그식의; *performance, behavior* iltchŏnghaji anŭn 일정하지 않은
error chalmot 잘못
error message COMPUT erŏ meseji 에러 메세지
erupt (*of volcano*) punch'urhada 분출하다; (*of violence*) palbarhada 발발하다; (*of person*) pokpparhada 폭발하다
eruption (*of volcano*) punhwa 분화; (*of violence*) palbal 발발
escalate hwakttaehada 확대하다
escalation hwakttae 확대
escalator esŭk'ŏlleitŏ 에스컬레이터
escape 1 *n* (*of prisoner, animal*) tomang 도망; (*of gas*) nuch'ul 누출; COMPUT isŭk'eip'ŭ 이스케이프; ***have a narrow ~*** (*from death*) kakkasŭro saranamtta 가까스로 살아남다; (*from arrest*) kakkasŭro ppajyŏnagada 가까스로 빠져나가다 **2** *v/i* (*of prisoner, animal*) tomanggada 도망가다; (*of gas*) nuch'uldoeda 누출되다 **3** *v/t*: ***the word ~s me*** kŭ mari saenggangnaji anssŭmnida 그 말이 생각나지 않습니다
escape chute pisangnyong hwalgangno 비상용 활강로
escort 1 *n* tongbanja 동반자; (*guard*) kyŏnghowŏn 경호원 **2** *v/t* (*socially*) paraedajuda 바래다주다; (*act as guard to*) kyŏnghohada 경호하다
especial → ***special***
especially t'ŭkppyŏrhi 특별히
espionage sŭp'ai haeng-wi 스파이 행위
essay *n* changmun 작문; (*at university*) lep'ot'ŭ 레포트
essential *adj* (*necessary*) p'ilssŭujŏgin 필수적인; (*very important*) haeksshimjŏgin 핵심적인
essentially ponjiltchŏgŭro 본질적으로
establish *company* sŏllip'ada 설립하다; (*create*) mandŭlda 만들다; (*determine*) iptchŭnghada 입증하다; ***~ oneself as*** …(ŭ)ro yumyŏnghaejida …(으)로 유명해지다
establishment (*firm, store etc*) shisŏl 시설; ***the Establishment*** kwŏllyŏk chipttan 권력 집단
estate (*land*) ttang 땅; (*of dead person*) yusan 유산
esthetic shimmijŏgin 심미적인
estimate 1 *n* kyŏnjŏk 견적 **2** *v/t* pyŏngkkahada 평가하다
estimation: ***he has gone up / down in my ~*** kŭedaehan naŭi p'yŏngganŭn tŏ nop'ajyŏt-tta / najajyŏt-tta 그에대한 나의 평가는 더 높아졌다 / 낮아졌다; ***in my ~*** naega pogienŭn 내가 보기에는
estranged *wife, husband* sowŏnhaejin 소원해진
estuary nŏlbŭn kang-ŏgwi 넓은 강어귀
ETA (= ***estimated time of arrival***) toch'ak yejŏng shigan 도착 예정 시간
etching ech'ing 에칭
eternal yŏngwŏnhan 영원한
eternity yŏngwŏn 영원
ethical yullijŏgin 윤리적인
ethics yulli 윤리
ethnic minjogŭi 민족의
ethnic group minjokchipttan 민족집단
ethnic minority sosu minjok 소수 민족
euphemism wan-gogŏ 완곡어
euphoria k'ŭn haengbok-kkam 큰

행복감
Europe Yurŏp 유럽
European 1 *adj* Yurŏbŭi 유럽의 **2** *n* Yurŏbin 유럽인
euthanasia allakssa 안락사
evacuate (*clear people from*) taep'ishik'ida 대피시키다; (*leave*) taep'ihada 대피하다
evade kyomyohi hoep'ihada 교묘히 회피하다
evaluate p'yŏngkkahada 평가하다
evaluation p'yŏngkka 평가
evangelist pogŭm chŏndosa 복음 전도사
evaporate (*of water*) chŭngbarhada 증발하다; (*of confidence*) yŏngich'ŏrŏm sarajida 연기처럼 사라지다
evasion (*of responsibilities etc*) hoep'i 회피
evasive aemaehan 애매한
eve chŏnya 전야
even 1 *adj* (*regular*) korŭn 고른; (*level*) p'yŏngp'yŏnghan 평평한; *number* tchakssuŭi 짝수의; ***get ~ with*** ...ege anggap'ŭmŭl hada ...에게 앙갚음을 하다 **2** *adv* choch'ado 조차도; ***~ my father*** naŭi abŏji choch'ado 나의 아버지 조차도; ***~ bigger/better*** tŏuk tŏ k'ŭn/naŭn 더욱 더 큰/나은; ***not*** ~ choch'a ant'a 조차 않다; ***~ so*** kŭrŏt'a hadŏrado 그렇다 하더라도; ***~ if ...*** pirok ...l/ŭltchirado 비록 ...ㄹ/을지라도 **3** *v/t*: ***~ the score*** tongtchŏmŭl mandŭlda 동점을 만들다
evening chŏnyŏk 저녁; ***in the ~*** chŏnyŏge 저녁에; ***this*** ~ onŭl chŏnyŏk 오늘 저녁; ***good ~*** annyŏnghaseyo 안녕하세요
evening classes yagan suŏp 야간 수업; **evening dress** (*for woman, man*) yahoebok 야회복; **evening paper** sok-kkan shinmun 석간 신문
evenly (*regularly*) korŭge 고르게
event haengsa 행사; SP shihap 시합; ***at all ~s*** amut'ŭn 아무튼
eventful tasahan 다사한
eventual kunggŭktchŏgin 궁극적인
eventually kunggŭktchŏgŭro 궁극적으로
ever *adv* ◊ (*with if, in future*) ŏnjen-ga 언젠가; ***if you ~ visit here, please call me*** ŏnjen-ga yŏgi oshimyŏn chege chŏnhwarŭl chuseyo 언제가 여기 오시면 제게 전화를 주세요 ◊ (*with past tense*) chigŭmkkaji 지금까지; ***have you ~ been to Korea?*** chigŭmkkaji Han-guge kabon chŏgi issŏyo? 지금까지 한국에 가본 적이 있어요? ◊: ***for ~*** ŏnjena 언제나; ***~ since*** kŭ hu chulgot 그 후 줄곧
evergreen *n* sangnokssu 상록수
everlasting yŏng-wŏnhan 영원한
every modŭn 모든; onŭ ...(i)na ta 어느 ...(이)나 다; ***~ day/week/month/year*** maeil/maeju/maewŏl/maenyŏn 매일/매주/매월/매년; ***~ other day*** it'ŭlmada 이틀마다; ***~ now and then*** ttaettaero 때때로
everybody → ***everyone***
everyday ilsangjŏgin 일상적인
everyone nuguna 누구나, modu 모두
everything modŭn kŏt 모든 것
everywhere modŭn kot 모든 곳; (*wherever*) ŏdidŭnji 어디든지
evict tchoch'anaeda 쫓아내다
evidence chŭnggŏ 증거; LAW chŭngŏn 증언; ***give*** ~ chŭng-ŏnhada 증언하다
evident myŏngbaek'an 명백한
evidently punmyŏnghi 분명히
evil 1 *adj* ak'an 악한 **2** *n* ak 악
evoke *image* hwan-gishik'ida 환기시키다
evolution chinhwa 진화
evolve *v/i* (*of animals*) chinhwahada 진화하다; (*develop*) paltchŏnhada 발전하다
ewe amnyang 암양
ex- ijŏnŭi 이전의
ex *n* F (*former wife*) chŏnbuin 전부인; (*former husband*) chŏnnamp'yŏn 전남편
exact *adj* chŏnghwak'an 정확한
exactly chŏnghwak'i 정확히; ***~!*** paro kŭrŏssŭmnida! 바로 그렇습니다!; ***not ~*** pandŭshi kŭroch'inŭn anssŭmnida 반드시 그렇지는

않습니다
exaggerate *v/t & v/i* kwajanghada 과장하다
exaggeration kwajang 과장
exam shihŏm 시험; ***take an ~*** shihŏmŭl poda 시험을 보다; ***pass / fail an ~*** shihŏme put-tta / ttŏrŏjida 시험에 붙다 / 떨어지다
examination (*of facts, patient*) kŏmsa 검사; EDU shihŏm 시험
examine (*study*) chosahada 조사하다; *patient* chinch'arhada 진찰하다; EDU shihŏmhada 시험하다
examiner EDU shihŏmgwan 시험관
example ye 예; ***for ~*** yerŭl tŭrŏsŏ 예를 들어서; ***set a good / bad ~*** choŭn / nappŭn yega toeda 좋은 / 나쁜 예가 되다
exasperated hwanan 화난
excavate *v/t* (*dig*) p'ada 파다; (*of archeologist*) palgurhada 발굴하다
excavation palgul 발굴
excavator kulch'ak-kki 굴착기
exceed (*be more than*) ch'ogwahada 초과하다; (*go beyond*) nŏmŏsŏda 넘어서다
exceedingly taedanhi 대단히
excel 1 *v/i* ttwiŏnada 뛰어나다; ***~ at*** ...e ttwiŏnada ...에 뛰어나다 **2** *v/t*: ***~ oneself*** chagi nŭngnyŏk isang-ŭl parhwihada 자기 능력 이상을 발휘하다
excellence ttwiŏnam 뛰어남
excellent ttwiŏnan 뛰어난
except ...ŭl / rŭl cheoehago ...을 / 를 제외하고; ***~ for*** ...i / ga ŏpssŭmyŏn ...이 / 가 없으면; ***~ that ...*** ...ranŭn kosŭl cheoehamyŏn ...라는 것을 제외하면
exception yeoe 예외; ***with the ~ of*** ...ŭl / rŭl cheoehagonŭn ...을 / 를 제외하고는; ***take ~ to*** ...e taehan iŭirŭl shinch'ŏnghada ... 에 대한 이의를 신청하다
exceptional (*very good*) iryejŏgŭro ttwiŏnan 이례적으로 뛰어난; (*special*) t'ŭkppyŏrhan yeoeŭi 특별한 예외의
exceptionally (*extremely*) maeu yeoejogŭro 매우 예외적으로
excerpt palch'we 발췌
excess 1 *n*: ***eat to ~*** p'oksshik'ada 폭식하다; ***drink to ~*** p'ogŭmhada 폭음하다; ***in ~ of*** ...ŭl / rŭl ch'ogwahanŭn ...을 / 를 초과하는 **2** *adj* kwadahan 과다한
excess baggage ch'ogwa suhamul 초과 수하물
excess fare ch'ogwa yogŭm 초과 요금
excessive chinach'in 지나친
exchange 1 *n* (*of views, between schools*) kyohwan 교환; ***in ~*** kyohwanŭro 교환으로; ***in ~ for*** ...wa / kwa kyohwanŭro ...와 / 과 교환으로 **2** *v/t* (*in store*) pakkuda 바꾸다, kyohwanhada 교환하다; *addresses* matpakkuda 맞바꾸다, kyohwanhada 교환하다; *currency* hwanjŏnhada 환전하다; ***~ X for Y*** Xŭl / rŭl Y(ŭ)ro kyohwanhada X을 / 를 Y(으)로 교환하다
exchange rate FIN hwannyul 환율
excitable shwipkke hŭngbunhanŭn 쉽게 흥분하는
excite (*make enthusiastic*) hŭngbunshik'ida 흥분시키다
excited hŭngbundoen 흥분된; ***get ~*** hŭngbunhada 흥분하다; ***get ~ about*** ...e hŭngbunhada ...에 흥분하다
excitement hŭngbun 흥분
exciting hŭngbunshik'inŭn 흥분시키는
exclaim oech'ida 외치다
exclamation kamt'an 감탄
exclamation point nŭkkimp'yo 느낌표
exclude (*not include*) cheoehada 제외하다; *possibility* paejehada 배제하다; (*from club etc*) tŭrŏoji mot'age hada 들어오지 못하게 하다
excluding ...ŭn / nŭn cheoehago ...은 / 는 제외하고
exclusive *restaurant etc* paet'ajŏgin 배타적인; *rights, interview* toktchŏmjŏgin 독점적인
excruciating *pain* komun pannŭn tŭt'an 고문 받는 듯한
excursion tchalbŭn yŏhaeng 짧은 여행
excuse 1 *n* pyŏnmyŏng 변명 **2** *v/t* (*forgive*) yongsŏhada 용서하다;

(*allow to leave*) ttŏnage hada 떠나게 하다; ~ ***X from Y*** Xŭl / rŭl Yesŏ myŏnjehae chuda X을 / 를 Y에서 면제해 주다; ~ ***me*** (*to get attention, to get past, interrupting s.o.*) shillyehamnida 실례합니다; (*apologizing*) choesonghamnida 죄송합니다; ~ ***me?*** (*what did you say?*) mwŏragoyo? 뭐라고요?

execute *criminal* sahyŏng chip'aenghada 사형 집행하다; *plan* shirhaenghada 실행하다

execution (*of criminal*) sahyŏng chip'aeng 사형 집행; (*of plan*) shirhaeng 실행

executioner sahyŏng chip'aeng-in 사형 집행인

executive *n* kanbu 간부

executive briefcase kanbuyong sŏryu kabang 간부용 서류 가방

executive washroom kanbuyong hwajangshil 간부용 화장실

exemplary mobŏmjŏgin 모범적인

exempt: ***be ~ from*** …(ŭ)ro put'ŏ myŏnjedoeda …(으)로 부터 면제되다

exercise 1 *n* (*physical*) undong 운동; EDU yŏnsŭp 연습; MIL hullyŏn 훈련; ***take some*** ~ undonghada 운동하다 **2** *v/t dog* undongshik'ida 운동시키다; *muscle* tallyŏnshik'ida 단련시키다; *caution, restraint* sayonghada 사용하다 **3** *v/i* undonghada 운동하다

exercise book EDU yŏnsŭptchang 연습장

exert *authority* parhwihada 발휘하다; ~ ***oneself*** noryŏk'ada 노력하다

exertion noryŏk 노력

exhale naeshwida 내쉬다

exhaust 1 *n* (*fumes*) paech'ul 배출; (*pipe*) paegigwan 배기관 **2** *v/t* (*tire*) nokch'oro mandŭlda 녹초로 만들다; (*use up*) ta ssŏ pŏrida 다 써 버리다

exhausted (*tired*) nokch'oga toen 녹초가 된

exhaust fumes paegi kasŭ 배기 가스

exhausting nokch'oga toege hanŭn 녹초가 되게 하는

exhaustion kŭkttoŭi p'iro 극도의 피로

exhaustive ch'ŏltchŏhan 철저한

exhaust pipe paegigwan 배기관

exhibit 1 *n* (*in exhibition*) chŏnship'um 전시품 **2** *v/t* (*of gallery, artist*) chŏnshihada 전시하다; (*give evidence of*) poida 보이다

exhibition chŏnshi 전시; (*of bad behavior*) ch'ut'ae 추태; (*of skill*) parhwi 발휘

exhibitionist chagi sŏnjŏn-ga 자기 선전가

exhilarating kibunŭl todunŭn 기분을 돋우는

exile 1 *n* (*forced*) ch'ubang 추방; (*political, voluntary*) mangmyŏng 망명; (*person*) ch'ubangja 추방자; (*person: voluntary*) mangmyŏngja 망명자 **2** *v/t* ch'ubanghada 추방하다

exist chonjaehada 존재하다; ~ ***on*** …(ŭ)ro saragada …(으)로 살아가다

existence chonjae 존재; (*life*) saenghwal 생활; ***in*** ~ hyŏnjonhanŭn 현존하는; ***come into*** ~ saenggida 생기다

existing hyŏnjonhanŭn 현존하는

exit *n* ch'ulgu 출구

exonerate mujoerŭl chŭngmyŏnghada 무죄를 증명하다

exorbitant sangsang-ŭl ch'owŏrhanŭn 상상을 초월하는

exotic iguktchŏgin 이국적인

expand 1 *v/t* nŏlp'ida 넓히다 **2** *v/i* nŭlda 늘다; (*of metal*) p'aengch'anghada 팽창하다

♦**expand on** tŏ chasehi sŏlmyŏnghada 더 자세히 설명하다

expanse: ***a vast ~ of*** nŏlkke p'yŏlch'yŏjin 넓게 펼쳐진

expansion hwaktchang 확장; (*of metal*) p'aengch'ang 팽창

expansion card COMPUT hwakchang k'adŭ 확장카드

expect 1 *v/t* kidaehada 기대하다; *baby* imshinhada 임신하다; (*suppose*) ch'uch'ŭk'ada 추측하다; (*demand*) yoguhada 요구하다 **2** *v/i*: ***be ~ing*** imshinjung-ida 임신 중이다; ***I ~ so*** kŭrŏl kŏyeyo 그럴 거예요

expectant yegihago innŭn 예기하고 있는

expectant mother imshinbu 임신부

expectation kidae 기대; **~s** (*demands*) changnaeŭi hŭimang 장래의 희망
expedient *n* p'yŏnppŏp 편법
expedition t'amhŏm 탐험; (*group*) t'amhŏmdae 탐험대; (*to do shopping, sightseeing*) tchalbŭn yŏhaeng 짧은 여행
expel *person* tchoch'anaeda 쫓아내다
expend *energy* sobihada 소비하다
expendable *person* hŭisaengdoel su innŭn 희생될 수 있는
expenditure chich'ul 지출
expense piyong 비용; ***at the company's ~*** hoesa piyong-ŭro 회사 비용으로; ***a joke at my ~*** narŭl tugo han nongdam 나를 두고 한 농담; ***at the ~ of his health*** kŭŭi kŏn-gang-ŭl haech'imyŏnsŏ 그의 건강을 해치면서
expense account piyong myŏngse 비용 명세
expenses kyŏngbi 경비
expensive pissan 비싼
experience 1 *n* (*event*) ch'ehŏm 체험; (*in life*) kyŏnghŏm 경험; (*in particular field*) kyŏngnyŏk 경력 **2** *v/t pain, pleasure* nŭkkida 느끼다; *difficulty* kyŏktta 겪다
experienced kyŏnghŏminnŭn 경험있는
experiment 1 *n* shirhŏm 실험 **2** *v/i* shirhŏmhada 실험하다; ***~ on animals*** tongmul shirhŏmŭl hada 동물 실험을 하다; ***~ with*** (*try out*) ...ŭl / rŭl shirhŏmhaeboda ...을 / 를 실험해보다
experimental shirhŏmŭi 실험의
expert 1 *adj* sungnyŏndoen; ***~ advice*** chŏnmun-gaŭi ch'unggo 전문가의 충고 **2** *n* chŏnmun-ga 전문가
expertise chŏnmun chishik / kisul 전문 지식 / 기술
expire man-gidoeda 만기되다
expiry kihan mallyo 기한 만료
expiry date yuhyo mallyoil 유효 만료일
explain *v/t & v/i* sŏlmyŏnghada 설명하다
explanation sŏlmyŏng 설명
explicit *instructions* myŏngbaek'an 명백한
explicitly *state* myŏngbaek'i 명백히; *forbid* punmyŏnghi 분명히
explode 1 *v/i* (*of bomb*) p'okpparhada 폭발하다 **2** *v/t bomb* p'okp'ashik'ida 폭파시키다
exploit[1] *n* wiŏp 위업
exploit[2] *v/t person* ch'akch'wihada 착취하다; *resources* kaebarhayŏ iyonghada 개발하여 이용하다
exploitation (*of person*) ch'akch'wi 착취
exploration t'amhŏm 탐험
exploratory *surgery* kŏmsa 검사
explore *country etc* tapssahada 답사하다; *possibility* t'amsaek'ada 탐색하다
explorer t'amhŏmga 탐험가
explosion p'okppal 폭발; (*in population*) kŭptchŭng 급증
explosive *n* p'okppalmul 폭발물
export 1 *n* (*action*) such'ul 수출; (*item*) such'ulp'um 수출품 **2** *v/t goods* such'urhada 수출하다; COMPUT chŏnsonghada 전송하다
export campaign such'ul k'aemp'ein 수출 캠페인
exporter (*person*) such'urŏptcha 수출업자; (*country*) such'ulguk 수출국
expose (*uncover*) tŭrŏnaeda 드러내다; *scandal* p'ongnohada 폭로하다; *person* poyojuda 보여주다; ***he's been ~d as ...*** kŭga ... imi tŭrŏnat-tta 그가 ... 임이 드러났다; ***~ X to Y*** Xŭl / rŭl Ye noch'ulshik'ida X을 / 를 Y에 노출시키다
exposure noch'ul 노출; (*of dishonest behavior*) t'allo 탄로; (*part of film*) chang 장
express 1 *adj* (*fast*) kŭp'aeng-ŭi 급행의; (*explicit*) myŏngbaek'an 명백한; ***~ train / bus*** kŭp'aeng yŏlch'a / pŏssŭ 급행 열차 / 버스 **2** *n* kŭp'aeng 급행 **3** *v/t* (*speak of, voice*) mallo p'yohyŏnhada 말로 표현하다; *feelings* p'yohyŏnhada 표현하다; ***~ oneself well / clearly*** chagi chashinŭl chal / punmyŏnghi p'yohyŏnhada 자기 자신을 잘 / 분명히 표현하다

express elevator kosok ellibeit'ŏ 고속 엘리베이터
expression (*voicing, phrase*) p'yohyŏn 표현; (*on face*) p'yojŏng 표정; ***with ~*** p'yohyŏni p'ungbuhage 표현이 풍부하게
expressive p'yohyŏni p'ungbuhan 표현이 풍부한; *face* p'yojŏng-i p'ungbuhan 표정이 풍부한
expressly (*explicitly*) myŏnghwak'i 명확히; (*deliberately*) ilburŏ 일부러
expressway kosokttoro 고속도로
expulsion (*from school*) t'oehak 퇴학; (*of diplomat*) ch'ubang 추방
exquisite (*beautiful*) chŏlmyohan 절묘한
extend 1 *v/t* nŏlp'ida 넓히다; *runway, path* nŭrida 늘이다; *contract, visa* yŏnjanghada 연장하다; *thanks, congratulations* p'yohyŏnhada 표현하다 **2** *v/i* (*of garden etc*) ppŏdŏit-tta 뻗어있다
extension (*to house*) hwaktchang 확장; (*of contract, visa*) yŏnjang 연장; TELEC naesŏn 내선
extension cable yŏnjang k'eibŭl 연장 케이블
extensive kwangbŏmwihan 광범위한
extent pŏmwi 범위; ***to such an ~ that*** ... ...ranŭn hankkajinŭn ...라는 한까지는; ***to a certain ~*** ŏnŭ chŏngdokkaji 어느 정도까지
exterior 1 *adj* oegwansang-ŭi 외관상의 **2** *n* (*of building*) oegwan 외관; (*of person*) kŏnmosŭp 겉모습
exterminate *vermin* chŏnmyŏlshik'ida 전멸시키다; *race* myŏltchongshik'ida 멸종시키다
external (*outside*) oebuŭi 외부의
extinct *species* myŏltchongdoen 멸종된
extinction (*of species*) myŏltchong 멸종
extinguish *fire, light* kkŭda 끄다
extinguisher sohwagi 소화기
extort: ***~ money from*** ...(ŭ)robut'ŏ tonŭl kangyohada ...(으)로부터 돈을 강요하다
extortion kangt'al 강탈
extortionate t'ŏmuniŏpsshi manŭn 터무니없이 많은
extra 1 *n* ch'ugaŭi kŏt 추가의 것 **2** *adj* ch'ugaŭi 추가의; ***be ~*** (*cost more*) ch'ugaida 추가이다 **3** *adv* t'ŭkppyŏrhi 특별히
extra charge ch'uga yogŭm 추가 요금
extract 1 *n* inyong 인용 **2** *v/t* kkŏnaeda 꺼내다; *coal, oil* p'anaeda 파내다; *tooth* ppoptta 뽑다; *information* ŏryŏpkke ŏdŏnaeda 어렵게 얻어내다
extraction (*of oil, coal*) ch'uch'ul 추출; (*of tooth*) ppopkki 뽑기
extradite indohada 인도하다
extradition pŏmjoein indo 범죄인 인도
extradition treaty pŏmjoein indo hyŏptchŏng 범죄인 인도 협정
extramarital kant'ong-ŭi 간통의
extraordinarily ŏmch'ŏngnage 엄청나게
extraordinary ŏmch'ŏngnan 엄청난
extravagance sach'i 사치
extravagant (*with money*) sach'isŭrŏun 사치스러운
extreme 1 *n* kŭkttan 극단 **2** *adj* kŭksshimhan 극심한; *views* kŭkttanjŏgin 극단적인
extremely taedanhi 대단히
extremist *n* kwagyŏngnonja 과격론자
extricate kuch'urhada 구출하다
extrovert *n* oehyangtchŏgin saram 외향적인 사람
exuberant hwalgiga ch'ungmanhan 활기가 충만한
exult kippŏnalttwida 기뻐날뛰다
eye 1 *n* nun 눈; (*of needle*) panŭlgwi 바늘귀; ***keep an ~ on*** (*look after*) ...ŭl / rŭl chik'yŏboda ...을 / 를 지켜보다; (*monitor*) ...ŭl / rŭl kamshihada ...을 / 를 감시하다 **2** *v/t* poda 보다
eyeball nunal 눈알; **eyebrow** nunssŏp 눈썹; **eyeglasses** an-gyŏng 안경; **eyelash** songnunssŏp 속눈썹; **eyelid** nunkkŏp'ul 눈꺼풀; **eyeliner** airainŏ 아이라이너; **eyeshadow** aishyaedou 아이섀도우; **eyesight** shiryŏk 시력; **eyesore** pogi hyunghan kŏt 보기 흉한 것; **eye strain** nunŭi p'iro 눈의 피로; **eyewitness** mok-kkyŏktcha 목격자

F

F (= ***Fahrenheit***) Hwasshi 화씨; ***45° ~*** Hwasshi 45to 화씨 45도
fabric chingmul 직물
fabulous koengjanghan 굉장한
façade (*of building*) chŏngmyŏn 정면; (*of person*) kŏnmosŭp 겉모습
face 1 *n* ŏlgul 얼굴; (*look, expression*) p'yojŏng 표정; ***~ to ~*** taemyŏnhago 대면하고; ***lose ~*** ch'emyŏnŭl ilt'a 체면을 잃다 **2** *v/t person, the sea* majuboda 마주보다; *fact* chingmyŏnhada 직면하다
facelift churŭm chegŏsul 주름 제거술
face value aengmyŏnkka 액면가; ***take at ~*** kŏnmosŭburo p'andanhada 겉모습으로 판단하다
facilitate shwipkke hada 쉽게 하다
facilities shisŏl 시설
fact sashil 사실; ***in ~, as a matter of ~*** sashirŭn 사실은
factor yoin 요인; MATH insu 인수
factory kongjang 공장
faculty (*hearing etc*) nŭngnyŏk 능력; (*at university*) hakppu 학부; (*teaching staff*) kyojigwŏn 교직원
fade *v/i* (*of colors*) paraeda 바래다; (*of sounds, memories*) hŭimihaejida 희미해지다
faded *color, jeans* paraen 바랜
fag F (*homosexual*) homo 호모
Fahrenheit Hwasshi 화씨
fail *v/i* shilp'aehada 실패하다; (*in exam*) ttŏrŏjida 떨어지다
failure shilp'ae 실패
faint 1 *adj* hŭimihan 희미한; ***feel ~*** ŏjirŏptta 어지럽다 **2** *v/i* kijŏrhada 기절하다
fair[1] *n* (*trade show*) muyŏk pangnamhoe 무역 박람회; (*agricultural*) p'ump'yŏnghoe 품평회
fair[2] *adj hair* kŭmbarŭi 금발의; *complexion* palgŭn 밝은; (*just*) kongjŏnghan 공정한; ***it's not ~*** kŭgŏsŭn kongjŏnghaji anssŭmnida 그것은 공정하지 않습니다
fairly *treat* kongjŏnghage 공정하게; (*quite*) kkwae 꽤
fairness (*of treatment*) kongjŏngham 공정함
fairy yojŏng 요정
fairy tale tonghwa 동화
faith shilloe 신뢰; REL shinang 신앙
faithful ch'ungshirhan 충실한; ***be ~ to one's partner*** sangdaeege ch'ungshirhada 상대에게 충실하다
fake 1 *n* katcha 가짜 **2** *adj* katchaŭi 가짜의
fall[1] **1** *v/i* (*of person, price, temperature etc*) ttŏrŏjida 떨어지다; (*stumble*) nŏmŏjida 넘어지다; (*of building, government*) munŏjida 무너지다; (*of tree*) ssŭrŏjida 쓰러지다; (*of night*) oda 오다; ***my birthday ~s on a Tuesday this year*** nae saeng-irŭn orhae hwayoirida 내 생일은 올해 화요일이다; ***~ ill*** pyŏng-e kŏllida 병에 걸리다 **2** *n* (*from high place*) ch'urak 추락; (*stumble*) nŏmŏjim 넘어짐; (*of government*) punggoe 붕괴; (*in temperature*) hagang 하강; (*of minister*) saim 사임; (*in price*) harak 하락
♦**fall back on** pisangshie sayonghada 비상시에 사용하다
♦**fall down** (*trip*) nŏmŏjida 넘어지다; (*because ill*) ssŭrŏjida 쓰러지다; (*of wall, building*) munŏjida 무너지다
♦**fall for** *person* …wa / kwa sarang-e ppajida …와 / 과 사랑에 빠지다; (*be deceived by*) …ŭi sogimsue kŏllida …의 속임수에 걸리다
♦**fall out** (*of hair*) ppajida 빠지다; (*argue*) saiga t'ŭrŏjida 사이가 틀어지다
♦**fall over** (*of person*) nŏmŏjida 넘어지다; (*of tree*) ssŭrŏjida 쓰러지다
♦**fall through** (*of plans*) shilp'aero

kkŭnnada 실패로 끝나다
fall[2] *n* (*autumn*) kaŭl 가을
fallout pangsasŏng naktchin 방사성 낙진
false kŭrŭttoen 그릇된
false teeth t'ŭlli 틀니
falsify wijohada 위조하다
fame myŏngsŏng 명성
familiar *adj* (*intimate*) ch'in-gŭnhan 친근한; (*well-known*) chal anŭn 잘 아는; *form of address* hŏmul ŏmnŭn 허물 없는; ***be ~ with X*** Xŭl / rŭl chal alda X을 / 를 잘 알다
familiarity (*with subject etc*) chŏngt'ong 정통; (*of behavior*) hŏmul ŏpssŭm 허물 없음
familiarize ik'ida 익히다; ***~ oneself with*** …wa / kwa ikssuk'aejida …와 / 과 익숙해지다
family kajok 가족
family doctor chuch'iŭi 주치의; **family name** sŏng 성; **family planning** kajok kyehoek 가족 계획
famine kigŭn 기근
famous yumyŏnghan 유명한; ***be ~ for*** …(ŭ)ro yumyŏnghada …(으)로 유명하다
fan[1] *n* (*supporter*) p'aen 팬
fan[2] **1** *n* (*for cooling: electric*) sŏnp'unggi 선풍기; (*handheld*) puch'ae 부채; (*on cooker*) hwanp'unggi 환풍기 **2** *v/t*: ***~ oneself*** puch'aejirhada 부채질하다
fanatic *n* kwangshinja 광신자
fanatical kwangshinjŏgin 광신적인
fan belt MOT p'aen pelt'ŭ 팬 벨트
fancy *adj design* mŏtchin 멋진
fancy dress kajang mudobok 가장 무도복
fancy-dress party kajang mudohoe 가장 무도회
fan dance puch'aech'um 부채춤
fang ŏmni 엄니
fanny pack hŏri chigap 허리 지갑
fantastic (*very good*) hwansangjŏgin 환상적인; (*very big*) ŏmch'ŏngnan 엄청난
fantasy hwansang 환상
far *adv* mŏlli 멀리; (*much*) tŏ 더; ***~ away*** mŏlli ttŏrŏjin 멀리 떨어진; ***how ~ is it to …?*** … kkaji ŏlmana mŏn-gayo? … 까지 얼마나 먼가요?; ***as ~ as the corner / hotel*** kusŏkkaji / hot'elkkaji 구석까지 / 호텔까지; ***as ~ as I can see*** naega pol su innŭn han 내가 볼 수 있는 한; ***as ~ as I know*** naega anŭn han 내가 아는 한; ***you've gone too ~*** (*in behavior*) nega nŏmu chinach'yŏtta 네가 너무 지나쳤다; ***so ~ so good*** chigŭmkkajinŭn choayo 지금까지는 좋아요
farce (*ridiculous goings-on*) utkkinŭn chit 웃기는 짓
fare *n* (*for travel*) yogŭm 요금
Far East Kŭkttong 극동
farewell *n* ibyŏl 이별
farewell party sŏngbyŏrhoe 송별회
farfetched murihan 무리한; ***a ~ story*** hŏhwangdoen iyagi 허황된 이야기
farm *n* nongjang 농장
farmer nongbu 농부
farmhouse nongga 농가
farmworker nongjang-ŭi ilkkun 농장의 일꾼
farsighted sŏn-gyŏnjimyŏng-i innŭn 선견지명이 있는; (*optically*) wŏnshiŭi 원시의
fart F **1** *n* panggwi 방귀 **2** *v/i* panggwi kkwida 방귀 뀌다
farther *adv* tŏ mŏlli 더 멀리
farthest *travel etc* kajang mŏlli 가장 멀리
fascinate *v/t* maehoksshik'ida 매혹시키다; ***be ~d by*** …e maehokttoeda …에 매혹되다
fascinating maehoktchŏgin 매혹적인
fascination (*with subject*) yŏlgwang 열광
fascism p'asshijŭm 파시즘
fascist **1** *n* p'asshisŭt'ŭ 파시스트 **2** *adj* p'asshijŭmŭi 파시즘의
fashion *n* yuhaeng 유행; (*in clothes*) p'aesshyŏn 패션; (*manner*) pangshik 방식; ***in ~*** yuhaenghanŭn 유행하는; ***out of ~*** yuhaeng-i chinan 유행이 지난
fashionable *clothes* yuhaeng-ŭl ttarŭnŭn 유행을 따르는; *idea, restaurant* inkkiinnŭn 인기있는; *person* mŏsŭl chal naenŭn 멋을 잘 내는

fashion-conscious yuhaeng-e mingamhan 유행에 민감한
fashion designer p'aesshyŏn tijainŏ 패션 디자이너
fast[1] **1** *adj* pparŭn 빠른; ***be ~*** (*of clock*) pparŭda 빠르다 **2** *adv* pparŭge 빠르게; ***stuck ~*** tandanhi pak'in 단단히 박힌; ***~ asleep*** kip'i chamdŭn 깊이 잠든
fast[2] *n* (*not eating*) kŭmshik 금식
fasten 1 *v/t* (*fix*) kojŏnghada 고정하다; *belt*, *zipper* chaeuda 채우다; *dress*, *bag* chamgŭda 잠그다; *lid*, *window* tat-tta 닫다; ***~ your seatbelt*** anjŏnbelt'ŭrŭl ch'agyonghashio 안전벨트를 착용하시오; ***~ X onto Y*** Xŭl / rŭl Ye kojŏnghada X을 / 를 Y에 고정하다 **2** *v/i* (*of dress etc*) chamgida 잠기다
fastener (*for dress*, *lid*) chamgŭnŭn kŏt 잠그는 것
fast food chŭkssŏk shikp'um 즉석 식품; (*hamburger*, *fried chicken*) p'aesŭt'ŭp'udŭ 패스트푸드; **fast-food restaurant** p'aesŭt'ŭp'udŭjŏm 패스트푸드점; **fast forward 1** *n* (*on video etc*) kosok kamkki 고속 감기 **2** *v/i* kosogŭro kamtta 고속으로 감다; **fast lane** (*on road*) kosok ch'asŏn 고속 차선; **fast train** kosok yŏlch'a 고속 열차
fat 1 *adj* ttungttunghan 뚱뚱한 **2** *n* (*on meat*) chibang 지방
fatal *illness*, *error* ch'imyŏngjŏgin 치명적인
fatality samangja 사망자
fatally: ***~ injured*** ch'imyŏngsang-ŭi 치명상의
fate unmyŏng 운명
father *n* abŏji 아버지
fatherhood abŏji toegi 아버지 되기
father-in-law (*husband's father*) shiabŏji 시아버지; (*wife's father*) chang-in 장인
fatherly abŏji kat'ŭn 아버지 같은
fathom *n* NAUT kil 길
fatigue *n* p'iro 피로
fatso *n* F ttungttungbo 뚱뚱보
fatty 1 *adj* chibang-i manŭn 지방이 많은 **2** *n* F (*person*) ttungbo 뚱보
faucet mulkkoktchi 물꼭지
fault *n* (*defect*) kyŏltchŏm 결점; ***it's your / my ~*** nŏŭi / naŭi chalmoshida 너의 / 나의 잘못이다; ***find ~ with*** …ŭl / rŭl hŭmjaptta …을 / 를 흠잡다
faultless *person*, *performance* hŭmjabŭlde ŏmnŭn 흠잡을데 없는
faulty *goods* kyŏltchŏm innŭn 결점 있는
favor hoŭi 호의; ***in ~ of*** (*resign*, *withdraw*) …ŭl / rŭl wihayŏ …을 / 를 위하여; ***be in ~ of*** …e ch'ansŏnghada …에 찬성하다; ***do s.o. a ~*** nuguege hoŭirŭl pep'ulda 누구에게 호의를 베풀다; ***do me a ~!*** (*don't be stupid*) utkkinŭn sori hajima! 웃기는 소리 하지마!
favorable *reply etc* hoŭijŏgin 호의적인
favorite 1 *n* (*thing*) cheil choahanŭn kŏt 제일 좋아하는 것; (*person*) cheil choahanŭn saram 제일 좋아하는 사람; (*food*) cheil choahanŭn ŭmshik 제일 좋아하는 음식 **2** *adj* cheil choahanŭn 제일 좋아하는
fax 1 *n* (*machine*) p'aekssŭ 팩스; (*document*) p'aekssŭ munsŏ 팩스 문서; ***send X by ~*** p'aekssŭro Xŭl / rŭl ponaeda 팩스로 X을 / 를 보내다 **2** *v/t* p'aekssŭroponaeda 팩스로 보내다; ***~ X to Y*** Xŭl / rŭl p'aekssŭroYege ponaeda X을 / 를 팩스로 Y에게 보내다
FBI (= ***Federal Bureau of Investigation***) Yŏnbang Susaguk 연방 수사국
fear 1 *n* turyŏum 두려움 **2** *v/t* turyŏwŏhada 두려워하다
fearless turyŏum ŏmnŭn 두려움 없는
feasibility study t'adangsŏng chosa 타당성 조사
feasible shirhaeng kanŭnghan 실행 가능한
feast *n* (*meal*) manch'an 만찬; (*event*) ch'uktche 축제
feat wiŏp 위업
feather kit'ŏl 깃털
feature 1 *n* (*on face*, *of city*, *style etc*) t'ŭktching 특징; (*article in paper*) kisa 기사; (*movie*) changp'yŏn yŏnghwa 장편 영화; ***make a ~ of*** …ŭl / rŭl t'ŭktching-ŭro hada

...을/를 특징으로 하다 **2** *v/t* (*of movie*) chuyŏnŭro hada 주연으로 하다
February iwŏl 이월
federal (*allied*) yŏnhabŭi 연합의; *court, police* yŏnbang chŏngbuŭi 연방 정부의; ***~ government*** yŏnbang chŏngbu 연방 정부
federation (*alliance*) yŏnhap 연합
fed up *adj* F chillin 질린; ***be ~ with*** ...e(ge) chillida ...에(게) 질리다
fee (*of doctor*) chillyobi 진료비; (*of consultant*) sangdambi 상담비; (*for entrance*) iptchangnyo 입장료; (*for school*) ip'akkŭm 입학금; (*for membership*) hoewŏnnyo 회원료
feeble *person* yŏnyak'an 연약한; *attempt* miyak'an 미약한; *laugh* himŏmnŭn 힘없는
feed *v/t* mŏgida 먹이다; *animal* mŏgirŭl chuda 먹이를 주다
feedback p'idŭbaek 피드백
feel 1 *v/t* (*touch*) manjida 만지다; *pain, pleasure, sensation* nŭkkida 느끼다; (*think*) saenggak'ada 생각하다 **2** *v/i* (*of cloth etc*) nŭkkimi it-tta 느낌이 있다; ***it ~s like silk / cotton*** shilk'ŭwa / myŏn-gwa kat'ŭn kamch'ogida 실크와 / 면과 같은 감촉이다; ***your hand ~s hot / cold*** tangshin soni ttŭgŏpkkunyo / ch'agapkkunyo 당신 손이 뜨겁군요 / 차갑군요; ***I ~ hungry / tired*** nanŭn paegop'ŭda / p'igonhada 나는 배고프다 / 피곤하다; ***how are you ~ing today?*** onŭl kibuni ŏttŏseyo? 오늘 기분이 어떠세요?; ***how does it ~ to be rich?*** pujaga toenikka ŏttŏn kibuni tŭseyo? 부자가 되니까 어떤 기분이 드세요?; ***do you ~ like a drink / meal?*** mwŏ mashirŏ / mŏgŭrŏ kallaeyo? 뭐 마시러 / 먹으러 갈래요?; ***I ~ like going / staying*** nanŭn kago / mŏmulgo ship'ŏyo 나는 가고 / 머물고 싶어요; ***I don't ~ like it*** pyŏllo naek'iji anneyo 별로 내키지 않네요
♦**feel up to** ...hal su issŭl kŏt kat-tta ...할 수 있을 것 같다
feeler (*of insect*) tŏdŭmi 더듬이
feelgood factor hoŭng 호응
feeling (*of happiness etc*) nŭkkim 느낌; (*emotion*) kamjŏng 감정; (*sensation*) kamgak 감각; ***what are your ~s about it?*** igŏse taehayŏ ŏttŏk'e saenggak'ashimnikka? 이것에 대하여 어떻게 생각하십니까?; ***I have mixed ~s about him*** nanŭn kŭege ch'aktchap'an shimjŏng-ŭl kajigo it-tta 나는 그에게 착잡한 심정을 가지고 있다
fellow *n* (*man*) saram 사람
fellow citizen kat'ŭn shimin 같은 시민; **fellow countryman** tongp'o 동포; **fellow man** kat'ŭn in-gan 같은 인간
felony chungjoe 중죄
felt *n* p'elt'ŭ 펠트
felt tip, felt-tip(ped) pen p'elt'ŭp'en 펠트펜
female 1 *adj animal, plant* amk'ŏsŭi 암컷의; (*relating to people*) yŏsŏng-ŭi 여성의 **2** *n* (*of animals, plants*) amk'ŏt 암컷; (*person*) yŏsŏng 여성; (*pej: woman*) kyejip 계집
feminine 1 *adj qualities* yŏsŏngjŏgin 여성적인; GRAM yŏsŏng-ŭi 여성의; ***she's very ~*** kŭnyŏnŭn aju yŏsŏngjŏgida 그녀는 아주 여성적이다 **2** *n* GRAM yŏsŏng 여성
feminism yŏkkwŏnjuŭi 여권주의, p'eminijŭm 페미니즘
feminist 1 *n* yŏkkwŏnjuŭija 여권주의자, p'eminisŭt'ŭ 페미니스트 **2** *adj group* yŏkkwŏnjuŭijaŭi 여권주의자의; *ideas* yŏkkwŏnjuŭiŭi 여권주의의
fence *n* ult'ari 울타리
♦**fence in** *land* ult'ariro tullŏ ssada 울타리로 둘러 싸다
fencing SP p'enshing 펜싱
fend: ***~ for oneself*** che himŭro kkuryŏnagada 제 힘으로 꾸려나가다
fender MOT p'endŏ 펜더
ferment[1] *v/i* (*of liquid*) parhyohada 발효하다
ferment[2] *n* (*unrest*) puran 불안
fermentation parhyo 발효
fermented soya paste toenjang 된장
fern yangch'iryu 양치류

ferocious *animal* hyungp'ohan 흉포한; *attack* chaninhan 잔인한
ferry *n* narutppae 나룻배
fertile *soil* piok'an 비옥한; *woman, animal* tasanŭi 다산의
fertility (*of soil*) piok 비옥; (*of woman, animal*) tasan 다산
fertility drug paeran ch'oktchinje 배란 촉진제
fertilize *v/t ovum* sujŏngshik'ida 수정시키다
fertilizer (*for soil*) piryo 비료
fervent *admirer* yŏllyŏrhan 열렬한
fester *v/i* (*of wound*) komtta 곪다
festival ch'uktche 축제
festive ch'uktcheŭi 축제의; ***the ~ season*** sŏngt'anjŏl kigan 성탄절 기간
festivities ch'uk'a haengsa 축하 행사
fetch *person* terigo oda 데리고 오다; *thing* kajyŏ oda 가져 오다; *price* …e p'allida …에 팔리다
fetus t'aea 태아
feud *n* purhwa 불화
fever yŏl 열
feverish yŏri innŭn 열이 있는; *fig*: *excitement* yŏlgwangtchŏgin 열광적인
few 1 *adj* (*not many*) manch'i anŭn 많지 않은; ***a ~*** (*things*) chogŭmŭi 조금의; ***quite a ~, a good ~*** (*a lot*) kkwae manŭn 꽤 많은; ***we have ~ friends*** urinŭn ch'in-guga manch'i ant'a 우리는 친구가 많지 않다; ***we have a ~ friends*** urinŭn ch'in-guga chom it-tta 우리는 친구가 좀 있다 **2** *pron* (*not many people*) chŏgŭn suŭi saram 적은 수의 사람; (*not many: things*) chŏgŭn suŭi kŏt 적은 수의 것; ***a ~*** (*people*) myŏnmyŏt saram 몇몇 사람; (*things*) myŏnmyŏsŭi kŏt 몇몇의 것; ***quite a ~, a good ~*** (*people*) kkwae manŭn saram 꽤 많은 사람; (*things*) kkwae manŭn kŏt 꽤 많은 것
fewer *adj* tŏ chagŭn 더 작은; ***~ than*** … poda chagŭn … 보다 작은
fiancé yak'onja 약혼자
fiancée yak'onnyŏ 약혼녀
fiasco taeshilp'ae 대실패
fib *n* sasohan kŏjinmal 사소한 거짓말
fiber *n* sŏmnyu 섬유
fiberglass *n* sŏmnyu yuri 섬유 유리; **fiber optic** kwangsŏmnyuŭi 광섬유의; **fiber optics** kwangsŏmnyu 광섬유
fickle pyŏndŏkssŭrŏun 변덕스러운
fiction (*novels*) sosŏl 소설; (*made-up story*) kkumin iyagi 꾸민 이야기
fictitious hŏguŭi 허구의
fiddle 1 *n* F (*violin*) kkaengkkaeng-i 깽깽이 **2** *v/i*: ***~ around with*** …ŭl / rŭl majijak-kkŏrida …을 / 를 만지작거리다 **3** *v/t accounts* sogida 속이다
fidelity ch'ungshil 충실
fidget *v/i* anjŏlbujŏl mot'ada 안절부절 못하다
field *n* tŭlp'an 들판; (*for crops*) pat 밭; (*for animals*) mokch'oji 목초지; (*of rice*) non 논; (*for sport*) kyŏnggijang 경기장; (*competitors in race*) kyŏnggi ch'amgaja 경기 참가자; (*of research, knowledge etc*) punya 분야; ***that's not my ~*** che punyaga animnida 제 분야가 아닙니다
field events p'ildŭ kyŏnggi 필드 경기
fierce sanaun 사나운
fiery *personality, temper* pul kat'ŭn 불 같은
fifteen yŏldasŏt 열 다섯, shibo 십오
fifteenth yŏldasŏt pŏntchaeŭi 열 다섯 번째의
fifth tasŏt pŏntchaeŭi 다섯 번째의
fiftieth shwin pŏntchaeŭi 쉰 번째의
fifty shwin 쉰, oship 오십
fifty-fifty *adv* oship tae oshibŭro 오십 대 오십으로
fig muhwagwa 무화과
fight 1 *n* ssaum 싸움; *in war* chŏnt'u 전투; *fig* (*for survival, championship etc*) t'ujaeng 투쟁; (*in boxing*) kyŏnggi 경기 **2** *v/t enemy, person, disease, injustice* …wa / kwa ssauda …와 / 과 싸우다; (*in boxing*) …wa / kwa kyŏruda …와 / 과 겨루다 **3** *v/i* ssauda 싸우다
♦ **fight for** *one's rights, a cause* …ŭl / rŭl wihae ssauda …을 / 를 위해 싸우다
fighter chŏnsa 전사; (*airplane*)

chŏnt'ugi 전투기; (*boxer*) sŏnsu 선수; ***she's a*** ~ kŭnyŏnŭn pulgurŭi ŭijirŭl kajigo it-tta 그녀는 불굴의 의지를 가지고 있다
figurative *use of word* piyujŏgin 비유적인; *art* chohyŏngjŏgin 조형적인
figure 1 *n* (*digit*) sutcha 숫자; (*of person*) mommae 몸매; (*form, shape*) hyŏngsang 형상 **2** *v/t* F (*think*) saenggak'ada 생각하다
♦**figure on** F (*plan*) kyehoek'ada 계획하다
♦**figure out** (*understand*) ihaehada 이해하다; *calculation* kyesanhada 계산하다
figure skating p'igyŏ sŭk'eit'ing 피겨 스케이팅
file[1] **1** *n* (*of documents*) sŏryuch'ŏl 서류철; COMPUT hwail 화일 **2** *v/t documents* ch'ŏrhada 철하다
♦**file away** *documents* ch'ŏrhayŏ pogwanhada 철하여 보관하다
file[2] *n* (*for wood, fingernails*) chul 줄
file cabinet sŏryuham 서류함
file manager COMPUT hwail maenijŏ 화일 매니저
filial piety hyo 효
Filipino 1 *adj* P'illip'inŭi 필리핀의 **2** *n* (*person*) P'illip'in saram 필리핀 사람
fill 1 *v/t* ch'aeuda 채우다 **2** *n*: ***eat one's*** ~ chanttŭk mŏktta 잔뜩 먹다
♦**fill in** *form* kiip'ada 기입하다; *hole* meuda 메우다
♦**fill in for** ...ŭl/rŭl taeshinhada ...을/를 대신하다
♦**fill out 1** *v/t form* kiip'ada 기입하다 **2** *v/i* (*get fatter*) saltchida 살찌다
♦**fill up 1** *v/t* kadŭk ch'aeuda 가득 채우다 **2** *v/i* (*of stadium, theater*) kadŭk ch'ada 가득 차다
fillet *n* ppyŏ parŭn saltchŏm 뼈 바른 살점
fillet steak p'ille sŭt'eik'ŭ 필레 스테이크
filling 1 *n* (*in sandwich*) sok 속; (*in tooth*) p'illing 필링 **2** *adj food* paeburŭge hanŭn 배부르게 하는
filling station chuyuso 주유소
film 1 *n* (*for camera*) p'illŭm 필름; (*movie*) yŏnghwa 영화 **2** *v/t person, event* ch'waryŏnghada 촬영하다
film-maker yŏnghwa chejaktcha 영화 제작자
film star yŏnghwa sŭt'a 영화 스타
filter 1 *n* p'ilt'ŏ 필터, yŏgwagi 여과기 **2** *v/t coffee, liquid* kŏrŭda 거르다
♦**filter through** (*of news reports*) saeŏ naoda 새어 나오다
filter tip (*cigarette*) p'ilt'ŏ 필터
filth pulgyŏrhan kŏt 불결한 것
filthy pulgyŏrhan 불결한; *language etc* sangsŭrŏun 상스러운
fin (*of fish*) chinŭrŏmi 지느러미
final 1 *adj* (*last*) majimagŭi 마지막의; *decision* ch'oejŏng-ŭi 최종의 **2** *n* SP kyŏlssŭng 결승
finalist kyŏlssŭngjŏn ch'ultchŏn sŏnsu 결승전 출전 선수
finalize mamurihada 마무리하다
finally majimagŭro 마지막으로; (*at last*) mach'imnae 마침내
finance 1 *n* chaejŏng 재정; (*provision of funds*) kŭmnyung 금융 **2** *v/t* ...e chagŭm chiwŏnŭl hada ...에 자금 지원을 하다
financial chaejŏng-ŭi 재정의; ***a ~ magazine*** kyŏngje chaptchi 경제 잡지
financial year hoegye yŏndo 회계 연도
financier chaejŏngga 재정가
find *v/t* ch'at-tta 찾다; ***if you ~ it too hot*** *weather* nŏmu tŏpttago saenggakttoemyŏn 너무 덥다고 생각되면; *food* nŏmu ttŭgŏpttago saenggakttoemyŏn 너무 뜨겁다고 생각되면; ***~ s.o. innocent / guilty*** LAW nugurŭl mujoero / yujoero p'an-gyŏrhada 누구를 무죄로 /유죄로 판결하다
♦**find out 1** *v/t* aranaeda 알아내다 **2** *v/i* (*inquire*) palk'yŏnaeda 밝혀내다; (*discover*) aranaeda 알아내다
fine[1] *adj day, weather* malgŭn 맑은; *wine, performance, city* hullyunghan 훌륭한; *distinction* misehan 미세한; *line* kanŭn 가는; *powder* koun 고운; *print* chŏnggyohan 정교한; ***how's that? – that's ~*** ŏttŏssŭmnikka? –

chossŭmnida 어떻습니까? – 좋습니다; ***that's ~ by me*** nanŭn choŭndeyo 나는 좋은데요; ***how are you? – ~*** ŏttŏk'e chinaeseyo? – chal issŭmnida 어떻게 지내세요? – 잘 있습니다

fine[2] *n* pŏlgŭm 벌금

finger *n* sonkkarak 손가락

fingernail sont'op 손톱; **fingerprint** *n* chimun 지문; **fingertip** sonkkarak kkŭt 손가락 끝; ***have X at one's ~s*** Xŭl / rŭl hwŏnhi alda X을 / 를 훤히 알다

finicky *person* kkadaroun 까다로운; *design* chinach'ige sŏmsehan 지나치게 섬세한

finish 1 *v/t* kkŭnnaeda 끝내다; ***~ doing sth*** muŏt'agirŭl kkŭnnaeda 무엇하기를 끝내다 **2** *v/i* kkŭnnada 끝나다 **3** *n* (*of product*) kkŭnmaejŭm 끝맺음; (*of race*) kyŏlssŭngjŏm 결승점

♦**finish off** *v/t* kkŭnmach'ida 끝마치다

♦**finish up** *v/t* ta kkŭnnaebŏrida 다 끝내버리다; ***he finished up liking it / living there*** kŭnŭn kŭgŏsŭl choahage toego / kŭgose salge toego marat-tta 그는 그것을 좋아하게 되고 / 그곳에 살게 되고 말았다

♦**finish with** *boyfriend etc* ...wa / kwaŭi kwan-gyerŭl kkŭnnaeda ...와 / 과의 관계를 끝내다

finishing line kyŏlssŭngsŏn 결승선

Finland P'illandŭ 핀란드

Finn P'illandŭ saram 핀란드 사람

Finnish 1 *adj* P'illandŭŭi 핀란드의 **2** *n* (*language*) P'illandŭŏ 핀란드어

fir chŏnnamu 전나무

fire 1 *n* pul 불; (*electric*, *gas*) nanbang 난방; (*blaze*) hwajae 화재; ***be on ~*** pul t'ago it-tta 불 타고 있다; ***catch ~*** pur put-tta 불 붙다; ***set X on ~***, ***set ~ to X*** Xe purŭl puch'ida X에 불을 붙이다 **2** *v/i* (*shoot*) ssoda 쏘다 **3** *v/t* F (*dismiss*) haegohada 해고하다; ***be ~d*** haegodoeda 해고되다

fire alarm hwajae kyŏngbogi 화재 경보기; **firearm** ch'ong 총; **fire department** sobangsŏ 소방서; **fire escape** hwajae p'inan changch'i 화재 피난 장치; **fire extinguisher** sohwagi 소화기; **firefighter**, **fireman** sobangsu 소방수; **fireplace** pyŏngnallo 벽난로; **fire truck** sobangch'a 소방차; **firewood** ttaelnamu 땔나무; **fireworks** pulkkonnori 불꽃놀이

firm[1] *adj grip*, *handshake* himinnŭn 힘있는; *flesh*, *muscles* tandanhan 단단한; *voice*, *decision* hwakkohan 확고한; ***a ~ deal*** hwaksshirhage toen kŏrae 확실하게 된 거래

firm[2] *n* COM hoesa 회사

first 1 *adj* ch'ŏŭmŭi 처음의; ***who's ~ please?*** ŏnŭ pun mŏnjŏimnikka? 어느 분 먼저입니까? **2** *n* (*person*) ch'ŏŭmŭi saram 처음의 사람; (*thing*) ch'ŏŭmŭi kŏt 처음의 것; ***~, please*** ch'ŏŭm pun oshipsshio 처음 분 오십시오 **3** *adv arrive*, *finish* ch'ŏŭmŭro 처음으로; (*beforehand*) mŏnjŏ 먼저; ***~ of all*** (*for one reason*) usŏnŭn 우선은; ***at ~*** ch'ŏŭme 처음에

first aid ŭnggŭp ch'iryo 응급 치료; **first-aid box**, **first-aid kit** kugŭmnyak sangja 구급약 상자; **first birthday** tol 돐; **first-born** *adj* majiro t'aeŏnan 맏이로 태어난; **first class 1** *adj ticket* ilttŭngshirŭi 일등실의; (*very good*) ch'oegogŭbŭi 최고급의 **2** *adv travel* ilttŭngshillo 일등실로; **first floor** ilch'ŭng 일층; **firsthand** *adj* chiktchŏptchŏgin 직접적인

firstly usŏn 우선

first name irŭm 이름

first-rate illyuŭi 일류의

fiscal *policy*, *measures* choseŭi 조세의

fiscal year hoegye yŏndo 회계 연도

fish 1 *n* mulkkogi 물고기; (*to eat*) saengsŏn 생선 **2** *v/i* naksshihada 낚시하다

fishbone saengsŏnppyŏ 생선뼈

fisherman ŏbu 어부

fishing naksshi 낚시

fishing boat ŏsŏn 어선; **fishing line** naksshitchul 낚싯줄; **fishing rod** naksshit-ttae 낚싯대

fishmonger saengsŏn changsu 생선 장수

fish stick saengsŏn t'wigim 생선 튀김
fishy F (*suspicious*) susanghan 수상한
fist chumŏk 주먹
fit[1] *n* MED paltchak 발작; ***a ~ of rage / jealousy*** sun-ganjŏgin pokssushim / chilt'ushim 순간적인 복수심 / 질투심
fit[2] *adj* (*physically*) kŏn-ganghan 건강한; (*morally*) chŏk'ap'an 적합한; ***keep ~*** kŏn-gang-ŭl yujihada 건강을 유지하다
fit[3] **1** *v/t* (*of clothes*) …ege mat-tta …에게 맞다; (*attach*) talda 달다 **2** *v/i* (*of clothes*) mat-tta 맞다; (*of piece of furniture etc*) tŭrŏ mat-tta 들어 맞다 **3** *n*: ***it's a good ~*** chal mat-tta 잘 맞다; ***it's a tight ~*** kkok mat-tta 꼭 맞다
♦**fit in** (*of person in group*) murie ŏullida 무리에 어울리다; ***it fits in with our plans*** kŭgŏsŭn uriŭi kyehoege tŭrŏ mannŭnda 그것은 우리의 계획에 들어 맞는다
fitful *sleep* sŏlch'in 설친
fitness (*physical*) kŏn-gangham 건강함
fitness center helssŭ k'ŭllŏp 헬스 클럽
fitted kitchen match'um puŏk 맞춤 부엌
fitter *n* chŏngbigong 정비공
fitting *adj* chŏktchŏrhan 적절한
fittings kŏnmul naebu changch'i 건물 내부 장치
five tasŏt 다섯, o 오
fix 1 *n* (*solution*) haegyŏl 해결; ***be in a ~*** F kon-gyŏng-e ch'ŏhae it-tta 곤경에 처해 있다 **2** *v/t* (*attach*) kojŏnghada 고정하다; (*repair*) koch'ida 고치다; (*arrange*: *meeting etc*) ilsshirŭl chŏnghada 일시를 정하다; *lunch* chunbihada 준비하다; (*dishonestly*: *match etc*) chojak'ada 조작하다; ***~ X onto Y*** Xŭl / rŭl Ye kojŏngshik'ida X을 / 를 Y에 고정시키다; ***I'll ~ you a drink*** chega mashil kŏsŭl mandŭrŏ tŭrigessŭmnida 제가 마실 것을 만들어 드리겠습니다
♦**fix up** *meeting* ilsshirŭl chŏnghada 일시를 정하다; ***it's all fixed up*** ta chŏnghaejyŏt-tta 다 정해졌다
fixed *part*, *exchange rate* kojŏngdoen 고정된
fixture (*in room*) sŏlbi 설비; SP chŏnggijŏn 정기전
flab (*on body*) kunsal 군살
flabbergast: ***be ~ed*** F ch'unggyŏgŭl pat-tta 충격을 받다
flabby *muscles*, *stomach* nŭrŏjin 늘어진
flag[1] *n* kitppal 깃발; (*national ~*) kukki 국기
flag[2] *v/i* (*tire*) chich'ida 지치다
flair (*talent*) chaenŭng 재능; ***have a natural ~ for*** …e t'agonan chaenŭng-i it-tta …에 타고난 재능이 있다
flake *n* yalbŭn chogak 얇은 조각
♦**flake off** *v/i* pŏtkkyŏjyŏ ttŏrŏjida 벗겨져 떨어지다
flaky *adj* pŏtkkyŏjigi shwiun 벗겨지기 쉬운; F (*odd*) pyŏllan 별난
flaky pastry p'asak'an p'aiyong panjuk 파삭한 파이용 반죽
flamboyant *personality* chashini nŏmch'yŏboinŭn 자신이 넘쳐보이는
flame *n* pulkkot 불꽃; **~s** pulkkil 불길
flammable kayŏnssŏng-ŭi 가연성의
flan op'ŭn p'ai 오픈 파이
flank 1 *n* (*of horse etc*) yŏpkkuri 옆구리; MIL taeyŏrŭi ch'ŭngmyŏn 대열의 측면 **2** *v/t*: ***be ~ed by*** (*by person*) …ŭl / rŭl yangnyŏp'e kŏnŭrida …을 / 를 양옆에 거느리다; (*by building*, *person etc*) …ŭl / rŭl yangnyŏp'e tuda …을 / 를 양옆에 두다
flap 1 *n* (*of envelope*, *pocket*) ttukkŏng 뚜껑; ***be in a ~*** F anjŏlbujŏl mot'ada 안절부절 못하다 **2** *v/t wings* p'ŏllŏgida 펄럭이다 **3** *v/i* (*of flag etc*) p'ŏllŏgida 펄럭이다; F (*panic*) ch'ojohaehada 초조해하다
flare 1 *n* (*distress signal*) chomyŏngt'an 조명탄; (*in dress*) p'ŭlleŏ 플레어 **2** *v/t nostrils* pŏrida 벌이다
♦**flare up** (*of violence*, *illness*) tolbarhada 돌발하다; (*of fire*) t'aorŭda 타오르다; (*get very angry*) hwaga ch'isot-tta 화가 치솟다

flash 1 *n* (*of light*) sŏmgwang 섬광; PHOT p'ŭllaeshwi 플래쉬; ***in a ~*** F nun kkamtchak'al saie 눈 깜짝할 사이에; ***have a ~ of inspiration*** yŏnggami pŏntchŏk ttorŭda 영감이 번쩍 떠오르다; ***~ of lightning*** pŏngaetppurŭi pŏntchŏgim 번갯불의 번쩍임 **2** *v/i* (*of light*) pich'ida 비치다 **3** *v/t headlights* pich'uda 비추다
flashback *n* (*in movie*) kwagŏ hoesang changmyŏn 과거 회상 장면
flashbulb sŏmgwang chŏn-gu 섬광 전구
flasher MOT chadong chŏmmyŏl changch'i 자동 점멸 장치
flashlight hoejung chŏndŭng 회중 전등; PHOT p'ŭllaeshwi 플래쉬
flashy *pej* yoranhan 요란한
flask pyŏng 병
flat 1 *adj surface, land* p'yŏngp'yŏnghan 평평한; *beer* kim ppajin 김 빠진; *battery, tire* ta tarŭn 다 닳은; *shoes* najŭn kubŭi 낮은 굽의; MUS panŭm naerimŭi 반음 내림의; ***and that's ~*** F tŏ isang-ŭn marhaji ank'essŏ 더 이상은 말하지 않겠어 **2** *adv* MUS panŭm naerimŭro 반음 내림으로; ***~ out*** chŏnsongnyŏgŭro hada 전속력으로 하다
flat-chested kasŭmi pinyak'an 가슴이 빈약한
flat rate iltchŏng-aek 일정액
flatten *v/t land, road* p'yŏngp'yŏnghage hada 평평하게 하다; (*by bombing, demolition*) munŏttŭrida 무너뜨리다
flatter *v/t* ach'ŏmhada 아첨하다
flattering *comments* ach'ŏmhanŭn 아첨하는; *color, clothes* shilmulboda totppoige hanŭn 실물보다 돋보이게 하는
flattery ach'ŏm 아첨
flavor 1 *n* mat 맛 **2** *v/t food* mannaeda 맛내다
flavoring chomiryo 조미료
flaw *n* hŭm 흠
flawless hŭmŏmnŭn 흠없는
flea pyŏruk 벼룩
flee *v/i* tomangch'ida 도망치다
fleet *n* NAUT hamdae 함대
fleeting *visit etc* chamkkan tong-anŭi 잠깐 동안의; ***catch a ~ glimpse of*** ŏlp'it poda 얼핏 보다
flesh (*of people, fruit etc*) sal 살; ***the ~*** yukch'e 육체; ***meet / see a person in the ~*** nugurŭl shiltchero mannada / poda 누구를 실제로 만나다 / 보다
flex *v/t muscles* such'ukshik'ida 수축시키다
flexible *material* kuburigi shwiun 구부리기 쉬운; *arrangement, hours* yungt'ongssŏng innŭn 융통성 있는; ***I'm quite ~ about the timing*** chŏnŭn amu ttaerado chossŭmnida 저는 아무 때라도 좋습니다
flick *v/t tail* hwidurŭda 휘두르다; ***he ~ed a fly off his hand*** kŭnŭn sonŭl hwidullŏsŏ p'arirŭl naetchoch'at-tta 그는 손을 휘둘러서 파리를 내쫓았다; ***she ~ed her hair out of her eyes*** kŭnŭn shiyarŭl karinŭn mŏrik'aragŭl ssŭrŏnŏmgyŏt-tta 그는 시야를 가리는 머리카락을 쓸어넘겼다
♦**flick through** *book, magazine* taegang hult'ŏboda 대강 훑어보다
flicker *v/i* (*of light, screen*) kkamppagida 깜박이다
flies (*on pants*) paji ammun 바지 앞문
flight (*in airplane*) pihaeng 비행; (*flying*) nalgi 날기; (*fleeing*) tomang 도망; ***~ (of stairs)*** han churŭi kyedan 한 줄의 계단; ***three ~s a day*** iril samhoeŭi hanggongp'yŏn 1일 3회의 항공편; ***a direct ~*** chik'ang 직항; ***it's a long ~*** igŏsŭn kin yohaeng-iyeyo 이것은 긴 여행이예요; ***when is your ~?*** tangshinŭi pihaenggi shiganŭn ŏnjeimnikka? 당신의 비행기 시간은 언제입니까?
flight crew sŭngmuwŏn 승무원; **flight deck** (*in airplane*) chojongshil 조종실; **flight number** hanggongp'yŏn pŏnho 항공편 번호; **flight path** pihaeng kyŏngno 비행 경로; **flight recorder** pŭllaek pakssŭ 블랙 박스; **flight time** (*departure*) ch'ulbal shigan 출발 시간; (*duration*) yŏhaeng shigan 여행 시간

flighty pyŏndŏkssŭrŏun 변덕스러운
flimsy *structure*, *furniture* yak'an 약한; *dress* yalbŭn 얇은; *material* tchijŏjigi shwiun 찢어지기 쉬운; *excuse* pinyak'an 빈약한
flinch umtchirhada 움찔하다
fling *v/t* naedŏnjida 내던지다; **~ open** kŏch'ilge yŏlda 거칠게 열다; **~ oneself into a chair** ŭijae t'ŏlssŏk ant'a 의자에 털썩 앉다
♦ **flip through** *book*, *magazine* taegang hult'ŏboda 대강 훑어보다
flipper (*for swimming*) mulgalk'wi 물갈퀴
flirt 1 *v/i* saeronggŏrida 새롱거리다 **2** *n* saeronggŏrinŭn saram 새롱거리는 사람
flirtatious saeronggŏrinŭn 새롱거리는
float *v/i* ttŭda 뜨다; FIN pyŏndong shisega toeda 변동 시세가 되다
flock *n* (*of sheep*) tte 떼
flog *v/t* (*whip*) ch'aetchiktchirhada 채찍질하다
flood 1 *n* hongsu 홍수; (*of river*) pŏmnam 범람 **2** *v/t* (*of river*) pŏmnamhada 범람하다; **~ its banks** kangttugi nŏmch'ida 강둑이 넘치다
flooding pŏmnam 범람
floodlight *n* t'ugwang chomyŏng 투광 조명
floor *n* (*of room*) marutppadak 마룻바닥; (*story*) ch'ŭng 층
floorboard padangnŏl 바닥널; **floor cloth** maru kŏlle 마루 걸레; **floor lamp** sŭt'aendŭ 스탠드
flop 1 *v/i* t'ŏlssŏk momŭl tŏnjida 털썩 몸을 던지다; F (*fail*) shilp'aejagida 실패작이다 **2** *n* F (*failure*) shilp'aejak 실패작
floppy *adj* (*not stiff*) hŏllŏnghan 헐렁한; (*weak*) narŭnhan 나른한
floppy (disk) p'ŭllop'i tisŭk'ŭ 플로피 디스크
florist kkotchangsu 꽃장수
flour milkkaru 밀가루
flourish *v/i* (*of plants*) chal charada 잘 자라다; (*of business*) pŏnch'anghada 번창하다; (*of civilization*) pŏnyŏnghada 번영하다
flourishing *business*, *trade* pŏnch'anghanŭn 번창하는
flow 1 *v/i* (*of river*) hŭrŭda 흐르다; (*of electric current*) t'onghada 통하다; (*of traffic*) sot'ongdoeda 소통되다; (*of work*) chinhaengdoeda 진행되다; ***the traffic ~s better*** kyot'ong sot'ong-i wŏnhwarhaejida 교통 소통이 원활해지다 **2** *n* (*of river*, *information*) hŭrŭm 흐름; (*of ideas*) kyohwan 교환
flowchart chagŏp kongjŏngdo 작업 공정도
flower 1 *n* kkot 꽃 **2** *v/i* kkoch'i p'ida 꽃이 피다
flowerbed hwadan 화단; **Flower Garland Sutra** Hwaŏmgyŏng 화엄경; **flowerpot** hwabyŏng 화병
flowery *pattern* kkŏnmunŭiŭi 꽃무늬의; *style of writing* misayŏguŭi 미사여구의
flu tok-kkam 독감
fluctuate *v/i* pyŏndonghada 변동하다
fluctuation pyŏndong 변동
fluency yuch'angham 유창함
fluent *adj speaker* yuch'anghan 유창한; ***he speaks ~ Korean*** kŭnŭn Han-gungmarŭl yuch'anghage handa 그는 한국말을 유창하게 한다
fluently *speak* yuch'anghage 유창하게; *write* yuryŏhage 유려하게
fluff: ***a bit of ~*** (*material*) yakkanŭi pop'ul 약간의 보풀
fluffy *adj material*, *hair* somt'ŏlgat'ŭn 솜털같은; **~ *clouds*** somt'ŏl kurŭm 솜털 구름
fluid *n* (*in body*) aek 액; (*for brakes*) yudong-aek 유동액
flunk *v/t* F (*subject*) …e naktcherŭl pat-tta …에 낙제를 받다
fluorescent hyŏnggwang-ŭi 형광의
flush 1 *v/t toilet* …ŭi murŭl naerida …의 물을 내리다; **~ *X down the toilet*** Xŭl / rŭl pyŏn-gie naeryŏ ponaeda X을 / 를 변기에 내려 보내다 **2** *v/i* (*of toilet*) muri naeryŏgada 물이 내려가다; (*go red in the face*) ppalgaejida 빨개지다 **3** *adj* (*level*) kat'ŭn nop'iŭi 같은 높이의; ***be ~ with*** …wa / kwa kat'ŭn nop'iida …와 / 과 같은 높이이다
♦ **flush away** (*down toilet*) pyŏn-gie

naeryŏ ponaeda 변기에 내려 보내다
♦**flush out** *rebels etc* naogehada 나오게 하다
fluster *v/t* tanghwanghage hada 당황하게 하다; ***get ~ed*** tanghwanghada 당황하다
flute p'ŭllut'ŭ 플루트; (*large*) taegŭm 대금; (*bamboo*) tanso 단소
flutter *v/i* (*of bird, wings*) p'ŏdŏkkŏrida 퍼덕거리다; (*of flag*) p'ŏllŏgida 펄럭이다; (*of heart*) tugŭn-gŏrida 두근거리다
fly[1] *n* (*insect*) p'ari 파리
fly[2] *n* (*on pants*) paji ammun 바지 앞문
fly[3] **1** *v/i* (*of bird, airplane*) nalda 날다; (*in airplane*) pihaenggiro yŏhaenghada 비행기로 여행하다; (*of flag*) keyangdoeda 게양되다; (*rush*) ttwiŏ nagada 뛰어 나가다; ***~ into a rage*** pŏlk'ŏk sŏngnaeda 벌컥 성내다 **2** *v/t airplane* chojonghada 조종하다; *airline* t'ada 타다; (*transport by air*) hanggong unsonghada 항공 운송하다
♦**fly away** naragada 날아가다
♦**fly back** *v/i* (*travel back*) pihaenggiro toragada 비행기로 돌아가다
♦**fly in 1** *v/i* (*of airplane, passengers*) toch'ak'ada 도착하다 **2** *v/t supplies etc* pihaenggiro unbanhada 비행기로 운반하다
♦**fly off** (*of hat etc*) naragada 날아가다
♦**fly out** *v/i* naragada 날아가다
♦**fly past** (*in formation*) kongjung pihaenghada 공중 비행하다; (*of time*) ssonsalgach'i chinagada 쏜살같이 지나가다
flying *n* pihaeng 비행
foam *n* (*on liquid*) kŏp'um 거품
foam rubber sŭp'onji komu 스폰지 고무
FOB (= ***free on board***) ponsŏn indo 본선 인도
focus *n* (*of attention*), PHOT ch'otchŏm 초점; ***be in ~ / out of ~*** PHOT ch'otchŏmi mat-tta / mat-tchi ant'a 초점이 맞다 /맞지 않다
♦**focus on** *also fig* ...e ch'otchŏmŭl match'uda ...에 초점을 맞추다
fodder saryo 사료
fog an-gae 안개
foggy an-gae kkin 안개 낀
foil[1] *n* (*silver ~ etc*) hoil 호일
foil[2] *v/t* (*thwart*) chwajŏlsshik'ida 좌절시키다
fold 1 *v/t paper* chŏptta 접다; *cloth* kaeda 개다; ***~ one's arms*** p'altchang-ŭl kkida 팔짱을 끼다 **2** *v/i* (*of business*) manghada 망하다 **3** *n* (*in cloth etc*) chŏbŭn chari 접은 자리
♦**fold up 1** *v/t* chŏptta 접다 **2** *v/i* (*of chair, table*) chŏp'ida 접히다
folder *also* COMPUT p'oldŏ 폴더
folding *adj* chŏmnŭn 접는
foliage ip 잎
folk (*people*) saram 사람; ***my ~s*** (*family*) nae kajok 내 가족; ***come in, ~s*** F tŭrŏoseyo, yŏrŏbun 들어오세요, 여러분
folk dance (*traditional*) minsok ch'um 민속 춤; (*western*) p'ok'ŭttaensŭ 포크댄스; **folk medicine** min-gan yoppŏp 민간 요법; **folk music** minsok ŭmak 민속 음악; **folk painting** minhwa 민화; **folk singer** minyo kasu 민요 가수; **folk song** minyo 민요
follow 1 *v/t person, road* ttaragada 따라가다; *guidelines, instructions* ttarŭda 따르다; *TV series, news* kyesok shich'ŏnghada 계속 시청하다; (*understand*) ihaehada 이해하다; ***~ me*** (*come*) chŏrŭl ttaraoseyo 저를 따라오세요 **2** *v/i* ttaragada 따라가다; (*logically*) sŏngnip'ada 성립하다; ***it ~s from this that ...*** kŭraesŏ ...ranŭn mari mat-tta 그래서 ...라는 말이 맞다; ***as ~s*** taŭmgwa kat'ŭn 다음과 같은
♦**follow up** *v/t inquiry* poganghada 보강하다
follower (*of politician etc*) chijija 지지자; (*of football team*) p'aen 팬; (*of TV program*) shich'ŏngja 시청자
following 1 *adj day, night* kŭ taŭmŭi 그 다음의; *pages* taŭmŭi 다음의 **2** *n* (*people*) chijija 지지자; ***the ~*** taŭmŭi kŏt 다음의 것

follow-up meeting pogang hoeŭi 보강 회의
follow-up visit chaebangmun 재방문; (*to doctor*) chaejin 재진
folly (*madness*) ŏrisŏgŭn chit 어리석은 짓
fond (*loving*) tajŏnghan 다정한; *memory* arŭmdaun 아름다운; ***be ~ of*** ...ŭl/rŭl choahada ...을/를 좋아하다
fondle *v/t* ssŭdadŭmtta 쓰다듬다
fondness aejŏng 애정; (*for wine, food*) aeho 애호
font (*in printing*) kŭltchach'e 글자체
food ŭmshik 음식
food freak F misshik-kka 미식가; **food mixer** miksso 믹서; **food poisoning** shiktchungdok 식중독
fool *n* pabo 바보; ***make a ~ of oneself*** usŭmkkŏriga toeda 웃음거리가 되다
♦**fool around** changnanch'ida 장난치다; (*sexually*) param p'iuda 바람피우다
♦**fool around with** *knife, drill etc* ...ŭl/rŭl kajigo changnanch'ida ...을/를 가지고 장난치다
foolish ŏrisŏgŭn 어리석은
foolproof chalmot toel suga ŏmnŭn 잘못 될 수가 없는
foot pal 발; (*measurement*) p'it'ŭ 피트; ***on ~*** kŏrŏsŏ 걸어서; ***at the ~ of the page / hill*** chang-ŭi/ŏndŏgŭi mit'e 장의/언덕의 밑에; ***put one's ~ in it*** F k'ŭn shilssurŭl hada 큰 실수를 하다
football (*soccer*) ch'uk-kku 축구; (*American-style*) mishik ch'uk-kku 미식 축구; (*ball*) ch'uk-kkugong 축구공; **football player** (*soccer*) ch'uk-kku sŏnsu 축구 선수; (*American-style*) mishik ch'uk-kku sŏnsu 미식 축구 선수; **footbridge** yukkyo 육교; **foothills** san-gisŭlgŭi chagŭn ŏndŏk 산기슭의 작은 언덕
footing (*basis*) kiban 기반; ***lose one's ~*** hŏt-ttidida 헛디디다; ***be on the same / a different ~*** tongdŭnghan/tarŭn chagyŏgida 동등한/다른 자격이다; ***be on a friendly ~ with*** ...wa/kwa uhojŏk kwan-gyerŭl kajida ...와/과 우호적 관계를 가지다
footlights kak-kkwang 각광; **footnote** kaktchu 각주; **footpath** indo 인도; **footprint** paltchaguk 발자국; **footstep** paltchaguk sori 발자국 소리; ***follow in s.o.'s ~s*** nuguŭi sŏllyerŭl ttarŭda 누구의 선례를 따르다; **footwear** shinbal 신발
for ◊ (*purpose, destination*) ...ŭl/rŭl wihan ...을/를 위한; ***clothes ~ children*** aidŭrŭl wihan ot 아이들을 위한 옷; ***I did it ~ John*** Jonŭl wihaesŏ hassŏyo 존을 위해서 했어요; ***a train ~ Seoul*** Sŏullo kanŭn kich'a 서울로 가는 기차; ***it's too big / small ~ you*** kŭgŏsŭn nŏege nŏmu k'ŭda/chaktta 그것은 너에게 너무 크다/작다; ***here's a letter ~ you*** yŏgi nŏege on p'yŏnjiga it-tta 여기 너에게 온 편지가 있다; ***this is ~ you*** ikŏsŭn nŏrŭl wihan kŏshida 이것은 너를 위한 것이다; ***what is there ~ lunch?*** chŏmshimŭro muŏshi issŭmnikka? 점심으로 무엇이 있습니까?; ***the steak is ~ me*** kŭ sŭt'eik'ŭnŭn che kŏshimnida 그 스테이크는 제 것입니다; ***what is this ~?*** ikŏsŭn muŏse sayongdoennŭn kŏshimnikka? 이것은 무엇에 사용되는 것입니까?; ***what ~?*** wae kŭron-gayo? 왜 그런가요? ◊ (*time*) ... tong-an ... 동안; ***~ three days / two hours*** sam il/tu shikan tong-an 삼 일/두 시간 동안; ***please get it done ~ Monday*** wŏryoire kkŭnnaejuseyo 월요일에 끝내주세요 ◊ (*distance*): ***I walked ~ a mile*** nanŭn il mairŭl kŏrŏtssŏyo 나는 일 마일을 걸었어요; ***it stretches ~ 100 miles*** kŭgŏsŭn 100mairina ppŏdŏ issŏyo 그것은 100마일이나 뻗어 있어요 ◊ (*in favor of*): ***I am ~ the idea*** nanŭn kŭ saenggagi choayo 나는 그 생각이 좋아요 ◊ (*instead of, in behalf of*): ***let me do that ~ you*** chega taeshin haedŭrigessŭmnida 제가 대신 해드리겠습니다; ***we are agents ~ ...*** urinŭn ...ŭl/rŭl taehaenghamnida 우리는 ...을/를 대행합니다 ◊ (*in

exchange for): ***I bought it ~ $25*** 25tallŏrŭl chugo sat-tta 25달러를 주고 샀다; ***how much did you sell it ~?*** kŭgŏsŭl ŏlmae p'aratssŭmnikka? 그것을 얼마에 팔았습니까?

forbid kŭmjihada 금지하다; ***~ X to do Y*** Xege Yhanŭn kŏsŭl kŭmjihada X에게 Y하는 것을 금지하다

forbidden *adj* kŭmjidoen 금지된; ***~ city*** chagŭmsŏng 자금성; ***it's ~*** kŭgŏsŭn kŭmjidoeŏ issŭmnida 그것은 금지되어 있습니다; ***smoking / parking ~*** kŭmnyŏn / chuch'a kŭmji 금연 / 주차 금지

forbidding hŏmak'an 험악한

force 1 *n* (*violence*) p'ongnyŏk 폭력; (*of explosion, wind, punch*) him 힘; ***come into ~*** (*of law etc*) yuhyohaejida 유효해지다; ***the ~s*** MIL chŏn-gun 전군 **2** *v/t door, lock* pusuda 부수다; ***~ X to do Y*** Xege Yhal kŏsŭl kangyohada X에게 Y할 것을 강요하다; ***~ X open*** Xŭl / rŭl ŏktchiro yŏlda X을 / 를 억지로 열다

forced *laugh, smile* ŏktchiŭi 억지의; *confession* kangjejŏgin 강제적인

forced landing pisang ch'angnyuk 비상 착륙

forceful *argument* himch'an 힘찬; *speaker* sŏldŭngnyŏk innŭn 설득력 있는; *character* wŏn-giwangsŏnghan 원기왕성한

forceps kyŏmja 겸자

forcible *entry* kangjejŏgin 강제적인; *argument* kangnyŏk'an 강력한

ford *n* yat'ŭn yŏul 얕은 여울

fore: ***come to the ~*** yumyŏnghaejida 유명해지다

foreboding pulgirhan yegam 불길한 예감; **forecast 1** *n* yesang 예상; (*of weather*) kisang yebo 기상 예보 **2** *v/t* yesanghada 예상하다; **forecourt** (*of service station*) kŭbyuhanŭn kot 급유하는 곳; **forefathers** chosang 조상; **forefinger** chipkke sonkkarak 집게 손가락; **foregone**: ***that's a ~ conclusion*** kŭgŏsŭn ch'ŏŭmbut'ŏ ppŏnhan kyŏllonida 그것은 처음부터 뻔한 결론이다; **foreground** chŏn-gyŏng 전경; **forehand** (*in tennis*) p'ohaendŭ 포핸드; **forehead** ima 이마

foreign oegugŭi 외국의

foreign affairs oemu 외무

foreign currency oehwa 외화

foreigner oegugin 외국인

foreign exchange oeguk'wan 외국환; **foreign language** oegugŏ 외국어; **Foreign Office** *Br* Oemubu 외무부; **foreign policy** oemu chŏngch'aek 외무 정책; **Foreign Minister** *Br* oemu changgwan 외무 장관

foreman kongjangjang 공장장; LAW paeshimwŏnjang 배심원장; **foremost** kajang chungnyohan 가장 중요한; **forerunner** sŏndu chuja 선두 주자; **foresee** yegyŏnhada 예견하다; **foreseeable** yegyŏnhal su innŭn 예견할 수 있는; ***in the ~ future*** kakkaun changnaee 가까운 장래에; **foresight** sŏn-gyŏnjimyŏng 선견지명

forest sup 숲

forestry imhak 임학

foretaste sajŏn kyŏnghŏm 사전 경험

foretell yeŏnhada 예언하다

forever yŏng-wŏnhi 영원히

foreword sŏmun 서문

forfeit *v/t* sangshirhada 상실하다

forge *v/t* (*counterfeit*) mojohada 모조하다; *signature* wijohada 위조하다

forger wijoja 위조자

forgery (*bank bill, document*) wijo 위조

forget it-tta 잊다

forgetful chal ijŏbŏrinŭn 잘 잊어버리는

forget-me-not (*flower*) mulmangch'o 물망초

forgive *v/t & v/i* yongsŏhada 용서하다

forgiveness yongsŏ 용서

fork *n* p'ok'ŭ 포크; (*in road*) pun-gitchŏm 분기점

♦**fork out** *v/i* F (*pay*) tonŭl naeda 돈을 내다

forklift (**truck**) chigech'a 지게차

form 1 *n* (*shape*) hyŏngt'ae 형태; (*document*) yangshik 양식 **2** *v/t* (*in clay etc*) mandŭlda 만들다; *friendship* maet-tta 맺다; *opinion* seuda 세우다; *past tense etc*

hwaryonghada 활용하다 **3** *v/i* (*take shape*, *develop*) kuch'ehwadoeda 구체화되다
formal hyŏngshiktchŏgin 형식적인; *recognition etc* kongtchŏgin 공적인
formality hyŏngshik 형식; ***it's just a ~*** kŭnyang hyŏngshigil ppunimnida 그냥 형식일 뿐입니다
formally *adv speak*, *behave* hyŏngshiktchŏgŭro 형식적으로; *recognized* kongtchŏgŭro 공적으로
format 1 *v/t diskette* p'omaet'ada 포맷하다; *document* yangshik'wahada 양식화하다 **2** *n* (*size*: *of magazine*, *paper etc*) k'ŭgi 크기; (*make-up*: *of program*) hyŏngshik 형식
formation (*act of forming*) hyŏngsŏng 형성; **~ *flying*** p'yŏndae pihaeng 편대 비행
formative hyŏngsŏnghanŭn 형성하는; ***in his ~ years*** kŭŭi in-gyŏk hyŏngsŏnggie 그의 인격 형성기에
former chŏnŭi 전의; ***the*** ~ chŏnja 전자
formerly ijŏne 이전에
formidable musŏun 무서운
formula MATH, CHEM kongshik 공식; (*for success etc*) pangbŏp 방법
formulate (*express*) myŏnghwak'i p'yohyŏnhada 명확히 표현하다
fort MIL yosae 요새
forth: ***back and ~*** apttwiro 앞뒤로; ***and so ~*** kit'a tŭngdŭng 기타 등등
forthcoming (*future*) tagaonŭn 다가오는; *personality* saenggagŭl t'ŏnonnŭn 생각을 터놓는
fortieth mahŭn pŏntchaeŭi 마흔 번째의
fortnight *Br* tu chu 두 주
fortress MIL yosae 요새
fortunate un choŭn 운 좋은
fortunately un chok'edo 운 좋게도
fortune un 운; (*lot of money*) k'ŭn ton 큰 돈; ***good ~*** haeng-un 행운
fortune-teller chŏmjaeng-i 점쟁이
forty mahŭn 마흔, saship 사십
forward 1 *adv* ap'ŭro 앞으로 **2** *adj pej*: *person* kŏnbangjin 건방진 **3** *n* SP p'owŏdŭ 포워드 **4** *v/t letter* hoesonghada 회송하다
forwarding agent COM unsuŏptcha 운수업자
fossil hwasŏk 화석
foster child ibyang-a 입양아
foster parents yangbumo 양부모
foul 1 *n* SP panch'ik 반칙 **2** *adj smell*, *taste* yŏkkyŏun 역겨운; *weather* chidok'an 지독한 **3** *v/t* SP panch'igŭro panghaehada 반칙으로 방해하다
found *v/t school etc* sŏllip'ada 설립하다
foundation (*of theory etc*) kŭn-gŏ 근거; (*organization*) chaedan 재단
foundations (*of building*) kich'o 기초
founder *n* sŏlliptcha 설립자
foundry chujo kongjang 주조 공장
fountain punsu 분수
four net 넷, sa 사
four-star *hotel* mugunghwa nesŭi 무궁화 넷의
four-stick game yut 윷
fourteen yŏllet 열 넷, shipssa 십사
fourteenth yŏlne pŏntchaeŭi 열 네 번째의
fourth ne pŏntchaeŭi 네 번째의
fowl kagŭmnyu 가금류
fox *n* yŏu 여우
fraction ilbubun 일부분; (*decimal*) punsu 분수
fracture 1 *n* kŭm 금 **2** *v/t* …e kŭmgage hada …에 금가게 하다
fragile kkaejigi shwiun 깨지기 쉬운
fragment *n* (*of vase etc*) chogak 조각; (*of story*, *conversation*) tanp'yŏn 단편
fragmentary tanp'yŏntchŏgin 단편적인
fragrance hyanggi 향기
fragrant hyangginanŭn 향기나는
frail yak'an 약한
frame 1 *n* (*of picture*, *window*) t'ŭl 틀; (*of eyeglasses*) t'e 테; (*of bicycle*) ppyŏdae 뼈대; **~ *of mind*** kibun 기분 **2** *v/t picture* t'ŭre kkiuda 틀에 끼우다; F *person* numyŏng ssŭiuda 누명 씌우다
framework kusang 구상
France P'ŭrangssŭ 프랑스
frank soltchik'an 솔직한
frankly soltchik'i 솔직히

frantic mich'in tŭt'an 미친 듯한
fraternal hyŏngjeŭi 형제의
fraud sagi 사기; (*person*) sagikkun 사기꾼
fraudulent sagiŭi 사기의
frayed *cuffs* p'ullin 풀린
freak 1 *n* (*unusual event*) pyŏndŏk 변덕; (*two-headed person, animal etc*) kihyŏng 기형; F (*strange person*) pyŏltchong 별종; ***movie / jazz ~*** F (*fanatic*) yŏnghwagwang / chaejŭgwang 영화광 / 재즈광 **2** *adj storm etc* toryŏnhan 돌연한; ***~ wind*** tolp'ung 돌풍
freckle chugŭnkkae 주근깨
free 1 *adj* (*at liberty*) chayuŭi 자유의; (*no cost*) muryŏŭi 무료의; *room, table* pin 빈; ***are you ~ this afternoon?*** onŭl ohue shigan issŭseyo? 오늘 오후에 시간 있으세요?; ***~ and easy*** yŏyuroun 여유로운; ***for ~*** muryoro 무료로 **2** *v/t prisoners* sŏkppanghada 석방하다
freebie F tŏm 덤
freedom chayu 자유
freedom of the press ŏllonŭi chayu 언론의 자유
free kick (*in soccer*) p'ŭrik'ik 프리킥; **freelance 1** *adj* chayu kyeyagŭi 자유 계약의 **2** *adv work* chayu kyeyagŭro 자유 계약으로; **freelancer** p'ŭriraensŏ 프리랜서; **free market economy** chayu shijang kyŏngje 자유 시장 경제; **free sample** muryo kyŏnbon 무료 견본; **free speech** ŏllonŭi chayu 언론의 자유; **freeway** kosokttoro 고속도로; **freewheel** *v/i* (*on bicycle*) p'edarŭl tteda 페달을 떼다
freeze 1 *v/t food, river* ŏllida 얼리다; *wages, bank account* tonggyŏrhada 동결하다; *video* sun-gan chŏngjishik'ida 순간 정지시키다 **2** *v/i* (*of water*) ŏlda 얼다
♦**freeze over** (*of river*) sumyŏni orŏbut-tta 수면이 얼어붙다
freezer naengdongshil 냉동실
freezing 1 *adj* mopsshi ch'uun 몹시 추운; *water* mopsshi ch'agaun 몹시 차가운; ***it's ~ (cold)*** (*of weather*) mopsshi ch'upssŭmnida 몹시 춥습니다; (*of water*) mopsshi ch'agapssŭmnida 몹시 차갑습니다; ***I'm ~ (cold)*** chŏnŭn mopsshi ch'uwŏyo 저는 몹시 추워요 **2** *n* naengdong 냉동; ***10 below ~*** yŏngha 10to 영하 10도
freezing compartment naengdongshil 냉동실
freezing point pingtchŏm 빙점
freight *n* hwamul 화물; (*costs*) hwamul unsongnyo 화물 운송료
freight car hwamulch'a 화물차
freighter (*ship*) hwamulsŏn 화물선; (*airplane*) hwamul pihaenggi 화물 비행기
freight train hwamul yŏlch'a 화물 열차
French 1 *adj* P'ŭrangssŭŭi 프랑스의 **2** *n* (*language*) P'ŭrangssŭŏ 프랑스어; ***the ~*** P'ŭrangssŭin 프랑스인
French doors ssang-yŏdaji yurimun 쌍여닫이 유리문; **French fries** kamja t'wigim 감자 튀김; (*fast food*) hurench'ihurai 후렌치후라이; **Frenchman** P'ŭrangssŭ namja 프랑스 남자; **Frenchwoman** P'ŭrangssŭ yŏja 프랑스 여자
frequency pinbŏnham 빈번함; RAD chup'asu 주파수; ***the increasing ~ of X*** Xi / ga palsaenghanŭn hoessuŭi chŭngga X이 / 가 발생하는 횟수의 증가
frequent[1] *adj* chajŭn 잦은; *visitor* chaju onŭn 자주 오는
frequent[2] *v/t bar* chaju ch'at-tta 자주 찾다
frequently chaju 자주
fresh *air, water, food* shinsŏnhan 신선한; *complexion* saenggiinnŭn 생기있는; (*cold*) ssalssarhan 쌀쌀한; *start* saeroun 새로운; (*impertinent*) kŏnbangjin 건방진; ***feel ~*** sangk'waehada 상쾌하다
♦**freshen up 1** *v/i* sshit-tta 씻다 **2** *v/t room, paintwork* saedanjanghada 새단장하다
freshman shinipssaeng 신입생
freshness (*of fruit, meat*) shinsŏndo 신선도; (*of style, approach*) shinsŏnham 신선함; (*of weather*) ssalssarham 쌀쌀함

freshwater *adj* minmurŭi 민물의
fret *v/i* kominhada 고민하다
friction mach'al 마찰
friction tape chŏn-gisŏnyong komut'eip'ŭ 전기선용 고무테이프
Friday kŭmnyoil 금요일
fridge naengjanggo 냉장고
friend ch'in-gu 친구; ***make ~s*** (*of one person*) ch'in-gurŭl sagwida 친구를 사귀다; (*of two people*) ch'in-guga toeda 친구가 되다; ***make ~s with X*** Xwa / kwa ch'in-guga toeda X와 / 과 친구가 되다
friendly *adj atmosphere* tajŏnghan 다정한; *person* ch'inhan 친한; (*easy to use*) shwiun 쉬운; ***be ~ with X*** (*be friends*) Xwa / kwa ch'inhage toeda X와 / 과 친하게 되다
friendship ujŏng 우정
fries hurench'ihurai 후렌치후라이
fright kkamtchak nollam 깜짝 놀람; ***give X a ~*** Xŭl / rŭl kkamtchak nollage hada X을 / 를 깜짝 놀라게 하다
frighten *v/t* kŏptchuda 겁주다; ***be ~ed*** kŏmnada 겁나다; ***don't be ~ed*** kŏmnaeji maseyo 겁내지 마세요; ***be ~ed of*** ... i / ga kŏmnada ...이 / 가 겁나다
frightening kŏmnanŭn 겁나는
frigid (*sexually*) pulgamtchŭng-ŭi 불감증의
frill (*on dress etc*) p'ŭril 프릴; (*fancy extra*) pugamul 부가물
fringe (*on dress, curtains etc*) sul 술; (*in hair*) ammŏri 앞머리; (*edge*) kajangjari 가장자리
frisk *v/t* momsusaek'ada 몸수색하다
frisky *puppy etc* kiun chok'e ttwiŏdaninŭn 기운 좋게 뛰어다니는
♦**fritter away** *time, fortune* hŏbihada 허비하다
frivolous shirŏmnŭn 실없는
frizzy *hair* kopssŭlgŏrinŭn 곱슬거리는
frog kaeguri 개구리
frogman chamsubu 잠수부
from ◊ (*in time*) ...(esŏ)but'ŏ ...(에서)부터; ***~ 9 to 5 (o'clock)*** ahopsshibut'ŏ tasŏsshikkaji 9시부터 5시까지; ***~ the 18th century*** 18segibut'ŏ 18세기부터; ***~ today on*** onŭlbut'ŏ 오늘부터; ***~ next Tuesday*** taŭm chu hwayoilbut'ŏ 다음 주 화요일부터 ◊ (*in space*) ...esŏ(but'ŏ) ...에서(부터); ***~ here to there*** yŏgiesŏ chŏgiro 여기에서 저기로; ***we drove here ~ Seoul*** urinŭn Sŏuresŏ yŏgikkaji unjŏnhae wassŭmnida 우리는 서울에서 여기까지 운전해 왔습니다 ◊ (*origin: of people*) ...(ŭ)robut'ŏ ...(으)로부터; ***a letter ~ Jo*** Chorobut'ŏ on p'yŏnji 조로부터 온 편지; ***a gift ~ the management*** kyŏng-yŏngjinŭrobut'ŏŭi sŏnmul 경영진으로부터의 선물; ***it doesn't say who it's ~*** igŏsŭn nuguegesŏ on kŏshinji palk'yŏit-tchi ant'a 이것은 누구에게서 온 것인지 밝혀있지 않다; ***I am ~ New Jersey*** chŏnŭn Nyujŏji ch'ulsshinimnida 저는 뉴저지 출신입니다; ***made ~ bananas*** pananaro mandŭn 바나나로 만든 ◊ (*because of*) ...(ŭ)ro ...(으)로; ***tired ~ the journey*** yŏhaeng-ŭro chich'in 여행으로 지친; ***it's ~ overeating*** nŏmu mani mŏgŏsŏ kŭrŏt'a 너무 많이 먹어서 그렇다
front 1 *n* (*of building, book*) ap 앞; (*cover organization*) kanp'an 간판; MIL, (*of weather*) chŏnsŏn 전선; ***a cold / warm ~*** hannaeng / onnan chŏnsŏn 한랭 / 온난 전선; ***in ~*** ap'e(sŏ) 앞에(서); (*in a race*) sŏndue(sŏ) 선두에(서); ***in ~ of*** ...ŭi aptchoge(sŏ) ...의 앞쪽에(서); ***at the ~*** ap'e(sŏ) 앞에(서); ***at the ~ of*** ...ŭi aptchoge(sŏ) ...의 앞쪽에(서) **2** *adj wheel, seat* aptchogŭi 앞쪽의 **3** *v/t TV program* chinhaenghada 진행하다
front cover p'yoji 표지; **front door** ammun 앞문; **front entrance** chŏngmun 정문
frontier kuk-kkyŏng 국경; *fig* (*of knowledge, science*) ch'oech'ŏmdan 최첨단
front page (*of newspaper*) ilmyŏn 일면; **front page news** ilmyŏn kisa 일면 기사; **front row** aptchul 앞줄; **front seat passenger** (*in car*) aptchwasŏk sŭnggaek 앞좌석 승객; **front-wheel drive** ap-ppak'wi

kullim 앞바퀴 굴림
frost sŏri 서리
frostbite tongsang 동상
frostbitten tongsang-e kŏllin 동상에 걸린
frosted glass pult'umyŏnghan yuri 불투명한 유리
frosting (*on cake*) sŏlt'ang-ŭl ip'im 설탕을 입힘
frosty *weather* sŏriga naerinŭn 서리가 내리는; *welcome* naengdamhan 냉담한
froth *n* kŏp'um 거품
frothy *cream etc* kŏp'umi manŭn 거품이 많은
frown 1 *n* tchip'urin ŏlgul 찌푸린 얼굴 **2** *v/i* tchip'urida 찌푸리다
frozen ŏrŭn 얼은; *wastes of Siberia* kŭk'anŭi 극한의; ***I'm ~*** F ch'uwŏsŏ ŏl chigyŏng-iyeyo 추워서 얼 지경이에요; ***a ~ chicken / pizza*** naengdong tak / p'ija 냉동 닭 / 피자
frozen food naengdong shikp'um 냉동 식품
fruit kwail 과일
fruitful *discussions etc* sŏngkkwaga manŭn 성과가 많은
fruit juice kwail chussŭ 과일 쥬스
fruit salad kwail saellŏdŭ 과일 샐러드
frustrate *v/t person, plans* chwajŏlsshik'ida 좌절시키다
frustrated *look, sigh* chwajŏldoen 좌절된
frustrating tchajŭngnanŭn 짜증나는
frustratingly *slow, hard* tchajŭngnadorok 짜증나도록
frustration chwajŏlgam 좌절감; ***sexual ~*** sŏngtchŏk yok-kku pulman 성적 욕구 불만; ***the ~s of modern life*** hyŏndaejŏk salme taehan chwajŏl 현대적 삶에 대한 좌절
fry *v/t* chijida 지지다; (*stir-~*) poktta 볶다; (*deep-~*) t'wigida 튀기다
fried egg kyeran hurai 계란 후라이
fried potatoes kamja t'wigim 감자 튀김
frying pan huraip'aen 후라이팬
fuck *v/t* V ...wa / kwa sŏnggyohada ...와 / 과 성교하다; ***~!*** sshibal 씨발!; ***~ him / that!*** sshibal nom / nomŭi kŏt! 씨발 놈 / 놈의 것!
♦**fuck off** V kkŏjida 꺼지다; ***~!*** kkojyŏbŏryŏ! 꺼져버려!
fucking V **1** *adj* chidok'an 지독한 **2** *adv* chidok'age 지독하게
fuel *n* yŏllyo 연료
fugitive *n* tomangja 도망자
fulfill shirhaenghada 실행하다; ***feel ~ed*** (*in job, life*) manjok'ada 만족하다
fulfilling *job* manjokssŭrŏun 만족스러운
fulfillment (*of contract etc*) shirhaeng 실행; (*spiritual*) manjok-kkam 만족감
full *bottle* kadŭk ch'an 가득 찬; *hotel, bus, diskette* kkwak ch'an 꽉 찬; *account, report* sangsehan 상세한; *life* pappŭn 바쁜; *schedule, day* ppadŭt'an 빠듯한; ***~ of*** ...(ŭ)ro kadŭk'an ...(으)로 가득한; ***~ up*** *hotel etc* kadŭk ch'ada 가득 차다; (*with food*) paeburŭda 배부르다; ***pay in ~*** chŏnaegŭl naeda 전액을 내다; ***sorry, we're ~*** (*at hotel*) choesonghajiman, ta ch'assŭmnida 죄송하지만, 다 찼습니다
full cover (*insurance*) chonghap pohŏm 종합 보험; **full-grown** ta charan 다 자란; **full-length** *dress* chŏnshindaeŭi 전신대의; *movie* changp'yŏnŭi 장편의; **full moon** porŭmttal 보름달; **full stop** mach'imp'yo 마침표; **full-time 1** *adj worker, job* chŏnshiganjeŭi 전시간제의 **2** *adv work* chŏnshiganjero 전시간제로
fully ta 다, wanjŏnhi 완전히; *describe* sangsehi 상세히
fumble *v/t catch* sŏt'urŭge chaptta 서투르게 잡다
♦**fumble around** tŏdŭmgŏrimyŏ ch'at-tta 더듬거리며 찾다
fume: ***be fuming*** F kyŏngnohada 격노하다
fumes maeyŏn 매연
fun chaemi 재미; ***it was great ~*** kŭgŏsŭn chŏngmal chaemiissŏssŏyo 그것은 정말 재미있었어요; ***bye, have ~!*** annyŏnghi kyeseyo, chaemiitkke chinaeseyo! 안녕히

계세요, 재미있게 지내세요!; ***for ~*** chaemiro 재미로; ***make ~ of*** …ŭl/rŭl nollida …을/를 놀리다

function 1 *n* (*of employee*) chingnŭng 직능; (*of machine part*) kinŭng 기능; (*reception etc*) haengsa 행사 **2** *v/i* chakttonghada 작동하다; ***~ as*** …ŭi kinŭng-ŭl hada …의 기능을 하다

function key COMPUT kinŭngk'i 기능키

fund 1 *n* chagŭm 자금 **2** *v/t project etc* …e chagŭmŭl chegonghada …에 자금을 제공하다

fundamental (*basic*) kibonjŏgin 기본적인; (*substantial*) ponjiltchŏgin 본질적인; (*crucial*) chung-yohan 중요한

fundamentally *different, altered* ponjiltchŏgŭro 본질적으로

funeral changnyeshik 장례식

funeral home yŏng-anso 영안소

funfair yuwŏnji 유원지

funicular (**railway**) k'eibŭl ch'ŏltto 케이블 철도

funnel *n* (*of ship*) kulttuk 굴뚝

funnily (*oddly*) isanghage 이상하게; (*comically*) utkkige 웃기게; ***~ enough*** isanghagedo 이상하게도

funny (*comical*) usŭun 우스운; (*odd*) isanghan 이상한

fur (*of coat, animal*) t'ŏl 털

furious (*angry*) kyŏngnohanŭn 격노하는; ***at a ~ pace*** maengnyŏrhan sokttoro 맹렬한 속도로

furnace hwadŏk 화덕; (*for metal*) yonggwangno 용광로

furnish *room* …e kagurŭl tŭryŏ not'a …에 가구를 들여 놓다; (*supply*) konggŭp'ada 공급하다

furniture kagu 가구; ***a piece of ~*** kagu han chŏm 가구 한 점

furry *animal, coat* t'ŏri p'ungsŏnghan 털이 풍성한

further 1 *adj* (*additional*) tto tarŭn 또 다른; (*more distant*) tŏ mŏn 더 먼; ***until ~ notice*** ch'uhu t'ongjiga issŭl ttaekkaji 추후 통지가 있을 때까지; ***have you anything ~ to say?*** tŏ marhal kŏshi issŭshimnikka? 더 말할 것이 있으십니까? **2** *adv walk, drive* tŏ 더; ***~, I want to say …*** chega tŏtppuch'yŏ marhago ship'ŭn kŏsŭn … imnida 제가 덧붙여 말하고 싶은 것은 … 입니다; ***2 miles ~ (on)*** 2mailboda tŏ mŏn 2마일보다 더 먼 **3** *v/t cause etc* chojanghada 조장하다

furthest 1 *adj* kajang mŏn 가장 먼 **2** *adv* kajang mŏlli 가장 멀리

furtive *glance* ŭnmirhan 은밀한

fury (*anger*) kyŏngno 격노

fuse ELEC **1** *n* p'yujŭ 퓨즈 **2** *v/i* p'yujŭga kkŭnk'ida 퓨즈가 끊기다 **3** *v/t* p'yujŭrŭl kkŭnt'a 퓨즈를 끊다

fusebox tukkŏbijip 두꺼비집

fuselage tongch'e 동체

fuse wire tohwasŏn 도화선

fusion yunghap 융합

fuss *n* nallibŏpssŏk 난리법석; ***make a ~*** (*complain*) nallich'ida 난리치다; (*behave in exaggerated way*) nallibŏpssŏk ttŏlda 난리법석 떨다; ***make a ~ of*** (*be very attentive to*) …ege modŭn kwanshimŭl ssot-tta …에게 모든 관심을 쏟다

fussy *person* kkadaroun 까다로운; *design etc* chinach'ige kkumin 지나치게 꾸민; ***be a ~ eater*** shikssŏng-i kkadaroptta 식성이 까다롭다

futile ssŭltte ŏmnŭn 쓸데 없는

future *n* mirae 미래; GRAM miraehyŏng 미래형; ***in ~*** miraeenŭn 미래에는

futures FIN sŏnmul kyeyak 선물 계약

futures market FIN sŏnmul shijang 선물 시장

futuristic *design* ch'ohyŏndaejŏgin 초현대적인

fuzzy *hair* kopssŭlgopssŭrhan 곱슬곱슬한; (*out of focus*) hŭrit'an 흐릿한

G

gadget kanttanhan togu 간단한 도구
gag 1 *n* chaegal 재갈; (*joke*) kaegŭ 개그 **2** *v/t person* …ege chaegarŭl mullida …에게 재갈을 물리다; *the press* ogap'ada 억압하다
gain *v/t* (*acquire*) ŏt-tta 얻다; **~ *speed*** sokttorŭl naeda 속도를 내다; **~ 5 *pounds*** op'aundŭga nŭlda 5파운드가 늘다
gale kangp'ung 강풍
gall bladder ssŭlgae 쓸개
gallery (*for art*) hwarang 화랑; (*in theater*) maen wich'ŭng kwallamsŏk 맨 위층 관람석
galley (*on ship*) chubang 주방
gallon kaellŏn 갤런
gallop *v/i* chiltchuhada 질주하다
gallows kyosudae 교수대
gallstone tamsŏk 담석
gamble tobak'ada 도박하다
gambler tobak-kkun 도박꾼
gambling tobak 도박
game *n* shihap 시합; (*of baseball, football*) kyŏnggi 경기; (*children's*) nori 놀이; (*in tennis*) keim 게임
gang p'aegŏri 패거리; (*of criminals*) kaeng 갱
♦**gang up on** p'aejiŏ konggyŏk'ada 패지어 공격하다
gangster nappŭn muri 나쁜 무리
gangway t'ongno 통로
gap (*in wall, teeth*) t'ŭm 틈; (*for parking, in figures*) pin-got 빈 곳; (*in time, conversation*) kongbaek 공백; (*between opinions, characters*) ch'ai 차이
gape *v/i* (*of person*) ibŭl ttak pŏlligo paraboda 입을 딱 벌리고 바라보다
♦**gape at** ibŭl ttak pŏllin ch'ae nŏkssŭl ilk'o ch'yŏdaboda 입을 딱 벌린 채 넋을 잃고 쳐다보다
gaping: **~ *hole*** k'ŭge pŏrŏjin kumŏng 크게 벌어진 구멍
garage (*for parking*) ch'ago 차고; (*for gas*) chuyuso 주유소; (*for repairs*) chadongch'a suriso 자동차 수리소
garbage ssŭregi 쓰레기; *fig* (*useless stuff*) ssŭlmoŏmnŭn kŏt 쓸모없는 것; (*poor quality item*) pullyangp'um 불량품; (*nonsense*) maldo an toenŭn sori 말도 안 되는 소리; ***don't talk ~!*** mal katchi anŭn sori hajido mara! 말 같지 않은 소리 하지도 마라!
garbage can ssŭregi t'ong 쓰레기 통; **garbage collection** ssŭregi sujip 쓰레기 수집; **garbage dump** ssŭregi p'yegijang 쓰레기 폐기장
garden chŏng-wŏn 정원, ttŭl 뜰
gardener (*professional*) chŏng-wŏnsa 정원사; ***he's an enthusiastic ~*** kŭnŭn chŏng-wŏnesŏ irhanŭn kŏsŭl choahaeyo 그는 정원에서 일하는 것을 좋아해요
gardening wŏnye 원예
gargle *v/i* ibanŭl kashida 입안을 가시다
garish chinach'ige hwaryŏhan 지나치게 화려한
garland *n* hwahwan 화환
garlic manŭl 마늘
garment ŭibok 의복
garnish *v/t* komyŏng-ŭro changshik'ada 고명으로 장식하다
garrison *n* (*place*) kun chudunji 군 주둔지; (*troops*) chudun-gun 주둔군
garter kat'ŏ 가터
gas *n* kich'e 기체; (*for cooking*) kasŭ 가스; (*gasoline*) hwibaryu 휘발유
gash *n* kilgo kipkke pein sangch'ŏ 길고 깊게 베인 상처
gasket kasŭk'et 가스켓
gasoline hwibaryu 휘발유
gasp 1 *n* hŏlttŏk-kkŏrim 헐떡거림; ***with a ~*** hŏlttŏk-kkŏrimyŏ 헐떡거리며 **2** *v/i* hŏlttŏk-kkŏrida 헐떡거리다; **~ *for breath*** sumŭl

hŏlttŏgida 숨을 헐떡이다
gas pedal aekssellŏreit'ŏ p'edal 액셀러레이터 페달; **gas pump** chuyu p'ŏmp'ŭ 주유 펌프; **gas station** chuyuso 주유소
gate taemun 대문; (*at airport*) t'apssŭnggu 탑승구
gatecrash ch'odaebat-tchi ank'o kada 초대받지 않고 가다
gateway (*entrance*) ipkku 입구; (*passage*) t'ongno 통로; *fig* kwanmun 관문
gather 1 *v/t facts, information* moŭda 모으다; ~ ***speed*** songnyŏgŭl nŭllyŏgada 속력을 늘려가다; ***am I to ~ that …?*** …rago ihaehamyŏn matssŭmnikka? …라고 이해하면 맞습니까? **2** *v/i* (*understand*) ch'uch'ŭk'ada 추측하다
♦**gather up** *possessions* …ŭl/rŭl chuwŏ moŭda …을/를 주워 모으다
gathering *n* (*group of people*) moim 모임
gaudy ch'onsŭrŏpkke hwaryŏhan 촌스럽게 화려한
gauge 1 *n* kyegi 계기 **2** *v/t pressure* ch'ŭktchŏnghada 측정하다; *opinion* p'andanhada 판단하다
gaunt such'ŏk'an 수척한
gauze kŏjŭ 거즈
gay 1 *n* (*homosexual*) tongsŏngaeja 동성애자 **2** *adj* tongsŏngaeŭi 동성애의
gaze 1 *n* ŭngshi 응시 **2** *v/i* ŭngshihada 응시하다
♦**gaze at** …ŭl/rŭl ŭngshihada …을/를 응시하다
GB (= ***Great Britain***) Yŏngguk 영국
GDP (= ***gross domestic product***) kungnae ch'ongsaengsan 국내 총생산
gear *n* (*equipment*) yonggu 용구; (*in vehicles*) kiŏ 기어
gear shift kiŏ chŏnhwan changch'i 기어 전환 장치
gel (*for hair*) chel 젤; (*for shower*) mulbinu 물비누
gem posŏk 보석; *fig* (*book etc*) myŏngjak 명작; (*person*) pobaegat'ŭn saram 보배같은 사람
gender sŏng 성
gene yujŏnja 유전자; ***it's in his ~s*** kŭ saramŭi ch'ŏnsŏng-ida 그 사람의 천성이다
genealogy book chokppo 족보
general 1 *n* (*in army*) changgun 장군; ***in ~*** ilbanjŏgŭro 일반적으로 **2** *adj* ilbanjŏgin 일반적인; (*overall*) chŏnch'ejŏgin 전체적인
general anesthetic chŏnshin mach'wi 전신 마취
general election ch'ongsŏn-gŏ 총선거
generalization ilbanhwa 일반화
generalize ilbanhwahada 일반화하다
generally ilbanjŏgŭro 일반적으로
generate (*create*) nat-tta 낳다; *electricity* palssaengshik'ida 발생시키다; (*in linguistics*) saengsŏnghada 생성하다; *feeling* irŭk'ida 일으키다; *accident, new situation etc* yagihada 야기하다
generation (*of family*) sedae 세대
generation gap sedae ch'ai 세대 차이
generator paltchŏn-gi 발전기
generosity nŏgŭrŏum 너그러움
generous (*with money*) inshim choŭn 인심 좋은; (*not too critical*) kwandaehan 관대한; *portion etc* p'ungbuhan 풍부한
genetic yujŏnjŏgin 유전적인
genetically yujŏnjŏgŭro 유전적으로
genetic engineering yujŏn konghak 유전 공학
genetic fingerprint yujŏnja chimun 유전자 지문
geneticist yujŏnhaktcha 유전학자
genetics yujŏnhak 유전학
genial *person, company* tajŏnghan 다정한
genitals saengshikki 생식기
genius ch'ŏnjae 천재
gentle pudŭrŏun 부드러운; *person* onhwahan 온화한
gentleman shinsa 신사
gents (*toilet*) namja hwajangshil 남자 화장실
genuine chintchaŭi 진짜의; *person* chinshirhan 진실한
geographical *features* chirijŏk 지리적
geography (*of area, subject*) chiri

지리
geological *features* chijirŭi 지질의; *survey* chijirhaktchŏk 지질학적
geologist chijirhaktcha 지질학자
geology (*of area*) chijil 지질; (*subject*) chijirhak 지질학
geometric(al) kihahaktchŏk 기하학적
geometry kihahak 기하학
geriatric 1 *adj* noinppyŏng-ŭi 노인병의 **2** *n* noin 노인
germ segyun 세균; (*of idea etc*) ssak 싹
German 1 *adj* Togirŭi 독일의 **2** *n* (*person*) Togirin 독일인; (*language*) Togirŏ 독일어
Germany Togil 독일
germ warfare segyunjŏn 세균전
gesticulate sontchisŭro marhada 손짓으로 말하다
gesture *n* (*with hand*) sontchit 손짓; *fig* (*of friendship*) ŭisa p'yoshi 의사 표시
get 1 *v/t* ◊ (*obtain*) ŏt-tta 얻다; (*fetch*) kajyŏoda 가져오다; (*receive*) pat-tta 받다; (*catch*: *bus*, *train etc*) t'ada 타다; (*understand*) alda 알다; ***I don't ~ it*** (*don't understand*) ihaehal su ŏpssŏyo 이해할 수 없어요 ◊ (*become*) ...haejida ...해지다; ***~ tired*** / ***careless*** p'igonhaejida / pujuŭihaejida 피곤해지다 / 부주의해지다; ***be ~ting older*** / ***warmer*** chŏmjŏm nŭlgŏgada / tŏwŏjida 점점 늙어가다 / 더워지다 ◊ (*causative*): ***~ sth done*** muŏsŭl hage hada 무엇을 하게 하다; ***~ s.o. to do sth*** nuguege muŏsŭl harago hada 누구에게 무엇을 하라고 하다; ***you must ~ him to agree*** kŭrŭl pandŭshi sŏlttŭkshik'yŏya hamnida 그를 반드시 설득시켜야 합니다; ***~ one's hair cut*** mŏrirŭl charŭda 머리를 자르다; ***~ the car washed*** sech'ashik'ida 세차시키다; ***~ the car fixed*** ch'arŭl surishik'ida 차를 수리시키다; ***~ sth ready*** muŏsŭl hal chunbirŭl kach'uda 무엇을 할 준비를 갖추다; ***~ going*** (*leave*) ttŏnada 떠나다 ◊ (*have opportunity*): ***~ to do sth*** muŏsŭl haepoda 무엇을 해보다; ***~ to know*** alge toeda 알게 되다 ◊: ***have got*** kajida 가지다; ***I've got some money*** tonŭl chom kajigo issŏyo 돈을 좀 가지고 있어요; ***I've got something for you*** tangshinhant'e chul kŏshi issŏyo 당신한테 줄 것이 있어요; ***I've got a headache*** mŏriga ap'ayo 머리가 아파요 ◊ (*have ~ to*) ...haeya hada ...해야 하다; ***I have got to study*** / ***see him*** nanŭn kongbuhaeya hamnida / kŭrŭl mannaboaya hamnida 나는 공부해야 합니다 / 그를 만나보아야 합니다; ***I don't want to, but I've got to*** wŏnhajinŭn anch'iman haeyahamnida 원하지는 않지만 해야합니다 **2** *v/i* (*arrive*) toch'ak'ada 도착하다
◆**get about** (*travel*) yŏgijŏgi yŏhaenghada 여기저기 여행하다; (*be mobile*) toratanida 돌아다니다
◆**get along** (*progress*) chinaeda 지내다; (*to party etc*) kada 가다; (*with s.o.*) saiga chot'a 사이가 좋다
◆**get at** (*criticize*) pinjŏngdaeda 빈정대다; (*imply*, *mean*) marharyŏhada 말하려하다
◆**get away 1** *v/i* (*leave*) ttŏnada 떠나다 **2** *v/t*: ***get sth away from s.o.*** nuguegesŏ muŏsŭl ppaeat-tta 누구에게서 무엇을 빼앗다
◆**get away with** *crime etc* pŏl pat-tchi ank'o haenaeda 벌 받지 않고 해내다
◆**get back 1** *v/i* toraoda 돌아오다; ***I'll ~ to you on that*** kŭgŏse taehan ŭngdabŭl tŭrigessŭmnida 그것에 대한 응답을 드리겠습니다 **2** *v/t* (*obtain again*) toech'at-tta 되찾다
◆**get by** (*pass*) chinagada 지나가다; (*financially*) kkuryŏnagada 꾸려나가다
◆**get down 1** *v/i* (*from ladder etc*) naeryŏgada 내려가다; (*duck etc*) ŏpttŭrida 엎드리다 **2** *v/t* (*depress*) uurhaehada 우울해하다
◆**get down to** *work* shijak'ada 시작하다; *real facts* tat'a 닿다
◆**get in 1** *v/i* (*of train*, *plane*) toch'ak'ada 도착하다; (*come home*)

chibe tŭrŏoda 집에 들어오다; (*to car*) t'ada 타다; ***how did they ~?*** (*of thieves, snakes etc*) ŏttŏk'e tŭrŏgassŭlkkayo? 어떻게 들어갔을까요? **2** *v/t* (*to suitcase etc*) chibŏ nŏt'a 집어 넣다

♦**get off 1** *v/i* (*from bus etc*) naerida 내리다; (*finish work*) iri kkŭnnada 일이 끝나다; (*not be punished*) pŏrŭl myŏnhada 벌을 면하다 **2** *v/t clothes, hat, footwear* pŏt-tta 벗다; *lid, top* pŏtkkida 벗기다; ***~ the grass!*** chandie tŭrŏgaji mashio! 잔디에 들어가지 마시오!

♦**get off with** *Br* (*sexually*) ...wa / kwa chŭlgida ...와 / 과 즐기다; ***~ a small fine*** kabyŏun pŏlgŭmŭro momyŏnhada 가벼운 벌금으로 모면하다

♦**get on 1** *v/i* (*to bike, bus, train*) t'ada 타다; (*be friendly*) saiga chot'a 사이가 좋다; (*become old*) naidŭrŏ kada 나이들어 가다; (*make progress*) chinch'ŏkttoeda 진척되다; ***it's getting on*** (*late*) shigani nŭjŏjinda 시간이 늦어진다; ***he's getting on*** kŭnŭn kkwae naidŭrŏganda 그는 꽤 나이들어간다; ***he's getting on for 50*** kŭnŭn nai oshibi ta toeŏt-tta 그는 나이 50이 다 되었다; ***he's getting on well at school*** kŭnŭn hak-kkyoesŏ chal haenagago it-tta 그는 학교에서 잘 해나가고 있다 **2** *v/t lid, top of box* ssŭiuda 씌우다; *boots* shintta 신다; ***~ the bus / one's bike*** pŏssŭe / chajŏn-gŏe t'ada 버스에 / 자전거에 타다; ***I can't get these pants on*** i pajirŭl ibŭl suga ŏpssŭmnida 이 바지를 입을 수가 없습니다

♦**get out 1** *v/i* (*from car etc*) naerida 내리다; (*of prison*) naoda 나오다; ***~!*** nagayo! 나가요!; ***let's ~ of here*** yŏgiesŏ nagapsshida 여기에서 나갑시다; ***I don't ~ much these days*** yojŭm pyŏllo pakke nagaji ansŭmnida 요즘 별로 밖에 나가지 않습니다 **2** *v/t nail, sth jammed, gun, pen* ppaenaeda 빼내다; *stain* ŏpssaeda 없애다

♦**get over** *fence, disappointment etc* igyŏnaeda 이겨내다, kŭkppok'ada 극복하다; *lover* it-tta 잊다

♦**get over with**: ***let's get it over with*** kŭnyang huttak haebŏripsshida 그냥 후딱 해버립시다

♦**get through** (*on telephone*) t'onghwahada 통화하다; (*make self understood*) ihaeshik'ida 이해시키다

♦**get up 1** *v/i* (*in morning, from chair etc*) irŏnada 일어나다; (*of wind*) ilda 일다 **2** *v/t hill* orŭda 오르다

getaway (*from robbery*) tomang 도망; ***~ car*** toju ch'aryang 도주 차량

get-together ch'in-gyo moim 친교 모임

ghastly (*horrible*) chidok'an 지독한

gherkin chagŭn oi 작은 오이

ghetto pinmin-ga 빈민가

ghost kwishin 귀신

ghostly kwishin-gat'ŭn 귀신같은

giant 1 *n* kŏin 거인; *fig* kŏjang 거장 **2** *adj* kŏdaehan 거대한

gibberish hoengsŏlsusŏl 횡설수설

giblets choryuŭi naejang 조류의 내장

giddiness hyŏn-gitchŭng 현기증

giddy ŏjirŏun 어지러운

gift sŏnmul 선물; (*natural ability*) t'agonan chaenŭng 타고난 재능

gifted t'agonan chaenŭng-i innŭn 타고난 재능이 있는

giftwrap *v/t* p'ojanghada 포장하다

gigabyte COMPUT kigabait'ŭ 기가바이트

gigantic pangdaehan 방대한

giggle 1 *v/i* kkilkkil ut-tta 낄낄 웃다 **2** *n* kkilkkil usŭm 낄낄 웃음

gill (*of fish*) agami 아가미

gilt *n* kŭmbak 금박; ***~s*** FIN uryangju 우량주

gimmick (*promotional*) suppŏp 수법; (*new invention*) koanmul 고안물

gin chin 진; ***~ and tonic*** chint'onik 진토닉

ginger *n* (*spice*) saenggang 생강

gingerbeer chinjŏ piŏ 진저 비어; **gingerbread** saenggangppang 생강빵; **ginger tea** saenggangch'a 생강차

ginseng insam 인삼

gipsy chipsshi 집시

giraffe kirin 기린

girder *n* taedŭlbo 대들보
girl yŏja 여자; (*young*) sonyŏ 소녀
girl friend yŏja ch'in-gu 여자 친구; (*lover*) aein 애인
girl guide sonyŏ tanwŏn 소녀단원
girlie magazine p'orŭno chaptchi 포르노 잡지
girl scout kŏlsŭk'aut'ŭ 걸스카우트
gist yotchŏm 요점
give chuda 주다; *fml* tŭrida 드리다; (*supply: electricity etc*) konggŭp'ada 공급하다; *~ a talk* iyagirŭl haejuda 이야기를 해주다; *~ a cry* ulda 울다; *~ a groan* shinŭmhada 신음하다; *~ her my regards* kŭnyŏege anburŭl chŏnhaejuseyo 그녀에게 안부를 전해주세요
♦**give away** (*as present*) chuda 주다; (*betray*) paebanhada 배반하다; ***give oneself away*** uyŏnhi p'ongnohada 우연히 폭로하다
♦**give back** tollyŏjuda 돌려주다
♦**give in 1** *v/i* (*surrender*) kulbok'ada 굴복하다 **2** *v/t* (*hand in*) chech'urhada 제출하다
♦**give off** *smell, fumes* naeda 내다
♦**give onto** (*open onto*) …(ŭ)ro t'onghada …(으)로 통하다
♦**give out 1** *v/t leaflets etc* paebuhada 배부하다 **2** *v/i* (*of supplies, strength*) tahada 다하다
♦**give up 1** *v/t smoking etc* kkŭnt'a 끊다; ***give oneself up to the police*** kyŏngch'are chasuhada 경찰에 자수하다 **2** *v/i* (*cease habit*) kkŭnt'a 끊다; (*stop making effort*) p'ogihada 포기하다
♦**give way** (*of bridge etc*) munŏjida 무너지다
given name *sŏng-ŭl cheoehan irŭm* 성을 제외한 이름
glacier pingha 빙하
glad kippŭn 기쁜; *~ to see you* mannasŏ pan-gapssŭmnida 만나서 반갑습니다; ***yes, I will be ~ to*** ye, kikkŏi hagessŏyo 예, 기꺼이 하겠어요
gladly kikkŏi 기꺼이
glamor maeryŏk 매력
glamorous maeryŏgi nŏmch'inŭn 매력이 넘치는
glance 1 *n* hŭlgŭt pom 흘긋 봄 **2** *v/i*: *~ at* …ŭl/rŭl hŭlgŭt poda …을/를 흘긋 보다
gland sŏn 선
glandular fever sŏnyŏl 선열
glare 1 *n* (*of sun, headlights*) nunbushinŭn pit 눈부시는 빛 **2** *v/i* (*of sun, headlights*) nunbushige pinnada 눈부시게 빛나다
♦**glare at** noryŏboda 노려보다
glaring *adj mistake* nune hwak ttŭinŭn 눈에 확 띄는
glass (*material*) yuri 유리; (*for drink*) k'ŏp 컵
glasses an-gyŏng 안경
glaze *n* yuyak 유약
♦**glaze over** (*of eyes*) nune saenggirŭl ilt'a 눈에 생기를 잃다
glazed *expression* hŭrit'an 흐릿한
glazier yuriŏptcha 유리업자
glazing (*glass*) yuri 유리
gleam 1 *n* ŏsŭrehan pit 어스레한 빛 **2** *v/i* ŏsŭrehage pich'ida 어스레하게 비치다
glee kippŭm 기쁨
gleeful kippŏhanŭn 기뻐하는
glib ipsshim choŭn 입심 좋은
glide (*of bird, plane*) hwalgonghada 활공하다; (*of person, furniture*) mikkŭrojida 미끄러지다
glider SP kŭllaidŏ 글라이더
gliding *n* SP kŭllaidŏ kyŏnggi 글라이더 경기
glimmer 1 *n* (*of light*) hŭimihan pit 희미한 빛; *~ of hope* shillalgat'ŭn hŭimang 실날같은 희망 **2** *v/i* kkamppagida 깜빡이다
glimpse 1 *n* hŭlkkŭt pom 흘끗 봄; ***catch a ~ of*** …ŭl/rŭl hŭlkkŭt poda …을/를 흘끗 보다 **2** *v/t* hŭlkkŭt poda 흘끗 보다
glint 1 *n* pantchak 반짝 **2** *v/i* (*of light*) pantchak pinnada 반짝 빛나다; (*of eyes*) pŏnttŭgida 번득이다
glisten *v/i* pantchak-kkŏrida 반짝거리다
glitter *v/i* pantchakpantchak pinnada 반짝반짝 빛나다
glitterati sagyogye saramdŭl 사교계 사람들
gloat *v/i* kosohaehada 고소해하다; ~

over kosohaehada 고소해하다
global (*worldwide*) chŏnsegyeŭi 전세계의; (*without exception*) t'onggwaljŏgin 통괄적인
global economy segye kyŏngje 세계 경제
globalization segyehwa 세계화
global market segye shijang 세계 시장
global warming segye onnanhwa 세계 온난화
globe (*the earth*) chigu 지구; (*model of earth*) chigubon 지구본
gloom (*darkness*) ŏduk'ŏmk'ŏmham 어두컴컴함; (*mood*) uul 우울
gloomy *room* ŏduk'ŏmk'ŏmhan 어두컴컴한; *mood*, *person* uurhan 우울한
glorious *weather* malgŭn 맑은; *victory* yŏnggwangsŭrŏun 영광스러운
glory *n* yŏnggwang 영광
gloss *n* (*shine*) yun 윤; (*general explanation*) chusŏk 주석
glossary yong-ŏ p'uri 용어 풀이
gloss paint kwangt'aek p'eint'ŭ 광택 페인트
glossy 1 *adj paper* kwangt'aek nanŭn 광택 나는 **2** *n* (*magazine*) kogŭp chaptchi 고급 잡지
glove changgap 장갑; (*in baseball*) yagu kŭllŏbŭ 야구 글러브
glow 1 *n* (*of light*) paengnyŏl 백열; (*of fire*) t'aorŭm 타오름; (*in cheeks*) taraorŭm 달아오름 **2** *v/i* (*light*) pich'ŭl naeda 빛을 내다; (*fire*) t'ada 타다 **2** *v/i* (*cheeks*) taraorŭda 달아오르다
glowing *description* yŏllyŏrhan 열렬한
glue 1 *n* p'ul 풀 **2** *v/t* p'ullo puch'ida 풀로 붙이다; **~ *X to Y*** Xŭl / rŭl Ye p'ullo puch'ida X을 / 를 Y에 풀로 붙이다
glum shimuruk'an 시무룩한
glutinous rice ch'apssal 찹쌀
glutton taeshikka 대식가
gluttony p'oksshik 폭식
GMT (= ***Greenwich Mean Time***) segye p'yojunshi 세계 표준시
gnarled *branch* madit'usŏng-iin 마디투성이인; *hands* kŏch'in 거친
gnat kakttagwi 각다귀
gnaw *v/t bone* kaltta 갉다
GNP (= ***gross national product***) kungmin ch'ongsaengsan 국민 총생산
Go (*game*) Paduk 바둑
go 1 *n*: ***on the ~*** chulgot irhayŏ 줄곧 일하여 **2** *v/i* kada 가다; (*leave*: *of train*, *plane*) ch'ulbarhada 출발하다; (*leave*: *of people*) ttŏnada 떠나다; (*work*, *function*) chakttonghada 작동하다; (*become*) …haejida …해지다; (*come out*: *of stain etc*) ŏpssŏjida 없어지다; (*cease*: *of pain etc*) sarajida 사라지다; (*match*: *of colors etc*) ŏullida 어울리다; **~ *quiet*** choyonghaejida 조용해지다; **~ *shopping* / *jogging*** shyop'ingharŏ / chogingharŏ kada 쇼핑하러 / 조깅하러 가다; ***I must be ~ing*** ije kayaman hamnida 이제 가야만 합니다; ***let's ~!*** kapsshida! 갑시다!; **~ *for a walk*** sanch'aek'ada 산책하다; **~ *to bed*** charŏ kada 자러 가다; **~ *to school*** hak-kkyoe kada 학교에 가다; ***how's the work ~ing?*** iri ŏttŏk'e toeŏgamnikka? 일이 어떻게 되어갑니까?; ***they're ~ing for $50*** kŭgŏsŭn 50tallŏe p'amnida 그것은 50달러에 팝니다; ***hamburger to ~*** haembŏgo p'ojanghaejuseyo 햄버거 포장해주세요; ***it's all gone*** ta ŏpssŏjyŏt-tta 다 없어졌다; ***be ~ing to do sth*** muŏsŭl hal kŏshida 무엇을 할 것이다
♦**go ahead** kŭrŏk'e haseyo 그렇게 하세요
♦**go ahead with** *plans etc* ch'ujinhada 추진하다
♦**go along with** *suggestion* …e ttarŭda …에 따르다
♦**go at** (*attack*) tŏmbyŏdŭlda 덤벼들다
♦**go away** (*of person*) ttŏnada 떠나다; (*of rain*) kŭch'ida 그치다; (*of pain*, *clouds*) sarajida 사라지다
♦**go back** (*return*) toragada 돌아가다; (*date back*) kŏsŭllŏ ollagada 거슬러 올라가다; **~ *to sleep*** tashi chada 다시 자다; ***we ~ a long way*** urinŭn orae algo chinaen saiyeyo 우리는

오래 알고 지낸 사이에요
♦**go by** (*go past*) chinagada 지나가다
♦**go down 1** *v/t stairs etc* naeryŏgada 내려가다 **2** *v/i* (*of sun*) chida 지다; (*of ship, swelling*) karaantta 가라앉다; **~ *well / badly*** (*of suggestion etc*) chok'e / nappŭge padadŭryŏjida 좋게 / 나쁘게 받아들여지다
♦**go for** (*attack*) tŏmbyŏdŭlda 덤벼들다; (*like*) choahada 좋아하다
♦**go in** (*to room, of sun*) turŏgada 들어가다; (*fit: of part etc*) mat-tta 맞다
♦**go in for** *competition, race* ch'ultchŏnhada 출전하다; (*like*) chŭlgida 즐기다
♦**go off 1** *v/i* (*leave*) kabŏrida 가버리다; (*of bomb*) p'okpparhada 폭발하다; (*of gun*) palssadoeda 발사되다; (*of alarm*) ullida 울리다; (*of milk etc*) sanghada 상하다 **2** *v/t* (*stop liking*) …i / ga shirŏjida …이 / 가 싫어지다
♦**go on** (*continue*) kyesok'ada 계속하다; (*happen*) irŏnada 일어나다; ***~, do it!*** (*encouraging*) kwaench'anayo, haeboseyo! 괜찮아요, 해보세요!; ***what's going on?*** musŭn il issŏyo? 무슨 일 있어요?; **~ *about*** ...e taehae kyesok ttŏdŭrŏdaeda ...에 대해 계속 떠들어대다
♦**go on at** (*nag*) …ege chansorihada …에게 잔소리하다; *husband* …ŭl / rŭl pagaji kŭltta …을 / 를 바가지 긁다
♦**go out** (*of person*) nagada 나가다; (*of light, fire*) kkŏjida 꺼지다
♦**go over** *v/t* (*check*) kŏmt'ohada 검토하다
♦**go through** *v/t illness, hard times* kyŏktta 겪다; (*check*) myŏnmirhi chosahada 면밀히 조사하다; (*read through*) t'ongdok'ada 통독하다
♦**go under** (*sink*) karaantta 가라앉다; (*of company*) manghada 망하다
♦**go up** (*climb, in price*) ollagada 올라가다
♦**go without 1** *v/t food etc* … ŏpsshi saragada … 없이 살아가다 **2** *v/i* ŏpsshi chinaeda 없이 지내다
goad *v/t* koerop'ida 괴롭히다
go-ahead 1 *n* hŏga 허가; ***get the ~*** hŏgabat-tta 허가받다 **2** *adj* (*enterprising, dynamic*) chinch'wijŏgin 진취적인
goal SP (*target*) kol 골; (*points*) tŭktchŏm 득점; (*objective*) mokp'yo 목표
goalkeeper kolk'ip'ŏ 골키퍼
goalpost kolttae 골대
goat yŏmso 염소
♦**gobble up** kegŏlsŭrŏpkke mŏktta 게걸스럽게 먹다
go-between chunggaeja 중개자
God Hanŭnim 하느님; ***thank ~!*** a, sarat-tta 아, 살았다; ***oh ~!*** sesang-e! 세상에!
god shin 신
goddess yŏshin 여신
godfather taebu 대부
godforsaken *place, town* hwangnyanghan 황량한
goggles poan-gyŏng 보안경; (*for skiing*) kogŭl 고글; (*for swimming*) muran-gyŏng 물안경
going *adj price etc* hyŏnjaeŭi 현재의; **~ *concern*** sujiga mannŭn saŏp 수지가 맞는 사업
goings-on pinan padŭl manhan haeng-wi 비난 받을 만한 행위
gold 1 *n* kŭm 금 **2** *adj* kŭmŭi 금의
golden *hair* kŭmsaegŭi 금색의
golden handshake t'oejikkŭm 퇴직금
golden wedding anniversary kŭmhonshik 금혼식
goldfish kŭmbung-ŏ 금붕어; **gold medal** kŭmmedal 금메달; **goldsmith** kŭmsegongsa 금세공사
golf kolp'ŭ 골프
golf club (*organization, stick*) kolp'ŭ k'ŭllŏp 골프 클럽
golf course kolp'ŭjang 골프장
golfer kolp'ŭ ch'inŭn saram 골프 치는 사람
gong (*iron*) ching 징; (*brass*) kkwaenggwari 꽹과리
good choŭn 좋은; ***a ~ many*** aju manŭn 아주 많은; ***be ~ at*** …ŭl / rŭl charhada …을 / 를 잘하다; ***be ~ for***

s.o. nuguege chot'a 누구에게 좋다
goodbye annyŏng 안녕; (*polite: to the person who is leaving*) annyŏnghi kaseyo 안녕히 가세요; (*polite: to the person who is staying*) annyŏnghi kyeseyo 안녕히 계세요; ***say ~ to s.o.*** nuguege chakppyŏl insarŭl hada 누구에게 작별 인사를 하다
good-for-nothing *n* amu ssŭlmo ŏmnŭn saram 아무 쓸모없는 사람; **Good Friday** Sŏnggŭmnyoil 성금요일; **good-humored** myŏngnanghan 명랑한; **good-looking** chal saenggin 잘 생긴; **good-natured** sŏnggyŏgi choŭn 성격이 좋은
goodness (*moral*) tŏk 덕; (*nutritional*) yŏngnyangbun 영양분; ***thank ~!*** komawŏra! 고마워라!
goods COM sangp'um 상품
goodwill hoŭi 호의
goody-goody *n* F ch'ak'an ch'ŏk'anŭn saram 착한 척하는 사람
gooey kkŭnjŏk-kkŭnjok'an 끈적끈적한
goof *v/i* F pabojisŭl hada 바보짓을 하다
goose kŏwi 거위
gooseberry kujŭberi 구즈베리
gooseflesh: ***it gives me ~*** narŭl sorŭmkkich'ige handa 나를 소름끼치게 한다
gorge 1 *n* hyŏpkkok 협곡 **2** *v/t*: ***~ oneself on sth*** muŏsŭl p'oshik'ada 무엇을 포식하다
gorgeous *weather* hwach'anghan 화창한; *dress, woman, hair, smell* kŭnsahan 근사한
gorilla korilla 고릴라
go-slow t'aeŏp 태업
Gospel (*in Bible*) Pogŭmsŏ 복음서
gossip 1 *n* chapttam 잡담; (*person*) hŏmdam 험담 **2** *v/i* chapttamhada 잡담하다
govern *country* tasŭrida 다스리다
government chŏngbu 정부
governor (*of province*) chisa 지사
gown (*long dress*) kin kŏt'ot 긴 겉옷; (*wedding dress*) weding tŭresŭ 웨딩 드레스; (*of judge*) pŏp-ppok 법복; (*of surgeon*) kaun 가운
grab *v/t* puyŏjaptta 부여잡다; ***~ something to eat*** kanshigŭl mŏktta 간식을 먹다; ***~ a nap*** hansum chada 한숨 자다
grace (*quality*) ua 우아
graceful uahan 우아한
gracious *person, style, living* p'umwi innŭn 품위 있는; ***good ~!*** chŏrŏn! 저런!
grade 1 *n* (*quality*) tŭnggŭp 등급; (*year in school*) hangnyŏn 학년; (*in exam*) sŏngjŏk 성적 **2** *v/t* tŭnggŭbŭl maegida 등급을 매기다; EDU *papers* sŏngjŏgŭl ŏt-tta 성적을 얻다;
grade crossing RAIL sup'yŏng kŏnnŏlmok 수평 건널목
gradient kyŏngsado 경사도
gradual chŏmch'ajŏgin 점차적인
gradually chŏmch'ajŏgŭro 점차적으로
graduate 1 *n* chorŏpssaeng 졸업생; (*at graduate school*) taehagwŏn hakssaeng 대학원 학생 **2** *v/i* chorŏp'ada 졸업하다
graduate school taehagwŏn 대학원
graduation chorŏp 졸업
graffiti naksso 낙서
graft *n* BOT chŏppuch'igi 접붙이기; MED ishik chojik 이식 조직; F (*corruption*) pujŏng pup'ye 부정 부패
grain nadal 낟알; (*in wood*) namutkkyŏl 나뭇결; ***go against the ~*** sŏngjire mat-tchi ant'a 성질에 맞지 않다
gram kŭraem 그램
grammar munppŏp 문법
grammatical munppŏpssang-ŭi 문법상의
grand 1 *adj* ungjanghan 웅장한; F (*very good*) widaehan 위대한 **2** *n* F (*$1000*) ch'ŏn tallŏ 천 달러
grandad haraboji 할아버지; **grandchild** (*male*) sonja 손자; (*female*) sonnyŏ 손녀; **granddaughter** sonnyŏ 손녀
grandeur ungjangham 웅장함
grandfather harabŏji 할아버지; **grandma** halmŏni 할머니; **grandmother** halmŏni 할머니; **grandpa** harabŏji 할아버지; **grandparents** chobumo 조부모; **grand piano**

kŭraendŭ p'iano 그랜드 피아노; **grandson** sonja 손자; **grandstand** t'ŭkppyŏl kwallamsŏk 특별 관람석
granite hwagang-am 화강암
granny halmŏni 할머니
grant 1 *n* (*money*) pojogŭm 보조금; (*for university, school*) changhak-kkŭm 장학금 **2** *v/t wish, peace* tŭrŏjuda 들어주다; *visa* hŏgahada 허가하다; *request* sŭng-inhada 승인하다; ***take sth for ~ed*** muŏsŭl tang-yŏnhan illo yŏgida 무엇을 당연한 일로 여기다; ***take s.o. for ~ed*** nugurŭl tang-yŏnhage yŏgida 누구를 당연하게 여기다
granule chagŭn algaeng-i 작은 알갱이
grape p'odo 포도
grapefruit kŭreip'ŭp'ŭrut'ŭ 그레이프프루트; **grapefruit juice** kŭreip'ŭp'ŭrut'ŭ chusŭ 그레이프프루트 주스; **grapevine**: ***hear sth through the ~*** muŏsŭl somunŭro tŭt-tta 무엇을 소문으로 듣다
graph top'yo 도표
graphic 1 *adj* (*vivid*) saengsaenghan 생생한 **2** *n* COMPUT kŭraep'ik 그래픽
graphics COMPUT kŭraep'ikssŭ 그래픽스
♦ **grapple with** *attacker* ...wa / kwa matpput'ŏ ssauda ...와 / 과 맞붙어 싸우다; *problem etc* ...wa / kwa sshirŭmhada ...와 / 과 씨름하다
grasp 1 *n* (*physical*) umk'yŏjapkki 움켜잡기; (*mental*) ihaeryŏk 이해력 **2** *v/t* (*physically*) umk'yŏjaptta 움켜잡다; (*understand*) ihaehada 이해하다
grass p'ul 풀
grasshopper mettugi 메뚜기; **grass widow** kwabugat'ŭn shinse 과부같은 신세; **grass widower** horabigat'ŭn shinse 홀아비같은 신세
grassy p'uri ugŏjin 풀이 우거진
grate[1] *n* (*metal*) soesalttae 쇠살대
grate[2] **1** *v/t carrots etc* pibyŏ pusŭrŏttŭrida 비벼 부스러뜨리다 **2** *v/i* (*of sound*) kŏsŭllida 거슬리다
grateful komapkke yŏginŭn 고맙게 여기는; ***be ~ to*** ...ŭl / rŭl komapkke yŏgida ...을 / 를 고맙게 여기다
grater kangp'an 강판
gratification manjoksshik'igi 만족시키기
gratify manjoksshik'ida 만족시키다
grating 1 *n* soe kyŏktcha ttukkŏng 쇠격자 뚜껑 **2** *adj sound, voice* kwie kŏsŭllinŭn 귀에 거슬리는
gratitude kamsa 감사
gratuity t'ip 팁
grave[1] *n* mudŏm 무덤
grave[2] *adj error* chungdaehan 중대한; *face, voice* kŭnŏmhan 근엄한
gravel *n* chagal 자갈
gravestone chagal 자갈
graveyard myoji 묘지
gravity PHYS chungnyŏk 중력
gravy yuktchŭp 육즙
gray *adj* hoesaegŭi 회색의; ***be going ~*** paekppari toeda 백발이 되다
gray-haired paekpparŭi 백발의
grayhound kŭreihaundŭ 그레이하운드
graze[1] *v/i* (*of cow, horse*) p'urŭl ttŭdŏmŏktta 풀을 뜯어먹다
graze[2] **1** *v/t arm etc* kabyŏpkke sŭch'ida 가볍게 스치다 **2** *n* (*on arm etc*) ch'algwasang 찰과상
grease (*for cooking*) yuji 유지; (*for car*) yunhwalyu 윤활유
greasy kirŭmkki manŭn 기름기 많은
great (*in size*) koengjanghi k'ŭn 굉장히 큰; (*in amount*) koengjanghi manŭn 굉장히 많은; (*outstanding*) hyŏnjŏhan 현저한; (*very important*) chungdaehan 중대한; *composer, writer* tae... 대...; F (*very good*) koengjanghi choŭn 굉장히 좋은; ~ ***composer*** taejak-kkok-kka 대작곡가; ***how was it? - ~*** ŏttaessŏyo? – koengjanghi choassŏyo 어땠어요? – 굉장히 좋았어요; ~ ***to see you!*** mannasŏ nŏmu pan-gapssŭmnida! 만나서 너무 반갑습니다!
Great Britain Yŏngguk 영국
Great Han Empire Taehanjeguk 대한제국
greatly koengjanghi 굉장히
greatness widaeham 위대함
greed yoksshim 욕심
greedy yoksshim manŭn 욕심 많은

green nokssaegŭi 녹색의; (*environmentally*) hwan-gyŏng pohoŭi 환경 보호의
greenhorn F p'unnaegi 풋내기; **greenhouse** onshil 온실; **greenhouse effect** onshil hyokkwa 온실 효과; **greenhouse gas** isanhwat'anso 이산화탄소; **green tea** nokch'a 녹차
greet insahada 인사하다
greeting insa 인사
grenade suryut'an 수류탄
grid kyŏktcha 격자
gridiron SP mishik ch'uk-kku kyŏnggijang 미식 축구 경기장
gridlock (*in traffic*) kyot'ongmang chŏngch'e 교통망 정체
grief pit'ong 비통
grievance pulp'yŏngkkŏri 불평거리
grieve pit'onghaehada 비통해하다; **~ *for s.o.*** nugurŭl irŏ pit'onghaehada 누구를 잃어 비통해하다
grill 1 *n* (*on window*) soech'angssal 쇠창살 **2** *v/t* (*interrogate*) shimmunhada 심문하다
grille soech'angssal 쇠창살
grim *look*, *person* ŏmhan 엄한; *prospect*, *future* naenghok'an 냉혹한
grimace *n* ŏlgurŭl tchip'urim 얼굴을 찌푸림
grime ttae 때
grimy ttaemudŭn 때묻은
grin 1 *n* shinggŭt usŭm 싱긋 웃음 **2** *v/i* shinggŭt ut-tta 싱긋 웃다
grind *v/t coffee*, *meat* kalda 갈다
grip 1 *n* (*on rope etc*) kkwak chabŭm 꽉 잡음; ***be losing one's ~*** (*losing one's skills*) nŭngnyŏgi ŏpssŏjida 능력이 없어지다 **2** *v/t* kkwak chaptta 꽉 잡다
gristle yŏn-gol 연골
grit *n* (*dirt*) mŏnji 먼지; (*for roads*) chan morae 잔 모래
groan 1 *n* shinŭm sori 신음 소리 **2** *v/i* shinŭmhada 신음하다
grocer shingnyo chap'wasang 식료 잡화상
groceries shingnyo chap'waryu 식료 잡화류
grocery store shingnyo chap'wajŏm 식료 잡화점
groin sat'aguni 사타구니
groom 1 *n* (*for bride*) shillang 신랑; (*for horse*) mabu 마부 **2** *v/t horse* sonjirhada 손질하다; (*train*, *prepare*) hullyŏnshik'ida 훈련시키다; ***well ~ed*** (*in appearance*) chal sonjildoen 잘 손질된
groove *n* hŭm 홈
grope 1 *v/i* (*in the dark*) sonŭro tŏdŭmtta 손으로 더듬다 **2** *v/t* (*sexually*) sonŭro tŏdŭmtta 손으로 더듬다
♦**grope for** *door*, *word* ch'at-tta 찾다
gross *adj* (*coarse*, *vulgar*) sangsŭrŏun 상스러운; *exaggeration* ŏmch'ŏngnan 엄청난; FIN ch'onggye 총계
gross domestic product kungnae ch'ongsaengsan 국내 총생산
gross national product kungmin ch'ongsaengsan 국민 총생산
ground 1 *n* ttang 땅; (*reason*) kŭn-gŏ 근거; ELEC chŏptchi 접지; ***on the ~*** hyŏnjang-e(sŏ) 현장에(서) **2** *v/t* ELEC chŏptchihada 접지하다
ground control chisang kwanje 지상 관제
ground crew chisang kŭnmuwŏn 지상 근무원
groundless kŭn-gŏ ŏmnŭn 근거 없는
ground meat kan kogi 간 고기; **groundnut** ttangk'ong 땅콩; **ground plan** p'yŏngmyŏndo 평면도; **ground staff** SP chŏngbiwŏn 정비원; (*at airport*) chisang kŭnmuwŏn 지상 근무원; **groundwork** kich'o chagŏp 기초 작업
group 1 *n* muri 무리; (*of companies*) kŭrup 그룹 **2** *v/t* murijit-tta 무리짓다
grow 1 *v/i* charada 자라다; (*of number*, *amount*) k'ŏjida 커지다; (*of business*) sŏngjanghada 성장하다; **~ *old* / ~ *tired*** nŭlgŏjida / p'igonhaejida 늙어지다 / 피곤해지다 **2** *v/t flowers* kirŭda 기르다
♦**grow up** (*of person*) charanada 자라나다; (*of city*) paltchŏnhada 발전하다; ***~!*** nai kapssŭl hae! 나이 값을 해!
growl 1 *n* ŭrŭrŏnggŏrinŭn sori 으르렁거리는 소리 **2** *v/i* ŭrŭrŏnggŏrida 으르렁거리다

grown-up 1 *n* ŏrŭn 어른 **2** *adj* ŏrŭnsŭrŏun 어른스러운
growth (*of person, company*) sŏngjang 성장; (*increase*) chŭngga 증가; MED chongyang 종양
grub (*of insect*) ttangbŏlle 땅벌레
grubby tŏrŏun 더러운
grudge 1 *n* yugam 유감; ***bear a ~*** yugamŭl kajida 유감을 가지다 **2** *v/t*: ***I don't ~ him his success*** kŭga sŏnggonghaedo pae anap'ayo 그가 성공해도 배 안아파요
grudging insaek'an 인색한
grueling *climb, task* nokch'oro mandŭnŭn 녹초로 만드는
gruff kulkko t'ak'an mokssori 굵고 탁한 목소리
grumble *v/i* t'udŏlgŏrida 투덜거리다
grumbler t'udŏlgŏrinŭn saram 투덜거리는 사람
grunt 1 *n* (*of pig*) kkulkkulgŏrim 꿀꿀거림; (*of person*) kŏch'in shinŭm 거친 신음 **2** *v/i* (*of pig*) kkulkkulgŏrida 꿀꿀거리다; (*of person*) kŏch'ilge shinŭmhada 거칠게 신음하다
guarantee 1 *n* pojŭng 보증; ***~ period*** pojŭng kigan 보증 기간 **2** *v/t* pojŭnghada 보증하다
guarantor pojŭng-in 보증인
guard 1 *n* (*security ~*) kyŏngbiwŏn 경비원; MIL poch'o 보초; (*in prison*) kyodogwan 교도관; ***be on one's ~ against*** ...ŭl / rŭl kyŏnggyehada ...을 / 를 경계하다 **2** *v/t* chik'ida 지키다
♦**guard against** ...ŭl / rŭl choshimhada ...을 / 를 조심하다
guarded *reply* choshimsŏng innŭn 조심성 있는
guardian LAW hugyŏnin 후견인
guerrilla kerilla 게릴라
guess 1 *n* ch'uch'ŭk 추측 **2** *v/t answer* ch'uch'ŭk'ada 추측하다; ***I ~ so*** kŭrŏn kŏt kat'ayo 그런 것 같아요; ***I ~ not*** kŭrŏch'i anŭn kŏt kat'ayo 그렇지 않은 것 같아요 **2** *v/i* ch'uch'ŭk'ada 추측하다
guesswork ŏrimjimjak 어림짐작
guest sonnim 손님
guesthouse yŏgwan 여관
guestroom sonnimnyong ch'imshil 손님용 침실
guffaw 1 *n* kaptchakssŭrŏn k'ŭn usŭm 갑작스런 큰 웃음 **2** *v/i* kaptchagi k'ŭge ut-tta 갑자기 크게 웃다
guidance annae 안내
guide 1 *n* (*person*) annaeja 안내자; (*book*) annaesŏ 안내서 **2** *v/t* annaehada 안내하다
guidebook annaesŏ 안내서
guided missile yudot'an 유도탄
guided tour kaidŭ t'uŏ 가이드 투어
guidelines chich'im 지침
guilt LAW pŏmjoe 범죄; (*moral*) choe 죄; (*guilty feeling*) choech'aek-kkam 죄책감
guilty LAW yujoeŭi 유죄의; (*responsible*) choe chiŭn 죄 지은; *look, smile* choe chiŭndŭt'an 죄 지은듯한; ***have a ~ conscience*** choech'aek-kkamŭl nŭkkida 죄책감을 느끼다
guinea pig morŭmot'ŭ 모르모트; *fig* shirhŏm chaeryo 실험 재료
guitar kit'a 기타
guitarist kit'a yŏnjuga 기타 연주가
gulf man 만; *fig* kip'ŭn t'ŭm 깊은 틈
gull kalmaegi 갈매기
gullet shiktto 식도
gullible sok-kki shwiun 속기 쉬운
gulp 1 *n* (*of water etc*) kkulkkŏk-kkulkkŏk mashim 꿀꺽꿀꺽 마심 **2** *v/i* (*in surprise*) sumŭl chugida 숨을 죽이다
♦**gulp down** *drink*, kkulkkŏk-kkulkkŏk mashida 꿀꺽꿀꺽 마시다; *breakfast, food* kŭp'i mŏktta 급히 먹다
gum[1] (*in mouth*) inmom 잇몸
gum[2] *n* (*glue*) chŏmsŏng komu 점성 고무; (*chewing ~*) kkŏm 껌
gun ch'ong 총
♦**gun down** ssoa nomŏttŭrida 쏘아 넘어뜨리다
gunfire p'ogyŏk 포격; **gunman** ch'onggi hyudaeja 총기 휴대자; (*robber*) mujang kangdo 무장 강도; **gunpowder** hwayak 화약; **gunshot** palp'o 발포; ***~ wound*** ch'ongsang 총상

gurgle *v/i* (*of baby*) mogŭl kkolttak-kkŏrida 목을 꼴딱거리다; (*of drain*) k'walk'wal hŭllŏnaoda 콸콸 흘러나오다
gush *v/i* (*of liquid*) p'ŏngp'ŏng sosanaoda 펑펑 솟아나오다
gushy F (*very enthusiastic*) chinach'ige kamsangjŏgin 지나치게 감상적인
gust *n* tolp'ung 돌풍
gusty *weather* parami shimhan 바람이 심한; ~ ***wind*** tolp'ung 돌풍
gut 1 *n* ch'angja 창자; F (*stomach*) pae 배; **~s** F (*courage*) yonggi 용기 **2** *v/t* (*of fire*) t'aewŏbŏrida 태워버리다
gutter (*on sidewalk*) torang 도랑; (*on roof*) homt'ong 홈통
guy F namja 남자; ***hey, you ~s*** ŏi, yŏrŏbun 어이, 여러분
gym ch'eyuk-kkwan 체육관
gymnasium ch'eyuk-kkwan 체육관
gymnast ch'eyuk kyosa 체육 교사
gymnastics ch'ejo 체조
gynecologist sanbuinkkwa ŭisa 산부인과 의사
gypsy chipsshi 집시

H

habit p'orŭt 버릇, sŭpkkwan 습관
habitable kŏjuhal su innŭn 거주할 수 있는
habitat sŏshiktchi 서식지
habitual sŭpkkwanjŏgin 습관적인; *smoker, drinker* sangsŭptchŏgin 상습적인
hack *n* (*poor writer*) samnyu chakkka 삼류 작가
hacker COMPUT haek'ŏ 해커
hackneyed chinbuhan 진부한
haddock taeguŭi iltchong 대구의 일종
haggard such'ŏk'an 수척한
haggle (*over price*) kkaktta 깎다
hail *n* ubak 우박
hair t'ŏl 털; (*on person's head*) mŏri 머리; (*single human* ~) mŏrik'arak 머리카락; ***short* ~ / *long* ~** tchalbŭn / kin mŏri 짧은 / 긴 머리
hairbrush mŏri sol 머리 솔; **haircut**: ***have a* ~** mŏrirŭl charŭda 머리를 자르다; **hairdo** mŏrihyŏng 머리형; **hairdresser** miyongsa 미용사; ***at the ~'s*** miyongshiresŏ 미용실에서; **hairdrier**, **hairdryer** heŏdŭraiŏ 헤어드라이어
hairless t'ŏri ŏmnŭn 털이 없는
hairpin mŏrip'in 머리핀; **hairpin curve** Uchahyŏng k'ŏbŭ U자형 커브; **hair-raising** mŏrikkŭch'i tchuppyŏt'aejinŭn 머리끝이 쭈뼛해지는; **hair remover** chemoyongp'um 제모용품; **hair-splitting** *n*: ***that's just* ~** sasohan ire shin-gyŏngssŭnŭn kŏshiyeyo 사소한 일에 신경쓰는 것이에요; **hairstyle** mŏrihyŏng 머리형
hairy *arm, animal* t'ori manŭn 털이 많은; F *frightening* musŏun 무서운
half 1 *n* pan 반; **~ (*past*) *ten*** yŏlshi pan 열시 반; **~ *an hour*** pan shigan 반 시간; **~ *a pound*** pan p'aundŭ 반 파운드 **2** *adj* panŭi 반의 **3** *adv*: ***~ eaten / finished*** panŭn mŏgŭn / kkŭnnan 반은 먹은 / 끝난; ***only ~ understood*** panman ihaedoen 반만 이해된
half-hearted maŭmi naek'iji annŭn 마음이 내키지 않는; **half time** *n* SP chunggan hyushik 중간 휴식; **halfway 1** *adj stage, point* chunggan chijŏmŭi 중간 지점의 **2** *adv* chunggane 중간에
hall (*large room*) hol 홀; (*hallway in house*) poktto 복도
halo wŏn-gwang 원광
halt 1 *v/i* mŏmch'uda 멈추다 **2** *v/t* mŏmch'ugehada 멈추게하다 **3** *n* chŏngji 정지; ***come to a* ~** mŏmch'uda 멈추다
halve *v/t* panŭro hada 반으로 하다
ham haem 햄
hamburger haembŏgŏ 햄버거
hammer 1 *n* mangch'i 망치 **2** *v/i* mangch'ijirhada 망치질하다; **~ *at the door*** munŭl k'wangk'wang tudŭrida 문을 쾅쾅 두드리다
hammock haemŏk 해먹
hamper[1] *n* (*for food*) paguni 바구니
hamper[2] *v/t* (*obstruct*) panghaehada 방해하다
hamster haemsŭt'ŏ 햄스터
hand 1 *n* son 손; (*of clock*) shigye panŭl 시계 바늘; (*worker*) ilsson 일손; ***at ~, to ~*** kakkaie 가까이에; ***at first ~*** chiktchŏptchogŭro 직접적으로; ***by ~*** sonŭro 손으로; *deliver* inp'yŏnŭro 인편으로; ***on the one ~ ..., on the other ~*** hanp'yŏnŭronŭn ..., tarŭn hanp'yŏnŭronŭn 한편으로는 ..., 다른 한편으로는; ***in ~*** (*being done*) kkŭnnanŭn chung-in 끝나는 중인; ***on your right ~*** orŭntchok panghyang-ŭro 오른쪽 방향으로; ***~s off!*** son tteseyo! 손 떼세요!; ***~s up!*** son tŭrŏ! 손 들어!; ***change ~s***

imjaga pakkwida 임자가 바뀌다
♦**hand down** *heirloom etc* mullyŏjuda 물려주다
♦**hand in** chech'urhada 제출하다
♦**hand on** chŏnhada 전하다
♦**hand out** nanuŏ chuda 나누어 주다
♦**hand over** kŏnnejuda 건네주다; (*to authorities*) nŏmgyŏjuda 넘겨주다
handbag *Br* son-gabang 손가방, haendŭbag 핸드백; **handbook** annaech'aektcha 안내책자; **handcuffs** sugap 수갑
handicap *n* (*physical*) shinch'e chang-ae 신체 장애; *fig* pullihan chokkŏn 불리한 조건
handicapped (*physically*) shinch'e chang-aeja innŭn 신체 장애가 있는; (*mentally*) chŏngshin chang-aeja innŭn 정신 장애가 있는; **~ *by a lack of funds*** chagŭm pujogŭro pullihan 자금 부족으로 불리한
handicraft sugong-ye 수공예
handiwork sugong 수공; (*handmade goods*) sugongp'um 수공품
handkerchief sonsugŏn 손수건
handle 1 *n* sonjabi 손잡이 **2** *v/t* taruda 다루다; ***let me ~ this*** chega tarugessŭmnida 제가 다루겠습니다
handlebars chajŏn-gŏ haendŭl 자전거 핸들
hand luggage suhwamul 수화물; **handmade** sugong-ŭi 수공의; **handrail** nan-gan 난간; **handshake** akssu 악수
hands-off kansŏp'aji annŭn 간섭하지 않는
handsome chal saenggin 잘 생긴
hands-on shilmurŭl chiktchŏp'anŭn 실무를 직접하는; ***get some ~ experience*** chiktchŏp kyŏnghŏmŭl ŏttta 직접 경험을 얻다
handwriting yukp'il 육필
handwritten sonŭro ssŭn 손으로 쓴
handy *tool, device* p'yŏllihan 편리한; ***it might come in ~*** ama ssŭlmo issŭl kŏshida 아마 쓸모 있을 것이다
hang 1 *v/t picture* kŏlda 걸다; *person* mok maedalda 목 매달다 **2** *v/i* (*of dress, hair*) nŭrŏjida 늘어지다 **3** *n*: ***get the ~ of*** ...ŭl/rŭl ihaehage toeda ...을/를 이해하게 되다
♦**hang around** ŏsŭllŏnggŏrida 어슬렁거리다
♦**hang on** *v/i* (*wait*) kidarida 기다리다
♦**hang on to** (*keep*) kyesok ...ŭl/rŭl kajigo it-tta 계속 ...을/를 가지고 있다
♦**hang up** *v/i* TELEC chŏnhwarŭl kkŭnt'a 전화를 끊다
hangar kyŏngnapkko 격납고
hanger (*for clothes*) otkkŏri 옷걸이
hang glider (*person*) haenggŭllaidŏrŭl t'anŭn saram 행글라이더를 타는 사람; (*device*) haenggŭllaidŏ 행글라이더; **hang gliding** haenggŭllaidŏ pihaeng 행글라이더 비행; **hangover** sukch'wi 숙취; (*idea, attitude*) yŏp'a 여파
♦**hanker after** ... ŭl/rŭl mopsshi katkko ship'ŏhada ...을/를 몹시 갖고 싶어하다
hankie, hanky F sonsugŏn 손수건
Han River Han-gang 한강
haphazard magujabiŭi 마구잡이의
happen irŏnada 일어나다; ***if you ~ to see him*** manyak nega kŭrŭl uyŏnhi mannandamyŏn 만약 네가 그를 우연히 만난다면; ***what has ~ed to you?*** musŭn iri issŏssŭmnikka? 무슨 일이 있었습니까?
♦**happen across** uyŏnhi palgyŏnhada 우연히 발견하다
happening palssaeng 발생
happily haengbok'age 행복하게; (*gladly*) kippŭge 기쁘게; (*luckily*) un chok'e 운 좋게
happiness haengbok 행복
happy haengbok'an 행복한
happy-go-lucky nakch'ŏnjŏgin 낙천적인
happy hour t'ŭkbyŏl yŏmkka pongsa kigan 특별 염가 봉사 기간
harass koerop'ida 괴롭히다
harassed shidallin 시달린
harassment koerop'im 괴롭힘; ***sexual ~*** sŏnghŭirong 성희롱
harbor 1 *n* hanggu 항구 **2** *v/t criminal* sumgida 숨기다; *grudge* maŭme p'umtta 마음에 품다
hard tandanhan 단단한; (*difficult*) ŏryŏun 어려운; *facts, evidence* hwak-

kkohan 확고한; **~ *of hearing*** kwiga mŏn 귀가 먼
hardback changjŏngbon 장정본; **hard-boiled egg** talgyal wansuk 달걀 완숙; **hard copy** hadŭ k'ap'i 하드 카피; **hard core** *n* haeksshimch'ŭng 핵심층; (*pornography*) nogoltchŏgin p'orŭno 노골적인 포르노; **hard currency** kyohwan kanŭng t'onghwa 교환 가능 통화; **hard disk** hadŭ tisŭk'ŭ 하드 디스크
harden 1 *v/t* kuch'ida 굳히다 **2** *v/i* (*of glue*) kut-tta 굳다; (*of attitude*) kanghaejida 강해지다
hardheaded naengjŏnghan 냉정한
hardliner kanggyŏngnonja 강경론자
hardly kŏŭi ...haji ant'a 거의 ...하지 않다; ***he ~ ever studies*** kŭnŭn kŏŭi kongbuhaji anayo 그는 거의 공부하지 않아요; ***I can ~ hear*** kŏŭi tŭlliji anayo 거의 들리지 않아요; ***did you agree? - ~!*** tong-ŭihaessŏyo? – ch'ŏnmaneyo! 동의했어요? – 천만에요!
hardness kutkki 굳기; (*difficulty*) ŏryŏum 어려움
hard sell chŏkkŭk p'anmae 적극 판매
hardship kollan 곤란
hard shoulder toroŭi taep'isŏn 도로의 대피선; **hard up** toni kunghan 돈이 궁한; **hardware** ch'ŏlmul 철물; COMPUT hadŭweŏ 하드웨어; **hardware store** ch'ŏlmultchŏm 철물점; **hard-working** yŏlsshimhi irhanŭn 열심히 일하는
hardy kanghan 강한
hare sant'okki 산토끼
harm 1 *n* hae 해; ***it wouldn't do any ~ to ...*** ... haedo kwaench'anŭl kŏshida ... 해도 괜찮을 것이다 **2** *v/t* haech'ida 해치다
harmful haeroun 해로운
harmless muhaehan 무해한
harmonious chohwadoen 조화된
harmonize chohwashik'ida 조화시키다
harmony MUS hwasŏng 화성; (*in relationship etc*) chohwa 조화
harp hap'ŭ 하프
♦**harp on about** F kyesok ...ŭl / rŭl toep'uri marhada 계속 ...을 / 를 되풀이 말하다
harpoon *n* chakssal 작살
harsh *criticism, words* kahok'an 가혹한; *color, light* kŏsŭllinŭn 거슬리는
harvest *n* ch'usu 추수
Harvest Festival Ch'usŏk 추석
hash: ***make a ~ of*** F ...ŭl / rŭl ŏngmang-ŭro mandŭlda ...을 / 를 엉망으로 만들다
hash browns kamja t'wigim 감자 튀김
hashish taemach'o 대마초
haste sŏdurŭm 서두름
hasty kŭp'an 급한
hat moja 모자
hatch *n* (*for serving food*) ch'anggu 창구; (*on ship*) haech'i 해치
♦**hatch out** (*of eggs*) puhwahada 부화하다
hatchback haech'ibaek 해치백
hatchet sondokki 손도끼
hate 1 *n* mium 미움 **2** *v/t* miwŏhada 미워하다
hatred chŭng-o 증오
haughty kŏmanhan 거만한
haul 1 *n* (*of fish*) ŏhoengnyang 어획량 **2** *v/t* (*pull*) chabattanggida 잡아당기다
haulage unban 운반
haulage company unsong hoesa 운송 회사
haulier unsong hoesa 운송 회사
haunch tunbu 둔부
haunt 1 *v/t* nat'anada 나타나다; (*of memory*) ttŏorŭda 떠오르다; ***this place is ~ed*** igosŭn yuryŏng-i nat'ananŭn koshida 이곳은 유령이 나타나는 곳이다 **2** *n* (*place*) chŭlgyŏ ch'annŭn kot 즐겨 찾는 곳
haunting *tune* noerirŭl ttŏnaji annŭn 뇌리를 떠나지 않는
have ◊ kajida 가지다; ***I ~ some money*** tonŭl chom kajigo issŏyo 돈을 좀 가지고 있어요; ***I ~ something for you*** tangshinhant'e chul kŏshi issŏyo 당신한테 줄 것이 있어요; ***I ~ a headache*** mŏriga ap'ayo 머리가 아파요; ***~ a cold***

kamgie kŏllida 감기에 걸리다; ***can I ~ ...?*** (*please give me*) ...ŭl / rŭl chushigetssŭmnikka? ...을 / 를 주시겠습니까?; ***do you ~ ...?*** ...i / ka issŭmnikka? ...이 / 가 있습니까?; ***I ~ no family*** nanŭn kajogi amudo ŏptta 나는 가족이 아무도 없다; ***I had no choice*** sŏnt'aegŭi yŏjiga ŏpssŏt-tta 선택의 여지가 없었다 ◊ (*own*) kajida 가지다, soyuhada 소유하다 ◊ *breakfast, lunch* mŏktta 먹다 ◊: ~ ***to*** (*must*) ...haeya hada ...해야 하다; ***I ~ to study / see him*** nanŭn kongbuhaeya hamnida / kŭrŭl mannaboaya hamnida 나는 공부해야 합니다 / 그를 만나보아야 합니다; ***you ~ to try*** nŏnŭn noryŏk'aeya hahanda 너는 노력해야 한다 ◊ (*causative*): ~ ***sth done*** muŏsŭl haet-tta 무엇을 했다; ***I had my hair cut*** nanŭn mŏrirŭl challat-tta 나는 머리를 잘랐다; ~ ***sth cleaned*** muŏsŭl set'agŭl matkkida 무엇을 세탁을 맡기다 ◊ (*auxiliary*): ***I ~ decided*** nanŭn kyŏltchŏnghaet-tta 나는 결정했다; ~ ***you seen her?*** kŭnyŏrŭl pon chŏgi issŭmnikka? 그녀를 본 적이 있습니까?

♦**have back** tollyŏbat-tta 돌려받다; ***when can I have it back?*** ŏnje kŭgŏsŭl tollyŏbadŭl su issŭmnikka? 언제 그것을 돌려받을 수 있습니까?

♦**have on** (*wear*) iptta 입다; (*have planned*) kyehoek'aet-tta 계획했다; ***do you have anything on for tonight?*** onŭl pame mwŏ hal il issŭmnikka? 오늘 밤에 뭐 할 일 있습니까?

haven *fig* anshikch'ŏ 안식처

havoc ŏngmangjinch'ang 엉망진창; ***play ~ with*** ...ŭl / rŭl ŏngmang-ŭro mandŭlda ...을 / 를 엉망으로 만들다

hawk mae 매; *fig* kanggyŏngnonja 강경론자

hay kŏnch'o 건초

hay fever kŏnch'oyŏl 건초열

hazard *n* wihŏm yoso 위험 요소

hazard lights MOT pisangdŭng 비상등

hazardous wihŏmhan 위험한

haze ajirang-i 아지랑이

hazel (*tree*) kaeamnamu 개암나무

hazelnut kaeam 개암

hazy *view, memories* hŭrin 흐린; ***I'm a bit ~ about it*** nanŭn kugŏse taehayŏ punmyŏnghaji ant'a 나는 그것에 대하여 분명하지 않다

he kŭ 그; ~ ***is American*** kŭnŭn Miguk saramiyeyo 그는 미국 사람이예요 ◊ (*omission of pronoun*): ***who is ~? - ~ is my teacher*** nuguyeyo? - che sŏsaengnimiyeyo 누구예요? – 제 선생님이예요

head **1** *n* mŏri 머리; (*boss, leader*) udumŏri 우두머리; (*on beer*) kŏp'um 거품; (*of nail*) monmŏri 못머리; (*of queue, line*) sŏndu 선두; ***$15 a ~*** han saram tang 15tallŏ 한 사람 당 15달러; ***~s or tails?*** ammyŏn animyŏn twinmyŏn? 앞면 아니면 뒷면?; ***at the ~ of the list*** myŏngdanŭi ch'ŏnmŏrie 명단의 첫머리에; ~ ***over heels*** *fall* kokkurajida 고꾸라지다; *fall in love* holttak 홀딱; ***lose one's ~*** (*go crazy*) che chŏngshinŭl ilt'a 제 정신을 잃다 **2** *v/t* (*lead*) ikkŭlda 이끌다; *ball* mŏriro pat-tta 머리로 받다

headache tut'ong 두통

header (*in soccer*) heding 헤딩; (*in document*) mŏrinmal 머릿말

headhunter COM injae sŭk'aut'ŭ tamdangja 인재 스카우트 담당자

heading (*in list*) p'yoje 표제

headlamp, **headlight** hedŭrait'ŭ 헤드라이트; **headline** mŏritkkisa 머릿기사; ***make the ~s*** mŏritkkisaro k'ŭge ch'wigŭpttoeda 머릿기사로 크게 취급되다; **headlong** *adv fall* kŏndubaktchillo 곤두박질로; **headmaster** kyojang 교장; **headmistress** yŏgyojang 여교장; **head office** (*of company*) ponsa 본사; **head-on** **1** *adv crash* chŏngmyŏnch'ungdorŭro 정면충돌으로 **2** *adj crash* chŏngmyŏnch'ungdorŭi 정면충돌의; **headphones** hedŭp'on 헤드폰; **headquarters** ponbu 본부; **headrest** mŏri patch'im 머리 받침; **headroom** (*under bridge*) wit kongganŭi nop'i 윗 공간의 높이; (*in car*) ch'ŏnjang-ŭi nop'i 천장의 높이;

headscarf mŏri sŭk'ap'ŭ 머리 스카프; **headstrong** wan-gohan 완고한; **head waiter** susŏk weit'ŏ 수석 웨이터; **headwind** matpparam 맞바람

heady *wine etc* ppalli ch'wihage hanŭn 빨리 취하게 하는

heal 1 *v/t* natkke hada 낫게 하다 **2** *v/i* nat-tta 낫다

health kŏn-gang 건강; ***your ~!*** tangshinŭi kŏn-gang-ŭl wihae! 당신의 건강을 위해!

health club helssŭ k'ullŏp 헬스 클럽; **health food** kŏn-gang shikp'um 건강 식품; **health food store** kŏn-gang shikp'umjŏm 건강 식품점; **health insurance** kŏn-gang pohŏm 건강 보험; **health resort** poyangji 보양지

healthy *person* kŏn-ganghan 건강한; *food, lifestyle* kŏn-gang-e choŭn 건강에 좋은; *economy* t'ŭnt'ŭnhan 튼튼한

heap *n* ssaa ollin tŏmi 쌓아 올린 더미

♦**heap up** ssaa ollida 쌓아 올리다

hear tŭt-tta 듣다

♦**hear about** ...e kwanhae tŭt-tta ...에 관해 듣다

♦**hear from** ...(ŭ)ro put'ŏ soshigŭl tŭt-tta ...(으)로 부터 소식을 듣다

hearing ch'ŏngnyŏk 청력; LAW shimni 심리; ***within ~*** tŭllinŭn pŏmwi ane(sŏ) 들리는 범위 안에(서); ***out of ~*** tŭllinŭn pŏmwi pakke(sŏ) 들리는 범위 밖에(서)

hearing aid poch'ŏnggi 보청기

hearsay: ***by ~*** p'ungmunŭro 풍문으로

hearse yŏngguch'a 영구차

heart shimjang 심장; (*emotional senses*) maŭm 마음; (*of problem*) haeksshim 핵심; (*of city, organization*) haeksshimbu 핵심부; ***know sth by ~*** muŏsŭl oeugo it-tta 무엇을 외우고 있다

heart attack shimjang mabi 심장 마비; **heartbeat** shimjang pakttong 심장 박동; **heartbreaking** aekkŭlk'e hanŭn 애끓게 하는; **heartburn** kasŭmari 가슴앓이; **heart failure** shimjang mabi 심장 마비; **heartfelt** *sympathy* chinshimesŏ urŏnan 진심에서 우러난

hearth pyŏngnallo padak 벽난로 바닥

heartless maejŏnghan 매정한

heartrending *plea, sight* pit'onghan 비통한

hearts (*in cards*) hat'ŭ 하트

heart throb F tonggyŏng-ŭi taesang 동경의 대상

heart transplant shimjang ishik 심장 이식

hearty *appetite* wangsŏnghan 왕성한; *meal* p'ungsŏnghan 풍성한; *person* tajŏngdagamhan 다정다감한

heat *n* yŏl 열

♦**heat up** teuda 데우다

heated *discussion* kyŏk'an 격한; ***~ floor*** ondol 온돌; ***~ swimming pool*** onsu suyŏngjang 온수 수영장

heater nanbang changch'i 난방 장치

heathen *n* igyodo 이교도

heating nanbang changch'i 난방 장치

heatproof, heat-resistant naeyŏlssŏng-ŭi 내열성의; **heat-stroke** yŏlssabyŏng 열사병; **heat-wave** yŏlp'a 열파

heave *v/t* (*lift*) tŭrŏollida 들어올리다

heaven ch'ŏnguk 천국; ***good ~s!*** chŏrŏn 저런!

heavy mugŏun 무거운; *rain* manŭn 많은; *traffic, cold, bleeding* shimhan 심한; *accent* kanghan 강한; *food* sohwaga chal andoenŭn 소화가 잘 안되는; *financial loss* shimgak'an 심각한; *loss of life* maksshimhan 막심한; ***~ smoker*** kolch'o 골초; ***~ drinker*** sulgorae 술고래

heavy-duty aju t'ŭnt'ŭnhan 아주 튼튼한

heavyweight SP hebikkŭp 헤비급

heckle *v/t* yayuhada 야유하다

hectic mopsshi pappŭn 몹시 바쁜

hedge *n* ult'ari 울타리

hedgehog kosŭmdoch'i 고슴도치

heed: ***pay ~ to*** yunyŏmhada 유념하다

heel (*of foot*) twikkumch'i 뒤꿈치; (*of shoe*) twich'uk 뒤축

heel bar kudu susŏntchip 구두 수선집

hefty mugŏun 무거운

height nop'i 높이; (*of person*) k'i 키; (*of airplane*) kodo 고도; (*of season*) chŏltchŏng 절정

heighten *effect, tension* nop'ida 높이다
heir sangsogin 상속인
heiress yŏja sangsogin 여자 상속인
helicopter hellik'opt'ŏ 헬리콥터
hell chiok 지옥; ***what the ~ are you doing / do you want?*** F todaech'e muŏsŭl hanŭn / wŏhanŭn kŏmnikka? 도대체 무엇을 하는 / 원하는 겁니까?; ***go to ~!*** F kkŏjyŏ pŏryŏ! 꺼져 버려!; ***a ~ of a lot*** F ŏmch'ŏng manŭn 엄청 많은; ***one ~ of a nice guy*** F koengjanghi choŭn saram 굉장히 좋은 사람
hello (*polite, to older people*) annyŏnghashimnikka 안녕하십니까; (*to friend, younger people*) annyŏng 안녕; TELEC yŏboseyo 여보세요; (*on entry phone*) nuguseyo 누구세요
helm NAUT k'i chojong changch'i 키 조종 장치
helmet helmet 헬멧
help 1 *n* toum 도움 **2** *v/t* toptta 돕다; ***~ oneself*** (*to food*) maŭmkkŏt tŭlda 마음껏 들다; ***I can't ~ it*** ŏtchŏl su ŏpssŏyo 어쩔 수 없어요; ***I couldn't ~ laughing*** utchi anŭl su ŏpssŏssŏyo 웃지 않을 수 없었어요
helper towajunŭn saram 도와주는 사람
help file COMPUT toummal p'ail 도움말 파일
helpful toumi toenŭn 도움이 되는
helping (*of food*) han kŭrŭt 한 그릇
helpless (*unable to cope*) honjasŏ ŏtchŏl su ŏmnŭn 혼자서 어쩔 수 없는; (*powerless*) muryŏk'an 무력한
help screen COMPUT toummal hwamyŏn 도움말 화면
hem *n* (*of dress etc*) ot-ttan 옷단
hemisphere pan-gu 반구
hemorrhage 1 *n* ch'urhyŏl 출혈 **2** *v/i* ch'urhyŏrhada 출혈하다
hemp taema 대마
hen amt'ak 암탉; (*of any bird*) amsae 암새
henchman *pej* shimbok 심복
henpecked yŏja sone chwiyŏ sanŭn 여자 손에 쥐여 사는; ***~ husband*** kongch'ŏga 공처가
hepatitis kannyŏm 간염
her 1 *adj* kŭnyŏŭi 그녀의; ***~ ticket*** kŭnyŏŭi p'yo 그녀의 표 **2** *pron* kŭnyŏrŭl 그녀; ***I know ~*** nanŭn kŭnyŏrŭl anda 나는 그녀를 안다; ***this is for ~*** igŏsŭn kŭnyŏŭi kŏshida 이것은 그녀의 것이다
herb shigyong p'ullip 식용 풀잎, hŏbŭ 허브
herb(al) tea hŏbŭ ch'a 허브 차
herd *n* tte 떼
here yŏgie(sŏ) 여기에(서); ***~'s to you!*** (*as toast*) kŏnbae! 건배!; ***~ you are*** (*giving sth*) yŏgi issŭmnida 여기 있습니다; ***~ we are!*** (*finding sth*) yŏgi itkkuna! 여기 있구나!
hereditary *disease* yujŏndoenŭn 유전되는
heritage yusan 유산
hermit ŭndunja 은둔자
hernia MED t'altchang 탈장
hero yŏng-ung 영웅
heroic yŏng-ungjŏgin 영웅적인
heroin heroin 헤로인
heroine yŏjangbu 여장부
heron waegari 왜가리
herpes MED p'ojin 포진
herring ch'ŏng-ŏ 청어
hers kŭnyŏŭi kot 그녀의 것; ***it's ~*** igosŭn kunyŏŭi kŏshida 이것은 그녀의 것이다; ***a cousin of ~*** kŭnyŏŭi sach'on 그녀의 사촌
herself kŭnyŏ chashin 그녀 자신; ***she hurt ~*** kŭnyŏga tach'yŏt-tta 그녀가 다쳤다; ***by ~*** kŭnyŏ sŭsŭro 그녀 스스로
hesitate mangsŏrida 망설이다
hesitation mangsŏrim 망설임
heterosexual *adj* isŏng-aeŭi 이성애의
heyday chŏnsŏnggi 전성기
hi annyŏng 안녕
hibernate tongmyŏnhada 동면하다
hiccup *n* ttalkkuktchil 딸꾹질; (*minor problem*) yak-kkanŭi munje 약간의 문제; ***have the ~s*** ttalkkuktchirhada 딸꾹질하다
hick *pej* F shigolttŭgi 시골뜨기
hick town *pej* F shigol 시골
hidden *meaning, treasure* sumgyŏjin 숨겨진, kamchwŏjin 감춰진
hide[1] **1** *v/t* sumgida 숨기다, kamch'uda 감추다 **2** *v/i* sumtta 숨다

hide[2] *n* (*of animal*) kajuk 가죽
hide-and-seek sumbakkoktchil 숨바꼭질
hideaway ŭnshinch'ŏ 은신처
hideous *weather*, *taste* kkŭmtchik'an 끔찍한; *crime* hyung-ak'an 흉악한; *face* hyunghan 흉한
hiding[1] (*beating*) maejil 매질
hiding[2]: ***be in ~*** ŭnshinhada 은신하다; ***go into ~*** sumtta 숨다
hiding place sumnŭn kot 숨는 곳
hierarchy kyegŭp chojik 계급 조직
hi-fi haip'ai 하이파이
high 1 *adj* nop'ŭn 높은; *wind* kanghan 강한; (*on drugs*) ch'wihan 취한; ***have a ~ opinion of s.o.*** nugurŭl nop'i p'yŏngkkahada 누구를 높이 평가하다; ***it is ~ time …*** ijen kŭman … hal ttaeda 이젠 그만 … 할 때다 **2** *n* MOT koso kiŏ 고속 기어; (*in statistics*) nop'ŭn sujun 높은 수준; EDU kodŭnghak-kkyo 고등학교 **3** *adv* nopkke 높게; ***~ in the sky*** hanŭl nopkke 하늘 높게; ***that's as ~ as we can go*** uriga hal su innŭn ch'oedaehanimnida 우리가 할 수 있는 최대한입니다
highbrow *adj* chishiginŭi 지식인의; **highchair** yuayong nop'ŭn ŭija 유아용 높은 의자; **highclass** kogŭbŭi 고급의; **high diving** taibing 다이빙; **high-frequency** kojup'a 고주파; **high-grade** kogŭbŭi 고급의; **high-handed** koaptchŏgin 고압적인; **high-heeled** nop'ŭn kubŭi 높은 굽의; **high jump** nop'i ttwigi 높이 뛰기; **high-level** kowi kogwanŭi 고위 고관의; **high life** sangnyu sahoeŭi saenghwal 상류 사회의 생활; **highlight 1** *n* (*main event*, *in hair*) hailait'ŭ 하이라이트 **2** *v/t* (*with pen*) kangjohada 강조하다; COMPUT pŭllogŭl ssŭiuda 블록을 씌우다; **highlighter** (*pen*) hyŏnggwangp'en 형광펜
highly *desirable*, *likely* k'ŭge 크게; ***be ~ paid*** nop'ŭn ponggŭbŭl pat-tta 높은 봉급을 받다; ***think ~ of s.o.*** nugurŭl nop'i p'yŏngkkahada 누구를 높이 평가하다
high-performance *drill*, *battery* kosŏngnŭng 고성능; **high-pitched** koŭmŭi 고음의; **high point** (*of life*, *career*, *program*) chŏltchŏng 절정; **high-powered** *engine* kosŏngnŭngŭi 고성능의; *intellectual* t'ŭkch'urhan 특출한; *salesman* kkŭnjilgin 끈질긴; **high pressure 1** *n* (*weather*) kogiap 고기압 **2** *adj* TECH koabŭi 고압의; *salesman* kangnyohanŭn 강요하는; *job*, *lifestyle* kodoŭi kinjang-ŭl yohanŭn 고도의 긴장을 요하는; **high priest** taejesajang 대제사장; *fig* (*of fashion etc*) chidoja 지도자; **high school** kodŭnghak-kkyo 고등학교; **high society** sangnyu sahoe 상류 사회; **high-speed train** kosok yŏlch'a 고속 열차; **high strung** mingamhan 민감한; **high tech 1** *n* ch'ŏmdan kisul 첨단 기술 **2** *adj* ch'ŏmdan kisurŭi 첨단 기술의; **high technology** ch'ŏmdan kisul 첨단 기술; **high-tension** *cable* koabŭi 고압의; **high tide** manjo 만조; **high water** ch'oego suwi 최고 수위; **highway** kosokttoro 고속도로; **high wire** (*in circus*) chult'agi chul 줄타기 줄
hijack 1 *v/t plane* kongjung napch'ihada 공중 납치하다; *bus* t'alch'wihada 탈취하다 **2** *n* (*of plane*) kongjung napch'i 공중 납치; (*of bus*) t'alch'wi 탈취
hijacker (*of plane*) kongjung napch'ibŏm 공중 납치범; (*of bus*) t'alch'wibŏm 탈취범
hike[1] **1** *n* toboyŏhaeng 도보여행 **2** *v/i* toboyŏhaenghada 도보여행하다
hike[2] *n* (*in prices*) insang 인상
hiker toboyŏhaengja 도보여행자
hilarious usŭmŭl chaanaenŭn 웃음을 자아내는
hill ŏndŏk 언덕; (*slope*) samyŏn 사면
hillbilly *pej* F sansaram 산사람
hillside ŏndŏgŭi samyŏn 언덕의 사면
hilltop ŏndŏk kkokttaegi 언덕 꼭대기
hilly kurŭngjidaeŭi 구릉지대의
hilt charu 자루
him kŭrŭl 그를; ***I know ~*** nanŭn kŭrŭl anda 나는 그를 안다; ***this is for ~*** igŏsŭn kŭŭi kŏshida 이것은 그의 것이다

himself kŭ chashin 그 자신; ***he hurt ~*** kŭnŭn tach'yŏt-tta 그는 다쳤다; ***by ~*** kŭ sŭsŭro 그 스스로
hinder panghaehada 방해하다
hindrance chang-ae 장애
hindsight twinŭjŭn kkaedarŭm 뒤늦은 깨달음; ***with ~*** twinŭjŭn kkaedarŭmŭro 뒤늦은 깨달음으로
hinge kyŏngch'ŏp 경첩
hint (*clue*) hint'ŭ 힌트; (*piece of advice*) choŏn 조언; (*implied suggestion*) amshi 암시; (*of red, sadness etc*) miyak'an chinghu 미약한 징후
hip kungdungi 궁둥이, ŏngdŏng-i 엉덩이
hip pocket twittchumŏni 뒷주머니
hippopotamus hama 하마
hire *v/t room, car* tonŭl chugo pillida 돈을 주고 빌리다; *person* koyonghada 고용하다
his 1 *adj* kuŭi 그의; ***~ ticket*** kuŭi p'yo 그의 표 **2** *pron* kuŭi kŏt 그의 것; ***it's ~*** igosŭn kuŭi kŏshida 이것은 그의 것이다; ***a cousin of ~*** kŭŭi sach'on 그의 사촌
hiss *v/i* (*of snake*) shwit sorirŭl naeda 쉿 소리를 내다; (*of audience*) yayurŭl ponaeda 야유를 보내다
historian sahaktcha 사학자
historic yŏkssasang-ŭro chungnyohan 역사상으로 중요한
historical yŏkssajŏgin 역사적인
history yŏkssa 역사
hit 1 *v/t* ch'ida 치다; (*collide with*) ch'ungdorhada 충돌하다; ***he was ~ by a bullet*** kŭnŭn t'anarŭl majat-tta 그는 탄알을 맞았다; ***it suddenly ~ me*** (*I realized*) nanŭn kaptchagi kkaedarat-tta 나는 갑자기 깨달았다; ***~ town*** (*arrive*) tongnee todarhada 동네에 도달하다 **2** *n* (*blow*) t'agyŏk 타격; MUS hit'ŭ 히트; (*success*) sŏnggong 성공
♦**hit back** toebadach'ida 되받아치다
♦**hit on** *idea* saenggak'aenaeda 생각해내다
♦**hit out at** (*criticize*) maengnyŏrhi pinanhada 맹렬히 비난하다
hit-and-run *adj*: ***~ accident*** ppaengsoni sago 뺑소니 사고; ***~ driver*** ppaengsoni unjŏnsu 뺑소니 운전수
hitch 1 *n* (*problem*) chang-ae 장애; ***without a ~*** chang-aeŏpsshi 장애없이 **2** *v/t* kŏrŏmaeda 걸어매다; ***~ X to Y*** Xŭl / rŭl Ye kŏrŏmaeda X을 / 를 Y에 걸어매다; ***~ a ride*** p'yŏnsŭnghada 편승하다 **3** *v/i* (*hitchhike*) p'yŏnsŭnghada 편승하다
♦**hitch up** *trailer* kkŭrŏollida 끌어올리다
hitchhike p'yŏnsŭnghada 편승하다
hitchhiker p'yŏnsŭng yŏhaengja 편승여행자
hitchhiking p'yŏnsŭnghagi 편승하기
hi-tech 1 *n* ch'ŏmdan kisul 첨단 기술 **2** *adj* ch'ŏmdan kisurŭi 첨단 기술의
hitlist taesangja myŏngdan 대상자 명단; **hitman** ch'ŏngbu sarinja 청부 살인자; **hit-or-miss** toenŭndaeroŭi 되는대로의; **hit squad** amsalttan 암살단
HIV Inch'e Myŏnyŏk Kyŏlp'ip Pairŏsŭ 인체 면역 결핍 바이러스
hive (*for bees*) pŏlt'ong 벌통
♦**hive off** *v/t* (COM: *separate off*) pullihada 분리하다
HIV-positive Eijŭ yangsŏng panŭng 에이즈 양성 반응
hoard 1 *n* pich'uk 비축 **2** *v/t* pich'uk'ada 비축하다
hoarse moksshwin 목쉰
hoax *n* sogimsu 속임수
hobble *v/i* chŏllŭmgŏrida 절름거리다
hobby ch'wimi 취미
hobo ttŭnaegi 뜨내기; (*itinerant worker*) ttŭnaegi ilkkun 뜨내기 일꾼
hockey (*ice ~*) aisŭ hak'i 아이스 하키
hog *n* (*pig*) twaeji 돼지
hoist 1 *n* kijunggi 기중기 **2** *v/t* kkŭrŏ ollida 끌어 올리다
hokum (*nonsense*) hŏt'ŭn sori 허튼 소리; (*sentimental stuff*) ssaguryŏmul 싸구려물
hold 1 *v/t* (*in hands*) chaptta 잡다, chibŏdŭlda 집어들다; (*support, keep in place*) chit'aenghada 지탱하다; *passport, job* kajida 가지다; *prisoner, suspect* puttchaptta 붙잡다; (*contain*) tamtta 담다; *course* yujihada 유지하다; ***~ one's breath*** sumŭl

chugida 숨을 죽이다; ***he can ~ his drink*** kŭnŭn surŭl kyesok mashil su it-tta 그는 술을 계속 마실 수 있다; ~ ***s.o. responsible*** nuguege ch'acgimit-ttago saenggak'ada 누구에게 책임있다고 생각하다; ~ ***that …*** (*believe, maintain*) …ranŭn saenggagŭl kosuhada …라는 생각을 고수하다; ~ ***the line*** TELEC kkŭntchimalgo kidariseyo 끊지말고 기다리세요 **2** *n* (*in ship, plane*) hwamulsshil 화물실; ***catch ~ of sth*** muŏsŭl chaptta 무엇을 잡다; ***lose one's ~ on sth*** (*on rope*) muŏsŭl noch'ida 무엇을 놓치다

♦**hold against**: ***hold X against Y*** Xttaemune Yŭl / rŭl wŏnmanghada X때문에 Y을 / 를 원망하다

♦**hold back 1** *v/t crowds* maktta 막다; *facts, information* sumgida 숨기다 **2** *v/i* (*not tell all*) ta marhaji ant'a 다 말하지 않다

♦**hold on** *v/i* (*wait*) kidarida 기다리다; TELEC kkŭntchiank'o it-tta 끊지않고 있다; ***now ~ a minute!*** chamkkanman kidaryŏ poseyo! 잠깐만 기다려 보세요!

♦**hold on to** (*keep*) kyesok kajigo it-tta 계속 가지고 있다; *belief* kosuhada 고수하다

♦**hold out 1** *v/t hand* naemilda 내밀다; *prospect* cheanhada 제안하다 **2** *v/i* (*of supplies*) kyesok namait-tta 계속 남아있다; (*survive*) pŏt'ida 버티다

♦**hold up** *v/t hand* tŭrŏ ollida 들어 올리다; *bank etc* kangt'arhada 강탈하다; (*make late*) chich'ehage hada 지체하게 하다; ***hold sth up as an example*** muŏsŭl yero cheshihada 무엇을 예로 제시하다

♦**hold with** (*approve of*) injŏnghada 인정하다

holder (*container*) kwak 곽; (*of passport, ticket etc*) soyuja 소유자; (*of record*) poyuja 보유자

holding company mohoesa 모회사

holdup (*robbery*) kangdo 강도; (*delay*) chich'e 지체

hole kumŏng 구멍

holiday (*single day*) hyuil 휴일; (*period*) hyuga 휴가

Holland Nedŏllandŭ 네덜란드

hollow *object* sogi pin 속이 빈; *cheeks* ump'uk tŭrŏgan 움푹 들어간; *words* konghŏhan 공허한

holly horanggashinamu 호랑가시나무

holocaust Yut'aein taehakssal 유태인 대학살

hologram hollograem 홀로그램

holster kwŏnch'ongjip 권총집

holy sŏngsŭrŏun 성스러운

Holy Spirit Sŏngnyŏng 성령

Holy Week Sŏng Chugan 성 주간

home 1 *n* kajŏng 가정, chip 집; (*native country*) koguk 고국; (*town, part of country*) kohyang 고향; (*for old people*) yangnowŏn 양로원; ***at ~*** (*in my house*) nae chibe 내 집에; (*in my country*) nae koguge 내 고국에; SP hom kyŏnggijang-esŏ 홈 경기장에서; ***make oneself at ~*** p'yŏnanhi hada 편안히 하다; ***at ~ and abroad*** kungnaeoeesŏ 국내외에서; ***work from ~*** chat'aek kŭnmu 자택 근무 **2** *adv* chibe 집에; (*in own country*) koguge 고국에; (*in own town, part of country*) kohyang-e 고향에; ***go ~*** chibe kada 집에 가다; (*to own country*) koguge kada 고국에 가다; (*to town, part of country*) kohyang-e kada 고향에 가다

home address chiptchuso 집주소; **homecoming** kwiga 귀가; **home computer** kajŏngnyong k'ŏmp'yut'ŏ 가정용 컴퓨터; **home education** kajŏng kyoyuk 가정 교육; **home game** hom kyŏnggi 홈 경기

homeless 1 *adj* chibŏmnŭn 집없는 **2** *n*: ***the ~*** mujut'aektcha 무주택자

homeloving kajŏngjŏgin 가정적인

homely (*homeloving*) kajŏngjŏgin 가정적인; (*not good-looking*) motssaenggin 못생긴

homemade chibesŏ mandŭn 집에서 만든; **home movie** chaga chejak yŏnghwa 자가 제작 영화; **home page** COMPUT homp'eiji 홈페이지

homeopathy tongjongnyoppŏp 동종요법

homesick: ***be ~*** hyangsuppyŏng-ŭl

alt'a 향수병을 앓다; **home town** kohyang 고향; **home tutor** kajŏng kyosa 가정 교사; **homeward** *adv* (*to own house*) kwiga kire 귀가 길에; (*to own country*) kwiguk kire 귀국 길에; **homework** EDU suktche 숙제; **homeworking** COM chat'aek kŭnmu 자택 근무
homicide (*crime*) sarin 살인; (*police department*) kyŏngch'al sarin chŏndam pusŏ 경찰 살인 전담 부서
homograph tonghyŏng-iŭiŏ 동형이의어
homophobia tongsŏng-ae hyŏmotchŭng 동성애 혐오증
homosexual 1 *adj* tongsŏng-aeŭi 동성애의 **2** *n* tongsŏng-aeja 동성애자
honest chŏngjik'an 정직한
honestly soltchik'age 솔직하게; ***~!*** chŏngmalloyo! 정말로요!
honesty chŏngjik 정직
honey kkul 꿀; F (*darling*) chagi 자기; (*to husband*) yŏbo 여보
honeycomb pŏltchip 벌집
honeymoon *n* shinhon yŏhaeng 신혼 여행
Hong Kong Hongk'ong 홍콩
honk *v/t horn* ullida 울리다
honor 1 *n* myŏng-ye 명예 **2** *v/t* yeuhada 예우하다
honorable *person* torirŭl anŭn 도리를 아는; *thing to do* torie mannŭn 도리에 맞는
honorific kyŏng-ŏppŏbŭi 경어법의
hood (*over head*) ose tallin moja 옷에 달린 모자; (*over cooker*) tŏpkkae 덮개; MOT enjin ttukkŏng 엔진 뚜껑; F (*gangster*) kkangp'ae 깡패
hoodlum kkangp'ae 깡패
hoof palkkup 발굽
hook kalgori 갈고리; (*to hang clothes on*) kori 고리; (*for fishing*) naksshippanŭl 낚시바늘; ***off the ~*** TELEC suhwagirŭl pŏsŏna 수화기를 벗어나
hooked: ***be ~ on*** (*on drugs, fig*) …e ppajida …에 빠지다
hooker F ch'angnyŏ 창녀
hooky: ***play ~*** mudan kyŏlssŏk'ada 무단 결석하다
hooligan pullyangbae 불량배
hooliganism pullyangbae kijil 불량배 기질
hoop t'e 테
hoot 1 *v/t horn* uusorirŭl naeda 우우소리를 내다 **2** *v/i* (*of car*) kyŏngjŏgŭl ullida 경적을 울리다; (*of owl*) puŏngbuŏng ulda 부엉부엉 울다
hop[1] *n* (*plant*) hop 홉
hop[2] *v/i* kabyŏpkke twiŏ orŭda 가볍게 뛰어 오르다
hope 1 *n* hŭimang 희망; ***there's no ~ of that*** chŏnhyŏ kŭrŏl kamang-i ŏptta 전혀 그럴 가망이 없다 **2** *v/i* parada 바라다, hŭimanghada 희망하다; ***~ for sth*** muŏsŭl parada 무엇을 바라다; ***I ~ so*** kŭrŏgil paramnida 그러길 바랍니다; ***I ~ not*** kŭrŏch'i ank'irŭl paramnida 그렇지 않기를 바랍니다 **3** *v/t*: ***I ~ you like it*** maŭme tŭlmyŏn chok'essŏyo 마음에 들면 좋겠어요
hopeful hŭimang-e ch'an 희망에 찬; (*promising*) kamang-innŭn 가망있는
hopefully *say, wait* kidaehamyŏ 기대하며; (*I / we hope*) paragŏnde 바라건데
hopeless *position, propect* hŭimang-ŭl irŭn 희망을 잃은; (*useless: person*) kamang ŏmnŭn 가망 없는
horizon (*on land*) chip'yŏngsŏn 지평선; (*at sea*) sup'yŏngsŏn 수평선
horizontal sup'yŏng-ŭi 수평의
hormone horŭmon 호르몬
horn (*of animal*) ppul 뿔; MOT kyŏngjŏk 경적
hornet malbŏl 말벌
horn-rimmed spectacles ppult'e an-gyŏng 뿔테 안경
horny (*sexually*) sŏngtchŏgŭro hŭngbunhan 성적으로 흥분한
horoscope chŏmsŏngsul 점성술
horrible chidok'an 지독한
horrify: ***I was horrified*** ch'unggyŏktchŏgiŏssŏyo 충격적이었어요
horrifying *experience* kkŭmtchik'an 끔찍한; *idea, prices* ch'unggyŏktchŏgin 충격적인
horror kongp'o 공포; ***the ~s of war*** chŏnjaeng-ŭi ch'amsa 전쟁의 참사

horror movie kongp'o yŏnghwa 공포 영화
hors d'oeuvre chŏnch'ae 전채
horse mal 말
horseback: ***on ~*** marŭl t'ago 말을 타고; **horse chestnut** maronie yŏlmae 마로니에 열매; **horsehair hat** kat 갓; **horsepower** maryŏk 마력; **horse race** kyŏngma 경마; **horseshoe** malgup 말굽
horticulture wŏnye 원예
hose hosŭ 호스
hospice yoyangso 요양소
hospitable hwandaehanŭn 환대하는
hospital pyŏng-wŏn 병원; ***go into the ~*** ibwŏnhada 입원하다
hospitality hwandae 환대
host *n* (*at party*, *reception*) chuin 주인; (*of TV program*) sahoeja 사회자
hostage injil 인질; ***be taken ~*** injillo chap'ida 인질로 잡히다
hostage taker injilbŏm 인질범
hostel (*inexpensive accommodations*) yŏgwan 여관; (*youth ~*) yusŭhŏsŭt'el 유스호스텔
hostess (*at party*, *reception*) antchuin 안주인; (*on airplane*) sŭt'yuŏdissŭ 스튜어디스; (*in bar*) yŏjong-ŏbwŏn 여종업원; (*prostitute*) hosŭt'essŭ 호스테스
hostile chŏkttaejŏgin 적대적인
hostility (*of attitude*) chŏkttaeshim 적대심; ***hostilities*** chŏnt'u 전투
hot *water*, *food* ttŭgŏun 뜨거운; *weather* tŏun 더운; (*spicy*) maeun 매운; F (*good*) maeu chal hanŭn 매우 잘 하는; ***I'm ~*** tŏwŏyo 더워요; ***it's so ~ today*** onŭl nalsshiga maeu tŏpkkunnyo 오늘 날씨가 매우 덥군요
hot dog hattogŭ 핫도그
hotel hot'el 호텔
hotplate yoriyong ch'ŏlp'an 요리용 철판
hot spot (*military*, *political*) punjaeng chiyŏk 분쟁 지역
hour shigan 시간
hourglass drum changgo 장고
hourly *adj* shiganmadaŭi 시간마다의
house *n* chip 집; ***at your ~*** nŏŭi chibesŏ 너의 집에서
houseboat chugŏyong pae 주거용 배; **housebreaking** kat'aek ch'imip 가택 침입; **household** kajok 가족; **household name** chal allyŏjin irŭm 잘 알려진 이름; **house husband** kasarŭl tolbonŭn namp'yŏn 가사를 돌보는 남편; **housekeeper** kajŏngbu 가정부; **housekeeping** (*activity*) kasa 가사; (*money*) kagye 가계; **House of Representatives** Hawŏn 하원; **housewarming** (**party**) chipttŭri 집들이; **housewife** chubu 주부; **housework** chiban il 집안 일
housing chut'aek 주택; TECH t'ŭl 틀
housing conditions chut'aek sajŏng 주택 사정
hovel nuch'uhan chip 누추한 집
hover pingbing maemdolda 빙빙 맴돌다
hovercraft hobŏk'ŭrap'ŭt'ŭ 호버크라프트
how ŏttŏk'e 어떻게; ***~ are you?*** annyŏnhaseyo? 안녕하세요?; ***~ about ...?*** ...hanŭn kŏshi ŏttŏgessŭmnikka? ...하는 것이 어떻겠습니까?; ***~ much?*** ŏlmank'ŭm? 얼만큼?; ***~ much do you want?*** ŏlmank'ŭm wŏnhaseyo? 얼만큼 원하세요?; ***~ much is it?*** ŏlmaimnikka? 얼마입니까?; ***~ many?*** ŏlmana mani? 얼마나 많이?; ***~ often?*** ŏlmana chaju? 얼마나 자주?; ***~ funny!*** ŏlmana chaemiinnŭnji! 얼마나 재미있는지!
however kŭrŏna 그러나; ***~ big / rich they are*** amuri k'ŭda / puyuhada hadŏrado 아무리 크다 / 부유하다 하더라도
howl *v/i* (*of dog*, *person in pain*) ulbujit-tta 울부짖다; (*with laughter*) sorinop'yŏ ut-tta 소리높여 웃다
hub (*of wheel*) pak'wiŭi chungshimbu 바퀴의 중심부
hubcap chadongch'aŭi hwilk'aep 자동차의 휠캡
♦**huddle together** tterŭl chiŏ moida 떼를 지어 모이다
huff: ***be in a ~*** palkkŭn hwarŭl naeda 발끈 화를 내다

hug *v/t* p'o-onghada 포옹하다, antta 안다
huge kŏdaehan 거대한; (*in amount*) makttaehan 막대한
hull *n* sŏnch'e 선체
hullabaloo soran 소란
hum 1 *v/t song, tune* k'onnoraero purŭda 콧노래로 부르다 **2** *v/i* (*of person*) k'onnoraerŭl purŭda 콧노래를 부르다; (*of machine*) wing-winggŏrida 윙윙거리다
human 1 *n* in-gan 인간, saram 사람 **2** *adj species, characteristics* in-ganŭi 인간의; *weakness* in-ganjŏgin 인간적인; ~ ***error*** saramŭi shilssu 사람의 실수
human being in-gan 인간
humane injŏng-innŭn 인정있는
humanitarian indojuŭiŭi 인도주의의
humanity (*human beings*) illyu 인류; (*of attitude etc*) saramdaum 사람다움, in-ganssŏng 인간성
human race illyu 인류
human resources insakkwa 인사과
humble *attitude, person* kyŏmsonhan 겸손한; *origins* ch'ŏnhan 천한; *meal, house* ch'orahan 초라한
humdrum maeu p'yŏngbŏmhan 매우 평범한
humid sŭp'an 습한
humidifier kasŭpkki 가습기
humidity sŭpkki 습기; ***90%*** ~ kuship p'ŏsent'ŭŭi sŭpdo 구십 퍼센트의 습도
humiliate kuryogŭl chuda 굴욕을 주다
humiliating kuryoktchŏgin 굴욕적인
humiliation kuryŏk 굴욕
humility kyŏmson 겸손
humor haehak 해학, usŭgae sori 우스개 소리; (*mood*) kibun 기분; ***sense of*** ~ yumŏ kamgak 유머 감각
humorous usŭun 우스운
hump 1 *n* (*of camel, person*) hok 혹; (*on road*) hŏmp'ŭ 험프, *sokttorŭl churige hagi wihan toro sang-ŭi changch'i* 속도를 줄이게 하기 위한 도로 상의 장치 **2** *v/t* (*carry*) chilmŏjida 짊어지다
hunch (*idea*) yegam 예감
hundred paek 백
hundred day ceremony (*after birth*) paegil 백일
hundredth *adj* paek pŏntchaeŭi 백 번째의
hundredweight 100p'aundŭ 100파운드; *Br* 112p'aundŭ 112파운드
Hungarian 1 *adj* Hŏnggariŭi 헝가리의 **2** *n* (*person*) Hŏnggari saram 헝가리 사람 (*language*) Hŏnggariŏ 헝가리어
Hungary Hŏnggari 헝가리
hunger paegop'ŭm 배고픔
hung-over sukch'wiŭi 숙취의
hungry paegop'ŭn 배고픈; ***I'm*** ~ paega kop'ayo 배가 고파요
hunk: ***great*** ~ F (*man*) mŏtchin namja 멋진 남자
hunky-dory F mansa p'yŏnanhan 만사 편안한
hunt 1 *n* (*for animals*) sanyang 사냥; (*for new leader, actor*) ch'ajŭm 찾음; (*for criminal, missing child*) susaek 수색 **2** *v/t animal* sanyanghada 사냥하다
♦**hunt for** ch'at-tta 찾다
hunter sanyangkkun 사냥꾼
hunting sanyang 사냥
hurdle SP chang-aemul 장애물; *fig* (*obstacle*) chang-ae 장애
hurdler SP chang-aemul kyŏngjuja 장애물 경주자
hurdles SP chang-aemul kyŏngju 장애물 경주
hurl himkkŏt naedŏnjida 힘껏 내던지다
hurray hwanhoŭi sori 환호의 소리; ~***!*** manse! 만세!
hurricane t'aep'ung 태풍
hurried sŏdurŭn 서두른
hurry 1 *n* sŏdurŭm 서두름; ***be in a*** ~ sodullŏ hada 서둘러 하다 **2** *v/i* sodurŭda 서두르다
♦**hurry up 1** *v/i* sŏdurŭda 서두르다; ~***!*** sŏdurŭseyo! 서두르세요! **2** *v/t* chaech'ok'ada 재촉하다
hurt 1 *v/i* ap'ŭda 아프다; ***my leg ~s*** tariga ap'ayo 다리가 아파요; ***does it ~?*** ap'ŭmnikka? 아픕니까? **2** *v/t* tach'ige hada 다치게 하다; (*emotionally*) ...ŭi maŭmŭl sanghage hada ...의 마음을 상하게

하다
husband namp'yŏn 남편
hush *n* choyongham 조용함; *~!* choyonghi! 조용히!
♦ **hush up** *scandal etc* shwishwihaebŏrida 쉬쉬해버리다
husk (*of grain*) kkŏptchil 껍질
husky *adj* shwin mokssoriŭi 쉰 목소리의, hŏsŭk'iŭi 허스키의
hustle 1 *n*: *~ and bustle* hwalgich'an honjap 활기찬 혼잡 **2** *v/t person* sŏdurŭge hada 서두르게 하다
hut odumak 오두막
hyacinth hiashinsŭ 히아신스
hybrid *n* (*plant*, *animal*) chaptchong 잡종
hydrant kŭpssugwan 급수관; *fire ~* sohwajŏn 소화전
hydraulic (*using water*) suabŭi 수압의; (*using oil*) yuabŭi 유압의
hydroelectric suryŏk chŏn-giŭi 수력 전기의
hydrofoil (*boat*) sujung-iksŏn 수중익선
hydrogen suso 수소
hydrogen bomb suso p'okt'an 수소 폭탄
hygiene wisaeng 위생
hygienic wisaengsang-ŭi 위생상의
hymn ch'ansongga 찬송가, sŏngga 성가
hype *n* kwadae sŏnjŏn 과대 선전
hyperactive chinach'ige sŏlch'inŭn 지나치게 설치는; **hypermarket** taehyŏng shyup'ŏmak'et 대형 슈퍼마켓; **hypersensitive** kwaminhan 과민한; **hypertension** kohyŏrap 고혈압; **hypertext** COMPUT haip'ŏt'ekssŭt'ŭ 하이퍼텍스트
hyphen iŭmp'yo 이음표
hypnosis ch'oemyŏnsul 최면술
hypnotherapy ch'oemyŏn yoppŏp 최면 요법
hypnotize ch'oemyŏnsurŭl kŏlda 최면술을 걸다
hypochondriac *n* uultchŭng hwanja 우울증 환자
hypocrisy wisŏn 위선
hypocrite wisŏnja 위선자
hypocritical wisŏnŭi 위선의
hypothermia chŏch'eontchŭng 저체온증
hypothesis kasŏl 가설
hypothetical kasŏrŭi 가설의
hysterectomy chagung chŏkch'ulssul 자궁 적출술
hysteria hisŭt'eri 히스테리
hysterical *person* pyŏngtchok hŭngbun sangt'aeŭi 병적 흥분 상태의, hisŭt'erisŏng-ŭi 히스테리성의; *laughter* paltchaktchŏgin 발작적인; (*very funny*) ŏmch'ŏngnage usŭun 엄청나게 우스운; *become ~* pyŏngtchŏk hŭngbunsangt'aega toeda 병적 흥분상태가 되다
hysterics hisŭt'eri 히스테리; (*laughter*) paltchaktchŏgin usŭm 발작적인 웃음

I

I ◊ na 나; H chŏ 저; ~ ***am American*** / ***a student*** nanŭn Migugin / hakssaengiyeyo 나는 미국인 / 학생이에요; ***can ~ buy you a drink?*** chega han chan sado toelkkayo? 제가 한 잔 사도 될까요? ◊ (*omission of pronoun*): ~ ***can't see*** pol su ŏpssŏyo 볼 수 없어요; ~ ***don't know*** mollayo 몰라요

ice ŏrŭm 얼음; ***break the ~*** *fig* ŏsaek'an punwigirŭl kkaeda 어색한 분위기를 깨다

♦**ice up** (*of engine etc*) tonggyŏldoeda 동결되다

iceberg pingsan 빙산; **icebox** aisŭ pakssŭ 아이스 박스; **icebreaker** (*ship*) swaebingsŏn 쇄빙선; **ice cream** aisŭ k'ŭrim 아이스 크림; **ice-cream parlor** aisŭ k'ŭrim kage 아이스 크림 가게; **ice cube** kak ŏrŭm 각 얼음

iced *drink* ŏrŭmŭl nŏhŭn 얼음을 넣은

iced coffee aisŭ k'ŏp'i 아이스 커피

ice hockey aisŭ hak'i 아이스 하키

ice rink sŭk'eit'ŭjang 스케이트장

icicle kodŭrŭm 고드름

icon (*cultural*) sang 상; COMPUT aik'on 아이콘

icy *road*, *surface* ŏrŭmi ŏrŭn 얼음이 얼은; *welcome* ssalssarhan 쌀쌀한

idea saenggak 생각; ***good ~!*** choŭn saenggagiya! 좋은 생각이야!; ***I have no ~*** nan chal morŭgennŭndeyo 난 잘 모르겠는데요; ***it's not a good ~ to …*** …hanŭn kŏsŭn choŭn saenggagi animnida …하는 것은 좋은 생각이 아닙니다

ideal (*perfect*) isangjŏgin 이상적인

idealistic isangjuŭijŏgin 이상주의적인

identical tong-irhan 동일한; ~ ***twins*** illanssŏng ssangdung-i 일란성 쌍둥이

identification hwagin 확인; (*papers etc*) chŭngmyŏngsŏ 증명서

identify hwaginhada 확인하다

identity shinwŏn 신원; ***their sense of national ~*** kŭdŭrŭi kungmin chuch'eŭishik 그들의 국민 주체의식

identity card shinbun chŭngmyŏngsŏ 신분 증명서

ideological inyŏmjŏgin 이념적인

ideology ideollogi 이데올로기

idiom (*saying*) kwanyong-ŏ 관용어

idiomatic kwanyongjŏgin 관용적인

idiosyncrasy t'ŭktchil 특질

idiot pabo 바보

idiotic ŏrisŏgŭn 어리석은

idle 1 *adj person* nat'aehan 나태한; *threat* ssŭltteŏmnŭn 쓸데없는; *machinery* nolgo innŭn 놀고 있는; ***in an ~ moment*** hangahan ttaee 한가한 때에 **2** *v/i* (*of engine*) kongjŏnhada 공전하다

♦**idle away** *time etc* pindunggŏrida 빈둥거리다

idol usang 우상

idolize sungbaehada 숭배하다

idyllic nagwŏn-gat'ŭn 낙원같은

if manyak ...myŏn 만약 ...면; (*whether or not*) ...inji aninji ...인지 아닌지; ~ ***you catch a cold*** manyak kamgie kŏllimyŏn 만약 감기에 걸리면; ***ask him ~ he will be there*** kŭege kŏgi issŭl kŏshinji aninji murŏposeyo 그에게 거기 있을 것인지 아닌지 물어보세요

igloo igŭllu 이글루

ignite *v/t* purŭl puch'ida 불을 붙이다

ignition (*in car*) chŏmhwa changch'i 점화 장치; ~ ***key*** igŭnishyŏn k'i 이그니션 키

ignorance muji 무지

ignorant morŭnŭn 모르는; (*rude*) muryehan 무례한

ignore mushihada 무시하다

ill ap'ŭn 아픈; ***fall ~***, ***be taken ~*** pyŏngdŭlda 병들다

illegal pulppŏbŭi 불법의

illegible ilkki ŏryŏun 읽기 어려운

illegitimate pulppŏpŭi 불법의; ***an ~ child*** sasaeng-a 사생아
ill-fated purunhan 불운한
illicit wibŏbŭi 위법의
illiterate munmaeng-ŭi 문맹의
ill-mannered muryehan 무례한
ill-natured sŏngmiga koyak'an 성미가 고약한
illness pyŏng 병
illogical pinollijŏgin 비논리적인
ill-tempered sŏngkkal innŭn 성깔 있는
illtreat hakttaehada 학대하다
illuminate *building etc* chomyŏnghada 조명하다
illuminating *remarks etc* punmyŏnghage hanŭn 분명하게 하는
illusion hwanyŏng 환영
illustrate *book* sap'warŭl kŭrida 삽화를 그리다; (*with examples*) yeshihada 예시하다
illustration kŭrim 그림; (*example*) shillye 실례
illustrator sap'waga 삽화가
ill will agŭi 악의
image (*picture*) imiji 이미지; (*exact likeness*) ppaedalmŭn mosŭp 빼닮은 모습; (*of politician, company*) insang 인상
image-conscious ch'emyŏnŭl ch'arinŭn 체면을 차리는
imaginable sangsanghal su innŭn 상상할 수 있는; ***the biggest / smallest size ~*** sangsanghal su innŭn ch'oedaeŭi / ch'oesoŭi k'ŭgi 상상할 수 있는 최대의 / 최소의 크기
imaginary kasang-ŭi 가상의
imagination sangsang 상상; ***it's all in your ~*** kŭgŏsŭn chŏnbu tangshinŭi sangsang-imnida 그것은 전부 당신의 상상입니다
imaginative sangsangnyŏgi p'ungbuhan 상상력이 풍부한
imagine sangsanghada 상상하다; ***I can just ~ it*** sangsang-i kamnida 상상이 갑니다; ***you're imagining things*** tangshini sangsanghanŭn kŏyeyo 당신이 상상하는 거에요
imbecile chŏngshin pagyaktcha 정신 박약자
IMF (= ***International Monetary Fund***) Kuktche T'onghwa Kigŭm 국제 통화 기금, Aiemep'ŭ 아이엠에프
imitate mobanghada 모방하다
imitation (*copying*) mobang 모방; (*something copied*) mojop'um 모조품
Imjin River Imjin-gang 임진강
immaculate t'i ŏmnŭn 티 없는
immaterial sanggwanŏmnŭn 상관없는
immature misŏngsugŭi 미성숙의
immediate chŭksshiŭi 즉시의; ***the ~ family*** *paeuja ttonŭn pumo hyŏngje, chashik* 배우자 또는 부모 형제, 자식; ***in the ~ neighborhood*** injŏp'an kose 인접한 곳에
immediately chŭksshiro 즉시로; ***~ after the bank / church*** ŭnhaeng / kyohoe paro yŏp'e 은행 / 교회 바로 옆에
immense ŏmch'ŏngnan 엄청난
immerse tamgŭda 담그다; ***~ oneself in*** molttuhada 몰두하다
immersion heater t'uip chŏnyŏlgi 투입 전열기
immigrant *n* ijuja 이주자
immigrate ijuhada 이주하다
immigration (*act*) iju 이주
Immigration Bureau Ch'urip Kwalliguk 출입 관리국
imminent chŏlbak'an 절박한
immobilize *factory* kadonghaji mot'age hada 가동하지 못하게 하다; *person* umjigiji mot'age hada 움직이지 못하게 하다; *car* kadongshik'iji mot'age hada 가동시키지 못하게 하다
immoderate mujŏltchehan 무절제한
immoral pudodŏk'an 부도덕한
immorality pudodŏk 부도덕
immortal pulmyŏrŭi 불멸의
immortality pulmyŏl 불멸
immune (*to illness, infection*) myŏnyŏgŭi 면역의; (*from ruling, requirement*) myŏnjedoen 면제된
immune system MED myŏnyŏk ch'egye 면역 체계
immunity (*to infection*) myŏnyŏk 면역; (*from ruling*) myŏnje 면제; ***diplomatic ~*** oegyomyŏnch'aek 외교면책

impact *n* (*of meteorite, vehicle*) ch'ungdol 충돌; (*of new manager etc*) yŏnghyangnyŏk 영향력; (*effect*) yŏnghyang 영향
impair haech'ida 해치다
impaired sonsangdoen 손상된
impartial kongjŏnghan 공정한
impassable *road* t'onghaenghal su ŏmnŭn 통행할 수 없는
impasse (*in negotiations etc*) kongyŏng 곤경
impassioned *speech, plea* yŏltchŏngjŏgin 열정적인
impassive naengjŏnghan 냉정한
impatience sŏnggŭp'am 성급함
impatient sŏnggŭp'an 성급한
impatiently sŏnggŭp'age 성급하게
impeccable *turnout* namural te ŏmnŭn 나무랄 데 없는; *English* wanbyŏk'an 완벽한
impeccably *dressed* namural te ŏpsshi 나무랄 데 없이; *speak Korean* wanbyŏk'age 완벽하게
impede panghaehada 방해하다
impediment (*in speech*) tŏdŭmgŏrim 더듬거림
impending imbak'an 임박한
impenetrable hearil su ŏmnŭn 헤아릴 수 없는
imperative 1 *adj* kkok haeya hal 꼭 해야 할; ***it is ~ that we go now*** urinŭn chigŭm kkok kaya handa 우리는 지금 꼭 가야 한다 **2** *n* GRAM myŏngnyŏngppŏp 명령법
imperceptible nŏmu chaga kamjihal su ŏmnŭn 너무 작아 감지할 수 없는
imperfect 1 *adj* purwanjŏnhan 불완전한 **2** *n* GRAM miwallyo 미완료
imperial chegugŭi 제국의
impersonal piin-ganjŏgin 비인간적인
impersonate (*as a joke*) hyungnaenaeda 흉내내다; (*illegally*) wijanghada 위장하다
impertinence kŏnbangjim 건방짐
impertinent kŏnbangjin 건방진
imperturbable ch'abunhan 차분한
impervious: **~ *to*** ...e mudŏmdŏmhan ...에 무덤덤한
impetuous ch'ungdongjŏgin 충동적인
impetus (*of campaign etc*) yŏse 여세
implement 1 *n* togu 도구 **2** *v/t measures etc* shirhaenghada 실행하다
implicate: **~ *s.o. in sth*** nugurŭl muŏse yŏllu shik'ida 누구를 무엇에 연루 시키다
implication hamch'uk 함축
implicit hamch'uktchŏgin 함축적인; *trust* chŏlttaejŏgin 절대적인
implore kanch'ŏnghada 간청하다
imply amshihada 암시하다
impolite pŏrŭt ŏmnŭn 버릇 없는
import 1 *n* suip 수입 **2** *v/t* suip'ada 수입하다
importance chungnyosŏng 중요성
important chungnyohan 중요한
importer suiptcha 수입자
impose *tax* pugwahada 부과하다; **~ *oneself on s.o.*** nuguege pudamŭl chuda 누구에게 부담을 주다
imposing insangjŏgin 인상적인
impossibility pulganŭng 불가능
impossible pulganŭnghan 불가능한
impostor sagikkun 사기꾼
impotence sŏng pullŭng 성 불능
impotent muryŏk'an 무력한; MED sŏng pullŭng-ŭi 성 불능의
impoverished pin-gone tchidŭn 빈곤에 찌든
impractical *person, suggestion* pihyŏnshiltchŏgin 비현실적인
impress kammyŏng chuda 감명 주다; ***be ~ed by s.o. / sth*** nuguege / muŏse kammyŏng pat-tta 누구에게 / 무엇에 감명 받다; ***I'm not ~ed*** chŏrŭl shilmangshik'inŭn-gunyo 저를 실망시키는군요
impression nŭkkim 느낌; (*impersonation*) hyungnaenaegi 흉내내기; ***make a good / bad ~ on s.o.*** nuguege choŭn / nappŭn insangŭl chuda 누구에게 좋은 / 나쁜 인상을 주다; ***get the ~ that ...*** ...ranŭn insang-ŭl pat-tta ...라는 인상을 받다
impressionable kamsusŏng-i yeminhan 감수성이 예민한
impressive insangjŏgin 인상적인
imprint *n* (*of credit card*) nullŏ tchigŭn chaguk 눌러 찍은 자국
imprison t'uok'ada 투옥하다
imprisonment t'uok 투옥
improbable irŏnal kŏt kattchi anŭn

일어날 것 같지 않은
improper *behavior* pujŏktchŏrhan 부적절한
improve 1 *v/t* hyangsangshik'ida 향상시키다 **2** *v/i* hyangsanghada 향상하다
improvement hyangsang 향상
improvise *v/i* (*in music*) chŭk'ŭngŭro hada 즉흥으로 하다; (*in plans*) chŭkssŏgesŏ mandŭlda 즉석에서 만들다
impudent ppŏnppŏnsŭrŏun 뻔뻔스러운
impulse ch'ungdong 충동; ***do sth on an ~*** ch'ungdongjŏgŭro muŏsŭl hada 충동적으로 무엇을 하다; ***~ buy*** ch'ungdong kumae 충동 구매
impulsive ch'ungdongjŏgin 충동적인
impunity: ***with ~*** pŏrŭl pat-tchi ank'o 벌을 받지 않고
impure pulssunhan 불순한
in 1 *prep* ...e(sŏ) …에(서); ***~ Washington / Seoul*** Wŏshingt'ŏne(sŏ) / Sŏure(sŏ) 워싱턴에(서) / 서울에(서); ***~ the street*** kŏrie(sŏ) 거리에(서); ***wounded ~ the leg / arm*** tarie / pare pusang-ŭl ibŭn 다리에 / 팔에 부상을 입은 ◊ (*inside*) ... ane / soge ...안에 / 속에; ***~ the box*** sangja ane 상자 안에; ***put it ~ your pocket*** chumŏni soge nŏŏ twŏra 주머니 속에 넣어 둬라 ◊: ***~ his novel*** kŭŭi sosŏl soge(sŏ) 그의 소설 속에(서); ***~ Faulkner*** P'ok'ŭnŏŭi chakp'um soge(sŏ) 포크너의 작품 속에(서) ◊ (*time*) ...e …에; ***~ 1999*** 1999nyŏne 1999년에; ***~ two hours*** (*from now*) tu shigan ane 두 시간 안에, tu shigan inaee 두 시간 이내에; ***~ the morning*** ach'ime 아침에; ***~ the summer*** yŏrŭme 여름에; ***~ August*** p'arwŏre 팔월에 ◊ (*manner*) …(ŭ)ro …(으)로; ***~ English / Korean*** Yŏng-ŏro / Han-gugŏro 영어로 / 한국어로; ***~ a loud voice*** k'ŭn mokssoriro 큰 목소리로; ***~ yellow*** noransaegŭro 노란색으로 ◊ (*while*): ***~ crossing the road*** kirŭl kŏnnŏnŭn tojung-e 길을 건너는 도중에; ***~ agreeing to this*** (*by virtue of*) igŏse tong-ŭihamŭrossŏ 이것에 동의함으로써 ◊: ***three ~ all*** t'ongt'ŭrŏ se kae 통틀어 세 개; ***one ~ ten*** yŏl kae chung han kae 열 개 중 한 개 **2** *adv*: ***be ~*** (*at home, in the building etc*) ane it-tta 안에 있다; (*arrived: of train*) toch'ak'an 도착한; ***when the diskette is ~*** tisŭk'eshi ane issŭl ttae 디스켓이 안에 있을 때; ***~ here*** yŏgie 여기에 **3** *adj* (*fashionable, popular*) yuhaenghanŭn 유행하는; ***pink is ~*** punhongsaegi yuhaeng-iyeyo 분홍색이 유행이예요
inability munŭng 무능
inaccessible chŏpkkŭnhagi ŏryŏun 접근하기 어려운
inaccurate pujŏnghwak'an 부정확한
inactive hwalttonghaji annŭn 활동하지 않는
inadequate pujŏkttanghan 부적당한
inadvisable kwŏnhal su ŏmnŭn 권할 수 없는
inanimate musaengmurŭi 무생물의
inapplicable chŏgyonghal su ŏmnŭn 적용할 수 없는
inappropriate pujŏkttanghan 부적당한
inarticulate marŭl ttokttok'i mot'anŭn 말을 똑똑히 못하는
inattentive pujuŭihan 부주의한
inaudible tŭlliji annŭn 들리지 않는
inaugural *speech* ch'wiimŭi 취임의
inaugurate *new building* kaegwanhada 개관하다; *new era* yŏlda 열다; *president* …ŭi ch'wiimshigŭl kŏhaenghada …의 취임식을 거행하다
inborn t'agonan 타고난
inbreeding tongjong pŏnshik 동종 번식
inc. (= ***incorporated***) pŏbin hoesa 법인 회사
incalculable *damage* makttaehan 막대한
incapable nŭngnyŏgi ŏmnŭn 능력이 없는; ***be ~ of doing sth*** muŏsŭl hanŭn kŏse munŭnghada 무엇을 하는 것에 무능하다
incendiary device panghwajangch'i 방화장치
incense[1] *n* hyang 향

incense[2] *v/t* maeu hwanage hada 매우 화나게 하다
incentive tonggi 동기
incessant kkŭnimŏmnŭn 끊임없는
incessantly kkŭnimŏpsshi 끊임없이
incest kŭnch'insanggan 근친상간
inch *n* inch'i 인치
incident sakkŏn 사건
incidental uyŏnhi irŏnanŭn 우연히 일어나는; ~ ***remark*** uyŏnhi naon mal 우연히 나온 말; ~ ***expenses*** chap-ppi 잡비
incidentally mari nan-gime 말이 난김에
incinerator sogangno 소각로
incision chŏlgae 절개
incisive *mind*, *analysis* nalk'aroun 날카로운
incite kyŏngnyŏhada 격려하다; ~ ***s.o. to do sth*** nuguege muŏsŭl hadorok kyŏngnyŏhada 누구에게 무엇을 하도록 격려하다
inclement *weather* hŏmak'an 험악한
inclination (*tendency*, *liking*) sŏnghyang 성향
incline: ***be ~d to do sth*** muŏsŭl hanŭn kyŏnghyang-i it-tta 무엇을 하는 경향이 있다
inclose → ***enclose***
include p'ohamhada 포함하다
including *prep* …ŭl / rŭl p'ohamhayŏ …을 / 를 포함하여
inclusive 1 *adj price* p'ohamhan 포함한 **2** *prep* p'ohamhayŏ 포함하여; ~ ***of*** …ŭl / rŭl p'ohamhayŏ …을 / 를 포함하여 **3** *adv* ilch'erŭl p'ohamhayŏ 일체를 포함하여; ***from Monday to Thursday*** ~ wŏryoilbut'ŏ mogyoilkkaji 월요일부터 목요일까지
incoherent tusŏŏmnŭn 두서없는
income sodŭk 소득
income tax sodŭksse 소득세
incoming *flight* toch'ak'anŭn 도착하는; *phone call* kŏllyŏonŭn 걸려오는; *president* huimŭi 후임의; ~ ***tide*** milmul 밀물
incomparable pihal te ŏmnŭn 비할 데 없는
incompatibility (*of personalities*) yangnip'al su ŏpssŭm 양립할 수 없음; (*of systems*) hohwan pulganŭng 호환 불가능
incompatible *personalities* yangnip'al su ŏmnŭn 양립할 수 없는; *formats*, *systems* hohwandoeji annŭn 호환되지 않는
incompetence munŭngnyŏk 무능력
incompetent munŭngnyŏk'an 무능력한
incomplete purwanjŏnhan 불완전한
incomprehensible ihaehal su ŏmnŭn 이해할 수 없는
inconceivable saenggakhal su choch'a ŏmnŭn 생각할 수 조차 없는
inconclusive kyŏltchŏngjŏgiji anŭn 결정적이지 않은
incongruous chohwadoeji annŭn 조화되지 않는
inconsiderate saryŏŏmnŭn 사려없는
inconsistent mosundoenŭn 모순되는
inconsolable wirohal kil ŏmnŭn 위로할 길 없는
inconspicuous nune ttŭiji annŭn 눈에 띄지 않는
inconvenience *n* pulp'yŏn 불편
inconvenient pulp'yŏnhan 불편한
incorporate p'ohamhada 포함하다
incorporated COM pŏbin hoesa 법인 회사
incorrect t'ŭllin 틀린
incorrectly t'ŭllige 틀리게
incorrigible ŏtchŏl su ŏmnŭn 어쩔 수 없는
increase 1 *v/t* chŭnggashik'ida 증가시키다 **2** *v/i* chŭnggahada 증가하다 **3** *n* chŭngga 증가
increasing chŭnggahanŭn 증가하는
increasingly kalssurok tŏ 갈수록 더
incredible (*amazing*, *very good*) midŏjiji annŭn 믿어지지 않는
incriminate choerŭl ssŭiuda 죄를 씌우다; ~ ***oneself*** choerŭl chainhada 죄를 자인하다
in-crowd naebu haeksshim chipttan 내부 핵심 집단
incubator ink'yubeit'ŏ 인큐베이터
incur ch'oraehada 초래하다
incurable pulch'iŭi 불치의
indebted: ***be ~ to s.o.*** nuguege shinserŭl chida 누구에게 신세를 지다
indecent chŏmjanch'i mot'an 점잖지

못한
indecisive kyŏlttanssŏng-i ŏmnŭn 결단성이 없는
indecisiveness uyubudan 우유부단
indeed (*in fact*) chinshillo 진실로; (*yes, agreeing*) kŭraeyo 그래요; ***very much*** ~ chŏngmal kŭraeyo 정말 그래요
indefinable magyŏnhan 막연한
indefinite muhanjŏnghan 무한정한; ~ ***article*** GRAM pujŏng kwansa 부정 관사
indefinitely mugihanŭro 무기한으로
indelicate mushin-gyŏnghan 무신경한
indent 1 *n* (*in text*) anŭro tŭryŏssŭgi 안으로 들여쓰기 **2** *v/t line* anŭro tŭryŏsŏ ssŭda 안으로 들여서 쓰다
independence tongnip 독립
Independence Day Tongnip Kinyŏmil 독립 기념일
independent tongniptchŏgin 독립적인
independently *deal with* tongniptchŏgŭro 독립적으로; ~ ***of*** pyŏlgaero 별개로
indescribable hyŏng-ŏnhal su ŏmnŭn 형언할 수 없는
indescribably *bad, beautiful* hyŏng-ŏnhal su ŏpttorok 형언할 수 없도록
indestructible p'agoehal su ŏmnŭn 파괴할 수 없는
indeterminate pujŏnghwak'an 부정확한
index (*for book*) saegin 색인
index card saegin k'adŭ 색인 카드
index finger chipkke sonkkarak 집게 손가락
India Indo 인도
Indian 1 *adj* Indoŭi 인도의 **2** *n* Indoin 인도인; (*American*) Indian 인디안
Indian summer hwach'anghan nalssi 화창한 날씨
indicate 1 *v/t* karik'ida 가리키다 **2** *v/i* (*when driving*) (tonŭn panghyang-ŭl) p'yoshihada (도는 방향을) 표시하다
indication p'yoshi 표시
indicator (*on car*) p'yoshidŭng 표시등
indict kisohada 기소하다
indifference mugwanshim 무관심
indifferent mugwanshimhan 무관심한; (*mediocre*) pot'ong-ŭi 보통의
indigestible sohwahagi ŏryŏun 소화하기 어려운
indigestion sohwa pullyang 소화 불량
indignant pun-gaehan 분개한
indignation pun-gae 분개
indirect kanjŏptchŏgin 간접적인
indirectly kanjŏptchŏgŭro 간접적으로
indiscreet mubunbyŏrhan 무분별한
indiscretion (*act*) mubunbyŏl 무분별
indiscriminate much'abyŏrŭi 무차별의
indispensable p'ilssuŭi 필수의
indisposed (*not well*) momi pulp'yŏnhan 몸이 불편한
indisputable nonŭiŭi yŏjiga ŏmnŭn 논의의 여지가 없는
indisputably ŭishimhal yŏji ŏpsshi 의심할 여지 없이
indistinct tturyŏt'aji anŭn 뚜렷하지 않은
indistinguishable pun-gan hal su ŏmnŭn 분간 할 수 없는
individual 1 *n* kaein 개인 **2** *adj* (*separate*) kaegaeŭi 개개의; (*personal*) kaeinŭi 개인의
individualist kaeinjuŭija 개인주의자
individually kaebyŏltchŏgŭro 개별적으로
indivisible pulgabunŭi 불가분의
indoctrinate chuip'ada 주입하다
indolence keŭrŭm 게으름
indolent nat'aehan 나태한
Indochina Indoch'aina 인도차이나
Indochinese *adj* Indoch'ainaŭi 인도차이나의
Indonesia Indoneshia 인도네시아
Indonesian 1 *adj* Indoneshiaŭi 인도네시아의 **2** *n* (*person*) Indoneshiain 인도네시아인
indoor shillaeŭi 실내의
indoors shillaee(sŏ) 실내에(서)
induction ceremony orient'eishyŏn 오리엔테이션
indulge 1 *v/t* (*oneself, one's tastes*) t'amnik'ada 탐닉하다 **2** *v/i*: ~ ***in sth*** muŏse ppajida 무엇에 빠지다
indulgence (*of tastes, appetite etc*) t'amnik 탐닉; (*laxity*) ŭngsŏk padŭm

응석 받음
indulgent (*not strict enough*) kwandaehan 관대한
industrial sanŏbŭi 산업의
industrial action nodong chaeng-ŭi haeng-wi 노동 쟁의 행위
industrial dispute nosaganŭi purhwa 노사간의 불화
industrialist shirŏpkka 실업가
industrialize 1 *v/t* sanŏp'wahada 산업화하다 **2** *v/i* sanŏp'wadoeda 산업화되다
industrial park kong-ŏpttanji 공업 단지
industrial waste sanŏpp'yegimul 산업폐기물
industrious kŭnmyŏnhan 근면한
industry sanŏp 산업
ineffective *person* munŭnghan 무능한; *measures, device* hyokkwaga ŏmnŭn 효과가 없는
ineffectual *person* munŭnghan 무능한
inefficient pinŭngnyultchŏgin 비능률적인
ineligible chagyŏgi ŏmnŭn 자격이 없는
inept nŭngnyŏgi ŏmnŭn 능력이 없는
inequality pulp'yŏngdŭng 불평등
inescapable p'ihal su ŏmnŭn 피할 수 없는
inestimable hearil su ŏmnŭn 헤아릴 수 없는
inevitable p'ihal su ŏmnŭn 피할 수 없는
inevitably p'ihal su ŏpsshi 피할 수 없이
inexcusable pyŏnmyŏnghal su ŏmnŭn 변명할 수 없는
inexhaustible *person* chich'il tchul morŭnŭun 지칠 줄 모르는; *supply* mujinjanghan 무진장한
inexpensive kapsshi ssan 값이 싼
inexperienced kyŏnghŏmi ŏmnŭn 경험이 없는
inexplicable sŏlmyŏnghal su ŏmnŭn 설명할 수 없는
inexpressible *joy* hyŏngŏnhal su ŏmnŭn 형언할 수 없는
infallible chŏlttae t'ŭllilli ŏmnŭn 절대 틀릴리 없는
infamous angmyŏng nop'ŭn 악명 높은
infancy yuagi 유아기; *fig* ch'ogi 초기
infant yua 유아
infantile *pej* yuch'ihan 유치한
infantry pobyŏngdae 보병대
infantry soldier pobyŏng 보병
infatuated: ***be ~ with s.o.*** nuguege holttak panhada 누구에게 홀딱 반하다
infect kamyŏmshik'ida 감염시키다; (*of person*) muldŭrida 물들이다; *food, water* oyŏmshik'ida 오염시키다; ***become ~ed*** (*of person*) muri tŭlda 물이 들다; (*of wound*) kamyŏmdoeda 감염되다
infected *wound* kamyŏmdoen 감염된
infection kamyŏm 감염
infectious *disease* chŏnyŏmssŏng-ŭi 전염성의; *laughter* omgyŏjigi shwiun 옮겨지기 쉬운
infer: ***~ X from Y*** Yesŏ Xŭl / rŭl ch'uronhada Y에서 X을 / 를 추론하다
inferior *quality* iryuŭi 이류의; (*in rank*) hagŭbŭi 하급의; (*in company*) hawiŭi 하위의
inferiority (*in quality*) iryu 이류
inferiority complex yŏlttŭng ŭishik 열등 의식
infertile *soil* pulmoŭi 불모의; *woman* purimŭi 불임의
infertility (*of soil*) pulmo 불모; (*of woman*) purim 불임
infidelity pujŏng 부정
infiltrate *v/t* ch'imip'ada 침입하다
infinite muhanhan 무한한
infinitive GRAM pujŏngsa 부정사
infinity muhan 무한
infirm hŏyak'an 허약한
infirmary (*in boarding school*) yanghoshil 양호실; MIL chillyoso 진료소
infirmity hŏyak 허약
inflame pul t'aorŭge hada 불 타오르게 하다
inflammable inhwassŏng-ŭi 인화성의
inflammation MED yŏmtchŭng 염증
inflatable *dinghy* komu pot'ŭ 고무 보트
inflate *v/t tire, dinghy* pup'ullida 부풀리다; *economy* t'onghwa

p'aengch'angshik'ida 통화 팽창시키다
inflation inp'ŭlle(ishyŏn) 인플레(이션)
inflationary (*of inflation*) inp'ŭlleishyŏnŭi 인플레이션의; (*causing inflation*) inp'ŭlleishyŏnŭl yubarhanŭn 인플레이션을 유발하는
inflection (*of voice*) ŏgyang 억양
inflexible *attitude*, *person* kup'il su ŏmnŭn 굽힐 수 없는
inflict: ~ ***X on Y*** Xŭl / rŭl Yege kahada X을 / 를 Y에게 가하다
in-flight pihaeng chung-ŭi 비행 중의; ~ ***entertainment*** kinaeorak 기내오락
influence 1 *n* yŏnghyang 영향; (*power to influence*) yŏnghyangnyŏk 영향력; ***be a good / bad ~ on s.o.*** nuguege choŭn / nappŭn yŏnghyang-ŭl chuda 누구에게 좋은 / 나쁜 영향을 주다 **2** *v/t s.o.'s thinking* yŏnghyang kkich'ida 영향 끼치다; *decision* yŏnghyang chuda 영향 주다
influential yŏnghyangnyŏk innŭn 영향력 있는
influenza tok-kkam 독감
inform 1 *v/t* allida 알리다; ~ ***X of Y*** Xege Yrŭl allyŏjuda X에게 Y를 알려주다; ***please keep me ~ed*** kyesok'aesŏ allyŏjuseyo 계속해서 알려주세요 **2** *v/i* shin-gohada 신고하다; ~ ***on s.o.*** nugurŭl shin-gohada 누구를 신고하다
informal *meeting*, *conversation* pigongshigŭi 비공식의; *form of address*, *agreement* yaksshigŭi 약식의; *dress* p'yŏngsangbok ch'arimŭi 평상복 차림의
informality (*of meeting*, *conversation*) pigongshik 비공식; (*of form of address*, *agreement*) yaksshik 약식
informant chŏngbo chegongja 정보 제공자
information chŏngbo 정보
information science chŏngbo kwahak 정보 과학; **information scientist** chŏngbo kwahaktcha 정보 과학자; **information technology** chŏngbo kisul 정보 기술
informative chŏngboga manŭn 정보가 많은
informer milgoja 밀고자
infra-red *adj* chŏgoesŏnŭi 적외선의
infrastructure (*of economy*, *society*) kigan shisŏl 기간 시설; (*of organization*) habu chojik 하부 조직
infrequent tŭmun 드문
infuriate kyŏngno shik'ida 격노 시키다; ***be ~ed at*** ...e nobaldaebarhada ...에 노발대발하다
infuriating kyŏngnok'e hanŭn 격노케 하는
infuse *v/i* (*of tea*) urida 우리다
infusion (*herb tea*) uryŏnaem 우려냄
ingenious tokch'angjŏgin 독창적인
ingenuity tokch'angnyŏk 독창력
ingot (*gold*) kŭmgoe 금괴; (*silver*) ŭn-goe 은괴
ingratiate: ~ ***oneself with s.o.*** nuguŭi piwirŭl match'uda 누구의 비위를 맞추다
ingratitude paeŭnmangdŏk 배은망덕
ingredient chaeryo 재료; *fig* yoso 요소
inhabit kŏjuhada 거주하다
inhabitable sal su innŭn 살 수 있는
inhabitant kŏjuja 거주자
inhale 1 *v/t* pparadŭrida 빨아들이다 **2** *v/i* (*when smoking*) hŭbip'ada 흡입하다
inhaler hŭbipkki 흡입기
inherit sangsok'ada 상속하다
inheritance sangsok 상속; (*characteristics*) yujŏn 유전
inhibit *growth*, *conversation etc* ŏktchehada 억제하다
inhibited ŏktchedoen 억제된
inhibition ŏktche 억제
inhospitable *city*, *people* pulch'injŏrhan 불친절한; *climate* hwangp'yehan 황폐한
in-house 1 *adj* sanaeŭi 사내의 **2** *adv work* sanaee(sŏ) 사내에(서)
inhuman injŏng ŏmnŭn 인정 없는
initial 1 *adj* ch'oech'oŭi 최초의 **2** *n* inishyŏl 이니셜 **3** *v/t* (*write initials on*) inishyŏllo ssŭda 이니셜로 쓰다
initially ch'ŏŭmbut'ŏ 처음부터
initiate kaeshihada 개시하다
initiation kaeshi 개시
initiative chudo 주도; ***do sth on one's own ~*** muŏsŭl solssŏnhaesŏ

hada 무엇을 솔선해서 하다
inject *medicine*, *drug* chusahada 주사하다; *fuel* nŏt'a 넣다; *capital* t'uip'ada 투입하다
injection MED chusa 주사; (*of fuel*) chuip 주입; (*of capital*) t'uip 도입
injure sangch'ŏ ip'ida 상처 입히다
injured 1 *adj leg*, *feelings* sangch'ŏ ibŭn 상처 입은 **2** *n*: ***the*** ~ pusangja 부상자
injury pusang 부상
injustice pujŏng 부정
ink ingk'ŭ 잉크
inkjet (**printer**) ingk'ŭ chet p'ŭrint'ŏ 잉크 젯 프린터
inland *sea* yuktchi tchogŭi 육지 쪽의; *mail*, *areas*, *trade* naeryugŭi 내륙의
in-laws inch'ŏk 인척
inlay *n* sanggam 상감
inlet (*of sea*) humi 후미; (*in machine*) chuipkku 주입구
inmate (*of prison*) sugamja 수감자; (*of mental hospital*) ibwŏn hwanja 입원 환자
inn yŏgwan 여관
innate t'agonan 타고난
inner naebuŭi 내부의; *thoughts* naetchŏgin 내적인
inner city toshi chungshimŭi (pinmin) chiyŏk 도시 중심의 (빈민) 지역
innermost kajang kipssuk'an 가장 깊숙한
inner tube (chajŏn-gŏ) t'yubŭ (자전거) 튜브
innocence LAW kyŏlbaek 결백; (*of child*) sunjinham 순진함
innocent LAW kyŏlbaek'an 결백한; *child* sunjinhan 순진한
innovation hyŏksshin 혁신
innovative hyŏksshinjŏgin 혁신적인
innovator (*person*) hŏksshin-ga 혁신가; (*company*) hyŏksshinhanŭn hoesa 혁신하는 회사
innumerable musuhan 무수한
inoculate yebang chŏptchonghada 예방 접종하다
inoculation yebang chŏptchong 예방 접종
inoffensive *animal* muhaehan 무해한; *person*, *attitude* agŭiga ŏmnŭn 악의가 없는
inorganic mugiŭi 무기의
in-patient ibwŏnhwanja 입원환자
input 1 *n* (*into project etc*) t'uip 투입; COMPUT imnyŏk 입력 **2** *v/t* (*into project*) t'uip'ada 투입하다; COMPUT imnyŏk'ada 입력하다
input port COMPUT imnyŏk tanja 입력 단자
inquest wŏnin kyumyŏng 원인 규명
inquire munŭihada 문의하다; ~ ***into sth*** muŏse taehae chosahada 무엇에 대해 조사하다
inquiry munŭi 문의
inquisitive t'amgujŏgin 탐구적인
insane mich'in 미친
insanitary piwisaengjŏgin 비위생적인
insanity chŏngshin isang 정신 이상
insatiable t'amyokssŭrŏun 탐욕스러운
inscription (*in book*) chemyŏng 제명
inscrutable pulgasaŭihan 불가사의한
insect konch'ung 곤충
insecticide salch'ungje 살충제
insect repellent pangch'ungje 방충제
insecure puranhan 불안한
insecurity puranjŏng 불안정
insensitive mugamgak'an 무감각한
insensitivity mugamgak 무감각
inseparable *two issues* pullihal su ŏmnŭn 분리할 수 없는; *two people* heŏjil su ŏmnŭn 헤어질 수 없는
insert 1 *n* (*in magazine etc*) sabip kwanggo 삽입 광고 **2** *v/t* kkiwŏ nŏt'a 끼워 넣다; ~ ***X into Y*** Xŭl/rŭl Ye kkiwŏ nŏt'a X을/를 Y에 끼워 넣다
insertion (*act*) sabip 삽입
inside 1 *n* (*of house*, *box*) naebu 내부; (*of road*) antchok 안쪽; ***somebody on the*** ~ naebuin 내부인; ~ ***out*** twijibŏsŏ 뒤집어서; ***turn sth*** ~ ***out*** muŏsŭl twijiptta 무엇을 뒤집다; ***know sth*** ~ ***out*** muŏsŭl wanbyŏk'age alda 무엇을 완벽하게 알다 **2** *prep* ane(sŏ) 안에(서); ~ ***the house*** chibane(sŏ) 집안에(서); ~ ***of 2 hours*** tushigan inae 두시간 이내 **3** *adv stay*, *remain* naebue(sŏ) 내부에(서); *go*, *carry* anŭro 안으로; ***we went*** ~ urinŭn anŭro tŭrŏgat-tta

우리는 안으로 들어갔다 **4** *adj* naebue innŭn 내부에 있는; **~ *information*** naebu chŏngbo 내부 정보; **~ *lane*** SP antchoklein 안쪽 레인; (*on road*) antchok kil 안쪽 길; **~ *pocket*** antchumŏni 안주머니

insider naebuin 내부인

insider trading FIN insaidŏ kŏrae 인사이더 거래

insides wijang 위장

insidious *disease* chamhaengssŏng-ŭi 잠행성의

insight t'ongch'al 통찰

insignificant *amount* chagŭmahan 자그마한; *person*, *problem* hach'anŭn 하찮은

insincere musŏng-ŭihan 무성의한

insincerity musŏng-ŭi 무성의

insinuate (*imply*) nŏnjishi pich'ida 넌지시 비치다

insist chujanghada 주장하다; ***please keep it, I ~*** sayangch'i mashigo kajiseyo 사양치 마시고 가지세요

♦**insist on** kangyohada 강요하다

insistent chibyohan 집요한

insolent kŏnbangjin 건방진

insoluble *problem* haegyŏrhal su ŏmnŭn 해결할 수 없는; *substance* yonghaedoeji annŭn 용해되지 않는

insolvent chibul pullŭng-ŭi 지불 불능의

insomnia pulmyŏntchŭng 불면증

inspect *work*, *tickets*, *baggage* chŏmgŏmhada 점검하다; *building*, *factory*, *school* shich'arhada 시찰하다

inspection (*of work*, *tickets*, *baggage*) chŏmgŏm 점검; (*of building*, *factory*, *school*) shich'al 시찰

inspector (*in factory etc*) kamch'altcha 감찰자

inspiration yŏnggam 영감; (*very good idea*) kibarhan saenggak 기발한 생각

inspire *respect etc* pullŏ irŭk'ida 불러 일으키다; ***be ~d by s.o.*** / ***sth*** nuguege / muŏse yŏnggamŭl pat-tta 누구에게 / 무엇에 영감을 받다

instability puranjŏng 불안정

instal(l) *equipment*, *software* sŏlch'ihada 설치하다

installation (*of equipment*, *software*) sŏlch'i 설치; ***military ~*** kunsashisŏl 군사시설

installment (*of story*, *TV drama etc*) (yŏnjaeŭi) il hoebun (연재의) 일 회분; (*payment*) punhal purip 분할 불입; ***monthly ~s*** wŏlbu 월부

installment plan punhal purip pangshik 분할 불입 방식

instance (*example*) ye 예; ***for ~*** yerŭl tŭrŏ 예를 들어

instant 1 *adj* chŭk-kkaktchŏgin 즉각적인 **2** *n* sun-gan 순간; ***in an ~*** sunshik-kkane 순식간에

instantaneous sunshik-kkanŭi 순식간의

instant coffee insŭt'ŏnt'ŭ k'ŏp'i 인스턴트 커피

instantly chŭksshi 즉시

instead taeshine 대신에; **~ *of*** … taeshine … 대신에

instep palttŭng 발등

instinct ponnŭng 본능

instinctive ponnŭngjŏgin 본능적인

institute 1 *n* yŏn-guso 연구소; (*academic*) hak'oe 학회; (*special home*) konggong kigwan 공공 기관 **2** *v/t inquiry* shijak'ada 시작하다

institution (*governmental*) kigwan 기관; (*something traditional*) kwansŭp 관습; (*setting up*) sŏltchŏng 설정

instruct (*order*) chishihada 지시하다; (*teach*) karŭch'ida 가르치다; **~ *X to do Y*** (*order*) Xege Y hal kŏsŭl chishihada X에게 Y할 것을 지시하다

instruction chishi sahang 지시 사항; ***~s for use*** sayongppŏp 사용법

instruction manual sayong sŏlmyŏngsŏ 사용 설명서

instructive kyoyuktchŏgin 교육적인

instructor kangsa 강사; (*in martial arts*) sabŏm 사범

instrument MUS ak-kki 악기; (*gadget*, *tool*) togu 도구

insubordinate pulboktchonghanŭn 불복종하는

insufficient pulch'ungbunhan 불충분한

insulate ELEC chŏryŏnhada 절연하다; (*against cold*) panghanhada 방한하다

insulation ELEC chŏryŏn 절연;

(against cold) panghan 방한
insulin inshyullin 인슐린
insult 1 *n* moyok 모욕 **2** *v/t* moyok'ada 모욕하다
insurance pohŏm 보험
insurance company pohŏm hoesa 보험 회사
insurance policy pohŏm chŭngsŏ 보험 증서
insure pohŏme tŭlda 보험에 들다; ***be ~ed*** pohŏme tŭrŏit-tta 보험에 들어있다
insurmountable kŭkppok'al su ŏmnŭn 극복할 수 없는
intact *(not damaged)* sonsangdoeji anŭn 손상되지 않은
intake *(of college etc)* suyong inwŏn 수용 인원
integrate *v/t* t'onghap'ada 통합하다
integrated circuit chiptchŏk hoero 집적 회로
integrity *(honesty)* chŏngjik 정직
intellect chisŏng 지성
intellectual 1 *adj* chitchŏgin 지적인 **2** *n* chisŏng-in 지성인
intelligence chinŭng 지능; *(news)* chŏngbo 정보
intelligence service chŏngbo kigwan 정보 기관
intelligent ttokttok'an 똑똑한
intelligible chal ihaehal su innŭn 잘 이해할 수 있는
intend … hal chaktchŏng-ida … 할 작정이다; ***~ to do sth*** *(do on purpose)* muŏsŭl ŭidohada 무엇을 의도하다; *(plan to do)* muŏsŭl hal chaktchŏng-ida 무엇을 할 작정이다; ***that's not what I ~ed*** kŭgŏn naega ŭidohan ke animnida 그건 내가 의도한 게 아닙니다
intense *sensation, pleasure* kangnyŏrhan 강렬한; *heat, pressure* kangnyŏk'an 강력한; *personality, concentration* kanghan 강한
intensify 1 *v/t effect, pressure* sege hada 세게 하다 **2** *v/i (of pain)* kanghaejida 강해지다; *(of fighting)* kyŏngnyŏrhaejida 격렬해지다
intensive *study, training, treatment* chiptchungjŏgin 집중적인
intensity *(of sensation, heat, pain)* kangdo 강도; *(of fighting)* kyŏngnyŏl 격렬
intensive care (unit) chunghwanjashil 중환자실
intensive course *(of language study)* chiptchung k'osŭ 집중 코스
intent: ***be ~ on doing sth*** *(determined to do)* muŏsŭl haryŏgo chaktchŏnghada 무엇을 하려고 작정하다; *(concentrating on)* muŏsŭl hanŭnde yŏltchunghada 무엇을 하는데 열중하다
intention ŭido 의도; ***I have no ~ of*** *(refuse to)* nanŭn … hal ŭidoga ŏpssŏyo 나는 … 할 의도가 없어요
intentional ŭidojŏgin 의도적인
intentionally koŭijŏgŭro 고의적으로
interaction sangho chagyong 상호 작용
interactive sangho chagyonghanŭn 상호 작용하는
intercede chungjaehada 중재하다
intercept *ball* karoch'aeda 가로채다; *message* yŏt-tŭt-tta 엿듣다; *missile* yogyŏk'ada 요격하다
interchange *n (of highways)* int'ŏch'einji 인터체인지
interchangeable pakkul su innŭn 바꿀 수 있는
intercom int'ŏk'ŏm 인터컴
intercourse *(sexual)* sŏnggyo 성교
interdependent sangho ŭijonhanŭn 상호 의존하는
interest 1 *n* kwanshim 관심; *(financial)* ija 이자; ***take an ~ in sth*** muŏse hŭngmirŭl kajida 무엇에 흥미를 가지다 **2** *v/t* hŭngmirŭl irŭk'ige hada 흥미를 일으키게 하다; ***does that offer ~ you?*** kŭ cheŭiga maŭme tŭmnikka? 그 제의가 마음에 듭니까
interested kwanshimi innŭn 관심이 있는; ***be ~ in sth*** muŏse kwanshimŭl kajida 무엇에 관심을 가지다; ***thanks, but I'm not ~*** komaptchiman, chŏn kwanshimi ŏmnŭndeyo 고맙지만, 전 관심이 없는데요
interesting chaemiinnŭn 재미있는
interest rate ijayul 이자율
interface 1 *n* chŏpch'ok yŏng-yŏk

접촉 영역, int'ŏpeisŭ 인터페이스 **2** *v/i* chŏpssok'ada 접속하다
interfere kansŏp'ada 간섭하다
♦**interfere with** *controls, plans* panghaehada 방해하다
interference kansŏp 간섭; RAD honsŏn 혼선
interior 1 *adj* shillaeŭi 실내의 **2** *n* (*of house*) shillae 실내; (*of country*) naeryuk 내륙; ***Department of the Interior*** Naemubu 내무부
interior decorator shillae changshik-kka 실내 장식가; **interior design** int'eriŏ tijain 인테리어 디자인; **interior designer** int'eriŏ tijainŏ 인테리어 디자이너
interlude (*at theater, concert*) mak-kkan 막간; (*period*) kigan 기간
intermediary *n* chungjaeja 중재자
intermediate *adj* chungganŭi 중간의
intermission (*in theater, movie theater*) hyuge shigan 휴게 시간
intern *v/t* kusok'ada 구속하다
internal *measurements* anŭi 안의; *trade* kung-naeŭi 국내의; (*within organization*) naebuŭi 내부의
internal combustion engine naeyŏn kigwan 내연 기관
internally (*in body*) ch'enaee(sŏ) 체내에(서); (*within organization*) naebujŏgŭro 내부적으로
Internal Revenue (Service) Kukssech'ŏng 국세청
international *adj* kuktchejŏgin 국제적인
International Court of Justice Kuktche Sabŏp Chaep'anso 국제 사법 재판소
internationally kuktchejŏgŭro 국제적으로
International Monetary Fund Kuktche T'onghwa Kigŭm 국제 통화 기금
Internet Int'ŏnet 인터넷; ***on the ~*** Int'ŏnet sangesŏ 인터넷 상에서
internist naekkwa chŏnmun ŭisa 내과 전문 의사
interpret 1 *v/t* (*linguistically*) t'ongyŏk'ada 통역하다; *music, comment etc* haesŏk'ada 해석하다 **2** *v/i* t'ongyŏk'ada 통역하다
interpretation (*linguistic*) t'ongyŏk 통역; (*of music, of meaning*) haesŏk 해석
interpreter t'ongyŏk-kka 통역가
interrelated *facts* sŏro kwan-gyega innŭn 서로 관계가 있는
interrogate shimmunhada 심문하다
interrogation shimmun 심문
interrogative *n* GRAM ŭimunsa 의문사
interrogator shimmunja 심문자
interrupt 1 *v/t speaker* chungdanshik'ida 중단시키다 **2** *v/i* chungdanhada 중단하다
interruption chungdan 중단
intersect kyoch'ahada 교차하다
intersection (*crossroads*) kyoch'a 교차
interstate *n* chugan kosok toro 주간 고속 도로
interval shigan kan-gyŏk 시간 간격; (*in theater, at concert*) hyuge shigan 휴게 시간
intervene (*of person, police etc*) chungjaehada 중재하다
intervention chungjae 중재
interview 1 *n* (*on TV, in paper*) int'ŏbyu 인터뷰; (*for job*) myŏnjŏp 면접 **2** *v/t* (*on TV, for paper*) int'ŏbyuhada 인터뷰하다; (*for job*) myŏnjŏp'ada 면접하다
interviewee (*on TV*) int'ŏbyu pannŭn saram 인터뷰 받는 사람; (*for job*) myŏnjŏp pannŭn saram 면접 받는 사람
interviewer (*on TV, for paper*) int'ŏbyuhanŭn saram 인터뷰하는 사람; (*for job*) myŏnjŏpkkwan 면접관
intestine ch'angja 창자
intimacy (*of friendship*) ch'insuk'am 친숙함; (*sexual*) kip'ŭn sai 깊은 사이
intimate *friend* ch'insuk'an 친숙한; (*sexually*) kip'ŭn saiin 깊은 사이인; *thoughts* kaeintchŏgin 개인적인
intimidate hyŏp-ppak'ada 협박하다
intimidation hyŏp-ppak 협박
into anŭro 안으로; (*change, transition*) ...(ŭ)ro ...(으)로; ***he put it ~ his suitcase*** kŭnŭn kŭgŏsŭl otkkabang anŭro nŏŏt-tta 그는 그것을 옷가방

안으로 넣었다; ***translate ~ English*** Yŏng-ŏro pŏnyŏk'ada 영어로 번역하다; ***be ~ sth*** F (*like*) muŏsŭl choahada 무엇을 좋아하다; (*be interested in*) muŏse kwanshimi it-tta 무엇에 관심이 있다; ***when you're ~ the job*** nega chomdŏ kŭ ire ikssuk'aejil ttae 네가 좀더 그 일에 익숙해질 때
intolerable ch'amŭl su ŏmnŭn 참을 수 없는
intolerant ch'amŭlssŏng ŏmnŭn 참을성 없는
intoxicated sul ch'wihan 술 취한
intransitive chadongsaŭi 자동사의
intravenous chŏngmaeng-naeŭi 정맥내의
intrepid taedamhan 대담한
intricate twiŏlk'in 뒤얽힌
intrigue 1 *n* ŭmmo 음모 **2** *v/t* hŭngmi kkŭlda 흥미 끌다; ***I would be ~d to know …*** chŏnŭn …ŭl / rŭl algo shipssŭmnida 저는 …을 / 를 알고 싶습니다
intriguing hogishimŭl chagŭk'anŭn 호기심을 자극하는
introduce sogaehada 소개하다; *new technique etc* toip'ada 도입하다; ***may I ~ …?*** …ŭl / rŭl sogaehaedo toelkkayo? …을 / 를 소개해도 될까요?
introduction (*to person, new food, sport etc*) sogae 소개; (*in book*) sŏron 서론; (*of new techniques etc*) toip 도입
introvert *n* naehyangtchŏgin saram 내향적인 사람
intrude ch'imbŏmhada 침범하다
intruder ch'imiptcha 침입자
intrusion ch'imbŏm 침범
intuition chik-kkwan 직관
invade ch'imnyak'ada 침략하다
invalid[1] *adj* muhyoŭi 무효의
invalid[2] *n* MED pyŏngja 병자
invalidate *claim, theory* muhyohwahada 무효화하다
invaluable *help* kapssŭl hearil su ŏmnŭn 값을 헤아릴 수 없는
invariably (*always*) hangsang 항상
invasion ch'imnyak 침략
invent palmyŏnghada 발명하다
invention palmyŏng 발명
inventive ch'ang-ŭijŏgin 창의적인
inventor palmyŏngga 발명가
inventory mongnok 목록
inverse *adj order* kŏkkuro toen 거꾸로 된
invert kŏkkuro hada 거꾸로 하다
inverted commas inyong puho 인용 부호
invertebrate *n* much'ŏkch'u tongmul 무척추 동물
invest 1 *v/t* t'ujadoeda 투자되다 **2** *v/i* t'ujahada 투자하다
investigate chosahada 조사하다
investigation chosa 조사
investigative journalism toktchajŏgin chosa podo 독자적인 조사 보도
investment t'uja 투자
investor t'ujaja 투자자
invigorating *climate* kiuni nage hanŭn 기운이 나게 하는
invincible mujŏgŭi 무적의
invisible nune poiji annŭn 눈에 보이지 않는
invitation ch'odae 초대
invite ch'odaehada 초대하다
invoice 1 *n* inboisŭ 인보이스 **2** *v/t customer* kumaesŏrŭl ponaeda 구매서를 보내다
involuntary muŭishiktchŏgin 무의식적인; (*forced*) kangjejŏgin 강제적인
involve *hard work, expense* subanhada 수반하다; (*concern*) kwan-gyehada 관계하다; ***what does it ~?*** kŭgŏsŭn muŏsŭl subanhamnikka? 그것은 무엇을 수반합니까?; ***get ~d with sth*** muŏse kwan-gyedoeda 무엇에 관계되다; (*negative*) muŏse yŏlludoeda 무엇에 연루되다; ***get ~d with s.o.*** nuguwa kwan-gyedoeda 누구와 관계되다
involved (*complex*) poktchap'an 복잡한
involvement (*in a project etc*) kwallyŏn 관련; (*in a crime, accident*) yŏllu 연루
invulnerable haech'il su ŏmnŭn 해칠 수 없는
inward 1 *adj* antchogŭi 안쪽의 **2** *adv*

antchŏgŭro 안쪽으로
inwardly maŭmsogŭro 마음속으로
iodine yoodŭ 요오드
IOU (= ***I owe you***) yaksshik ch'ayong chŭngsŏ 약식 차용 증서
IQ (= ***intelligence quotient***) aik'yu 아이큐
Iran Iran 이란
Iranian 1 *adj* Iranŭi 이란의 **2** *n* (*person*) Iranin이란인; (*language*) Iranŏ 이란어
Iraq Irak'ŭ 이라크
Iraqi 1 *adj* Irak'ŭŭi 이라크의 **2** *n* (*person*) Irak'ŭin 이라크인
Ireland Aillaendŭ 아일랜드
iris (*of eye*) hongch'ae 홍채; (*flower*) airisŭ 아이리스
Irish *adj* Aillaendŭŭi 아일랜드의
Irishman Aillaendŭ namja 아일랜드 남자
Irishwoman Aillaendŭ yŏja 아일랜드 여자
iron 1 *n* (*substance*) soe 쇠; (*for clothes*) tarimi 다리미 **2** *v/t shirts etc* tarimjirhada 다림질하다
ironic(al) panŏjŏgin 반어적인
ironing tarimjil 다림질; ***do the ~*** tarimjirhada 다림질하다
ironing board tarimjilttae 다림질대
ironworks ch'ŏlgongso 철공소
irony airŏni 아이러니; (*in prose style*) p'ungja 풍자
irrational purhamnihan 불합리한
irreconcilable hwahaehal su ŏmnŭn 화해할 수 없는
irrecoverable hoebok'al su ŏmnŭn 회복할 수 없는
irregular *intervals, sizes* pulgyuch'iktchŏgin 불규칙적인; *behavior* panch'igŭi 반칙의
irrelevant kwallyŏni ŏmnŭn 관련이 없는
irreparable koch'il su ŏmnŭn 고칠 수 없는
irreplaceable *object, person* taech'ehal su ŏmnŭn 대체할 수 없는
irrepressible *sense of humor* ŏngnurŭl su ŏmnŭn 억누를 수 없는; *person* mallil su ŏmnŭn 말릴 수 없는
irreproachable namural te ŏmnŭn 나무랄 데 없는
irresistible *offer* sayanghal su ŏmnŭn 사양할 수 없는; *pleasure* ŏktchehal su ŏmnŭn 억제할 수 없는
irrespective: ***~ of*** ...e kwan-gyeŏpsshi ...에 관계없이
irresponsible much'aegimhan 무책임한
irretrievable torik'il su ŏmnŭn 돌이킬 수 없는
irreverent pulssonhan 불손한
irrevocable ch'wisohal su ŏmnŭn 취소할 수 없는
irrigate kwan-gaehada 관개하다
irrigation kwan-gae 관개
irrigation canal kwan-gaeyong suro 관개용 수로
irritable tchajŭng-ŭl chal naenŭn 짜증을 잘 내는
irritate tchajŭngnage hada 짜증나게 하다
irritating tchajŭngnage hanŭn 짜증나게 하는
irritation ch'ajŭngnanŭn kŏt 짜증나는 것
Islam (*religion*) Isŭllamgyo 이슬람교; (*race*) Isŭllam minjok 이슬람 민족; (*Islamic state*) Isŭllam kuk-kka 이슬람 국가
Islamic Isŭllamŭi 이슬람의
island sŏm 섬
islander sŏmssaram 섬사람
isolate (*from society*) koripshik'ida 고립시키다; (*separate*) pullihada 분리시키다; (*in prison, hospital*) kyŏngnishik'ida 격리시키다; (*identify*) ppobanaeda 뽑아내다
isolated *house* oettan 외딴; *occurrence* ttaro 따로
isolation (*of a region*) korip 고립; ***in ~*** kyŏngnihayŏ 따로 분리해서
isolation ward kyŏngni pyŏngdong 격리 병동
Israel Isŭrael 이스라엘
Israeli 1 *adj* Isŭraerŭi 이스라엘의 **2** *n* Isŭraerin 이스라엘인
issue 1 *n* (*matter*) chaengtchŏm 쟁점; (*topic*) nontchŏm 논점; (*of magazine*) ho 호 **2** *v/t passport, visa* palgŭp'ada 발급하다; *coins* parhaenghada 발행하다; *supplies* chigŭp'ada 지급하다; *warning*

kongp'yohada 공표하다; ***the point at ~*** nonŭi sahang 논의 사항; ***take ~ with s.o.*** / ***sth*** nugue / muŏse iŭirŭl chegihada 누구에 / 무엇에 이의를 제기하다

IT (= ***information technology***) chŏngbo kisul 정보 기술

it ◊ (*as subject*) kŭgŏsun 그것은; (*as object*) kŭgŏsŭl 그것을 ◊ (*not translated*): ***what is ~? - ~'s a novel*** muŏshiyeyo? - sosŏriyeyo 무엇이에요? - 소설이에요; ***~'s on the table*** ch'aekssang-wie issŏyo 책상위에 있어요; ***~'s me*** / ***him*** chŏyeyo / kŭyeyo 저예요 / 그예요; ***~'s Charlie here*** TELEC chŏ, Ch'alliyeyo 저, 찰리예요; ***~'s your turn*** tangshin ch'aryeyeyo 당신 차례예요; ***that's ~!*** (*that's right*) majayo! 맞아요!; (*I've finished*) twaessŏyo! 됐어요!

Italian 1 *adj* It'alliaŭi 이탈리아의 **2** *n* (*person*) It'alliain 이탈리아인; (*language*) It'alliaŏ 이탈리아어

italic it'aellikch'eŭi 이탤릭체의

italics: ***in ~*** it'aellikch'aero 이탤릭체로

Italy It'allia 이탈리아

itch 1 *n* karyŏum 가려움 **2** *v/i* karyŏptta 가렵다

item hangmok 항목

itemize *invoice* myŏngserŭl palk'ida 명세를 밝히다

itinerary yŏjŏng 여정

its kŭgŏsŭi 그것의

itself kŭgŏt chach'e 그것 자체; ***by ~*** (*alone*) hollo 홀로; (*automatically*) chŏjŏllo 저절로

ivory (*substance*) sang-a 상아

ivy tamjaeng-i 담쟁이

J

jab *v/t* k'uk tchirŭda 쿡 찌르다
jack MOT chaek 잭; (*in cards*) chaek 잭
♦jack up MOT chaegŭro mirŏ ollida 잭으로 밀어 올리다
jacket chaek'it 재킷; (*of book*) k'ŏbŏ 커버
jacket potato kuun kamja yori 구운 감자 요리
jack-knife *v/i* chaengnaip'ŭch'ŏrŏm kuburŏjida 잭나이프처럼 구부러지다
jackpot kŏaegŭi sanggŭm 거액의 상금; ***hit the ~*** kŏaegŭi sanggŭmŭl t'ada 거액의 상금을 타다
jade *n* pich'wi 비취
jagged t'omni moyang-ŭi 톱니 모양의
jail kyodoso 교도소
jam[1] chaem 잼
jam[2] **1** *n* MOT kyot'ong honjap 교통 혼잡; F (*difficulty*) kon-gyŏng 곤경; ***be in a ~*** kon-gyŏng-e ch'ŏhada 곤경에 처하다 **2** *v/t* (*ram*) ssushyŏ nŏt'a 쑤셔 넣다; *broadcast* panghaehada 방해하다; ***be ~med*** (*of roads*) kkwak ch'ait-tta 꽉 차있다; (*of door, window*) umjigiji ank'e toeda 움직이지 않게 되다 **3** *v/i* (*stick*) umjigiji ant'a 움직이지 않다; (*squeeze*) ttemilgo tŭrŏgada 떼밀고 들어가다
jam-packed ppaekppaek'age kkwak ch'an 빽빽하게 꽉 찬
janitor suwi 수위
January irwŏl 일월
Japan Ilbon 일본
Japanese 1 *adj* Ilbonŭi 일본의 **2** *n* (*person*) Ilbon saram 일본 사람; (*language*) Ilbonŏ 일본어
jar[1] *n* (*container*) tanji 단지
jar[2] *v/i* (*of noise*) ppigŏk-kkŏrida 삐걱거리다; ***~ on*** …e kŏsŭllida …에 거슬리다
jargon chŏnmun yong-ŏ 전문 용어
jaundice hwangdal 황달
jaw *n* t'ŏk 턱
jaywalker mudan hwoengdanhanŭn saram 무단 횡단하는 사람
jazz chaejŭ 재즈
♦jazz up F tach'aeropkke hada 다채롭게 하다
jealous chilt'uhanŭn 질투하는; ***be ~ of*** …ŭl / rŭl chilt'uhada …을 / 를 질투하다
jealousy chilt'u 질투
jeans ch'ŏngbaji 청바지
jeep chip'ŭch'a 지프차
jeer 1 *n* yayu 야유 **2** *v/i* yayuhada 야유하다; ***~ at*** …ŭl / rŭl usŭpkke yŏgida …을 / 를 우습게 여기다
Jehovah's Witness Yŏhowaŭi Chŭng-in 여호와의 증인
jelly chaem 잼
jelly bean chelli kwaja 젤리 과자
jellyfish haep'ari 해파리
jeopardize wit'aeropkke hada 위태롭게 하다
jeopardy: ***be in ~*** wit'aeroptta 위태롭다
jerk[1] **1** *n* kaptchagi umjigim 갑자기 움직임 **2** *v/t* kaptchagi umjigida 갑자기 움직이다
jerk[2] *n* F (*fool*) mŏngch'ŏng-i 멍청이
jerky *movement* kaptchagi umjiginŭn 갑자기 움직이는
jest 1 *n* nongdam 농담; ***in ~*** nongdamŭro 농담으로 **2** *v/i* nongdamhada 농담하다
Jesus Yesu(nim) 예수(님)
jet 1 *n* (*of water*) punch'ul 분출; (*nozzle*) punch'ulgu 분출구; (*airplane*) chet'ŭgi 제트기 **2** *v/i* (*travel*) chet'ŭgiro yŏhaenghada 제트기로 여행하다
jet-black saekkaman 새까만; **jet engine** chet'ŭ enjin 제트 엔진; **jet-lag** shich'aro inhan p'iro 시차로 인한 피로
jettison t'uhahada 투하하다; *fig*

pŏrida 버리다
jetty pudu 부두
Jew Yut'aein 유태인
jewel posŏk 보석; *fig* (*person*) pobae 보배
jeweler posŏkssang 보석상
jewelry posŏngnyu 보석류
Jewish *religion* Yut'aegyoŭi 유태교의; *people* Yut'aeinŭi 유태인의
jiffy: ***in a ~*** F kot 곧
jigsaw (puzzle) chogak kŭrim match'ugi 조각 그림 맞추기
jilt ch'abŏrida 차버리다
jingle 1 *n* (*song*) kwanggoyong ŭmak 광고용 음악 **2** *v/i* (*of keys, coins*) ttallanggŏrida 딸랑거리다
jinx (*person*) chaesuŏmnŭn saram 재수없는 사람; (*bad luck*) ma 마; ***there's a ~ on this project*** i kihoegenŭn maga kkiŏt-tta 이 기획에는 마가 끼었다
jitters: ***get the ~*** F anjŏlbujŏl mot'ada 안절부절 못하다
jittery F anjŏlbujŏl mot'anŭn 안절부절 못하는
job (*employment*) chigŏp 직업; (*task*) il 일; ***out of a ~*** shiltchik'ayŏ 실직하여; ***it's a good ~ you ...*** nega ... hagil charhaet-tta 네가 ... 하길 잘했다; ***you'll have a ~*** (*it'll be difficult*) himdŭl kŏyeyo 힘들 거예요
job description chingmu naeyong sŏlmyŏngsŏ 직무 내용 설명서
job hunt: ***be job hunting*** chigŏbŭl kuhago it-tta 직업을 구하고 있다
jobless shiltchik'an 실직한
job satisfaction chigŏp manjoktto 직업 만족도
Job's tears tea yulmuch'a 율무차
jockey *n* kisu 기수
jog 1 *n* choging 조깅; ***go for a ~*** chogingharŏ kada 조깅하러 가다 **2** *v/i* (*as exercise*) choginghada 조깅하다 **3** *v/t elbow etc* saltchak milch'ida 살짝 밀치다; ***~ one's memory*** kiŏgŭl toesallida 기억을 되살리다
jogger (*person*) choginghanŭn saram 조깅하는 사람; (*shoe*) choging shyujŭ 조깅 슈즈
jogging choging 조깅; ***go ~*** chogingharŏ kada 조깅하러 가다
jogging suit chogingbok 조깅복
john F (*toilet*) hwajangshil 화장실
join 1 *n* iŭn chari 이은 자리 **2** *v/i* (*of roads, rivers*) hapch'yŏjida 합쳐지다; (*become a member*) kaip'ada 가입하다 **3** *v/t* (*connect*) yŏn-gyŏrhada 연결하다; *person* hamnyuhada 합류하다; *club* ip'oehada 입회하다; (*go to work for*) ipssahada 입사하다; (*of road*) mannada 만나다
♦**join in** kach'i hada 같이 하다
joiner mokssu 목수
joint 1 *n* ANAT kwanjŏl 관절; (*in woodwork*) chŏp'ap pubun 접합 부분; (*of meat*) k'ŭn kogit-ttŏng-ŏri 큰 고깃덩어리; F (*place*) kot 곳; (*of cannabis*) marihwana 마리화나 **2** *adj* (*shared*) kongdong-ŭi 공동의
joint account kongdong kujwa 공동 구좌; **joint-stock company** haptcha hoesa 합자 회사; **joint venture** haptchak t'uja 합작 투자
joke 1 *n* (*story*) nongdam 농담; (*practical ~*) chitkkujŭn changnan 짓궂은 장난; ***play a ~ on*** ...ŭl / rŭl nollida ...을 / 를 놀리다; ***it's no ~*** usŭl iri anida 웃을 일이 아니다 **2** *v/i* (*pretend*) ikssalburida 익살부리다; (*have a ~*) nongdamhada 농담하다
joker *pej* utkkinŭn nom 웃기는 놈; (*in cards*) chok'ŏ 조커
joking: ***~ apart*** nongdam kŭmanhago 농담 그만하고
jokingly nongdamŭro 농담으로
jolly *adj* yuk'waehan 유쾌한
jolt 1 *n* (*jerk*) tŏlk'ŏk-kkŏrim 덜컥거림 **2** *v/t* (*push*) sege ch'ida 세게 치다
jostle *v/t* nanp'ok'age milda 난폭하게 밀다
♦**jot down** chŏgŏduda 적어두다
journal (*magazine*) chaptchi 잡지; (*diary*) ilgi 일기
journalism (*writing*) ŏllon 언론; (*profession* ŏllon-gye 언론계
journalist kija 기자
journey *n* yŏhaeng 여행
joy kippŭm 기쁨
jubilant hwanhohanŭn 환호하는

jubilation hwanho 환호
judge 1 *n* LAW p'ansa 판사; (*in competition*) shimsa wiwŏn 심사 위원 **2** *v/t* p'andanhada 판단하다; *competition* shimsahada 심사하다; (*estimate*) taegang miruŏ poda 대강 미루어 보다
judgment LAW chaep'an 재판; (*opinion*) p'andan 판단; (*good sense*) p'andannyŏk 판단력
judicial sabŏbŭi 사법의
judicious punbyŏl innŭn 분별 있는
judo yudo 유도
juggle yosurŭl purida 요술을 부리다; *fig* chaejurŭl purida 재주를 부리다
juggler yosuljaeng-i 요술쟁이
juice chusŭ 쥬스
juicy chŭbi manŭn 즙이 많은; *news, gossip* hŭngmijinjinhan 흥미진진한
July ch'irwŏl 칠월
jumble *n* twibŏmbŏk 뒤범벅
♦**jumble up** twibŏmbŏgŭl mandŭlda 뒤범벅을 만들다
jump 1 *n* ttwiŏ orŭm 뛰어 오름; (*increase*) kŭpssangssŭng 급상승; ***give a ~*** (*of surprise*) (nollasŏ) p'ŏltchŏk ttwida (놀라서) 펄쩍 뛰다 **2** *v/i* ttwiŏ orŭda 뛰어 오르다; (*in surprise*) p'ŏltchŏk ttwida 펄쩍 뛰다; (*increase*) kŭpssangssŭnghada 급상승하다; ***~ to one's feet*** pŏlttŏk irŏnada 벌떡 일어나다; ***~ to conclusions*** kŭp'age kyŏllon chit-tta 급하게 결론 짓다 **3** *v/t fence etc* ttwiŏ nŏmtta 뛰어 넘다; F (*attack*) tŏmbyŏdŭlda 덤벼들다
♦**jump at** *opportunity* k'waehi ŭnghada 쾌히 응하다
jumper SP toyak sŏnsu 도약 선수; (*horse*) chang-aemul kyŏngjuma 장애물 경주마; COMPUT chŏmp'ŏ 점퍼
jumpy shin-gyŏng kwaminŭi 신경 과민의
junction (*of roads*) kyoch'ajŏm 교차점
June yuwŏl 유월
jungle millim 밀림
junior 1 *adj* (*subordinate*) sonaraeŭi 손아래의; (*younger*) ŏrin 어린 **2** *n* (*subordinate*) sonaraet saram 손아랫 사람; ***she is ten years my ~*** kŭnyŏnŭn naboda yŏl sal ŏrida 그녀는 나보다 열 살 어리다
junk (*garbage*) komul 고물
junk food chŏngk'ŭ p'udŭ 정크 푸드
junkie chungdoktcha 중독자
junk mail ssŭregi up'yŏnmul 쓰레기 우편물
junkyard komul sujipsso 고물 수집소
jurisdiction LAW sabŏpkkwŏn 사법권
juror paeshimwŏn 배심원
jury paeshimwŏndan 배심원단; (*panel*) shimsawiwŏndan 심사위원단
just 1 *adj law* kongjŏnghan 공정한; *war, cause* t'adanghan 타당한 **2** *adv* (*barely*) kyŏu 겨우; (*exactly*) mach'im 마침; (*only*) tanji 단지; ***I've ~ seen her*** mak kŭnyŏrŭl poassŏyo 막 그녀를 보았어요; ***~ about*** (*almost*) kŏŭi 거의; ***I was ~ about to leave*** nanŭn mak ttŏnaryŏdŏn ch'amiŏssŏyo 나는 막 떠나려던 참이었어요; ***~ like that*** (*abruptly*) kŭnyang kŭrŏk'e 그냥 그렇게; (*exactly like that*) paro kŭrŏk'e 바로 그렇게; ***~ now*** (*a few moments ago*) panggŭm 방금; (*at the moment*) paro chigŭm 바로 지금; ***~ you wait!*** nŏ tugo poja! 너 두고 보자!; ***~ be quiet!*** chom choyonghi hae! 좀 조용히 해!
justice chŏng-ŭi 정의; (*of cause*) t'adang 타당
justifiable chŏngdanghwa hal su innŭn 정당화할 수 있는
justifiably chŏngdanghage 정당하게
justification chŏngdanghwa 정당화
justify chŏngdanghwahada 정당화하다; *text* match'uda 맞추다
justly (*fairly*) chŏngdanghage 정당하게; (*deservedly*) mattanghage 마땅하게
♦**jut out** *v/i* tolch'urhada 돌출하다
juvenile 1 *adj* sonyŏnŭi 소년의; *pej* misuk'an 미숙한 **2** *n fml* sonyŏn 소년
juvenile delinquency sonyŏn pŏmjoe 소년 범죄
juvenile delinquent sonyŏn pŏmjoeja 소년 범죄자

K

k (= ***kilobyte***) k'ilobait'ŭ 킬로바이트; (= ***thousand***) ch'ŏn 천
Kanghwa Island Kanghwado 강화도
karaoke karaok'e 가라오케
karaoke room noraebang 노래방
karate k'arat'e 카라테
karate chop k'arat'e ilgyŏk 카라테 일격
KBS (= ***Korean Broadcasting System***) Han-guk Pangsong Kongsa 한국 방송 공사
keel *n* NAUT yonggol 용골
keen (*intense*) kanghan 강한
keep 1 *n*: ***for ~s*** F ŏnjekkajina 언제까지나 **2** *v/t* pogwanhada 보관하다; (*not give back*) chagi kŏsŭro hada 자기 것으로 하다; (*not lose*) yujihada 유지하다; (*detain*) put-ttŭrŏ tuda 붙들어 두다; (*store*) kansuhada 간수하다; *family* puyanghada 부양하다; *animals* kirŭda 기르다; **~ *a promise*** yakssogŭl chik'ida 약속을 지키다; **~ *... waiting*** ...ŭl / rŭl kyesok kidarige hada ...을 / 를 계속 기다리게 하다; **~ *... to oneself*** (*not tell*) ...ŭl / rŭl alliji ant'a ...을 / 를 알리지 않다; **~ *X from Y*** Xŭl / rŭl Yege alliji ant'a X을 / 를 Y에게 알리지 않다; **~ (*on*) *trying*** kyesok noryŏk'ada 계속 노력하다; **~ (*on*) *interrupting*** kyesok panghaehada 계속 방해하다 **3** *v/i* (*remain*) ... it-tta ... 있다; (*of food, milk*) ssŏktchi ank'o kyŏndida 썩지 않고 견디다; **~ *calm*** ch'imch'ak'age it-tta 침착하게 있다
♦**keep away 1** *v/i* mullŏna it-tta 물러나 있다; **~ *from*** ...(ŭ)robut'ŏ mullŏna it-tta ...(으)로부터 물러나 있다 **2** *v/t* kakkai kaji mot'age hada 가까이 가지 못하게 하다
♦**keep back** *v/t* (*hold in check*) maktta 막다; *information* kamch'uda 감추다
♦**keep down** *v/t voice, noise* natch'uda 낮추다; *costs, inflation etc* chinjŏngshik'ida 진정시키다; *food* padadŭrida 받아들이다
♦**keep in** (*in hospital*) kyesok ibwŏnhae itkke hada 계속 입원해 있게 하다; (*in school*) put-ttŭro tuda 붙들어 두다
♦**keep off 1** *v/t* (*avoid*) p'ihada 피하다; **~ *the grass!*** chandirŭl paltchi mashiyo! 잔디를 밟지 마시요! **2** *v/i* (*of rain*) oji ant'a 오지 않다
♦**keep out** *v/i* tŭrogaji ant'a 들어가지 않다; **~*!*** (*as sign*) tŭrogaji mashiyo! 들어가지 마시요!
♦**keep out of** *argument, trouble* ...e kkiŏ tŭrŏgaji ant'a ...에 끼어 들어가지 않다
♦**keep to** *path, rules* chik'ida 지키다
♦**keep up 1** *v/i* (*when running etc*) twijiji ank'o ttaragada 뒤지지 않고 따라가다 **2** *v/t pace, payments* yujihada 유지하다; *bridge, pants* chit'aenghada 지탱하다
♦**keep up with** ...e twittŏrŏjiji ant'a ...에 뒤떨어지지 않다; (*stay in touch with*) ...wa / kwa kyesok yŏllak'ada ...와 / 과 계속 연락하다
keeping: ***in ~ with*** ...wa / kwa chohwahayŏ ...와 / 과 조화하여; (*with promises*) ...wa / kwa ilch'ihayŏ ...와 / 과 일치하여
kennel kaejip 개집
kennels kae sayuktchang 개 사육장
kernel haek 핵
kerosene tŭng-yu 등유
ketchup k'ech'ŏp 케첩
kettle chujŏnja 주전자
key 1 *n* (*to door, drawer*) yŏlsoe 열쇠; COMPUT, (*on piano*) k'i 키; MUS cho 조 **2** *adj* (*vital*) maeu chungnyohan 매우 중요한 **3** *v/t* COMPUT k'irŭl ch'ida 키를 치다

◆**key in** *data* imnyŏk'ada 입력하다
keyboard COMPUT, MUS k'ibodŭ 키보드; (*of piano*) kŏnban 건반; **keyboarder** COMPUT charyorŭl imnyŏk'anŭn saram 자료를 입력하는 사람; **keycard** k'adŭro toen yŏlsoe 카드로 된 열쇠
keyed-up kinjangdoen 긴장된
keyhole yŏlsoe kumŏng 열쇠 구멍; **keynote speech** kijo yŏnsŏl 기조 연설; **keyring** yŏlsoe kori 열쇠 고리
kick 1 *n* ch'agi 차기; F (*thrill*) hŭngbun 흥분; ***get a ~ out of ...*** ...i / ga ssŏk chaemiit-tta ...이 / 가 썩 재미있다; (***just***) ***for ~s*** chaemiro 재미로 **2** *v/t* ch'ada 차다; F *habit* kkŭnt'a 끊다 **3** *v/i* ch'ada 차다
◆**kick around** *ball* molgo tanida 몰고 다니다; (*treat harshly*) hamburo taruda 함부로 다루다; F (*discuss*) yŏrŏmoro kŏmt'ohada 여러모로 검토하다
◆**kick in 1** *v/t* F (*money*) naeda 내다 **2** *v/i* (*of boiler etc*) chakttonghada 작동하다
◆**kick off** *v/i* k'ik'op'ŭhada 킥오프하다; F (*start*) shijak'ada 시작하다
◆**kick out** *v/t* tchoch'anaeda 쫓아내다; ***~ of the company / army*** hoesaesŏ / kundaeesŏ tchotkkyŏnada 회사에서 / 군대에서 쫓겨나다
kickback F (*bribe*) chŏngch'i hŏn-gŭm 정치 헌금
kickoff k'ik'op'ŭ 킥오프
kid F **1** *n* (*child*) ai 아이; ***~ brother / sister*** namdongsaeng / yŏdongsaeng 남동생 / 여동생 **2** *v/t* nollida 놀리다 **3** *v/i* nongdamhada 농담하다; ***I was only ~ding*** kŭnyang nongdamiyeyo 그냥 농담이예요
kidder F nongdam chal hanŭn saram 농담 잘 하는 사람
kidnap napch'ihada 납치하다; *child* yugoehada 유괴하다
kidnap(p)er napch'ibŏm 납치범; (*of child*) yugoebŏm 유괴범
kidnap(p)ing napch'i 납치; (*of child*) yugoe 유괴
kidney ANAT shinjang 신장; (*to eat*) k'ongp'at 콩팥
kill *v/t also time* chugida 죽이다; ***be ~ed in an accident*** sagoro chuktta 사고로 죽다; ***~ oneself*** chasarhada 자살하다
killer sarinja 살인자; (*cause of death*) sain 사인
killing sarhae 살해; ***make a ~*** (*lots of money*) tte tonŭl pŏlda 떼 돈을 벌다
kiln kama 가마
kilo k'illo 킬로
kilobyte k'illobait'ŭ 킬로바이트
kilogram k'illogŭraem 킬로그램
kilometer k'illomit'ŏ 킬로미터
kimchee kimch'i 김치
kimono k'imono 키모노
kind[1] *adj* ch'injŏrhan 친절한
kind[2] *n* chongnyu 종류; ***what ~ of ...?*** ŏttŏn chongnyuŭi ...? 어떤 종류의 ...?; ***what ~ of dog is that?*** chŏgŏsŭn ŏttŏn chongnyuŭi kaeimnikka? 저것은 어떤 종류의 개입니까?; ***all ~s of people*** oman chongnyuŭi saram 오만 종류의 사람; ***nothing of the ~*** kyŏlk'o kŭrŏn kŏshi anida 결코 그런 것이 아니다; ***~ of sad / strange*** F ŏnŭ chŏngdo sŭlp'ŭda / isanghada 어느 정도 슬프다 / 이상하다
kindergarten yuch'iwŏn 유치원
kind-hearted maŭmsshi koun 마음씨 고운
kindly 1 *adj* ch'injorhan 친절한 **2** *adv* ch'injŏrhage 친절하게; (*please*) chebal 제발
kindness ch'injŏl 친절
king wang 왕
kingdom wangguk 왕국
king-size(d) F k'ing saijŭ 킹 사이즈
kink (*in hose etc*) kkoim 꼬임
kinky F pyŏnt'aejŏgin 변태적인
kiosk kani maejŏm 간이 매점
kiss 1 *n* k'isŭ 키스 **2** *v/t* k'isŭhada 키스하다 **3** *v/i* k'isŭhada 키스하다
kit (*equipment*) changbi 장비; (*for assembly*) chorimnyongp'um 조립용품
kitchen puŏk 부엌
kite yŏn 연
kite flying yŏnnalligi 연날리기
kitten saekki koyang-i 새끼 고양이

kitty (*money*) kongdong chŏngnipkkŭm 공동 적립금
klutz F (*clumsy*) tŏllŏng-i 덜렁이
knack yoryŏng 요령
knead *dough* panjuk'ada 반죽하다
knee *n* murŭp 무릎
kneecap *n* sŭlgaegol 슬개골
kneel murŭp kkult'a 무릎 꿇다
knick-knacks chajilgurehan changshin-gu 자질구레한 장신구
knife 1 *n* k'al 칼 **2** *v/t* k'allo tchirŭda 칼로 찌르다
knit 1 *v/t* t'ŏlshillo ttŭda 털실로 뜨다 **2** *v/i* ttŭgaejirhada 뜨개질하다
♦**knit together** (*of bone*) itta 잇다
knitting (*sth being knitted*) p'yŏnmul 편물; (*activity*) ttŭgaejil 뜨개질
knitwear nit'ŭ weŏ 니트 웨어
knob (*on door*) sonjabi 손잡이
knock 1 *n* (*on door*) mun tudŭrinŭn sori 문 두드리는 소리; (*blow*) t'agyŏk 타격 **2** *v/t* (*hit*) ch'ida 치다; F (*criticize*) kkalboda 깔보다 **3** *v/i* (*on the door*) nok'ŭhada 노크하다; **~ *at the door*** munŭl nok'ŭhada 문을 노크하다
♦**knock around 1** *v/t* (*beat*) magu tudŭlgyŏ p'aeda 마구 두들겨 패다 **2** *v/i* F (*travel*) magu toradanida 마구 돌아다니다
♦**knock down** (*of car*) ch'iŏ nŏmŏttŭrida 치어 넘어뜨리다; *object, building etc* hŏrŏ nŏmŏttŭrida 헐어 넘어뜨리다; F (*reduce the price of*) ...ŭi kapssŭl naerida ...의 값을 내리다
♦**knock out** (*make unconscious*) naga ttŏrŏjige hada 나가 떨어지게 하다; (*of medicine*) chamdŭlge hada 잠들게 하다; *power lines etc* munŏttŭrida 무너뜨리다
♦**knock over** nŏmŏttŭrida 넘어뜨리다; (*of car*) ch'io nŏmŏttŭrida 치어 넘어뜨리다
knockout *n* SP nogaut'ŭ 녹아우트
knot 1 *n* maedŭp 매듭 **2** *v/t* maeda 매다
knotty *problem* haegyŏri kollanhan 해결이 곤란한
know 1 *v/t* alda 알다; *language* ...e chŏngt'onghada ...에 정통하다; (*recognize*) araboda 알아보다 **2** *v/i* algo it-tta 알고 있다; ***I don't ~*** mollayo 몰라요; ***yes, I ~*** ye, algo issŏyo 예, 알고 있어요 **3** *n*: ***be in the ~*** naebu sajŏng-ŭl chal algo it-tta 내부 사정을 잘 알고 있다
knowhow nohau 노하우
knowing alget-ttanŭn shigŭi 알겠다는 식의
knowingly (*wittingly*) algosŏdo 알고서도; *smile etc* anŭn tŭt'an 아는 듯한
know-it-all F anŭn ch'e hanŭn saram 아는 체 하는 사람
knowledge chishik 지식; ***to the best of my ~*** naega algo itkkironŭn 내가 알고 있기로는; ***have a good ~ of*** ...e chŏngt'onghada ...에 정통하다
knowledgeable chishigi innŭn 지식이 있는
knuckle sonkkarak madi 손가락 마디
♦**knuckle down** chinjihage ch'akssuhada 진지하게 착수하다
♦**knuckle under** kulbok'ada 굴복하다
KO k'ei ou 케이 오우
Koje Island Kŏjedo 거제도
Korea (*South*) Han-guk 한국; (*North*) Puk'an 북한
Korean 1 *adj* (*South*) Han-gugŭi 한국의; (*North*) Puk'anŭi 북한의 **2** *n* (*South*) Han-guk saram 한국 사람; (*North*) Puk'an saram 북한 사람; (*language*) Han-gugŏ 한국어
Korean Broadcasting System Han-guk Pangsong Kongsa 한국 방송 공사; **Korean chess** changgi 장기; **Korean costume** hanbok 한복; **Korean oboe** p'iri 피리; **Korean script** Han-gŭl 한글; **Korean Strait** Taehanhaehyŏp 대한해협, Namhae 남해; **Korean-style hotel** yŏgwan 여관; **Korean-style mattress** yo 요; **Korean War** Han-guk Chŏnjaeng 한국 전쟁; **Korean wrestling** sshirŭm 씨름
kosher REL Yut'aein yulppŏbe mannŭn 유태인 율법에 맞는; F chŏngdanghan 정당한
kudos yŏng-ye 영예
Kum River Kŭmgang 금강

L

lab shirhŏmshil 실험실
label 1 *n* kkorip'yo 꼬리표 **2** *v/t baggage* kkorip'yorŭl puch'ida 꼬리표를 붙이다
labor *n* nodong 노동; (*giving birth*) punman 분만; ***be in ~*** punman chung-ida 분만 중이다
laboratory shirhŏmshil 실험실
laboratory technician shirhŏmshil kisultcha 실험실 기술자
labored *style, speech* ŏsaek'an 어색한
laborer nodongja 노동자
laborious himdŭnŭn 힘드는
labor union nodong chohap 노동 조합
labor ward punmanshil 분만실
lace *n* leisŭ 레이스; (*for shoe*) kkŭn 끈
♦**lace up** *shoes* kkŭnŭl maeda 끈을 매다
lack 1 *n* pujok 부족 **2** *v/t* ...i / ga ŏptta ...이 / 가 없다; ***he ~s confidence*** kŭnŭn chashin-gami ŏptta 그는 자신감이 없다 **3** *v/i*: ***be ~ing*** pujok'ada 부족하다
lacquer *n* (*for hair*) heŏsŭp'ŭrei 헤어스프레이
lacquerware ch'ilgi 칠기
lad chŏlmŭn namja 젊은 남자
ladder sadari 사다리
laden chŏktchaehan 적재한
ladies' room yŏja hwajangshil 여자 화장실
ladle *n* kuktcha 국자
lady sungnyŏ 숙녀
ladybug mudangbŏlle 무당벌레
lag *v/t pipes* p'iboktchaero ssada 피복재로 싸다
♦**lag behind** twittŏrŏjida 뒤떨어지다
lager lagŏ piŏ 라거 비어
lagoon sŏk'o 석호
laidback nŭgŭt'an 느긋한
lake hosu 호수
lamb saekkiyang 새끼양; (*meat*) yanggogi 양고기
lame *person* chŏllŭmbariŭi 절름발이의; *excuse* ŏsŏlp'ŭn 어설픈
lament 1 *n* pit'an 비탄 **2** *v/t* sŭlp'ŏhada 슬퍼하다
lamentable sŏgŭlp'ŭn 서글픈
laminated k'ot'inghan 코팅한; ***~ glass*** yalbŭn p'anyuri 얇은 판유리
lamp tŭngppul 등불
lamppost karodŭng kidung 가로등 기둥
lampshade chŏndŭnggat 전등갓
land 1 *n* ttang 땅; (*shore*) yuktchi 육지; (*country*) nara 나라; ***by ~*** yungnoro 육로로; ***on ~*** yuktchie(sŏ) 육지에(서); ***work on the ~*** (*as farmer*) nongsa chitkko salda 농사 짓고 살다 **2** *v/t airplane* ch'angnyukshik'ida 착륙시키다; *job* ŏt-tta 얻다 **3** *v/i* (*of airplane*) ch'angnyuk'ada 착륙하다; (*of ball, sth thrown*) ttorŏjida 떨어지다
landing (*of airplane*) ch'angnyuk 착륙; (*top of staircase*) ch'ŭnggyech'am 층계참
landing field pihaengjang 비행장; **landing gear** ch'angnyuk changch'i 착륙 장치; **landing strip** kasŏl hwaltchuro 가설 활주로
landlady (*of hostel etc*) yŏjuin 여주인; **landlord** (*of hostel etc*) chuin 주인; **landmark** *yumyŏnghan kŏnch'ungmul* 유명한 건축물; *fig* hoek-kkijŏgin sakkŏn 획기적인 사건; **land owner** chiju 지주; **landscape 1** *n* kyŏngch'i 경치; (*painting*) p'unggyŏnghwa 풍경화 **2** *adv print* karo panghyang-ŭro 가로 방향으로; **landslide** sansat'ae 산사태; ***~ victory*** apssŭng 압승
lane (*in country*) shigolkkil 시골길; (*alley*) chobŭn kil 좁은 길; (*on highway*) ch'asŏn 차선
language ŏnŏ 언어
lank *hair* kirŭmgi kkin 기름기 낀

lanky *person* horihorihan 호리호리한
lantern tŭng 등
Lao (*language*) Laosŭŏ 라오스어
Laos Laosŭ 라오스
Laotian 1 *adj* Laosŭŭi 라오스의 **2** *n* (*person*) Laosŭin 라오스인
lap[1] *n* (*of racetrack*) han pak'wi 한 바퀴
lap[2] *n* (*of water*) chanmulkkyŏrŭi sori 잔물결의 소리
♦**lap up** *milk* halt'amŏktta 핥아먹다; *flattery* koji kot-ttaero padadŭrida 곧이 곧대로 받아들이다
lap[3] *n* (*of person*) murŭp 무릎
lapel chŏbŭn otkkit 접은 옷깃
laptop COMPUT laept'ap 랩탑
larceny chŏlttotchoe 절도죄
large k'ŭn 큰; ***at ~*** (*criminal, wild animal*) t'alch'urhan 탈출한
largely (*mainly*) churo 주로
lark (*bird*) chongdalssae 종달새
larva yuch'ung 유충
laryngitis huduyŏm 후두염
larynx hudu 후두
laser leijyŏ 레이저
laser beam leijyŏ kwangsŏn 레이저 광선
laser printer leijyŏ p'urint'ŏ 레이저 프린터
lash[1] *v/t* (*with whip*) ch'aetchiktchirhada 채찍질하다
lash[2] *n* (*eyelash*) songnunssŏp 속눈썹
♦**lash down** (*with rope*) tandanhi muktta 단단히 묶다
last[1] *adj* (*in series*) majimak 마지막; (*preceding*) chŏnbŏnŭi 전번의; ***~ but one*** majimagesŏ tu pŏntchae 마지막에서 두 번째; ***~ night*** ŏjetppam 어젯밤; ***~ but not least*** kkŭch'ijiman chungnyohage tŏtppuch'inŭn kŏsŭn 끝이지만 중요하게 덧붙이는 것은; ***at ~*** mach'imnae 마침내
last[2] *v/i* chisokttoeda 지속되다
lastly majimagŭro 마지막으로
latch *n* kŏlssoe 걸쇠
late (*behind time*) nŭjŭn 늦은; (*at night*) pam nŭjŭn 밤 늦은; ***it's getting ~*** nŭjŏjinda 늦어진다; ***of ~*** ch'oegŭne 최근에; ***the ~ 19th / 20th century*** shipkku / iship segi mal 십구 / 이십 세기 말; ***sleep ~*** nŭttcham chada 늦잠자다
lately ch'oegŭne 최근에
later *adv* najung-e 나중에; ***see you ~!*** najung-e poja! 나중에 보자!; ***~ on*** najung-e 나중에
latest *news, developments* ch'oeshinŭi 최신의; *girlfriend* ch'oegŭnŭi 최근의
lathe *n* sŏnban 선반
lather (*from soap*) kŏp'um 거품
Latin America Nammi 남미
Latin American 1 *adj* Lat'in Amerik'aŭi 라틴 아메리카의 **2** *n* Lat'in Amerik'ain 라틴 아메리카인
latitude (*geographical*) wido 위도; (*freedom to maneuver*) hŏyong pŏmwi 허용 범위
latter hujaŭi 후자의
laugh 1 *n* usŭm 웃음; ***it was a ~*** chaemiissŏt-tta 재미있었다 **2** *v/i* uttta 웃다
♦**laugh at** (*mock*) …ŭl / rŭl piut-tta …을 / 를 비웃다
laughing stock: ***make oneself a ~*** sŭsŭrorŭl usŭmkkŏriro mandŭlda 스스로를 웃음거리로 만들다; ***become a ~*** usŭmkkŏriga toeda 웃음거리가 되다
laughter usŭm 웃음
launch 1 *n* (*boat*) chinsusŏn 진수선; (*of rocket*) palssa 발사; (*of ship*) chinsu 진수; (*of new product*) palmae 발매 **2** *v/t rocket* palssahada 발사하다; *ship* chinsuhada 진수하다; *product* palmaehada 발매하다
launch(ing) ceremony (*for ship*) chinsushik 진수식; (*for product*) palmae ch'uk'ayŏn 발매 축하연
launch(ing) pad palssadae 발사대
launder set'ak'ada 세탁하다
laundromat selp'ŭ set'aksso 셀프세탁소
laundry (*place*) set'aksso 세탁소; (*clothes*) set'angmul 세탁물; ***get one's ~ done*** set'ak'age hada 세탁하게 하다
laurel wŏlgyesu 월계수
lavatory hwajangshil 화장실
lavender labendŏ 라벤더
laver (*seaweed*) kim 김
lavish *adj* p'ungbuhan 풍부한

law pŏp 법; (*as subject*) pŏp'ak 법학; ***against the ~*** pulppŏbin 불법인; ***forbidden by ~*** pŏbŭro kŭmjidoen 법으로 금지된
law court pŏptchŏng 법정
lawful hap-ppŏptchŏgin 합법적인
lawless mubŏbŭi 무법의
lawn chandi 잔디
lawn mower chandi kkangnŭn kigye 잔디 깎는 기계
lawsuit sosong 소송
lawyer pyŏnhosa 변호사
lax nŭsŭnhan 느슨한
laxative *n* pyŏnbiyak 변비약
lay *v/t* (*put down*) not'a 놓다; *eggs* nat'a 낳다; V (*sexually*) sŏnggyohada 성교하다
♦**lay into** (*attack*) konggyŏk'ada 공격하다
♦**lay off** *workers* haegohada 해고하다
♦**lay on** (*provide*) maryŏnhada 마련하다
♦**lay out** *objects* chinyŏrhada 진열하다; *page* leiausŭl hada 레이아웃을 하다
layer *n* ch'ŭng 층
layman amach'uŏ 아마추어
layout paech'i 배치
♦**laze around** pindŭnggŏrida 빈둥거리다
lazy *person* keŭrŭn 게으른; *day* harirŏmnŭn 하릴없는
lb (= ***pound(s)***) p'aundŭ 파운드
LCD (= ***liquid crystal display***) aektchŏng p'yoshi changch'i 액정 표시 장치
lead[1] **1** *v/t procession*, *race* sŏndue sŏda 선두에 서다; *company*, *team* ikkŭlda 이끌다; (*guide*, *take*) indohada 인도하다 **2** *v/i* (*in race*, *competition*) sŏndue sŏda 선두에 서다; (*provide leadership*) t'ongsorhada 통솔하다; ***a street ~ing off the square*** kwangjangesŏ ppŏdŏnaonŭn kil 광장에서 뻗어나오는 길; ***where is this ~ing?*** ŏdiro hŭllŏgago innŭn kŏmnikka? 어디로 흘러가고 있는 겁니까? **3** *n* (*in race*) sŏndu 선두; ***be in the ~*** sŏndue it-tta 선두에 있다; ***take the ~*** sŏndue tŭrŏsŏda 선두에 들어서다; ***lose the ~*** sŏnduesŏ millyŏnada 선두에서 밀려나다
♦**lead on** (*go in front*) aptchang sŏda 앞장 서다
♦**lead up to** …(ŭ)ro ikkŭlgo kada …(으)로 이끌고 가다
lead[2] *n* (*for dog*) kae chul 개 줄
lead[3] *n* (*metal*) nap 납
leader chidoja 지도자
leadership (*of party etc*) t'ongsollyŏk 통솔력; ***under his ~*** kŭŭi chido ha-e 그의 지도 하에; ***~ skills*** chidoryŏk 지도력
leadership contest chidoja sŏn-gŏ hoeŭi 지도자 선거 회의
lead-free *gas* muyŏnŭi 무연의
leading *runner* sŏnduŭi 선두의; *company*, *product* chudojŏgin 주도적인
leading-edge *adj company*, *technology* ch'ŏmdanŭi 첨단의
leaf ip 잎
♦**leaf through** taech'ung pomyŏ nŏmgida 대충 보며 넘기다
leaflet chŏndan 전단
league yŏnmaeng 연맹
leak 1 *n* saeŏ naom 새어 나옴; (*of information*) nuch'ul 누출 **2** *v/i* saeda 새다
♦**leak out** (*of air*, *gas*) saeŏ naoda 새어 나오다; (*of news*) nusŏldoeda 누설되다
leaky *pipe*, *boat* saenŭn 새는
lean[1] **1** *v/i* (*be at an angle*) kidaeda 기대다; ***~ against sth*** muŏse kidaeda 무엇에 기대다 **2** *v/t* kidaedorok hada 기대도록 하다; ***~ sth against sth*** muŏsŭl muŏse kidaeŏ not'a 무엇을 무엇에 기대어 놓다
lean[2] *adj meat* salk'ogiŭi 살코기의; *style*, *prose* kundŏdŏgi ŏmnŭn 군더더기 없는
leap 1 *n* toyak 도약; ***a great ~ forward*** tae chinbo 대 진보 **2** *v/i* hultchŏk ttwida 훌쩍 뛰다
leap year yunnyŏn 윤년
learn paeuda 배우다; ***~ how to do sth*** muŏsŭl hanŭn pangbŏbŭl paeuda 무엇을 하는 방법을 배우다

learner paeunŭn saram 배우는 사람
learning *n* (*knowledge*) chishik 지식; (*act*) hakssŭp 학습
learning curve hakssŭp kokssŏn 학습 곡선; ***be on the ~*** shin-gisurŭl sŭpttŭk'aeya handa 신기술을 습득해야 한다
lease 1 *n* imdae 임대 **2** *v/t apartment, equipment* imdaehada 임대하다
♦**lease out** imdaehada 임대하다
leash *n* (*for dog*) kae chul 개 줄
least 1 *adj* (*slightest*) kajang chagŭn 가장 작은 **2** *adv* kajang an 가장 안; ***~ difficult*** kajang anŏryŏun 가장 안어려운 **3** *n* ch'oesoryang 최소량; ***not in the ~ surprised*** / ***disappointed*** chogŭmdo nollaji / shilmanghaji annŭn 조금도 놀라지 / 실망하지 않은; ***at ~*** chŏgŏdo 적어도
leather 1 *n* kajuk 가죽 **2** *adj* kajugŭi 가죽의
leave 1 *n* (*vacation*) hyuga 휴가; ***on ~*** hyugarŭl ŏdŏ 휴가를 얻어 **2** *v/t city, place, person* ttŏnada 떠나다; *husband, wife* pŏrida 버리다; *food on plate* namgyŏ tuda 남겨 두다; *scar, memory, message* namgida 남기다; (*forget, leave behind*) ijŏbŏrigo tŭgo kada 잊어버리고 두고 가다; ***let's ~ things as they are*** kŭnyang kŭdaero tugiro hapsshida 그냥 그대로 두기로 합시다; ***how did you ~ things with him?*** kŭ saramgwaŭi irŭn ŏttŏk'e hagiro haessŭmnikka? 그 사람과의 일은 어떻게 하기로 했습니까?; ***~ alone*** (*not touch*) kŭnyang kŭdaero tŭda 그냥 그대로 두다; (*not interfere with*) kansŏp'aji ant'a 간섭하지 않다; (*not damage*) haerŭl ip'iji ant'a 해를 입히지 않다; ***be left*** namtta 남다; ***there is nothing left*** namŭn kŏshi ŏpssŭmnida 남은 것이 없습니다 **2** *v/i* (*of person*) ttŏnada 떠나다; (*of plane, train, bus*) ch'ulbarhada 출발하다
♦**leave behind** *person* twie namgida 뒤에 남기다; *object* tugo kada 두고 가다; (*forget*) ijŏ pŏrigo tŭgo kada 잊어 버리고 두고 가다
♦**leave on** *hat* ssŭn ch'aero tuda 쓴 채로 두다; *coat* ibŭn ch'aero tuda 입은 채로 두다; *TV, computer* k'yŏn ch'aero tuda 켠 채로 두다
♦**leave out** *word* saengnyak'ada 생략하다; (*not put away*) naenoŭn ch'ae pŏryŏduda 내놓은 채 버려두다; ***leave me out of this*** chŏnŭn i iresŏ cheoeshik'yŏ chushipsshio 저는 이 일에서 제외시켜 주십시오
leaving party songbyŏrhoe 송별회
lecture 1 *n* kang-ŭi 강의 **2** *v/i* (*at university*) kang-ŭihada 강의하다
lecture hall kang-ŭishil 강의실
lecturer kangsa 강사
LED (= ***light-emitting diode***) palgwang taiodŭ 발광 다이오드
ledge t'ŏk 턱
ledger COM wŏntchang 원장
leek puch'u 부추
leer *n* (*sexual*) ch'up'a 추파
left 1 *adj* oentchogŭi 왼쪽의; POL chwaigŭi 좌익의 **2** *n* oentchok 왼쪽; POL chwaik 좌익; ***on the ~*** oentchoge(sŏ) 왼쪽에(서); ***on the ~ of sth*** muŏsŭi oentchoge(sŏ) 무엇의 왼쪽에(서); ***to the ~*** *turn, look* oentchogŭro 왼쪽으로 **3** *adv turn, look* oentchogŭro 왼쪽으로
left-hand *bend* oenp'yŏnŭro hanŭn 왼편으로 하는; **left-hand drive** chwach'ŭk haendŭl unjŏn 좌측 핸들 운전; **left-handed** oensonjabi 왼손잡이; **left-overs** (*food*) namŭn kŏt 남은 것; **left-wing** POL chwaik 좌익
leg tari 다리; ***pull s.o.'s ~*** nugurŭl nollida 누구를 놀리다
legacy yusan 유산
legal (*allowed*) hap-ppŏptchŏgin 합법적인; (*relating to the law*) pŏptchŏgin 법적인
legal adviser pŏptchŏk choŏnja 법적 조언자
legality hap-ppŏp 합법
legalize hap-ppŏp'wahada 합법화하다
legend chŏnsŏl 전설
legendary chŏnsŏljŏgin 전설적인
legible ilkki shwiun 읽기 쉬운
legislate chejŏnghada 제정하다
legislation (*laws*) pŏmyul 법률;

(*passing of laws*) ip-ppŏp 입법
legislative *powers*, *assembly* ip-ppŏbŭi 입법의
legislature POL ip-ppŏp-ppu 입법부
legitimate *claim* chŏkppŏbŭi 적법의; *complaint*, *cause* chŏngdanghan 정당한; *child* chŏkch'urŭi 적출의
leg room: ***there's no ~*** tarirŭl p'yŏnhage noŭl su ŏpssŏyo 다리를 편하게 놓을 수 없어요
leisure yŏga 여가; ***at your ~*** tangshini p'yŏnhan shigane 당신이 편한 시간에
leisure center lejŏ sent'ŏ 레저 센터
leisurely *pace* nŭgŭt'an 느긋한
leisure time yŏga shigan 여가 시간
lemon lemon 레몬
lemonade lemoneidŭ 레모네이드
lemon juice lemon chusŭ 레몬 주스
lemon tea lemonch'a 레몬차
lend: ***~ s.o. sth*** nuguege muŏsŭl pillyŏjuda 누구에게 무엇을 빌려주다
length kiri 길이; ***at ~*** *describe*, *explain* kilge 길게; (*eventually*) mach'imnae 마침내
lengthen nŭllida 늘리다
lengthy *speech*, *stay* kin 긴
lenient kwandaehan 관대한
lens lenjŭ 렌즈
lens cover lenjŭ ttukkŏng 렌즈 뚜껑
Lent sasunjŏl 사순절
lentil lenjŭ k'ong 렌즈 콩
lentil soup lenjŭ k'ong sŭp'ŭ 렌즈 콩 스프
leopard p'yobŏm 표범
leotard ch'ejobok 체조복
lesbian 1 *n* lejŭbiŏn 레즈비언 **2** *adj* lejŭbiŏnŭi 레즈비언의
less: ***eat / talk ~*** tŏl mŏktta / marhada 덜 먹다 / 말하다; ***~ interesting / serious*** tŏl hŭngmiroun / shimgak'an 덜 흥미로운 / 심각한; ***it cost ~*** toni tŏl tŭnda 돈이 덜 든다; ***~ than $200*** 200tallŏ miman 200달러 미만
lesson suŏp 수업
let *v/t* (*allow*): ***~ s.o. do sth*** nuga muŏt'age haejuda 누가 무엇하게 해주다; ***~ me go!*** noajwŏ! 놓아줘!; ***~ him come in*** kŭrŭl tŭrŏoge haseyo 그를 들어오게 하세요; ***~'s go / stay*** kaja / mŏmŭlja 가자 / 머물자; ***~'s not argue*** ssauji malja 싸우지 말자; ***~ alone*** … kinŭn k'ŏnyŏng …기는 커녕; ***he can't read, ~ alone write*** kŭnŭn ssŭginŭn k'ŏnyŏng iltchido mot'anda 그는 쓰기는 커녕 읽지도 못한다; ***~ go of sth*** (*of rope*, *handle*) muŏsŭl noa pŏrida 무엇을 놓아 버리다
♦**let down** *hair* p'urŏ naerida 풀어 내리다; *shades* naerida 내리다; (*disappoint*) shilmangshik'ida 실망시키다; (*make longer*) tanŭl naerida 단을 내리다
♦**let in** (*to house*) tŭrŏgada 들어가다
♦**let off** (*not punish*) yongsŏhada 용서하다; (*from car*) naeryŏ chuda 내려 주다; ***let a student off homework*** hakssaeng-ege suktcherŭl myŏnjehae chuda 학생에게 숙제를 면제해 주다
♦**let out** (*of room*, *building*) nagage hada 나가게 하다; *jacket etc* nŭllida 늘리다; *groan*, *yell* ip ppakkŭro naeda 입 밖으로 내다
♦**let up** *v/i* (*stop*) mŏt-tta 멎다
lethal ch'imyŏngjŏgin 치명적인
lethargic nogonhan 노곤한
letter (*of alphabet*) kŭltcha 글자; (*in mail*) p'yŏnji 편지
letterhead (*heading*) *p'yŏnjiji wiŭi inswae munkku* 편지지 위의 인쇄 문구; (*headed paper*) wit pubune inswae munkkuga innŭn p'yŏnjiji 윗 부분에 인쇄 문구가 있는 편지지
letter of credit COM shinyongtchang 신용장
letter of guarantee pojŭngsŏ 보증서
lettuce sangch'u 상추
letup: ***without a ~*** shwiji ank'o 쉬지 않고
leukemia paek'yŏlppyŏng 백혈병
level 1 *adj field*, *surface* p'yŏngp'yŏnghan 평평한; (*in competition*, *scores*) kat'ŭn sujunŭi 같은 수준의; ***draw ~ with s.o.*** nuguwa makssangmak'a-e irŭda 누구와 막상막하에 이르다 **2** *n* (*on scale*, *in hierarchy*) sujun 수준; (*amount*, *quantity*) yang 양; ***on the***

~ (*on ~ ground*) p'yŏngp'yŏnghan kose(sŏ) 평평한 곳에(서); ***be on the ~*** F (*honest*) chŏngjik'ada 정직하다
level-headed punbyŏl innŭn 분별 있는
lever 1 *n* chire 지레 **2** *v/t* chirero umjigida 지레로 움직이다; ~ ***sth open*** muŏsŭl pijibŏ yŏlda 무엇을 비집어 열다
leverage chireŭi chagyong 지레의 작용; (*influence*) seryŏk 세력
levy *v/t taxes* chingsuhada 징수하다
lewd ch'ujap'an 추잡한
liability (*responsibility*) ch'aegim 책임
liability insurance ch'aegim pohŏm 책임 보험
liable (*answerable*) ch'aegimjyŏya hanŭn 책임져야 하는; ***be ~ to*** (*likely*) ...hanŭn kyŏnghyang-i it-tta ...하는 경향이 있다
♦**liaise with** yŏllagŭl ch'wihada 연락을 취하다
liaison (*contacts*) yŏllak 연락
liar kŏjitmaljaeng-i 거짓말쟁이
libel 1 *n* munsŏe ŭihan myŏng-ye hweson 문서에 의한 명예 훼손 **2** *v/t* myŏng-ye hwesonhada 명예 훼손하다
liberal *adj* (*broad-minded*) maŭmi nŏlbŭn 마음이 넓은; *portion etc* insaek'aji anŭn 인색하지 않은; POL chayujuŭiŭi 자유주의의
liberate haebangshik'ida 해방시키다
liberated *woman* haebangdoen 해방된
Liberation Day Kwangboktchŏl 광복절
liberty chayu 자유; ***at ~*** (*prisoner etc*) chayuro 자유로; ***be at ~ to do sth*** muŏsŭl maŭmdaero hada 무엇을 마음대로 하다
librarian sasŏ 사서
library tosŏgwan 도서관
Libya Libia 리비아
Libyan 1 *adj* Libiaŭi 리비아의 **2** *n* Libiain 리비아인
license 1 *n* (*for car*) myŏnhŏtchŭng 면허증; (*for imports, exports, TV, gun*) hŏgatchŭng 허가증 **2** *v/t*: ***be ~d*** (*of car*) myŏnhŏ pat-tta 면허 받다; (*of gun, equipment*) hŏga pat-tta 허가 받다
license number tŭngnok pŏnho 등록 번호
license plate pŏnhop'an 번호판
lick 1 *n* halkki 핥기 **2** *v/t* haltta 핥다; ~ ***one's lips*** immasŭl tashida 입맛을 다시다
licking: ***get a ~*** F (*defeat*) chida 지다
lid ttukkŏng 뚜껑
lie[1] **1** *n* (*untruth*) kŏjinmal 거짓말 **2** *v/i* kŏjinmarhada 거짓말하다
lie[2] *v/i* (*of person*) nuptta 눕다; (*of object*) it-tta 있다; (*be situated*) wich'ihada 위치하다
♦**lie down** nuptta 눕다
lieutenant: ***first ~*** chung-wi 중위; ***second ~*** sowi 소위
life saengmyŏng 생명; (*living*) saenghwal 생활; (~ *span*) sumyŏng 수명; ***all her ~*** kŭnyŏ p'yŏngsaeng-e 그녀 평생에; ***that's ~!*** insaeng-iran kŭrŏn kŏshimnida! 인생이란 그런 것입니다!
life belt kumyŏng tti 구명 띠; **lifeboat** kumyŏngjŏng 구명정; **life expectancy** yesang sumyŏng 예상 수명; **lifeguard** kujowŏn 구조원; **life history** saenghwalsa 생활사; **life insurance** saengmyŏng pohŏm 생명 보험; **life jacket** kumyŏng chokki 구명 조끼
lifeless saengmyŏng ŏmnŭn 생명 없는
lifelike sara innŭn tŭt'an 살아 있는 듯한; **lifelong** p'yŏngsaeng-ŭi 평생의; **life preserver** (*for swimmer*) kumyŏnggu 구명구; **life-saving** *adj equipment* kumyŏng-ŭi 구명의; *medicine, drug* saengmyŏng-ŭl kuhanŭn 생명을 구하는; **lifesized** shilmul k'ŭgiŭi 실물 크기의; **life-threatening** saengmyŏng-ŭl wihyŏp'anŭn 생명을 위협하는; **lifetime** p'yŏngsaeng 평생; ***in my ~*** nae p'yŏngsaeng-e 내 평생에
lift 1 *v/t* tŭrŏ ollida 들어 올리다 **2** *v/i* (*of fog*) kŏch'ida 걷히다 **3** *n* (*in car*) t'aeugi 태우기; *Br* (*elevator*) ellibeit'ŏ 엘리베이터; ***give s.o. a ~*** nugurŭl t'aewŏ chuda 누구를 태워 주다

♦**lift off** *v/i* (*of rocket*) sosa orŭda 솟아 오르다
liftoff (*of rocket*) iryuk 이륙
ligament indae 인대
light[1] **1** *n* pit 빛; (*lamp*) tŭng 등; ***in the ~ of*** …e pich'uŏsŏ …에 비추어서; ***have you got a ~?*** pul issŭmnikka? 불 있습니까? **2** *v/t fire, cigarette* pul puch'ida 불 붙이다; (*illuminate*) chomyŏnghada 조명하다 **3** *adj* (*not dark*) palgŭn 밝은
light[2] **1** *adj* (*not heavy*) kabyŏun 가벼운 **2** *adv*: ***travel ~*** chimŭl mani kajiji ank'o yŏhaenghada 짐을 많이 가지지 않고 여행하다
♦**light up 1** *v/t* (*illuminate*) palkke hada 밝게 하다 **2** *v/i* (*start to smoke*) puri nada 불이 나다
light bulb paegyŏl chŏn-gu 백열 전구
lighten[1] *v/t color* palkke hada 밝게 하다
lighten[2] *v/t load* kabyŏpkke hada 가볍게 하다
♦**lighten up** (*of person*) kibun p'ulda 기분 풀다
lighter (*for cigarettes*) lait'ŏ 라이터
light-headed (*dizzy*) ŏjirŏun 어지러운
light-hearted maŭm kabyŏun 마음 가벼운
lighthouse tŭngdae 등대
lighting chomyŏng 조명
lightly *touch* kabyŏpkke 가볍게; ***get off ~*** kabyŏpkke momyŏnhada 가볍게 모면하다
lightness[1] (*of room*) palgŭm 밝음
lightness[2] (*in weight*) kabyŏum 가벼움
lightning pŏn-gae 번개
lightning conductor p'iroech'im 피뢰침
light pen lait'ŭ p'en 라이트 펜
lightweight (*in boxing*) lait'ŭkkŭp sŏnsu 라이트급 선수
light year kwangnyŏn 광년
likable hogami kanŭn 호감이 가는
like[1] **1** *prep* kat'ŭn 같은; ***be ~ s.o.*** nuguwa tamtta 누구와 닮다; ***be ~ sth*** muŏtkkwa kat-tta 무엇과 같다; ***what is she ~?*** kŭ yŏjanŭn ŏttŏn saramimnikka? 그 여자는 어떤 사람입니까?; ***it's not ~ him*** (*not his character*) kŭ saramdaptchi anssŭmnida 그 사람답지 않습니다; ***do it ~ this*** irŏk'e haseyo 이렇게 하세요 **2** *conj* F: ***~ I said*** naega marhaettŭshi 내가 말했듯이
like[2] *v/t* choahada 좋아하다; ***I ~ her*** nanŭn kŭnyŏrŭl choahamnida 나는 그녀를 좋아합니다; ***I would ~ …*** nanŭn …ŭl / rŭl wŏnhamnida 나는 …을 / 를 원합니다; ***I would ~ a bigger room*** nanŭn tŏ k'ŭn pang-ŭl wŏnhaeyo 나는 더 큰 방을 원해요; ***I would ~ to …*** nanŭn ...hago shipssŭmida 나는 …하고 싶습니다; ***I would ~ to leave*** nanŭn ttŏnago ship'ŏyo 나는 떠나고 싶어요; ***would you ~ …?*** …ŭl wŏnhamnikka? …을 / 를 원합니까?; ***would you ~ to …?*** ...hago shipssŭmnikka? …하고 싶습니까?; ***~ to do sth*** muŏsŭl hago shiptta 무엇을 하고 싶다; ***if you ~*** tangshini chot'amyŏn 당신이 좋다면
likeable hogami kanŭn 호감이 가는
likelihood kanŭngssŏng 가능성; ***in all ~*** shiptchungp'algu 십중팔구
likely (*probable*) amado 아마도; ***not ~!*** maldo andoemnida! 말도 안됩니다!
likeness (*resemblance*) yusa 유사
liking: ***to your ~*** tangshin maŭme tŭnŭn 당신 마음에 드는; ***take a ~ to s.o.*** nuguga choajida 누구가 좋아지다
lilac (*flower, color*) laillak 라일락
lily paek'ap 백합
lily of the valley ŭnbang-ul kkot 은방울 꽃
limb sonbal 손발
lime[1] (*fruit, tree*) laim 라임
lime[2] (*substance*) sŏk'oe 석회
limegreen laim nokssaek 라임 녹색
limelight: ***be in the ~*** mut saramŭi chumogŭl pat-tta 뭇 사람의 주목을 받다
limit 1 *n* han-gye 한계; (*of s.o.'s land*) kyŏnggye 경계; ***within ~s*** chŏkttanghage 적당하게; ***off ~s*** ch'urip kŭmji 출입 금지; ***that's the ~!*** ijen tŏ isang ch'amŭl suga ŏpssŏyo! 이젠 더 이상 참을 수가

없어요! **2** *v/t* hanjŏnghada 한정하다
limitation han-gye 한계
limited company *Br* yuhan ch'aegim hoesa 유한 책임 회사
limo, **limousine** limujin 리무진
limp[1] *adj* hŭnŭjŏk-kkŏrinŭn 흐느적거리는
limp[2] *n* chŏlttuk-kkŏrim 절뚝거림; ***he has a ~*** kŭnŭn parŭl chŏlttuk-kkŏrinda 그는 발을 절뚝거린다
line[1] *n* (*on paper*, *road*, *for telephone*) sŏn 선; (*of people*, *text*, *trees*) chul 줄; (*of business*) saŏp 사업; ***the ~ is busy*** t'onghwa chung imnida 통화 중 입니다; ***hold the ~*** chamshiman kidariseyo 잠시만 기다리세요; ***draw the ~ at sth*** muŏsŭl handoro chŏnghada 무엇을 한도로 정하다; ***~ of inquiry*** chosaŭi panghyang 조사의 방향; ***~ of reasoning*** ch'uron 추론; ***stand in ~*** churŭl sŏda 줄을 서다; ***in ~ with*** (*conforming with*) …e sunŭnghayŏ …에 순응하여
line[2] *v/t* (*with material*) …(ŭ)ro anŭl taeda …(으)로 안을 대다
♦**line up** *v/i* chul sŏda 줄 서다
linen (*material*, *sheets etc*) linen 리넨
liner (*ship*) chŏnggisŏn 정기선
linesman SP sŏnshim 선심
linger nama it-tta 남아 있다
lingerie lanjeri 란제리
linguist ŏnŏhaktcha 언어학자; (*good at languages*) ŏhage nŭnghan saram 어학에 능한 사람
linguistic ŏhagŭi 어학의
lining (*of clothes*) ankkam 안감; (*of pipe*, *brakes*) laining 라이닝
link 1 *n* (*connection*) yŏn-gwan 연관; (*in chain*) kori 고리; (*of friendship*) yudae kwan-gye 유대 관계 **2** *v/t* yŏn-gyŏrhada 연결하다
♦**link up** *v/i* mannada 만나다; TV yŏn-gyŏrhada 연결하다
lion saja 사자
lip ipssul 입술
lipread *v/t & v/i* immoyang-ŭro iltta 입모양으로 읽다
lipstick lipssŭt'ik 립스틱
liqueur lik'yurŭ 리큐르
liquid 1 *n* aekch'e 액체 **2** *adj* aekch'eŭi 액체의
liquidation ch'ŏngsan 청산; ***go into ~*** ch'ŏngsanhada 청산하다
liquidity FIN yudong chasan 유동 자산
liquor sul 술
liquorice kamch'o 감초
liquor store churyu p'anmaejŏm 주류 판매점
lisp 1 *n* hyŏ tchalbŭn sori 혀 짧은 소리 **2** *v/i* hyŏ tchalbŭn soriro marhada 혀 짧은 소리로 말하다
list 1 *n* mongnok 목록 **2** *v/t* mongnoge ollida 목록에 올리다
listen tŭt-tta 듣다
♦**listen in** yŏt-ttŭt-tta 엿듣다
♦**listen to** *radio*, *person* …ŭl / rŭl tŭt-tta …을 / 를 듣다
listener (*to radio*) ch'ŏngch'wija 청취자; ***he's a good ~*** kŭnŭn saram marŭl chal tŭrŏjumnida 그는 사람 말을 잘 들어줍니다
listings magazine pangsong p'ŭrogŭraem chaptchi 방송 프로그램 잡지
listless maŭm naek'iji annŭn 마음 내키지 않는
liter lit'ŏ 리터
literal *adj* kŭltcha kŭdaeroŭi 글자 그대로의
literary munhagŭi 문학의
literate: ***be ~*** kŭrŭl ilkko ssŭl chul anda 글을 읽고 쓸 줄 안다
literature munhak 문학
litter ssŭregi 쓰레기; (*of young animals*) han pae saekki 한 배 새끼
little 1 *adj* chagŭn 작은; ***the ~ ones*** aidŭl 아이들 **2** *n* chogŭm 조금; ***the ~ I know*** naega kŏŭi morŭnŭn kŏt 내가 거의 모르는 것; ***a ~*** chogŭm 조금; ***a ~ bread / wine*** ppang / p'odoju chogŭm 빵 / 포도주 조금; ***a ~ is better than nothing*** chogŭmirado innŭn kŏshi ŏmnŭn kotppoda nat-tta 조금이라도 있는 것이 없는 것보다 낫다 **3** *adv* chogŭmŭn 조금은; ***~ by ~*** chogŭmsshik 조금씩; ***a ~ better / bigger*** chogŭm tŏ choŭn / k'ŭn 조금 더 좋은 / 큰; ***a ~ before 6*** yŏsŏtshi chogŭm chŏne 6시 조금 전에
live[1] *v/i* salda 살다

♦**live on 1** *v/t rice, bread* ...ŭl / rŭl mŏk-kko salda ...을 / 를 먹고 살다 **2** *v/i* (*continue living*) kyesok salda 계속 살다
♦**live up**: ***live it up*** sach'issŭrŏpkke salda 사치스럽게 살다
♦**live up to** ...e mannŭn saenghwarŭl hada ...에 맞는 생활을 하다
♦**live with** *person* ...wa / kwa tonggŏhada ...와 / 과 동거하다
live[2] *adj* (*living*) sara innŭn 살아 있는; ELEC chŏn-giga t'onghago innŭn 전기가 통하고 있는; ~ ***ammunition*** shilt'an 실탄; ~ ***broadcast*** saengbangsong 생방송
livelihood saenggye 생계
lively hwalgi ch'an 활기 찬
liver ANAT kanjang 간장; (*food*) kan 간
livestock kach'uk 가축
livid (*angry*) nobaldaebarhan 노발대발한
living 1 *adj* sara innŭn 살아 있는 **2** *n* saenghwal 생활; (*means of support*) saenggye 생계; ***earn one's*** ~ saenghwalbirŭl pŏlda 생활비를 벌다
living room kŏshil 거실
lizard tomabaem 도마뱀
load 1 *n* chim 짐; ELEC puha 부하; ~***s of*** manŭn 많은 **2** *v/t car, truck* chimŭl shilt'a 짐을 싣다; *camera* p'illŭmŭl nŏt'a 필름을 넣다; *gun* changjŏnhada 장전하다; *software* lodŭhada 로드하다; ~ ***sth onto sth*** muŏsŭl muŏse shilt'a 무엇을 무엇에 싣다
loaded F (*very rich*) toni manŭn 돈이 많은; (*drunk*) ch'wihan 취한
loaf tŏng-ŏri 덩어리; ***a ~ of bread*** ppang han tŏng-ŏri 빵 한 덩어리
♦**loaf around** nolgo chinaeda 놀고 지내다
loafer (*shoe*) kanp'yŏnhwa 간편화
loan 1 *n* taebu 대부; ***on*** ~ pillin 빌린 **2** *v/t*: ~ ***s.o. sth*** nuguege muŏsŭl pillyŏjuda 누구에게 무엇을 빌려주다
loathe mopsshi shirŏhada 몹시 싫어하다
lobby (*in hotel*) lobi 로비; (*in theater*) hyugeshil 휴게실; POL amnyŏk tanch'e 압력 단체
lobster padatkkajae 바닷가재
local 1 *adj* chibang-ŭi 지방의; ***I'm not*** ~ nanŭn igot sarami aniyeyo 나는 이곳 사람이 아니예요 **2** *n* (*person*) chibang saram 지방 사람
local anesthetic kukppu mach'wi 국부 마취; **local call** TELEC shinae t'onghwa 시내 통화; **local government** chibang chach'i 지방 자치
locality changso 장소
locally *live, work* kakkaie(sŏ) 가까이에(서)
local produce chibang t'ŭkssanmul 지방 특산물
local time hyŏnji shigan 현지 시간
locate *new factory etc* wich'irŭl chŏnghada 위치를 정하다; (*identify position of*) wich'irŭl aranaeda 위치를 알아내다; ***be ~d*** wich'ihada 위치하다
location (*siting*) wich'i sŏnjŏng 위치 선정; (*identifying position of*) wich'irŭl aranaem 위치를 알아냄; ***on*** ~ *movie* yaoe ch'waryŏngjung 야외 촬영중
lock[1] (*of hair*) t'arae 타래
lock[2] **1** *n* (*on door*) chamulssoe 자물쇠 **2** *v/t door* chamgŭda 잠그다; ~ ***sth in position*** muŏsŭl chejarie kojŏngshik'ida 무엇을 제자리에 고정시키다
♦**lock away** chamulssoerŭl ch'aewŏ nŏt'a 자물쇠를 채워 넣다
♦**lock in** *person* kaduda 가두다
♦**lock out** (*of house*) mot tŭrŏoge chamgŭda 못 들어오게 잠그다; ***I was locked out of my office*** yŏlssoega ŏpssŏsŏ samushire mot tŭrŏgassŏyo 열쇠가 없어서 사무실에 못 들어갔어요
♦**lock up** (*in prison*) kamgŭmhada 감금하다
locker lok'ŏ 로커
locksmith chamulssoe chejogong 자물쇠 제조공
locust mettugi 메뚜기
lodge 1 *v/t complaint* chech'urhada 제출하다 **2** *v/i* (*of bullet, ball*) pak'ida 박히다
lodger hasugin 하숙인
loft tarakppang 다락방; (*apartment*)

kŏnmul maen wich'ŭng-ŭi chugŏ konggan 건물 맨 윗층의 주거 공간
lofty *heights* maeu nop'ŭn 매우 높은; *ideals* chigohan 지고한
log (*wood*) t'ongnamu 통나무; (*written record*) iltchi 일지
♦**log off** chongnyohada 종료하다
♦**log on** shijak'ada 시작하다
♦**log on to** ...ŭl / rŭl shijak'ada ...을 / 를 시작하다
logbook iltchi 일지
log cabin t'ongnamu odumaktchip 통나무 오두막집
logic nolli 논리
logical nollijŏgin 논리적인
logistics MIL pyŏngch'am ŏmmu 병참 업무; COM sangsehan kyehoek 상세한 계획
logo logo 로고
loiter pindunggŏrida 빈둥거리다
London Lŏndŏn 런던
loneliness oeroum 외로움; (*of place*) korip 고립
lonely *person* oeroun 외로운; *place* koripttoen 고립된
loner *honja itkki choahanŭn saram* 혼자 있기 좋아하는 사람
long[1] **1** *adj* kin 긴; ***it's a ~ way*** mŏrŏyo 멀어요; ***for a ~ time*** oraettong-an 오랫동안 **2** *adv* orae 오래; ***don't be ~*** kkumulgŏriji mara 꾸물거리지 마라; ***5 weeks is too ~*** tasŏt chunŭn nŏmu kilda 다섯 주는 너무 길다; ***will it take ~?*** orae kŏllyŏyo? 오래 걸려요?; ***that was ~ ago*** aju orae chŏniyeyo 아주 오래 전이예요; ***~ before then*** hwŏlsshin kŭ chŏne 훨씬 그 전에; ***before ~*** kot 곧; ***we can't wait any ~er*** urinŭn tŏ isang kidaril su ŏpssŏyo 우리는 더 이상 기다릴 수 없어요; ***he no ~er works here*** kŭnŭn tŏ isang yŏgi irhaji anayo 그는 더 이상 여기 일하지 않아요; ***so ~ as*** (*provided*) ...hanŭn han ...하는 한; ***so ~!*** annyŏng! 안녕!
long[2] *v/i*: ***~ for sth*** muŏsŭl aet'age parada 무엇을 애타게 바라다; ***be ~ing to do sth*** muŏt hanŭn kŏsŭl aet'age parada 무엇 하는 것을 애타게 바라다
long-distance *adj phonecall, race, flight* changgŏriŭi 장거리의
longing *n* kalmang 갈망
longitude kyŏngdo 경도
long jump nŏlbi ttwigi 넓이 뛰기; **long-range** *missile* wŏn-gŏriŭi 원거리의; *forecast* changgijŏgin 장기적인; **long-sighted** sŏn-gyŏnjimyŏng-i innŭn 선견지명이 있는; **long-sleeved** kin somaeŭi 긴 소매의; **long-standing** orae kyesokttoenŭn 오래 계속되는; **long-term** *adj* changgiŭi 장기의; **long wave** changp'a 장파
loo *Br* hwajangshil 화장실
look 1 *n* (*appearance*) moyang 모양; (*glance*) pom 봄; ***give s.o. / sth a ~*** muŏsŭl / nugurŭl hult'ŏboda 무엇을 / 누구를 훑어보다; ***have a ~ at sth*** (*examine*) muŏsŭl salp'yŏboda 무엇을 살펴보다; ***can I have a ~?*** pwado toelkkayo? 봐도 될까요?; ***can I have a ~ around?*** (*in store etc*) tullŏbwado toelkkayo? 둘러봐도 될까요?; ***~s*** (*beauty*) yongmo 용모 **2** *v/i* poda 보다; (*search*) ch'ajaboda 찾아보다; (*seem*) poida 보이다; ***you ~ tired / different*** nŏnŭn p'igonhae / talla poinda 너는 피곤해 / 달라보인다
♦**look after** ...ŭl / rŭl posalp'ida ...을 / 를 보살피다
♦**look around** *museum, city* ...ŭl / rŭl tullŏboda ...을 / 를 둘러보다
♦**look at** ...ŭl / rŭl poda ...을 / 를 보다; (*examine*) ...ŭl / rŭl salp'yŏboda ...을 / 를 살펴보다; (*consider*) ...ŭl / rŭl koch'arhada ...을 / 를 고찰하다
♦**look back** twidoraboda 뒤돌아보다
♦**look down on** (*despise*) ...ŭl / rŭl natch'uŏ poda ...을 / 를 낮추어 보다
♦**look for** ...ŭl / rŭl ch'at-tta ...을 / 를 찾다
♦**look forward to** ...ŭl / rŭl kidaehada ...을 / 를 기대하다
♦**look in on** (*visit*) ...ŭl / rŭl pangmunhada ...을 / 를 방문하다
♦**look into** (*investigate*) ...ŭl / rŭl chosahada ...을 / 를 조사하다
♦**look on 1** *v/i* (*watch*)

panggwanhada 방관하다 **2** *v/t*: ~ ***s.o.*** / ***sth as*** (*consider*) nugurŭl / muŏsŭl …(ŭ)ro kanjuhada 누구를 / 무엇을 …(으)로 간주하다
♦**look onto** *garden*, *street* …(ŭ)ro myŏnhada …(으)로 면하다
♦**look out** (*of window etc*) pakkach'ŭl naedaboda 바깥을 내다보다; (*pay attention*) chuŭihada 주의하다; ~**!** choshimhae! 조심해!
♦**look out for** …ŭl / rŭl ch'ajaboda …을 / 를 찾아보다; (*be on guard against*) …ŭl / rŭl kyŏnggyehada …을 / 를 경계하다
♦**look out of** *window* pakkach'ŭl naedaboda 바깥을 내다보다
♦**look over** *house*, *translation* …ŭl / rŭl taech'ung hult'ŏboda …을 / 를 대충 훑어보다
♦**look through** *magazine*, *notes* …ŭl / rŭl ch'ŏltchŏhi chosahada …을 / 를 철저히 조사하다
♦**look to** (*rely on*) …e ŭijihada …에 의지하다
♦**look up 1** *v/i* (*from paper etc*) ch'ajaboda 찾아보다; (*improve*) paltchŏnhada 발전하다; ***things are looking up*** iri choajigo it-tta 일이 좋아지고 있다 **2** *v/t word*, *phone number* ch'ajaboda 찾아보다; (*visit*) pangmunhada 방문하다
♦**look up to** (*respect*) chon-gyŏnghada 존경하다
lookout (*person*) mangbogi 망보기; ***be on the ~ for*** …ŭl / rŭl kyŏnggyehada …을 / 를 경계하다
♦**loom up** ŏryŏmp'ushi nat'anada 어렴풋이 나타나다
loony F **1** *n* mich'igwang-i 미치광이 **2** *adj* mich'in 미친
loop *n* kori 고리
loophole (*in law etc*) hŏtchŏm 허점
loose *connection*, *button* nŭsŭnhan 느슨한; *clothes* hŏlgŏun 헐거운; *morals* pangjonghan 방종한; *wording* sanmanhan 산만한; ***~ change*** chandon pusŭrŏgi 잔돈 부스러기; ***tie up the ~ ends*** kyŏlmarŭl chit-tta 결말을 짓다
loosely *tied* hŏlgŏpkke 헐겁게; *worded* sanmanhage 산만하게
loosen *collar*, *knot* nŭsŭnhage hada 느슨하게 하다
loot 1 *n* yakt'alp'um 약탈품 **2** *v/i* yakt'arhada 약탈하다
looter yakt'altcha 약탈자
♦**lop off** sak-kkamhada 삭감하다
lop-sided hantchogŭro kiurŏjin 한쪽으로 기울어진
Lord (*God*) Chu 주; ***~'s Prayer*** Chu Kidomun 주 기도문
lorry *Br* t'ŭrŏk 트럭
lose 1 *v/t object* ilt'a 잃다; *match* chida 지다 **2** *v/i* SP chida 지다; (*of clock*) nŭjŏjida 늦어지다; ***I'm lost*** nanŭn kirŭl irŏbŏryŏssŏyo 나는 길을 잃어버렸어요; ***get lost!*** kkŏjyŏbŏryŏ! 꺼져버려!
♦**lose out** shilp'aehada 실패하다
loser SP p'aeja 패자; (*in life*) shilp'aeja 실패자
loss (*of object*) sonshil 손실; (*of loved one*) sangshil 상실; (*in business*) sonhae 손해; ***make a ~*** sonhaerŭl iptta 손해를 입다; ***be at a ~*** ŏtchihal parŭl morŭda 어찌할 바를 모르다
lost irŭn 잃은
lost-and-found (office) punshilmul sent'ŏ 분실물 센터
lot: ***a ~ of***, ***~s of*** manŭn 많은; ***a ~***, ***~s*** *eat*, *talk etc* mani 많이; ***a ~ better*** / ***easier*** hwŏlsshin toe choŭn / shiun 훨씬 더 좋은 / 쉬운
lotion loshyŏn 로션
loud shikkŭrŏun 시끄러운; *color* yoranhan 요란한
loudspeaker hwakssŏnggi 확성기
lounge launji 라운지
♦**lounge around** pindunggŏrida 빈둥거리다
louse i 이
lousy F (*bad*) hyŏngp'yonŏmnŭn 형편없는
lout shigolttŭgi 시골뜨기
lovable sarangsŭrŏun 사랑스러운
love 1 *n* sarang 사랑; (*in tennis*) mudŭktchŏm 무득점; ***be in ~*** saranghago it-tta 사랑하고 있다; ***fall in ~*** sarang-e ppajida 사랑에 빠지다; ***make ~*** sŏng kwan-gyerŭl kajida 성 관계를 가지다; ***yes my ~*** kŭraeyo yŏbo 그래요 여보 **2** *v/t person*,

country saranghada 사랑하다; **~ *to do sth*** muŏt hanŭn kŏsŭl koengjanghi choahada 무엇 하는 것을 굉장히 좋아하다

love affair yŏnae sakkŏn 연애 사건; **love life** sŏngsaenghwal 성생활; **love letter** yŏnae p'yŏnji 연애 편지

lovely *face, hair, color, tune* arŭmdaun 아름다운; *person, character* sarangsŭrŏun 사랑스러운; *holiday, weather, meal* mŏtchin 멋진; ***we had a ~ time*** urinŭn chŏngmal chŭlgŏpkke ponaessŏyo 우리는 정말 즐겁게 보냈어요

love marriage yŏnae kyŏrhon 연애 결혼

lover aein 애인

loving *adj* aejŏng-i innŭn 애정이 있는

low 1 *adj bridge, wall, voice, quality* najŭn 낮은; *price* ssan 싼; *salary* chagŭn 작은; ***be feeling ~*** ch'imurhage nŭkkida 침울하게 느끼다; ***be ~ on gas / tea*** kasŭga / ch'aga kŏŭi ta ttŏrŏjida 가스가 / 차가 거의 다 떨어지다 **2** *n* (*in weather*) chŏgiap 저기압; (*in sales, statistics*) chŏjo 저조

lowbrow *adj movie, writing* sujuni najŭn 수준이 낮은; *person* kyoyang-i ŏmnŭn 교양이 없는; **low-calorie** chŏk'alloriŭi 저칼로리의; **low-cut** *dress* kasŭmi mani p'ain 가슴이 많이 파인

lower *v/t boat, sth to the ground* naerida 내리다; *flag, hemline* natch'uda 낮추다; *pressure, price* ttŏrŏttŭrida 떨어뜨리다

low-fat chŏjibang-ŭi 저지방의; **lowkey** chajehanŭn 자제하는; **lowlands** chŏji 저지; **low-pressure area** chŏgiap chidae 저기압 지대; **low season** pisugi 비수기; **low tide** ssŏlmul 썰물

loyal ch'ungsŏngsŭrŏun 충성스러운

lozenge (*shape*) marŭmmokkol 마름모꼴; (*tablet*) marŭmmokkol chŏngje 마름모꼴 정제

Ltd (= ***limited***) yuhanhoesa 유한회사

lubricant *n* yunhwaltche 윤활제

lubricate mikkŭrŏpkke hada 미끄럽게 하다

lubrication mikkŭrŏpkke ham 미끄럽게 함

lucid (*clear*) algi shwiun 알기 쉬운; (*sane*) chejŏngshinŭi 제정신의

luck un 운; ***bad ~*** purun 불운; ***hard ~!*** chaesuŏpkkun! 재수없군!; ***good ~*** haeng-un 행운; ***good ~!*** haeng-unŭl pimnida! 행운을 빕니다!

♦**luck out** F uni chot'a 운이 좋다

luckily un chok'e 운 좋게

lucky *person* un choŭn 운 좋은; *day, number* haeng-unŭl kajyŏonŭn 행운을 가져오는; *coincidence* unttaega mannŭn 운때가 맞는; ***you were ~*** nŏn uni choassŏ 넌 운이 좋았어; ***he's ~ to be alive*** kŭnŭn un chok'edo sara namat-tta 그는 운 좋게도 살아 남았다; ***that's ~!*** kŭgŏ un chŏassŏyo! 그거 운 좋았어요!

ludicrous pabosŭrŏun 바보스러운

luggage suhwamul 수화물

lukewarm *water* mijigŭnhan 미지근한; *reception* naengdamhan 냉담한

lull 1 *n* (*in storm, fighting*) chinjŏng 진정; (*in conversation*) chamshi chungdandoem 잠시 중단됨 **2** *v/t*: **~ *s.o. into a false sense of security*** nugurŭl kŏjisŭro anshimshik'ida 누구를 거짓으로 안심시키다

lullaby chajangga 자장가

lumbago yot'ong 요통

lumber *n* (*timber*) chaemok 재목

luminous pich'ŭl naenŭn 빛을 내는

lump (*of sugar*) chogak 조각; (*swelling*) hok 혹

♦**lump together** ilgwaljŏgŭro ch'wigŭp'ada 일괄적으로 취급하다

lump sum ilsshibul 일시불

lumpy *liquid, sauce* tŏng-ŏri t'usŏng-iŭi 덩어리 투성이의; *mattress* ult'ungbult'unghan 울퉁불퉁한

lunacy mich'in chit 미친 짓

lunar tarŭi 달의

lunar calendar ŭmnyŏk 음력

Lunar New Year Sŏllal 설날

lunatic *n* mich'igwang-i 미치광이

lunch chŏmshim 점심; ***have ~*** chŏmshimŭl mŏktta 점심을 먹다

lunch box toshirak 도시락; **lunch**

break, **lunchtime** chŏmshimshigan 점심시간
lung p'ye 폐
lung cancer p'yeam 폐암
♦**lunge at** tchirŭda 찌르다
lurch *v/i* pit'ŭlgŏrida 비틀거리다
lure 1 *n* maeryŏk 매력 **2** *v/t* sogimsuro yuhok'ada 속임수로 유혹하다
lurid *color* yoranhan 요란한; *details* mushimushihan 무시무시한
lurk (*of person*) chambok'ada 잠복하다; (*of doubt*) chamjaehada 잠재하다
luscious *fruit*, *dessert* talk'omhan 달콤한; *woman*, *man* kwannŭngjŏgin 관능적인
lust *n* yongmang 욕망
luxurious sach'isŭrŏun 사치스러운
luxury 1 *n* sach'i 사치 **2** *adj* sach'isŭrŏun 사치스러운
lymph gland limp'ŭsaem 림프샘
lynch chipttan p'ok'aeng-ŭl kahada 집단 폭행을 가하다
lynx sŭrasoni 스라소니
lyricist chakssaga 작사가
lyrics kasa 가사

M

MA (= ***Master of Arts***) munhak sŏkssa 문학 석사
ma'am (*to married woman*) samonim 사모님; (*to unmarried woman*) agasshi 아가씨
machine 1 *n* kigye 기계 **2** *v/t* (*on sewing machine*) chaebongt'ŭllo paktta 재봉틀로 박다; TECH kigyero saengsanhada 기계로 생산하다
machine gun *n* kigwanch'ong 기관총
machine-readable k'ŏmp'yut'ŏ ch'ŏriga kanŭnghan 컴퓨터 처리가 가능한
machinery (*machines*) kigyeryu 기계류; (*of government, organization*) kigwan 기관
machismo *namjadaumŭl kangjoham* 남자다움을 강조함
macho *namjadaumŭl kangjohan* 남자다움을 강조한
mackintosh pangsu oet'u 방수 외투
macro COMPUT maek'ŭro 매크로
mad (*insane*) mich'in 미친; F (*angry*) mich'il tŭshi hwanan 미칠 듯이 화난; ***be ~ about*** F (*enthusiastic*) …ŭl / rŭl mich'idŭshi choahada …을 / 를 미치듯이 좋아하다; ***drive s.o. ~*** nugurŭl mich'igehada 누구를 미치게 하다; ***go ~*** (*become insane*) mich'yŏgada 미쳐가다; (*with enthusiasm*) kippŏsŏ mich'in tŭshi nalttwida 기뻐서 미친 듯이 날뛰다; ***like ~*** F *run*, *work* mich'in tŭshi 미친 듯이
madden (*infuriate*) mich'il tŭshi hwanage hada 미칠 듯이 화나게 하다
maddening hwaga nasŏ mich'ige hanŭn 화가 나서 미치게 하는
made-to-measure match'umŭi 맞춤의
madhouse *fig* nanjangp'an 난장판
madly mich'in tŭshi 미친 듯이; ***~ in love*** sarang-e mich'yŏsŏ 사랑에 미쳐서
madman mich'igwang-i 미치광이
madness kwangkki 광기
Mafia: ***the ~*** Map'ia chojik 마피아 조직
magazine (*printed*) chaptchi 잡지
maggot kudŏgi 구더기
magic 1 *n* masul 마술; (*tricks*) yosul 요술; ***like ~*** yosulgach'i 요술같이 **2** *adj* masurŭi 마술의
magical masuljŏgin 마술적인; *moment* shinbiroun 신비로운
magician (*performer*) masulssa 마술사
magic spell chumun 주문
magic trick yosul 요술
magnanimous kwandaehan 관대한
magnet chasŏk 자석
magnetic chagiŭi 자기의; *personality* maehoktchŏgin 매혹적인
magnetism chagi 자기; (*of person*) maehok 매혹
magnificence changnyŏham 장려함
magnificent changnyŏhan 장려한; ***what a ~ day!*** ŏlmana mŏtchin nariyeyo! 얼마나 멋진 날이예요!
magnify hwakttaehada 확대하다; *difficulties* kwajanghada 과장하다
magnifying glass totppogi 돋보기
magnitude kyumo 규모
mah-jong majak 마작
maid (*servant*) hanyŏ 하녀; (*in hotel*) hot'el chong-ŏbwŏn 호텔 종업원
maiden name kyŏrhon chŏnŭi sŏng 결혼 전의 성
maiden voyage ch'ŏnyŏ hanghae 처녀 항해
mail 1 *n* up'yŏn 우편; ***put sth in the ~*** muŏsŭl up'yŏnŭro ponaeda 무엇을 우편으로 보내다 **2** *v/t letter* p'yŏnjihada 편지하다
mailbox (*in street*) uch'et'ong 우체통; (*of house*) up'yŏnham 우편함; COMPUT meilbakssŭ 메일박스

mailing list chusorok 주소록
mailman uch'ebu 우체부; **mail-order catalog** t'ongshin p'anmae ch'aektcha 통신 판매 책자; **mail-order firm** t'ongshin p'anmae hoesa 통신 판매 회사
maim pulguro mandŭlda 불구로 만들다
main *adj* chudoen 주된
mainboard COMPUT meinbodŭ 메인보드; **mainframe** *n* k'ŏmp'yut'ŏ ponch'e 컴퓨터 본체; **mainland** pont'o 본토; ***on the ~*** pont'oesŏ 본토에서; **mainland China** Chungguk pont'o 중국 본토
mainly churo 주로
main road chudoro 주도로
main street chungshimga 중심가
maintain *law and order*, *speed*, *machine*, *house* yujihada 유지하다; *relationship* chisok'ada 지속하다; *old building* pojonhada 보존하다; *family* puyanghada 부양하다; *innocence*, *guilt* chujanghada 주장하다; ***~ that ...*** ...ranŭn kosŭl chujanghada ...라는 것을 주장하다
maintenance (*of machine*, *house*, *law and order*) yuji 유지; (*of old building*) pojon 보존; (*money*) puyangbi 부양비
Maitreya Buddha Mirŭkppul 미륵불
majestic ungdaehan 웅대한
major 1 *adj* (*significant*) chuyohan 주요한; ***in C ~*** MUS ta changjo 다 장조 **2** *n* MIL soryŏng 소령
♦**major in** ... ŭl/rŭl chŏn-gonghada ...을/를 전공하다
majority taedasu 대다수; POL kwabansu 과반수; ***be in the ~*** kwabansuida 과반수이다
make 1 *n* (*brand*) sangp'yo 상표 **2** *v/t* mandŭlda 만들다; (*earn*) pŏlda 벌다; MATH ida 이다; ***two and two ~ four*** i tŏhagi inŭn saida 이 더하기 이는 사이다; ***~ a decision*** kyŏltchŏng-ŭl hada 결정을 하다; ***~ a telephone call*** chŏnhwarŭl hada 전화를 하다; ***made in Korea*** Han-gukssan 한국산; ***~ it*** (*catch bus*, *train*) che shigane t'ada 제 시간에 타다; (*come*) oda 오다; (*succeed*) sŏnggonghada 성공하다; (*survive*) saranada 살아나다; ***I just made it to the station*** kyŏu che shigane yŏge toch'akaessŏyo 겨우 제 시간에 역에 도착했어요; ***what time do you ~ it?*** tangshin shigyenŭn myŏt shiimnikka? 당신 시계는 몇 시입니까?; ***~ believe*** ...inch'ehada ...인체 하다; ***~ do with*** ...(ŭ)ro manjok'ada ...(으)로 만족하다; ***what do you ~ of it?*** tangshinŭi saenggagŭn ŏttŏsŭmnikka? 당신의 생각은 어떻습니까? ◊: ***~ s.o. do sth*** (*force to*) nuguege muŏsŭl shik'ida 누구에게 무엇을 시키다; (*cause to*) nugurŭl muŏt'age hada 누구를 무엇하게 하다; ***you can't ~ me do it!*** tangshini nahant'e kŭgŏsŭl shik'il su ŏpssŏyo! 당신이 나한테 그것을 시킬 수 없어요! ◊: ***~ s.o. happy / angry*** nugurŭl haengbok'age / hwanage hada 누구를 행복하게 / 화나게 하다
♦**make for** (*go toward*) ...ro kada ...로 가다
♦**make off** taranada 달아나다
♦**make off with** (*steal*) humch'ida 훔치다
♦**make out** *v/t list* chakssŏnghada 작성하다; *check* ssŭda 쓰다; (*see*) poda 보다; (*imply*) nŏnjishi pich'uda 넌지시 비추다
♦**make over**: ***make X over to Y*** Xrŭl Yege mullyŏjuda X를 Y에게 물려주다
♦**make up 1** *v/i* (*of woman*, *actor*) hwajanghada 화장하다; (*after quarrel*) hwahaehada 화해하다 **2** *v/t story*, *excuse* kkumida 꾸미다; *face* hwajanghada 화장하다; (*constitute*) kusŏnghada 구성하다; ***be made up of*** ...(ŭ)ro kusŏngdoeŏ itta ...(으)로 구성되어 있다; ***~ one's mind*** maŭmŭl chŏnghada 마음을 정하다; ***make it up*** (*after quarrel*) hwahaehada 화해하다
♦**make up for** (*compensate for*) pŏlch'unghada 벌충하다
make-believe *n* kkumin kŏt 꾸민 것
maker saengsanja 생산자
makeshift imshi sudan 임시 수단

make-up (*cosmetics*) hwajangp'um 화장품
maladjusted chŏgŭng-ŭl mot'anŭn 적응을 못하는
Malay (*language*) Malleiŏ 말레이어; (*person*) Malleishia saram 말레이시아 사람
Malaysia Malleishia 말레이시아
Malaysian Malleishiain 말레이시아인
male 1 *adj* (*masculine*) namsŏng-ŭi 남성의; *animal*, *bird*, *fish* suk'ŏsŭi 수컷의 **2** *n* (*man*) namja 남자; (*animal*, *bird*, *fish*) suk'ŏt 수컷
male chauvinist (pig) namsŏng uwŏltchuŭija 남성 우월주의자
male nurse namja kanhosa 남자 간호사
malevolent agŭi innŭn 악의 있는
malfunction 1 *n* chakttong pullyang 작동 불량 **2** *v/i* chakttong-i chal toeji ant'a 작동이 잘 되지 않다
malice agŭi 악의
malicious agŭi innŭn 악의 있는
malignant *tumor* akssŏng-ŭi 악성의
mall (*shopping ~*) sangga 상가
malnutrition yŏngnyang shiltcho 영양 실조
malpractice kwashil 과실
maltreat hakttaehada 학대하다
maltreatment hakttae 학대
mammal p'oyu tongmul 포유 동물
mammoth *adj* (*enormous*) kŏdaehan 거대한
man *n* namja 남자; (*human being*) saram 사람; (*humanity*) illyu 인류; (*in chess*, *checkers*) mal 말
manage 1 *v/t business* kwallihada 관리하다; *big company* kyŏngnyŏnghada 경영하다; *money* kkuryŏgada 꾸려가다; *bags* taruda 다루다; **~ to ...** irŏktchŏrŏk ... haenaeda 이럭저럭 ... 해내다 **2** *v/i* (*cope*) kyŏndida 견디다; (*financially*) kkuryŏnagada 꾸려나가다; ***can you ~?*** tangshini hal su issŭmnikka? 당신이 할 수 있습니까?
manageable tarugi shwiun 다루기 쉬운
management kwalli 관리; (*of big company*) kyŏngnyŏng 경영; (*managers*) kyŏngnyŏngjin 경영진; ***under his ~*** kuŭi kwalliha-e 그의 관리하에; (*of big company*) kuŭi kyŏngnyŏngha-e 그의 경영하에
management buyout kyŏngnyŏngkkwŏn maemae 경영권 매매; **management consultant** kyŏngnyŏng sangdamja 경영 상담자; **management studies** kyŏngnyŏnghak 경영학; **management team** kyŏngnyŏngt'im 경영팀
manager (*of department*) kwalliin 관리인; (*of factory*, *of people*) kwallija 관리자; (*of company*) kyŏngnyŏngja 경영자; (*executive*) kyŏngnyŏng-in 경영인; (*of shop*, *restaurant*, *hotel*) chibaein 지배인
managerial kwalliŭi 관리의
managing director pujang 부장
Mandarin (*language*) Chungguk Pukkyŏng-ŏ 중국 북경어
mandarin (*in China*) kwalli 관리
mandarin orange kyul 귤
mandate (*authority*) kwŏnhan puyŏ 권한 부여; (*task*) immu 임무
mandatory ŭimujŏgin 의무적인
mane (*of horse*) kalgi 갈기
maneuver 1 *n* umjigim 움직임; *fig* ch'aengnyak 책략 **2** *v/t* kyomyohi umjigida 교묘히 움직이다
mangle *v/t* (*crush*) tchiburŏttŭrida 찌부러뜨리다
manhandle *person* kŏch'ilge taehada 거칠게 대하다; *object* illyŏgŭro umjigida 인력으로 움직이다
manhood (*maturity*) sŏngnyŏn 성년; (*virility*) namjadaum 남자다움
man-hour *irindang han shiganŭi nodongnyang* 일인당 한 시간의 노동량
manhunt pŏmin susaek 범인 수색
mania (*craze*): **~ *for ...*** ...kwang ...광
maniac mich'in saram 미친 사람
manicure *n* maenik'yuŏ 매니큐어
manifest 1 *adj* myŏngbaek'an 명백한 **2** *v/t* myŏngbaek'age hada 명백하게 하다; **~ *itself*** nat'anada 나타나다
manipulate *person* chojonghada 조종하다; *bones* kyojŏnghada 교정하다
manipulation (*of person*) chojong

조종; (*of bones*) kyojŏng 교정
manipulative chojonghanŭn 조종하는
mankind illyu 인류
manly namjadaun 남자다운
man-made in-gong 인공
mannequin (*for clothes*) manek'ing 마네킹
manner (*of doing sth*) pangshik 방식; (*attitude*) t'aedo 태도
manners: ***good / bad ~*** yeŭi parŭm / ŏpssŭm 예의 바름 / 없음; ***have no ~*** yeŭiga ŏptta 예의가 없다
manpower illyŏk 인력
mansion chŏt'aek 저택
mantelpiece pyŏngnallo wiŭi sŏnban 벽난로 위의 선반
manual 1 *adj* sonŭro hanŭn 손으로 하는; ***~ labor*** sonil 손일; ***a ~ worker*** yukch'e nodongja 육체 노동자 **2** *n* sŏlmyŏngsŏ 설명서
manufacture 1 *n* chejoŏp 제조업 **2** *v/t equipment* chejohada 제조하다
manufacturer chejoŏptcha 제조업자
manufacturing (*industry*) kong-ŏp 공업
manure piryo 비료
manuscript wŏn-go 원고; ***original ~*** wŏnbon 원본
many 1 *adj* manŭn 많은; ***~ times*** yŏrŏ pŏn 여러 번; ***not ~ people / taxis*** kŭri manch'i anŭn saram / t'aeksshi 그리 많지 않은 사람 / 택시; ***too ~ problems / beers*** nŏmu manŭn munjedŭl / maektchu 너무 많은 문제들 / 맥주 **2** *pron* manŭn kŏt 많은 것; (*people*) manŭn saram 많은 사람; ***a great ~***, ***a good ~*** taedanhi manŭn 대단히 많은; ***how ~ do you need?*** ŏlmana mani p'iryohashimnikka? 얼마나 많이 필요하십니까?
map *n* chido 지도
♦**map out** *career etc* sangsehi kyehoek'ada 상세히 계획하다
maple tanp'ungnamu 단풍나무
mar mangch'yŏnot'a 망쳐놓다
marathon (*race*) marat'on 마라톤
marble (*material*) taerisŏk 대리석
March samwŏl 삼월; ***1st ~ Memorial Day*** Samiltchŏl 삼일절; ***~ First Movement*** Samil Undong 삼일 운동
march 1 *n* haengjin 행진; (*demonstration*) temo haengjin 데모 행진 **2** *v/i* haengjinhada 행진하다; (*in protest*) temo haengjinhada 데모 행진하다
Mardi Gras Osunjŏrŭi Hwayoil 오순절의 화요일
mare ammal 암말
margarine magarin 마가린
margin (*of page*) yŏbaek 여백; (*profit ~*) imun 이문; ***by a narrow ~*** kyŏu 겨우
marginal (*slight*) chŏgŭn 적은
marginally (*slightly*) chogŭm 조금
marihuana, **marijuana** taemach'o 대마초
marina yot'ŭ kyeryujang 요트 계류장
marinade *n* maerineidŭ 매리네이드
marinate chŏrida 절이다
marine 1 *adj* padaŭi 바다의 **2** *n* MIL haegun 해군
Marine Corps Haebyŏngdae 해병대
marital kyŏrhonŭi 결혼의
maritime haeyangŭi 해양의
mark 1 *n* (*stain*) ŏlluk 얼룩; (*sign, token*) p'yoshi 표시; (*trace*) chach'wi 자취; EDU sŏngjŏk 성적; ***leave one's ~*** yŏnghyang-ŭl namgida 영향을 남기다 **2** *v/t* (*stain*) chagugŭl naeda 자국을 내다; EDU sŏngjŏgŭl ŏt-tta 성적을 얻다; (*indicate*) p'yoshihada 표시하다; (*commemorate*) kinyŏmhada 기념하다 **3** *v/i* (*of fabric*) chagungnada 자국나다
♦**mark down** *price* kagyŏgŭl naerida 가격을 내리다
♦**mark out** (*with a line etc*) sŏnŭl kŭt-tta 선을 긋다; *fig* (*set apart*) karŭda 가르다
♦**mark up** *price* kagyŏgŭl ollida 가격을 올리다; *goods* p'yoshihada 표시하다
marked (*definite*) hwaksshirhan 확실한
marker (*highlighter*) hyŏnggwangp'en 형광펜
market 1 *n* shijang 시장; (*stock ~*) chushik shijang 주식 시장; ***on the ~*** shijang-e 시장에 **2** *v/t* p'anmaehada 판매하다

market economy shijang kyŏngje 시장 경제
market forces shijangnyŏk 시장력
marketing maemae 매매
market leader shijang-ŭi sŏndujuja 시장의 선두주자; **marketplace** (*in town*) shijang 시장; (*for commodities*) maemae changso 매매 장소; **market research** shijang chosa 시장 조사; **market share** shijang chŏmnyuyul 시장 점유율
mark-up kagyŏk insang 가격 인상
marmalade mamalleidŭ 마말레이드
marquee taehyŏng ch'ŏnmak 대형 천막
marriage (*institution*) kyŏrhon 결혼; (*state of being married*) kyŏrhon saenghwal 결혼 생활; (*event*) kyŏrhonshik 결혼식
marriage certificate kyŏrhon chŭngmyŏngsŏ 결혼 증명서
marriage counselor kyŏrhon sangdamwŏn 결혼 상담원
married kihonŭi 기혼의, kyŏrhonhan 결혼한; ***a ~ man*** kihon namsŏng 기혼 남성, yubunam 유부남; ***be ~ to ...*** ...wa / kwa kyŏrhonhada ...와 / 과 결혼하다
marry kyŏrhonhada 결혼하다; (*perform ceremony*) churyehada 주례하다; ***get married*** kyŏrhonhada 결혼하다
marsh sŭptchi 습지
marshal *n* (*police officer*) kyŏngch'algwan 경찰관; (*official*) haengsa wiwŏn 행사 위원
marshmallow mashimaello 마시멜로
marshy sŭptchiŭi 습지의
martial arts musul 무술
martial law kyeŏmnyŏng 계엄령
martyr *n* sun-gyoja 순교자; *fig* hŭisaengja 희생자
marvel *n* nollaŭn kŏt 놀라운 것; ***you're a ~*** tangshinŭn taedanhagunyo 당신은 대단하군요
♦**marvel at** ...e nollada ...에 놀라다
marvelous koengjanghi choŭn 굉장히 좋은
Marxism Marŭk'ŭsŭjuŭi 마르크스주의
Marxist 1 *adj* Marŭk'ŭsŭjuŭiŭi 마르크스주의의 **2** *n* Marŭk'ŭsŭjuŭija 마르크스주의자
mascara masŭk'ara 마스카라
mascot haeng-unŭl kajyŏonŭn kŏt 행운을 가져오는 것, masŭk'ot'ŭ 마스코트
masculine *also* GRAM namsŏngjŏgin 남성적인
masculinity namsŏngmi 남성미
mash *v/t* ŭkkaeda 으깨다
mashed potatoes ŭkkaen kamja 으깬 감자, maeshit'ŭ p'ot'eit'o 매시트 포테이토
mask 1 *n* kamyŏn 가면 **2** *v/t feelings* kamch'uda 감추다
mask dance t'alch'um 탈춤
masochism maejŏk'ijŭm 매저키즘
masochist maejŏk'isŭt'ŭ 매저키스트
mason sŏkssu 석수
masonry tol segong 돌 세공
masquerade 1 *n fig* kajang 가장 **2** *v/i*: ***~ as*** ... in ch'ŏk'ada ... 인 척하다
mass[1] **1** *n* (*great amount*) taryang 다량; (*body*) k'ŭn tŏng-ŏri 큰 덩어리; ***a solid ~*** koch'e 고체; ***the ~es*** taejung 대중; ***~es of*** aju manŭn 아주 많은 **2** *v/i* moida 모이다
mass[2] REL misa 미사
massacre 1 *n* taeryang hakssal 대량 학살; F (*in sport*) ch'amp'ae 참패 **2** *v/t* hakssarhada 학살하다; F (*in sport*) ch'ampaeshik'ida 참패시키다
massage 1 *n* anma 안마, masaji 마사지 **2** *v/t* anmahada 안마하다; *figures* ŏlbŏmurida 얼버무리다
massage parlor *euph* maech'un-gul 매춘굴
masseur (namja) anmasa (남자) 안마사
masseuse (yŏya) anmasa (여자) 안마사
massive kŏdaehan 거대한
mass media taejung maech'e 대중 매체; **mass-produce** taeryang saengsanhada 대량 생산하다; **mass-production** taeryang saengsan 대량 생산
mast (*of ship*) tot-ttae 돛대; (*for radio*) taehyŏng ant'ena 대형 안테나
master 1 *n* (*of dog*) chuin 주인; (*of ship*) sŏnjang 선장; ***be a ~ of*** ...e

chŏngt'onghada ..에 정통하다 **2** *v/t* *skill*, *language* chŏngt'onghada 정통하다; *situation* t'ongjehada 통제하다
master bedroom anppang 안방
master key masŭt'ŏk'i 마스터키
masterly hullyunghan 훌륭한
mastermind 1 *n* ch'idoja 지도자 **2** *v/t* twiesŏ chidohada 뒤에서 지도하다; **Master of Arts** munhak sŏkssa 문학 석사; **master of ceremonies** sahoeja 사회자; **masterpiece** myŏngjak 명작; **master's (degree)** sŏkssa(hagwi) 석사(학위)
mastery chŏngbok 정복
masturbate chawihada 자위하다
mat *n* (*for floor*) chari 자리, maet'ŭ 매트; (*for table*) t'eibŭl po 테이블 보
match[1] (*for cigarette*) sŏngnyang 성냥
match[2] **1** *n* (*competition*) shihap 시합; ***be no ~ for s.o.*** nuguŭi sandaega andoeda 누구의 상대가 안되다; ***meet one's ~*** hojŏkssurŭl mannada 호적수를 만나다 **2** *v/t* (*go with*) ŏullida 어울리다; (*equal*) …e p'iltchŏk'ada …에 필적하다 **3** *v/i* (*of colors*, *patterns*) ŏullida 어울리다
matchbox sŏngnyangkkap 성냥갑
matching *adj* ŏullinŭn 어울리는
mate 1 *n* (*of animal*) tchak 짝; NAUT hanghaesa 항해사 **2** *v/i* tchaktchit-tta 짝짓다
material 1 *n* (*fabric*) otkkam 옷감; (*substance*) chaeryo 재료 **2** *adj* multchirŭi 물질의; (*not spiritual*) sesoktchŏgin 세속적인
materialism yumullon 유물론
materialist yumullonja 유물론자
materialistic yumullonjŏgin 유물론적인
materialize shilch'ehwahada 실체화하다
materials charyo 자료
maternal ŏmŏniŭi 어머니의; *relative* mogyeŭi 모계의; ***~ grandfather*** oeharabŏji 외할아버지
maternity mosŏng 모성
maternity dress imsanbok 임산복; **maternity hospital** sanbuinkkwa 산부인과; **maternity leave** ch'ulsan hyuga 출산 휴가; **maternity ward** sanbuinkkwa pyŏngdong 산부인과 병동
math suhak 수학
mathematical *calculations*, *formula* suhagŭi 수학의; *mind*, *person* suhage nŭnghan 수학에 능한
mathematician suhaktcha 수학자
mathematics suhak 수학
matinée (*of play*) chugan kongnyŏn 주간 공연; (*of movie*) chugan sangnyŏng 주간 상영
matriarch yŏgajang 여가장
matrimony kyŏrhon 결혼
matt kwangt'aegi ŏmnŭn 광택이 없는
matter (*affair*) sakkŏn 사건; PHYS multchil 물질; ***as a ~ of course*** tangnyŏnhi 당연히; ***as a ~ of fact*** sashirŭn 사실은; ***what's the ~?*** musŭn iri issŭmnikka? 무슨 일이 있습니까?; ***no ~ what she says*** kunyŏga muŏshirago marhadŭn kane 그녀가 무엇이라고 말하든 간에 **2** *v/i* chungnyohada 중요하다; ***it doesn't ~*** kŭgŏsŭn sanggwanŏptta 그것은 상관없다
matter-of-fact tamdamhan 담담한
mattress maet'ŭrisŭ 매트리스
mature 1 *adj* sŏngsuk'an 성숙한 **2** *v/i* (*of person*) sŏngsuk'ada 성숙하다; (*of insurance policy etc*) man-giga toeda 만기가 되다
maturity (*adulthood*) sŏngsuk-kki 성숙기; (*in behavior*, *attitude*) sŏngsuk'am 성숙함
maximize ch'oedaehwahada 최대화하다
maximum 1 *adj* ch'oedaeŭi 최대의 **2** *n* ch'oedae 최대
May owŏl 오월
may ◊ (*possibility*) ...iltchido morŭnda ...일지도 모른다; ***it ~ rain*** piga oltchido morŭnda 비가 올지도 모른다; ***you ~ be right*** nega majŭl chido morŭnda 네가 맞을 지도 모른다; ***it ~ not happen*** irŏnaji annŭl jido mŏrŭnda 일어나지 않을 지도 모른다 ◊ (*permission*) ...haedo chot'a ...해도 좋다; ***you ~ go now*** inje kado chossŭmnida 인제 가도 좋습니다; ***~ I help?*** towa tŭrilkkayo? 도와 드릴까요?; ***~ I***

smoke? tambae p'iwodo toegessŭmnikka? 담배 피워도 되겠습니까?; ***you ~ if you like*** wŏnhashindamyŏn, hasyŏdo kwanch'ansŭmnida 원하신다면, 하셔도 괜찮습니다 ◊ (*wish, hope*) ...hagirŭl parada ...하기를 바라다; ***~ you both be very happy*** tubuni hamkke hangsang haengbok'ashigirŭl paramnida 두분이 함께 항상 행복하시기를 바랍니다

maybe amado 아마도

May Day Nodongjŏl 노동절

mayo, mayonnaise mayonejŭ 마요네즈

mayor shijang 시장

maze miro 미로

MB (= ***megabyte***) megabait'ŭ 메가바이트

MBA (= ***Master's in Business Administration***) kyŏngnyŏnghak sŏkssa 경영학 석사

MBO (= ***management buyout***) kyŏngnyŏngkkwŏn maemae 경영권 매매

MD (= ***Doctor of Medicine***) ŭihak pakssa 의학 박사

me na 나; H chŏ 저; ***it's ~*** nada 나다; H chŏimnida 저입니다; ***he knows ~*** kŭnŭn narŭl anda 그는 나를 안다; ***that's for ~*** naŭi kŏshida 나의 것이다

meadow ch'owŏn 초원

meager pulch'ŭngbunhan 불충분한

meal shikssa 식사

mealtime shikssa shigan 식사 시간

mean[1] (*with money*) insaek'an 인색한; (*nasty*) mot-ttoen 못된

mean[2] **1** *v/t* (*intend*) ŭidohada 의도하다; (*signify*) ŭimihada 의미하다; ***~ to do sth*** muŏsŭl haryŏgo hada 무엇을 하려고 하다; ***be ~t for*** ...ŭl/rŭl wihan kŏshida ...을/를 위한 것이다; (*of remark*) ...ŭl/rŭl tugo marhada ...을/를 두고 말하다; ***doesn't it ~ anything to you?*** (*doesn't it matter?*) tangshinege amu sanggwan ŏpssŏyo? 당신에게 아무 상관 없어요? **2** *v/i*: ***~ well*** choŭn ŭidorŭl kajida 좋은 의도를 가지다

meaning (*of word*) ŭimi 의미

meaningful (*comprehensible*) ihaeganŭn 이해가는; *glance* ŭimiinnŭn 의미있는

meaningless muŭimihan 무의미한

means (*financial*) chaesan 재산; (*way*) sudan 수단; ***~ of transport*** kyot'ong sudan 교통 수단; ***by all ~*** (*certainly*) mullon 물론; ***by no ~ poor*** kyŏlk'o kananhaji ant'a 결코 가난하지 않다; ***by ~ of*** ...ŭl/rŭl ssŏsŏ ...을/를 써서

meantime: ***in the ~*** kŭ saie 그 사이에

measles hongnyŏk 홍역

measure 1 *n* (*step*) pangch'aek 방책; (*certain amount*) ŏnŭ chŏngdo 어느 정도 **2** *v/t* ch'issurŭl chaeda 치수를 재다 **3** *v/i* chaeŏjida 재어지다

♦**measure out** pullyang-ŭl chaeda 분량을 재다

♦**measure up to** ... mank'ŭm chal hada ... 만큼 잘 하다

measurement (*action*) ch'ŭktchŏng 측정; ***~s*** (*dimensions*) ch'issu 치수; ***system of ~*** ch'ŭktchŏngppŏp 측정법

meat kogi 고기

meatball kogi wanja 고기 완자

meatloaf mitŭ lopŭ 미트 로프, *chŏmin kogiwa ppanggaru, kyeranŭl nŏk'o obŭne kuun tŏng-ŏri* 저민 고기와 빵가루, 계란을 넣고 오븐에 구운 덩어리

mechanic kigyegong 기계공

mechanical *device* kigyeŭi 기계의; *gesture* kigyejŏgin 기계적인

mechanically *do sth* kigyejŏgŭro 기계적으로

mechanism kigye changch'i 기계 장치

mechanize kigyehwahada 기계화하다

medal medal 메달

medalist susangja 수상자

meddle kansŏp'ada 간섭하다; ***~ with*** ...ŭl/rŭl manjijak-kkŏrida ...을/를 만지작거리다

media: ***the ~*** maesŭk'ŏm 매스컴

media hype maesŭk'ŏmŭi kwajang 매스컴의 과장

median strip chung-ang pullidae 중앙

분리대
mediate chungjaehada 중재하다
mediation chungjae 중재
mediator chungjaein 중재인
medical 1 *adj* ŭihagŭi 의학의; **~ *treatment*** ch'iryo 치료; **~ *insurance*** ŭiryo pohŏm 의료 보험; **~ *problem*** kŏn-gang munje 건강 문제 **2** *n* shinch'e kŏmsa 신체 검사
medical certificate chindansŏ 진단서
Medicare noin ŭiryo pojang chedo 노인 의료 보장 제도
medicated yagyong-ŭi 약용의
medication yak 약
medicinal yagŭi 약의
medicine (*science*) ŭihak 의학; (*medication*) yak 약
medieval chungseŭi 중세의; *fig* kushigŭi 구식의
mediocre chillajŭn 질낮은
mediocrity (*of work etc*) chillajŭm 질낮음; (*person*) chŏjil 저질
meditate myŏngsanghada 명상하다; (*of Christian*) mukssanghada 묵상하다; (*of Buddhist monk*) ch'amsŏnhada 참선하다
meditation myŏngsang 명상; (*in Christianity*) mukssang 묵상; (*in Buddhism*) ch'amsŏn 참선
medium 1 *adj* (*average*) chungganŭi 중간의; *steak* pantchŭm ik'in 반쯤 익힌 **2** *n* (*in size*) chunggan k'ŭgi 중간 크기; (*vehicle*) maech'e 매체; (*spiritualist*) yŏngmae 영매
medium-sized chunggan k'ŭgiŭi 중간 크기의
medium wave RAD chungp'a 중파
medley (*mixture*) kagyanggakssaek 각양각색; (*of songs*) medŭlli 메들리
meek yamjŏnhan 얌전한
meet 1 *v/t* mannada 만나다; (*collect*) majungnagada 마중나가다; (*in competition*) matssŏda 맞서다; (*of eyes*) majuch'ida 마주치다; (*satisfy*) ch'ungjokshik'ida 충족시키다 **2** *v/i* mannada 만나다; (*in competition*) taejŏnhada 대전하다; (*of eyes*) majuch'ida 마주치다; (*of committee etc*) moida 모이다 **3** *n* SP kyŏnggi 경기
♦**meet with** *person* …wa / kwa mannada …와 / 과 만나다; *approval* pat-tta 받다; *success, failure* majihada 맞이하다
meeting mannam 만남; (*of committee, in business*) hoeŭi 회의; ***he's in a ~*** kŭnŭn hoeŭi chung-ida 그는 회의 중이다
meeting place yakssok changso 약속 장소
megabyte COMPUT megabait'ŭ 메가바이트
melancholy *adj* ultchŏk'an 울적한
mellow 1 *adj* kammiroun 감미로운; *fruit, wine* sukssŏnghan 숙성한; *color* pudŭrŏun 부드러운; *person* wŏnsuk'an 원숙한 **2** *v/i* (*of person*) wŏnsuk'ada 원숙하다
melodious koktchoga arŭmdaun 곡조가 아름다운
melodramatic melodŭramagat'ŭn 멜로드라마같은
melody melodi 멜로디, sŏnnyul 선율
melon melon 멜론
melt 1 *v/i* noktta 녹다 **2** *v/t* nogida 녹이다
♦**melt away** *fig* sŏsŏhi sarajida 서서히 사라지다
♦**melt down** *metal* nogida 녹이다
melting pot *fig* togani 도가니
member irwŏn 일원; **~ *of Congress*** kuk'oe ŭiwŏn 국회 의원
membership hoewŏn chagyŏk 회원 자격; (*number of members*) hoewŏn su 회원 수
membership card hoewŏntchŭng 회원증
membrane mak 막
memento kinyŏmmul 기념물
memo memo 메모, kirok 기록
memoirs hoegorok 회고록
memorable kiŏk'al manhan 기억할 만한
memorial 1 *adj* kinyŏmŭi 기념의 **2** *n* kinyŏmbi 기념비
Memorial Day Hyŏnch'ung-il 현충일
memorize amgihada 암기하다
memory (*recollection*) kiŏk 기억; (*emotionally tinged*) ch'uŏk 추억; (*power of recollection*) kiŏngnyŏk 기억력; COMPUT yongnyang 용량, memori 메모리; ***have a good / bad***

~ kiŏngnyŏgi chot'a / nappŭda 기억력이 좋다 / 나쁘다; ***in ~ of*** ...ŭl / rŭl kinyŏmhamyŏ ...을 / 를 기념하며
menace 1 *n* (*threat*) wihyŏp 위협; (*person*) wihŏm inmul 위험 인물 **2** *v/t* wihyŏp'ada 위협하다
menacing wihyŏp'anŭn 위협하는
mend 1 *v/t* koch'ida 고치다; *clothes*, *shoes* susŏnhada 수선하다 **2** *n*: ***be on the ~*** (*after illness*) tŏ naajida 더 나아지다
menial *adj* ch'ŏnhan 천한
meningitis noemangnyŏm 뇌막염
menopause p'yegyŏnggi 폐경기
men's room namja hwajangshil 남자 화장실
menstruate wŏlgyŏnghada 월경하다, saengnihada 생리하다
menstruation wŏlgyŏng 월경, saengni 생리
mental chŏngshinŭi 정신의; *torture*, *suffering* maŭmŭi 마음의; F (*crazy*) chŏngshinppyŏng-ŭi 정신병의
mental arithmetic amsan 암산; **mental cruelty** chŏngshintchŏk hakttae 정신적 학대; **mental hospital** chŏngshin pyŏng-wŏn 정신 병원; **mental illness** chŏngshinppyŏng 정신병
mentality chŏngshin sangt'ae 정신 상태
mentally (*inwardly*) maŭm sogŭro 마음 속으로; *calculate* chitchŏgŭro 지적으로; ***~ handicapped*** chŏngshintchŏk chang-aeja innŭn 정신적 장애가 있는; ***~ ill*** chŏngshinppyŏng-i innŭn 정신병이 있는
mention 1 *n* ŏn-gŭp 언급 **2** *v/t* ŏn-gŭp'ada 언급하다; ***don't ~ it*** (*you're welcome*) ch'ŏnmaneyo 천만에요
mentor choryŏktcha 조력자
menu (*for food*) shikttan 식단, menyu 메뉴; COMPUT menyu 메뉴
mercenary 1 *adj* tonŭl moktchŏgŭro hanŭn 돈을 목적으로 하는 **2** *n* MIL yongbyŏng 용병
merchandise sangp'um 상품
merchant sang-in 상인
merciful chabiroun 자비로운
mercifully (*thankfully*) tahaengsŭrŏpkkedo 다행스럽게도
merciless mujabihan 무자비한
mercury suŭn 수은
mercy chabi 자비; ***be at s.o.'s ~*** nuguŭi maŭmdaero toeda 누구의 마음대로 되다
mere tanji 단지
merely tanji 단지
merge *v/i* (*of two lines etc*) hapch'ida 합치다; (*of companies*) hap-ppyŏnghada 합병하다
merger COM hap-ppyŏng 합병
merit 1 *n* (*worth*) kach'i 가치; (*advantage*) changtchŏm 장점 **2** *v/t* ...hal kach'iga it-tta ...할 가치가 있다
merry yuk'waehan 유쾌한; ***Merry Christmas!*** chŭlgŏun Sŏngt'ani toegirŭl paramnida! 즐거운 성탄이 되기를 바랍니다!
merry-go-round hoejŏn mongma 회전 목마
mesh *n* kŭmul 그물
mess *n* (*untidiness*) ŏngmang-in kŏt 엉망인 것; (*trouble*) kon-gyŏng 곤경; ***be a ~*** (*of room*, *desk*, *hair*) ŏngmang-ida 엉망이다; (*of situation*, *s.o.'s life*) hollansŭropt-tta 혼란스럽다
♦**mess around 1** *v/i* pindanggŏrida 빈둥거리다 **2** *v/t person* hollanshik'ida 혼란시키다
♦**mess around with** ...ŭl / rŭl katkko nolda ...을 / 를 갖고 놀다; *s.o.'s wife* ...wa / kwa param p'iuda ...와 / 과 바람 피우다
♦**mess up** *room*, *papers* ŏjirŭda 어지르다; *plans*, *marriage* mangch'yŏ not'a 망쳐 놓다
message chŏnhanŭn mal 전하는 말, mesiji 메시지; (*of movie*, *book*) kyohun 교훈
messenger meshinjŏ 메신저; (*courier*) paedalbu 배달부
messy *room* ŏjiroun 어지러운; *person* hollanhage hanŭn 혼란하게 하는; *job* chijŏbunhan 지저분한; *divorce*, *situation* nanch'ŏhan 난처한
metabolism shinjindaesa 신진대사
metal 1 *n* kŭmsok 금속 **2** *adj*

kŭmsogŭi 금속의
metallic kŭmsokssŏng-ŭi 금속성의
meteor yusŏng 유성
meteoric *fig* yusŏnggat'ŭn 유성같은
meteorite unsŏk 운석
meteorological kisanghagŭi 기상학의
meteorologist kisanghaktcha 기상학자
meteorology kisanghak 기상학
meter[1] (*for gas etc*) kyeryanggi 계량기; (*parking ~, in cab*) yogŭm kyesan-gi 요금 계산기
meter[2] (*unit of length*) mit'ŏ 미터
method pangbŏp 방법
methodical iltchŏnghan pangshige ttarŭn 일정한 방식에 따른
methodically iltchŏnghan pangshigŭro 일정한 방식으로
Methodist Church Kamni Kyohoe 감리 교회
meticulous seshimhan 세심한
metric mit'ŏppŏbŭi 미터법의
metropolis taedoshi 대도시; (*capital city*) sudo 수도
metropolitan *adj* taedoshiŭi 대도시의
mew → ***miaow***
Mexican 1 *adj* Meksshik'oŭi 멕시코의 **2** *n* Meksshik'oin 멕시코인
Mexico Meksshik'o 멕시코
mezzanine (floor) chungch'ŭng 중층
miaow 1 *n* yaong 야옹 **2** *v/i* yaonghago ulda 야옹하고 울다
mickey mouse *adj* F *pej*: *course, qualification* kach'iŏmnŭn 가치없는
microchip maik'ŭroch'ip 마이크로칩; **microcosm** souju 소우주; **microelectronics** kŭksso chŏnja konghak 극소 전자 공학; **microfilm** maik'ŭrop'illŭm 마이크로필름; **microphone** maik'ŭ 마이크; **microprocessor** maik'ŭrop'ŭrosesŏ 마이크로프로세서; **microscope** hyŏnmigyŏng 현미경; **microscopic** kŭk'i chagŭn 극히 작은; **microwave** (*oven*) chŏnjarenji 전자렌지
midair: ***in ~*** kongjung-esŏ 공중에서
midday chŏng-o 정오
middle 1 *adj* chungganŭi 중간의 **2** *n* kaunde 가운데; ***in the ~ of*** (*floor, room*) …ŭi chung-ang-esŏ …의 중앙에서; (*period of time*) … chung-e … 중에; ***in the ~ of the night*** hanbam chung-e 한밤 중에; ***be in the ~ of doing sth*** muŏsŭl hanŭn chung-ida 무엇을 하는 중이다
middle-aged chungnyŏnŭi 중년의; **Middle Ages** Chungse 중세; **middle-class** *adj* chungsanch'ŭng-ŭi 중산층의; **middle class(es)** chungsanch'ŭng 중산층; **Middle East** Chungdong 중동; **middleman** chunggan sang-in 중간 상인; **middle name** chunggan irŭm 중간 이름; **middleweight** *n* (*boxer*) chunggankkŭp 중간급
middling kŭjŏ kŭrŏn 그저 그런
midget *adj* ch'osohyŏng-ŭi 초소형의
midnight chajŏng 자정; ***at ~*** chajŏng-e 자정에; **midsummer** hannyŏrŭm 한여름; **midway** chungdo-e 중도에; **midweek** *adv* chujung-e 주중에; **Midwest** Chungsŏbu 중서부; **midwife** chosanwŏn 조산원; **midwinter** hangyŏul 한겨울
might[1] ...iltchido morŭnda ...일지도 모른다; ***I ~ be late*** chŏnŭn ama nŭjŭltchido morŭgessumnida 저는 아마 늦을지도 모르겠습니다; ***it ~ rain*** piga oltchido morŭgessŭmnida 비가 올지도 모르겠습니다; ***it ~ never happen*** kŭgŏsŭn ama tashinŭn irŏnaji anŭl kŏshimnida 그것은 아마 다시는 일어나지 않을 것입니다; ***I ~ have lost it*** chŏnŭn kŭgŏsŭl irŏporyŏnnŭnjido morŭgessŭmnida 저는 그것을 잃어버렸는지도 모르겠습니다; ***he ~ have left*** hoksshi kŭga ttŏnassŭltchi morŭgessŭmnida 혹시 그가 떠났을지 모르겠습니다; ***you ~ as well spend the night here*** tanshindo yŏgisŏ pamŭl ponaeya haltchi morŭmnida 당신도 여기서 밤을 보내야 할지 모릅니다; ***you ~ have told me!*** chinjak naege marŭl haessŏyaji! 진작 내게 말을 했어야지!
might[2] *n* (*power*) him 힘
mighty 1 *adj* himinnŭn 힘있는 **2** *adv* F (*extremely*) maeu 매우
migraine p'yŏndŭt'ong 편두통
migrant worker iju nodongja 이주 노동자

migrate ijuhada 이주하다
migration iju 이주
mike maik'ŭ 마이크
mild *weather, climate, person* onhwahan 온화한; *taste* sunhan 순한; *voice* pudŭrŏun 부드러운
mildly pudŭrŏpkke 부드럽게
mildew komp'ang-i 곰팡이
mildness (*of weather, person*) onhwaham 온화함; (*of voice*) pudŭrŏum 부드러움; (*of taste*) sunham 순함
mile mail 마일; **~s *better/easier*** F hwŏlsshin naŭn / shwiun 훨씬 나은 / 쉬운
mileage mail su 마일 수
milestone *fig* ijŏngp'yo 이정표
militant 1 *adj* t'ujaengtchŏgin 투쟁적인 **2** *n* t'usa 투사
military 1 *adj* kunŭi 군의 **2** *n*: ***the ~*** kun 군
military academy yuk-kkun sagwan hak-kkyo 육군 사관 학교
militia shimin-gun 시민군
milk 1 *n* uyu 우유 **2** *v/t* chŏjŭl tchada 젖을 짜다
milk chocolate milk'ŭ chyok'olit 밀크 쵸콜릿
milk shake milk'ŭ shweik'ŭ 밀크 쉐이크
mill *n* (*factory*) kongjang 공장; (*for grinding*) punswaegi 분쇄기
♦ **mill around** mujilssŏhage umjigida 무질서하게 움직이다
millennium ch'ŏnnyŏn 천년
milligram milligŭraem 밀리그램
millimeter millimit'ŏ 밀리미터
million paengman 백만
millionaire paengman changja 백만 장자
mime *v/t* tongjagŭro p'yohyŏnhada 동작으로 표현하다
mimic 1 *n* hyungnae 흉내 **2** *v/t* hyungnaenaeda 흉내내다
mince *v/t* chŏmida 저미다
mincemeat minsŭ p'ai sok 민스 파이 속
mince pie minsŭ p'ai 민스 파이
mind 1 *n* chŏngshin 정신; ***it's all in your ~*** kŭgŏsŭn ta nŏŭi sangsang-ida 그것은 다 너의 상상이다; ***be out of one's ~*** chŏngshini nagada 정신이 나가다; ***bear sth in ~*** muŏsŭl kiŏk'ago it-tta 무엇을 기억하고 있다; ***change one's ~*** maŭmŭl pakkuda 마음을 바꾸다; ***it didn't enter my ~*** kŭgŏsŭn na-ege sangsangdo kaji anat-tta 그것은 나에게 상상도 가지 않았다; ***give s.o. a piece of one's ~*** nugurŭl namurada 누구를 나무라다; ***make up one's ~*** maŭmŭl chŏnghada 마음을 정하다; ***have sth on one's ~*** (*be worried*) muŏsŭl kŭnshimhada 무엇을 근심하다; ***keep one's ~ on*** …e chŏnnyŏmhada …에 전념하다 **2** *v/t* (*look after*) tolboda 돌보다; (*object to*) ŏntchanahada 언짢아하다; (*heed*) maŭme tuda 마음에 두다; ***I don't ~ what we do*** nanŭn uriga muŏsŭl hadŭn sanggwanŏptta 나는 우리가 무엇을 하든 상관없다; ***do you ~ if I smoke?*** tambaerŭl p'iwŏdo kwaench'ank'essŭmnikka? 담배를 피워도 괜찮겠습니까?; ***would you ~ opening the window?*** ch'angmunŭl yŏrŏ chushigessŭmnikka? 창문을 열어 주시겠습니까?; ***no, I don't ~*** anio, kwaench'ansŭmnida 아니오, 괜찮습니다; ***~ the step!*** kyedanŭl choshimhaseyo! 계단을 조심하세요! **3** *v/i*: ***~!*** (*be careful*) choshimhaseyo! 조심하세요!; ***never ~!*** shin-gyŏng ssŭl kŏt ŏpssŭmnida! 신경 쓸 것 없습니다!; ***I don't ~*** chŏnŭn sanggwanopssŭmnida 저는 상관없습니다
mind-boggling nollaun 놀라운
mindless *violence* saenggagŏmnŭn 생각없는
mine[1] *pron* naŭi kŏt 나의 것; H chŏŭi kŏt 저의 것; ***a cousin of ~*** naŭi sach'on 나의 사촌; H chŏŭi sach'on 저의 사촌
mine[2] **1** *n* (*for coal etc*) kwangsan 광산 **2** *v/i* (*for coal etc*) p'ada 파다; **~ *for*** ch'aegurhada 채굴하다
mine[3] **1** *n* (*explosive*) chiroe 지뢰 **2** *v/t* …e chiroerŭl sŏlch'ihada …에 지뢰를 설치하다
minefield MIL chiroepat 지뢰밭; *fig*

wihŏmjidae 위험 지대
miner kwangbu 광부
mineral *n* kwangmul 광물
mineral water kwangch'ŏnsu 광천수, saengsu 생수
minesweeper NAUT chiroe t'amsaekssŏn 지뢰 탐색선
mingle *v/i* (*of sounds, smells*) sŏktta 섞다; (*at party*) *toradanimyŏ manŭn saramdŭrege marhada* 돌아다니며 많은 사람들에게 말하다
mini → ***miniskirt***
miniature *adj* sohyŏng-ŭi 소형의
minibus sohyŏng pŏsŭ 소형 버스
minimal ch'oesoŭi 최소의
minimize ch'oesohwahada 최소화하다; (*downplay*) kwaso p'yŏngkkahada 과소 평가하다
minimum 1 *adj* ch'oesohanŭi 최소한의 **2** *n* ch'oeso 최소
minimum wage ch'oejŏ ponggŭp 최저 봉급
mining kwang-ŏp 광업
miniskirt mini sŭk'ot'ŭ 미니 스커트
minister POL changgwan 장관; REL mokssa 목사
ministerial changgwan-ŭi 장관의
ministry POL pu 부; (*in US, Japan*) sŏng 성
mink (*fur*) mingk'ŭ 밍크; (*coat*) mingk'ŭ k'ot'ŭ 밍크 코트
minor 1 *adj* poda chagŭn 보다 작은; ***in G ~*** MUS sa tantchoŭi 사 단조의 **2** *n* LAW misŏngnyŏnja 미성년자
minority sosup'a 소수파; ***be in the ~*** sosup'aida 소수파이다
mint *n* (*herb*) pak'a 박하, mint'ŭ 민트; (*chocolate*) mint'ŭ chyok'ollit 민트 쵸콜릿; (*hard candy*) pak'a sat'ang 박하 사탕
minus 1 *n* (*~ sign*) ppaegi puho 빼기 부호 **2** *prep* ŭmŭi 음의; ***42 ~ 18 is 24*** sashibi ppaegi shipp'arŭn ishipssaida 42 빼기 18은 24이다; ***temperatures of ~ 18 degrees*** yŏngha shipp'alto 영하 18도
minuscule aju chagŭn 아주 작은
minute[1] *n* (*of time*) pun 분; ***in a ~*** (*soon*) kot 곧; ***just a ~*** chamshiman kidariseyo 잠시만 기다리세요
minute[2] *adj* (*tiny*) aju chogŭman 아주 조그만; (*detailed*) sangsehan 상세한; ***in ~ detail*** sangsehi 상세히
minutely (*in detail*) sangsehage 상세하게
minutes (*of meeting*) ŭisarok 의사록
miracle kijŏk 기적
miraculous kijŏktchŏgin 기적적인
miraculously kijŏkkach'i 기적같이
mirage shin-giru 신기루
mirror 1 *n* kŏul 거울; MOT paengmirŏ 백미러 **2** *v/t* pich'uda 비추다
misanthropist saramŭl shirŏhanŭn saram 사람을 싫어하는 사람
misapprehension: ***be under a ~*** chalmot saenggak'ada 잘못 생각하다
misbehave nappŭge haengdonghada 나쁘게 행동하다
misbehavior nappŭn haengdong 나쁜 행동
miscalculate *v/t & v/i* chalmot kyesanhada 잘못 계산하다
miscalculation osan 오산
miscarriage MED yusan 유산; ***~ of justice*** oshim 오심
miscarry (*of plan*) shilp'aehada 실패하다
miscellaneous kajigakssaegŭi 가지각색의
mischief (*naughtiness*) chitkkujŭn changnan 짓궂은 장난
mischievous *child* changnankkurŏgiŭi 장난꾸러기의; *behavior* chitkkujŭn 짓궂은
misconception ohae 오해
misconduct pujŏng haeng-wi 부정 행위
misconstrue chalmot haesŏk'ada 잘못 해석하다
misdemeanor kyŏngbŏmtchoe 경범죄; ***youthful ~s*** ch'ŏngsonyŏn pihaeng 청소년 비행
miser kudusoe 구두쇠
miserable (*unhappy*) purhaenghan 불행한; *weather* koyak'an 고약한; *performance* hyŏngp'yŏnŏmnŭn 형편없는
miserly insaek'an 인색한
misery (*unhappiness*) purhaeng 불행; (*wretchedness*) pich'amham 비참함
misfire (*of joke, scheme*) pinnagada 빗나가다

misfit (*in society*) pujŏgŭngja 부적응자
misfortune purhaeng 불행
misgiving yŏmnyŏ 염려
misguided chalmot chidodoen 잘못 지도된
mishandle chalmot taruda 잘못 다루다
mishap sago 사고
misinterpret chalmot haesŏk'ada 잘못 해석하다
misinterpretation chalmot-ttoen haesŏk 잘못된 해석
misjudge *person, situation* chalmot p'andanhada 잘못 판단하다
mislay tun kosŭl ijŏbŏrida 둔 곳을 잊어버리다
mislead odohada 오도하다
misleading odohanŭn 오도하는
mismanage chalmot unyŏnghada 잘못 운영하다
mismanagement chalmot-ttoen unyŏng 잘못된 운영
mismatch chalmot match'uda 잘못 맞추다
misplaced *loyalty* chalmot chun 잘못 준
misprint *n* chalmot-ttoen inswae 잘못된 인쇄
mispronounce t'ŭllin parŭmŭl hada 틀린 발음을 하다
mispronunciation t'ŭllin parŭm 틀린 발음
misread *word, figures* chalmot iltta 잘못 읽다; *situation* ohaehada 오해하다
misrepresent t'ŭllige chŏnhada 틀리게 전하다
miss[1]: ***Miss Smith*** Sŭmisŭ yang 스미스 양; *~!* agasshi! 아가씨!
miss[2] **1** *n* SP shiltchŏm 실점; ***give sth a ~*** *meeting, party etc* muŏse ppajida 무엇에 빠지다 **2** *v/t* (*not hit*) noch'ida 놓치다; (*not meet*) ŏtkkallida 엇갈리다; (*emotionally*) kŭriwŏhada 그리워하다; *bus, train, plane* noch'ida 놓치다; (*not notice*) arach'aeji mot'ada 알아채지 못하다; (*not be present at*) …e ppajida …에 빠지다 **3** *v/i* noch'ida 놓치다
misshapen pijŏngsangtchŏgin moyang-ŭi 비정상적인 모양의
missile (*rocket*) misail 미사일
missing irŏbŏrin 잃어버린; ***be ~*** ŏpssŏjida 없어지다
mission (*task*) samyŏng 사명; (*people*) sajŏl 사절
missionary REL sŏn-gyosa 선교사
misspell chalmot ch'ŏltchahada 잘못 철자하다
mist an-gae 안개
♦**mist over** (*of eyes*) hŭryŏjida 흐려지다
♦**mist up** (*of mirror, window*) kimi sŏrida 김이 서리다
mistake 1 *n* shilssu 실수; ***make a ~*** shilssuhada 실수하다; ***by ~*** shilssuro 실수로 **2** *v/t* ch'ak-kkak'ada 착각하다; ***~ X for Y*** Xŭl/rŭl Y(ŭ)ro chak-kkak'ada X을/를 Y(으)로 착각하다
mistaken: ***be ~*** t'ŭllin 틀린
mister → ***Mr***
mistress (*lover*) chŏngbu 정부; (*of servant*) yŏjuin 여주인; (*of dog*) chuin 주인
mistrust 1 *n* pulsshin 불신 **2** *v/t* pulsshinhada 불신하다
misty *weather* an-gae kkin 안개 낀; *eyes* hŭryŏjin 흐려진; *color* hŭrin 흐린
misunderstand ohaehada 오해하다
misunderstanding (*mistake*) ohae 오해; (*argument*) ŭigyŏn ch'ai 의견 차이
misuse 1 *n* oyong 오용 **2** *v/t* chalmot sayonghada 잘못 사용하다
mitigating circumstances kyŏnggam sayu 경감 사유
mitt (*in baseball*) mit'ŭ 미트
mitten pŏng-ŏri changgap 벙어리 장갑
mix 1 *n* (*mixture*) sŏkkŭn kŏt 섞은 것; (*in cooking*) honhammul 혼합물; (*ready to use*) *miri mandŭrŏjin yori chaeryo* 미리 만들어진 요리 재료 **2** *v/t* sŏktta 섞다 **3** *v/i* (*socially*) ŏullida 어울리다
♦**mix up** (*confuse*) hŏtkkallida 헛갈리다; (*muddle up*) sŏkkŏ not'a 섞어 놓다; ***mix X up with Y*** Xŭl/rŭl Ywa/kwa hondonghada X을/를

Y와 / 과 혼동하다; ***be mixed up*** (*emotionally*) hollansŭrŏwŏ hada 혼란스러워 하다; (*of figures, papers*) twisŏk-kkida 뒤섞이다; ***be mixed up in*** …e kwallyŏndoeda …에 관련되다; ***get mixed up with*** …wa / kwa kwan-gyehada …와 / 과 관계하다

♦**mix with** (*associate with*) …wa / kwa ŏullida …와 / 과 어울리다

mixed *feelings* hollanhan 혼란한; *reactions, reviews* sŏk-kkin 섞인

mixed marriage kuktche kyŏrhon 국제 결혼

mixer (*for food*) miksŏ 믹서; (*drink*) k'akt'eillyong mualk'ool ŭmnyo 칵테일용 무알코올 음료; ***she's a good ~*** kŭnyŏnŭn sagyossŏng-i chot'a 그녀는 사교성이 좋다

mixture honhap 혼합; (*medicine*) mulyak 물약

mix-up hollan 혼란

moan 1 *n* (*of pain*) shinŭm sori 신음 소리; (*complaint*) pulp'yŏng 불평 **2** *v/i* (*in pain*) shinŭmhada 신음하다; (*complain*) pulp'yŏnghada 불평하다

mob 1 *n* p'oktto 폭도 **2** *v/t* tterŭl chiŏ tallyŏdŭlda 떼를 지어 달려들다

mobile[1] *adj person* umjigil su innŭn 움직일 수 있는

mobile[2] *n* (*for decoration*) mobil 모빌

mobile home idongshik chut'aek 이동식 주택

mobile phone *Br* haendŭp'on 핸드폰, idong chŏnhwa 이동 전화

mobility idong 이동

mobster p'ongnyŏk tanwŏn 폭력 단원

mock 1 *adj* hyungnaenaen 흉내낸; *exams, elections* moŭiŭi 모의의 **2** *v/t* hyungnaenaemyŏ choronghada 흉내내며 조롱하다

mockery chorong 조롱; (*travesty*) chojak 조작

mock-up (*model*) mohyŏng 모형

mode (*form*) pangshik 방식; COMPUT modŭ 모드

model 1 *adj employee, husband* mobŏmŭi 모범의; *boat, plane* mohyŏng-ŭi 모형의 **2** *n* (*miniature*) mohyŏng 모형; (*pattern*) ponbogi 본보기; (*fashion ~*) model 모델; ***male ~*** namja model 남자 모델 **3** *v/t* …ŭi moderŭl hada …의 모델을 하다 **4** *v/i* (*for designer*) moderida 모델이다; (*for artist, photographer*) moderŭl hada 모델을 하다

modem modem 모뎀

moderate 1 *adj* chŏkttanghan 적당한, almajŭn 알맞은; POL on-gŏnhan 온건한 **2** *n* POL on-gŏnp'a 온건파 **3** *v/t* chŏkttanghi hada 적당히 하다

moderately chŏkttanghage 적당하게

moderation (*restraint*) chungnyong 중용; ***in ~*** chŏkttanghage 적당하게

modern hyŏndaeŭi 현대의

modernization hyŏndaehwa 현대화

modernize 1 *v/t* hyŏndaejŏgŭro pakkuda 현대적으로 바꾸다 **2** *v/i* (*of business, country*) hyŏndaehwahada 현대화하다

modest *house, apartment* susuhan 수수한; (*small*) chogŭmahan 조그마한; (*not conceited*) kyŏmsonhan 겸손한

modesty (*of house, apartment*) susuham 수수함; (*of wage, improvement*) chogŭmaham 조그마함; (*lack of conceit*) kyŏmson 겸손

modification sujŏng 수정

modify sujŏnghada 수정하다

modular *furniture* choribŭi 조립의

module chorip tanwi 조립 단위; (*space ~*) sŏn 선

moist sŭpkki innŭn 습기 있는, ch'ukch'uk'an 축축한

moisten ch'ukch'uk'age hada 축축하게 하다

moisture sŭpkki 습기

moisturizer (*for skin*) moisch'yŏraijŏ 모이스처라이저

molar ŏgŭmni 어금니

molasses tangmil 당밀

mold[1] *n* (*on food*) komp'ang-i 곰팡이

mold[2] **1** *n* t'ŭl 틀 **2** *v/t clay etc* t'ŭre nŏŏ mandŭlda 틀에 넣어 만들다; *character, person* hyŏngsŏngshik'ida 형성시키다

moldy *food* komp'ang-i p'in 곰팡이 핀

mole (*on skin*) chŏm 점

molecular punjaŭi 분자의

molecule punja 분자
molest *child, woman* sŏngtchŏgŭro hŭironghada 성적으로 희롱하다
mollycoddle chinach'ige posalp'ida 지나치게 보살피다
molten nogŭn 녹은
mom F ŏmma 엄마
moment sun-gan 순간; ***at the ~*** chigŭmŭn 지금은; ***at that ~*** kŭ ttaeenŭn 그 때에는; ***at the very ~*** paro kŭ sun-gane 바로 그 순간에; ***for the ~*** tangbun-gan 당분간
momentarily (*for a moment*) chamshi tong-an 잠시 동안; (*in a moment*) kot 곧
momentary sun-ganŭi 순간의
momentous chungdaehan 중대한
momentum him 힘
monarch kunju 군주
monastery sudowŏn 수도원
monastic sudosŭng kat'ŭn 수도승 같은
Monday wŏryoil 월요일
monetary kŭmnyung-ŭi 금융의
money ton 돈
money-lender taegŭmŏptcha 대금업자; **money market** kŭmnyung shijang 금융 시장; **money order** up'yŏnhwan 우편환
Mongolia Monggo 몽고
Mongolian 1 *adj* Monggoŭi 몽고의 **2** *n* (*person*) Monggoin 몽고인
mongrel chaptchonggyŏn 잡종견
monitor 1 *n* COMPUT monit'ŏ 모니터 **2** *v/t* chik'yŏboda 지켜보다
monk sudosa 수도사
monkey wŏnsung-i 원숭이; F (*child*) ŏrin nom 어린 놈
♦ **monkey around with** F …ŭl/rŭl kajigo changnanch'ida …을/를 가지고 장난치다
monkey wrench mŏngk'i sŭp'aenŏ 멍키 스패너
monogram *n* yaktcha 약자
monogrammed yaktchaga saegyŏjin 약자가 새겨진
monolog tokppaek 독백
monopolize toktchŏmhada 독점하다
monopoly toktchŏm 독점
monotonous tanjoroun 단조로운
monotony tanjoroum 단조로움
monsoon monsun 몬순
monsoon season monsun kyejŏl 몬순 계절
monster *n* koemul 괴물
monstrosity hyungmul 흉물
monstrous (*frightening*) koemulgat'ŭn 괴물같은; (*enormous*) kŏdaehan 거대한; (*shocking*) ch'unggyŏktchŏgin 충격적인
month tal 달, wŏl 월
monthly 1 *adj* maedarŭi 매달의 **2** *adv* maedalmada 매달마다 **3** *n* (*magazine*) wŏlganji 월간지
monument kinyŏmbi 기념비; (*sculpture*) kinyŏm tongsang 기념 동상
mood (*frame of mind*) kibun 기분; (*bad ~*) kibuni nappŭn sangt'ae 기분이 나쁜 상태; (*of meeting, country*) punwigi 분위기; ***be in a good/bad ~*** kibuni chot'a/nappŭda 기분이 좋다/나쁘다; ***be in the ~ for …*** hago ship'ŭn kibunida …하고 싶은 기분이다
moody kibuni chaju pyŏnhanŭn 기분이 자주 변하는; (*bad-tempered*) kibuni nappŭn 기분이 나쁜
moon *n* tal 달
moonlight 1 *n* talppit 달빛 **2** *v/i* F pame puŏbŭl hada 밤에 부업을 하다
moonlit talppich'i ŏrin 달빛이 어린
moor *v/t boat* chŏngbaksshik'ida 정박시키다
moorings chŏngbaktchang 정박장
moose k'ŭn sasŭm 큰 사슴
mop 1 *n* taegŏlle 대걸레 **2** *v/t floor* taegŏllero taktta 대걸레로 닦다; *eyes, face* taktta 닦다
♦ **mop up** taktta 닦다; MIL sot'anghada 소탕하다
mope uurhaehada 우울해하다
moral 1 *adj person, behavior etc* todŏktchŏgin 도덕적인 **2** *n* (*of story*) kyohun 교훈; **~s** todŏk kwannyŏm 도덕 관념
morale sagi 사기
morality todŏkssŏng 도덕성
morbid pyŏngtchŏgin 병적인
more 1 *adj* tŏ manŭn 더 많은; ***some ~ tea?*** ch'arŭl chom tŏ tŭshigessŭmnikka? 차를 좀 더

드시겠습니까?; **~ *and* ~ *students / time*** chŏmjŏm tŏ manŭn hakssaengdŭl / shigan 점점 더 많은 학생들 / 시간 **2** *adv* tŏŭk 더욱; **~ *important*** tŏ chung-yohan 더 중요한; **~ *often*** tŏuk chaju 더욱 자주; **~ *and*** ~ tŏuk tŏ 더욱 더; **~ *or less*** (*about*) chŏngdo 정도; (*virtually*) sashilssang 사실상; ***once*** ~ hanbŏn tŏ 한번 더; **~ *than*** ... poda tŏ mani ... 보다 더 많이; **~ *than 80 people were injured*** 80myŏngboda tŏ manŭn sarami pusang-ŭl tanghaet-tta 80명보다 더 많은 사람이 부상을 당했다; ***I don't live there any*** ~ nanŭn tŏ isang kŏgi salji ansŭmnida 나는 더 이상 거기 살지 않습니다 **3** *pron* tŏ 더; ***do you want some ~?*** tŏ wŏnhashimnikka? 더 원하십니까?; ***a little*** ~ chogŭm tŏ 조금 더

moreover kŏgidaga 거기다가

morgue yŏng-anshil 영안실

Mormonism Molmon-gyo 몰몬교

morning ach'im 아침; ***in the*** ~ (*early*) ach'ime 아침에; (*before noon*) ojŏne 오전에; (*tomorrow*) naeil ach'im 내일 아침; ***four o'clock in the*** ~ ojŏn neshi 오전 네시; ***this*** ~ onŭl ach'im 오늘 아침; ***tomorrow*** ~ naeil ach'im 내일 아침; ***good*** ~ annyŏnghaseyo 안녕하세요; (*on waking up*) annyŏnghi chumusyŏssŏyo 안녕히 주무셨어요

moron pabo 바보

morose uurhan 우울한

morphine morŭp'in 모르핀

morsel: ***a ~ of*** han chogagŭi 한 조각의

mortal 1 *adj* chugŏyahal unmyŏng-ŭi 죽어야할 운명의; *blow* ch'imyŏngjŏgin 치명적인; **~ *enemy*** pulgu taech'ŏnŭi wŏnsu 불구 대천의 원수 **2** *n* pot'ong saram 보통 사람

mortality chugŭl unmyŏng 죽을 운명; (*death rate*) samangnyul 사망률

mortar[1] MIL pakkyŏkp'o 박격포

mortar[2] (*cement*) hoebanjuk 회반죽

mortgage 1 *n* chŏdang 저당 **2** *v/t* chŏdang chap'ida 저당 잡히다

mortician chang-ŭisa 장의사

mortuary yŏng-anshil 영안실

mosaic mojaik'ŭ 모자이크

mosquito mogi 모기

mosquito coil mogihyang 모기향

mosquito net mogijang 모기장

moss ikki 이끼

mossy ikki kkin 이끼 낀

most 1 *adj* taebubunŭi 대부분의; **~ *people would agree with you*** taebubunŭi saramdŭri tangshin ŭigyŏne tong-ŭihal kŏshimnida 대부분의 사람들이 당신 의견에 동의할 것입니다 **2** *adv* kajang 가장; (*very*) maeu 매우; ***the ~ beautiful / interesting*** kajang arŭmdaun / chaemiinnŭn 가장 아름다운 / 재미있는; ***that's the one I like*** ~ kŭgŏshi naega kajang choahanŭn kŏshida 그것이 내가 가장 좋아하는 것이다; **~ *of all*** muŏtppodado 무엇보다도 **3** *pron* taebubun 대부분; (*maximum*) ch'oedaehanŭi kŏt 최대한의 것; ***at (the)*** ~ manaya 많아야; ***make the ~ of*** ch'oedaehan hwaryonghada 최대한 활용하다

mostly taebubunŭn 대부분은, churo 주로

motel mot'el 모텔

moth nabang 나방

mother 1 *n* ŏmŏni 어머니 **2** *v/t* ŏmŏnigach'i tolboda 어머니같이 돌보다

motherboard COMPUT madŏbodŭ 마더보드; **motherhood** ŏmŏniim 어머니임; **mother-in-law** shiŏmŏni 시어머니

motherly ŏmŏnigat'ŭn 어머니같은

mother-of-pearl chagae 자개; **~ *inlay*** chagae changshik 자개 장식; **Mother's Day** ŏmŏninal 어머니날; **mother tongue** mogugŏ 모국어

motif chuje 주제

motion 1 *n* umjigim 움직임; (*of the body*) tongjak 동작; (*proposal*) chean 제안; ***set things in*** ~ ch'ujinhada 추진하다 **2** *v/t*: ***he ~ed me forward*** kŭga na-ege ap'ŭro orago sonjit'aet-tta 그가 나에게 앞으로 오라고 손짓했다

motionless umjigiji annŭn 움직이지

않는
motivate *person* tonggirŭl puyŏhada 동기를 부여하다; ***I don't feel very ~d*** nanŭn pyŏllo ŭiyogi annanda 나는 별로 의욕이 안난다
motivation tonggi puyŏ 동기 부여
motive tonggi 동기
motor naeyŏn-gigwan 내연기관, mot'ŏ 모터
motorbike ot'obai 오토바이; **motorboat** mot'ŏbot'ŭ 모터보트; **motorcade** chadongch'a haengnyŏl 자동차 행렬; **motorcycle** ot'obai 오토바이; **motorcyclist** ot'obairŭl t'anŭn saram 오토바이를 타는 사람; **motor home** idong chut'aekch'a 이동 주택차
motorist unjŏnja 운전자
motorscooter sŭk'ut'ŏ 스쿠터
motor vehicle chadongch'a 자동차
motto chwaumyŏng 좌우명, mot'o 모토; ***school ~*** kyohun 교훈
mound (*hillock*) chagŭn ŏndŏk 작은 언덕; (*in baseball*) maundŭ 마운드; (*pile*) sandŏmi 산더미
mount 1 *n* (*mountain*) san 산; (*horse*) sŭngma 승마 **2** *v/t steps* orŭda 오르다; *horse*, *bicycle* t'ada 타다; *campaign* ch'akssuhada 착수하다; *photo etc* tandanhan tee puch'ida 단단한 데에 붙이다 **3** *v/i* orŭda 오르다
♦**mount up** nŭlda 늘다
mountain san 산
mountain bike sanak chajŏn-gŏ 산악 자전거
mountaineer tŭngsan-ga 등산가, sanagin 산악인
mountaineering tŭngsan 등산
mountainous sanjiŭi 산지의
mountain spirits sanshin 산신
mourn 1 *v/t* ch'udohada 추도하다 **2** *v/i*: **~ for** ...ŭi chugŭmŭl sŭlp'ŏhada ...의 죽음을 슬퍼하다
mourner chogaek 조객
mournful sŭlp'ŭme chamgin 슬픔에 잠긴
mourning sang 상; ***be in ~*** sang chung-ida 상 중이다; ***wear ~*** sangbogŭl iptta 상복을 입다
mouse chwi 쥐; COMPUT mausŭ 마우스
mouse mat COMPUT mausŭ maet'ŭ 마우스 매트
mouth *n* ip 입; (*of river*) ŏgwi 어귀, hagu 하구
mouthful han ip kadŭk 한 입 가득
mouthorgan hamonik'a 하모니카; **mouthpiece** (*of instrument*) ibe taego punŭn pubun 입에 대고 부는 부분; (*spokesperson*) taebyŏnin 대변인; **mouthwash** yangch'iaek 양치액; **mouthwatering** kunch'im tolge hanŭn 군침 돌게 하는
move 1 *n* (*in chess*, *checkers*) su 수; (*step*, *action*) umjigim 움직임; (*change of house*) isa 이사; ***get a ~ on!*** sŏdŭrŭshipsshio! 서두르십시오!; ***don't make a ~!*** umjigiji ma! 움직이지 마!; ***it's your ~*** (*in chess etc*) tangshin ch'aryeimnida 당신 차례입니다 **2** *v/t object* umjigida 움직이다; (*transfer*) omgida 옮기다; (*emotionally*) kamdongshik'ida 감동시키다 **3** *v/i* umjigida 움직이다; (*transfer*) omgida 옮기다; ***~ house*** isahada 이사하다
♦**move around** (*in room*) toradanida 돌아다니다; (*from place to place*) idonghada 이동하다
♦**move away** mullŏnada 물러나다; (*move house*) isahada 이사하다
♦**move in** isaoda 이사오다
♦**move on** (*to another town*) isahada 이사하다; (*to another job*) chŏnjinhada 전직하다; (*to another subject*) pakkuda 바꾸다
♦**move out** (*of house*) isanagada 이사나가다; (*of area*) ttŏnada 떠나다
♦**move up** (*be promoted*) sŭngjinhada 승진하다; (*make room*) charirŭl mandŭlda 자리를 만들다; ***they have moved up to second position*** kŭdŭrŭn che iwie ollat-tta 그들은 제 이위에 올랐다
movement umjigim 움직임; (*organization*) undong 운동; MUS aktchang 악장
movers isatchim unsong-ŏptcha 이삿짐 운송업자
movie yŏnghwa 영화; ***go to a ~ / the ~s*** yŏnghwa porŏ kada 영화 보러 가다

moviegoer: ***be a big ~*** yŏnghwa porŏ kanŭn kŏsŭl maeu choahada 영화 보러 가는 것을 매우 좋아하다
movie theater yŏnghwagwan 영화관
moving (*which can move*) umjiginŭn 움직이는; (*emotionally*) kamdongjŏgin 감동적인
mow *grass* peda 베다
mower p'ulbenŭn kigye 풀베는 기계
moxibustion ssukttŭm 쑥뜸
MP (= ***Military Policeman***) hŏnbyŏng 헌병
mph (= ***miles per hour***) shisok 시속; ***at 50 ~*** shisok 50maillo 시속 50마일로
Mr: ***~ Kevin Brown*** K'ebin Pŭraunsshi 케빈 브라운씨
Mrs: ***~ Margo MacDonald*** Mago Maekttonaldŭ yŏsa 마고 맥도날드 여사
Ms: ***~ Sunmi Lee*** I Sunmisshi 이 순미씨
much 1 *adj* manŭn 많은; ***I have as ~ time as you need*** shiganŭn ŏlmadŭnji issŏyo 시간은 얼마든지 있어요; ***there's not ~ difference*** pyŏllo tarŭji anayo 별로 다르지 않아요 **2** *adv* mani 많이; ***very ~*** aju mani 아주 많이; ***too ~*** nŏmu mani 너무 많이; ***do you like it? - not ~*** kŭgŏsŭl choahaeyo? - pyŏlloyo 그것을 좋아해요? - 별로요; ***as ~ as ...*** ...mank'ŭm mani ...만큼 많이; ***I thought as ~*** nado kŭrŏk'e saenggak'aessŏyo 나도 그렇게 생각했어요 **3** *pron* manŭn kŏt 많은 것; ***he earns as ~ as me*** kŭnŭn namank'ŭm tonŭl pŏnda 그는 나만큼 돈을 번다; ***nothing ~*** pyŏllo 별로
muck (*dirt*) tŏrŏun kŏt 더러운 것
mucus chŏmaek 점액; (*in nose*) k'onmul 콧물
mud chinhŭk 진흙
muddle 1 *n* (*mess*) ŏmmang-in sangt'ae 엉망인 상태; (*confusion*) hollan 혼란 **2** *v/t* hŏllanshik'ida 혼란시키다
♦**muddle up** ŏngmang-ŭro mandŭlda 엉망으로 만들다; (*confuse*) hŏtkkallida 헛갈리다
muddy *adj* chinhŭkt'usŏng-iŭi 진흙투성이의
muffin mŏp'in 머핀
muffle chal andŭllige hada 잘 안들리게 하다
♦**muffle up** *v/i* ttattŭt'age kamssada 따뜻하게 감싸다
muffler MOT pang-ŭm changch'i 방음 장치; (*scarf*) mokttori 목도리
mug[1] *n* (*for tea, coffee*) mŏgŭjan 머그잔; F (*face*) ŏlgul 얼굴
mug[2] *v/t* (*attack*) nosang kangdojirŭl hada 노상 강도질을 하다
mugger nosang kangdo 노상 강도
mugging nosang kangdo haeng-wi 노상 강도 행위
muggy hut'ŏptchigŭnhan 후텁지근한
mule nosae 노새; (*slipper*) myul 뮬, twiga t'ŭin kudu 뒤가 트인 구두
♦**mull over** chuŭi kipkke saenggak'ada 주의 깊게 생각하다
multilingual tagugŏŭi 다국어의
multimedia *n* mŏlt'imidiŏ 멀티미디어, tajung maech'e 다중 매체
multinational 1 *adj* taguktchŏgŭi 다국적의 **2** *n* COM taguktchŏk kiŏp 다국적 기업
multiple *adj* tayanghan 다양한
multiplication MATH kopssem 곱셈
multiply 1 *v/t* kop'ada 곱하다 **2** *v/i* chŭnggahada 증가하다
mumble 1 *n* chung-ŏlgŏrim 중얼거림 **2** *v/t & v/i* chung-ŏlgŏrida 중얼거리다
mumps ihasŏnnyŏm 이하선염
munch *v/t & v/i* ujŏkujŏk sshiptta 우적우적 씹다
municipal shiŭi 시의
mural *n* pyŏk'wa 벽화
murder 1 *n* sarin 살인 **2** *v/t person* sarinhada 살인하다; *song* mangch'yŏ not'a 망쳐 놓다
murderer sarinja 살인자
murderous *rage, look* sarinhal kŏt kat'ŭn 살인할 것 같은
murmur 1 *n* sokssagim 속삭임 **2** *v/t* sokssagida 속삭이다
muscle kŭnyuk 근육
muscular *pain, strain* kŭnyugŭi 근육의; *person* kŭnyuktchirŭi 근육질의
muse *v/i* saenggage chamgida 생각에

잠기다
museum pangmulgwan 박물관
mushroom 1 *n* pŏsŏt 버섯 **2** *v/i* ppalli charada 빨리 자라다
music ŭmak 음악; (*written*) akppo 악보
musical 1 *adj* ŭmagŭi 음악의; *person* ŭmaktchŏgin 음악적인; *voice* ŭmakkat'ŭn 음악같은 **2** *n* myujik'ŏl 뮤지컬
musical instrument akki 악기
musician ŭmak-kka 음악가
mussel honghap 홍합
must ◊ (*necessity*) ...haeya hada ...해야 하다; ***I ~ be on time*** nanŭn pandŭshi cheshigane issŏya handa 나는 반드시 제시간에 있어야 한다; ***I ~*** kŭraeyaman handa 그래야만 한다; ***I ~n't be late*** nanŭn nŭjŏsŏnŭn andoenda 나는 늦어서는 안된다 ◊ (*probability*): ***it ~ be about 6 o'clock*** 6shi tchŭm toessŭl kŏyeyo 6시 쯤 됐을 거예요; ***they ~ have arrived by now*** kŭdŭrŭn chigŭmimyŏn toch'ak'aekketchyo 그들은 지금이면 도착했겠죠
mustache k'otssuyŏm 콧수염
mustard kyŏja 겨자
musty komp'angnae nanŭn 곰팡내 나는
mute *adj* muŏnŭi 무언의
muted *color* pudŭrŏun 부드러운; *opposition*, *criticism* yak'an 약한
mutilate *person* sanghaerŭl ip'ida 상해를 입히다; *thing* hwesonhada 훼손하다
mutiny 1 *n* pallan 반란 **2** *v/i* pallanŭl irŭk'ida 반란을 일으키다
mutter *v/t & v/i* chung-ŏlgŏrida 중얼거리다
mutual sanghoganŭi 상호간의
muzzle 1 *n* (*of animal*, *dog*) chudung-i 주둥이; (*device*) immagae 입마개 **2** *v/t*: ***~ the press*** ŏllon podorŭl maktta 언론 보도를 막다
my ◊ naŭi 나의; H chŏŭi 저의; ***~ decision / money*** naŭi kyŏltchŏng / ton 나의 결정 / 돈; ***~ leg hurts*** tariga ap'ayo 다리가 아파요 ◊ (*referring to family*, *groups etc*, *Korean usually uses the pronoun 'our'*) uriŭi 우리의; ***~ house / mother*** uri chip / ŏmŏni 우리 집 / 어머니; ***~ family*** uri kajok 우리 가족; ***~ country / company*** uri nara / hoesa 우리 나라 / 회사
myopic kŭnshianŭi 근시안의
myself na chashin 나 자신; ***by ~*** (*alone*) honja 혼자; (*without any help*) sŭsŭro 스스로
mysterious shinbihan 신비한
mysteriously shinbihage 신비하게
mystery shinbi 신비; (*fact which is mysterious*) pulgasaŭi 불가사의
mystify pulgahaehage mandŭlda 불가해하게 만들다; ***I'm mystified*** ihaehal su ŏpssŏyo 이해할 수 없어요
myth shinhwa 신화; *fig* mangsang 망상
mythical shinhwaŭi 신화의
mythology shinhwahak 신화학

N

nab (*take for oneself*) nakka ch'aeda 낚아 채다
nag *v/t & v/i* chansorihada 잔소리하다; **~ s.o. to do sth** nuguege muŏsŭl harago chansorihada 누구에게 무엇을 하라고 잔소리하다
nagging *person* chansorihanŭn 잔소리하는; *doubt* sŏnggashin 성가신; *pain* kkŭnjilgin 끈질긴
nail (*for wood*) mot 못; (*on finger, toe*) sont'op 손톱
nail clippers sont'opkkak-kki 손톱깎이; **nail file** sont'optchul 손톱줄; **nail polish** maenik'yuŏ 매니큐어; **nail polish remover** maenik'yuŏ chiunŭn yak 매니큐어 지우는 약; **nail scissors** sont'op kkangnŭn kawi 손톱 깎는 가위; **nail varnish** maenik'yuŏ 매니큐어
naive sunjinhan 순진한
naked pŏlgŏbŏsŭn 벌거벗은; *truth, aggression* chŏngnarahan 적나라한; **to the ~ eye** yuganŭronŭn 육안으로는
name 1 *n* irŭm 이름; (*on document*) sŏngmyŏng 성명; ***what's your ~?*** irŭmi muŏsshimnikka? 이름이 무엇입니까?; (*polite*) sŏnghami ŏttŏk'e toeshimnikka? 성함이 어떻게 되십니까?; ***what's his ~?*** kŭŭi irŭmŭn muŏshimnikka? 그의 이름은 무엇입니까?; ***call s.o. ~s*** nugurŭl yok'ada 누구를 욕하다; ***make a ~ for oneself*** yumyŏnghaejida 유명해지다 **2** *v/t* irŭmŭl chit-tta 이름을 짓다
♦**name for**: ***name X for Y*** Yŭi irŭmŭl ttasŏ Xŭi irŭmŭl chit-tta Y의 이름을 따서 X의 이름을 짓다
namely chŭk 즉
namesake tongmyŏng-iin 동명이인
nametag irŭmp'yo 이름표
Namhae Island Namhaedo 남해도
nanny *n* yumo 유모
nap *n* nattcham 낮잠; ***have a ~*** nattchamŭl chada 낮잠을 자다
nape: **~ of the neck** mokttŏlmi 목덜미
napkin (*table ~*) naepk'in 냅킨; (*sanitary ~*) saengnidae 생리대
narcotic *n* mayak 마약
narcotics agent mayak tansokppan 마약 단속반
narrate iyagihada 이야기하다
narration (*telling*) iyagihagi 이야기하기
narrative 1 *n* (*story*) iyagi 이야기 **2** *adj poem, style* iyagishigŭi 이야기식의
narrator iyagihanŭn saram 이야기하는 사람
narrow *street, bed, views* chobŭn 좁은; *victory* kakkasŭro ŏdŭn 가까스로 얻은
narrowly *win, escape* kakkasŭro 가까스로
narrow-minded maŭmi chobŭn 마음이 좁은
nasal *voice* k'ŏssoriŭi 콧소리의
nasty *person, thing to say* mot-ttoen 못된; *smell, weather* pulk'waehan 불쾌한; *cut, wound, disease* shimhan 심한
nation kuk-kka 국가, nara 나라
national 1 *adj* kuk-kkaŭi 국가의, naraŭi 나라의 **2** *n* kungmin 국민
national anthem kuk-kka 국가; (*South Korean*) Aeguk-kka 애국가; **National Assembly** Kuk'oe 국회; **national debt** kukch'ae 국채; **national flag** (*South Korean*) t'aegŭk-kki 태극기; **National Foundation Day** Kaech'ŏnjŏl 개천절
nationalism minjoktchuŭi 민족주의
nationality kuktchŏk 국적
nationalize *industry etc* kugyŏnghwahada 국영화하다

national park kungnip kong-wŏn 국립 공원
native 1 *adj* ch'ulssaeng-ŭi 출생의; ~ ***language*** mogugŏ 모국어 **2** *n* ch'ulsshinŭi saram 출신의 사람; (*tribesman*) wŏnjumin 원주민
native country ch'ulssaengguk 출생국
native speaker wŏnŏmin 원어민
NATO (= ***North Atlantic Treaty Organization***) Pukttaesŏyang Choyak Kigu 북대서양 조약 기구
natural *resources* chayŏnŭi 자연의; *flavor* sunsuhan 순수한; (*obvious*) tangnyŏnhan 당연한; ~ ***blonde*** t'agonan kŭmbal 타고난 금발; ~ ***death*** chayŏnsa 자연사
natural gas ch'ŏnyŏn kassŭ 천연 가스
naturalist saengt'aehaktcha 생태학자
naturalize: ***become ~d*** kwihwahada 귀화하다
naturally (*of course*) tangnyŏnhi 당연히; *behave*, *speak* chayŏnsŭrŏpkke 자연스럽게; (*by nature*) pollae 본래
natural science chayŏn kwahak 자연 과학
natural scientist chayŏn kwahaktcha 자연 과학자
nature chayŏn 자연; (*of person*) ch'ŏnsŏng 천성; (*of problem*) sŏngkkyŏk 성격
nature reserve chayŏn pohogu 자연 보호구
naughty chitkkujŭn 짓궂은; *photograph*, *word etc* yahan 야한
nausea mesŭkkŏum 메스꺼움; *fig* yŏk-kkyŏum 역겨움
nauseate *fig* (*disgust*) yŏk-kkyŏpkke hada 역겹게 하다
nauseating *fig* yŏk-kkyŏun 역겨운
nauseous: ***feel*** ~ t'ohal kŏt kat-tta 토할 것 같다
nautical hanghaeŭi 항해의
nautical mile haeri 해리
naval haegunŭi 해군의
naval base haegun kiji 해군 기지
navel paekkop 배꼽
navigable *river* hanghaehal su innŭn 항해할 수 있는
navigate *v/i* (*in ship*, *airplane*) hanghaehada 항해하다; (*in car*) kil annaerŭl hada 길 안내를 하다; COMPUT kŏmsaek'ada 검색하다
navigation hanghaesul 항해술; (*in car*) kil annaehagi 길 안내하기
navigator (*in ship*, *airplane*) hanghaesa 항해사; (*in car*) kil annaerŭl hanŭn saram 길 안내를 하는 사람
navy haegun 해군
navy blue 1 *n* namsaek 남색 **2** *adj* namsaegŭi 남색의
near 1 *adv* kakkai 가까이 **2** *prep* kakkaie 가까이에; ~ ***the bank*** ŭnhaeng kakkaie 은행 가까이에; ***do you go ~ the bank?*** ŭnhaeng kŭnch'ŏro kamnikka? 은행 근처로 갑니까? **3** *adj* kakkaun 가까운; ***the ~est bus stop*** kajang kakkaun pŏssŭ chŏngnyujang 가장 가까운 버스 정류장; ***in the ~ future*** kakkaun mirae-e 가까운 미래에
nearby *adv live* kakkapkke 가깝게
nearly kŏŭi 거의
near-sighted kŭnshiŭi 근시의
neat *room*, *desk* kkaekkŭt'an 깨끗한; *person* tanjŏnghan 단정한; *whiskey* sunsuhan 순수한; *solution* hyŏnmyŏnghan 현명한; F (*terrific*) kŭnsahan 근사한
necessarily pandŭshi 반드시
necessary p'iryohan 필요한; ***it is ~ to …*** …hal p'iryoga it-tta …할 필요가 있다
necessitate p'iryoro hada 필요로 하다
necessity p'iryossŏng 필요성; (*sth necessary*) p'ilssup'um 필수품
neck mok 목
necklace mok-kkŏri 목걸이; **neck-line** (*of dress*) moksŏn 목선; **neck-tie** nekt'ai 넥타이
née mihon ttaeŭi sŏng 미혼 때의 성
need 1 *n* p'iryo 필요; ***if ~ be*** p'iryohadamyŏn 필요하다면; ***in ~*** toumŭi p'iryohan 도움이 필요한; ***be in ~ of sth*** muŏshi p'iryohada 무엇이 필요하다; ***there's no ~ to be upset*** kibun nappahal p'iryonŭn

hanado ŏptta 기분 나빠할 필요는 하나도 없다 **2** *v/t* p'iryohada 필요하다; ***you'll ~ to buy one*** nŏnŭn hanarŭl sayahal kŏshida 너는 하나를 사야할 것이다; ***you don't ~ to wait*** kidaril p'iryoga ŏptta 기다릴 필요가 없다; ***I ~ to talk to you*** tangshin-gwa iyagihaeyagessŏyo 당신과 이야기해야겠어요; ***~ I say more?*** tŏ marhal p'iryoga issŭmnikka? 더 말할 필요가 있습니까?

needle (*for sewing*, *on dial*) panŭl 바늘; (*for injection*) chusa panŭl 주사 바늘

needlework panŭjil 바느질

needy pin-gunghan 빈궁한

negative 1 *adj* GRAM pujŏng-ŭi 부정의; *attitude*, *person* pujŏngjŏgin 부정적인; ELEC ŭmgŭgŭi 음극의 **2** *n*: ***answer in the ~*** anirago taedap'ada 아니라고 대답하다

neglect 1 *n* pangch'i 방치 **2** *v/t garden*, *one's health* tolboji ant'a 돌보지 않다; ***~ to do X*** Xŭl / rŭl haji ant'a X을 / 를 하지 않다

neglected *garden*, *author* pŏryŏjin 버려진; ***feel ~*** pŏryŏjin tŭt'an nŭkkimi tŭlda 버려진 듯한 느낌이 들다

negligence t'aeman 태만

negligent sohorhan 소홀한

negligible *amount* mushihaedo choŭn 무시해도 좋은

negotiable *salary*, *terms* hyŏpssanghal su innŭn 협상할 수 있는

negotiate 1 *v/i* hyŏpssanghada 협상하다 **2** *v/t deal*, *settlement* hyŏpssanghada 협상하다; *obstacles* ttulkko nagada 뚫고 나가다; *curve* chal tolda 잘 돌다

negotiation hyŏpssang 협상

negotiator hyŏpssangga 협상가

Negro Hŭgin 흑인

neigh *v/i* hinghinggŏrida 힝힝거리다

neighbor iut saram 이웃 사람; (*at table*) yŏp saram 옆 사람

neighborhood iut 이웃; ***in the ~ of*** *fig* … kakkai … 가까이

neighboring *house*, *state* iushin 이웃인

neighborly iutkkach'i tajŏnghan 이웃같이 다정한

neither 1 *adj* ŏnŭ ...to anin 어느 ...도 아닌 (+ *negative verb*); ***~ applicant was any good*** ŏnŭn hubojado mattanghaji anat-tta 어느 후보자도 마땅하지 않았다 **2** *pron* ŏnŭ tchoktto ... 어느 쪽도 ... (+ *negative verb*); ***which do you want? --, thanks*** ŏttŏn kŏsŭl wŏnhaseyo? – komaptchina, ŏnŭ tchoktto animnida 어떤 것을 원하세요? - 고맙지만, 어느 쪽도 아닙니다 **3** *adv*: ***~ X nor Y ...*** Xto Yto ... X도 Y도 ... (+ *negative verb*); ***~ Jane nor Sally knew where it was*** Cheindo Saellido kŭgŏshi ŏdi innŭnji mollat-tta 제인도 샐리도 그것이 어디 있는지 몰랐다 **4** *conj*: ***~ do I*** nadoyo 나도요, chŏdoyo 저도요; ***I don't like it - ~ do I*** nanŭn kŭgŏt choahaji anayo – nado choahaji anayo 나는 그것 좋아하지 않아요 - 나도 좋아하지 않아요; ***I can't see it - ~ can I*** nanŭn anboinŭn teyo - chŏdo anboyŏyo 나는 안보이는 데요 - 저도 안보여요

neon light neon ssain 네온 싸인

Nepal Nep'al 네팔

Nepalese 1 *adj* Nep'arŭi 네팔의 **2** *n* (*person*) Nep'arin 네팔인

nephew chok'a 조카

nerd F ŏlgani 얼간이

nerve shin-gyŏng 신경; (*courage*) yonggi 용기; (*impudence*) ppŏnppŏnham 뻔뻔함; ***it's bad for my ~s*** shin-gyŏng ssŭige handa 신경 쓰이게 한다; ***get on s.o.'s ~s*** nuguŭi shin-gyŏng-ŭl kŏndŭrida 누구의 신경을 건드리다

nerve-racking chomajomahage hanŭn 조마조마하게 하는

nervous *person* shin-gyŏng-i kwaminhan 신경이 과민한; ***be ~ about doing sth*** muŏt hanŭn kŏsŭl puranhaehada 무엇 하는 것을 불안해하다

nervous breakdown shin-gyŏng soeyak 신경 쇠약

nervous energy shin-gyŏng enŏji 신경 에너지
nervousness shin-gyŏngtchil 신경질
nervous wreck shin-gyŏng soeyaktcha 신경 쇠약자
nervy (*fresh*) ppŏnppŏnhan 뻔뻔한
nest *n* tungji 둥지
♦**nestle up to**: ~ ***s.o.*** nuguege momŭl p'yŏnhi kidaeda 누구에게 몸을 편히 기대다
net[1] (*for fishing*) kŭmul 그물; (*for tennis*) net'ŭ 네트
net[2] *adj amount* sunsuhan 순수한; *price* chŏngkka 정가; *weight* p'ojangŭl cheoehan 포장을 제외한
net curtain mangsa k'ŏt'ŭn 망사 커튼
net profit suniik 순이익
nettle *v/t* shin-gyŏngtchilnage hada 신경질나게 하다
network (*of contacts, cells*) kŭmulmang 그물망; COMPUT net'ŭwŏk'ŭ 네트워크
neurologist shin-gyŏngkkwa ŭisa 신경과 의사
neurosis shin-gyŏngtchŭng 신경증
neurotic *adj* shin-gyŏng kwaminŭi 신경 과민의
neuter *v/t animal* kŏsehada 거세하다
neutral 1 *adj country* chungnibŭi 중립의; *color* chunggansaegŭi 중간색의 **2** *n* (*gear*) chungnip wich'i 중립 위치; ***in ~*** chungnibe 중립에
neutrality chungnipssŏng 중립성
neutralize muryŏk'age hada 무력하게 하다
never chŏlttae (+ *negative verb*) 절대; ***you're ~ going to believe this*** tangshinŭn chŏlttaero kŭgŏsŭl midŭl su ŏpssŭl kŏshimnida 당신은 절대로 그것을 믿을 수 없을 것입니다; ***you ~ promised, did you?*** tangshinŭn chŏlttaero yakssok'aji anatchyo? 당신은 절대로 약속하지 않았죠? ◊ (*past*) han pŏndo (+ *negative verb*) 한 번도; ***I have ~ eaten kimchee*** han pŏndo kimch'irŭl mŏgŏbon chŏgi ŏpssŏyo 한 번도 김치를 먹어본 적이 없어요
never-ending kkŭdŏmnŭn 끝없는
nevertheless kŭrŏmedo pulguhago 그럼에도 불구하고
new saeroun 새로운; ***this system is still ~ to me*** i pangshigŭn na-ege yŏjŏnhi saerop-tta 이 방식은 나에게 여전히 새롭다; ***I'm ~ to the job*** nanŭn kŭ ire ikssuk'aji ant'a 나는 그 일에 익숙하지 않다; ***that's nothing ~*** saeroun kŏsŭn amu kŏt-tto ŏptta 새로운 것은 아무 것도 없다
newborn *adj* kannan 갓난
newcomer saero on saram 새로 온 사람; (*to organization*) shinip 신입
newly (*recently*) ch'oegŭn 최근
newly-weds shinhon pubu 신혼 부부
new moon ch'ossŭngttal 초승달
news soshik 소식; (*on TV, radio*) nyusŭ 뉴스; ***that's ~ to me*** kŭmshi ch'omunida 금시 초문이다
news agency t'ongshinsa 통신사; **newscast** TV nyusŭ pangsong 뉴스 방송; **newscaster** TV nyusŭ pangsonghanŭn saram 뉴스 방송하는 사람; **news dealer** shinmun p'anmaeso 신문 판매소; **news flash** sokppo 속보; **newspaper** shinmun 신문; **newsreader** TV *etc* nyusŭ pangsonghanŭn saram 뉴스 방송하는 사람; **news report** nyusŭ podo 뉴스 보도; **newsstand** shinmun kap'andae 신문 가판대; **newsvendor** shinmun p'anmaewŏn 신문 판매원
New Year Saehae 새해; (*public holiday*) Shinjŏng 신정; ***Happy ~!*** Saehae pok mani padŭseyo! 새해 복 많이 받으세요!; **New Year's Day** Saehae Ch'ŏnnal 새해 첫날; (*lunar*) Sŏllal 설날; **New Year's Eve** Sŏttal Kŭmŭmnal 섣달 그믐날; **New York** Nyuyok 뉴욕; **New Zealand** Nyujillaendŭ 뉴질랜드; **New Zealander** Nyujillaendŭin 뉴질랜드인
next 1 *adj* taŭmŭi 다음의; ***the ~ week / month he came back again*** taŭm chu / tare kŭga tashi torawat-tta 다음 주 / 달에 그가 다시 돌아왔다; ***who's ~?*** taŭm pun? 다음 분? **2** *adv* taŭme 다음에; ***~ to*** (*beside*) …ŭi yŏp'ye …의 옆에; (*in comparison with*) …e iŏsŏ …에 이어서
next-door 1 *adj neighbor* yŏptchibŭi

옆집의 **2** *adv live* yŏptchibe 옆집에
next of kin kŭnch'in 근친
nibble *v/t* kalga mŏktta 갉아 먹다; *s.o.'s ear* saltchak kkaemulda 살짝 깨물다
nice mŏtchin 멋진; ***be ~ to your father*** ne abŏjihant'e charhae 네 아버지한테 잘해; ***that's very ~ of you*** chŏngmal ch'injŏrhagunnyo 정말 친절하군요
nicely *written, presented* chal 잘; (*pleasantly*) kippŭge 기쁘게
niceties: ***social ~*** sagyoppŏp 사교법
niche (*in market*) t'ŭmsae 틈새; (*special position*) chŏktchŏrhan changso 적절한 장소
nick *n* (*cut*) hŭm 흠; ***in the ~ of time*** paro che ttaee 바로 제 때에
nickel nik'el 니켈; (*coin*) ossent'ŭtchari tongjŏn 오센트짜리 동전
nickname *n* pyŏlmyŏng 별명
niece yŏja chok'a 여자 조카
niggardly *adj* insaek'an 인색한
night pam 밤; (*in hotel*) pak 박; ***tomorrow ~*** naeil pam 내일 밤; (*evening*) naeil chŏnyŏk 내일 저녁; ***11 o'clock at ~*** pam yŏrhanshi 밤 11시; ***travel by ~*** pam yŏhaeng 밤 여행; ***during the ~*** pam saie 밤 사이에; ***stay the ~*** pamŭl chinaeda 밤을 지내다; ***a room for 3 ~s*** samil pamŭl mugŭl pang 3일 밤을 묵을 방; ***work ~s*** yagan kŭnmuida 야간 근무이다; ***good ~*** annyŏnghi chumushipsshiyo 안녕히 주무십시요, F chal cha 잘 자
nightcap (*drink*) *chagi chŏne mashinŭn sul* 자기 전에 마시는 술; **nightclub** nait'ŭ k'ŭllŏp 나이트클럽; **nightdress** chamot 잠옷; **nightfall**: ***at ~*** ch'ojŏnyŏge 초저녁에; **night flight** pambihaenggi 밤비행기; **nightgown** chamot 잠옷
nightingale nait'inggeil 나이팅게일
nightlife pam yuhŭng 밤 유흥
nightly 1 *adj* maeil pamŭi 매일 밤의 **2** *adv* maeil pame 매일 밤에
nightmare angmong 악몽; *fig* angmonggat'ŭn kŏt 악몽같은 것
night porter yagŭn poi 야근 보이; **night school** yagan hak-kkyo 야간 학교; **night shift** yagan kŭnmu 야간 근무; **nightshirt** chamot 잠옷; **nightspot** nait'ŭ k'ŭllop 나이트 클럽; **nighttime**: ***at ~, in the ~*** pame 밤에
nimble chaepparŭn 재빠른
nine ahop 아홉, ku 구
nineteen yŏrahop 열 아홉, shipkku 십구
nineteenth yŏrahop pŏntchaeŭi 열 아홉 번째의
ninetieth ahŭn pŏntchaeŭi 아흔 번째의
ninety ahŭn 아흔, kuship 구십
ninth ahop pŏntchaeŭi 아홉 번째의
nip *n* (*pinch*) kkojipk-kki 꼬집기; (*bite*) mulgi 물기
nipple chŏtkkoktchi 젖꼭지, yudu 유두
nitrogen chilso 질소
no 1 *adv* ◊ aniyo 아니오 ◊ (*using 'yes', ie yes, that is right*): ***you don't know the answer, do you? – ~, I don't*** tabŭl morŭjyo? - ye, mollayo 답을 모르죠? - 예, 몰라요 **2** *adj*: ***there's ~ coffee / tea left*** namŭn k'ŏp'i / ch'aga ŏptta 남은 커피 / 차가 없다; ***I have ~ family*** nanŭn kajogi amudo ŏptta 나는 가족이 아무도 없다; ***I'm ~ linguist*** nanŭn ŏnŏhaktchaga anida 나는 언어학자가 아니다; ***~ smoking / ~ parking*** kŭmyŏn / chuch'agŭmji 금연 / 주차금지; ***~ man is perfect*** nugudo wanjŏnhaji ant'a 누구도 완전하지 않다
nobility kip'um 기품; ***the ~*** kwijok 귀족
noble *adj* kogwihan 고귀한
nobody amudo (+ *negative verb*) 아무도; ***~ knows*** amudo morŭnda 아무도 모른다; ***there was ~ at home*** chibenŭn amudo ŏpssŏt-tta 집에는 아무도 없었다; ***who was there? - ~*** kŏgi nuga issŏssŏyo? - amudo ŏpssŏssŏyo 거기 누가 있었어요? - 아무도 없었어요
nod 1 *n* kkŭdŏgim 끄덕임 **2** *v/i* kogaerŭl kkŭdŏgida 고개를 끄덕이다
♦**nod off** (*fall asleep*) kkubŏk-kkubŏk cholda 꾸벅꾸벅 졸다

no-hoper F munŭngnyŏktcha 무능력자
noise sori 소리; (*loud, unpleasant*) soŭm 소음
noisy shikkŭrŏun 시끄러운
nominal *amount* irŭmppunin 이름뿐인
nominate (*appoint*) immyŏnghada 임명하다; ***~ s.o. for a post*** (*propose*) nugurŭl kongch'ŏnhada 누구를 공천하다
nomination (*appointing*) immyŏng 임명; (*proposal*) kongch'ŏn 공천; (*person proposed*) kongch'ŏnja 공천자
nominee (*person proposed*) kongch'ŏnja 공천자; (*for prize*) hubo 후보; (*person appointed*) immyŏngja 임명자
nonalcoholic alk'oori ŏmnŭn 알코올이 없는
nonaligned chungniptchŏgin 중립적인
nonchalant t'aeyŏnhan 태연한
noncommissioned officer yuk-kkun hasagwan 육군 하사관
noncommittal *response* aemaemohohan 애매모호한; ***he was very ~*** kŭnŭn koengjanghi aemaemohohan t'aedorŭl chihaet-tta 그는 굉장히 애매모호한 태도를 취했다
nondescript t'ŭktching-ŏmnŭn 특징없는
none amu kŏtto (+ *negative verb*) 아무 것도; (*person*) amudo (+ *negative verb*) 아무도; ***~ of the students is American*** hakssaengdŭl chung amudo Miguk sarami anida 학생들 중 아무도 미국 사람이 아니다; ***~ of the chocolate was sold*** amu ch'yok'ollitto p'alliji anat-tta 아무 쵸콜릿도 팔리지 않았다; ***there is / are ~ left*** amu kŏtto namŭn kŏshi ŏptta 아무 것도 남은 것이 없다
nonentity pojal kŏt omnŭn 보잘 것 없는
nonetheless kŭrŏmedo pulguhago 그럼에도 불구하고
nonexistent chonjaehaji annŭn 존재하지 않는; **nonfiction** nonp'iksshyŏn 논픽션; **non(in)flammable** puryŏnsŏng-ŭi 불연성의; **noninterference, nonintervention** pulgansŏp 불간섭; **noniron** *shirt* tarimjiri p'iryoŏmnŭn 다림질이 필요없는
no-no F: ***that's a ~*** kŭgŏsŭn haesŏnŭn andoenda 그것은 해서는 안된다
no-nonsense *approach* hyŏnshiltchŏgin 현실적인
nonpayment mibul 미불; **nonpolluting** mugonghaeŭi 무공해의; **nonresident** *n* pigŏjuja 비거주자; **nonreturnable** *deposit* hwanbul pulgaŭi 환불 불가의
nonsense maldo andoenŭn kŏt 말도 안되는 것; ***don't talk ~*** maldo andoenŭn sori haji mara 말도 안되는 소리 하지 마라; ***~, it's easy!*** musŭn sori, shwiun kŏshiya! 무슨 소리, 쉬운 것이야!
nonskid *tires* mikkŭrŏjiji annŭn 미끄러지지 않는; **nonslip** *surface* mikkŭrŏjiji annŭn 미끄러지지 않는; **nonsmoker** (*person*) pihŭbyŏnja 비흡연자; **nonstandard** p'yojune mat-tchi annŭn 표준에 맞지 않는; **nonstick** *pan* nurŏputtchi annŭn 눌어붙지 않는; **nonstop 1** *adj flight, train* chik'aengŭi 직행의; *chatter* chungdan ŏmnŭn 중단 없는 **2** *adv fly, travel* chik'aeng-ŭro 직행으로; *chatter, argue* chungdan ŏpsshi 중단 없이; **nonswimmer** suyŏng-ŭl mot'anŭn saram 수영을 못하는 사람; **nonunion** *adj* chohabe kaip'aji anŭn 조합에 가입하지 않은; **nonviolence** pip'ongnyŏk 비폭력; **nonviolent** pip'ongnyŏgŭi 비폭력의
noodles kukssu 국수; (*instant*) ramyŏn 라면; (*chilled*) naengmyŏn 냉면
nook kusŏk 구석
noon chŏng-o 정오; ***at ~*** chŏng-o-e 정오에
noose olgami 올가미
nor …to ttohan (+ *negative verb*) …도 또한; ***~ do I*** nado anida 나도 아니다
norm chŏngsang 정상

normal chŏngsang-ŭi 정상의
normality chŏngsang sangt'ae 정상 상태
normalize *relationships* chŏngsanghwahada 정상화하다
normally (*usually*) pot'ong-ŭro 보통으로; (*in a normal way*) chŏngsang-ŭro 정상으로
north 1 *n* puk 북; ***to the ~ of*** …ŭi puktchoge …의 북쪽에 **2** *adj* puktchogŭi 북쪽의 **3** *adv travel* puktchogŭro 북쪽으로; **~ of** …ŭi pukppang-e …의 북방에
North America Pungmi 북미
North American 1 *adj* Pungmiŭi 북미의 **2** *n* Pungmiin 북미인
northeast *n* tongbuk 동북
northerly *adj* puk'yang-ŭi 북향의
northern pukppuŭi 북부의
northerner pukppu chibang saram 북부 지방 사람
North Korea Puk'an 북한
North Korean 1 *adj* Puk'anŭi 북한의 **2** *n* Puk'an saram 북한 사람
North Pole Pukkŭk 북극
northward *travel* puktchogŭro 북쪽으로
northwest *n* pukssŏ 북서
Norway Norŭwei 노르웨이
Norwegian 1 *adj* Norŭweiŭi 노르웨이의 **2** *n* (*person*) Norŭweiin 노르웨이인; (*language*) Norŭweiŏ 노르웨이어
nose k'o 코; ***it was right under my ~!*** paro nae nun ap'esŏ irŏnat-tta! 바로 내 눈 앞에서 일어났다!
♦**nose around** k'aeda 캐다
nosebleed k'op'i 코피
nostalgia hyangsu 향수
nostalgic hyangsuŭi 향수의
nostril k'otkkumŏng 콧구멍
nosy ch'amgyŏnhagi choahanŭn 참견하기 좋아하는
not: ***~ this one, that one*** igŏshi anira chŏgŏt 이것이 아니라 저것, igŏt malgo chŏgŏt 이것 말고 저것; ***~ now*** chigŭm malgo 지금 말고; ***~ there*** kŭgot malgo 그곳 말고; ***~ before Tuesday / next week*** hwayoil / taŭm chu chŏnenŭn andoego 화요일 / 다음 주 전에는 안되고; ***~ for me, thanks*** komaptchiman, chŏnŭn kwanch'anssŭmnida 고맙지만, 저는 괜찮습니다; ***~ a lot*** pyŏllo 별로 ◊ (*with verbs*): ***it's ~ ready / allowed*** igŏsŭn chunbitoeji / hŏgadoeji anat-tta 그것은 준비되지 / 허가되지 않았다; ***I don't know*** nanŭn morŭnda 나는 모른다; ***I am ~ American*** nanŭn Migugini animnida 나는 미국인이 아닙니다; ***he didn't help*** kŭnŭn toptchi anat-tta 그는 돕지 않았다; ***don't do it like that*** kŭrŏk'e haji maseyo 그렇게 하지 마세요
notable chumok'al manhan 주목할 만한
notary kongjŭng-in 공증인
notch *n* pen chaguk 벤 자국
note *n* (*short letter*) tchalbŭn p'yŏnji 짧은 편지; MUS ŭmp'yo 음표; (*to self*) memo 메모; (*comment on text*) chu 주; ***take ~s*** chŏktta 적다; ***take ~ of sth*** muŏsŭl arach'aeda 무엇을 알아채다
♦**note down** chŏgŏduda 적어두다
notebook kongch'aek 공책; COMPUT not'ŭbuk 노트북
noted allyŏjin 알려진
notepad memojich'ŏp 메모지첩
notepaper p'yŏnjiji 편지지
nothing amu kŏt-tto (+ *negative verb*) 아무 것도; ***there's ~ left*** amu kŏt-tto namtchi anat-tta 아무 것도 남지 않았다; ***what did you do? - ~*** muŏsŭl mŏgŏssŏyo? - amu kŏt-tto 무엇을 먹었어요? - 아무 것도; ***~ for me thanks*** chŏnŭn kwaench'anayo 저는 괜찮아요; ***~ can change it*** ŏttŏn kŏt-tto kŭgŏsŭl pakkul su ŏptta 어떤 것도 그것을 바꿀 수 없다; ***~ but...*** ...il ppun ...일 뿐; ***he's ~ but trouble*** kŭnŭn munjekkŏriil ppunida 그는 문제거리일 뿐이다; ***~ much*** pyŏllo 별로; ***for ~*** (*for free*) muryoro 무료로; (*for no reason*) amu iyu ŏpsshi 아무 이유 없이; ***I'd like ~ better*** naega cheil choahanŭn kŏshida 내가 제일 좋아하는 것이다
notice 1 *n* (*on bulletin board, in street*) keshi 게시; (*advance warning*)

chuŭi 주의; (*in newspaper*) konggo 공고; (*to leave job, to leave house*) t'ongji 통지; ***at short ~*** tchalbŭn shihanŭl namgin ch'ae 짧은 시한을 남긴 채; ***until further ~*** ch'uhu t'ongjiga issŭl ttaekkaji 추후 통지가 있을 때까지; ***give s.o. his / her ~*** (*to quit job*) nuguege haeim t'ongjirŭl hada 누구에게 해임 통지를 하다; ***hand in one's ~*** (*to employer*) sajik'al kŏsŭl allida 사직할 것을 알리다; ***four weeks' ~*** saju chŏne t'ongjihanŭn kŏt 사주 전에 통지하는 것; ***take ~ of*** …e chuŭihada …에 주의하다; ***take no ~ of*** …e amurŏn chuŭirŭl haji ant'a …에 아무런 주의를 하지 않다 **2** *v/t* arach'aeda 알아채다

noticeable chumok'al manhan 주목할 만한

notify konggohada 공고하다

notion saenggak 생각

notions panŭjil yongp'um 바느질 용품

notorious angmyŏng nop'ŭn 악명 높은

nougat nuga 누가

noun myŏngsa 명사

nourishing yŏngnyang-innŭn 영양있는

nourishment yŏngnyangbun 영양분

novel *n* sosŏl 소설

novelist sosŏlga 소설가

novelty (*being novel*) chamshinham 참신함; (*sth novel*) saeroum 새로움

November shibirwŏl 십일월

novice ch'oshimja 초심자

now chigŭm 지금; ***~ and again, ~ and then*** ttaettaero 때때로; ***by ~*** chigŭmtchŭm 지금쯤; ***from ~ on*** chigŭmbut'ŏ 지금부터; ***right ~*** paro chigŭm 바로 지금; ***just ~*** (*at this moment*) chigŭm paro 지금 바로; (*a little while ago*) paro chŏne 바로 전에; ***~, ~!*** cha, cha! 자, 자!; ***~, where did I put it?*** ŏ, naega kŭgŏsŭl ŏdie tuŏssŭlkka? 어, 내가 그것을 어디에 두었을까?

nowadays yojŭŭm 요즈음

nowhere amu kosedo 아무 곳에도; ***it's ~ near finished*** hanado kkŭnnaji anat-tta 하나도 끝나지 않았다

nozzle kkŭt 끝

nuclear haegŭi 핵의, haek 핵

nuclear energy haek enŏji 핵 에너지; **nuclear fission** haek punnyŏl 핵 분열; **nuclear-free** pihaegŭi 비핵의; **nuclear physics** haek mullihak 핵 물리학; **nuclear power** wŏnjaryŏk 원자력; **nuclear power station** wŏnjaryŏk paltchŏnso 원자력 발전소; **nuclear reactor** wŏnjaro 원자로; **nuclear waste** haek p'yegimul 핵 폐기물; **nuclear weapons** haek mugi 핵 무기

nude 1 *adj* almomŭi 알몸의 **2** *n* (*painting*) nach'ehwa 나체화; ***in the ~*** nach'ero 나체로

nudge *v/t* p'alkkumch'iro k'ukk'uk tchirŭda 팔꿈치로 쿡쿡 찌르다

nudist *n* nach'ejuŭija 나체주의자

nuisance kwich'anŭn kŏt 귀찮은 것; ***make a ~ of oneself*** namege p'yerŭl kkich'ida 남에게 폐를 끼치다; ***what a ~!*** irŏk'e kwich'anŭl suga! 이렇게 귀찮을 수가!

nuke *v/t* haek konggyŏk'ada 핵 공격하다

null and void muhyoŭi 무효의

numb kamgagŏmnŭn 감각없는; (*emotionally*) mugamgak'an 무감각한

number 1 *n* (*figure, quantity*) su 수; (*of hotel room, house, phone ~ etc*) pŏnho 번호; ***quite a ~ of*** manŭn 많은; ***a small ~ of*** chŏgŭn 적은 **2** *v/t* (*put a number on*) pŏnhorŭl maegida 번호를 매기다

numeral sutcha 숫자

numerate kyesanŭl hal su innŭn 계산을 할 수 있는

numeric keys COMPUT sutchap'an 숫자판

numerous manŭn 많은

nun sunyŏ 수녀

nurse kanhosa 간호사

nursery yugashil 육아실; (*for plants*) onshil 온실

nursery rhyme tongnyo 동요; **nursery school** poyugwŏn 보육원; **nursery school teacher** poyugwŏn

kyosa 보육원 교사
nursing kanho ŏmmu 간호 업무
nursing home (*for old people*) yangnowŏn 양로원
nut kyŏn-gwa 견과; (*for bolt*) nŏt'ŭ 너트; **~s** F (*testicles*) pural 불알
nutcrackers hodu kkanŭn kigu 호두 까는 기구
nutrient yŏngnyangbun 영양분
nutrition yŏngnyang 영양
nutritious yŏngnyang-i innŭn 영양이 있는
nuts *adj* F (*crazy*) mich'in 미친; ***be ~ about s.o.*** nugue mich'ida 누구에 미치다
nutshell: ***in a ~*** aju kanttanhage 아주 간단하게
nutty *taste* kyŏn-gwa mashi nanŭn 견과 맛이 나는; F (*crazy*) mich'in 미친
nylon 1 *n* naillon 나일론 **2** *adj* naillonŭi 나일론의

O

oak (*tree*) ok'ŭnamu 오크나무; (*wood*) ok'ŭ 오크
oar no 노
oasis oashissŭ 오아시스; *fig* hyushikch'ŏ 휴식처
oath LAW sŏnsŏ 선서; (*swearword*) yokssŏl 욕설; ***you are on ~*** tangshinŭn sŏnsŏrŭl haessŭmnida 당신을 선서를 했습니다
oatmeal ot'ŭmil 오트밀
oats kwiri 귀리
obedience sunjong 순종
obedient sunjonghanŭn 순종하는
obey ...e sunjonghada ...에 순종하다
obituary *n* pugo 부고
object[1] *n* (*thing*) mulch'e 물체; (*of love, pity*) taesang 대상; (*aim*) moktchŏk 목적; GRAM moktchŏgŏ 목적어
object[2] *v/i* pandaehada 반대하다
♦**object to** ...e pandaehada ...에 반대하다
objection pandae 반대
objectionable (*unpleasant*) pulk'waehan 불쾌한
objective 1 *adj* kaekkwanjŏgin 객관적인 **2** *n* mokp'yo 목표
obligation ŭimu 의무; ***be under an ~ to s.o.*** nuguege ŭnhyerŭl ipkko it-tta 누구에게 은혜를 입고 있다
obligatory ŭimuŭi 의무의
oblige: ***much ~d!*** chŏngmal komawŏyo! 정말 고마워요!
obliging chal tolbwajunŭn 잘 돌봐주는
oblique 1 *adj reference* kanjŏptchŏgin 간접적인 **2** *n* (*in punctuation*) pitkkŭm 빗금
obliterate *city* wanjŏnhi p'agoehada 완전히 파괴하다; *memory* chiuda 지우다
oblivion ich'yŏjin sangt'ae 잊혀진 상태; ***fall into ~*** ich'yŏjida 잊혀지다
oblivious: ***be ~ of*** ...ŭl/rŭl arach'ariji mot'ada ...을/를 알아차리지 못하다
oblong *adj* chikssagak'yŏng-ŭi 직사각형의
obnoxious aju pulk'waehan 아주 불쾌한
obscene ŭmnanhan 음란한; *poverty* kkŭmtchik'an 끔찍한
obscure (*hard to see*) chal poiji annŭn 잘 보이지 않는; (*hard to understand*) nanhaehan 난해한; (*little known*) mumyŏng-ŭi 무명의
observance (*of festival*) haengsa 행사
observant kwanch'allyŏgi yerihan 관찰력이 예리한
observation (*of nature*) kwanch'al 관찰; (*comment*) kwanch'al kyŏlgwa 관찰 결과
observatory kwanch'ŭksso 관측소
observe (*notice*) nunch'ich'aeda 눈치채다; *natural phenomena* kwanch'arhada 관찰하다; ***he was ~d leaving the ...*** kŭga ...ŭl/rŭl ttŏnanŭn kŏshi mok-kkyŏkttoeŏt-tta 그가 ...을/를 떠나는 것이 목격되었다
observer kwanch'altcha 관찰자; (*at conference, elections*) ip'oein 입회인
obsess: ***be ~ed with*** ...e(ge) sarojap'ida ...에(게) 사로잡히다
obsession kangbak kwannyŏm 강박 관념
obsessive kangbak kwanyŏme sarojap'in 강박 관념에 사로잡힌
obsolete p'yemuri toen 폐물이 된
obstacle chang-ae 장애; (*to progress etc*) panghae 방해
obstetrician sanbuinkkwa ŭisa 산부인과 의사
obstinacy kojip 고집
obstinate kojibi sen 고집이 센
obstruct *road, passage* maktta 막다; *investigation, police* panghaehada 방해하다
obstruction (*on road etc*)

panghaemul 방해물
obstructive *tactics* panghaehanŭn 방해하는
obtain hoekttŭk'ada 획득하다; *advice* ŏt-tta 얻다
obtainable *products* kuibi kanŭnghan 구입이 가능한
obvious myŏngbaek'an 명백한; (*not subtle*) nogoltchŏgin 노골적인
obviously myŏngbaek'age 명백하게; *~!* mullonijiyo! 물론이지요!
occasion ttae 때
occasional kakkŭmŭi 가끔의
occasionally ttaettaero 때때로
occult 1 *adj* mabŏbŭi 마법의 **2** *n*: ***the ~*** mabŏp 마법
occupant (*of vehicle*) sŭnggaek 승객; (*of house*) chugŏja 주거자
occupation (*job*) chigŏp 직업; (*of country*) chŏmnyŏng 점령
occupy ch'ajihada 차지하다; *country* chŏmnyŏnghada 점령하다
occur irŏnada 일어나다; ***it ~red to me that ...*** na-ege ...ranŭn saenggagi ttollat-tta 나에게 ...라는 생각이 떠올랐다
occurrence sakkŏn 사건
ocean pada 바다
o'clock: ***at five / six ~*** tasŏt / yŏsot shie 다섯 / 여섯 시에
October shiwŏl 시월
octopus munŏ 문어; (*very small*) naktchi 낙지
odd (*strange*) isanghan 이상한; (*not even*) holssu 홀수; ***the ~ one out*** (*person*) yubyŏlnan saram 유별난 사람; (*thing*) yubyŏlnan kŏt 유별난 것
odds: ***be at ~ with*** ...wa / kwa ch'ungdorhada ...와 / 과 충돌하다
odds and ends chapttongsani 잡동사니; (*to do*) chapttahan kŏttŭl 잡다한 것들
odometer chuhaeng kŏrigye 주행 거리계
odor naemsae 냄새
of (*possession*) ...ŭi ...의; ***the color ~ the car*** kŭ ch'aŭi saek 그 차의 색; ***the works ~ Dickens*** Tik'insŭŭi chakp'um 디킨스의 작품; ***five / ten minutes ~ twelve*** yŏldushi obun / shippun jŏn 열두시 오분 / 십분 전; ***die ~ cancer / pneumonia*** amŭro / p'yeryŏmŭro chuktta 암으로 / 폐렴으로 죽다; ***love ~ money / adventure*** tone / mohŏme taehan sarang 돈에 / 모험에 대한 사랑; ***~ the three this is ...*** set chung-e igŏshi ...ida 셋 중에 이것이 ...이다
off 1 *prep* ...esŏ ttŏrŏjyŏsŏ ...에서 떨어져서; ***~ the main road*** (*away from*) chudoroesŏ ttŏrŏjyŏ 주도로에서 떨어져; (*leading off*) chudoroesŏ pŏsŏna 주도로에서 벗어나; ***$20 ~ the price*** 20tallŏ harinhayŏ 20달러 할인하여; ***he's ~ his food*** kŭnŭn immasŭl irŏt-tta 그는 입맛을 잃었다 **2** *adv*: ***be ~*** (*of light, TV, machine*) kkŏjyŏ it-tta 꺼져 있다; (*of brake*) p'ullyŏ it-tta 풀려 있다; (*of lid*) yŏllyŏ it-tta 열려 있다; (*not at work*) shwida 쉬다; (*canceled*) ch'wisodoeda 취소되다; ***we're ~ tomorrow*** (*leaving*) urinŭn naeil ttŏnanda 우리는 내일 떠난다; ***I'm ~ to New York*** nanŭn Nyuyoge kal kŏshida 나는 뉴욕에 갈 것이다; ***with his pants / hat ~*** pajirŭl / mojarŭl pŏsŭnch'ae 바지를 / 모자를 벗은채; ***take a day ~*** haru shwida 하루 쉬다; ***it's 3 miles ~*** 3mail ttŏrŏjyŏ it-tta 3마일 떨어져 있다; ***it's a long way ~*** (*in the distance*) mŏlli ttŏrojyŏ it-tta 멀리 떨어져 있다; (*in the future*) mŏn amnarŭi irida 먼 앞날의 일이다; ***drive / walk ~*** ch'arŭl molgo / kŏrŏsŏ ka pŏrida 차를 몰고 / 걸어서 가 버리다 **3** *adj*: ***the ~ switch*** chŏngji pŏt'ŭn 정지 버튼
offend *v/t* (*insult*) kibun sanghage hada 기분 상하게 하다
offender LAW pŏmjoeja 범죄자
offense LAW wibŏp 위법
offensive 1 *adj* pulk'waehan 불쾌한 **2** *n* MIL konggyŏk 공격; ***go onto the ~*** konggyŏk'ada 공격하다
offer 1 *n* chegong 제공 **2** *v/t* chegonghada 제공하다; ***~ s.o. sth*** nuguege muŏsŭl kwŏnhada 누구에게 무엇을 권하다
offhand *adj attitude* amurŏk'ena

hanŭn 아무렇게나 하는
office (*building*) samushillyong kŏnmul 사무실용 건물; (*room*) samushil 사무실; (*position*) kwanch'ŏng 관청
office block samushillyong koch'ŭng piltting 사무실용 고층 빌딩
office hours ŏmmu shigan 업무 시간
officer MIL changgyo 장교; (*in police*) kyŏnggwan 경관
official 1 *adj organization, statement* kongshigŭi 공식의; *view, theory* kongtchŏgin 공적인; (*confirmed*) kongshik'wadoen 공식화된 **2** *n* kongmuwŏn 공무원
officially (*strictly speaking*) kongshiktchŏgŭro 공식적으로
off-line *adj* chŏpssogŭl anhan sangt'aeŭi 접속을 안한 상태의; ***go ~*** chŏpssogŭl kkŭnt'a 접속을 끊다
off-peak *rates* hansanhan ttaeŭi 한산한 때의; *season* pisugiŭi 비수기의
off-season 1 *adj* pisugiŭi 비수기의 **2** *n* pisugi 비수기
offset *v/t losses* sangswaehada 상쇄하다
offside 1 *adj wheel etc* ch'ado tchogŭi 차도 쪽의 **2** *adv* SP op'ŭsaidŭ 오프사이드
offspring chashik 자식
off-white *adj* misaegŭi 미색의
often chaju 자주
oil 1 *n* kirŭm 기름; (*for machine*) sŏgyu 석유; (*for skin*) oil 오일 **2** *v/t hinges, bearings* kirŭmch'irŭl hada 기름칠을 하다
oil company sŏgyu hoesa 석유 회사; **oil painting** yuhwa 유화; **oil rig** sŏgyu kulch'ak changch'i 석유 굴착 장치; **oil tanker** yujosŏn 유조선; **oil well** yujŏng 유정
oily kirŭmkki manŭn 기름기 많은
ointment yŏn-go 연고
ok: ***can I? - ~*** haedo toelkkayo? - kŭraeyo 해도 될까요? - 그래요; ***is it ~ with you if ...?*** ... haedo kwaench'angessŭmnikka? ... 해도 괜찮겠습니까?; ***that's ~ by me*** nanŭn kwaench'anayo 나는 괜찮아요; ***are you ~?*** (*well, not hurt*) kwaench'anŭseyo? 괜찮으세요?; ***are you ~ for Friday?*** kŭmnyoire kwaench'anŭseyo? 금요일에 괜찮으세요?; ***he's ~*** (*is a good guy*) kŭnŭn kwaench'anŭn saramida 그는 괜찮은 사람이다; ***is this bus ~ for ...?*** i pŏssŭ ...e kamnikka? 이 버스 ...에 갑니까?; ***the car's going ~ now*** ch'aga ijenŭn chal kanda 차가 이제는 잘 간다
old *person* nŭlgŭn 늙은; *building, car etc* oraedoen 오래된; *custom* oraen 오랜; (*previous*) yejŏnŭi 예전의; (*no longer fresh*) nalgŭn 낡은; ***how ~ are you / is he?*** tangshinŭn / kŭnŭn myŏtssarimnikka? 당신은 / 그는 몇살입니까?
old age nonyŏn 노년
Old Choson Kojosŏn 고조선
old-fashioned kushigŭi 구식의
olive ollibŭ 올리브
olive oil ollibŭ kirŭm 올리브 기름
Olympic Games Ollimp'ik Keim 올림픽 게임
omelet omŭllet 오믈렛
ominous pulgirhan 불길한
omission (*act*) t'aeman 태만; (*that omitted*) ppajin kŏt 빠진 것
omit ppaeda 빼다; ***~ to do sth*** muŏsŭl hagirŭl it-tta 무엇을 하기를 잊다
on 1 *prep* ... wie ... 위에; ***~ the table*** t'eibŭl wie 테이블 위에; ***~ the wall*** pyŏge 벽에; ***~ the bus / train*** pŏsŭe / kich'a-e 버스에 / 기차에; ***~ TV / the radio*** t'ibŭiro / radioro TV로 / 라디오로; ***~ Sunday*** iryoire 일요일에; ***~ the 1st of ...*** ...ŭi ch'ŏtchaenare ..의 첫째날에; ***this is ~ me*** (*I'm paying*) chega naegessŭmnida 제가 내겠습니다; ***~ his arrival / departure*** kŭga toch'ak'aja / ch'ulbarhaja kot 그가 도착하자 / 출발하자 곧 **2** *adv* ***be ~*** (*of light, TV, computer etc*) k'yŏjyŏ it-tta 켜져 있다; (*of brake*) kŏllyŏ it-tta 걸려 있다; (*of lid, top*) tach'yŏ it-tta 닫혀 있다; (*of program*) pangsongdoeda 방송되다; (*of meeting etc: be scheduled to happen*) itkket-tta 있겠다; ***what's ~ tonight?***

(*on TV etc*) onŭrŭn muŏsŭl hamnikka? 오늘은 무엇을 합니까?; (*what's planned?*) onŭrŭn muŏsŭl hal kŏsimnikka? 오늘은 무엇을 할 것입니까?; ***with his jacket / hat ~*** oet'urŭl ipkko / mojarŭl ssŭgo 외투를 입고 / 모자를 쓰고; ***you're ~*** (*I accept your offer etc*) chossŭmnida 좋습니다; ***~ you go*** (*go ahead*) kyesok'ahipsshio 계속하십시오; ***walk / talk ~*** kyesok kŏt-tta / iyagi hada 계속 걷다 / 이야기 하다; ***and so ~*** kit'adŭngdŭng 기타 등등; ***~ and ~ talk etc*** kkŭnimŏpsshi kyesok'aesŏ 끊임없이 계속해서 **3** *adj*: ***the ~ switch*** shijak pŏt'ŭn 시작 버튼

once 1 *adv* (*one time*) han pŏn 한 번; (*formerly*) hanttaee 한때에; ***~ again, ~ more*** tashi han pŏn 다시 한 번; ***at ~*** (*immediately*) chŭksshi 즉시; ***all at ~*** (*suddenly*) kaptchagi 갑자기; ***(all) at ~*** (*together*) hankkŏbŏne 한꺼번에; ***~ upon a time there was ...*** yennal yettchŏge ... i issŏt-tta 옛날 옛적에 ... 이 있었다 **2** *conj*: ...hal ttae ...할 때; ***~ you have finished*** nega ta kkŭnnaessŭl ttae 네가 다 끝냈을 때

one 1 (*number*) hana 하나, il 일 **2** *adj* hanaŭi 하나의; ***~ day*** ŏnŭ nal 어느 날 **3** *pron* hana 하나; ***which ~?*** (*person*) ŏnŭ saram? 어느 사람?; (*thing*) ŏnŭ kŏt? 어느 것?; ***~ by ~*** *enter, deal with* hanasshik 하나씩; ***~ another*** sŏro 서로; ***what can ~ say / do?*** nuga muŏsŭl marhal / hal su itkketssŭmnikka? 누가 무엇을 말할 / 할 수 있겠습니까?; ***the little ~s*** aidŭl 아이들

one-off *n* (*unique event, person*) yuirhan kŏt 유일한 것; (*exception*) yeoeŏpsshi han pŏn ppunin kŏt 예외없이 한 번 뿐인 것

one-parent family p'yŏnch'in kajŏng 편친 가정

oneself chagi chashin 자기 자신; ***do sth by ~*** muŏsŭl sŭsŭro hada 무엇을 스스로 하다

one-sided *discussion, fight* ilbangjŏgin 일방적인; **one-way street** ilbang t'onghaengno 일방통행로; **one-way ticket** p'yŏndo sŭngch'akkwŏn 편도 승차권

onion yangp'a 양파

on-line *adj* ollainŭi 온라인의; ***go ~ to*** ...wa / kwa chŏpssok'ada ...와 / 과 접속하다

on-line service COMPUT ollain sŏbissŭ 온라인 서비스

onlooker kugyŏngkkun 구경꾼

only 1 *adv* tanji 단지; ***not ~ X but Y also*** Xppunman anira Ydo ttohan X뿐만 아니라 Y도 또한; ***~ just*** kanshinhi 간신히, kyŏu 겨우 **2** *adj* yuirhan 유일한; ***~ son*** oeadŭl 외아들; ***~ daughter*** oedongttal 외동딸

onset shijak 시작

onside *adv* SP chŏnggyuŭi wich'ie 정규의 위치에

onto: ***put X ~ Y*** (*on top of*) Xŭl / rŭl Ywie not'a X을 / 를 Y위에 놓다

onward ap'ŭro 앞으로; ***from ... ~*** ...esŏbut'ŏ ...에서부터

ooze 1 *v/i* (*of liquid, mud*) sŭmyŏnaoda 스며나오다 **2** *v/t*: ***he ~s charm*** kŭegenŭn nŏmch'yŏnanŭn maeryŏgi it-tta 그에게는 넘쳐나는 매력이 있다

opaque *glass* pult'umyŏnghan 불투명한

OPEC (= ***Organization of Petroleum Exporting Countries***) Sŏgyu Such'ulguk Kigu 석유 수출국 기구

open 1 *adj door, shop, window* yŏllyŏ innŭn 열려 있는; *flower* p'in 핀; COMPUT *file* yŏllin 열린; (*honest, frank*) sumgimŏmnŭn 숨김없는; *market, society* kaebangdoen 개방된; *relationship* sŏro kusok'aji annŭn 서로 구속하지 않는; *countryside* hwŏnhi t'ŭin 훤히 트인; ***in the ~ air*** yaoeesŏ 야외에서 **2** *v/t also* COMPUT *file* yŏlda 열다; *book, paper* p'ida 피다; *bank account* t'ŭda 트다; *meeting* shijak'ada 시작하다 **3** *v/i* (*of door, shop*) yŏllida 열리다; (*of flower*) p'ida 피다

♦ **open up** *v/i* (*of person*) songmaŭmŭl t'ŏnot'a 속마음을 터놓다

open-air *adj meeting, concert* yaoeŭi 야외의; *pool* ogoeŭi 옥외의

open-ended *contract etc* handoga ŏmnŭn 한도가 없는
opening (*in wall etc*) t'ŭm 틈; (*of movie, novel etc*) appubun 앞부분; (*job going*) kongsŏk 공석
openly (*honestly, frankly*) sumgimŏpsshi 숨김없이
open-minded hŏshimt'anhoehan 허심탄회한; **open plan office** op'ŭn p'ŭllaen samushil 오픈 플랜 사무실, *kubunŏpsshi yŏrŏshi hamkke ssŭnŭn samushil* 구분없이 여럿이 함께 쓰는 사무실; **open ticket** op'ŭnt'ik'et 오픈티켓, *sayong-irŭl chehanhaji annŭn p'yo* 사용일을 제한하지 않은 표
opera op'era 오페라
opera glasses op'era mang-wŏn-gyŏng 오페라 망원경; **opera house** op'era haussŭ 오페라 하우스; **opera singer** op'era kasu 오페라 가수
operate 1 *v/i* (*of company*) unyŏngdoeda 운영되다; (*of airline etc*) chojongdoeda 조종되다; (*of machine*) chakttonghada 작동하다; MED susurŭl hada 수술을 하다 **2** *v/t machine* chojonghada 조종하다
♦**operate on** MED susurhada 수술하다
operating instructions sayongppŏp 사용법; **operating room** MED susulshil 수술실; **operating system** COMPUT op'ŏreit'ing shisŭt'em 오퍼레이팅 시스템
operation MED susul 수술; (*of machine*) chojong 조종; **~s** (*of company*) unyŏng 운영; ***have an ~*** MED susurŭl pat-tta 수술을 받다
operator TELEC kyohwansu 교환수; (*of machine*) kisa 기사; (*tour ~*) kwan-gwang-ŏptcha 관광업자
ophthalmologist an-kkwa ŭisa 안과 의사
opinion ŭigyŏn 의견; ***in my ~*** naŭi ŭigyŏnŭronŭn 나의 의견으로는
opponent (*in game*) sangdae 상대; (*of tax reforms etc*) pandaeja 반대자
opportunity kihoe 기회
oppose pandaehada 반대하다; ***be ~d to*** ...e pandaehada ...에 반대하다; ***as ~d to*** ...wa / kwa pandaero ...와 / 과 반대로
opposite 1 *adj side, direction, meaning* pandaeŭi 반대의; *views, characters* sangbandoen 상반된; ***the ~ sex*** isŏng 이성 **2** *n* pandae 반대
opposition (*to plan*) pandae 반대; POL yadang 야당
oppress *the people* appak'ada 압박하다
oppressive *rule* kahok'an 가혹한; *dictator* p'oak'an 포악한; *weather* uurhagehanŭn 우울하게하는
optical illusion ch'aksshi 착시
optician an-gyŏngsang 안경상
optimism nakch'ŏnjuŭi 낙천주의
optimist nakch'ŏnjuŭija 낙천주의자
optimistic *attitude, person* nakch'ŏnjŏgin 낙천적인; *view, speech* nakkwanjŏgin 낙관적인
optimum 1 *adj* ch'oejŏgŭi 최적의 **2** *n* ch'oejŏk 최적
option sŏnt'aek-kkwŏn 선택권
optional sŏnt'aegŭi 선택의
optional extras opsshŏn sangp'um 옵션 상품
or hogŭn 혹은, ttonŭn 또는; ***~ else!*** kŭroch'i anŭmyŏn! 그렇지 않으면!
oral *exam* kusurŭi 구술의; *hygiene* kugang-ŭi 구강의; ***~ sex*** oral sekssŭ 오랄 섹스
orange 1 *adj* (*color*) chuhwangsaegŭi 주황색의 **2** *n* (*fruit*) orenji 오렌지; (*color*) chuhwangsaek 주황색
orange juice orenji chusŭ 오렌지 쥬스
orator yŏnsŏlga 연설가
orbit 1 *n* (*of earth*) kwedo 궤도; ***send sth into ~*** muŏsŭl kwedo-e ollida 무엇을 궤도에 올리다 **2** *v/t* kongjŏnhada 공전하다
orchard kwasuwŏn 과수원
orchestra ok'esŭt'ŭra 오케스트라
orchid nanch'o 난초
ordeal shiryŏn 시련
order 1 *n* (*command*) myŏngnyŏng 명령; (*sequence*) sunsŏ 순서; (*being well arranged*) paeyŏl 배열; (*for goods, in restaurant*) chumun 주문; ***in ~ to*** ... hagi wihayŏ ... 하기 위하여; ***out of ~*** (*not functioning*) kojangnan 고장난; (*not in sequence*)

sunsŏga pakkwin 순서가 바뀐 **2** *v/t* (*put in sequence*, *layout*) sunsŏdaero chŏngnihada 순서대로 정리하다; *goods*, *meal* chumunhada 주문하다; **~ *s.o. to do sth*** nuguege muŏsŭl harago myŏngnyŏnghada 누구에게 무엇을 하라고 명령하다 **3** *v/i* (*in restaurant*) chumunhada 주문하다
orderly 1 *adj lifestyle* parŭn 바른 **2** *n* (*in hospital*) pyŏng-wŏnŭi chabyŏkppu 병원의 잡역부
ordinary pot'ong-ŭi 보통의
ore kwangsŏk 광석
organ ANAT chojik 조직; MUS orŭgan 오르간
organic *food* yugi nongppŏbŭi 유기 농법의; *fertilizer* yugiŭi 유기의
organism saengmul 생물
organization kigu 기구; (*organizing*) chojik 조직
organize chojik'ada 조직하다
organizer (*person*) chojiktcha 조직자
orgasm orŭgajŭm 오르가즘
Orient Tongnyang 동양
orient *v/t*: ***the teacher ~ed me toward …*** sŏnsaengnimi naŭi kwanshimŭl … tchogŭro ikkŭro chuŏt-tta 선생님이 나의 관심을 … 쪽으로 이끌어 주었다; **~ *oneself*** (*get bearings*) chagi wich'irŭl ttokpparo alda 자기 위치를 똑바로 알다
Oriental 1 *adj* tongnyang-ŭi 동양의 **2** *n* Tongnyang saram 동양 사람
origin kiwŏn 기원; ***person of Chinese ~*** Chunggugesŏ on saram 중국에서 온 사람
original 1 *adj* (*not copied*) chintchaŭi 진짜의; (*first*) ch'oech'oŭi 최초의 **2** *n* (*painting etc*) wŏnjak 원작
originality tokch'angssŏng 독창성
originally wŏllaenŭn 원래는; (*at first*) ch'ŏŭmenŭn 처음에는
originate 1 *v/t scheme*, *idea* shijak'ada 시작하다 **2** *v/i* (*of idea*, *belief*) pirot'ada 비롯하다; (*of family*) ch'ulsshinida 출신이다
originator (*of scheme etc*) ch'angshija 창시자; ***he's not an ~*** kŭnŭn ch'angŭijŏgin sarami anida 그는 창의적인 사람이 아니다
ornament *n* changsshikp'um 장식품
ornamental changshingnyong-ŭi 장식용의
ornate *style*, *architecture* hwaryŏhage changshik'an 화려하게 장식한
orphan *n* koa 고아
orphanage koawŏn 고아원
orthopedic chŏnghyŏng oekkwaŭi 정형 외과의
ostentatious kwashihanŭn 과시하는
other 1 *adj* tarŭn 다른; ***the ~ day*** (*recently*) chinan pŏne 지난 번에; ***every ~ day*** haru kŏnnŏ 하루 건너; ***every ~ person*** han myŏng kŏnnŏ 한 명 건너 **2** *n* (*thing*) tarŭn hanaŭi kŏt 다른 하나의 것; (*person*) tarŭn han myŏng 다른 한 명; ***the ~s*** (*objects*) namŏji kŏt 나머지 것; (*people*) namŏji saram 나머지 사람
otherwise kŭrŏch'i anŭmyŏn 그렇지 않으면; (*differently*) tarŭge 다르게
otter sudal 수달
ought ...haeya hada ...해야 하다; ***I / you ~ to know ...*** nanŭn / nŏnŭn ...ŭl / rŭl araya handa 나는 / 너는 ...을 / 를 알아야 한다; ***you ~ to have done it*** nŏnŭn kŭgŏsŭl haessŏya haet-tta 너는 그것을 했어야 했다
ounce onsŭ 온스
our uriŭi 우리의
ours uriŭi kŏt 우리의 것; ***an idea of ~*** uri saenggak 우리 생각
ourselves uri chashin 우리 자신; ***by ~*** uri chashinŭro 우리 자신으로
oust (*from office*) naetchot-tta 내쫓다
out: ***be ~*** (*of light*, *fire*) kkŏjyŏ it-tta 꺼져 있다; (*of flower*, *sun*) chyŏ it-tta 져 있다; (*not at home*, *not in building*) ŏptta 없다; (*of calculations*) t'ŭllida 틀리다; (*be published*) ch'ulp'andoeda 출판되다; (*of secret*) t'allonada 탄로나다; (*no longer in competition*) t'allak'ada 탈락하다; (*no longer in fashion*) yuhaeng-e twijida 유행에 뒤지다; ***~ here in Dallas*** i kot Tallasŭesŏ 이 곳 달라스에서; ***he's ~ in the garden*** kŭnŭn chŏng-wŏne nagait-tta 그는 정원에 나가있다; (***get***) ***~!*** nagaseyo! 나가세요!; (***get***) ***~ of my room!*** naebang-esŏ nagaseyo! 내

방에서 나가세요!; ***that's ~!*** (*out of the question*) maldo andoenda! 말도 안된다!; ***he's ~ to win*** (*fully intending to*) kŭnŭn igigoja handa 그는 이기고자 한다
outboard motor sŏnoe mot'ŏ 선외 모터
outbreak (*of violence, war*) tolbal 돌발
outburst kamjŏng-ŭi p'okppal 감정의 폭발
outcast so-oeja 소외자
outcome kyŏlkkwa 결과
outcry kangnyŏrhan hang-ŭi 강렬한 항의
outdated kushigŭi 구식의
outdo poda tŏ charhada 보다 더 잘하다
outdoor *toilet, activities, life* yaoeŭi 야외의
outdoors *adv* yaoeesŏ 야외에서
outer *wall etc* oebuŭi 외부의
outer space uju 우주
outfit (*clothes*) ŭisang 의상; (*company, organization*) chojik 조직
outgoing *flight* ttŏnaganŭn 떠나가는; *personality* oehyangtchŏgin 외향적인
outgrow *old ideas* pŏsŏnada 벗어나다
outing (*trip*) sop'ung 소풍
outlet (*of pipe*) paech'ulgu 배출구; (*for sales*) maejang 매장; ELEC sok'et 소켓
outline 1 *n* (*of person, building etc*) yun-gwak 윤곽; (*of plan, novel*) kaeyo 개요 **2** *v/t plans etc* ...ŭi yun-gwagŭl chaptta ...의 윤곽을 잡다
outlive poda tŏ orae salda 보다 더 오래 살다
outlook (*prospects*) chŏnmang 전망
outlying *areas* oejin 외진
outnumber poda suga mant'a 보다 수가 많다
out of ◊ (*motion*) ...esŏ pakkŭro ...에서 밖으로; ***run ~ the house*** chibesŏ pakkŭro tallyŏnaoda 집에서 밖으로 달려나오다 ◊ (*position*) ...(ŭ)robut'ŏ ttŏrŏjin ...(으)로부터 떨어진; ***20 miles ~ Detroit*** Tit'ŭroit'ŭro put'ŏ 20mail ttŏrŏjin 디트로이트로 부터 20마일 떨어진 ◊ (*cause*) ttaemune 때문에; ***~ jealousy / curiosity*** chilt'ushim / hogishim ttaemune 질투심 / 호기심 때문에 ◊ (*without*) ta ttŏrŏjin 다 떨어진; ***we're ~ beer*** urinŭn maektchuga ta ttŏrŏjyŏt-tta 우리는 맥주가 다 떨어졌다; ***we're ~ gas*** urinŭn hwiballyuga ta ttŏrŏjyŏt-tta 우리는 휘발유가 다 떨어졌다 ◊ (*from a group*): ***5 ~ 10*** yŏl chung tasŏt 10중 5
out-of-date kushigŭi 구식의
out-of-the-way oejin 외진
outperform poda ttwiŏnada 보다 뛰어나다
output 1 *n* (*of factory*) saengsan 생산; COMPUT ch'ullyŏk 출력 **2** *v/t* (*produce*) saengsanhada 생산하다; COMPUT *signal* ch'ullyŏk'ada 출력하다
outrage 1 *n* (*feeling*) pun-gae 분개; (*act*) p'ongnyŏk 폭력 **2** *v/t* maeu hwanage hada 매우 화나게 하다; ***I was ~d to hear ...*** nanŭn ...ŭl / rŭl tŭtkko mopsshi hwaga nat-tta 나는 ...을 / 를 듣고 몹시 화가 났다
outrageous *acts* p'ongnyŏktchŏgin 폭력적인; *prices* t'ŏmuniŏmnŭn 터무니없는
outright 1 *adj winner* wanjŏnhan 완전한 **2** *adv win* wanjŏnhi 완전히; *kill* chŭksshi 즉시
outrun poda ppalli tallida 보다 빨리 달리다
outset shijak 시작; ***from the ~*** shijak'al ttaebut'ŏ 시작할 때부터
outside 1 *adj surface, wall, lane* pakkach'ŭi 바깥의 **2** *adv sit* pakkat'e 바깥에; *go* pakkŭro 밖으로 **3** *prep* ...ŭi pakke ...의 밖에; (*apart from*) ... oeŭi ... 외의; ***~ Seoul*** Sŏul oegwage 서울 외곽에 **4** *n* (*of building, case etc*) pakkat myŏn 바깥 면; ***at the ~*** ch'oedaehanŭro 최대한으로
outside broadcast sŭt'yudio pakkŭi pangsong 스튜디오 밖의 방송
outsider oebusaram 외부사람
outsize *adj clothing* t'ŭkttaehyŏng-ŭi 특대형의
outskirts pyŏnduri 변두리
outspoken soltchik'an 솔직한

outstanding t'ŭkch'urhan 특출한; FIN *invoice, sums* miburŭi 미불의
outward *adj appearance* oegwanŭi 외관의; ~ ***journey*** ttŏnanŭn yŏhaeng 떠나는 여행
outwardly kŏt'ŭronŭn 겉으로는
outweigh poda chungnyohada 보다 중요하다
outwit sŏnsuch'ida 선수치다
oval *adj* talgyarhyŏng-ŭi 달걀형의
ovary (*of animals, people*) nanso 난소
oven obŭn 오븐
over 1 *prep* (*above*) ...ŭi witchoge ...의 윗쪽에; (*across*) ...ŭi chŏtchok p'yŏne ...의 저쪽 편에; (*more than*) poda tŏ 보다 더; (*during*) tong-ane 동안에; ***travel all ~ Korea*** Han-guk chŏnyŏgŭl yŏhaenghada 한국 전역을 여행하다; ***you find them all ~ Korea*** kŭgŏsŭn Han-guk ŏdiena it-tta 그것은 한국 어디에나 있다; ***let's talk ~ a drink / meal*** mashimyŏnsŏ / mŏgŭmyŏnsŏ iyagihapsshida 마시면서 / 먹으면서 이야기합시다; ***we're ~ the worst*** urinŭn ch'oeagŭi sanghwang-ŭl nŏmgyŏt-tta 우리는 최악의 상황을 넘겼다 **2** *adv*: ***be ~*** (*finished*) kkŭnnada 끝나다; (*left*) namtta 남다; ~ ***to you*** (*your turn*) nŏŭi ch'arye 너의 차례; ~ ***in Europe*** Yurŏbesŏnŭn 유럽에서는; ~ ***here / there*** yŏgie / chŏgie 여기에 / 저기에; ***it hurts all ~*** onmomi ssushida 온몸이 쑤시다; ***painted white all ~*** chŏnbu hayak'e p'eit'ŭ ch'irhaejin 전부 하얗게 페인트 칠해진; ***it's all ~*** ta kkŭnnat-tta 다 끝났다; ~ ***and ~ again*** myŏtppŏnigo toep'urihaesŏ 몇번이고 되풀이해서; ***do sth ~ (again)*** muŏsŭl tashi toep'urihada 무엇을 다시 되풀이하다
overall 1 *adj length* chŏnch'eŭi 전체의 **2** *adv modify* chŏnbanjŏgin 전반적인
overawe: ***be ~d by s.o. / sth*** nuguege / muŏse kŏmmŏktta 누구에게 / 무엇에 겁먹다
overboard: ***man ~!*** sarami ppajyŏt-tta! 사람이 빠졌다!; ***go ~ for s.o. / sth*** nuguege / muŏsege ppajida 누구에게 / 무엇에게 빠지다
overcast *day, sky* hŭrin 흐린
overcharge *v/t customer* pagaji ssŭiuda 바가지 씌우다
overcoat oet'u 외투
overcome *difficulties* kŭkppok'ada 극복하다; ***be ~ by emotion*** kamjŏng-ŭl ŏngnurŭji mot'ada 감정을 억누르지 못하다
overcrowded nŏmu honjap'an 너무 혼잡한
overdo (*exaggerate*) chinach'ige hada 지나치게 하다; (*in cooking*) nŏmu ik'ida 너무 익히다; ***you're ~ing things*** tangshinŭn irŭl chinach'ige hanŭn-gunnyo 당신은 일을 지나치게 하는군요
overdone *meat* chinach'ige ik'in 지나치게 익힌
overdose *n* kwaing pogyong 과잉 복용
overdraft chanaegŭl ch'ogwahanŭn inch'ul 잔액을 초과하는 인출; ***have an ~*** chanaekppoda tŏ inch'urhada 잔액보다 더 인출하다
overdraw *account* …esŏ chanaekppoda tŏ inch'ulshik'ida …에서 잔액보다 더 인출시키다; ***be $800 ~n*** chanaekppoda p'albaektallŏrŭl tŏ inch'ulshik'ida 잔액보다 800달러를 더 인출시키다
overdrive MOT obŏdŭraibŭ 오버드라이브
overdue *apology, change* nŭjŭn 늦은
overestimate *abilities, value* kwadae p'yŏngkkahada 과대 평가하다
overexpose *photograph* chinach'ige noch'urhada 지나치게 노출하다
overflow 1 *n* (*pipe*) nŏmch'im 넘침 **2** *v/i* (*of water*) nŏmch'ida 넘치다
overgrown *garden* musŏnghan 무성한; ***he's an ~ baby*** kŭnŭn aich'ŏrŏm kunda 그는 아이처럼 군다
overhaul *v/t engine* chŏngmil kŏmsahada 정밀 검사하다; *plans* chŏngmilkŏmt'ohada 정밀 검토하다
overhead 1 *adj lights* mŏri wiesŏ 머리 위에서; *railroad* kokkaŭi 고가의 **2** *n* FIN kanjŏppi 간접비
overhear uyŏnhi tŭt-tta 우연히 듣다
overjoyed taedanhi kippŭn 대단히 기쁜

overland 1 *adj route* yungnoŭi 육로의 **2** *adv travel* yungnoro 육로로
overlap *v/i* (*of tiles etc*) pubunjŏgŭro kyŏpch'ida 부분적으로 겹치다; (*of periods, theories*) chungbokdoeda 중복되다
overload *v/t vehicle* nŏmu mani shil-tta 너무 많이 싣다; ELEC kwabuhahada 과부하하다
overlook (*of building etc*) naeryŏdaboda 내려다보다; (*not see*) motppoda 못보다; (*pretend not to see*) nun-gama chuda 눈감아 주다
overly chinach'ige 지나치게; ***not ~ ...*** chinach'iji ank'e ... 지나치지 않게 ...
overnight *adv travel* pamsae 밤새; ***stay ~*** haruppamŭl chinaeda 하룻밤을 지내다
overnight bag chagŭn yŏhaeng-yong kabang 작은 여행용 가방
overpaid kwadahage chibuldoen 과다하게 지불된
overpass (*for car*) kokka toro 고가 도로; (*for people*) yukkyo 육교
overpower *v/t* (*physically*) muryŏk'age hada 무력하게 하다
overpowering *smell* aju kanghan 아주 강한; *sense of guilt* aju k'ŭn 아주 큰
overpriced nŏmu pissan 너무 비싼
overrated kwadae p'yŏngkkadoen 과대 평가된
overrule *decision* muhyohwahada 무효화하다
overrun *country* wanjŏnhi ch'imnyak'ada 완전히 침략하다; *time* ch'ogwahada 초과하다; ***be ~ with*** ...(ŭ)ro tŭlkkŭlt'a ...(으)로 들끓다
overseas 1 *adv* haeoero 해외로 **2** *adj* haeoeŭi 해외의
overseas Koreans haeoe kyop'o 해외 교포
oversee kamdok'ada 감독하다
oversight kan-gwaro inhan shilssu 간과로 인한 실수
oversleep nŭttcham chada 늦잠자다
overtake (*in work, development*) ttarajaptta 따라잡다; *Br* MOT ch'uwŏrhada 추월하다
overthrow chŏnbok 전복
overtime 1 *n* ch'ogwa kŭnmu 초과 근무; SP yŏnjangjŏn 연장전 **2** *adv work* kŭnmu shigan oero 근무 시간 외로
overture MUS sŏgok 서곡; ***make ~s to*** ...ege cheŭihada ...에게 제의하다
overturn 1 *v/t object* twiŏptta 뒤엎다; *government* chŏnbok'ada 전복하다 **2** *v/i* (*of vehicle*) twijip'ida 뒤집히다
overweight *baggage* chungnyang ch'ogwaŭi 중량 초과의; *person* ch'ejung kwadaŭi 체중 과다의
overwhelm (*with work*) apttohada 압도하다; (*with emotion*) kaptchagi tanghwanghage hada 갑자기 당황하게 하다; ***be ~ed by*** (*by response*) ...(ŭ)ro ŏtchŏl chul morŭda ...(으)로 어쩔 줄 모르다
overwork 1 *n* kwaro 과로 **2** *v/i* kwarohada 과로하다 **3** *v/t* kwaroshik'ida 과로시키다
owe *v/t* pitchida 빚지다; ***~ s.o. $500*** nuguege 500tallŏrŭl pitchida 누구에게 500달러를 빚지다; ***~ s.o. an apology*** nuguege sagwahal kŏshi it-tta 누구에게 사과할 것이 있다; ***how much do I ~ you?*** chega tangshinege ŏlmana tŏ tŭryŏya hamnikka? 제가 당신에게 얼마나 더 드려야 합니까?
owing to ...ttaemune ...때문에; ***~ the weather*** nalsshittaemune 날씨때문에
owl olppaemi 올빼미
own[1] *v/t* soyuhada 소유하다
own[2] **1** *adj* soyuŭi 소유의 **2** *pron*: ***a car/an apartment of my ~*** nae soyuŭi ch'a/ap'at'ŭ 내 소유의 차/아파트; ***on my/his ~*** honja 혼자
♦**own up** mojori chabaek'ada 모조리 자백하다
owner chuin 주인; (*of hotel, company etc*) soyuja 소유자
ownership soyukkwŏn 소유권
ox hwangso 황소
oxide sanhwamul 산화물
oxygen sanso 산소
oyster kul 굴
ozone ojon 오존
ozone layer ojonch'ŭng 오존층

P

pace 1 *n* (*step*) kŏrŭm 걸음; (*speed*) soktto 속도 **2** *v/i*: **~ *up and down*** watta katta hada 왔다 갔다 하다

pacemaker MED maekppak chojŏnggi 맥박 조정기; SP sŏndu chuja 선두 주자

Pacific: ***the* ~ (*Ocean*)** T'aep'yŏng-yang 태평양

Pacific Rim: ***the* ~** T'aep'yŏng-yang yŏnan 태평양 연안; **~ *countries*** T'aep'yŏng-yang yŏnan kuk-kka 태평양 연안 국가

pacifier komu chŏtkkoktchi 고무 젖꼭지

pacifism p'yŏnghwajuŭi 평화주의

pacifist *n* p'yŏnghwajuŭija 평화주의자

pacify chinjŏngshik'ida 진정시키다

pack 1 *n* (*back~*) paenang 배낭; (*of cereal*, *food*) t'ong 통; (*of cigarettes*,*cards*) kap 갑 **2** *v/t bag*, *item of clothing*, *groceries etc* ssada 싸다; *goods* p'ojanghada 포장하다 **3** *v/i* chim kkurida 짐 꾸리다

package 1 *n* sop'o 소포; (*of offers etc*) ilgwal 일괄 **2** *v/t* (*in packs*, *for promotion*) p'ojanghada 포장하다

package deal ilgwal kŏrae 일괄 거래

package tour p'aek'iji kwangwang 패키지 관광

packaging (*of product*) p'ojang 포장; (*of rock star etc*) sangp'umhwa 상품화

packed (*crowded*) honjap'an 혼잡한

packet pongji 봉지; (*of envelopes*) mukkŭm 묶음

pact kyeyak 계약

pad[1] **1** *n* (*piece of cloth etc*) ch'ŏntchogak 천조각; (*for writing*) chong-i mukkŭm 종이 묶음 **2** *v/t* (*with material*) taeda 대다; *speech*, *report* kilge nŭllida 길게 늘리다

pad[2] *v/i* (*move quietly*) soriŏpsshi kŏt-tta 소리없이 걷다

padded: **~ *jacket*** nubi chaek'it 누비 재킷; **~ *shoulders*** ŏkkaeshimŭl taen 어깨심을 댄

padding (*material*) p'aeding 패딩; (*in speech etc*) pulp'iryohan sabibŏgu 불필요한 삽입어구

paddle[1] **1** *n* (*for canoe*) no 노 **2** *v/i* (*in canoe*) chŏt-tta 젓다

paddle[2] *v/i* (*in water*) multchangnanŭl ch'ida 물장난을 치다

paddock ul ch'in chandipat 울 친 잔디밭

padlock 1 *n* chamulsoe 자물쇠 **2** *v/t* chamulsoero chamgŭda 자물쇠로 잠그다; **~ *X to Y*** Xŭl / rŭl Ykkaji chamgŭda X을 / 를 Y까지 잠그다

page[1] *n* (*of book etc*) p'eiji 페이지; **~ *number*** tchok pŏnho 쪽 번호

page[2] *v/t* (*call*) hoch'urhada 호출하다

pager hoch'ulgi 호출기

pagoda t'ap 탑

paid employment yugŭp koyong 유급 고용

pail yangdong-i 양동이

pain ap'ŭm 아픔; ***be in* ~** ap'ahada 아파하다; ***take ~s to …*** … hagi wihae mopsshi aessŭda … 하기 위해 몹시 애쓰다; ***a ~ in the neck*** F nunŭi kashi 눈의 가시

painful *arm*, *leg etc* ap'ŭn 아픈; (*distressing*) kot'ongsŭrŏun 고통스러운; (*laborious*) himdŭn 힘든

painfully (*extremely*, *acutely*) kot'ongsŭrŏpkke 고통스럽게

painkiller chint'ongje 진통제

painless mut'ong-ŭi 무통의

painstaking *work* himdŭnŭn 힘드는; *worker* sugorŭl akkiji annŭn 수고를 아끼지 않는

paint 1 *n* (*for wall*, *car*) p'eint'ŭ 페인트; (*for artist*) mulkkam 물감 **2** *v/t wall etc* ch'irhada 칠하다; *picture* kŭrida 그리다 **3** *v/i* (*as art form*) kŭrida 그리다

paintbrush (*for wall, ceiling etc*) p'eint'ŭ sol 페인트 솔; (*of artist*) kŭrim put 그림 붓
painter (*decorator*) changshik-kka 장식가; (*artist*) hwaga 화가
painting (*activity*) kŭrim kŭrigi 그림 그리기; (*picture*) hoehwa chakp'um 회화 작품
paintwork tojang 도장
pair (*of people, animals, objects*) ssang 쌍; (*of shoes*) k'yŏlle 켤레; ***a ~ of shoes / sandals*** shinbal / saendŭl han k'yŏlle 신발 / 샌들 한 켤레; ***a ~ of pants*** paji han pŏl 바지 한 벌
pajama jacket chamot wit-ttori 잠옷 윗도리
pajama pants chamot paji 잠옷 바지
pajamas chamot 잠옷
Pakistan P'ak'isŭt'an 파키스탄
Pakistani 1 *adj* P'ak'isŭt'anŭi 파키스탄의 **2** *n* P'ak'isŭt'anin 파키스탄인
pal F (*friend*) ch'in-gu 친구; ***hey ~, got a light?*** ŏi, igŏt pwa, pul chom issŏ? 어이, 이것 봐, 불 좀 있어?
palace kunggwŏl 궁궐
palate kugae 구개; *fig* migak 미각
palatial kunggwŏlgat'ŭn 궁궐같은
pale *person* ch'angbaek'an 창백한; ***~ pink / blue*** yŏt'ŭn punhongsaek / p'aransaek 옅은 분홍색 / 파란색
pallet hwamul unbanttae 화물 운반대
pallor ch'angbaek 창백
palm[1] (*of hand*) sonppadak 손바닥
palm[2] (*tree*) yajanamu 야자나무
palpitations MED shimgyehangjin 심계항진
paltry chwikkorimanhan 쥐꼬리만한
pamper aejijungjihada 애지중지하다
pamphlet p'amp'ŭllet 팜플렛
pan 1 *n* (*for cooking*) nambi 남비 **2** *v/t* F (*criticize*) hokp'yŏnghada 혹평하다
♦**pan out** (*develop*) chŏn-gaehada 전개하다
pancake p'aenk'eik'ŭ 팬케이크; (*Korean-style*) chŏn 전
panda p'aendŏ kom 팬더 곰
pandemonium asurajang 아수라장
pane (*of glass*) ch'ang-yuri 창유리
panel (*section*) k'an 칸; (*in TV discussion*) p'aenŏl 패널; (*investigating*) chosadan 조사단; (*committee*) wiwŏndan 위원단
paneling p'annerhagi 판넬하기
panhandle *v/i* F kugŏrhada 구걸하다
panic 1 *n* tanghwang 당황 **2** *v/i* tanghwanghada 당황하다; ***don't ~*** tanghwanghaji mara 당황하지 마라
panic selling FIN pisangshiŭi kŭmmae 비상시의 급매
panic-stricken kŏbe chillin 겁에 질린
panorama p'anorama 파노라마
panoramic *view* hwak t'ŭin 확 트인
pansy (*flower*) p'aenji 팬지
pant *v/i* sumi ch'ada 숨이 차다
panties p'aent'i 팬티
pantihose → ***pantyhose***
pants paji 바지; ***a pair of ~*** paji han pŏl 바지 한 벌
pantyhose p'aent'i sŭt'ak'ing 팬티 스타킹
paper 1 *n* (*material*) chong-i 종이; (*news~*) shinmun 신문; (*wall~*) pyŏktchi 벽지; (*academic*) nonmun 논문; (*examination ~*) shihŏmji 시험지; ***~s*** (*documents*) sŏryu 서류; (*identity ~s*) shinbuntchŭng 신분증; ***a piece of ~*** chong-i han chang 종이 한 장 **2** *adj* chong-iro mandŭn 종이로 만든 **3** *v/t room, walls* tobaehada 도배하다
paperback chong-ip'yojiŭi yŏmkkap'an ch'aek 종이표지의 염가판 책; **paper bag** chong-i kabang 종이 가방; **paper clip** k'ŭllip 클립; **paper cup** chong-ik'ŏp 종이컵; **paperwork** munsŏ ŏmmu 문서 업무
par (*in golf*) p'a 파; ***be on a ~ with*** ...wa / kwa kat-tta ...와 / 과 같다; ***feel below ~*** k'ŏndishyŏni nappŭda 컨디션이 나쁘다
parachute 1 *n* nak'asan 낙하산 **2** *v/i* nak'asanŭro naeryŏoda 낙하산으로 내려오다 **3** *v/t troops, supplies* nak'asanŭro t'uhahada 낙하산으로 투하하다
parachutist nak'asankanghaja 낙하산강하자
parade 1 *n* (*procession*) p'ŏreidŭ 퍼레이드 **2** *v/i* haengjinhada 행진하다

3 *v/t* (*show off*) kwashihada 과시하다
paradise nagwŏn 낙원
paradox yŏkssŏl 역설
paradoxical yŏkssŏltchŏgin 역설적인
paradoxically yŏlssŏltchŏgŭro 역설적으로
paragraph mundan 문단
parallel 1 *n* p'yŏnghaeng 평행; (*of latitude*) wido 위도; *fig* yusattchŏm 유사점; ***do two things in ~*** tugaji irŭl tongshie hada 두가지 일을 동시에 하다 **2** *adj lines* p'yŏnghaenghanŭn 평행하는; *fig* tongshie irŏnanŭn 동시에 일어나는 **3** *v/t* (*match*) p'iltchŏk'ada 필적하다
paralysis mabi 마비
paralyze mabishik'ida 마비시키다; *fig* muryŏkk'ehada 무력케하다
paramedic chun ŭiryo hwalttong chongsaja 준 의료 활동 종사자
parameter chehan pŏmwi 제한 범위
paramilitary 1 *adj* chun kunsajŏgin 준 군사적인 **2** *n* chun kunsayowŏn 준 군사요원
paramount kajang chung-yohan 가장 중요한; ***be ~*** kajang chung-yohada 가장 중요하다
paranoia p'ihae mangsang 피해 망상
paranoid *adj* p'ihae mangsang-ŭi 피해 망상의
paraphernalia chapttongsani 잡동사니
paraphrase *n* pakkuŏ ssŭgi 바꾸어 쓰기
paraplegic *n* habanshin mabihwanja 하반신 마비환자
parasite kisaeng tongshingmul 기생 동식물; *fig* kisaengch'unggat'ŭn saram 기생충같은 사람
parasol p'arasol 파라솔
paratrooper nak'asanbyŏng 낙하산병
parcel *n* sop'o 소포
♦**parcel up** kkurŏmiro ssada 꾸러미로 싸다
parch *v/t*: ***be ~ed*** (*of person*) mogi t'ada 목이 타다
pardon 1 *n* LAW samyŏn 사면; ***I beg your ~?*** (*what did you say?*) mwŏrago hashyŏttchyo? 뭐라고 하셨죠?; ***I beg your ~*** (*I'm sorry*) choesonghamnida 죄송합니다 **2** *v/t* yongsŏhada 용서하다; LAW samyŏnhada 사면하다; ***~ me?*** mwŏraguyo? 뭐라구요?
pare (*peel*) kkŏptchirŭl pŏtkkida 껍질을 벗기다
parent pumo 부모
parental pumo-ŭi 부모의
parent company mohoesa 모회사; **Parents' Day** Ŏbŏinal 어버이날; **parent-teacher association** sach'inhoe 사친회
park[1] (*area*) kong-wŏn 공원
park[2] *v/i & v/t* MOT chuch'ahada 주차하다
parka p'ak'a 파카
parking MOT chuch'a 주차; ***no ~*** chuch'agŭmji 주차금지
parking brake sudong pŭreik'ŭ 수동 브레이크; **parking garage** ch'ago 차고; **parking lot** chuch'ajang 주차장; **parking meter** chuch'a yogŭmgi 주차 요금기; **parking place** chuch'a changso 주차 장소; **parking ticket** chuch'a wiban ttaktchi 주차 위반 딱지
parliament ŭihoe 의회; (*in Korea*) Kuk'oe 국회
parliamentary ŭihoeŭi 의회의; ***~ buildings*** kuk'oe ŭisadang 국회 의사당
parole 1 *n* kasŏkppang 가석방; ***be on ~*** kasŏkppangdoeda 가석방되다 **2** *v/t* kasŏkppanghada 가석방하다
parrot aengmusae 앵무새
parsley p'asŭlli 파슬리
part 1 *n* (*portion*) pubun 부분; (*section*) p'yŏn 편; (*area*) chiyŏk 지역; (*of machine*) pup'um 부품; (*in play, movie*) yŏk 역; MUS p'at'ŭ 파트; (*in hair*) karŭma 가르마; ***take ~ in*** ch'amyŏhada 참여하다 **2** *adv* (*partly*) pubuntchŏgŭro 부분적으로 **3** *v/i* heŏjida 헤어지다 **4** *v/t*: ***~ one's hair*** karŭmarŭl t'ada 가르마를 타다
♦**part with** ch'ŏbunhada 처분하다
part exchange ton taeshin mulgŏnŭro chugo patkki 돈 대신 물건으로 주고 받기; ***take sth in ~*** ton taeshin mulgŏnŭl kajida 돈 대신 물건을 가지다
partial (*incomplete*) purwanjŏnhan

불완전한; ***be ~ to*** choahada 좋아하다
partially pubuntchŏgŭro 부분적으로
participant ch'amgaja 참가자
participate ch'amgahada 참가하다; ~ ***in sth*** muŏse ch'amgahada 무엇에 참가하다
participation ch'amga 참가
particle PHYS soriptcha 소립자; (*small amount*) kŭkssoryang 극소량
particular (*specific*) t'ŭktchŏnghan 특정한; (*special*) t'ŭkppyŏrhan 특별한; (*fussy*) kkadaroun 까다로운; ***in*** ~ t'ŭkppyŏrhi 특별히
particularly t'ŭkppyŏrhage 특별하게
parting (*of people*) ibyŏl 이별
partition 1 *n* (*screen*) k'anmagi 칸막이; (*of country*) pulli 분리 **2** *v/t country* pullihada 분리하다
♦**partition off** k'anmagirŭl hada 칸막이를 하다
partly pubuntchŏgŭro 부분적으로
partner COM tong-ŏptcha 동업자; (*personal*) paeuja 배우자; (*professional*) tong-ŏptcha 동업자; (*in particular activity*) tchak 짝
partnership COM tong-ŏp 동업; (*in particular activity*) hyŏmnyŏk kwan-gye 협력 관계
part of speech p'umsa 품사; **part owner** kongdong soyuja 공동 소유자; **part-time 1** *adj* shiganjeŭi 시간제의 **2** *adv work* shiganjero 시간제로
party 1 *n* (*celebration*) p'at'i 파티; POL chŏngdang 정당; (*group of people*) muri 무리; ***be a ~ to*** yŏlludoeda 연루되다 **2** *v/i* F p'at'irŭl hada 파티를 하다
pass 1 *n* (*permit*), SP p'aesŭ 패스; (*in mountains*) sankkil 산길; ***make a ~ at*** kuaehada 구애하다 **2** *v/t* (*hand*) chŏnhaejuda 전해주다; (*go past*) chinagada 지나가다; MOT ch'uwŏrhada 추월하다; (*go beyond*) nŏmŏsŏda 넘어서다; (*approve*) sŭng-in pat-tta 승인 받다; SP p'aesŭhada 패스하다; ~ ***an exam*** shihŏme hapkkyŏk'ada 시험에 합격하다; ~ ***sentence*** LAW p'an-gyŏrŭl naerida 판결을 내리다; ~ ***the time*** shiganŭl ponaeda 시간을 보내다 **3** *v/i* (*of time*) ponaeda 보내다; (*in exam*) shihŏme put-tta 시험에 붙다; SP p'aesŭhada 패스하다; (*go away*) ŏpssŏjida 없어지다
♦**pass around** tollida 돌리다
♦**pass away** (*die*) sesang-ŭl ttŭda 세상을 뜨다
♦**pass by** *v/t & v/i* (*go past*) chinagada 지나가다
♦**pass on 1** *v/t information, book* chŏnhada 전하다; *costs, savings* tollyŏjuda 돌려주다 **2** *v/i* (*die*) sesang-ŭl ttŭda 세상을 뜨다
♦**pass out** (*faint*) kijŏrhada 기절하다
♦**pass through** *town* t'onghae chinagada 통해 지나가다
♦**pass up** *chance* noch'ida 놓치다
passable *road* chinagal su innŭn 지나갈 수 있는; (*acceptable*) kwaench'anŭn 괜찮은
passage (*corridor*) poktto 복도; (*from poem*) chŏl 절; (*from book*) tallak 단락; (*of time*) kyŏnggwa 경과
passageway t'ongno 통로
passenger sŭnggaek 승객
passenger seat sŭnggaeksŏk 승객석
passer-by t'onghaengin 통행인
passion (*emotion*) kyŏngnyŏrhan kamjŏng 격렬한 감정; (*sexual desire*) yoktchŏng 욕정; (*fervor*) yŏltchŏng 열정
passionate *lover* chŏngnyŏltchŏgin 정열적인; (*fervent*) yŏltchŏngjŏgin 열정적인
passive 1 *adj* sudongjŏgin 수동적인 **2** *n* GRAM sudongt'ae 수동태; ***in the*** ~ sudongt'aero 수동태로
pass mark hapkkyŏktchŏm 합격점; **passport** yŏkkwŏn 여권; **passport control** yŏkkwŏn kwalli 여권 관리; **password** amho 암호
past 1 *adj* (*former*) mŏnjŏtppŏnŭi 먼젓번의; ***the ~ few days*** chinan myŏch'il 지난 며칠; ***that's all ~ now*** kŭgŏn ije ta chinagassŏyo 그건 이제 다 지나갔어요 **2** *n* kwagŏ 과거; ***in the*** ~ kwagŏe 과거에 **3** *prep* (*in time*) nŏmŏ 넘어; (*in position*) chinasŏ 지나서; ***it's ~ 7 o'clock*** ilgop shiga nŏmŏssŏyo 일곱 시가 넘었어요; ***it's half ~ two*** tushi

paniyeyo 두시 반이예요 **4** *adv*: ***run*** / ***walk*** ~ ttwiŏsŏ / kŏrŏsŏ chinagada 뛰어서 / 걸어서 지나가다
paste 1 *n* (*adhesive*) p'ul 풀 **2** *v/t* (*stick*) puch'ida 붙이다
pastel 1 *n* (*color*) p'asŭt'el 파스텔 **2** *adj* p'asŭt'erŭi 파스텔의
pastime ch'wimi 취미
pastor kyogu mokssa 교구 목사
past participle kwagŏ punsa 과거 분사
pastrami hunje soegogi 훈제 쇠고기
pastry (*for pie*) milkkaru panjuk 밀가루 반죽; (*small cake*) p'aesŭch'yuri 패스츄리
past tense kwagŏ shije 과거 시제
pasty *adj complexion* ch'angbaek'an 창백한
pat 1 *n* kabyŏpkke tudŭrigi 가볍게 두드리기; ***give s.o. a ~ on the back*** *fig* nugurŭl ch'uk'ahada 누구를 축하하다 **2** *v/t* kabyŏpkke tudŭrida 가볍게 두드리다
patch 1 *n* (*on clothes*) hŏnggŏp 헝겊; (*period*) kigan 기간; (*area*) kot 곳; (*of fog*) charak 자락; ***not be a ~ on*** ...wa / kwa pigyodo toeji ant'a ...와 / 과 비교도 되지 않다 **2** *v/t clothes* hŏnggŏp'ŭl taeda 헝겊을 대다
♦**patch up** (*repair*) mibongjŏgŭro koch'ida 미봉적으로 고치다; *quarrel* haegyŏrhada 해결하다
patchwork 1 *n* (*needlework*) p'aech'iwŏk'ŭ 패치워크 **2** *adj quilt* p'aech'iwŏk'ŭŭi 패치워크의
patchy *quality*, *work* korŭji mot'an 고르지 못한
patent 1 *adj* (*obvious*) punmyŏnghan 분명한 **2** *n* (*for invention*) t'ŭk'ŏ 특허 **3** *v/t invention* t'ŭk'ŏrŭl ŏt-tta 특허를 얻다
patent leather enamel kajuk 에나멜 가죽
patently (*clearly*) punmyŏnghi 분명히
paternal *relative* pugyeŭi 부계의; *pride*, *love* pusŏngŭi 부성의
paternalism kajoktchuŭi 가족주의
paternalistic kajoktchŏgin 가족적인
paternity pusŏng 부성
path kil 길; *fig* chillo 진로
pathetic aech'ŏroun 애처로운; F (*very bad*) hyŏngp'yŏnŏmnŭn 형편없는
pathological pyŏngtchŏgin 병적인
pathologist pyŏngnihaktcha 병리학자
pathology pyŏngnihak 병리학
patience ch'amŭlssŏng 참을성
patient 1 *n* hwanja 환자 **2** *adj* ch'amŭlssŏng innŭn 참을성 있는; ***just be ~!*** ch'amara! 참아라!
patiently ch'amŭlssŏng itkke 참을성 있게
patio anttŭl 안뜰
patriot aeguktcha 애국자
patriotic aeguktchŏgin 애국적인
patriotism aeguksshim 애국심
patrol 1 *n* sunch'al 순찰; ***be on ~*** sunch'arhada 순찰하다 **2** *v/t streets*, *border* sunch'arhada 순찰하다
patrol car sunch'alch'a 순찰차; **patrolman** sunch'algwan 순찰관; **patrol wagon** choesu hosongch'a 죄수 호송차
patron (*of store*, *movie house*) kogaek 고객; (*of artist*, *charity etc*) huwŏnja 후원자
patronize *store* tan-gollo tanida 단골로 다니다; *person* sŏnshimŭl ssŭnŭn tŭt'ada 선심을 쓰는 듯하다
patronizing sŏnshimŭl ssŭnŭn tŭt'an 선심을 쓰는 듯한
patter 1 *n* (*of rain etc*) hududuk'anŭn sori 후두둑하는 소리; F (*of salesman*) ppalli chikkŏrinŭn mal 빨리 지껄이는 말 **2** *v/i* hududuk ttŏrŏjida 후두둑 떨어지다
pattern *n* (*fabric*) munŭi 무늬; (*for knitting*, *sewing*) p'aet'ŏn 패턴; (*model*) ponbogi 본보기; (*in behavior*, *events*) yangshik 양식
patterned munŭi innŭn 무늬 있는
paunch ttongppae 똥배
pause 1 *n* chungdan 중단 **2** *v/i* chungdanhada 중단하다 **3** *v/t tape* chungdanshik'ida 중단시키다
pave kkalda 깔다; ***~ the way for*** ...eŭi kirŭl yŏlda ...에의 길을 열다
pavement (*asphalt*) asŭp'alt'ŭ 아스팔트
paving stone p'osŏk 포석
paw 1 *n* (*of animal*) pal 발; F (*hand*)

son 손 **2** *v/t* F sonŭro manjida 손으로 만지다
pawn[1] *n* (*in chess*) chol 졸; *fig* iyong tanghanŭn saram 이용 당하는 사람
pawn[2] *v/t* chŏdang-ŭl chap'ida 저당을 잡히다
pawnbroker chŏndangp'o chuin 전당포 주인
pawnshop chŏndangp'o 전당포
pay 1 *n* posu 보수; ***in the ~ of*** koyongdoen 고용된 **2** *v/t employee* posurŭl chuda 보수를 주다; *sum* chiburhada 지불하다; *bill* nap-ppuhada 납부하다; ***~ attention*** chuŭirŭl kiurida 주의를 기울이다; ***~ s.o. a compliment*** nuguege ch'ingch'anŭl hada 누구에게 칭찬을 하다 **3** *v/i* chiburhada 지불하다; (*be profitable*) sujiga matta 수지가 맞다; ***it doesn't ~ to …*** … hanŭn kŏshi tŭgi toeji anayo … 하는 것이 득이 되지 않아요; ***~ for*** *purchase* sada 사다; ***you'll ~ for this!*** *fig* i ire taehan taetkkarŭl ch'irŭge toelkkŏyeyo! 이 일에 대한 댓가를 치르게 될꺼예요!
♦**pay back** *person* kaptta 갚다; *loan* pyŏnjehada 변제하다; (*get revenge on*) anggap'ŭmŭl hada 앙갚음을 하다
♦**pay in** (*bank*) yegŭmhada 예금하다
♦**pay off 1** *v/t debt* kaptta 갚다; *corrupt official* noemurŭl chuda 뇌물을 주다 **2** *v/i* (*be profitable*) idŭgi toeda 이득이되다
♦**pay up** chiburhada 지불하다
payable chiburhaeya hal 지불해야 할
pay check ponggŭp 봉급
payday ponggŭmnal 봉급날
payee such'wiin 수취인
pay envelope ponggŭp pongt'u 봉급 봉투
payer chiburin 지불인
payment (*of bill*) nabip 납입; (*money*) chibul 지불
pay phone kongjung chŏnhwa 공중 전화
payroll (*money*) chibul ponggŭp ch'ongaek 지불 봉급 총액; (*employees*) chongŏbwŏn ch'ongsu 종업원 총수; ***be on the ~*** koyongdoeda 고용되다
PC (= ***personal computer***) p'isshi 피씨; (= ***politically correct***) p'yŏn-gyŏni omnŭn 편견이 없는
pea wanduk'ong 완두콩
peace (*not war*) p'yŏnghwa 평화; (*quietness*) koyo 고요
peaceable *person* onsunhan 온순한
Peace Corps P'yŏnghwa Pongsadan 평화 봉사단
peaceful p'yŏnghwaroun 평화로운
peacefully p'yŏnghwaropkke 평화롭게
peach pokssung-a 복숭아
peacock kongjakssae 공작새
peak 1 *n* (*of mountain*) chŏngsang 정상; (*mountain*) san 산; *fig* ch'oegoch'i 최고치 **2** *v/i* ch'oegoch'ie tarhada 최고치에 달하다
peak consumption ch'oedae sobiryang 최대 소비량
peak hours p'ik'ŭ shigan 피크 시간
peanut ttangk'ong 땅콩; ***get paid ~s*** F chwikkorimank'ŭm tonŭl pannŭnda 쥐꼬리만큼 돈을 받는다; ***that's ~s to him*** F kŭ saramegen sae parŭi p'iyeyo 그 사람에겐 새 발의 피예요
peanut butter ttangk'ong pŏt'ŏ 땅콩 버터
pear pae 배
pearl chinju 진주
peasant nongmin 농민
pebble chagal 자갈
pecan p'ik'an 피칸
peck 1 *n* (*bite*) tchogi 쪼기; (*kiss*) ppoppo 뽀뽀 **2** *v/t* (*bite*) tchoda 쪼다; (*kiss*) ppoppohada 뽀뽀하다
peculiar (*strange*) kimyohan 기묘한; ***~ to*** (*special*) ...t'ŭgŭi ...특유의
peculiarity (*strangeness*) kimyoham 기묘함; (*special feature*) tokt'ŭk'am 독특함
pedal 1 *n* p'edal 페달 **2** *v/i* (*turn ~s*) p'edarŭl paltta 페달을 밟다; (*cycle*) chajŏn-gŏrŭl t'ada 자전거를 타다
pedantic hyŏnhaktchŏgin 현학적인
pedestal (*for statue*) (chogagŭi) patch'imttae (조각의) 받침대
pedestrian *n* pohaengja 보행자
pedestrian precinct pohaengja

chŏnyong kuyŏk 보행자 전용 구역
pediatrician soakkwa ŭisa 소아과 의사
pediatrics soakkwa 소아과
pedicab samnyun t'aekssi 삼륜 택시
pedigree 1 *n* hyŏlt'ong 혈통 **2** *adj* hyŏlt'ong-i punmyŏnghan 혈통이 분명한
pee *v/i* F ojum nuda 오줌 누다
peek 1 *n* saltchak yŏtppogi 살짝 엿보기 **2** *v/i* saltchak yŏtppoda 살짝 엿보다
peel 1 *n* kkŏptchil 껍질 **2** *v/t fruit, vegetables* kkŏptchirŭl pŏtkkida 껍질을 벗기다 **3** *v/i* (*of nose, shoulders*) kkŏptchiri pŏtkkyŏjida 껍질이 벗겨지다
peep → ***peek***
peephole tŭryŏda ponŭn kumŏng 들여다 보는 구멍
peer[1] *n* (*in status*) taedŭnghan saram 대등한 사람; (*in age*) tongbae 동배
peer[2] *v/i* chasehi poda 자세히 보다; **~ *through the mist*** an-gae sogŭl tturŏjige poda 안개 속을 뚫어지게 보다; **~ *at*** tturŏjige poda 뚫어지게 보다
peeved F shin-gyŏng-i kŏsŭllinŭn 신경이 거슬리는
peg *n* (*for coat*) mot 못; (*for tent*) malttuk 말뚝; ***off the ~*** kisŏngbok 기성복
pejorative kyŏngmyŏrŏ 경멸어
pellet chagŭn kong 작은 공; (*air rifle bullet*) chagŭn ch'ong-al 작은 총알
pelt 1 *v/t*: **~ *X with Y*** Xege Yŭl / rŭl tŏnjida X에게 Y을 / 를 던지다 **2** *v/i*: ***they ~ed along the road*** kŭdŭrŭn kirŭl ttarasŏ kŭp'i kat-tta 그들은 길을 따라서 급히 갔다; ***it's ~ing down*** piga sech'age naeryŏch'yŏyo 비가 세차게 내려쳐요
pelvis kolbanppyŏ 골반뼈
pen[1] *n* (*ballpoint ~*) polp'en 볼펜; (*fountain ~*) mannyŏnp'il 만년필
pen[2] (*enclosure*) uri 우리
pen[3] → ***penitentiary***
penalize ch'ŏbŏrhada 처벌하다
penalty ch'ŏbŏl 처벌; SP p'aenŏlt'i 패널티
penalty area SP p'aenŏlt'i kuyŏk 패널티 구역
penalty clause (kyeyakŭi) wiyak pŏlch'ik chohang (계약의) 위약 벌칙 조항
pencil yŏnp'il 연필
pencil sharpener yŏnp'il kkak-kki 연필 깍기
pendant (*necklace*) mok-kkŏri 목걸이
pending 1 *prep* …ŭl / rŭl ttaekkaji …을 / 를 때까지 **2** *adj*: ***be ~*** (*awaiting decision*) kyŏltchŏngi naogikkaji kidarinŭn 결정이 나오기까지 기다리는; (*about to happen*) imbak'an 임박한
penetrate kwant'onghada 관통하다; *market* chinch'urhada 진출하다
penetrating *stare, sound* nalk'aroun 날카로운; *analysis* kanp'ahanŭn 간파하는
penetration ch'imt'u 침투; (*of market*) chinch'ul 진출
pen friend p'enp'al ch'in-gu 펜팔 친구
penicillin p'enishillin 페니실린
peninsula pando 반도
penis ŭmgyŏng 음경
penitence huhoe 후회
penitent *adj* nwiuch'inŭn 뉘우치는
penitentiary kyodoso 교도소
pen name p'ilmyŏng 필명
pennant samgak-kki 삼각기
penniless muilp'unŭi 무일푼의
penpal p'enp'al ch'in-gu 펜팔 친구
pension yŏn-gŭm 연금
♦ **pension off** myŏng-ye t'oejiksshik'ida 명예 퇴직시키다
pension fund yŏn-gŭmchohap 연금 조합
pension scheme yŏn-gŭm chedo 연금 제도
pensive saenggage chamgin 생각에 잠긴
Pentagon: ***the ~*** Miguk kukppangssŏng 미국 국방성
penthouse p'aent'ŭhausŭ 팬트하우스
pent-up ŏngnullin 억눌린
penultimate ŏmiesŏ tubŏntchae ŭmjŏrŭi 어미에서 두번째 음절의
people saram 사람; (*race, tribe*) minjok 민족; ***the ~*** kungmin 국민; ***the American ~*** Miguk kungmin

미국 국민; ~ ***say ...*** saramdŭrŭn ... rago marhanda 사람들은 ... 라고 말한다
pepper (*spice*) huch'u 후추; (*chilli*) koch'u 고추; (*pimiento*) p'imang 피망
peppermint (*candy*) pak'asat'ang 박하사탕; (*flavoring*) pak'ahyang 박하향
pep talk kyŏngnyŏ yŏnsŏl 격려 연설
per tang 당; ~ ***annum*** illyŏne 일년에
perceive (*with senses*) kamjihada 감지하다; (*view, interpret*) arach'arida 알아차리다
percent p'ŏsent'ŭ 퍼센트; ***10/20*** ~ ship/iship p'ŏsent'ŭ 십/이십 퍼센트
percentage piyul 비율
perceptible chigak'al su innŭn 지각할 수 있는
perceptibly arach'aril su itkke 알아차릴 수 있게
perception (*through senses*) kamji 감지; (*of situation*) inji 인지; (*insight*) chigak 지각
perceptive t'ongch'allyŏk innŭn 통찰력 있는
perch 1 *n* (*for bird*) hwaet-ttae 횃대 **2** *v/i* (*of bird*) hwaet-ttaee antta 횃대에앉다; (*of person*) chamshi antta 잠시 앉다
percolate *v/i* (*of coffee*) k'ŏp'irŭl naerida 커피를 내리다
percolator k'ŏp'i meik'ŏ 커피 메이커
percussion t'aak-kki 타악기
percussion instrument t'aak-kki 타악기
perfect 1 *n* GRAM wallyohyŏng 완료형 **2** *adj* wanbyŏk'an 완벽한 **3** *v/t* wanjŏnhage hada 완전하게 하다
perfection wanbyŏk 완벽; ***to*** ~ wanbyŏk'i 완벽히
perfectionist *n* wanbyŏkjuŭija 완벽주의자
perfectly wanbyŏk'age 완벽하게; (*totally*) wanjŏnhage 완전하게
perforated *line* chŏmsŏni tchik'in 점선이 찍힌
perforations chŏlch'wisŏn 절취선
perform 1 *v/t* (*carry out*) tahada 다하다; (*of actor, musician*) kong-yŏnhada 공연하다 **2** *v/i* (*of actor, musician, dancer*) kong-yŏnhada 공연하다; (*of machine*) chakttonghada 작동하다
performance (*by actor, musician*) kong-yŏn 공연; (*of employee, company etc*) ŏmmu suhaeng 업무 수행; (*by machine*) sŏngnŭng 성능
performance car sŏngnŭng-i usuhan ch'a 성능이 우수한 차
performer kong-yŏnja 공연자
perfume hyangsu 향수; (*of flower*) hyanggi 향기
perfunctory hyŏngshiktchŏgin 형식적인
perhaps amado 아마도
peril wihŏm 위험
perilous wihŏmhan 위험한
perimeter chubyŏn 주변; (*of circle*) chuwi 주위
perimeter fence kyŏnggyesŏn ult'ari 경계선 울타리
period (*time*) kigan 기간; (*menstruation*) saengni 생리; (*punctuation mark*) mach'imp'yo 마침표; ***I don't want to,*** ~***!*** tŏ isang marhal p'iryodo ŏpsshi nan hago shiptchi anayo! 더 이상 말할 필요도 없이 난 하고 싶지 않아요!
periodic chugijŏgin 주기적인
periodical *n* chŏnggi kanhaengmul 정기 간행물
periodically chŏnggijŏgŭro 정기적으로
peripheral 1 *adj* (*not crucial*) taesuroptchi anŭn 대수롭지 않은 **2** *n* COMPUT chubyŏn changch'i 주변 장치
periphery chuwi 주위
perish (*of rubber*) ssŏktta 썩다; (*of person*) sesang-ŭl ttŭda 세상을 뜨다
perishable ssŏk-kki shwiun 썩기 쉬운
perjure: ~ ***oneself*** wijŭnghada 위증하다
perjury wijŭng 위증
perk *n* (*of job*) itchŏm 이점
♦**perk up 1** *v/t* saenggi tolge hada 생기 돌게 하다 **2** *v/i* saenggiga nada 생기가 나다
perky (*cheerful*) kiun ch'an 기운 찬
perm 1 *n* p'ama 파마 **2** *v/t* p'ama hada 파마 하다

permanent yŏnggujŏgin 영구적인
permanently yŏngguhi 영구히
permissible hŏyongdoel su innŭn 허용될 수 있는
permission hŏrak 허락
permissive kwandaehan 관대한
permit 1 *n* hŏgasŏ 허가서 **2** *v/t* hŏrak'ada 허락하다; ***~ X to do Y*** Xi / ga Yhanŭn kŏsŭl hŏrak'ada X이 / 가 Y하는 것을 허락하다
perpendicular *adj* sujigŭi 수직의
perpetual kkŭnimŏmnŭn 끊임없는
perpetually kyesok'aesŏ 계속해서
perpetuate yŏng-wŏnhage hada 영원하게 하다
perplex tanghok'age hada 당혹하게 하다
perplexed tanghok'an 당혹한
perplexity tanghok 당혹
persecute pak'aehada 박해하다
persecution pak'ae 박해
perseverance kkŭn-gi 끈기
persevere kyesok'aesŏ hada 계속해서 하다
persist chisok'ada 지속하다; ***~ in*** kkŭndŏktchige toep'urihada 끈덕지게 되풀이하다
persistence (*perseverance*) kkŭn-gi 끈기; (*continuation*) chisok 지속
persistent *person, questions* kkŭndŏktchige toep'urihanŭn 끈덕지게 되풀이하는; *rain, unemployment etc* chisoktchŏgin 지속적인
persistently (*continually*) kyesok'aesŏ 계속해서
person saram 사람; ***in ~*** ponini chiktchŏp 본인이 직접
personal (*private*) kaeintchŏgin 개인적인; (*relating to a particular individual*) kaeinŭi 개인의; ***don't make ~ remarks*** satchŏgin marŭn haji maseyo 사적인 말은 하지 마세요
personal assistant kaeinbisŏ 개인 비서; **personal computer** kaeinnyong k'ŏmp'yut'ŏ 개인용 컴퓨터; **personal hygiene** kaein wisaeng 개인 위생
personality sŏngkkyŏk 성격; (*celebrity*) yumyŏng-in 유명인
personally (*for my part*) narossŏnŭn 나로서는; (*in person*) chiktchŏp 직접; ***don't take it ~*** tangshin mariragonŭn saenggak'aji maseyo 당신 말이라고는 생각하지 마세요
personal pronoun inch'ing taemyŏngsa 인칭 대명사; **personal seal**, **personal stamp** tojang 도장; **personal stereo** kaeinyong sŭt'ereo 개인용 스테레오
personnel (*employees*) chigwŏn 직원; (*department*) insakkwa 인사과
personnel manager insa tamdang pujang 인사 담당 부장
perspiration ttam 땀
perspire ttamŭl hŭllida 땀을 흘리다
persuade sŏlttŭk'ada 설득하다; ***~ s.o. to do sth*** nugurŭl muŏt'adorok sŏlttŭk'ada 누구를 무엇하도록 설득하다
persuasion sŏlttŭk 설득
persuasive sŏlttŭngnyŏk innŭn 설득력 있는
pertinent chŏktchŏrhan 적절한
perturb uryŏhada 우려하다
perturbing uryŏdoenŭn 우려되는
pervasive *influence, ideas* nŏlli p'ŏjyŏ innŭn 널리 퍼져 있는
perverse (*awkward*) isanghan 이상한
perversion (*sexual*) pyŏnt'ae 변태
pervert *n* (*sexual*) pyŏnt'ae sŏngnyŏktcha 변태 성욕자
pessimism pigwanjuŭi 비관주의
pessimist pigwanjuŭija 비관주의자
pessimistic pigwanjŏgin 비관적인
pest yuhaehan kŏt 유해한 것; F (*person*) koltchitkkŏri 골칫거리
pest control pyŏngch'unghae kwalli 병충해 관리
pester kwich'ank'e kulda 귀찮게 굴다; ***~ s.o. to do sth*** nuguege muŏsŭl hae tallago chorŭda 누구에게 무엇을 해 달라고 조르다
pesticide salch'ungje 살충제
pet 1 *n* (*animal*) aewandongmul 애완동물; (*favorite person*) t'ŭk'i choahanŭn saram 특히 좋아하는 사람 **2** *adj* (*favorite*) t'ŭk'i choahanŭn 특히 좋아하는 **3** *v/t animal* ssŭdadŭmtta 쓰다듬다 **4** *v/i* (*of couple*) aemuhada 애무하다

petal kkonnip 꽃잎
♦**peter out** chŏmch'ajŏgŭro ŏpssŏjida 점차적으로 없어지다
petite momtchibi chagŭn 몸집이 작은
petition *n* ch'ŏng-wŏnsŏ 청원서
petrified sosŭrach'in 소스라친
petrify sosŭrach'ige hada 소스라치게 하다
petrochemical sŏgyu hwahak chep'um 석유 화학 제품
petroleum sŏgyu 석유
petty *person, behavior* piyŏrhan 비열한; *details* shishihan 시시한
petty cash ssamjit-tton 쌈짓돈
petulant sŏngmarŭn 성마른
pew kyohoeŭi shindosŏk 교회의 신도석
pewter paengnap 백랍
pharmaceutical cheyagŭi 제약의
pharmaceuticals cheyak 제약
pharmacist (*in store*) yakssa 약사
pharmacy (*store*) yak-kkuk 약국
phase shigi 시기
♦**phase in** tan-gyejŏgŭro t'uip'ada 단계적으로 투입하다
♦**phase out** tan-gyejŏgŭro chegŏhada 단계적으로 제거하다
PhD (= ***Doctor of Philosophy***) pakssa 박사
phenomenal koengjanghan 굉장한
phenomenally koengjanghi 굉장히
phenomenon hyŏnsang 현상
philanthropic injŏng-i manŭn 인정이 많은
philanthropist chasŏn-ga 자선가
philanthropy chasŏn 자선
Philippines: ***the*** ~ P'illip'in 필리핀
philistine *n* kyoyang ŏmnŭn saram 교양 없는 사람
philosopher ch'ŏrhaktcha 철학자
philosophical ch'ŏrhaktchŏgin 철학적인
philosophy ch'ŏrhak 철학
phobia kongp'otchŭng 공포증
phone 1 *n* chŏnhwa 전화 **2** *v/t* chŏnhwa kŏlda 전화 걸다 **3** *v/i* chŏnhwahada 전화하다
phone book chŏnhwabŏnhobu 전화번호부; **phone booth** kongjung chŏnhwa pakssŭ 공중 전화 박스; **phonecall** chŏnhwa 전화; **phone number** chŏnhwa pŏnho 전화 번호
phon(e)y *adj* katchaŭi 가짜의; ***a ~ ten dollar bill*** ship tallŏ tchari wijo chip'ye 십 달러 짜리 위조 지폐
photo *n* sajin 사진
photo album sajinaelbŏm 사진앨범; **photocopier** pokssagi 복사기; **photocopy 1** *n* pokssa 복사 **2** *v/t* pokssahada 복사하다
photogenic sajini chal pannŭn 사진이 잘 받는
photograph 1 *n* sajin 사진 **2** *v/t* sajin tchiktta 사진 찍다
photographer sajinsa 사진사
photography sajin ch'waryŏng 사진 촬영
phrase 1 *n* munkku 문구 **2** *v/t* mallo p'yohyŏnhada 말로 표현하다
phrasebook sugŏjip 숙어집
physical 1 *adj* (*relating to the body*) yukch'eŭi 육체의 **2** *n* MED shinch'e kŏmsa 신체 검사
physical handicap shinch'e chang-ae 신체 장애
physically yukch'ejŏgŭro 육체적으로
physician naekkwa ŭisa 내과 의사
physicist mullihaktcha 물리학자
physics mullihak 물리학
physiotherapist mulli ch'iryosa 물리 치료사
physiotherapy mulli ch'iryo 물리 치료
physique mommae 몸매
pianist p'ianisŭt'ŭ 피아니스트
piano p'iano 피아노
pick 1 *n*: ***take your*** ~ korŭseyo 고르세요 **2** *v/t* (*choose*) sŏnt'aek'ada 선택하다; *flowers, fruit* ttada 따다; ~ ***one's nose*** k'orŭl hubida 코를 후비다 **3** *v/i*: ~ ***and choose*** korŭda 고르다
♦**pick at**: ~ ***one's food*** saech'ŏrŏm chogŭmsshik mŏktta 새처럼 조금씩 먹다
♦**pick on** (*treat unfairly*) ch'abyŏrhada 차별하다; (*select*) kollanaeda 골라내다
♦**pick out** (*identify*) araboda 알아보다
♦**pick up 1** *v/t* chibŏ tŭlda 집어 들다; (*from ground*) chuwŏ ollida 주워

올리다; *person, the kids etc* teryŏoda 데려오다; *dry cleaning etc* kajyŏoda 가져오다; *information* ipssuhada 입수하다; (*from airport etc*) majung naoda 마중 나오다; (*in car*) ch'a-e t'aeuda 차에 태우다; (*sexually*) ch'inhaejida 친해지다; *language, skill* paeuda 배우다; *habit* sŭpttŭk'ada 습득하다; *illness* ...-e kŏllida ...에 걸리다; (*buy*) sada 사다; *criminal* ch'ep'ohada 체포하다 **2** *v/i* (*improve*) hojŏndoeda 호전되다; (*of weather*) choajida 좋아지다

picket 1 *n* (*of strikers*) p'ik'et 피켓 **2** *v/t* kamshihada 감시하다

picket fence malttuk ult'ari 말뚝 울타리

picket line p'ik'et lain 피켓 라인

pickle *v/t* (sogŭm / shikch'oe) chŏrida (소금 / 식초에) 절이다

pickles p'ik'ŭl 피클

pickpocket somaech'igi 소매치기

pick-up (truck) t'ŭrŏk 트럭

picky F kkadaroun 까다로운

picnic 1 *n* sop'ung 소풍 **2** *v/i* sop'ung kada 소풍 가다

picture 1 *n* (*photo*) sajin 사진; (*painting*) hoehwa 회화; (*illustration*) kŭrim 그림; ***keep s.o. in the ~*** nuguege allyŏjuda 누구에게 알려주다 **2** *v/t* sangsanghada 상상하다

picture book kŭrimch'aek 그림책

picturesque kŭrimgwa kat'ŭn 그림과 같은

pie p'ai 파이

piece (*fragment*) chogak 조각; (*component*) pup'um 부품; (*in board game*) mal 말; ***a ~ of pie / bread*** p'ai / ppang han chogak 파이 / 빵 한 조각; ***a ~ of advice*** ch'unggo han madi 충고 한 마디; ***go to ~s*** chwajŏrhada 좌절하다; ***take to ~s*** punhaehada 분해하다

♦**piece together** *broken plate* chogagŭl moŭda 조각을 모으다; *facts, evidence* tcha match'uda 짜 맞추다

piecemeal *adv* han pŏne han kajisshik 한 번에 한 가지씩

piecework *n* sangnil 삯일

pierce (*penetrate*) kwant'onghada 관통하다; *ears* ttult'a 뚫다

piercing *noise* kwirŭl tchinnŭn tŭt'an 귀를 찢는 듯한; *eyes* nalk'aroun 날카로운; *wind* maesŏun 매서운

pig twaeji 돼지; (*unpleasant person*) twaejigat'ŭn nom 돼지같은 놈

pigeon pidulgi 비둘기

pigheaded wan-gohan 완고한; **pigpen** twaejiuri 돼지우리; *fig* chijŏbunhago pulgyŏrhan kot 지저분하고 불결한 곳; **pigskin** twaeji kajuk 돼지 가죽; **pigtail** ttaŭn mŏri 땋은 머리

pile tŏmi 더미; ***a ~ of work*** santtŏmigach'i manŭn il 산더미같이 많은 일

♦**pile up 1** *v/i* (*of work, bills*) moida 모이다 **2** *v/t* ssat'a 쌓다

piles MED ch'ijil 치질

pile-up MOT yŏnswae ch'ungdol 연쇄 충돌

pilfering chomttoduktchil 좀도둑질

pilgrim sullyeja 순례자

pilgrimage sullye 순례

pill aryak 알약; ***the ~*** mŏngnŭn p'iimnyak 먹는 피임약; ***be on the ~*** p'iimhada 피임하다

pillar kidung 기둥

pillion (*of motorbike*) twitjwasŏk 뒷좌석

pillow *n* pegae 베개

pillowcase pegaennit 베갯잇

pilot 1 *n* (*of airplane*) chojongsa 조종사 **2** *v/t airplane* chojonghada 조종하다

pilot plant shihŏm kongjang 시험 공장

pilot scheme yebi kyehoek 예비 계획

pimp *n* p'oju 포주

pimple yŏdŭrŭm 여드름

PIN (= ***personal identification number***) kaein hwagin pŏnho 개인 확인 번호

pin 1 *n* (*for sewing*) p'in 핀; (*in bowling*) pollingp'in 볼링핀; (*badge*) paetchi 배지; ***a 2-~ electric plug*** p'ini tu kaein p'ŭllŏgŭ 핀이 두 개인 플러그 **2** *v/t* (*hold down*) kkomtchak mot'age nurŭda 꼼짝 못하게 누르다;

(*attach*) kkot-tta 꽂다
♦**pin down**: ***pin s.o. down to a date*** nugurŭl t'ŭktchŏng naltcha-e tongŭihadorok mandŭlda 누구를 특정 날짜에 동의하도록 만들다
♦**pin up** *notice* puch'ida 붙이다
pincers p'ench'i 펜치; (*of crab*) chipkkebal 집게발
pinch 1 *n* kkojipkki 꼬집기; (*of salt, sugar etc*) *son-garagŭro chogŭm chipkki* 손가락으로 조금 집기; ***at a ~*** yusashie 유사시에 **2** *v/t* kkojiptta 꼬집다 **3** *v/i* (*of shoes*) kkok kkida 꼭 끼다
pine[1] *n* (*tree, wood*) sonamu 소나무
pine[2] *v/i*: **~ *for*** kŭriwŏhada 그리워하다
pineapple p'ainaep'ŭl 파인애플
ping *n* p'inghanŭn sori 핑하는 소리
ping-pong t'ak-kku 탁구
pink (*color*) punhongsaegŭi 분홍색의
pinnacle *fig* chŏngsang 정상
pinpoint chŏnghwak'i aranaeda 정확히 알아내다
pins and needles chŏrim 저림
pinstripe *adj* kanŭn serojul munŭiŭi 가는 세로줄 무늬의
pint p'aint'ŭ 파인트
pin-up (girl) p'in ŏp(yŏja) 핀 업(여자)
pioneer 1 *n fig* sŏn-guja 선구자 **2** *v/t* kaech'ŏk'ada 개척하다
pioneering *adj* sŏn-gujŏgin 선구적인
pious kyŏnggŏnhan 경건한
pip *n* (*of fruit*) sshi 씨
pipe 1 *n* (*for smoking*) p'aip'ŭ 파이프; (*for water, gas, sewage*) kwan 관 **2** *v/t* kwanŭro ponaeda 관으로 보내다
♦**pipe down** choyonghi hada 조용히 하다
piped music shillae kyŏng-ŭmak 실내 경음악
pipeline p'aip'ŭrain 파이프라인; ***in the ~*** chinhaeng chung-in 진행 중인
piping hot kimi solsol nage ttŭgŏun 김이 솔솔 나게 뜨거운
pirate *v/t software* p'yojŏrhada 표절하다
piss *v/i* V (*urinate*) ojum nuda 오줌 누다
pissed F (*annoyed*) hwaga nan 화가 난; *Br* (*drunk*) ch'ihan 취한
pistol kwŏnch'ong 권총
piston p'isŭt'on 피스톤
pit *n* (*hole*) kumŏng 구멍; (*coal mine*) kaeng 갱; (*in fruit*) sshi 씨
pitch[1] *n* MUS karak 가락
pitch[2] **1** *v/i* (*in baseball*) t'uguhada 투구하다 **2** *v/t tent* ch'ida 치다; *ball* tŏnjida 던지다
pitch black ch'irhŭk 칠흑
pitcher[1] (*baseball player*) t'usu 투수
pitcher[2] (*container*) chujŏnja 주전자
piteous pulssanghan 불쌍한
pitfall hamjŏng 함정
pith (*of citrus fruit*) shim 심
pitiful *sight* yŏnminŭl cha-anaenŭn 연민을 자아내는; *excuse, attempt* hanshimhan 한심한
pitiless maejŏnghan 매정한
pittance aju chŏgŭn ton 아주 적은 돈
pity 1 *n* tongjŏng 동정; ***it's a ~ that …*** … hadani aesŏk'agunyo … 하다니 애석하군요; ***what a ~!*** andwaetkkunyo! 안됐군요!; ***take ~ on*** pulssanghi yŏgida 불쌍히 여기다 **2** *v/t person* tongjŏnghada 동정하다
pivot *v/i* hoejŏnhada 회전하다
pixel COMPUT p'iksel 픽셀
pizza p'ija 피자
placard pyŏkppo 벽보
place 1 *n* changso 장소; (*restaurant*) shikttang 식당; (*bar*) sultchip 술집; (*apartment, house*) chip 집; (*in book*) ikttŏn kot 읽던 곳; (*in race, competition*) tŭngssu 등수; (*seat*) chari 자리; ***at my / his ~*** naŭi / kŭŭi chibesŏ 나의 / 그의 집에서; ***in ~ of*** taeshine 대신에; ***feel out of ~*** pulp'yŏnhada 불편하다; ***take ~*** yŏllida 열리다; ***in the first ~*** (*firstly*) ch'ŏt-tchaero 첫째로; (*in the beginning*) ch'ŏŭmenŭn 처음에는 **2** *v/t* (*put*) not'a 놓다; (*identify*) ŏttŏk'e algo innŭn saraminji aranaeda 어떻게 알고 있는 사람인지 알아내다; **~ *an order*** chumunhada 주문하다
place mat shikt'agyong maet'ŭ 식탁용 매트
placid ch'abunhan 차분한

plague 1 *n* chŏnyŏmppyŏng 전염병 **2** *v/t* (*bother*) koerop'ida 괴롭히다
plain[1] *n* p'yŏng-ya 평야
plain[2] **1** *adj* (*clear, obvious*) myŏngbaek'an 명백한; (*not fancy*) p'yŏngbŏmhan 평범한; (*not pretty*) motssaenggin 못생긴; (*not patterned*) mujiŭi 무지의; (*blunt*) soltchik'an 솔직한; ~ ***chocolate*** p'ŭllein ch'ok'ollit 플레인 초콜릿 **2** *adv crazy etc* wanjŏnhi 완전히
plain clothes: ***in*** ~ sabogŭi 사복의
plainly (*clearly*) punmyŏnghage 분명하게; (*bluntly*) soltchik'age 솔직하게; (*simply*) kanttanhi 간단히
plain-spoken soltchik'i marhanŭn 솔직히 말하는
plaintiff wŏn-go 원고
plaintive kusŭlp'ŭn 구슬픈
plait 1 *n* (*in hair*) ttaŭn mŏri 땋은 머리 **2** *v/t hair* ttat'a 땋다
plan 1 *n* (*project, intention*) kyehoek 계획; (*drawing*) sŏlgyedo 설계도 **2** *v/t* (*prepare*) chunbihada 준비하다; (*design*) tijainhada 디자인하다; ~ ***to do*** ...hal kŏsŭl kyehoek'ada ...할 것을 계획하다 **3** *v/i* kyehoek'ada 계획하다
plane[1] *n* (*airplane*) pihaenggi 비행기
plane[2] *n* (*tool*) taep'ae 대패
planet haengsŏng 행성
plank nŏlppanji 널빤지; *fig* (*of policy*) chŏngdang kangnyŏng hangmok 정당 강령 항목
planning chunbi 준비; ***at the ~ stage*** chunbihanŭn tan-gye-esŏ 준비하는 단계에서
plant[1] **1** *n* shingmul 식물 **2** *v/t* shimtta 심다
plant[2] *n* (*factory*) kongjang 공장; (*equipment*) changbi 장비
plantation p'ŭllaent'eishyŏn 플랜테이션
plaque[1] (*on wall*) kinyŏm aektcha 기념 액자
plaque[2] (*on teeth*) ch'isŏk 치석
plaster 1 *n* (*on wall, ceiling*) hoebanjuk 회반죽 **2** *v/t wall, ceiling* hoebanjugŭl parŭda 회반죽을 바르다; ***be ~ed with*** ... (ŭ)ro ttŏkch'iri toeda ... (으)로 떡칠이 되다
plaster cast sŏk-kkosang 석고상, kibsŭ 깁스
plastic 1 *n* p'ŭllasŭt'ik 플라스틱 **2** *adj* (*made of* ~) p'ullasŭt'igŭi 플라스틱의
plastic bag pinil pongji 비닐 봉지; **plastic money** shinyong k'adŭ 신용 카드; **plastic surgeon** sŏnghyŏng ŭisa 성형 의사; **plastic surgery** sŏnghyŏng susul 성형 수술
plate *n* (*for food*) chŏpssi 접시; (*sheet of metal*) p'an-gŭm 판금
plateau kowŏn 고원
platform (*stage*) tansang 단상; RAIL p'ŭllaetp'om 플랫폼; *fig* (*political*) chŏngdang kangnyŏng 정당 강령
platinum 1 *n* paek-kkŭm 백금 **2** *adj* paek-kkŭmŭi 백금의
platitude chinbuhan mal 진부한 말
platonic *relationship* chŏngshintchŏgin 정신적인
platoon (*of soldiers*) sodae 소대
platter (*for food*) taehyŏng chŏpssi 대형 접시
plausible kŭrŏl ttŭt'an 그럴 듯한
play 1 *n* (*in theater, on TV*) yŏn-gŭk 연극; (*of children*) nori 놀이; TECH tongnŏk 동력; SP kyŏnggi 경기 **2** *v/i* (*of children*) nolda 놀다; (*of musician*) yŏnjuhada 연주하다; (SP: *perform*) undonghada 운동하다; (SP: *take part*) ch'amgahada 참가하다 **3** *v/t musical instrument, piece of music* yŏnjuhada 연주하다; *game* hada 하다; *opponent* kyŏruda 겨루다; *Macbeth etc* yŏn-gihada 연기하다; ~ ***a joke on*** nollida 놀리다
♦**play around** (*be unfaithful*) paramŭl p'iuda 바람을 피우다
♦**play down** kyŏngshihada 경시하다
♦**play up** (*of machine*) kojang-i nada 고장이 나다; (*of child*) yadanbŏpsŏgŭl p'iuda 야단법석을 피우다; (*of tooth etc*) sangt'aega nappajida 상태가 나빠지다
playact (*pretend*) ch'ŏk'ada 척하다; **playback** chaesaeng 재생; **playboy** paramdung-i 바람둥이
player SP kyŏnggija 경기자; MUS yŏnjuja 연주자; THEA yŏn-gija 연기자

playful *punch etc* changnanŭi 장난의
playground norit'ŏ 놀이터
playing card k'adŭ 카드
playing field kyŏnggijang 경기장
playmate norich'in-gu 놀이친구
playwright kŭktchak-kka 극작가
plaza (*for shopping*) p'ŭllaja 플라자
plea *n* kanch'ŏng 간청
plead *v/i*: ~ ***for*** kanch'ŏnghada 간청하다; ~ ***guilty / not guilty*** yujoe / mujoerŭl hangbyŏnhada 유죄 / 무죄를 항변하다; ~ ***with*** kanch'ŏnghada 간청하다
pleasant yuk'waehan 유쾌한
please 1 *adv* chebal 제발; ***more tea? - yes,*** ~ ch'a tŏ hashigessŏyo? - ne, tŏ chuseyo 차 더 하시겠어요? - 네, 더 주세요; ~ ***do*** mullonimnida 물론입니다 **2** *v/t* kippŭge hada 기쁘게 하다; ~ ***yourself*** cho-ŭshil taero haseyo 좋으실 대로 하세요
pleased kippŭn 기쁜; (*satisfied*) manjok'an 만족한; ***be*** ~ ***with sth*** musŏse manjok'ada 무엇에 만족하다; ~ ***to meet you*** mannasŏ pan-gapssŭmnida 만나서 반갑습니다
pleasing chŭlgŏun 즐거운
pleasure (*happiness, satisfaction*) manjok 만족; (*not business*) orak 오락; (*delight*) kippŭmŭl chunŭn kŏt 기쁨을 주는 것; ***it's a*** ~ (*you're welcome*) ch'ŏnmaneyo 천만에요; ***with*** ~ kikkŏi 기꺼이
pleat *n* (*in skirt*) churŭm 주름
pledge 1 *n* (*promise*) yakssok 약속; ***Pledge of Allegiance*** kuk-kkie taehan maengse 국기에 대한 맹세 **2** *v/t* (*promise*) yakssok'ada 약속하다
plentiful nŏngnŏk'an 넉넉한
plenty (*abundance*) p'ung-yo 풍요; ~ ***of*** manŭn 많은; ***that's*** ~ twaessŏyo 됐어요; ***there's*** ~ ***for everyone*** moduege toragal mank'ŭm ch'ungbunhamnida 모두에게 돌아갈 만큼 충분합니다
pliable hwigi shwiun 휘기 쉬운
pliers p'ench'i 펜치; ***a pair of*** ~ p'ench'i han pŏl 펜치 한 벌
plight kon-gyŏng 곤경
plod *v/i* (*walk*) mugŏun kŏrŭmŭro ch'ŏnch'ŏnhi kŏt-tta 무거운 걸음으로 천천히 걷다
♦**plod along, plod on** (*with a job*) yŏrŭi ŏpsshi kŭrŏktchŏrŏk hada 열의 없이 그럭저럭 하다
plodder (*at work, school*) kkujunhi irhanŭn saram 꾸준히 일하는 사람
plot[1] *n* (*land*) chagŭn kuhoegŭi ttang 작은 구획의 땅
plot[2] **1** *n* (*conspiracy*) kyeryak 계략; (*of novel*) kusŏng 구성 **2** *v/t* hoekch'aek'ada 획책하다 **3** *v/i* ŭmmohada 음모하다
plotter ŭmmoja 음모자; COMPUT p'ŭllot'ŏ 플로터
plow 1 *n* chaenggi 쟁기 **2** *v/t* kalda 갈다 **3** *v/i* kyŏngjak'ada 경작하다
♦**plow back** *profits* chaet'ujahada 재투자하다
pluck *v/t eyebrows* ppoptta 뽑다; *chicken* t'ŏrŭl chaba ppoptta 털을 잡아 뽑다
♦**pluck up**: ~ ***courage*** yonggirŭl naeda 용기를 내다
plug 1 *n* (*for sink, bath*) magae 마개; (*electrical*) p'ŭllŏgŭ 플러그; (*spark* ~) chŏmhwa p'ullŏgŭ 점화 플러그; (*for new book etc*) sŏnjŏnyong ch'uch'ŏnsa 선전용 추천사 **2** *v/t hole* t'ŭrŏ maktta 틀어 막다; *new book etc* sŏnjŏnhada 선전하다
♦**plug away** F yŏlsshimhi kkujunhage hada 열심히 꾸준하게 하다
♦**plug in** *v/t* p'ŭllŏgŭrŭl kkot-tta 플러그를 꽂다
plum 1 *n* chadu 자두 **2** *adj job* taeuga t'ukppyŏrhan 대우가 특별한
plumage kitt'ŏl 깃털
plumb *adj* sujigŭi 수직의
plumber paegwangong 배관공
plumbing (*pipes*) paegwan 배관
plummet (*of airplane*) sujigŭro ttŏrŏjida 수직으로 떨어지다; (*of prices*) chik kangha 직 강하
plump *adj* p'odongp'odonghan 포동포동한
♦**plump for** korŭda 고르다
plunge 1 *n* ttwiŏdŭm 뛰어듦; (*in prices*) harak 하락; ***take the*** ~ mohŏmŭl hada 모험을 하다 **2** *v/i* torip'ada 돌입하다; (*of prices*)

harak'ada 하락하다 **3** *v/t* tchirŭda 찌르다; ***the city was ~d into darkness*** toshiga ŏduum sogŭro ppajyŏ tŭrŏt-tta 도시가 어둠 속으로 빠져 들었다; ***the news ~d him into despair*** kŭ soshigŭro, kŭnŭn chŏlmang-e ppajyŏt-tta 그 소식으로, 그는 절망에 빠졌다
plunging *neckline* kip'i p'ajin 깊이 파진
plural 1 *adj* pokssuŭi 복수의 **2** *n* pokssuhyŏng 복수형
plus 1 *prep* tŏhayŏ 더하여 **2** *adj* isang-ŭi 이상의; ***$500 ~*** 500 tallŏ isang 오백 달러 이상 **3** *n* (*symbol*) tŏhagi 더하기; (*advantage*) ittchŏm 이점 **4** *conj* (*moreover*) tŏugi 더욱이
plush hwaryŏhan 화려한
plywood happ'an 합판
p.m. ohu 오후
pneumatic kich'eŭi 기체의
pneumatic drill konggi tŭril 공기 드릴
pneumonia p'yeryŏm 폐렴
poach[1] *v/t* (*cook*) ttŭgŏun mure samtta 뜨거운 물에 삶다
poach[2] **1** *v/i* millyŏp'ada 밀렵하다 **2** *v/t* (*hunt*) *salmon etc* mollae chaptta 몰래 잡다
poached egg suran 수란
P.O. Box sasŏham 사서함
pocket 1 *n* hojumŏni 호주머니; ***line one's own ~s*** chagi hojumŏnirŭl ch'aeuda 자기 호주머니를 채우다; ***be out of ~*** pint'ŏlt'ŏriga toeda 빈털터리가 되다 **2** *adj* (*miniature*) sohyŏng-ŭi 소형의 **3** *v/t* sŭltchŏk kajida 슬쩍 가지다
pocketbook (*purse*) chagŭn sonkkabang 작은 손가방; (*billfold*) chigap 지갑; (*book*) p'ok'etyong ch'aek 포켓용 책; **pocket calculator** p'ok'etyong kyesan-gi 포켓용 계산기; **pocketknife** chumŏnik'al 주머니칼
podium yŏndan 연단
poem shi 시
poet shiin 시인
poetic shittchŏgin 시적인
poetic justice sap'ilgwijŏng 사필귀정
poetry shi 시
poignant kamdongjŏgin 감동적인
point 1 *n* (*of pencil, knife*) kkŭt 끝; (*in competition, exam*) chŏmsu 점수; (*purpose*) moktchŏk 목적; (*moment*) sun-gan 순간; (*in argument, discussion*) yotchŏm 요점; (*in decimals*) sosutchŏm 소수점; ***5~3*** otchŏm sam 오점 삼; ***beside the ~*** yotchŏmŭl pŏsŏnan 요점을 벗어난; ***be on the ~ of*** mak haryŏgo hada 막 하려고 하다; ***get to the ~*** yotchŏmŭl marhada 요점을 말하다; ***the ~ is ...*** yotchŏmŭn ... 요점은...; ***there's no ~ in waiting / trying*** kidaril / shidohal iyuga ŏpssŏyo 기다릴 / 시도할 이유가 없어요 **2** *v/i* sonkkaragŭro karik'ida 손가락으로 가리키다 **3** *v/t gun* kyŏnuda 겨누다
♦ **point at** (*with finger*) karik'ida 가리키다
♦ **point out** *sights, advantages* chijŏk'ada 지적하다
♦ **point to** (*with finger*) sonkkaragŭro karik'ida 손가락으로 가리키다; *fig* (*indicate*) amshihada 암시하다
point-blank 1 *adj refusal* nogoltchŏgin 노골적인; ***at ~ range*** chikssa kŏriesŏ 직사 거리에서 **2** *adv refuse* nogoltchŏgŭro 노골적으로
pointed *remark* nalk'aroun 날카로운
pointer (*for teacher*) kyop'yŏn 교편; (*hint*) choŏn 조언; (*sign, indication*) amshi 암시
pointless soyongŏmnŭn 소용없는; ***it's ~ trying*** noryŏk'aedo soyong-ŏpssŏyo 노력해도 소용없어요
point of sale (*place*) maejang 매장; (*promotional material*) sŏnjŏnyong mulp'um 선전용 물품
point of view kwantchŏm 관점
poise ch'imch'ak 침착
poised *person* ch'imch'ak'an 침착한
poison 1 *n* tok 독 **2** *v/t* tokssarhada 독살하다; *water* togŭl t'ada 독을 타다; *fig*: *relationship* mangch'ida 망치다
poisonous yudok'an 유독한
poke 1 *n* tchirŭgi 찌르기 **2** *v/t* (*prod*) ssushida 쑤시다; (*stick*) k'uk tchirŭda 쿡 찌르다; ***~ fun at*** nollida 놀리다; ***~ one's nose into*** ch'amgyŏnhada

참견하다
♦**poke around** (*in a place*) twijida 뒤지다; (*ask about a person*) kkoch'ikkoch'i k'aeda 꼬치꼬치 캐다
poker (*card game*) p'okŏ 포커
poky (*cramped*) pijobŭn 비좁은
Poland P'ollandŭ 폴란드
polar kŭktchiŭi 극지의
polar bear puk-kkŭk kom 북극 곰
polarize *v/t* yangbunhwahada 양분화하다
Pole P'ollandŭin 폴란드인
pole[1] (*of wood, metal*) kidung 기둥
pole[2] (*of earth*) kŭk 극
polevault changttae nop'i ttwigi 장대 높이 뛰기
police *n* kyŏngch'al 경찰
policeman kyŏngch'algwan 경찰관; **police state** kyŏngch'al kuk-kka 경찰 국가; **police station** kyŏngch'alsŏ 경찰서; **policewoman** yŏgyŏng 여경
policy[1] chŏngch'aek 정책
policy[2] (*insurance ~*) yak-kkwan 약관
polio soamabi 소아마비
Polish 1 *adj* P'ollandŭŭi 폴란드의 **2** *n* P'ollandŭŏ 폴란드어
polish 1 *n* kwangt'aektche 광택제; (*nail ~*) maenik'yuŏ 매니큐어 **2** *v/t* kwangnaeda 광내다; *speech* tadŭmtta 다듬다
♦**polish off** *food* ta mŏgŏ ch'iuda 다 먹어 치우다
♦**polish up** *skill* kalgo tadŭmtta 갈고 다듬다
polished *performance* chal tadŭmŏjin 잘 다듬어진
polite kongsonhan 공손한
politely kongsonhage 공손하게
politeness kongsonham 공손함
political chŏngch'ijŏgin 정치적인
politically correct p'yŏn-gyŏni ŏmnŭn 편견이 없는
politician chŏngch'iga 정치가
politics chŏngch'i 정치; ***what are his ~?*** kŭ saramŭi chŏngch'ijŏk sogyŏni mwŏn-gayo? 그 사람의 정치적 소견이 뭔가요?
poll 1 *n* (*survey*) yŏron chosa 여론 조사; ***the ~s*** (*election*) sŏn-gŏ 선거; ***go to the ~s*** t'up'yohada 투표하다 **2** *v/t people* yŏronŭl mut-tta 여론을 묻다; *votes* tŭkp'yohada 득표하다
pollen hwabun 화분
pollen count hwabunnyang 화분량
polling booth kip'yoso 기표소
pollster yŏron chosawŏn 여론 조사원
pollutant oyŏmmultchil 오염물질
pollute oyŏmshik'ida 오염시키다
pollution oyŏm 오염
polo neck t'ŏt'ŭlnek 터틀넥
polo shirt p'olo shyŏch'ŭ 폴로 셔츠
polyethylene p'olliet'illen 폴리에틸렌
polyester p'olliesŭt'erŭ 폴리에스테르
polystyrene p'ollisŭt'iren 폴리스티렌
polyunsaturate kodo pulp'ohwa multchil 고도 불포화 물질
pompous kŏdŭrŭm p'iunŭn 거드름 피우는
pond yŏnmot 연못
ponder *v/i* komgomi saenggak'ada 곰곰이 생각하다
pony chorangmal 조랑말
ponytail twiro mungnŭn mŏri 뒤로 묶는 머리
poodle p'udŭl 푸들
pool[1] (*swimming ~*) suyŏngjang 수영장; (*of water, blood*) ungdŏng-i 웅덩이
pool[2] (*game*) Miguksshik tanggu 미국식 당구
pool[3] **1** *n* (*fund*) kongdonggigŭm 공동기금 **2** *v/t resources* kongdong ikkwŏnŭro hada 공동 이권으로 하다
pool hall tanggujang 당구장
pool table tanggudae 당구대
pooped F nokch'oga toen 녹초가 된
poor 1 *adj* (*not wealthy*) kananhan 가난한; (*not good*) sŏt'urŭn 서투른; (*unfortunate*) purhaenghan 불행한; ***be in ~ health*** kŏn-gang-i choch'i antta 건강이 좋지 않다; ***~ old Tony!*** pulssanghan T'oni! 불쌍한 토니! **2** *n*: ***the ~*** pinja 빈자
poorly 1 *adv* hyŏngp'yŏnŏpssi 형편없이 **2** *adj* (*unwell*) momi choch'i anŭn 몸이 좋지 않은
pop[1] **1** *n* (*noise*) p'ŏng hanŭn sori 펑 하는 소리 **2** *v/i* (*of balloon etc*) p'ŏng hanŭn soriga nada 펑 하는 소리가 나다 **3** *v/t cork* ttada 따다; *balloon* p'ŏng hago t'ŏjida 펑 하고 터지다

pop[2] **1** *n* MUS taejunggayo 대중가요 **2** *adj* taejung-ŭi 대중의
pop[3] F (*father*) appa 아빠
pop[4] F (*put*) noa tuda 놓아 두다
♦**pop up** *v/i* (*appear suddenly*) pulssuk nat'anada 불쑥 나타나다
popcorn p'apk'on 팝콘
pope kyohwang 교황
poppy yanggwibi 양귀비
Popsicle® aisŭ k'eik'ŭ 아이스 케이크
pop song p'apssong 팝송
popular inkki innŭn 인기 있는; *belief, support* taejungtchŏgin 대중적인
popularity inkki 인기
populate kŏjuhada 거주하다
population in-gu 인구
porcelain 1 *n* tojagi 도자기 **2** *adj* tojagiŭi 도자기의
porch peranda 베란다
porcupine hojŏ 호저
pore (*of skin*) mogong 모공
♦**pore over** chasehi poda 자세히 보다
pork twaejigogi 돼지고기
porn *n* p'orŭno 포르노
porn(o) *adj* p'orŭnoŭi 포르노의
pornographic oesŏltchŏgin 외설적인
pornography p'orŭno 포르노
porous t'ugwassŏngi choŭn 투과성이 좋은
port[1] *n* (*town*) hanggu 항구; (*area*) pudu 부두
port[2] *adj* (*left-hand*) chwach'ugŭi 좌측의
port[3] COMPUT p'ot'ŭ 포트
portable 1 *adj* hyudaeyong-ŭi 휴대용의 **2** *n* COMPUT, TV p'ot'ŏbŭl 포터블
porter unbanin 운반인; (*doorkeeper*) munjigi 문지기
porthole NAUT hyŏnch'ang 현창
portion *n* pubun 부분; (*of food*) inbun 인분
portrait 1 *n* (*painting, photograph*) ch'osanghwa 초상화; (*depiction*) myosa 묘사 **2** *adv print* seroro 세로로
portray (*of artist, photographer*) ch'osanghwarŭl kŭrida / tchiktta 초상화를 그리다 / 찍다; (*of actor*) yŏn-gihada 연기하다; (*of author*) myosahada 묘사하다
portrayal (*by actor*) yŏn-gi 연기; (*by author*) myosa 묘사
Portugal P'orŭt'ugal 포르투갈
Portuguese 1 *adj* P'orŭt'ugarŭi 포르투갈의 **2** *n* (*person*) P'orŭt'ugarin 포르투갈인; (*language*) P'orŭt'ugarŏ 포르투갈어
pose 1 *n* (*pretense*) kŏtch'ire 겉치레 **2** *v/i* (*for artist, photographer*) p'ojŭ ch'wihada 포즈 취하다; **~ *as*** (*of person*) ... in ch'ŏk'ada ... 인 척하다 **3** *v/t*: ***~ a problem / a threat*** munje / wihyŏbŭl yagihada 문제 / 위협을 야기하다
position 1 *n* (*location*) wich'i 위치; (*stance*) chase 자세; (*in race, competition*) wi 위; (*occupied by soldiers*) chinji 진지; (*point of view*) kwantchŏm 관점; (*situation*) iptchang 입장; (*job*) chigŏp 직업; (*status*) chiwi 지위 **2** *v/t* paech'ihada 배치하다
positive *attitude* chŏk-kkŭktchŏgin 적극적인; *response* kŭngjŏngjŏgin 긍정적인; *test results* yangsŏng-ŭi 양성의; GRAM wŏnkkŭbŭi 원급의; ELEC yanggŭgŭi 양극의; ***be ~*** (*sure*) hwaksshinhada 확신하다
positively (*decidedly*) punmyŏnghi 분명히; (*definitely*) hwakssirhi 확실히
possess soyuhada 소유하다
possession (*ownership*) soyu 소유; (*thing owned*) soyumul 소유물; ***~s*** chaesan 재산
possessive *person* soyuyogi kanghan 소유욕이 강한; GRAM soyukkyŏk 소유격
possibility kanŭngssŏng 가능성
possible kanŭnghan 가능한; ***the quickest ~ ...*** kanŭnghan kajang pparŭn ... 가능한 가장 빠른 ...; ***the best ~ ...*** kanŭnghan ch'oesŏnŭi ... 가능한 최선의 ...
possibly (*perhaps*) amado 아마도; ***how could I ~ have known that?*** chega kwayŏn ŏttŏk'e kŭgŏsŭl al su issŏtkkessŭmnikka? 제가 과연 어떻게 그것을 알 수 있었겠습니까?; ***that can't ~ be right*** kŭgŏn chŏlttaero orŭl li ŏpssŏyo 그건

절대로 샐을 리 없어요; ***could you ~ tell me ...?*** ...ŭl/rŭl malssŭmhae chushil su innŭnjiyo? ...을/를 말씀해 주실 수 있는지요?
post[1] **1** *n* (*of wood*, *metal*) kidung 기둥 **2** *v/t notice* keshihada 게시하다; *profits* kongshihada 공시하다; ***keep s.o. ~ed*** nuguege kyesok soshigŭl chŏnhada 누구에게 계속 소식을 전하다
post[2] **1** *n* (*place of duty*) pusŏ 부서 **2** *v/t soldier*, *employee* paesok'ada 배속하다; *guards* paech'ihada 배치하다
postage up'yŏn yogŭm 우편 요금
postal up'yŏnŭi 우편의
postcard yŏpssŏ 엽서
postdate shiltcheboda naltcharŭl nŭtch'uŏ chŏktta 실제보다 날짜를 늦추어 적다
poster p'osŭt'ŏ 포스터
posterior *n* F kungdung-i 궁둥이
posterity hudae 후대
postgraduate 1 *n* taehagwŏn hakssaeng 대학원 학생 **2** *adj* taehagwŏnŭi 대학원의
posthumous sahuŭi 사후의; ***a ~ child*** yuboktcha 유복자
posthumously sahue 사후에
posting (*assignment*) immyŏng 임명
postmark soin 소인
postmortem kŏmshi 검시
post office uch'eguk 우체국
postpone yŏn-gihada 연기하다
postponement yŏn-gi 연기
posture chase 자세
postwar chŏnhuŭi 전후의
pot[1] (*for cooking*) naembi 냄비; (*for coffee*, *tea*) chujŏnja 주전자; (*for plant*) hwabun 화분
pot[2] F (*marijuana*) taemach'o 대마초
potato kamja 감자
potato chips kamja ch'ip 감자 칩
potent kangnyŏk'an 강력한
potential 1 *adj* chamjaejŏgin 잠재적인 **2** *n* chamjaeryŏk 잠재력
potentially chamjaejŏgŭro 잠재적으로
pothole (*in road*) p'aein kumŏng 패인 구멍
potter *n* togong 도공
pottery (*activity*) toye 도예; (*items*) togi 도기; (*place*) toyeji 도예지
potty *n* (*for baby*) yuayong pyŏn-gi 유아용 변기
pouch (*bag*) chagŭn chumŏni 작은 주머니
poultry (*birds*) kagŭm 가금; (*meat*) kagŭm kogi 가금 고기
pounce *v/i* (*of animal*) tŏmbida 덤비다; *fig* tŏpch'ida 덮치다
pound[1] *n* (*weight*) p'aundŭ 파운드
pound[2] (*for strays*) uri 우리; (*for cars*) ch'aryang kyŏninso 차량 견인소
pound[3] *v/i* (*of heart*) ttwida 뛰다; ***~ on*** (*hammer on*) magu tudŭrida 마구 두드리다
pound sterling p'aundŭ ton 파운드 돈
pour 1 *v/t liquid* ssoda put-tta 쏟아 붓다 **2** *v/i*: ***it's ~ing*** (***with rain***) (piga) ŏkssugach'i p'ŏbunnŭnda (비가) 억수같이 퍼붓는다
♦**pour out** *liquid* ttarŭda 따르다; *troubles* t'ŏ not'a 터 놓다
pout *v/i* ppurut'unghada 뿌루퉁하다
poverty kanan 가난
poverty-stricken tchijŏjige kananhan 찢어지게 가난한
powder 1 *n* karu 가루; (*for face*) pun 분 **2** *v/t face* pun parŭda 분 바르다
powder room hwajangshil 화장실
power 1 *n* (*strength*) him 힘; (*authority*) kwŏllyŏk 권력; (*energy*) enŏji 에너지; (*electricity*) chŏn-gi 전기; ***in ~*** POL chipkkwŏnhanŭn 집권하는; ***fall from ~*** POL kwŏnjwaesŏ ttŏrŏjida 권좌에서 떨어지다 **2** *v/t*: ***be ~ed by*** ...(ŭ)ro umjigida ...(으)로 움직이다
power cut chŏngjŏn 정전
powerful kangnyŏk'an 강력한
powerless muryŏk'an 무력한; ***be ~ to ...*** tojŏhi ...hal su ŏptta 도저히 ...할 수 없다
power line chŏn-gisŏn 전기선; **power outage** chŏngjŏn 정전; **power station** paltchŏnso 발전소; **power steering** p'awŏ sŭt'iŏring 파워 스티어링; **power unit** (*of computer*) p'awŏ yunit 파워 유닛; (*motor*) enjin 엔진
PR (= ***public relations***) hongbo 홍보

practical *experience* shiltchejŏgin 실제적인; *person* shillijŏgin 실리적인; (*functional*) shiryongjŏgin 실용적인
practical joke haengdong-ŭro hanŭn mot-ttoen changnan 행동으로 하는 못된 장난
Practical Learning Shirhak 실학
practically *behave*, *think* shillijŏgŭro 실리적으로; (*almost*) kŏŭi 거의
practice 1 *n* shiltche 실제; (*training*) yŏnssŭp 연습; (*rehearsal*) lihŏsŏl 리허설; (*custom*) sŭpkkwan 습관; ***in ~*** (*in reality*) hyŏnshiltchŏgŭro 현실적으로; ***be out of ~*** sŏt'urŭda 서투르다 **2** *v/i* hullyŏnhada 훈련하다 **3** *v/t* yŏnssŭp'ada 연습하다; *law*, *medicine* chongsahada 종사하다
pragmatic shillijŏgin 실리적인
pragmatism shiryongjuŭi 실용주의
prairie taech'owŏn 대초원
praise 1 *n* ch'ingch'an 칭찬 **2** *v/t* ch'ingch'anhada 칭찬하다
praiseworthy ch'ingch'an hal manhan 칭찬 할 만한
prank changnan 장난
prattle *v/i* chaejalgŏrida 재잘거리다
pray kidohada 기도하다
prayer kido 기도
preach 1 *v/i* REL sŏlgyohada 설교하다; (*moralize*) t'airŭda 타이르다 **2** *v/t* sŏlgyohada 설교하다
preacher sŏlgyoja 설교자
precarious puranjŏnghan 불안정한
precariously puranjŏnghage 불안정하게
precaution yebang 예방
precautionary *measure* yebang-ŭi 예방의
precede *v/t* (*in time*) miri haenghaejida 미리 행해지다; (*walk in front of*) apssŏ kada 앞서 가다
precedence: ***take ~*** usŏnhada 우선하다; ***take ~ over*** ...e usŏnhada ...에 우선하다
precedent sŏllye 선례
preceding *week etc* chŏn(ŭi) 전(의); *chapter* ap'ŭi 앞의
precinct (*district*) haengjŏng kuyŏk 행정 구역
precious kwijunghan 귀중한
precipitate *v/t crisis* yagishik'ida 야기시키다
précis *n* yoyak 요약
precise chŏnghwak'an 정확한
precisely chŏnghwak'age 정확하게
precision chŏnghwak 정확
precocious *child* chosuk'an 조숙한
preconceived *idea* sŏnibŭi 선입의
precondition p'ilssu chokkŏn 필수 조건
predator (*animal*) yuksshik tongmul 육식 동물
predecessor (*in job*) chŏnimja 전임자; (*machine*) ijŏn model 이전 모델
predestination unmyŏng yejŏngsŏl 운명 예정설
predicament kungji 궁지
predict yegyŏnhada 예견하다
predictable yegyŏnhal su innŭn 예견할 수 있는
prediction yegyŏn 예견
predominant chuyohan 주요한
predominantly churo 주로
predominate chuga toeŏ it-tta 주가 되어 있다
prefabricated choripsshigŭi 조립식의
preface *n* sŏmun 서문
prefer sŏnhohada 선호하다; ***~ X to Y*** Xŭl / rŭl Ypoda tŏ choahada X을 / 를 Y보다 더 좋아하다; ***~ to do*** ohiryŏ ...nŭn kŏshi natkket-tta 오히려 ...는 것이 낫겠다
preferable ohiryŏ naŭn 오히려 나은; ***be ~ to*** poda nat-tta 보다 낫다
preferably toedorok imyŏn 되도록 이면
preference sŏnho 선호
preferential udaehanŭn 우대하는
prefix *n* chŏpttusa 접두사
pregnancy imshin 임신
pregnant imshinhan 임신한
prehistoric sŏnsashidaeŭi 선사시대의; *fig* shidaee aju twittŏrŏjin 시대에 아주 뒤떨어진
prejudice 1 *n* sŏnipkkyŏn 선입견 **2** *v/t person* p'yŏn-gyŏnŭl p'umkke hada 편견을 품게 하다; *chances* sonsangshik'ida 손상시키다
prejudiced p'yŏn-gyŏnŭl kajin 편견을 가진
preliminary *adj* yebiŭi 예비의

premarital honjŏnŭi 혼전의; ~ ***sex*** honjŏn sŏnggyo 혼전 성교
premature shigisangjoŭi 시기상조의; ~ ***baby*** misuga 미숙아; ~ ***death*** yojŏl 요절
premeditated kyehoektchŏgin 계획적인
premier *n* POL susang 수상
première *n* ch'oyŏn 초연
premises kunae 구내
premium *n* (*in insurance*) p'ŭrimiŏm 프리미엄
premonition yegam 예감
prenatal ch'ulssaeng chŏnŭi 출생 전의
preoccupied molttuhan 몰두한
preparation (*act*) chunbi 준비; ***in ~ for*** ...ŭl / rŭl chunbihaesŏ ...을 / 를 준비해서; ~***s*** chunbi 준비
prepare 1 *v/t room, meal* chunbihada 준비하다; ***be ~d to do sth*** (*willing*) muŏsŭl hal chunbiga toeŏ it-tta 무엇을 할 준비가 되어 있다 **2** *v/i* chunbihada 준비하다
preposition chŏnch'isa 전치사
preposterous t'ŏmuni ŏmnŭn 터무니 없는
prerequisite chŏnjejokkŏn 전제조건
Presbyterian Church Changno Kyohoe 장로 교회
prescribe (*of doctor*) ch'ŏbanghada 처방하다
prescription MED ch'ŏbangjŏn 처방전
presence issŭm 있음; ***in the ~ of*** myŏnjŏnesŏ 면전에서
presence of mind ch'imch'ak'am 침착함
present[1] **1** *adj* (*current*) hyŏnjaeŭi 현재의; ***be*** ~ ch'amsŏk'ada 참석하다 **2** *n*: ***the*** ~ hyŏnjae 현재; GRAM hyŏnjaehyŏng 현재형; ***at*** ~ chigŭm 지금
present[2] **1** *n* (*gift*) sŏnmul 선물 **2** *v/t award, bouquet* suyŏhada 수여하다; *program* sogaehada 소개하다; ~ ***X with Y*** Yŭl / rŭl Xege chŭngjŏnghada Y을 / 를 X에게 증정하다
presentation (*to audience*) palp'yo 발표
present-day onŭlnarŭi 오늘날의
presently (*now*) hyŏnjaeronŭn 현재로는; (*soon*) kot 곧
preservation pojon 보존
preservative *n* pangbuje 방부제
preserve 1 *n* (*domain*) yŏngyŏk 영역 **2** *v/t standards, peace etc* pojonhada 보존하다; *wood etc* pohohada 보호하다; *food* chŏjanghada 저장하다
preside *v/i* (*at meeting*) sahoe poda 사회 보다; ~ ***over*** *meeting* ŭijang norŭt'ada 의장 노릇하다
presidency (*term*) taet'ongnyŏng imgi 대통령 임기; (*office*) taet'ongnyŏngjik 대통령직
president POL taet'ongnyŏng 대통령; (*of company*) sajang 사장
presidential taet'ongnyŏngŭi 대통령의
press 1 *n*: ***the*** ~ ŏllon 언론 **2** *v/t button* nurŭda 누르다; (*urge*) kangyohada 강요하다; *hand* kkwak chwida 꽉 쥐다; *grapes* tchada 짜다; *clothes* tarimjirhada 다림질하다 **3** *v/i*: ~ ***for*** chorŭda 조르다
press conference kijahoegyŏn 기자회견
pressing *adj* chŏlsshirhan 절실한
pressure 1 *n* amnyŏk 압력; (*air* ~) kiap 기압; (*of work, demands*) amnyŏk 압력; ***be under ~*** sŭt'ŭresŭga it-tta 스트레스가 있다; ***be under ~ to ...*** ... haeya hal wigie mollyŏit-tta ... 해야 할 위기에 몰려있다 **2** *v/t* amnyŏgŭl kahada 압력을 가하다
prestige myŏngsŏng 명성
prestigious myŏngsŏng-i nainnŭn 명성이 나있는
presumably amado 아마도
presume ch'ujŏnghada 추정하다; ~ ***to ...*** ... kamhi...hada 감히 ...하다
presumption (*of innocence, guilt*) ch'ujŏng 추정
presumptuous kŏnbangjin 건방진
pre-tax segŭmŭl p'ohamhan 세금을 포함한
pretend 1 *v/t* ... in ch'ŏk'ada ... 인 척하다 **2** *v/i* ch'ŏk'ada 척하다
pretense kŏjit 거짓
pretentious challan ch'ŏk'anŭn 잘난 척하는

pretext p'inggye 핑계
pretty 1 *adj* yeppŭn 예쁜 **2** *adv* (*quite*) sangdanghi 상당히
prevail igida 이기다
prevailing usehan 우세한
prevent maktta 막다; **~ *X* (*from*) *doing Y*** Xi / ga Yhanŭn kŏsŭl mot'age hada X이 / 가 Y하는 것을 못하게 하다
prevention yebang 예방
preventive yebangŭi 예방의
preview *n* (*of movie*) shisa 시사; (*of exhibition*) shiyŏn 시연
previous ijŏnŭi 이전의
previously chŏne 전에
prewar chŏnjaeng chŏnŭi 전쟁 전의
prey *n* mŏgi 먹이
♦**prey on** chabamŏktta 잡아먹다; *fig* (*of conman etc*) tŭngch'yŏmŏktta 등쳐먹다
price 1 *n* kagyŏk 가격 **2** *v/t* COM kagyŏgŭl maegida 가격을 매기다
priceless kapssŭl maegil su ŏmnŭn 값을 매길 수 없는
price war kagyŏk harin kyŏngjaeng 가격 할인 경쟁
prick[1] **1** *n* (*pain*) tchirŭm 찌름 **2** *v/t* (*jab*) tchirŭda 찌르다
prick[2] *n* V (*penis*) chot 좆; (*person*) yabihan nom 야비한 놈
♦**prick up**: **~ *one's ears*** (*of dog*) kwirŭl tchonggŭt seuda 귀를 쫑긋 세우다; (*of person*) kwi kiurida 귀 기울이다
prickle (*on plant*) kashi 가시
prickly *beard*, *plant* ttakkŭmgŏrinŭn 따끔거리는; (*irritable*) sŏngmarŭn 성마른
pride 1 *n* (*in person*, *achievement*) charang 자랑; (*self-respect*) chajonshim 자존심 **2** *v/t*: **~ *oneself on*** charangsŭrŏpkke yŏgida 자랑스럽게 여기다
priest sŏngjiktcha 성직자; (*Catholic*) shinbu 신부
primarily ponjiltchŏgŭro 본질적으로
primary 1 *adj* chuyohan 주요한 **2** *n* POL yebisŏn-gŏ 예비선거
prime 1 *n*: ***be in one's* ~** hanch'ang ttaeida 한창 때이다 **2** *adj example*, *reason* kajang chungnyohan 가장 중요한; ***of* ~ *importance*** aju chungdaehan 아주 중대한
prime minister kungmuch'ongni 국무총리
prime time TV hwanggŭmshiganttae 황금시간대
primitive wŏnshiŭi 원시의; *conditions* wŏnshijŏgin 원시적인
prince wangja 왕자
princess kongju 공주
principal 1 *adj* chuyohan 주요한 **2** *n* (*of school*) kyojang 교장
principally taegae 대개
principle (*in moral sense*) toŭi 도의; (*rule*) wŏnch'ik 원칙; ***on* ~** toŭisang 도의상; ***in* ~** wŏnch'iktchŏgŭro 원칙적으로
print 1 *n* (*in book*, *newspaper etc*) inswae 인쇄; (*photograph*) inhwa 인화; ***out of* ~** chŏlp'andoen 절판된 **2** *v/t book*, *newspaper* parhaenghada 발행하다; COMPUT inswaehada 인쇄하다; (*using block capitals*) taemuntcharo ssŭda 대문자로 쓰다
♦**print out** inswaehada 인쇄하다
printed matter inswaemul 인쇄물
printer (*person*) inswaeŏptcha 인쇄업자; (*machine*) p'ŭrint'ŏ 프린터
printing press inswaegi 인쇄기
printout p'ŭrint'ŭdoen kŏt 프린트된 것
prior 1 *adj* ijŏnŭi 이전의 **2** *prep*: **~ *to*** chŏne 전에
prioritize (*put in order of priority*) usŏn sunwirŭl maegida 우선 순위를 매기다; (*give priority to*) usŏnkkwŏnŭl chuda 우선권을 주다
priority ch'oeusŏn sahang 최우선 사항; ***have* ~** usŏnkkwŏni it-tta 우선권이 있다
prison kamok 감옥
prisoner choesu 죄수; ***take s.o.* ~** nugurŭl p'ororo chaptta 누구를 포로로 잡다
prisoner of war chŏnjaeng p'oro 전쟁 포로
privacy sasaenghwal 사생활
private 1 *adj* satchŏgin 사적인 **2** *n* MIL sabyŏng 사병; ***in* ~** naemirhage 내밀하게
privately (*in private*) naemirhage

내밀하게; *funded, owned* min-gane ŭihae 민간에 의해; (*inwardly*) maŭm sogŭro 마음 속으로
private sector min-gan pumun 민간 부문
privilege (*special treatment*) t'ŭktchŏn 특전; (*honor*) yŏnggwang 영광
privileged t'ŭk-kkwŏnŭl kajin 특권을 가진; (*honored*) yŏnggwangsŭrŏun 영광스러운
prize 1 *n* sang 상 **2** *v/t* kach'i itkke yŏgida 가치 있게 여기다
prizewinner susangja 수상자
prizewinning ipssanghan 입상한
pro[1] *n*: ***the ~s and cons*** ch'anban yangnon 찬반 양론
pro[2] → ***professional***
pro[3]: ***be ~ …*** (*in favor of*) …e ch'ansŏnghada …에 찬성하다
probability kamangsŏng 가망성
probable kŭrŏlttŭt'an 그럴듯한
probably ama 아마
probation (*in job*) kyŏnsŭp 견습; LAW chip'aeng yuye 집행 유예
probation officer poho kamch'algwan 보호 감찰관
probation period (*in job*) kyŏnsŭpkkigan 견습기간
probe 1 *n* (*investigation*) ch'ŏltchŏhan chosa 철저한 조사; (*scientific*) t'amsa 탐사 **2** *v/t* (*investigate*) chasehi chosahada 자세히 조사하다
problem munje 문제; ***no ~*** muje ŏpssŏyo 문제 없어요
procedure chŏlch'a 절차
proceed 1 *v/i* (*of people*) kada 가다; (*of work etc*) chinhaengdoeda 진행되다; ***~ with the lesson*** tashi suŏbŭl kyesok'ada 다시 수업을 계속하다 **2** *v/t*: ***~ to do sth*** kŭrigonasŏ muŏsŭl hada 그리고나서 무엇을 하다
proceedings (*events*) haengsa 행사
proceeds suik 수익
process 1 *n* kwajŏng 과정; ***in the ~*** (*while doing it*) kŭrŏnŭn kwajŏng-e 그러는 과정에 **2** *v/t food, raw materials* kagonghada 가공하다; *data, application etc* ch'ŏrihada 처리하다
procession haengjin 행진
processor COMPUT p'ŭrosesŏ 프로세서
proclaim sŏnŏnhada 선언하다
prod 1 *n* tchirŭgi 찌르기 **2** *v/t* ssushida 쑤시다
prodigy: (***child***) ~ shindong 신동
produce 1 *n* nongsanmul 농산물 **2** *v/t commodity* saengsanhada 생산하다; (*bring about*) yagihada 야기하다; (*bring out*) kkŏnaeda 꺼내다; *play, movie, TV program* chejak'ada 제작하다
producer (*of commodity*) saengsanja 생산자; (*of play, movie, TV program*) chejaktcha 제작자
product saengsanmul 생산물; (*result*) kyŏlgwa 결과
production saengsan 생산; (*of play, movie, TV program*) chejak 제작
production capacity saengsannyŏk 생산력
production costs saengsanbi 생산비
productive saengsanjŏgin 생산적인
productivity saengsanssŏng 생산성
profane *language* pulgyŏnghan 불경한
profess …in ch'ŏk'ada …인 척하다
profession chigŏp 직업
professional 1 *adj* (*not amateur*) p'ŭroŭi 프로의; *advice, help* chigŏbtchŏgin 직업적인; *piece of work* chŏnmunjŏgin 전문적인; ***turn ~*** p'ŭroro chŏnhyanghada 프로로 전향하다 **2** *n* (*doctor, lawyer etc*) chŏnmunjik chongsaja 전문직 종사자; (*not an amateur*) p'ŭro 프로
professionally *play sport* p'ŭro sŏnsuro 프로 선수로; (*well, skillfully*) chŏnmunjŏgŭro 전문적으로
professor kyosu 교수
proficiency nŭngsuk 능숙
proficient nŭngsuk'an 능숙한
profile (*of face*) yŏm mosŭp 옆 모습; (*description*) p'ŭrop'il 프로필
profit 1 *n* iik 이익 **2** *v/i*: ***~ from*** …(ŭ)ro iigŭl ŏt-tta …(으)로 이익을 얻다
profitability suikssŏng 수익성
profitable suigi choŭn 수익이 좋은

profit margin sunsuik 순수익
profound *shock* kip'ŭn 깊은; *hatred* ppuri kip'ŭn 뿌리 깊은; ***a ~ thinker*** shimohan sasaek-kka 심오한 사색가
profoundly kipkke 깊게
prognosis yeji 예지
program 1 *n* kyehoek 계획; RAD, TV, COMPUT, THEA pŭrogŭraem 프로그램 **2** *v/t* COMPUT pŭrogŭraem tchada 프로그램 짜다
programmer COMPUT pŭrogŭraemŏ 프로그래머
progress 1 *n* chinhaeng 진행; ***make ~*** (*of patient*) ch'adorŭl poida 차도를 보이다; (*of building work*) chinch'ŏkdoeda 진척되다; ***in ~*** chinhaeng chung-in 진행 중인 **2** *v/i* (*in time*) chinhaengdoeda 진행되다; (*move on*) chindoga nagada 진도가 나가다; (*improve*) hyangsanghada 향상하다; ***how is the work ~ing?*** irŭn ŏttŏk'e toeŏ kago issŏyo? 일은 어떻게 되어 가고 있어요?
progressive *adj* (*enlightened*) chinbojŏgin 진보적인; *disease* chinhaenghanŭn 진행하는
progressively chŏmch'ajŏgŭro 점차적으로
prohibit kŭmjihada 금지하다
prohibition kŭmji 금지; ***Prohibition*** Kŭmjuppŏp 금주법
prohibitive *prices* koengjanghi pissan 굉장히 비싼
project[1] *n* (*plan*) kyehoek 계획; (*undertaking*) saŏp 사업; EDU kwaje 과제; (*housing area*) chut'aek tanji 주택 단지
project[2] **1** *v/t figures, sales* yesanhada 예산하다; *movie* yŏngsahada 영사하다 **2** *v/i* (*stick out*) t'wiŏnaoda 튀어나오다
projection (*forecast*) yesan 예산
projector (*for slides*) yŏngsagi 영사기
prolific *writer, artist* tajagŭi 다작의
prolong yŏnjanghada 연장하다
prom (*school dance*) hak-kkyo ch'uktche 학교 축제
prominent *nose, chin* t'uk t'wiŏ naon 툭 튀어 나온; (*significant*) t'agwŏrhan 탁월한
promiscuity hon-gyo 혼교
promiscuous nanjap'an 난잡한
promise 1 *n* yakssok 약속 **2** *v/t* yakssok'ada 약속하다; ***~ to …*** … hagiro yakssok'ada … 하기로 약속하다; ***~ X to Y*** Xege Yŭl / rŭl yakssok'ada X에게 Y을 / 를 약속하다 **3** *v/i* yakssok'ada 약속하다
promising chŏndoga ch'angch'anghan 전도가 창창한
promote *employee* sŭngjinhada 승진하다; (*encourage, foster*) ch'oktchinhada 촉진하다; COM sŏnjŏnhada 선전하다
promoter (*of sports event*) p'ŭromot'ŏ 프로모터
promotion (*of employee*) sŭngjin 승진; (*of scheme, idea*) sŏnjŏn 선전; COM p'anmae ch'oktchin 판매 촉진
prompt 1 *adj* (*on time*) shiganŭl chik'inŭn 시간을 지키는; (*speedy*) chŭk-kkaktchŏgin 즉각적인 **2** *adv*: ***at two o'clock ~*** chŏnggak tu shie 정각 두 시에 **3** *v/t* (*cause*) yubalshik'ida 유발시키다; *actor* taesarŭl illŏjuda 대사를 일러주다 **4** *n* COMPUT p'ŭromp'ŭt'ŭ 프롬프트
promptly (*on time*) cheshigane 제시간에; (*immediately*) chŭksshi 즉시
prone: ***be ~ to do …*** … hagi shwiptta … 하기 쉽다
pronoun taemyŏngsa 대명사
pronounce *word* parŭmhada 발음하다; (*declare*) kongp'yohada 공표하다
pronounced *accent* kanghan 강한; *views* hwak-kkohan 확고한
pronunciation parŭm 발음
proof *n* chŭnggŏ 증거; (*of book*) kyojŏngswae 교정쇄
prop 1 *v/t* kidaeŏ not'a 기대어 놓다 **2** *n* (*in theater*) sop'um 소품
♦**prop up** ollyŏ patch'ida 올려 받치다; *regime* chijihada 지지하다
propaganda sŏnjŏn hwalttong 선전 활동
propel ch'ujinhada 추진하다
propellant (*in aerosol*) koap kkassŭ 고압 가스
propeller (*of boat*) p'ŭrop'ellŏ 프로펠러

proper (*real*) chŏngshigŭi 정식의; (*correct*) parŭn 바른; (*fitting*) almajŭn 알맞은
properly (*correctly*) chedaero 제대로; (*fittingly*) chŏk'ap'age 적합하게
property soyumul 소유물; (*land*) ttang 땅
property developer t'oji kaebarŏptcha 토지 개발업자
prophecy yeŏn 예언
prophesy yeŏnhada 예언하다
proportion (*ratio*) piyul 비율; (*number, amount*) pubun 부분; **~s** (*dimensions*) yongjŏk 용적
proportional piryehanŭn 비례하는
proposal (*suggestion*) chean 제안; (*of marriage*) ch'ŏnghon 청혼
propose 1 *v/t* (*suggest*) cheanhada 제안하다; (*plan*) kyehoek'ada 계획하다 **2** *v/i* (*make offer of marriage*) ch'ŏnghonhada 청혼하다
proposition 1 *n* cheŭi 제의 **2** *v/t woman* yuhok'ada 유혹하다
proprietor kyŏngnyŏng-in 경영인
proprietress yŏsŏng kyŏngnyŏng-in 여성 경영인
prose sanmun 산문
prosecute *v/t* LAW kisohada 기소하다
prosecution LAW kiso 기소; (*lawyers*) kisojach'ŭk 기소자측
prosecutor kŏmsa 검사
prospect 1 *n* (*chance, likelihood*) kamang 가망; (*thought of something in the future*) yesang 예상; **~s** chŏnmang 전망 **2** *v/i*: **~ for** *gold* shigurhada 시굴하다
prospective kidaedoenŭn 기대되는
prosper (*of person*) sŏnggonghada 성공하다; (*of business, city*) pŏnch'anghada 번창하다
prosperity pŏnch'ang 번창
prosperous *person* sŏnggonghan 성공한; *businesss, city* pŏnch'anghanŭn 번창하는
prostitute *n* maech'unbu 매춘부; ***male*** **~** namch'ang 남창
prostitution maech'un 매춘
prostrate: ***be ~ with grief*** sŭlp'ŭme ppajyŏ it-tta 슬픔에 빠져 있다
protect pohohada 보호하다
protection poho 보호
protection money poho pannŭn taekkaro ttŭtkkinŭn ton 보호 받는 대가로 뜯기는 돈
protective pohohanŭn 보호하는
protector suhoja 수호자
protein tanbaektchil 단백질
protest 1 *n* hang-ŭi 항의; (*demonstration*) temo 데모 **2** *v/t* hang-ŭihada 항의하다; (*object to*) iŭirŭl chegihada 이의를 제기하다 **3** *v/i* panbak'ada 반박하다; (*demonstrate*) temohada 데모하다
Protestant 1 *n* Shin-gyodo 신교도 **2** *adj* Shin-gyodoŭi 신교도의
Protestantism Kaeshin-gyo 개신교
protester temoja 데모자
protocol ŭirye 의례
prototype wŏnhyŏng 원형
protracted orae kkŭnŭn 오래 끄는
protrude *v/i* pulssuk t'wiŏ naoda 불쑥 튀어 나오다
proud charangsŭrŏun 자랑스러운; (*independent*) chajonshimi kanghan 자존심이 강한; ***be ~ of*** charangsŭrŏpkke yŏgida 자랑스럽게 여기다
proudly charangsŭrŏpkke 자랑스럽게
prove chŭngmyŏnghada 증명하다
proverb sokttam 속담
provide chegonghada 제공하다; ***~ Y to X, ~ X with Y*** Xege Yŭl / rŭl chegonghada X에게 Y을 / 를 제공하다; ***~d*** (***that***) ***...*** ...ranŭn chokkŏnŭro ...라는 조건으로
♦ **provide for** *family* puyanghada 부양하다; (*of law etc*) kyujŏnghada 규정하다
province chibang 지방
provincial *city* chibang-ŭi 지방의; *pej* ch'onssŭrŏun 촌스러운
provision (*supply*) konggŭp 공급; (*of law, contract*) chohang 조항
provisional imshijŏgin 임시적인
proviso tansŏ 단서
provocation hwanage hanŭn kŏt 화나게 하는 것
provocative (*intended to annoy*) chagŭk'anŭn 자극하는; (*controversial*) nonjaengjŏgin 논쟁적인; (*sexually*) chagŭktchŏgin 자극적인
provoke (*cause*) yubarhada 유발하다;

(*annoy*) sŏnggashige hada 성가시게 하다
prow NAUT paenmŏri 뱃머리
prowess ttwiŏnan somsshi 뛰어난 솜씨
prowl *v/i* (*of tiger etc*) ŏsŭllŏnggŏrida 어슬렁거리다; (*of burglar*) sŏsŏngdaeda 서성대다
prowler sŏsŏngdaenŭn saram 서성대는 사람
proximity kŭnjŏp 근접
proxy (*authority*) taerikkwŏn 대리권; (*person*) taeriin 대리인
prude ssungmaek 쑥맥
prudence shinjung 신중
prudent punbyŏl innŭn 분별 있는
prudish ssungmaegin 쑥맥인
prune[1] *n* mallin chadu 말린 자두
prune[2] *v/t plant* (kajirŭl) ch'ida (가지를) 치다; *expenditure*, *labor force* sak-kkamhada 삭감하다; *essay* kan-gyŏrhi hada 간결히 하다
pry k'aego tanida 캐고 다니다
♦**pry into** kkoch'ikkoch'i k'aemutkko tanida 꼬치꼬치 캐묻고 다니다
PS (= ***postscript***) ch'ushin 추신
pseudonym ka-myŏng 가명
psychiatric chŏngshinkkwaŭi 정신과의
psychiatrist chŏngshinkkwa ŭisa 정신과 의사
psychiatry chŏngshinŭihak 정신의학
psychic *adj* shimnyŏng-ŭi 심령의
psychoanalysis chŏngshin punsŏk 정신 분석
psychoanalyst chŏngshin punsŏk haktcha 정신 분석 학자
psychoanalyze chŏngshin punsŏk'ada 정신 분석하다
psychological shimnijŏgin 심리적인
psychologically shimnijŏgŭro 심리적으로
psychologist shimnihaktcha 심리학자
psychology shimnihak 심리학
psychopath chŏngshinppyŏngja 정신병자
puberty sach'un-gi 사춘기
pubic hair ŭmmo 음모
public 1 *adj* (*in ~*) konggaejŏgin 공개적인; (*of the masses*) taejung-ŭi 대중의; (*open to the ~*) konggong-ŭi 공공의 **2** *n*: ***the ~*** taejung 대중; ***in ~*** kongtchŏgin changso-e(sŏ) 공적인 장소에(서)
publication (*of book*, *report*) ch'ulp'an 출판; (*by newspaper*) parhaeng 발행; (*book*) ch'ulp'an 출판; (*newspaper*) parhaeng 발행
publicity sŏnjŏn 선전
publicize (*make known*) sŏnjŏnhada 선전하다; COM kwanggohada 광고하다
publicly konggaejŏgŭro 공개적으로
public prosecutor kŏmch'algwan 검찰관; **public relations** hongbo 홍보; **public school** kongnip hakkyo 공립 학교; **public sector** konggong pumun 공공 부문
publish ch'ulp'anhada 출판하다
publisher (*person*) ch'ulp'anŏptcha 출판업자; (*company*) ch'ulp'ansa 출판사
publishing ch'ulp'anŏp 출판업
publishing company ch'ulp'ansa 출판사
puddle *n* ungdŏng-i 웅덩이
puff 1 *n* (*of wind*, *smoke*) hanbŏn huk pulgi 한번 훅 불기 **2** *v/i* (*pant*) hŏlttŏk-kkŏrida 헐떡거리다
puffy *eyes*, *face* puŏorŭn 부어오른
pull 1 *n* (*on rope*) chaba tanggigi 잡아 당기기; F (*appeal*) hoŭng 호응; F (*influence*) yŏnghyangnyŏk 영향력 **2** *v/t* kkŭlda 끌다; *rope*, *hair* chaba tanggida 잡아 당기다; *tooth* ppoptta 뽑다; *muscle* murihage ssŭda 무리하게 쓰다 **3** *v/i* tanggida 당기다
♦**pull apart** (*separate*) tteŏnaeda 떼어내다
♦**pull away** *v/t* chabach'aeda 잡아채다
♦**pull down** naerida 내리다; (*demolish*) hŏmulda 허물다
♦**pull in** (*of bus*, *train*) toch'ak'ada 도착하다
♦**pull off** *leaves etc* tteŏnaeda 떼어내다; *coat etc* pŏt-tta 벗다; F *deal etc* sŏnggongjŏgŭro haenaeda 성공적으로 해내다
♦**pull out 1** *v/t* kkŏnaeda 꺼내다;

troops hut'oeshik'ida 후퇴시키다 **2** *v/i* (*of an agreement*) ch'ŏrhoehada 철회하다; (*of a competition*) ppajida 빠지다; (*of troops*) hut'oehada 후퇴하다; (*of ship*) ch'urhanghada 출항하다
♦**pull through** (*from an illness*) wank'waehada 완쾌하다
♦**pull together 1** *v/i* (*cooperate*) hyŏpttonghada 협동하다 **2** *v/t*: ***pull oneself together*** maŭmŭl karaanch'ida 마음을 가라앉히다
♦**pull up 1** *v/t* kkŭrŏollida 끌어올리다; *plant*, *weeds* chaba ppoptta 잡아 뽑다 **2** *v/i* (*of car etc*) sŏda 서다
pulley torŭrae 도르래
pulp kwayuk 과육; (*for paper-making*) p'ŏlp'ŭ 펄프
pulpit sŏlgyodan 설교단
pulsate (*of heart*, *blood*) kodongch'ida 고동치다; (*of rhythm*) chindonghada 진동하다
pulse maekppak 맥박
pulverize karuro mandŭlda 가루로 만들다
pump 1 *n* p'ŏmp'ŭ 펌프 **2** *v/t water* p'ŏmp'ŭro p'ŏ ollida 펌프로 퍼 올리다; *air* mirŏnaeda 밀어내다
♦**pump up** konggirŭl chuip'ada 공기를 주입하다
pumpkin hobak 호박
pun tong-ŭmiŭiŭi maltchangnan 동음이의의 말장난
punch 1 *n* (*blow*) chumŏktchil 주먹질; (*implement*) kumŏng ttullŭn kigu 구멍 뚫는 기구 **2** *v/t* (*with fist*) huryŏch'ida 후려치다; *hole* kumŏng-ŭl ttult'a 구멍을 뚫다; *ticket* kaech'arhada 개찰하다
punch line *nongdam chung utkkinŭn taemok* 농담 중 웃기는 대목
punctual shiganŭl ŏmsuhanŭn 시간을 엄수하는
punctuality shigan ŏmsu 시간 엄수
punctually chŏnghwak'i 정확히
punctuate kuduttchŏmŭl tchiktta 구두점을 찍다
punctuation kudutppŏp 구두법
punctuation mark kuduttchŏm 구두점
puncture 1 *n* kumŏng 구멍 **2** *v/t* kumŏng ttult'a 구멍 뚫다
pungent chagŭk'anŭn 자극하는
punish *person* ch'ŏbŏrhada 처벌하다
punishing *pace*, *schedule* chich'ige hanŭn 지치게 하는
punishment ch'ŏbŏl 처벌
puny *person* hŏyak'an 허약한
pup (*young dog*) kang-aji 강아지
pupil[1] (*of eye*) nunttongja 눈동자
pupil[2] (*student*) hakssaeng 학생
puppet kkokttugaksshi 꼭두각시
puppet government koeroe chŏngbu 괴뢰 정부
puppy kang-aji 강아지
purchase[1] **1** *n* kumae 구매 **2** *v/t* kumaehada 구매하다
purchase[2] (*grip*) sone chwida 손에 쥐다
purchaser maeiptcha 매입자
pure *silk* sunsuhan 순수한; *air*, *water* kkaekkŭt'an 깨끗한; *sound* malgŭn 맑은; (*morally*) kyŏlbaek'an 결백한; ~ ***wool*** / ***gold*** / ***white*** sunmo / sungŭm / sunbaek 순모 / 순금 / 순백
purely wanjŏnhi 완전히
purge 1 *n* (*of political party*) sukch'ŏng 숙청 **2** *v/t* sukch'ŏnghada 숙청하다
purify *water* chŏnghwahada 정화하다
puritan ch'ŏnggyodo 청교도
puritanical ŏmkkyŏk'an 엄격한
purity ch'ŏnggyŏl 청결; (*moral*) kyŏlbaek 결백
purple *adj* chajuppich'ŭi 자주빛의
Purple Heart MIL myŏng-ye sang-i hunjang 명예 상이 훈장
purpose moktchŏk 목적; ***on ~*** koŭijŏgŭro 고의적으로
purposeful tanhohan 단호한
purposely ilburŏ 일부러
purr *v/i* (*of cat*) kŭrŭrŏng-gŏrida 그르렁거리다
purse *n* (*pocketbook*) haendŭbaek 핸드백
pursue *v/t person* ch'ujŏk'ada 추적하다; *career* ch'uguhada 추구하다; *course of action* kyesok'ada 계속하다
pursuer ch'ujŏktcha 추적자
pursuit (*chase*) ch'ujŏk 추적; (*of happiness etc*) ch'ugu 추구; (*activity*)

il 일
pus korŭm 고름
Pusan Pusan 부산
push 1 *n* (*shove*) milgi 밀기; (*of button*) nurŭgi 누르기 **2** *v/t* (*shove*) milda 밀다; *button* nurŭda 누르다; (*pressure*) kaap'ada 가압하다; *drugs* mayak milmaehada 마약 밀매하다; ***be ~ed for*** mojarada 모자라다; ***be ~ing 40*** kŏŭi mahŭni ta toeda 거의 마흔이 다 되다 **3** *v/i* milda 밀다
♦**push along** *cart etc* milgo kada 밀고 가다
♦**push away** mirŏ chech'ida 밀어 제치다
♦**push off 1** *v/t lid* mirŏnaeda 밀어내다 **2** *v/i* F (*leave*) ttŏnada 떠나다; ***~!*** chŏri ka! 저리 가!
♦**push on** *v/i* (*continue*) kyesok'ada 계속하다
♦**push up** *prices* ollida 올리다
push-button nurŭm tanch'ushigŭi 누름 단추식의
pusher (*of drugs*) mayak milmaeja 마약 밀매자
push-up p'al kup'yŏ p'yŏgi 팔 굽혀 펴기
pushy ppŏnppŏnsŭrŏun 뻔뻔스러운
puss, pussy (cat) koyang-i 고양이
put not'a 놓다; *question* mut-tta 묻다; ***~ the cost at ...*** ...(ŭ)ro kagyŏgŭl ŏrimjaptta ...(으)로 가격을 어림잡다
♦**put aside** *money* chŏgŭmhada 저금하다; *work* chŏbŏduda 접어두다
♦**put away** (*in closet etc*) ch'iuda 치우다; (*in institution*) kamgŭmhada 감금하다; *drink* mashida 마시다; *money* chŏgŭmhada 저금하다; *animal* allakssashik'ida 안락사시키다
♦**put back** (*replace*) chejarie tollyŏnot'a 제자리에 돌려놓다
♦**put by** *money* chŏgŭmhada 저금하다
♦**put down** not'a 놓다; *deposit* sŏnburhada 선불하다; *rebellion* chinap'ada 진압하다; (*belittle*) nach'uda 낮추다; (*in writing*) ssŭda 쓰다; ***put one's foot down*** (*in car*) kasok'ada 가속하다; (*be firm*) kutkke kyŏlsshimhada 굳게 결심하다; ***put X down to Y*** (*attribute*) Xŭl / rŭl Yŭi t'asŭro tollida X을 / 를 Y의 탓으로 돌리다
♦**put forward** *idea etc* cheanhada 제안하다
♦**put in** nŏt'a 넣다; *time* ponaeda 보내다; *request, claim* cheshihada 제시하다
♦**put in for** yoch'ŏnghada 요청하다
♦**put off** *light, radio, TV* kkŭda 끄다; (*postpone*) yŏn-gihada 연기하다; (*deter*) tannyŏmshik'ida 단념시키다; (*repel*) pulk'waehada 불쾌하다; ***put X off Y*** Xi / ga Yŭl / rŭl tannyŏmhage hada X이 / 가 Y을 / 를 단념하게 하다
♦**put on** *light, radio, TV* k'yŏda 켜다; *tape, music* t'ŭlda 틀다; *jacket* iptta 입다; *shoes* shintta 신다; *eyeglasses* ssŭda 쓰다; *make-up* hada 하다; *brake* chakttongshik'ida 작동시키다; (*perform*) kongyŏnhada 공연하다; (*assume*) kajanghada 가장하다; ***~ weight*** ch'ejung-ŭl nŭrida 체중을 늘이다; ***she's just putting it on*** kŭ yŏjanŭn kŭ-nyang kŭrŏn ch'ŏk'ago innŭn kŏyeyo 그 여자는 그냥 그런 척하고 있는 거예요
♦**put out** *hand* naemilda 내밀다; *fire* sohwahada 소화하다; *light* kkŭda 끄다
♦**put through** (*on phone*) pakkwŏ chuda 바꿔 주다
♦**put together** (*assemble*) chorip'ada 조립하다; (*organize*) chojik'ada 조직하다
♦**put up** *hand* tŭlda 들다; *person* chaewŏjuda 재워주다; (*erect*) seuda 세우다; *prices* ollida 올리다; *poster, notice* puch'ida 붙이다; *money* naeda 내다; ***~ for sale*** p'allyŏgo naenot'a 팔려고 내놓다
♦**put up with** (*tolerate*) ch'amtta 참다
putty yuri chŏp'aptche 유리 접합제
puzzle 1 *n* (*mystery*) susukkekki 수수께끼; (*game*) p'ŏjŭl 퍼즐 **2** *v/t* yŏngmunŭl morŭge hada 영문을 모르게 하다
puzzling yŏngmun morŭl 영문 모를
PVC p'i pŭi sshi 피 브이 씨
pylon koapssŏnnyong ch'ŏlt'ap 고압선용 철탑
P'yongyang P'yŏngnyang 평양

Q

quack[1] **1** *n* (*of duck*) kkwaek-kkwaek unŭn sori 꽥꽥 우는 소리 **2** *v/i* kkwaek-kkwaek ulda 꽥꽥 울다
quack[2] F (*bad doctor*) tolp'ari ŭisa 돌팔이 의사
quadrangle (*figure*) sagak'yŏng 사각형; (*courtyard*) anttŭl 안뜰
quadruped ne pal chimsŭng 네 발 짐승
quadruple *v/i* ne paero hada 네 배로 하다
quadruplets ne ssangdung-i 네 쌍둥이
quaint *cottage* yeppŭjanghan 예쁘장한; *ideas etc* kimyohan 기묘한
quake 1 *n* (*earth~*) chijin 지진 **2** *v/i* (*of earth*) hŭndŭllida 흔들리다; (*with fear*) tŏdŏl ttŏlda 덜덜 떨다
qualification (*from university etc*) chagyŏk 자격; (*of remark etc*) chehan 제한; ***have the right ~s for a job*** ottŏn chigŏbe chŏk'ap'an chagyŏgŭl kajida 어떤 직업에 적합한 자격을 가지다
qualified *doctor, engineer etc* chagyŏktchŭng-i innŭn 자격증이 있는; (*restricted*) chehandoen 제한된; ***I am not ~ to judge*** nanŭn p'andanhal chagyŏgi ŏpssŭmnida 나는 판단할 자격이 없습니다
qualify 1 *v/t* (*of degree, course etc*) chagyŏgŭl chuda 자격을 주다; *remark etc* chehanhada 제한하다 **2** *v/i* (*get degree etc*) chagyŏgŭl ŏt-tta 자격을 얻다; (*in competition*) yesŏnŭl t'onggwahada 예선을 통과하다; ***our team has qualified for the semi-final*** uri t'imŭn chun-gyŏlssŭngjŏne chinch'urhaet-tta 우리 팀은 준결승전에 진출했다; ***that doesn't ~ as ...*** kŭgŏsŭn ...(ŭ)rosŏ chagyŏgi ŏptta 그것은 ...(으)로서 자격이 없다
quality p'umjil 품질; (*characteristic*) sŏngjil 성질
quality control p'umjil kwalli 품질 관리
qualm yangshimŭi kach'aek 양심의 가책; ***have no ~s about*** ...e taehae yangshimŭi kach'aegŭl pat-tchi ant'a ...에 대해 양심의 가책을 받지 않다
quantify yang-ŭl chaeda 양을 재다
quantity yang 양
quarantine (*for animals*) kŏmnyŏk 검역; (*for people*) kyŏngni 격리
quarrel 1 *n* tat'um 다툼 **2** *v/i* tat'uda 다투다
quarrelsome tat'ugi choahanŭn 다투기 좋아하는
quarry (*for mining*) ch'aesŏktchang 채석장
quart yak 0.95lit'ŏ 약 0.95리터
quarter 1 *n* sabunŭi il 사분의 일; (*25 cents*) ishibossent'ŭ tongjŏn 이십오센트 동전; (*part of town*) chiyŏk 지역; ***a ~ of an hour*** shibobun 십오분; ***a ~ of 5*** tasŏtsshi shibobun chŏn 다섯시 십오분 전; ***~ after 5*** tashŏtsshi shibobun 다섯시 십오분 **2** *v/t* saro nanuda 사로 나누다
quarterback SP k'wŏt'ŏbaek 쿼터백; **quarterfinal** chunjun-gyŏlssŭng 준준결승; **quarterfinalist** chunjun-gyŏlssŭng chinch'ultcha 준준결승 진출자
quarterly 1 *adj* kyeganŭi 계간의 **2** *adv* kyeganŭro 계간으로
quarter note MUS sabun ŭmp'yo 사분 음표
quarters MIL pyŏngnyŏng 병영
quartet MUS sajungju 사중주
quartz sŏgyŏng 석영
quaver 1 *n* (*in voice*) ttŏllinŭn sori 떨리는 소리 **2** *v/i* (*of voice*) ttŏllida 떨리다
queen yŏwang 여왕
queen bee yŏwangbŏl 여왕벌
queer (*peculiar*) kimyohan 기묘한

quench *thirst* kashige hada 가시게 하다; *flames* kkŭda 끄다
query 1 *n* ŭimun 의문 **2** *v/t* (*express doubt about*) ŭimunŭl chegihada 의문을 제기하다; (*check*) hwaginhada 확인하다; ***~ X with Y*** Yege Xe kwanhan ŭimunŭl chegihada Y에게 X에 관한 의문을 제기하다
question 1 *n* chilmun 질문; (*matter*) munje 문제; ***in ~*** (*being talked about*) munjeŭi 문제의; (*in doubt*) ŭishimtchŏgŭn 의심쩍은; ***it's a ~ of money / time*** tonŭi / shiganŭi munjeyeyo 돈의 / 시간의 문제예요; ***out of the ~*** chŏnhyŏ pulganŭnghan 전혀 불가능한 **2** *v/t person* chilmunhada 질문하다; LAW shimmunhada 심문하다; (*doubt*) ŭishimhada 의심하다
questionable *honesty, figures* ŭishimsŭrŏun 의심스러운
questioning *look, tone* ŭishimtchŏgŏ hanŭn 의심쩍어 하는
question mark murŭmp'yo 물음표
questionnaire chilmunsŏ 질문서
quick pparŭn 빠른; ***be ~!*** ppalli hae! 빨리 해!; ***let's have a ~ drink*** ttak han chanman mashija 딱 한 잔만 마시자; ***can I have a ~ look?*** chamkkan pwado toelkkayo? 잠깐 봐도 될까요?; ***that was ~!*** ppalli haenneyo! 빨리 했네요!
quicksand yusa 유사; **quicksilver** suŭn 수은; **quickwitted** chaech'i innŭn 재치 있는
quiet choyonghan 조용한; *life, town* koyohan 고요한; ***keep ~ about*** ...ŭl / rŭl pimillo haeduda ...을 / 를 비밀로 해두다; ***~!*** choyonghi hae! 조용히 해!
♦**quieten down 1** *v/t children, class* choyonghage hada 조용하게 하다 **2** *v/i* (*of children*) choyonghaejida 조용해지다; (*of political situation*) chinjŏngdoeda 진정되다
quilt (*on bed*) nubi ibul 누비 이불
quinine k'inine 키니네
quip 1 *n* chaech'i innŭn mal 재치 있는 말 **2** *v/i* nollida 놀리다
quirky pyŏllan 별난
quit 1 *v/t job* kŭmanduda 그만두다; ***~ doing sth*** muŏt hanŭn kŏsŭl kŭmanduda 무엇 하는 것을 그만두다 **2** *v/i* (*leave job*) chiktchang-ŭl kŭmanduda 직장을 그만두다; COMPUT kkŭnnaeda 끝내다; ***get one's notice to ~*** (*from landlord*) chip piuranŭn t'ongjirŭl pat-tta 집 비우라는 통지를 받다
quite (*fairly*) kkwae 꽤; (*completely*) wanjŏnhi 완전히; ***not ~ ready*** chunbiga wanjŏnhi toeji anŭn 준비가 완전히 되지 않은; ***I didn't ~ understand*** ta ihaehal su ŏpssŏssŏyo 다 이해할 수 없었어요; ***is that right? - not ~*** majayo? – kŏŭi 맞아요? – 거의; ***~!*** chŏngmal! 정말!; ***~ a lot*** kkwae manŭn 꽤 많은; ***it was ~ a surprise / change*** kkwae nollaun iriŏssŏyo / kkwae k'ŭn pyŏnhwayŏssŏyo 꽤 놀라운 일이었어요 / 꽤 큰 변화였어요
quits: ***be ~ with*** ...wa / kwa p'ijangp'ajang-i toeda ...와 / 과 피장파장이 되다
quiver *v/i* hŭndŭllida 흔들리다
quiz 1 *n* k'wijŭ 퀴즈 **2** *v/t* murŏboda 물어보다
quiz program k'wijŭ p'ŭro 퀴즈 프로
quota mok 몫
quotation (*from author*) inyong 인용; (*price*) kyŏnjŏk 견적
quotation marks inyong puho 인용 부호
quote 1 *n* (*from author*) inyongmun 인용문; (*price*) kyŏnjŏk 견적; (*quotation mark*) inyong puho 인용 부호; ***give X a ~ for Y*** Xege Yŭi piyong-ŭl kyŏnjŏk'ada X에게 Y의 비용을 견적하다 **2** *v/t text* inyonghada 인용하다; *price* kyŏnjŏk'ada 견적하다 **3** *v/i* inyonghada 인용하다; ***~ from an author*** chak-kkaŭi kŭrŭl inyonghada 작가의 글을 인용하다

R

rabbit t'okki 토끼
rabies kwanggyŏnppyŏng 광견병
raccoon miguk nŏguri 미국 너구리
race[1] *n* (*of people*) injong 인종
race[2] **1** *n* SP kyŏngju 경주; ***the ~s*** (*horse ~s*) kyŏngma 경마 **2** *v/i* (*run fast*) chiltchuhada 질주하다; SP kyŏngjuhada 경주하다; ***he ~d through his meal / work*** kŭnŭn kŭp'i shikssarŭl / irŭl haet-tta 그는 급히 식사를 / 일을 했다 **3** *v/t*: ***I'll ~ you*** kyŏngjuhaja 경주하자
racecourse kyŏngju k'osŭ 경주 코스; **racehorse** kyŏngjuma 경주마; **racetrack** (*for cars, athletics*) kyŏngjujang 경주장
racial injong-ŭi 인종의; ~ ***equality*** injong p'yŏngdŭng 인종 평등
racing kyŏngju 경주
racing car kyŏngjuch'a 경주차
racing driver kyŏngjuja 경주자
racism injong ch'abyŏltchuŭi 인종 차별주의
racist 1 *n* injong ch'abyŏltchuŭija 인종 차별주의자 **2** *adj* injong ch'abyŏltchŏgin 인종 차별적인
rack 1 *n* (*for parking bikes*) chuch'adae 주차대; (*for bags on train*) sŏnban 선반; (*for CDs*) kkoji 꽂이; (*for coats*) kŏri 걸이 **2** *v/t*: ~ ***one's brains*** mŏrirŭl tchada 머리를 짜다
racket[1] SP lak'et 라켓
racket[2] (*noise*) soŭm 소음; (*criminal activity*) pujŏnghan tonppŏri 부정한 돈벌이
radar leida 레이다
radiant *smile, appearance* hwanhi pinnanŭn 환히 빛나는
radiate *v/i* (*of heat, light*) pich'ŭl parhada 빛을 발하다
radiation PHYS pangsasŏn 방사선
radiator (*in room*) nanbanggi 난방기; (*in car*) ladiet'ŏ 라디에이터
radical 1 *adj* kŭnbonjŏgin 근본적인; POL *views* kŭptchinjŏgin 급진적인 **2** *n* POL kŭptchinjuŭija 급진주의자
radicalism POL kŭptchinjuŭi 급진주의
radically kŭnbonjŏgŭro 근본적으로
radio ladio 라디오; ***on the ~*** ladioe(sŏ) 라디오에(서); ***by ~*** mujŏnŭro 무전으로
radioactive pangsanŭng-i innŭn 방사능이 있는; **radioactivity** pangsanŭng 방사능; **radio station** ladio pangsongguk 라디오 방송국; **radiotherapy** pangsanŭng yoppŏp 방사능 요법
radish mu 무
radius panjirŭm 반지름
raffle *n* chebi ppopkki 제비 뽑기
raft ttenmok 뗏목
rafter sŏkkarae 서까래
rag (*for cleaning etc*) hŏnggŏptchogak 헝겊조각
rage 1 *n* kyŏngno 격노; ***be in a ~*** kyŏngnohada 격노하다; ***all the ~*** taeyuhaeng 대유행 **2** *v/i* (*of person*) kyŏngnohada 격노하다; (*of storm*) sanapkke morach'ida 사납게 몰아치다
ragged *edge* tŭltchungnaltchuk'an 들쭉날쭉한; *appearance* namnuhan 남루한; *clothes* tchijŏjin 찢어진
raid 1 *n* (*by troops, police*) kŭpssŭp 급습; (*by robbers*) ch'imip 침입; FIN ilje maedo 일제 매도 **2** *v/t* (*of troops, police*) kŭpssŭp'ada 급습하다; (*of robbers*) ch'imip'ada 침입하다
raider (*bank robber etc*) ch'imiptcha 침입자
rail (*on track*) ch'ŏltto 철도; (*hand~*) nan-gan 난간; (*for towel*) sugŏn kŏri 수건 걸이; ***by ~*** kich'aro 기차로
railings (*around park etc*) ult'ari 울타리
railroad ch'ŏltto 철도
railroad station kich'ayŏk 기차역

rain 1 *n* pi 비; ***in the ~*** pitssoge(sŏ) 빗속에(서); ***the ~s*** changma 장마 **2** *v/i* piga oda 비가 오다; ***it's ~ing*** piga onda 비가 온다
rainbow mujigae 무지개; **raincheck**: ***can I take a ~ on that?*** ŏnjen-ga taŭme hamyŏn andoelkkayo? 언젠가 다음에 하면 안될까요?; **raincoat** ubi 우비; **raindrop** pitppang-ul 빗방울; **rainfall** kang-u 강우; **rain forest** urim 우림; ***tropical ~*** yŏlttae urim 열대 우림; **rainstorm** p'okp'ung-u 폭풍우
rainy piga onŭn 비가 오는; ***it's ~*** piga onnŭn-gunnyo 비가 오는군요
rainy season changmach'ŏl 장마철
raise 1 *n* (*in salary*) insang 인상 **2** *v/t shelf etc* ollida 올리다; *offer* nŭllida 늘리다; *children* k'iuda 키우다; *question* chegihada 제기하다; *money* moŭda 모으다
raisin kŏnp'odo 건포도
rake *n* (*for garden*) kalk'wi 갈퀴
rally *n* (*meeting, reunion*) taehoe 대회; MOT, (*in tennis*) laelli 랠리
♦**rally around 1** *v/i* tourŏ moida 도우러 모이다 **2** *v/t* ...ŭl / rŭl tourŏ tallyŏoda ...을 / 를 도우러 달려오다
RAM (= ***random access memory***) laem 램
ram 1 *n* sunnyang 숫양 **2** *v/t ship, car* puditch'ida 부딪히다
ramble 1 *n* (*walk*) sanch'aek 산책 **2** *v/i* (*walk*) sanch'aek'ada 산책하다; (*when speaking, talk incoherently*) tusŏŏpsshi iyagihada 두서없이 이야기하다
rambler (*walker*) sanch'aek'anŭn saram 산책하는 사람
rambling 1 *n* (*walking*) sanch'aek 산책; (*in speech*) hoengsŏlsusŏl 횡설수설 **2** *adj speech* tusŏŏmnŭn 두서없는
ramp hanggonggiŭi t'ŭraep 항공기의 트랩; (*for raising vehicle*) raemp'ŭ 램프]
rampage 1 *v/i* nalttwimyŏ toradanida 날뛰며 돌아다니다 **2** *n*: ***go on the ~*** nalttwimyŏ toradanida 날뛰며 돌아다니다
rampart sŏngbyŏk 성벽
ramshackle *building* kŭmbang-irado munŏjil tŭt'an 금방이라도 무너질 듯한; *car* kŭmbang-irado pusŏjil tŭt'an 금방이라도 부서질 듯한
ranch moktchang 목장
rancher moktchangju 목장주
rancid ssŏgŭn 썩은
rancor wŏnhan 원한
R & D (= ***research and development***) yŏn-gu kaebal 연구 개발
random 1 *adj* mujagwiŭi 무작위의; ***~ sample*** mujagwi saemp'ŭl 무작위 샘플 **2** *n*: ***at ~*** mujagwiro 무작위로
range 1 *n* (*of products*) pŏmwi 범위; (*of voice*) ŭmnyŏk 음역; (*of airplane*) hangssok kŏri 항속 거리; (*of gun, missile*) sajŏng kŏri 사정 거리; (*of mountains*) sanmaek 산맥 **2** *v/i*: ***~ from X to Y*** Xesŏ Ykkaji irŭda X에서 Y까지 이르다
ranger (*forest ~*) sallim kyŏngbiwŏn 산림 경비원
rank 1 *n* MIL kyegŭp 계급; (*in society*) shinbun 신분; ***the ~s*** MIL ilban sabyŏng 일반 사병 **2** *v/t* tŭnggŭbŭl maegida 등급을 매기다
♦**rank among** ...(ŭ)ro p'yŏngkkahada ...(으)로 평가하다
ransack satssach'i twijida 샅샅이 뒤지다
ransom momkkap 몸값; ***hold s.o. to ~*** nugurŭl ŏngnyuhayŏ momkkapssŭl yoguhada 누구를 억류하여 몸값을 요구하다
rant: ***~ and rave*** koraegorae sorich'ida 고래고래 소리치다
rap 1 *n* (*at door etc*) t'okt'ok tudŭrigi 톡톡 두드리기; MUS laep 랩 **2** *v/t table etc* t'okt'ok tudŭrida 톡톡 두드리다
♦**rap at** *window etc* t'okt'ok tudŭrida 톡톡 두드리다
rape 1 *n* kanggan 강간 **2** *v/t* kangganhada 강간하다
rape victim kanggan p'ihaeja 강간 피해자
rapid shinssok'an 신속한
rapidity shinssok 신속
rapids kŭmnyu 급류
rapist kangganbŏm 강간범

rapturous yŏlgwangtchŏgin 열광적인
rare tŭmun 드문; *antique, skills* chin-gihan 진기한; *steak* tŏl igŭn 덜 익은
rarely tŭmulge 드물게
rarity chinp'um 진품
rascal changnankkurŏgi 장난꾸러기
rash[1] MED paltchin 발진
rash[2] *action, behavior* sŏnggŭpp'an 성급한
raspberry namuttalgi 나무딸기
rat *n* chwi 쥐
rate 1 *n* (*of birth, death etc*) piyul 비율; (*of exchange*) hwannyul 환율; (*price*) yogŭm 요금; (*speed*) chindo 진도; ***an hourly ~*** (*of pay*) shigandang 시간당; ***a weekly ~*** (*of pay*) chudang 주당; ***~ of interest*** FIN ijayul 이자율; ***at this ~*** (*at this speed*) i chŏngdo sokttomyŏn 이 정도 속도면; (*carrying on like this*) kyesok irŏn sangt'aeramyŏn 계속 이런 상태라면 **2** *v/t* (*consider, rank*) p'yŏngkkahada 평가하다
rather (*somewhat*) taso 다소; (*preferably*) ohiryŏ 오히려; ***I would ~ stay here*** nanŭn ohiryŏ yŏgi innŭn p'yŏni natkkessŏyo 나는 오히려 여기 있는 편이 낫겠어요; ***or would you ~ have coffee?*** animyŏn ohiryŏ k'ŏp'iro hagessŏyo? 아니면 오히려 커피로 하겠어요?
ration 1 *n* paegŭmnyang 배급량 **2** *v/t supplies* paegŭp'ada 배급하다
rational hamnijŏgin 합리적인
rationality hamnisŏng 합리성
rationalization (*of production etc*) hyoyurhwa 효율화
rationalize 1 *v/t production* hyoyurhwahada 효율화하다; *actions etc* hamnihwahada 합리화하다 **2** *v/i* hamnihwahada 합리화하다
rat race kwada kyŏngjaeng sahoe 과다 경쟁 사회
rattle 1 *n* (*noise*) tŏlk'ŏk-kkŏrinŭn sori 덜컥거리는 소리 **2** *v/t* tŏlk'ŏk-kkŏrida 덜컥거리다 **3** *v/i* tŏlk'ŏk-kkŏrida 덜컥거리다
♦**rattle off** *poem, list of names* kŏch'imŏpsshi chikkŏrida 거침없이 지껄이다
rattlesnake pang-ulbaem 방울뱀
ravage: ***~d by war*** chŏnjaeng-ŭro hwangp'yehaejin 전쟁으로 황폐해진
rave *v/i* (*talk deliriously*) hŏtssorihada 헛소리하다; (*talk wildly*) chŏngshinŏpsshi chikkŏrida 정신없이 지껄이다; ***~ about sth*** (*be very enthusiastic*) muŏse yŏlgwanghada 무엇에 열광하다
raven kkamagwi 까마귀
ravenous *appetite* kegŏlssŭrŏun 게걸스러운
rave review kŭkch'anŭi p'yŏng 극찬의 평
ravine chobŭn koltchagi 좁은 골짜기
raving mad wanjŏnhi mich'in 완전히 미친
ravishing maehoktchŏgin 매혹적인
raw *meat, vegetables* nalkkŏsŭi 날것의; *sugar, iron* kagonghaji anŭn 가공하지 않은
raw fish hoe 회
raw materials wŏllyo 원료
ray pit 빛; ***a ~ of hope*** han kadak hŭimang 한 가닥 희망
razor myŏndok'al 면도칼
razor blade myŏndonal 면도날
re COM …e kwanhayŏ …에 관하여
reach 1 *n*: ***within ~*** (*close to hand*) soni tannŭn kose 손이 닿는 곳에; (*easily accessible*) kakkaun kose 가까운 곳에; ***out of ~*** soni tach'i annŭn kose 손이 닿지 않는 곳에 **2** *v/t city etc* toch'ak'ada 도착하다; (*go as far as*) …e tat'a …에 닿다; *decision, agreement* …e irŭda …에 이르다
♦**reach out** *v/i* sonŭl ppŏtch'ida 손을 뻗치다
react panjagyonghada 반작용하다; (*to news etc*) panŭnghada 반응하다
reaction panjagyong 반작용; (*to news etc*) panŭng 반응
reactionary 1 *n* pandongjuŭija 반동주의자 **2** *adj* pandong-ŭi 반동의
reactor (*nuclear*) wŏnjaro 원자로
read 1 *v/t* iltta 읽다; *diskette* …ŭi chŏngborŭl iltta …의 정보를 읽다 **2** *v/i* iltta 읽다; ***~ to s.o.*** nuguege ilgŏ chuda 누구에게 읽어 주다
♦**read out** *v/t* (*aloud*) k'ŭn soriro iltta 큰 소리로 읽다

♦**read up on** …ŭl / rŭl yŏn-guhada …을 / 를 연구하다
readable ilgŭl su innŭn 읽을 수 있는
reader (*person*) tokssŏga 독서가
readily *admit*, *agree* sŏnttŭt 선뜻
readiness (*for action*) chunbiga toeŏ issŭm 준비가 되어 있음; (*willingness*) kikkŏi hanŭn maŭm 기꺼이 하는 마음
reading (*activity*) tokssŏ 독서; (*from meter etc*) ch'ŭktchŏng 측정
reading matter ilgŭl kŏri 읽을 거리
readjust 1 *v/t equipment*, *controls* chaejŏngnihada 재정리하다 **2** *v/i* (*to conditions*) chaejŏgŭnghada 재적응하다
read-only file COMPUT p'andok chŏnyong p'ail 판독 전용 파일
read-only memory COMPUT p'andok chŏnyong kiŏk changch'i 판독 전용 기억 장치
ready (*prepared*) chunbidoen 준비된; (*willing*) kikkŏi …handa 기꺼이 …하다; ***he is always ~ to listen*** kŭnŭn hangsang kikkŏi tŭnnŭnda 그는 항상 기꺼이 듣는다; ***get*** (***one-self***) ~ chunbihada 준비하다; ***get … ready*** …ŭl / rŭl chunbihada …을 / 를 준비하다
ready-made *meal* miri mandŭrŏjyŏ innŭn 미리 만들어져 있는; *solution* chinbuhan 진부한
ready-to-wear kisŏngbok 기성복
real chintcha-ŭi 진짜의
real estate pudongsan 부동산
realism hyŏnshiltchuŭi 현실주의; (*in literature*, *art*) sashiltchuŭi 사실주의
realist hyŏnshiltchuŭija 현실주의자; (*in literature*, *art etc*) sashiltchuŭija 사실주의자
realistic hyŏnshiltchŏgin 현실적인
reality hyŏnshil 현실
realization (*of goal*) shirhyŏn 실현; (*understanding*) kkaedarŭm 깨달음
realize *v/t* kkaedat-tta 깨닫다; FIN …ŭi iigŭl poda …의 이익을 보다; ***I ~ now that …*** nanŭn ijeya …ranŭn kŏsŭl kkaedannŭnda 나는 이제야 …라는 것을 깨닫는다
really chŏngmallo 정말로; (*very*) taedanhi 대단히; ~***?*** chŏngmariyeyo? 정말이예요?; ***not ~*** (*not much*) pyŏlloyeyo 별로예요
real time COMPUT shilsshigan 실시간
real-time COMPUT shilsshiganŭi 실시간의
realtor pudongsan chunggaein 부동산 중개인
reap suhwak'ada 수확하다
reappear tashi nat'anada 다시 나타나다
rear 1 *n* paehu 배후 **2** *adj* twiŭi 뒤의; *lights* twittchogŭi 뒷쪽의
rearm 1 *v/t* chaemujangshik'ida 재무장시키다 **2** *v/i* chaemujanghada 재무장하다
rearmost maen twittchogŭi 맨 뒷쪽의
rearrange *flowers*, *chairs* chaebaeyŏrhada 재배열하다; *schedule* chaejŏngnihada 재정리하다
rear-view mirror paengmirŏ 백미러
reason 1 *n* (*faculty*) isŏng 이성; (*cause*) iyu 이유 **2** *v/i*: ***~ with s.o.*** nugurŭl shŏlttŭk'ae poda 누구를 설득해 보다
reasonable *person*, *behavior* punbyŏl innŭn 분별 있는; *price* chŏkttanghan 적당한; ***a ~ number of people*** sangdanghi manŭn saramdŭl 상당히 많은 사람들
reasonably *act*, *behave* ich'ie matkke 이치에 맞게; (*quite*) sangdanghi 상당히
reassure anshimshik'ida 안심시키다
reassuring anshimhage hanŭn 안심하게 하는
rebate (*money back*) hwanbul 환불
rebel *n* panyŏktcha 반역자; ***~ troops*** pallan-gun 반란군
rebellion pallan 반란
rebellious panhangjŏgin 반항적인
rebound *v/i* (*of ball etc*) toet'wida 되튀다
rebuff *n* kŏjŏl 거절
rebuild kaech'uk'ada 개축하다; *relationship* hoebok'ada 회복하다
rebuke *v/t* chilch'aek'ada 질책하다
recall *v/t ambassador* sohwanhada 소환하다; (*remember*) sanggihada 상기하다
recapture *v/t* MIL t'arhwan 탈환; *criminal* chaech'ep'ohada

재체포하다
receding *hair* pŏtkkyŏjinŭn 벗겨지는
receipt yŏngsujŭng 영수증; ***acknowledge ~ of*** …ŭl / rŭl padassŭmŭl injŏnghada …을 / 를 받았음을 인정하다; **~s** FIN suip 수입
receive pat-tta 받다
receiver (*of letter*) such'wiin 수취인; TELEC suhwagi 수화기; RAD sushingi 수신기
receivership: ***be in ~*** chaesan kwalli sangt'aee noyŏ it-tta 재산 관리 상태에 놓여 있다
recent ch'oegŭnŭi 최근의
recently ch'oegŭne 최근에
reception (*in hotel, company*) p'ŭront'ŭ 프론트; (*formal party*) lisepsshyŏn p'at'i 리셉션 파티; (*welcome*) hwanyŏng 환영; RAD sushin 수신
reception desk annae tesŭk'ŭ 안내 데스크
receptionist chŏpssuwŏn 접수원
receptive: ***be ~ to*** …ŭl / rŭl chal padadŭrida …을 / 를 잘 받아들이다
recess (*in wall etc*) ump'uk tŭrŏgan kot 움푹 들어간 곳; EDU shwinŭn shigan 쉬는 시간; (*of legislature*) hyuhoe 휴회
recession pulgyŏnggi 불경기
recharge *battery* ch'ungjŏnhada 충전하다
recipe choribŏp 조리법
recipient (*of parcel etc*) such'wiin 수취인; (*of payment*) suryŏng-in 수령인
reciprocal sanghoganŭi 상호간의
recital MUS lisait'ŭl 리사이틀
recite *poem* nangsonghada 낭송하다; *details, facts* yŏlgŏhada 열거하다
reckless mumohan 무모한
reckon (*think, consider*) …rago saenggak'ada …라고 생각하다
♦**reckon with**: ***have s.o. / sth to ~*** nugurŭl / muŏsŭl koryŏe nŏt'a 누구를 / 무엇을 고려에 넣다
reclaim *land from sea* kanch'ŏk'ada 간척하다
recline *v/i* kidaeda 기대다
recluse ŭndunja 은둔자
recognition (*of state, achievements*) injŏng 인정; (*of person*) arabom 알아봄; ***change beyond ~*** arabol su ŏpssŭl chŏngdoro pyŏnhada 알아볼 수 없을 정도로 변하다
recognizable arabol su innŭn 알아볼 수 있는
recognize *person, voice, tune* araboda 알아보다; (*distinguish*) pun-ganhada 분간하다; POL *state* sŭng-inhada 승인하다; ***it can be ~d by …*** …(ŭ)ro pun-gandoel su it-tta …(으)로 분간될 수 있다
recollect hoesanghada 회상하다
recollection hoesang 회상
recommend ch'uch'ŏnhada 추천하다
recommendation ch'uch'ŏn 추천
reconcile *people* hwahaeshik'ida 화해시키다; *differences* chohwashik'ida 조화시키다; *facts* ilch'ishik'ida 일치시키다; ***~ oneself to …*** …ŭl / rŭl kamsuhada …을 / 를 감수하다; ***be ~d*** (*of two people*) hwahaehada 화해하다
reconciliation (*of people*) hwahae 화해; (*of differences*) chohwa 조화; (*of facts*) ilch'i 일치
recondition …ŭl / rŭl surihada …을 / 를 수리하다
reconnaissance MIL chŏngch'al 정찰
reconsider *v/t & v/i* chaegohada 재고하다
reconstruct *city* chaegŏnhada 재건하다; *one's life* tashi ch'usŭrida 다시 추스리다; *crime* chaehyŏnhada 재현하다
record 1 *n* MUS lek'odŭ 레코드; SP *etc* kyŏnggi kirok 경기 기록; (*written document etc*) kirok munsŏ 기록 문서; (*in database*) hanbŏrŭi teit'ŏ 한벌의 데이터; **~s** (*archives*) kirok munsŏ 기록 문서; ***say sth off the ~*** muŏsŭl pigongshigŭro marhada 무엇을 비공식으로 말하다; ***have a criminal ~*** chŏnkkwaga it-tta 전과가 있다; ***have a good ~ for …*** …i / ga chot'anŭn p'yŏngp'anŭl kajigo it-tta …이 / 가 좋다는 평판을 가지고 있다 **2** *v/t* (*on tape etc*) nogŭmhada 녹음하다
record-breaking kirogŭl kkaenŭn

기록을 깨는
recorder MUS lik'odŏ 리코더
record holder kirok poyuja 기록 보유자
recording nogŭm 녹음
recording studio nogŭmshil 녹음실
record player nogŭmgi 녹음기
recoup *losses* toech'at-tta 되찾다
recover 1 *v/t* (*get back*) toech'at-tta 되찾다 **2** *v/i* (*from illness*) hoebok'ada 회복하다
recovery (*of sth lost, stolen goods*) toech'ajŭm 되찾음; (*from illness*) hoebok 회복; ***he has made a good ~*** kŭŭi hoebogŭn sunjorowat-tta 그의 회복은 순조로왔다
recreation orak 오락
recruit 1 *n* MIL shinbyŏng 신병; (*to company*) shinip sawŏn 신입 사원 **2** *v/t new staff* mojip'ada 모집하다
recruitment shin-gyu mojip 신규 모집
recruitment drive shin-gyu mojip k'aemp'ein 신규 모집 캠페인
rectangle chikssagak'yŏng 직사각형
rectangular chikssagak'yŏng-ŭi 직사각형의
recuperate hoebok'ada 회복하다
recur chaebarhada 재발하다
recurrent chaebarhanŭn 재발하는
recycle chaesaeng iyonghada 재생 이용하다
recycling chaesaeng iyong 재생 이용
red ppalgan 빨간; *hair* pulgŭn 붉은; ***in the ~*** chŏktchaga nada 적자가 나다
Red Cross Chŏksshiptcha 적십자
redden *v/i* (*blush*) pulgŏjida 붉어지다
redecorate *v/t* sae tanjanghada 새 단장하다
redeem *debt* sanghwanhada 상환하다; *sinners* kuwŏnhada 구원하다
redeeming: ***~ feature*** *kyŏltchŏmŭl powanhae chunŭn changtchŏm* =결점을 보완해 주는 장점
redevelop *part of town* chaegaebarhada 재개발하다
red-handed: ***catch ~*** hyŏnhaengbŏmŭro chaptta 현행범으로 잡다; **redhead** mŏrik'aragi pulgŭn saram 머리카락이 붉은 사람; **red-hot** saeppalgak'e tan 새빨갛게 단; **red light** ppalgan pul 빨간 불; **red light district** hongdŭngga 홍등가; **red meat** pulgŭn saegi tonŭn kogi 붉은 색이 도는 고기; **red tape** kwallyojŏk hyŏngshiktchuŭi 관료적 형식주의
reduce churida 줄이다
reduction kamso 감소
redundant (*unnecessary*) pulp'iryohan 불필요한
reed BOT kalttae 갈대
reef (*in sea*) amch'o 암초
reef knot ongmaedŭp 옭매듭
reek *v/i* naemsaega nada 냄새가 나다; ***~ of*** …ŭi naemsaega nada …의 냄새가 나다
reel *n* (*of film*) lil 릴; (*of thread*) shilp'ae 실패
refer *v/t*: ***~ a decision / problem to*** …ege kyŏltchŏng-ŭl / mun-jerŭl nŏmgida …에게 결정을 / 문제를 넘기다
♦**refer to** (*allude to*) …ŭl / rŭl ŏn-gŭp'ada …을 / 를 언급하다; *dictionary etc* …e chohoehada …에 조회하다
referee SP shimp'an 심판; (*for job*) shinwŏn pojŭng-in 신원 보증인
reference (*allusion*) ŏn-gŭp 언급; (*for job*) ch'uch'ŏnsŏ 추천서; (*~ number*) chohoe 조회; ***with ~ to*** …e kwallyŏnhayŏ …에 관련하여
reference book ch'amgo tosŏ 참고 도서
referendum kungmin t'up'yo 국민 투표
refill *v/t tank, glass* tashi ch'aeuda 다시 채우다
refine *oil, sugar* chŏngjehada 정제하다; *technique* chŏnggyohage hada 정교하게 하다
refined *manners, language* seryŏndoen 세련된
refinery chŏngjeso 정제소
reflation t'onghwa chaep'aengch'ang 통화 재팽창
reflect 1 *v/t light* pansahada 반사하다; ***be ~ed in …*** …e pich'wŏjida …에 비춰지다 **2** *v/i* (*think*) komgomhi saenggak'ada 곰곰히 생각하다

reflection (*in water*, *glass etc*) pansadoen kŭrimja 반사된 그림자; (*consideration*) shimsasuk-kko 심사숙고
reflex (*in body*) pansa shin-gyŏng 반사 신경
reflex reaction pansa undong 반사 운동
reform 1 *n* kaehyŏk 개혁 **2** *v/t* kaehyŏk'ada 개혁하다
refrain[1] *v/i* samgahada 삼가하다; ***please ~ from smoking*** tambaerŭl samgahae chushigi paramnida 담배를 삼가해 주시기 바랍니다
refrain[2] *n* (*in song etc*) huryŏm 후렴
refresh *person* kiun ch'arige hada 기운 차리게 하다; ***feel ~ed*** sangk'waehage nŭkkida 상쾌하게 느끼다
refresher course chaegyoyuk kwajŏng 재교육 과정
refreshing *experience* ch'amshinhan 참신한; ***~ drink*** ch'ŏngnyang ŭmnyo 청량 음료
refreshments tagwa 다과
refrigerate naengjanghada 냉장하다
refrigerator naengjanggo 냉장고
refuel 1 *v/t airplane* yŏllyorŭl konggŭp'ada 연료를 공급하다 **2** *v/i* (*of airplane*) yŏllyorŭl pogŭp pat-tta 연료를 보급 받다
refuge p'inanch'ŏ 피난처; ***take ~*** (*from storm etc*) p'inanhada 피난하다
refugee nanmin 난민
refund 1 *n* hwanbul 환불 **2** *v/t* hwanburhada 환불하다
refusal kŏjŏl 거절
refuse kŏjŏrhada 거절하다; ***~ to ...*** ...hagirŭl kŏjŏrhada ...하기를 거절하다
regain *control*, *the lead* toech'at-tta 되찾다
regard 1 *n*: ***have great ~ for*** ...ŭl / rŭl chon-gyŏnghada ...을 / 를 존경하다; ***in this ~*** i chŏme kwanhaesŏnŭn 이 점에 관해서는; ***with ~ to*** ...e kwanhaesŏ ...에 관해서; (***kind***) ***~s*** anbu 안부; ***give my ~s to Mina*** Minaege anbu chŏnhaejuseyo 민아에게 안부 전해주세요; ***with no ~ for*** ...ŭl / rŭl koryŏhaji ank'o ...을 / 를 고려하지 않고 **2** *v/t*: ***~ X as Y*** Xŭl / rŭl Y(ŭ)ro kanjuhada X을 / 를 Y(으)로 간주하다; ***as ~s*** ...e kwanhaesŏnŭn ...에 관해서는
regarding ...e taehaesŏ ...에 대해서
regardless ŏtchaet-ttŭn 어쨌든; ***~ of*** ...e kaeŭich'i ank'o ...에 개의치 않고
regime (*government*) chŏngkkwŏn 정권
regiment *n* yŏndae 연대
region chibang 지방; ***in the ~ of*** yak... 약 ...; ***in the ~ of $5,000*** yak 5,000tallŏ 약 5,000달러
regional chiyŏgŭi 지역의
register 1 *n* tŭngnok 등록 **2** *v/t birth*, *death* shin-gohada 신고하다; *vehicle* tŭngnok'ada 등록하다; *letter* tŭngkkiro puch'ida 등기로 부치다; *emotion* nat'anaeda 나타내다; ***send a letter ~ed*** pyŏnjirŭl tŭngkkiro ponaeda 편지를 등기로 보내다 **3** *v/i* (*at university*) ip'ak tŭngnogŭl hada 입학 등록을 하다; (*for a course*) tŭngnogŭl hada 등록을 하다; (*with police*) shin-gohada 신고하다
registered letter tŭngkki up'yŏn 등기 우편
registration (*at university*) ip'ak tŭngnok 입학 등록; (*for course*) tŭngnok'ada 등록하다
regret 1 *v/t* huhoehada 후회하다 **2** *n* yugam 유감
regrettable yugamsŭrŏun 유감스러운
regrettably yugamsŭrŏpkkedo 유감스럽게도
regular 1 *adj* kyuch'iktchŏgin 규칙적인; *pattern*, *shape* iltchŏnghan 일정한; (*normal*) pot'ong-ŭi 보통의 **2** *n* (*at bar etc*) tan-gol 단골
regulate kyujehada 규제하다
regulation (*rule*) kyuch'ik 규칙
rehabilitate *ex-criminal* sahoero pok-kkwishik'ida 사회로 복귀시키다
rehearsal lihŏsŏl 리허설
rehearse *v/t & v/i* lihŏsŏrhada 리허설하다
reign 1 *n* kullim 군림 **2** *v/i* kullimhada 군림하다

reimburse ...ŭi piyong-ŭl kaptta ...의 비용을 갚다
rein koppi 고삐
reincarnation hwansaeng 환생
reinforce *structure* poganghada 보강하다; *beliefs* kanghwahada 강화하다
reinforced concrete ch'ŏlgŭn k'onk'ŭrit'ŭ 철근 콘크리트
reinforcements MIL chŭng-wŏn-gun 증원군
reinstate *person in office* poktchiksshik'ida 복직시키다; *paragraph in text* pogwŏnhada 복원하다
reject *v/t* kŏjŏrhada 거절하다
rejection kŏjŏl 거절
relapse MED chaebal 재발; ***have a ~*** pyŏng-i chaebarhada 병이 재발하다
relate 1 *v/t story* iyagihada 이야기하다; ***~ X to Y*** Xŭl / rŭl Yege yŏn-gyŏlshik'ida X을 / 를 Y에게 연결시키다 **2** *v/i*: ***~ to ...*** (*be connected with*) ...wa / kwa kwallyŏni it-tta ...와 / 과 관련이 있다; ***he doesn't ~ to people*** kŭnŭn saramdŭlgwa chal sŏk-kkijil mot'anda 그는 사람들과 잘 섞이질 못한다
related (*by family*) ch'inch'ŏgi toenŭn 친척이 되는; *events, ideas etc* kwallyŏni innŭn 관련이 있는
relation (*in family*) ch'inch'ŏk 친척; (*connection*) kwan-gye 관계; ***business / diplomatic ~s*** saŏp / oegyo kwan-gye 사업 / 외교 관계
relationship kwan-gye 관계; (*sexual*) sŏnggwan-gye 성관계
relative 1 *n* ch'inch'ŏk 친척 **2** *adj* sangdaejŏgin 상대적인; ***X is ~ to Y*** Xŭn / nŭn Ye piryehanda X은 / 는 Y에 비례한다
relatively sandaejŏgŭro 상대적으로
relax 1 *v/i* p'yŏnhi shwida 편히 쉬다; ***~!, don't get angry*** maŭm p'yŏnhage saenggak'ae! hwanaeji mallagu 마음 편하게 생각 해! 화내지 말라구 **2** *v/t muscle* himŭl ppaeda 힘을 빼다; *pace* nŭtch'uda 늦추다; *laws* wanhwashik'ida 완화시키다
relaxation kinjang wanhwa 긴장 완화
relay 1 *v/t message* chŏnhada 전하다; *radio, TV signals* chunggyehada 중계하다 **2** *n*: ~ (***race***) kyeju kyŏnggi 계주 경기
release 1 *n* (*from prison*) sŏkppang 석방; (*of CD etc*) palmae 발매; (*of news, information*) palp'yo 발표 **2** *v/t prisoner* sŏkppanghada 석방하다; *CD* palmaehada 발매하다; *parking brake* p'ulda 풀다; *information* konggaehada 발표하다
relent maŭmi nugŭrŏjida 마음이 누그러지다
relentless (*determined*) tanhohan 단호한; *rain etc* sajŏng-ŏmnŭn 사정없는
relevance kwallyŏnssŏng 관련성
relevant kwallyŏndoen 관련된
reliability shilloessŏng 신뢰성
reliable shilloehal su innŭn 신뢰할 수 있는
reliably hwaksshirhage 확실하게; ***I am ~ informed that ...*** nanŭn ...ranŭn kosŭl hwakssirhage chŏnhae tŭrŏtta 나는 ...라는 것을 확실하게 전해 들었다
reliance ŭijon 의존; ***~ on s.o. / sth*** nugue / muŏse taehan ŭijon 누구에/무엇에 대한 의존
relic yumul 유물
relief anshim 안심; ***that's a ~*** anshimi toemnida 안심이 됩니다
relieve *pressure, pain* churida 줄이다; (*take over from*) kyodaehada 교대하다; ***be ~d*** (*at news etc*) anshimi toeda 안심이 되다
religion chonggyo 종교
religious chonggyojŏgin 종교적인; *person* shinangshim-i kip'ŭn 신앙심이 깊은
religiously (*conscientiously*) yangshimjŏgŭro 양심적으로
relish 1 *n* (*sauce*) yangnyŏm 양념 **2** *v/t idea, prospect* chŭlgida 즐기다
relive *the past* sanggihada 상기하다
relocate *v/i* (*of business*) ijŏnhada 이전하다; (*of employee*) chaebaech'ihada 재배치하다
reluctance naek'iji anŭm 내키지 않음
reluctant naek'iji annŭn 내키지 않는;

be ~ to do sth muŏsŭl hanŭn kŏshi naek'iji ant'a 무엇을 하는 것이 내키지 않다
reluctantly maji mot'ae 마지 못해
♦**rely on** ŭijihada 의지하다; ***~ s.o. to do sth*** nuguege muŏt hanŭn kŏsŭl ŭijihada 누구에게 무엇 하는 것을 의지하다
remain (*be left*) namgyŏjida 남겨지다; (*stay*) kyesok … it-tta 계속 … 있다; ***they ~ed silent*** kŭdŭrŭn kyesok choyonghage issŏt-tta 그들은 계속 조용하게 있었다
remainder *also* MATH namŏji 나머지
remains (*of body*) yuhae 유해
remand 1 *v/t*: ***~ s.o. in custody*** nugurŭl kuryushik'ida 누구를 구류시키다 **2** *n*: ***be on ~*** kuryu chung-ida 구류 중이다
remark 1 *n* ŏn-gŭp 언급 **2** *v/t* ŏn-gŭp'ada 언급하다
remarkable chumok'al manhan 주목할 만한
remarkably taedanhi 대단히
remarry *v/i* chaehonhada 재혼하다
remedy *n* MED ch'iryo 치료; *fig* kujech'aek 구제책
remember 1 *v/t* kiŏk'ada 기억하다; ***~ to lock the door*** mun chamgŭnŭn kŏl, ittchi marayo 문 잠그는 걸, 잊지 말아요; ***~ me to her*** kŭnyŏege nae anburŭl chŏnhaejuseyo 그녀에게 내 안부를 전해주세요 **2** *v/i* kiŏk'ada 기억하다; ***I don't ~*** chŏnŭn kiŏgi naji anayo 저는 기억이 나지 않아요
remind: ***~ s.o. of sth*** (*bring to their attention*) nuguege muŏsŭl ilkkaewŏjuda 누구에게 무엇을 일깨워주다; (*make remember*) nuguege muŏsŭl kiŏng nage hada 누구에게 무엇을 기억 나게 하다; ***~ s.o. of s.o.*** nugurŭl pomyŏn nugun-gaga saenggangnada 누구를 보면 누군가가 생각나다
reminder saegangnage hanŭn kŏt 생각나게 하는 것; COM tokch'oktchang 독촉장
reminisce hoesang 회상
reminiscent: ***be ~ of sth*** muŏsŭl yŏnsangshik'ida 무엇을 연상시키다
remnant yumul 유물
remorse chach'aek 자책
remorseless *person* mujabihan 무자비한; *demands* kkŭnimŏmnŭn 끊임없는; *pace* mŏmch'ul su ŏmnŭn 멈출 수 없는
remote *village* oettan 외딴; *possibility*, *connection* hŭibak'an 희박한; (*aloof*) ch'oyŏnhan 초연한; *ancestor* mŏn 먼
remote access COMPUT wŏnkkyŏk chŏpkkŭn 원격 접근
remote control wŏnkkyŏk chojong 원격 조종
remotely *connected* mŏlli 멀리; ***just ~ possible*** kanŭngssŏng-i kŏŭi hŭibak'an 가능성이 거의 희박한
removal chegŏ 제거
remove ch'iuda 치우다; *top*, *lid* pŏtkkida 벗기다; *coat etc* pŏt-tta 벗다; *doubt*, *suspicion* ŏpssaeda 없애다
remuneration posu 보수
remunerative posuga ch'ungbunhan 보수가 충분한
rename kaemyŏnghada 개명하다
render haenghada 행하다; ***~ a service*** pongsahada 봉사하다; ***~ s.o. helpless*** / ***unconscious*** nugurŭl mugiryŏk'age / ŭishigŭl ilk'e hada 누구를 무기력하게 / 의식을 잃게 하다
rendering (*of music*) yŏnju 연주
rendez-vous (*romantic*) langdebu 랑데부; MIL chipkkyŏltchi 집결지
renew *contract*, *license* kaengshinhada 갱신하다; *discussions* chaegaehada 재개하다
renewal (*of contract etc*) kaengshin 갱신; (*of discussions*) chaegae 재개
renounce *v/t title*, *rights* p'ogihada 포기하다
renovate *building* kaejohada 개조하다
renovation (*of building*) kaejo 개조
renown yumyŏng 유명
renowned yumyŏnghan 유명한
rent 1 *n* imdaeryo 임대료; ***for ~*** imdaeyong 임대용 **2** *v/t apartment*, *car* imdaehada 임대하다
rental (*money*) imdae kŭmaek 임대 금액
rental agreement imdae kyeyaksŏ

임대 계약서
rental car imdae chadongch'a 임대 자동차
rent-free *adv* imdaeryoga ŏpsshi 임대료가 없이
reopen 1 *v/t store* chaegaejanghada 재개장하다; *business, negotiations, case* chaegaehada 재개하다 **2** *v/i* (*of theater etc*) chaegaejanghada 재개장하다
reorganization chaep'yŏnsŏng 재편성
reorganize chaep'yŏnsŏnghada 재편성하다
rep COM seiljŭ maen 세일즈 맨
repaint tashi ch'irhada 다시 칠하다
repair 1 *v/t* koch'ida 고치다 **2** *n*: ***in a good/bad state of ~*** suriga chal toen/chal toeji anŭn 수리가 잘 된/잘 되지 않은
repairman surigong 수리공
repatriate songwanhada 송환하다
repay *money, person* kaptta 갚다
repayment pyŏnje 변제
repeal *v/t law* p'yejihada 폐지하다
repeat 1 *v/t something said* panbok'ada 반복하다; *performance, experience* toep'urihada 되풀이하다; ***am I ~ing myself?*** chŏne marhaettŏn chŏgi innayo? 전에 말했던 적이 있나요? **2** *v/i* panbok'ada 반복하다; ***I ~, do not touch it*** tashi marhanŭnde, kŭgŏsŭl manjiji maseyo 다시 말하는데, 그것을 만지지 마세요 **3** *n* (*TV program*) chaebangsong 재방송
repeat business COM chaegŏrae 재거래
repeated panboktoenŭn 반복되는
repeat order COM chaejumun 재주문
repel *v/t invaders, attack* kyŏkt'oehada 격퇴하다; *insects* moranaeda 몰아내다; (*disgust*) pulk'waegamŭl irŭk'ida 불쾌감을 일으키다
repellent 1 *n* (*insect ~*) *pŏllee mulliji ank'e hanŭn yak* 벌레에 물리지 않게 하는 약 **2** *adj* pulk'waehan 불쾌한
repent huhoehada 후회하다
repercussions p'agŭp hyokkwa 파급 효과
repetition (*of word, event etc*) panbok 반복
repetitive toep'uridoenŭn 되풀이되는
replace (*put back*) toedollyŏnot'a 되돌려놓다; (*take the place of*) taeshinhada 대신하다
replacement (*person*) huimja 후임자; (*thing*) taech'ep'um 대체품
replacement part taech'ebup'um 대체부품
replay 1 *n* (*recording*) chaesaeng 재생; (*match*) chaeshihap 재시합 **2** *v/t match* chaeshihap'ada 재시합하다
replica poktchep'um 복제품
reply 1 *n* taedap 대답 **2** *v/t & v/i* taedap'ada 대답하다
report 1 *n* (*account*) pogosŏ 보고서; (*by journalist*) podo 보도 **2** *v/t* pogohada 보고하다; ***~ one's findings to s.o.*** nuguege chosa kyŏlgwarŭl pogohada 누구에게 조사 결과를 보고하다; ***~ a person to the police*** saramŭl kyŏngch'are kobarhada 사람을 경찰에 고발하다; ***he is ~ed to be in Hong Kong*** kŭnŭn hongk'onge innŭn kŏsŭro pogodoeŏtta 그는 홍콩에 있는 것으로 보고되었다 **3** *v/i* (*of journalist*) podohada 보도하다; (*present oneself*) ch'ulttuhada 출두하다
♦**report to** (*in business*) ...ege pogohada ...에게 보고하다
report card sŏngjŏkp'yo 성적표
reporter kija 기자
repossess COM *miwanbuldoen sangp'umŭl hoesuhada* 미완불된 상품을 회수하다
reprehensible pinan padŭlmanhan 비난 받을만한
represent (*act for*) taerihada 대리하다; (*stand for*) taep'yohada 대표하다; (*of images in painting etc*) myosahada 묘사하다
representative 1 *n* taeriin 대리인; COM taep'yoja 대표자; POL taebyŏnja 대변자 **2** *adj* (*typical*) chŏnhyŏngjŏgin 전형적인
repress *revolt* ŏgap'ada 억압하다;

feelings, *natural urges* ŏngnurŭda 억누르다; *laugh* ch'amtta 참다
repression POL chinap 진압
repressive POL ŏgaptchŏgin 억압적인
reprieve 1 *n* LAW chip'aeng yuye 집행 유예; *fig* ilshijŏk yŏn-gi 일시적 연기 **2** *v/t prisoner* chip'aeng-ŭl yuyehada 집행을 유예하다
reprimand *v/t* chilch'aek'ada 질책하다
reprint 1 *n* chaep'an 재판 **2** *v/t* chaep'anhada 재판하다
reprisal pokssu 복수; ***take ~s*** pokssuhada 복수하다
reproach 1 *n* pinan 비난; ***be beyond ~*** pinanŭi yŏjiga ŏptta 비난의 여지가 없다 **2** *v/t* pinanhada 비난하다
reproachful pinanhanŭn 비난하는
reproduce 1 *v/t atmosphere*, *mood* chaehyŏnhada 재현하다 **2** *v/i* BIO chaesaengshik'ada 재생식하다
reproduction BIO chaesaengshik 재생식; (*of sound*, *images*) chaesaeng 재생; (*piece of furniture*) poktche 복제
reproductive BIO chaesaengshik'anŭn 재생식하는
reptile p'ach'ungnyu 파충류
republic konghwaguk 공화국
Republic of Korea Taehanmin-guk 대한민국
republican 1 *n* konghwadangjuŭija 공화당주의자; ***Republican*** POL Konghwadang-wŏn 공화당원; (*supporter*) Konghwadang chijija 공화당 지지자 **2** *adj* Konghwadang-ŭl chijihanŭn 공화당을 지지하는
repudiate (*deny*) kŏjŏrhada 거절하다
repulsive mesŭkkŏun 메스꺼운
reputable p'yŏngp'ani choŭn 평판이 좋은
reputation p'yŏngp'an 평판; ***have a good / bad ~*** p'yŏngp'ani chot'a / nappŭda 평판이 좋다 / 나쁘 다
request 1 *n* yoch'ŏng 요청; ***on ~*** yoch'ŏnge ttara 요청에 따라 **2** *v/t* ch'ŏnghada 청하다
require (*need*) p'iryohada 필요하다; ***it ~s great care*** seshimhan chuŭiga p'iryohamnida 세심한 주의가 필요합니다; ***as ~d by law*** pŏbŭro chŏnghaejyŏ it-ttŭshi 법으로 정해져 있듯이; ***guests are ~d to ...*** sonnimdŭrŭn ...ŭl / rŭl haeya hamnida 손님들은 ...을 / 를 해야 합니다
required (*necessary*) p'iryohan 필요한
requirement (*need*) yogu 요구; (*condition*) chokkŏn 조건
reroute *airplane etc* k'osŭrŭl pyŏn-gyŏnghada 코스를 변경하다
rerun *tape* chaesangyŏnghada 재상영하다
rescue 1 *n* kujo 구조; ***come to s.o.'s ~*** nugurŭl kujoharŏ oda 누구를 구조하러 오다 **2** *v/t* kujohada 구조하다
rescue party kujodae 구조대
research *n* yŏn-gu 연구
♦**research into** ...e taehan yŏn-gu ...에 대한 연구
research and development yŏn-gu kaebal 연구 개발
research assistant yŏn-gu pojowŏn 연구 보조원
researcher yŏn-guwŏn 연구원
research project yŏn-gu kyehoek 연구 계획
resemblance yusa 유사
resemble tamtta 닮다
resent ...e pun-gaehada ...에 분개하다
resentful pun-gaehan 분개한
resentment pun-gae 분개
reservation (*of room*, *table*) yeyak 예약; (*mental*) ŭigushim 의구심; (*special area*) t'ŭkppyŏl poryuji 특별 보류지; ***I have a ~*** nanŭn yeyagŭl haet-tta 나는 예약을 했다
reserve 1 *n* (*store*) pich'uk 비축; (*aloofness*) naengdam 냉담; SP hubo sŏnsu 후보 선수; **~s** FIN poyugŭm 보유금; ***keep sth in ~*** muŏsŭl pich'uk'ada 무엇을 비축하다 **2** *v/t seat*, *table* yeyak'ada 예약하다; *judgment* poryuhada 보류하다
reserved *person*, *manner* malssuga chŏgŭn 말수가 적은; *table*, *seat* yeyaktoen 예약된
reservoir (*for water*) chŏsuji 저수지
reside kŏjuhada 거주하다

residence (*house etc*) kŏjuji 거주지; (*stay*) ch'eryu 체류
residence permit kŏju hŏga 거주 허가
resident 1 *n* kŏjuja 거주자 **2** *adj manager etc* sangjuhanŭn 상주하는
residential *district* chugŏŭi 주거의
residue chanyŏmul 잔여물
resign 1 *v/t position* saimhada 사임하다; **~ *oneself to*** ch'enyŏmhago ...hagiro hada 체념하고 ...하기로 하다 **2** *v/i* (*from job*) sagjik'ada 사직하다
resignation (*from job*) sajik 사직; (*mental*) tannyŏm 단념
resigned ch'enyŏmhanŭn 체념하는; ***we have become ~ to the fact that ...*** urinŭn ...ranŭn sashire tannyŏmhage toeŏtta 우리는 ...라는 사실에 단념하게 되었다
resilient *personality* k'waehwarhan 쾌활한; *material* naegussŏng-i kanghan 내구성이 강한
resin suji 수지
resist 1 *v/t enemy, s.o.'s advances* chŏhanghada 저항하다; *new measures* pandaehada 반대하다; *temptation* kyŏndida 견디다 **2** *v/i* pŏt'ida 버티다
resistance chŏhang 저항
resistant *material* chŏhangnyŏgi innŭn 저항력이 있는
resolute ŭijiga kudŭn 의지가 굳은
resolution (*decision*) kyŏlsshim 결심; (*determination*) kyŏryŏnham 결연함
resolution (*of problem*) haegyŏl 해결; (*of image*) sŏnmyŏngdo 선명도
resolve *problem, mystery* haegyŏrhada 해결하다; **~ *to do sth*** muŏsŭl hagi wihae kyŏlsshimhada 무엇을 하기 위해 결심하다
resort 1 *n* (*place*) hyuyangji 휴양지; ***as a last ~*** majimak sudanŭro 마지막 수단으로
resounding *success* wanjŏnhan 완전한
resource chawŏn 자원
resourceful kiryagi p'ungbuhan 기략이 풍부한
respect 1 *n* chon-gyŏng 존경; (*consideration*) paeryŏ 배려; ***show ~ to*** kyŏngŭirŭl p'yohada 경의를 표하다; ***with ~ to*** ...e taehayŏ ...에 대하여; ***in this / that ~*** irŏhan / chŏrŏhan kwantchŏmesŏ 이러한 / 저러한 관점에서; ***in many ~s*** yŏrŏ myŏnesŏ 여러 면에서; ***pay one's last ~s to s.o.*** nuguege ch'oehuŭi kyŏng-ŭirŭl p'yohada 누구에게 최후의 경의를 표하다 **2** *v/t person, opinion* chon-gyŏnghada 존경하다; *law, privacy* chonjunghada 존중하다
respectable hullyunghan 훌륭한
respectful chon-gyŏnghanŭn 존경하는
respectfully chŏngjunghage 정중하게
respective kak-kkagŭi 각각의
respectively kak-kki 각기
respiration hohŭp 호흡
respirator MED in-gong hohŭpkki 인공 호흡기
respite hyushik 휴식; ***without ~*** shwim ŏpsshi 쉼 없이
respond (*answer*) taedap'ada 대답하다; (*react*) panŭnghada 반응하다
response (*answer*) taedap 대답; (*reaction*) panŭng 반응
responsibility ch'aegim 책임; (*duty*) ŭimu 의무; ***accept ~ for*** ch'aegimŭl chida 책임을 지다
responsible chaegimi innŭn 책임이 있는; (*trustworthy*) shilloehal su innŭn 신뢰할 수 있는; *job* ch'aegimi mugŏun 책임이 무거운
responsive *audience, brakes* panŭnghanŭn 반응하는
rest[1] **1** *n* hyushik 휴식 **2** *v/i* shwida 쉬다; **~ *on*** (*be based on*) ...e kich'ohada ...에 기초하다; (*lean against*) ...e kidaeda ...에 기대다; ***it all ~s with him*** modŭn kŏn kŭ saram sone tallyŏ issŭmnida 모든 건 그 사람 손에 달려 있습니다 **3** *v/t* (*lean, balance etc*) kidaeda 기대다
rest[2]: ***the ~*** namŏji 나머지
restaurant shikttang 식당
restaurant car RAIL shikttangch'a 식당차
rest cure anjŏng yoppŏp 안정 요법
rest home yoyangso 요양소
restless kamanit-tchi mot'anŭn

가만있지 못하는; ***have a ~ night*** cham mot irunŭn pamŭl ponaeda 잠 못 이루는 밤을 보내다
restoration pok-kku 복구
restore *building etc* pok-kkuhada 복구하다
restrain *dog*, *troops* cheap'ada 제압하다; *emotions* ŏngnurŭda 억누르다; ***~ oneself*** chajehada 자제하다
restraint (*moderation*) ŏktche 억제
restrict chehanhada 제한하다; ***I'll ~ myself to …*** chŏnŭn …man hagessŭmnida 저는 …만 하겠습니다
restricted *view* hanjŏngdoen 한정된
restricted area MIL chehan-guyŏk 제한구역
restriction chehan 제한
rest room hwajangshil 화장실
result *n* kyŏlgwa 결과; ***as a ~ of this*** igŏsŭi kyŏlgwaro 이것의 결과로
♦**result from** …e kiinhada …에 기인하다
♦**result in** …(ŭ)ro kkŭnnada …(으)로 끝나다
resume *v/t* chaegaehada 재개하다
résumé iryŏkssŏ 이력서
resurface 1 *v/t roads* chaep'ojanghada 재포장하다 **2** *v/i* (*reappear*) chaehyŏndoeda 재현되다
resurrection REL puhwal 부활
resuscitate sosaengshik'ida 소생시키다
retail 1 *adv* somaero 소매로 **2** *v/i*: ***~ at*** …e somaero p'alda …에 소매로 팔다
retailer somae sangin 소매 상인
retail price somae kagyŏk 소매 가격
retain kyesok yujihada 계속 유지하다; *lawyer* koyonghada 고용하다
retainer FIN suimnyo 수임료
retaliate pokssuhada 복수하다
retaliation pokssu 복수
retarded (*mentally*) chŏnŭnghan 저능한
retire *v/i* (*from work*) ŭnt'oehada 은퇴하다
retired ŭnt'oehan 은퇴한
retirement ŭnt'oe 은퇴
retirement age chŏngnyŏn 정년
retiring naehyangjŏgin 내향적인
retort 1 *n* panbak 반박 **2** *v/i* panbak'ada 반박하다
retrace *footsteps* toedoragada 되돌아가다
retract *v/t claws* omŭrida 오므리다; *undercarriage* kkŭrŏdanggida 끌어당기다; *statement* ch'ŏrhoehada 철회하다
retreat 1 *v/i* MIL hut'oehada 후퇴하다; (*in discussion etc*) mullŏsŏda 물러서다 **2** *n* MIL hut'oe 후퇴; (*place*) p'inanch'ŏ 피난처
retrieve toech'at-tta 되찾다
retriever (*dog*) lit'ŭribŏ 리트리버
retroactive *law etc* sogŭp'anŭn 소급하는
retrograde *move* t'oebohada 퇴보하다; *decision* chŏrhoehada 철회하다
retrospect: ***in ~*** hoegohae pomyŏn 회고해 보면
retrospective (*of movies*) hoegojŏn 회고전
return 1 *n* (*coming back*, *going back*) kwihwan 귀환; (*giving back*) panhwan 반환; COMPUT shirhaeng 실행; (*in tennis*) pan-gyŏk 반격; ***by ~ (of post)*** pannŭn chŭksshiro 받는 즉시로; ***~s*** (*profit*) iik 이익; ***many happy ~s (of the day)*** saeng-irŭl ch'uk'ahamnida 생일을 축하합니다 **2** *v/t* (*give back*) tollyŏjuda 돌려주다; (*put back*) tollyŏnot'a 돌려놓다; *favor*, *invitation* podap'ada 보답하다 **3** *v/i* (*go back*) toedoragada 되돌아가다; (*come back*) toedoraoda 되돌아오다; (*of good times*, *doubts etc*) chaehyŏnhada 재현하다
return flight wangbok pihaenggi 왕복 비행기
return journey wangbok yŏhaeng 왕복 여행
reunification t'ong-il 통일
reunion chaehoe 재회
reunite *v/t country* chaet'onghap'ada 재통합하다; *old friends* chaehoehada 재회하다
reusable chaesayong-i kanŭnghan 재사용이 가능한
reuse chaesayonghada 재사용하다
rev *n* hoejŏn 회전; ***~s per minute***

pun tang hoejŏn 분 당 회전
♦**rev up** *v/t engine* sokttorŭl pparŭge hada 속도를 빠르게 하다
revaluation p'yŏngkkajŏlssang 평가절상
reveal (*make visible*) tŭrŏnaeda 드러내다; (*make known*) palk'ida 밝히다
revealing *remark* palk'yŏjunŭn 밝혀주는; *dress* noch'uldoen 노출된
revelation p'ongno 폭로
revenge *n* pobok 보복; ***take one's ~*** pobok'ada 보복하다
revenue seip 세입
reverberate (*of sound*) ullyŏ p'ŏjida 울려 퍼지다
Reverend sŏngjiktcha 성직자
reverent kyŏngŏnhan 경건한
reverse 1 *adj sequence* kŏkkurodoen 거꾸로된 **2** *n* (*opposite*) pandae 반대; (*back*) twittchang 뒷장; (*of envelope*) twinmyŏn 뒷면; MOT hujin 후진 **3** *v/t sequence* kŏkkuro hada 거꾸로 하다; *vehicle* hujinhada 후진하다 **4** *v/i* MOT hujinhada 후진하다
review 1 *n* (*of book*, *movie*) pip'yŏng 비평; (*of troops*) yŏlbyŏngshik 열병식; (*of situation etc*) chaegŏmt'o 재검토 **2** *v/t book*, *movie* nonp'yŏnghada 논평하다; *troops* sayŏrhada 사열하다; *situation etc* chaegŏmt'ohada 재검토하다; EDU pokssŭp'ada 복습하다
reviewer (*of movie etc*) p'yŏngnon-ga 평론가
revise *v/t opinion*, *text* sujŏnghada 수정하다
revision (*of opinion*, *text*) sujŏng 수정
revisionism POL sujŏngjuŭi 수정주의
revival (*of custom*, *old style etc*) puhwal 부활; (*of patient*) sosaeng 소생
revive 1 *v/t custom*, *old style etc* puhwarhada 부활하다; *patient* sosaengshik'ida 소생시키다 **2** *v/i* (*of business etc*) hoeboktoeda 회복되다
revoke *law*, *license* muhyoro hada 무효로 하다
revolt 1 *n* pallan 반란 **2** *v/i* pallanhada 반란하다
revolting (*disgusting*) hyŏmogamŭl nŭkkige hanŭn 혐오감을 느끼게 하는
revolution POL hyŏngmyŏng 혁명; (*turn*) hoejŏn 회전
revolutionary 1 *n* POL hyŏngmyŏngga 혁명가 **2** *adj spirit*, *forces* hyŏngmyŏng-ŭi 혁명의; *ideas* hyŏngmyŏngjŏgin 혁명적인
revolutionize hyŏngmyŏng-ŭl irŭk'ida 혁명을 일으키다
revolve *v/i* hoejŏnhada 회전하다
revolver kwŏnch'ong 권총
revolving door hoejŏnmun 회전문
revue THEA shisap'ungjagŭk 시사풍자극
revulsion kyŏkppyŏn 격변
reward 1 *n* posang 보상; (*financial*) posu 보수 **2** *v/t* (*financially*) posurŭl chuda 보수를 주다
rewarding porami innŭn 보람이 있는
rewind *v/t film*, *tape* tashi kamtta 다시 감다
rewrite *v/t* tashi ssŭda 다시 쓰다
rhetoric susa 수사
rheumatism lyumat'ijŭm 류마티즘
rhinoceros k'otppulsso 코뿔소
rhubarb changgunp'ul 장군풀
rhyme 1 *n* un 운 **2** *v/i* chakssihada 작시하다; ***~ with*** …wa / kwa uni mattta …와 / 과 운이 맞다
rhythm lidŭm 리듬
rib *n* kalbippyŏ 갈비뼈
ribbon libon 리본
rice ssal 쌀; (*cooked*) pap 밥
rice bowl pap kŭrŭt 밥 그릇; **rice cake** ttŏk 떡; **rice cooker** chŏn-gi papssot 전기 밥솥; **ricefield**, **rice paddy** non 논; **rice planting** monaegi 모내기; **rice wine** makkkŏlli 막걸리
rich 1 *adj* puyuhan 부유한; *food* mashi chinhan 맛이 진한 **2** *n*: ***the ~*** puja 부자
rid: ***get ~ of*** ŏpssaeda 없애다
riddle susukkekki 수수께끼
ride 1 *n* t'am 탐; (*journey*) yŏhaeng 여행; ***do you want a ~ into town?*** shinaee t'aewŏ chulkkayo? 시내에 태워 줄까요? **2** *v/t horse*, *bike* t'ada 타다 **3** *v/i* (*on horse*) sŭngmahada

승마하다; (*on bike, in vehicle*) t'ada 타다
rider (*on horse*) kisu 기수; (*on bike*) chajŏn-gŏ t'anŭn saram 자전거 타는 사람
ridge (*raised strip*) ollagan t'ŏk 올라간 턱; (*of mountain*) santtŭngsŏng-i 산등성이; (*of roof*) chibung kkokttaegi 지붕 꼭대기
ridicule 1 *n* choso 조소 **2** *v/t* choronghada 조롱하다
ridiculous t'ŏmuniŏmnŭn 터무니없는
ridiculously t'ŏmuniŏpsshi 터무니없이
riding (*on horseback*) sŭngma 승마
rifle *n* soch'ong 소총
rift (*in earth*) tanch'ŭng 단층; (*in party etc*) kyunyŏl 균열
rig 1 *n* (*oil* ~) kulch'ak changch'i 굴착 장치; (*truck*) t'ŭrŏk 트럭 **2** *v/t elections* chojak'ada 조작하다
right 1 *adj* (*correct*) mannŭn 맞는; (*proper, just*) olbarŭn 올바른; (*suitable*) chŏktchŏrhan 적절한; (*not left*) orŭntchogŭi 오른쪽의; **be ~** (*of answer, person*) mat-tta 맞다; (*of clock*) chŏnghwak'ada 정확하다; ***that's ~!*** paro kŭgŏya! 바로 그거야!; ***put things ~*** irŭl haegyŏrhada 일을 해결하다; ***that's not ~*** (*not fair*) kŭgŏsŭn andoel irida 그것은 안될 일이다; → ***alright*** **2** *adv* (*directly*) paro 바로; (*correctly*) olbarŭge 올바르게; (*completely*) wanjŏnhi 완전히; (*not left*) orŭntchogŭro 오른쪽으로; ***~ now*** (*immediately*) tangjang 당장; (*at the moment*) chigŭm 지금 **3** *n* (*civil, legal etc*) kwŏlli 권리; (*not left*) orŭntchok 오른쪽; POL uik 우익; ***on the ~*** orŭntchoge(sŏ) 오른쪽에(서); POL uige(sŏ) 우익에(서); ***turn to the ~, take a ~*** orŭntchogŭro toshio 오른쪽으로 도시오; ***be in the ~*** torie mat-tta 도리에 맞다; ***know ~ from wrong*** olk'o kŭrŭmŭl kubyŏrhada 옳고 그름을 구별하다
right-angle chik-kkak 직각; ***at ~s to*** …wa / kwa chik-kkagŭro …와 / 과 직각으로
righteous army ŭibyŏng 의병
rightful *heir, owner etc* happŏptchŏgin 합법적인
right-hand *adj* orŭntchogŭi 오른쪽의; ***on the ~ side*** orŭnp'yŏne 오른편에; **right-hand drive** MOT uch'ŭk haendul unjŏn 우측 핸들 운전; **right-handed** orŭnsonjabiŭi 오른손잡이의; **right-hand man** shimbok 심복; **right of way** (*in traffic*) t'onghaeng usŏnkkwŏn 통행 우선권; (*across land*) t'onghaengkkwŏn 통행권; **right wing** *n* POL uik 우익; SP uch'ŭk konggyŏkssu 우측 공격수; **right-wing** *adj* POL uigŭi 우익의; **right-winger** POL uik chijija 우익 지지자; **right-wing extremism** POL kŭgup'a 극우파
rigid *material* tandanhan 단단한; *principles* ŏmkkyŏk'an 엄격한; *attitude* wangohan 완고한
rigor (*of discipline*) ŏmkkyŏk 엄격; ***the ~s of winter*** kyŏurŭi hokttok'am 겨울의 혹독함
rigorous *discipline* ŏmkkyŏk'an 엄격한; *tests, analysis* myŏnmirhan 면밀한
rim (*of wheel*) t'eduri 테두리; (*of cup*) kajangjari 가장자리; (*of eyeglasses*) t'e 테
ring[1] (*circle*) wŏnhyŏng 원형; (*on finger*) panji 반지; (*in boxing, at circus*) ling 링
ring[2] **1** *n* (*of bell*) ullim 울림; (*of voice*) ullinŭn sori 울리는 소리 **2** *v/t bell* ullida 울리다 **3** *v/i* (*of bell*) ullida 울리다; ***please ~ for attention*** chong-ŭl ch'yŏsŏ pullŏjuseyo 종을 쳐서 불러주세요
ringleader chumoja 주모자
ring-pull chabadangginŭn kori 잡아당기는 고리
rink chang 장
rinse 1 *n* (*for hair color*) linssŭ 린스 **2** *v/t clothes, dishes* hengguda 헹구다; *hair* linssŭhada 린스하다
riot 1 *n* p'okttong 폭동 **2** *v/i* p'okttongŭl irŭk'ida 폭동을 일으키다
rioter p'okttongja 폭동자
riot police kyŏngch'al kidongdae 경찰 기동대

rip 1 *n* (*in cloth etc*) tchijŏjin kot 찢어진 곳 **2** *v/t cloth etc* tchit-tta 찢다; ~ ***sth open*** muŏsŭl tchijŏ yŏlda 무엇을 찢어 열다
♦**rip off** F (*cheat*) sogida 속이다; *customers* p'ongnirŭl ch'wihada 폭리를 취하다
ripe *fruit* igŭn 익은
ripen *v/i* (*of fruit*) iktta 익다
ripeness (*of fruit*) sukssŏng 숙성
rip-off *n* F sagi 사기
ripple *n* (*on water*) mulkkyŏl 물결
rise 1 *v/i* (*from chair etc*) irŏnada 일어나다; (*of sun*) ttŏorŭda 떠오르다; (*of rocket*) sosaorŭda 솟아오르다; (*of price, temperature, water level*) orŭda 오르다 **2** *n* (*in price, salary*) insang 인상; (*in water level, temperature*) sangsŭng 상승
risk 1 *n* wihŏm 위험; ***take a ~*** wihŏmŭl murŭpssŭda 위험을 무릅쓰다 **2** *v/t* wishŏme ppattŭrida 위험에 빠뜨리다; ***let's ~ it*** kamhaenghae popsshida 감행해 봅시다
risky wihŏmhan 위험한
ritual 1 *n* ŭishik 의식 **2** *adj* ŭishigŭi 의식의
rival 1 *n* kyŏngjaengja 경쟁자 **2** *v/t* …wa / kwa kyŏngjaenghada …와 / 과 경쟁하다; ***I can't ~ that*** i isang tŏ chal hal sunŭn ŏpssŏyo 이 이상 더 잘 할 수는 없어요
rivalry kyŏngjaeng 경쟁
river kang 강
riverbed kangppadak 강바닥
riverside kangbyŏn 강변
rivet 1 *n* taemot 대못 **2** *v/t* taemosŭro paktta 대못으로 박다
road kil 길; ***it's just down the ~*** paro chŏtchoge issŏyo 바로 저쪽에 있어요
roadblock parik'eidŭ 바리케이드; **road hog** nanp'ok unjŏnja 난폭 운전자; **road holding** (*of vehicle*) chuhaeng anjŏngssŏng 주행 안정성; **road map** toro chido 도로 지도; **roadside**: ***at the ~*** kilkkae 길가에; **roadsign** toro p'yojip'an 도로 표지판; **roadway** toro 도로; **road works** toro kongsa 도로 공사; **roadworthy** torochuhaeng-e almajŭn 도로 주행에 알맞은
roam toradtanida 돌아다니다
roar 1 *n* (*of traffic, engine*) urŭrŭnggŏrinŭn sori 우르릉거리는 소리; (*of lion*) p'ohyo 포효; (*of person*) koham 고함 **2** *v/i* (*of engine*) urŭrŭnggŏrida 우르릉거리다; (*of lion*) p'ohyohada 포효하다; (*of person*) kohamch'ida 고함치다; ~ ***with laughter*** k'ŭge ut-tta 크게 웃다
roast 1 *n* (*of beef etc*) kuun ŭmshik 구운 음식 **2** *v/t* kuptta 굽다 **3** *v/i* (*of food*) kuwŏjida 구워지다; ***we're ~ing*** F tchidŭshi tŏptta 찌듯이 덥다
roast beef kuun soegogi 구운 쇠고기
roast pork kuun twaejigogi 구운 돼지고기
rob *person, bank* kangt'arhada 강탈하다; ***I've been ~bed*** kangdo tanghaessŏyo 강도 당했어요
robber kangdo 강도
robbery kangdojil 강도질
robe (*of judge*) pŏp-ppok 법복; (*of priest*) yebok 예복; (*bath~*) mogyok kkaun 목욕 가운
robin kaettong chippagwi sae 개똥 지빠귀 새
robot lobot 로봇
robust t'ŭnt'ŭnhan 튼튼한
rock 1 *n* tol 돌; MUS lak 락; ***on the ~s*** *drink* ŏrŭmŭl kyŏt-ttŭryŏ 얼음을 곁들여; *marriage* p'at'ane irŭrŏ 파탄에 이르러 **2** *v/t baby, cradle* choyonghi hŭndŭlda 조용히 흔들다; (*surprise*) nollage hada 놀라게 하다 **3** *v/i* (*on chair*) hŭndŭlgŏrida 흔들거리다; (*of boat*) chindonghada 진동하다
rock bottom: ***reach ~*** mitppadagŭro ttŏrŏjida 밑바닥으로 떨어지다
rock-bottom *adj prices* ch'oejŏŭi 최저의
rocket 1 *n* (*space ~*) lok'et 로켓; (*firework*) ssoaollinŭn pulkkot 쏘아올리는 불꽃 **2** *v/i* (*of prices etc*) ch'isot-tta 치솟다
rocking chair hŭndŭl ŭija 흔들 의자
rock'n' roll lakk'ŭllol 락큰롤
rock star laksŭt'a 락스타
rocky *beach, path* pawiga manŭn

바위가 많은
rod makttae 막대; (*for fishing*) nakkshit-ttae 낚싯대
rodent sŏlch'iryu 설치류
rogue kŏndal 건달
ROK (= ***Republic of Korea***) Taehanmin-guk 대한민국
role yŏk'al 역할
role model ponbogiga toenŭn saram 본보기가 되는 사람
roll 1 *n* (*bread*) lolppang 롤빵; (*of film*) lol 롤; (*of thunder*) ullim 울림; (*list*, *register*) mongnok 목록 **2** *v/i* (*of ball etc*) kurŭda 구르다; (*of boat*) hŭndŭlgŏrida 흔들거리다 **3** *v/t*: ~ ***sth into a ball*** muŏsŭl kongch'ŏrŏm kullida 무엇을 공처럼 굴리다
♦**roll over 1** *v/i* twinggulda 뒹굴다 **2** *v/t person*, *object* kullyŏ nŏmŏttŭrida 굴려 넘어뜨리다; (*renew*) kiganŭl yŏnjangshik'ida 기간을 연장시키다; (*extend*) nŭllida 늘리다
♦**roll up 1** *v/t sleeves* kŏdŏollida 걷어올리다 **2** *v/i* F (*arrive*) toch'ak'ada 도착하다
roll call chŏmho 점호
roller (*for hair*) mŏri manŭn lol 머리 마는 롤
roller blade *n* lollŏ pŭlleidŭ 롤러 블레이드; **roller coaster** lollŏ k'osŭt'ŏ 롤러 코스터; **roller skate** *n* lollŏ sŭk'eit'ŭ 롤러 스케이트
rolling pin panjugŭl minŭn pangmangi 반죽을 미는 방망이
ROM (= ***read only memory***) lom 롬
Roman Catholic 1 *n* Loma K'at'ollik 로마 카톨릭 **2** *adj* Loma K'at'ollik-kkyoŭi 로마 카톨릭교의
Roman Catholicism Ch'ŏnjugyo 천주교
romance (*affair*) lomaensŭ 로맨스; (*novel*, *movie*) yŏnae 연애
romantic lomaent'ik'an 로맨틱한
roof chibung 지붕
roof rack MOT lup'ŭraek 루프랙
room pang 방; (*space*) changso 장소; ***there's no ~ for ...*** ...ŭl / rŭl wihan changsoga ŏptta ...을 / 를 위한 장소가 없다
room clerk kaekssil tamdangja 객실 담당자; **roommate** lum meit'ŭ 룸메이트; **room service** lum ssŏbissŭ 룸 서비스
roomy *house etc* nŏlbŭn 넓은; *clothes* hŏllŏnghan 헐렁한
root ppuri 뿌리; (*of word*) kŭnwŏn 근원; ~***s*** (*of person*) kohyang 고향
♦**root out** (*get rid of*) chegŏhada 제거하다; (*find*) ch'at-tta 찾다
root directory COMPUT ŭddŭm tirekt'ori 으뜸 디렉토리
rope pattchul 밧줄
♦**rope off** churŭl ch'ida 줄을 치다
rose BOT changmi 장미
Rose of Sharon Mugunghwa 무궁화
rostrum yŏndan 연단
rosy *cheeks* hongjorŭl ttin 홍조를 띤; *future* yumanghan 유망한
rot 1 *n* (*in wood*, *teeth*) ssŏgŭm 썩음 **2** *v/i* (*of food*, *wood*, *teeth*) ssŏktta 썩다
rota tangbŏn 당번
rotate *v/i* hoejŏnhada 회전하다
rotation (*around the sun etc*) hoejŏn 회전; ***do sth in ~*** muŏsŭl kyodaero hada 무엇을 교대로 하다
rotten *food*, *wood etc* ssŏgŭn 썩은; *trick*, *thing to do* pup'aehan 부패한; *weather*, *luck* pulk'waehan 불쾌한
rough 1 *adj surface* ult'ungbult'unghan 울퉁불퉁한; *hands*, *skin*, *voice* kŏch'in 거친; (*violent*) nanp'ok'an 난폭한; *crossing*, *seas* sananun 사나운; (*approximate*) taegang-ŭi 대강의; ~ ***draft*** ch'ogo 초고 **2** *adv*: ***sleep ~*** nosuk'ada 노숙하다 **3** *n* (*in golf*) lŏp'ŭ 러프 **4** *v/t*: ~ ***it*** pulp'yŏnhan saenghwarŭl hada 불편한 생활을 하다
roughage (*in food*) sŏmnyujil 섬유질
roughly (*approximately*) taeryak 대략
roulette lullet 룰렛
round 1 *adj* tunggŭn 둥근; ***in ~ figures*** kkŭtchŭl charŭn sutcharo 끝을 자른 숫자로 **2** *n* (*of mailman*) paedal kuyŏk 배달 구역; (*of toast*) tchok 쪽; (*of drinks*) ch'a 차; (*of competition*) hoe 회; (*in boxing match*) laundŭ 라운드 **3** *v/t the corner* tolda 돌다 **4** *adv*, *prep* → **around**

♦**round off** *edges* tunggŭlge hada 둥글게 하다; *meeting etc* mamurihada 마무리하다
♦**round up** *figure* kkŭtchŭl challa ollida 끝을 잘라 올리다; *suspects, criminals* kŏmgŏhada 검거하다
roundabout *adj route* uhoeŭi 우회의; *way of saying sth* kanjŏptchŏgin 간접적인; **round trip** wangbok yŏhaeng 왕복 여행; **round trip ticket** wangbok yŏhaengp'yo 왕복 여행표; **round-up** (*of cattle*) mori 몰이; (*of suspects, criminals*) kŏmgŏ 검거; (*of news*) yoyak 요약
rouse (*from sleep*) kkaeda 깨다; *interest, emotions* chagŭk'ada 자극하다
rousing *speech etc* kŭktchŏgin 극적인
route kil 길
routine 1 *adj* ilssangjŏgin 일상적인 **2** *n* ilgwa 일과; ***as a matter of ~*** ilssangjŏgŭro 일상적으로
row[1] (*line*) yŏl 열; ***5 days in a ~*** tatssae yŏniŏsŏ 닷새 연이어서
row[2] **1** *v/t boat* no chŏt-tta 노 젓다 **2** *v/i* chŏŏgada 저어가다
rowboat chŏnnŭn pae 젓는 배
rowdy nanp'ok'an 난폭한
row house yollip chut'aek 연립 주택
royal *adj* wang-ŭi 왕의
royalty (*royal persons*) wangjok 왕족; (*on book, recording*) loyŏlt'i 로열티
rub *v/t* munjirŭda 문지르다; (*to polish*) yun naeda 윤 내다
♦**rub down** (*clean*) ch'ŏngsohada 청소하다
♦**rub off 1** *v/t dirt* munjillŏ ŏpssaeda 문질러 없애다; *paint etc* pŏtkkida 벗기다 **2** *v/i*: ***it rubs off on you*** tangshinege yŏnghyang-ŭl kkich'imnida 당신에게 영향을 끼칩니다
♦**rub out** (*with eraser*) chiuda 지우다
rubber 1 *n* (*material*) komu 고무 **2** *adj* komuŭi 고무의
rubble chapssŏk 잡석
ruby (*jewel*) lubi 루비
rucksack paenang 배낭
rudder paeŭi k'i 배의 키
ruddy *complexion* pulgŭn 붉은
rude muryehan 무례한; ***it is ~ to …*** …hanŭn kŏsŭn muryehada …하는 것은 무례하다; ***I didn't mean to be ~*** muryehage haryŏgo haet-ttŏn ke aniyeyo 무례하게 하려고 했던 게 아니예요
rudeness murye 무례
rudimentary kich'oŭi 기초의
rudiments kich'o 기초
ruffian purhandang 불한당
ruffle 1 *n* (*on dress*) churŭm changshik 주름 장식 **2** *v/t hair* hŏngk'ŭrŏjige hada 헝클어지게 하다; *person* sŏngnage hada 성나게 하다; ***get ~d*** sŏng-i nada 성이 나다
rug kkalgae 깔개; (*blanket*) tamnyo 담요
rugged *scenery, cliffs* pawi t'usŏng-iŭi 바위 투성이의; *face* kŏch'in 거친; *resistance* wan-ganghan 완강한
ruin 1 *n* p'agoe 파괴; ***~s*** yujŏk 유적; ***in ~s*** (*of city, building*) p'agoedoen 파괴된; (*of plans, marriage*) p'amyŏrhan 파멸한 **2** *v/t party, birthday, vacation* mangch'ida 망치다; *plans* manggattŭrida 망가뜨리다; *reputation* p'agoehada 파괴하다; ***be ~ed*** (*financially*) p'asanhada 파산하다
rule 1 *n* (*of club, game*) kyuch'ik 규칙; (*of monarch*) chibae 지배; (*for measuring*) cha 자; ***as a ~*** taech'ero 대체로 **2** *v/t country* tasŭrida 다스리다; ***the judge ~d that …*** p'ansanŭn …rago p'an-gyŏrhaet-tta 판사는 …라고 판결했다 **3** *v/i* (*of monarch*) t'ongch'ihada 통치하다
♦**rule out** choeoehada 제외하다
ruler (*for measuring*) cha 자; (*of state*) t'ongch'ija 통치자
ruling 1 *n* p'an-gyŏl 판결 **2** *adj party* chibaehanŭn 지배하는
rum (*drink*) lŏm 럼
rumble *v/i* (*of stomach*) kkorŭrŭkkŏrida 꼬르륵거리다; (*of train in tunnel*) yoranhan sorirŭl naeda 요란한 소리를 내다
♦**rummage around** twijyŏ ch'ajanaeda 뒤져 찾아내다
rummage sale chapttongsani p'anmae 잡동사니 판매
rumor 1 *n* somun 소문 **2** *v/t*: ***it is ~ed***

that ... ...rago somuni nada ...라고 소문이 나다
rump (*of animal*) ŏngdŏngi 엉덩이
rumple *clothes, paper* kugida 구기다
rumpsteak lŏmp'ŭ sŭt'eik'ŭ 럼프 스테이크
run 1 *n* (*on foot*) talligi 달리기; (*in pantyhose*) orŭi p'ullim 올의 풀림; (*of play*) yŏnsok kong-yŏn 연속 공연; ***go for a ~*** choginghada 조깅하다; ***make a ~ for it*** tomangch'ida 도망치다; ***a criminal on the ~*** tomang chungin pŏmjoeja 도망 중인 범죄자; ***in the short / long ~*** tchalkke / kilge pomyŏn 짧게 / 길게 보면; ***a ~ on the dollar*** tallŏ kangse 달러 강세 **2** *v/i* (*of person, animal*) tallida 달리다; (*of river*) hŭrŭda 흐르다; (*of trains etc*) unhaengdoeda 운행되다; (*of paint, make-up*) pŏnjida 번지다; (*of nose, eyes*) hŭrŭda 흐르다; (*of faucet*) hŭrŭda 흐르다; (*of play*) yŏnsok kong-yŏndoeda 연속 공연되다; (*of engine, machine*) umjigida 움직이다; (*of software*) shirhaengtoeji ant'a 실행되지 않다; (*in election*) ch'ulmahada 출마하다; ***~ for President*** taet'ongnyŏnge ch'ulmahada 대통령에 출마하다 **3** *v/t race* kyŏngjuhada 경주하다; *3 miles etc* tallida 달리다; *business, hotel, project etc* unyŏnghada 운영하다; *software* shirhaenghada 실행하다; ***he ran his eye down the page*** kŭnŭn kŭ p'eijirŭl taegang hult'ŏ poat-tta 그는 그 페이지를 대강 훑어 보았다
♦**run across** (*meet*) uyŏnhi mannada 우연히 만나다; (*find*) ch'at-tta 찾다
♦**run away** taranada 달아나다
♦**run down 1** *v/t* (*knock down*) tŭribat-tta 들이받다; (*criticize*) hŏlttŭt-tta 헐뜯다; *stocks* kach'irŭl ttŏrŏttŭrida 가치를 떨어뜨리다 **2** *v/i* (*of battery*) taltta 닳다
♦**run into** (*meet*) uyŏnhi mannada 우연히 만나다; *difficulties* ch'ŏhada 처하다; *car* tŭribat-tta 들이받다
♦**run off 1** *v/i* tomangch'ida 도망치다 **2** *v/t* (*print*) inswaehada 인쇄하다
♦**run out** (*of contract*) man-giga toeda 만기가 되다; (*of time*) ta hada 다 하다; (*of supplies*) ttŏrŏjida 떨어지다
♦**run out of** *time, patience* ta ssŏbŏrida 다 써버리다; *supplies* ttŏrŏjida 떨어지다; ***I ran out of gas*** kassŭga ttŏrŏjyŏssŏyo 가스가 떨어졌어요
♦**run over 1** *v/t* (*knock down*) tŭribat-tta 들이받다; ***can we ~ the details again?*** tashi hanbŏn chasehan sahange taehae arabolkkayo? 다시 한번 자세한 사항에 대해 알아볼까요? **2** *v/i* (*of water etc*) nŏmch'ida 넘치다
♦**run through** (*rehearse*) shiyŏnhada 시연하다; (*go over, check*) kŏmt'ohada 검토하다
♦**run up** *v/t debts* ssat'a 쌓다; *clothes* mandŭlda 만들다
run-down *person* chich'in 지친; *part of town, building* hŏrŭmhan 허름한
rung (*of ladder*) tan 단
runner (*athlete*) kyŏngjuja 경주자
runner-up ch'attchŏmja 차점자
running 1 *n* SP talligi 달리기; (*of business*) kyŏngyŏng kwalli 경영 관리 **2** *adj*: ***for two days ~*** yŏniŏ it'ŭl ttong-ane 연이어 이틀 동안에
running water (*supply*) yusu 유수
runny *liquid, nose* hŭrŭnŭn 흐르는
run-up SP toumdatkki 도움닫기; ***in the ~ to*** paro chiktchŏne 바로 직전에
runway hwaltchuro 활주로
rupture 1 *n* (*in pipe*), MED p'ayŏl 파열; (*in relations*) tanjŏl 단절 **2** *v/i* (*of pipe etc*) p'ayŏldoeda 파열되다
rural shigorŭi 시골의
rush 1 *n* mopsshi sŏdurŭm 몹시 서두름; ***do sth in a ~*** sodullŏ muŏsŭl hada 서둘러 무엇을 하다; ***be in a ~*** mopsshi sŏdurŭda 몹시 서두르다; ***what's the big ~?*** wae kŭrŏk'e kŭp'aeyo? 왜 그렇게 급해요? **2** *v/t person* sŏdurŭge hada 서두르게 하다; *meal* sŏdullŏ mŏktta 서둘러 먹다; ***~ s.o. to the hospital*** nugurŭl pyŏng-wŏnŭro kŭpssonghada 누구를 병원으로 급송하다 **3** *v/i* sŏdurŭda 서두르다

rush hour ch'ult'oegŭn shigan 출퇴근 시간
Russia Lŏshia 러시아
Russian 1 *adj* Lŏshiaŭi 러시아의 **2** *n* Lŏshiain 러시아인; (*language*) Lŏshiaŏ 러시아어
rust 1 *n* nok 녹 **2** *v/i* nokssŭlda 녹슬다
rustle *n* (*of silk, leaves*) pasŭrakkkŏrinŭn sori 바스락거리는 소리
♦**rustle up** F *meal* chaeppalli mandŭlda 재빨리 만들다
rust-proof *adj* nogi sŭlji annŭn 녹이 슬지 않는
rust remover nok chegŏje 녹 제거제
rusty nogi sŭn 녹이 슨; *French, math etc* sŏt'un 서툰; ***I'm a little ~*** chŏnŭn yakkan sŏt'umnida 저는 약간 서툽니다
rut (*in road*) hom 홈; ***be in a ~*** p'ane pak'in saenghwarŭl hada 판에 박힌 생활을 하다
ruthless kach'aŏmnŭn 가차없는
ruthlessness kach'aŏpssŭm 가차없음
rye homil 호밀
rye bread homil ppang 호밀 빵

S

sabbatical *n* (*of academic*) anshingnyŏn 안식년

sabotage 1 *n* kyehoektchŏgin p'agoe 계획적인 파괴 **2** *v/t* kyehoektchŏgŭro p'agoehada 계획적으로 파괴하다

saccharin *n* sak'arin 사카린

sachet (*of shampoo etc*) pongji 봉지

sack 1 *n* (*bag*) p'odae 포대 **2** *v/t* F haegohada 해고하다

sacred *music* chonggyojŏgin 종교적인; *building*, *place* shinsŏnghan 신성한

sacrifice 1 *n* chemul 제물; (*act*) hŭisaeng 희생; ***make ~s*** *fig* hŭisaenghada 희생하다 **2** *v/t* pach'ida 바치다; *one's freedom etc* hŭisaenghada 희생하다

sad sŭlp'ŭn 슬픈

saddle *n* anjang 안장

sadism sadijŭm 사디즘

sadist sadisŭt'ŭ 사디스트

sadistic sadisŭt'ŭjŏgin 사디스트 적인

sadly *say etc* sŭlp'ŭge 슬프게; (*regrettably*) huhoesŭrŏpkkedo 후회스럽게도

sadness sŭlp'ŭm 슬픔

safe 1 *adj* anjŏnhan 안전한; *investment*, *prediction* anshimhal su innŭn 안심할 수 있는 **2** *n* kŭmgo 금고

safeguard 1 *n* pohoch'aek 보호책; ***as a ~ against*** …e taehan pohoch'aegŭro …에 대한 보호책으로 **2** *v/t* pohohada 보호하다

safekeeping: ***give sth to s.o. for ~*** anjŏnhage pogwanŭl wihae muŏsŭl nuguege chuda 안전한 보관을 위해 무엇을 누구에게 주다

safely *arrive* musahi 무사히; *complete tests etc* munjeŏpsshi 문제없이; *drive* anjŏnhage 안전하게; *assume* chalmot toel kŏktchŏng ŏpsshi 잘못 될 걱정 없이

safety anjŏn 안전; (*of investment*) anjŏnssŏng 안전성; ***be in ~*** musahada 무사하다

safety-conscious anjŏnŭl saenggak'anŭn 안전을 생각하는; **safety first** anjŏn usŏn 안전 우선; **safety pin** anjŏnp'in 안전핀

sag 1 *n* (*in ceiling etc*) nŭrŏjim 늘어짐 **2** *v/i* (*of ceiling*, *rope*) ch'uk ch'ŏjida 축 처지다; (*of output*, *tempo*) chulda 줄다

sage (*herb*) saelbiŏ 샐비어

sail 1 *n* tot 돛; (*voyage*) hanghae 항해; (*in small boat*) paennori 뱃놀이 **2** *v/t* *yacht* ttŭiuda 띄우다 **3** *v/i* hanghaehada 항해하다; (*depart*) ch'urhanghada 출항하다

sailboard 1 *n* windŭ sŏp'ing podŭ 윈드 서핑 보드 **2** *v/i* windŭ sŏp'inghada 윈드 서핑하다

sailboarding windŭ sŏp'ing 윈드 서핑

sailboat yot'ŭ 요트

sailing SP yot'ŭ kyŏnggi 요트 경기

sailing ship pŏmsŏn 범선

sailor (*in the navy*) subyŏng 수병; SP yot'ŭ kyŏnggija 요트 경기자; ***be a good / bad ~*** paenmŏlmirŭl haji ant'a / hada 뱃멀미를 하지 않다 / 하다

saint sŏng-in 성인

sake: ***for my / your ~*** narŭl / nŏrŭl wihaesŏ 나를 / 너를 위해서; ***for the ~ of*** …ŭl / rŭl wihayŏ …을 / 를 위하여

salad saellŏdŭ 샐러드

salad dressing sallŏdŭ tŭreshing 샐러드 드레싱

salary wŏlgŭp 월급

salary scale ponggŭp sujun 봉급 수준

sale p'anmae 판매; (*reduced prices*) harin p'anmae 할인 판매; ***for ~*** (*sign*) maemae 매매; ***is this for ~?*** igŏ p'anŭn kŏmnikka? 이거 파는 겁니까?; ***be on ~*** p'anmae chung-ida 판매 중이다; (*at reduced prices*) seil

chung-ida 세일 중이다
sales (*department*) p'anmaebusŏ 판매부서
sales clerk (*in store*) p'anmae chŏmwŏn 판매 점원; **sales figures** p'anmae kŭmaek 판매 금액; **salesman** seiljŭmaen 세일즈맨; **sales manager** p'anmae pujang 판매 부장; **sales meeting** p'anmae hoeŭi 판매 회의
saliva ch'im 침
salmon yŏnŏ 연어
saloon (*bar*) sultchip 술집
salt sogŭm 소금
saltcellar sogŭm kŭrŭt 소금 그릇
salty tchan 짠
salutary *experience* yuik'an 유익한
salute 1 *n* MIL kyŏngnye 경례; ***take the ~*** kyŏngnyerŭl pat-tta 경례를 받다 **2** *v/t v/i* MIL kyŏngnyehada 경례하다
salvage *v/t* (*from wreck*) kujohada 구조하다
salvation REL kuwŏn 구원; *fig* kujo 구조
Salvation Army Kusegun 구세군
same 1 *adj* kat'ŭn 같은 **2** *pron*: ***the ~*** kat'ŭn kŏt 같은 것; ***Happy New Year – the ~ to you*** saehae pok mani padŭseyo - saehae pok mani padŭseyo 새해 복 많이 받으세요 - 새해 복 많이 받으세요; ***he's not the ~ any more*** kŭ saram, yejŏn katchi anayo 그 사람, 예전 같지 않아요; ***all the ~*** kŭraedo 그래도; ***men are all the ~*** namjadŭrŭn ta ttokkat'ayo 남자들은 다 똑같아요; ***it's all the ~ to me*** chŏn, sanggwanŏpssŏyo 전, 상관없어요 **3** *adv*: ***smell / sound the ~*** naemsaega / soriga ttok-kkat'ayo 냄새가 / 소리가 똑같아요
sample *n* (*for inspection*) kyŏnbon 견본; (*of behavior, work*) p'yobon 표본
sanatorium yoyangso 요양소
sanction 1 *n* (*approval*) hŏga 허가; (*penalty*) chejae 제재; ***economic ~s*** kyŏngje chejae 경제 제재 **2** *v/t* (*approve*) hŏgahada 허가하다
sanctity shinsŏng 신성
sanctuary REL sŏngjŏn 성전; (*for animals*) poho kuyŏk 보호 구역
sand 1 *n* morae 모래 **2** *v/t* (*with sandpaper*) sap'oro munjirŭda 사포로 문지르다
sandal saendŭl 샌들
sandbag morae chumŏni 모래 주머니
sand dune morae ŏndŏk 모래 언덕
sander (*tool*) sap'oro tangnŭn changch'i 사포로 닦는 장치
sandpaper 1 *n* sap'o 사포 **2** *v/t* sap'oro taktta 사포로 닦다; **sandpit** moraep'an 모래판; **sandstone** saam 사암
sandwich 1 *n* saendŭwich'i 샌드위치 **2** *v/t*: ***be ~ed between two ...*** tu ... saie kkida 두 ... 사이에 끼이다
sandy *beach*, *soil* moraeŭi 모래의; *hair* moraesaegŭi 모래색의
sane chejŏngshinŭi 제정신의
sanitarium yoyangso 요양소
sanitary *conditions* wisaeng-ŭi 위생의; *installations* wisaengjŏgin 위생적인
sanitary napkin saengnidae 생리대
sanitation (*sanitary installations*) wisaengsŏlbi 위생설비; (*removal of waste*) wisaengch'ŏri 위생처리
sanitation department ch'ŏngsokkwa 청소과
sanity chejŏngshin 제정신
Santa Claus Sant'ak'ŭllosŭ 산타클로스
sap 1 *n* (*in tree*) suaek 수액 **2** *v/t s.o.'s energy* yak'washik'ida 약화시키다
sapphire *n* (*jewel*) sap'aiŏ 사파이어
sarcasm p'ungja 풍자
sarcastic pinjŏngdaenŭn 빈정대는
sardine chŏng-ŏri 정어리
sash (*on dress*, *uniform*) tti 띠; (*in window*) saesshi 새시
Satan Sat'an 사탄
satellite in-gong-wisŏng 인공위성
satellite dish in-gong-wisŏng chŏpsshi 인공위성 접시
satellite TV wisŏng t'ibŭi 위성 티브이
satin kongdan 공단
satire p'ungja 풍자
satirical p'ungjajŏgin 풍자적인
satirist p'ungjaga 풍자가
satisfaction manjok 만족; ***get ~ out of sth*** muŏesŏ manjogŭl nŭkkida

무엇에서 만족을 느끼다; ***a feeling of ~*** manjok-kkam 만족감; ***is that to your ~?*** maŭme tŭshimnikka? 마음에 드십니까?
satisfactory manjok'an 만족한; (*just good enough*) kŭjŏ kŭrŏn 그저 그런; ***this is not ~*** igŏsŭronŭn ch'ungbunch'i anayo 이것으로는 충분치 않아요
satisfy *customers* manjoksshik'ida 만족시키다; *hunger, sexual desires, conditions* ch'ungjokshik'ida 충족시키다; ***I am satisfied*** (*had enough to eat*) chŏnŭn ch'ungbunhi mŏgŏssŏyo 저는 충분히 먹었어요; ***I am satisfied that …*** (*convinced*) …ranŭn-gŏshi napttŭg kamnida …라는 것이 납득 갑니다; ***I hope you're satisfied!*** sogi shiwŏnhajiyo! 속이 시원하지요!
Saturday t'oyoil 토요일
sauce sossŭ 소스
saucepan naembi 냄비
saucer pach'im chŏpsshi 받침 접시
saucy *person* kŏnbangjin 건방진; *dress* mŏtchin 멋진
Saudi Arabia Saudi Arabia 사우디 아라비아
Saudi (Arabian) 1 *adj* Saudi Arabiaŭi 사우디 아라비아의 **2** *n* (*person*) Saudi Arabiain 사우디 아라비아인
sauna sauna 사우나
saunter *v/i* ŏsŭllŏnggŏrida 어슬렁거리다
sausage soshiji 소시지
savage *adj animal* yasaeng-ŭi 야생의; *attack* chaninhan 잔인한; *criticism* hokttok'an 혹독한
save 1 *v/t* (*rescue*) kuhada 구하다; (*put aside*: *money*) moanot'a 모아놓다; (*in bank*) chŏch'uk'ada 저축하다; *time, money* chŏryak'ada 절약하다; (*collect*) moŭda 모으다; COMPUT chŏjanghada 저장하다; *goal* chŏjihada 저지하다; ***you could ~ yourself a lot of effort*** tŏl himdŭrŏssŭl sudo issŏnnŭnde 덜 힘들었을 수도 있었는데 **2** *v/i* (*put money aside*) chŏgŭmhada 저금하다; SP maganaeda 막아내다 **3** *n* SP tŭktchŏm maganaegi 득점 막아내기
♦**save up for** …e taebihae moŭda …에 대비해 모으다
saving (*amount saved*) chŏryakpun 절약분; (*activity*) chŏryak 절약
savings yegŭm 예금
savings account pot'ong yegŭm 보통 예금
savings bank chŏch'uk ŭnhaeng 저축 은행
Savior REL Kuseju 구세주
savor *v/t* ŭmmihada 음미하다
savory *adj* (*not sweet*) tchaptcharhan 짭짤한
saw 1 *n* (*tool*) t'op 톱 **2** *v/t* t'obŭro charŭda 톱으로 자르다
♦**saw off** t'obŭro k'yŏda 톱으로 켜다
sawdust t'op-ppap 톱밥
saxophone saekssŏp'on 색소폰
say 1 *v/t* marhada 말하다; ***can I ~ something?*** chega muŏl chom yaegihaedo toelkkayo? 제가 뭘 좀 얘기해도 될까요?; ***that is to ~*** chŭk 즉; ***what do you ~ to that?*** kŭgŏse taehae ŏttŏk'e saenggak'anayo? 그것에 대해 어떻게 생각하나요? **2** *n*: ***have one's ~*** hago ship'ŭn marŭl hada 하고 싶은 말을 하다
saying sokttam 속담
scab (*on wound*) ttaktchi 딱지
scaffolding palp'an 발판
scald *v/t*: ***be ~ed*** teda 데다
scale[1] (*on fish*) pinŭl 비늘
scale[2] **1** *n* (*size*) kyumo 규모; (*on thermometer etc*) nunkkŭm 눈금; (*of map*) ch'ukch'ŏk 축척; MUS ŭmgye 음계; ***on a larger / smaller ~*** chomdŏ k'ŭn / chagŭn kyumoro 좀더 큰 / 작은 규모로 **2** *v/t cliffs etc* orŭda 오르다
scale drawing ch'ukch'ŏk tomyŏn 축척 도면
scales (*for weighing*) chŏul 저울
scalp *n* mŏritkkajuk 머리가죽
scalpel oekkwayong mesŭ 외과용 메스
scalper amp'yosang 암표상
scam F sagi 사기
scan 1 *v/t horizon, page* chasehi salp'yŏboda 자세히 살펴보다; MED chŏngmil chosahada 정밀 조사하다;

COMPUT sŭk'aenhada 스캔하다 **2** *n* MED ch'enae pangsanŭng punp'o sajin 체내 방사능 분포 사진

♦**scan in** COMPUT sŭk'aenhada 스캔하다

scandal sŭk'aendŭl 스캔들

scandalous *affair* such'isŭrŏun 수치스러 운; *prices* t'ŏmuniŏmnŭn 터무니없는

scanner MED, COMPUT sŭk'aenŏ 스캐너

scantily *adv*: ~ ***clad*** osŭl chedaero katch'wo iptchi anŭn 옷을 제대로 갖춰 입지 않은

scanty *clothes* sonppadangmanhan 손바닥만한

scapegoat hŭisaengnyang 희생양

scar 1 *n* hyungt'ŏ 흉터 **2** *v/t* hyungt'ŏrŭl namgida 흉터를 남기다

scarce (*in short supply*) mojaranŭn 모자라는; ***make oneself*** ~ sŭltchŏk nagada 슬쩍 나가다

scarcely: ***I had ~ begun to speak when ...*** nanŭn ...hajamaja marhagi shijak'aet-tta 나는 ...하자마자 말하기 시작했다; ***I ~ know her*** chŏn, kŭ yŏjarŭl kŏŭi mollayo 전, 그 여자를 거의 몰라요; ~ ***any*** kŏŭi ŏptta 거의 없다

scarcity pujok 부족

scare 1 *v/t* kŏptchuda 겁주다; ***be ~d of*** musŏwŏhada 무서워하다 **2** *n* (*panic*, *alarm*) puran 불안; ***give s.o. a*** ~ nuguege kŏptchuda 누구에게 겁주다

♦**scare away** kŏptchuŏ tchoch'anaeda 겁주어 쫓아내다

scarecrow hŏsuabi 허수아비

scaremonger hŏtssomunŭl p'ŏttŭrinŭn saram 헛소문을 퍼뜨리는 사람

scarf (*around neck*) mokttori 목도리; (*over head*) sŭk'ap'ŭ 스카프

scarlet chuhongsaek 주홍색

scarlet fever sŏnghongnyŏl 성홍열

scary mushimushihan 무시무시한

scathing t'ongnyŏrhan 통렬한

scatter 1 *v/t leaflets*, *seeds* ppurida 뿌리다; ***be ~ed all over the room*** pang chŏnch'e-e ppuryŏjyŏ it-tta 방 전체에 뿌려져 있다 **2** *v/i* (*of crowd etc*) hŭt'ŏjida 흩어지다

scatterbrained mŏriga sanmanhan 머리가 산만한

scattered *showers* sanbaltchŏgin 산발적인; *family*, *villages* hŭt'ŏjin 흩어진

scenario shinario 시나리오

scene THEA chang 장; (*view*, *sight*) changmyŏn 장면; (*of accident*, *crime etc*) hyŏnjang 현장; (*setting*: *of novel*, *in a movie*) paegyŏng 배경; (*part of movie*) changmyŏn 장면; (*argument*) soran 소란; ***make a*** ~ soranŭl p'iuda 소란을 피우다; ***~s*** THEA mudae paegyŏng 무대 배경; ***jazz ~ / drugs*** ~ F chaejŭgye / mayak-kkye 재즈계 / 마약계; ***behind the ~s*** *fig* nam morŭge 남 모르게

scenery p'unggyŏng 풍경; THEA mudae paegyŏng 무대 배경

scent *n* (*smell*) hyanggi 향기; (*perfume*) hyangsu 향수; (*of animal*) naemsae 냄새

schedule 1 *n* (*of events*) yejŏng 예정; (*of work*) iltchŏng 일정; (*for trains*, *of lessons*) shiganp'yo 시간표; ***be on*** ~ yejŏngdaeroida 예정대로이다; ***be behind*** ~ yejŏngboda nŭt-tta 예정보다 늦다 **2** *v/t* (*put on* ~) yejŏnghada 예정하다; ***it's ~d for completion next month*** taŭmttare kkŭnmach'igiro toeŏ issŏyo 다음달에 끝마치기로 되어 있어요

scheduled flight chŏnggi hanggongp'yŏn 정기 항공편

scheme 1 *n* (*plan*) kyehoek 계획; (*wicked plot*) moŭi 모의 **2** *v/i* (*plot*) moŭihada 모의하다

scheming *adj* kyohwarhan 교활한

schizophrenia chŏngshin punyŏltchŭng 정신 분열증

schizophrenic 1 *n* chŏngshin punyŏltchŭng hwanja 정신 분열증 환자 **2** *adj* chŏngshin punyŏltchŭng-ŭi 정신 분열증의

scholar haktcha 학자

scholarship (*scholarly work*) hangmun 학문; (*financial award*) changhak-kkŭm 장학금

school hak-kkyo 학교; (*university*) taehak 대학

schoolbag ch'aek-kkabang 책가방; **schoolboy** namhakssaeng 남학생; **schoolchildren** hakttong 학동; **school days** suŏbil 수업일; **schoolgirl** yŏhakssaeng 여학생; **schoolteacher** hak-kkyo sŏnsaengnim 학교 선생님
sciatica chwagol shin-gyŏngt'ong 좌골 신경통
science kwahak 과학
science fiction kongsang kwahak sosŏl 공상 과학 소설
scientific kwahaktchŏgin 과학적인
scientist kwahaktcha 과학자
scissors kawi 가위
scoff[1] *v/t* (*eat fast*) kegŏlsŭrŏpkke mŏktta 게걸스럽게 먹다; (*eat whole lot*) ta mŏgŏ ch'iuda 다 먹어 치우다
scoff[2] *v/i* nollida 놀리다
♦**scoff at** ...ŭl/rŭl piut-tta ...을/를 비웃다
scold *v/t child, husband* kkujit-tta 꾸짖다
scoop 1 *n* (*for food*) kuktcha 국자; (*for mud, coal*) sap 삽; (*in journalism*) t'ŭktchong 특종 **2** *v/t* p'uda 푸다; *ice cream* ttŭda 뜨다
♦**scoop up** p'ŏ ollida 퍼 올리다; *kids, books* ana ollida 안아 올리다
scooter (*with motor*) sŭk'ut'ŏ 스쿠터; (*child's*) oe pal sŭk'eit'ŭ 외 발 스케이트
scope pŏmwi 범위; (*opportunity*) kihoe 기회; (*latitude*) yŏji 여지
scorch *v/t* kŭsŭllida 그슬리다
scorching hot tchinŭn tŭshi tŏun 찌는 듯이 더운
score 1 *n* SP tŭktchŏm 득점; (*written music*) akppo 악보; (*of movie etc*) ŭmak 음악; ***what's the ~?*** chŏmsuga ŏttaeyo? 점수가 어때요?; ***have a ~ to settle with s.o.*** nuguege ssain wŏnhanŭl p'ulda 누구에게 쌓인 원한을 풀다 **2** *v/t goal, point* chŏmsurŭl kirok'ada 점수를 기록하다; (*cut: line*) saegim nunŭl naeda 새김 눈을 내다 **3** *v/i* tŭktchŏmhada 득점하다; (*keep the score*) chŏmsurŭl kirok'ada 점수를 기록하다; ***that's where he ~s*** kŭge kŭ namjaŭi kangtchŏmiyeyo 그게 그 남자의 강점이예요
scorer (*of goal, point*) tŭktchŏmja 득점자; (*score-keeper*) chŏmsu kirogwŏn 점수 기록원
scorn 1 *n* kyŏngmyŏl 경멸; ***pour ~ on sth*** muŏsŭl kyŏngmyŏrhada 무엇을 경멸하다 **2** *v/t idea, suggestion* kyŏngmyŏrhada 경멸하다
scornful kyŏngmyŏrhanŭn 경멸하는
Scot Sŭk'ot'ŭllaendŭin 스코틀랜드인
Scotch (*whiskey*) sŭk'ach'i 스카치
Scotland Sŭk'ot'ŭllaendŭ 스코틀랜드
Scottish Sŭk'ot'ŭllaendŭŭi 스코틀랜드의
scot-free: ***get off ~*** pŏrŭl momyŏnhada 벌을 모면하다
scoundrel akttang 악당
scour[1] (*search*) ch'aja tanida 찾아 다니다
scour[2] *pans* munjillŏ taktta 문질러 닦다
scout *n* (*boy ~*) sŭk'aut'ŭ 스카우트
scowl 1 *n* tchinggŭrin ŏlgul 찡그린 얼굴 **2** *v/i* tchinggŭrida 찡그리다
scram F tomanggada 도망가다
scramble 1 *n* (*rush*) punmang 분망 **2** *v/t message* ilburŏ twisŏktta 일부러 뒤섞다 **3** *v/i* (*climb*) chaepparŭge kiŏ orŭda 재빠르게 기어 오르다; ***he ~d to his feet*** kŭnŭn chaeppalli irŏnat-tta 그는 재빨리 일어났다
scrambled eggs sŭk'ŭraembŭrhan talgyal yori 스크램블한 달걀 요리
scrap 1 *n* (*metal*) p'yech'ŏl 폐철; (*fight*) ssaum 싸움; (*little bit*) chogŭm 조금 **2** *v/t project etc* p'yegishik'ida 폐기시키다; *paragraph etc* chiuda 지우다
scrapbook sŭk'ŭraep puk 스크랩 북
scrape 1 *n* (*on paintwork etc*) kŭlk'in chaguk 긁힌 자국 **2** *v/t paintwork, one's arm etc* kŭktta 긁다; *vegetables* k'allo tadŭmtta 칼로 다듬다; ***~ a living*** irŏktchŏrŏk saenghwarhada 이럭저럭 생활하다
♦**scrape through** (*in exam*) kanshinhi hapkkyŏk'ada 간신히 합격하다
scrap heap ssŭregi tŏmi 쓰레기 더미; ***good for the ~*** amu tchagedo ssŭlmo ŏmnŭn 아무 짝에도 쓸모

없는
scrap metal p'yech'ŏl 폐철
scrappy *work* chirimyŏllŏrhan 지리멸렬한
scratch 1 *n* (*to stop itching*) kŭlkki 긁기; (*by cat etc*) halk'wigi 할퀴기; (*on paintwork*) kŭlk'in chaguk 긁힌 자국; ***have a ~*** (*to stop itching*) kŭktta 긁다; ***start from ~*** ch'ŏŭmbut'ŏ shijak'ada 처음부터 시작하다; ***not up to ~*** manjoksŭrŏptchi mot'an 만족스럽지 못한 **2** *v/t* (*to stop itching*) kŭktta 긁다; (*by cat etc*) halk'wida 할퀴다 **3** *v/i* (*of cat, nails*) kŭktta 긁다
scrawl 1 *n* hwigalgyŏ ssŭn kŭltcha 휘갈겨 쓴 글자 **2** *v/t* hwigalgyŏ ssŭda 휘갈겨 쓰다
scream 1 *n* oech'imsori 외침소리 **2** *v/i* sorich'ida 소리치다
screech 1 *n* (*of tires*) kkik'anŭn sori 끽하는 소리; (*scream*) pimyŏng sori 비명 소리 **2** *v/i* (*of tires*) kkik'anŭn soriga nada 끽하는 소리가 나다; (*scream*) pimyŏngŭl chirŭda 비명을 지르다
screen 1 *n* (*in room, hospital*) k'anmagi 칸막이; (*protective*) magi 막이; (*in movie theater*) sŭk'ŭrin 스크린; COMPUT hwamyŏn 화면; ***on the ~*** (*in movie*) ŭnmage 은막에; ***on*** (***the***) ~ COMPUT hwamyŏnsang-e 화면상에 **2** *v/t* (*protect, hide*) kamch'uda 감추다; *movie* sang-yŏnghada 상영하다; (*for security reasons*) sŏnbyŏrhada 선별하다
screenplay kakppon 각본; **screen saver** COMPUT hwamyŏn pohogi 화면 보호기; **screen test** sŭk'ŭrin t'esŭt'ŭ 스크린 테스트
screw 1 *n* nasamot 나사못; V (*sex*) sŏnggyo 성교 **2** *v/t* V sŏnggyorŭl hada 성교를 하다; F (*cheat*) sogida 속이다; ***~ sth to sth*** muŏsŭl muŏse nasamosŭro kojŏngshik'ida 무엇을 무엇에 나사못으로 고정시키다
♦**screw up 1** *v/t eyes* tchinggŭrida 찡그리다; *piece of paper* toldol mungch'ida 돌돌 뭉치다; F (*make a mess of*) mangch'ida 망치다 **2** *v/i* F (*make a bad mistake*) k'ŭn shilssuro ŏngmang-i toege hada 큰 실수로 엉망이 되게 하다
screwdriver tŭraibŏ 드라이버
screwed up F (*psychologically*) pitturŏjin 비뚤어진
screw top (*on bottle*) pit'ŭrŏ yŏnŭn magae 비틀어 여는 마개
scribble 1 *n* kalgyŏ ssŭgi 갈겨 쓰기 **2** *v/t* (*write quickly*) kalgyŏ ssŭda 갈겨 쓰다 **3** *v/i* kalgyŏ ssŭda 갈겨 쓰다
script (*for play etc*) taebon 대본; (*form of writing*) kŭltchach'e 글자체
Scripture: ***the*** (***Holy***) ***~s*** Kyŏngjŏn 경전
scriptwriter chak-kka 작가
scroll *n* (*manuscript*) turumari 두루마리
♦**scroll down** *v/i* COMPUT araero naerida 아래로 내리다
♦**scroll up** *v/i* COMPUT wiro ollida 위로 올리다
scrounger kŏjŏ ŏnnŭn saram 거저 얻는 사람
scrub *v/t floors, hands* munjirŭda 문지르다
scrubbing brush sol 솔
scruffy chijŏbunhan 지저분한
♦**scrunch up** *plastic cup etc* pusŏjida 부서지다
scruples todŏk kwannyŏm 도덕 관념; ***have no ~ about doing sth*** muŏsŭl hanŭn te issŏ todŏktchŏk chujŏhami ŏptta 무엇을 하는 데 있어 도덕적 주저함이 없다
scrupulous (*with moral principles*) todŏktchŏgin 도덕적인; (*thorough*) pint'ŭmŏmnŭn 빈틈없는; *attention to detail* kkomkkomhan 꼼꼼한
scrutinize chasehi chosahada 자세히 조사하다
scrutiny chosa 조사; ***come under ~*** semirhi chosadoeda 세밀히 조사되다
scuba diving sŭk'ubŏ taibing 스쿠버 다이빙
scuffle *n* nant'u 난투
sculptor chogak-kka 조각가
sculpture *n* (*art*) chogak 조각; (*sth sculpted*) chogakp'um 조각품
scum (*on liquid*) tchikkŏgi 찌꺼기; *pej* ssŭregi 쓰레기

scythe *n* nat 낫
sea pada 바다; ***by the*** ~ pada yŏp'e 바다 옆에
seafaring *nation* haeyang-ŭi 해양의; **seafood** haesanmul 해산물; **seafront** patatkka 바닷가; **seagoing** *vessel* wŏnyang-ŭi 원양의; **seagull** kalmaegi 갈매기
seal[1] *n* (*animal*) mulkkae 물개
seal[2] **1** *n* (*on document*) pong-in 봉인; TECH milbong 밀봉 **2** *v/t container* milbonghada 밀봉하다
♦**seal off** *area* pongswaehada 봉쇄하다
sea level: ***above / below*** ~ haesumyŏn wie / araee 해수면 위에 / 아래에
seam *n* (*on garment*) solgi 솔기; (*of ore*) kwangch'ŭng 광층
seaman sŏnwŏn 선원; **seaport** hanggudoshi 항구도시; **sea power** (*nation*) haegun-guk 해군국
search 1 *n* (*for missing person, object*) susaek 수색; (*for solution*) t'amsaek 탐색; COMPUT sŏch'i 서치; (*for happiness*) ch'ugu 추구 **2** *v/t forest, room* ch'at-tta 찾다; COMPUT sŏchi'hada 서치하다
♦**search for** *sth missing* ch'at-tta 찾다; *missing person* susaek'ada 수색하다; *solution* t'amsaek'ada 탐색하다; COMPUT sŏchi'hada 서치하다; *happiness* ch'uguhada 추구하다
searching *adj look* susaek'anŭn 수색하는; *question* nalk'aroun 날카로운
searchlight t'amjodŭng 탐조등; **search party** susaekttae 수색대; **search warrant** susaek yŏngtchang 수색 영장
seasick paemŏlmiga nan 배멀미가 난; ***get*** ~ paemŏlmihada 배멀미하다; **seaside** haebyŏnkka 해변가; ***at the*** ~ haebyŏne 해변에; ***go to the*** ~ haebyŏnŭro kada 해변으로 가다; **seaside resort** haebyŏn lijot'ŭ 해변 리조트; **sea slug** haesam 해삼
season *n* (*winter etc*) kyejŏl 계절; (*for tourism etc*) ch'ŏl 철
seasoned *wood* chal kŏnjodoen 잘 건조된; *traveler etc* kyŏnghŏmŭl ssahŭn 경험을 쌓은
seasoning chomiryo 조미료
season ticket (*for transportation*) chŏnggi sŭngch'akkwŏn 정기 승차권; (*for stadium, opera*) chŏnggi iptchangkkwŏn 정기 입장권
seat 1 *n* chari 자리; (*of pants*) kungdung-i 궁둥이; ***please take a*** ~ ch'akssŏk'ayŏ chushipsshio 착석하여 주십시오 **2** *v/t* (*have seating for*) chwasŏgŭl kajigo it-tta 좌석을 가지고 있다; ***please remain ~ed*** ch'akssŏk'ayŏ kyeshigil paramnida 착석하여 계시길 바랍니다
seat belt chwasŏk pelt'ŭ 좌석 벨트
sea urchin sŏngge 성게
seaweed haech'o 해초; ***edible*** ~ kim 김
secluded mŏlli ttŏrŏjyŏ hanjŏk'an 멀리 떨어져 한적한
seclusion mŏlli ttŏrŏjim 멀리 떨어짐
second 1 *n* (*of time*) ch'o 초; ***just a*** ~ chamkkanmanyo 잠깐만요 **2** *adj* tu pŏntchaeŭi 두 번째의; ~ ***biggest*** tu pŏntchaero k'ŭn 두 번째로 큰 **3** *adv come in* tu pŏntchaero 두 번째로 **4** *v/t motion* ch'ansŏnghada 찬성하다
secondary pojojŏgin 보조적인; ***of*** ~ ***importance*** ich'ajŏgŭro chungyohan 이차적으로 중요한
secondary education chungdŭng kyoyuk 중등 교육
second-best *adj* tu pŏntchaero chal hanŭn 두 번째로 잘 하는; **second class** *adj ticket* idŭngsŏgŭi 이등석의; **second gear** MOT idan kiŏ 이단 기어; **second hand** (*on clock*) ch'och'im 초침; **secondhand 1** *adj* chunggoŭi 중고의 **2** *adv buy* chunggoro 중고로
secondly tultchaero 둘째로
second-rate iryuŭi 이류의
second thoughts: ***I've had*** ~ chŏn, saenggagŭl pakkwŏssŏyo 전, 생각을 바꿨어요
secrecy kimil 기밀
secret 1 *n* pimil 비밀; ***do sth in*** ~ muŏsŭl pimillie hada 무엇을 비밀리에 하다 **2** *adj garden, passage*

ŭnmirhan 은밀한; *work, department* pimirŭi 비밀의
secret agent kanch'ŏp 간첩
secretarial *tasks, job* pisŏŭi 비서의
secretary pisŏ 비서; POL changgwan 장관
Secretary of State Kungmubu Changgwan 국무부 장관
secrete (*give off*) punbihada 분비하다; (*hide*) sumgida 숨기다
secretion (*of liquid*) punbiaek 분비액; (*liquid secreted*) punbimul 분비물; (*concealment*) ŭnnik 은닉
secretive t'ŏ noch'i annŭn 터 놓지 않는
secretly ŭnmirhi 은밀히
secret police pimil kyŏngch'al 비밀 경찰
secret service pimil chŏngbo kigwan 비밀 정보 기관
sect punp'a 분파
section (*of book, text*) kwa 과; (*of apple*) chogak 조각; (*of building*) kuhoek 구획; (*of company*) pusŏ 부서
sector yŏngnyŏk 영역
secular sesogŭi 세속의
secure 1 *adj shelf, job* anjŏnhan 안전한; *feeling* anshimhanŭn 안심하는 **2** *v/t shelf etc* anjŏnhage hada 안전하게 하다; *s.o.'s help, funding* ŏt-tta 얻다
security (*in job*) anjŏnssŏng 안전성; (*for investment*) pojang 보장; (*at airport etc*) poan 보안; (*department responsible for ~*) poankkwa 보안과; (*of beliefs etc*) hwaksshin 확신; ***securities*** FIN yukka chŭngkkwŏn 유가 증권; ***securities market*** FIN yukka chŭngkkwŏn shijang 유가 증권 시장
security alert poan kyŏnggye 보안 경계; **security check** poan hwagin 보안 확인; **security-conscious** poanŭl chungshihanŭn 보안을 중시하는; **security forces** anjŏn-gun 안전군; **security guard** kyŏngbiwŏn 경비원; **security risk** (*person*) wihŏm inmul 위험 인물
sedan MOT ssallongch'a 쌀롱차
sedative *n* chinjŏngje 진정제
sediment ch'imjŏnmul 침전물
seduce (*sexually*) yuhok'ada 유혹하다
seduction (*sexual*) yuhok 유혹
seductive *dress* maeryŏktchŏgin 매력적인; *offer* yuhoktchŏgin 유혹적인
see poda 보다; (*understand*) alda 알다; ***can I ~ the manager?*** ch'aegimjarŭl mannal su issŭlkkayo? 책임자를 만날 수 있을까요?; ***you should ~ a doctor*** tangshinŭn ŭisahant'e kabwaya toemnida 당신은 의사한테 가봐야 됩니다; ***~ s.o. home*** nuga chibe musahi wannŭnjirŭl hwaginhada 누가 집에 무사히 왔는지를 확인하다; ***I'll ~ you to the door*** munkkaji paraeda chulkkeyo 문까지 바래다 줄께요; ***~ you!*** tto mannayo! 또 만나요!; ***I ~*** algessŏyo 알겠어요
♦**see about** (*look into*) salp'yŏboda 살펴보다
♦**see off** (*at airport etc*) paeunghada 배웅하다; (*chase away*) tchoch'a ponaeda 쫓아 보내다
♦**see to**: ***~ sth*** muŏshi chal ch'ŏri toeŏnnŭnji hwaginhada 무엇이 잘 처리 되었는지 확인하다; ***~ it that sth gets done*** muŏsŭl kkŭnnaenŭn kŏsŭl t'ŭllimŏpsshi hada 무엇을 끝내는 것을 틀림없이 하다
seed sshi 씨; (*in tennis*) sidŭ 시드; ***go to ~*** (*of person, district*) t'oerak'ada 퇴락하다
seedling (*of tree*) myomok 묘목; (*of plant*) myojong 묘종
seedy *bar, district* p'yŏngp'ani nappŭn 평판이 나쁜
seeing (that) …(i)gi ttaemune …(이)기 때문에
seeing-eye dog maengdogyŏn 맹도견
seek 1 *v/t employment* ch'at-tta 찾다; *truth* ch'uguhada 추구하다 **2** *v/i* t'amsaek'ada 탐색하다
seem …kŏt kat-tta …것 같다; ***it ~s that*** …in kŏt kat'a poida …인 것 같아 보이다
seemingly pogienŭn 보기에는
seep (*of liquid*) saeda 새다

♦ **seep out** (*of liquid*) saeŏnaoda 새어나오다
seesaw shiso 시소
see-through *dress, material* pich'inŭn 비치는
segment (*of chart, structure*) pubun 부분; (*of orange*) chogak 조각
segmented pubuntchŏgin 부분적인
segregate pullihada 분리하다
segregation pulli 분리
seismology chijinhak 지진학
seize chaptta 잡다; *opportunity* p'och'ak'ada 포착하다; (*of customs, police etc*) amnyuhada 압류하다
♦ **seize up** (*of engine*) mŏmch'uda 멈추다
seizure MED paltchak 발작; (*of drugs etc*) amnyu 압류
seldom tŭmulge 드물게
select 1 *v/t* sŏnt'aek'ada 선택하다 **2** *adj* (*exclusive*) chŏngsŏnhan 정선한
selection (*choice*) sŏnt'aek 선택; (*that chosen*) sŏnt'aekttoen kŏt 선택된 것; (*people chosen*) sŏnt'aekttoen saram 선택된 사람; (*assortment*) kusaek 구색
selection process sŏnbal kwajŏng 선발 과정
selective anmogi nop'ŭn 안목이 높은
self chaa 자아
self-addressed envelope ponin chusorŭl chŏgŭn pongt'u 본인 주소를 적은 봉투; **self-assured** chashin innŭn 자신 있는; **self-catering** *sŭsŭro ŭmshigŭl haemŏngnŭn* 스스로 음식을 해먹는; **self-centered** chagi ponwiŭi 자기 본위의; **self-confessed** chainhanŭn 자인하는; **self-confidence** chashin 자신; **self-confident** chashin innŭn 자신 있는; **self-conscious** chaŭishigi kanghan 자의식이 강한; **self-contained** *apartment* tongnipshigŭi 독립식의; **self-control** chaje 자제; **self-defense** chagi pang-ŏ 자기 방어; **self-discipline** chagi suyang 자기 수양; **self-doubt** chagi pulsshin 자기 불신; **self-employed** chayŏng-ŭi 자영의; **self-evident** chamyŏnghan 자명한; **self-interest** sarisayok 사리사욕
selfish igijŏgin 이기적인
selfless yoksshimi ŏmnŭn 욕심이 없는
self-made man chasusŏnggahan saram 자수성가한 사람; **self-possessed** ch'imch'ak'an 침착한; **self-reliant** tongniptchŏgin 독립적인; **self-respect** chajonshim 자존심; **self-righteous** *pej* tokssŏnjŏgin 독선적인; **self-satisfied** *pej* chagi manjogŭi 자기 만족의; **self-service** *adj* selp'ŭssŏbisŭŭi 셀프서비스의; **self-service restaurant** selp'ŭssŏbisŭ shikttang 셀프서비스 식당
sell 1 *v/t* p'alda 팔다; ***you have to ~ yourself*** ne chashinŭl sŏnjŏnhaeya twaeyo 네 자신을 선전해야 돼요 **2** *v/i* (*of products*) p'anmaedoeda 판매되다
seller p'anmaeja 판매자
selling *n* COM p'anmae 판매
selling point COM p'anmae kangjotchŏm 판매 강조점
semen chŏng-aek 정액
semester hak-kki 학기
semi (*truck*) t'ŭrŏk 트럭
semicircle panwŏn 반원; **semicircular** panwŏnhyŏngŭi 반원형의; **semiconductor** ELEC pandoch'e 반도체; **semifinal** chun-gyŏlssŭng 준결승
seminar semina 세미나
semiskilled pan sungnyŏnŭi 반 숙련의
senate sang-wŏn 상원
senator sang-wŏnŭiwŏn 상원의원
send *v/t* ponaeda 보내다; ~ ***sth to s.o.*** nuguege muŏsŭl ponaeda 누구에게 무엇을 보내다; ~ ***s.o. to s.o.*** nugurŭl nuguege ponaeda 누구를 누구에게 보내다; ~ ***her my best wishes*** kŭnyŏege anbu chŏnhae chuseyo 그녀에게 안부 전해 주세요
♦ **send back** *letter* pansonghada 반송하다; *person, food* tollyŏ ponaeda 돌려 보내다
♦ **send for** *doctor, help* purŭrŏ ponaeda 부르러 보내다

♦**send in** *troops* ponaeda 보내다; *next interviewee* tŭryŏ ponaeda 들여 보내다; *application form* chech'urhada 제출하다
♦**send off** *letter, fax etc* palssonghada 발송하다
♦**send up** (*mock*) nollida 놀리다
sender (*of letter*) palssong-in 발송인
senile nosoehan 노쇠한
senility nosoe 노쇠
senior (*older*) sonwiŭi 손위의; (*in rank*) sanggŭbŭi 상급의; ***be ~ to X*** (*in rank*) Xboda wittcharie innŭn X보다 윗자리에 있는
senior citizen ŏrŭshin 어르신
sensation (*feeling*) kamgak 감각; (*event*) sensseisyŏn 센세이션; (*person*) sŏnp'ungjŏgŭro inkki innŭn saram 선풍적으로 인기 있는 사람; (*thing*) sŏnp'ungjŏgŭro inkki innŭn kŏt 선풍적으로 인기 있는 것
sensational *news, discovery* sesangŭl ttŏdŭlssŏk'age hanŭn 세상을 떠들썩하게 하는; (*very good*) nunbushin 눈부신
sense 1 *n* (*meaning*) ttŭt 뜻; (*purpose, point*) ŭimi 의미; (*common ~*) sangshik 상식; (*of sight, smell etc*) kamgak 감각; (*feeling*) nŭtkkim 느낌; ***in a ~*** ŏttŏn ŭimiesŏnŭn 어떤 의미에서는; ***talk ~, man!*** ŏi, ich'ie mannŭn marŭl hae! 어이, 이치에 맞는 말을 해!; ***it doesn't make ~*** kŭgŏn mari andwaeyo 그건 말이 안돼요; ***there's no ~ in waiting / trying*** kidaril / shidohal iyuga ŏpssŏyo 기다릴 / 시도할 이유가 없어요 **2** *v/t s.o.'s presence* arach'aeda 알아채다
senseless (*pointless*) muŭimihan 무의미한
sensible *person, decision* punbyŏri innŭn 분별이 있는; *advice* hyŏnmyŏnghan 현명한
sensitive *skin* min-gamhan 민감한; *person* yeminhan 예민한
sensitivity min-gamham 민감함
sensual kwangnŭngtchŏgin 관능적인
sensuality kwangnŭng 관능
sensuous kamgaktchŏgin 감각적인
sentence 1 *n* GRAM munjang 문장; LAW p'an-gyŏl 판결 **2** *v/t* LAW p'an-gyŏrŭl naerida 판결을 내리다
sentiment (*emotion*) kamsang 감상; (*opinion*) sogam 소감
sentimental kamsangtchŏgin 감상적인
sentimentality kamsang 감상
sentry poch'o 보초
Seoul Sŏul 서울
separate 1 *adj* pyŏlgaeŭi 별개의; ***keep X ~ from Y*** Xwa / kwa Yŭl / rŭl pullihada X와 / 과 Y을 / 를 분리하다 **2** *v/t* pullihada 분리하다; ***~ X from Y*** Xŭl / rŭl Yesŏ pullihada X을 / 를 Y에서 분리하다 **3** *v/i* (*of couple*) pyŏlgŏhada 별거하다
separated *couple* pyŏlgŏhan 별거한
separately *pay, treat, deal with* ttaro 따로
separation pulli 분리; (*of couple*) pyŏlgŏ 별거
September kuwŏl 구월
septic pup'aessŏng-ŭi 부패성의; ***go ~*** komtta 곪다
sequel sokp'yŏn 속편
sequence *n* sunsŏ 순서; ***in ~*** sunsŏdaero 순서대로; ***out of ~*** sunsŏe mat-tchi ank'e 순서에 맞지 않게; ***the ~ of events*** sakkŏnŭi sunsŏ 사건의 순서
serene *person* ch'abunhan 차분한; *lake, smile* p'yŏng-onhan 평온한
sergeant chungsa 중사
serial *n* yŏnsongmul 연속물
serialize *novel on TV* yŏnsok pangyŏnghada 연속 방영하다
serial killer yŏnsok sarhaebŏm 연속 살해범; **serial number** (*of product*) illyŏnbŏnho 일련번호; **serial port** COMPUT sshiriŏl p'ot'ŭ 씨리얼 포트
series (*of numbers, events*) yŏnsok 연속
serious *illness, situation, damage* shimgak'an 심각한; (*person: earnest*) chinjihan 진지한; *company* shinmang innŭn 신망 있는; ***I'm ~*** chinshimiyeyo 진심이예요; ***we'd better take a ~ look at it*** uri kŭgŏse taehae chinjihage ponŭn ke choŭl kŏt kat'ayo 우리 그것에 대해 진지하게 보는 게 좋을 것 같아요

seriously *injured* shimhage 심하게; *understaffed* chinjŏngŭro 진정으로; ~ ***intend to ...*** chinjihage ...haryŏgo hada 진지하게 ...하려고 하다; ***~?*** chŏngmallo? 정말로?; ***take s.o. ~*** nugurŭl chinjihage saenggak'ada 누구를 진지하게 생각하다

sermon sŏlgyo 설교

servant koyongin 고용인

serve 1 *n* (*in tennis*) sŏbŭ 서브 **2** *v/t food, meal* naeda 내다; *person, guests* shijungdŭlda 시중들다; *customer in shop* moshida 모시다; *one's country, the people* pongsahada 봉사하다; ***it ~s you / him right*** nŏnŭn / kŭnŭn hapttanghan taeurŭl padat-tta 너는 / 그는 합당한 대우를 받았다 **3** *v/i* ch'arida 차리다; (*in post, job*) kŭnmuhada 근무하다; (*in tennis*) sŏbŭhada 서브하다

♦**serve up** *meal* ch'aryŏnaeda 차려내다

server (*in tennis*) sŏbŭhanŭn saram 서브하는 사람; COMPUT sŏbŏ 서버

service 1 *n* sŏbissŭ 서비스; (*in tennis*) sŏbŭhanŭn kkŏt 서브하는 것; ***the ~s*** kundae 군대 **2** *v/t vehicle, machine* sŏbissŭhada 서비스하다

service area hyugeso 휴게소; **service charge** (*in restaurant, club*) sŏbissŭryo 서비스료; **service industry** sŏbissŭ sanŏp 서비스 산업; **serviceman** MIL kunin 군인; **service provider** COMPUT sŏbissŭ chegonghoesa 서비스 제공회사; **service sector** sŏbissŭ sanŏp pubun 서비스 산업 부분; **service station** chuyuso 주유소

session (*of parliament*) kaejŏng chungim 개정 중임; (*with psychiatrist, consultant etc*) mit'ing 미팅

set 1 *n* (*of tools, books etc, in tennis, scenery*) set'ŭ 세트; (*group of people*) chipttan 집단; MATH chip'ap 집합; (*where a movie is made*) ch'waryŏngjangso 촬영장소; ***television ~*** t'ellebijŏn set'ŭ 텔레비전 세트 **2** *v/t* (*place*) not'a 놓다; *movie, novel etc* ...ŭi paegyŏng-ŭl chŏnghada ...의 배경을 정하다; *date, time, limit* chŏnghada 정하다; *mechanism* chojŏnghada 조정하다; *alarm clock* match'uŏ not'a 맞추어 놓다; *broken limb* umjigiji ank'e kojŏnghada 움직이지 않게 고정하다; *jewel* paganŏt'a 박아넣다; (*type~*) shiktchahada 식자하다; ***~ the table*** sang-ŭl ch'arida 상을 차리다; ***~ a task for s.o.*** nuguege ch'aegimŭl pugwahada 누구에게 책임을 부과하다 **3** *v/i* (*of sun*) chida 지다; (*of glue*) ŭnggohada 응고하다 **4** *adj views, ideas* hwak-kkohan 확고한; ***be dead ~ on X*** X hanŭn kŏsŭl hwakssirhi maŭm mŏktta X 하는 것을 확실히 마음 먹다; ***be very ~ in one's ways*** chagi pangshingmanŭl kojip'ada 자기 방식만을 고집하다; ***~ book / reading*** (*in course*) sojŏngŭi ch'aek / ilgŭlkkŏri 소정의 책 / 읽을거리; ***~ meal*** chŏngshik 정식

♦**set apart**: ***set X apart from Y*** Xŭl / rŭl Ywa / kwa kubyŏrhada X을 / 를 Y와 / 과 구별하다

♦**set aside** (*for future use*) ch'aenggyŏduda 챙겨두다

♦**set back** (*in plans etc*) twich'yŏjige hada 뒤쳐지게 하다; ***it set me back $400*** nanŭn kŭgŏse 400tallŏrŭl ssŏt-tta 나는 그것에 400달러를 썼다

♦**set off 1** *v/i* (*on journey*) ch'ulbarhada 출발하다 **2** *v/t explosion* chŏmhwahada 점화하다; *chain reaction* shijak'age hada 시작하게 하다

♦**set out 1** *v/i* (*on journey*) ch'ulbarhada 출발하다; ***~ to do X*** (*intend*) X hanŭn kŏsŭl chaktchŏnghada X 하는 것을 작정하다 **2** *v/t ideas, proposal* sŏlmyŏnghada 설명하다; *goods* naenot'a 내놓다

♦**set to** (*start on a task*) shijak'ada 시작하다

♦**set up 1** *v/t new company* sŏllip'ada 설립하다; *system* seuda 세우다; *equipment, machine* chorip'ada 조립하다; *market stall* set'inghada 세팅하다; F (*frame*) ummorŭl kkumida 음모를 꾸미다 **2** *v/i* (*in*

business) kaeŏp'ada 개업하다
setback hut'oe 후퇴
setting (*of novel etc*) paegyŏng 배경; (*of house*) wich'i 위치
settle 1 *v/i* (*of bird*) antta 앉다; (*of liquid*) malgajida 맑아지다; (*of dust*) karaantta 가라앉다; (*to live*) chŏngch'ak'ada 정착하다 **2** *v/t dispute, argument* hwahaeshik'ida 화해시키다; *uncertainty* haegyŏrhada 해결하다; *s.o.'s debts* ch'ŏngsanhada 청산하다; *check* chiburhada 지불하다; ***that ~s it!*** kŭgŏsŭro irŭn kyŏltchŏngdwaessŏyo! 그것으로 일은 결정됐어요!
♦**settle down** (*stop being noisy*) choyonghaejida 조용해지다; (*stop wild living*) charijaptta 자리잡다; (*in an area*) chŏngch'ak'ada 정착하다
♦**settle for** padadŭrida 받아들이다
settlement (*of claim, debt*) ch'ŏngsan 청산; (*of dispute*) hwahae 화해; (*payment*) chibul 지불; (*of building*) ch'imha 침하
settler (*in new country*) ijuja 이주자
set-up (*structure*) kujo 구조; (*relationship*) kwan-gye 관계; F (*frame-up*) kkumyŏjin il 꾸며진 일
seven ilgop 일곱, ch'il 칠
seventeen yŏrilgop 열 일곱, shipch'il 십칠
seventeenth yŏrilgop pŏntchaeŭi 열 일곱 번째의
seventh ilgop pŏntchaeŭi 일곱 번째의
seventieth irhŭn pŏntchaeŭi 일흔 번째의
seventy irhŭn 일흔, ch'ilsship 칠십
sever *v/t arm, cable etc* chŏlttanhada 절단하다; *relations* chŏryŏnhada 절연하다
several 1 *adj* myŏnmyŏch'ŭi 몇몇의 **2** *pron* myŏt kae 몇 개
severe *illness, penalty* shimhan 심한; *teacher, face* ŏmkkyŏk'an 엄격한; *winter, weather* mojin 모진
severely shimhage 심하게; *speak, stare* ŏmhage 엄하게
severity (*of illness*) shimham 심함; (*of penalty*) kahok 가혹; (*of look*) ŏmkkyŏk 엄격; (*of winter*) mojim 모짐
sew 1 *v/t* kkwemaeda 꿰매다 **2** *v/i* panŭjirhada 바느질하다
♦**sew on** *button* kkwemaeŏ talda 꿰매어 달다
sewage hasu 하수
sewage plant hasu ch'ŏrijang 하수 처리장
sewer hasugwan 하수관
sewing (*skill*) panŭjil 바느질; (*that being sewn*) panŭjilkkŏri 바느질거리
sewing machine chaebongt'ŭl 재봉틀
sex (*act*) sŏnggyo 성교; (*gender*) sŏng 성; ***have ~ with s.o.*** nuguwa sŏnggyohada 누구와 성교하다
sexual sŏngtchŏgin 성적인
sexual intercourse sŏnggyo 성교
sexually transmitted disease sŏngppyŏng 성병
sexy ssekssihan 섹시한
shabby *coat etc* nalgŭn 낡은; *treatment* piyŏrhan 비열한
shack odumaktchip 오두막집
shade 1 *n* ŭngdal 응달; (*for lamp*) karigae 가리개; (*of color*) saektcho 색조; (*on window*) pŭllaindŭ 블라인드; ***in the ~*** ŭngdare(sŏ) 응달에(서) **2** *v/t* (*from sun, light*) karida 가리다
shadow *n* kŭrimja 그림자
shady *spot* kŭnŭljin 그늘진; *character, dealings etc* ŭishimsŭrŏun 의심스러운
shaft (*of axle, hammer*) charu 자루; (*of mine*) sugaeng 수갱
shaggy *hair, dog* tŏpssuruk'an 덥수룩한
shake 1 *n*: ***give X a good ~*** Xŭl / rŭl toege hŭndŭlda X을 / 를 되게 흔들다 **2** *v/t* hŭndŭlda 흔들다; ***~ hands*** akssuhada 악수하다; ***~ hands with X*** Xwa / kwa akssuhada X와 / 과 악수하다; ***~ one's head*** kogaerŭl chŏt-tta 고개를 젖다 **3** *v/i* (*of hands, voice*) ttŏlda 떨다; (*of building*) hŭndŭllida 흔들리다
shaken (*emotionally*) hollansŭrŏun 혼란스러운
shake-up kujo chojŏng 구조 조정
shaky *table etc* hŭndŭlgŏrinŭn 흔들거리는; (*after illness, shock*)

pit'ŭlgorinŭn 비틀거리는; *grasp of sth, grammar etc* puranjŏnghan 불안정한
shall (*future*) …hal kŏshida …할 것이다; ***I ~ do my best*** nanŭn ch'oesŏnŭl tahal kŏshida 나는 최선을 다할 것이다 ◊ (*determined*) …hagessŭmnida …하겠습니다; ***I shan't see them*** nanŭn kŭdŭrŭl mannaji ank'essŭmnida 나는 그들을 만나지 않겠습니다 ◊ (*suggesting*): ***~ we go now?*** uri chigŭm kalkkayo? 우리 지금 갈까요?
shallow *water* yat'ŭn 얕은; *person* ch'ŏnbak'an 천박한
shaman mudang 무당
shaman rite kut 굿
shaman song muga 무가
Shamanism Musok Shinang 무속 신앙
shamanistic music muak 무악
shame 1 *n* such'ishim 수치심; ***bring ~ on*** …e such'ishimŭl an-gyŏjuda …에 수치심을 안겨주다; ***what a ~!*** chŏngmal andwaessŏyo! 정말 안됐어요!; ***~ on you!*** pukkŭrŏptchido anni! 부끄럽지도 않니! **2** *v/t* mangshinshik'ida 망신시키다; ***~ X into doing Y*** X(ŭ)ro hayŏgŭm pukkŭrŏwŏ Yhage hada X(으)로 하여금 부끄러워 Y하게 하다
shameful such'isŭrŏun 수치스러운
shameless p'aryŏmch'ihan 파렴치한
shampoo *n* shyamp'u 샴푸
shape 1 *n* moyang 모양 **2** *v/t clay* moyang-ŭl mandŭlda 모양을 만들다; *s.o.'s life, the future* sŏlgyehada 설계하다
shapeless *dress etc* polp'umŏmnŭn 볼품없는
shapely *figure* mommaega choŭn 몸매가 좋은
share 1 *n* mok 몫; FIN chushik 주식; ***do one's ~ of the work*** chagi mokssŭi irŭl hada 자기 몫의 일을 하다 **2** *v/t* punbaehada 분배하다; *room, bed* hamkke ssŭda 함께 쓰다; *s.o.'s feelings, opinions* hamkke hada 함께 하다 **3** *v/i* hamkke nanuda 함께 나누다
♦**share out** kyundŭnghage nanuda 균등하게 나누다
shareholder chuju 주주
shark sangŏ 상어
sharp 1 *adj knife* nalk'aroun 날카로운; *mind* myŏngminhan 명민한; *pain* sarŭl enŭn tŭt'an 살을 에는 듯한; *taste* chagŭktchŏgin 자극적인; ***~ tongue*** tokssŏl 독설 **2** *adv* MUS panŭm nopkke 반음 높게; ***at 3 o'clock ~*** seshi chŏnggage 세시 정각에
sharpen *knife* kalda 갈다; *skills* yŏnmahada 연마하다; *pencil* kkaktta 깎다
shatter 1 *v/t glass* pusuda 부수다; *illusions* kkaejida 깨지다 **2** *v/i* (*of glass*) pusŏjida 부서지다
shattered F (*exhausted*) chich'in 지친; (*very upset*) tandanhi ch'unggyŏgŭl padŭn 단단히 충격을 받은
shattering *news, experience* ch'imyŏngjŏgin 치명적인; *effect* ŏmch'ŏngnan 엄청난
shave 1 *v/t & v/i* myŏndohada 면도하다 **2** *n* myŏndo 면도; ***have a ~*** myŏndohada 면도하다; ***that was a close ~*** kanshinhi myŏnhaet-tta 간신히 면했다
♦**shave off** *beard* kkakkabŏrida 깎아버리다; *piece of wood* kkakanaeda 깎아내다
shaven *head* sakpparhan 삭발한
shaver (*electric*) myŏndogi 면도기
shaving brush myŏndoyong sol 면도용 솔
shaving soap myŏndoyong pinu 면도용 비누
shawl shyol 숄
she kŭnyŏ 그녀, kŭ yŏja 그 여자; ***~ is American*** kŭnyŏnŭn Miguk saramiyeyo 그녀는 미국 사람이에요 ◊ (*omission of pronoun*): ***who is ~? - ~ is my teacher*** nuguyeyo? – che sŏnsaengnimiyeyo 누구에요? – 제 선생님이에요
shears k'ŭn kawi 큰 가위
sheath *n* (*for knife*) k'altchip 칼집; (*contraceptive*) k'ondom 콘돔
shed[1] *v/t blood, tears* hŭllida 흘리다; *leaves* ttŏrŏttŭrida 떨어뜨리다; ~

light on *fig* haemyŏnghada 해명하다
shed[2] *n* ch'anggo 창고
sheep yang 양
sheepdog yang chik'inŭn kae 양 지키는 개
sheepish tanghwanghanŭn 당황하는
sheepskin *adj lining* yanggajuk 양가죽
sheer *adj madness*, *luxury* wanjŏnhan 완전한; *drop* kŏŭi sujigin 거의 수직인; *cliffs* kap'arŭn 가파른
sheet (*for bed*) shit'ŭ 시트; (*of paper*) chang 장; (*of metal*, *glass*) p'an 판
shelf sŏnban 선반; ***shelves*** yŏrŏgaeŭi sŏnban 여러개의 선반
shell 1 *n* (*of mussel*, *egg etc*) kkŏptchil 껍질; (*of tortoise*) tŭngttaktchi 등딱지; MIL yut'an 유탄; ***come out of one's ~*** *fig* maŭmŭl t'ŏnot'a 마음을 터놓다 **2** *v/t peas* pŏtkkida 벗기다; MIL p'ogyŏk'ada 포격하다
shellfire p'ohwa 포화; ***come under ~*** p'ogyŏgŭl pat-tta 포격을 받다
shellfish kapkkangnyu 갑각류
shelter 1 *n* (*refuge*) p'inanch'ŏ 피난처; (*against air raids*) taep'iho 대피호; (*at bus stop*) chŏngnyujang 정류장 **2** *v/i* (*from rain*, *bombing etc*) p'ihada 피하다 **3** *v/t* (*protect*) pohohada 보호하다
sheltered *place* p'ihal su innŭn 피할 수 있는; ***lead a ~ life*** ŭndunsaenghwarŭl hada 은둔생활을 하다
shepherd *n* yangch'i-gi 양치기
sherry seriju 세리주
shield 1 *n* pangp'ae 방패; (*sports trophy*) usŭngp'ae 우승패; TECH magi 막이 **2** *v/t* (*protect*) pohohada 보호하다
shift 1 *n* (*in attitude*, *thinking*) pyŏnhwa 변화; (*switchover*) pyŏn-gyŏng 변경; (*in direction of wind etc*) idong 이동; (*period of work*) kyodae 교대 **2** *v/t* (*move*) omgida 옮기다; *stains etc* ŏpssaeda 없애다; ***~ the emphasis onto*** ...(ŭ)ro kangjotchŏmŭl idonghada ...(으)로 강조점을 이동하다 **3** *v/i* (*move*) omgida 옮기다; (*of attitude*, *opinion*) pyŏnhada 변하다; (*of wind*) idonghada 이동하다; ***that's ~ing!*** F kkwae pparŭgunyo! 꽤 빠르군요!
shift key COMPUT ship'ŭt'ŭ k'i 시프트 키
shift work kyodae kŭnmu 교대 근무
shifty *pej* kansahan 간사한
shifty-looking *pej* kansahae poinŭn 간사해 보이는
shimmer *v/i* arŭn-gŏrida 아른거리다
shin *n* chŏnggang-i 정강이
shine 1 *v/i* (*of sun*, *moon*) pinnada 빛나다; (*of shoes*) pantchagida 반짝이다; *fig* (*of student etc*) ttwiŏnada 뛰어나다 **2** *v/t flashlight etc* pich'uda 비추다 **3** *n* (*on shoes etc*) pantchak-kkŏrim 반짝거림
shingle (*on beach*) chagal 자갈
shingles MED taesangp'ojin 대상포진
shiny *surface* pantchak-kkŏrinŭn 반짝거리는
ship 1 *n* pae 배 **2** *v/t* (*send*) ponaeda 보내다; (*send by sea*) sŏnjŏk'ada 선적하다
shipment (*consignment*) hwamul 화물
shipowner sŏnbak soyuja 선박 소유자
shipping (*sea traffic*) haesang kyot'ong 해상 교통; (*sending*) palssong 발송; (*sending by sea*) sŏnjŏk 선적
shipping company haeunhoesa 해운회사
shipshape *adj* chŏngdondoen 정돈된; **shipwreck 1** *n* nanp'a 난파 **2** *v/t* nanp'ashik'ida 난파시키다; ***be ~ed*** nanp'adoeda 난파되다; **shipyard** chosŏnso 조선소
shirk keŭllihada 게을리하다
shirt shyŏch'ŭ 셔츠
shirt sleeves: ***in his ~*** usosŭl pŏtkko 웃옷을 벗고
shit F **1** *n* ttong 똥; (*bad quality goods*, *work*) ssŭregi 쓰레기; ***I need a ~*** hwajangsire kayagessŏ 화장실에 가야겠어 **2** *v/i* yongbyŏnboda 용변보다 **3** *interj*: ***~!*** chegiral! 제기랄!
shitty F chinjŏlmŏri nanŭn 진절머리 나는

shiver *v/i* ttŏlda 떨다
shock 1 *n* ch'unggyŏk 충격; ELEC shyok'ŭ 쇼크; ***be in ~*** MED ch'unggyŏgesŏ pŏsŏnaji mot'ada 충격에서 벗어나지 못하다 **2** *v/t* nollage hada 놀라게 하다; ***be ~ed by*** ch'unggyŏgŭl pat-tta 충격을 받다
shock absorber MOT wanch'unggi 완충기
shocking ch'unggyŏktchŏgin 충격적인; F (*very bad*) chidok'i choch'i anŭn 지독히 좋지 않은
shoddy *goods* p'umjiri nappŭn 품질이 나쁜; *behavior* such'isŭrŏun 수치스러운
shoe shinbal 신발
shoelace shinbalkkŭn 신발끈; **shoestore** shinbalkkage 신발가게; **shoestring**; ***do X on a ~*** Xŭl / rŭl aju chŏgŭn yesanŭro hada X을 / 를 아주 적은 예산으로 하다
♦ **shoo away** shwitsori naeŏ tchoch'abŏrida 쉿소리 내어 쫓아버리다
shoot 1 *n* BOT ŏrin-gaji 어린가지 **2** *v/t* ssoda 쏘다; (*and kill*) ch'ongsarhada 총살하다; *movie* ch'waryŏnghada 촬영하다; ***~ X in the leg*** Xŭi tarirŭl ssoda X의 다리를 쏘다 **3** *v/i* ch'ongŭl ssoda 총을 쏘다
♦ **shoot down** *airplane* ssoa ttŏrŏttŭrida 쏘아 떨어뜨리다; *suggestion* kŏjŏrhada 거절하다
♦ **shoot off** (*rush off*) taranada 달아나다
♦ **shoot up** (*of prices*) ch'isot-tta 치솟다; (*of children*) ssukssuk charada 쑥쑥 자라다; (*of buildings etc*) tanshigane chiŏjida 단시간에 지어지다; (*of new suburbs*) pulssuk saenggida 불쑥 생기다
shooting star yusŏng 유성
shop 1 *n* sangjŏm 상점; ***talk ~*** il iyagiman hada 일 이야기만 하다 **2** *v/i* shijangboda 시장보다; ***go ~ping*** changborŏ kada 장보러 가다
shopkeeper somaesang-in 소매상인
shoplifter somaech'igi 소매치기
shopper shyop'inghanŭn saram 쇼핑하는 사람
shopping (*activity*) shyop'ing 쇼핑; (*items*) chang pon mulgŏn 장 본 물건; ***do one's ~*** changboda 장보다
shopping mall shyop'ingssent'ŏ 쇼핑센터
shop steward nodongjohabŭi chiktchangwiwŏn 노동조합의 직장위원
shore mulkka 물가; ***on ~*** (*not at sea*) yukssang-e(sŏ) 육상에(서)
short 1 *adj* (*in height*) k'iga chagŭn 키가 작은; *road*, *distance* tchalbŭn 짧은; (*in time*) oraedoeji anŭn 오래되지 않은; ***be ~ of*** mojarada 모자라다 **2** *adv*: ***cut a vacation / meeting ~*** hyugarŭl / hoeŭirŭl yejŏngboda ppalli kkŭnnaeda 휴가를 / 회의를 예정보다 빨리 끝내다; ***stop a person ~*** sarami marhanŭn kŏsŭl kkŭnŏborida 사람이 말하는 것을 끊어버리다; ***go ~ of*** chogŭm mojarŭge chinaeda 조금 모자르게 지내다; ***in ~*** yoyak'amyŏn 요약하면
shortage pujok 부족
short circuit *n* tallak 단락; **shortcoming** kyŏltchŏm 결점; **shortcut** chirŭmkkil 지름길
shorten *v/t dress*, *vacation*, *workday etc* churida 줄이다; *hair* tchalkke hada 짧게 하다; ***~ a movie*** yŏnghwaŭi pullyang-ŭl churida 영화의 분량을 줄이다
shortfall pujok 부족; **shorthand** *n* sok-kki 속기; **shortlist** *n* (*of candidates*) ch'oejong myŏngdan 최종 명단; **short-lived** tanmyŏnghan 단명한
shortly (*soon*) kot 곧; ***~ before that*** kŭ chŏne paro 그 전에 바로
shorts panbaji 반바지; (*underwear*) sogot 속옷
shortsighted kŭnshiŭi 근시의; *fig* kŭnshianjŏgin 근시안적인; **short-sleeved** panp'arŭi 반팔의; **short-staffed** chigwŏni mojaranŭn 직원이 모자라는; **short story** tanp'yŏnsosŏl 단편소설; **short-tempered** sŏnggŭp'an 성급한; **short-term** tangigan 단기간; **short time**: ***be on ~*** (*of workers*) choŏp tanch'uk'ada 조업 단축하다; **short wave** tanp'a

단파

shot (*from gun*) ch'ongssori 총소리; (*photograph*) sajin 사진; (*injection*) chusa 주사; ***be a good/poor ~*** ch'ong-ŭl chal/mot ssonŭn saramida 총을 잘/못 쏘는 사람이다; ***like a ~*** *accept, run off* ch'ong-algatchi 총알같이

shotgun yŏpch'ong 엽총

should haeya hada 해야 하다; ***what ~ I do?*** nanŭn musŭn irŭl haeya hamnikka? 나는 무슨 일을 해야 합니까?; ***you ~n't do that*** tangshinŭn kŭrŏk'e hamyŏn andoemnida 당신은 그렇게 하면 안됩니다; ***that ~ be enough*** kŭgŏllo ch'ungbunhagetchyo 그걸로 충분하겠죠; ***you ~ have heard him!*** nŏnŭn kŭga ttŏdŭnŭn kŏl turossŏya haessŏ! 너는 그가 떠드는 걸 들었어야 했어!

shoulder *n* ŏkkae 어깨

shoulder blade kyŏngapkkol 견갑골

shout 1 *n* pimyŏngsori 비명소리 **2** *v/i* sorich'ida 소리치다 **3** *v/t order* myŏngnyŏnghada 명령하다

♦**shout at** …e taego sorijirŭda …에 대고 소리지르다

shouting *n* sorijirŭm 소리지름

shove 1 *n* ttemilgi 떼밀기 **2** *v/t* mirŏnaeda 밀어내다 **3** *v/i* milda 밀다

♦**shove in** *v/i* (*in line-up*) saech'igihada 새치기하다

♦**shove off** *v/i* F (*go away*) ka pŏrida 가 버리다

shovel *n* sap 삽

show 1 *n* THEA, TV shyo 쇼; (*display*) p'yohyŏn 표현; ***on ~*** (*at exhibition*) chŏnshi chung-in 전시 중인; ***it's all done for ~*** *pej* kŭgŏ shyohanŭn kŏeyo 그거 쇼하는 거에요 **2** *v/t passport, ticket* poyŏjuda 보여주다; *interest, emotion* nat'anaeda 나타내다; (*at exhibition*) chŏnshihada 전시하다; *movie* sangyŏnghada 상영하다; ***~ X to Y*** Xrŭl Yege poyŏjuda X를 Y에게 보여주다 **3** *v/i* (*be visible*) poida 보이다; (*of movie*) sangyŏngdoeda 상영되다

♦**show off 1** *v/t skills* parhwihada 발휘하다 **2** *v/i pej* uttchuldaeda 우쭐대다

♦**show up 1** *v/t shortcomings etc* hwagyŏnhi poyŏjuda 확연히 보여주다; ***don't show me up in public*** saramdŭl ap'esŏ narŭl tanghwanghage haji maseyo 사람들 앞에서 나를 당황하게 하지 마세요 **2** *v/i* (*arrive*) nat'anada 나타나다; (*be visible*) poyŏjida 보여지다

show business shyo pijŭnisŭ 쇼 비즈니스

showdown han p'an taegyŏl 한 판 대결

shower 1 *n* (*of rain*) sonagi 소나기; (*to wash*) shyawŏ 샤워; ***take a ~*** shyawŏhada 샤워하다 **2** *v/i* shyawŏhada 샤워하다 **3** *v/t*: ***~ X with compliments/praise*** Xege ch'ansarŭl/ch'ingch'anŭl p'ŏbut-tta X에게 찬사를/칭찬을 퍼붓다

shower bath shyawŏ 샤워; **shower cap** shyawŏ k'aep 샤워 캡; **shower curtain** shyawŏ k'ŏt'ŭn 샤워 커튼; **showerproof** pangsuŭi 방수의

show jumping chang-aemul ttwiŏnŏmkki 장애물 뛰어넘기

show-off hŏp'ungjang-i 허풍장이

showroom shyo rum 쇼 룸; ***in ~ condition*** hanbŏndo sayongdoeji anŭn 한번도 사용되지 않은

showy *jacket, behavior* nŏmu nune ttŭinŭn 너무 눈에 띄는

shred 1 *n* (*of paper etc*) chogak 조각; (*of evidence etc*) tanp'yŏn 단편 **2** *v/t paper* kalgari tchijŏbŏrida 갈가리 찢어버리다; (*in cooking*) chogak naeda 조각 내다

shredder (*for documents*) sŏryu chŏlttan-gi 서류 절단기

shrewd pint'ŭm ŏmnŭn 빈틈 없는

shriek 1 *n* pimyŏng 비명 **2** *v/i* pimyŏngŭl chirŭda 비명을 지르다

shrimp saeu 새우

shrine sŏnggorham 성골함

shrink *v/i* (*of material*) churŏdŭlda 줄어들다; (*of support etc*) kamsohada 감소하다

shrink-wrap such'uk p'ojanghada 수축 포장하다

shrink-wrapping such'uk p'ojang

수축 포장
shrivel tchugŭlgŏrige hada 쭈글거리게 하다
shrub, shrubbery kwanmok 관목
shrug 1 *n* ŏkkaerŭl ŭssŭk-kkŏrim 어깨를 으쓱거림 **2** *v/t & v/i*: ~ (***one's shoulders***) ŏkkaerŭl ŭssŭk-kkŏrida 어깨를 으쓱거리다
shudder 1 *n* (*of fear, disgust*) momsŏri ch'im 몸서리 침; (*of earth etc*) ttŏllim 떨림 **2** *v/i* (*with fear, disgust*) momsŏrich'ida 몸서리치다; (*of earth, building*) ttŏllida 떨리다
shuffle 1 *v/t cards* twisŏktta 뒤섞다 **2** *v/i* (*in walking*) chiljil kkŭlmyŏ kada 질질 끌며 가다
shun *person* p'ihada 피하다; *drugs etc* kkŏrida 꺼리다
shut 1 *v/t* tat-tta 닫다 **2** *v/i* tatch'ida 닫히다; ***the shop was*** ~ kagega munŭl tadat-tta 가게가 문을 닫았다
♦**shut down 1** *v/t business* p'yeŏp'ada 폐업하다; *computer* chongnyonaeda 종료내다 **2** *v/i* (*of business*) p'yeŏp'ada 폐업하다; (*of computer*) chongnyohada 종료하다
♦**shut up** *v/i* (*be quiet*) choyonghi hada 조용히 하다; ~**!** choyonghi hae! 조용히 해!
shutter (*on window*) tŏnmun 덧문; PHOT shyŏt'ŏ 셔터
shuttle *v/i* wangbok'ada 왕복하다
shuttlebus (*at airport*) shyŏt'ŭlppŏsŭ 셔틀버스; **shuttlecock** SP paedŭmint'ŏn kong 배드민턴 공; **shuttle service** shyŏt'ŭl sŏbissŭ 셔틀 서비스
shy *person* sujubŏhanŭn 수줍어하는; *animal* sunhan 순한
shyness sujubŭm 수줍음; (*of animal*) sunham 순함
Siamese twins shyam ssangdung-i 샴 쌍둥이
sick ap'ŭn 아픈; *sense of humor* pulk'waehan 불쾌한; *society* kuyŏktchil nanŭn 구역질 나는; ***I'm going to be*** ~ (*vomit*) t'ohallaeyo 토할래요; ***be*** ~ ***of*** (*fed up with*) chigyŏptta 지겹다
sicken 1 *v/t* (*disgust*) yŏk-kkyŏwŏ hada 역겨워 하다 **2** *v/i*: ***be*** ~***ing for*** chŭngsangŭl poida 증상을 보이다
sickening pulk'waehan 불쾌한
sickle wŏnhyŏng nat 원형 낫
sick leave pyŏngga 병가; ***be on*** ~ pyŏngga chung-ida 병가 중이다
sickly *person* pyŏngyak'an 병약한; *color* hyŏlssaegi nappŭn 혈색이 나쁜
sickness pyŏng 병
side *n* (*of box, house*) yŏmmyŏn 옆면; (*of room, field*) ch'ungmyŏn 측면; (*of mountain*) kyŏngsa-myŏn 경사면; (*of person*) yŏpkkuri 옆구리; SP t'im 팀; ***take*** ~***s*** (*favor one side*) p'yŏnŭl tŭlda 편을 들다; ***take*** ~***s with*** …ŭi p'yŏnŭl tŭlda …의 편을 들다; ***I'm on your*** ~ tangshin p'yŏniyeyo 당신 편이예요; ~ ***by*** ~ naranhi 나란히; ***at the*** ~ ***of the road*** kilkkae(sŏ) 길가에(서); ***on the big / small*** ~ k'ŭn / chagŭn p'yŏn 큰 / 작은 편
♦**side with** chijihada 지지하다
sideboard ch'antchang 찬장; **side dish** panch'an 반찬; **side effect** pujagyong 부작용; **sidelight** MOT ch'ap'okttŭng 차폭등; **sideline 1** *n* puŏp 부업 **2** *v/t*: ***feel*** ~***d*** panggwanjach'ŏrŏm nŭkkida 방관자처럼 느끼다; **side street** kolmok-kkil 골목길; **sidetrack** *v/t* …ŭi chuŭirŭl tollida …의 주의를 돌리다; ***he got*** ~***ed into talking about politics again*** kŭnŭn tto tashi yŏpkkilo ppajyŏ chŏngch'ie taehae iyagihaet-tta 그는 또 다시 옆길로 빠져 정치에 대해 이야기했다; **sidewalk** indo 인도; **sidewalk café** noch'ŏn k'ap'e 노천 카페; **sideways** *adv* yŏp'ŭro 옆으로
siege p'owi konggyŏk 포위 공격; ***lay*** ~ ***to*** p'owi konggyŏk'ada 포위 공격하다
sieve *n* ch'e 체
sift *v/t corn, ore* ch'ero ch'ida 체로 치다; *data* kŏllŏnaeda 걸러내다
♦**sift through** *details, data* chosahayŏ kŏllŏnaeda 조사하여 걸러내다
sigh 1 *n* hansum 한숨; ***heave a*** ~ ***of relief*** andoŭi hansumŭl shwida 안도의 한숨을 쉬다 **2** *v/i* hansum chit-tta 한숨 짓다
sight *n* kwanggyŏng 광경; (*power of*

♦**size up** p'yŏngkkahada 평가하다
sizeable *house* sangdanghi k'ŭn 상당히 큰; *meal, order* kkwae manŭn 꽤 많은
sizzle chigŭlgŏrida 지글거리다
skate 1 *n* sŭk'eit'ŭ 스케이트 **2** *v/i* sŭk'eit'ŭ t'ada 스케이트 타다
skateboard *n* sŭk'eit'ŭbodŭ 스케이트보드
skater sŭk'eit'ŭ t'anŭn saram 스케이트 타는 사람
skating sŭk'eit'ŭ t'agi 스케이트 타기
skeleton haegol 해골
skeleton key kyŏtssoe 곁쇠
skeptic hoeŭironja 회의론자
skeptical hoeŭijŏgin 회의적인
skepticism hoeŭiron 회의론
sketch 1 *n* sŭk'ech'i 스케치; THEA ch'ongŭk 촌극 **2** *v/t* sŭk'ech'ihada 스케치하다
sketchbook sŭk'ech'ibuk 스케치북
sketchy *knowledge etc* tanp'yŏntchŏgin 단편적인
ski 1 *n* sŭk'i 스키 **2** *v/i* sŭk'i t'ada 스키 타다
skid 1 *n* mikkŭrŏm 미끄럼 **2** *v/i* mikkŭrŏjida 미끄러지다
skier sŭk'i t'anŭn saram 스키 타는 사람
skiing sŭk'i t'agi 스키 타기
ski lift sŭk'i lip'ŭt'ŭ 스키 리프트
skill kisul 기술
skilled sungnyŏndoen 숙련된
skilled worker sungnyŏn-gong 숙련공
skillful nŭngsuk'an 능숙한
skim *surface* sŭch'idŭt chinagada 스치듯 지나가다
♦**skim off** *the best* sŏnch'wihada 선취하다
♦**skim through** *text* taech'ung hult'ŏboda 대충 훑어보다
skimmed milk t'altchi uyu 탈지 우유
skimpy *account etc* pinyak'an 빈약한; *little dress* kkwak choenŭn 꽉 죄는
skin 1 *n* (*of person*) p'ibu 피부; (*of animal*) kajuk 가죽; (*of fish*) kkŏptchil 껍질 **2** *v/t* ...ŭi kkŏptchirŭl pŏtkkida ...의 껍질을 벗기다
skin diving sŭk'in taibing 스킨 다이빙
skinny kkangmarŭn 깡마른
skin-tight mome kkok mannŭn 몸에 꼭 맞는
skip 1 *n* (*little jump*) ttwiŏ orŭm 뛰어 오름 **2** *v/i* kkangch'unggŏrimyŏ ttwiŏdanida 깡충거리며 뛰어다니다 **3** *v/t* (*omit*) ppattŭrida 빠뜨리다
ski pole sŭk'i chip'ang-i 스키 지팡이
skipper NAUT sŏnjang 선장; (*of team*) chujang 주장
skirt *n* ch'ima 치마
ski run sŭk'i hwaltchuro 스키 활주로
ski tow sŭk'it'o 스키토
skull tugaegol 두개골
sky hanŭl 하늘
skylight ch'aegwangch'ang 채광창; **skyline** sŭk'airain 스카이라인; **skyscraper** mach'ŏllu 마천루
slab (*of stone*) sŏkp'an 석판; (*of cake etc*) tut'umhage k'ŭn chogak 두툼하게 큰 조각
slack *discipline, rope* nŭsŭnhan 느슨한; *person, work* pujuŭihan 부주의한; *period* pulgyŏnggiŭi 불경기의
slacken *v/t rope* nŭsŭnhage hada 느슨하게 하다; *pace* nŭtch'uda 늦추다
♦**slacken off** *v/i* (*of trading*) yak'wadoeda 약화되다; (*of pace*) nŭtch'uŏjida 늦추어지다
slacks paji 바지
slam 1 *v/t door* k'wang tat-tta 쾅 닫다 **2** *v/i* (*of door etc*) k'wang tach'ida 쾅 닫히다
♦**slam down** t'ŏlssŏk naeryŏnot'a 털썩 내려놓다
slander 1 *n* chungsang 중상 **2** *v/t* chungsanghada 중상하다
slang sogŏ 속어; (*of a specific group*) ŭnŏ 은어
slant 1 *v/i* kiulda 기울다 **2** *n* kyŏngsa 경사; (*given to a story*) kwantchŏm 관점
slanting *roof* pisŭdŭmhan 비스듬한; *eyes* ch'ik'yŏ ollagan 치켜 올라간
slap 1 *n* (*blow*) ch'igi 치기 **2** *v/t* ch'alssak ttaerida 찰싹 때리다
slash 1 *n* (*cut*) pegi 베기; (*in punctuation*) sŭllaeshwi 슬래쉬 **2** *v/t skin etc* naeribeda 내리베다; *prices, costs* sak-kkamhada 삭감하다; ~

one's wrists tongmaegŭl peda 동맥을 베다
slate *n* sŭlleit'ŭ 슬레이트
slaughter 1 *n* (*of animals*) tosal 도살; (*of people*, *troops*) hakssal 학살 **2** *v/t animals* tosarhada 도살하다; *people*, *troops* hakssarhada 학살하다
slave *n* noye 노예
slay sarhaehada 살해하다
slaying (*murder*) sarhae 살해
sleazy *bar*, *character* t'arak'an 타락한
sled(ge) *n* ssŏlmae 썰매
sledge hammer taehyŏng mangch'i 대형 망치
sleep 1 *n* cham 잠; ***go to ~*** chami tŭlda 잠이 들다; ***I need a good ~*** ch'ungbunhage chaya haeyo 충분하게 자야 해요; ***I couldn't get to ~*** chal suga ŏpssŏssŏyo 잘 수가 없었어요 **2** *v/i* chada 자다
♦**sleep on** *v/t proposal*, *decision* ch'ungbunhi saenggak'ada 충분히 생각하다
♦**sleep with** (*have sex with*) ...wa / kwa kach'i chada ...와 / 과 같이 자다
sleeping bag sŭllip'ing paek 슬리핑 백; **sleeping car** ch'imdaech'a 침대차; **sleeping pill** sumyŏnje 수면제
sleepless *night* cham mot irunŭn 잠 못 이루는
sleepwalker mongnyuppyŏngja 몽유병자
sleepy *yawn* chollin 졸린; *town* choyonghan 조용한; ***I'm ~*** chollyŏyo 졸려요
sleet *n* ssaragi nun 싸라기 눈
sleeve (*of jacket etc*) somae 소매
sleeveless somaega ŏmnŭn 소매가 없는
sleight of hand kamtchok-kkat'ŭn sonnollim 감쪽같은 손놀림
slender *figure*, *arms* kanyalp'ŭn 가냘픈; *chance* hŭibak'an 희박한; *income*, *margin* ŏlma andoenŭn 얼마 안되는
slice 1 *n* (*of bread*, *tart*) chogak 조각; (*of profits etc*) pubun 부분 **2** *v/t loaf etc* yalkke charŭda 얇게 자르다
sliced bread challanoŭn ppang 잘라놓은 빵
slick 1 *adj performance* nŭngsuk'an 능숙한; *pej* (*cunning*) kyomyohan 교묘한 **2** *n* (*of oil*) mak 막
slide 1 *n* (*for kids*) mikkŭrŏmt'ŭl 미끄럼틀; PHOT sŭllaidŭ 슬라이드 **2** *v/i* mikkŭrojida 미끄러지다; (*of exchange rate etc*) ttŏrŏjida 떨어지다 **3** *v/t* mirŏnŏt'a 밀어넣다
sliding door midaji mun 미닫이 문
slight 1 *adj person*, *figure* kanyalp'ŭn 가냘픈; *difference etc* yakkanŭi 약간의; ***no, not in the ~est*** anio, chogŭmdo animnida 아니오, 조금도 아닙니다 **2** *n* (*insult*) moyok 모욕
slightly yakkan 약간
slim 1 *adj* nalsshinhan 날씬한; *chance* hŭibak'an 희박한 **2** *v/i* sal ppaeda 살 빼다
slime kkŭnjŏk-kkŭnjŏk'an kŏt 끈적끈적한 것
slimy *liquid* chilch'ŏk'an 질척한; *person* allanggŏrinŭn 알랑거리는
sling 1 *n* (*for arm*) samgak-kkŏn 삼각건 **2** *v/t* (*throw*) tŏnjida 던지다
slip 1 *n* (*on ice etc*) mikkŭrŏjim 미끄러짐; (*mistake*) shilssu 실수; ***a ~ of paper*** chagŭn chong-i 작은 종이; ***a ~ of the tongue*** shirŏn 실언; ***give s.o. the ~*** nugurŭl ttadollida 누구를 따돌리다 **2** *v/i* (*on ice etc*) mikkŭrŏjida 미끄러지다; (*of quality etc*) chŏhadoeda 저하되다; ***he ~ped out of the room*** kŭnŭn saltchak pangŭl nagat-tta 그는 살짝 방을 나갔다 **3** *v/t* (*put*) saltchak not'a 살짝 놓다; ***he ~ped it into his briefcase*** kŭnŭn sŏryugabang-e kŭgŏsŭl salmyŏshi nŏŏt-tta 그는 서류가방에 그것을 살며시 넣었다
♦**slip away** (*of time*) sunshik-kkane chinagada 순식간에 지나가다; (*of opportunity*) kŭnyang sarajida 그냥 사라지다; (*die quietly*) choyonghi sesang-ŭl ttŭda 조용히 세상을 뜨다
♦**slip off** *v/t jacket etc* pŏt-tta 벗다
♦**slip out** *v/i* (*go out*) ppajyŏ nagada 빠져 나가다
♦**slip up** *v/i* (*make mistake*) shilssuhada 실수하다
slipped disc ch'uganp'an 추간판

slipper sŭllip'ŏ 슬리퍼
slippery mikkŭrŏun 미끄러운
slipshod kkomkkomhaji anŭn 꼼꼼하지 않은
slit 1 *n* (*tear*) tchijŏjin kot 찢어진 곳; (*hole*) kumŏng 구멍; (*in skirt*) kilge t'ŭn kot 길게 튼 곳 **2** *v/t* tchijŏ yŏlda 찢어 열다; *throat* peda 베다
slither *v/i* mikkŭrŏjida 미끄러지다
slobber *v/i* kunch'im hŭllida 군침 흘리다
slogan sŭllogŏn 슬로건
slop *v/t* ppurida 뿌리다
slope 1 *n* (*of roof*) kyŏngsa 경사; (*of handwriting*) kiulgi 기울기; (*of mountain*) kisŭk 기슭; ***built on a ~*** kisŭlge sewŏjin 기슭에 세워진 **2** *v/i* kyŏngsajida 경사지다; ***the road ~s down to the sea*** kiri padatchogŭro kyŏngsajyŏ it-tta 길이 바다쪽으로 경사져 있다
sloppy *work* pujuŭihan 부주의한; (*in dress*) tangjŏngch'i mot'an 단정치 못한; (*too sentimental*) chinach'ige kamsangjŏgin 지나치게 감상적인
sloshed F (*drunk*) sul ch'wihan 술 취한
slot *n* t'ŭmsae 틈새; (*in schedule*) tcham 짬, piŏinnŭn shigan 비어있는 시간
♦**slot in 1** *v/t* kkiuda 끼우다 **2** *v/i* kkiwŏjida 끼워지다
slot machine (*for vending*) chap'an-gi 자판기; (*for gambling*) sŭllot mŏshin 슬롯 머신
slouch *v/i* momŭl kuburida 몸을 구부리다
slovenly tanjŏngch'i mot'an 단정치 못한
slow nŭrin 느린; ***be ~*** (*of clock*) nŭrida 느리다
♦**slow down 1** *v/t* nŭrige hada 느리게 하다 **2** *v/i* nŭryŏjida 느려지다
slowdown (*in production*) t'aeŏp 태업
slow motion: ***in ~*** nŭrin tongjagŭro 느린 동작으로
slug *n* (*animal*) mindalp'aeng-i 민달팽이
sluggish *pace* nŭrin 느린; *river* wanmanhan 완만한; *start* hwalbarhaji mot'an 활발하지 못한
slum *n* pinmin-ga 빈민가
slump 1 *n* (*in trade*) pulgyŏnggi 불경기 **2** *v/i* (*of economy*) soet'oehada 쇠퇴하다; (*collapse*: *of person*) ssŭrŏjida 쓰러지다
slur 1 *n* (*on s.o.'s character*) pibang 비방 **2** *v/t words* punmyŏnghaji ank'e marhada 분명하지 않게 말하다
slurred *speech* parŭmi punmyŏngch'i anŭn 발음이 분명치 않은
slush nok-kki shijak'an nun 녹기 시작한 눈; *pej* (*sentimental stuff*) nunmul tchage hanŭn kŏt 눈물 짜게 하는 것
slush fund pijagŭm 비자금
slut p'umhaeng-i nappŭn yŏja 품행이 나쁜 여자
sly kyohwarhan 교활한; ***on the ~*** nam mollae saltchak 남 몰래 살짝
smack 1 *n* sonppadagŭro han tae ttaerigi 손바닥으로 한 대 때리기 **2** *v/t child, bottom* sonppadagŭro ch'alssak ttaerida 손바닥으로 찰싹 때리다
small 1 *adj* (*in size*) chagŭn 작은; (*in amount*) chŏgŭn 적은 **2** *n*: ***the ~ of the back*** hŏri tŭngtchogŭi chilluk'an pubun 허리 등쪽의 질록한 부분
small change chandon 잔돈; **small hours** shimnya 심야; **smallpox** ch'ŏnyŏndu 천연두; **small print** (*on a contract*) sebu chohang 세부 조항; **small talk** chapttam 잡담
smart 1 *adj* (*elegant*) mŏtchin 멋진; (*intelligent*) ttokttok'an 똑똑한; *pace* sangdanghi pparŭn 상당히 빠른; ***get ~ with*** (*fresh*) ...ege kŏnbangjige kulda ...에게 건방지게 굴다 **2** *v/i* (*hurt*) ssushida 쑤시다
smart card chŏnja k'adŭ 전자 카드
♦**smarten up** *v/t* malssuk'age hada 말쑥하게 하다
smash 1 *n* (*noise*) pusŏjinŭn sori 부서지는 소리; (*car crash*) ch'ungdol 충돌; (*in tennis*) sŭmaeshi 스매시 **2** *v/t* (*break*) pusuda 부수다; (*hit hard*) kangt'ahada 강타하다; ***~ X to pieces*** Xŭl / rŭl sansanjogak naeda

X을/를 산산조각 내다 **3** *v/i* (*break*) pusŏjida 부서지다; ***the driver ~ed into …*** unjŏnjanŭn …e ch'ungdorhaet-tta 운전자는 …에 충돌했다
smash hit F taehit'ŭ 대히트
smashing F kkŭnnaejunŭn 끝내주는
smattering (*of a language*) ŏsŏlp'ŭn shillyŏk 어설픈 실력
smear 1 *n* (*of ink etc*) ŏlluk 얼룩; MED tomal p'yobon kŏmsa 도말 표본 검사; (*on character*) otchŏm 오점 **2** *v/t paint etc* parŭda 바르다; *character* tŏrŏp'ida 더럽히다
smear campaign chungsang moryak 중상 모략
smell 1 *n* naemsae 냄새; ***sense of ~*** hugak 후각 **2** *v/t* …ŭi naemsaerŭl mat-tta …의 냄새를 맡다 **3** *v/i* (*unpleasantly*) naemsaega nada 냄새가 나다; (*sniff*) naemsaerŭl mat-tta 냄새를 맡다; ***what does it ~ of?*** ŏttŏn naemsaega nanŭndeyo? 어떤 냄새가 나는데요?; ***you ~ of beer*** tangshinhant'esŏ maektchu naemsaega nayo 당신한테서 맥주 냄새가 나요
smelly naemsae nanŭn 냄새 나는
smile 1 *n* miso 미소 **2** *v/i* misojit-tta 미소짓다
♦**smile at** …ege misojit-tta …에게 미소짓다
smirk 1 *n* nŭnggŭlmajŭn usŭm 능글맞은 웃음 **2** *v/i* nŭnggŭlmatkke ut-tta 능글맞게 웃다
smog sŭmogŭ 스모그
smoke 1 *n* yŏn-gi 연기; ***have a ~*** tambaerŭl p'iuda 담배를 피우다 **2** *v/t cigarettes* p'iuda 피우다; *bacon* hunjehada 훈제하다 **3** *v/i* yŏn-giga nada 연기가 나다; ***I don't ~*** chŏn, tambaerŭl p'iuji anayo 전, 담배를 피우지 않아요
smoker (*person*) hŭbyŏnja 흡연자
smoking hŭbyŏn 흡연; ***no ~*** kŭmyŏn 금연
smoky *air* yŏn-giga chauk'an 연기가 자욱한
smolder (*of fire*) yŏn-giman p'iuda 연기만 피우다; (*with anger*) sogŭro ssaida 속으로 쌓이다; (*with desire*) tŭlkkŭlt'a 들끓다
smooth 1 *adj surface, skin, sea* maekkŭrŏun 매끄러운; *ride* pudŭrŏun 부드러운; *transition* sunjoroun 순조로운; *pej: person* chinach'ige yejŏl parŭn 지나치게 예절 바른 **2** *v/t hair* ssŭdadŭmda 쓰다듬다
♦**smooth down** (*with sandpaper etc*) pudŭrŏpkke mandŭlda 부드럽게 만들다
♦**smooth out** *paper, cloth* p'yŏda 펴다
♦**smooth over**: ***smooth things over*** wŏnmanhage haegyŏrhada 원만하게 해결하다
smother *flames* tŏp'ŏ kkŭda 덮어 끄다; *person* chilsshik shik'ida 질식 시키다; ***~ X with kisses*** Xege k'isŭrŭl p'ŏbut-tta X에게 키스를 퍼붓다
smudge 1 *n* ŏlluk 얼룩 **2** *v/t* tŏrŏp'ida 더럽히다
smug chal nan ch'ehanŭn 잘 난 체하는
smuggle *v/t* milssuhada 밀수하다
smuggler milssuŏptcha 밀수업자
smuggling milssu 밀수
smutty *joke* ŭmnanhan 음란한
snack *n* kanshik 간식
snack bar kani shikttang 간이 식당
snag (*problem*) ttŭt'aji anŭn chang-ae 뜻하지 않은 장애
snail talp'aeng-i 달팽이
snake *n* paem 뱀
snap 1 *n* ttak'anŭn sori 딱하는 소리; PHOT sŭnaep sajin 스냅 사진 **2** *v/t* (*break*) purŏttŭrida 부러뜨리다; (*say sharply*) ttakttak-kkŏrida 딱딱거리다 **3** *v/i* (*break*) purŏjida 부러지다 **4** *adj decision, judgment* sunshik-kkanŭi 순식간의
♦**snap up** *bargain* ŏllŭn sada 얼른 사다
snappy *person, mood* sŏnggŭp'an 성급한; *decision, response* minch'ŏp'an 민첩한; (*elegant*) uahan 우아한
snapshot sŭnaep sajin 스냅 사진
snarl 1 *n* (*of dog*) ŭrŭrŏnggŏrim 으르렁거림 **2** *v/i* ŭrŭrŏnggŏrida

으르렁거리다
snatch 1 *v/t* chabach'aeda 잡아채다; (*steal*) humch'ida 훔치다; (*kidnap*) yugoehada 유괴하다 **2** *v/i* chabach'aeda 잡아채다
snazzy seryŏndoen 세련된
sneak 1 *v/t* (*remove*, *steal*) sŭltchŏk kajyŏgada 슬쩍 가져가다; ~ ***a glance at*** kyŏnnunjirhada 곁눈질하다 **2** *v/i*: ~ ***into the room / out of the room*** sŭlgŭmŏni pang-ŭro tŭrŏgada / pang-esŏ nagada 슬그머니 방으로 들어가다 / 방에서 나가다
sneakers undonghwa 운동화
sneaking: ***have a ~ suspicion that ...*** ...ranŭn ŭishimŭl ŭn-gŭnhi kajida ...라는 의심을 은근히 가지다
sneaky F (*crafty*) kyomyohan 교묘한
sneer 1 *n* piusŭm 비웃음 **2** *v/i* piut-tta 비웃다
sneeze 1 *n* chaech'aegi 재채기 **2** *v/i* chaech'aegihada 재채기하다
sniff 1 *v/i* (*to clear nose*) k'orŭl hultchŏk-kkŏrida 코를 훌쩍거리다; (*to catch scent*) k'orŭl k'ŭngk'ŭnggŏrida 코를 킁킁거리다 **2** *v/t* (*smell*) k'oro tŭrishwida 코로 들이쉬다
sniper chŏgyŏkppyŏng 저격병
snitch F **1** *n* (*telltale*) kojajiltchaeng-i 고자질쟁이 **2** *v/i* kojajirhada 고자질하다
snob songmul 속물
snobbish songmurŭi 속물의
snooker tanggu 당구
♦**snoop around** kiutkkŏrimyŏ toradanida 기웃거리며 돌아다니다
snooty kŏmanhan 거만한
snooze 1 *n* cholgi 졸기; ***have a ~*** cholda 졸다 **2** *v/i* cholda 졸다
snore *v/i* k'o kolda 코 골다
snoring *n* k'o kolgi 코 골기
snorkel sŭnok'ŭl 스노클
snort *v/i* (*of animal*) k'otkkimŭl naeppumtta 콧김을 내뿜다; (*of person: disdainfully*) k'otppanggwi kkwida 콧방귀 뀌다
snout (*of pig*) chudung-i 주둥이
snow 1 *n* nun 눈 **2** *v/i* nuni naerida 눈이 내리다
♦**snow under**: ***be snowed under with ...*** ...(ŭ)ro apttodanghada ...(으)로 압도당하다
snowball *n* nunttŏng-i 눈덩이; **snowbound** nune katch'in 눈에 갇힌; **snow chains** MOT sŭnou ch'ein 스노우 체인; **snowdrift** ssain nundŏmi 쌓인 눈더미; **snowdrop** anemone 아네모네; **snowflake** nunsong-i 눈송이; **snowman** nunssaram 눈사람; **snowplow** chesŏlgi 제설기; **snowstorm** nunbora 눈보라
snowy *weather* nuni onŭn 눈이 오는; *roads*, *hills* nuni ssain 눈이 쌓인
snub 1 *n* naengdae 냉대 **2** *v/t* naengdaehada 냉대하다
snub-nosed chumŏk k'oŭi 주먹코의
snug anŭk'an 아늑한; (*tight-fitting*) kkok mannŭn 꼭 맞는
♦**snuggle down** p'ogŭnhage momŭl mut-tta 포근하게 몸을 묻다
♦**snuggle up to** ...ŭl / rŭl kkŭrŏ antta ...을 / 를 끌어 안다
so 1 *adv* nŏmu 너무; ~ ***hot / cold*** nŏmu tŏun / ch'uun 너무 더운 / 추운; ***not ~ much*** nŏmu manch'i ank'e 너무 많지 않게; ~ ***much better / easier*** hwŏlsshin tŏ choŭn / shwiun 훨씬 더 좋은 / 쉬운; ***eat / drink ~ much*** nŏmu mani mŏktta / mashida 너무 많이 먹다 / 마시다; ***I miss you ~*** nega koengjanghi pogo shiptta 네가 굉장히 보고 싶다; ~ ***am I / do I*** nado kŭraeyo / kŭrŏk'e haeyo 나도 그래요 / 그렇게 해요; ~ ***is she / does she*** kŭ yŏjado kŭraeyo / kŭrŏk'e haeyo 그 여자도 그래요 / 그렇게 해요; ***and ~ on*** kit'a tŭngdŭng 기타 등등; ~ ***what?*** kŭraesŏ ŏtchaet-ttanŭn kŏya? 그래서 어쨌다는 거야? **2** *pron*: ***I hope ~ / think ~*** kŭrŏk'e toegil paramnida / kŭrŏk'e saenggak'amnida 그렇게 되길 바랍니다 / 그렇게 생각합니다; ***you didn't tell me - I did ~*** nahant'e marhaji anassŏ - ani, marhaessŏ 나한테 말하지 않았어 - 아니, 말했어; ***50 or ~*** oship chŏngdo 오십 정도 **3** *conj* (*for that reason*)

kŭgŏsŭro inhaesŏ 그것으로 인해서; (*in order that*) kŭraesŏ 그래서; ***and ~ I missed the train*** kŭraesŏ nanŭn kich'arŭl notch'ŏt-tta 그래서 나는 기차를 놓쳤다; ~ (***that***) ***I could come too*** kŭrŏk'e haesŏ na yŏkssi ol su itssŏtta 그렇게 해서 나 역시 올 수 있었다
soak *v/t* (*steep*) tamgŭda 담그다; (*of water, rain*) chŏksshida 적시다
♦**soak up** *liquid* pparadŭrida 빨아들이다
soaked hŭmppŏk chŏjŭn 흠뻑 젖은
so-and-so F (*unknown person*) amugae 아무개; (*annoying person*) shirŭn nom 싫은 놈
soap *n* (*for washing*) pinu 비누
soap (opera) yŏnsok tŭrama 연속 드라마
soapy *water* pinuŭi 비누의
soar (*of rocket etc*) sosa orŭda 솟아 오르다; (*of prices*) ch'isot-tta 치솟다
sob 1 *n* hŭnŭkkim 흐느낌 **2** *v/i* hŭnŭkkyŏ ulda 흐느껴 울다
sober (*not drunk*) ch'wihaji anŭn 취하지 않은; (*serious*) chinjihan 진지한
♦**sober up** suri kkaeda 술이 깨다
so-called (*referred to as*) lago hanŭn kŏsŭn 라고 하는 것은; *pej* sowi 소위
soccer ch'uk-kku 축구
sociable sagyojŏgin 사교적인
social *adj* sahoeŭi 사회의; (*recreational*) ch'inmogŭi 친목의
socialism sahoejuŭi 사회주의
socialist 1 *adj* sahoejuŭijŏgin 사회주의적인 **2** *n* sahoejuŭija 사회주의자
socialize saramgwa sagwida 사람과 사귀다
social work sahoe saŏp 사회 사업
social worker sahoe saŏpkka 사회 사업가
society sahoe 사회; (*organization*) tanch'e 단체
sociology sahoehak 사회학
sock[1] (*for wearing*) yangmal 양말
sock[2] **1** *n* (*punch*) kangt'a 강타 **2** *v/t* (*punch*) sege ch'ida 세게 치다
socket ELEC sok'et 소켓; (*of eye*) angu 안구; (*of arm*) kwanjŏl 관절
soda (~ *water*) t'ansansu 탄산수; (*ice-cream* ~) k'ŭrimsoda 크림소다; (*soft drink*) ch'ŏngnyang ŭmnyo 청량 음료
sofa sop'a 소파
sofa bed sop'ashik ch'imdae 소파식 침대
soft *pillow, chair* p'ukssinhan 푹신한; *voice, music, skin, color* pudŭrŏun 부드러운; *light* onhwahan 온화한; (*lenient*) kwandaehan 관대한; ***have a ~ spot for*** …ŭl / rŭl koengjanghi choahada …을 / 를 굉장히 좋아하다
soft drink ch'ŏngnyang ŭmnyo 청량 음료
soften 1 *v/t* pudŭrŏpkke hada 부드럽게 하다, wanhwahada 완화하다 **2** *v/i* (*of butter, ice cream*) pudŭrŏwŏjida 부드러워지다
softly pudŭrŏpkke 부드럽게
software sop'ŭt'ŭweŏ 소프트웨어
soggy chŏjŭn 젖은; *pastry* sŏlguwŏjin 설구워진
soil 1 *n* (*earth*) hŭk 흙 **2** *v/t* tŏrŏp'ida 더럽히다
solar energy t'aeyang enŏji 태양 에너지
solar panel t'aeyang chŏnjip'an 태양 전지판
soldier kunin 군인
sole[1] *n* (*of foot, shoe*) padak 바닥
sole[2] *adj* tan hanaŭi 단 하나의
solely ojik 오직
solemn (*serious*) ŏmssuk'an 엄숙한
solid *adj* (*hard*) tandanhan 단단한; (*without holes*) kyŏn-gohan 견고한; *gold, silver* sun 순; (*sturdy*) t'ŭnt'ŭnhan 튼튼한; *evidence* hwakkohan 확고한; *support* kangnyŏk'an 강력한
solidarity tan-gyŏl 단결
solidify *v/i* kudŏjida 굳어지다
solitaire (*card game*) sollit'erŭ 솔리테르
solitary *life, activity* kodok'an 고독한; (*single*) tan hanaŭi 단 하나의
solitude kodok 고독
solo 1 *n* MUS (*of vocalist*) tokch'ang 독창; (*of instrumentalist*) toktchu 독주 **2** *adj* honjaŭi 혼자의
soloist (*vocalist*) tokch'angja 독창자;

(*instrumentalist*) toktchuja 독주자
soluble *substance* kayongssŏng-ŭi 가용성의; *problem* haegyŏrhal su innŭn 해결할 수 있는
solution haedap 해답; (*mixture*) honhap 혼합
solve p'ulda 풀다
solvent *adj* (*financially*) chibul nŭngnyŏgi innŭn 지불 능력이 있는
somber (*dark*) kŏmusŭrŭmhan 거무스름한; (*serious*) ch'imurhan 침울한
some 1 *adj* ŏttŏn 어떤, ŏlmaganŭi 얼마간의; ***~ people say that ...*** ŏttŏ saramdŭrŭn ... rago malhanda 어떤 사람들은 ... 라고 말한다; ***would you like ~ water / cookies?*** mul / kwaja chom tŭshigessŏyo? 물 / 과자 좀 드시겠어요? **2** *pron* (*people*) ŏttŏn saramdŭl 어떤 사람들; (*things*) ŏttŏn kŏt 어떤 것; ***~ of the group*** kŭrubŭi ŏttŏn idŭl 그룹의 어떤 이들; ***would you like ~?*** chom hashigessŏyo? 좀 하시겠어요?; ***give me ~*** chogŭm chuseyo 조금 주세요 **3** *adv* (*a bit*) chogŭm 조금; ***we'll have to wait ~*** urin chogŭm kidaryŏya hae 우린 조금 기다려야 해
somebody nugun-ga 누군가
someday ŏnjen-ga 언젠가
somehow (*by one means or another*) ŏttŏk'edŭnji 어떻게든지; (*for some unknown reason*) ŏtchŏnji 어쩐지
someone → ***somebody***
someplace → ***somewhere***
somersault 1 *n* chaeju nŏmkki 재주 넘기 **2** *v/i* chaeju nŏmtta 재주 넘다
something muŏshin-ga 무엇인가; ***would you like ~ to drink / eat?*** mashil / ŏgŭl kŏt chom hashigessŏyo? 마실 / 먹을 것 좀 하시겠어요?; ***is ~ wrong?*** muŏshi chalmot toeŏssŭmnikka? 무엇이 잘못 되었습니까?
sometime ŏnjen-ga 언젠가; ***~ last year*** changnyŏn ŏnjen-ga 작년 언젠가
sometimes ttaettaero 때때로
somewhere 1 *adv* ŏdin-gae 어딘가에 **2** *pron*: ***let's go ~ quiet*** ŏdi choyonghan kosŭro kapsshida 어디 조용한 곳으로 갑시다; ***is there ~ to park?*** ŏdie chuch'ahal koshi issŏyo? 어디 주차할 곳이 있어요?
son adŭl 아들
song norae 노래
songwriter chakssa chak-kkok-kka 작사 작곡가
son-in-law sawi 사위
son of a bitch F kaesaekki 개새끼
soon kot 곧; ***as ~ as*** ...haja maja ...하자 마자; ***as ~ as possible*** kanŭnghan han ppalli 가능한 한 빨리; ***~er or later*** choman-gan 조만간; ***the ~er the better*** pparŭmyŏn pparŭlssurok choayo 빠르면 빠를수록 좋아요
soot kŭŭrŭm 그을음
soothe chinjŏngshik'ida 진정시키다
sophisticated *person, tastes* seryŏndoen 세련된; *machine* chŏnggyohan 정교한
sophomore ihangnyŏn 이학년
soprano *n* sop'ŭrano 소프라노
sordid *affair, business* tŏrŏun 더러운
sore 1 *adj* (*painful*) ap'ŭn 아픈; F (*angry*) hwaga nan 화가 난; ***is it ~?*** ap'ayo? 아파요? **2** *n* sangch'ŏ 상처
sorrow *n* sulp'ŭm 슬픔
sorry (*sad*) *day* sŭlp'ŭn 슬픈; *sight* pulssanghan 불쌍한; **(*I'm*) ~** (*apologizing*) mianhae 미안해; (*polite*) mianhamnida 미안합니다; **(*I'm*) *~ but I can't help*** (*regretting*) mianhajiman, chega toul suga ŏmneyo 미안하지만, 제가 도울 수가 없네요; ***I will be ~ to leave Seoul*** Sŏurŭl ttŏnani yugamimnida 서울을 떠나니 유감입니다; ***I won't be ~ to go home*** chŏnŭn chibe kanŭn ke natkkessŏyo 저는 집에 가는 게 낫겠어요; ***I feel ~ for her*** kŭ yŏjaga andwaetkkunyo 그 여자가 안됐군요
sort 1 *n* chongnyu 종류; ***~ of ...*** F taso ... 다소 ...; ***is it finished? – ~ of*** F kkŭnnassŏyo? - kŭrŏndaeroyo 끝났어요? - 그런대로요 **2** *v/t* pullyuhada 분류하다; COMPUT kubunhada 구분하다
♦**sort out** *papers* karyŏnaeda 가려내다; *problem* haegyŏrhada 해결하다

so-so *adv* kŭjŏ kŭrŏn 그저 그런
soul REL yŏnghon 영혼; *fig* (*of a nation etc*) chŏngshin 정신; (*character*) t'ukssŏng 특성; (*person*) saram 사람
sound[1] *adj* (*sensible*) punbyŏl innŭn 분별 있는; (*healthy*) kŏn-ganghan 건강한; **~ *sleep*** sungmyŏn 숙면
sound[2] **1** *n* sori 소리 **2** *v/t* (*pronounce*) parŭmhada 발음하다; MED ch'ŏngjinhada 청진하다; **~ *one's horn*** kyŏngjŏgŭl ullida 경적을 울리다 **3** *v/i*: ***that ~s interesting*** chaemiissŭl kŏt kat'ayo 재미있을 것 같아요; ***that ~s like a good idea*** choŭn saenggak kat'ayo 좋은 생각 같아요; ***she ~ed unhappy*** kŭ yŏjanŭn purhaenghage tŭllyŏtta 그 여자는 불행하게 들렸다
sound card COMPUT saundŭ k'adŭ 사운드 카드
soundly *sleep* kip'i 깊이; *beaten* wanbyŏk'age 완벽하게
soundproof *adj* pang-ŭmŭi 방음의
soundtrack paegyŏng ŭmak 배경 음악
soup (*western*) sup'ŭ 수프; (*Korean*) kuk 국
soup bowl (*western*) sup'ŭ chŏpsshi 수프 접시; (*Korean*) kuk kŭrŭt 국 그릇
sour *adj apple* shin 신; *milk* sanghan 상한; *comment* shimsulgujŭn 심술궂은
source *n* wŏnch'ŏn 원천; (*of river*) suwŏnji 수원지; (*person*) chŏngbo chegongja 정보 제공자
south 1 *adj* namtchogŭi 남쪽의 **2** *n* namtchok 남쪽; (*of country*) namtchok chibang 남쪽 지방; ***to the ~ of*** ...ŭi namtchoge ...의 남쪽에 **3** *adv* namtchogŭro 남쪽으로
South Africa Namap'ŭrik'a 남아프리카; **South African 1** *adj* Namap'ŭrik'aŭi 남아프리카의 **2** *n* Namap'ŭrik'ain 남아프리카인; **South America** Nammi 남미; **South American 1** *adj* Nammiŭi 남미의 **2** *n* Nammiin 남미인; **southeast 1** *n* namdongtchok 남동쪽 **2** *adj* namdongtchogŭi 남동쪽의 **3** *adv* namdongtchogŭro 남동쪽으로; ***it's ~ of*** ...ŭi namdongtchoge it-tta ...의 남동쪽에 있다; **Southeast Asia** Tongnam Ashia 동남 아시아; **Southeast Asian** *adj* Tongnam Ashiaŭi 동남 아시아의; **southeastern** namdongtchogŭi 남동쪽의
southerly *adj* namhyang-ŭi 남향의
southern nambuŭi 남부의
South Korea Namhan 남한
South Korean 1 *adj* Namhanŭi 남한의 **2** *n* (*person*) Namhanin 남한인
southward *adv* namtchogŭro 남쪽으로
southwest 1 *n* namsŏtchok 남서쪽 **2** *adj* namsŏtchogŭi 남서쪽의 **3** *adv* namsŏtchogŭro 남서쪽으로; ***it's ~ of*** ...ŭi namsŏtchoge it-tta ...의 남서쪽에 있다
southwestern namsŏtchogŭi 남서쪽의
souvenir kinyŏmp'um 기념품
sovereign *adj state* tongnibŭi 독립의
sovereignty (*of state*) tongnipkkuk 독립국
Soviet Union Soryŏn 소련
sow[1] *n* (*female pig*) amt'waeji 암퇘지
sow[2] *v/t seeds* ppurida 뿌리다
soy bean k'ong 콩; **soy milk** tuyu 두유; **soy sauce** kanjang 간장
spa onch'ŏn 온천
space *n* (*atmosphere*) uju 우주; (*area*) pin k'an 빈 칸; (*room*) konggan 공간
♦**space out** iltchŏnghan kan-gyŏgŭl tuda 일정한 간격을 두다
spacebar COMPUT sŭp'eisŭ pa 스페이스 바; **spacecraft, spaceship** ujusŏn 우주선; **space shuttle** uju wangbokssŏn 우주 왕복선; **space station** uju chŏnggŏjang 우주 정거장; **spacesuit** ujubok 우주복
spacious tŭnŏlbŭn 드넓은
spade sap 삽; **~*s*** (*in card game*) sŭp'eidŭ 스페이드
Spain Sŭp'ein 스페인
span *v/t* (*in time, of bridge*) kŏlch'ida 걸치다
Spaniard Sŭp'ein saram 스페인 사람
Spanish 1 *adj* Sŭp'einŭi 스페인의 **2** *n* (*language*) Sŭp'einŏ 스페인어

spank sonppadagŭro ttaerida 손바닥으로 때리다
spare 1 *v/t money* pillida 빌리다; *time* naeda 내다; (*do without*) ŏpsshi chinaeda 없이 지내다; ***can you ~ the time?*** shiganŭl nael su issŏyo? 시간을 낼 수 있어요?; ***there were 5 to ~*** 5kaega nama issŏssŏyo 5개가 남아 있었어요 **2** *adj* yebiŭi 예비의 **3** *n* (*part*) yebip'um 예비품
spare ribs kalbi 갈비; **spare room** yebi pang 예비 방; **spare time** namnŭn shigan 남는 시간; **spare tire** MOT yebi t'aiŏ 예비 타이어; **spare wheel** yebi pak'wi 예비 바퀴
spark *n* pulkkot 불꽃
sparkle *v/i* pinnada 빛나다
sparkling wine shyamp'ein 샴페인
spark plug chŏmhwajŏn 점화전
sparrow ch'amsae 참새
sparse *vegetation* sanjaehanŭn 산재하는
sparsely: ***~ populated*** in-guga hŭibak'an 인구가 희박한
spatter *v/t mud*, *paint* t'wigida 튀기다
speak 1 *v/i* marhada 말하다; (*make a speech*) yŏnsŏrhada 연설하다; ***we're not ~ing (to each other)*** urinŭn sŏro maldo anhaeyo 우리는 서로 말도 안해요; ***~ing*** TELEC chŏndeyo 전데요 **2** *v/t foreign language* marhada 말하다; ***~ one's mind*** songmaŭmŭl t'ŏnot'a 속마음을 터놓다
♦**speak for** …ŭl / rŭl taep'yohada …을 / 를 대표하다
♦**speak out** kŏrikkimŏpsshi marhada 거리낌없이 말하다
♦**speak up** (*speak louder*) k'ŭn soriro marhada 큰 소리로 말하다
speaker (*at conference*) yŏnsŏltcha 연설자; (*orator*) ungbyŏn-ga 웅변가; (*of sound system*) sŭp'ik'ŏ 스피커
spearmint sŭp'iamint'ŭ 스피아민트
special t'ŭkppyŏrhan 특별한; (*particular*) t'ŭktchŏnghan 특정한
specialist chŏnmun-ga 전문가
specialize (*of company*) chŏnmunŭro hada 전문으로 하다; (*of student*) chŏn-gonghada 전공하다; ***~ in*** (*of company*) …ŭl / rŭl chŏnmunŭro hada …을 / 를 전문으로 하다; (*of student*) …ŭl / rŭl chŏn-gonghada …을 / 를 전공하다
specially → ***especially***
specialty chŏnmun 전문
species chong 종
specific t'ŭktchŏnghan 특정한
specifically t'ŭk'i 특히
specifications (*of machine etc*) myŏngsesŏ 명세서
specify myŏnggihada 명기하다
specimen (*of work*) kyŏnbon 견본; MED p'yobon 표본
speck (*of dust*, *soot*) chagŭn ŏlluk 작은 얼룩
spectacle (*impressive sight*) changgwan 장관
spectacular *adj* nunbushin 눈부신 *profit* kwalmok'al manhan 괄목할 만한
spectator kwan-gaek 관객
spectrum *fig* pŏmwi 범위
speculate *v/i* ch'uch'ŭk'ada 추측하다; FIN t'ugihada 투기하다
speculation ch'uch'ŭk 추측; FIN t'ŭgi 투기
speculator FIN t'ŭgiŏptcha 투기업자
speech (*address*) yŏnsŏl 연설; (*in play*) taesa 대사; (*ability to speak*) marhanŭn nŭngnyŏk 말하는 능력; (*way of speaking*) malt'u 말투
speechless hal marŭl irŭn 할 말을 잃은
speech defect ŏnŏ chang-ae 언어 장애; **speech therapist** ŏnŏ ch'iryo chŏnmun-ga 언어 치료 전문가; **speech writer** yŏnsŏlmun chakssŏngja 연설문 작성자
speed 1 *n* soktto 속도; ***at a ~ of 150 mph*** shisok 150mairŭi sokttoro 시속 150마일의 속도로 **2** *v/i* ppalli kada 빨리 가다; (*drive too quickly*) kwasok'ada 과속하다
♦**speed by** ppalli chinagada 빨리 지나가다
♦**speed up 1** *v/i* ppalli hada 빨리 하다 **2** *v/t* ppalli hage hada 빨리 하게 하다
speedboat k'waesoktchŏng 쾌속정
speedily pparŭge 빠르게
speeding *n* (*when driving*) kwasok 과속

speeding fine kwasok pŏlgŭm 과속 벌금
speed limit soktto chehan 속도 제한
speedometer sokttogye 속도계
speedy pparŭn 빠른
spell[1] *v/t & v/i* ch'ŏltchahada 철자하다
spell[2] *n* (*period of time*) kigan 기간
spellbound mabŏbe kŏllin 마법에 걸린; **spellcheck** COMPUT ch'ŏltcha hwagin 철자 확인; ***do a ~ on*** …ŭi ch'ŏltcharŭl hwaginhada …의 철자를 확인하다; **spellchecker** COMPUT ch'ŏltcha hwagin togu 철자 확인 도구
spelling ch'ŏltcha 철자
spend *money* ssŭda 쓰다; *time* ponaeda 보내다
spendthrift *adj* nangbibyŏgi shimhan 낭비벽이 심한
sperm chŏngja 정자; (*semen*) chŏngaek 정액
sperm bank chŏngja ŭnhaeng 정자 은행
sphere ku 구; *fig* punya 분야; ***~ of influence*** seryok-kkwŏn 세력권
spice *n* (*seasoning*) yangnyŏm 양념
spicy *food* maeun 매운
spider kŏmi 거미
spiderweb kŏmijul 거미줄
spike *n* ppyojuk'an kkŭt 뾰죽한 끝; (*on railings*) taemot 대못
spill 1 *v/t* ŏptchirŭda 엎지르다 **2** *v/i* ŏptchillŏjida 엎질러지다
spin[1] **1** *n* (*turn*) hoejŏn 회전 **2** *v/t* hoejŏnshik'ida 회전시키다 **3** *v/i* (*of wheel*) hoejŏnhada 회전하다; ***my head is ~ning*** moriga tol chigyŏng-iyeyo 머리가 돌 지경이예요
spin[2] *v/t wool, cotton* pangjŏk'ada 방적하다; *web* tchada 짜다
♦ **spin around** (*of person, car*) chaepparŭge tolda 재빠르게 돌다
♦ **spin out** kkŭlda 끌다
spinach shigŭmch'i 시금치
spinal ch'ŏkch'uŭi 척추의; *problem, defect* chungch'ujŏgin 중추적인
spinal column ch'ŏkch'u 척추
spin doctor taebyŏnin 대변인; **spin-dry** *v/t* t'alssuhada 탈수하다; **spin-dryer** t'alssugi 탈수기
spine ch'ŏkch'u 척추; (*of book*) tŭng 등; (*on plant, hedgehog*) kashi 가시
spineless (*cowardly*) kŏbi manŭn 겁이 많은
spin-off pusanmul 부산물
spiral 1 *n* nasŏnhyŏng-ŭi 나선형의 **2** *v/i* (*rise quickly*) kŭpssok'i orŭda 급속히 오르다
spiral staircase nasŏnhyŏng-ŭi ch'ŭnggye 나선형의 층계
spire ppyojokt'ap 뾰족탑
spirit *n* (*attitude*) chŏngshin 정신; (*soul*) yŏnghon 영혼; (*energy*) hwalgi 활기; (*courage*) yonggi 용기
spirited *performance* hwalbarhan 활발한
spirit level kip'o sujun-gi 기포 수준기
spirits[1] (*alcohol*) chŭngnyuhayŏ mandŭn sul 증류하여 만든 술
spirits[2] (*morale*) sagi 사기; ***be in good / poor ~*** kibuni chot'a / p'uri chugŏit-tta 기분이 좋다 / 풀이 죽어있다
spiritual *adj* chŏngshintchŏgin 정신적인
spiritualism shimnyŏngjuŭi 심령주의
spiritualist *n* shimnyŏngjuŭija 심령주의자
spit *v/i* (*of person*) ch'imŭl paet-tta 침을 뱉다; ***it's ~ting with rain*** posŭlbiga ogo it-tta 보슬비가 오고 있다
♦ **spit out** *food, liquid* naebaet-tta 내뱉다
spite *n* agŭi 악의; ***in ~ of*** pulguhago 불구하고
spiteful agŭi innŭn 악의 있는
spitting image: ***be the ~ of s.o.*** nuguwa ttok-kkat-tta 누구와 똑같다
splash 1 *n* (*noise*) mul t'winŭn sori 물 튀는 소리; (*small amount of liquid*) soryang 소량; ***a ~ of red / blue*** ppalgan / p'aran taejo saekssang 빨간 / 파란 대조 색상 **2** *v/t* t'wigida 튀기다 **3** *v/i* murŭl t'wigida 물을 튀기다; (*of water*) t'wida 튀다
♦ **splash down** (*of spacecraft*) susang ch'angnyuk'ada 수상 착륙하다
♦ **splash out 1** *v/t money* ssŭda 쓰다 **2** *v/i*: ***I splashed out on a round the world trip*** nanŭn segye iltchu hanŭnde tonŭl mani ssŏssŏyo 나는

세계 일주 하는데 돈을 많이 썼어요
splendid mŏtchin 멋진
splendor hwaryŏham 화려함
splint *n* MED pumok 부목
splinter 1 *n* kashi 가시 **2** *v/i* chogangnada 조각나다
splinter group punp'a 분파
split 1 *n* (*in wood*) tchogaejim 쪼개짐; (*in leather*) tchijŏjim 찢어짐; (*disagreement*) purhwa 불화; (*division, share*) mok 몫 **2** *v/t logs* tchogaeda 쪼개다; *leather* tchit-tta 찢다; (*cause disagreement in*) punyŏlsshik'ida 분열시키다; (*divide*) nanuda 나누다 **3** *v/i* (*of wood*) tchogaejida 쪼개지다; (*of leather*) tchijŏjida 찢어지다; (*disagree*) punyŏldoeda 분열되다
♦**split up** *v/i* (*of couple*) heŏjida 헤어지다
split personality PSYCH ijung inkkyŏk 이중 인격
splitting: ~ ***headache*** ppagaejinŭn tŭt'an tut'ong 빠개지는 듯한 두통
spoil *v/t* mangch'ida 망치다; *child* pŏrŭdŏpsshi mandŭlda 버릇없이 만들다
spoilsport F punwigi kkaenŭn saram 분위기 깨는 사람
spoilt *adj child* pŏrŭtŏmnŭn 버릇없는; ***be ~ for choice*** nŏmu manasŏ korŭl suga ŏptta 너무 많아서 고를 수가 없다
spoke (*of wheel*) sal 살
spokesman, spokesperson, spokeswoman taebyŏnin 대변인
sponge *n* sŭp'onji 스폰지
♦**sponge off** F pilbut'ŏ salda 빌붙어 살다
sponger F pilbut'ŏ sanŭn saram 빌붙어 사는 사람
sponsor 1 *n* (*for membership etc*) pojŭngin 보증인; (*for sports, cultural event*) huwŏnja 후원자 **2** *v/t* (*for membership etc*) pojŭnghada 보증하다; (*for sports, cultural event*) huwŏnhada 후원하다
sponsorship huwŏn 후원
spontaneous chabaltchŏgin 자발적인
spooky F mushimushihan 무시무시한
spool *n* (*for film*) ril 릴; (*for thread*) shilp'ae 실패
spoon *n* sutkkarak 숟가락; ***~ and chopsticks*** sujŏ 수저
spoonfeed *fig* chinach'ige pohohada 지나치게 보호하다
spoonful han sutkkarak 한 숟가락
sporadic sanbaltchŏgin 산발적인
sport *n* sŭp'och'ŭ 스포츠
sporting *event* undong-ŭi 운동의; (*fair, generous*) kwandaehan 관대한
sportscar sŭp'och'ŭ k'a 스포츠 카; **sportscoat** undong-yong chaek'it 운동용 재킷; **sports journalist** sŭp'och'ŭ kija 스포츠 기자; **sportsman** namja undongga 남자 운동가; **sports news** sŭp'och'ŭ nyusŭ 스포츠 뉴스; **sports page** sŭp'och'ŭran 스포츠란; **sportswoman** yŏja undongga 여자 운동가
sporty *person* sŭp'och'ŭrŭl choahanŭn 스포츠를 좋아하는; *clothes* sŭp'ot'ihan 스포티한
spot[1] (*pimple*) yŏdŭrŭm 여드름; (*from measles etc*) panjŏm 반점; (*part of pattern*) mulppang-ul munŭi 물방울 무늬
spot[2] (*place*) changso 장소; ***on the ~*** (*in the place in question*) hyŏnjang-esŏ 현장에서; (*immediately*) chŭksshi 즉시; ***put s.o. on the ~*** nugurŭl kollanhan ch'ŏjie not'a 누구를 곤란한 처지에 놓다
spot[3] *v/t* (*notice*) arach'aeda 알아채다; (*identify*) shikppyŏrhada 식별하다
spot check mujagwi ch'uch'ul kŏmsa 무작위 추출 검사; ***carry out spot checks*** mujagwiro kŏmsahada 무작위로 검사하다
spotless mŏnji han chŏm ŏmnŭn 먼지 한 점 없는
spotlight *n* sŭp'otŭrait'ŭ 스포트라이트
spotted *fabric* mulppang-ul munŭiŭi 물방울 무늬의
spotty (*with pimples*) yŏdŭrŭmi nan 여드름이 난
spouse *fml* paeuja 배우자
spout 1 *n* chudung-i 주둥이 **2** *v/i* (*of liquid*) punch'uldoeda 분출되다
sprain 1 *n* ppim 삠 **2** *v/t* ppida 삐다
sprawl *v/i* k'ŭn taetcharo ppŏt-tta 큰

대자로 뻗다; (*of city*) sabang-ŭro ppŏt-tta 사방으로 뻗다; ***send s.o. ~ing*** nugurŭl ttaeryŏ nup'ida 누구를 때려 눕히다
sprawling *city, suburbs* ppŏdŏnagago innŭn 뻗어나가고 있는
spray 1 *n* (*of sea water, from fountain*) mulbora 물보라; (*paint, for hair*) sŭp'ŭrei 스프레이 **2** *v/t* ppurida 뿌리다; ~ ***X with Y*** Xe Yŭl/rŭl ppurida X에 Y을/를 뿌리다
spraygun punmugi 분무기
spread 1 *n* (*of disease, etc*) manyŏn 만연; (*of religion*) pogŭp 보급; F (*big meal*) chanch'itssang 잔칫상 **2** *v/t* (*lay*) p'yŏlch'ida 펼치다; *butter, jam* parŭda 바르다; *news, rumor, disease* p'ŏttŭrida 퍼뜨리다; *arms, legs* pŏllida 벌리다 **3** *v/i* p'ŏjida 퍼지다; (*of butter*) pallajida 발라지다
spreadsheet COMPUT sŭp'ŭredŭshit'ŭ 스프레드시트
spree: ***go on a ~*** F shinnage surŭl mashimyŏ nolda 신나게 술을 마시며 놀다; ***go on a shopping ~*** hŭngch'ŏngmangch'ŏng shyop'ing-ŭl hada 흥청망청 쇼핑을 하다
sprightly wŏn-giwangsŏnghan 원기왕성한
spring[1] *n* (*season*) pom 봄
spring[2] *n* (*device*) yongsuch'ŏl 용수철
spring[3] **1** *n* (*jump*) ttwigi 뛰기; (*stream*) saem 샘 **2** *v/i* irŏsŏda 일어서다; ~ ***from*** ...esŏ pirot-ttoeda ...에서 비롯되다
springboard taibing tae 다이빙 대; **spring chicken**: ***she's no ~*** (*hum*) kŭnyŏnŭn kŭrŏk'e chŏmtchi anayo 그녀는 그렇게 젊지 않아요; **spring-cleaning** pommaji taech'ŏngso 봄맞이 대청소; **springtime** pomch'ŏl 봄철
springy *ground* t'ansŏng-i innŭn 탄성이 있는; *walk, mattress* t'allyŏgi innŭn 탄력이 있는
sprinkle *v/t* ppurida 뿌리다; ~ ***X with Y*** Xe Yŭl/rŭl ppurida X에 Y을/를 뿌리다
sprinkler (*for garden*) salssugi 살수기; (*in ceiling*) chadong sohwa changch'i 자동 소화 장치
sprint 1 *n* SP tan-gŏri yukssang kyŏnggi 단거리 육상 경기; (*for the bus etc*) chiltchu 질주 **2** *v/i* chiltchuhada 질주하다
sprinter SP tan-gŏri yukssang sŏnsu 단거리 육상 선수
sprout 1 *v/i* (*of seed*) t'ŭda 트다 **2** *n*: (***Brussels***) **~s** ssagyangbaech'u 싹양배추
spruce *adj* maepsshi innŭn 맵시 있는
spur *n fig* chagŭk 자극; ***on the ~ of the moment*** ch'ungdongtchŏgŭro 충동적으로
♦**spur on** (*encourage*) chagŭk'ada 자극하다
spurt 1 *n* (*in race*) punbal 분발; ***put on a ~*** soktto naeda 속도 내다 **2** *v/i* (*of liquid*) ppumŏjyŏ naoda 뿜어져 나오다
spy 1 *n* kanch'ŏp 간첩 **2** *v/i* kanch'ŏp norŭsŭl hada 간첩 노릇을 하다 **3** *v/t* yŏtppoda 엿보다
♦**spy on** kamshihada 감시하다
squabble 1 *n* maldat'um 말다툼 **2** *v/i* maldat'umhada 말다툼하다
squalid chijŏbunhan 지저분한
squalor nuch'uham 누추함
squander *money* nangbihada 낭비하다
square 1 *adj* (*in shape*) sagak'yŏng-ŭi 사각형의; ~ ***mile/yard*** p'yŏngbang mail/yadŭ 평방 마일/야드 **2** *n* (*shape*) sagak'yŏng 사각형; (*in town*) kwangjang 광장; (*in board game*) k'an 칸; MATH chegop 제곱; ***we're back to ~ one*** urinŭn wŏntchŏmŭro torawat-tta 우리는 원점으로 돌아왔다
square root chegopkkŭn 제곱근
squash[1] *n* (*vegetable*) hobak 호박
squash[2] *n* (*game*) sŭk'wŏshi 스쿼시
squash[3] *v/t* (*crush*) nullŏ tchigŭrŏttŭrida 눌러 찌그러뜨리다
squat 1 *adj* (*in shape*) ttangttalmak'an 땅딸막한 **2** *v/i* (*sit*) ungk'ŭrigo antta 웅크리고 앉다; (*illegally*) mudan kŏjuhada 무단 거주하다
squatter mudan kŏjuja 무단 거주자
squeak 1 *n* (*of mouse*) tchiktchk-kkŏrinŭn sori 찍찍거리는 소리; (*of

hinge) ppigok-kkŏrinŭn sori 삐걱거리는 소리 **2** *v/i* (*of mouse*) tchiktchk-kkŏrida 찍찍거리다; (*of hinge, shoes*) ppigŏk-kkŏrida 삐걱거리다

squeal 1 *n* kkaek-kkaek-kkŏrinŭn sori 깩깩거리는 소리 **2** *v/i* kkaek-kkaek-kkŏrida 깩깩거리다

squeamish mŏlmiga chal nanŭn 멀미가 잘 나는

squeeze 1 *n* (*of hand, shoulder*) kkwak chwim 꽉 쥠 **2** *v/t* (*press*) kkwak chwida 꽉 쥐다; (*remove juice from*) tchada 짜다

♦**squeeze in 1** *v/i* (*to a car etc*) kkwak kkiida 꽉 끼이다 **2** *v/t* kkiŏ nŏt'a 끼어 넣다

♦**squeeze up** *v/i* (*to make space*) mirŏ puch'ida 밀어 붙이다

squid ojing-ŏ 오징어

squint *n* sap'alnun 사팔눈

squirm (*wriggle*) pŏdunggŏrida 버둥거리다; (*in embarrassment*) pibi kkoda 비비 꼬다

squirrel *n* taramjwi 다람쥐

squirt 1 *v/t* ppumŏnaeda 뿜어내다 **2** *n pej* F p'unnaegi 풋내기

stab 1 *n* F shido 시도 **2** *v/t person* tchirŭda 찌르다

stability anjŏngssŏng 안정성

stabilize 1 *v/t prices, currency* anjŏngshik'ida 안정시키다; *boat* kojŏngshik'ida 고정시키다 **2** *v/i* (*of prices etc*) anjŏngdoeda 안정되다

stable[1] *n* (*for horses*) magutkkan 마구간

stable[2] *adj* anjŏngdoen 안정된

stack 1 *n* (*pile*) tŏmi 더미; (*smoke~*) kulttuk 굴뚝 **2** *v/t* ssaaollida 쌓아올리다

stadium kyŏnggijang 경기장

staff *n* (*employees*) chigwŏn 직원; (*teachers*) kyosa 교사

staffroom (*in school*) kyomushil 교무실

stage[1] (*in life, project etc*) tan-gye 단계; (*of journey*) yŏjŏng 여정

stage[2] **1** *n* THEA mudae 무대; ***go on the ~*** paeuga toeda 배우가 되다 **2** *v/t play* kong-yŏnhada 공연하다; *demonstration, strike* pŏrida 벌이다

stage door punjangshil ipkku 분장실 입구

stagger 1 *v/i* hwich'ŏnggŏrida 휘청거리다 **2** *v/t* (*amaze*) kkamtchak nollage hada 깜짝 놀라게 하다; *coffee breaks etc* sŏro ŏtkkallige hada 서로 엇갈리게 하다

staggering kiga mak'inŭn 기가 막히는

stagnant *water* koeŏ innŭn 괴어 있는; *economy* ch'imch'ehan 침체한

stagnate (*of person, mind*) ch'imch'ehada 침체하다

stag party ch'onggak p'at'i 총각 파티

stain 1 *n* (*dirty mark*) ŏlluk 얼룩; (*for wood*) ch'akssaek 착색 **2** *v/t* (*dirty*) tŏrŏp'ida 더럽히다; *wood* ch'akssaek'ada 착색하다 **3** *v/i* (*of wine etc*) ŏllugi saenggida 얼룩이 생기다; (*of fabric*) tŏrŏwŏjida 더러워지다

stained glass sŭt'eindŭ kŭllasŭ 스테인드 글라스

stainless steel 1 *n* sŭt'einlesŭ 스테인레스 **2** *adj* sŭt'einlesŭŭi 스테인레스의

stain remover ŏlluk chegŏje 얼룩 제거제

stair kyedan 계단; ***the ~s*** ch'ŭnggye 층계

staircase ch'ŭnggye 층계

stake 1 *n* (*of wood*) malttuk 말뚝; (*when gambling*) p'antton 판돈; (*investment*) t'uja 투자; ***be at ~*** wigie ch'ŏhada 위기에 처하다 **2** *v/t tree* malttugŭro chijihada 말뚝으로 지지하다; *money* kŏlda 걸다; *person* kyŏngjejŏgŭro wŏnjohada 경제적으로 원조하다

stale *bread* shinsŏnhaji anŭn 신선하지 않은; *air* k'wik'wihan 퀴퀴한; *news* chinbuhan 진부한

stalemate (*in chess*) suga modu mak'im 수가 모두 막힘; *fig* chint'oeyangnan 진퇴양난

stalk[1] *n* (*of fruit, plant*) chulgi 줄기

stalk[2] *v/t animal* ch'ujŏk'ada 추적하다; *person* twirŭl paltta 뒤를 밟다

stalker (*of person*) sŭt'ok'ŏ 스토커

stall[1] *n* (*at market*) chinyŏlttae 진열대;

(*for cow, horse*) han k'an 한 칸
stall[2] **1** *v/i* (*of vehicle, plane, engine*) mŏmch'uda 멈추다; (*play for time*) kyomyohage shiganŭl kkŭlda 교묘하게 시간을 끌다 **2** *v/t engine* kkŭda 끄다; *people* chiyŏnshik'ida 지연시키다
stallion chongma 종마
stalwart *adj* tŭndŭnhan 든든한
stamina ch'eryŏk 체력
stammer 1 *n* maldŏdŭm 말더듬 **2** *v/i* marŭl tŏdŭmtta 말을 더듬다
stamp[1] **1** *n* (*for letter*) up'yo 우표; (*device*) tojang 도장; (*mark made with device*) tojang chaguk 도장 자국 **2** *v/t letter* up'yo puch'ida 우표 붙이다; *document, passport* tojang tchiktta 도장 찍다
stamp[2] *v/t*: *~ one's feet* parŭl kurŭda 발을 구르다
♦**stamp out** (*eradicate*) kŭnjŏrhada 근절하다
stampede *n* (*of cattle etc*) ururu taranam 우루루 달아남; (*of people*) swaedo 쇄도
stance (*position*) iptchang 입장
stand 1 *n* (*at exhibition*) kwallamsŏk 관람석; (*witness ~*) chŭng-insŏk 증인석; (*support, base*) patch'imttae 받침대; ***take the ~*** LAW chŭnggŏrŭl chech'urhada 증거를 제출하다 **2** *v/i* (*be situated: of person*) sŏda 서다; (*of object, building*) wich'ihada 위치하다; (*as opposed to sit*) sŏda 서다; (*rise*) irŏsŏda 일어서다; ***~ still*** umjigiji ank'o sŏ it-tta 움직이지 않고 서 있다; ***where do I ~ with you?*** urinŭn ŏttŏn kwan-gyein-gayo? 우리는 어떤 관계인가요? **3** *v/t* (*tolerate*) ch'amtta 참다; (*put*) not'a 놓다; ***you don't ~ a chance*** tangshinhant'enŭn kamang ŏpssŏyo 당신한테는 가망 없어요; ***~ one's ground*** mullŏsŏji ant'a 물러서지 않다
♦**stand back** mullŏna it-tta 물러나 있다
♦**stand by 1** *v/i* (*not take action*) panggwanhada 방관하다; (*be ready*) taegihada 대기하다 **2** *v/t person* chijihada 지지하다; *decision* kojip'ada 고집하다
♦**stand down** (*withdraw*) mullŏnada 물러나다
♦**stand for** (*tolerate*) ch'amtta 참다; (*represent*) p'yoshihada 표시하다
♦**stand in for** taeshinhada 대신하다
♦**stand out** nune ttŭida 눈에 띄다
♦**stand up 1** *v/i* irŏsŏda 일어서다 **2** *v/t* F param mach'ida 바람 맞히다
♦**stand up for** pang-ŏhada 방어하다
♦**stand up to** matssŏda 맞서다
standard 1 *adj* (*usual*) pot'ong-ŭi 보통의 **2** *n* (*level of excellence*) kijun 기준; (*expectation*) kidae 기대; TECH p'yojun 표준; ***be up to ~*** p'yojune tarhada 표준에 달하다; ***not be up to ~*** p'yojune midarhada 표준에 미달하다
standardize *v/t* kyugyŏk'wahada 규격화하다
standard of living saenghwal sujun 생활 수준
standby: ***on ~*** (*for flight*) taegihago innŭn 대기하고 있는
standby passenger t'apssŭng taegija 탑승 대기자
standing *n* (*in society etc*) chiwi 지위; (*repute*) myŏngsŏng 명성; ***a musician of some ~*** p'yŏngp'ani choŭn ŭmak-kka 평판이 좋은 음악가
standing room ipssŏk 입석
standoffish ssalssarhan 쌀쌀한;
standpoint kwantchŏm 관점;
standstill: ***be at a ~*** mŏmch'un 멈춘; ***bring to a ~*** mŏmch'uge hada 멈추게 하다
staple[1] *n* (*foodstuff*) chuyo shikp'um 주요 식품
staple[2] **1** *n* (*fastener*) hoch'ik'isŭ al 호치키스 알 **2** *v/t* hoch'ik'isŭro tchiktta 호치키스로 찍다
staple diet chuyoshikttan 주요식단
staple gun sŭt'eip'ŭl kŏn 스테이플 건
stapler hoch'ik'isŭ 호치키스
star 1 *n* pyŏl 별; *fig* sŭt'a 스타 **2** *v/t* (*of movie*) chuyŏnŭro hada 주연으로 하다 **3** *v/i* (*in movie*) chuyŏnhada 주연하다
starboard *adj* uch'ŭgŭi 우측의
stare 1 *n* ppanhi ch'yŏdabom 빤히 쳐다봄 **2** *v/i* ppanhi ch'yŏdaboda

빤히 쳐다본다; **~ at** …ŭl / rŭl ppanhi ch'yŏdaboda …을 / 를 빤히 쳐다보다
starfish pulgasari 불가사리
stark 1 *adj landscape* sangmak'an 삭막한; *reminder*, *contrast etc* chŏngnarahan 적나라한 **2** *adv*: **~ naked** holttak pŏsŭn 홀딱 벗은
starling tchirŭregi 찌르레기
Stars and Stripes sŏngjogi 성조기
start 1 *n* shijak 시작; ***get off to a good / bad ~*** (*in race*) choŭn / nappŭn ch'ulbarŭl hada 좋은 / 나쁜 출발을 하다; (*in marriage*, *career*) choŭn / nappŭn shijagŭl hada 좋은 / 나쁜 시작을 하다; ***from the ~*** ch'ŏŭmbut'ŏ 처음부터; ***well, it's a ~!*** kŭraedo shijagŭn han semijiyo! 그래도 시작은 한 셈이지요! **2** *v/i* shijakdoeda 시작되다; (*set off*) ch'ulbarhada 출발하다; (*of engine*, *car*) shidongdoeda 시동되다; ***~ing from tomorrow*** naeilbut'ŏ shijak'aesŏ 내일부터 시작해서 **3** *v/t* shijak'ada 시작하다; *engine*, *car* shidongshik'ida 시동시키다; *business* seuda 세우다; ***~ to do X*** Xhagi shijak'ada X하기 시작하다
starter (*part of meal*) ep'it'aijyŏ 에피타이저; (*of car*) shidongjangch'i 시동장치
starting point (*for walk*) ch'ulbaltchŏm 출발점; (*for discussion*, *thesis*) kitchŏm 기점
starting salary ch'ŏtwŏlgŭp 첫 월급
startle kkamtchak nollage hada 깜짝 놀라게 하다
startling kkamtchak nollage hanŭn 깜짝 놀라게 하는
starvation kia 기아
starve *v/i* kumjurida 굶주리다; ***~ to death*** kulmŏchuktta 굶어 죽다; ***I'm starving*** F pae kop'a chukkessŏyo 배 고파 죽겠어요
state[1] 1 *n* (*of car*, *house etc*) sangt'ae 상태; (*part of country*) chu 주; (*country*) kuk-kka 국가; ***the States*** Miguk 미국 **2** *adj capital etc* chu(rib)ŭi 주(립)의; *banquet etc* kongshiktchŏgin 공식적인
state[2] *v/t* kongshiktchŏguro parŏnhada 공식적으로 발언하다
State Department (Mi)Kungmusŏng (미)국무성
statement (*to police*) chinsul 진술; (*announcement*) palp'yo 발표; (*bank ~*) (ŭnhaeng) t'ongjang (은행) 통장
state of emergency pisangsat'ae 비상사태
state-of-the-art *adj* ch'oech'ŏmdanŭi 최첨단의
statesman chŏngch'iga 정치가
state trooper churip kyŏngch'al 주립 경찰
state visit kongsshik pangmun 공식 방문
static (electricity) chŏngjŏn-gi 정전기
station 1 *n* RAIL yŏk 역; RAD, TV pangsongguk 방송국 **2** *v/t guard etc* paech'ihada 배치하다; ***be ~ed at*** (*of soldier*) …e paech'idoeda …에 배치되다
stationary chŏngjihan 정지한
stationery munbanggu 문방구
stationery store munbanggujŏm 문방구점
station wagon waegŏn 왜건
statistical t'onggyeŭi 통계의
statistically t'onggyejŏguro 통계적으로
statistics (*science*) t'onggyehak 통계학; (*figures*) t'onggye 통계
statue sang 상
Statue of Liberty chayuŭi yŏshinsang 자유의 여신상
status chiwi 지위
status symbol shinbunŭi sangjing 신분의 상징
statute pŏmnyŏng 법령
staunch *adj* ch'ungshirhan 충실한
stay 1 *n* ch'eryu 체류 **2** *v/i* (*in a place*) mŏmurŭda 머무르다; (*in a condition*) yujihada 유지하다; ***~ in a hotel*** hot'ere muktta 호텔에 묵다; ***~ right there!*** kŏgisŏ kkomtchaktto hajima! 거기서 꼼짝도 하지마!; ***~ put*** ŏdiro ka pŏriji ant'a 어디로 가 버리지 않다
♦**stay away** ttŏrŏjyŏ it-tta 떨어져 있다
♦**stay away from** …put'ŏ ttŏrŏjyŏ it-

tta …부터 떨어져 있다
♦**stay behind** twie namtta 뒤에 남다
♦**stay up** (*not go to bed*) (chaji ank'o) irŏna it-tta (자지 않고) 일어나 있다
steadily *improve etc* chŏmch'ajŏgŭro 점차적으로
steady 1 *adj* (*not shaking*) ttŏlliji annŭn 떨리지 않는; (*regular*) iltchŏnghan 일정한; (*continuous*) kkŭnimŏmnŭn 끊임없는 **2** *adv*: ***be going ~*** iltchŏnghage sagwida 일정하게 사귀다; ***~ on!*** ch'imch'ak'age hae! 침착하게 해! **3** *v/t* anjŏngshik'ida 안정시키다
steak sŭt'eik'ŭ 스테이크
steal 1 *v/t money etc* humch'ida 훔치다 **2** *v/i* (*be a thief*) toduktchirhada 도둑질하다; ***~ into / out of*** (*move quietly*) salgŭmŏni tŭrŏgada / ppajyŏnagada 살그머니 들어가다 / 빠져나가다
stealthy mollae hanŭn 몰래 하는
steam 1 *n* kim 김 **2** *v/t food* tchida 찌다
♦**steam up 1** *v/i* (*of window*) kimi sŏrida 김이 서리다 **2** *v/t*: ***be steamed up*** F yŏl pat-tta 열 받다
steamer (*for cooking*) tchimt'ong 찜통
steam iron sŭt'im tarimi 스팀 다리미
steel 1 *n* kangch'ŏl 강철 **2** *adj* kangch'ŏllo mandŭn 강철로 만든
steep[1] *adj hill etc* kap'arŭn 가파른; F *prices* pissan 비싼
steep[2] *v/t* (*soak*) tamgŭda 담그다
steeplechase (*in athletics*) chang-aemul kyŏnggi 장애물 경기
steer[1] *n* (*animal*) kŏsehan hwangso 거세한 황소
steer[2] *v/t car, boat* chojonghada 조종하다; *person, conversation* ikkŭlda 이끌다
steering (*of motor vehicle*) sŭt'ŏring 스터링
steering wheel haendŭl 핸들
stem[1] *n* (*of plant*) chulgi 줄기; (*of glass*) sonjabi 손잡이; (*of pipe*) tae 대; (*of word*) ŏgan 어간
♦**stem from** …esŏ yuraehada …에서 유래하다
stem[2] *v/t* (*block*) ŏktchehada 억제하다
stemware sultchan 술잔
stench akch'wi 악취
step 1 *n* (*pace*) kŏrŭm 걸음; (*stair*) kyedan 계단; (*measure*) choch'i 조치; ***~ by ~*** ch'arye ch'aryero 차례 차례로 **2** *v/i* han-gŏrŭm naedidida 한걸음 내디디다; ***don't ~ on it*** paltchi mara 밟지 마라
♦**step down** (*from post etc*) mullŏnada 물러나다
♦**step out** *v/i* (*go out for a short time*) chamkkan nagada 잠깐 나가다
♦**step up** *v/t* (*increase*) chŭnggashik'ida 증가시키다
stepbrother ŭibut'yŏngje 의붓형제; **stepdaughter** ŭibut-ttal 의붓딸; **stepfather** kyebu 계부; **stepladder** palp'an tallin sadari 발판 달린 사다리; **stepmother** kyemo 계모
stepping stone tidimttol 디딤돌; *fig* palp'an 발판
stepsister ŭibut-chamae 의붓자매
stepson ŭibudadŭl 의붓아들
stereo *n* (*sound system*) sŭt'ereo 스테레오
stereotype *n* chŏnhyŏng 전형
sterile *woman, man* purimŭi 불임의; *equipment* salgyundoen 살균된
sterilize *woman* purimk'ehada 불임케 하다; *equipment* sodok'ada 소독하다
sterling *n* FIN p'aundŭ 파운드
stern *adj* ŏmkkyŏk'an 엄격한
steroids sŭt'eroidŭ 스테로이드
stethoscope ch'ŏngjin-gi 청진기
Stetson® k'auboi moja 카우보이 모자
stevedore pudu nodongja 부두 노동자
stew *n* sŭt'yu 스튜
steward (*on plane, ship*) samujang 사무장
stewardess (*on plane, ship*) sŭt'yuŏdisŭ 스튜어디스
stick[1] *n* (*wood*) makttaegi 막대기; (*of policeman*) konbong 곤봉; (*walking ~*) chip'ang-i 지팡이; ***the ~s*** F tumesankkol 두메산골
stick[2] **1** *v/t* (*with adhesive*) puch'ida 붙이다; F (*put*) nŏt'a 넣다 **2** *v/i* (*jam*)

tallabut-tta 달라붙다; (*adhere*) put-tta 붙다
♦**stick around** F mŏmullŏ it-tta 머물러 있다
♦**stick by** F ...ege ch'ungshirhada ...에게 충실하다
♦**stick out** *v/i* (*protrude*) pulssuk naoda 불쑥 나오다; (*be noticeable*) nune ttŭida 눈에 띄다
♦**stick to** (*adhere to*) ...e tallabut-tta ...에 달라붙다; *plan etc* ...e ch'ungshirhada ...에 충실하다; *path* chal ttaragada 잘 따라가다; *story* kosuhada 고수하다; F (*follow*) ttarŭda 따르다
♦**stick together** F kach'i put'ŏit-tta 같이 붙어있다
♦**stick up** *poster* puch'ida 붙이다
♦**stick up for** onghohada 옹호하다
sticker sŭt'ik'ŏ 스티커
sticking plaster panch'anggo 반창고
stick-in-the-mud kut'ae-ŭiyŏnhan saram 구태의연한 사람
sticky *hands*, *surface* kkŭnjŏk-kkŏrinŭn 끈적거리는; *label* punnŭn 붙는
sticky rice ch'apssal 찹쌀
stiff 1 *adj brush*, *leather* ppŏtppŏt'an 뻣뻣한; *muscle*, *body* ppŏgŭnhan 뻐근한; *mixture*, *paste* toen 된; (*in manner*) ttakttak'an 딱딱한; *drink* tok'an 독한; *competition* shimhan 심한; *penalty* kwajunghan 과중한 **2** *adv*: ***be scared ~*** F koengjanghi kŏbe chillida 굉장히 겁에 질리다; ***be bored ~*** F koengjanghi chiruhaejida 굉장히 지루해지다
stiffen *v/i* ttattak'aejida 딱딱해지다
♦**stiffen up** (*of muscle*) ppŏtppŏt'age hada 뻣뻣하게 하다
stifle *v/t yawn*, *laugh* kkuk ch'amtta 꾹 참다; *criticism*, *debate* ŏktchehada 억제하다
stifling tapttap'an 답답한
stigma omyŏng 오명
stilettos ppyojok kudu 뾰족 구두
still[1] **1** *adj* koyohan 고요한 **2** *adv* kamanhi 가만히; ***keep ~!*** kamanhi issŏ! 가만히 있어!; ***stand ~!*** kamanhi sŏ issŏ 가만히 서 있어!
still[2] *adv* (*yet*) ajiktto 아직도; (*nevertheless*) kŭraedo 그래도; ***do you ~ want it?*** ajiktto kŭgŏsŭl kajigo ship'ŏyo? 아직도 그것을 가지고 싶어요?; ***she ~ hasn't finished*** kŭnyŏnŭn ajiktto kkŭnnaeji anassŏyo 그녀는 아직도 끝내지 않았어요; ***she might ~ come*** kŭnyŏnŭn kŭraedo oltchi morŭmnida 그녀는 그래도 올지 모릅니다; ***they are ~ my parents*** kŭdŭrŭn kŭraedo na-ŭi pumonimimnida 그들은 그래도 나의 부모님입니다; ***~ more*** tŏ-uk tŏ 더욱 더
stillborn: ***be ~*** sasandoeda 사산되다
stilted ttakttak'an 딱딱한
stilts (*under house*) kidung 기둥
stimulant chakŭktche 자극제
stimulate *person*, *growth*, *demand* chagŭk'ada 자극하다
stimulating chagŭktchŏgin 자극적인
stimulation hŭngbun 흥분
stimulus (*incentive*) chagŭk 자극
sting 1 *n* (*from bee*, *jellyfish*) ssoin sangch'ŏ 쏘인 상처 **2** *v/t* (*of bee*, *jellyfish*) ssoda 쏘다 **3** *v/i* (*of eyes*, *scratch*) ttakkŭmgŏrida 따끔거리다
stinging *remark*, *criticism* shillarhan 신랄한
stingy F insaek'an 인색한
stink 1 *n* akch'wi 악취; F (*fuss*) malssŏng 말썽; ***make a ~*** F malssŏng-ŭl purida 말썽을 부리다 **2** *v/i* koyak'an naemsaega nada 고약한 냄새가 나다; F (*be very bad*) hyŏngp'yŏnŏpsshi nappŭda 형편없이 나쁘다
stint *n* (*period*) iltchŏng kigan 일정 기간
♦**stint on** ...ŭl / rŭl akkida ...을 / 를 아끼다
stipulate kyujŏnghada 규정하다
stipulation kyujŏng 규정
stir 1 *n*: ***give the soup a ~*** kugŭl hwijŏt-tta 국을 휘젓다; ***cause a ~*** *fig* sodong-ŭl irŭk'ida 소동을 일으키다 **2** *v/t* hwijŏt-tta 휘젓다 **3** *v/i* (*of sleeping person*) twich'ŏgida 뒤척이다
♦**stir up** *crowd* sŏndonghada 선동하다; *bad memories* irŭk'ida

일으키다
stir-crazy: ***be ~*** F mŏriga saltchak ton 머리가 살짝 돈
stir-fry *v/t* poktta 볶다
stirring *music*, *speech* changk'waehan 장쾌한
stitch 1 *n* (*in sewing*) panŭlttam 바늘땀; (*in knitting*) k'o 코; ***~es*** MED panŭl 바늘; ***take the ~es out*** MED shirŭl ppoptta 실을 뽑다; ***have a ~*** ssushida 쑤시다 **2** *v/t sew* kkwemaeda 꿰매다
♦**stitch up** *wound* kkwemaeda 꿰매다
stitching (*stitches*) panŭjil 바느질
stock 1 *n* (*reserves*) chŏjang 저장; (COM: *of store*) sangp'um 상품; (*animals*) kach'uk 가축; FIN chushik 주식; (*ingredient*) sup'ŭ chaeryo 수프 재료; ***in ~*** maejang-e innŭn 매장에 있는; ***out of ~*** (*of products*) maejindoen 매진된; ***we are out of ~*** ta p'allyŏnnŭndeyo 다 팔렸는데요; ***take ~*** kŏmt'ohada 검토하다 **2** *v/t* COM katch'uda 갖추다
♦**stock up on** tŭryŏnot'a 들여놓다
stockbroker chushik chungmae-in 주식 중매인; **stock exchange** chŭngkkwŏn kŏraeso 증권 거래소; **stockholder** chuju 주주
stocking sŭt'ak'ing 스타킹
stock market chŭngkkwŏn shijang 증권 시장; **stockmarket crash** chŭngkkwŏn shijang punggoe 증권 시장 붕괴; **stockpile 1** *n* (*of food*, *weapons*) pich'uk 비축 **2** *v/t* pich'uk'ada 비축하다; **stockroom** ch'angggo 창고; **stock-still**: ***stand ~*** kkomtchagank'o innŭn 꼼짝않고 있는; **stocktaking** chaego josa 재고 조사
stocky ttangttalmak'an 땅딸막한
stodgy *food* sohwaga chal andoenŭn 소화가 잘 안되는
stomach 1 *n* (*organ*) wi 위; (*abdomen*) pae 배 **2** *v/t* (*tolerate*) ch'amtta 참다
stomach-ache pokt'ong 복통
stone *n* (*material*) sŏktcho 석조; (*pebble*) tol 돌; ***precious ~*** posŏk 보석
stoned F (*on drugs*) ch'wihan 취한
stone-deaf aju kwiga mŏgŭn 아주 귀가 먹은
stonewall *v/i* F ŏlbŏmurida 얼버무리다
stony *ground*, *path* tori manŭn 돌이 많은
stool (*seat*) (tŭng-i ŏmnŭn) kŏlssang (등이 없는) 걸상
stoop[1] **1** *n*: ***he has a ~*** kŭnŭn tŭng-i kuburŏjyŏssŏyo 그는 등이 구부러졌어요 **2** *v/i* (*bend down*) ungk'ŭrida 웅크리다; (*have bent back*) tŭng-i kuptta 등이 굽다
stoop[2] *n* (*porch*) hyŏn-gwan ipkku-ŭi ch'ŭngch'ŭngdae 현관 입구의 층층대
stop 1 *n* (*for train*) yŏk 역; (*for bus*) chŏngnyujang 정류장; ***come to a ~*** mŏmch'uda 멈추다; ***put a ~ to*** …ŭl / rŭl mŏmch'uda …을 / 를 멈추다 **2** *v/t* (*put an end to*) mŏmch'uda 멈추다; (*prevent*) mot'age hada 못하게 하다; (*cease*) kŭmanduda 그만두다; *person in street* seuda 세우다; *car*, *bus*, *train*, *etc*: *of driver* mŏmch'uge hada 멈추게 하다; ***~ talking immediately!*** yaegirŭl chŭksshi kŭmanduseyo! 얘기를 즉시 그만두세요!; ***I ~ped her from leaving*** nanŭn kŭnyŏrŭl mot-ttŏnage haet-tta 나는 그녀를 못떠나게 했다; ***it has ~ped raining*** piga kŭch'yŏt-tta 비가 그쳤다; ***~ a check*** chiburŭl chŏngjishik'ida 지불을 정지시키다 **3** *v/i* (*come to a halt*) mŏmch'uda 멈추다; (*of snow*, *rain*) kŭch'ida 그치다; (*in a particular place*: *of bus*, *train*) sŏda 서다
♦**stop by** (*visit*) tŭllŭda 들리다
♦**stop off** tojung-e tŭllŭda 도중에 들리다
♦**stop over** chamshi mŏmurŭda 잠시 머무르다
♦**stop up** *sink* maktta 막다
stopgap imshi pyŏnt'ong 임시 변통; **stoplight** (*traffic light*) ppalgan pul 빨간 불; (*brake light*) sŭt'op lait'ŭ 스톱 라이트; **stopover** chamshi mŏmum 잠시 머뭄
stopper (*for bath*, *basin*) kumŏng magae 구멍 마개; (*for bottle*) pyŏng

magae 병 마개
stopping: ***no*** ~ (*sign*) mŏmch'um chŏngji 멈춤 정지
stop sign mŏmch'um shinho 멈춤 신호
stopwatch sŭt'op wŏch'i 스톱 워치
storage pogwan 보관; ***put in*** ~ ...ŭl/rŭl ch'anggo-e nŏ-ŏ pogwanhada ...을/를 창고에 넣어 보관하다; ***be in*** ~ pogwan chung-ida 보관 중이다
storage capacity COMPUT kiŏk yongnyang 기억 용량; **storage jar** hang-ari 항아리; **storage space** pogwan changso 보관 장소
store 1 *n* kage 가게; (*stock*) chŏjang 저장; (*storehouse*) ch'anggo 창고 **2** *v/t* chŏjanghada 저장하다; COMPUT kiŏk'ada 기억하다
storefront sangjŏmŭi chŏngmyŏn 상점의 정면; **storehouse** ch'anggo 창고; **storekeeper** kage chuin 가게 주인; **storeroom** ch'anggo 창고; **store window** shyowindo 쇼윈도
storm *n* p'okp'ung 폭풍; (*with rain*) p'okp'ung-u 폭풍우
storm drain paesuro 배수로; **storm window** tŏt-ch'angmun 덧창문; **storm warning** p'okp'ungju-ŭibo 폭풍주의보
stormy *weather* p'okp'ung-u-ga ch'inŭn 폭풍우가 치는; *relationship* kyŏngnyŏrhan 격렬한
story[1] (*tale, account*) iyagi 이야기; (*newspaper article*) kisa 기사; F (*lie*) chiŏnaen iyagi 지어낸 이야기
story[2] (*of building*) ch'ŭng 층
stout *adj person* ttungttunghan 뚱뚱한; *boots* chilgin 질긴
stove (*for cooking*) yoriyong konno 요리용 곤로; (*for heating*) sŭt'obŭ 스토브
stow chibŏnŏt'a 집어넣다
♦**stow away** *v/i* mirhanghada 밀항하다
stowaway mirhangja 밀항자
straight 1 *adj line, hair* kodŭn 곧은; *back* kkotkkot'an 꼿꼿한; (*honest, direct*) soltchik'an 솔직한; (*not criminal*) chŏnkkwaga ŏmnŭn 전과가 없는; *whiskey etc* sŭt'ŭreit'ŭ 스트레이트; (*tidy*) chŏngdondoen 정돈된; (*conservative*) kojishik'an 고지식한; (*not homosexual*) tongsŏng-yŏnaejaga anin 동성연애자가 아닌; ***be a ~ A student*** sŏngjŏgi maeu usuhan hakssaeng 성적이 매우 우수한 학생 **2** *adv* (*in a straight line*) ttokpparo 똑바로; (*directly, immediately*) kot-tchang 곧장; ***stand up ~!*** paro sŏ! 바로 서!; ***look ... ~ in the eye*** ...ŭi nunŭl ttokpparo ch'yŏdaboda ...의 눈을 똑바로 쳐다보다; ***go*** ~ F (*of criminal*) ch'aksshirhan saenghwarŭl hada 착실한 생활을 하다; ***give it to me*** ~ F naege ttokpparo yaegihaejuseyo! 내게 똑바로 얘기해주세요!; ~ ***ahead*** *be situated* paro ap'e 바로 앞에; *walk, drive* ttokpparo 똑바로; *look* ttokpparŭn 똑바른; ***carry ~ on*** (*of driver etc*) ttokpparo kada 똑바로 가다; ~***away***, ~ ***off*** chŭksshi 즉시; ~ ***out*** soltchik'age 솔직하게; ~ ***up*** (*without ice*) sŭt'ŭreit'ŭ 스트레이트
straighten *v/t* ttokpparŭge hada 똑바르게 하다
♦**straighten out 1** *v/t situation* haegyŏrhada 해결하다 **2** *v/i* (*of road*) pallajida 발라지다
♦**straighten up** hŏrirŭl p'yŏda 허리를 펴다
straightforward (*honest, direct*) soltchik'an 솔직한; (*simple*) kanttanhan 간단한
strain[1] **1** *n* (*on rope*) p'aengp'aengham 팽팽함; (*on engine, heart*) muri 무리; (*on person*) kinjang 긴장 **2** *v/t* (*injure*) murirŭl hada 무리를 하다; *finances, budget* pudamŭl chuda 부담을 주다
strain[2] *v/t vegetables* murŭl kŏrŭda 물을 거르다; *oil, fat etc* kŏllŏnaeda 걸러내다
strainer (*for vegetables etc*) ch'e 체
strait haehyŏp 해협
straitlaced ŏmkkyŏk'an 엄격한
strand[1] *n* (*of hair, wool, thread*) kadak 가닥
strand[2] *v/t* odogado mot'age hada 오도가도 못하게 하다; ***be ~ed***

odogado mot'ada 오도가도 못하다
strange (*odd*, *curious*) isanghan 이상한; (*unknown*, *foreign*) morŭnŭn 모르는
strangely (*oddly*) isanghage 이상하게; ~ ***enough*** isanghagedo 이상하게도
stranger (*person you don't know*) natssŏn saram 낯선 사람; ***I'm a ~ here myself*** yŏginŭn nado chal morŭnŭn koshimnida 여기는 나도 잘 모르는 곳입니다
strangle *person* kyosarhada 교살하다
strap *n* (*of purse*) kajuk-kkŭn 가죽끈; (*of bra*, *dress*, *shoe*) kkŭn 끈; (*of watch*) chul 줄
♦**strap in** kojŏngshik'ida 고정시키다
strapless ŏkkaekkŭni ŏmnŭn 어깨끈이 없는
strategic chŏllyaktchŏgin 전략적인
strategy MIL chŏllyak 전략; (*plan*) kyehoek 계획
straw[1] miltchip 밀짚; ***that's the last ~!*** innaeŭi han-gyerŭl nŏmkke hanŭn kŏshida! 인내의 한계를 넘게 하는 것이다!
straw[2] (*for drink*) sŭt'ŭro 스트로
strawberry ttalgi 딸기
stray 1 *adj animal* chuin ŏmnŭn 주인 없는; *bullet* pinnagan 빗나간 **2** *n* (*dog*, *cat*) ttŏdori chimsŭng 떠돌이 짐승 **3** *v/i* (*of animal*) kirŭl ilt'a 길을 잃다; (*of child*) yŏp killo pinnagada 옆 길로 빗나가다; (*of eyes*, *thoughts*) hemaeda 헤매다
streak *n* (*of dirt*, *paint*) chulmunŭi ŏlluk 줄무늬 얼룩; (*of nastiness etc*) kimi 기미 **2** *v/i* (*move quickly*) pŏn-gaech'ŏrŏm tallida 번개처럼 달리다 **3** *v/t*: ***be ~ed with*** …(ŭ)ro churi chida …(으)로 줄이 지다
stream 1 *n* kaeul 개울; (*of people*) mulkkyŏl 물결; ***come on ~*** saengsanŭl kadonghada 생산을 가동하다 **2** *v/i* hŭrŭda 흐르다; ***~ out of*** …esŏ nŏmch'yŏ hŭrŭda …에서 넘쳐 흐르다; ***sunlight ~ed into the room*** haetppich'i pang-anŭro nŏmch'yŏ tŭrŏwat-tta 햇빛이 방안으로 넘쳐 들어왔다
streamer ch'uktcheyong chong-i t'eip'ŭ 축제용 종이 테이프
streamline *v/t fig* nŭngnyultchŏgŭro hada 능률적으로 하다
streamlined *car*, *plane* yusŏnhyŏng-ŭi 유선형의; *fig*: *organization* nŭngnyultchŏgin 능률적인
street kŏri 거리
streetcar chŏnch'a 전차; **streetlight** karodŭng 가로등; **streetpeople** purangja 부랑자; **streetwalker** ch'angnyŏ 창녀; **streetwise** *adj* sesang multchŏng-e palgŭn 세상 물정에 밝은
strength him 힘; *fig* (*strong point*) changtchŏm 장점; (*of wind*, *current*) kangdo 강도; (*of emotion*, *friendship etc*) kangham 강함; (*of currency*) kangse 강세
strengthen 1 *v/t* kanghage hada 강하게 하다 **2** *v/i* kanghaejida 강해지다
strenuous himdŭn 힘든
stress 1 *n* (*emphasis*) akssent'ŭ 악센트; (*tension*) sŭt'ŭresŭ 스트레스; ***be under ~*** sŭt'ŭresŭrŭl pat-tta 스트레스를 받다 **2** *v/t syllable* akssent'ŭrŭl chuda 악센트를 주다; *importance etc* kangjohada 강조하다; ***I must ~ that …*** nanŭn …ranŭn kŏsŭl kangjohaeyagessŭmnida 나는 …라는 것을 강조해야겠습니다
stressed out F sŭt'ŭresŭrŭl shimhage pannŭn 스트레스를 심하게 받는
stressful sŭt'ŭresŭga shimhan 스트레스가 심한
stretch 1 *n* (*of land*, *water*, *road*) p'yŏlch'yŏjim 펼쳐짐; ***at a ~*** (*non-stop*) tansume 단숨에 **2** *adj fabric* shinch'ukssŏng innŭn 신축성 있는 **3** *v/t material* nŭrida 늘이다; *small income* akkyŏ ssŭda 아껴 쓰다; F *rules* hwakttae chŏgyonghada 확대 적용하다; ***he ~ed out his hand*** kŭnŭn sonŭl naemirŏt-tta 그는 손을 내밀었다; ***a job that ~es me*** nae nŭngnyŏgŭl hankkŏt parhwihage hanŭn chigŏp 내 능력을 한껏 발휘하게 하는 직업 **4** *v/i* (*to relax muscles*) tchuk ppŏt-tta 쭉 뻗다; (*to reach sth*) naemilda 내밀다; (*extend*) ppŏtch'ida 뻗치다; (*of fabric*: *give*)

nŭrŏnada 늘어나다; (*of fabric*: *sag*) nŭrŏjida 늘어지다; ***~ from X to Y*** (*extend*) Xesŏ Ykkaji ppŏdŏ it-tta X에서 Y까지 뻗어 있다

stretcher tŭlkkŏt 들것

strict *person* ŏmhan 엄한; *instructions*, *rules* ŏmkkyŏk'an 엄격한

strictly ŏmkkyŏk'age 엄격하게; ***it is ~ forbidden*** kŭgŏsŭn ŏmkkyŏk'age kŭmjidoeŏ it-tta 그것은 엄격하게 금지되어 있다

stride 1 *n* k'ŭn kŏrŭm 큰 걸음; ***lengthen one's ~*** songnyŏgŭl naeda 속력을 내다; ***take sth in one's ~*** muŏsŭl shwipkke ttwiŏnŏmtta 무엇을 쉽게 뛰어넘다 **2** *v/i* sŏngk'ŭmsŏngk'ŭm kŏt-tta 성큼성큼 걷다

strident kwie kŏsŭllinŭn 귀에 거슬리는; *demands* soranhan 소란한

strike 1 *n* (*of workers*) p'aŏp 파업; (*in baseball*) sŭt'ŭraik'ŭ 스트라이크; (*of oil*) palgyŏn 발견; ***be on ~*** tongmaeng p'aŏp chung-ida 동맹 파업 중이다; ***go on ~*** tongmaeng p'aŏbŭl kyŏrhaenghada 동맹 파업을 결행하다 **2** *v/i* (*of workers*) tongmaeng p'aŏp'ada 동맹 파업하다; (*attack*) konggyŏk'ada 공격하다; (*of disaster*) ttŏrŏjida 떨어지다; (*of clock*) ch'ida 치다 **3** *v/t person* ttaerida 때리다; *object* pudich'ida 부딪히다; *fig* (*of disaster*, *illness*) kaptchagi tŏpch'ida 갑자기 덮치다; *match* kŭt-tta 긋다; (*of idea*, *thought*) ttŏ-orŭda 떠오르다; *oil* palgyŏnhada 발견하다; ***she struck me as being ...*** kŭnyŏnŭn naege ...(ŭ)ro poyŏt-tta 그녀는 내게 ...(으)로 보였다

♦**strike out** *v/t* (*delete*) saktchehada 삭제하다

strikebreaker p'aŏp panghaeja 파업 방해자

striker (*person on strike*) p'aŏptcha 파업자

striking (*marked*) tudŭrŏjinŭn 두드러지는; (*eye-catching*) insangjŏgin 인상적인

string *n* (*cord*) kkŭn 끈; (*of violin*, *tennis racket etc*) chul 줄; ***~s*** (*musicians*) hyŏnak-kki yŏnjuja 현악기 연주자; ***pull ~s*** paehu-esŏ chojonghada 배후에서 조종하다; ***a ~ of*** (*series*) illyŏnŭi 일련의

♦**string along 1** *v/i* ttaragada 따라가다 **2** *v/t*: ***string X along*** (*deceive*) Xŭl / rŭl sogida X을 / 를 속이다

♦**string up** F kyosuhyŏng-e ch'ŏhada 교수형에 처하다

stringed instrument hyŏnak-kki 현악기

stringent ŏmjunghan 엄중한

string player hyŏnak-kki yŏnjuja 현악기 연주자

strip 1 *n* kanŭlgo kin chogak 가늘고 긴 조각; (*comic ~*) manhwaran 만화란 **2** *v/t* (*remove*) pŏtkkida 벗기다; *leaves from tree* ttŏrŏttŭrida 떨어뜨리다; (*undress*) osŭl pŏtkkida 옷을 벗기다; ***~ X of Y*** Xegesŏ Yŭl / rŭl ppaeat-tta X에게서 Y을 / 를 빼앗다 **3** *v/i* (*undress*) osŭl pŏt-tta 옷을 벗다; (*of stripper*) sŭt'ŭripsshorŭl hada 스트립쇼를 하다

strip club sŭt'ŭripsshorŭl hanŭn kot 스트립쇼를 하는 곳

stripe chulmunŭi 줄무늬; (*indicating rank*) kyegŭp 계급

striped chulmunŭi-ŭi 줄무늬의

stripper sŭt'ŭrip'ŏ 스트리퍼

strip show sŭt'ŭripssho 스트립쇼

striptease sŭt'ŭripssho 스트립쇼

strive 1 *v/t*: ***~ to do ...*** ...ŭl / rŭl haryŏgo noryŏk'ada ...을 / 를 하려고 노력하다 **2** *v/i*: ***~ for*** ...ŭl / rŭl ŏdŭryŏgo noryŏk'ada ...을 / 를 얻으려고 노력하다

stroke 1 *n* MED noejol 뇌졸; (*in writing*, *painting*) hoek 획; (*style of swimming*) suyŏngpppŏp 수영법; ***~ of luck*** ttŭtppakkŭi haeng-un 뜻밖의 행운; ***she never does a ~ (of work)*** kŭnyŏnŭn sonkkaraktto kkadak'aji annŭnda 그녀는 손가락도 까닥하지 않는다 **2** *v/t* ssŭdadŭmtta 쓰다듬다

stroll 1 *n* sanch'aek 산책 **2** *v/i* sanch'aek'ada 산책하다; ***she ~ed over to the radio*** kŭnyŏnŭn ladio

innŭn tchogŭro ŏsullŏnggŏrimyŏ kŏrŏgat-tta 그녀는 라디오 있는 쪽으로 어슬렁거리며 걸어갔다
stroller (*for baby*) yumoch'a 유모차
strong *person* himssen 힘센; *feeling* kanghan 강한; *structure* kyŏn-gohan 견고한; *candidate* yuryŏk'an 유력한; *support, supporter* kangnyŏk'an 강력한; *wind* ssen 센; *tea, coffee* chinhan 진한; *alcoholic drink* tok'an 독한; *taste, perfume* kangnyŏrhan 강렬한; *smell* chidok'an 지독한; *views, objections* kanggyŏnghan 강경한; *currency* kangseŭi 강세의
stronghold *fig* kŭn-gŏji 근거지
strongly *object, feel* kanghage 강하게
strong-minded shimjiga kujŭn 심지가 굳은
strong-willed ŭijiga kanghan 의지가 강한
structural kujosang-ŭi 구조상의
structure 1 *n* (*sth built*) kŏnch'ungmul 건축물; (*mode of construction*) kujo 구조 **2** *v/t* tchada 짜다
struggle 1 *n* (*fight*) ssa-um 싸움; (*for power*) t'ujaeng 투쟁; (*hard time*) aktchŏn kot'u 악전 고투 **2** *v/i* (*with a person*) momburimch'ida 몸부림치다; (*have a hard time*) aktchŏn kot'uhada 악전 고투하다; (*mentally*) aessŭda 애쓰다 **3** *v/t*: **~ *to do*** ...ŭl / rŭl haryŏgo momburimch'ida ...을 / 를 하려고 몸부림치다; ***she was struggling to understand*** kŭnyŏnŭn ihaeharyŏgo aessŏt-tta 그녀는 이해하려고 애썼다
strum kabyŏpkke ch'ida 가볍게 치다
strut *v/i* kŏdŭlmŏk-kkŏrimyŏ kŏt-tta 거들먹거리며 걷다
stub 1 *n* (*of cigarette*) kkongch'o 꽁초; (*of check, ticket*) tteŏjugo namŭn tchok 떼어주고 남은 쪽 **2** *v/t*: **~ *one's toe*** palkkŭch'ŭl ch'ae-ida 발끝을 채이다
♦**stub out** pibyŏ kkŭda 비벼 끄다
stubble (*on man's face*) kkach'irhaejin suyŏm 까칠해진 수염
stubborn kojibi ssen 고집이 센; *refusal, defense* wan-ganghan 완강한
stubby mungttuk'an 뭉뚝한
stuck: ***be ~ on ...*** F (*romantically*) ...ege panhae it-tta ...에게 반해 있다
stuck-up F kŏmanhan 거만한
student hakssaeng 학생
student movement hakssaeng undong 학생 운동; **student nurse** kanho shilssŭpssaeng 간호 실습생; **student teacher** kyoyuk shilssŭpssaeng 교육 실습생, kyosaeng 교생
studio (*of artist, sculptor*) chagŏpsshil 작업실; (*recording ~*) nogŭmshil 녹음실; (*film ~*) yŏnghwa ch'waryŏngso 영화 촬영소; (*TV ~*) pangsongshil 방송실
studious yŏlsshimhi kongbuhanŭn 열심히 공부하는
study 1 *n* (*room*) sŏjae 서재; (*learning*) kongbu 공부; (*research*) yŏn-gu 연구 **2** *v/t* (*at school, university*) kongbuhada 공부하다; (*examine*) chal salp'yŏboda 잘 살펴보다 **3** *v/i* kongbuhada 공부하다
stuff 1 *n* (*things*) mulgŏn 물건; (*belongings*) chim 짐 **2** *v/t turkey* sogŭl ch'ae-uda 속을 채우다; **~ *X into Y*** Xŭl / rŭl Ye ch'aewŏ nŏt'a X을 / 를 Y에 채워 넣다
stuffed toy inhyŏng 인형
stuffing (*for turkey*) sok 속; (*in chair, teddy bear*) sogŭl ch'aeunŭn chaeryo 속을 채우는 재료
stuffy *room* t'ongp'ung-i chal andoenŭn 통풍이 잘 안되는; *person* ttattak'an 딱딱한
stumble hŏt-ttidida 헛디디다
♦**stumble across** uyŏnhi majuch'ida 우연히 마주치다
♦**stumble over** ...e kŏllyŏ nŏmŏjida ...에 걸려 넘어지다; *words* tŏdŭmtta 더듬다
stumbling block chang-aemul 장애물
stump 1 *n* (*of tree*) kŭrut'ŏgi 그루터기 **2** *v/t* (*of question, questioner*) nanch'ŏhage hada 난처하게 하다
♦**stump up** F tonŭl naeda 돈을 내다
stun (*with a blow*) kijŏlsshik'ida 기절시키다; (*by news*) ŏribŏngbŏnghage hada 어리벙벙하게 하다

stunning (*amazing*) koengjanghan 굉장한; (*very beautiful*) maeu mŏshinnŭn 매우 멋있는
stunt *n* (*for publicity*) *imogŭl kkŭlgi wihan haengdong* 이목을 끌기 위한 행동; (*in movie*) wihŏmhan changmyŏn 위험한 장면
stuntman sŭt'ŏnt'ŭmaen 스턴트맨
stupefy mŏnghage hada 멍하게 하다
stupendous koengjanghan 굉장한; (*very large*) ŏmch'ŏngnan 엄청난
stupid ŏrisŏgŭn 어리석은; *book, movie* shishihan 시시한
stupidity ŏrisŏgŭm 어리석음
stupor (*drunken*) insa pulssŏng 인사 불성
sturdy ŏkssen 억센; *object* t'ŭnt'ŭnhan 튼튼한
stutter *v/i* marŭl tŏdŭmtta 말을 더듬다
style *n* (*method, manner*) pangbŏp 방법; (*of writing*) munch'e 문체; (*of architecture*) yangshik 양식; (*fashion*) yuhaeng 유행; (*elegance*) p'umkkyŏk 품격; ***go out of ~*** yuhaeng-i chinada 유행이 지나다
stylish mŏshinnŭn 멋있는
stylist (*hair ~*) sŭt'aillisŭt'ŭ 스타일리스트
subcommittee punkkwa wiwŏnhoe 분과 위원회
subcompact (car) sohyŏng chadongch'a 소형 자동차
subconscious: ***the ~*** (***mind***) muŭishik 무의식
subcontract *v/t* hach'ŏnghada 하청하다
subcontractor hach'ŏng-ŏptcha 하청업자
subdirectory COMPUT ttallin tirekt'ori 딸린 디렉토리
subdivide *v/t* sebunhada 세분하다
subdued kara-anjŭn 가라앉은; *lighting* natch'un 낮춘
subheading chagŭn chemok 작은 제목
subject 1 *n* (*of country*) kungmin 국민; (*topic*) chuje 주제; (*branch of learning*) kwamok 과목; GRAM chuŏ 주어; ***change the ~*** hwajerŭl pakkŭda 화제를 바꾸다 **2** *adj*: ***be ~ to*** ...hagi shwiun ...하기 쉬운; ***~ to availability*** yŏbuni nama innŭn hando naeesŏ 여분이 남아 있는 한도 내에서 **3** *v/t*: ***~ s.o. to*** nuguege ...ŭl/rŭl kyŏk-kke hada 누구에게 ...을/를 겪게 하다
subjective chugwanjŏgin 주관적인
sublet *v/t* chŏndaehada 전대하다
submachine gun kigwan tanch'ong 기관 단총
submarine chamsuham 잠수함
submerge 1 *v/t* chamgige hada 잠기게 하다 **2** *v/i* (*of submarine*) chamsuhada 잠수하다
submission (*surrender*) hangbok 항복; (*to committee etc*) chech'uran 제출안
submissive sunjongjŏgin 순종적인
submit *v/t plan, proposal* chech'urhada 제출하다
subordinate 1 *adj* arae-ŭi 아래의 **2** *n* araet saram 아랫 사람
subpoena 1 *n* sohwantchang 소환장 **2** *v/t person* sohwanhada 소환하다
♦**subscribe to** *magazine etc* chŏnggi kudok'ada 정기 구독하다; *theory* ...e tong-ŭihada ...에 동의하다
subscriber (*to magazine*) chŏnggi kudoktcha 정기 구독자
subscription chŏnggi kudok 정기 구독
subsequent ttarasŏ irŏnan 따라서 일어난
subsequently kŭ hu-e 그 후에
subside (*of flood waters*) ppajida 빠지다; (*of winds, fears*) karaantta 가라앉다; (*of building*) naeryŏantta 내려앉다
subsidiary *n* chahoesa 자회사
subsidize pojogŭmŭl chigŭp'ada 보조금을 지급하다
subsidy pojogŭm 보조금
♦**subsist on** ... (ŭ)ro sara nagada ... (으)로 살아 나가다
subsistence farmer chagumnong 자급농
subsistence level ch'oejŏ saenghwal sujun 최저 생활 수준
substance (*matter*) multchil 물질
substandard p'yojun midarŭi 표준 미달의

substantial sangdanghan 상당한
substantially (*considerably*) sangdanghage 상당하게; (*in essence*) shiltchiltchŏgŭro 실질적으로
substantiate chŭnggŏrŭl taeda 증거를 대다
substantive *adj* shiltchiltchŏgin 실질적인
substitute 1 *n* (*for person*) taeriin 대리인; (*for commodity*) taeyongp'um 대용품; SP pogyŏl sŏnsu 보결 선수 **2** *v/t* taeshinŭro ssŭda 대신으로 쓰다; **~ *X for Y*** X(ŭ)ro Yŭl/rŭl taeshinhada X(으)로 Y을/를 대신하다 **3** *v/i*: **~ *for s.o.*** nugurŭl taeshinhada 누구를 대신하다
substitution (*act*) taeyong 대용; ***make a ~*** SP taeshin kiyonghada 대신 기용하다
subtitle 1 *n* chamak 자막 **2** *v/t movie* chamagŭl talda 자막을 달다
subtle mimyohan 미묘한
subtract *v/t number* ppaeda 빼다; **~ *X from Y*** Yesŏ Xŭl/rŭl ppaeda Y에서 X을/를 빼다
suburb kyo-oe 교외; ***the ~s*** kŭn-gyo 근교
suburban kŭn-gyo-ŭi 근교의
subversive 1 *adj* chŏnbokshik'inŭn 전복시키는 **2** *n* chŏnbok 전복
subway chihach'ŏl 지하철
subzero *adj* yŏnghaŭi 영하의
succeed 1 *v/i* (*be successful*) sŏnggonghada 성공하다; (*to the throne*) kyesŭnghada 계승하다; (*in office*) in-gyehada 인계하다; **~ *in doing*** …ŭl/rŭl hanŭn te sŏnggonghada …을/를 하는 데 성공하다 **2** *v/t* (*come after*) huimjaga toeda 후임자가 되다; *monarch* kyesŭnghada 계승하다
succeeding twiiŭn 뒤이은
success sŏnggong 성공; ***be a ~*** taesŏnggong-ida 대성공이다
successful sŏnggongtchŏgin 성공적인
successfully sŏnggongtchŏgŭro 성공적으로
succession (*sequence*) yŏnsok 연속; (*to the throne*) kyesŭng 계승; (*to office*) in-gye 인계; ***in ~*** kyesok'aesŏ 계속해서
successive it-ttarŭn 잇따른
successor huimja 후임자
succinct kan-gyŏrhan 간결한
succulent *meat*, *fruit* chŭbi manŭn 즙이 많은
succumb (*give in*) kulbok'ada 굴복하다; **~ *to temptation*** yuhoge kulbok'ada 유혹에 굴복하다
such 1 *adj* (*of that kind*) kŭrŏn 그런; **~ *a*** (*to that extent*) kŭ chŏngdo-ŭi 그 정도의; **~ *as*** …wa/kwa kat'ŭn …와/과 같은; ***there is no ~ word as …*** …wa/kwa kat'ŭn marŭn ŏptta …와/과 같은 말은 없다 **2** *adv* kŭrŏk'e 그렇게; ***as ~*** kŭrosŏ 그로서; ***it was ~ a hot day*** kŭrŏk'e tŏun nariŏssŏyo 그렇게 더운 나랴이었어요
suck *candy* ppara mŏktta 빨아 먹다; **~ *one's thumb*** sonkkaragŭl ppalda 손가락을 빨다; **~ *X from Y*** Yesŏ Xŭl/rŭl ppalda Y에서 X을/를 빨다
♦**suck up 1** *v/t* pparadŭrida 빨아들이다 **2** *v/i*: **~ *to s.o.*** nuguege ach'ŏmhada 누구에게 아첨하다
sucker F (*person*) chal songnŭn saram 잘 속는 사람; (*lollipop*) makttaegi sat'ang 막대기 사탕
sucking pig chŏnmŏgi twaeji 젖먹이 돼지
suction hŭbip 흡입
sudden kaptchakssŭrŏn 갑작스런; ***all of a ~*** kaptchagi 갑자기
suddenly kaptchagi 갑자기
suds (*soap ~*) kŏp'um 거품
sue *v/t* kosohada 고소하다
suede *n* sŭweidŭ 스웨이드
suffer 1 *v/i* (*be in pain*) kosaenghada 고생하다; (*deteriorate*) nappajida 나빠지다; (*of school work etc*) chijang-ŭl pat-tta 지장을 받다; ***be ~ing from*** …ranŭn pyŏng-ŭl kajigo it-tta …라는 병을 가지고 있다 **2** *v/t*: **~ *a loss*** sonhaerŭl iptta 손해를 입다; **~ *a setback*** panghaerŭl pat-tta 방해를 받다
suffering *n* kot'ong 고통
sufficient ch'ungbunhan 충분한
sufficiently ch'ungbunhage 충분하게

suffocate 1 *v/i* chilsshikssahada 질식사하다 **2** *v/t* chilsshiksshik'ida 질식시키다
suffocation chilsshik 질식
sugar 1 *n* sŏlt'ang 설탕 **2** *v/t* sŏlt'ang-ŭl nŏt'a 설탕을 넣다
sugar bowl sŏlt'ang-t'ong 설탕통
sugar cane sat'ang susu 사탕 수수
suggest *v/t* cheanhada 제안하다; ***I ~ that we stop now*** nanŭn uriga chigŭm kŭmandul kŏsŭl cheanhamnida 나는 우리가 지금 그만둘 것을 제안합니다
suggestion chean 제안
suicide chasal 자살; ***commit ~*** chasarhada 자살하다
suit 1 *n* yangbok han pŏl 양복 한 벌; (*in cards*) tchakp'ae han pŏl 짝패 한 벌 **2** *v/t* (*of clothes, color*) ŏullida 어울리다; ***~ yourself!*** maŭmdaero haseyo! 마음대로 하세요!; ***be ~ed for*** ...e chŏk'ap'ada ...에 적합하다
suitable ŏullinŭn 어울리는; *choice of words, time* chŏkttanghan 적당한
suitcase yŏhaeng kabang 여행 가방
suite (*of rooms*) sŭwit'ŭ 스위트; (*furniture*) sop'a sett'ŭ 소파 셋트; MUS chogok 조곡
sulfur yuhwang 유황
sulk *v/i* purut'unghaejida 부루퉁해지다
sulky purut'unghan 부루퉁한
sullen ch'imurhan 침울한
sultry *climate* hut'ŏptchigŭnhan 후텁지근한; (*sexually*) kwannŭngjŏgin 관능적인
sum (*total*) ch'onggye 총계; (*amount*) kŭmaek 금액; (*in arithmetic*) kyesan 계산; ***a large ~ of money*** manŭn ton 많은 돈; ***the ~ insured*** hwaktchŏng kŭmaek 확정 금액; ***the ~ total of his efforts*** kŭŭi noryŏgŭi ch'ongch'e 그의 노력의 총체
♦**sum up 1** *v/t* (*summarize*) yoyak'ada 요약하다; (*assess*) p'yŏngkkahada 평가하다 **2** *v/i* LAW *p'ansaga kaegwarhayŏ marhada* 판사가 개괄하여 말하다
summarize *v/t* yoyak'ada 요약하다
summary *n* yoyak 요약
summer yŏrŭm 여름
summit (*of mountain*) chŏngsang 정상; *fig* chŏltchŏng 절정; POL sunoe hoedam 수뇌 회담
summon sojip'ada 소집하다
♦**summon up** *strength* pullŏ irŭk'ida 불러 일으키다
summons LAW sohwantchang 소환장
sump (*for oil*) kirŭmt'ong 기름통
sun t'aeyang 태양; ***in the ~*** haetppyŏch'e(sŏ) 햇볕에(서); ***out of the ~*** kŭnŭre(sŏ) 그늘에(서); ***he has had too much ~*** kŭnŭn haetppyŏch'ŭl nŏmu tchoe-ŏt-tta 그는 햇볕을 너무 쬐었다
sunbathe ilgwangnyogŭl hada 일광욕을 하다; **sunblock** haetppyŏt ch'adannyong k'ŭrim 햇볕 차단용 크림; **sunburn** haetppyŏch'e t'am 햇볕에 탐; **sunburnt** haetppyŏch'e t'an 햇볕에 탄
Sunday iryoil 일요일
sundial haeshigye 해시계
sundries chap-ppi 잡비
sunglasses saegan-gyŏng 색안경
sunken *cheeks* holtchuk'an 홀쭉한
sunny *day* hwach'anghan 화창한; *disposition* myŏngnanghan 명랑한; ***it's ~*** hwach'anghan narimnida 화창한 날입니다
sunrise ilch'ul 일출; **sunset** ilmol 일몰; **sunshade** p'arasol 파라솔; **sunshine** haetppit 햇빛; **sunstroke** ilssappyŏng 일사병; **suntan** haetppyŏch'e t'am 햇볕에 탐; ***get a ~*** haetppyŏch'e t'aeuda 햇볕에 태우다
super 1 *adj* F ch'oegoŭi 최고의 **2** *n* (*of apartment block*) kwalliin 관리인
superb koengjanghi ttwiŏnan 굉장히 뛰어난
superficial *analysis* p'yomyŏnjŏgin 표면적인; *person* ch'ŏnbak'an 천박한; *wounds* yat'ŭn 얕은
superfluous pulp'iryohan 불필요한
superhuman *efforts* ch'oinjŏgin 초인적인
superintendent (*of apartment block*) kwalliin 관리인
superior 1 *adj* (*better*) poda ttwiŏnan 보다 뛰어난; *pej*: *attitude* kŏmanhan

거만한 **2** *n* (*in organization, society*) witssaram 윗사람
supermarket sup'ŏmak'et 수퍼마켓;
supernatural 1 *adj powers* ch'ojayŏnjŏgin 초자연적인 **2** *n*: ***the ~*** ch'ojayŏnjŏgin hyŏnsang 초자연적인 현상; **superpower** POL ch'ogangdaeguk 초강대국; **supersonic** ch'oŭmsogŭi 초음속의
superstition mishin 미신
superstitious *person* mishinŭl minnŭn 미신을 믿는
supervise kamdok'ada 감독하다
supervisor (*at work*) kamdoktcha 감독자
supper chŏnyŏk shikssa 저녁 식사
supple yuyŏnhan 유연한
supplement (*extra payment*) ch'ugaaek 추가액
supplier COM konggŭbwŏn 공급원
supply 1 *n* konggŭp 공급; ***~ and demand*** konggŭpkkwa suyo 공급과 수요; ***supplies*** konggŭpp'um 공급품 **2** *v/t goods* konggŭp'ada 공급하다; ***~ X with Y*** Xege Yŭl / rŭl konggŭp'ada X에게 Y을 / 를 공급하다; ***be supplied with*** …i / ga naejangdoeŏ it-tta …이 / 가 내장되어 있다
support 1 *n* (*structural*) t'odae 토대; (*backing*) chiji 지지 **2** *v/t building, structure* chit'aenghada 지탱하다; (*financially*) puyanghada 부양하다; (*back*) chijihada 지지하다
supporter chijija 지지자; (*of football team etc*) huwŏnja 후원자
supportive chal towajunŭn 잘 도와주는
suppose (*imagine*) kajŏnghada 가정하다; ***I ~ so*** ama kŭrŏk'etchi 아마 그렇겠지; ***be ~d to …*** (*be meant to*) …hagiro toeŏit-tta …하기로 되어있다; (*be said to be*) …(ŭ)ro allyŏjyŏ it-tta …(으)로 알려져 있다; ***you are not ~d to …*** (*not allowed to*) …haji ank'iro toeŏit-tta …하지 않기로 되어있다
suppository MED chwayak 좌약
suppress *rebellion etc* chinap'ada 진압하다
suppression chinap 진압
supremacy chudokkwŏn 주도권
supreme *being, commander* ch'oegowiŭi 최고위의; *effort, courage, delight* kŭkttoŭi 극도의
Supreme Court Kodŭng Pŏbwŏn 고등 법원
surcharge *n* puga yogŭm 부가 요금
sure 1 *adj* hwaksshinhanŭn 확신하는; ***I'm ~*** hwaksshinhamnida 확신합니다; ***I'm not ~*** kŭlsseyo 글쎄요; ***be ~ about*** …e taehae hwaksshinhada …에 대해 확신하다; ***make ~ that*** …ranŭn kŏsŭl hwaksshirhage hada …라는 것을 확실하게 하다 **2** *adv*: ***~ enough*** chŏngmallo 정말로; ***it ~ is hot today*** F onŭrŭn hwaksshirhi tŏpkkunnyo 오늘은 확실히 덥군요; ***~!*** mullon! 물론!
surely (*certainly*) pandŭshi 반드시; (*gladly*) kikkŏi 기꺼이; (*slight doubt*) sŏlma 설마; (*strong doubt*) kyŏlk'o 결코; ***~ you don't mean that*** sŏlma chinjŏngŭro kŭrŏk'e marhanŭn kŏn anigetchiyo 설마 진정으로 그렇게 말하는 건 아니겠지요; ***~ that can't be right*** kyŏlk'o majŭl li ŏpssŏyo 결코 맞을 리 없어요
surf 1 *n* (*on sea*) millyŏdŭnŭn p'ado 밀려드는 파도 **2** *v/t*: ***~ the Net*** int'ŏnesŭl tullŏboda 인터넷을 둘러보다
surface 1 *n* (*of table, object*) p'yomyŏn 표면; (*of water*) sumyŏn 수면; ***on the ~*** *fig* kŏt'ŭronŭn 겉으로는 **2** *v/i* (*of swimmer, submarine*) ttŏorŭda 떠오르다; (*appear*) nat'anada 나타나다
surface mail yukssang up'yŏnmul 육상 우편물
surfboard sŏp'ing podŭ 서핑 보드
surfer (*on sea*) sŏp'inghanŭn saram 서핑하는 사람
surfing sŏp'ing 서핑; ***go ~*** sŏp'ingharŏ kada 서핑하러 가다
surge *n* ELEC chŏllyuŭi tongnyo 전류의 동요; (*in demand etc*) kŭpssangssŭng 급상승
♦**surge forward** (*of crowd*) millyŏnagada 밀려나가다
surgeon oekkwa ŭisa 외과 의사

surgery susul 수술; ***undergo ~*** susurŭl pat-tta 수술을 받다
surgical susurŭi 수술의
surly muttukttuk'an 무뚝뚝한
surmount *difficulties* kŭkppok'ada 극복하다
surname sŏng 성
surpass nŭnggahada 능가하다
surplus 1 *n* ing-yŏ 잉여 **2** *adj* namŏjiŭi 나머지의
surprise 1 *n* nollaum 놀라움; ***it'll come as no ~*** nollaptchi anŭn iri toel kŏshida 놀랍지 않은 일이 될 것이다 **2** *v/t* nollage hada 놀라게 하다; ***be / look ~d*** nollada / nolla poida 놀라다 / 놀라 보이다
surprising nollaun 놀라운
surprisingly nollapkke 놀랍게
surrender 1 *v/i* MIL hangbok'ada 항복하다 **2** *v/t* (*hand in*: *weapons etc*) nŏmgyŏjuda 넘겨주다 **3** *n* hangbok 항복; (*handing in*) indo 인도
surrogate mother taerimo 대리모
surround *v/t* tullŏ ssada 둘러 싸다; ***be ~ed by*** …(ŭ)ro tullŏssaida …(으)로 둘러싸이다
surrounding *adj* chuwiŭi 주위의
surroundings hwan-gyŏng 환경
survey 1 *n* (*of modern literature etc*) kaekwan 개관; (*of building*) chosa 조사 **2** *v/t* (*look at*) tullŏboda 둘러보다; *building* chosahada 조사하다
surveyor kŏnmul chosawŏn 건물 조사원
survival saranamŭm 살아남음; ***struggle for ~*** saengjon kyŏngjaeng 생존 경쟁; ***~ of the fittest*** chŏktcha saengjon 적자 생존
survive 1 *v/i* (*of species*, *patient*) saranamtta 살아남다; ***how are you? – surviving*** ŏttŏseyo? – kŭjŏ kŭraeyo 어떠세요? - 그저 그래요; ***his two surviving daughters*** kŭga namgin tu ttal 그가 남긴 두 딸 **2** *v/t* *accident*, *operation* saranamtta 살아남다; (*outlive*) poda orae salda 보다 오래 살다
survivor saengjonja 생존자; ***he's a ~*** *fig* kŭnŭn saengjonnyŏgi kanghada 그는 생존력이 강하다
susceptible (*emotionally*) kamsusŏng-i kanghan 감수성이 강한; ***be ~ to the cold / heat*** ch'uwie / yŏre min-gamhada 추위에 / 열에 민감하다
suspect 1 *n* hyŏmŭija 혐의자 **2** *v/t* *person* ŭishimhada 의심하다; (*suppose*) chimjak'ada 짐작하다
suspected *murderer* hyŏmŭirŭl pannŭn 혐의를 받는; *cause*, *heart attack etc* chimjakttoenŭn 짐작되는
suspend (*hang*) maedalda 매달다; (*from office*, *duties*) chŏngjishik'ida 정지시키다
suspenders (*for pants*) melppang 멜빵
suspense sŏsŭp'ensŭ 서스펜스
suspension (*in vehicle*) sŏsŭp'enshyŏn 서스펜션; (*from duty*) chŏngji 정지
suspension bridge hyŏnsugyo 현수교
suspicion ŭishim 의심
suspicious (*causing suspicion*) susanghan 수상한; (*feeling suspicion*) ŭishimsŭrŏun 의심스러운; ***be ~ of*** …ŭl / rŭl ŭishimhada …을 / 를 의심하다
sustain *pressure etc* chit'aenghada 지탱하다; *injuries* pat-tta 받다
swab *v/t* kŏllejirhada 걸레질하다
swagger *n* ppomnaenŭn kŏrŭm 뽐내는 걸음
swallow[1] *v/t & v/i* samk'ida 삼키다
swallow[2] *n* (*bird*) chebi 제비
swamp 1 *n* nŭp 늪 **2** *v/t*: ***be ~ed with*** …(ŭ)ro mirŏdakch'yŏ it-tta …(으)로 밀어닥쳐 있다
swampy *ground* nŭp kat'ŭn 늪 같은
swan paektcho 백조
swap 1 *v/t*: ***~ X for Y*** Xŭl / rŭl Ywa / kwa pakkuda X을 / 를 Y와 / 과 바꾸다 **2** *v/i* pakkuda 바꾸다
swarm 1 *n* (*of bees*) tte 떼 **2** *v/i* (*of ants*, *tourists etc*) tterŭl chit-tta 떼를 짓다; ***the town was ~ing with tourists*** toshinŭn kwan-gwanggaegŭro ttejiŏ issŏt-tta 도시는 관광객으로 떼지어 있었다
swarthy kŏmusŭrehan 거무스레한
swat *v/t* *insect*, *fly* ch'alssak ch'ida

찰싹 치다

sway 1 *n* (*influence, power*) seryŏk 세력 **2** *v/i* hŭndŭlgŏrida 흔들리다

swear *v/i* (*use swearword*) yogŭl hada 욕을 하다; (*promise*) maengsehada 맹세하다; LAW sŏnsŏhada 선서하다; ***~ at*** …ege yogŭl hada …에게 욕을 하다

♦**swear in**: ***~ as a witness*** chŭnginŭro sŏnsŏhada 증인으로 선서하다

swearword yok 욕

sweat 1 *n* ttam 땀; ***covered in ~*** ttamt'usŏng-iin 땀투성이인 **2** *v/i* ttamŭl hŭllida 땀을 흘리다

sweater sŭwet'ŏ 스웨터

sweatshirt sŭwet'ŭ shyŏch'ŭ 스웨트 셔츠

sweaty *hands* ttami paen 땀이 밴; *smell* ttamnae nanŭn 땀내 나는

Swede Sŭweden saram 스웨덴 사람

Sweden Sŭweden 스웨덴

Swedish 1 *adj* Sŭwedenŭi 스웨덴의 **2** *n* Sŭweden mal 스웨덴 말

sweep 1 *v/t floor, leaves* ssŭlda 쓸다 **2** *n* (*long curve*) man-gok 만곡

♦**sweep up** *v/t mess, crumbs* ssurŏ moŭda 쓸어 모으다

sweeping *adj generalization, statement* taegang-ŭi 대강의; *changes* chŏnmyŏnjŏgin 전면적인

sweet *adj taste, tea* tan 단; F (*kind*) ch'injŏrhan 친절한; F (*cute*) kwiyŏun 귀여운

sweet and sour *adj* saek'omdalk'omhan 새콤달콤한

sweetcorn okssusu 옥수수

sweeten *v/t drink, food* talgehada 달게 하다

sweetener (*for drink*) kammiryo 감미료

sweetheart aein 애인

swell 1 *v/i* (*of limb*) put-tta 붓다 **2** *adj* F (*good*) mŏtchin 멋진 **3** *n* (*of the sea*) kubich'im 굽이침

swelling *n* MED pugi 부기

sweltering tchinŭn tŭt'an 찌는 듯한

swerve *v/i* (*of driver, car*) pinnagada 빗나가다

swift *adj* pparŭn 빠른

swim 1 *v/i* suyŏnghada 수영하다; ***go ~ming*** suyŏngharŏ kada 수영하러 가다; ***my head is ~ming*** hyŏngijŭng-i nanda 현기증이 난다 **2** *n* suyŏng 수영; ***go for a ~*** suyŏngharŏ kada 수영하러 가다

swimmer suyŏnghanŭn saram 수영하는 사람

swimming suyŏng 수영

swimming pool suyŏngjang 수영장

swimsuit suyŏngbok 수영복

swindle 1 *n* sagi 사기 **2** *v/t* sagirŭl ch'ida 사기를 치다; ***~ X out of Y*** Xegesŏ Yŭl / rŭl sach'wihada X에게서 Y을 / 를 사취하다

swine F (*person*) saekki 새끼

swing 1 *n* (*of pendulum*) hŭndŭllim 흔들림; (*for child*) kŭne 그네; ***there has been a ~ to the Democrats*** yŏroni Minjudang tchogŭro kiulgo it-tta 여론이 민주당 쪽으로 기울고 있다 **2** *v/t* hŭndŭlda 흔들다 **3** *v/i* hŭndŭlgŏrida 흔들거리다; (*turn*) hoejŏnshik'ida 회전시키다; (*of public opinion etc*) kiulda 기울다

swing-door hoejŏnmu 회전문

Swiss *adj* Sŭwisŭŭi 스위스의

switch 1 *n* (*for light*) sŭwich'i 스위치; (*change*) chŏnhwan 전환 **2** *v/t* (*change*) pakkuda 바꾸다 **3** *v/i* (*change*) pakkwida 바뀌다

♦**switch off** *v/t lights, engine, PC* kkŭda 끄다

♦**switch on** *v/t lights, engine, PC* k'yŏda 켜다

switchboard paejŏnban 배전반

switchover (*to new system*) chŏnhwan 전환

Switzerland Sŭwisŭ 스위스

swivel *v/i* hoejŏnhada 회전하다

swollen puŭn 부은

swoop *v/i* (*of bird*) naeri tŏpch'ida 내리 덮치다

♦**swoop down on** *prey* ...ŭl/rŭl hyanghae naeri tŏpch'ida ...을/를 향해 내리 덮치다

♦**swoop on** (*of police etc*) tŏpch'ida 덮치다

sword kŏm 검

sycamore k'ŭn tanp'ungnamu 큰 단풍나무

syllable ŭmjŏl 음절

syllabus kaeyo 개요
symbol (*character*) kiho 기호; (*in poetry etc*) sangjing 상징
symbolic sangjingjŏgin 상징적인
symbolism sangjingjuŭi 상징주의
symbolize sangjinghada 상징하다
symmetric(al) taech'ingjŏgin 대칭적인
symmetry taech'ing 대칭
sympathetic (*showing pity*) tongjŏnghanŭn 동정하는; (*understanding*) chal arajunŭn 잘 알아주는; ***be ~ toward a person / an idea*** nugurŭl / saenggagŭl chal ihaehada 누구를 / 생각을 잘 이해하다
♦**sympathize with** *person*, *views* chal ihaehada 잘 이해하다
sympathizer POL tongjoja 동조자
sympathy (*pity*) tongjŏngshim 동정심; (*understanding*) ihae 이해; ***don't expect any ~ from me!*** naege ihaebadŭl saenggagŭn ilch'e haji mara 내게 이해받을 생각은 일체 하지 마라
symphony kyohyanggok 교향곡
symptom MED, *fig* chŭnghu 증후
symptomatic: ***be ~ of*** …ŭi chŭnghurŭl poida …의 증후를 보이다
synchronize shiganŭl match'uda 시간을 맞추다
synonym tong-ŭiŏ 동의어
syntax munjangnon 문장론
synthetic hapssŏng-ŭi 합성의
syphilis maedok 매독
syringe chusagi 주사기
syrup shirŏp 시럽
system ch'egye 체계; (*structure: political etc*) chojik 조직; (*method*) pangshik 방식; (*orderliness*) sunsŏ 순서; (*computer*) shisŭt'em 시스템; ***the braking / fuel injection ~*** pŭreik'ŭ changch'i / yŏllyo konggŭp changch'i 브레이크 장치 / 연료 공급 장치; ***digestive ~*** sohwa kyet'ong 소화 계통
systematic *approach* chojiktchŏgin 조직적인
systematically *study* ch'egejŏgŭro 체계적으로; *destroy* kyehoektchŏgŭro 계획적으로
systems analyst COMPUT shisŭt'em punsŏk-kka 시스템 분석가

T

tab *n* ttagae 따개; (*in text*) t'aep 탭; ***pick up the ~*** hant'ŏk naeda 한턱 내다
table *n* sang 상; (*of figures*) p'yo 표
tablecloth shikt'akppo 식탁보
tablespoon k'ŭn sutkkarak 큰 숟가락
tablet MED allyak 알약, chŏngje 정제
table tennis t'ak-kku 탁구
tabloid *n* (*newspaper*) t'abŭlloidŭp'an shinmun 타블로이드판 신문
taboo *adj* kŭmgiŭi 금기의
tacit muŏnŭi 무언의
tack 1 *n* (*nail*) aptchŏng 압정 **2** *v/t* (*sew*) shich'imjirhada 시침질하다 **3** *v/i* (*of yacht*) kaltchitchahyŏng-ŭro naagada 갈짓자형으로 나아가다
tackle 1 *n* (*gear*) togu 도구; SP t'aek'ŭl 태클 **2** *v/t* SP t'aek'ŭrhada 태클하다; *problem* ...wa / kwa sshirŭmhada ...와 / 과 씨름하다; *intruder* ...e tallyŏdŭlda ...에 달려들다
tacky *paint, glue* kkŭnjŏk-kkŭnjŏk'an 끈적끈적한; (*cheap, poor quality*) polp'um ŏmnŭn 볼품 없는; *behavior* ch'ŏnbak'an 천박한
tact chaech'i 재치
tactful chaech'i innŭn 재치 있는
tactical chŏnsultchŏgin 전술적인
tactics chŏnsul 전술
tactless chaech'i ŏmnŭn 재치 없는
tadpole olch'aeng-i 올챙이
Taedong River Taedonggang 대동강
T'aekwondo T'aekkwŏndo 태권도
tag (*label*) kkorip'yo 꼬리표
tail *n* kkori 꼬리
tail light midŭng 미등
tailor chaebongsa 재봉사
tailor-made *suit* match'umŭi 맞춤의; *solution* ansŏng match'umŭi 안성 맞춤의
tail wind sunp'ung 순풍
tainted *food* ssŏgŭn 썩은; *reputation, atmosphere* tŏrŏp'yŏjin 더럽혀진
Taiwan Taeman 대만
Taiwanese 1 *adj* Taemanŭi 대만의 **2** *n* Taemanin 대만인; (*dialect*) Taemanŏ 대만어
take *v/t* (*remove*) kajigo kada 가지고 가다; (*steal*) humch'ida 훔치다; (*transport*) t'aewŏ chuda 태워 주다; (*accompany*) terigo kada 데리고 가다; (*accept: money, gift, credit cards*) pat-tta 받다; (*study: math, French*) suganghada 수강하다; *exam* ch'ida 치다; *degree* ch'widŭk'ada 취득하다; *s.o.'s temperature* chaeda 재다; (*endure*) ch'amtta 참다; (*require*) p'iryoro hada 필요로 하다; ***this bus will ~ you to the center*** i pŏsŭrŭl t'amyŏn sent'ŏkkaji kal su issŭmnida 이 버스를 타면 센터까지 갈 수 있습니다; ***~ a photograph of s.o.*** nuguŭi sajinŭl tchiktta 누구의 사진을 찍다; ***~ a photocopy*** pokssahada 복사하다; ***~ a stroll*** sanch'aek'ada 산책하다; ***it ~s 2 hours*** 2shigani kŏllida 2시간이 걸리다; ***how long does it ~?*** ŏlmana kŏllimnikka? 얼마나 걸립니까?; ***I'll ~ it*** (*when shopping*) igŏsŭro hagessŭmnida 이것으로 하겠습니다
♦**take after** ...wa / kwa tamtta ...와 / 과 닮다
♦**take away** *pain* ŏpssaeda 없애다; *object* kajigo kada 가지고 가다; MATH ppaeda 빼다; ***take sth away from s.o.*** (*by force*) nugurobut'ŏ muŏsŭl ppaeasakada 누구로부터 무엇을 빼앗아가다
♦**take back** (*return: object*) toedollyŏjuda 되돌려주다; *person* teryŏdajuda 데려다주다; (*accept back: husband etc*) tashi padadŭrida 다시 받아들이다; ***that takes me back*** yennal saenggagi nage handa 옛날 생각이 나게 한다
♦**take down** (*from shelf*) naerida

내리다; *scaffolding* haech'ehada 해체하다; *pants* pŏt-tta 벗다; (*lengthen*) nŭrida 늘이다; (*write down*) pada chŏktta 받아 적다
♦**take in** (*take indoors*) chibanŭro tŭrida 집안으로 들이다; (*give accommodation*) mukke hada 묵게 하다; (*make narrower*) churida 줄이다; (*deceive*) sogida 속이다; (*include*) p'ohamhada 포함하다
♦**take off 1** *v/t clothes, hat* pŏt-tta 벗다; *10% etc* kkaktta 깍다; (*mimic*) hyungnaenaeda 흉내내다; ***can you take a bit off here?*** (*to barber*) yŏgirŭl chogŭmman challa chushigessŭmnikka? 여기를 조금만 잘라 주시겠습니까?; ***take a day/week off*** harurŭl/iltchuirŭl shwida 하루를/일주일을 쉬다 **2** *v/i* (*of airplane*) iryuk'ada 이륙하다; (*become popular*) inkkirŭl ŏt-tta 인기를 얻다
♦**take on** *job* mat-tta 맡다; *staff* koyonghada 고용하다
♦**take out** (*from bag, pocket*) kkŏnaeda 꺼내다; *stain* chiuda 지우다; *appendix, tooth* ppoptta 뽑다; *word from text* ppaenaeda 빼내다; *money from bank* inch'urhada 인출하다; (*to dinner etc*) terigo nagada 데리고 나가다; *insurance policy* …e tŭlda …에 들다; ***take it out on s.o.*** nuguege hwap'urihada 누구에게 화풀이하다
♦**take over 1** *v/t company etc* insuhada 인수하다; ***tourists ~ the town*** kwan-gwanggaekttŭri toshirŭl kadŭk ch'aeuda 관광객들이 도시를 가득 채우다 **2** *v/i* (*of new management etc*) chang-ak'ada 장악하다; (*do sth in s.o.'s place*) taeshinhada 대신하다
♦**take to** (*like*) choahage toeda 좋아하게 되다; (*form habit of*) …hanŭn sŭpkkwani tŭlda …하는 습관이 들다
♦**take up** *carpet etc* turŏ ollida 들어 올리다; (*carry up*) wiro unbanhada 위로 운반하다; (*shorten*) churida 줄이다; *hobby, new job* shijak'ada 시작하다; *judo, new language* paeugi shijak'ada 배우기 시작하다; *offer* surak'ada 수락하다; *space, time* ch'ajihada 차지하다; ***I'll take you up on your offer*** tangshinŭi cheŭirŭl padadŭrigessŭmnida 당신의 제의를 받아들이겠습니다

take-home pay shilssuip 실수입;
takeoff (*of airplane*) iryuk 이륙; (*impersonation*) hyungnae 흉내;
takeover COM insu 인수; **takeover bid** konggae maeip 공개 매입
takings maesanggo 매상고
talcum powder ttamtti karu 땀띠 가루
tale iyagi 이야기
talent chaenŭng 재능
talented chaenŭng-i innŭn 재능이 있는
talk 1 *v/i* marhada 말하다; ***can I ~ to …?*** …wa/kwa marhal su issŭmnikka? …와/과 말할 수 있습니까?; ***I'll ~ to him about it*** chega kŭege kŭgŏse kwanhae iyagi hagessŏyo 제가 그에게 그것에 관해 이야기 하겠어요 **2** *v/t English* marhada 말하다; *business* ŭinonhada 의논하다; ***~ s.o. into sth*** nugurŭl sŏlttŭk'ayŏ muŏsŭl shik'ida 누구를 설득하여 무엇을 시키다 **3** *n* (*conversation*) taehwa 대화; (*lecture*) kangnyŏn 강연; ***he's all ~*** kŭnŭn hŏp'ungjang-iyeyo 그는 허풍장이예요
♦**talk over** ŭinonhada 의논하다
talkative mari manŭn 말이 많은
talk show chwadamhoe 좌담회
tall k'iga k'ŭn 키가 큰
tall order murihan yogu 무리한 요구
tall story hŏp'ung 허풍
tame *adj animal* kildŭryŏjin 길들여진; *joke etc* shishihan 시시한
♦**tamper with** manjijak-kkŏrida 만지작거리다; (*deliberately interfere with*) hamburo manjida 함부로 만지다
tampon t'amp'on 탐폰
tan 1 *n* (*from sun*) ssŏnt'en 썬텐; (*color*) hwanggalssaek 황갈색 **2** *v/i* (*in sun*) haetppyŏch'e t'ada 햇볕에 타다 **3** *v/t leather* mudujirhada 무두질하다

tandem (*bike*) 2insŭng chajŏn-gŏ 2인승 자전거
tangerine milgam 밀감, kyul 귤
tangle *n* ŏngk'im 엉킴
♦**tangle up**: ***get tangled up*** (*of string etc*) ŏngk'ida 엉키다
tango *n* t'aenggo 탱고
tank chŏjang t'aengk'ŭ 저장 탱크; MOT, MIL, (*for skin diver*) t'aengk'ŭ 탱크
tanker (*ship*) yujosŏn 유조선; (*truck*) yujoch'a 유조차
tanned (*sun-~*) haetppyŏch'e t'an 햇볕에 탄
tantalizing kamjilnage hanŭn 감질나게 하는
tantamount: ***be ~ to*** ...wa / kwa tongdŭnghada ...와 / 과 동등하다
tantrum tchatchŭng 짜증
Taoism Togyo 도교
tap 1 *n* kkoktchi 꼭지 **2** *v/t* (*knock*) kabyŏpkke tudŭrida 가볍게 두드리다; *phone* toch'ŏnghada 도청하다
♦**tap into** *resources* iyonghagi shijak'ada 이용하기 시작하다
tap dance *n* t'aepttaensŭ 탭댄스
tape 1 *n* (*for recording, sticky*) t'eip'ŭ 테이프 **2** *v/t conversation etc* nogŭmhada 녹음하다; (*video*) nok'wahada 녹화하다; (*with sticky tape*) t'eip'ŭro puch'ida 테이프로 붙이다
tape deck k'aset'ŭ p'ŭlleiŏ 카셋트 플레이어; **tape drive** COMPUT paegŏp tŭraibŭ 백업 드라이브; **tape measure** chulja 줄자
taper *v/i* chŏmjŏm kanŭrŏjida 점점 가늘어지다
♦**taper off** (*of production, figures*) chŏmjŏm churŏdŭlda 점점 줄어들다
tape recorder nogŭmgi 녹음기
tape recording t'eip'ŭ nogŭm 테이프 녹음
tapestry t'aep'isŭt'ŭri 태피스트리
tar *n* t'arŭ 타르
tardy nŭjŭn 늦은
target 1 *n* (*in shooting*) kwanyŏk 과녁, p'yojŏk 표적; (*for sales, production*) mokp'yo 목표 **2** *v/t market* mokp'yoro hada 목표로 하다
target date mokp'yo magamil 목표 마감일; **target group** COM mokp'yo kŭrup 목표 그룹; **target market** p'yojŏk shijang 표적 시장
tariff (*price*) yogŭmp'yo 요금표; (*tax*) kwanse 관세
tarmac (*at airport*) hwaltchuro 활주로
tarnish *v/t metal* pyŏnsaeksshik'ida 변색시키다; *reputation* sonsangshik'ida 손상시키다
tarpaulin pangsup'o 방수포
tart *n* kwail p'ai 과일 파이
task immu 임무
task force t'ŭkppyŏl chosadan 특별 조사단; MIL t'ŭkssu kidongdae 특수 기동대
tassel sul 술
taste 1 *n* (*sense*) migak 미각; (*of food etc*) mat 맛; (*in clothes, art etc*) ch'wihyang 취향; ***he has no ~ in clothes*** kŭnŭn amurŏn p'aeshyŏn kamgagi ŏptta 그는 아무런 패션 감각이 없다 **2** *v/t also fig* matppoda 맛보다
tasteful kamgaginnŭn 감각있는
tasteless *food* ammu mat ŏmnŭn 아무 맛 없는; *remark, person* mŏdŏmnŭn 멋없는
tasty mashinnŭn 맛있는
tattered *clothes, book* tchijŏjin 찢어진
tatters: ***in ~*** *also fig* nudŏgiga toeŏ 누더기가 되어
tattoo munshin 문신
taunt 1 *n* chorong 조롱 **2** *v/t* choronghada 조롱하다
taut p'aengp'aenghan 팽팽한
tax 1 *n* segŭm 세금; ***before / after ~*** segŭmŭl p'ohamhan / kongjehan 세금을 포함한 / 공제한 **2** *v/t people* ...ege segŭmŭl pugwahada ...에게 세금을 부과하다; *product* ...e segŭmŭl pugwahada ...에 세금을 부과하다
taxation kwase 과세; (*collection of taxes*) chingse 징세
tax code segŭm kiho 세금 기호; **tax-deductible** segŭm kongjega kanŭnghan 세금 공제가 가능한; **tax evasion** t'alsse 탈세; **tax-free** myŏnseŭi 면세의
taxi t'aeksshi 택시

taxidriver t'aeksshi unjŏnsa 택시 운전사
tax inspector semu chosagwan 세무 조사관
taxi rank t'aeksshi sŭngch'ajang 택시 승차장
tax payer napsseja 납세자
tax return (*form*) napsse shin-gosŏ 납세 신고서
tea (*drink*) ch'a 차; (*meal*) tagwa 다과; ***green ~*** nokch'a 녹차; ***black ~*** hongch'a 홍차
teabag ch'a pongji 차 봉지
teach 1 *v/t person*, *subject* karŭch'ida 가르치다; ***~ s.o. to do sth*** nuguege muŏt hanŭn kŏsŭl karŭch'ida 누구에게 무엇 하는 것을 가르치다 **2** *v/i* karŭch'ida 가르치다
teacher sŏnsaeng 선생; (*form of address*) sŏnsaengnim 선생님; (*describing profession*) kyosa 교사
Teachers' Day Sŭsŭng-ŭi nal 스승의 날
teacher training kyosa hullyŏn 교사 훈련
teaching (*profession*) kyojik 교직
teaching aid pojo kyojae 보조 교재
teaching assistant kangsa 강사
tea cloth marŭn haengju 마른 행주; **teacup** ch'atchan 찻잔; **tea drinker** ch'a aehoga 차 애호가
teak t'ik'ŭ namu 티크 나무
tea leaves ch'annip 찻잎
team t'im 팀
team spirit tanch'e chŏngshin 단체 정신
teamster t'ŭrŏk unjŏnsa 트럭 운전사
teamwork hyŏpttong chagŏp 협동 작업
teapot chattchujŏnja 찻주전자
tear[1] **1** *n* (*in cloth etc*) tchijŏjin t'ŭm 찢어진 틈 **2** *v/t paper*, *cloth* tchit-tta 찢다; ***be torn between two alternatives*** tu taean saiesŏ mangsŏrida 두 대안 사이에서 망설이다 **3** *v/i* (*go fast*) chiltchuhada 질주하다
♦**tear up** *paper* kalgigalgi tchit-tta 갈기갈기 찢다; *agreement* ch'wisohada 취소하다
tear[2] (*in eye*) nunmul 눈물; ***burst into ~s*** urŭmŭl t'ŏttŭrida 울음을 터뜨리다; ***be in ~s*** nunmurŭl hŭllida 눈물을 흘리다
teardrop nunmul pang-ŭl 눈물 방울
tearful nunmul ŏrin 눈물 어린
tear gas ch'oerugasŭ 최루가스
tearoom chattchip 찻집
tease *v/t* (*maliciously*) koerop'ida 괴롭히다; (*for fun*) nollida 놀리다
tea service, **tea set** ch'attchan set'ŭ 찻잔 세트; **teaspoon** ch'atssutkkarak 찻숟가락
teat chŏtkkoktchi 젖꼭지
technical kisultchŏgin 기술적인; (*relating to particular field*) chŏnmunŭi 전문의
technicality (*technical nature*) chŏnmunsŏng 전문성; LAW sasohan sahang 사소한 사항; ***that's just a ~*** kŭgŏsŭn kŭnyang sasohan iril ppunida 그것은 그냥 사소한 일일 뿐이다
technically kisultchŏgŭro 기술적으로; (*strictly speaking*) ŏmmirhi marhamyŏn 엄밀히 말하면
technician kisultcha 기술자
technique kisul 기술; (*of performer*) kigyo 기교
technological kwahak kisulsang-ŭi 과학 기술상의
technology kwahak kisul 과학 기술
technophobia kwahak kisul kongp'otchŭng 과학 기술 공포증
tedious chiruhan 지루한
tee *n* (*in golf*) t'i 티
teem: ***be ~ing with rain*** p'oguga ssodajigo it-tta 폭우가 쏟아지고 있다; ***be ~ing with tourists / ants*** kwan-gwanggaekttŭllo / kaemidŭllo nŏmch'ida 관광객들로 / 개미들로 넘치다
teenage *fashions* ship taeŭi 십 대의
teenager t'ineijŏ 틴에이저
teens: ***be in one's ~*** ship taeida 십 대이다; ***reach one's ~*** ship taega toeda 십 대가 되다
telecommunications t'ongshin 통신
telegram chŏnbo 전보
telegraph pole chŏnshinju 전신주
telepathic chŏngshin kamŭng-ŭi 정신 감응의; ***you must be ~!*** maŭmi t'onghaetkkunyo! 마음이 통했군요!

telepathy chŏngshin kamŭng 정신 감응

telephone 1 *n* chŏnhwa 전화; ***be on the ~*** (*be speaking*) t'onghwa chung-ida 통화 중이다; (*possess a phone*) chŏnhwaga it-tta 전화가 있다 **2** *v/t person* …ege chŏnhwarŭl kŏlda …에게 전화를 걸다 **3** *v/i* chŏnhwahada 전화하다

telephone booth kongjung chŏnhwa pakssŭ 공중 전화 박스; **telephone call** chŏnhwa 전화; **telephone directory** chŏnhwa pŏnhobu 전화 번호부; **telephone exchange** chŏnhwa kyohwan-guk 전화 교환국; **telephone number** chŏnhwa pŏnho 전화 번호

telephoto lens mang-wŏn lenjŭ 망원 렌즈

telesales chŏnhwa p'anmae 전화 판매

telescope mang-wŏn-gyŏng 망원경

televise pang-yŏnghada 방영하다

television t'ellebijŏn 텔레비전; (*set*) t'ellebijŏn susanggi 텔레비전 수상기; ***on ~*** t'ellebijŏne(sŏ) 텔레비전에(서); ***watch ~*** t'ellebijŏnŭl poda 텔레비전을 보다

television program t'ellebijŏn p'ŭrogŭraem 텔레비전 프로그램; **television set** t'ellebijŏn susanggi 텔레비전 수상기; **television studio** t'ellebijŏn nok'washil 텔레비전 녹화실

tell 1 *v/t story* marhada 말하다; *lie* kŏjinmarhada 거짓말하다; *the difference* kubyŏrhada 구별하다; ***~ s.o. sth*** nuguege muŏsŭl marhada 누구에게 무엇을 말하다; ***don't ~ Mom*** ŏmmahant'e marhajima 엄마한테 말하지마; ***could you ~ me the way to …?*** …(ŭ)ro kanŭn kirŭl karŭch'yŏ chushigessŏyo? …(으)로 가는 길을 가르쳐 주시겠어요?; ***~ s.o. to do sth*** nuguege muŏsŭl harago marhada 누구에게 무엇을 하라고 말하다; ***you're ~ing me!*** chŏngmal kŭraeyo! 정말 그래요! **2** *v/i* (*have effect*) yŏnghyang-ŭl mich'ida 영향을 미치다; ***the heat is ~ing on him*** kŭnŭn tŏwirŭl mŏkkko it-tta 그는 더위를 먹고 있다; ***time will ~*** shigani chinamyŏn kkaedatkke toel kŏshida 시간이 지나면 깨닫게 될 것이다

♦**tell off** (*reprimand*) kkujit-tta 꾸짖다

teller ŭnhaeng ch'ullabwŏn 은행 출납원

telltale 1 *adj signs* sashirŭl tŭrŏnaenŭn 사실을 드러내는 **2** *n* kojajiljaeng-i 고자질쟁이

temp 1 *n* (*employee*) imshi chigwŏn 임시 직원 **2** *v/i* imshijigŭro irhada 임시직으로 일하다

temper (*bad ~*) sŏngjil 성질, kibun 기분; ***be in a ~*** hwarŭl naego it-tta 화를 내고 있다; ***keep one's ~*** hwarŭl ch'amtta 화를 참다; ***lose one's ~*** hwarŭl naeda 화를 내다

temperament kijil 기질

temperamental (*moody*) pyŏndŏkssŭrŏun 변덕스러운

temperature ondo 온도; (*fever*) yŏl 열; ***have a ~*** yŏri it-tta 열이 있다

temple[1] REL sawŏn 사원

temple[2] ANAT kwanjanori 관자놀이

tempo MUS paktcha 박자; (*of work*) soktto 속도

temporarily ilsshijŏgŭro 일시적으로

temporary ilsshijŏgin 일시적인

tempt yuhok'ada 유혹하다

temptation yuhok 유혹

tempting yuhoktchŏgin 유혹적인

ten yŏl 열, ship 십

tenacious wan-ganghan 완강한

tenant ch'ayongja 차용자

tend[1] *v/t* (*look after*) tolboda 돌보다

tend[2]: ***~ to do sth*** muŏt hanŭn p'yŏnida 무엇 하는 편이다; ***~ toward sth*** muŏsŭi kyŏnghyang-i it-tta 무엇의 경향이 있다

tendency kyŏnghyang 경향

tender[1] *adj* (*sore*) manjimyŏn ap'ŭn 만지면 아픈; (*affectionate*) tajŏnghan 다정한; *steak* yŏnhan 연한

tender[2] *n* COM ipch'al 입찰

tenderness (*soreness*) manjimyŏn ap'ŭm 만지면 아픔; (*of kiss etc*) tajŏngham 다정함; (*of steak*) yŏnham 연함

tendon himtchul 힘줄

tennis t'enissŭ 테니스
tennis ball t'enissŭ kong 테니스 공; **tennis court** t'enissŭ chang 테니스 장; **tennis player** t'enissŭ sŏnsu 테니스 선수; **tennis racket** t'enissŭ lak'et 테니스 라켓
tenor *n* MUS t'enŏ 테너
tense[1] *n* GRAM shije 시제
tense[2] *adj muscle* kinjangdoen 긴장된; *voice*, *person* kinjanghan 긴장한; *moment* kinjangdoenŭn 긴장되는
♦**tense up** kinjangdoeda 긴장되다
tension (*of rope*) p'aengp'aengham 팽팽함; (*in atmosphere*, *voice*) kinjang 긴장; (*in movie*, *novel*) kinbak-kkam 긴박감
tent ch'ŏnmak 천막
tentacle ch'okssu 촉수
tentative chujŏhanŭn 주저하는
tenterhooks: ***be on ~*** chobashimhada 조바심하다
tenth yŏl pŏntchaeŭi 열 번째의
tepid *water*, *reaction* mijigŭnhan 미지근한
term (*period of time*) kigan 기간; (*condition*) kiil 기일; (*word*) yong-ŏ 용어; ***be on good / bad ~s with s.o.*** nuguwa choŭn / nappŭn kwan-gyeida 누구와 좋은 / 나쁜 관계이다; ***in the long / short ~*** changgijŏgŭro / tan-gijŏgŭro 장기적으로 / 단기적으로; ***come to ~s with sth*** muŏsŭl padadŭrida 무엇을 받아들이다
terminal 1 *n* (*at airport*, *for buses*) t'ŏminŏl 터미널; (*for containers*) chip'atchang 집하장; ELEC tanja 단자; COMPUT tanmal changch'i 단말 장치 **2** *adj illness* pulch'iŭi 불치의
terminally *adv*: ***~ ill*** pulch'ippyŏng-ŭi 불치병의
terminate 1 *v/t contract* wanjŏnhi kkŭnnaeda 완전히 끝내다; ***~ a pregnancy*** nakt'aeshik'ida 낙태시키다 **2** *v/i* kkŭnnada 끝나다
termination (*of contract*) man-gi 만기; (*of pregnancy*) nakt'ae 낙태
terminology chŏnmun yong-ŏ 전문 용어
terminus (*for buses*, *trains*) chongtchŏm 종점
terrace (*on hillside*) kyedanshik pat 계단식 밭; (*patio*) t'erasŭ 테라스
terra cotta t'erak'ot'a 테라코타
terrain chihyŏng 지형
terrestrial 1 *n* chiguin 지구인 **2** *adj television* chisang-ŭi 지상의
terrible kkŭmtchik'an 끔찍한
terribly (*very*) mopsshi 몹시
terrific koengjanghan 굉장한
terrifically (*very*) koengjanghage 굉장하게
terrify kŏmnage hada 겁나게 하다; ***be terrified*** kŏbe chillida 겁에 질리다
terrifying kŏmnage hanŭn 겁나게 하는
territorial yŏngt'oŭi 영토의
territorial waters yŏnghae 영해
territory yŏngt'o 영토; *fig* kuyŏk 구역
terror kongp'o 공포
terrorism t'erŏrijŭm 테러리즘
terrorist t'erŏbŏm 테러범
terrorist organization t'erŏ chojik 테러 조직
terrorize wihyŏp'ada 위협하다
test 1 *n* shihŏm 시험 **2** *v/t* shihŏmhada 시험하다; *new product*, *drug etc* shirhŏmhada 실험하다
testament (*to a person*, *life etc*) kinyŏmmul 기념물; ***Old / New Testament*** REL Kuyak / Shinyak Sŏngsŏ 구약 / 신약 성서
testicle kohwan 고환
testify *v/i* LAW chŭng-ŏnhada 증언하다
testimonial ch'uch'ŏntchang 추천장
test tube shihŏmgwan 시험관
test-tube baby shihŏmgwan agi 시험관 아기
testy sŏngmi kŭp'an 성미 급한
tetanus p'asangp'ung 파상풍
tether 1 *v/t horse* maeda 매다 **2** *n*: ***be at the end of one's ~*** han-gyee irŭda 한계에 이르다
text ponmun 본문
textbook kyokkwasŏ 교과서
text file COMPUT t'eksŭt'ŭ p'ail 텍스트 파일
textile chingmul 직물
texture (*of skin*, *material*) kyŏl 결; (*of

food) sship'inŭn nŭkkim 씹히는 느낌

Thai 1 *adj* T'aegugŭi 태국의 **2** *n* (*person*) T'aegugin 태국인; (*language*) T'aegugŏ 태국어

Thailand T'aiguk 태국

than ...poda ...보다; ***bigger / faster ~ me*** naboda tŏ k'ŭn / pparŭn 나보다 더 큰 / 빠른

thank *v/t* kamsahada 감사하다; ***~ you*** (*polite*) kamsahamnida 감사합니다, komapssŭmnida 고맙습니다; F komawŏ 고마워; ***no ~ you*** komaptchiman, kwaench'ansŭmnida 고맙지만, 괜찮습니다

thanks kamsa 감사, komaum 고마움; ***~!*** komapssŭmnida! 고맙습니다!; (*to friend, to younger people*) komawŏ! 고마워!; ***~ to*** ...tŏkt'aege ...덕택에

thankful kamsahanŭn 감사하는

thankfully kamsahagedo 감사하게도, komapkkedo 고맙게도; (*luckily*) tahaenghido 다행히도

thankless *task* poram ŏmnŭn 보람 없는

Thanksgiving (Day) Ch'usu Kamsajŏl 추수 감사절

that 1 *adj* chŏ 저; ***~ one*** (*thing*) chŏgŏt 저것; (*person*) chŏ saram 저 사람 **2** *pron* (*thing*) chŏgŏt 저것; 사람; ***what is ~?*** chŏgŏsŭn muŏshimnikka? 저것은 무엇입니까?; ***who is ~?*** chŏ saramŭn nuguimnikka? 저 사람은 누구입니까?; ***~'s mine*** kŭgŏsŭn che kŏshimnida 그것은 제 것입니다; ***~'s tea*** kŭgŏsŭn ch'aimnida 그것은 차입니다; ***~'s very kind*** kŭgŏsŭn chŏngmal ch'injorhan irimnida 그것은 정말 친절한 일입니다 ◊ (*relative*) ...hanŭn ...하는; ***the person / car ~ you see*** tangshini pogo innŭn saram / ch'a 당신이 보고 있는 사람 / 차 **3** *conj*: ***I think ~ ...*** jŏnŭn ...rago saenggak'amnida 저는 ...라고 생각합니다 **4** *adv* (*so*) kŭrŏk'e 그렇게; ***~ big*** kŭrok'e k'ŭn 그렇게 큰

thaw *v/i* (*of snow, frozen food*) noktta 녹다

the ◊ (*no equivalent in Korean*): ***~ border*** kuk-kkyŏng 국경 ◊ (*identifying or with previous reference*) kŭ 그; ***~ doctor who treated me*** narŭl ch'iryohan kŭ ŭisa 나를 치료한 그 의사; ***is that ~ ring he gave you?*** igŏshi kŭga tangshinege chun kŭi panjiyeyo? 이것이 그가 당신에게 준 그 반지예요?; ***~ blue bag is mine*** kŭ p'aran kabang-i che kŏshiyeyo 그 파란 가방이 제 것이예요 ◊: ***~ sooner ~ better*** pparŭmyŏn pparŭlsurok chot'a 빠르면 빠를수록 좋다

theater yŏn-gŭk 연극; (*building*) kŭktchang 극장

theatrical yŏn-gŭgŭi 연극의; (*overdone*) kwajangdoen 과장된

theft toduktchil 도둑질

their kŭdŭrŭi 그들의; (*his or her*): ***somebody has left ~ coat behind*** nugun-ga k'ot'ŭrŭl nwadugo kassŏyo 누군가 코트를 놔두고 갔어요

theirs kŭdŭrŭi kŏt 그들의 것; ***a friend of ~*** kŭdŭrŭi ch'in-gu 그들의 친구

them kŭdŭl 그들; ***that's for ~*** kŭdŭrŭi kŏshimnida 그들의 것입니다; ***who's that? - it's ~ again*** nuguyeyo? - tto kŭdŭriyeyo 누구예요? - 또 그들이예요 ◊ (*him or her*): ***nobody had a car with ~*** amudo ch'arŭl kajigo oji anassŏyo 아무도 차를 가지고 오지 않았어요

theme t'ema 테마

theme park t'ema kong-wŏn 테마 공원

theme song chujega 주제가

themselves kŭdŭl chashin 그들 자신; ***by ~*** (*alone*) kŭdŭl sŭsŭro 그들 스스로

then (*at that time*) kŭ ttae 그 때; (*after that*) kŭrigo nasŏ 그리고 나서; (*deducing*) kŭrŏt'amyŏn 그렇다면; ***by ~*** kŭ ttaeenŭn 그 때에는

theology shinhak 신학

theoretical ironŭi 이론의; ***~ physics*** iron mullihak 이론 물리학

theory iron 이론; ***in ~*** ironsang-ŭro 이론상으로

therapeutic ch'iryoŭi 치료의

therapist ch'iryo chŏnmun-ga 치료 전문가
therapy ch'iryo 치료
there kŭ kose 그 곳에; ***over ~ / down ~*** chŏ wie / araee 저 위에 / 아래에; ***~ is*** ...i it-tta ...이 있다; ***~ are*** ...tŭri it-tta ...들이 있다; ***is / are ~ ...?*** ...i / tŭri issŭmnikka? ...이 / 들이 있습니까?; ***isn't / aren't ~ ...?*** ...i / tŭri ŏpssŭmnikka? ...이 / 들이 없습니까?; ***~ you are*** (*giving sth*) yogi issŭmnida 여기 있습니다; (*finding sth*) yŏgi issŏkkunyo 여기 있었군요; (*completing sth*) twaessŭmnida 됐습니다; ***$50 ~ and back*** wangbok 50tallŏimnida 왕복 50달러입니다; ***~ he is!*** kŭga chŏgi itkkunyo 그가 저기 있군요!; ***~, ~!*** cha, cha! 자, 자!
thereabouts kŭ chŏngdo 그 정도
therefore ttarasŏ 따라서, kŭrŏmŭro 그러므로
thermometer ondogye 온도계
thermos flask poonbyŏng 보온병
thermostat chadong ondo chojŏl changch'i 자동 온도 조절 장치
these 1 *adj* igŏttŭrŭi 이것들의, i ...dŭl 이 ...들 **2** *pron* igŏttŭl 이것들
thesis nonmun 논문
they kŭdŭl 그들; (*things*) kŭgŏttŭl 그것들 ◊ (*he or she*): ***if anyone knows ~ should say so*** manyak nugurado andamyŏn, kŭrŏk'e yegihaeya hamnida 만약 누구라도 안다면, 그렇게 얘기해야 합니다 ◊ (*impersonal*): ***~ say that ...*** kŭdŭri ...rago marhada 그들이 ...라고 말하다; ***~ are going to change the law*** kŭdŭrŭn pobŭl pakkul kŏshida 그들은 법을 바꿀 것이다
thick tukkŏun 두꺼운; F (*stupid*) tunhan 둔한; *fog* chit'ŭn 짙은; *soup* kŏltchuk'an 걸쭉한; ***~ hair*** such'i manŭn mŏri 숱이 많은 머리
thicken *sauce* kŏltchuk'age hada 걸쭉하게 하다
thickset ttangttalmak'an 땅딸막한
thickskinned *fig* ppŏnppŏnsŭrŏun 뻔뻔스러운
thief totuk 도둑
thigh nŏptchŏkttari 넓적다리
thimble kolmu 골무
thin *material* yalbŭn 얇은; *hair, line* kanŭn 가는; *person* marŭn 마른; *soup* mulgŭn 묽은
thing samul 사물; ***~s*** (*belongings*) soyumul 소유물; ***how are ~s?*** ŏttŏk'e chinaeseyo? 어떻게 지내세요?; ***good ~ you told me*** naege marŭl chal haet-tta 내게 말을 잘 했다; ***what a ~ to do / say!*** musŭn chishiya / mariya! 무슨 짓이야 / 말이야!
thingumajig F kŭ mwŏrago hanŭn kŏt 그 뭐라고 하는 것; (*person*) kŭ mwŏrago hanŭn saram 그 뭐라고 하는 사람
think saenggak'ada 생각하다; ***I ~ so*** kŭrŏn kŏt kat'ayo 그런 것 같아요; ***I don't ~ so*** kŭroch'i anŭn kŏt kat'ayo 그렇지 않은 것 같아요; ***I ~ so too*** chŏdo kŭrŏk'e saenggak'aeyo 저도 그렇게 생각해요; ***what do you ~?*** ŏttŏk'e saenggak'aseyo? 어떻게 생각하세요?; ***what do you ~ of it?*** kŭgŏsŭl ŏttŏk'e saenggak'aeyo? 그것을 어떻게 생각해요?; ***I can't ~ of anything more*** kŭ isang-ŭn saenggangnaji anayo 그 이상은 생각나지 않아요; ***~ hard!*** chal saenggak'ae pwa! 잘 생각해 봐!; ***I'm ~ing about emigrating*** nanŭn imin-ganŭn kŏsŭl saenggak chung-ida 나는 이민가는 것을 생각 중이다
♦**think over** suk-kkohada 숙고하다
♦**think through** yomojomo saenggak'ae poda 요모조모 생각해 보다
♦**think up** *plan* saenggak'aenaeda 생각해내다
third 1 *adj* chesamŭi 제3의, se pŏntchaeŭi 세 번째의 **2** *n* (*in sequence*) chesam 제3, se pŏntchae 세 번째; (*fraction*) sambunŭi il 삼분의 일
thirdly se pŏntchaeronŭn 세 번째로는
third-party insurance ch'aegim pohŏm 책임 보험; **third-rate** samnyuŭi 삼류의; **Third World** Chesam Segye 제3 세계
thirst kaltchŭng 갈증
thirsty mongmarŭn 목마른; ***be ~***

mongmarŭda 목마르다
thirteen yŏlsset 열 셋, shipssam 십삼
thirteenth yŏlsse pŏntchaeŭi 열 세 번째의
thirtieth sŏrŭn pŏntchaeŭi 서른 번째의
thirty sŏrŭn 서른, samship 삼십
Thirty-Eighth Parallel Samp'alssŏn 삼팔선
this 1 *adj* i 이; ~ ***one*** igŏt 이것 **2** *pron* igŏt 이것; ~ ***is good*** igŏsŭn chota 이것은 좋다; ~ ***is*** (*introducing*) i saramŭn ...imnida 이 사람은 ...입니다; TELEC chŏnŭn ...imnida 저는 ...입니다 **3** *adv*: ~ ***big*** / ***high*** i chŏngdoro k'ŭda / noptta 이 정도로 크다 / 높다
thorn kashi 가시
thorough *search*, *person* ch'ŏltchŏhan 철저한; *knowledge* wanjŏnhan 완전한
thoroughbred sunjong 순종
those 1 *adj people* kŭdŭrŭi 그들의; *things*, *animals* kŭgŏttŭrŭi 그것들의; ***in ~ days*** kŭ tangshienŭn 그 당시에는 **2** *pron* (*people*) kŭdŭl 그들; (*things*, *animals*) kŭgŏttŭl 그것들
though 1 *conj* (*although*) …ijiman …이지만; ***even ~ …*** …handa hadŏrado …한다 하더라도; ***~ it might fail*** shilp'aehagetchiman 실패하겠지만; ***as ~*** mach'i …ch'ŏrŏm 마치 …처럼 **2** *adv* kŭrŏt'ŏrado 그렇더라도; ***it's not finished ~*** kŭrŏt'arado ajik kkŭnnan kŏsŭn anida 그렇더라도 아직 끝난 것은 아니다
thought (*single*) sago 사고, saenggak 생각; (*collective*) sasang 사상
thoughtful saenggagi kip'ŭn 생각이 깊은; *book* shimsasuk-kkohan 심사숙고한; (*considerate*) saryŏ kip'ŭn 사려 깊은
thoughtless namŭl koryŏhaji annŭn 남을 고려하지 않는
thousand ch'ŏn 천; ***~s of*** su ch'ŏnŭi 수 천의; ***ten ~*** man 만; ***hundred ~*** shim man 십만
thousandth *adj* ch'ŏn pŏntchaeŭi 천 번째의
thrash *v/t* magu ttaerida 마구 때리다; SP ch'amp'aeshik'ida 참패시키다
♦**thrash around** (*with arms etc*) momburimch'ida 몸부림치다
♦**thrash out** *solution* nonŭihaesŏ haegyŏrhada 논의해서 해결하다
thrashing ch'aetchiktchil 채찍질; SP ch'amp'ae 참패
thread 1 *n* shil 실; (*of screw*) nasasan 나사산 **2** *v/t needle*, *beads* …e shirŭl kkweda …에 실을 꿰다
threadbare tarŭn 닳은
threat wihyŏp 위협
threaten wihyŏp'ada 위협하다
threatening *gesture*, *tone* wihyŏp'anŭn 위협하는; *sky* tchip'urin 찌푸린; ***a ~ letter*** hyŏppak p'yŏnji 협박 편지
three set 셋, sam 삼
Three Han Samhan 삼한; **Three Kingdoms** Samguk 삼국; **three-quarters** *n* sabunŭi sam 사분의 삼
thresh *v/t corn* t'algok'ada 탈곡하다
threshold (*of house*) muntchibang 문지방; (*of new age*) ch'ulbaltchŏm 출발점; ***on the ~ of*** …ŭi ch'ulbaltchŏme …의 출발점에
thrift chŏryak 절약
thrifty chŏryak'anŭn 절약하는
thrill 1 *n* chŏnyul 전율 **2** *v/t*: ***be ~ed*** kamgyŏk'ada 감격하다
thriller sŭrillŏmul 스릴러물
thrilling kamgyŏk'age hanŭn 감격하게 하는
thrive (*of plant*) ulch'anghage charada 울창하게 자라다; (*of economy*) pŏnch'anghada 번창하다
throat mokkumŏng 목구멍
throat lozenges mok sat'ang 목 사탕
throb 1 *n* (*of heart*) maekppak 맥박; (*of music*) ttŏllimŭm 떨림음 **2** *v/i* (*of heart*) ttwida 뛰다; (*of music*) ttŏllida 떨리다
thrombosis hyŏltchŏntchŭng 혈전증
throne wangjwa 왕좌
throttle 1 *n* (*on motorbike*, *boat*) soktto chojŏl changch'i 속도 조절 장치 **2** *v/t* (*strangle*) moktchorŭda 목조르다
♦**throttle back** *v/i* kamsok'ada 감속하다
through 1 *prep* ◊ (*across*) …ŭl

t'onghayŏ …을 통하여; ***go ~ the city*** toshirŭl chinagada 도시를 지나가다 ◊ (*during*) …ŭi tong-an naenae …의 동안 내내; ***~ the winter / summer*** kyŏul / yŏrŭm tong-an naenae 겨울 / 여름 동안 내내; ***Monday ~ Friday*** wŏryoilbut'ŏ kŭmnyoil tong-an naenae 월요일부터 금요일 동안 내내 ◊ (*thanks to*) … tŏkppune … 덕분에; ***arranged ~ him*** kŭ tŏkppune 그 덕분에 **2** *adv*: ***wet ~*** mongttang chŏjŏt-tta 몽땅 젖었다; ***watch a movie ~*** yŏnghwarŭl kkŭtkkaji poda 영화를 끝까지 보다; ***read a book ~*** ch'aegŭl kkŭtkkaji iltta 책을 끝까지 읽다 **3** *adj*: ***be ~*** (*of couple*) kwan-gyega kkŭnnada 관계가 끝나다; (*have arrived*: *of news etc*) toch'ak'ada 도착하다; ***you're ~*** TELEC yŏn-gyŏldwaessŭmnida 연결됐습니다; ***I'm ~ with*** *person* nanŭn …wa / kwa kwan-gyerŭl kkŭnnaet-tta 나는 …와 / 과의 관계를 끝냈다; (*no longer need*) nanŭn …ŭl / rŭl ta ssŏt-tta 나는 …을 / 를 다 썼다

through flight chik'aeng pihaenggi 직행 비행기

throughout 1 *prep journey*, *night* …tong-an naenae …동안 내내; *novel* …ŭi toch'ŏe …의 도처에 **2** *adv* (*in all parts*) chŏnch'ejŏgŭro 전체적으로

through train chik'aeng yŏlch'a 직행 열차

throw 1 *v/t* tŏnjida 던지다; (*of horse*) naep'aenggaech'ida 내팽개치다; (*disconcert*) tanghwanghage hada 당황하게 하다; *party* yŏlda 열다 **2** *n* tŏnjigi 던지기

♦**throw away** pŏrida 버리다

♦**throw out** *old things* naebŏrida 내버리다; *person* naetchot-tta 내쫓다; *plan* pugyŏrhada 부결하다

♦**throw up 1** *v/t ball* wiro tŏnjida 위로 던지다; ***~ one's hands*** tu son tŭlda 두 손 들다 **2** *v/i* (*vomit*) t'ohada 토하다

throw-away *remark* amurŏch'i ank'e han 아무렇지 않게 한; (*disposable*) irhoeyong 일회용

throw-in SP sŭroin 스로인

thru → ***through***

thrush (*bird*) kaettongjippagwi 개똥지빠귀

thrust *v/t* (*push hard*) sege tchirŭda 세게 찌르다; ***~ sth into s.o.'s hands*** muŏsŭl nuguŭi sone ŏktchiro ttŏmatkkida 무엇을 누구의 손에 억지로 떠맡기다; ***~ one's way through the crowd*** kunjung sogŭl hech'igo naagada 군중 속을 헤치고 나아가다

thud *n* k'unghanŭn sori 쿵하는 소리

thug hyung-akppŏm 흉악범

thumb 1 *n* ŏmji sonkkarak 엄지 손가락 **2** *v/t*: ***~ a ride*** p'yŏnsŭnghada 편승하다

thumbtack app'in 압핀

thump 1 *n* (*blow*) chumŏktchil 주먹질; (*noise*) k'unghanŭn sori 쿵하는 소리 **2** *v/t person* ch'ida 치다; ***~ one's fist on the table*** t'eibŭrŭl chumŏgŭro tudŭrida 테이블을 주먹으로 두드리다 **3** *v/i* (*of heart*) tugŭndugŭn ttwida 두근두근 뛰다; ***~ on the door*** mune k'unghago puditch'ida 문에 쿵하고 부딪치다

thunder *n* ch'ŏndung 천둥

thunderstorm noeu 뇌우

thundery *weather* ch'ŏndung-i morach'il tŭt'an 천둥이 몰아칠 듯한

Thursday mogyoil 목요일

thus ttarasŏ 따라서

thwart *person*, *plans* panghaehada 방해하다

thyroid (gland) kapssangsŏn 갑상선

Tibet T'ibet'ŭ 티베트

Tibetan 1 *adj* T'ibet'ŭŭi 티베트의 **2** *n* (*person*) T'ibet'ŭin 티베트인; (*language*) T'ibet'ŭŏ 티베트어

tick 1 *n* (*of clock*) ttokttak sori 똑딱 소리; (*checkmark*) chŏmgŏm p'yoshi 점검 표시 **2** *v/i* (*of clock*) ttokttak-kkŏrida 똑딱거리다

♦**tick off** (*reprimand*) chuŭi chuda 주의 주다

ticket p'yo 표

ticket collector kaech'arwŏn 개찰원; **ticket inspector** p'yo kŏmsawŏn 표 검사원; **ticket machine** p'yo chadong p'anmaegi 표 자동 판매기; **ticket office** (*at station*) maep'yoso 매표소

tickle 1 *v/t person* kanjirŏp'ida 간지럽히다 **2** *v/i* (*of material*) kanjilkanjirhada 간질간질하다; (*of person*) kanjirida 간질이다

ticklish *person* kanjirŏumŭl chal t'anŭn 간지러움을 잘 타는

tidal wave chosŏkp'a 조석파

tide chosu 조수; ***high ~*** manjo 만조; ***low ~*** kanjo 간조; ***the ~ is in / out*** milmurida / ssŏlmurida 밀물이다 / 썰물이다

tidy *person*, *habits* tanjŏnghan 단정한; *room*, *house* chŏngdondoen 정돈된

♦**tidy up 1** *v/t room*, *shelves* chŏngdonhada 정돈하다; ***tidy oneself up*** tanjŏnghi hada 단정히 하다 **2** *v/i* chŏngdonhada 정돈하다

tie 1 *n* (*necktie*) nekt'ai 넥타이; (SP: *even result*) tongtchŏm 동점; ***he doesn't have any ~s*** kŭnŭn amu yŏn-gojado ŏptta 그는 아무 연고자도 없다 **2** *v/t knot* choida 조이다; *hands* muktta 묶다; ***~ two ropes together*** tu kaeŭi kkŭnŭl hamkke muktta 두 개의 끈을 함께 묶다 **3** *v/i* SP tongtchŏmi toeda 동점이 되다

♦**tie down** (*with rope*) mukkŏ not'a 묶어 놓다; (*restrict*) kusok'ada 구속하다

♦**tie up** muktta 묶다; *boat* maeda 매다; ***I'm tied up tomorrow*** nanŭn naeil yakssogi it-tta 나는 내일 약속이 있다

tier ch'ŭng 층

tiger horang-i 호랑이

tight 1 *adj clothes* kkok kkinŭn 꼭 끼는; *security* tandanhan 단단한; (*hard to move*) kkok kkiin 꼭 끼인; (*properly shut*) kkok tach'in 꼭 닫힌; (*not leaving much time*) ch'okppak'an 촉박한; F (*drunk*) ch'wihan 취한 **2** *adv hold* tandanhi 단단히; *shut* kkok 꼭

tighten *screw* tandanhi choida 단단히 조이다; *control*, *security* kanghwahada 강화하다; ***~ one's grip on sth*** muŏsŭl chang-ak'ada 무엇을 장악하다

♦**tighten up** *v/i* (*in discipline*, *security*) ŏmhage hada 엄하게 하다

tight-fisted insaek'an 인색한

tightrope p'aengp'aenghan chul 팽팽한 줄

tile t'ail 타일

till[1] → ***until***

till[2] (*cash register*) ton sŏrap 돈 서랍

till[3] *v/t soil* kyŏngjak'ada 경작하다

tilt 1 *v/t* kiurida 기울이다 **2** *v/i* kiulda 기울다

timber moktchae 목재

time shigan 시간; (*occasion*) pŏn 번; ***~ is up*** ije shigani ta twaet-tta 이제 시간이 다 됐다; ***for the ~ being*** tangbun-gan 당분간; ***have a good ~*** choŭn shiganŭl ponaeda 좋은 시간을 보내다; ***have a good ~!*** choŭn shiganŭl ponaeseyo! 좋은 시간을 보내세요!; ***what's the ~?*** myŏt shiimnikka? 몇 시입니까?; ***the first ~*** ch'oŭmŭro 처음으로; ***four ~s*** ne pŏn 네 번; ***~ and again*** myŏt pŏnina kyesok 몇 번이나 계속; ***all the ~*** nŭl 늘; ***three at a ~*** han pŏne set 한 번에 셋; ***at the same ~*** *speak*, *reply etc* tongshie 동시에; (*however*) kŭrŏmyŏnsŏdo 그러면서도; ***in ~*** shiganŭl match'uŏ 시간을 맞추어; ***on ~*** chŏnggage 정각에; ***in no ~*** kot 곧

time bomb shihan p'okt'an 시한 폭탄; **time clock** (*in factory*) ch'ult'oegŭn shigan kirok-kkye 출퇴근 시간 기록계; **time-consuming** manŭn shigani kŏllinŭn 많은 시간이 걸리는; **time lag** shich'a 시차; **time limit** chehan shigan 제한 시간

timely chŏksshiŭi 적시의

time out SP t'aim aut 타임 아웃

timer t'aimŏ 타이머

timesaving *n* shigan chŏryak 시간 절약; **timescale** (*of project*) shigi 시기; **time switch** t'aim sŭwich'i 타임 스위치; **timetable** shiganp'yo 시간표; **timewarp** waegokttoen shigandae 왜곡된 시간대; **time zone** p'yojun shiganttae 표준 시간대

timid *person*, *animal* kŏmmanŭn

겁많은; *smile* kŏmmŏgŭn 겁먹은
timing (*choosing a time*) shigirŭl match'ugi 시기를 맞추기; (*of actor, dancer*) t'aiming 타이밍
tin (*metal*) chusŏk 주석
tinfoil ŭnjong-i 은종이
tinge *n* (*of color*) yŏt'ŭn saektcho 엷은 색조; (*of sadness*) kisaek 기색
tingle *v/i* ttakkŭmgŏrida 따끔거리다
♦**tinker with** manjijak-kkŏrida 만지작거리다
tinkle *n* (*of bell*) ttallangttallang 딸랑딸랑
tinsel pantchak-kkŏrinŭn kŭmsok changshik 반짝거리는 금속 장식
tint 1 *n* (*of color*) yŏnhan saektcho 연한 색조; (*in hair*) yŏmsaek 염색 **2** *v/t hair* yŏmsaek'ada 염색하다
tinted *glasses* saek-kkal innŭn 색깔 있는
tiny chogŭmahan 조그마한
tip[1] *n* (*of stick, finger*) kkŭt 끝; (*of mountain*) chŏngsang 정상; (*of cigarette*) p'ilt'ŏ 필터
tip[2] **1** *n* (*piece of advice*) pigyŏl 비결; (*money*) t'ip 팁 **2** *v/t waiter etc* ...ege t'ibŭl chuda ...에게 팁을 주다
♦**tip off** pimil chŏngborŭl chuda 비밀 정보를 주다
♦**tip over** *jug, liquid* twiŏptta 뒤엎다; ***he tipped water all over me*** kŭnŭn na-ege murŭl ont'ong twijibŏ ssŭiwŏt-tta 그는 나에게 물을 온통 뒤집어 씌웠다
tipped *cigarettes* p'ilt'ŏ innŭn tambae 필터 있는 담배
tippy-toe: ***on ~*** palkkŭt'ŭro 발끝으로
tipsy ŏlk'ŭnhage ch'wihan 얼큰하게 취한
tire[1] *n* t'aiŏ 타이어
tire[2] **1** *v/t* chich'ige hada 지치게 하다 **2** *v/i* chich'ida 지치다; ***he never ~s of it*** kŭnŭn kŭgŏsŭl kyŏlk'o shiltchŭng naeji annŭnda 그는 그것을 결코 싫증 내지 않는다
tired p'igonhan 피곤한; ***be ~ of s.o.*** / ***sth*** nugue / muŏse shiltchŭng nada 누구에 / 무엇에 싫증 나다
tireless *efforts* chich'il chul morŭnŭn 지칠 줄 모르는
tiresome kwich'anŭn 귀찮은, sŏnggashin 성가신
tiring chich'ige hanŭn 지치게 하는
tissue ANAT chojik 조직; (*handkerchief*) hwajangji 화장지
tissue paper p'ojangji 포장지
tit[1] (*bird*) pakssae 박새
tit[2]: ***~ for tat*** matppadach'igi 맞받아치기
tit[3] V (*breast*) chŏtkkasŭm 젖가슴
title (*of novel etc*) chemok 제목; (*of person*) chik'am 직함; LAW kwŏlli 권리
titter *v/i* k'ikk'ik-kkŏrida 킥킥거리다
to 1 *prep* ...(ŭ)ro ...(으)로; ***~ Korea*** Han-gugŭro 한국으로; ***~ Chicago*** Shik'agoro 시카고로; ***go ~ my place*** uri chibŭro kada 우리 집으로 가다; ***walk ~ the station*** yŏgŭro kŏrŏgada 역으로 걸어가다; ***~ the north / south of*** ...ŭi puktchogŭro / namtchogŭro ...의 북쪽으로 / 남쪽으로; ***give sth ~ s.o.*** muŏsŭl nuguege chuda 무엇을 누구에게 주다; ***from Monday ~ Wednesday*** wŏryoilbut'ŏ suyoilkkaji 월요일부터 수요일까지; ***from 10 ~ 15 people*** 10myŏng-esŏ 15myŏng-ŭi saramdŭl 10명에서 15명의 사람들 **2** (*with verbs*) ...hagi wihae ...하기 위해, ...hanŭn kŏt ...하는 것; ***~ speak*** marhanŭn kŏt 말하는 것; ***learn ~ drive*** unjŏnhanŭn kŏsŭl paeuda 운전하는 것을 배우다; ***nice ~ eat*** mŏk-kkie choŭn 먹기에 좋은; ***too heavy ~ carry*** unbanhagie nŏmu mugŏun 운반하기에 너무 무거운; ***~ be honest with you*** nŏhant'e soltchik'i marhajamyŏn 너한테 솔직히 말하자면 **3** *adv*: ***~ and fro*** apttwiro 앞뒤로
toad tukkŏbi 두꺼비
toadstool tokppŏsŏt 독버섯
toast 1 *n* t'osŭt'ŭ 토스트; (*when drinking*) kŏnbae 건배; ***propose a ~ to s.o.*** nugurŭl wihae kŏnbaehajago hada 누구를 위해 건배하자고 하다 **2** *v/t person* kŏnbaehada 건배하다
tobacco tambae 담배
toboggan *n* ssŏlmae 썰매
today onŭl 오늘

toddle (*of child*) ajang-ajang kŏt-tta 아장아장 걷다
toddler ajang-ajang kŏnnŭn ai 아장아장 걷는 아이
toe 1 *n* palkkarak 발가락; (*of shoe*) palkkŭt pubun 발끝 부분 **2** *v/t*: **~ *the line*** kyuch'igŭl ttarŭda 규칙을 따르다
toffee t'op'i 토피
tofu tubu 두부
together hamkke 함께; (*at the same time*) tongshie 동시에
toil *n* nogo 노고
toilet hwajangshil 화장실; ***go to the ~*** hwajangshire kada 화장실에 가다
toilet paper hwajangji 화장지, hyuji 휴지
toiletries semyŏn yongp'um 세면 용품
Tok Island Toktto 독도
token (*sign*) p'yoshi 표시; (*gift ~*) sangp'umkkwŏn 상품권; (*for slot machine*) t'ok'ŭn 토큰
Tokyo Tonggyŏng 동경
tolerable *pain etc* ch'amŭl su innŭn 참을 수 있는; (*quite good*) kkwae kwaench'anŭn 꽤 괜찮은
tolerance kwanyong 관용
tolerant kwanyong innŭn 관용 있는
tolerate *noise*, *person* ch'amtta 참다; ***I won't ~ it!*** igŏsŭn ch'amŭl suga ŏpssŏyo! 이것은 참을 수가 없어요!
toll[1] *v/i* (*of bell*) ch'ŏnch'ŏnhi kyesok'aesŏ ullida 천천히 계속해서 울리다
toll[2] (*deaths*) hŭisaeng 희생
toll[3] (*for bridge*, *road*) t'onghaengnyo 통행료; TELEC t'onghwaryo 통화료
toll booth yogŭm chingsuso 요금 징수소; **toll-free** TELEC muryo t'onghwa 무료 통화; **toll road** yuryo toro 유료 도로
tomato t'omat'o 토마토
tomato ketchup t'omat'o k'ech'ap 토마토 케찹
tomb mudŏm 무덤
tomboy malgwallyang-i 말괄량이
tombstone pisŏk 비석
tomcat suk'oyang-i 수코양이
tomorrow naeil 내일; ***the day after ~*** more 모레; **~ *morning*** naeil ach'im 내일 아침
ton t'on 톤
tone (*of color*) saektcho 색조; (*of musical instrument*) ŭmsaek 음색; (*of conversation etc*) ŏjo 어조; (*of neighborhood*) punwigi 분위기; **~ *of voice*** mokssori 목소리
♦**tone down** *demands*, *criticism* pudŭrŏpkke hada 부드럽게 하다
toner t'onŏ 토너
tongs chipkke 집게; (*for hair*) mŏri indu 머리 인두
tongue *n* hyŏ 혀
tonic MED kangjangje 강장제
tonic (water) t'onik wŏt'ŏ 토닉 워터
tonight onŭl pam 오늘 밤
tonsillitis p'yŏndosŏnnyŏm 편도선염
tonsils p'yŏndosŏn 편도선
too (*also*) ttohan 또한, to 도; (*excessively*) nŏmu 너무; ***me ~*** chŏdoyo 저도요; **~ *big* / *hot*** nŏmu k'ŭn / ttŭgŏun 너무 큰 / 뜨거운; **~ *much food*** nŏmu manŭn ŭmshik 너무 많은 음식; ***eat ~ much*** nŏmuna mani mŏktta 너무 많이 먹다
tool togu 도구
tooth i 이
toothache ch'it'ong 치통; **toothbrush** ch'itssol 칫솔; **toothless** iga ŏmnŭn 이가 없는; **toothpaste** ch'iyak 치약; **toothpick** issushigae 이쑤시개
top 1 *n* (*upper part*) witppubun 윗부분; (*of mountain*, *tree*) kkokttaegi 꼭대기; (*lid*: *of bottle etc*, *pen*) ttukkŏng 뚜껑; (*of class*, *league*) sangnyu 상류; (*clothing*) sang-ŭi 상의; (MOT: *gear*) t'opkkiŏ 톱기어; ***on ~ of*** …ŭi wie …의 위에; ***at the ~ of*** …ŭi witchoge …의 위쪽에; ***get to the ~*** (*of company etc*) chŏngsang-e orŭda 정상에 오르다; ***be over the ~*** (*exaggerated*) kwajangdoeda 과장되다 **2** *adj branches* kkokttaegiŭi 꼭대기의; *floor* maenwiŭi 맨위의; *management*, *official* sangbuŭi 상부의; *player* ch'oesang-ŭi 최상의; *speed*, *note* ch'oegoŭi 최고의 **3** *v/t*: ***~ped with cream*** k'ŭrimŭro tŏp'in 크림으로 덮힌

♦**top up** *glass, tank* kadŭk ch'aeuda 가득 채우다
top hat chungsanmo 중산모
topheavy puranjŏnghan 불안정한
topic hwaje 화제
topical hwajeŭi 화제의
topless *adj* kasŭmŭl tŭrŏnaen 가슴을 드러낸, t'op'ŭllisŭ 토플리스
topmost *branches, floor* ch'oesang-ŭi 최상의
topping (*on pizza*) t'op'ing 토핑
topple 1 *v/i* ssŭrŏjida 쓰러지다 **2** *v/t government* ssŭrŏttŭrida 쓰러뜨리다
top secret kŭkppi 극비
topsy-turvy *adj* (*in disorder*) twijukppaktchugin 뒤죽박죽인; *world* hollansŭrŏun 혼란스러운
torch (*with flame*) hwaetppul 횃불
torment 1 *n* kot'ong 고통 **2** *v/t person, animal* koerop'ida 괴롭히다; ***~ed by doubt*** ŭishimŭro koerowahanŭn 의심으로 괴로와하는
tornado hoeori param 회오리 바람
torrent kŭmnyu 급류; (*of lava*) punch'ul 분출; (*of abuse, words*) yŏnbal 연발
torrential *rain* ŏkssugat'ŭn 억수같은
tortoise kŏbuk 거북
torture 1 *n* komun 고문 **2** *v/t* komunhada 고문하다
toss 1 *v/t ball* kabyŏpkke tŏnjida 가볍게 던지다; *rider* ttŏrŏttŭrida 떨어뜨리다; *salad* pŏmurida 버무리다; ***~ a coin*** tongjŏnŭl tŏnjyŏ chŏnghada 동전을 던져 정하다 **2** *v/i*: ***~ and turn*** twich'ŏk-kkŏrida 뒤척거리다
total 1 *n* hapkkye 합계 **2** *adj sum, amount* chŏnch'eŭi 전체의; *disaster, idiot, stranger* wanjŏnhan 완전한; ***~ amount of money*** ch'ong-aek 총액 **3** *v/t* F (*car*) wanjŏnhi pusuda 완전히 부수다
totalitarian chŏnch'ejuŭiŭi 전체주의의
totally wanjŏnhi 완전히
tote bag taehyŏng haendŭbaek 대형 핸드백
totter (*of person*) pit'ŭlgŏrida 비틀거리다
touch 1 *n* (*act of touching*) chŏpch'ok 접촉; (*sense*) ch'ok-kkam 촉감; (*little bit*) yakkan 약간; SP t'ŏch'i 터치; ***lose ~ with s.o.*** nuguwa yŏllagi kkŭnkkida 누구와 연락이 끊기다; ***keep in ~ with s.o.*** nuguwa kyesok yŏllak'ada 누구와 계속 연락하다; ***be out of ~*** chopch'ok'aji ank'o chinaeda 접촉하지 않고 지내다 **2** *v/t* manjida 만지다; (*emotionally*) kamdongshik'ida 감동시키다 **3** *v/i* manjida 만지다; (*of two lines etc*) chŏpch'ok'ada 접촉하다
♦**touch down** (*of airplane*) ch'angnyuk'ada 착륙하다; SP tŭktchŏmhada 득점하다
♦**touch on** (*mention*) kandanhi ŏn-gŭp'ada 간단히 언급하다
♦**touch up** *photo* sonjirhada 손질하다
touchdown (*of airplane*) ch'angnyuk 착륙; SP t'ŏch'idaun 터치다운
touching *adj* kamdongshik'inŭn 감동시키는
touchline SP t'ŏch'irain 터치라인
touchy *person* chinach'ige yeminhan 지나치게 예민한
tough *person* ŏkssen 억센; *meat* chilgin 질긴; *question, exam* ŏryŏun 어려운; *material* kŏch'in 거친; *punishment* ŏmhan 엄한
tough guy ŏkssen sanai 억센 사나이
tour 1 *n* kwan-gwang 관광 **2** *v/t area* kwan-gwanghada 관광하다
tourism kwan-gwang-ŏp 관광업
tourist kwan-gwanggaek 관광객
tourist (information) office kwan-gwang annaeso 관광 안내소
tournament shihap 시합
tour operator kwan-gwang-ŏptcha 관광업자
tousled *hair* hŏngk'ŭrŏjin 헝클어진
tow 1 *v/t car, boat* kkŭlda 끌다 **2** *n* kkŭlgi 끌기; ***give s.o. a ~*** nugurŭl kkŭrŏjuda 누구를 끌어주다
♦**tow away** *car* kyŏninhada 견인하다
toward *prep* …ŭl / rŭl hyanghayŏ …을 / 를 향하여; (*in behavior, attitude*) …ege …에게
towel sugŏn 수건
tower *n* t'ap 탑
town toshi 도시
town council shi ŭihoe 시 의회

town hall shich'ŏng 시청
township myŏn 면
towrope kyŏninnyong patchul 견인용 밧줄
toxic toksŏng-ŭi 독성의
toy changnankkam 장난감
♦**toy with** *object* kajigo nolda 가지고 놀다; *idea* halkkamalkka saenggak'ada 할까말까 생각하다
trace 1 *n* (*of substance*) hŭnjŏk 흔적 **2** *v/t* (*find*) susaek'ada 수색하다; (*follow*: *footsteps*) ch'ujŏk'ada 추적하다; (*draw*) kŭrida 그리다
track *n* (*path*) kil 길; (*on race course*) t'ŭraek 트랙; (*race course*) k'osŭ 코스; RAIL ch'ŏltto 철도; ~ ***10*** RAIL 10ppŏn sŏllo 10번 선로; ***keep ~ of sth*** muŏshi kirogŭl namgida 무엇의 기록을 남기다
♦**track down** twitchoch'a ch'ajanaeda 뒤쫓아 찾아내다
tracksuit poon undongbok 보온 운동복
tractor t'ŭraekt'ŏ 트랙터
trade 1 *n* (*commerce*) sang-ŏp 상업; (*between countries*) muyŏk 무역; (*profession, craft*) chigŏp 직업 **2** *v/i* (*do business*) changsahada 장사하다; ~ ***in sth*** musŭn changsarŭl hada 무슨 장사를 하다 **3** *v/t* (*exchange*) kyohwanhada 교환하다; ~ ***sth for sth*** muŏtkkwa muŏsŭl kyohwanhada 무엇과 무엇을 교환하다
♦**trade in** *v/t* (*when buying*) *uttonŭl naego shinp'umgwa kyohwanhada* 웃돈을 내고 신품과 교환하다
trade fair muyŏk chŏnshihoe 무역 전시회; **trademark** tŭngnok sangp'yo 등록 상표; **trade mission** muyŏk-kkwan 무역관
trader sang-in 상인
trade secret kiŏp pimil 기업 비밀
tradesman (*plumber etc*) surigong 수리공; (*deliveryman etc*) paedarwŏn 배달원
trade(s) union nodong chohap 노동 조합
tradition chŏnt'ong 전통
traditional chŏnt'ongjŏgin 전통적인
traditionally chŏnt'ongjŏgŭro 전통적으로
traffic *n* kyot'ong 교통; (*in drugs*) milssu 밀수
♦**traffic in** *drugs* milssuhada 밀수하다
traffic circle lot'ŏri 로터리; **traffic cop** F kyot'ong sun-gyŏng 교통 순경; **traffic jam** kyot'ong ch'ejŭng 교통 체증; **traffic light** shinhodŭng 신호등; **traffic police** kyot'ong sun-gyŏng 교통 순경; **traffic sign** kyot'ong shinho 교통 신호; **traffic violation** kyot'ong wiban 교통 위반
tragedy pigŭk 비극
tragic pigŭktchŏgin 비극적인
trail 1 *n* (*path*) kil 길; (*of blood*) hŭnjŏk 흔적 **2** *v/t* (*follow*) ttaragada 따라가다; (*tow*) kkŭlda 끌다 **3** *v/i* (*lag behind*) kkŭllida 끌리다
trailer (*pulled by vehicle*) t'ŭreillŏ 트레일러; (*mobile home*) idong chut'aek 이동 주택; (*of movie*) yegop'yŏn 예고편
train[1] *n* kich'a 기차; ***go by ~*** kich'aro kada 기차로 가다
train[2] **1** *v/t team, athlete, dog* hullyŏnshik'ida 훈련시키다; *employee* kyoyukshik'ida 교육시키다 **2** *v/i* (*of team, athlete*) yŏnssŭp'ada 연습하다; (*of teacher etc*) kyoyukpat-tta 교육받다
trainee kyŏnsŭpssaeng 견습생
trainer SP k'och'i 코치; (*of dog*) hullyŏnsa 훈련사
trainers *Br* (*shoes*) undonghwa 운동화
training (*of new staff*) kyoyuk 교육; SP hullyŏn 훈련; ***be in ~*** SP hullyŏn chung-ida 훈련 중이다; ***be out of ~*** SP hullyŏn chung-i anida 훈련 중이 아니다
training course kyŏnsŭp kwajŏng 견습 과정
training scheme hullyŏn kyehoek 훈련 계획
train station kich'ayŏk 기차역
trait t'ŭkssŏng 특성
traitor paebanja 배반자
tramp 1 *n pej* (*woman*) kŏlle 걸레; *Br* (*hobo*) ttŏdori 떠돌이 **2** *v/i* k'ungk'ung kŏt-tta 쿵쿵 걷다

trample *v/t*: ***be ~d to death*** palp'yŏ chuktta 밟혀 죽다; ***be ~d underfoot*** magu chitppalp'ida 마구 짓밟히다
♦**trample on** *person, object* palba munggaeda 밟아 뭉개다
trampoline t'ŭraemp'ollin 트램폴린
trance honsu sangt'ae 혼수 상태; ***go into a ~*** honsu sangt'aee ppajida 혼수 상태에 빠지다
tranquil p'yŏng-onhan 평온한
tranquility p'yŏng-on 평온
tranquilizer chinjŏngje 진정제
transact *deal, business* ch'ŏrihada 처리하다
transaction kŏrae 거래
transatlantic Taesŏyang hoengdanŭi 대서양 횡단의
transcendental ch'owŏltchŏgin 초월적인
transcript (*of meeting, trial*) sabon 사본
transfer 1 *v/t* omgida 옮기다; *money* songgŭmhada 송금하다; *player* ijŏk'ada 이적하다 **2** *v/i* (*switch*) pakkuda 바꾸다 (*when traveling*) omgyŏt'ada 옮겨타다 **3** *n* idong 이동; (*in travel*) karat'agi 갈아타기; (*of money*) songgŭmhwan 송금환
transferable *ticket* yangdohal su innŭn 양도할 수 있는
transform *v/t* pyŏnhyŏngshik'ida 변형시키다
transformation pyŏnhyŏng 변형
transformer ELEC pyŏnapkki 변압기
transfusion chuip 주입
transistor t'ŭraenjisŭt'ŏ 트랜지스터; (*radio*) t'ŭraenjisŭt'ŏ ladio 트랜지스터 라디오
transit: ***in ~*** *goods* susong chung-in 수송 중인; ***~ passenger*** t'onggwa yŏgaek 통과 여객
transition pyŏnhwa 변화
transitional kwadojŏgin 과도적인; ***~ period*** kwadogi 과도기
transit lounge (*at airport*) t'onggwa yŏgaek taehapsshil 통과 여객 대합실
translate pŏnyŏk'ada 번역하다
translation pŏnyŏk 번역
translator pŏnyŏkka 번역가
transliterate ŭmnyŏk'ada 음역하다
transmission (*of news, program*) pangsong 방송; (*of disease*) chŏnyŏm 전염; MOT pyŏnsokki 변속기
transmit *program* pangsonghada 방송하다; *disease* chŏnyŏmshik'ida 전염시키다
transmitter RAD, TV songshin-gi 송신기
transpacific T'aep'yŏngyang hoengdanŭi 태평양 횡단의
transparency PHOT sŭllaidŭ 슬라이드
transparent t'umyŏnghan 투명한; *blouse* sogi pich'inŭn 속이 비치는; (*obvious*) myŏngbaek'an 명백한
transplant MED **1** *v/t* ishik'ada 이식하다 **2** *n* ishik susul 이식 수술
transport 1 *v/t goods, people* susonghada 수송하다 **2** *n* (*of goods, people*) susong 수송
transportation (*of goods, people*) susong 수송; ***means of ~*** kyot'ong sudan 교통 수단; ***public ~*** taejung kyot'ong 대중 교통; ***Department of Transportation*** Kyot'ongbu 교통부
transvestite *isŏng-ŭi osŭl ipkki choahanŭn saram* 이성의 옷을 입기 좋아하는 사람
trap 1 *n* (*for animal*) tŏt 덫; (*question, set-up etc*) hamjŏng 함정; ***set a ~ for s.o.*** nugurŭl hamjŏng-e ppattŭrida 누구를 함정에 빠뜨리다 **2** *v/t animal* tŏch'ŭro chaptta 덫으로 잡다; *person* hamjŏng-e ppattŭrida 함정에 빠뜨리다; ***be ~ped*** hamjŏng-e ppajida 함정에 빠지다; (*in marriage, bad job etc*) tŏch'e kŏllida 덫에 걸리다
trapdoor tŭlch'angmun 들창문
trapeze kogyeyong kŭne 곡예용 그네
trappings (*of power*) pugamul 부가물
trash (*garbage*) ssŭregi 쓰레기; (*poor product*) pullyangp'um 불량품; (*book, movie etc*) choltchak 졸작; (*despicable person*) in-gan ssŭregi 인간 쓰레기
trashcan ssŭregi t'ong 쓰레기 통
trashy *goods, novel* ssŭlmoŏmnŭn 쓸모없는
traumatic chŏngshinjŏgŭro k'ŭn ch'unggyŏgŭl chunŭn 정신적으로 큰 충격을 주는

travel 1 *n* yŏhaeng 여행; **~s** yŏhaeng 여행 **2** *v/i* yŏhaenghada 여행하다 **3** *v/t miles* yŏhaenghayŏ chinagada 여행하여 지나가다
travel agency yŏhaengsa 여행사
travel bag yŏhaeng kabang 여행 가방
traveler yŏhaenggaek 여행객
traveler's check yŏhaengja sup'yo 여행자 수표; **travel expenses** yŏhaeng piyong 여행 비용; **travel insurance** yŏhaeng pohŏm 여행 보험
trawler t'ŭrol ŏsŏn 트롤 어선
tray (*for food etc*) chaengban 쟁반; (*to go in oven*) p'an 판; (*in printer, copier*) holdŏ 홀더
treacherous paebanhanŭn 배반하는; *currents, roads* wihŏmhan 위험한
treachery paeban 배반
tread 1 *n* palkkŏrŭm 발걸음; (*of staircase*) tidimp'an 디딤판; (*of tire*) t'ŭredŭ 트레드 **2** *v/i* paltta 밟다
♦**tread on** paltta 밟다
treason panyŏk 반역
treasure 1 *n* pomul 보물; (*person*) sojunghan saram 소중한 사람 **2** *v/t gift etc* sojunghi hada 소중히 하다
treasurer hoegye tamdangja 회계 담당자
Treasury Department Chaemusŏng 재무성
treat 1 *n* (*pleasure*) k'ŭn kippŭm 큰 기쁨; ***it was a real ~*** chŏngmal kippŏssŏ 정말 기뻤어; ***I have a ~ for you*** tangshinŭl nollage hae tŭril iri issŭmnida 당신을 놀라게 해 드릴 일이 있습니다; ***it's my ~*** (*I'm paying*) chega hant'ŏk naegessŭmnida 제가 한턱 내겠습니다 **2** *v/t materials* taruda 다루다; *illness* ch'iryohada 치료하다; (*behave toward*) taeuhada 대우하다; ***~ s.o. to sth*** nuguege muŏsŭl taejŏp'ada 누구에게 무엇을 대접하다
treatment (*of materials*) ch'wigŭp 취급; (*of illness*) ch'iryo 치료; (*of people*) taeu 대우
treaty choyak 조약
treble[1] MUS ch'oegoŭmbuŭi 최고음부의
treble[2] **1** *adv*: ***~ the price*** sebaero ttwin kagyŏk 세배로 뛴 가격 **2** *v/i* sebaero chŭnggahada 세배로 증가하다
tree namu 나무
tremble (*of person*) ttŏlda 떨다; (*of hand, voice*) ttŏllida 떨리다; (*of building*) hŭndŭllida 흔들리다
tremendous (*very good*) koengjanghan 굉장한; (*enormous*) aju kŏdaehan 아주 거대한
tremendously (*very*) koengjanghi 굉장히; (*a lot*) maeu 매우
tremor (*of earth*) yaktchin 약진
trench ch'amho 참호
trend kyŏnghyang 경향; (*fashion*) yuhaeng-ŭi kyŏnghyang 유행의 경향
trendy ch'oeshin yuhaeng-ŭi 최신 유행의; *person* yuhaeng-ŭl ttarŭnŭn 유행을 따르는
trespass ch'imip'ada 침입하다; ***no ~ing*** ch'urip kŭmji 출입 금지
♦**trespass on** *land* …e ch'imip'ada …에 침입하다; *privacy* …ŭl / rŭl ch'imhaehada …을 / 를 침해하다; *s.o.'s time* …ŭl / rŭl ppaeat-tta …을 / 를 빼앗다
trespasser pulppŏp ch'imiptcha 불법 침입자
trial LAW kongp'an 공판; (*of equipment*) shihŏm 시험; ***on ~*** LAW kongp'an chung 공판 중; ***have sth on ~*** *equipment* muŏsŭl shihŏmhae poda 무엇을 시험해 보다
trial period (*for employee*) kyŏnsŭp kigan 견습 기간; (*for equipment*) shihŏm kigan 시험 기간
triangle samgak'yŏng 삼각형; MUS t'ŭraiaenggŭl 트라이앵글
triangular samgak'yŏng-ŭi 삼각형의
tribe pujok 부족
tribunal shimp'an wiwŏnhoe 심판 위원회
tributary (*river*) chiryu 지류
trick 1 *n* (*to deceive*) sogimsu 속임수; (*knack*) kigyo 기교; ***play a ~ on s.o.*** nuguege changnanjirŭl hada 누구에게 장난질을 하다 **2** *v/t* sogida 속이다; ***~ s.o. into doing sth*** nugurŭl sogyŏsŏ muŏsŭl shik'ida 누구를 속여서 무엇을 시키다
trickery sagi 사기

trickle *v/i* ttokttok ttŏrŏjida 똑똑 떨어지다
trickster sagikkun 사기꾼
tricky (*difficult*) tarugi himdŭn 다루기 힘든; *person* kyohwarhan 교활한
tricycle sebal chajŏn-gŏ 세발 자전거
trifle (*triviality*) hach'anŭn kŏt 하찮은 것
trifling hach'anŭn 하찮은
trigger *n* pang-asoe 방아쇠; (*on camcorder*) shijak pŏt'ŭn 시작 버튼; (*cause*) yubal yoin 유발 요인
♦**trigger off** yubarhada 유발하다
trim 1 *adj* (*neat*) malkkŭmhan 말끔한; *figure* nŭlsshinhan 늘씬한 **2** *v/t hair*, *hedge* sonjirhada 손질하다; *budget*, *costs* sak-kkamhada 삭감하다; (*decorate*: *dress*) changshik'ada 장식하다 **3** *n* (*cut*) saltchak charŭm 살짝 자름; ***just a ~, please*** (*to hairdresser*) kŭnyang saltchak tadŭmŏ chuseyo 그냥 살짝 다듬어 주세요; ***in good ~*** *car*, *machine*, *boxer* chal chŏngbidoen 잘 정비된; *house* chal kakkuŏjin 잘 가꾸어진
trimming (*on clothes*) tŏtppuch'in changshik 덧붙인 장식; ***with all the ~s*** modŭn pugaŭi kŏttŭlgwa 모든 부가의 것들과
trinket chajilgurehan changshin-gu 자질구레한 장신구
trio MUS samjungju 삼중주
trip 1 *n* (*journey*) yŏhaeng 여행 **2** *v/i* (*stumble*) kŏllyŏ nŏmŏjida 걸려 넘어지다 **3** *v/t person* kŏrŏ nŏmŏttŭrida 걸어 넘어뜨리다
♦**trip up 1** *v/t* (*cause to fall*) kŏrŏ nŏmŏttŭrida 걸어 넘어뜨리다; (*cause to go wrong*) shilp'aehage hada 실패하게 하다 **2** *v/i* (*fall*) nŏmŏjida 넘어지다; (*make a mistake*) shilssuhada 실수하다
tripe (*food*) yang 양
Tripitaka Koreana REL P'almandaejanggyŏng 팔만대장경
triple → ***treble***[2]
triplets se ssangdung-i 세 쌍둥이
tripod PHOT samgakttae 삼각대
trite chinbuhan 진부한
triumph *n* sŭngni 승리
trivial sasohan 사소한
triviality sasohan kŏt 사소한 것
trombone t'ŭrŏmbon 트럼본
troops kundae 군대
trophy usŭngk'ŏp 우승컵
tropic hoegwisŏn 회귀선
tropical yŏlttaeŭi 열대의
tropics yŏlttae chibang 열대 지방
trot *v/i* ch'ongch'ong kŏrŭmŭro kada 총총 걸음으로 가다
trouble 1 *n* (*difficulties*) munje 문제; (*inconvenience*) pulp'yŏn 불편; (*disturbance*) malssŏng 말썽; ***go to a lot of ~ to do sth*** muŏsŭl hagi wihae manŭn sugorŭl hada 무엇을 하기 위해 많은 수고를 하다; ***no ~*** munje ŏpssŭmnida 문제 없습니다; ***get into ~*** malssŏng-i nada 말썽이 나다 **2** *v/t* (*worry*) kŏktchŏngshik'ida 걱정시키다; (*bother*, *disturb*) kwich'ank'e hada 귀찮게 하다; (*of back*, *liver etc*) koerop'ida 괴롭히다
trouble-free kojang-i ŏmnŭn 고장이 없는; **troublemaker** malssŏngkkun 말썽꾼; **troubleshooter** (*problem solver*) munje haegyŏlssa 문제 해결사; (*mediator*) punjaeng chojŏngja 분쟁 조정자; **troubleshooting** (*problem solving*) munje haegyŏl 문제 해결; (*for faulty equipment*) kojang suri 고장 수리
troublesome kolch'i ap'ŭn 골치 아픈
trousers *Br* paji 바지
trout song-ŏ 송어
truce hyujŏn 휴전
truck hwamulch'a 화물차
truck driver t'ŭrŏk unjŏnsa 트럭 운전사; **truck farm** ship'anyong nongsanmul chaebae nongga 시판용 농산물 재배 농가; **truck farmer** ship'anyong nongsanmul chaebae nongbu 시판용 농산물 재배 농부; **truck stop** t'ŭrŏk unjŏnsa shikttang 트럭 운전사 식당
trudge 1 *v/i* mŏlgo ŏryŏpkke kada 멀고 어렵게 가다 **2** *n* mŏlgo ŏryŏun kil 멀고 어려운 길
true chŏngmarŭi 정말의; *friend*, *American* chintchaŭi 진짜의; ***come ~*** (*of hopes*, *dream*) shirhyŏndoeda 실현되다

truly chŏngmallo 정말로; ***Yours ~*** ...ollim ...올림

trumpet *n* t'ŭrŏmp'et 트럼펫

trunk (*of tree*) chulgi 줄기; (*of body*) momttung-i 몸뚱이; (*of elephant*) k'o 코; (*container*, *of car*) t'ŭrŏngk'ŭ 트렁크

trust 1 *n* (*in person*, *car etc*) shilloe 신뢰; (*in an organization*) shinyong 신용; FIN witak 위탁 **2** *v/t* shilloehada 신뢰하다; ***I ~ you*** tangshinŭl shilloehamnida 당신을 신뢰합니다

trusted shilloehal su innŭn 신뢰할 수 있는

trustee p'ishint'agin 피신탁인

trustful, **trusting** shilloehanŭn 신뢰하는

trustworthy shilloehal su innŭn 신뢰할 수 있는

truth chinshil 진실; (*fact*) sashil 사실

truthful chinshirhan 진실한; *account* chintchaŭi 진짜의

try 1 *v/t* noryŏk'ada 노력하다; *food* mŏgŏboda 먹어보다; *plan*, *route* shidohada 시도하다; LAW chaep'anhada 재판하다; ***~ to do sth*** muŏsŭl haryŏgo hada 무엇을 하려고 하다 **2** *v/i* haeboda 해보다; ***you must ~ harder*** tangshinŭn tŏ yŏlshimhi noryŏk'aeya hamnida 당신은 더 열심히 노력해야 합니다 **3** *n* shido 시도; ***can I have a ~?*** (*of food*) hanbŏn matppwado toelkkayo? 한번 맛봐도 될까요?; (*at doing sth*) hanbŏn haebwado toelkkayo? 한번 해봐도 될까요?

♦**try on** *clothes* ibŏboda 입어보다

♦**try out** *machine*, *method* shihŏmhae poda 시험해 보다

trying (*annoying*) tchajŭngnanŭn 짜증나는

T-shirt t'ishyŏch'ŭ 티셔츠

tub (*bath*) yoktcho 욕조; (*of liquid*) t'ong 통; (*for yoghurt*, *ice cream*) kwak 곽

tubby *adj* t'ongt'onghan 통통한

tube (*pipe*) kwan 관; (*of toothpaste*, *ointment*) t'yubŭ 튜브

tubeless *tire* t'yubŭga ŏmnŭn 튜브가 없는

tuberculosis kyŏrhaek 결핵

tuck 1 *n* (*in dress*) tan 단 **2** *v/t* (*put*) kkiwŏ nŏt'a 끼워 넣다

♦**tuck away** (*put away*) ch'iuda 치우다; (*eat quickly*) sunshik-kkane mŏgŏch'iuda 순식간에 먹어치우다

♦**tuck in 1** *v/t children* iburŭl tŏp'ŏjuda 이불을 덮어주다; *sheets* ...ŭi kkŭch'ŭl chŏbŏ nŏt'a ...의 끝을 접어 넣다 **2** *v/i* (*start eating*) mŏk-kki shijak'ada 먹기 시작하다

♦**tuck up** *sleeves etc* kŏdŏ ollida 걷어 올리다; ***tuck s.o. up in bed*** nugurŭl ch'imdaee nŏk'o iburŭl tŏp'ŏjuda 누구를 침대에 넣고 이불을 덮어주다

Tuesday hwayoil 화요일

tuft sul 술; (*of grass*) sup'ul 수풀

tug 1 *n* (*pull*) chaba tanggim 잡아 당김; NAUT yeinsŏn 예인선 **2** *v/t* (*pull*) chaba tanggida 잡아 당기다

tuition suŏp 수업; ***private ~*** kaein kyosŭp 개인 교습

tulip t'yullip 튤립

tumble *v/i* kullŏ ttŏrŏjida 굴러 떨어지다; (*of wall*) munŏjida 무너지다

tumbledown munŏjilttŭt'an 무너질 듯한

tumbler (*for drink*) chan 잔; (*in circus*) kogyesa 곡예사

Tumen River Tuman-gang 두만강

tummy pae 배

tummy ache pokt'ong 복통

tumor chongnyang 종양

tumult soran 소란

tumultuous soransŭrŏun 소란스러운

tuna ch'amch'i 참치

tune 1 *n* koktcho 곡조; ***in ~*** ŭmjŏng-i mannŭn 음정이 맞는; ***out of ~*** ŭmjŏng-i t'ŭllin 음정이 틀린 **2** *v/t instrument* choyurhada 조율하다

♦**tune in** *v/i* RAD, TV ch'aenŏrŭl match'uda 채널을 맞추다

♦**tune in to** (*on radio*) ch'ŏngch'wihada 청취하다; (*on TV*) shich'ŏnghada 시청하다

♦**tune up 1** *v/i* (*of orchestra*, *players*) ak-kkiŭi ŭmŭl match'uda 악기의 음을 맞추다 **2** *v/t engine* chojŏrhada 조절하다

tuneful arŭmdaun sŏnyurŭi 아름다운 선율의

tuner (*hi-fi*) t'yunŏ 튜너
tunic EDU kyobok sang-ŭi 교복 상의
tunnel *n* t'ŏnŏl 터널
turbine t'ŏbin 터빈
turbot kajami 가자미
turbulence (*in air travel*) nan-giryu 난기류
turbulent *love affair* kyŏngnyŏrhan 격렬한; *meeting, life* tongnyohanŭn 동요하는; *weather* kŏch'in 거친
turf chandibat 잔디밭; (*piece*) chandi 잔디
Turk T'ŏk'iin 터키인
Turkey T'ŏk'i 터키
turkey ch'ilmyŏnjo 칠면조
Turkish 1 *adj* T'ŏk'iŭi 터키의 **2** *n* (*language*) T'ŏk'iŏ 터키어
turmoil hollan 혼란
turn 1 *n* (*rotation*) hoejŏn 회전; (*in road*) mot'ung-i 모퉁이; (*in vaudeville*) ch'arye 차례; ***take ~s doing sth*** muŏsŭl kyodaero hada 무엇을 교대로 하다; ***it's my ~*** che ch'aryeimnida 제 차례입니다; ***it's not your ~ yet*** ajik tangshin sunsŏga animnida 아직 당신 순서가 아닙니다; ***take a ~ at the wheel*** ch'arŭl kyodaero unjŏnhada 차를 교대로 운전하다; ***do s.o. a good ~*** nuguege ch'injŏrhage hada 누구에게 친절하게 하다 **2** *v/t key, screw etc* tollida 돌리다; *wheel* hoejŏnshik'ida 회전시키다; *corner* tolda 돌다; *food, sheets* twijiptta 뒤집다; *pages of book* nŏmgida 넘기다; ***~ one's back on s.o.*** nuguege tŭng-ŭl tollida 누구에게 등을 돌리다 **3** *v/i* (*of driver, car*) tolda 돌다; (*of wheel*) hoejŏnhada 회전하다; ***~ right / left here*** yŏgisŏ orŭntchogŭro / oentchogŭro toseyo 여기서 오른쪽으로 / 왼쪽으로 도세요; ***it has ~ed sour / cold*** shiŏjyŏt-tta / ch'uwŏjyŏt-tta 시어졌다 / 추워졌다; ***he has ~ed 40*** kŭnŭn sashibi nŏmŏt-tta 그는 40이 넘었다
♦**turn around 1** *v/t object* tollida 돌리다; *company* hojŏnshik'ida 호전시키다; (COM: *deal with*) chumune match'uda 주문에 맞추다 **2** *v/i* (*of person, driver*) tolda 돌다
♦**turn away 1** *v/t* (*send away*) tchoch'abŏrida 쫓아버리다 **2** *v/i* (*walk away*) chinach'yŏ kada 지나쳐 가다; (*look away*) oemyŏnhada 외면하다
♦**turn back 1** *v/t edges, sheets* twijiptta 뒤집다 **2** *v/i* (*of walkers etc*) toedoragada 되돌아가다; (*in course of action*) mullŏsŏda 물러서다
♦**turn down** *v/t offer, invitation* kŏjŏrhada 거절하다; *volume, TV, heating* churida 줄이다; *edge, collar* chŏptta 접다
♦**turn in 1** *v/i* (*go to bed*) chamjarie tŭlda 잠자리에 들다 **2** *v/t* (*to police*) shin-gohada 신고하다
♦**turn off 1** *v/t TV, heater, engine* kkŭda 끄다; *water* chamgŭda 잠그다; F (*sexually*) sŏngtchŏk hŭngmirŭl ilk'e hada 성적 흥미를 잃게 하다 **2** *v/i* (*in driving etc*) tarŭn killo tŭrŏsŏda 다른 길로 들어서다; (*of machine*) kkŏjida 꺼지다
♦**turn on 1** *v/t TV, heater, engine* k'yŏda 켜다; *water* t'ŭlda 틀다; F (*sexually*) sŏngtchŏgŭro hŭngbunshik'ida 성적으로 흥분시키다 **2** *v/i* (*of machine*) k'yŏjida 켜지다
♦**turn out 1** *v/t lights* kkŭda 끄다 **2** *v/i*: ***as it turned out*** kyŏlguk 결국
♦**turn over 1** *v/i* (*in bed*) twich'ŏkkŏrida 뒤척거리다; (*of vehicle*) twijibŏjida 뒤집어지다 **2** *v/t* (*put upside down*) twijiptta 뒤집다; *page* nŏmgida 넘기다; FIN …ŭi maesangŭl ollida …의 매상을 올리다
♦**turn up 1** *v/t collar* seuda 세우다; *volume, heating* nop'ida 높이다 **2** *v/i* (*arrive*) nat'anada 나타나다
turning mot'ung-i 모퉁이
turning point chŏnhwanjŏm 전환점
turnip sunmu 순무
turnout (*people*) ch'amsŏktcha 참석자; **turnover** FIN maesanggo 매상고; **turnpike** yuryo kosokttoro 유료 고속도로; **turnstile** shiptchahyŏng hoejŏnshik mun 십자형 회전식 문; **turntable** (*of record player*) t'ŏnt'eibŭl 턴테이블
turquoise *adj* ch'ŏngnokssaegŭi

청록색의
turret (*of castle*) t'ap 탑; (*of tank*) p'ot'ap 포탑
turtle kŏbuk 거북
turtleneck (sweater) t'ŏt'ŭllek sŭwet'ŏ 터틀넥 스웨터
turtle ship kŏbukssŏn 거북선
tusk ŏmni 엄니
tutor: (***private***) ~ kaein kyosa 개인 교사
tutorial *n* kaebyŏl chido shigan 개별 지도 시간
tuxedo t'ŏksshido 턱시도
TV t'ibi 티비, t'ellebi 텔레비; ***on ~*** t'ibie 티비에
TV program t'ibi p'ŭrogŭraem 티비 프로그램
twang 1 *n* (*in voice*) k'otssori 콧소리 **2** *v/t guitar string* t'winggida 튕기다
tweezers choktchipkke 족집게
twelfth *adj* yŏldu pŏntchaeŭi 열 두 번째의
twelve yŏldul 열 둘, shibi 십이
twentieth *adj* sŭmu pŏntchaeŭi 스무 번째의
twenty sŭmul 스물, iship 이십
twice tu pŏn 두 번; ***~ as much*** tu paeŭi yang-ŭro 두 배의 양으로
twiddle manjijak-kkŏrida 만지작거리다; ***~ one's thumbs*** pindunggŏrida 빈둥거리다
twig *n* kaji 가지
twilight noŭl 노을
twin han ssang-ŭi hantchok 한 쌍의 한쪽; ***~s*** ssangdung-i 쌍둥이
twin beds t'ŭwin pedŭ 트윈 베드
twinge (*of pain*) ssushinŭn tŭt'an ap'ŭm 쑤시는 듯한 아픔
twinkle *v/i* (*of stars*) pantchagida 반짝이다; (*of eyes*) pinnada 빛나다
twin town chamae toshi 자매 도시
twirl 1 *v/t* pingbing tollida 빙빙 돌리다 **2** *n* (*of cream etc*) soyongdori kkorŭi changshik 소용돌이 꼴의 장식
twist 1 *v/t* kkoda 꼬다; ***~ one's ankle*** palmogŭl ppida 발목을 삐다 **2** *v/i* (*of road, river*) kuburŏjida 구부러지다 **3** *n* (*in rope*) kkoim 꼬임; (*in road*) kulgok 굴곡; (*in plot, story*) ttŭt pakkŭi chŏn-gae 뜻 밖의 전개
twisty *road* kkubulkkuburhan 꾸불꾸불한
twit F pabo 바보
twitch 1 *n* (*nervous*) kyŏngnyŏn 경련 **2** *v/i* (*jerk*) kyŏngnyŏni ilda 경련이 일다
twitter *v/i* (*of birds*) chijŏgwida 지저귀다
two tul 둘, i 이; ***the ~ of them*** kŭdŭl tul 그들 둘
two-faced ijung in-gyŏgŭi 이중 인격의; **two-stroke** *adj engine* ihaengjŏng ssaik'ŭrŭi 이행정 싸이클의; **two-way traffic** yangbanghyang t'onghaengno 양방향 통행로
tycoon kŏmul 거물
type 1 *n* (*sort*) yuhyŏng 유형; ***what ~ of ...?*** ŏttŏn yuhyŏng-ŭi ...? 어떤 유형의 ...? **2** *v/i* (*use a keyboard*) t'aja ch'ida 타자 치다 **3** *v/t* (*with a typewriter*) t'ajagiro ch'ida 타자기로 치다
typewriter t'ajagi 타자기
typhoid (fever) changt'ip'usŭ 장티푸스
typhoon t'aep'ung 태풍
typhus paltchint'ip'usŭ 발진티푸스
typical chŏnhyŏngjŏgin 전형적인; ***that's ~ of him!*** kŭnŭn hangsang kŭrŏch'anayo! 그는 항상 그렇잖아요!
typically ilbanjŏgŭro 일반적으로; ~ ***American*** chŏnhyŏngjŏgin Migugin 전형적인 미국인
typist t'aip'isŭt'ŭ 타이피스트
tyrannical p'okkunjŏgin 폭군적인
tyrannize aptchehada 압제하다
tyranny chŏnje chŏngch'i 전제 정치
tyrant p'ok-kkun 폭군

U

ugly hyunghan 흉한; *situation* kkŭmtchik'an 끔찍한
UK (= ***United Kingdom***) Yŏngguk 영국
ulcer kweyang 궤양
Ullung Island Ullŭngdo 울릉도
ultimate (*best, definitive*) ch'oesang-ŭi 최상의; (*final*) kunggŭktchŏgin 궁극적인; (*fundamental*) kibonjŏgin 기본적인
ultimately (*in the end*) kyŏlguk 결국
ultimatum ch'oehu t'ongch'ŏp 최후 통첩
ultrasound MED ch'oŭmp'a 초음파
ultraviolet *adj* chaoeŭi 자외의; ***~ rays*** chaoesŏn 자외선
umbilical cord t'aetchul 탯줄
umbrella usan 우산
umpire *n* shimp'an 심판
umpteen F musuhan 무수한
UN (= ***United Nations***) Kuktche Yŏnhap 국제 연합
unable: ***be ~ to do X*** (*not know how to*) Xŭl / rŭl hal churŭl morŭnda X을 / 를 할 줄을 모른다; (*not be in a position to*) Xŭl / rŭl hal su ŏptta X을 / 를 할 수 없다
unacceptable padadŭril su ŏmnŭn 받아들일 수 없는; *poverty* issŭl su ŏmnŭn 있을 수 없는; ***it is ~ that...*** ...ranŭn kŏsŭn padadŭril su ŏptta ...라는 것은 받아들일 수 없다
unaccountable sŏlmyŏnghal su ŏmnŭn 설명할 수 없는
unaccustomed: ***be ~ to X*** Xe ikssuk'aji ant'a X에 익숙하지 않다
unadulterated *fig* (*absolute*) sunjŏnhan 순전한
un-American panmiguktchŏgin 반미국적인
unanimous *verdict* manjang-ilch'iŭi 만장일치의; ***be ~ on*** ...e manjang-ilch'ihada ...에 만장일치하다
unanimously *vote, decide* manjang-ilch'iro 만장일치로
unapproachable *person* kakkaihagi ŏryŏun 가까이하기 어려운
unarmed *person* pimujang-ŭi 비무장의; ***~ combat*** yukt'anjŏn 육탄전
unassuming kyŏmsonhan 겸손한
unattached (*without a partner*) toksshinin 독신인
unattended naebŏryŏdun 내버려둔; ***leave X ~*** Xŭl / rŭl naebŏryŏduda X을 / 를 내버려두다
unauthorized muhŏgaŭi 무허가의
unavoidable p'ihal su ŏmnŭn 피할 수 없는
unavoidably: ***be ~ detained*** pulgap'ihage nŭjŏjida 불가피하게 늦어지다
unaware: ***be ~ of*** ...ŭl / rŭl kkaedatchi mot'ada ...을 / 를 깨닫지 못하다
unawares: ***catch X ~*** Xŭl / rŭl pulsshie sŭpkkyŏk'ada X을 / 를 불시에 습격하다
unbalanced kyunhyŏng-ŭl irŭn 균형을 잃은; PSYCH puranjŏnghan 불안정한
unbearable kyŏndil su ŏmnŭn 견딜 수 없는; ***he's ~*** kŭnŭn kyŏndil su ŏmnŭn saramiyeyo 그는 견딜 수 없는 사람이에요
unbeatable *team, quality* amudo ttaraol su ŏmnŭn 아무도 따라올 수 없는
unbeaten *team* ch'ŏnhamujŏgŭi 천하무적의
unbeknown(st): ***~ to his parents*** kŭŭi pumonim mollae 그의 부모님 몰래
unbelievable midŭl su ŏmnŭn 믿을 수 없는; F (*heat, value*) ŏmch'ŏngnan 엄청난; ***he's ~*** F (*very good / bad*) kŭnŭn koengjanghi choŭn / mot-ttoen saramimnida 그는

굉장히 좋은/못된 사람입니다
unbias(s)ed p'yŏn-gyŏnŏmnŭn 편견없는
unblock *pipe* ttult'a 뚫다
unborn ajik t'aeŏnaji anŭn 아직 태어나지 않은; ***an ~ baby*** t'aea 태아
unbreakable *plate, world's record* kkaejiji annŭn 깨지지 않는
unbutton p'ulda 풀다
uncalled-for chujenŏmŭn 주제넘은
uncanny *skill, feeling* myohan 묘한; ***have an ~ resemblance to*** ...ŭl/rŭl myohage tamtta ...을/를 묘하게 닮다
unceasing kkŭnimŏmnŭn 끊임없는
uncertain *future, weather* purhwaksshirhan 불확실한; *origins* pulmyŏnghwak'an 불명확한; ***be ~ about X*** Xŭl/rŭl hwaksshinhaji mot'ada X을/를 확신하지 못하다; ***it's ~*** hwaksshirhaji anssŭmnida 확실하지 않습니다
uncertainty (*of the future*) purhwaksshilssŏng 불확실성; ***there is still ~ about ...*** ...ŭn/nŭn ajik purhwaksshirhamnida ...은/는 아직 불확실합니다
unchecked: ***go ~*** chŏjidoeji ant'a 저지되지 않다
uncle (*in general*) ajŏsshi 아저씨; (*father's brother, single*) samch'on 삼촌; (*mother's brother, single*) oesamch'on 외삼촌; (*father's sister's husband*) komobu 고모부; (*mother's sister's husband*) imobu 이모부
uncomfortable pulp'yŏnhan 불편한: ***feel ~ about X*** (*about decision etc*) Xi/ga kkŏrimchik'ada X이/가 꺼림직하다; ***I feel ~ with him*** nanŭn kŭga pulp'yŏnhada 나는 그가 불편하다
uncommon hŭnhaji anŭn 흔하지 않은; ***it's not ~*** kŭgŏsŭn hŭnhaji anŭn irida 그것은 흔하지 않은 일이다
uncompromising t'ahyŏp'aji annŭn 타협하지 않는
unconcerned shin-gyŏngssŭji annŭn 신경쓰지 않는; ***be ~ about X*** Xe shin-gyŏngssŭji annŭnda X에 신경 쓰지 않는다
unconditional mujokkŏnŭi 무조건의
unconscious MED muŭishik sangt'aeŭi 무의식 상태의; PSYCH muŭishiktchŏgin 무의식적인; ***knock ~*** ch'yŏsŏ kijŏlshik'ida 쳐서 기절시키다; ***be ~ of X*** (*not aware*) Xŭl/rŭl kkaedatchi mot'ada X을/를 깨닫지 못하다
uncontrollable *anger, desire* chajehal su ŏmnŭn 자제할 수 없는; *children* kamdanghal su ŏmnŭn 감당할 수 없는
unconventional pigwansŭptchŏgin 비관습적인
uncooperative pihyŏptchojŏgin 비협조적인
uncork *bottle* magaerŭl ppoptta 마개를 뽑다
uncover (*remove covering from*) tŏpkkaerŭl pŏtkkida 덮개를 벗기다; (*discover*) palgurhada 발굴하다; *plot* palk'yŏnaeda 밝혀내다
undamaged sonsangdoeji anŭn 손상되지 않은
undaunted: ***carry on ~*** kurhaji ank'o haenaeda 굴하지 않고 해내다
undecided *matter* chŏnghaji anŭn 정하지 않은; ***be ~ about X*** Xŭl/rŭl kyŏltchŏnghaji mot'ada X을/를 결정하지 못하다
undelete COMPUT twesalligi 되살리기
undeniable pujŏnghal su ŏmnŭn 부정할 수 없는
undeniably pujŏnghal su ŏpsshi 부정할 수 없이
under 1 *prep* (*beneath*) ...ŭi arae ...의 아래에; (*less than*) ... miman ... 미만; ***~ $500*** 500tallŏ miman 500달러 미만; ***~ the water*** mul mit'e 물 밑에; ***it is ~ review/investigation*** kŭgŏsŭn kŏmt'o/chosa chung-ida 그것은 검토/조사 중이다 **2** *adv* (*anesthetized*): ***the patient is still ~*** hwanjanŭn ajik mach'iesŏ kkaeŏnaji anassŭmnida 환자는 아직 마취에서 깨어나지 않았습니다
underage *drinking etc* misŏngnyŏnŭi 미성년의; ***be ~*** misŏngnyŏnjaida 미성년자이다
underarm *adv throw* mit'ŭro tŏnjyŏ 밑으로 던져

undercarriage ch'angnyuk changch'i 착륙 장치
undercover *adj agent* pimillie sumgyŏjin 비밀리에 숨겨진
undercut *v/t* COM poda tŏ kkakka chegonghada 보다 더 깎아 제공하다
underdog yaktcha 약자
underdone *meat* tŏl ik'in 덜 익힌; ***I prefer my steak ~*** chŏnŭn tŏl ik'in sŭt'eik'ŭga chossŭmnida 저는 덜 익힌 스테이크가 좋습니다
underestimate *v/t person, skills, task* kwasop'yŏngkkahada 과소평가하다
underexposed PHOT noch'uri pujok'an 노출이 부족한
underfed yŏngnyangbujogŭi 영양부족의
undergo *surgery, treatment* pat-tta 받다; *experiences* kyŏktta 겪다
underground 1 *adj passages etc* chihaŭi 지하의; POL *resistance, newpaper etc* pimirŭi 비밀의; ***~ activities*** POL chiha undong 지하 운동 **2** *adv work* chiha-esŏ 지하에서; ***go ~*** POL chiharo ŭnnik'ada 지하로 은닉하다
undergrowth tŏmbul 덤불
underhand *adj (devious)* ŭmhŏmhan 음험한
underlie *v/t* ...ŭi kŭn-gŏga toeda ...의 근거가 되다
underline *v/t text* mitchul kŭt-tta 밑줄 긋다
underlying *causes, problems* kŭnwŏnjŏgin 근원적인
undermine *v/t s.o.'s position* mollae hwesonhada 몰래 훼손하다; *theory* hŭndŭlda 흔들다
underneath 1 *prep* ...ŭi mit'e ...의 밑에 **2** *adv* mit'e 밑에
underpants p'aench'ŭ 팬츠
underpass (*for pedestrians*) chihado 지하도
underprivileged hyet'aekpat-tchi mot'an 혜택받지 못한
underrate *v/t* kwasop'yŏngkkahada 과소평가하다
undershirt rŏning shyŏch'ŭ 러닝 셔츠
undersized pot'ongboda chagŭn 보통보다 작은
underskirt sokch'ima 속치마
understaffed chŏgŭn suŭi chigwŏnŭl kajin 적은 수의 직원을 가진
understand 1 *v/t* ihaehada 이해하다; ***I ~ that you ...*** naega algienŭn tangshini ... 내가 알기에는 당신이 ...; ***they are understood to be in Canada*** kŭdŭrŭn K'aenadae innŭn kŏsŭro allyŏjyŏit-tta 그들은 캐나다에 있는 것으로 알려져있다 **2** *v/i* ihaehada 이해하다
understandable ihaehal su innŭn 이해할 수 있는
understandably ihaehal su itkke 이해할 수 있게
understanding 1 *adj person* ihaeshiminnŭn 이해심있는 **2** *n (of problem, situation)* ihae 이해; (*agreement*) tong-ŭi 동의; ***on the ~ that*** ...ranŭn chokkŏn ha-e ...라는 조건 하에
understatement ŏktchedoen p'yohyŏn 억제된 표현
undertake *task* surak'ada 수락하다; ***~ to do X*** (*agree to*) Xŭl/rŭl hal kŏsŭl surak'ada X을/를 할 것을 수락하다
undertaking (*enterprise*) saŏp 사업; (*promise*) yakssok 약속
undervalue *v/t* kwaso p'yŏngkkahada 과소 평가하다
underwear sogot 속옷, naeŭi 내의
underweight *adj person* ch'ejung midarŭi 체중 미달의
underworld (*criminal*) amhŭk-kka 암흑가; (*in mythology*) chŏsŭng 저승
underwrite *v/t* FIN pojŭnghada 보증하다
undeserved padŭl kach'iga ŏmnŭn 받을 가치가 없는
undesirable *features, changes* paramjik'aji annŭn 바람직하지 않은; *person* pulk'waehan 불쾌한; ***~ element*** nune kashi 눈에 가시
undisputed *champion, leader* amudo nŏmboji mot'al 아무도 넘보지 못할
undo *parcel, wrapping, buttons* p'ulda 풀다; *s.o. else's work* soyong-ŏpkke hada 소용없게 하다
undoubtedly ŭishimhal yŏji ŏpsshi 의심할 여지 없이
undreamt-of *riches* kkumdo mot kkul chŏngdoŭi 꿈도 못 꿀 정도의

undress 1 *v/t* pŏtkkida 벗기다; ***get ~ed*** osŭl pŏt-tta 옷을 벗다 **2** *v/i* ot pŏtkkida 옷 벗기다
undue (*excessive*) chinach'in 지나친
unduly chinach'ige 지나치게
unearth *ancient remains* palgurhada 발굴하다; *fig* (*find*) palgyŏnhada 발견하다; *secret* p'ahech'ida 파헤치다
unearthly: ***at this ~ hour*** ŏngttunghan shigane 엉뚱한 시간에
uneasy *relationship*, *peace* puranhan 불안한; ***feel ~ about*** ...ŭl / rŭl puranhae hada ...을 / 를 불안해 하다
uneatable mŏgŭl su ŏmnŭn 먹을 수 없는
uneconomic iigi andoenŭn 이익이 안되는
uneducated kyoyukppat-tchi mot'an 교육받지 못한
unemployed shiltchik'an 실직한; ***the ~*** shirŏptcha 실업자
unemployment shirŏp 실업
unending kkŭdŏmnŭn 끝없는
unequal ttokkatchi anŭn 똑같지 않은; *pay* pulgongp'yŏnghan 불공평한; ***be ~ to the task*** kŭ irŭl hal nŭngnyŏgi ŏptta 그 일을 할 능력이 없다
unerring *judgment*, *instinct* t'ŭllimŏmnŭn 틀림없는
uneven *quality* kyunirhaji anŭn 균일하지 않은; *surface*, *ground* korŭji anŭn 고르지 않은
unevenly *distributed*, *applied* korŭji ank'e 고르지 않게; ***~ matched*** sangdaega andoenŭn 상대가 안되는
uneventful *day*, *journey* pyŏril ŏmnŭn 별일 없는
unexpected yesanghaji mot'an 예상하지 못한
unexpectedly yesang pakke 예상 밖에
unfair pulgongjŏnghan 불공정한
unfaithful *husband*, *wife* pujŏnghan 부정한; ***be ~ to X*** X morŭge paramŭl p'iuda X 모르게 바람을 피우다
unfamiliar ikssuk'aji anŭn 익숙하지 않은; ***be ~ with X*** Xe ikssuk'aji ant'a X에 익숙하지 않다
unfasten *belt* p'ulda 풀다
unfavorable *weather conditions* hogami an-ganŭn 호감이 안가는; *report*, *review* hoŭijŏgi anin 호의적이 아닌
unfeeling *person* mujŏnghan 무정한
unfinished kkŭnnaeji anŭn 끝내지 않은; ***leave X ~*** Xŭl / rŭl kkŭnnaeji anŭn ch'aero tuda X을 / 를 끝내지 않은 채로 두다
unfit (*physically*) undong pujogin 운동 부족인; (*not morally suited*) pujŏkkyŏgin 부적격인; ***be ~ to eat / drink*** mŏk-kkie / mashigie pujŏkttanghada 먹기에 / 마시기에 부적당하다
unfix *part* pullihada 분리하다; *screw* ppaenaeda 빼내다
unflappable ch'imch'ak'an 침착한
unfold 1 *v/t sheets*, *letter*, *one's arms* p'yŏda 펴다 **2** *v/i* (*of story*, *view etc*) p'yŏlch'ŏjida 펼쳐지다
unforeseen yesanghaji mot'an 예상하지 못한
unforgettable ijŭl su ŏmnŭn 잊을 수 없는
unforgivable yongsŏhal su ŏmnŭn 용서할 수 없는; ***that was ~ of you*** kŭgŏsŭn yongsŏpat-tchi mot'al irida 그것은 용서받지 못할 일이다
unfortunate *people* un ŏmnŭn 운 없는; *choice of words*, *event* chalmot-ttoen 잘못된; ***that's ~ for you*** kŭgŏt chŏngmal andwaetkkunyo 그것 정말 안됐군요
unfortunately purhaenghi 불행히
unfounded kŭn-gŏmnŭn 근거없는
unfriendly pulch'injŏrhan 불친절한; *software* tarugi ŏryŏun 다루기 어려운
unfurnished kaguga ŏmnŭn 가구가 없는
ungodly: ***at this ~ hour*** ŏngttunghan shigane 엉뚱한 시간에
ungrateful kamsahal chul morŭnŭn 감사할 줄 모르는
unhappiness purhaeng 불행
unhappy purhaenghan 불행한; (*not satisfied*) pulmansŭrŏun 불만스러운; ***be ~ with the service*** sŏbissŭe pulmanida 서비스에 불만이다
unharmed musahan 무사한
unhealthy *person* kŏn-ganghaji

mot'an 건강하지 못한; *conditions* choch'i anŭn 좋지 않은; *food, atmosphere* kŏn-gang-e choch'i anŭn 건강에 좋지 않은; *economy, balance sheet* choch'i mot'an 좋지 못한
unheard-of chŏllye ŏmnŭn 전례 없는
unhurt tach'iji anŭn 다치지 않은
unhygienic piwisaengjŏgin 비위생적인
unification t'ong-il 통일
uniform 1 *n* MIL chebok 제복; (*of school pupil*) kyobok 교복; (*of sportsman, air hostess*) yunip'om 유니폼 **2** *adj* iltchŏnghan 일정한
unify t'ong-irhada 통일하다
unilateral ilbangjŏgin 일방적인
unimaginable sangsanghal su ŏmnŭn 상상할 수 없는
unimaginative sangsangnyŏgi ŏmnŭn 상상력이 없는
unimportant chungnyohaji anŭn 중요하지 않은
uninhabitable sal su ŏmnŭn 살 수 없는
uninhabited sarami salji annŭn 사람이 살지 않는
uninjured sangch'ŏ ŏmnŭn 상처 없는
unintelligible ihaehal su ŏmnŭn 이해할 수 없는
unintentional koŭiga anin 고의가 아닌
unintentionally ŭidoch'i ank'e 의도치 않게
uninteresting chaemi ŏmnŭn 재미 없는
uninterrupted *sleep, two hours' work* kkŭnimŏmnŭn 끊임없는
union POL yŏnhap 연합; (*labor ~*) nojo 노조
unique tokt'ŭk'an 독특한; ***with his own ~ humor / style*** kŭ t'ŭgyuŭi yumŏro / sŭt'aillo 그 특유의 유머로 / 스타일로
unit (*of measurement*) tanwi 단위; (*section: of machine, structure*) pup'um 부품; (*department*) pusŏ 부서; MIL pudae 부대
unit cost COM tanwi wŏnkka 단위 원가
unite 1 *v/t* kyŏrhap'ada 결합하다; *company* hap-ppyŏnghada 합병하다 **2** *v/i* hanaga toeda 하나가 되다
united hanaga toen 하나가 된; *group, organization, country* yŏnhapttoen 연합된
United Kingdom Yŏngguk 영국
United Nations Kuktche Yŏnhap 국제 연합 ~ ***troops*** Yuen-gun 유엔군
United People's Party T'ong-il Kungmindang 통일 국민당
United States (of America) Miguk 미국, Mihaptchungguk 미국미합중국 *fml*
unity t'ong-il 통일; (*of all being*) tanilssŏng 단일성
universal (*general*) pop'yŏnjŏgin 보편적인; *language* kongt'ong-ŭi 공통의
universally pop'yŏnjŏgŭro 보편적으로
universe uju 우주
university taehak-kkyo 대학교; ***he is at ~*** kŭnŭn taehakssaeng-ida 그는 대학생이다
unjust pulgongjŏnghan 불공정한
unkempt tanjŏnghaji mot'an 단정하지 못한
unkind pulch'injŏrhan 불친절한
unknown 1 *adj* allyŏjiji anŭn 알려지지 않은 **2** *n*: ***a journey into the ~*** mijiroŭi yŏhaeng 미지로의 여행
unleaded (gasoline) muyŏn hwibaryu 무연 휘발유
unless …haji anŭmyŏn …하지 않으면; ***~ he pays us tomorrow*** kŭga naeilkkaji tonŭl chuji anŭmyŏn 그가 내일까지 돈을 주지 않으면
unlike *prep* kach'i anŭn 같지 않은; ***it's ~ him to drink so much*** kŭrŏk'e mani mashidani kŭdaptchi ant'a 그렇게 많이 마시다니 그답지 않다; ***the photograph was completely ~ her*** kŭ sajinŭn kŭnyŏgach'i anboinda 그 사진은 그녀같이 안보인다
unlikely issŭl kŏt kach'i anŭn 있을 것 같지 않은; ***he is ~ to win*** kŭnŭn igil kŏt kach'i ant'a 그는 이길 것 같지 않다; ***it is ~ that*** …hal kŏt kach'i ant'a …할 것 같지 않다
unlimited hanŏmnŭn 한없는

unload (*baggage etc*) naerida 내리다
unlock chamulsoerŭl yŏlda 자물쇠를 열다
unluckily unŏpkke 운없게
unlucky *day*, *choice*, *person* unŏmnŭn 운없는; ***that was so ~ for you!*** chŏngmal uni ŏpssŏtkkunyo! 정말 운이 없었군요!
unmade-up *face* hwajanghaji anŭn 화장하지 않은
unmanned *spacecraft* muinŭi 무인의
unmarried mihonŭi 미혼의
unmistakable t'ŭllimŏmnŭn 틀림없는
unmoved (*emotionally*) tongnyo ŏmnŭn 동요 없는
unmusical *person* ŭmaktchŏk sojiri ŏmnŭn 음악적 소질이 없는; *sounds* kwie kŏsŭllinŭn 귀에 거슬리는
unnatural pujayŏnsŭrŏun 부자연스러운; ***it's not ~ to be annoyed*** hwanaenŭn kŏt-tto tangnyŏnhamnida 화내는 것도 당연합니다
unnecessary pulp'iryohan 불필요한
unnerving kŏmnage hanŭn 겁나게 하는
unnoticed: ***it went ~*** nune ttŭiji anassŏyo 눈에 띄지 않았어요
unobtainable *goods* ŏdŭl su ŏmnŭn 얻을 수 없는; TELEC yŏn-gyŏri andoenŭn 연결이 안되는
unobtrusive nune ttŭiji annŭn 눈에 띄지 않는
unoccupied *building*, *house*, *post* piŏinnŭn 비어있는; *room* amudo ŏmnŭn 아무도 없는; *person* hal il ŏmnŭn 할 일 없는
unofficial pigongshiktchŏgin 비공식적인
unofficially pigongshiktchŏgŭro 비공식적으로
unpack *v/t & v/i* p'ulda 풀다
unpaid *work* mugŭbŭi 무급의
unpleasant pulk'waehan 불쾌한; ***he was very ~ to her*** kŭnŭn kŭnyŏŭi kibunŭl sanghage haet-tta 그는 그녀의 기분을 상하게 했다
unplug *v/t TV*, *computer* ...ŭi p'ŭllŏgŭrŭl ppoptta ...의 플러그를 뽑다
unpopular *person* inkkiŏmnŭn 인기없는; *decision* chijipat-tchi mot'anŭn 지지받지 못하는
unprecedented chŏllye ŏmnŭn 전례 없는; ***it was ~ for a woman to ...*** yojaga ...hanŭn kŏsŭn ijŏnenŭn ŏpttŏn iriŏt-tta 여자가 ...하는 것은 이전에는 없던 일이었다
unpredictable *person*, *weather* yech'ŭk'al su ŏmnŭn 예측할 수 없는
unprincipled *pej* pidodŏktchŏgin 비도덕적인
unpretentious hŏshigŏmnŭn 허식없는
unproductive *meeting*, *discussion* pisaengsanjŏgin 비생산적인
unprofessional *person*, *behavior* chŏnmunindaptchi anŭn 전문인답지 않은; *workmanship* pip'ŭrojŏgin 비프로적인
unprofitable iigi ŏmnŭn 이익이 없는
unpronounceable parŭmhal su ŏmnŭn, parŭmi pulganŭnghan 발음할 수 없는, 발음이 불가능한
unprotected *borders* mubangbiŭi 무방비의; *machine* pohodoeji anŭn 보호되지 않은; **~ *sex*** *k'ondomŭl sayonghaji ank'o hanŭn sŏnggyo* 콘돔을 사용하지 않고 하는 성교
unprovoked *attack* tobaldoeji anŭn 도발되지 않은
unqualified *worker*, *doctor etc* chagyŏgi ŏmnŭn 자격이 없는
unquestionably (*without doubt*) murŏ pol p'iryodo ŏpsshi 물어 볼 필요도 없이
unquestioning ŭishimŏmnŭn 의심없는
unravel *v/t string*, *mystery* p'ulda 풀다
unreadable *book* ilkki ŏryŏun 읽기 어려운
unreal *creature* shiltchaehaji annŭn 실재하지 않는; (*unrealistic*) pihyŏnsshiltchŏgin 비현실적인; ***this is ~!*** F midŭl su ŏpssŏyo! 믿을 수 없어요!
unrealistic pihyŏnsshiltchŏgin 비현실적인
unreasonable pihamnijŏgin 비합리적인
unrelated kwan-gyeŏmnŭn 관계없는

unrelenting kkujunhan 꾸준한
unreliable midŭl su ŏmnŭn 믿을 수 없는
unrest puran 불안
unrestrained *emotions* ŏktchedoeji anŭn 억제되지 않은
unroadworthy *wihŏmhal chŏngdoro kojangna innŭn* 위험할 정도로 고장나 있는
unroll *v/t carpet, scroll* p'ida 피다
unruly tarugi himdŭn 다루기 힘든
unsafe anjŏnhaji anŭn 안전하지 않은; **~ *to drink / eat*** mashigie / mŏk-kkie anjŏnhaji anŭn 마시기에 / 먹기에 안전하지 않은
unsanitary piwisaengjŏgin 비위생적인
unsatisfactory manjokssŭrŏptchi mot'an 만족스럽지 못한
unsavory *person, reputation* pulk'waehan 불쾌한; *district* hŏmak'an 험악한
unscathed tach'in te ŏmnŭn 다친 데 없는; (*not damaged*) hŭmtchibŏmnŭn 흠집없는
unscrew nasarŭl p'ulda 나사를 풀다; *top* magaerŭl yŏlda 마개를 열다
unscrupulous pudodŏk'an 부도덕한
unselfish it'ajŏgin 이타적인
unsettled *issue* kyŏltchŏngdoeji anŭn 결정되지 않은; *weather, stock market* pyŏnhagi shwiun 변하기 쉬운; *lifestyle* iltchŏngch'i anŭn 일정치 않은; *bills* migyŏltcheŭi 미결제의; *of stomach* paet'allan 배탈난
unshaven myŏndohaji anŭn 면도하지 않은
unsightly pogi hyunghan 보기 흉한
unskilled misuk'an 미숙한; **~ *labor*** misungnyŏn nodongja 미숙련 노동자
unsociable pisagyojŏgin 비사교적인
unsophisticated tansunhan 단순한
unstable *person, structure* puranjŏnghan 불안정한; *area, economy* puranhan 불안한
unsteady (*on one's feet*) pit'ŭlgŏrinŭn 비틀거리는; *ladder* hŭndŭlgŏrinŭn 흔들거리는
unstinting: ***be ~ in one's efforts*** noryŏgŭl akkiji ant'a 노력을 아끼지 않다
unstuck: ***come ~*** (*of notice etc*) ttŏrŏjida 떨어지다; (*of plan etc*) manghada 망하다
unsuccessful *writer, party etc* shilp'aehan 실패한; *candidate* nakssŏndoen 낙선된; *attempt* sŏngonghaji mot'an 성공하지 못한; ***he tried but was ~*** kŭnŭn noryŏk'aet-tchiman shilp'aehaet-tta 그는 노력했지만 실패했다
unsuccessfully *try, apply* sŏngongjŏgiji mot'age 성공적이지 못하게
unsuitable pujŏkttanghan 부적당한
unsuspecting ŭichimhaji annŭn 의심하지 않는
unswerving *loyalty, devotion* hwakkobudonghan 확고부동한
unthinkable saenggak'al su choch'a ŏmnŭn 생각할 수 조차 없는
untidy chijŏbunhan 지저분한
untie *knot, laces* p'ulda 풀다; *prisoner* p'urŏjuda 풀어주다
until 1 *prep* kkaji 까지; ***from Monday ~ Friday*** wŏryoilbut'ŏ kŭmnyoilkkaji 월요일부터 금요일까지; ***I can wait ~ tomorrow*** naeilkkaji kidaril su issŭmnida 내일까지 기다릴 수 있습니다; ***not ~ Friday*** kŭmnyoil chŏnenŭn malgo 금요일 전에는 말고; ***it won't be finished ~ July*** ch'irwŏlkkajinŭn mot kkŭnnael kŏt kassŭmnida 칠월까지는 못 끝낼 것 같습니다
2 *conj* hal ttaekkaji 할 때까지; ***can you wait ~ I'm ready?*** chega chunbidoel ttaekkaji kidaril su itkkessŭmnikka? 제가 준비될 때까지 기다릴 수 있겠습니까?; ***they won't do anything ~ you say so*** tangshini kŭrŏrago hal ttaekkaji kŭdŭrŭn amu kŏtto haji anŭl kŏshimnida 당신이 그러라고 할 때까지 그들은 아무 것도 하지 않을 것입니다
untimely *death* ttae anin 때 아닌
untiring *efforts* chich'iji annŭn 지치지 않는
untold *riches, suffering* makttaehan 막대한; *story* palk'yŏjiji anŭn 밝혀지지 않은
untranslatable pŏnyŏk'al su ŏmnŭn

번역할 수 없는
untrue sashiri anin 사실이 아닌
unused[1] *goods* sayonghaji anŭn 사용하지 않은
unused[2]: ***be ~ to sth*** muŏse ikssuk'aji ant'a 무엇에 익숙하지 않다; ***be ~ to doing sth*** muŏsŭl hanŭn kŏshi ikssuk'aji ant'a 무엇을 하는 것이 익숙하지 않다
unusual tŭmun 드문
unusually tŭmulge 드물게
unveil *memorial*, *statue etc* pŏtkkida 벗기다; *plans* konggaehada 공개하다
unwell (*physically*) momi choch'i anŭn 몸이 좋지 않은; (*mentally*) kibuni choch'i anŭn 기분이 좋지 않은
unwilling: ***be ~ to do sth*** muŏsŭl hanŭn kŏsŭl naek'yŏhaji ant'a 무엇을 하는 것을 내켜하지 않다
unwind 1 *v/t tape* p'ulda 풀다 **2** *v/i* (*of tape*, *story*) p'ullida 풀리다; (*relax*) kinjang-ŭl p'ulda 긴장을 풀다
unwise hyŏnmyŏnghaji mot'an 현명하지 못한
unwrap *gift* p'urŏ poda 풀어 보다
unwritten *rule* kwansŭptchŏgin 관습적인; ***~ law*** kwansŭppŏp 관습법
unzip *v/t dress etc* chip'ŏrŭl yŏlda 지퍼를 열다; COMPUT apch'ugŭl p'ulda 압축을 풀다
up 1 *adv* wie 위에; ***~ in the sky / on the roof*** hanŭl / chibung wie 하늘 / 지붕 위에; ***~ here / there*** yŏgi / chŏgi wie 여기 / 저기 위에; ***be ~*** (*out of bed*) irŏna it-tta 일어나 있다; (*of sun*) ttŏolla it-tta 떠올라 있다; (*be built*) sewŏjyŏ it-tta 세워져 있다; (*of shelves*) sŏlch'idoeŏ it-tta 설치되어 있다; (*of prices*, *temperature*) olla it-tta 올라 있다; (*have expired*) kkŭnnada 끝나다; ***what's ~?*** musŭn il issŭmnikka? 무슨 일 있습니까?; ***~ to the year 1989*** 1989nyŏnkkaji 1989년까지; ***he came ~ to me*** kŭnŭn na-ege tagawat-tta 그는 나에게 다가왔다; ***what are you ~ to these days?*** yojŭm musŭn irŭl hamyŏ chinaeshimnikka? 요즘 무슨 일을 하며 지내십니까?; ***what are those kids ~ to?*** aidŭri musŭn chisŭl hago it-tchi? 아이들이 무슨 짓을 하고 있지?; ***be ~ to something*** (***bad***) mot-ttoen chisŭl hago it-tta 못된 짓을 하고 있다; ***I don't feel ~ to it*** nanŭn kŭrŏl kibuni tŭlji anssŭmnida 나는 그럴 기분이 들지 않습니다; ***it's ~ to you*** tangshinhant'e tallyŏssŏyo 당신한테 달렸어요; ***it's ~ to them to solve it*** kŭdŭri haegyoerhaeyajiyo 그들이 해결해야지요; ***be ~ and about*** (*after illness*) hoebok'ayŏ toradanida 회복하여 돌아다니다 **2** *prep*: ***further ~ the mountain*** sanŭi tŏ nop'ŭn tchoge 산의 더 높은 쪽에; ***he climbed ~ a tree*** kŭnŭn namurŭl t'ago ŏllagat-tta 그는 나무를 타고 올라갔다; ***they ran ~ the street*** kŭdŭrŭn kirŭl ttara tallyŏt-tta 그들은 길을 따라 달렸다; ***the water goes ~ this pipe*** murŭl i kwanŭl ttara hŭrŭmnida 물은 이 관을 따라 흐릅니다; ***we traveled ~ to Kang-wondo*** urinŭn Kang-wŏndokkaji yŏhaenghae ollagat-tta 우리는 강원도까지 여행해 올라갔다 **3** *n*: ***~s and downs*** kibok 기복
upbringing kajŏng kyoyuk 가정 교육
upcoming *adj* tagaonŭn 다가오는
update 1 *v/t file*, *records* ch'oeshinŭi kŏsŭro pakkuda 최신의 것으로 바꾸다; ***~ s.o. on sth*** nuguege muŏse kwanhan ch'oeshin chŏngborŭl chuda 누구에게 무엇에 관한 최신 정보를 주다 **2** *n* (*of files*, *records*) ch'oeshin kŏsŭroŭi kyoch'e 최신 것으로의 교체; ***can you give me an ~ on the situation?*** kajang ch'oegŭnŭi sanghwang-ŭl allyŏjushigessŭmnikka? 가장 최근의 상황을 알려주시겠습니까?
upgrade 1 *v/t computers*, *ticket etc* ŏpkkŭreidŭhada 업그레이드하다; (*replace with new version*) saeroun kŏsŭrŏ kyoch'ehada 새로운 것으로 교체하다; *product* hyangsangshik'ida 향상시키다 **2** *n* (*software version*) ŏpkkŭreidŭ 업그레이드
upheaval (*emotional*, *physical*) k'ŭn pyŏnhwa 큰 변화; (*political*, *social*) kyŏkppyŏn 격변

uphill 1 *adv walk* ŏndŏk wiro 언덕 위로; ***the road goes ~*** orŭmak kirida 오르막 길이다 **2** *adj struggle* himdŭnŭn 힘드는
uphold *traditions, rights* yujihada 유지하다; (*vindicate*) hwaginhada 확인하다
upholstery (*fabric*) kagu changshik 가구 장식; (*padding*) kaguŭi sok 가구의 속
upkeep *n* (*of buildings, parks etc*) yuji 유지
upload *v/t* COMPUT ŏprodŭhada 업로드하다
upmarket *adj restaurant, hotel* kop'umkkyŏgŭi 고품격의
upon → ***on***
upper *part of sth* wi tchogŭi 위 쪽의; *stretches of a river* sangnyuŭi 상류의; *atmosphere* wiŭi 위의; ***~ deck*** sanggapp'an 상갑판
upper-class sangnyuch'ŭng-ŭi 상류층의
upper classes sangnyuch'ŭng 상류층
UPP (= ***United People's Party***) T'ongil Kungmindang 통일국민당
upright 1 *adj citizen* parŭn 바른 **2** *adv sit* ttokpparo 똑바로
upright (piano) ŏmnait'ŭ p'iano 업라이트 피아노
uprising p'okttong 폭동
uproar (*loud noise*) soran 소란; (*protest*) hang-ŭi 항의
upset 1 *v/t drink, glass* twijiptta 뒤집다; (*emotionally*) kibun sanghagehada 기분 상하게하다 **2** *adj* (*emotionally*) kibun sanghan 기분 상한; ***get ~ about sth*** muŏse kibun sanghada 무엇에 기분 상하다; ***have an ~ stomach*** paet'allada 배탈나다
upsetting sokssanghan 속상한
upshot (*result, outcome*) kyŏlgwa 결과
upside down *adv* kŏkkuro 거꾸로; ***turn sth ~*** *box etc* muŏsŭl kŏkkuro twijiptta 무엇을 거꾸로 뒤집다
upstairs 1 *adv* wich'ŭng-e 위층에 **2** *adj room* wich'ŭng-ŭi 위층의
upstart pyŏrak ch'ulssehan nom 벼락 출세한 놈
upstream *adv* sangnyuro 상류로
uptight F (*nervous*) anjŏlbujŏl mot'anŭn 안절부절 못하는; (*inhibited*) kinjang-ŭro ttakttak'aejin 긴장으로 딱딱해진
up-to-date *fashions, data* ch'oeshinŭi 최신의
upturn (*in economy*) hojŏn 호전
upward *adv fly, move* wiro 위로; ***~ of 10,000*** man isang-ŭro 만 이상으로
uranium uranyum 우라늄
urban toshiŭi 도시의
urbanization toshihwa 도시화
urchin kkoma 꼬마
urge 1 *n* ch'ungdong 충동; ***I felt an ~ to hit him*** nanŭn kŭrŭl ttaerigo ship'ŭn ch'ungdong-ŭl nŭkkyŏt-tta 나는 그를 때리고 싶은 충동을 느꼈다 **2** *v/t*: ***~ X to do Y*** Xege Y(ŭ)rago puch'ugida X에게 Y(으)라고 부추기다
♦**urge on** kyŏngyŏhada 격려하다
urgency (*of situation*) kin-gŭp 긴급
urgent *job, letter* kŭp'an 급한; ***be in ~ need of*** …i / ga kŭp'age p'iryohada …이/가 급하게 필요하다; ***is it ~?*** kŭp'an kŏshimnikka? 급한 것입니까?
urinate sobyŏnŭl poda 소변을 보다
urine sobyŏn 소변
urn tanji 단지
us uri 우리; ***that's for ~*** uri kŏshimnida 우리 것입니다; ***who's that? - it's ~*** nuguseyo? - uriyeyo 누구세요? - 우리예요
US(A) (= ***United States*** (***of America***)) Miguk 미국, Mihaptchungguk 미국미합중국 *fml*
usable ssŭl su innŭn 쓸 수 있는
usage (*linguistic*) ŏppŏp 어법
use 1 *v/t* ssŭda 쓰다, sayonghada 사용하다; *pej*: *person* iyonghada 이용하다; ***I could ~ a drink*** F mwŏ chom mashyŏyagessŏyo 뭐 좀 마셔야겠어요 **2** *n* sayong 사용, ssŭgi 쓰기, iyong 이용; ***be of great ~ to s.o.*** nuguege k'ŭge ssŭlmo it-tta 누구에게 크게 쓸모 있다; ***be of no ~ to s.o.*** nuguege ssŭlmo ŏptta 누구에게 쓸모 없다; ***is that of any ~?*** ssŭlmo issŭmnikka? 쓸모

있습니까?; ***it's no ~*** soyong ŏmnŭn irimnida 소용 없는 일입니다; ***it's no ~ trying / waiting*** haebwaya / kidaryŏbwaya soyong ŏpssŭmnida 해봐야 / 기다려봐야 소용 없습니다
♦**use up** ta ssŏbŏrida 다 써버리다
used[1] *car etc* ch'unggo 중고
used[2]: ***be ~ to s.o. / sth*** nugue / muŏse ikssuk'aejyŏ it-tta 누구에 / 무엇에 익숙해져 있다; ***get ~ to s.o. / sth*** nugue / muŏse ikssuk'aejida 누구에 / 무엇에 익숙해지다; ***be ~ to doing sth*** muŏsŭl hanŭn kŏse ikssuk'aejyŏ it-tta 무엇을 하는 것에 익숙해져 있다; ***get ~ to doing sth*** muŏsŭl hanŭn kŏse ikssuk'aejida 무엇을 하는 것에 익숙해지다
used[3]: ***I ~ to like / know him*** hanttae nanŭn kŭrŭl choahaessŏt-tta / arassŏt-tta 한때 나는 그를 좋아했었다 / 알았었다; ***I don't work there now, but I ~ to*** chigŭmŭn anijiman, yejŏnenŭn kŭ gosesŏ irhaessŏssŏyo 지금은 아니지만, 예전에는 그 곳에서 일했었어요; ***I ~ to work with him*** nanŭn kŭwa kach'i irhaessŏssŭmnida 나는 그와 같이 일했었습니다
useful ssŭlmoinnŭn 쓸모있는
usefulness ssŭlmo 쓸모
useless ssŭlmoŏmnŭn 쓸모없는; F *person* mojaran 모자란; ***it's ~ trying*** noryŏk'aebwattcha ssŭlmoŏmnŭn chishida 노력해봤자 쓸모없는 짓이다
user (*of product*) sayongja 사용자
user-friendly sayonghagi shwiun 사용하기 쉬운
usher *n* (*at wedding*) annaeja 안내자
♦**usher in** *new era* ...(ŭ)ro indohada ...(으)로 인도하다
usual pot'ong-ŭi 보통의; ***as ~*** pot'ong ttaech'ŏrŏm 보통 때처럼; ***the ~, please*** nŭl hanŭn kŏsŭro chushipsshio 늘 하는 것으로 주십시오
usually pot'ong 보통
utensil yonggu 용구
uterus chagung 자궁
utility (*usefulness*) yuyongssŏng 유용성; (*software*) yut'illit'i 유틸리티; ***public utilities*** kong-ik saŏp 공익 사업
utilize yuyonghage hada 유용하게 하다
utmost 1 *adj* ch'oedaehanŭi 최대한의 **2** *n*: ***do one's ~*** ch'oesŏnŭl tahada 최선을 다하다
utter 1 *adj* wanjŏnhan 완전한 **2** *v/t sound* parhada 발하다
utterly wanjŏnhi 완전히
U-turn yut'ŏn U턴; *fig* (*in policy*) wanjŏnhan t'albakkum 완전한 탈바꿈

V

vacant *building* piŏ innŭn 비어 있는; *position* kongsŏgin 공석인; *look* mŏnghan 멍한
vacate *room* piuda 비우다
vacation *n* hyuga 휴가; ***be on ~*** hyuga chung-ida 휴가 중이다; ***go to ... on ~*** hyugaro ...e kada 휴가로 ...에 가다; ***take a ~*** hyugarŭl kat-tta 휴가를 갖다
vacationer hyuga yŏhaenggaek 휴가 여행객
vaccinate yebang chŏptchonghada 예방 접종하다; ***be ~d against ...*** yebang chŏptchong chusarŭl mat-tta ... 예방 접종 주사를 맞다
vaccination yebang chŏptchong 예방 접종
vaccine paeksshin 백신
vacuum 1 *n* PHYS chin-gong 진공; *fig* (*in one's life*) konghŏ 공허 **2** *v/t* *floors* chin-gong ch'ŏngsogiro ch'ŏngsohada 진공 청소기로 청소하다
vacuum cleaner chin-gong ch'ŏngsogi 진공 청소기; **vacuum flask** chin-gonggwan 진공관; **vacuum-packed** chin-gongp'ojang-ŭi 진공포장의
vagina chil 질
vaginal chirŭi 질의
vague mohohan 모호한; *feeling* ŏryŏmp'ut'an 어렴풋한; *taste of sth*, *resemblance* hŭrit'an 흐릿한; ***he was very ~ about it*** kŭnŭn kŭ ire taehae mohohan t'aedorŭl ch'wihaet-tta 그는 그 일에 대해 모호한 태도를 취했다
vaguely *answer* mohohage 모호하게; (*slightly*) yakkan 약간
vain 1 *adj person* hŏyŏngshimi manŭn 허영심이 많은; *hope* hŏt-ttoen 헛된 **2** *n*: ***in ~*** hŏt-ttoege 헛되게; ***their efforts were in ~*** kŭdŭrŭi noryŏgŭn hŏtssugoro torakat-tta 그들의 노력은 헛수고로 돌아갔다
valet (*person*) shijung tŭnŭn saram 시중 드는 사람
valet service (*for clothes*) set'ak sŏbissŭ 세탁 서비스; (*for cars*) sech'a sŏbissŭ 세차 서비스
valiant yonggamhan 용감한
valid *passport*, *document* yuhyohan 유효한; *reason*, *argument* t'adanghan 타당한
validate (*with official stamp*) yuhyohage hada 유효하게 하다; (*back up*) chŭngmyŏnghada 증명하다
validity t'adangsŏng 타당성
valley koltchagi 골짜기
valuable 1 *adj* kwijunghan 귀중한 **2** *n*: **~s** kwijungp'um 귀중품
valuation kamjŏng 감정; ***at his ~*** kŭga kamjŏnghan paronŭn 그가 감정한 바로는
value 1 *n* kach'i 가치; ***be good ~*** kŭmanhan kach'iga it-tta 그만한 가치가 있다; ***get ~ for money*** ton mank'ŭmŭi kach'irŭl ŏt-tta 돈 만큼의 가치를 얻다; ***rise / fall in ~*** kach'iga orŭda / ttŏrŏjida 가치가 오르다 / 떨어지다 **2** *v/t s.o.'s friendship*, *one's freedom* sojunghi yŏgida 소중히 여기다; ***I ~ your advice*** tangshiŭi ch'unggorŭl sojunghi saenggak'aeyo 당신의 충고를 소중히 생각해요; ***have an object ~d*** ŏttŏn mulgŏnŭi kapssŭl p'yŏngkkabat-tta 어떤 물건의 값을 평가받다
valve paelbŭ 밸브
van ponggoch'a 봉고차
vandal koŭijŏgŭro konggongmurŭl pusunŭn saram 고의적으로 공공물을 부수는 사람
vandalism koŭijŏk p'agoe 고의적 파괴
vandalize koŭijŏgŭro p'agoehada 고의적으로 파괴하다

vanilla 1 *n* panilla 바닐라 **2** *adj* panillaŭi 바닐라의
vanish sarajida 사라지다
vanity chamanshim 자만심; (*of hopes*) konghŏham 공허함
vanity case hwajangp'um kabang 화장품 가방
vantage point (*on hill etc*) chŏnmang-i choŭn chijŏm 전망이 좋은 지점
vapor chŭnggi 증기
vaporize *v/t* (*of bomb*) chŭngbalshik'ida 증발시키다
vapor trail pihaeng-un 비행운
variable 1 *adj amount* kabyŏnŭi 가변의; *moods*, *weather* pyŏndŏkssŭrŏun 변덕스러운 **2** *n* MATH, COMPUT pyŏnssu 변수
variation pyŏndong 변동
varicose vein nojang chŏngmaek 노장 정맥
varied *range*, *diet* tayanghan 다양한
variety pyŏnhwa 변화; (*type*) tayangssŏng 다양성; ***a ~ of things to do*** yŏrŏ kaji hal il 여러 가지 할 일
various (*several*) yŏrŏ 여러; (*different*) kaji kakssaegŭi 가지 각색의
varnish 1 *n* nisŭ 니스 **2** *v/t* nisŭrŭl ch'irhada 니스를 칠하다
vary 1 *v/i* pakkwida 바뀌다; ***it varies*** ch'ŏnch'amanbyŏrijiyo 천차만별이지요 **2** *v/t* pakkuda 바꾸다
vase kkotppyŏng 꽃병
vast *desert*, *city* kwanghwarhan 광활한; *collection*, *knowledge* pangdaehan 방대한
vaudeville shyo 쇼
vault[1] *n* (*in roof*) tunggŭn ch'ŏnjang 둥근 천장; **~s** (*cellar*) chiha ch'anggo 지하 창고
vault[2] **1** *n* SP toyak 도약 **2** *v/t beam etc* ttwiŏnŏmtta 뛰어넘다
VCR (= ***video cassette recorder***) pŭi ssi al 브이 시이 알
veal songaji kogi 송아지 고기
vegan 1 *n* ch'ŏltchŏhan ch'aeshiktchuŭija 철저한 채식주의자 **2** *adj* ch'ŏltchŏhan ch'aeshigŭi 철저한 채식의
vegetable yach'ae 야채
vegetarian 1 *n* ch'aeshiktchuŭija 채식주의자 **2** *adj* ch'aeshigŭi 채식의
vehicle unban sudan 운반 수단; (*for information etc*) chŏndal sudan 전달 수단
veil 1 *n* peil 베일 **2** *v/t* karida 가리다
vein (*in leg etc*) chŏngmaek 정맥
Velcro® *n* tchiktchigi 찍찍이
velocity soktto 속도
velvet pelbet 벨벳
vending machine chadong p'anmaegi 자동 판매기
vendor LAW maegagin 매각인
veneer (*on wood*) peniŏ happ'an 베니어 합판; (*of politeness etc*) hŏshik 허식
venereal disease sŏngppyŏng 성병
venetian blind penishyŏn pŭllaidŭ 베니션 블라인드
vengeance pokssu 복수; ***with a ~*** kyŏngnyŏrhage 격렬하게
venison sasŭm kogi 사슴 고기
venom (*of snake*) tok 독
vent *n* (*for air*) t'onggi kumŏng 통기 구멍; ***give ~ to*** *feelings* t'ŏttŭrida 터뜨리다
ventilate *room* hwan-gihada 환기하다
ventilation t'onggi 통기
ventilation shaft hwan-gigaeng 환기갱
ventilator hwan-gi changch'i 환기 장치
ventriloquist pok'wasulssa 복화술사
venture 1 *n* (*undertaking*) mohŏm 모험; COM t'ugijŏk saŏp 투기적 사업 **2** *v/i* kwagamhi haeboda 과감히 해보다
venue (*for meeting etc*) changso 장소
veranda peranda 베란다
verb tongsa 동사
verdict LAW p'yŏnggyŏl 평결; (*opinion*, *judgment*) p'andan 판단
verge *n* (*of road*) kajangjari 가장자리; kyŏnggye 경계; ***be on the ~ of*** *ruin*, *collapse*, *tears* … ilbo chiktchŏne it-tta … 일보 직전에 있다
♦**verge on** kŏŭi kat-tta 거의 같다
verification iptchŭng 입증; (*confirmation*) hwagin 확인
verify (*check out*) chŭngmyŏnghada

증명하다; (*confirm*) hwaginhada 확인하다
vermicelli perŭmich'elli 베르미첼리
vermin haech'ung 해충
vermouth perŭmut'ŭju 베르무트주
vernacular *n* ilssang-yong-ŏ 일상용어
versatile *person* tajaedanŭnghan 다재다능한; *equipment, mind* mannŭng-ŭi 만능의
versatility (*of person*) tajaedanŭng 다재다능; (*of equipment, mind*) mannŭng 만능
verse (*poetry*) shi 시; (*part of poem, song*) chŏl 절
versed: ***be well ~ in a subject*** han chujee chŏngt'onghada 한 주제에 정통하다
version (*of song, book*) p'an 판; ***what is your ~ of what happened?*** kŭ sakkŏne taehae ŏttŏk'e saenggak'aeyo? 그 사건에 대해 어떻게 생각해요?
versus SP, LAW tae 대
vertebra ch'ŏkch'ugol 척추골
vertebrate *n* ch'ŏkch'udongmul 척추동물
vertical sujigŭi 수직의
vertigo hyŏn-gitchŭng 현기증
very 1 *adv* taedanhi 대단히; ***was it cold? – not ~*** ch'uwŏssŏyo? - maninŭn aniŏssŏyo 추웠어요? - 많이는 아니었어요; ***the ~ best*** kajang choŭn 가장 좋은 **2** *adj* paro 바로; ***in the ~ act*** hyŏnhaengbŏmŭro 현행범으로; ***that's the ~ thing I need*** chŏgŏshi paro naega p'iryoro hanŭn kŭ mulgŏniyeyo 저것이 바로 내가 필요로 하는 그 물건이에요; ***the ~ thought*** paro kŭ saenggak 바로 그 생각; ***right at the ~ top / bottom*** kkokttaegi / padag-ŭi paro kŏgie 꼭대기 / 바닥의 바로 거기에
vessel NAUT pae 배
vest chokki 조끼
vestige (*of previous civilization etc*) yujŏk 유적; (*of truth*) hŭnjŏk 흔적
vet[1] *n* (*for animals*) suŭisa 수의사
vet[2] *v/t applicants etc* chŏmgŏmhada 점검하다
vet[3] *n* MIL koch'ambyŏng
veteran 1 *n* pet'erang 베테랑 **2** *adj* (*old*) orae sayonghan 오래 사용한; (*experienced*) pet'erang-ŭi 베테랑의
veterinarian suŭisa 수의사
veto 1 *n* kŏbukkwŏn 거부권 **2** *v/t* kŏbuhada 거부하다
vexed (*worried*) komindoenŭn 고민되는; ***the ~ question of ...*** nollanŭi yŏjiga manŭn … munje 논란의 여지가 많은 … 문제
via kyŏngnyuhayŏ 경유하여
viable *life form, company* saengjonhal su innŭn 생존할 수 있는; *alternative, plan* hyoryŏgi innŭn 효력이 있는
vibrate *v/i* hŭndŭllida 흔들리다
vibration chindong 진동
vice ak 악; ***the problem of ~*** sahoeagŭi munje 사회악의 문제
vice president (*of company*) pusajang 부사장; (*of state*) put'ongnyŏng 부통령
vice squad p'unggi sabŏm tansokppan 풍기 사범 단속반
vice versa pandaero 반대로
vicinity kŭnch'ŏ 근처; ***in the ~ of*** …ŭi kŭnch'ŏe(sŏ) …의 근처에(서); (*with figures*) taeryak … 대략 …
vicious *dog* sŏngjiri koyak'an 성질이 고약한; *attack, temper, criticism* chidok'an 지독한
victim hŭisaeng 희생
victimize hŭisaengshikida 희생시키다
victor sŭngnija 승리자
victorious sŭngnihan 승리한
victory sŭngni 승리; ***win a ~ over*** …e taehae sŭngnihada …에 대해 승리하다
video 1 *n* pidio 비디오; ***have X on ~*** Xŭl / rŭl pidioe tamtta X을 / 를 비디오에 담다 **2** *v/t* pidioro ch'waryŏnghada 비디오로 촬영하다
video camera pidio k'amera 비디오 카메라; **video cassette** pidio k'aset'ŭ 비디오 카세트; **video cassete recorder** pidio k'aset'ŭ nok'wagi 비디오 카세트 녹화기; **video conference** TELEC hwasang hoeŭi 화상 회의; **video game** chŏnja orak 전자 오락; **videophone** pidio chŏnhwa 비디오 전화; **video**

recorder pidio nok'wagi 비디오 녹화기; **video recording** pidio nok'wa 비디오 녹화; **videotape** pidio t'eip'ŭ 비디오 테이프
Vietnam Pet'ŭnam 베트남, Wŏlnam 월남
Vietnamese 1 *adj* Pet'ŭnamŭi 베트남의, Wŏlnamŭi 월남의 **2** *n* Pet'ŭnamin 베트남인, Wŏlnamin 월남인; (*language*) Pet'ŭnamŏ 베트남어, Wŏlnamŏ 월남어
view 1 *n* kyŏngch'i 경치; (*of situation*) kyŏnhae 견해; ***in ~ of***...ŭl / rŭl salp'yŏbomyŏn ...을 / 를 살펴보면; ***be on ~*** (*of paintings*) chŏnshi chung-ida 전시 중이다; ***with a ~ to*** ...hal moktchŏgŭro ...할 목적으로 **2** *v/t events, situation* paraboda 바라보다; *TV program* shich'ŏnghada 시청하다; *house for sale* tullŏboda 둘러보다 **3** *v/i* (*watch TV*) shich'ŏnghada 시청하다
viewer TV shich'ŏngja 시청자
viewfinder PHOT p'aindŏ 파인더
viewpoint kwantchŏm 관점
vigor (*energy*) hwalgi 활기
vigorous *person* hwalbarhan 활발한; *shake* kyŏksshimhan 격심한; *denial* kangnyŏk'an 강력한
vile *smell* mopsshi yŏk-kkyŏun 몹시 역겨운; *thing to do* piyŏrhan 비열한
village maŭl 마을
villager maŭl saram 마을 사람
villain akttang 악당
vindicate ...ŭi chinshirŭlip-tchŭnghada ...의 진실을 입증하다; ***I feel ~d*** kyŏlbaek'aejin nŭkkimiyeyo 결백해진 느낌이예요
vindictive poboktchŏgin 보복적인
vine p'odonamu 포도나무
vinegar shikch'o 식초
vineyard p'odowŏn 포도원
vintage 1 *n* (*of wine*) ch'oegogŭp p'odoju 최고급 포도주 **2** *adj* (*classic*) oraedoeŏ kabŏch'iga innŭn 오래되어 값어치가 있는
violate *rules, treaty* wibanhada 위반하다; *sanctity of place* modok'ada 모독하다
violation (*of rules, treaty, traffic*) wiban 위반; (*of sanctity*) modok 모독
violence (*of person, movie*) p'ongnyŏk 폭력; (*of emotion, reaction*) kyŏngnyŏrham 격렬함; (*of gale*) kangnyŏrham 강렬함; ***outbreak of ~*** p'ongnyŏk sat'aeŭi palssaeng 폭력 사태의 발생
violent *person, movie* nanp'okhan 난폭한; *emotion, reaction* kyŏngnyŏrhan 격렬한; *gale* kangnyŏrhan 강렬한; ***have a ~ temper*** sŏngkkyŏgi nanp'ok'ada 성격이 난폭하다
violently *react* nanp'ok'age 난폭하게; *object* kangnyŏk'age 강력하게; ***fall ~ in love with s.o.*** nuguwa kyŏktchŏngjŏgŭro sarange ppajida 누구와 격정적으로 사랑에 빠지다
violet (*color*) poratppit 보라빛; (*plant*) chebikkot 제비꽃
violin paiollin 바이올린
violinist paiollin yŏnjuja 바이올린 연주자
VIP pŭi ai p'i 브이 아이 피이
viral *infection* pairŏsŭŭi 바이러스의
virgin (*female*) ch'ŏnyŏ 처녀; (*male*) sutch'onggak 숫총각
virginity tongjŏng 동정; ***lose one's ~*** sun-gyŏrŭl ilt'a 순결을 잃다
virile *man* namjadaun 남자다운; *prose* kanggŏnhan 강건한
virility namsŏngdaum 남성다움; (*sexual*) saengshik nŭngnyŏk 생식 능력
virtual sashilssang-ŭi 사실상의
virtual reality kasang hyŏnshil 가상 현실
virtually kŏŭi 거의
virtue tŏk 덕; ***in ~ of*** ttaemune 때문에
virtuoso MUS kŏjang 거장
virtuous kogyŏrhan 고결한
virulent *disease* yudok'an 유독한
virus MED, COMPUT pairŏsŭ 바이러스
visa pija 비자
visibility nune poim 눈에 보임; (*range of vision*) shiya 시야
visible *object* poinŭn 보이는; *difference* nune ttŭinŭn 눈에 띄는; *anger* myŏngbaek'an 명백한; ***not ~ to the naked eye*** yuganŭronŭn poiji annŭn 육안으로는 보이지 않는
visibly *different* nune ttŭige 눈에

띄게; ***he was ~ moved*** kŭnŭn kamdong padŭn kŏshi yŏngnyŏk'aet-tta 그는 감동 받은 것이 역력했다
vision (*eyesight*) shiryŏk 시력; REL *etc* hwanyŏng 환영
visit 1 *n* pangmun 방문; ***pay a ~ to the doctor / dentist*** ŭisa / ch'ikkwaŭisarŭl ch'ajagada 의사 / 치과의사를 찾아가다; ***pay s.o. a ~*** nugurŭl pangmunhada 누구를 방문하다 **2** *v/t* pangmunhada 방문하다
visiting card myŏngham 명함
visiting hours (*at hospital*) myŏnhoe shigan 면회 시간
visitor (*guest*) sonnim 손님; (*to museum etc*) kwallamgaek 관람객; (*tourist*) kwan-gwanggaek 관광객
visor ch'aeng 챙
visual shigaktchŏgin 시각적인
visual aid shigak kyojae 시각 교재
visual display unit yŏngsang p'yoshi changch'i 영상 표시 장치
visualize maŭm soge ttŏollida 마음 속에 떠올리다; (*foresee*) yegyŏnhada 예견하다
visually shigaktchŏgŭro 시각적으로
visually impaired shigaktchŏgŭro sonsangdoen 시각적으로 손상된
vital (*essential*) p'ilssujŏgin 필수적인; ***it is ~ that*** ...ranŭn kŏsŭn kŭk'i chungdaehamnida ...라는 것은 극히 중대합니다
vitality (*of person, city etc*) hwallyŏk 활력
vitally: ***~ important*** kŭk'i chungdaehan 극히 중대한
vital organs chungyo shinch'e kigwan 중요 신체 기관
vital statistics (*of woman*) mommae ch'itssu 몸매 치수
vitamin pit'amin 비타민
vitamin pill pit'amin chŏngje 비타민 정제
vivacious k'waehwarhan 쾌활한
vivacity k'waehwal 쾌활
vivid *color* kangnyŏrhan 강렬한; *memory* sŏnmyŏnghan 선명한; *imagination* saengsaenghan 생생한
V-neck Vchahyŏng mokssŏn V자형 목선
vocabulary ŏhwi 어휘
vocal mokssoriŭi 목소리의; (*expressing opinions*) sori nop'yŏ chujanghanŭn 소리 높여 주장하는
vocal cords sŏngdae 성대
vocal group MUS pok'ŏl kŭrup 보컬 그룹
vocalist MUS pok'ŏllisŭt'ŭ 보컬리스트
vocation (*calling*) samyŏng 사명; (*profession*) chigŏp 직업
vocational *guidance* chigŏpssang-ŭi 직업상의
vodka podŭk'a 보드카
vogue yuhaeng 유행; ***be in ~*** yuhaeng chung-ida 유행 중이다
voice 1 *n* mokssori 목소리 **2** *v/t opinions* p'yomyŏnghada 표명하다
voicemail ŭmsŏng up'yŏn 음성 우편
void 1 *n* pin konggan 빈 공간 **2** *adj*: ***~ of*** ...i / ga ŏmnŭn ...이 / 가 없는
volatile *personality, moods* pyŏndŏkssŭrŏun 변덕스러운
volcano hwasan 화산
volley *n* (*of shots*) iltchesagyŏk 일제사격; (*in tennis*) palli 발리
volleyball paegu 배구
volt polt'ŭ 볼트
voltage chŏnap 전압
volume (*of container*) ip-ppang yongjŏk 입방 용적; (*of work, business, liquid etc*) yang 양; (*of book*) han kwŏn 한 권; (*of radio etc*) ŭmnyang 음량
volume control ŭmnyang chojŏlgi 음량 조절기
voluntary *adj* chabaltchŏgin 자발적인
volunteer 1 *n* chawŏnja 자원자 **2** *v/i* chajinhaesŏ hada 자진해서 하다
voluptuous yuk-kkamjŏgin 육감적인
vomit 1 *n* kut'o 구토 **2** *v/i* t'ohada 토하다
♦**vomit up** t'ohada 토하다
vomiting t'oham 토함
voracious *appetite* wangsŏnghan 왕성한
vote 1 *n* t'up'yo 투표; ***have the ~*** t'up'yokkwŏnŭl kajida 투표권을 가지다 **2** *v/i* POL t'up'yohada 투표하다; ***~ for / against*** ...e ch'ansŏng / pandae t'up'yohada ...에

찬성/반대 투표하다 **3** *v/t*: ***they ~d him President*** kŭdŭrŭn kŭrŭl taet'ongnyŏng-ŭro t'up'yohaet-tta 그들은 그를 대통령으로 투표했다; ***they ~d to stay behind*** kŭdŭrŭn twiro mullŏsŏ itkkirŭl t'up'yohaet-tta 그들은 뒤로 물러서 있기를 투표했다
♦**vote in** *new member* sŏnch'urhada 선출하다
♦**vote on** *issue* p'yogyŏrhada 표결하다
♦**vote out** (*of office*) t'up'yoe ŭihae ch'ubanghada 투표에 의해 추방하다
voter yukkwŏnja 유권자
voting t'up'yo 투표
voting booth kip'yoso 기표소
vouch for *person*, *truth* pojŭnghada 보증하다
voucher harinkkwŏn 할인권
vow 1 *n* sŏyak 서약 **2** *v/t*: ~ ***to do sth*** muŏt hal kŏsŭl maengsehada 무엇 할 것을 맹세하다
vowel moŭm 모음
voyage (*by sea*) hanghae 항해; (*in space*) ujuyŏhaeng 우주여행
vulgar *person*, *language* chŏsok'an 저속한
vulnerable (*to attack*) konggyŏk tanghagi shwiun 공격 당하기 쉬운; (*to criticism etc*) sangch'ŏ patkki shwiun 상처 받기 쉬운
vulture tokssuri 독수리

W

wad *n* (*of paper*) tabal 다발; (*of absorbent cotton etc*) mungch'i 뭉치; ***a ~ of $100 bills*** paek talla chip'ye han tabal 백 달라 지폐 한 다발
waddle *v/i* twittunggŏrimyŏ kŏt-tta 뒤뚱거리며 걷다
wade kŏrŏsŏ kŏnnŏda 걸어서 건너다
♦**wade through** *book*, *documents* himdŭlge haenagada 힘들게 해나가다
wafer (*cookie*) weip'ŏ 웨이퍼; REL chebyŏng 제병
waffle[1] *n* (*to eat*) wap'ŭl 와플
waffle[2] *v/i* pujirŏmnŭn marŭl hada 부질없는 말을 하다
wag 1 *v/t tail*, *finger* hŭndŭlda 흔들다 **2** *v/i* (*of tail*) hŭndŭlgŏrida 흔들거리다
wage[1] *v/t war* ch'irŭda 치르다
wage[2] *n* wŏlgŭp 월급
wage earner kajang 가장
wage freeze imgŭm tonggyŏl 임금 동결
wage packet wŏlgŭp pongt'u 월급 봉투
wager *n* naegi 내기
waggle *v/t hips*, *ears* hŭndŭlda 흔들다; *loose screw*, *tooth etc* hŭndŭlgŏrida 흔들거리다
wagon: ***be on the ~*** F surŭl kkŭnt'a 술을 끊다
wail 1 *n* (*of person*, *baby*) ulbujijŭm 울부짖음; (*of siren*) kusŭlp'ŭn sori 구슬픈 소리 **2** *v/i* (*of person*, *baby*) ulbujit-tta 울부짖다; (*of siren*) kusŭlp'ŭn sorirŭl naeda 구슬픈 소리를 내다
waist hŏri 허리
waistline hŏrisŏn 허리선
wait 1 *n* kidarim 기다림 **2** *v/i* kidarida 기다리다; ***we'll ~ until he's ready*** urinŭn kŭga chunbidoel ttaekkaji kidaril kŏshimnida 우리는 그가 준비될 때까지 기다릴 것입니다 **2** *v/t meal* miruda 미루다; ***~ table*** shikttang kŭpssa norŭsŭl hada 식당 급사 노릇을 하다
♦**wait for** …ŭl / rŭl kidarida …을 / 를 기다리다; ***~ me!*** narŭl kidaryŏ chuseyo! 나를 기다려 주세요!
♦**wait on** *person* …ŭi shijung-ŭl tŭlda …의 시중을 들다
♦**wait up** chaji ank'o kidarida 자지 않고 기다리다
waiter weit'ŏ 웨이터; ***~!*** weit'ŏ! 웨이터!
waiting *n* kidarinŭn kŏt 기다리는 것; ***no ~ sign*** kidariji mashio 기다리지 마시오
waiting list taegija myŏngdan 대기자 명단
waiting room taegishil 대기실
waitress weit'ŭrisŭ 웨이트리스
waive (*relinquish*) p'ogihada 포기하다; (*dispense with*) ch'ŏrhoehada 철회하다
wake (*of ship*) paega chinagan chari 배가 지나간 자리; ***in the ~ of*** *fig* …ŭl / rŭl it-ttara …을 / 를 잇따라; ***follow in the ~ of*** …ŭl / rŭl it-ttarŭda …을 / 를 잇따르다
♦**wake up 1** *v/i* chami kkaeda 잠이 깨다 **2** *v/t* kkaeuda 깨우다
wake-up call moning k'ol 모닝 콜
Wales Weiljŭ 웨일즈
walk 1 *n* kŏtkki 걷기; (*in front of house*) *toroesŏ chipkkajiŭi kil* 도로에서 집까지의 길; ***it's a five-minute ~ from the station*** yŏgesŏ kŏrŏ o pun kŏriida 역에서 걸어 오 분 거리이다; ***it's a long / short ~ to the office*** samushilkkajinŭn kŏrŏsŏ mŏn / kakkaun kŏriida 사무실까지는 걸어서 먼 / 가까운 거리이다; ***go for a ~*** sanch'aekhada 산책하다 **2** *v/i* kŏt-tta 걷다; (*as opposed to taking the car / bus etc*) kŏrŏsŏ kada 걸어서 가다; (*hike*) tobo yŏhaenghada 도보

여행하다; ~ ***up to*** tagagada 다가가다 **3** *v/t dog* sanch'aekshik'ida 산책시키다; ~ ***the streets*** (*walk around*) kŏrirŭl toradanida 거리를 돌아다니다

♦**walk out** (*on spouse, of room etc*) kaptchagi ttŏnada 갑자기 떠나다; (*go on strike*) tongmaeng p'aŏp'ada 동맹 파업하다

♦**walk out on** *spouse, family* ...ŭl/rŭl pŏrida ...을/를 버리다

walker (*hiker*) pohaengja 보행자; (*for baby, old person*) pohaenggi 보행기; ***be a slow/fast*** ~ kŏrŭmi nŭrida/pparŭda 걸음이 느리다 /빠르다

walkie-talkie mujŏn-gi 무전기

walk-in closet taehyŏng ot-tchang 대형 옷장

walking (*as opposed to driving*) kŏnnŭn kŏt 걷는 것; (*hiking*) tobo yŏhaeng 도보 여행; ***be within ~ distance*** kŏrŏsŏ kal su innŭn kŏriida 걸어서 갈 수 있는 거리이다

walking stick chip'ang-i 지팡이

walking tour tobo yŏhaeng 도보 여행

Walkman® wŏk'ŭmaen 워크맨; **walkout** (*strike*) tongmaeng p'aŏp 동맹 파업; **walkover** (*easy win*) nakssŭng 낙승; **walk-up** *n* *ellibeit'ŏga ŏmnŭn ap'at'ŭ* 엘리베이터가 없는 아파트

wall (*of room, house*) pyŏk 벽; (*around garden*) tam 담; *fig* (*of silence etc*) pyŏk 벽; ***go to the*** ~ (*of company*) p'asanhada 파산하다; ***drive ... up the*** ~ F ...ŭl/rŭl mich'ige hada ...을/를 미치게 하다

wallet chigap 지갑

wallop F **1** *n* (*to ball*) kangt'a 강타; ***get a*** ~ shimhage mat-tta 심하게 맞다 **2** *v/t* ttaerida 때리다; *ball* ch'ida 치다; (*defeat*) ch'amp'aeshik'ida 참패시키다

wallpaper 1 *n* pyŏktchi 벽지 **2** *v/t* pyŏktchirŭl parŭda 벽지를 바르다

Wall Street Wŏl Sŭt'ŭrit'ŭ (*Miguk kŭmyunggye*) 월 스트리트 (미국 금융계)

wall-to-wall carpet match'um k'ap'et 맞춤 카펫

walnut hodu 호두

waltz *n* walch'ŭ 왈츠

wan *face* ch'angbaek'an 창백한

wander *v/i* (*roam*) ttŏdoradanida 떠돌아다니다; (*of tourist*) toradanida 돌아다니다; (*stray*) hemaeda 헤매다; (*of attention*) sanmanhaejida 산만해지다

♦**wander around** yŏgijŏgi toradanida 여기저기 돌아다니다

wane (*of interest, enthusiasm*) chŏmjŏm churŏdŭlda 점점 줄어들다

wangle *v/t* F yongk'e kuhada 용케 구하다

want 1 *n*: ***for ~ of*** ...i/ga ŏpssŏsŏ ...이/가 없어서 **2** *v/t* (*desire*) wŏnhada 원하다; (*need*) p'iryohada 필요하다; ~ ***to do sth*** muŏsŭl hago shiptta 무엇을 하고 싶다; ***I ~ to stay here*** nanŭn yŏgi mŏmulgo shipssŭmnida 나는 여기 머물고 싶습니다; ***do you ~ to go too? - no, I don't ~ to*** tangshindo kago ship'ŏyo?- aniyo, nanŭn kago shiptchi anayo 당신도 가고 싶어요? - 아니요, 나는 가고 싶지 않아요; ***you can have whatever you ~*** tangshini wŏnhanŭn kŏsŭn muŏshidŭn kajil su issŏyo 당신이 원하는 것은 무엇이든 가질 수 있어요; ***it's not what I ~ed*** kŭgŏn naega wŏnhaet-ttŏn kŏshi aniyeyo 그건 내가 원했던 것이 아니예요; ***she ~s you to go back*** kŭnyŏnŭn tangshini toragagil wŏnhaeyo 그녀는 당신이 돌아가길 원해요; ***he ~s a haircut*** kŭnŭn mŏrirŭl challayagessŏyo 그는 머리를 잘라야겠어요 **3** *v/i*: ~ ***for nothing*** pujok'ami ŏptta 부족함이 없다

want ad saenghwal kwanggo 생활 광고

wanted *adj* (*by police*) chimyŏng subaedoen 지명 수배된

wanting: ***be ~ in*** ...i/ga mojarada ...이/가 모자라다

wanton *adj* chemŏt-ttaeroin 제멋대로인

war *n* chŏnjaeng 전쟁; ***be at*** ~ kyojŏn chung-ida 교전 중이다

warble *v/i* (*of bird*) chijŏgwida

지저귀다
ward (*in hospital*) pyŏngdong 병동; (*child*) p'ihugyŏnin 피후견인
♦**ward off** *blow, attacker* p'ihada 피하다; *cold, illness* yebanghada 예방하다
warden (*of prison*) kyodosojang 교도소장
wardrobe (*for clothes*) ot-tchang 옷장; (*clothes*) otkkaji 옷가지
warehouse ch'anggo 창고
warfare chŏnjaeng 전쟁
warhead t'andu 탄두
warily choshimhaesŏ 조심해서
warm *adj welcome, smile etc* ttattŭt'an 따뜻한; *summer* tŏun 더운
♦**warm up 1** *v/t person, room* ttattŭt'age hada 따뜻하게 하다; *soup, plates* teuda 데우다 **2** *v/i* (*of person, room*) ttattŭt'aejida 따뜻해지다; (*of soup*) tewŏjida 데워지다; (*of athlete etc*) chunbi undong-ŭl hada 준비 운동을 하다
warmhearted ch'injŏrhan 친절한
warmly *dressed, welcome, smile* ttattŭt'age 따뜻하게
warmth on-gi 온기; (*of welcome, smile*) onjŏng 온정
warn kyŏnggohada 경고하다
warning *n* kyŏnggo 경고; ***without ~*** kaptchagi 갑자기
warp 1 *v/t wood* hwigehada 휘게 하다; *character* pitturŏjige hada 비뚤어지게 하다 **2** *v/i* (*of wood*) hwida 휘다
warped *fig* pitturŏjin 비뚤어진
warplane kunyonggi 군용기
warrant 1 *n* yŏngtchang 영장 **2** *v/t* (*deserve, call for*) chŏngdanghwahada 정당화하다
warranty pojŭng 보증; ***be under ~*** pojŭng kigan chung-ida 보증 기간 중이다
warrior chŏnsa 전사
warship kunham 군함
wart samagwi 사마귀
wartime chŏnshi 전시
wary *look, response* shinjunghan 신중한; ***keep a ~ eye on*** …ŭl / rŭl seshimhage poda …을 / 를 세심하게 보다; ***be ~ of*** …ŭl / rŭl ŭishimhada …을 / 를 의심하다
wash 1 *n*: ***have a ~*** sshit-tta 씻다; ***that jacket / shirt needs a ~*** chŏ chaek'isŭn / shyŏch'ŭnŭn pparaya handa 저 재킷은 / 셔츠는 빨아야 한다 **2** *v/t clothes* ppalda 빨다; *dishes* taktta 닦다; *one's hands* sshit-tta 씻다 **3** *v/i* sshit-tta 씻다
♦**wash up** (*wash one's hands and face*) sshit-tta 씻다
washable ppal su innŭn 빨 수 있는
washbasin, **washbowl** semyŏn-gi 세면기
washcloth sugŏn 수건
washed out kiuni ŏmnŭn 기운이 없는
washer (*for faucet etc*) washyŏ 와셔; → ***washing machine***
washing ppallae 빨래; ***do the ~*** ppallaerŭl hada 빨래를 하다
washing machine set'ak-kki 세탁기
Washington (*city*) Wŏshingt'ŏn 워싱턴
washroom hwajangshil 화장실
wasp (*insect*) malbŏl 말벌
waste 1 *n* nangbi 낭비; (*from industrial process*) p'yegimul 폐기물; ***it's a ~ of time / money*** kŭgŏsŭn shiganŭi / tonŭi nangbiyeyo 그것은 시간의 / 돈의 낭비예요 **2** *adj* ssŭlmo-ŏmnŭn 쓸모없는 **3** *v/t* nangbihada 낭비하다
♦**waste away** yawida 야위다
wasteful nangbiga shimhan 낭비가 심한
wasteland hwangp'ye chiyŏk 황폐 지역; **wastepaper** hyuji 휴지; **wastepaper basket** hyujit'ong 휴지통; **waste pipe** (*for water*) paesugwan 배수관; **waste product** p'yegimul 폐기물
watch 1 *n* (*timepiece*) shigye 시계; ***keep ~*** mangboda 망보다 **2** *v/t movie, TV* poda 보다; (*observe*) chal poda 잘 보다; (*spy on*) kamshihada 감시하다; (*look after*) tolbwajuda 돌봐주다 **3** *v/i* chik'yŏboda 지켜보다
♦**watch for**: ***he is watching for his father*** kŭnŭn abŏjiga onŭnji chikyŏbogo it-tta 그는 아버지가 오는지 지켜보고 있다

♦**watch out** choshimhada 조심하다; *~!* choshimhae! 조심해!
♦**watch out for** (*be careful of*) ...ŭl / rŭl choshimhada ...을 / 를 조심하다
watchful chu-ŭigip'ŭn 주의깊은
watchmaker shigye chejoin 시계 제조인
water 1 *n* mul 물; **~s** NAUT yŏnghae 영해 **2** *v/t plant* murŭl chuda 물을 주다 **3** *v/i* (*of eyes*) nunmuri nada 눈물이 나다; ***my mouth is ~ing*** ch'imŭl hŭllida 침을 흘리다
♦**water down** *drink* murŭl t'ada 물을 타다
watercolor (*paint*) such'aehwa mulkkam 수채화 물감; (*painting*) such'aehwa 수채화; **watercress** mulnaeng-i 물냉이; **waterfall** p'okp'o 폭포
watering can mulppurigae 물뿌리개
watering hole (*hum*) sultchip 술집
water level suwi 수위; **water lily** suryŏn 수련; **waterline** (*at shore*) hae-ansŏn 해안선; (*of ship*) holssusŏn 홀수선; **waterlogged** mure chamgin 물에 잠긴; **watermark** chip'yeŭi naebich'inŭn munŭi 지폐의 내비치는 무늬; **watermelon** subak 수박; **water polo** sugu 수구; **waterproof** *adj* pangsudoenŭn 방수되는; **watershed** punsuryŏng 분수령; **waterside** *n* mulkka 물가; ***at the ~*** mulkkae(sŏ) 물가에(서); **waterskiing** susangsŭk'i 수상스키; **watertight** *compartment* pangsuŭi 방수의; **waterway** suro 수로; **waterwings** suyŏng yŏnsŭmnyong t'yubŭ 수영 연습용 튜브
watery mulgŭn 묽은
watt wat'ŭ 와트
wave[1] *n* (*in sea*) p'ado 파도
wave[2] **1** *n* (*of hand*) sonŭl hŭndŭnŭn shinho 손을 흔드는 신호 **2** *v/i* (*with hand*) sonŭl hŭndŭlda 손을 흔들다; (*of flag*) p'ŏllŏgida 펄럭이다; ***~ to s.o.*** nuguege sonŭl hŭndŭlda 누구에게 손을 흔들다 **3** *v/t flag etc* hŭndŭlda 흔들다
wavelength RAD p'ajang 파장; ***be on the same ~*** *fig* chal t'onghada 잘 통하다
waver chujŏhada 주저하다
wavy *hair, line* kupssŭlgŏrinŭn 굽슬거리는
wax *n* (*for floor, furniture*) wakssŭ 왁스; (*in ear*) kwiji 귀지
way 1 *n* (*method*) pangbŏp 방법; (*~ of doing sth*) pangshik 방식; (*route*) kil 길; ***this ~*** (*like this*) irŏk'e 이렇게; (*in this direction*) itchogŭro 이쪽으로; ***by the ~*** (*incidentally*) kŭrŏnde 그런데; ***by ~ of*** (*via*) ...ŭl / rŭl kŏch'yŏsŏ ...을 / 를 거쳐서; (*in the form of*) ...ŭl / rŭl hal semŭro ...을 / 를 할 셈으로; ***in a ~*** (*in certain respects*) ŏttŏn myŏnesŏnŭn 어떤 면에서는; ***be under ~*** chinhaeng chung-ida 진행 중이다; ***give ~*** MOT yangbohada 양보하다; (*collapse*) munŏjida 무너지다; ***give ~ to*** (*be replaced by*) ...(ŭ)ro pakkwida ...(으)로 바뀌다; ***have one's (own) ~*** chagi maŭmdaero hada 자기 마음대로 하다; ***OK, we'll do it your ~*** choayo, tangshin pangshigŭro hagessŏyo 좋아요, 당신 방식으로 하겠어요; ***lead the ~*** (*go first*) apssŏ kada 앞서 가다; (*be the leader, pioneer*) solssŏnhada 솔선하다; ***lose one's ~*** kirŭl ilt'a 길을 잃다; ***make ~*** kirŭl pik'yŏjuda 길을 비켜주다; ***be in the ~*** panghaega toeda 방해가 되다; ***it's on the ~ to the station*** yŏgŭro kanŭn kire issŏyo 역으로 가는 길에 있어요; ***I was on my ~ to the station*** nanŭn yŏgŭro kanŭn chung-iŏssŏyo 나는 역으로 가는 중이었어요; ***no ~!*** ŏrimdo ŏpssŏ! 어림도 없어!; ***there's no ~ he can do it*** kŭnŭn kŭgosŭl kyŏlk'o hal su ŏpssŏyo 그는 그것을 결코 할 수 없어요 **2** *adv* F (*far*) nŏmu 너무; ***it's ~ too soon to decide*** kyŏltchŏnghagienŭn nŏmu illŏyo 결정하기에는 너무 일러요; ***they are ~ behind with their work*** kŭdŭrŭn iri nŏmu millyŏ issŏyo 그들은 일이 너무 밀려 있어요
way back yejŏne 예전에; **way in** ippku 입구; **way of life** saenghwal pangshik 생활 방식; **way out**

ch'ulgu 출구; *fig* (*from situation*) haegyŏlch'aek 해결책
we uri 우리; ~ ***are American*** urinŭn Miguk saramiyeyo 우리는 미국 사람이에요
weak yak'an 약한; *tea, coffee* yŏnhan 연한
weaken 1 *v/t* yak'agehada 약하게 하다 **2** *v/i* yak'aejida 약해지다
weakling yaktcha 약자
weakness yaktchŏm 약점; ***have a ~ for*** (*liking*) ...ege yak'ada ...에게 약하다
wealth pu 부; ***a ~ of*** p'ungbuhan 풍부한
wealthy puyuhan 부유한
wean *v/t* chŏjŭl tteda 젖을 떼다
weapon mugi 무기
wear 1 *n*: ~ (***and tear***) tarŭm 닳음; ***clothes for everyday ~ / evening ~*** ilssangbok / p'at'ibok 일상복 / 파티복 **2** *v/t* (*have on*) iptta 입다; (*damage*) talk'e hada 닳게 하다 **3** *v/i* (*of carpet, fabric*: ~ *out*) tarhajida 닳아지다; (*last*) kyŏndida 견디다
♦**wear away 1** *v/i* tarhajida 닳아지다 **2** *v/t* talk'e hada 닳게 하다
♦**wear off** (*of effect, feeling*) chŏmjŏm ŏpssŏjida 점점 없어지다
♦**wear out 1** *v/t* (*tire*) chich'ige hada 지치게 하다; *shoes* tara ttŏrŏjige hada 닳아 떨어지게 하다 **2** *v/i* (*of shoes, carpet*) tara ttŏrŏjida 닳아 떨어지다
wearily chich'yŏsŏ 지쳐서
wearing (*tiring*) chich'ige hanŭn 지치게 하는
weary chich'in 지친
weasel choktchebi 족제비
weather 1 *n* nalsshi 날씨; ***be feeling under the ~*** momi tchibudŭdŭhada 몸이 찌부드드하다 **2** *v/t crisis* ttulk'o nagada 뚫고 나가다
weather-beaten pibarame shidallin 비바람에 시달린; **weather chart** ilgido 일기도; **weather forecast** ilgi yebo 일기 예보; **weatherman** kisang yebowŏn 기상 예보원
weave 1 *v/t* tchada 짜다 **2** *v/i* (*move*) nubida 누비다
web tchasŏ mandŭn kŏt 짜서 만든 것; ***spider's ~*** kŏmijip 거미집; ***the Web*** Wep 웹
webbed feet mulgalk'wiga tallin pal 물갈퀴가 달린 발
web browser wep pŭraujŏ 웹 브라우저; **web page** wep p'eiji 웹 페이지; **website** wep sa-it'ŭ 웹 사이트
wedding kyŏrhonshik 결혼식
wedding anniversary kyŏrhon kinyŏmil 결혼 기념일; **wedding cake** weding k'eik'ŭ 웨딩 케이크; **wedding day** kyŏrhonshingnal 결혼식날; **wedding dress** weding tŭresŭ 웨딩 드레스; **wedding hall** yeshiktchang 예식장; **wedding ring** kyŏrhon panji 결혼 반지
wedge *n* (*to hold sth in place*) sswaegi 쐐기; (*of cheese etc*) sswaegi moyang 쐐기 모양
Wednesday suyoil 수요일
weed 1 *n* chapch'o 잡초 **2** *v/t* chapch'orŭl ppoptta 잡초를 뽑다
♦**weed out** ch'uryŏnaeda 추려내다
weedkiller chech'oje 제초제
week chu 주; ***a ~ tomorrow*** p'aril twie 팔일 뒤에
weekday p'yŏng-il 평일
weekend chumal 주말; ***on the ~*** chumare 주말에
weekly 1 *adj* maeju-ŭi 매주의; ~ ***payment*** chugŭp 주급 **2** *n* (*magazine*) chugan 주간 **3** *adv* maejumada 매주마다
weep ulda 울다
weeping willow suyang pŏdŭl 수양 버들
weigh 1 *v/t* mugerŭl talda 무게를 달다; ~ ***anchor*** tach'ŭl ollida 닻을 올리다 **2** *v/i* mugega nagada 무게가 나가다
♦**weigh down**: ***be weighed down with*** ...ŭi mugero nullyŏjida ...의 무게로 눌려지다; *with worries* kibuni karaantta 기분이 가라앉다
♦**weigh up** (*assess*) p'yŏngkkahada 평가하다
weight (*of person, object*) muge 무게
weightless mujungnyŏgŭi 무중력의
weightlessness mujungnyŏk 무중력
weightlifter yŏktto sŏnsu 역도 선수

weightlifting yŏktto 역도
weir tuk 둑
weird isanghan 이상한
weirdo *n* F isanghan saram 이상한 사람
welcome 1 *adj* hwanyŏng pannŭn 환영 받는; ***you're ~*** ch'ŏnmaneyo 천만에요; ***you're ~ to try some*** ŏlmadŭnji haseyo 얼마든지 하세요 **2** *n* (*for guests etc*) hwanyŏng 환영; (*to news, proposal*) kikkŏi padadŭrim 기꺼이 받아들임 **3** *v/t guests etc* hwanyŏnghada 환영하다; *decision etc* kikkŏi padadŭrida 기꺼이 받아들이다
weld *v/t* yongjŏp'ada 용접하다
welder yongjŏpkkong 용접공
welfare poktchi 복지; (*financial assistance*) saenghwal pojo 생활 보조; ***be on ~*** saenghwal pojorŭl pat-tta 생활 보조를 받다
welfare check saenghwal pojogŭm 생활 보조금; **welfare state** poktchi kuk-kka 복지 국가; **welfare work** poktchi saŏp 복지 사업; **welfare worker** poktchi saŏpkka 복지 사업가
well[1] *n* (*for water*) umul 우물; ***oil ~*** yujŏn 유전
well[2] **1** *adv* chal 잘; ***as ~*** (*too*) ...do ...도; ***as ~ as*** (*in addition to*) ...ppunmananira ...do ...뿐만아니라 ...도; ***he came as ~*** kŭdo wat-tta 그도 왔다; ***he has a motorbike as ~ as a car*** kŭnŭn ch'appunman anira ot'obaido kajigo it-tta 그는 차뿐만 아니라 오토바이도 가지고 있다; ***I can't swim as ~ as you*** nanŭn tangshinmank'ŭm suyŏng-ŭl chal hal su ŏpssŏyo 나는 당신만큼 수영을 잘 할 수 없어요; ***it's just as ~ you told me*** tangshini naege yaegihaesŏ mach'im chal toe-ŏssŭmnida 당신이 내게 얘기해서 마침 잘 되었습니다; ***very ~*** (*acknowledging an order*) chal algessŭmnida 잘 알겠습니다; (*reluctant agreement*) ŏtchaet-ttŭn chossŭmnida 어쨌든 좋습니다; ***~, ~!*** (*surprise*) irŏn, irŏn! 이런, 이런!; ***~ ...*** (*uncertainty, thinking*) kŭlsse ... 글쎄 ... **2** *adj*: ***be ~*** chal it-tta 잘 있다; ***feel ~*** momi chot'a 몸이 좋다; ***get ~ soon!*** ppalli na-ŭseyo! 빨리 나으세요!
well-balanced *person, meal, diet* kyunhyŏng chap'in 균형 잡힌; **well-behaved** p'umhaeng-i tanjŏnghan 품행이 단정한; **well-being** pongni 복리; (*feeling*) haengbok 행복; **well-done** *meat* chal igŭn 잘 익은; **well-dressed** choŭn osŭl ibŭn 좋은 옷을 입은; **well-earned** che himŭro ŏdŭn 제 힘으로 얻은; **well-heeled** puyuhan 부유한; **well-known** chal allyŏjin 잘 알려진; **well-made** chal mandŭrŏjin 잘 만들어진; **well-mannered** yeŭi parŭn 예의 바른; **well-meaning** sŏnŭiŭi 선의의; **well-off** puyuhan 부유한; **well-read** paksshik'an 박식한; **well-timed** ttaerŭl chal match'un 때를 잘 맞춘; **well-to-do** puyuhan 부유한; **well-worn** tarappajin 닳아빠진
west 1 *n* sŏtchok 서쪽; (*western part of a country*) sŏbu 서부; ***the West*** (*western nations*) Sŏyang 서양 **2** *adj* sŏ 서; ***~ wind*** sŏp'ung 서풍 **3** *adv* sŏtchogŭro 서쪽으로; ***~ of*** ...ŭi sŏtchoge ...의 서쪽에
West Coast (*of USA*) (Migugŭi) T'aep'yŏng-yang Yŏnan (미국의) 태평양 연안
westerly *direction* sŏtchogŭi 서쪽의; *wind* sŏtchogesŏ punŭn 서쪽에서 부는
western 1 *adj* sŏtchogŭi 서쪽의; ***Western*** Sŏyang-ŭi 서양의 **2** *n* (*movie*) sŏbugŭk 서부극
Westerner Sŏyang saram 서양 사람
westernized sŏyanghwadoen 서양화된
westward sŏtchogŭro 서쪽으로
wet *adj* chŏjŭn 젖은; (*rainy*) piga onŭn 비가 오는; ***"~ paint"*** ch'il chu-ŭi 칠 주의; ***be ~ through*** hamppak chŏt-tta 함빡 젖다
whack F **1** *n* (*blow*) ch'ŏlssŏk ttaerim 철썩 때림 **2** *v/t* ch'ŏlssŏk ttaerida 철썩 때리다
whale korae 고래
whaling koraejabi 고래잡이

wharf *n* pudu 부두
what 1 *pron* ◊ muŏt 무엇; **~ *is that?*** chŏgŏsŭn muŏshimnikka? 저것은 무엇입니까?; **~ *is it?*** (*what do you want?*) wae? 왜?; (*what did you say?*) mwŏrago? 뭐라고?; (*astonishment*) musŭn soriya? 무슨 소리야?; **~ *about some dinner?*** chŏnyŏgŭl mŏngnŭn kŏshi ŏttŏk'essŏyo? 저녁을 먹는 것이 어떻겠어요?; **~ *about heading home?*** chibŭro kanŭn kŏshi ŏttŏk'essŏyo? 집으로 가는 것이 어떻겠어요?; **~ *for?*** (*why?*) wae? 왜?; ***so ~?*** kŭraesŏ? 그래서? ◊ (*relative*) ...hanŭn kŏt ...하는 것; ***that's not ~ I meant*** kŭgŏn naega ŭimihanŭn kŏshi aniyeyo 그건 내가 의미하는 것이 아니예요; ***that's ~ I like*** kŭgŏshi chega choahanŭn kŏshiyeyo 그것이 제가 좋아하는 것이예요 **2** *adj* ◊ (*what kind of*) ŏttŏn 어떤; **~ *color is the car?*** kŭ ch'anŭn ŏttŏn saek-kkarimnikka? 그 차는 어떤 색깔입니까? ◊ (*which*) ŏnŭ 어느; **~ *university are you at?*** tangshinŭn ŏnŭ taehage tanigo issumnikka? 당신은 어느 대학에 다니고 있습니까? **3** *adv*: **~ *a lovely day!*** ŏlmana nalsshiga choŭn narinjiyŏ! 얼마나 날씨가 좋은 날인지요!
whatever 1 *pron* …hanŭn kosŭn muŏshidŭnji …하는 것은 무엇이든지; (*regardless of*) …i / ga …hal chirado …이 / 가 …할 지라도; **~ *people say, I believe her*** saramdŭri musŭn marŭl hal chirado, nanŭn kŭnyŏrŭl minnŭnda 사람들이 무슨 말을 할 지라도, 나는 그녀를 믿는다 **2** *adj* ŏttŏn …(i)rado 어떤 …(이)라도; ***you have no reason ~ to worry*** tangshinŭn hanado kŏktchŏnghal iyuga ŏpssŏyo 당신은 하나도 걱정할 이유가 없어요
wheat mil 밀
wheedle: **~ *X out of Y*** Yŭl / rŭl kkoshyŏsŏ Xŭl / rŭl ŏdŏnaeda Y을 / 를 꼬셔서 X을 / 를 얻어내다
wheel 1 *n* pak'wi 바퀴; (*steering ~*) haendŭl 핸들 **2** *v/t bicycle* mirŏ umjigida 밀어 움직이다 **3** *v/i* (*of birds*) pingbing tolda 빙빙 돌다
♦ **wheel around** panghyang-ŭl hwik pakkuda 방향을 휙 바꾸다
wheelbarrow illyunch'a 일륜차; **wheelchair** hwilch'eŏ 휠체어; **wheel clamp** *n* ch'aryang chomsoe 차량 좀쇠
wheeze *v/i* sshigŭn-gŏrida 씨근거리다
when 1 *adv* ŏnje 언제; **~ *is the baby due?*** ainŭn ŏnje t'aeŏnal yejŏng-ingayo? 아이는 언제 태어날 예정인가요? **2** *conj* ...hal ttae ...할 때; **~ *I was a child*** naega ŏryŏssŭl ttae 내가 어렸을 때
whenever (*each time*) …hal ttaemada …할 때마다; (*regardless of when*) …hal ttaenŭn ŏnjedŭnji …할 때는 언제든지; ***call me ~ you like*** hago ship'ŭl ttaenŭn ŏnjedŭnji naege chŏnhwahaseyo 하고 싶을 때는 언제든지 내게 전화하세요
where 1 *adv* ŏdi 어디; **~ *were you born?*** kohyang-i ŏdiimnikka? 고향이 어디입니까?; **~ *from?*** ŏdiesŏ wassŭmnikka? 어디에서 왔습니까?; **~ *to?*** ŏdiro kamnikka? 어디로 갑니까? **2** *conj* …hanŭn kot …하는 곳; ***this is ~ I used to live*** yŏgiga naega sarat-ttŏn koshimnida 여기가 내가 살았던 곳입니다
whereabouts *adv* ŏditchŭme(sŏ) 어디쯤에(서)
wherever 1 *conj* (*anywhere*) …hanŭn kosŭn ŏdidŭnji …하는 곳은 어디든지; (*regardless of where*) ŏdirŭl …(ha)dŏrado 어디를 …(하)더라도; **~ *you go, don't forget it*** ŏdirŭl kadŏrado kŭgŏsŭl ittchi maseyo 어디를 가더라도 그것을 잊지 마세요 **2** *adv* taech'e ŏdi-e 대체 어디에
whet *appetite* shigyogŭl totkkunŭn kŏt 식욕을 돋구는 것
whether …inji …인지; ***he asked ~ I knew you*** kŭnŭn naega tangshinŭl anŭnji murŏbwassŏyo 그는 내가 당신을 아는지 물어봤어요; **~ *or not*** …inji aninji …인지 아닌지; ***I don't know ~ to tell him or not*** kŭege marŭl haeya haltchi anhaeya haltchi

morŭgessŏyo 그에게 말을 해야 할지 안해야 할지 모르겠어요; **~ ... or ...** ...inji ...inji ...인지 ...인지; ***I don't know ~ he is a student or a teacher*** kŭga hakssaenginji sŏnsaengniminji morŭgessŏyo 그가 학생인지 선생님인지 모르겠어요; **~ ... or not** (*regardless*) ...inji anidŭnji kane ...인지 아니든지 간에
which 1 *adj* ŏnŭ 어느; ***~ one is yours?*** ŏnŭ kŏshi tangshin kŏshimnikka? 어느 것이 당신 것입니까? **2** *pron* (*interrogative*) ŏnŭ kŏt 어느 것; (*relative*) ...hanŭn ...하는; ***the subject ~ I'm studying*** naega kongbuhanŭn kwamok 내가 공부하는 과목; ***take one, it doesn't matter ~*** ŏnŭ kŏsŭl kajyŏdo sang-gwanŏpssŭmnida 어느 것을 가져도 상관없습니다
whichever 1 *adj* ŏnŭ ...irado 어느 ...이라도 **2** *pron* ...hanŭn kŏsŭn ŏnŭ kŏshidŭn ...하는 것은 어느 것이든
whiff (*smell*) huk p'unggim 훅 풍김
while 1 *conj* ...hanŭn tong-an ...하는 동안; (*although*) ...hal chirado ...할 지라도 **2** *n*: ***a long ~*** orae 오래; ***for a ~*** chamshi tong-an 잠시 동안; ***I'll wait a ~ longer*** nanŭn chomdŏ kidarigessŭmnida 나는 좀더 기다리겠습니다
♦**while away** pindungbindung chinaeda 빈둥빈둥 지내다
whim pyŏndŏk 변덕; ***on a ~*** kŭnyang kaptchagi 그냥 갑자기
whimper *v/i* hultchŏk-kkŏrida 훌쩍거리다; (*of animal*) kkingkking-gŏrida 낑낑거리다
whine *v/i* (*of dog*) kkingkking-gŏrida 낑낑거리다; F (*complain*) ch'ing-ŏlgŏrida 칭얼거리다
whip 1 *n* ch'aetchiktchil 채찍질 **2** *v/t* (*beat*) ch'aetchiktchirhada 채찍질하다; *cream* hwijŏŏ kŏp'umŭl naeda 휘저어 거품을 내다; F (*defeat*) kyŏkp'ahada 격파하다
♦**whip out** F (*take out*) hwik kkŭjibŏnaeda 휙 끄집어내다
♦**whip up** (*arouse*) tobalshik'ida 도발시키다
whipped cream saeng k'ŭrim 생 크림
whipping (*beating*) ch'aektchiktchil 채찍질; F (*defeat*) p'aebae 패배
whirl 1 *n*: ***my mind is in a ~*** nae maŭmi kalp'irŭl mot-tchamnŭnda 내 마음이 갈피를 못잡는다 **2** *v/i* p'ing tolda 핑 돌다
whirlpool (*in river*) soyongdori 소용돌이; (*for relaxation*) chak'uji 자쿠지
whirlwind hoe-oribaram 회오리바람
whir(r) *v/i* wingwing tolda 윙윙 돌다
whisk 1 *n* (*kitchen utensil*) hwijŏnnŭn kigu 휘젖는 기구 **2** *v/t eggs* hwijŏt-tta 휘젖다
♦**whisk away** ssak kajyŏgabŏrida 싹 가져가버리다
whiskers (*of man*) kurenarut 구레나룻; (*of animal*) suyŏm 수염
whiskey wisŭk'i 위스키
whisper 1 *n* sokssagim 속삭임 **2** *v/t & v/i* sokssagida 속삭이다
whistle 1 *n* (*sound*) hwip'aram 휘파람; (*device*) hogak 호각 **2** *v/i* hwip'aramŭl pulda 휘파람을 불다; (*of wind*) sshing pulda 씽 불다 **3** *v/t* hwip'aramŭro noraehada 휘파람으로 노래하다
white 1 *n* (*color*) hayan saek 하얀 색; (*of egg*) hŭinja 흰자; (*person*) paegin 백인 **2** *adj* hayan 하얀; *person* paegin 백인
white-collar worker samujik sawŏn 사무직 사원; **White House** Paegak-kkwan 백악관; **white lie** agŭi-ŏmnŭn kŏjinmal 악의없는 거짓말; **white meat** hŭin kogi 흰 고기; **whiteout** (*for text*) sujŏng-aek 수정액; **white-wash 1** *n* paekssaek toryo 백색 도료; *fig* tullŏdaenŭn kŏjinmal 둘러대는 거짓말 **2** *v/t* paekssaek toryorŭl ch'irhada 백색 도료를 칠하다; *fig* hodohada 호도하다; **white wine** paekp'odoju 백포도주
whittle *wood* kkakka tadŭmtta 깍아 다듬다
♦**whittle down** churida 줄이다
whizz *n*: ***be a ~ at*** F koengjanghi chal hada 굉장히 잘 하다
♦**whizz by** (*of time, car*) sshing chinagada 씽 지나가다

whizzkid F shindong 신동
who (*interrogative*) nugu 누구; (*relative*) ...hanŭn ...하는; ***~ is that over there?*** chŏ sarami nuguimnikka? 저 사람이 누구입니까?; ***the woman ~ saved the boy*** kŭsonyŏnŭl kuhan yŏja 그소년을 구한 여자
whodun(n)it ch'urimul 추리물
whoever …hanŭn nugudŭnji …하는 누구든지
whole 1 *adj* modŭn 모든; ***a ~ chicken*** t'ongdak han mari 통닭 한 마리; ***two ~ hours*** kkobak tu shigan 꼬박 두 시간; ***the ~ town / country*** maŭl / kuk-kka chŏnch'e 마을 / 국가 전체; ***it's a ~ lot easier / better*** kŭgosŭn hwolsshin shwiptta / nat-tta 그것은 훨씬 쉽다 / 낫다 **2** *n* chŏnch'e 전체; ***the ~ of the United States*** Miguk chŏnch'e 미국 전체; ***on the ~*** taech'ero 대체로
whole food chayŏn shikp'um 자연 식품; **whole-hearted** chinshimŭi 진심의; **wholemeal bread** t'ongmilppang 통밀빵; **wholesale 1** *adj* tomae-ŭi 도매의; *fig* taeryang-ŭi 대량의 **2** *adv* tomaekkapssŭro 도매값으로; **wholesaler** tomae-ŏptcha 도매업자; **wholesome** (*healthy*) kŏn-gang-e choŭn 건강에 좋은; *attitude etc* kŏnjŏnhan 건전한
wholly wanjŏnhi 완전히
wholly owned subsidiary chahoesa 자회사
whom *fml* nugurŭl 누구를
whooping cough paegirhae 백일해
whore *n* ch'angnyŏ 창녀
whose 1 *pron* (*interrogative*) nuguŭi kŏt 누구의 것; (*relative*) ...hanŭn ...하는; ***~ is this?*** igŏsŭn nuguŭi kŏshimnikka? 이것은 누구의 것입니까?; ***a country ~ economy is booming*** kyŏngje-ŭi pumi irŏnago innŭn nara 경제의 붐이 일어나고 있는 나라 **2** *adj* nuguŭi 누구의; ***~ bike is that?*** chŏgŏsŭn nuguŭi chajŏn-gŏ-imnikka? 저것은 누구의 자전거입니까?
why (*interrogative*) wae 왜; (*relative*) wae …hanŭnji 왜 …하는지; ***that's ~*** kŭraesŏ-ida 그래서이다; ***~ not?*** wae andwae? 왜 안돼?; (*agreeing to suggestion*) kŭrojyo 그러죠; ***I don't know ~ he left*** kŭga wae ttŏnannŭnji mollayo 그가 왜 떠났는지 몰라요
wick shimji 심지
wicked saak'an 사악한
wicker pŏdŭlgaji 버들가지
wicker chair pŏdŭllo mandŭn ŭija 버들로 만든 의자
wicket (*in station, bank etc*) ch'anggu 창구
wide *adj* nŏlbŭn 넓은; *experience* p'ong-nŏlbŭn 폭넓은; *range* kwangbŏmwihan 광범위한; ***be 12 foot ~*** p'ogi shibip'it'ŭ-ida 폭이 12피트이다
wide-awake wanjŏnhi chami kkaen 완전히 잠이 깬
widely *used, known* nŏlkke 넓게
widen 1 *v/t* nŏlp'ida 넓히다 **2** *v/i* nŏlbŏjida 넓어지다
wide-open *window* nŏlkke yŏllin 넓게 열린; *eyes* k'ŭge ttŭn 크게 뜬
widespread manyŏndoen 만연된
widow kwabu 과부
widower horabi 홀아비
width p'ok 폭
wield *weapon, power* hwidurŭda 휘두르다
wife anae 아내
wig kabal 가발
wiggle *v/t hips, loose screw* hŭndŭlda 흔들다
wild 1 *adj animal, flowers* yasaeng 야생; *teenager, party* kŏch'in 거친; *scheme* mich'in tŭt'an 미친 듯한; *applause* yŏlgwangtchŏgin 열광적인; ***be ~ about*** (*enthusiastic*) …e yŏltchunghada …에 열중하다; ***go ~*** yŏlgwanghada 열광하다; (*become angry*) mopsshi hŭngbunhada 몹시 흥분하다; ***run ~*** (*of children*) chemot-ttaero nolda 제멋대로 놀다; (*of plants*) magu charada 마구 자라다 **2** *n*: ***the ~s*** migaeji 미개지
wildcard character COMPUT amugaemunja 아무개문자
wilderness hwangmuji 황무지
wildfire: ***spread like ~*** sapsshigane

p'ŏjida 삽시간에 퍼지다; **wildgoose chase** ttŭn-gurŭm chapkki 뜬구름 잡기; **wildlife** yasaeng tongmul 야생 동물
will[1] *n* LAW yusŏ 유서
will[2] *n* (*willpower*) ŭiji 의지
will[3]: ***I ~ let you know tomorrow*** naeil allyŏdŭrigessŭmnida 내일 알려드리겠습니다; ***~ you be there?*** kŏgi issŭl kkŏyeyo? 거기 있을 꺼예요?; ***I won't be back until late*** nanŭn nŭtkkekkaji toraoji anŭl kkŏyeyo 나는 늦게까지 돌아오지 않을 꺼예요; ***you ~ call me, won't you?*** chege chŏnhwahashilkkŏjyo? 제게 전화하실꺼죠?; ***I'll pay for this - no you won't*** chega naegessŭmnida - ani, kŭrŏji maseyo 제가 내겠습니다 - 아니, 그러지 마세요; ***the car won't start*** ch'a-e shidong-i an-gŏllyo 차에 시동이 안걸려; ***~ you tell her that ...?*** tangshini kŭnyŏege ...rago marhae chushigessŭmnikka? 당신이 그녀에게 ...라고 말해 주시겠습니까?; ***~ you have some more tea?*** ch'arŭl tŏ tŭshigessŏyo? 차를 더 드시겠어요?; ***~ you stop that!*** kŭmandwŏ! 그만둬!
willfull *person* kojibi sen 고집이 센; *action* ilburŏ-ŭi 일부러의
willing: ***be ~ to do ...*** kikkŏi ...hada 기꺼이 ...하다
willingly kikkŏi 기꺼이
willingness kikkŏi hanŭn maŭm 기꺼이 하는 마음
willow pŏdŭnamu 버드나무
willpower ŭijiryŏk 의지력
willy-nilly (*at random*) mujagwiro 무작위로
wilt (*of plant*) shidŭlda 시들다
wily kkoega manŭn 꾀가 많은
wimp F mugiryŏk'an saram 무기력한 사람
win 1 *n* sŭng-ni 승리 **2** *v/t* igida 이기다; *lottery* tangch'ŏmdoeda 당첨되다; *money* ttada 따다; ***~ a prize*** susanghada 수상하다 **3** *v/i* igida 이기다
wince *v/i* ŏlgurŭl tchip'urida 얼굴을 찌푸리다
winch *n* kwŏnyanggi 권양기
wind[1] **1** *n* param 바람; (*flatulence*) hŏtppae purŭm 헛배 부름; ***get ~ of*** ...ŭi somunŭl tŭt-tta ...의 소문을 듣다 **2** *v/t*: ***be ~ed*** hŏlttŏgida 헐떡이다
wind[2] **1** *v/i* kubijida 굽이지다 **2** *v/t* kamtta 감다
♦ **wind down 1** *v/i* (*of party etc*) sŏsŏhi kkŭnnada 서서히 끝나다 **2** *v/t car window* naerida 내리다; *business* p'ye-ŏp'aryŏgo hada 폐업하려고 하다
♦ **wind up 1** *v/t clock* kamtta 감다; *car window* ollida 올리다; *speech, presentation* kkŭch'ŭl maet-tta 끝을 맺다; *affairs* kyŏlmarŭl chit-tta 결말을 짖다; *company* p'ye-ŏp'ada 폐업하다 **2** *v/i* (*finish*) kkŭnnada 끝나다; ***~ in the hospital*** kyŏlguk pyŏng-wŏn shinserŭl chida 결국 병원 신세를 지다
windfall hoengjae 횡재
winding *adj* kkubulkkuburhan 꾸불꾸불한
wind instrument kwanak-kki 관악기
windmill p'ungch'a 풍차
window ch'angmun 창문; COMPUT windou 윈도우; ***in the ~*** (*of store*) chinyŏldoen 진열된
windowpane ch'ang-yuri 창유리; **window-shop**: ***go ~ping*** aishyop'inghada 아이쇼핑하다; **windowsill** ch'angt'ŏk 창턱
windpipe sumt'ong 숨통; **windshield** (chadongch'a) amnyuri (자동차) 앞유리; **windshield wiper** waip'ŏ 와이퍼
windsurfer (*person*) windŭsŏp'inghanŭn saram 윈드서핑하는 사람; (*board*) windŭsŏp'ing podŭ 윈드서핑 보드
windsurfing windŭsŏp'ing 윈드서핑
windy *weather, day* param punŭn 바람 부는; ***it's getting ~*** parami pulgi shijak'anda 바람이 불기 시작한다
wine p'odoju 포도주
wine list p'odoju menyu 포도주 메뉴
wing *n* nalgae 날개; ***right ~ / left ~*** SP, *politics* uik / chwaik 우익 / 좌익

wink 1 *n* wingk'ŭ 윙크 **2** *v/i* (*of person*) wingk'ŭhada 윙크하다; ***~ at*** …ege wingk'ŭhada …에게 윙크하다
winner usŭngja 우승자; (*in election*) tangsŏnja 당선자; (*in lottery*) tangch'ŏmja 당첨자; (*of prize*) susangja 수상자
winning *adj* igin 이긴; *lottery ticket* tangch'ŏmdoen 당첨된
winning post kyŏlssŭngjŏm 결승점
winnings sanggŭm 상금
winter *n* kyŏul 겨울
winter sports kyŏul sŭp'och'ŭ 겨울 스포츠
wintry kyŏul kat'ŭn 겨울같은
wipe *v/t* taktta 닦다; *tape* chiuda 지우다
♦**wipe off** *dirty mark* takkanaeda 닦아내다; (*from tape*) chiuda 지우다
♦**wipe out** (*kill*, *destroy*) chŏnmyŏlshik'ida 전멸시키다; *debt* wanje 완제
wire ch'ŏlssa 철사; ELEC chŏngit-tchul 전깃줄
wireless musŏnŭi 무선의
wire netting ch'ŏlmang 철망
wiring ELEC paesŏn 배선
wiry *person* tandanhan 단단한
wisdom chihye 지혜
wisdom tooth sarang-ni 사랑니
wise hyŏnmyŏng-han 현명한
wisecrack *n* ppyŏga innŭn nongdam 뼈가 있는 농담
wise guy *pej* anŭn ch'ŏk'anŭn nom 아는 척하는 놈
wisely *act* hyŏnmyŏng-hage 현명하게
wish 1 *n* sowŏn 소원; ***best ~es*** modŭn iri chal toegirŭl paramnida 모든 일이 잘 되기를 바랍니다 **2** *v/t* …igirŭl parada …이기를 바라다; ***I ~ that …*** nanŭn …hagirŭl paramnida 나는 …하기를 바랍니다; ***~ s.o. well*** nuga chal toegirŭl parada 누가 잘 되기를 바라다; ***I ~ed him good luck*** nanŭn kŭŭi haeng-unŭl pirŏt-tta 나는 그의 행운을 빌었다
♦**wish for** parada 바라다
wishful thinking anihage nakkwanjŏgin saenggak 안이하게 낙관적인 생각
wishy-washy *person* shishihan 시시한; *color* hŭi-yŏmŏlgŏn 희여멀건
wisp (*of hair*) tabal 다발; (*of smoke*) chulgi 줄기
wistful tamnaenŭn tŭt'an 탐내는 듯한
wit (*humor*) chaech'i 재치; (*person*) chaech'i-innŭn saram 재치있는 사람; ***be at one's ~s' end*** ŏtchihal parŭl morŭda 어찌할 바를 모르다; ***keep one's ~s about one*** ch'imch'ak'age it-tta 침착하게 있다
witch manyŏ 마녀
witchcraft mabŏp 마법
with ◊ (*accompanied by*, *proximity*) ...wa / kwa hamkke ...와 / 과 함께; ***I live ~ my aunt*** nanŭn nae ajumŏniwa hamkke samnida 나는 내 아주머니와 함께 삽니다; ***compare X ~ Y*** Xŭl / rŭl Ywa / gwa pigyohada X을 / 를 Y와 / 과 비교하다; ***be connected ~*** …wa / kwa kwallyŏndoeda …와 / 과 관련되다; ***are you ~ me?*** (*do you understand?*) che marŭl aradŭrŭl su issŭmnikka? 제 말을 알아들을 수 있습니까?; ***~ no money*** ton ŏpssi 돈 없이 ◊ (*instrument*) ...(ŭ)ro ...(으)로; ***stabbed ~ a knife*** k'allo tchillin 칼로 찔린 ◊ (*cause*) ...(ŭ)ro ...(으)로; ***shivering ~ fear*** turyŏumŭro ttŏnŭn 두려움으로 떠는 ◊ (*possession*) ...i / ga innŭn ...이 / 가 있는; ***the house ~ the red door*** ppalgan muni innŭn kŭ chip 빨간 문이 있는 그 집 ◊: ***~ a smile / ~ a wave*** usŭmyŏnsŏ / sontchit'amyŏnsŏ 웃으면서 / 손짓하면서 ◊: ***be angry ~ s.o.*** nuguege hwaga nada 누구에게 화가 나다; ***be satisfied ~ sth*** musŏse manjok'ada 무엇에 만족하다
withdraw 1 *v/t complaint*, *application* ch'wisohada 취소하다; *money from bank* ppaenaeda 빼내다; *troops* ch'ŏlssushik'ida 철수시키다 **2** *v/i* (*of competitor*) mullŏnada 물러나다; (*of troops*) ch'ŏlssuhada 철수하다
withdrawal (*of complaint*, *application*) ch'wiso 취소; (*of money*) inch'ul 인출; (*of troops*) ch'ŏlssu 철수; (*from drugs*) kkŭnŭm 끊음
withdrawal symptoms kŭmdan hyŏnsang 금단 현상

withdrawn *adj person* naesŏngjŏgin 내성적인
wither shidŭlda 시들다
withhold poryuhada 보류하다
within *prep* (*inside*) …ane(sŏ) …안에(서); (*time*) …inae-e …이내에; (*distance*) …ane …안에; ***is it ~ walking distance?*** kŏrŏsŏ kal su innŭn kŏri-imnikka? 걸어서 갈 수 있는 거리입니까?; ***we kept ~ the budget*** urinŭn yesanŭl nŏmtchi anat-tta 우리는 예산을 넘지 않았다; ***~ my power / my capabilities*** nae him / nŭngnyŏgŭro hal su innŭn 내 힘 / 능력으로 할 수 있는; ***~ reach*** kakkaun kose 가까운 곳에
without …ŏpsshi …없이; ***~ looking / ~ asking*** poji ank'o / murŏboji ank'o 보지 않고 / 물어보지 않고
withstand kyŏndiŏnaeda 견디어내다
witness 1 *n* (*at trial*) chŭng-in 증인; (*of accident, crime*) mok-kkyŏktcha 목격자; (*to signature*) chŭng-inŭro sŏmyŏngham 증인으로 서명함 **2** *v/t accident, crime* mok-kkyŏk'ada 목격하다; *signature* chŭng-inŭro sŏmyŏnghada 증인으로 서명하다
witness stand chŭng-insŏk 증인석
witticism chaech'i 재치
witty chaech'i-innŭn 재치있는
wobble *v/i* hŭndŭlgŏrida 흔들거리다
wobbly hŭndŭlgŏrinŭn 흔들거리는; *voice* ttŏllinŭn 떨리는
wolf 1 *n* (*animal*) nŭkttae 늑대; *fig* (*womanizer*) paramdung-i 바람둥이 **2** *v/t*: **~ (down)** kyegŏlssŭre mŏktta 게걸스레 먹다
wolf whistle *n maeryŏktchŏgin yŏjarŭl pogo punŭn hwip'aram* 매력적인 여자를 보고 부는 휘파람
woman yŏja 여자
woman doctor yŏŭisa 여의사
womanizer paramdung-i 바람둥이
womanly yŏjadaun 여자다운
woman priest yŏja mokssa 여자 목사
womb chagung 자궁
women's lib yŏsŏng haebang undong 여성 해방 운동
women's libber yŏsŏng haebang undongga 여성 해방 운동가
won FIN wŏn 원
wonder 1 *n* (*amazement*) nollaum 놀라움; ***no ~!*** tang-yŏnhae! 당연해!; ***it's a ~ that*** …ranŭn kŏsŭn nollaun irida …라는 것은 놀라운 일이다 **2** *v/i* ŭi-ahage yŏgida 의아하게 여기다 **3** *v/t* kunggŭmhada 궁금하다; ***I ~ if you could help*** tangshini towajul su innŭnji kung-gŭmhamnida 당신이 도와줄 수 있는지 궁금합니다
wonderful nollaun 놀라운
wood namu 나무; (*forest*) sup 숲
wooded namuga ugŏjin 나무가 우거진
wooden namuro toen 나무로 된
woodpecker ttakttaguri 딱따구리
woodwind MUS mok-kkwanak-kki 목관악기
woodwork (*wooden parts*) moktcho pubun 목조 부분; (*activity*) mok-kkong 목공
wool yangmo 양모
woolen 1 *adj* mojik 모직 **2** *n* mojingmul 모직물
word 1 *n* tanŏ 단어; (*in Bible*) pogŭm 복음; (*news*) soshik 소식; (*promise*) yakssok 약속; ***I couldn't understand a ~ of what he said*** kŭga hanŭn marŭn hanado ihaehal su ŏpssŏssŏyo 그가 하는 말은 하나도 이해할 수 없었어요; ***is there any ~ from …?*** …(ŭ)robut'ŏ soshigi issŏyo? …(으)로부터 소식이 있어요?; ***you have my ~*** naega yakssok'agessŭmnida 내가 약속하겠습니다; ***~s*** (*of song*) kasa 가사; ***have ~s*** (*argue*) maldat'umhada 말다툼하다; ***have a ~ with*** …wa / kwa handu madi marhada …와 / 과 한두 마디 말하다 **2** *v/t article, letter* marŭl kollasŏ ssŭda 말을 골라서 쓰다
wording p'yohyŏn 표현
word processing wŏdŭ p'ŭrosesŭrŭl sayong 워드 프로세스를 사용
word processor (*software*) wŏdŭ p'ŭrosesŏ 워드 프로세서
work 1 *n* il 일; ***out of ~*** shiltchik'an 실직한; ***be at ~*** irhago it-tta 일하고 있다; (*at office*) chiktchang-e it-tta 직장에 있다; ***I go to ~ by bus*** nanŭn

pŏsŭro ch'ulgŭnhamnida 나는 버스로 출근합니다 **2** *v/i* (*of person*) irhada 일하다; (*of student*) kongbuhada 공부하다; (*of machine*) umjigida 움직이다; (*succeed*) chal toeda 잘 되다; ***how does it ~?*** (*of device*) ŏttŏk'e sayonghamnikka? 어떻게 사용합니까? **3** *v/t employee* irŭl shik'ida 일을 시키다; *machine* sayonghada 사용하다

♦**work off** *bad mood, anger ttan irŭl haesŏ ijŏbŏrige hada* 딴 일을 해서 잊어버리게 하다; *flab* undong-ŭro sarŭl ppaeda 운동으로 살을 빼다

♦**work out 1** *v/t problem* p'ulda 풀다; *solution* haegyŏrhada 해결하다 **2** *v/i* (*at gym*) undonghada 운동하다; (*of relationship etc*) chal toeda 잘 되다

♦**work out to** (*add up to*) naoda 나오다

♦**work up** *enthusiasm* pullŏ irŭk'ida 불러 일으키다; *appetite* totkkuda 돋구다; ***get worked up*** (*angry*) hwaga nada 화가 나다; (*nervous*) puranhaejida 불안해지다

workable *solution* shirhaeng kanŭnghan 실행 가능한

workaholic *n* ilppŏlle 일벌레

workday (*hours of work*) kŭnmu shigan 근무 시간; (*not a holiday*) p'yŏng-il 평일

worker nodongja 노동자; ***she's a good ~*** (*of student*) kŭnyŏnŭn kongburŭl yŏlsshimi handa 그녀는 공부를 열심히 한다

workforce (*of company*) chŏn chong-ŏbwŏn 전 종업원; (*of country*) nodong in-gu 노동 인구

work hours kŭnmu shigan 근무 시간

working class nodongja kyegŭp 노동자 계급; **working-class** nodongja kyegŭbŭi 노동자 계급의; **working knowledge** kibonjŏgin chishik 기본적인 지식

workload ŏmmuryang 업무량; **workman** chagŏp inbu 작업 인부; **workmanlike** somsshi innŭn 솜씨 있는; **workmanship** somsshi 솜씨; **work of art** yesulp'um 예술품; **workout** yŏnsŭp 연습; **work permit** nodong hŏga 노동 허가; **workshop** chagŏptchang 작업장; (*seminar*) wŏk'ŭshyop 워크숍; **work station** tongnip chagŏp konggan 독립 작업 공간

world segye 세계; (*social*) sesang 세상; ***the ~ of computers / the ~ of the theater*** k'ŏmpyut'ŏgye / yŏngŭk-kkye 컴퓨터계 / 연극계; ***out of this ~*** F tŏ hal nawiŏmnŭn 더 할 나위없는

worldly sesoktchŏgin 세속적인; *person* sesang multchŏng-e palgŭn 세상 물정에 밝은; ~ ***goods*** chaemul 재물

world power segyejŏk kangdaeguk 세계적 강대국; **world war** segye taejŏn 세계 대전; **worldwide 1** *adj* segyejŏgin 세계적인 **2** *adv* segyejŏgŭro 세계적으로

worm *n* pŏlle 벌레

worn-out *shoes, carpet, part* tarhappajin 닳아빠진; *person* chich'in 지친

worried kŏktchŏngsŭrŏn 걱정스런

worry 1 *n* kŏktchŏng 걱정 **2** *v/t* kŏktchŏngshik'ida 걱정시키다; (*upset*) puranhage hada 불안하게 하다 **3** *v/i* kŏktchŏnghada 걱정하다; ***it will be alright, don't ~!*** kwaench'anŭl kŏshimnida, kŏktchonghaji maseyo! 괜찮을 것입니다, 걱정하지 마세요!

worrying kŏktchŏngdoenŭn 걱정되는

worse 1 *adj* tŏ nappŭn 더 나쁜 **2** *adv* tŏ nappŭge 더 나쁘게

worsen *v/i* tŏ nappajida 더 나빠지다

worship 1 *n* sungbae 숭배 **2** *v/t* sungbaehada 숭배하다; *fig* maeu saranghada 매우 사랑하다

worst 1 *adj* kajang nappŭn 가장 나쁜 **2** *adv* kajang nappŭge 가장 나쁘게 **3** *n*: ***the ~*** ch'oe-ak 최악; ***if the ~ comes to ~*** ch'oe-agŭi sangt'ae-enŭn 최악의 상태에는

worth *adj*: ***$20 ~ of gas*** iship tallŏ ŏch'iŭi kasŭ 이십 달러 어치의 가스; ***be ~*** ...ŭi kach'iga it-tta ...의 가치가 있다; ***how much is it ~?*** kŭgŏsŭn ŏlmaimnikka? 그것은 얼마입니까?; ***be ~ reading / seeing*** ilgŭl / pol manhada 읽을 / 볼 만하다; ***be ~ it*** hal manhada 할 만하다

worthless *object* kach'iga ŏmnŭn 가치가 없는; *person* ssŭlmo ŏmnŭn 쓸모없는
worthwhile *cause* porami innŭn 보람이 있는; ***be ~*** (*beneficial*, *useful*) ssŭlmoit-tta 쓸모있다; (*worth the effort*) hal manhada 할 만하다
worthy chon-gyŏnghal manhan 존경할 만한; *cause* chijihal manhan 지지할 만한; ***be ~ of*** (*deserve*) ...ŭl/rŭl padŭl manhan ...을/를 받을 만한
would: ***I ~ help if I could*** towadŭril su issŭmyŏn towadŭrigettchiyo 도와드릴 수 있으면 도와드리겠지요; ***I said that I ~ go*** nanŭn kaget-ttago maraessŭmnida 나는 가겠다고 말했습니다; ***I told him I ~ not leave unless ...*** nanŭn kŭege ...haji annŭn han ttŏnaji ank'et-ttago maraessŭmnida 나는 그에게 ...하지 않는 한 떠나지 않겠다고 말했습니다; ***~ you like to go to the movies?*** yŏnghwa porŏ kalkkayo? 영화 보러 갈까요?; ***~ you mind if I smoked?*** tambaerŭl p'iwŏdo kwaench'anayo? 담배를 피워도 괜찮아요?; ***~ you tell her that ...?*** kŭnyŏege ...rago marhaejushigessŭmnikka? 그녀에게 ...라고 말해주시겠습니까?; ***~ you close the door?*** munŭl tadajushigessŭmnikka? 문을 닫아주시겠습니까?; ***I ~ have told you but ...*** tangshinege yaegihaessŏya haetchiman... 당신에게 얘기했어야 했지만...; ***I ~ not have been so angry if ...*** ...myŏn nanŭn kŭrŏk'e hwarŭl naeji anassŭl kŏshimnida ...면 나는 그렇게 화를 내지 않았을 것입니다
wound 1 *n* sangch'ŏ 상처; (*in war*) pusang 부상 **2** *v/t* (*with weapon*) sangch'ŏrŭl ip'ida 상처를 입히다; (*with remark*) sanghage hada 상하게 하다
wow *interj* wa 와
wrap *v/t parcel*, *gift* ssada 싸다; (*cover*, *wind*) kamtta 감다
♦**wrap up** *v/i* (*against the cold*) ttattŭt'age iptta 따뜻하게 입다
wrapper (*for product*, *candy*) p'ojangji 포장지
wrapping p'ojang chaeryo 포장 재료
wrapping paper p'ojangji 포장지
wrath punno 분노
wreath hwahwan 화환
wreck 1 *n* chanhae 잔해; ***be a nervous ~*** shin-gyŏng soeyagida 신경 쇠약이다 **2** *v/t* ŏngmang-ŭro p'agoehada 엉망으로 파괴하다; *plans*, *career*, *marriage* ŏngmang-ŭro mandŭlda 엉망으로 만들다
wreckage (*of car*, *plane*) chanhae 잔해; ***~ of marriage / career*** mangch'yŏjin kyŏrhon / kyŏngnyŏk 망쳐진 결혼 / 경력
wrecker kujoch'a 구조차
wrecking company ch'aryang kujo hoesa 차량 구조 회사
wrench 1 *n* (*tool*) lench'i 렌치; (*injury*) pp'im 삠 **2** *v/t* (*injure*) pit'ŭlda 비틀다; (*pull*) ŏktchiro ppaeda 억지로 빼다
wrestle sshirŭmhada 씨름하다
♦**wrestle with** *problems* ...wa / kwa sshirŭmhada ...와 / 과 씨름하다
wrestler (*Korean*) sshirŭm sŏnsu 씨름 선수; (*western*) lesŭlling sŏnsu 레슬링 선수
wrestling (*Korean*) sshirŭm 씨름; (*western*) lesŭlling 레슬링
wrestling contest (*Korean*) sshirŭm kyŏnggi 씨름 경기; (*western*) lesŭlling kyŏnggi 레슬링 경기
wriggle *v/i* (*squirm*) momburimch'ida 몸부림치다; (*along the ground*) kkumt'ŭlgŏrimyŏ naagada 꿈틀거리며 나아가다
♦**wriggle out of** hech'yŏnagada 헤쳐나가다
♦**wring out** *cloth* tchada 짜다
wrinkle 1 *n* churŭm 주름 **2** *v/t clothes* churŭmjige hada 주름지게 하다 **3** *v/i* (*of clothes*) churŭmjida 주름지다
wrist sonmok 손목
wristwatch sonmok shigye 손목 시계
writ LAW yŏngtchang 영장
write 1 *v/t* ssŭda 쓰다; *music* chak-kkok'ada 작곡하다 **2** *v/i* ssŭda 쓰다; (*of author*) kŭrŭl ssŭda 글을 쓰다; (*send a letter*) p'yŏnjirŭl ssŭda

편지를 쓰다
♦**write down** padajŏktta 받아적다
♦**write off** *debt* ch'ŏngsanhada 청산하다; *car* pakssallaeda 박살내다
writer chak-kka 작가; (*of song*) chak-kkok-kka 작곡가
write-up p'yŏngnon 평론
writhe momburimch'ida 몸부림치다
writing (*as career*) kŭl ssŭgi 글 쓰기; (*hand-~*) kŭlsshi 글씨; (*words*) ssŭgi 쓰기; (*script*) kirok 기록; ***in ~*** sŏmyŏnŭro 서면으로
writing desk ch'aekssang 책상
writing paper p'ilgi yongji 필기 용지
wrong 1 *adj* t'ŭllin 틀린; *decision, choice* chalmot-ttoen 잘못된; ***be ~*** (*of person*) t'ŭllida 틀리다; (*morally*) nappŭda 나쁘다; ***what's ~?*** musŭn iriyeyo? 무슨 일이에요?; ***there is something ~ with the car*** ch'a-e muŏshin-ga isang-i it-tta 차에 무엇인가 이상이 있다 **2** *adv* chalmot 잘못; ***go ~*** (*of person*) t'ŭllida 틀리다; (*of marriage, plan etc*) chalmot-ttoeda 잘못되다 **3** *n* chalmot 잘못; ***right and ~*** chaljalmot 잘잘못; ***be in the ~*** chalmoshida 잘못이다
wrongful pudanghan 부당한
wrongly pudanghage 부당하게
wrong number chalmot kŏllin chŏnhwa 잘못 걸린 전화
wry pikkonŭn 비꼬는

XY

xenophobia oegugin hyŏmo 외국인 혐오
X-ray 1 *n* Xsŏn X선 **2** *v/t* Xsŏn ch'waryŏng-ŭl hada X선 촬영을 하다

yacht yot'ŭ 요트
yachting yot'ŭ t'agi 요트 타기
yachtsman yot'ŭ chojongja 요트 조종자
Yalu River Amnok-kkang 압록강
Yank *n* F Miguk saram 미국 사람
yank *v/t* hwaek tanggida 홱 당기다
yap *v/i* (*of dog*) k'aengk'aeng chit-tta 캥캥 짖다; F (*talk a lot*) chaejalgŏrida 재잘거리다
yard[1] (*of prison, institution etc*) kunae 구내; (*behind house*) twinmadang 뒷마당; (*for storage*) mulgŏn tunŭn kot 물건 두는 곳
yard[2] (*measurement*) yadŭ 야드
yardstick *fig* ch'ŏktto 척도
yarn *n* (*thread*) shil 실; F (*story*) kkumyŏnaen iyagi 꾸며낸 이야기
yawn 1 *n* hap'um 하품 **2** *v/i* hap'umhada 하품하다
year nyŏn 년; ***for ~s*** F yŏrŏ hae tong-an 여러 해 동안
yearly 1 *adj* maenyŏnŭi 매년의 **2** *adv* maenyŏn 매년
yearn *v/i* kalmanghada 갈망하다
♦**yearn for** …ŭl/rŭl mopsshi parada …을/를 몹시 바라다
yearning *n* kalmang 갈망
yeast hyomo 효모
yell 1 *n* koham 고함 **2** *v/i* koham chirŭda 고함 지르다 **3** *v/t* kohamch'yŏ purŭda 고함쳐 부르다
yellow 1 *n* norang 노랑 **2** *adj* noran 노란
yellow pages ŏptchongbyŏl chŏnhwa pŏnhobu 업종별 전화 번호부
Yellow Sea Hwanghae 황해, Sŏhae 서해
yelp 1 *n* kkaengkkaenggŏrinŭn sori 깽깽거리는 소리 **2** *v/i* kkaengkkaenggŏrida 깽깽거리다
yen FIN en 엔
yes ye 예 ◊ (*using 'no', ie no, that is not right*): ***you don't know the answer, do you? – oh ~, I do*** tabŭl morŭjyo? - aniyo, arayo 답을 모르죠? - 아니요, 알아요
yesman *pej* ach'ŏmkkun 아첨꾼
yesterday ŏje 어제; ***the day before ~*** kŭjŏkke 그저께
yet 1 *adv* ajik 아직; (*so far*) chigŭmkkaji 지금까지; ***as ~*** ajik-kkaji 아직까지; ***have you finished ~?*** inje ta kkŭnnaessŏyo? 인제 다 끝냈어요?; ***he hasn't arrived ~*** kŭnŭn ajik toch'ak'aji anat-tta 그는 아직 도착하지 않았다; ***is he here? – not ~*** kŭnŭn yŏgi wassŏyo? – ajik anwassŏyo 그는 여기 왔어요? - 아직 안왔어요; ***~ bigger/longer*** tŏuk tŏ k'ŭn/kin 더욱 더 큰/긴 **2** *conj* (*all the same, still*) yŏjŏnhi 여전히; ***~ I'm not sure*** yŏjŏnhi hwaksshinhal su ŏpssŏyo 여전히 확신할 수 없어요
yield 1 *n* (*from fields etc*) sanch'ul 산출; (*from investment*) iik 이익 **2** *v/t* *fruit, good harvest* sanch'urhada 산출하다; *interest* iigŭl naeda 이익을 내다 **3** *v/i* (*give way*) yangbohada 양보하다
yin and yang ŭmyang 음양
YMCA (= ***Young Men's Christian Association***) Kidok-kkyo Ch'ŏngnyŏnhoe 기독교 청년회
yoghurt yogurŭt'ŭ 요구르트
yolk norŭnja 노른자
you ◊ nŏ 너; (*polite*) tangshin 당신; (*plural*) nŏhŭidŭl 너희들; (*plural polite*) yŏrŏbundŭl 여러분들; ***he knows ~*** kŭnŭn tangshinŭn arayo 그는 당신을 알아요; ***that's for ~*** naŭi kŏshida 나의 것이다 ◊ (*omission of pronoun*): ***when are***

~ ***coming back?*** ŏnje toraol kŏmnikka? 언제 돌아올 겁니까? ◊: ~ ***never know*** kyŏlk'o al su ŏmnŭn iriyeyo 결코 알 수 없는 일이예요; ~ ***can't trust him*** kŭnŭn midŭl su ŏpssŏyo 그는 믿을 수 없어요

young chŏlmŭn 젊은; *wine* sukssŏngdoeji anŭn 숙성되지 않은

youngster chŏlmŭni 젊은이

your nŏŭi 너의; (*polite*) tangshinŭi 당신의

yours nŏŭi kŏt 너의 것; (*polite*) tangshinŭi kŏt 당신의 것; ***a friend of*** ~ nŏŭi / tangshinŭi ch'in-gu 너의 / 당신의 친구; ***Yours ...*** (*at end of letter*) ...ollim ...올림

yourself ne chashin 네 자신; (*polite*) tangshin chashin 당신 자신; ***by*** ~ honjasŏ 혼자서

yourselves nŏhŭidŭl chashin 너희들 자신; (*polite*) tangshindŭl chashin 당신들 자신; ***by*** ~ nŏhŭidŭl sŭsŭro 너희들 스스로

youth (*age*) ch'ŏngch'un-gi 청춘기; (*young man*) chŏlmŭni 젊은이; (*young people*) chŏlmŭn saram 젊은 사람

youthful chŏlmŭn 젊은

youth hostel yusŭ hosŭt'el 유스 호스텔

Z

zap *v/t* (*delete*) saktchehada 삭제하다; F (*kill*) haech'iuda 해치우다; F (*hit*) ch'ida 치다
♦**zap along** F (*move fast*) chaepssage umjigida 잽싸게 움직이다
zapped F (*exhausted*) chich'in 지친
zappy F *car*, *pace* pparŭn 빠른; (*lively*, *energetic*) wŏn-giwangsŏnghan 원기왕성한
zeal yŏlsshim 열심
zebra ŏllungmal 얼룩말
Zen sŏn 선
Zen Buddhism sŏnbulgyo 선불교
zero kong 공, yŏng 영; ***10 below ~*** yŏngha 10to 영하 10도
♦**zero in on** (*identify*) aranaeda 알아내다
zero growth chero sŏngjang 제로 성장
zest yŏltchŏng 열정
zigzag 1 *n* chigŭjaegŭhyŏng 지그재그형 **2** *v/i* chigŭjaegŭro umjigida 지그재그로 움직이다
zilch F amu kŏt-tto opssŭm 아무 것도 없음
zinc ayŏn 아연
♦**zip up** *v/t* chip'ŏrŭl chamgŭda 지퍼를 잠그다; COMPUT apch'uk'ada 하다
zip code up'yŏn pŏnho 우편 번호
zipper chip'ŏ 지퍼
zither (*with seven strings*) ajaeng 아쟁; (*plucked*) kŏmun-go 거문고
zodiac hwangdodae 황도대; ***signs of the ~*** hwangdodaeŭi shibi kung 황도대의 십이 궁
zombie F (*barely human person*) nŏng nagan saram 넋 나간 사람; ***feel like a ~*** (*exhausted*) kijinmaektchinhan 기진맥진한
zone chidae 지대
zoo tongmurwŏn 동물원
zoological tongmurhakssang-ŭi 동물학상의
zoology tongmurhak 동물학
zoom F (*move fast*) kŭp'i kada 급히 가다
♦**zoom in on** PHOT chumnenjŭro match'uda 줌렌즈로 맞추다
zoom lens chumnenjŭ 줌렌즈

Numbers

	Korean		Sino-Korean	
0	kong	공	yŏng	영
1	hana	하나	il	일
2	tul	둘	i	이
3	set	셋	sam	삼
4	net	넷	sa	사
5	tasŏt	다섯	o	오
6	yŏsŏt	여섯	yuk	육
7	ilgop	일곱	ch'il	칠
8	yŏdŏl	여덟	p'al	팔
9	ahop	아홉	ku	구
10	yŏl	열	ship	십
11	yŏrhana	열 하나	shibil	십일
12	yŏldul	열 둘	shibi	십이
13	yŏlsset	열 셋	shipssam	십삼
14	yŏllet	열 넷	shipssa	십사
15	yŏldasŏt	열 다섯	shibo	십오
16	yŏlyŏsŏt	열 여섯	shimyuk	십육
17	yŏrilgop	열 일곱	shipch'il	십칠
18	yŏlyŏdŏl	열 여덟	shipp'al	십팔
19	yŏrahop	열 아홉	shipkku	십구
20	sŭmul	스물	iship	이십
21	sŭmul hana	스물 하나	ishibil	이십일
30	sŏrŭn	서른	samship	삼십
35	sŏrŭn tasŏt	서른 다섯	samshibo	삼십오
40	mahŭn	마흔	saship	사십
50	shwin	쉰	oship	오십
60	yesun	예순	yuksship	육십
70	irhŭn	일흔	ch'ilsship	칠십
80	yŏdŭn	여든	p'alsship	팔십
90	ahŭn	아흔	kuship	구십
100	*no native Korean*		paek	백
101	*numbers above 99*		paegil	백일
200			ibaek	이백
1,000			ch'ŏn	천
2,000			ich'ŏn	이천
10,000			man	만
20,000			iman	이만
100,000			shimman	십만
1,000,000			paengman	백만
2,000,000			ibaengman	이백만
10,000,000			ch'ŏnman	천만
100,000,000			ŏk	억
1,000,000,000			ship ŏk	십억
8,655			p'alch'ŏnyuk-paegoshibo	팔천육백오십오

	Korean	Sino-Korean
1st	ch'ŏt pŏntchaeŭi 첫 번째의	che irŭi 제 1의
2nd	tu pŏntchaeŭi 두 번째의	che iŭi 제 2의
3rd	se pŏntchaeŭi 세 번째의	che samŭi 제 3의
4th	ne pŏntchaeŭi 네 번째의	che saŭi 제 4의
5th	tasŏt pŏntchaeŭi 다섯 번째의	che oŭi 제 5의
6th	yŏsŏt pŏntchaeŭi 여섯 번째의	che yugŭi 제 6의
7th	ilgop pŏntchaeŭi 일곱 번째의	che ch'irŭi 제 7의
8th	yŏdŏl pŏntchaeŭi 여덟 번째의	che p'arŭi 제 8의
9th	ahop pŏntchaeŭi 아홉 번째의	che kuŭi 제 9의
10th	yŏl pŏntchaeŭi 열 번째의	che shipŭi 제 10의
11th	yŏrhan pŏntchaeŭi 열 한 번째의	che shibirŭi 제 11의
12th	yŏldu pŏntchaeŭi 열 두 번째의	che shibiŭi 제 12의
13th	yŏlsse pŏntchaeŭi 열 세 번째의	che shipsamŭi 제 13의
14th	yŏlne pŏntchaeŭi 열 네 번째의	che shipsaŭi 제 14의
15th	yŏldasŏt pŏntchaeŭi 열 다섯 번째의	che shiboŭi 제 15의
16th	yŏl yŏsŏt pŏntchaeŭi 열 여섯 번째의	che shimyugŭi 제 16의
17th	yŏrilgop pŏntchaeŭi 열 일곱 번째의	che shipch'irŭi 제 17의
18th	yŏlyŏdŏl pŏntchaeŭi 열 여덟 번째의	che shipp'arŭi 제 18의
19th	yŏrahop pŏntchaeŭi 열 아홉 번째의	che shipguŭi 제 19의
20th	sŭmu pŏntchaeŭi 스무 번째의	che ishibŭi 제 20의
21st	sŭmul han pŏntchaeŭi 스물 한 번째의	che ishibirŭi 제 21의
30th	sŏrŭn pŏntchaeŭi 서른 번째의	che samshibŭi 제 30의
40th	mahŭn pŏntchaeŭi 마흔 번째의	che sashibŭi 제 40의
50th	shwin pŏntchaeŭi 쉰 번째의	che oshibŭi 제 50의
60th	yesun pŏntchaeŭi 예순 번째의	che yuksshibŭi 제 60의
70th	irhŭn pŏntchaeŭi 일흔 번째의	che ch'ilsshibŭi 제 70의
80th	yŏdŭn pŏntchaeŭi 여든 번째의	che p'alsshibŭi 제 80의
90th	ahŭn pŏntchaeŭi 아흔 번째의	che kushibŭi 제 90의
100th	paek pŏntchaeŭi 백 번째의	che paekŭi 제 100의

Korean numbers are usually used with countwords such as **chan** 잔 (cup), **myŏng** 명 (person), **k'yŏlle** 켤레 (pair), **pŏn** 번 (time). When used in this way **hana**, **tul**, **set**, and **net** contract to **han**, **tu**, **se**, **ne**:

k'ŏp'i han chan
커피 한 잔
a cup of coffee

kyosu se myŏng
교수 세 명
three professors

Sino-Korean cardinal numbers are used with (amongst other things) dates, money and foreign loanwords. To tell the time, Korean numbers are used for hours and Sino-Korean for minutes and seconds:

ich'ŏnillyŏn irwŏl iril
이천일년 일월 일일
1st January 2001

samship k'illomit'ŏ
삼십 킬로미터
30 kilometers

ohu seshi samship-ppun
오후 세시 삼십분
3.30pm

han shigan shippun och'o
한 시간 십분 오초
1 hour, 10 minutes and 5 seconds